WHERE *to* SKI
AND *Snowboard*
W O R L D W I D E

The Reuters Guide
to the World's Best Winter Sports Resorts

DISCARDED

What do the world's top 350,000 traders have in common?

Every effort has been made by the editors and publishers to ensure that the information contained herein is as accurate and up to date as possible at the time the book went to press. However, they assume no liability for any loss, injury, accident or inconvenience sustained by anyone as a result of the advice and information given in this guide.

Skiing and snowboarding are hazardous sports and the mountains are an inherently hostile environment. You go skiing or riding at your own risk.

GET THE NEXT EDITION FREE!
BY SENDING US RESORT REPORTS
We are always grateful for feedback on the resorts our readers visit. The 100 most useful reports earn a free copy of the 2003 edition, in advance of publication in September 2002.

Send resort reports by e-mail to:
reports@snowfile.com

WHERE *to* SKI *AND* Snowboard
WORLDWIDE

The Reuters Guide
to the World's Best Winter Sports Resorts

Edited by
Chris Gill and **Dave Watts**

MOUNTAIN SPORTS PRESS

HarperSports
An imprint of HarperCollins*Publishers*

NortonWood

REUTERS

This edition published 2001

10 9 8 7 6 5 4 3 2 1

Editors Chris Gill and Dave Watts
Assistant editors Martin Hall, Mandy Crook, Minnie Burlton, Catherine Weakley, Emma Morris, Melanie Papworth, Robin Campbell
Australia/NZ editor Bronwen Gora
Contributors Chris Allan, Alan Coulson, Nicky Holford, James Hooke, Tim Perry, Adam Ruck, Helena Wiesner, Ian Porter

Design by Fox Design Consultants
Australian cover design by Luke Causby, HarperCollins Design Studio
Production by Guide Editors
Contents/cover photos by Snowpix.com / Chris Gill
Australian cover photo by Getty Images / Scott Markewitz
Production manager Ian Stratford
Printed and bound in Italy by Conti Tipocolor

Edited in the United Kingdom by NortonWood Publishing Ltd
The Old Forge
Norton St Philip
Bath BA2 7LW
United Kingdom
tel + 44 1373 835208
e-mail mailbox@snow-zone.co.uk

In Europe

ISBN 0 9536371 3 1

A CIP catalogue entry for this book is available from the British Library.

Published by
NortonWood Publishing Ltd
tel + 44 1373 835208
fax + 44 1373 834106
e-mail mailbox@snow-zone.co.uk

Book trade sales are handled by
Portfolio Books Ltd
Unit 5 Perivale Industrial Park
Horsenden Lane South
Greenford UB6 7RL
United Kingdom
tel + 44 20 8997 9000
fax + 44 20 8997 9097
e-mail sales@portfoliobooks.com

In the United States and Canada

ISBN 0 9676747 6 X

Published by
Mountain Sports Press
929 Pearl Street, Suite 200
Boulder, CO 80302
tel 303-448-7663
fax 303-448-7670
e-mail Bill.Grout@time4.com

Book trade sales are handled by
Publishers Group West

In Australia and New Zealand

ISBN 0 7322 7363 3

Published and distributed by
HarperCollins*Publishers* (Australia) Pty Limited
25 Ryde Road (PO Box 321)
Pymble, NSW 2073
tel + 61 2 9952 5000
fax + 61 2 9952 5444

Individual copies of the book can be purchased by credit card from www.amazon.com

WHERE *to* SKI
AND *Snowboard*
W O R L D W I D E

Contents

Resort chapters

9

About this book

it's simply the best

This is a new international guide to the world's best winter sports resorts, being published simultaneously in North America, Australasia and Europe. So how come the Sunday Times of London has already decided, as we say on the cover, that it *'can't be beaten'*?

The answer is that *Where to Ski and Snowboard Worldwide* is actually closely based on an existing British book, which is now in its sixth edition and is generally regarded as Britain's leading ski resort guide.

We believe that this is simply the best guide to ski and snowboard resorts that you can buy. Here's why:

• By making the most of technology we are able to go to press as late as the end of July and make the book **up to date for the season ahead** – the 2001/02 season. To see what we mean, check out our What's new chapter, crammed with new resort developments.

• To help you compile a shortlist of resorts, we work hard to make our information **reader-friendly**, with star-ratings for the main aspects of each resort and crystal-clear lists of resort plus-points and minus-points at the start of each chapter.

• We don't hesitate to express **critical views**. We learned our craft at the UK's principal consumer organization, Consumers' Association, where we both became editors of flagship magazines – so a consumerist attitude comes naturally to us.

• Our resort chapters give an **unrivalled level of detail** – including scale plans showing the extent and layout of each major resort, as well as all the facts you need to have at your fingertips.

• We use color printing fully, including not only mountain maps (over 125 of them) but also photographs, carefully chosen so that you can see for yourself what different resorts are like. For readers in North America, in particular, we expect this approach to come as something of a revelation: ski resort guides don't have to be printed in monochrome on rough paper.

Our ability to launch *Where to Ski and Snowboard Worldwide* is largely due to the support of Reuters, who also sponsor the parent book *Where to Ski and Snowboard.* We are grateful for that support, which has given us the confidence to make investments that would otherwise have seemed too risky.

We are uncompromising in our commitment to helping you, our readers, to make an informed choice; we're confident that you'll find the commitment shows in the finished product.

Enjoy your skiing and riding this season.

Chris Gill and Dave Watts
Norton St Philip, England 30 July 2001

What's new?

lifts and snow for 2002

The main news from the resorts of Europe and North America.

AUSTRIA

The new Ski Alliance Amadé joint lift ticket covers over 275 lifts in more than 30 ski resorts in eastern Austria: the Gastein valley and Grossarl; Salzburger Sportwelt (main areas: Flachau/ Wagrain/ St Johann and Zauchensee/ Kleinarl); Hochkönigs Winterreich (Maria Alm and neighbors). Buses, trains and road tolls between the resorts are also covered by the lift ticket.

BAD GASTEIN The parallel Weitmoser surface lifts on Schlossalm are being replaced by a six-pack.

ELLMAU 2000/01 saw a second six-pack to the Hartkaiser-Brandstadl area and another one was installed between Ellmau and Scheffau.

HINTERTUX-MAYRHOFEN Last season saw a gondola replace the old double chair-lift from the Hintertux base area, and the world's highest jumbo gondola was installed from 2660m/8,730ft to 3250m/10,660ft. For 2001/02 the Eggalm/Rastkogel area above Lanersbach is being linked with Mayrhofen's slopes, via a new six-pack from Rastkogel and a new 150-person tram from the Mayrhofen slopes. All this will mean a 40% increase in Mayrhofen's terrain to a total of 143km/90 miles. In the existing Mayrhofen area the old double chair up to Schafskopf will be replaced by a six-pack for 2001/02. Another new six-pack will be built in this area, opening up new trails.

ISCHGL For 2001/02 another fast eight-seater chair replaces a slow three-seater to Idjoch. Last season saw a quad upgraded to an eight-seater and another quad and six-pack installed to replace existing T-bars on the Ischgl side. Over in Samnaun, yet another six-pack replaced a T-bar. More snowmaking was also installed.

LECH For 2000/01 the Rüfikopf tram was modernized with new panoramic cabins, and the restaurant at the top refurbished. The Zuger Hochlicht tram was taken out of service.

OBERGURGL A new eight-seater gondola from Hochgurgl up to Wurmkogl is planned for 2001/02. In the Gaisberg sector, a quad chair-lift replaces the Übungs surface lift; and a six-pack replaces the Steinmann and Sattel surface lifts.

SAALBACH-HINTERGLEMM For 2000/01 two lifts on the south-facing slopes above Hinterglemm were replaced by fast chairs.

SCHLADMING The old gondola from Haus was upgraded to an eight-seater last season. The slow double chair-lift from Rohrmoos on Hochwurzen was also replaced, by a fast six-pack.

SÖLDEN A new gondola was installed last season on the Tiefenbach glacier. Also new was a six-pack from Langegg to the Rotkoglhütte.

SÖLL For 2000/01 the old single-seat chair to the Hohe Salve was replaced by an eight-seater gondola from Hochsöll. In Hopfgarten, a liftline-prone T-bar was replaced by an eight-seater chair.

Who do one billion people look to
for their daily news?

St Anton There's a new eight-person gondola from Nasserein to Gampen and a new fast quad from east of the central village to Fang. The old funicular has been demolished, widening the home run.

Zell am See For 2001/02, a quad chair will replace a T-bar up to Schmittenhöhe on the Sonnkogel side and snowmaking will cover 70% of the lower slopes. In Kaprun, a giant gondola will replace the funicular which suffered the tragic fire last year. It will eventually end at the Alpincenter at the top of the defunct funicular. But for 2001/02 only the first stage will be in place, ending near the top of the existing gondola. So for 2001/02 everyone will have to take a solitary fast quad to the main slopes from the top of the gondolas – expect huge liftlines.

FRANCE

As we went to press the Mont Blanc tunnel, closed since the tragic fire in 1999, was officially due to reopen in the fall of 2001. But the project has been delayed several times and locals predict that it won't open until December at the earliest, and maybe not until after the 2001/02 season.

Alpe-d'Huez For 2000/01, new developments included a second stage to the Marmottes gondola, the replacement of the old Chatelard surface lift to Auris by a two-seater chair, a lift from the Villard-Reculas car park up to the fast chair, increased capacity of the Alpette gondola at Oz, and a second automatic snowmaking plant. Plans for 2001/02 include replacement of the glacier double chair by a quad starting lower down on the glacier, and increased capacity on the first stage of the Marmottes gondola.

Avoriaz/Morzine For 2000/01 the gondola from Ardent to Les Lindarets was upgraded to increase its capacity. For 2001/02 another six-pack will replace the double surface lift from Les Lindarets up to Avoriaz. A new trail will be built at the top to join the existing trails down to Les Lindarets. In Morzine, the Belvédère and Mouilles double chairs were replaced by quads for 2000/01, and the area at the top of the Pleney gondola was rebuilt to make reaching the other lifts easier. More snowmaking was installed.

Chamonix The Charlanon surface lift, completing the Flégère-Brévent link, was upgraded to a fast quad last season.

Châtel In 2000/01 the three-person chair from Les Combes to Cornebois was replaced by a high-speed quad.

Courchevel For 2000/01 the slow chair from Les Creux to La Vizelle was replaced by a six-pack and the start of the Creux Noir chair was moved up the mountain to avoid congestion at Les Creux. For 2001/02 a new six-pack will replace the long Pralong surface lift from the beginner slopes above 1850. Another six-pack will replace three surface lifts in 1650, making the journey to Signal from 1850 quicker.

Les Deux-Alpes The old Jandri 3 gondola from mid-mountain to the glacier was dismantled last season. A new eight-seater chair, to replace the original gondola, should be ready for 2001/02.

Flaine France's first fast eight-seater chair was installed for 2000/01, from the village at Flaine Forêt to Les Grands Vans. We understood that a new gondola would be in place for 2001/02, going from Samoëns village to Samoëns 1600, but as this page went to press we heard that it has been delayed. A new fast quad from Morillon 1100 will serve the Bergin trail.

LES MENUIRES For 2001/02, a new six-pack will go from the center of the village to mid-mountain, and another new fast six-seater up to Mont de la Chambre and the links with Méribel and Val-Thorens. The top section of the rickety old gondola that used to be the main way up will be demolished.

MÉRIBEL For 2001/02, the slow old Plan des Mains chair, from the bottom of Mont Vallon up to the Plattières gondola, will be replaced by a six-pack.

LA PLAGNE For 2000/01, the liftline-prone Grande Rochette gondola from Plagne-Centre was replaced by a new gondola with three times the capacity. 2001/02 will see more snowmaking. The Biolley two-seater chair-lift from Plagne Centre and the two-seater from Plagne 1800 to Aime-la-Plagne are being upgraded to quads.

SERRE-CHEVALIER For 2001/02 a new six-pack will replace the parallel Prorel surface lifts, linking the Chantemerle section to the Briançon slopes. And snowmaking is being doubled.

VAL-D'ISÈRE 2000/01 saw a new high-speed chair replace the defunct Cascade and Pissaillas chairs on the Pissaillas glacier. For 2001/02 the old Bellevarde tram is being replaced by a giant gondola. And the Glacier chair, an essential link from Solaise towards the Col de L'Iseran and the Pissaillas glacier, is being upgraded to a six-pack.

VAL-THORENS For 2001/02 a new jumbo gondola will start from the bottom of the gondola towards Caron and take you to near the Col de la Montée du Fond, ending the need to walk to the Maurienne side (the Fourth Valley). Two new successive quads in the Fourth Valley will take you from Plan Bouchet at the top of the gondola up from the Maurienne valley to Pointe du Bouchet and three new trails.

ITALY

Turin has been chosen to host the 2006 Olympic Winter Games; most of the Alpine events will be held at Sansicario and Sestriere, with the freestyle competitions at Sauze d'Oulx.

BORMIO A new fast quad is to replace the Isabella chair from Bormio 2000 next season. Bormio has been chosen to host the World Alpine Ski Championships in 2005.

CERVINIA There's a new trail down into Zermatt from the top of the fast chair-lifts to the Swiss border.

LIVIGNO A new six-pack from Valfin on the Mottolino slopes to the top of Monte della Neve has opened up a couple of new black trails.

MONTEROSA SKI The area is in the middle of an ambitious programme to link Alagna properly by lifts and trail to Gressoney (the link has in the past involved skiing off-trail). For 2000/01 the ancient tram out of Alagna was replaced by a new gondola to Pianalunga, followed by a new chair-lift, which takes you to the top tram (still tiny and ancient) up to Punta Indren. 2000/01 also saw new fast chairs and more snowmaking at Antagnod and Orsia.

SELVA/SELLA RONDA For 2000/01 a fast quad replaced the surface lift from Piz Seteur, in Plan de Gralba, up to Passo Sella. And in Canazei, two chairs on Belvedere were upgraded – to a six-pack and a quad. There's a new gondola up to Col Pradat in Colfosco's local area, and a new quad chair at Bufaure di Sotto in Val di Fassa. The Marmolada glacier is now included in the Dolomiti Superski lift ticket.

SWITZERLAND

CHAMPÉRY The old Grand Paradis and Planachaux double chairs are being replaced by six-packs.

DAVOS For 2000/01 the Dorftälli surface lift to Weissfluhjoch was replaced by a six-pack starting at the mid-station of the funicular railway. Plans to replace the railway have been abandoned.

ST MORITZ The World Alpine Ski Championships are to be held in St Moritz in 2003. For 2001/02 on Corviglia, the Plateau Nair T-bar from Marguns will be replaced by a fast quad.

VERBIER The first two stages of the gondola from Le Châble to Les Attelas, via Verbier and Les Ruinettes, will be upgraded for 2001/02.

VILLARS For 2001/02 a six-seater chair will link from La Rasse to Chaux Ronde, replacing a surface lift and slow chair.

UNITED STATES

CALIFORNIA

HEAVENLY The new eight-person gondola from the center of South Lake Tahoe to the middle of Heavenly's slopes is now open. Work on the pedestrian village around the new gondola base is under way. Two new gladed trails are opening for 2001/02 in the upper Nevada area off Skyline Trail.

LAKE TAHOE At Squaw, work on a new base village is progressing. The first phase should be ready for 2001/02.

MAMMOTH MOUNTAIN Work has started on a new car-free village at the core of Mammoth Lakes, eventually with a gondola link to the slopes. A six-pack has replaced the two lifts up from Juniper Springs.

COLORADO

ASPEN After 54 years as a skiers-only mountain, snowboarding is now allowed on Aspen Mountain. At Highlands, even more steep terrain is to be added in Highland Bowl, and the base lodge at Highlands Village is ready.

COPPER MOUNTAIN The new car-free resort center is now open.

KEYSTONE 2000/01 saw a new six-pack on the back side of Keystone Mountain – speeding up the return from North Peak.

TELLURIDE For 2001/02 three new fast chairs will open an extra 733 acres of terrain (a massive 70% increase in the area of Telluride's slopes) and 20 new trails in Prospect Bowl. A new mountain restaurant with a Ute Indian theme (teepees etc) is also planned.

VAIL The 2000/01 season saw another fast quad and another 125 acres of terrain in Blue Sky Basin. Snowmaking has been upgraded.

WINTER PARK The first phase of the slope-side village is now complete.

UTAH

ALTA-SNOWBIRD For 2001/02, Alta is installing its first fast quad to replace the slow triple Sugarloaf lift. From the top of this you will be able to ski down into Snowbird's Mineral Basin to access the whole of Snowbird's terrain as well on a joint area lift ticket. A second fast quad in Mineral Basin will bring you back. The joint area will cover 4,700 acres, making it the biggest lift-linked area in Utah and one of the biggest in the US. The resorts will keep separate ownership and operation, and Alta is still refusing to allow snowboarding.

THE CANYONS For 2000/01 an open-air gondola opened from the parking area to the resort village and the new Dreamscape quad chair accessed the area's eighth mountain and 300 acres of new terrain. For

2001/02 a new triple chair between Dreamscape and Peak 5 opens five new intermediate trails.

DEER VALLEY A new day lodge at the bottom of the Empire and Ruby lifts will be open for 2001/02. The Quincy triple chair will be replaced by a high-speed quad. And snowmaking will be increased.

SNOWBASIN A new base lodge and skier services lodge will be ready for 2001/02. And there will be two plush new mountain restaurants. A new access road reduces the journey time from Salt Lake City.

THE REST OF THE WEST

JACKSON HOLE For 2000/01, the old Union Pass surface lift to the base area from the Hobacks was replaced by a quad chair. Another quad was built from the Moose Creek condo area of Teton Village to the Union Pass chair. In nearby Grand Targhee, 500 acres of former snowcat skiing will be served by a fast quad for 2001/02.

NEW ENGLAND

SMUGGLERS' NOTCH Snowmaking was extended by 40% for 2000/01 and a new water reservoir will increase the capacity further for 2001/02. Four new trails opened on Sterling Mountain last season and two more are planned for 2001/02.

CANADA

WESTERN CANADA

BANFF For 2001/02 Sunshine's old access gondola will be replaced by a new eight-seater, almost doubling the capacity and cutting the journey time to Sunshine Village to under 13 minutes. For 2000/01 the Wolverine fast quad replaced the old Wheeler chair and another quad replaced the Fireweed T-bar.

BIG WHITE Last season saw the opening of the new Happy Valley adventure area, with huge tubing hill, linked to the village by a new eight-person gondola. 2001/02 will see four new black trails off the Ridge Rocket chair.

FERNIE The Bear T-bar was replaced by a fast quad for 2000/01, improving access to both Lizard and Cedar Bowls.

JASPER A new quad chair-lift from mid-mountain to Eagle Ridge will open up twenty new trails for the 2001/02 season, and provide a more direct route to the Knob chair-lift.

KICKING HORSE The resort started operating last season, 2000/01. As this page goes to press it is confirmed that the chair-lift to Blue Heaven and the first developments at the mountain village will not be in place until 2002/03.

LAKE LOUISE For 2000/01 the Glacier chair from the base was replaced by an additional fast quad.

PANORAMA For 2000/01 new expert terrain was opened in Taynton Bowl. A new open-air gondola connects the lower and upper villages.

EASTERN CANADA

TREMBLANT A new beginner area by the village is planned for 2001/02.

ANDORRA

PAL-ARINSAL 2000/01 saw the resorts of Pal and Arinsal become one. The new link is via a 50-person tram from Coll de la Botella in Pal to the top of the Arinsal slopes. Snowmaking was also extended.

Pas de la Casa For 2000/01 the Font Negre surface lift above Pas de la Casa was replaced by a six-pack. Two surface lifts to Grau Roig from Encamp have also been upgraded to a six-pack. 2001/02 will see the expansion of the Pas de la Casa beginner area and new snowmaking.

Soldeu The new gondola from Canillo to El Forn is now open. There's a new beginner area at the top, and a new fast quad continues up to Portella, and the Soldeu El Tarter slopes. The Espiolets beginner area has been improved and snowmaking has been extended. For 2001/02, the Riba Escorxada beginners' area is being improved and further additions to the Espiolets beginner area are planned. Artificial snowmaking is to be extended.

SPAIN

Baqueira-Beret For 2000/01 a new fast chair and surface lift opened up the area facing the main Beret slopes. And a new chair in the Bonaigua sector has opened up two new blue trails. Snowmaking has increased.

SWEDEN

Åre For 2001/02 there will be two new red and two new blue slopes (all with snowmaking) in the central area above the town.

Dreams Are Not One-Size-Fits-All.

Do you dream of fresh powder? Breathtaking views? A night at the symphony? Whatever your favorite thing about a winter vacation is, you'll find more of it in Austria.

Enjoy a hearty Tyrolean lunch slopeside, instead of overpriced cafeteria food. Take a day off skiing to visit an ancient castle or cathedral. Ski the Alps, where it all began. All for a lot less than you might think. SkiEurope builds vacations that fit, **starting at $499** – an unforgettable week at an unbeatable price*.

Plan it now. Visit www.ski-europe.com for an immediate personalized proposal on how to make your skiing dreams come true.

WHERE DREAMS COME IN ALL SHAPES AND SIZES.
*This amazing price includes airfare, lodging, breakfast, transportation to and from the airport, local taxes and service charges.

800.333.5533   www.ski-europe.com

Transatlantic differences

bigger than you might expect

Are you thinking of giving the Rockies a miss and heading for the Alps this year? Or the other way round? Or are you sitting in Sydney wondering where to go for that ski-trip of a lifetime? If so, it's important to appreciate the differences between the North American and European skiing experiences. It's not that either one is better than the other – we love them both – but that you need to be prepared for what you're going to find, if you're going to get the best from your trip.

THE SLOPES

Europe's skiing mountains are generally much bigger than North America's. In many US resorts in this book, the vertical (the height difference between top of the lift system and the bottom of the slopes) is around 700m/2,300ft and very few exceed 1000m/3,300ft. Each lift usually serves several different (but often similar) trails cut through the trees. Many big-name Alpine resorts such as Chamonix, Davos, Val-d'Isère and Zermatt have verticals of around 2000m/ 6,600ft or more. This makes for much longer trails through very varied scenery, from craggy mountaintop bowls way above the tree-line down to low pastures and meadows where cattle may still be kept in wooden huts over the winter.

Ski areas are usually much bigger in Europe too. Comparisons are complicated by two things: the fact that European resorts talk in terms of the length of trails, whereas North American ones deal in skiable area; and the fact that in North America each lift tends to serve a variety of trails, whereas in the Alps it's not uncommon for a lift to serve only one or two identified trails – though it may also serve large areas of 'off-piste' terrain (discussed later).

There are several lift-linked circuits in the Alps that have around 100 lifts and more than 200km/125 miles of trails. The biggest of them all is the Trois Vallées, which has 200 lifts and over 600km/ 400 miles of trails. These dwarf the biggest US mountain (Vail, with 33 lifts and 5,000 acres of terrain).

Along with the bigger verticals of the European Alps comes more dramatic scenery. Most US ski areas are set among rolling hills, covered in trees, which give pleasant but unremarkable views compared with the Alps, where the dramatic peaks of the mountains tower high above many resorts (and often way above the top of the ski area too), giving stunning views.

Whereas in Europe it is common for most of the slopes to be above the tree-line (indeed some resorts have slopes that are entirely above the tree-line), in North America most ski trails are below the tree-line, and open areas such as Vail's Back Bowls and Whistler's top bowls are the exception rather than the rule. This isn't because American resorts are lower; it's because the tree-line is much higher.

One advantage of all these trees is that you normally have good visibility when it's snowing – while on open terrain bad visibility could be a severe problem. It is not unusual for most lifts and slopes of high European resorts to be closed (perhaps for a few days at a time) by heavy snowfalls or high winds. And because the mountains are bigger, often with snow-filled bowls high above the slopes, it can take longer after a snowfall for the ski patrol to eliminate avalanche danger and open the trails again.

The trees in North America have an added attraction too. You can often ski or board 'in the trees', treating them as slalom poles and enjoying the good powder that usually lies in the forests. Provided the spaces are wide enough, we find this great fun – and it's something we miss in Europe, where tree skiing in gladed terrain is virtually unknown and some resorts ban skiing in the trees for environmental reasons.

Because of the different nature of the mountain terrain, the roads are very different too. In North America, the roads to resorts are generally wide and good and driving to or between resorts is easy. In Europe, you encounter much narrower, more winding roads and more high mountain passes – all made scarier by crazy local drivers passing on blind curves and doing twice the speed limit.

THE SNOW

It snows a lot more in North America (in the western part at least) than it does in Europe. Comparisons between resorts in North America are simplified by the emphasis that is placed on snowfall – the total amount of precipitation in the season. So everyone know that on average Alta gets more snow than Park City, Winter Park more than Vail. In Europe, you rarely get anything more than the current base depth. But in our view the important thing is that it snows more frequently in North America. It is quite normal to get snowfalls two or three times a week, giving a good chance of hitting powder conditions. In Europe it tends to snow much less often, and most of a season's snowfall may come in two or three big dumps. What this means is that you encounter fresh powder conditions much less often in Europe than in western North America.

Another big difference is that snowmaking facilities are used much earlier in the season in North America to lay down a base in November or even October. So while many US and Canadian resorts are in full swing by Thanksgiving (late November), few Alpine resorts come to life before Christmas.

In general, North American resorts (certainly in the west) don't have to worry too much about having a decent snow base for most of the season. But in Europe things are much more varied – which is why we give resorts a snow reliability rating and often talk about whether they are snow-sure (which means 'likely to have acceptable snow when you visit'). Broadly, the higher elevation of the slopes, the more snow-sure they are. High French resorts usually have lots of snow, many low Austrian resorts often have problems.

THE TRAILS AND LIFTS

The classification of marked trails ('pistes' in Europe) is different in North America and Europe. North America uses green, blue and black gradings, while most of Europe uses blue, red and black (though France, Andorra, Norway and Sweden have green as well):

North America	Europe
green circle	easier blue runs (green in France)
blue square	steeper blue and easier red runs
black diamond	steeper red and most black runs
double black diamond	steepest blacks and many off-piste runs

A few US resorts have now introduced a grading between the normal blue and black (sometimes double blue square, sometimes a hybrid blue-black square). These roughly translate to European red runs.

Another big difference is what happens if you stray off the marked trails. In Europe, you are then going 'off-piste' and you do so at your own risk – even if you are on a slope that lies between two marked and groomed trails. The ski patrol takes no responsibility for your safety, the slope is highly unlikely to be protected against avalanche danger and it will not be patrolled at the end of the day; it is effectively like going into the backcountry in North America. US and Canadian resorts practically always have a boundary (often marked by a rope) and venturing beyond it is discouraged or forbidden. But within the boundaries there is often challenging terrain that is very much like being off-piste in Europe – with the important advantage that it is much safer, because it's patrolled and avalanche-controlled. This is a tremendous advantage of North America skiing for experts, who can have fun much more cheaply and safely than in the Alps. Some US resorts are adding areas that you have to hike to – or perhaps get a tow behind a snowcat part of the way. The reward is delightful isolation, untracked snow and security that you would not have in Europe.

European resorts are at last trying to match North American trail grooming. For years trail grooming wasn't really taken seriously by many Alpine resorts, and you were quite likely to find rock hard ridges on trails between the lines taken by grooming machines. Grooming is much better in many European resorts now – but few reach the normal North American standard and a much smaller proportion of trails is likely to be groomed each night.

The long liftlines that used to exist in many European resorts a few years ago have largely been eliminated by powerful new lifts. But in many cases little thought was given to the resulting overcrowding on the trails. North American trails seem blissfully quiet compared with many in Europe, where you sometimes have to look over your shoulder to make sure it's safe to make a turn.

Europe's liftlines come as a major culture shock for most North Americans – not because of their length but because of their disorganized, unruly nature. North American liftlines are highly disciplined, with people waiting patiently in several parallel lines, alternating with others; there are lift attendants organizing the line and making sure that all the spaces on the lift are filled by ushering people on from the special 'singles' lines. In Europe it's more of a free-for-all. Instead of several lanes guided by ropes leading to the lift, there's usually just one 'funnel', with the line starting 20 or 40 people wide and people shuffling forward trying to get to the front by elbowing, pushing and treading over other peoples' skis. You'll never hear a 'please go ahead' or an apology as you might in North America. Singles lines are rare – and where they do exist are nowhere near as well organized (partly because of communication difficulties – many people in the line don't speak the local language and can't understand the lift attendant's instructions).

Other service elements that don't exist in Europe include: mountain 'hosts' on hand to greet and help you, free guided tours of the trails, grooming maps, trail maps and boxes of tissues freely available at the bottom of most lifts. In general the lift attendants, ticket sellers and mountain employees are less likely to have a welcoming, enthusiastic attitude.

One area where we reckon Europe clearly beats North America is that the lifts are open longer. In North America it is common for lifts to shut as early as 3pm or 3.30pm, with the top lifts in some resorts closing at 2pm or even earlier. In Europe it is normal for the lifts to operate until 4.30pm (or maybe later from mid-February on). This early closing may explain why North Americans don't take lunch as seriously as many Europeans and why US and Canadian mountain restaurants tend to be huge self-service cafeterias serving fast food to allow people to refuel quickly and get back on the slopes. In Europe, there are places like that, but there are also many more atmospheric small huts, table-service restaurants and sunny terraces where lunch is to be lingered over along with a bottle of wine or a couple of beers.

Another European advantage is cost. At current exchange rates, lift tickets in Canada are typically 60 or 70 per cent more expensive than those in major resorts in the Alps, and tickets in the US are double the European price. We're comparing tickets for a week here – the comparison for day tickets is less dramatic, because in Europe weekly tickets offer bigger savings than those in North America.

THE SKI SCHOOLS

In North America, each resort has one ski school operated by the ski company that also operates the lifts and in some cases the whole resort. The schools are geared to the brief visits that North Americans typically make – so courses are short, people join and leave classes constantly, and there is no attempt to build any group spirit. In Europe, in contrast, most people join ski school classes for a full six-day week, and their whole vacation is likely to revolve around the class – they will spend time together as a group after skiing, and will expect to get to know their one instructor quite well during the week. American schools frequently disappoint European visitors because of this difference.

On the other hand, standards of instruction and particularly of communication in North American schools are generally higher, and much more consistent. In Europe, the management of schools is often very lax – the instructors are usually self-employed, and the whole culture is one in which supervision and management of performance is not encouraged. Standards of spoken English, in particular, may be poor.

Perhaps it's no surprise, in this context, that instruction in North America is appreciably more expensive than in Europe. And child-care is much more expensive

THE RESORTS

Resorts vary enormously in both Europe and North America. But in general in Austria and Switzerland they are based on old farming villages that have been there for centuries. Of course, they have expanded into resorts, but the old center is usually there, the expansion has been in the local style, with wooden chalet-style buildings, and they are still year-round communities run by local families who have lived there for generations. Many Austrian resorts have pretty floodlit onion-domed churches. Our favourite Swiss resorts include some beautiful traffic-free villages (such as Wengen, Mürren, Saas-Fee and Zermatt) set high-up on the mountain where they can be reached only by mountain railway.

French and Italian resorts are more varied. Especially in France, there are a lot of soulless purpose-built resorts (mainly consisting of apartment blocks) thrown up without much concern for the environment in the middle of the snowfields. But there are often traditional, more atmospheric villages lower down. And many resorts are based around such villages.

In North America, there are few old 'villages' but some delightful old towns (such as Aspen, Telluride, Jackson Hole and Stowe). Many resort villages have been purpose-built for skiing in a variety of styles. But some resorts have no real focus, having grown up to suit day visitors and weekenders who arrive and move around by car.

Just as the resorts vary, so does the après-ski. In general, Europeans take their après-ski more seriously than North Americans – and it is accompanied by much more alcohol. In Austria, in particular, you'll find lots of drinking and dancing going on from mid-afternoon (on the mountain) until 2am or 3am (in the lively bars and clubs) pretty much everywhere. In the other European countries the scene varies much more from resort to resort. In North America, again the scene varies but while bars tend to be lively as the slopes close, they tend to be quieter after dinner than they would be in Europe. Oh … and while smoking is banned from many public places in North America it is very common all over European resorts (including in restaurants and on the lifts).

Lodging tends to be much more spacious and luxurious in North America than in Europe. In particular, condos (condominiums – apartments that are individually owned but rented out through central agencies) are reliably large and comfortable. In France, in contrast, apartments tend to be tiny, and it is not unusual for a one-room studio to be sold on the basis that it sleeps four adults. Things are improving in Europe – in Les Arcs, for example, they are not only building much more spacious new apartments, but they are modifying existing buildings to join pairs of apartments together. But it is a slow business.

Every European resort has a tourist office that is the main channel of communication with the resort's potential visitors. Whatever you want to know about, you first of all ask the tourist office. Many operate some some sort of booking system or at least information system about available accommodations. In North America, the arrangements vary widely, depending on whether the resort is based on an existing town or has been created especially for skiing – in which case it will be under the same management as the lifts, and will operate a central accommodations booking service. Some resorts have a visitor bureau, but it rarely has the same central role as the European resort tourist office.

Because most Europeans visit the resorts of the Alps for a week, finding accommodations for a shorter period can be difficult. Apartments are almost always rented only by the week, but also many hotels will refuse shorter bookings at peak times, except at short notice when the management have to accept that they are not going to find a week-long booking. This is less true in resorts and valley towns with a big summer trade, where any booking in the winter is welcome – Chamonix is the prime example.

Get your
money back

Choosing your resort

get it right first time

Most people get to go skiing or boarding only once or twice a year – and then only for a few days at a time. So choosing the right resort is crucially important. This book is designed to help you get it right the first time. Here is some advice on how to use our information to best effect – particularly for the benefit of readers with relatively narrow experience of different resorts. Chamonix, Châtel and Courchevel are all French resorts, but they are as similar as chalk and Camembert.

Lots of factors need to be taken into account. The weight you attach to each of them depends on your own personal preferences, and on the make-up of the group you are going on vacation with.

Each resort chapter is organized in the same way, to help you choose the right resort. This short introduction takes you through the structure and what you will find under each heading we use.

YOUR KIND OF RESORT?

At the start of each chapter are four elements designed to give you a good idea of whether the resort is likely to suit *you,* and whether you should read our detailed analysis of it:

A one-line verdict – summing up the resort in a few words.

How it Rates – star-ratings of the resort from 11 points of view. (All these star-ratings are brought together in one comparative chart, which follows this chapter.)

Lists of good and bad points – key things to know about the resort and its slopes, picked out with ➊ and ➋ symbols.

A final summary – this is where we aim to weigh up the pros and cons, coming off the fence and giving our view of who might like it.

There's also a **What's new** section; this is likely to be of most use and interest in resorts you know from past experience.

We then look at each aspect in more detail.

THE RESORT

Resorts vary enormously in character and charm, especially in the Alps. At the extremes of the Alpine range are the handful of really hideous apartment-block French resorts thrown up hastily in the 1960s – Les Menuires, Plagne Centre and Flaine, for example – and the captivating old traffic-free mountain villages of which Switzerland has an unfair number. But some purpose-built places (such as Belle Plagne) can have a much friendlier feel than some long-established resorts with big, block-like buildings (eg Davos). Some places can be very sprawling (eg Kitzbühel) whereas others are surprisingly compact (eg Wengen). North America has managed to avoid the worst excesses of European resort building, but there is still the choice between purpose-built resorts (Vail, Whistler, Snowbird) and resorts based on existing towns (Aspen, Park City). You often have a choice: stay in the old town some distance from the slopes, or in modern accommodations built around the lift base – Steamboat, Crested Butte and Jackson are all examples.

In the Alps, the landscape can have an important impact –

whether the resort is at the bottom of a narrow, shady valley (eg Ischgl) or on a sunny shelf with panoramic views (eg Crans-Montana). Some places are working towns as well as ski resorts (eg Bormio, Jackson). Some are full of bars, discos and shops (eg St Anton, Whistler). Others are peaceful backwaters (eg Arabba, Smugglers' Notch). Traffic may fill the streets (eg Sölden, Jackson). Or the village may be traffic-free (eg Mürren).

THE MOUNTAINS

The slopes Some mountains and lift networks are vast and complex, while others are much smaller and lacking variety.

Snow reliability This varies enormously. Some resorts (including some very big names in the Alps) are notorious for treating their paying guests to ice, mud and slush. In the Alps in particular, whether a resort is likely to have decent snow on its slopes normally depends on the height, the direction most of the slopes face (north good, south bad), its snowfall record and the extent of its snowmaking. But bear in mind that in the Alps high resorts tend to have rocky terrain where the runs will need more snow than those on the pasture land of lower resorts. Bear in mind that snowmaking can operate only if temperatures are low enough (typically –2°C / 28°F or less), so it's much more useful in midwinter than in spring.

For experts, intermediates, beginners Most (though not all) resorts have something to offer **beginners**, but there are things to look out for. Will you have to buy a full price lift ticket? Will you have to walk a long way to the slopes each day, carrying the gear that experts seem to find so easily portable but beginners always struggle with? Are there easy longer runs to move on to if you graduate from the beginner slopes after a couple of days? Relatively few resorts will keep an **expert** happy for a week's holiday. We're sure experts can work out for themselves what they need to look for – but we would point out that for experts who don't want to go to the expense of hiring a guide to go off-trail ('off-piste' in eurospeak), there is much more fun to be had safely in North American resorts like Whistler and Aspen than in European ones like Val-d'Isère. As for **intermediates**, whether a resort will suit you really depends on your ability and appetite. Are you happy to ski the same few trails repeatedly, or do you want to cover a lot of ground? Do you want to be challenged by the slopes, or flattered?

For cross-country We don't pretend that this is a guide for avid cross-country skiers. But if you or one of your group wants to try it, our summary here will help you gauge whether the resort is worth considering or whether it is a waste of time.

Liftlines Another key factor. Most Alpine resorts have improved their lift systems enormously in the last 10 years, and monster liftlines are largely a thing of the past. Crowding on the trails is more of a worry in many Alpine resorts, and we mention problems of this kind here.

Mountain restaurants Here's a subject that generally divides people into two opposing camps. To some people (mostly Europeans), having decent lunches in civilized surroundings – either in the sun, contemplating amazing scenery, or in a cozy hut, sheltered from the elements – is a key part of the vacation. Others regard a prolonged mid-day stop as a waste of valuable skiing time, as well as money. We are firmly in the former camp. We get very disheartened by places with miserable restaurants and miserable food (many resorts in America); and there are some resorts that we go to partly because of the cozy huts and excellent cuisine (notably Zermatt).

Schools and guides This is an area where we rely heavily on readers' reports of their own or their friends' experiences. The only way to judge a ski school is by trying it. Reports on schools are always extremely valuable and frequently record disappointment, especially in Alpine resorts.

Facilities for children If you need nursery facilities, don't go to Italy. In other Alpine countries, facilities for looking after and teaching children can vary enormously between resorts. We say what is available in each resort. But, again, to be of real help we need reports from people who've used the facilities.

SNOWBOARDING

The Mountains section applies to both skiers and snowboarders. But because certain things are important to snowboarding that aren't relevant (or aren't as relevant) to skiing, we also include a special assessment for snowboarders. This covers issues such as whether the slopes present special attractions or problems (eg flat sections that snowboarders have to 'scoot' along), whether there is a good fun-park and half-pipe, how much you can expect to have to use surface-lifts and whether you'll find specialist snowboard schools and shops.

STAYING THERE

How to go The usual choice is between hotels and apartment/condo accommodations, although some resorts lack one or the other. (The catered chalet holiday remains a peculiarly British phenomenon, not dealt with in this edition.) Hotels, of course, can vary a lot but, especially in France and Switzerland, can work out very expensive. Apartments can be very economical but French ones, in particular, tend to be very small – it's not unusual for prices to be based on four people sleeping in a one-room studio, for example.

We list hotels that we can recommend, and we have given each a price rating from ① to ⑤ – the more coins, the more expensive.

Staying up the mountain / down the valley If there are interesting options for staying on the slopes above the resort village or in valley towns below it, we've picked them out.

Eating out The range of restaurants varies widely. Even some big resorts, such as Les Arcs, may have little choice because most of the clientele stay in their apartments or chalets. Others, such as Val-d'Isère, have a huge range, including national and regional cuisine, pizzas, fondues and international fare. American resorts generally have an excellent range of restaurants – most people eat out.

Après-ski Tastes and styles vary enormously. Most resorts have pleasant places in which to have an immediate post-skiing beer or hot chocolate. Some then go dead. Others have noisy bars and discos until dawn. We are largely dependent for this section on hearing from reporters who are keen après-skiers.

Off the slopes This is largely aimed at assessing how suitable a resort is for someone who doesn't intend to use the slopes – a non-skiing spouse or elderly relative or friend, for example. In some resorts, such as most French purpose-built places, there is really nothing to amuse them. In others, such Cortina or St Moritz, people walking, skating, curling or doing nothing outnumber people skiing or boarding. Excursion possibilities vary widely. And there are great variations in the practicality of meeting skiers and boarders for lunch up the mountain.

Resort ratings at a glance

The following six pages bring together the ratings we give each resort for 11 key characteristics. You'll find these ratings at the start of each resort chapter too. Use the tables here to compare resorts directly for the aspects that are most important to you. You'll be able to see at a glance which resorts come out top and bottom of the pile.

AUSTRIA – FRANCE

	Bad Gastein	Ellmau	Hintertux	Ischgl	Kitzbühel	Lech	Mayrhofen
Page	41	48	51	58	63	69	76
Snow	***	**	*****	****	**	****	***
Extent	****	****	**	****	****	****	***
Experts	***	*	***	***	***	****	*
Intermediates	****	****	***	****	****	****	***
Beginners	**	****	*	**	**	****	**
Convenience	**	***	**	***	**	***	*
Queues	***	****	***	***	**	***	*
Restaurants	****	**	**	**	****	**	****
Scenery	***	***	***	***	***	***	***
Resort charm	***	***	***	****	****	****	***
Off-slope	****	***	*	***	*****	***	****

	Obergurgl	Obertauern	Saalbach-Hinterglemm	Schladming	Sölden	Söll	St Anton
Page	81	86	88	94	98	100	107
Snow	*****	****	***	***	*****	**	****
Extent	**	**	***	***	***	****	****
Experts	**	***	**	**	***	*	*****
Intermediates	***	****	****	****	****	****	***
Beginners	****	*****	***	****	**	***	*
Convenience	****	****	****	***	***	**	***
Queues	*****	****	***	****	***	***	**
Restaurants	**	***	****	****	***	**	***
Scenery	***	***	***	***	***	***	***
Resort charm	****	**	****	****	**	***	****
Off-slope	**	**	**	****	**	**	***

	Zell am See		FRANCE Alpe-d'Huez	Les Arcs	Avoriaz	Chamonix
Page	114		122	130	135	139
Snow	**		****	****	***	****
Extent	**		****	***	*****	***
Experts	**		****	****	***	*****
Intermediates	***		****	****	****	**
Beginners	***		*****	****	****	*
Convenience	**		****	****	****	*
Queues	**		****	***	**	**
Restaurants	***		****	**	****	**
Scenery	***		****	***	***	*****
Resort charm	***		*	*	**	****
Off-slope	****		***	*	*	*****

FRANCE

	Châtel	La Clusaz	Courchevel	Les Deux-Alpes	Flaine	La Grave
Page	146	151	157	163	168	174
Snow	**	**	****	****	****	***
Extent	*****	***	*****	***	****	**
Experts	***	***	****	****	****	*****
Intermediates	****	****	*****	**	*****	*
Beginners	**	****	*****	***	*****	*
Convenience	**	***	****	***	*****	***
Queues	***	***	****	**	****	****
Restaurants	***	****	****	**	**	**
Scenery	***	****	***	****	****	****
Resort charm	***	****	**	**	*	***
Off-slope	**	***	***	**	*	*

	Megève	Les Menuires	Méribel	Morzine	La Plagne	Serre-Chevalier
Page	176	182	185	192	198	207
Snow	**	****	****	**	****	****
Extent	*****	*****	*****	*****	****	****
Experts	**	****	****	***	***	***
Intermediates	****	*****	*****	****	*****	****
Beginners	***	***	***	***	*****	****
Convenience	**	*****	***	**	*****	***
Queues	****	****	****	***	**	***
Restaurants	*****	***	****	***	**	***
Scenery	***	***	***	***	****	****
Resort charm	****	*	***	***	*	***
Off-slope	****	*	***	***	*	**

	Ste-Foy	St-Martin-de-Belleville	La Tania	Tignes	Val-d'Isère	Val-Thorens
Page	213	215	217	219	227	235
Snow	***	***	***	*****	*****	*****
Extent	*	*****	*****	*****	*****	*****
Experts	****	****	****	*****	*****	****
Intermediates	***	*****	*****	*****	*****	*****
Beginners	**	***	**	**	***	****
Convenience	***	***	****	****	***	*****
Queues	*****	****	****	****	****	***
Restaurants	*	****	****	**	**	****
Scenery	***	***	***	***	***	***
Resort charm	***	****	***	**	***	**
Off-slope	*	*	*	*	**	**

ITALY

	Bormio	Cervinia	Cortina d'Ampezzo	Courmayeur	Livigno	Monterosa Ski
Page	243	245	250	255	260	264
Snow	***	*****	***	****	****	***
Extent	**	***	***	**	**	****
Experts	*	*	**	***	**	***
Intermediates	***	****	***	****	***	****
Beginners	**	*****	*****	**	****	**
Convenience	***	***	*	*	**	****
Queues	***	***	***	****	****	****
Restaurants	****	***	****	****	***	**
Scenery	***	****	*****	****	***	****
Resort charm	****	**	****	****	***	***
Off-slope	****	*	*****	***	**	*

	Sauze d'Oulx	Selva	Sestriere
Page	267	272	280
Snow	**	****	***
Extent	*****	*****	****
Experts	**	***	***
Intermediates	****	*****	****
Beginners	**	****	***
Convenience	**	***	****
Queues	***	***	***
Restaurants	***	****	**
Scenery	***	*****	***
Resort charm	**	***	*
Off-slope	*	***	*

	Champéry	Crans-Montana	Davos	Flims	Grindelwald	Gstaad	Mürren
Page	286	288	293	300	305	309	311
Snow	**	**	****	***	**	*	***
Extent	*****	***	*****	****	***	****	*
Experts	***	**	****	***	**	**	***
Intermediates	****	****	*****	*****	*****	***	***
Beginners	**	***	**	****	***	***	**
Convenience	*	**	**	***	**	*	***
Queues	****	***	**	***	**	***	***
Restaurants	***	***	***	***	***	***	**
Scenery	****	****	****	***	*****	***	*****
Resort charm	****	**	**	***	****	****	*****
Off-slope	***	****	*****	***	****	****	***

	Saas-Fee	St Moritz	Verbier	Villars	Wengen	Zermatt
Page	315	320	326	334	336	341
Snow	*****	****	***	**	**	****
Extent	**	*****	*****	**	***	****
Experts	***	****	*****	**	**	*****
Intermediates	****	****	***	***	****	****
Beginners	*****	**	**	****	***	*
Convenience	***	**	**	***	***	*
Queues	***	**	***	***	***	***
Restaurants	***	****	***	***	****	*****
Scenery	****	****	****	***	*****	*****
Resort charm	*****	*	***	****	*****	*****
Off-slope	****	*****	***	****	****	****

	CALIFORNIA		COLORADO			Copper
	Heavenly	Mammoth	Aspen	Beaver Creek	Breckenridge	Mountain
Page	350	357	362	369	371	376
Snow	****	****	*****	*****	*****	*****
Extent	***	***	****	***	**	**
Experts	***	****	*****	****	****	****
Intermediates	****	****	*****	****	****	****
Beginners	****	****	*****	*****	****	****
Convenience	*	**	**	****	***	****
Queues	****	****	****	*****	****	****
Restaurants	*	*	****	**	**	*
Scenery	****	***	***	***	***	***
Resort charm	*	**	****	***	***	**
Off-slope	**	*	****	***	***	*

Ratings at a glance

UNITED STATES continued

COLORADO continued

	Crested Butte	Keystone	Steamboat	Telluride	Vail	Winter Park
Page	378	380	385	390	392	398
Snow	****	*****	****	****	*****	*****
Extent	**	**	***	**	****	***
Experts	****	***	***	****	****	****
Intermediates	***	****	****	***	*****	****
Beginners	****	****	*****	*****	*****	*****
Convenience	***	**	***	****	***	***
Queues	*****	****	****	*****	**	****
Restaurants	*	***	***	*	**	***
Scenery	***	***	***	****	***	***
Resort charm	****	**	**	****	***	**
Off-slope	**	**	**	**	***	*

UTAH

	Alta	The Canyons	Deer Valley	Park City	Snowbasin	Snowbird
Page	405	407	409	411	416	418
Snow	*****	****	****	****	*****	*****
Extent	***	***	**	***	***	***
Experts	*****	***	***	****	****	*****
Intermediates	***	***	****	****	****	***
Beginners	***	***	****	****	**	**
Convenience	****	****	****	***	*	*****
Queues	***	****	****	****	*****	**
Restaurants	**	***	****	**	*	*
Scenery	****	***	***	***	****	***
Resort charm	**	**	***	***	**	*
Off-slope	*	**	**	***	*	*

REST OF THE WEST / NEW ENGLAND

	Big Sky	Jackson	Sun Valley	Killington	Smugglers'	Stowe	Sunday River
Page	422	424	429	434	438	440	442
Snow	****	****	***	***	***	***	***
Extent	***	***	***	**	*	*	**
Experts	*****	*****	***	***	***	***	**
Intermediates	****	**	****	***	***	****	****
Beginners	****	***	***	****	****	****	****
Convenience	****	***	**	*	*****	*	***
Queues	*****	***	****	****	****	****	****
Restaurants	*	*	****	*	*	**	***
Scenery	***	***	***	***	***	***	***
Resort charm	**	****	***	**	**	****	**
Off-slope	**	***	***	*	*	*	*

CANADA – AND THE REST

WESTERN CANADA

	Banff	Big White	Fernie	Jasper	Kicking Horse	Lake Louise	Panorama
Page	447	453	455	459	461	463	468
Snow	****	****	****	****	****	****	***
Extent	****	***	***	*	***	****	**
Experts	****	*****	*****	**	****	****	****
Intermediates	****	****	**	**	***	****	***
Beginners	***	****	****	****	***	***	****
Convenience	*	****	****	*	*	*	****
Queues	****	*****	****	****	*****	****	****
Restaurants	***	*	*	**	**	**	*
Scenery	****	***	****	***	***	*****	***
Resort charm	***	**	**	***	*	***	**
Off-slope	*****	**	**	***	*	****	*

EASTERN CANADA / ANDORRA / SPAIN

	EASTERN CANADA		ANDORRA			SPAIN
	Whistler	Tremblant	Arinsal	Pas de la Casa	Soldeu	Baqueira
Page	470	478	484	486	488	493
Snow	****	****	***	***	***	***
Extent	****	**	*	***	**	***
Experts	*****	***	*	*	*	***
Intermediates	*****	***	**	***	***	****
Beginners	****	****	***	****	****	**
Convenience	****	****	***	****	***	***
Queues	***	***	***	***	***	***
Restaurants	**	**	**	***	*	**
Scenery	***	***	***	**	***	***
Resort charm	***	****	*	*	*	**
Off-slope	**	***	*	*	*	*

NORWAY / SWEDEN / NEW ZEALAND

	NORWAY	SWEDEN	NEW ZEALAND
	Hemsedal	Åre	Queenstown
Page	503	506	513
Snow	****	***	**
Extent	*	**	*
Experts	**	**	***
Intermediates	****	****	***
Beginners	***	****	***
Convenience	**	***	*
Queues	****	****	***
Restaurants	*	***	*
Scenery	**	***	****
Resort charm	**	***	**
Off-slope	*	***	*****

Resort chapters explained

FINDING A RESORT

The bulk of the book consists of chapters devoted to individual major resorts, some also covering minor resorts that share the same lift system. These chapters are ordered alphabetically and grouped by country – first, the four major Alpine countries in alphabetical order; then the US and Canada (where resorts are grouped by states or regions); then minor European countries; then Australasia.

There's a **chapter-by-chapter listing** in the detailed Contents at the start of the book.

Short cuts to the resorts that might suit you are provided by a table of comparative **star-ratings**, immediately preceding this page.

At the back of the book is an **index** to the resort chapters, combined with a **directory** giving basic information on hundreds of other minor resorts. Where the resort you are looking up is a minor resort covered in a chapter devoted mainly to a bigger resort, the page reference will take you to the start of that chapter, not to the page on which the minor resort is described.

There's further guidance on using our information in the chapter on Choosing your resort – designed to be helpful particularly to people with narrow experience of resorts, who may not appreciate how big the differences can be.

READING A CHAPTER

The **star-ratings** at the start of each chapter summarise our view of the resort in 11 respects, including how well it suits different standards of skier/boarder. The more stars, the better.

We give phone and fax numbers and internet addresses of the **tourist office** (and we now give phone numbers for recommended hotels, too).

Our **mountain maps** show the resorts' own classification of runs. Those for the US and Canada show green, blue and black runs; those for most of Europe show blue, red and black; those for France and one or two other places show green, blue, red and black. On many maps of resorts in North America we also follow the usual convention of using black diamonds to indicate open expert terrain where the runs are not precisely defined. We do not distinguish single-diamond terrain from the steeper double-diamond terrain.

We show all the lifts on the mountain, including any definitely planned for construction for the coming season. We use the following symbols to identify **fast or high-capacity lifts**:

Ⓥ fast chair-lift

ⓑ gondola

Ⓦ tram (cable-car)

Ⓧ funicular railroad

Austria is a completely different vacation experience from the other Alpine countries. If you have never been there you will notice a huge difference – many people who discover it fall in love with it and never want to go anywhere else. One essential ingredient is that the partying is as important as the skiing or riding in most Austrian resorts – après-ski starts early and finishes late. The other essential ingredient is the nature of the villages. There are none of the monstrous purpose-built block resorts of France and a few big resorts such as St Anton. But essentially Austria is the land of cute little villages clustered around onion-domed churches; of friendly wooded mountains, reassuring to beginners and timid intermediates in a way that bleak snowfields and craggy peaks will never be; of friendly people who don't find it demeaning to speak their guests' language; and of jolly beer-fuelled après-ski action, starting in many resorts in mid-afternoon with dancing in on-mountain restaurants and going on as long as you have the legs for it. And Austrian resorts have (rather belatedly) made great strides in their attempt to catch up on the snowmaking front – most have radically increased their snowmaking capacity in recent years. In midwinter, especially, lack of snow generally goes hand in hand with low night-time temperatures, even at low altitudes, and snowmaking comes into its own.

It's the après-ski that strikes most first-time visitors as being Austria's unique selling point. The few French resorts that have lively après-ski are dominated by British or Scandinavian holidaymakers (and resort workers and ski-bums). The French are noticeable by their absence and you could be in London or Stockholm rather than France.

But Austrian après-ski remains very Austrian. Huge quantities of beer and schnapps are drunk, German is the predominant language and German drinking songs are common. So is incredibly loud Europop music. People pack into mountain restaurants at the end of the day and dance in their ski boots on the dance floor, on the tables, on the bar, on the roof beams, wherever there's room. There are open-air ice bars on the mountain, umbrella bars and countless transparent 'igloos' in which to shelter from bad weather. In many

37

ISCHGL TOURIST OFFICE

One of the Austrian resorts that has it all – nightlife, charm and good snowy slopes ↓

resorts the bands don't stop playing or the DJs working until darkness falls, when the happy skiers slide off down the mountain in the dark to find another watering hole in town. After dinner the drinking and dancing starts again – for those who take time out for dinner, that is.

Of course, not all Austrian resorts conform to this image. But lots of big name ones with the best and most extensive slopes do. St Anton, Saalbach-Hinterglemm, Ischgl and Zell am See for example, fit this bill.

One thing that all Austrian resorts have in common is reliably comfortable accommodation – whether it's in four-star hotels with pools, saunas and spas, or in great-value family-run guest houses, of which Austria has thousands. The accommodations are very much

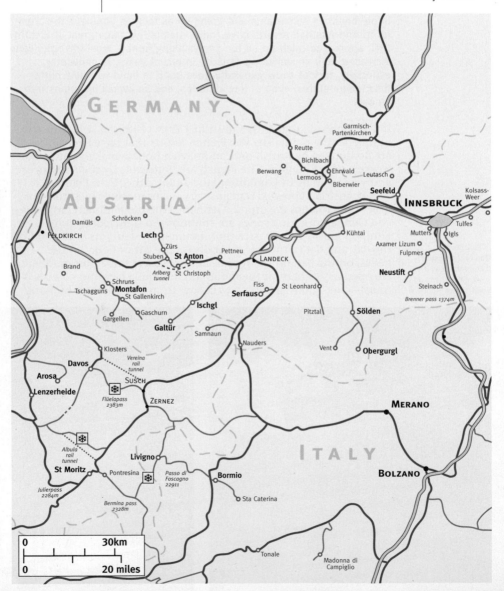

dominated by hotels and guest houses; apartments and condos are in general much less widely available .

Most Austrian resorts are real, friendly villages on valley floors, with skiing and boarding on the wooded slopes above them. They have expanded enormously since the Second World War, but practically all the development has been in traditional chalet style, and the villages generally look good even without the snow that is the saving grace of many French and even some Swiss resorts. Indeed, many Tirolean resorts are as busy in August as in February.

Outside the big-name resorts the skiing is often quite limited. There are many Austrian resorts that an avid skier could explore fully in half a day. Those who have tried the bigger areas of France and developed a taste for them may find the list of acceptable Austrian

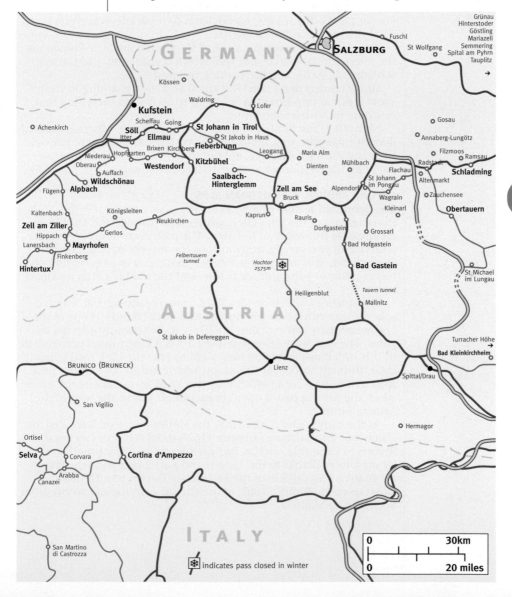

indicates pass closed in winter

resorts quite a short one.

Unfortunately, several of the resorts on that shortlist bring you up against another problem – low altitude, and therefore poor snow conditions. Kitzbühel is at 760m/2,500ft and Söll at 700m/2,300ft, for example. The top heights of Austrian resorts are relatively low, too – typically 1800m/5,900ft to 2000m/6,500ft; as we have noted above, snowmaking is becoming more widespread, but it works only when the conditions are right.

The resorts of the Arlberg area, at the western end of the Tirol – St Anton, Lech and Zürs – stand apart from these concerns, with excellent snow records and extensive skiing. And there are other resorts where you can be reasonably confident of good snow, such as Obergurgl, Obertauern and Ischgl, not to mention the year-round slopes on glaciers such as those at Hintertux, Neustift and Kaprun. But for most other resorts our advice is to book late, when you know what the snow conditions are like.

There are some extensive areas of slopes that are little-known on the international market and well worth considering. Bad Gastein, Schladming, Ischgl and Lech spring to mind.

Snowboarders don't need big areas; and snowboarding in slushy snow is not as unpleasant as skiing in it. So it's not surprising that boarding in Austria is booming.

Nightlife is not limited to drinking and dancing – there are lots of floodlit toboggan runs, for example. And not all resorts are raucous. Lech and Zürs, for example, are full of rich, cool, beautiful people enjoying the comfort of 4-star sophisticated hotels.

GETTING AROUND THE AUSTRIAN ALPS

The dominant feature of Austria for the skier with a car is the thoroughfare of the Inn valley, which runs through the Tirol from Landeck via Innsbruck to Kufstein. The motorway along it extends, with one or two breaks, westwards to the Arlberg pass and on to Switzerland. This artery is relatively reliable except in exceptionally bad conditions – the altitude is low, and the road is a vital transport link.

The Arlberg – which divides Tirol from Vorarlberg, but which is also the watershed between Austria and Switzerland – is one of the few areas where driving plans are likely to be seriously affected by snow. The east–west Arlberg pass itself has a long tunnel underneath it; this isn't cheap, and you may want to take the high road when it's clear, through Stuben, St Christoph and St Anton. The Flexen pass road to Zürs and Lech (which may be closed by avalanche risk even when the Arlberg pass is open) branches off just to the west of the Arlberg summit.

At the eastern end of the Tirol, the Gerlos pass road from Zell am Ziller over into Salzburg province (1628m/5,341ft) can be closed. Resorts in Carinthia, such as Bad Kleinkirchheim, are usually reached by motorway thanks to the Tauern and Katschberg tunnels. The alternative is to drive over the Radstädter Tauern pass through Obertauern (1740m/5,710ft), or use the car-carrying rail service from Böckstein to Mallnitz.

Bad Gastein

Spa-town resort with extensive slopes

HOW IT RATES

The slopes
Snow	★★★
Extent	★★★★
Experts	★★★
Intermediates	★★★★
Beginners	★★
Convenience	★★
Liftlines	★★★
Restaurants	★★★★

The rest
Scenery	★★★
Resort charm	★★★
Off-slope	★★★★

What's new

For 2000/01 the old chair-lift from the Graukogel base up to the mid-mountain station was replaced by a faster double chair-lift with a moving carpet loading system.

2001/02 will see the replacement of both of Schlossalm's Weitmoser parallel T-bars by a new six-pack.

For 2001/02, the old Gastein lift ticket has been replaced by the new Ski Alliance Amadé joint lift ticket – see separate box on lift tickets.

⊕ Four separate, varied areas with a huge number of slopes both above and below the tree line

⊕ Great for confident intermediates, with lots of long, challenging reds – and great cruising and carving in the Schlossalm sector

⊕ More reliable snow than in most low-altitude Austrian resorts, with high Sportgastein area as back-up

⊕ Lots of good, atmospheric, traditional mountain restaurants

⊕ Plenty of off-slope facilities, many related to its origins as a spa resort

⊕ New Ski Alliance Amadé lift ticket covers wide range of nearby resorts

⊖ Unless you have a car, you need to choose your location with care or budget for a lot of expensive cab rides – the lift bases are widely spread and using the public transport can be time-consuming and frustrating

⊖ Spa-town atmosphere is not to everyone's taste, and downtown Bad Gastein can suffer from local traffic on the narrow streets; more spacious Bad Hofgastein is a better base for many people

⊖ Near-beginners and timid intermediates must be wary of leaving the Schlossalm sector

The Gastein valley isn't widely known internationally. It deserves better: it's a great resort for competent intermediates who are happy on genuine red runs, and the list of drawbacks we've identified above is short.

With its grand hotels, trinket shops and cramped, steep setting, central Bad Gastein itself is a far cry from your standard chalet-style Austrian village. You might prefer it. If not, staying out of the center near the lifts offers a more normal winter-sports holiday experience, and both Bad Hofgastein and Dorfgastein, down the valley, are equally well worth considering as a base.

To make the most of the valley, you need a car. With five spread-out mountains, of which only two are linked, the valley needs a first class public transport system, and it doesn't have one – traveling from one end of the valley to the other can take over an hour and may involve a couple of changes.

BAD GASTEIN TO

Many of the slopes are above the tree-line – though there is a healthy amount of vertical below it →

MOUNTAIN FACTS

Figures relate to the Gastein valley and Grossarl areas only

Altitude	840m-2685m
	2,760ft-8,810ft
Lifts	51
Trails	200km/
	124 miles
Blue	24%
Red	66%
Black	10%
Snowmaking	60km
	37 miles
Recco detectors used

LIFT TICKETS

2001/02 prices in euros

Ski Alliance Amadé Ski ticket

The new joint lift ticket covers over 275 lifts in more than 30 ski resorts in this part of Austria: the Gastein valley and Grossarl; Salzburger Sportwelt (main areas: Flachau/ Wagrain/ St Johann and Zauchensee/ Kleinarl); Hochkönigs Winterreich (Maria Alm and neighbors). Buses, trains and road tolls between the resorts are covered by the ticket.

Main ticket

1-day ticket 32 (low season 29) 6-day ticket 150 (low-season 140)

Children

Under 15: 6-day ticket 75 (low season 70) 15–19: 6-day ticket 140 Under 6: free ticket

Notes Morning and afternoon tickets are also available (as are tickets from 11am, 1pm and 2pm on). 1½-day and 2½-day tickets are also possible.

The resort

Bad Gastein sits near the head of eastern Austria's Gastein valley. It is an old spa that had its heyday many years ago; it has now spread widely, but still has a compact core. Here, a bizarre combination of buildings (upscale, modern, hotel-shopping-casino complex; baroque town hall; concrete multi-story parking lot) are laid out in a cramped horseshoe, set in what is virtually a gorge, complete with waterfall crashing beneath the main street. It mainly attracts a quite formal German/Austrian clientele. The main road and railroad bypass the center – though it can still get choked with local traffic.

Up the hill above the center of the town, beside the railroad, is a modern suburb with more of a ski-resort feel. For easy access to the slopes, this is the place to be – a gondola gives direct access to Stubnerkogel. On the other side of the town is a second mountain, Graukogel, accessed by a chair-lift starting a bus-ride from the center.

A few miles down the valley is Bad Hofgastein – also a spa, but a more modern and less stuffy-feeling village in an open setting on the wide valley floor. The slopes of Schlossalm – linked to Stubnerkogel via the intervening valley of Angertal – are accessed by a funicular from the outskirts of Bad Hofgastein. But you need a bus to get to it from the wrong side of the sprawling resort.

Dorfgastein is a more relaxed and rustic village a little further down the valley. Dorfgastein has its own extensive slopes, accessed by chair-lifts starting well outside the village, linked with the slopes of Grossarl in the next valley to the east.

Sportgastein is a separate sector, at the head of the Gastein valley, with little in the way of resort development.

Buses and trains covered by the lift ticket run between the villages and lift stations. There is a confusing range of bus services running at least hourly throughout the day, half-hourly on some routes at peak times; this sounds inadequate, and reporters confirm that it is. A car is most definitely an asset if you want to get around easily.

The new Ski Alliance Amadé lift ticket covers over 30 resorts in five

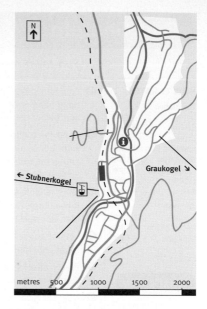

areas in eastern Austria – see margin. The linked resorts of Alpendorf, Wagrain and Flachau are easily reached by a regular train service to St Johann im Pongau, near Alpendorf. From there it's a short hop to the parallel linked area of Kleinarl, Flachauwinkl and Zauchensee. Further afield but worth a visit is Schladming (also linked by rail but involving at least one change). Drivers can also visit Maria Alm, to the north of the Gastein valley.

Also worth visiting but not included on the lift ticket are Zell am See (easily reached by rail) and snow-sure Obertauern and Kaprun.

The mountains

Most of the runs are on the open slopes above the tree line, though there are runs to the lift stations at valley level. The terrain is generally quite challenging without being at all extreme – only on Schlossalm is there an extensive area of genuinely easy slopes.

THE SLOPES
Extensive but fragmented

Most people based in Bad Gastein or Bad Hofgastein naturally spend most of their time on the extensive slopes of the main mountains, Stubnerkogel and Schlossalm.

Stubnerkogel is the more challenging mountain, with blue runs forced to take roundabout routes.

There are runs in all directions from the peak giving about 500m/1,600ft vertical on the open slopes above the tree line and rather more in the woods below it.

Schlossalm is better suited to timid skiers, with surface lifts and chair-lifts serving a wide area of gentle runs above mid-mountain. But the top lifts lead to some challenging terrain, and the Kleine Scharte tram takes you up a serious 750m/2,460ft vertical. The runs from Schlossalm down into Angertal are south-facing and low, but well covered by snowmaking, and there is always the option of riding down in the new gondola that serves this mountainside.

The separate and much smaller **Graukogel** is a steep, straightforward mountain. With trails running through the forest, the area is a great asset in bad weather and quiet at other times.

The higher, more exposed slopes of **Sportgastein**, 9km/6 miles south of Bad Gastein, have the best snow in the area and are served by an eight-person two-stage gondola; the descent totals an impressive 1065m/3,500ft, but there are few trails – basically, variants on the long run back down to the main lift.

Down the valley, the extensive slopes of **Dorfgastein** and **Grossarl**, linked via Kreuzkogel, offer a good choice of runs arranged in three tiers –

though there is no easy run to the valley. This area is unjustly neglected by those staying further up the valley.

SNOW RELIABILITY
Good for a low-altitude resort
Although the area is of typically Austrian low altitude, this part of the Alps has a relatively good snow record and there is a battery of snowmaking guns in crucial sections. There are a lot of lifts and runs above mid-station height, and the higher sector of Sportgastein is an important fallback.

FOR EXPERTS
More fast cruises than challenge
There are few black runs but there are long, challenging reds with steepish terrain for fast cruising or bump-bashing, depending on the conditions.

Graukogel has the World Cup slopes, and provides some challenge on its upper slopes. The other main sectors have plenty of opportunities to go off-trail, with or without hiking.

Sportgastein is worth the trip – there are off-trail possibilities on the front of the mountain, and a long off-trail run off the back drops around 1500m/4,900ft from Kreuzkogel to Heilstollen in the valley (on the bus route). Remember to check the bus times carefully or a long wait (or walk) could await you at the bottom. On the sunny opposite shoulder a reader

boarding

The Gastein valley is starting to embrace boarding, at least on the slopes. There's a snowboard park with a half-pipe at Haitzingalm on Schlossalm, and the valley plays host to lots of specialist snowboard events. The area is not ideal for beginners – there are few easy slopes and there's still a fairly high proportion of surface lifts (unavoidable when making the link between Bad Hofgastein and Bad Gastein, and between Dorfgastein and Grossarl). There's a fair bit to do in the evenings, but it's not as lively and as boarder-friendly as a lot of other Austrian resorts.

reports 'enormous' fields of corn snow in spring.

Dorfgastein has the least demanding slopes in the area, but there is a fine black run from mid-mountain to the village.

FOR INTERMEDIATES
Not for leisurely cruisers

Good intermediates will love all the areas on the lift ticket – more than enough to keep you happy for a week. A particular delight is the beautiful 8km/5 mile red run, well away from the lifts, from Höhe Scharte down to Bad Hofgastein. The open north-facing slopes of Stubnerkogel down into Angertal are good, for both interest and snow-cover – try the red down to Hartlgut at the end of the day and a train-ride home after a few beers. The same is true of the Graukogel runs.

For early intermediates, the area as a whole is uncomfortably challenging. But Grossarl (linked to Dorfgastein) and Schlossalm are less demanding than other sectors, and the open bowl around the main cluster of restaurants at Schlossalm is splendid cruising (and carving) territory.

FOR BEGINNERS
Unsuitable slopes

Beginner areas are scattered around the valley, but none combines convenience with reassuringly gentle gradients. The transition to longer runs is not an easy one, either.

FOR CROSS-COUNTRY
Extensive, but low and scattered

There are an impressive 90km/56miles of trails, but all are along the valley floor, making only the small loop at Sportgastein reasonably reliable for snow. Another drawback is the scattered nature of the loops. Bad Hofgastein is by far the best base for cross-country skiing, with long trails stretching almost to Bad Gastein.

LIFTLINES
Buses can be a problem

There are few problems outside the peak season in late February. The powerful gondola at Sportgastein has eliminated the liftlines that used to arise when conditions were poor elsewhere. Morning lines to get out of the valley and for the Bad Hofgastein mid-station tram are the worst. Peak period lines for the valley buses may be the biggest problem.

MOUNTAIN RESTAURANTS
One of the pleasures of this area

Numerous atmospheric, traditional huts are scattered around. Good value and good food are the norm. Bad Gastein's places are more expensive than the others. The Jungerstube has been recommended for its 'atmosphere and traditional food'.

Bad Hofgastein's smart Kleine Scharte at Schlossalm has a large terrace, plus yodelling! Lively places include Aeroplanstadl on the 8km/5 miles Höhe Scharte run, Hamburger Skiheim again at Schlossalm (with 'barbecue in the snow') and the Panoramastube in Dorfgastein. The Wengeralm, also above Dorf, is a cozy, upscale refuge with a good terrace. We've had good reports of the restaurants at Sportgastein.

SCHOOLS AND GUIDES
English widely spoken

The two schools have good reputations (for their English as well as the lessons). But we lack recent reports.

FACILITIES FOR CHILDREN
Reasonable

With its fragmented areas and rather serious slopes, Bad Gastein hardly seems an ideal resort for small children, but there are facilities for all-day care, of which the ski kindergarten at the Grüner Baum sounds the most inviting. There's a new 'Fun Center' with a variety of activities for kids at the top of the Stubnerkogel gondola.

SCHOOLS/GUIDES

2000/01 prices in euros

Bad Gastein
Manager Werner Pflaum
Classes 6 days
5hr: 10am-3pm, 1hr lunch; 3hr: 1pm-4pm
6 full days: 123
Private lessons
55 min
36 for 55 min; each additional person 9

Luigi
Manager Luigi Kravanja
Classes 6 days
5hr: 10am-3pm with 1hr lunch
6 full days: 113
Children's classes
Adults with children full-day: 36
3 full-days: 98
Private lessons
1hr or full-day
33 for 1hr; each additional person 18

CHILDCARE

Both ski schools run ski kindergartens.

There is a kindergarten at the Grüner Baum hotel, taking children aged 3 to 8, from 9.30 to 4pm. Skiing is available, with a special lift.

↑ Grand hotel and spa buildings in the center, chalets on the outskirts

Staying there

HOW TO GO

Hotels This is an upscale spa resort, and it has lots of smart hotels with good spa facilities – there are almost as many 4-star places as 3-star ones.

((((5) **Elisabethpark** (2551-0) Popular luxury hotel for those looking for excellent facilities, style, comfort and formality. Poorly placed for the slopes, but does run a courtesy bus.

((((4) **Salzburger Hof** (2037-0) 4-star with excellent spa facilities, a longish walk from the village gondola.

((((4) **Wildbad** (6434 3761) Luxurious 4-star within reasonable walking distance of the main lift.

((((4) **Schillerhof** (2581) Reliable 3-star in good position, opposite Graukogel lift.

((((4) **Grüner Baum** (2516-0) Splendidly secluded Relais & Châteaux place, tucked away in the Kötschachtal.

((((3) **Mozart** (2686-0) Well placed for buses. Good, filling food.

((((3) **Alpenblick** (2062-0) Good value, informal 3-star; well placed for the slopes.

Apartments/condos Plenty of apartments are available for rent but you have to book them directly.

EATING OUT
Something for most tastes

There is a fair range of restaurants, including surprisingly fine Chinese and seafood places. The Bellevue Alm, a short way up Stubnerkogel, is one of the liveliest places to eat at (it's a half-hour walk from the center of Bad Gastein or you can take the private chair-lift up) – there's a weekly folklore evening with traditional food and dancing. The à la carte menus at the 3-star hotels Nussdorferhof and Mozart are good value. The Medeterran in the town center has also been recommended.

Bad Gastein phone numbers

From elsewhere in Austria add the prefix 06434.

From abroad use the prefix +43 6434.

GETTING THERE

Air Salzburg, transfer 2hr. Linz or Munich, transfer 3½hr.

Rail Mainline station in resort.

ACTIVITIES

Indoor Fitness center (swimming, sauna, gym), thermal baths, squash, tennis, bowling, indoor golf, darts, casino, museum, theater, concerts

Outdoor Natural ice rinks (skating and curling), sleigh rides, horse-riding, ice-climbing, toboggan runs, snow bikes, 35km/ 22 miles cleared paths

TOURIST OFFICE

Postcode A-5640
t +43 (6434) 25310
f 253137
info@gastein.com
www.gastein.com

APRES-SKI
Varied, but no oom-pah-pah

There are elegant tea rooms, sophisticated dances, numerous bars, discos and casinos, but the general ambience is rather subdued. This part of Austria has not imported the informal Tirolean-style 'oom-pah-pah' jollity. There is tea-dancing at the Bellevue Alm though. The Elisabethpark, Salzburger Hof, Weismayr, Eden and Lindenhof bars are all pleasant for a quiet drink. The Hexenhaüsl is a more informal little wooden schnapps bar.

Haeggblom's has live music, gets full of young Swedes and is 'brilliant', says a reporter. The Bunny Bar is more sophisticated than its name suggests.

The Gatz and High Life are the main clubs. The casino gives you a generous amount of free chips, so those with will power and/or luck can have a surprisingly inexpensive couple of hours there. Organized bowling and casino trips are also available.

OFF THE SLOPES
Great variety of things to do

Provided you don't mind the style of the place, Bad Gastein has a lot to offer off the slopes, whether you're active or not. The spas are supposed to have a regenerative effect thanks to the high radon content. The Gastein Healing Gallery is a highlight – a train takes you down into an old gold-digging tunnel where you can lie on benches inhaling radon in steam-room-like heat and humidity for a couple of hours. We find all this a bit strange: radon is a radioactive, carcinogenic gas. The Rock Pool is a large indoor pool hewn out of the rock, heated naturally by hot springs.

Meeting up the mountain is no problem for pedestrians, though getting to the best mountain restaurants isn't easy.

There are organized coach trips to Kitzbühel, Salzburg and Goldegg Castle, and trains run to the resorts of Zell am See and St Johann im Pongau.

Bad Hofgastein
860m/2,820ft

Bad Hofgastein is a sizeable, quiet, old spa village set spaciously in a broad section of the valley. It has an impressive Gothic church, traditional-style buildings, elegant quiet hotels, narrow alleys and a babbling brook. Everything is kept in pristine order.

THE RESORT

Although rather sprawling, the village has a pleasant pedestrianized area which acts as a central focus. Because of the spa 'cures' there's a relatively high number of people just messing around during the day, notably at the curling rinks in Kurpark. The place looks very pretty in the evenings, under the soft glow of its lamps. The large spa building, the Kurzentrum, is rather a blot on the landscape.

The best location to stay is in the pedestrian zone, which is relatively handy for most things including the slopes. A high proportion of hotels are a long walk from the lift station – but there is a shuttle-bus.

THE MOUNTAINS

The Schlossalm sector above Bad Hofgastein is linked to the Stubnerkogel area via the Angertal valley, forming the largest body of slopes in the valley.

The slopes Bad Hofgastein's main access lift is a short funicular that takes you up to a mid-station at Kitzstein, above which most of the slopes are found. Here, you have a choice between a tram or two-stage chair up to Schlossalm.

Snowboarding The blue runs between Schlossalm and Angertal form the largest network of beginner runs in the area, however you need to negotiate a few surface lifts to ride them all.

Snow reliability Snowmaking is fairly extensive up to 2050m/6,730ft. But the low altitude of the town means that snow-cover down to the bottom is unreliable.

Experts There are no real challenges on the local trails but there is ample opportunity to go off-trail.

Intermediates Good intermediates will enjoy the local slopes, especially the long red run from Hohe Scharte back down to town.

Beginners From Bad Hofgastein, you have to catch a bus to the limited beginner area over at Angertal.

Cross-country Bad Hofgastein makes a fine base for cross-country when its lengthy valley-floor trails have snow.

Liftlines Both the funicular and the much lower capacity tram above it can generate big lines (30 minutes in the rush hour during peak season is not unusual). At such times, the chair is an obvious alternative to the tram and there's closed-circuit TV at the funicular base station which shows you the situation up at the tram.

Mountain restaurants The Schlossalm area boasts some of the best mountain huts in the valley (see earlier section).

Schools and guides We have received complimentary reports of the ski schools in the past, but haven't heard from recent visitors.

Facilities for children The Angertal school runs the village ski kindergarten, which can be very inconvenient for parents. Lack of many English-speaking children to play with may be another drawback.

STAYING THERE

How to go Bad Hofgastein is essentially a hotel resort. The hotels tend to be large and of good quality, and many have their own fine spa facilities. Some are within easy walking distance of the funicular, a few provide courtesy transport, and most of the rest are close to bus stops.

Hotels The Palace Gastein (6715-0) is a big 4-star with superb leisure facilities, including pool and thermal baths. The elegant Germania (6232-0) is similarly comfortable.

The high-quality Norica (8391-0) is atypically modern in design, but is well positioned in the pedestrian zone. The Alpina (8475-0) is another well located 4-star, five minutes from the slopes. The Astoria (6277-0) is well appointed but quite poorly positioned and doesn't supply courtesy transport.

The Kurpark (6301) has been recommended for its good food, service and central location.

Apartments/condos Accommodations can be organized through the tourist office.

Eating out There is a good range of restaurants, and many hotels offer good formal dining. The Moserkeller is an intimate restaurant, and Pension Maier one of the better informal places. The Pyrkerhöhe, on the slopes just above town, is worth an evening excursion, and Da Dino is a popular pizza and pasta place.

Après-ski It is very quiet by Austrian standards. Some reporters have been disappointed; others have loved the peacefulness. There are, however, a few animated places around. The Picolo ice bar in the center of town is lively immediately after the lifts close. Evergreen has a friendly atmosphere. Visions is a spacious modern disco, while Match Box and C'est la Vie have loud music and are full of teenagers.

Most of Bad Hofgastein's clientele prefer something more sedate. Café Weitmoser is an historic little castle popular for its cakes at tea-time. The outdoor bar of the Osterreichischer Hof is a pleasant spot to catch the last of the sun. Another atmospheric tea-time rendezvous is the Tennishalle. Later, the West End bar is a cozy place for a quiet drink. The Glocknerkeller in Hotel Zum Toni and the Rondo bar in Hotel Kärnten have live music in a low-key ambience.

The Bad Gastein casino provides cabs to and from Bad Hofgastein.

Off the slopes The Kurzentrum is at the center of things, and is arguably an even more impressive spa facility than that of Bad Gastein. It has a splendid thermal pool, and offers a range of therapies. Other off-slope amenities include artificial and natural ice skating, indoor tennis, squash, sleigh rides. There are lovely walks.

Dorfgastein 830m/2,720ft

Those who prefer not to stay in large, commercialized villages should consider Dorfgastein. Prices are lower, and the atmosphere is friendlier and more informal – a contrast to its rather cold setting, sheltered from the sun.

The extensive slopes are more suitable for early intermediates than the steeps above Bad Gastein. Runs are long and varied, amid lovely scenery. Unfortunately the low-altitude beginner areas can be cold and icy. Bad Hofgastein's funicular is 15 minutes away by bus.

There are a few shops and après-ski places, a short walk or bus-ride from the slopes. Café St Ruperb is a nice village pizzeria. The Kirchenwirt (7251) and Römerhof (7777) are comfortable hotels, while Pension Skihausl (7516) is cheaper, does good food, and is next to the slopes.

There is an outdoor heated pool with sauna-solarium, a bowling alley and a ski kindergarten.

Bad Hofgastein phone numbers
From elsewhere in Austria add the prefix 06432.
From abroad use the prefix +43 6432.

Dorfgastein phone numbers
From elsewhere in Austria add the prefix 06433.
From abroad use the prefix +43 6433.

A quiet base from which to access the extensive Ski Welt area

HOW IT RATES

The slopes

Snow	**
Extent	****
Experts	*
Intermediates	****
Beginners	****
Convenience	***
Liftlines	****
Restaurants	**

The rest

Scenery	***
Resort charm	***
Off-slope	***

- ➕ Part of Ski Welt, Austria's largest linked ski and snowboard area
- ➕ Pretty, easy slopes
- ➕ Excellent beginner areas (but snow reliability can be a problem)
- ➕ Massive recent investment in snowmaking has paid off
- ➕ Cheap by Austrian standards
- ➕ Quiet, charming family resort – more appealing than neighboring Söll

- ➖ Poor natural snow record but increased snowmaking does compensate
- ➖ Village a bus-ride from slopes
- ➖ Mostly short runs and little for experts or good intermediates
- ➖ Lack of varied nightlife
- ➖ Ski Welt slopes can get crowded on weekends and in high season

Like nearby Söll, Ellmau gives access to the large Ski Welt circuit, with good slopes for early intermediates. The resort is a pleasant, quiet alternative to Söll, and offers more amenities than other neighbors such as Scheffau.

Although Ellmau's natural snow record is poor, continuing investment in snowmaking has made a big difference. The snow may not always be in tip-top condition, but at least there'll be some. The new chairs that replace surface lifts at Hartkaiser make it possible to move around the mountain a bit quicker now, though of course the runs will still be short.

48

MOUNTAIN FACTS

Altitude	620m-1830m
	2,030ft-6,000ft
Lifts	93
Trails	250km
	155 miles
Blue	43%
Red	48%
Black	9%
Snowmaking	130km
	81 miles

THE RESORT
Ellmau sits at the north-eastern corner of the Ski Welt, between St Johann and Wörgl. Although a sizeable resort, and becoming more commercialized each year, it remains quiet, with traditional chalet-style buildings, welcoming bars and shops, and a picturesque old church. Buses around the resort, necessary if you stay in the village,

attract complaint for being infrequent.
Make sure you get an Ellmau guest card entitling you to various discounts, including to the Kaiserbad leisure center.

THE MOUNTAIN
The Ski Welt is the largest mountain circuit in Austria. It links Going, Scheffau, Söll, Itter, Hopfgarten and Brixen. Most runs are not difficult, but

What's new

The snowmaking capacity in the Ski Welt has been hugely increased in recent years. It now covers 130km/81 miles of trails (over half the trails in the Ski Welt) and is the largest snowmaking facility anywhere in Austria. Almost all the trails in the Ellmau– Going sector now have snowmaking.

For 2000/01 a high-speed six-seater chair-lift replaced a T-bar up to the Hartkaiser–Brandstadl area. This joins another six-pack that was installed for the previous season.

Another six-person chair replaced a T-bar on the link between Ellmau and Scheffau.

we receive complaints that it is slow to get about, due to the number of short connecting runs and the trail map. Westendorf is covered by the Ski Welt ticket, though its local slopes are not linked. Kitzbühel, Waidring, Fieberbrunn and St Johann are in easy reach for day trips and covered by the Kitzbüheler Alpenskiticket.

Slopes Ellmau is close to the best slopes in the area, above Scheffau. The funicular on the edge of the village takes you up to Hartkaiser, from where a fine long red (a favorite with reporters) leads down to Blaiken (Scheffau's lift station). A choice of gondola or two-stage chair goes back to Brandstadl, the start of three varied, long alternatives back to Blaiken.

Immediately beyond Brandstadl, an array of short runs and lifts link that point to Zinsberg. From there, excellent, long, south-facing trails lead down to Brixen. Then it's a short bus-ride to Westendorf's pleasant separate area. Part-way down to Brixen you can head towards Söll, or by conquering the Hohe Salve get access to a long, west-facing run to Hopfgarten.

Ellmau and Going share a pleasant little area of slopes on Astberg, slightly apart from the rest of the area, and well suited to the unadventurous and families. One trail leads to the funicular for access to the rest of Ski Welt. The main Astberg chair is rather inconveniently positioned, midway

between Ellmau and Going.

Snow reliability With a low average height, and important links that get a lot of sun, the snowmaking that the Ski Welt has installed is essential. And the Ellmau–Going sector now claims almost all its slopes are covered by snowmaking. This can, of course, only be used when it is cold enough and it cannot prevent slush and icy patches forming. The north-facing Eiberg area above Scheffau holds its snow well.

Snowboarding Ellmau is a good place to try boarding as the local slopes are easy. For decent boarders it is more limited, but there is a terrain-park and quarter-pipe near Söll.

Experts There's a steep plunge off the Hohe Salve summit, and a little bump field between Brandstadl and Neualm, but the area isn't really suitable except for those prepared to seek out off-trail opportunities. The ski route from Brandstadl down to Scheffau is a highlight and you can go off-trail with a guide from Brandstadl to Söll.

Intermediates With good snow, the Ski Welt is a paradise for early intermediates and those who love easy cruising. There are lots of blue runs and many of the reds deserve a blue grading. It is a big area and you get a feeling of traveling around. The main challenge is when the snow isn't perfect – ice and slush can make even gentle slopes seem tricky. In general the most difficult slopes are those

LIFT TICKETS

2001/02 prices in euros

Ski Welt Wilder Kaiser-Brixental
Covers all lifts in the Wilder Kaiser-Brixental area from Going to Westendorf, and the ski-bus.
Main ticket
1-day ticket 29
6-day ticket 143
Children
Under 16: 6-day ticket 81
Under 6: free ticket
Short-term tickets
Single ascent on some lifts, tickets from 11am, noon 2pm to the end of the day.
Alternative periods
5 in 7 days, 7 in 10 days, 10 in 14 days.
Alternative tickets
Söll ticket available (6-day ticket for adults 117, for children 68) covers 12 lifts, 34km/21 mile trail). Kitzbüheler Alpen-ski ticket covers five large ski areas – Schneewinkel (including St Johann), Ski Region Kitzbühel, Ski Welt Wilder Kaiser, Bergbahnen Wildschönau and Alpbachtal (adult 6-day 160).

CHILDCARE

Ist school has a playroom open from 9am. Hartkaiser school opened a ski nursery last season. Top school welcomes children and provides lunchtime care on request. There is also a village non-skiing kindergarten.

Phone numbers
From elsewhere in Austria add the prefix 05358.
From abroad use the prefix +43 5358.

TOURIST OFFICE

Postcode A-6352
t +43 (5358) 2301
f 3443
ellmau@netway.at
www.ellmau.com

from the mid-stations to the valleys. For timid intermediates the easy slopes of Astberg are on hand to Ellmau guests.
Beginners Ellmau has an array of good beginner areas, now covered by snowmaking. The main ones are at the Going end, but there are some by the road to the funicular. The Astberg chair opens up a more snow-sure plateau at altitude. The Brandstadl–Hartkaiser area has a section of short, easy runs, and a nice long trail running the length of the funicular which even near-beginners can manage.
Cross-country When there is snow, there are long, quite challenging trails, but trails at altitude are lacking.
Liftlines Continued introduction of new lifts has greatly improved this once line-prone area.
Mountain restaurants The smaller places are fairly consistent in providing good-value food in pleasant surroundings, but the larger restaurants should be avoided. The Rübezahl above Ellmau is our favorite in the whole Ski Welt and the hut at Neualm has also been recommended. The larger self-service restaurants are functional (the Jochstube at Eiberg is an exception) and suffer lines. Going is a good spot for a quiet lunch.
Schools and guides The three schools have good reputations – except that classes can be very large. We had a good report about the Top School this year: 'Both our six-year-old and our adult friend were very pleased with the service and the way they progressed'. As well as the main schools there are mountaineering schools that organize tours in the Wilder Kaiser and the Kitzbühel mountains.
Facilities for children Ellmau is an attractive resort for families. Kindergarten facilities seem to be satisfactory and include fun ideas such as a mini train to the lifts. We have had no recent reports, however.

STAYING THERE

Ellmau has a compact center, but its accommodations are scattered, and the bus service unreliable. Hotel position is quite important, so make sure you cater for your needs when booking.
How to go Ellmau is essentially a hotel and pension resort, though there are apartments that can be booked locally.
Hotels Bär (2395) is an elegant but relaxed Relais & Châteaux chalet, but twice the price of any other hotel. Hochfilzer (2501) is central, well equipped (it has an outdoor hot-tub) and popular with reporters.
Apartments/condos There is a wide variety. The Landhof apartments (with pool and sauna) were highly praised by a recent reporter: 'An absolute treasure'.
Après-ski Events include bowling, sleigh rides, Tirolean folklore and inner-tubing, but there is little else. The Memory bar and Dorfstüberl are favorites, though both are very quiet.
Eating out The hotel Hochfilzer has a reputation for good food and the Café Bettina, midway between the funicular and town, is good for afternoon coffee and cakes.
Off the slopes The Kaiserbad leisure center is good. There are many excursions available, including Innsbruck, Salzburg, Rattenburg and Vitipeno. St Johann in Tirol is a nice little town only a few miles away by bus. Valley walks are spoiled by the busy main road.

Going 775m/2,540ft

Going is a tiny, attractively rustic village, well placed for the limited but quiet slopes of the Astberg and for the vast beginner areas between here and Ellmau. Prices are low, but it's not an ideal place for covering the whole of the Ski Welt on the cheap.

Going is ideal for families looking for a quiet time, particularly if they have a car for transport to Scheffau or St Johann when the Astberg's low runs have poor snow.

Hintertux

1500m/4,920ft

Powerful new lifts and excellent snow in a bleak setting

➕ One of the best glaciers in the world, with some great runs for experts and intermediates on guaranteed good snow

➕ Some excellent off-trail opportunities

➕ Series of high-speed gondolas have speeded up access to the skiing

➕ Ziller Valley lift ticket covers other nearby resorts, including Mayrhofen

➕ Short transfers from Innsbruck

➖ Tiny village in bleak setting

➖ Little to do off the slopes

➖ Not really suitable for beginners

➖ Inadequate mountain restaurants

Hintertux has one of the best glaciers in the world and its slopes are open 365 days a year. It's popular with national ski teams for summer training. In winter, it provides guaranteed good snow even when lower resorts are suffering badly. The village itself is small, with few diversions. The traditional old villages of Madseit and Juns are pleasant, but Lanersbach is a more attractive option.

MOUNTAIN FACTS

for Hintertux, Eggalm and Rastkogel

Altitude	1300m-3250m
	4,270ft-10,660ft
Lifts	34
Trails	125km/78 miles
Blue	30%
Red	56%
Black	14%
Snowmaking	15km
	9 miles

TVB TUX / J P. FANKHAUSER

In good conditions you can ski down to the village from the glacier – a huge descent ↓

THE RESORT

Tiny Hintertux is bleakly set at the end of the Tux valley. Ringed by steep mountains except to the north, the village is often in shade. It is little more than a small collection of hotels and guest houses; there is another, smaller group of hotels near the lifts, which lie a 15-minute walk away from the village, across a parking lot that fills with day-visitors' cars and buses, especially when snow is poor in lower resorts. Lanersbach, the largest of the villages in the valley, is 5km/3 miles down the road. It has its own ski area, which has a new link with Mayrhofen's area (see separate chapter), and a regular free shuttle-bus to Hintertux.

THE MOUNTAINS

Hintertux's slopes are fairly extensive and, for a glacier, surprisingly challenging. We revisited it last season when it was raining in lower resorts and had a great time skiing powder.
Slopes A series of speedy new gondolas now takes you in three stages from the base at 1500m/4,920ft to the top of the glacier at 3250m/10,66oft in under 20 minutes. Two gondolas go from the base to Sommerbergalm. From here two more gondolas, including a 24-person jumbo, go up to Tuxer Ferner Haus, beside the glacier. Then a short slope takes you down to a further 24-person gondola, which whisks you up to Gefrorene Wand ('frozen face') at 3250m/10,66oft. From Sommerbergalm, a fast quad chair serves the slopes below Tuxer Joch; from the top of this sector, an excellent secluded off-trail run goes down to the base station. Between the top of the glacier and Tuxer Ferner Haus there are further chairs and surface lifts to play on and links across to another 1000m/3,28oft-vertical chain of lifts below Grosser Kaserer on the west. Behind Gefrorene Wand is the area's one sunny trail served by a triple chair. Descent to the valley involves a short ascent to Sommerbergalm on the way.

The Ziller Super Ski ticket covers all the lifts and buses in the Ziller valley.

What's new

Hintertux has invested millions in its lift system in recent years. For 2001/02 the big news is a link between the Eggalm/Rastkogel area above Lanersbach with Mayrhofen's slopes, via a high-speed six-seater chair from Rastkogel and with a new 150-person tram and a new trail to bring you back. This transforms the attraction of tiny Lanersbach as a place to stay by opening up 143km/89 miles of lift-linked trails.

This follows powerful new gondolas on the Hintertux glacier for the 2000/01 season which now whisk you from the base at 1500m/4,92oft to the top of the glacier at 3250m/10,66oft in under 20 minutes. These include the world's highest jumbo gondola, holding 24 people, going from 2660m/8,730ft to 3250m/10,66oft and a new eight-person gondola from the base area.

Snowboarding There is Europe's highest World Cup half-pipe on the glacier (a popular hang-out throughout the summer), and a terrain park. There are also great off-trail opportunities.

Snow reliability Snow does not come more reliable than this. Even off the glacier, the other slopes are high and face north, making for very reliable snow-cover. The runs from Tuxer Ferner Haus down to Sommerbergalm have snowmaking as well.

Experts There is more to amuse experts here than on any other glacier, with a couple of serious black runs at glacier level and steep slopes and ungroomed ski routes beneath.

Intermediates The area particularly suits good or aggressive intermediates. The long runs down from Gefrorene Wand and Kaserer are fun. And there is a pleasant, tree-lined ski route from the valley from Sommerbergalm and another from Tuxer Joch. Moderate intermediates will love the glacier.

Beginners This is not an ideal resort, but there are beginner areas down the valley at Madseit and Juns.

Cross-country There are 20km/12 miles of trails, along the Tux creek, between Madseit and Lanersbach.

Liftlines There used to be huge lines at Hintertux when snow was poor elsewhere. The splendid new lifts have largely solved this problem – but we have had one reporter complaining that there was a 'frightening' unruly crush with 'no liftline management' for the jumbo gondola when the chair-lifts were closed by high winds. The main runs can get crowded, when it is best to head over to the quieter Keserer lifts and runs.

Mountain restaurants The inadequate mountain restaurants tend to get very crowded and the big self-service places lack charm. The 90-year-old Spannagelhaus is an exception and there are great views from the Gletscherhütte, at the top.

Schools and guides The ski school has a good reputation.

Facilities for children There's a children's section of the ski school, and Lanersbach has a nursery.

STAYING THERE

How to go Most hotels are large and comfortable and have spa facilities, but there are also more modest pensions.

Hotels Close to lifts are the 4-star Neuhintertux (8580) and Vierjahreszeiten (8525). We stayed in the Hintertuxerhof (85300) a short walk away and found it welcoming, with good food, sauna and steam room.

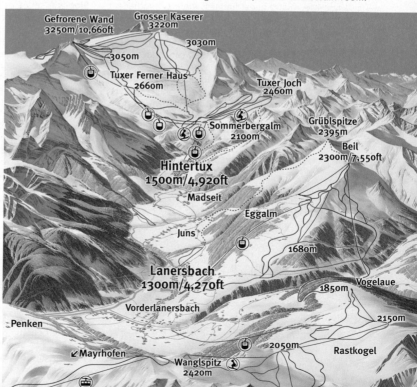

Phone numbers
From elsewhere in
Austria add the prefix
05287.
From abroad use the
prefix +43 5287.

TOURIST OFFICE

Postcode A-6293
t +43 (5287) 8506
f 8508
info@tux.at
www.tux.at

Pensions Kössler (87490) and Willeiter (87492) are in the heart of the village.
Apartments/condos There are plenty.
Eating out Restaurants are mainly hotel-based. The Vierjahreszeiten cafe is pleasant and informal.
Après-ski Nightlife is quiet, though there are some bars and discos in the valley and a night bus between Lanersbach and Hintertux runs until 2am. The Rindererhof has a lively tea dance and a new après-ski bar is due to open at the bottom of the gondola.
Off the slopes The spa facilities are excellent but, in general, you're much better off in Mayrhofen if you don't want to use the slopes.

Lanersbach 1300m/4,270ft

The attraction of staying in Lanersbach and neighboring Vorderlanersbach will be transformed by the new link for 2001/02 from the Rastkogel slopes above Vorderlanersbach directly into Mayrhofen's ski area. There are also regular free buses to Hintertux.

THE RESORT
Lanersbach is an attractive, spacious, traditional village spoiled only a little by the busy road up to Hintertux, which passes the main lift. Happily, the quiet center near the pretty church is bypassed by the road, yet within walking distance of the gondola up to Eggalm. The village is small and uncommercialised, but it has all you need in a resort. And prices are relatively low. Vorderlanersbach is even smaller with a gondola up to the Rastkogel area.
Slopes The slopes of Eggalm, accessed by the gondola from Lanersbach, have a high point of 2300m/7,550ft at Beil, and a small network of varied, mostly wooded trails served by three other lifts and leading back to the village and across to Vorderlanersbach. From there you can take the Rastkogel gondola, which gives access to the new high-speed, six-person chair-lift link with Mayrhofen's slopes. The area is also served by two old, slow chairs and two T-bars and reaches 2500m/8,200ft. There is no slope directly back to the village, but a trail leads to a chair in the Eggalm sector.
Snow reliability Snow conditions are usually good, at least in early season; by Austrian standards, these are high slopes and there is some snowmaking on Eggalm, but the Vorderlanersbach

sector, in particular, gets a lot of sun.
Snowboarding The Mayrhofen and Hintertux pipes and parks are easily accessed and floodlit boarding using the Hinterangerlift is popular.
Experts There are no trails to challenge experts, but there is a fine off-trail route starting a short walk from Beil and finishing at the village.
Intermediates From 2001/02, the link with Mayrhofen's slopes will mean you have access to 143km/89 miles in total.
Beginners Both areas have beginner areas but there are no ideal progression slopes.
Cross-country These are the best bases in the area for cross-country.
Liftlines Up to now the areas have been delightfully deserted. Whether hordes coming over from Mayrhofen will change that remains to be seen.
Mountain restaurants These are delightfully quiet.
Schools and guides The Lanersbach school now has a new rival in Luggi's, but we lack reports on either.
Facilities for children The non-ski nursery takes children from age two, the schools from four. Lanersbach is generally child-friendly, though a lack of other English-speaking children to play with could be a problem.

STAYING THERE
How to go Lanersbach is essentially a hotel resort.
Hotels The Lanersbachherof (87256) is a good 4-star with pool, sauna, steam and hot-tub close to the lifts, but it is also on the main road. The cheaper 3-star Pinzger (87541) and Alpengruss (87293) are similarly situated. In Vorderlanersbach the 3-star Kirchlerhof (8560) has 'comfortable rooms and excellent food' says a reporter.
Apartments/condos Quite a lot available.
Eating out Restaurants are mainly hotel-based.
Après-ski Nightlife is quiet by Austrian standards but there is a disco or two. We enjoyed the jolly Hühnerstall in Lanersbach (an old wooden building with traditional Austrian music) and the ancient wine bar in Vorderlanersbach.
Off the slopes Off-slope facilities are fairly good considering the size of the resort. Some hotels have pools, hot-tubs and fitness rooms open to non-residents. There is a tennis center which also has squash and bowling. Mayrhofen is a worthwhile excursion and Salzburg is just within range.

Innsbruck 575m/1,890ft

A cultured city base for a range of little ski resorts

Innsbruck is not a ski resort in the usual sense. It is an historic university city of 130,000 inhabitants, with a vibrant cultural life, set at a major Alpine crossroads, and a major tourist destination in summer. Its local slopes are of local interest. But the city has twice hosted the Olympic Winter Games, and it lies at the heart of a little group of resorts that share a lift ticket and are accessible by efficient bus services. Among them, as it happens, is one of the three or four best glacier areas in the Alps – the Stubaier Gletscher.

MOUNTAIN FACTS

Altitude	575m-3210m
	1,890ft-10,530ft
Lifts	63
Trails	130km/81 miles
Blue	35%
Red	42%
Black	23%
Snowmaking	34km
	21 miles

Innsbruck phone numbers
From elsewhere in Austria add the prefix 0512.
From abroad use the prefix +43 512.

The Inn valley is a broad, flat-bottomed trench here, but Innsbruck manages to fill it from side to side. It is a sizeable city, and as you would expect from its Olympic background it has an excellent range of winter sport facilities, as well as a captivating car-free medieval core. It has smart modern shopping areas, trendy bars and restaurants, museums (including, of course, one devoted to the Olympics), concert halls, theatres, a zoo and other attractions that you might seek out on a summer vacation, but normally wouldn't expect to find when going skiing.

Winter diversions off the slopes include 300km/186 miles of cross-country trails, some at valley level but others appreciably above it; curling and skating at the Olympic center, including public ice-hockey sessions; several toboggan runs totalling 50km/31 miles, the longest (above Birgitz) an impressive 10km/6 miles and 960m/3,150ft vertical; and rides on

a four-man bob at Igls.

Not the least of the attractions of staying in such a place is that you don't pay ski resort prices for anything.

There are hotels, inns and guest-houses of every standard and style, with 3-star and 4-star hotels forming the nucleus. Among the more distinctive hotels are the grand 5-star Europa Tyrol (5931), the ancient 4-star Goldener Adler (571111) and the 3-star Weisses Kreuz (59479), in the central pedestrian zone, and the 4-star art nouveau Best Western Neue Post (59476).

As well as the traditional Austrian restaurants there's a wide choice of Italian ones, plus a smattering of more exotic alternatives from Mexican to Japanese.

There is an impressive 1400m/4,590ft vertical of slopes on the south-facing slopes of **Seegrube-Nordkette**. The focus of the slopes at Seegrube (1905m/6,250ft) is reached by tram rising 1050m/3,450ft from

There are great views
from the top of Igls's
Olympic slopes →

INNSBRUCK TOURISMUS / MICHAEL
GILHAUS

Igls phone numbers
From elsewhere in
Austria add the prefix
0512.
From abroad use the
prefix +43 512.

LIFT TICKETS

2001/02 prices in
euros
**Innsbruck Gletscher
Ski ticket**
covers Seegrube–
Nordkette,
Patscherkofel (Igls),
Axamer Lizum,
Glungezer (Tulfes),
Schlick 2000
(Fulpmes), Stubaier
Gletscher
6-day ticket 141 for
adults
113 for over 60s
85 for children aged 7
to 15
Super-Ski ticket
covers all the above
plus one day in the
Arlberg (St Anton)
and one day in
Kitzbühel
5 days out of 6 ticket
(2000/01 prices)
175 for adults
120 for children aged
7 to 15

Hungerburg on the outskirts of the city
(with buses and a funicular up to the
tram departure station). Although there
are red runs to the valley, the snow is
not reliable – you normally ride the
tram to get access to the red runs of
370m/1,210ft vertical below Seegrube,
served by a chair-lift. A further stage of
the tram rises 350m/1,150ft vertical to
access the Karinne ski route, which is
said to be fearsomely steep (up to 70
per cent gradient). You can ski it with
a guide and collect not only a T-shirt
but a certificate to prove you did it.

But for visitors, if not for residents,
skiing usually means heading for the
opposite side of the Inn valley, to east
or west of the side valley that runs
southwards towards the Brenner pass
and Italy. The Brenner road is a major
pipeline for goods and tourists
traveling between Germany and Italy,
and opens up the possibility of
excursions to the Dolomites.

The standard Innsbruck lift ticket
covers the lifts in all the resorts dealt
with here, except Seefeld. The
extraordinary Super-Skiticket includes
days in Kitzbühel to the east and St
Anton to the west. Free ski-bus
services run to and from all the lift-
ticket-covered areas, but only at the
beginning and end of the day. A car
makes life in general more
convenient, especially if you are
staying in one of the outlying villages
rather than in downtown Innsbruck.

There are snowboard parks in the
Seegrube and Axamer Lizum sectors,
and at Schlick 2000 and the Stubaier
Gletscher.

IGLS 900m/2,950ft
**Igls seems almost a suburb of
Innsbruck – the city streetcars run out
to the village – but really it is a resort
in its own right. Its famous downhill
race course is an excellent trail.**
The village of Igls is small and quiet,
with not much in the way of diversions
apart from the beautiful walks, the
Olympic bob run and the tea shops.
You can stay in Igls, where the hotels
are mostly small, comfortable and
concentrated in the center of the
village, a bit of a walk from the tram
station. An exception is the family-run
5-star Sporthotel (377241), which
occupies the prime site, centrally
placed between the streetcar station
and the tram station: 'Excellent
facilities, good food and nice bar' said
a reporter this year.

The skiing on Patscherkofel revolves
around the excellent, varied, long red
run that formed the men's downhill
course in 1976, when Franz Klammer
took ski racing (and the Olympic gold
medal) by storm. There is a blue-run
variation on this run, and off-trail
possibilities. A tram rises
1050m/3,450ft from the village (and
you can take it down if the lower runs
are poor or shut). At the top, a chair
rises a further 275m/900ft to the
summit offering wonderful views over
Innsbruck. A fast quad and a couple of
surface lifts serve slopes below the
tram station. There is a short beginner
lift at village level, and another a short
bus-ride up the hill. We have received
mixed reports on the grooming of the
trails however.

In general the resort is very suitable
for families with good easy slopes at
village level.

Après-ski is quiet and the Pub is
the only place with much life.

AXAMER LIZUM 1580m/5,180ft
**The mountain outpost of the Inn-side
village of Axams is a simple ski station
and nothing more, but it does have
some good slopes and reliable snow
conditions.**
Axamer Lizum could scarcely offer a
sharper contrast to Igls. It offers much
more varied slopes and a network of
lifts, with the base station at a much
higher altitude. The slopes here hosted
all the Olympic Alpine events in 1976
except the men's downhill (which was
at Igls), and this is the standard local
venue for weekend sport – hence the
huge parking lot which is the most

**Axams phone
numbers**
From elsewhere in
Austria add the prefix
05234.
From abroad use the
prefix +43 5234.

**Neustift phone
numbers**
From elsewhere in
Austria add the prefix
05226.
From abroad use the
prefix +43 5226.

prominent feature of the 'resort'.

You can stay up here – there is a 4-star hotel at the lift base, the Lizumerhof (68244) – but it's difficult to see why you would want to. (If you want a holiday in a purely functional resort with nothing to amuse you in the evenings, you might as well go somewhere that has rather more extensive slopes than these.)

The main slopes on Hoadl and Pleisen are blues and reds, almost entirely above the trees but otherwise nicely varied. The vertical of the main east-facing slopes above the main lift station is 'only' 700m/2,300ft, but for good skiers at least there is the possibility of a 1300m/4,270ft descent at the end of the day from Pleisen to the outskirts of Axams – an easy 6.5km/4 mile black run.

On the opposite side of the base station, a chair-lift serves a fairly easy black slope. Beyond it are links to the slopes above Mutters, but the lifts here are closed for 2001/02 – see below.

There are accommodations not far away at lower altitude in Axams – including four 3-star hotels – and in other nearby villages such as Götzens (one 4-star hotel, two 3-star gasthofs) and Birgitz (two 3-star hotels).

INNSBRUCK TOURISMUS / MICHAEL GILHAUS

The historic city of Innsbruck makes an interesting, relatively cheap base from which to try the varied nearby slopes ↓

STUBAIER GLETSCHER 1750m/5,740ft

The Stubaier Gletscher is one of the best glacier ski and snowboard areas in the world and you can visit here in summer as well as winter. The nearest place to stay is picturesque Neustift, 20km/12 miles away and served by regular buses.

The glacier is accessed by two alternative two-stage gondolas from the huge parking lot at Mutterberg (1750m/5,740ft). On the glacier a variety of chair- and surface lifts allow fabulous high altitude cruising on blue and red runs, which normally have excellent snow on slopes between 3200m/10,500ft and 2300m/7,550ft. A lovely 10km/6 mile ungroomed ski-route down via a deserted bowl takes you to the valley – or if you start at the top, a descent of about 14km/9 miles and 1450m/4,760ft vertical is possible. There is also good off-trail on the glacier to be explored with a guide.

A new 100m/330ft half-pipe has been installed on the glacier for this season and continued improvements to the lift have virtually eliminated what used to be enormous lines.

Neustift is an attractive Tirolean village halfway along the Stubai valley, with the main road bypassing the village center. It has a small area of local slopes but what you go for is the glacier. There are lots of 4- and 3-star hotels in the village – the Sonnhof (2224) has been recommended by reporters. Most of the restaurants are hotel-based – reporters recommend Bellefonte's pizzas and the atmospheric Hoferwirt.

FULPMES 935m/3,070ft

Fulpmes is a sizeable village between Innsbruck and Neustift, on the way to the Stubaier Gletscher, with a fair-sized ski area of its own called Schlick 2000.
A two-stage gondola leads to a series of chair- and surface lifts serving a few mainly short blue and red runs on the 2230m/7,320ft Sennjoch. There are also a couple of tougher ungroomed ski-routes and a terrain park.

MUTTERS 830m/2,720ft

Almost as close to Innsbruck as Igls, Mutters is a charming rustic village at the foot of long slopes of 900m/2,950ft vertical. Its slopes are likely to be closed this season and re-opened for the 2002/03 season.
Four new lifts are being built here, including a new access lift from just

← Innsbruck is surrounded by pretty villages in delightful settings

INNSBRUCK TOURISMUS / MICHAEL GILHAUS

SEEFELD 1200m/3,940ft

Seefeld is a pretty all-round winter holiday resort with highly recommended cross-country trails and off-slope activities, and a couple of small, separate areas of downhill slopes.

A classic postwar Tirolean tourist development, Seefeld is well designed in traditional Tirolean style, with a large pedestrian-only center.

Seefeld's slopes are divided into two main sectors – Gschwandtkopf and Rosshütte. Both are on the outskirts and reached from most hotels by a regular free shuttle-bus.

Gschwandtkopf is a rounded hill with 300m/980ft of intermediate vertical down two main slopes, while Rosshütte is more extensive and has a terrain park and half-pipe. The top of Rosshütte can be reached by a funicular to 1800m/5,910ft and then a cable car to 2100m/6,890ft and runs end up in adjacent Hermannstall. From Rosshütte two new six-seater chairs go to the shoulder of Härmelekopf at 2050m/6,730ft – an improvement on the old tram, allowing repeated runs as well as the long red run down.

Rosshütte has some seriously steep off-trail challenges for experts and will offer intermediates an interesting day out from Innsbruck – but the terrain is of no interest for a week's stay. The beginner areas in the central village are broad and gentle, with extensive snowmaking facilities.

Seefeld's 200km/124 miles of excellent cross-country trails are some of the best in Europe and are one reason why Innsbruck has been able to hold the Winter Olympics twice and, more recently, the Nordic World Championships.

Seefeld is a very pleasant place to stay if you want a comfortable relaxed time without much downhill skiing or riding. Lots of people come here and don't venture onto the slopes. The upscale nature of the resort is reflected in the hotels – there are seven 5-stars and almost 30 4-stars. On our last visit we stayed at the 4-star Hiltpolt (2253), which was very comfortable with good food.

Seefeld phone numbers
From elsewhere in Austria add the prefix 05212.
From abroad use the prefix +43 5212.

---

outside the village. They will serve a couple of long red runs and one long blue right back to the valley as well as shorter runs near the top of the mountain. There are also a couple of good long toboggan runs.

The half-dozen hotels in the village divide equally into 3-star and 4-star categories. There is a lively après-ski scene and great off-slope facilities including tennis courts, saunas, skating rinks and 40 curling lanes.

TULFES 920m/3,020ft

Tulfes gets rather overshadowed by the Olympic resorts of Igls and Axamer Lizum, but it has some worthwhile runs.

The runs are on the north-facing slopes of Glungezer. A chair-lift from a parking lot above the village serves red and blue runs of 600m/1,970ft vertical. This leads to a surface lift up to the tree line serving a red run of 500m/1,640ft vertical. And this in turn leads to two surface lifts serving open red runs from the top height of 2305m/7,560ft – almost 1400m/4,590ft above the village.

Like Igls, the village sits on the shelf on the south side of the Inn valley. There are a dozen hotels and gasthofs, with the pick of them probably being the 3-star Neuwirt (78309).

Tulfes phone numbers
From elsewhere in Austria add the prefix 05223.
From abroad use the prefix +43 5223.

TOURIST OFFICE

Postcode A-6021 Innsbruck, Burggraben 3
t +43 (512) 59850
f 59850-7
info@innsbruck.tvb.co.at
www.innsbruck-tourismus

The most underrated resort we know. Cute, snow-sure, wild

HOW IT RATES

The slopes

Snow	★★★★
Extent	★★★★
Experts	★★★
Intermediates	★★★★
Beginners	★★
Convenience	★★★
Lines	★★★
Restaurants	★★

The rest

Scenery	★★★
Resort charm	★★★★
Off-slope	★★★

➕ Charming old Tirolean village, expanded in sympathetic fashion

➕ High slopes with reliable snow

➕ Lots of good intermediate runs, extending over the Swiss border to duty-free Samnaun

➕ Impressive lift system

➕ Very lively après-ski

➖ Not ideal for beginners, for various reasons

➖ Few tough runs for experts

➖ A few T-bars still to be eradicated

➖ Wild après-ski may not be to everyone's taste

Ischgl receives rave reviews from almost every reader who goes there but remains surprisingly unknown. It combines a pretty, largely traffic-free, traditional Tirolean village with extensive intermediate slopes, the most efficient lift system in Austria, some of the most reliable snow in Austria and some of the liveliest après-ski. Although there are some good-value basic pensions, it is dominated by pricey, upscale hotels and is popular with Germans and Scandinavians. The après-ski needs to be seen to be believed – scantily clad dancing girls on the bars of plush 4-star hotels, live music in many bars, and lots of clubs. The resort is quite trendy and attracts top-draw entertainers for end-of-season open-air concerts – Bob Dylan, Diana Ross, Madonna, Bon Jovi, Tina Turner, Elton John, Rod Stewart and, last season, Sting.

What's new

The lift system is being continuously improved and now boasts three gondolas and 14 high-speed chair-lifts. For 2001/02 another high-speed eight-seater chair replaces a slow three-seater to Idjoch. Parking facilities at the base area will also be greatly increased. Last season saw a quad upgraded to an eight-seater and another quad and six-pack installed to replace existing T-bars on the Ischgl side. Over in Samnaun, yet another six-pack replaced a T-bar.

More snowmaking was installed and the Idalp-Panorama and Höllboden restaurants were rebuilt and expanded.

The resort has introduced a unique refund service if the road to and from it is shut because of avalanche danger. Alternative accommodations will be paid for as long as the road is closed.

The resort

The village is in the long, narrow Paznaun valley and the lower, steep, north-facing slopes and the village get almost no sun in early season.

The main street is virtually traffic-free, with architecture that is a mixture of original buildings, traditional Tirolean-style hotels and shops and more recent additions built in the local style. The village is long and narrow, but you can walk from one end to the other in 10 minutes or so.

But it's far from flat – and the ups and downs can be quite treacherous. There's now an underground moving walkway (as in airports) from the center of town to the Fimba gondola, which cuts out some nasty hills.

There's a selection of lively bars, an excellent sports center and a fair number of shops to stroll round. But early evening drunks can be intrusive.

The mountains

Ischgl is a fair-sized, relatively high, snow-sure area ideal for intermediates. Most trails are red, with very few black or easy blue runs. Being able to cross over to duty-free Samnaun in Switzerland adds spice to the area. The local lift ticket covers Samnaun and the more expensive Silvretta ticket covers this area plus Galtür, and smaller Kappl and See – all linked by an infrequent bus service. Visiting St Anton is easy with a car.

THE SLOPES
Cross-border cruising

The main slopes start at the top of three gondolas. From both ends of the village you can get up to the sunny **Idalp** plateau, where the schools and guides meet. At the east end of town the third gondola goes about 300m/???ft higher to Pardatschgrat, from where it's an easy run down to Idalp – with the alternative of testing red and black runs towards Ischgl. Lifts

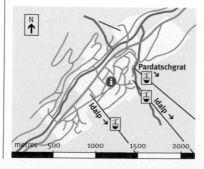

Pardatschgrat

MOUNTAIN FACTS

Altitude	1400m-2870m
	4,590ft-9,420ft
Lifts	42
Trails	200km/124 miles
Blue	25%
Red	60%
Black	15%
Snowmaking	48km
	30 miles
Recco detectors used	

radiate from Idalp, leading to a wide variety of mainly north-west- and west-facing intermediate runs. Idalp is the hub of the slopes and can get very crowded, especially at ski school meeting time and the end of the day.

A short trail brings you to the lifts serving the **Höllenkar** bowl, leading up to the area's south-western extremity at Palinkopf. There are further lifts beyond Höllenkar, on the Fimbatal.

The mountain ridge above Idalp forms the border with Switzerland. On the Swiss side the hub of activity is **Alp Trida**, surrounded by south- and east-facing runs with great views. From here an enjoyable, scenic red run goes down to tiny Compatsch, from where there is a bus to Ravaisch – for the cable-car back – and Samnaun.

From the Palinkopf area there is a very beautiful run to Samnaun itself, down an unspoilt valley. It is not difficult, but doesn't always have ideal snow conditions and is prone to closure because of avalanche risk.

SNOW RELIABILITY
Very good

All the slopes, except the runs back to the resort, are above 2000m/6,560ft and much of those on the Ischgl side are north-west- or north-facing. So snow conditions are often good here when they're poor in other resorts (which can lead to crowds when bus-loads of visitors arrive from lower resorts). There is snowmaking on some runs all the way from Idjoch to Ischgl.

FOR EXPERTS
Not much on-trail challenge

Ischgl can't compare with nearby St Anton for exciting slopes, and some of the runs marked black on the trail map barely deserve their rating. But there is plenty of beautiful off-trail to be found with a guide – and because there are few experts around, it doesn't get tracked out quickly. The wooded lower slopes of the Fimbatal are delightful in a snowstorm.

The best steep trail is the Fimba Nord run from Pardatschgrat towards Ischgl. If snow is poor near the bottom, you can do the top half of this repeatedly by catching the gondola at the mid-station. A variant will take you down a black to Velilltal, with return by chair-lift or, conditions permitting, an ungroomed ski-route back to Ischgl.

FOR INTERMEDIATES
Something for everyone

Most of the slopes are wide, forgiving and ideal for intermediates (though the high slopes can be windswept and bleak in bad weather). The extent and quality of the slopes have impressed all our intermediate reporters this year.

At the tough end of the spectrum our favorite runs are those from

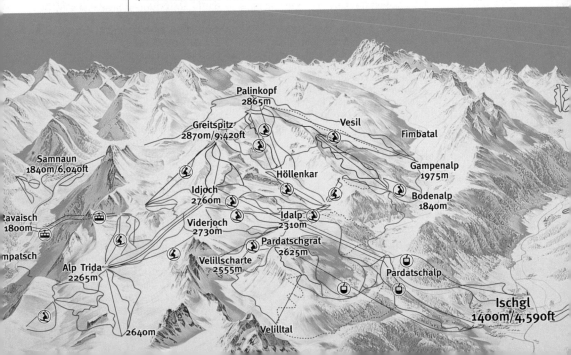

Palinkopf
2865m

Vesil

Fimbatal

Greitspitz
2870m/9,420ft

Gampenalp
1975m

Samnaun
1840m/6,040ft

Höllenkar

Bodenalp
1840m

Idjoch
2760m

Ravaisch
1800m

Idalp
2310m

Viderjoch
2730m

Pardatschgrat
2625m

mpatsch

Velillscharte
2555m

Pardatschalp

Alp Trida
2265m

2640m

Velilltal

Ischgl
1400m/4,590ft

← Most of Ischgl's slopes face north or north-west, so the snow keeps in excellent condition
ISCHGL TOURIST OFFICE

pleasant progression for fast learners. But away from this area there are few runs that are ideal for the near-beginner. You'd do better to learn elsewhere and come to Ischgl later.

FOR CROSS-COUNTRY
Plenty in the valley
There is 48km/30 miles of cross-country track in the Paznaun valley between Ischgl, Galtür and Wirl. This tends to be pretty sunless, especially in early season, and is away from the main slopes, which makes meeting downhillers for lunch rather inconvenient. We've also seen people doing cross-country high up in the Fimbatal, towards Gampenalp, though this isn't an official trail. Galtür is a better choice for cross-country skiers, with 60km/37 miles of loops.

LIFTLINES
An amazing transformation
Ischgl used to be renowned for its lines. But three gondolas now transport 6,700 people an hour out of the village and once on the mountain, fast chairs whizz you around. The double-decker tram from Samnaun has cut the lines there. The one bottleneck is getting back to Idjoch from Alp Trida on the Swiss side at peak times.

MOUNTAIN RESTAURANTS
Much improved
Mountain restaurants tend to be crowded but quite good quality, with over half now offering table-service. The Paznauner Taya, above Bodenalp, is an attractive, rustic chalet, but it gets very crowded. There is table-service upstairs and often a band playing on the terrace. Down in Fimbatal is the quieter rustic restaurant (with table-service) at Bodenalp.

The main restaurant at Idalp has a big self-service cafeteria, and a good table-service alternative (with a sunny outdoor terrace with great views).

LIFT TICKETS
2001/02 prices in euros

VIP Ski ticket
Covers all lifts in Ischgl and Samnaun and local buses.
Main ticket
1-day ticket 37
6-day ticket 159
Senior citizens
Over 60: 6-day ticket 126
Children
Under 16: 6-day ticket 95
Under 7: free ticket
Short-term tickets
Single and multi-ascent tickets for main lifts; half-day ticket from 11.30 (28); trial ticket from 2pm (17).
Alternative periods
5 skiing days in 7, 10 days in 14.
Notes VIP Ski ticket is available to those staying in Ischgl, Samnaun or Mathon only on presentation of a guest card. Discounts for physically disabled and groups.
Credit cards are not accepted at the lift ticket office.
Alternative tickets
Silvretta ski ticket covers Ischgl, Samnaun, Galtür, Kappl and See (adult 6-day 186), 66 lifts and use of ski-bus; See is 15km/9 miles away.

Palinkopf down to Gampenalp and on along the valley to the secluded restaurant at Bodenalp. You can do the top of these runs repeatedly, taking the chair-lift back up from Gampenalp.

There are also interesting and challenging black runs down the Hollspitz chair, and from both the top and bottom of the surface-lift from Idjoch up to Greitspitz. The reds from Pardatschgrat and Velillscharte down the beautiful valley to Velilltal and the red from Greitspitz into Switzerland are great for quiet, high-speed cruising.

For easier motorway cruising, there is lots of choice, including the Swiss side, where the runs from the border down to Alp Trida should prove ideal. So should the runs that take you back to Idalp on the return journey. But there are frequent moans from intermediates about the red runs down to Ischgl itself; neither is easy, conditions can be tricky, and it can be worryingly crowded at the end of the day with too many people skiing beyond their ability (perhaps helped by a schnapps or two too many).

FOR BEGINNERS
Not ideal
Beginners go up the mountain to Idalp, where there are good, sunny, snow-sure beginner areas and a short beginners' surface lift. The blue runs on the east side of the bowl offer

---

boarding *Ischgl has long been popular with boarders. Between Idalp, the main station above the town, and Idjoch, a chair-ride further up, is a big half-pipe and excellent fun-park. The lifts are generally boarder-friendly; where there is a surface lift, there's often a chair option. The area is well suited to beginners and intermediates; experts will love Ischgl after fresh snow, but nearby St Anton is even better. The town rocks at night, with very lively bars.*

SCHOOLS/GUIDES

2001/02 prices in euros

Ischgl-Silvretta
Classes 6 days
4hr: 10.30-12.30 and
1.30-3.30
5 full days: 145
Children's classes
Ages: from 6
6 full days including
lunch: 145
Private lessons
Half- (2hr) or full-day
(4hr) 105 for half-day;
each additional
person 15

Phone numbers
From elsewhere in
Austria add the prefix
05444.
From abroad use the
prefix +43 5444.

CHILDCARE

The childcare facilities
are all up the
mountain at Idalp.
There's a ski
kindergarten for
children aged 3 to 5;
from age 5 they go
into a slightly more
demanding regime in
an 'adventure
garden'; lunch is
included in both
arrangements, which
are open 6 days a
week. Toilet-trained
children can be left at
a non-ski nursery;
lunch is available.

There's also a smaller, crowded self-service nearby. The restaurant at Pardatschgrat tends to be quieter. The pizzeria at Schwarzwand has been recommended by a recent reporter.

The restaurants on the Swiss side at Alp Trida are pleasant. The Alp Bella has been recommended for a quiet time. The Marmotte has pricey table-service as well as self-service and a huge terrace. We have had a report of the remote Heidelberghütte towing lunchers 5km/3 miles to it behind a snowmobile: 'A memorable trip.'

SCHOOLS AND GUIDES
Good despite language problems
The school meets up at Idalp and starts very late (10.30 to 12.30 and 1.30 to 3.30) – perhaps to allow people to get over their hangovers from the nightlife! We've had a rave report of both adult and children's classes. 'Mixed language but the best instruction I've ever had,' said an adult intermediate. 'Mixed language but excellent – very patient and small group. Can stay with class through lunch,' said a satisfied parent.

As well as normal lessons the school organizes off-trail tours – this area is one of the best in the Alps for touring.

FACILITIES FOR CHILDREN
High-altitude options
The childcare facilities are all up at Idalp, but we have no first-hand reports of the service they provide. We have, however, heard from reporters who both stayed at hotel Sonne with six-month-old babies and were delighted with the private babysitter the hotel arranged.

Staying there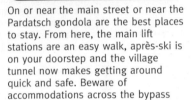

On or near the main street or near the Pardatsch gondola are the best places to stay. From here, the main lift stations are an easy walk, après-ski is on your doorstep and the village tunnel now makes getting around quick and safe. Beware of accommodations across the bypass road a long way from the lifts.

HOW TO GO
Very wide price range
Hotels There is a good selection from luxurious and expensive to basic B&Bs.
((((5) **Trofana Royal** (600) One of Austria's most luxurious hotels, with prices to match. Sumptuous spa facilities.
((((5) **Madlein** (5226) Convenient, modern family-run chalet. Pool, sauna, steam room. Nightclub and disco.
((((5) **Elisabeth** (5411) Right by the Pardatsch gondola with lively après-ski, pool, sauna and steam room.
((((5) **Solaria** (5205) Near the Madlein and just as luxurious, but with a 'friendly family atmosphere'.
((((5) **Piz Tasna** (5277) Up hill behind church: 'Quiet location, friendly, lovely views over village, excellent food.'
(((4) **Sonne** (5302) Highly rated by reporters. In the center of the village. Lively stube. Sauna, hot-tub, solarium.
(((3) **Jägerhof** (5206) 'Jewel of a hotel' says reporter this year. Friendly, good food, large rooms. Sauna and steam.
(((3) **Astoria** (5220) Comfortable B&B hotel that faces the Silvretta gondola.
(((3) **Christine** (5346) Probably the best B&B in town. Near the center of town.
(((3) **Erna** (5555) Small, central B&B. Firmly recommended by a reporter who has holidayed in Ischgl 20 times.

② **Alpenrose** (5255) Popular, good-value pension with 'basic rooms and food' close to Pardatschgratbahn.
② **Dorfschmeide** (5769) Small, central B&B recommended by reporter.
Apartments/condos Some attractive apartments are available.

EATING OUT
Plenty of choice

Our favorite places for dinner are the traditional Austrian restaurants and stubes, of which there's a wide choice. The Goldener Adler probably serves the best food around and has a fine traditional dining room. The Wippas stube in the Sonne is lively and serves good food. For pizza try the Nona or the Trofana-Alm, which is as much a bar as a restaurant, and for fondue the Kitzloch with its galleried tables overlooking the dance floor. La Bamba is a restaurant-bar serving Mexican specialities. The Grillalm, Salner and Tirol are also popular eateries.

APRES-SKI
Very lively

Ischgl is one of the liveliest resorts in the Alps, from early afternoon on. Lots of revelers are still in their ski boots late in the evening.

The Shatzi bar of the hotel Elisabeth by the Pardatschgratbahn is the place to head for after your last run – indoor and outdoor bars and scantily clad dancing girls. Niki's Stadl across the road is a great place to sing along to live versions of the local Austrian hits. The Kitzloch is said to have lost out a bit to these two places – but had dancing on tables and congas last time we were there. The Trofana Alm is the place to head for near the Silvrettabahn. The Post hotel with its casino also has a busy outdoor bar beneath a giant umbrella. The Sunn-Alm at the hotel Sonne gets crowded and has live music. The Kuhstahl under the Sporthotel Silvretta and Fire & Ice over the road are both lively all evening. Guxa and Allegra liven up after dinner and the Golden Eagle is 'good for live bands'. The dancing girls from the Elisabeth move to the Wunderbar club at the hotel Madlein in the evenings and wear even less. Our favorite club was the place underneath the hotel Post, which has ancient Roman theme decor.

OFF THE SLOPES
No sun but a nice pool

The village gets little sun in the middle of winter, and the resort is best suited to those keen to hit the slopes. But there's no shortage of off-slope activities. There are 24km/15 miles of marked walks, a floodlit toboggan run and a splendid sports center. It's easy to get around the valley by bus. But meeting on the slopes for lunch, except at the tops of the gondolas, is a problem for pedestrians.

STAYING DOWN THE VALLEY
Too far without a car

Ischgl is fairly isolated. Landeck is the nearest big town. It has good shopping and is well positioned for trips to the surrounding resorts, including Serfaus, Nauders, Sölden and St Anton.

Galtür 1585m/5,200ft

Galtür has hit the headlines in recent years because of avalanche disasters, but the village center has been rebuilt and fortified against further avalanches since the 1999 disaster.

It is a charming, peaceful, traditional village clustered around a pretty little church, amid impressive mountain scenery. Quieter, sunnier and cheaper than Ischgl, it is a good base for a quiet family holiday. There are good 3-star and 4-star hotels – the Almhof (5443 8253), Ballunspitz (5443 8214) and Flüchthorn (5443 8202) have been recommended. The nightlife is quiet, but there's a couple of jolly bars.

Galtür's own slopes are not particularly challenging, but its black runs are ideal for intermediates and there are fine beginner areas plus plenty of 'graduation' trails for improvers. The school has a high reputation – and we've had a good report about its teaching of children.

If you intend to visit Ischgl a lot, bear in mind that the bus service isn't very frequent and finishes early.

Off-slope facilities are limited, but there's a natural ice rink and a sports center with pool, tennis and squash.

Samnaun 1840m/6,040ft

Samnaun is a small, quiet village and its duty-free status makes it a useful stopover for restocking on booze and tobacco. A reporter warns that most duty-free outlets are closed on Sunday.

Kitzbühel

Wonderful town and extensive slopes, but unreliable snow

HOW IT RATES

The slopes

Snow	**
Extent	****
Experts	***
Intermediates	****
Beginners	**
Convenience	**
Liftlines	**
Restaurants	****

The rest

Scenery	***
Resort charm	****
Off-slope	*****

➕ Large, attractive, varied slopes offering a sensation of travel both on- and off-trail

➕ Beautiful medieval town center

➕ Vibrant nightlife

➕ Plenty of off-slope amenities, both for the energetic and the rest

➕ A surprisingly large amount of cheap and cheerful accommodation

➕ Lively mountain restaurants

➖ Unreliable snow especially on lower slopes (though increasing amount of snowmaking)

➖ Surprisingly little expert terrain

➖ Disjointed slopes, with quite a lot of bussing to get around them

➖ Disappointing beginner area

➖ Crowded trails

Kitzbühel is an impressive name to drop socially. Its Hahnenkamm race-course is the most spectacular and challenging on the World Cup downhill circuit, helping the resort to cultivate a reputation as a special place. But the race course is untypical of Kitzbühel and often its slopes are icy, slushy or just bare. We have visited Kitz countless times, and rarely found decent snow on the lower slopes. It does of course get good snow at times and has invested serious money in snowmaking (not least to prevent its famous race being cancelled due to lack of snow, with all the resulting bad publicity). But Kitzbühel's low altitude means that its problems won't go away.

The resort has a beautiful old traffic-free center complete with cobbled streets and lovely buildings. It has expensive, elegant hotels but there is also a huge amount of inexpensive hotel and guest-house accommodation, which attracts low-budget visitors, many of whom are young and like to party in its famous après-ski haunts.

What's new

Recent years have seen a massive investment in much-needed snowmaking. And several T-bars have been replaced by high-speed quads.

The resort

Set at a junction of broad, pretty valleys, Kitzbühel is a large, animated town, with separate areas of local slopes on each side. The beautiful walled medieval center – complete with quaint church, cobbled streets and attractively painted buildings – is traffic-free during the day and a

compelling place to stay.

But the much-publicized old town is only a small part of Kitzbühel; the resort spreads widely, and crowded roads surround the old town reducing the charm factor somewhat.

Visitors used to peaceful little Austrian villages are likely to be disappointed by its urban nature. But for those who like it, the sophisticated,

MOUNTAIN FACTS

Altitude	800m-2000m
	2,620ft-6,560ft
Lifts	60
Trails	158km/98 miles
Blue	50%
Red	42%
Black	8%
Snowmaking	57km
	35 miles
Recco detectors used	

glitzy, towny ambience and swanky shops and cafes are what 'make' Kitzbühel.

The bus service around town and to the outlying slopes has been highly praised by a regular visitor: 'More buses now, and extra ones at busy times.' But having a car is useful for visiting lots of other resorts covered by the Kitzbüheler Alpen-ski ticket. It is also handy for visiting Salzburg and Innsbruck, though you can reach these by train too (there's a station in town).

The mountains

Snow and liftlines permitting, the mountain suits intermediates well. Although experts can find things to do, there are many better places for them. Kitz's total area is large, and includes access to sizeable Kirchberg.

THE SLOPES
Big but fragmented
Kitzbühel's slopes are divided into four areas – three sizeable and one much smaller. Two of the major areas are connected by trail (almost) in one direction only.

The **Hahnenkamm** is by far the largest, and accessible from the town. It is reached via a gondola or two chair-lifts, from the top of which a choice of steep and gentle runs lead down into Ehrenbachgraben; from there several chair-lifts fan out. One takes you to the gentle peak of Steinbergkogel, the high point of the sector. Beyond is the slightly lower peak of Pengelstein. On the far side of Pengelstein several long runs lead down to the west of the resort; shuttle-buses link their end-points at Aschau and Skirast with Obwiesen, Kirchberg and Kitz. Another lift from Ehrenbachgraben goes up to Ehrenbachhöhe, the focal point of the sector, linked by lifts and runs to Kirchberg and Klausen, on the road between Kitzbühel and Kirchberg.

Pengelstein is the start of the 'ski safari' route to the higher area of **Jochberg–Pass Thurn**. The trail from Pengelstein finishes at Trampelpfad, a short walk or cab-ride from the Jochberg lifts. A parallel trail from Steinbergkogel ends at Hechenmoos – more than a walk from Jochberg, but you can get the shuttle-bus from here. Jochberg–Pass Thurn is well worth the excursion, with better snow and fewer crowds than the local slopes – but runs are short and there are lots of T-bars. Pass Thurn is the terminus of the shuttle-bus, where it is worth

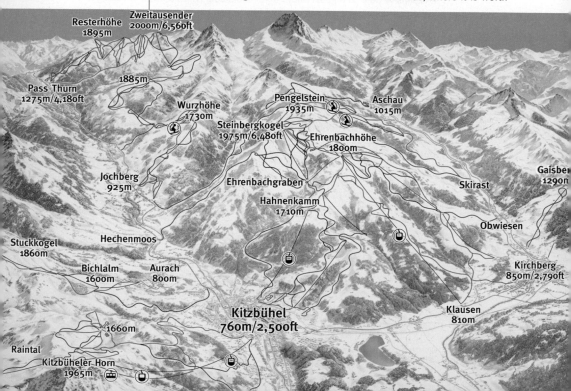

Resterhöhe 1895m

Zweitausender 2000m/6,56oft

Pass Thurn 1275m/4,18oft

1885m

Wurzhöhe 1730m

Pengelstein 1935m

Aschau 1015m

Steinbergkogel 1975m/6,48oft

Ehrenbachhöhe 1800m

Gaisber 1290m

Jochberg 925m

Ehrenbachgraben

Skirast

Hahnenkamm 1710m

Obwiesen

Stuckkogel 1860m

Hechenmoos

Bichlalm 1600m

Aurach 800m

Kirchberg 850m/2,790m

Klausen 81om

Kitzbühel 760m/2,500ft

1660m

Raintal

Kitzbüheler Horn 1965m

Mountain restaurants and extensive views are two of Kitzbühel's delights ➔

KITZBÜHEL TOURIST OFFICE

LIFT TICKETS

2001/02 prices in euros

Kitzbühel
Covers all lifts in Kitzbühel, Kirchberg, Jochberg, Pass Thurn, Bichlalm and Aschau, linking buses, and swimming pool.
Main ticket
1-day ticket 32
6-day ticket 155
(low season 143)
Senior citizens
Over 60: 6-day ticket 124
Children
Under 19: 6-day ticket 124
Under 15: 6-day ticket 97
Under 6: free ticket
Short-term tickets
Single ascent tickets for the major lifts; hourly refunds on day tickets; day tickets can be bought in half-hourly steps from 11am.
Notes 5% reduction for groups of over 15 people. The season ticket is valid in Gstaad.
Alternative tickets
Kitzbüheler Alpen-ski ticket covers five large ski areas – Schneewinkl (St Johann), Ski Region Kitzbühel, Ski Welt Wilder Kaiser, Bergbahnen Wildschönau and Alpbachtal (adult 6-day 160).

ending the day to ensure a bus seat.

The very small **Bichlalm** area is of little interest except for getting away from the crowds, sampling the restaurants and working on your suntan. When conditions are good, the top station (Stuckkogel) accesses an off-trail route to Fieberbrunn.

The **Kitzbüheler Horn** is equally sunny, with repercussions on snow-cover, but many slopes are above the 1270m/4,170ft-high mid-station, accessed by a modern gondola starting close to the railway station, but some way from the center. The second stage leads to the sunny Trattalm bowl at around 1660m/5,450ft, but the alternative tram takes you up to the summit of the Horn, from where a fine, solitary east-facing trail leads down into the Raintal on the far side, with a chair-lift returning to the ridge. There are widely spread blue, red and black runs back towards town.

The trail map has recently been greatly improved by the addition of altitudes and mountain restaurants. And a reporter praised 'the Bergbahn Info people in bright jackets at the main lift stations, who offer accurate advice on closures, directions etc'.

SNOW RELIABILITY
More snowmaking now
In a normal year, snow on the lower slopes can be thin or non-existent at times (though the snow at the top is often okay). The problem is that Kitzbühel's slopes have one of the lowest average heights in the Alps. The expansion of snowmaking in recent years has improved matters when it's cold enough to make snow – major runs right down to Kitzbühel, Kirchberg, Klausen and Jochberg are covered. But many slopes still remain unprotected. The best plan is to book at the last minute when snow-cover is known to be good. Otherwise, take a car for snow-searching excursions.

boarding *Kitzbühel was slow off the mark with boarding, keeping to its image of World Cup Downhill venue/skier party town. However, things have changed, and now there is a half-pipe, terrain park and boarder-cross course on the Kitzbüheler Horn, an area with few surface lifts. Many lifts in the main area are surface lifts, but all major lifts are gondolas and chair-lifts – the area suits beginners and intermediates well. The town is lively at night, with plenty of bars and clubs; the Londoner Pub is the main place with boarder appeal.*

Kitzbühel's Hahnenkamm Downhill race, held in mid-January each year, is the toughest as well as one of the most famous on the World Cup circuit. On the race weekend the town is packed and there is a real carnival atmosphere, with bands, people in traditional costumes and huge (and loud) cowbells everywhere.

The race itself starts with a steep icy section before you hit the famous Mausfalle and Steilhang, where even Franz Klammer used to get worried. The course (now thankfully served by snow-guns) starts near the top of the new gondola and drops 860m/2,820ft to finish amid the noise and celebrations right on the edge of town. Ordinary mortals can try all but the steepest parts of the course after the race weekend, whenever the snow is good enough – it's an ungroomed red ski route mostly. We tried it last season and found it steep and tricky in parts going slowly – it must be terrifying at race speeds of 80mph or more. The course is normally closed from the start of the season until after the race.

66

SCHOOLS/GUIDES

2001/02 prices in euros
Hahnenkamm
Classes 6 days
4hr: 2hr am and pm
6 full days 116
Children's classes
Ages: up to 14
6 full days 134
Private lessons
On request.

Kitzbüheler Horn
Classes 6 days
4hr: 2hr am and pm
6 full days 120
Children's classes
6 full days 130
Private lessons
On request.

Red Devils
Classes 6 days
4hr: 2hr am and pm
6 full days 116
Children's classes
Ages: 4 to 11
6 full days 134
Private lessons
On request.

Total
Classes 6 days
4hr: 9.30-11.30 and 1pm-3pm
6 full days 127
Children's classes
Ages: 4 to 11
6 full days 127
Private lessons
On request.

FOR EXPERTS
Plan to go off-trail
Steep trails are concentrated in the ring of runs down into the bowl of Ehrenbachgraben, the most direct of which are challenging bump runs. Nearby is the Streif red, the basis for the famous Hahnenkamm Downhill race – see the feature panel opposite. When conditions allow, there is plenty of off-trail potential – some of it safely close to trails, some requiring a guide.

FOR INTERMEDIATES
Lots of alternatives
The Hahnenkamm area is prime intermediate terrain. Good intermediates will want to do the World Cup downhill run, of course. And the long 1000m/3,280ft-vertical blue to Klausen from Ehrenbachhöhe is also satisfying. The long runs down to the Kirchberg–Aschau road make a fine end to the day; earlier, they are rather spoiled by the lack of return lifts.

The east-facing Raintal run on the Horn is an excellent slope for good intermediates to hone their skills on.

The runs above Jochberg are particularly good for mixed abilities. Less adventurous types have some fine runs either side of Pengelstein, including the safari route and the Hieslegg trail above Aschau. The short, high runs at the top of the Pass Thurn area are ideal if you're more timid. There are also easy reds down to both Pass Thurn and Jochberg. Much of the Horn and Bichlalm is good cruising.

FOR BEGINNERS
Not ideal
The Hahnenkamm beginner areas are no more than adequate, and prone to poor snow conditions. The Horn has a high, sunny nursery-like section, and precocious learners will soon be cruising home from there on the long Hagstein trail. There are plenty of other easy runs to progress to.

FOR CROSS-COUNTRY
Plentiful but low
There are nearly 35km/22 miles of trails scattered here and there, but all are at valley level and prone to lack of snow. When the snow is good, try the quiet Reith area.

LIFTLINES
Still a drawback
Replacing the old Hahnenkamm tram with a speedy six-person gondola has vastly reduced morning liftlines. However, once up the mountain there are some bottlenecks at slow old chairs and surface lifts. But we did have a report of a 'line-free week during the February semester break' last season. Both the Horn and the Hahnenkamm can have overcrowded trails. We have also received complaints from reporters about the warning signs for avalanche danger and closed or icy trails being in German only.

MOUNTAIN RESTAURANTS
A highlight
'One of the reasons we keep going back,' says one of our Kitz regulars. There are many restaurants, now thankfully marked on the trail map. Avoid the large self-service places and stick to the smaller huts. On the Horn the Hornköpfl-Hütte has good food and sunny terraces. Alpenhaus is good for a lively lunch, the Gipfelhaus (recently renovated) is quieter with 'good views and food'. The 'busy' Alderhütte has also been recommended. The Bichlalm

Kitzbühel phone numbers

From elsewhere in Austria add the prefix 05356.
From abroad use the prefix +43 5356.

CHILDCARE

Most schools cater for small children, offering lunchtime supervision as well as lessons on baby slopes – generally from age 3. There is no non-ski nursery, but babysitters and nannies can be hired.

GETTING THERE

Air Salzburg, transfer 1½hr. Munich, transfer 2hr. Innsbruck, transfer 1½hr.

Rail Mainline station in resort. Postbus every 15 min from station.

---

in the next-door sector is also good if you want some peace. At Jochberg–Pass Thurn the Jägerwurzhütte and Trattenbachalm are recommended, and Panoramaalm has great views. The Steinbergkogel, Sonnbühel, Ochsalm, Seidalm, Fleckalm and Brandseit in the Hahnenkamm sector are good – and there are many others. The pricey Hochkitzbühel table-service restaurant at the top of the gondola has good food, but service is 'not brilliant'.

SCHOOLS AND GUIDES
Off-trail guiding a bargain

There are now half-a-dozen competing schools. The original school, Rudi Sailer's famous Red Devils, got a scathing review from a reporter this year – when an instructor told a nervous woman to 'get down now', then left her after she fell. In contrast to the 200-strong Red Devils, the other schools emphasize their small scale and personal nature. The Total school is the best established of these and includes video analysis. A reporter says: 'Never seen so many British instructors. Good reports all round.'

FACILITIES FOR CHILDREN
Not an ideal choice

Provided your children are able and willing to take classes, you can deposit them at any of the schools. The Total school has supervision until 5pm.

Staying there

The size of Kitz makes choice of location important. The old town is charming, and gives you most options. It's reasonably equidistant from the two main lift stations either side of town – both are within walking distance. However, the Hahnenkamm is very much the larger (and more snow-sure) of the two areas, and many visitors prefer to be close to its gondola. But the Hahnenkamm beginner areas are often lacking in snow, and then novices are taken up the Horn.

HOW TO GO
Mainly hotels and pensions

Kitz is essentially a hotel resort.
Hotels There is an enormous choice, especially of 4-star and 3-star hotels.
(((((5) **Tennerhof** (63181) Luxuriously converted farmhouse in big garden with renowned restaurant. Beautiful panelled rooms.

(((((5) **Schloss Lebenberg** (6901) Modernised 'castle' with smart pool, and free shuttle-bus to make up for secluded but inconvenient location. Free nursery for kids aged 3-plus.
((((4) **Weisses Rössl** (625410) Smartly traditional exclusive 5-star apartment hotel, recently refurbished.
((((4) **Goldener Greif** (64311) Historic inn, elegantly renovated; vaulted lobby-sitting area, panelled bar, casino.
((((4) **Jägerwirt** (6981) Modern chalet with 'helpful staff and wonderful food'. Not ideally placed.
(((3) **Schweizerhof** (62735) Comfortable chalet right by Hahnenkamm gondola.
(((3) **Maria Theresia** (64711) Big, comfortable modern chalet.
(((3) **Hahnenhof** (62582) Small and traditional, with rustic charm.
(((3) **Strasshofer** (62285) An old favorite with a regular reporter – 'central, family-run, friendly, good food, quiet rooms at back'.
(1) **Mühlbergerhof** (62835) Small, friendly pension in good position.
Apartments/condos There are plenty of apartments in Kitz. Many of the best (and best-positioned) places are attached to hotels.

EATING OUT
Something for everyone

There is a wide range of restaurants to suit all pockets, including pizzerias and fast food outlets (even McDonald's). Some 4-star hotels have excellent restaurants; Zur Tenne ('top class hotel and food') and Maria Theresia have been recommended by reporters. But the Unterberger Stuben ('excellent but expensive' says a reporter) vies with Schwedenkapelle for the 'best in town' award. Good, cheaper places include the Huberbräu-Stüberl, Sportstüberl and Zinnkrug. Goldene Gams has both a traditional Austrian dining room and one serving modern Italian and French food. On Fridays and Saturdays you can dine at the top of the Hahnenkamm gondola.

APRES-SKI
A main attraction

Nightlife is a great selling point of Kitz. There's something for all tastes, from throbbing bars full of teenagers to quiet little places, nice cafes full of calories and self-consciously smart spots for fur-coat flaunting.

Much of the action starts quite late; immediately after the slopes close the town is jolly without being much

ACTIVITIES

Indoor Aquarena Center (2 pools, 2 slides, sauna, solarium, mud baths, aerated baths, underwater massage) – free entry with lift ticket, indoor tennis hall, 2 squash courts, fitness center, beauty center, bridge, indoor riding school, local theatre, library, museum, chess club, casino, three-screen cinema.

Outdoor Ice rink (curling and skating), horse-riding, sleigh rides, toboggan run, ballooning, ski-bobs, flying school, wildlife park, hang-gliding, paragliding, 40km/25 miles of cleared walking paths (free guided tours), copper mine tours

TOURIST OFFICE

Postcode A-6370
t +43 (5356) 621550
f 62307
info@kitzbuehel.com
www.kitzbuehel.com

Kirchberg phone numbers
From elsewhere in Austria add the prefix 05357.
From abroad use the prefix +43 5357.

livelier than many other Tirolean resorts – try the Mockingstube, near the gondola, which often has live music. Cafes Praxmair, Kortschak and Langer are among the most atmospheric tea-time places for cakes and pastries. Stamperl is a very lively bar. Later the lively Big Ben British pub, American-style Highways bar and Das Lichtl (with thousands of lights hanging from the ceiling) get packed. Seppi's Pub is recommended for sport on TV, pizzas and the eccentric owner with his 'huge moustache'. Royal, Olympia and Take 5 are the main discos. The Londoner Pub is the loudest, most crowded, smokiest place in town, with sing-along and dance-along music; you often have to wait to be allowed in as other people leave. There's a casino for more formal entertainment. A reporter says there's 'table dancing at the Go Go Bar Café Romantica 2km/1 mile out of town – we weren't tempted.'

OFF THE SLOPES
Plenty to do

The Aquarena leisure center is covered by the lift ticket and is very impressive, with two pools, sauna, solarium and various health activities. There's a museum, which was refurbished last season, and many concerts are organized. The railway also affords plenty of scope for excursions (eg to Salzburg and Innsbruck) and bus trips are available.

Kitzbühel's beautiful medieval center is the nicest place to stay ↓

Kirchberg 850m/2,790ft

THE RESORT
Kirchberg is a large, spread out, lively village. If you stay in the village center, it's a bus-ride to both the lifts up to the main slopes. If you stay near the lifts, don't expect nightlife.

THE MOUNTAIN
Slopes A gondola at Klausen on the road towards Kitzbühel takes you up into the main slopes that Kirchberg shares with Kitzbühel. The alternative route via three successive chair-lifts starts with a bus-ride in the opposite direction. The separate small Gaisberg area is on the other side of the valley.
Snow reliability Only about 90m/300ft higher than neighboring Kitzbühel, Kirchberg suffers from the same unreliable snow.
Snowboarding Boarders might prefer Kitzbühel for the Horn's terrain park.
Experts Few challenging slopes.
Intermediates The main slopes it shares with Kitzbühel are ideal for intermediates when snow is good.
Beginners There's a beginner lift and area at the foot of the Gaisberg slopes.
Cross-country Plenty of trails, but all at valley level so can be affected by lack of snow. The area above Aschau is said to be particularly good and there is a night-time track on Lake Schwarz.
Liftlines As with Kitzbühel poor snow conditions can cause overcrowding.
Mountain restaurants There are some good local huts.
Schools and guides There are three schools but we lack recent reports.
Facilities for children There are non-ski and ski kindergartens.

STAYING THERE
How to go There's a wide choice of chalet-style hotels and pensions.
Hotels The 4-star Klausen (2128) is close to the main gondola and has its own après-ski bar, the Sporthotel Tyrol (2787) is a bit out of the village center with pool and spa facilities.
Apartments/condos There are some available.
Après-ski There's a good toboggan run on Gaisberg. Nightlife is very lively both in discos and bars – the traditional Kupferstubn, the Londoner (with frequent live music), the Boomerang, Gismo and Fuchslokal.
Off the slopes A few of the hotels have swimming pools, saunas and solariums.

Charming luxury for the beautiful people

HOW IT RATES

The slopes

Snow	****
Extent	****
Experts	****
Intermediates	****
Beginners	****
Convenience	***
Lines	***
Restaurants	**

The rest

Scenery	***
Resort charm	****
Off-slope	***

➕ Picturesque Alpine village

➕ Fair-sized, largely intermediate trail network plus good off-trail terrain

➕ Easy access to the tougher slopes of St Anton and other Arlberg resorts

➕ Sunny slopes with excellent snow record and extensive snowmaking

➕ Lively après-ski scene

➕ Very chic resort, with some very comfortable hotels

➖ Very expensive, and credit cards not always accepted by hotels, shops, restaurants or lift pass office

➖ Surprising dearth of atmospheric mountain restaurants other than in the mini-resort of Oberlech

➖ Very few tough trails

➖ Blue runs back to the village are rather steep for nervous novices

➖ Still a few antiquated lifts

Lech and its higher neighbor Zürs are the most glamorous and expensive resorts in Austria. Their shared slopes could fairly easily be linked with those of St Anton – but then their rich and royal visitors would be forced to mingle with the hoi polloi from their equally famous but less exclusive neighbor.

Lech is for those who don't mind fur coats, do like well-groomed, snow-sure, cruising trails, and are content to enjoy a winter holiday in pampered comfort and style in a traditional Alpine village. There are challenging slopes available (mainly off-trail) and the tougher slopes of St Anton are only a short bus- or car-ride away. But it is the part-timer, who enjoys the après and the strolling as much as the winter sports, who will get the most out of the resort. It helps to have deep pockets.

What's new

A couple of years ago a new hands-free electronic lift pass system was introduced for the whole Arlberg region. And over the last few years a number of high-speed chair-lifts replaced slower ones. Sidewalks were also widened and roads narrowed in the center of the village.

For 2000/01 the Rüfikopf cable-car was modernised with new panoramic cabins and the restaurant at the top refurbished. The Hasensprung chair had a moving carpet installed to speed loading. The Zuger Hochlicht cable-car was taken out of service.

The resort

Like other glitz-and-glamour resorts, such as Courchevel and Zermatt, Lech and Zürs attract some visitors who simply want to be seen, but they also have great attractions for the rest of us.

The clientele is largely German and Austrian. The fur coat count is one of the highest in the Alps. And it helps to be able to afford a helicopter transfer out: Lech lies in a high valley reachable in winter only by driving over the Flexen Pass from Stuben (Zürs is just below the top). This road can be closed for days on end after an exceptional snowfall.

The village offers cozy old-world Austrian charm with modern convenience. While some of the best hotels are right in the center, they are not obtrusive. The village remains picturesque despite its growth and popularity – there is a domed church and covered wooden bridge over the gurgling river that runs down one side of the main street; on the other side are enticing and pricey shops. In good weather the center is a picture of open-air cafes, dancing in the street and a fashion show of fur coats and horse-drawn carriages, with good views of the mountains on all sides.

The top hotels are owned by a few families and have large numbers of regular guests who come back year after year.

Oberlech is a small, traffic-free collection of 4-star hotels and chalets set on the trail above Lech and served by a tram which works until 1am, allowing access to Lech's much livelier nightlife and shopping. If you stay there, luggage is delivered efficiently from Lech to your hotel via underground tunnels, leaving you unburdened for the short, snowy walk from the tram.

Zug is a hamlet, 3km/2 miles from

Schlegelkopf

Oberlech

Rüfikopf

metres	500	1000	1500	2000	2500	3000

boarding *Lech's upper class image has not stood in the way of its snowboarding development, and it continues to improve its facilities. Chairs and cable-cars, with hardly any surface lifts, and perfectly manicured trails make the area ideal for beginner and intermediate boarders – lessons are with the local ski school. There's also a good terrain park above the town at the Schlegelkopf, with jumps, a boarder-cross and a half-pipe. More confident boarders should hire a guide and track some powder. The town slips back to being an up-market ski destination in the evenings – bars tend to be in 4-star hotels populated by 'beautiful people'.*

MOUNTAIN FACTS

Altitude 1450m-2660m
4,760ft-8,730ft

Arlberg region

Lifts	83
Trails	260km/
	162 miles
Blue	25%
Red	50%
Black	25%
Snowmaking	65km/
	40 miles
Recco detectors used	

Lech, which connects with the Lech–Oberlech area. The few accommodations are mostly bed and breakfast with one 4-star hotel, the Rote Wand, which serves the best Kaiserschmarren (a delicious chopped pancake and fruit dessert) in the Arlberg. From Lech, Zug makes a good night out: you can take a horse-drawn sleigh for a fondue at the Rote Wand, Klösterle or Auerhahn, followed by a visit to the Rote Wand disco.

As well as Lech and Zürs, the Arlberg lift pass covers St Anton, St Christoph and Stuben, all reachable by car or bus.

The mountains

Lech and Zürs are working hard on improving their links. There are still some old two-seaters, but new fast chairs have improved the network considerably in recent years. The runs, with a lot of gentle wide blues and reds, flatter leisurely cruisers and suit most of the clientele. For such an up-market resort the trail map is surprisingly unclear – see remarks in the St Anton chapter.

THE SLOPES
One-way traffic

The main slopes center on **Oberlech**, 300m/980ft above Lech, and are reached from the village by chair-lifts

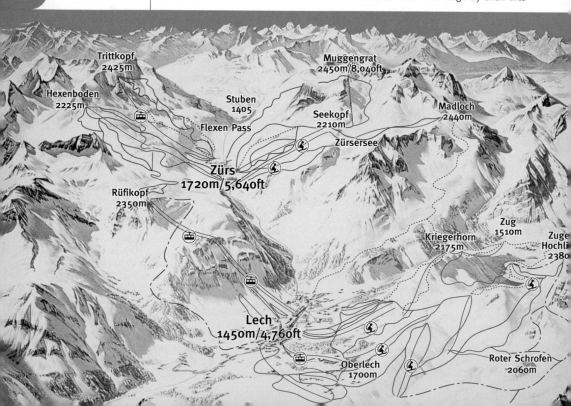

Trittkopf
2425m

Hexenboden
2225m

Muggengrat
2450m/8,040ft

Stuben
1405

Madloch
2440m

Flexen Pass

Seekopf
2210m

Zürsersee

Zürs
1720m/5,640ft

Rüfikopf
2350m

Zug
1510m

Zuge
Hochli
2380

Kriegerhorn
2175m

Lech
1450m/4,760ft

Oberlech
1700m

Roter Schrofen
2060m

A LITTLE HISTORY

The first settlers in Lech came from the Valais region of Switzerland in the 11th century. Skiing started in the early 1900s. The Lech ski school was founded in 1925 and the first T-bar was built in 1939. Patrick Ortlieb, Olympic Downhill champion at Albertville in 1992, was born and learned to ski in Oberlech.

LIFT TICKETS

2001/02 prices in euros

Arlberg Ski ticket
Covers all St Anton, St Christoph, Lech, Zürs and Stuben lifts, and linking bus between Rauz and Zürs.
Main ticket
1-day ticket 37
6-day ticket 171
Senior citizens
Over 65: 6-day ticket 146
Children
Under 15: 6-day ticket 103
Short-term tickets
Single ascent tickets on some lifts throughout Arlberg. Half-day tickets (adults 28) from noon, afternoon 'taster' tickets (16) from 3pm. Day tickets have by-the-hour reimbursement.
Notes Main ticket also covers Klösterle (10 lifts), 7km/4 miles west of Stuben. Discounts during wedel, firn and snow crystal weeks. Senior citizen ticket for women over 60.

as well as the tram. The wide, open trails are perfect for intermediates and there is also lots of off-trail potential for experts. **Zuger Hochlicht** is the highest point of this sector and views from here, and Kriegerhorn below, are stunning. As at St Anton, the toughest runs here are now classed as 'ski routes' or 'high-alpine touring routes' rather than trails, with all the resulting confusion (see the St Anton chapter). The only way down to Zug, for example, is by one of the ski routes.

The linked Lech–Zürs–Lech circuit can be done only in a clockwise direction. To get to Zürs you take the **Rüfikopf** tram from the center of Lech. From the top there are long cruisey trails, via a couple of lifts, down to Zürs. During school holidays and other busy periods the linking lifts and runs on the circuit can get crowded.

All the slopes at Zürs are above the tree-line, with two areas on either side of the village. The more difficult runs are off the top of **Trittkopf** – on the same side as the runs down from Lech. On the other side of the valley, chairs go up to **Seekopf** and **Zürsersee** with intermediate runs down. There's a chair up to **Muggengrat** (at 2450m/ 8,040ft the highest point of the Zürs area) from below Zürsersee. This has a blue run back under it and a lovely long red away from all the lifts back down to Zürs. But most people head for the Madloch chair. This accesses the long ski route all the way back to Lech. You can peel off part-way down and head for Zug and the chair-lift up to the Kriegerhorn above Oberlech.

SNOW RELIABILITY
One of Austria's best

Lech and Zürs both get a lot of snow, but Austrian weather station records show a big difference between them despite their proximity. Lech gets an average of around 8m/26ft of snow between December and March, almost twice as much as St Anton and three times as much as Kitzbühel, but Zürs gets half as much again as Lech. The altitude is high by Austrian resort standards and there is excellent snowmaking on Lech's sunny lower slopes.

This combination, together with excellent grooming, means that the Lech–Zürs area normally has good coverage from December until April. And the snow is frequently better here than on St Anton's predominantly south-facing slopes.

FOR EXPERTS
Off-trail is main attraction

There are only two black trails on the map, although there are the two types of off-trail route referred to above. The official recommendation is to visit these with a ski instructor or guide, though many ignore the advice. But experts will get a lot more out of the area if they do have a guide, as there is plenty of excellent off-trail other than the marked ski routes, much of it accessed by long traverses. Especially in fresh snow, it can be wonderful. A recent reporter found the lack of demanding runs that you can tackle on your own quite limited.

Many of the best runs start from the Steinmähder chair, which finishes just below Zuger Hochlicht. Some routes involve a short climb to access bowls of untracked powder. From the Kriegerhorn there are shorter off-trail runs down towards Lech and a very scenic long ski route down to Zug. Most runs, however, are south- or west-facing and can suffer from getting a lot of sun.

At the end of the season, when the snow is deep and settled, the off-trail off the shoulder of the Wöstertäli from the top of the Rüfikopf tram down to Lech can be superb. There are also good runs from the top of the Trittkopf tram in the Zürs sector, including a tricky one above the Flexen Pass down to Stuben.

Experts will also enjoy cruising some of the steeper red runs and will want to visit St Anton during the week, where there are more challenging trails as well as more off-trail.

Helicopter transport is available to a couple of remote spots.

FOR INTERMEDIATES
Flattering variety for all
The trails in the Oberlech area are nearly all immaculately groomed blue runs, the upper ones above the trees, the lower ones in wide expanses cut through them. It is ideal territory for leisurely cruisers not wanting surprises. And even low intermediates will be able to take on the circuit to Zürs and back, the only significant red involved being the beautiful long (and not at all difficult) 'ski route' back to Lech from the top of the Madloch chair in Zürs.

More adventurous intermediates should take the fast Steinmähder chair to just below Zuger Hochlicht and from there take the scenic red run all the way to Zug (the latter part on a 'ski route' rather than a trail). And if you feel ready to have a stab at some off-trail, Lech is a good place to try it.

Zürs has many more interesting red runs, on both sides of the valley. We particularly like the west-facing reds down from the Trittkopf tram and the usually quiet red run back to Zürs from the Muggengrat chair, which starts in a steep bowl.

FOR BEGINNERS
Easy slopes in all areas
The main beginners slopes are in Oberlech, but there is also a nice isolated area in the village dedicated purely to beginners. There are good, easy runs to progress to, both above and below Oberlech.

FOR CROSS-COUNTRY
Picturesque valley trail
There are two cross-country trails in Lech. The longer one is 15km; it begins in the center of town and leads through the beautiful Zug valley, following the Lech river and ending up outside Zug. The other begins behind the church and goes to Stubenbach (another hamlet in the Lech area). In Zürs there is a 3km/2 mile track starting at Zürs and going to the Flexen Pass. This starts at 1600m/5,250ft and climbs to 1800m/5,910ft.

LIFTLINES
No recent complaints
The region proudly boasts that it limits numbers on the slopes to 14,000 a day for a more enjoyable experience, and there have been significant lift improvements in recent years. On our last visit we thought traffic on the circuit through Zürs, particularly, has improved thanks to the fast Zürsersee quad chair-lift which has relieved pressure on the Seekopf chair. But there are one or two remaining problems – notably the Schlegelkopf fast quad out of Lech. The crucial Madloch chair at the top of the Zürs area must still generate lines of people on the one-way circuit going to Lech and so must the trams. But recent reporters have not complained of any problems.

MOUNTAIN RESTAURANTS
Few atmospheric places
There are surprisingly few cozy Alpine restaurants in the area. A lively area for lunch is at Oberlech, where there are several big sunny terraces set prettily around the trail; our favorite is the Goldener Berg (which has also been highly recommended by a recent reporter). Quite often you'll find a live band playing outside one of the restaurants.

One of the best mountain restaurants is Seekopf (reached by the Seekopf chair-lift) which has a lovely sun terrace. The traditional Schröfli Alm, not marked on the trail map but just above the bottom of the Seekopf lift, is a pleasant traditional chalet. Also popular is the self-service Palmenalpe above Zug, but it does get very crowded. The Mohnenfluh, at the top of the Lech beginner lift, does 'excellent' food.

Many people go back to the villages

SCHOOLS/GUIDES

**Lech and Oberlech
Classes** 6 days
4hr: 10am-noon and
1pm-3pm
6 full days 146
Children's classes
Ages: 3½ to 13
6 full days 134
Private lessons
Full day only
175 for 1 day; each
additional person 15

CHILDCARE

There are ski
kindergartens in Lech,
Zürs and Oberlech
taking children from
age 3, from 9am to
4.30.

GETTING THERE

Air Zürich, transfer
2½hr. Innsbruck,
transfer 1½hr.

Rail Langen (15km/9
miles); 9 buses daily
from station, buses
connect with
international trains.

for lunch. For a gourmet blow-out in Zürs, Chesa Verde in the hotel Edelweiss and the hotel Hirlanda's restaurant both feature in the Gault-Millau gourmet's guide (as does the Arlberg in Lech), and the Lorünser does a 'magnificent' buffet. The hotel Rote Wand in Zug serves more casual fare. Café Schneider in Lech serves good local dishes. Hus Nr 8, at the end of the route back from Zürs, is 300 years old and has good traditional food.

SCHOOLS AND GUIDES
Excellent in parts
The ski schools of Lech, Oberlech and Zürs all have good reputations and the instructors speak good English. Group lessons are divided into no fewer than 10 ability levels. One past visitor enjoyed 'the best lesson I have ever had'. In peak periods, you should book both instructors and guides well in advance, however, as many are booked regularly every year by an exclusive clientele.

FACILITIES FOR CHILDREN
Oberlech's fine, but expensive
Oberlech does make an excellent choice for families who can afford it, particularly as it's so convenient for the slopes. The Sonnenburg and the Goldener Berg have in-house kindergartens. Reporters tell us the Oberlech school is great for children, with small classes, good English spoken and lunch offered.

Staying there

Lech is big enough for some of the cheaper accommodations to be quite a walk from the lifts. Unless you're heavily into nightlife, staying up in Oberlech is very attractive – reporters recommend both the Goldener Berg (22050) and the Burg (22910) for food, comfort, facilities (pool and sauna) and views from your own balcony.

HOW TO GO
Surprising variety
There is quite a variety of accommodations from luxury hotels through to simple but spotless B&Bs.
Hotels There are three 5-star hotels, over 30 4-star and countless more modest places.
(((((5) **Arlberg** (2134) Patronised by royalty and celebrities. Elegantly rustic chalet, centrally placed. Pool.

The picturesque main street has a gurgling river running between it and the slopes →

Phone numbers
From elsewhere in Austria add the prefix 05583.
From abroad use the prefix +43 5583.

((((5) **Post** (2206) Lovely old Relais & Chateaux place on main street with pool and sauna.

((((4) **Krone** (2551) One of the oldest buildings in the village, in a prime spot by the river.

((((4) **Tannbergerhof** (2202) Splendidly atmospheric inn on main street, with outdoor bar and hugely popular disco (tea-time as well as later). Pool.

((((4) **Haldenhof** (2444) Friendly and well run, with antiques and a fine collection of prints and paintings.

((((4) **Sonnenburg** (Oberlech) (2147) Luxury on-trail chalet (popular for lunch). Good children's facilities. Pool.

((((4) **Monzabon** (2104) Excellent restaurant and wine cellar. Pool.

((2) **Haus Angerhof** (2418) Beautiful ancient pension, with wood panels and quaint little windows.

((2) **Haus Fernsicht** (2432) Pension with spa facilities.

((2) **Haus Rudboden** (2220) Right by the beginner areas.

Apartments/condos There are lots available through local agencies.

EATING OUT
Not necessarily expensive
There are over 50 restaurants in Lech, nearly all of them in hotels. For reasonably priced meals try the Montana, which serves French cuisine and has an excellent wine cellar, the Krone, Ambrosius (above a shopping arcade), or the Post, which serves Austrian nouvelle-type food. The Madlochblick has a typically Austrian restaurant, very cozy with good solid food. Hus Nr 8 is one of the best non-hotel restaurants (see mountain restaurants) and does good fondue. For pasta and other Italian fare there is Pizzeria Charly. In Oberlech there is a good fondue at the Alte Goldener Berg, a tavern built in 1432. In Zug the Rote Wand is excellent for fondues and a good night out. Also try the Alphorn, the Klösterle and the Olympia.

A reporter recommends Gasthaus Älpele near Zug, 3km/2miles from the road – up the valley on the cross-country route, for its atmosphere and good food. Transport is arranged by the restaurant in the form of covered wagons attached to a snowcat.

APRES-SKI
Good but pricey
The umbrella bar of the Burg hotel at Oberlech is popular immediately after the slopes close, as is the champagne bar in Oberlech's Hotel Montana. Then the 'beautiful people' head for the Hotel Krone's ice bar which has a lovely setting by the river, or to the outdoor bar of the Tannbergerhof.

ACTIVITIES

Indoor Tennis, hotel swimming pools and saunas, squash, museum, art gallery, hotel spas

Outdoor 30km/19 miles of cleared walking paths, toboggan run (from Oberlech), artificial ice rink (skating, curling), sleigh rides, billiards, helicopter rides

TOURIST OFFICE

Postcode A-6764
t +43 (5583) 21610
f 3155
info@lech-zuers.at
www.lech-zuers.at

Inside the Tannbergerhof, there's a tea dance disco. The bar in the Strolz store is good for people-watching in bad weather.

Later on, the Arlberg Hotel's Scotch Club disco (owned and run by former Olympic champion, Egon Zimmermann), and those in the hotels Almhof-Schneider and Krone liven up. The latter's Side Step specialises in 60s and 70s music. S'Pfefferkörndl is a good place for a drink, and you can get a steak or pizza there until late. The smart, modern-style Fux bar and restaurant has live music and is one of the latest trendy places.

For a change of scene, the Rote Wand in Zug has a disco.

Taxi James is a shared minibus cab, which charges a flat fare for any journey in Lech/Zürs – you phone and it picks you up within half an hour.

OFF THE SLOPES
Poseurs' paradise
Many visitors to Lech don't indulge in sports. If you're armed with limitless funds the shopping possibilities are enticing, and the main street is often filled with fur-clad browsers. Strolz's plush emporium in the center of town is a good place to up the rate at which you're spending euros.

It's easy for pedestrians to get to Oberlech or Zug to meet friends for lunch on the slopes – or for skiers and boarders to get back to the village. The village outdoor bars make ideal posing positions – but make sure you are immaculately groomed or you'll feel out of place. An excursion to St Anton, to see how the other half live, is possible, though Lech clientele may feel more at home getting off the bus at chic St Christoph. For the more active there are 30km/19miles of walking paths and a variety of sporting activities – the walk along the river to Zug is especially beautiful.

Zürs 1,720m/5,640ft

Ten minutes' drive towards St Anton from Lech, Zürs is almost on the Flexen Pass, with good snow virtually guaranteed. Zürs was a tiny hamlet used only for farming during the summer until (in the late 1890s) the Flexen Pass road was built and Zürs began to develop, entering the winter sports scene in the early 20th century.

The village is even more exclusive than Lech, with no hotels of less than 3-star standing, and a dozen 4-star and 5-star hotels around which life revolves. But the opulence is less overt here. There are few shops. Nightlife is quiet. There's a disco in the Edelweiss hotel (26620) and a piano bar in the Alpenhof (2191). Mathie's-Stüble and Kaminstüble are worth trying, as is Vernissage, at the Skiclub Alpenrose (22710), which is reported to be the best nightspot in town. Serious dining means the Zürserhof (25130) and the Lorünser (22540); make sure your wallet will stand a visit before you go – credit cards are not accepted. For something cheaper, try spaghetti in the basement of the Edelweiss. (Princess Caroline, who stays at the Lorünser, is reputed to have been successful in ordering it here as late as 5am.) All phone numbers given are for 4- or 5-star hotels.

Zürs has its own school, but many of the instructors are booked for the entire season by regular clients, and more than 80% of them are hired privately. The resort also has its own kindergarten.

Stuben 1405m/4,610ft

Stuben is linked by lifts and trails to St Anton, but is on the Vorarlberg side of the Arlberg pass (St Anton is over in the Tirol). There are infrequent but timetabled buses between the village and Lech and Zürs.

Dating back to the 13th century, Stuben is a small, unspoiled village where personal service and quiet friendliness are the order of the day. Modern developments are kept to a minimum. The only concessions to the new era are a few unobtrusive hotels, a school, two or three bars, a couple of banks and a few little shops. The old church and traditional buildings, usually snow-covered, make Stuben a really charming Alpine village.

The north-facing local slopes retain snow well, though the line-free but slow village chair can be a cold ride. A quicker and warmer way to get to St Anton in the morning, if you have a car, is to drive down the road to Rauz.

Stuben has sunny beginner areas separate from the main slopes, but lack of easy runs make it unsuitable for beginners. Evenings are quiet, but several places have a pleasant atmosphere. The charming old Post (7610) is a very comfortable 4-star renowned for its fine restaurant.

Mayrhofen

Bigger means better for 2002

HOW IT RATES

The slopes

Snow	***
Extent	***
Experts	*
Intermediates	***
Beginners	**
Convenience	*
Trails	*
Restaurants	****

The rest

Scenery	***
Resort charm	***
Off-slope	****

➕ New lifts for 2001/02 will increase local terrain by 40%

➕ Snow-sure by Tirol standards, plus the Hintertux glacier nearby

➕ Various nearby areas on the same lift pass, and reached by free bus

➕ Lively après-ski – though it's easily avoided if you prefer peace

➕ Excellent children's amenities

➕ Wide range of off-slope facilities

➖ Two widely separated areas of slopes and no runs back to the village itself from the main area

➖ Best beginner area served by a liftline-prone tram, itself a longish walk or bus-ride from town

➖ Slopes can be crowded, with some long liftlines

➖ Mainly short runs

➖ Little to challenge experts

While many young or youngish visitors like Mayrhofen for its lively nightlife, it is also an excellent family resort, with highly regarded kindergartens and ski schools and a fun pool with special children's area. The liveliest of the nightlife is confined to a few very popular places, easily avoided by families.

Two new lifts for the 2001/02 season will link Mayrhofen's existing slopes with those of Lanersbach and Vorderlanersbach, increasing the local trails by around 40% and giving some much needed longer runs – most of the existing runs are very short (typically 300m/98oft to 400m/1,310ft vertical). Intermediates who are willing to travel around on the free buses can have an enjoyably varied week visiting different ski areas on the Ziller valley lift ticket, including the excellent glacier up at Hintertux. But if you plan to spend a lot of time at the glacier, consider staying in Lanersbach, described in the Hintertux chapter.

Despite recent lift improvements, Mayrhofen itself is not a convenient resort – the main lift station is at one end of town and you have to catch the lift down as well as up, or end up a bus-ride from town.

What's new

Massive investment in lifts in recent years includes new high-capacity gondolas out of town and from Hippach and high-speed chairs on the mountain.

2001/02 will see a new 150-person tram from the slopes to link with Rastkogel above Vorderlanersbach, previously a bus-ride away. This area links to the Eggalm area above Lanersbach. The link back will be by a new high-speed six-pack. All this will mean a 40% increase in Mayrhofen's terrain to a total of 143km/89 miles.

Back in the existing Mayrhofen area the old double chair up to Schafskopf will be replaced by a high-speed six-pack for 2001/02. Another new six-pack will be built in this area, opening up new runs.

MAYRHOFEN TOURIST BOARD / K HRUSCHKA

Mayrhofen is prettily set in a wide valley, with mountains on three sides ➔

The resort

Mayrhofen is a fairly large resort sitting in the flat-bottomed Zillertal. Most shops, bars and restaurants are on the one main, long, largely pedestrianized, street, with hotels and pensions spread over a wider area. As the village has grown, architecture has been kept traditional.

Despite its reputation for lively après-ski, Mayrhofen is not dominated by loud drinkers. They exist, but tend to gather in a few easily avoided bars. The central hotels are mainly slightly upscale, and overall the resort feels pleasantly civilized.

The Penken lift station is towards one end of the main street, while the Ahorn tram is out in the suburbs, about 1km (less than a mile) from the center. The free bus service is frequent and efficient, though it finishes early (5pm).

MOUNTAIN FACTS

Altitude 630m-2500m/
2,070ft-8,200ft
Lifts 45
Pistes 143km/89 miles
Blue 29%
Red 59%
Black 12%
Snowmaking 78km/
48 miles

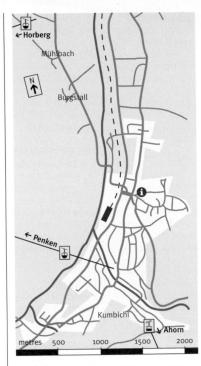

LIFT TICKETS

2001/02 prices in
euros
Mayrhofen/Zillertal
Coverage depends on
period – see notes.
Main ticket
1-day ticket 28
6-day ticket (including
glacier) 159
Children
15 to 18: 6-day ticket
(including glacier) 127
6 to 14: 6-day ticket
(including glacier)
95.50
Under 6: free ticket
Short-term tickets
tickets available from
11am, noon and 2pm.
Alternative periods
Zillertaler ski ticket
available for 4 days'
skiing in 6, 5 days in
7, 6 days in 7 and 10
days in 14.
Notes Up to 3-day
tickets covers Penken,
Horberg-Gerent,
Ahorn, Rastkogel and
Eggalm areas only; 4-
day and over includes
all 149 Ziller valley
lifts (including
Hintertux glacier),
478km/297 miles of
trail, ski-bus and
railway.
Alternative tickets
Zillertaler ski ticket
also available without
Hintertux glacier (6
days 132 for adults,
106 for 15- to 18-year
olds, 79 for 6- to 14-
year olds).

you often have to take them down as
well as up. The largest area is **Penken,**
accessed by the main jumbo gondola
from one end of town. It is also
accessible via the 8-person Hippach
gondola, a bus-ride away and by the
gondolas from Finkenberg and
Vorderlanersbach in the Hintertux
valley. You cannot get back to
Mayrhofen on snow – you either catch
the main gondola down or, if cover is
good, you can get back to both
Finkenberg and Hippach on snow (the
Finkenberg trail is a path, classified
red, and there's an ungroomed ski-
route to Hippach). The Penken area
will link via a new tram from the
2001/02 season with the **Rastkogel** and
Eggalm areas previously accessible
only by the valley bus, forming a
linked area of 128km/80 miles of trails
– see What's New and the Hintertux
chapter.

The only trail from the mountains to
Mayrhofen (the outskirts of it) is a
winding run down from **Ahorn** (black
on the map), so moving between
mountains or lunching in the village
means a serious waste of slope time.

SNOW RELIABILITY
Good by Austrian standards

Although the highest lift goes no
higher than 2500m/8,200ft, the area is
reasonably good for snow-cover
because (apart from the unreliable
valley runs) all of Mayrhofen's slopes
are above 1580m/5,180ft. Snowmaking
covers nearly all the main slopes in the
Penken/Horberg/Gerent area. And there
is one of the best glaciers in the Alps
within day-trip range, at Hintertux.

FOR EXPERTS
Not ideal

Mayrhofen itself doesn't have much for
experts. But there are worthwhile
challenges to be found, including off-
trail areas, you can go touring, and
reporters staying here and visiting the

The mountains

Of Mayrhofen's two areas of slopes
Penken/Rastkogel/Eggalm is mainly
suitable for intermediates, and Ahorn
mainly for beginners. Neither has much
for experts. A frequent free bus serves
other resorts covered by the pass,
notably Hintertux and Gerlos – but we
hear you may need to be up early to
beat the liftlines. If you buy a lift ticket
in advance through a tour operator,
make sure it covers the Hintertux
glacier. Signposting and marking of
runs is good.

THE SLOPES
Highly inconvenient

Lifts to the two main sectors are a
longish walk or a bus-ride apart, and

boarding *Mayrhofen is not ideal for learning to snowboard – the beginner
areas are inconvenient and the abundance of surface lifts adds to
the difficulty. For intermediates though, the slopes are good and the gondolas
and chair-lifts mean that few surface lifts have to be negotiated. There is a
terrain park and a half-pipe, where the British Championships have been held for
the last two seasons, in the Penken area. More advanced riders will enjoy the
Hintertux glacier, further up the valley – it's a boarder-friendly place (except for
the surface lifts), with Europe's highest World Cup half-pipe and some good off-
trail possibilities. Budget prices and lively nightlife make Mayrhofen a popular
boarder destination.*

other resorts on the valley lift pass have been more than happy. The long ungroomed trail to Hippach is the only challenging local slope, and is rarely in good order – as a report from a repeat visitor testifies: 'Snow conditions were the best I've known, yet some parts were extremely tricky due to poor snow cover.'

FOR INTERMEDIATES
On the tough side
Most of Mayrhofen's slopes are on the steep side of the usual intermediate range and so great for confident or competent intermediates. And the new expansion for 2001/02 means there will be more of them and some longer runs too, making the area more interesting for high-mileage cruisers. But most of the runs in the main Penken area are short. And there are few really gentle blue runs, making the area less than ideal for nervous intermediates. Overcrowding of many lifts and runs can add to the intimidation factor.

If you're willing to travel, each of the main mountains covered by the Ziller valley pass is large and varied enough for an interesting day out.

FOR BEGINNERS
Overrated: big drawbacks
Despite its reputation for teaching, Mayrhofen is not ideal for beginners. The Ahorn beginner areas are excellent – high, extensive and sunny – but it's a rather tiresome journey to reach them (and to get home again). The overcrowded slopes and restaurants add to the hassle. The Penken nursery area is less satisfactory. And there are few long blues to progress to from the beginner areas.

FOR CROSS-COUNTRY
Go to Lanersbach
In theory there is a fine 20km/12 mile trail along the valley to Zell am Ziller, plus small loops conveniently in, or close to, the village. But snow at 600m/1,970ft is not reliable. Vorderlanersbach has a much higher, more snow-sure trail running to Madseit.

LIFTLINES
Problems being tackled
The Penken jumbo-gondola opened in 1995, theoretically ending morning and evening liftlines that were among the worst in the Alps. But one peak-period visitor tells of a chaotic scramble for boarding. And there are still lengthy liftlines for the Ahorn tram.

The increased capacity of both the Penken and Hornberg lifts from the valley means the slopes can now get

SCHOOLS/GUIDES

Mayrhofen Red Profis
2001/02 prices in euros

Classes 5 days
2½hr: 10am-12.30 or 1pm-3.30
5 half days 89

Children's classes
Ages: 4 to 14
6 full days 158

Private lessons
Hourly and daily
36 for 1hr; each additional person 14

Mayrhofen Total
2000/01 prices in euros

Classes 6 days
4hr: 10am-noon and 1pm-3pm
6 full days 115

Children's classes
Ages: 4 to 14
6 full days including lunch 172

Private lessons
Hourly and daily
40 for 1hr

Mount Everest
2000/01 prices in euros

Classes 6 days
4hr: 10am-noon and 1pm-3pm
6 full days 112

Children's classes
Ages: 5 to 14
6 full days including lunch 169

Private lessons
Hourly
36 for 1hr; each additional person 15

Phone numbers
From elsewhere in Austria add the prefix 05285.
From abroad use the prefix +43 5285.

CHILDCARE

All three ski schools run children's classes for children aged 4 to 14 where lunch is provided. Two of them run ski kindergartens for children aged 1 to 4.

Wuppy's Kinderland non-skiing nursery at the fun pool complex takes children aged 3 months to 7 years, 9am to 5pm, Monday to Friday.

---

very crowded, causing some liftlines. Slow, old lifts are being quickly replaced by fast new ones but that has added to the crowds on the trails. The new expansion into the previously quiet Rastkogel and Eggalm areas may dissipate the crowds and solve this problem. Buses to and from the more out-of-town gondolas are often crowded, especially the Finkenberg one, which also serves Hintertux.

MOUNTAIN RESTAURANTS
Plenty of them
Most of Penken's many mountain restaurants are attractive and serve good-value food but can get crowded– Vroni's is highly recommended. The tiny Hiatamadl hut serves simple, wholesome home-cooked food. The Schneekar restaurant at the top of the Gerent section has been recommended. To get away from the crowds try the restaurants on Eggalm. The Ahorn's restaurants are inadequate for the hordes using them.

SCHOOLS AND GUIDES
Excellent reputation
Mayrhofen's popularity is founded on its three schools and a high proportion of guests take lessons. We have received many positive reports over the years and one recent reporter was delighted with her two-day private lesson with the Total school.

FACILITIES FOR CHILDREN
Good but inconvenient
Mayrhofen has put childcare at the center of its pitch, and all the facilities are excellent. But you may prefer to take your kids to resorts where they don't have to be bussed around and ferried up and down the mountain.

Staying there

The village is rather long and sprawling, and the lift stations are at one end of it. Although there is a free bus service, location is important. The original center, around the market, church, tourist office and bus/railway stations, is now on the edge of things. The most convenient area is on the main street, as close as possible to the Penken gondola station.

HOW TO GO
Choose your price range
Hotels There are dozens of cheap pensions, but most visitors stay in the

---

larger, better hotels. One reporter warns that it can be a bit noisy near the center of the resort.

《《《⑤ **Elisabeth** (6767) The resort's only 5-star hotel, an opulent chalet in a fair position near the post office.

《《《④ **Manni's** (63301-0) Well-placed, smartly designed; pool.

《《《④ **Kramerwirt** (6700) Lovely Tirolean hotel simply oozing character. A recent visitor reports 'friendly and helpful staff, comfortable rooms, varied and interesting half-board menu'.

《《③ **Strass** (6705) Best placed of the 4-stars, very close to the Penken gondola. Lively bars, disco, fitness center, solarium, pool and children's playroom, but rooms lack style.

《《③ **Rose** (62229) Well placed, a few minutes' walk from the center. Good food.

《《③ **Neue Post** (62131) Convenient family-run 4-star on the main street – 'good food and nice big rooms'.

《《③ **Waldheim** (62211) Smallish, cozy 3-star gasthof, not far from the Penken lift.

《《③ **St Georg** (62792-0) Poorly positioned for amenities, but ideal for those wanting a multi-facility quality hotel in peaceful surroundings.

《《③ **Jägerhof** (62540) Another peaceful hotel with good facilities, mid-way between the two lifts.

① **Claudia** (62361), **Monika** (62178) Cheap little twin guest houses in a good position.

① **Kumbichl** (62371), **Kumbichlhof** (62458) Adjoining pensions, next to the Ahorn tram.

EATING OUT
Wide choice
Most visitors are on half-board, but there is a large choice of restaurants catering for most tastes and budgets. The Hotel Rose has a particularly good, informal restaurant. The restaurants in the Kramerwirt, Neuhaus ('excellent standards of food and service'), and Gasthaus Ländenhof are also recommended. Manni's is good for pizzas ('a genuine pleasure to eat there') and Kaiser Brundl, opposite the Neuhaus, has been recommended for its extensive menu (traditional and international dishes) and good food, though one reporter complained of appalling service on one occasion. Wirthaus zum Griena is a 'wonderful old wooden building offering traditional farmhouse cuisine'.

GETTING THERE

Air Salzburg, transfer 3hr. Munich, transfer 2½hr. Innsbruck, transfer 1hr.

Rail Local line through to resort; regular buses from station.

ACTIVITIES

Indoor Bowling, adventure pool, 2 hotel pools open to the public, massage, sauna, squash, fitness center, indoor tennis center at Hotel Berghof (3 courts, coaching available), indoor riding-school, pool and billiards, cinema
Outdoor Ice-skating rink, curling, horse-riding, horse sleigh rides, 45km/28 miles cleared paths, hang-gliding, paragliding, tobogganing (2 runs of 2.5km/1.5 miles), snowrafting

TOURIST OFFICE

Postcode A-6290
t +43 (5285) 6760
f 6760 33
mayrhofen@zillertal.
tirol.at
www.mayrhofen.com

APRES-SKI
Lively but not rowdy

Nightlife is a great selling point. Mayrhofen has all the standard Tirolean-style entertainments, such as folk dancing, bier kellers and tea dances, along with bowling, sleigh rides, tobogganing, but also some seriously lively bars and discos.

At close of play, the Happy End umbrella bar, at the top of the Penken gondola, is lively and the Ice bar, in the hotel Strass (near the Penken gondola base station), gets packed out. Micky's is another recommended après-ski bar.

Some of the other bars in the Strass are rocking places later on – the Lobby bar has live music and the Sport's Arena club has a good atmosphere. Mo's American theme bar and Scotland Yard are also popular with reporters. The Schlussel disco can be 'wild'. Try Am Kamin (in the hotel Elisabeth) if you're after more Manhattan than Mayrhofen. The Neue Post bar and the Passage are recommended for a quiet drink.

OFF THE SLOPES
Good for all

The village travel agency arranges trips to Italy, and Innsbruck is easily reached by train. There are also good walks and sports amenities, including the swimming pool complex – with saunas, solariums and lots of other fun features. Pedestrians have no trouble getting up the mountain to meet friends for lunch.

Finkenberg 840m/2,760ft

Finkenberg is a much smaller, quieter village than Mayrhofen.

THE RESORT

Finkenberg is no more than a collection of traditional-style hotels, bars, cafes and private homes spread along the busy, steep main road between Mayrhofen and Lanersbach. Most hotels are within walking distance of the gondola, and many of the more distant ones run minibuses to the lift station.

THE MOUNTAIN

Finkenberg shares Mayrhofen's main Penken slopes. The gondola up to Ahorn is a short bus-ride away.
Slopes A gondola gives good direct access to the Penken slopes.
Snow reliability The local slopes are not as well-endowed with snowmaking as Mayrhofen's.
Snowboarding There are no special facilities.
Experts Not much challenge, though we did find a black run not marked on the trail map.
Intermediates The whole newly expanded area opens up from the top of the gondola.
Beginners The village beginner area, given good snow, means beginners do not need to buy the full lift ticket. But it's a sunless spot, and good conditions are far from certain.
Cross-country Cross-country skiers have to get a bus up to Lanersbach.
Liftlines The gondola gives line-free access to the Penken.
Mountain restaurants See the recommendations given for Mayrhofen.
Schools and guides There are two schools. The Finkenberg School has a particularly good reputation.
Facilities for children There's a non-ski childcare center, and the ski nursery takes children from age four.

STAYING THERE

Hotels There are a fair number. The Sporthotel Stock (6775) has great spa facilities and is owned by the family of the famous former downhill champion Leonard Stock.
Eating out Restaurants are mostly hotel-based.
Après-ski Finkenberg is quiet in the evenings. The main après-ski spots are the Laterndl Pub and Finkennest. Mayrhofen is a short cab-ride away.
Off the slopes Swimming, curling and ice-skating are available, and the local walks have been recommended.

Obergurgl

High, snow-sure slopes with loyal clientele

HOW IT RATES

The slopes

Snow	*****
Extent	**
Experts	**
Intermediates	***
Beginners	****
Convenience	****
Liftlines	*****
Restaurants	**

The rest

Scenery	***
Resort charm	****
Off-slope	**

➕ Glaciers apart, one of the Alps' most reliable resorts for snow – especially good for a late-season holiday

➕ Excellent area for beginners, timid intermediates and families

➕ Mainly liftline- and crowd-free

➕ Retains village charm despite modern development

➕ Lively tea-time après-ski

➕ Obergurgl and Hochgurgl slopes are now linked by gondola

➖ Small area with no tough trails

➖ Very bleak setting, with few sheltered slopes for bad weather

➖ Few off-slope amenities except in hotels

➖ Quiet nightlife by Austrian standards

➖ For a small Austrian resort, rather expensive

A loyal band of visitors go back every year to Obergurgl or Hochgurgl, booking a year in advance in recognition of the limited supply of beds. They love the high, snow-sure, easy intermediate slopes, the end-of-the-valley seclusion and the civilized atmosphere in the comfortable, expensive hotels.

Sceptics say that the villages and the slopes are too limited. They have a point. If we're going to a bleak, high, snow-sure resort where there is nothing to do but ski or board, we'd rather go somewhere with rather more skiing or boarding to do (like Tignes, for example).

What's new

The resort is planning three new lifts for 2001/02: a new eight-seater gondola from Hochgurgl up to Wurmkogl; in the Gaisberg sector, a four-seater chair-lift replacing the Übungs surface lift; and a six-pack in place of the Steinmann and Sattel surface lifts.

Guests can now buy their tickets at hotel reception desks – credit cards are still not accepted at the lift office.

Snowmaking was also extended last season.

There's a new casino at the Hochwirst hotel. And there's a new 24hr internet accommodations booking service.

The resort

Obergurgl is based on a traditional old village, set in a remote, bleak spot, the dead end of a long road up past Sölden. It is the highest parish in Austria and is usually under a blanket of snow from November until May. The surrounding mountains are bleak, with an array of avalanche barriers giving them a forbidding appearance.

Hochgurgl, a bus-ride (or gondola-ride) away across the mountainside, is little more than a handful of hotels at the foot of its own slopes.

Obergurgl has no through traffic and few day visitors. The village center is mainly traffic-free, and entirely so at night. Village atmosphere is lively during the day and immediately after the slopes close, but can be subdued later at night; there are some nightspots, but most people stay in their hotels. The resort is popular with families and well-heeled groups looking for a relaxing winter break.

Despite its small size, this is a village of parts. At the northern entrance to the resort is a cluster of hotels near the main Festkogel gondola, which takes you to all the local slopes. This area is good for

getting to the slopes and for ease of access by car, but it's a long walk or a shuttle-bus from the village center and the beginner areas. The road then passes another group of hotels around the ice rink, up the hillside to the east (beware steep, sometimes treacherous walks to and from other amenities). The village proper starts with an attractive little square with church, fountain, and the original village hotel (the Edelweiss und Gurgl). Just above are the Rosskar and Gaisberg chair-lifts to the local slopes. Drivers have underground parking right in the center of town.

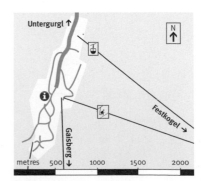

Hochgurgl, despite its location on the slopes at 2150m/7,050ft, is not conveniently arranged. From practically all the half-dozen hotels you have to negotiate roads and/or staircases to get to or from the snow. Hochgurgl is even quieter than Obergurgl at night.

For a day out, it's a short bus or car trip to Sölden (good, quite steep and extensive intermediate slopes), and a long car trip to Kühtai (a worthwhile high area near Innsbruck). Much closer is the tiny touring launch-pad of Vent.

The mountains

The slopes of Obergurgl and Hochgurgl are about 4km/2 miles apart but are now directly linked by gondola, as well as by road. Even so, the slopes are still surprisingly limited, and lacking interest or challenge for adventurous intermediates or experts. You don't get the sense of travel, as you do in bigger Alpine resorts.

Most of the slopes are very exposed and there are very few woodland runs to head to in poor conditions. Wind and white-outs can shut the lifts and, especially in early season, severe cold can curtail enthusiasm.

The lift ticket is quite expensive for the relatively small area.

THE SLOPES
Limited cruising

Obergurgl is the smaller of the two linked areas. It is in two sections, well linked by trail in one direction, more loosely in the other. The gondola and the Rosskar fast quad chair-lift from the village go to the higher Festkogl area. This is served by two surface lifts and a chair up to 3035m/9,960ft (you can join the Rosskar lift at its mid-station too). From here you can head back to the gondola base or over to Gaisberg, with its high point at Hohe Mut, reached by a long, slow chair. Two new high capacity chair-lifts are replacing the three surface lifts here for 2001/02. A chair up from Obergurgl's village square provides the other link on to the Gaisberg slopes.

The Top Express gondola is the obvious way to travel to **Hochgurgl** during the day. But there is still the alternative of a regular and reliable free shuttle-bus to Untergurgl. From there, a chair-lift goes up to Hochgurgl (also reachable by car, or by bus – once daily). From this season a new eight-person gondola will go up from here to the high point of Wurmkogl (3080m/10,100ft), replacing a chain of old chair-lifts. From Wurmkogl there are spectacular views of the Dolomites. A separate chair-lift from mid-mountain serves runs on the shoulder of Schermerspitze, and there are surface lifts serving other mid-mountain slopes to north and sound of the main axis.

A single tree-lined run leads down from Hochgurgl to the bottom of the Untergurgl chair.

SNOW RELIABILITY
Excellent

Obergurgl has high slopes and is arguably the most snow-sure of Europe's non-glacier resorts – even without its snowmaking, which is now impressively extensive. It has a justifiably popular mid-December white week, and regular late-season visitors who book well in advance.

MOUNTAIN FACTS

Altitude	1800m-3080m
	5,910ft-10,100ft
Lifts	23
Trails	110km/68 miles
Blue	32%
Red	50%
Black	18%
Snowmaking	25km/
	16 miles

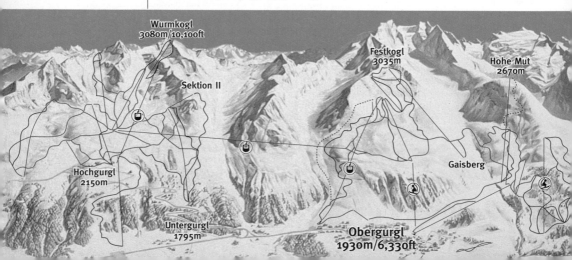

Wurmkogl
3080m/10,100ft

Festkogl
3035m

Hohe Mut
2670m

Sektion II

Hochgurgl
2150m

Gaisberg

Untergurgl
1795m

Obergurgl
1930m/6,330ft

Obergurgl

LIFT TICKETS

2001/02 prices in euros

Obergurgl ski ticket
Covers all lifts in Obergurgl and Hochgurgl, and local ski-bus.
Beginners Lift ticket or points card.
Main ticket
1-day ticket 35.5
6-day ticket 171.5
(low season 151)
Senior citizens
Over 60: 6-day ticket 104.5
Children
Under 16: 6-day ticket 104.5
Under 8: free ticket
Short-term tickets
Half-day (from 11am, noon, 1pm or 2pm).
Alternative periods
5 days' skiing in 7 and 11 days' skiing in14 tickets available.

FOR EXPERTS
Not generally recommendable

There is a fair amount of enjoyable off-trail to be found with a guide – especially from Obergurgl – and the top school groups often go off-trail when there is little avalanche danger. This is a well-known area for ski touring, and we have reports of very challenging expeditions on the glaciers at the head of the valley.

The most challenging official trail is the Hohe Mut bump run beneath the slow, old chair-lift at Gaisberg. But this is often irritatingly awkward rather than pleasurable, being icy, worn and difficult to follow in places. Other blacks are rather overrated – they could easily be red – and there are few challenges. Experts will soon tire of cruising the mainly short runs, no matter how powdery the snow.

FOR INTERMEDIATES
Good but limited

There is some perfect intermediate terrain here, made even better by the normally flattering snow conditions. The problem is, there's not much of it. Keen trail-bashers will quickly tire of travelling the same runs and be itching to catch the bus to Sölden, down the valley – unfortunately, there is no ticket-sharing arrangement.

Hochgurgl has the bigger area of easy runs, and these make good cruising. For more challenging intermediate runs, head to the Vorderer Wurmkogellift, on the right as you look at the mountain. Less confident intermediates may find the woodland trail down from Hochgurgl to the bus stop at Untergurgl tricky.

The Obergurgl area has more red than blue runs but most offer no great challenge to a confident intermediate. There is some easy cruising around mid-mountain on the Festkogel. The blue run from the top of the Festkogel gondola down to the village, via the Gaisberg sector, is one of the longest cruises in the area. And there's another long enjoyable run down the length of the gondola, with a scenic off-trail

boarding *Obergurgl is a traditional ski destination, attracting an affluent and (dare we say it?) 'older' clientele. But the resort is actually pretty good for snowboarding. There's a terrain-park and quarter pipe on the Festkogl in Obergurgl and a half-pipe on the Wurmkogl in Hochgurgl. Beginners will be pleased to find that much of the resort can be covered without having to ride surface lifts. And there's also some off-trail potential for more advanced riders. Evenings tend to be a bit tame but Sölden, 20 minutes by road, has stacks of lively bars.*

SCHOOLS/GUIDES

2001/02 prices in euros

Obergurgl
Classes 6 days
4hr: 10am-noon and 2pm-4pm
6 full days 143
Children's classes
Ages: from 5
6 full days including lunch 143
Private lessons
Half and full day
167 for full day
106 for half day; each additional person 8.

Hochgurgl
Classes 6 days
4hr: 10am-noon and 2pm-4pm
6 full days 143
Children's classes
Ages: from 5
6 full days 143
Private lessons
Hourly, half and full day
55 for 1hr, for 1 or 2 people; each additional person 15.
109 for half day, for 1 or 2 people; each additional person 15

CHILDCARE

The ski schools at Obergurgl and Hochgurgl take children over the age of 5. Children can join the ski kindergarten from age of 3.

The village kindergarten in Obergurgl also takes children from the age of 3.

The Alpina, Austria and Hochfirst hotels (among others) have in-house kindergartens.

---

variant in the adjoining valley.

In the Gaisberg area, there are very easy runs in front of the Nederhütte and back towards town. The bottom surface lifts here serve very short but sometimes surprisingly tricky and bumpy runs.

FOR BEGINNERS
Fine for first-timers or improvers

The inconveniently situated Mahdstuhl beginner area above Obergurgl is adequate for complete beginners. And the Gaisberg run – under the chair out of the village – and the wide blue run next to the Übungslift can be completed as soon as a modicum of control is achieved.

Near beginners can travel from the top of the four-person Wurmkogl chair to Hochgurgl village (600m/1,970ft vertical) without any problems. However, a recent reporter complained that the Hochgurgl beginner areas are inconveniently placed for complete beginners to have to walk to.

The quality of the snow makes the area a good (but relatively expensive) choice for beginners compared with most lower Austrian resorts.

CROSS-COUNTRY
Limited but snow-sure

Three small loops, one each at Obergurgl, Untergurgl and Hochgurgl, give just 12km/7 miles of trail. All are relatively snow-sure and pleasantly situated. Lessons are available.

LIFTLINES
Some peak-time bottlenecks

The resort is too remote to attract day trippers, and its authorities do not encourage 'bussing-in' when lower villages are struggling for snow. So major liftlines are rare – even at Christmas and New Year.

We have reports of short lines for the village lifts at the start of ski school but these tend to clear quickly (though one peak-season visitor tells of half-hour waits for the Rosskar lift as classes re-assemble after lunch). Liftlines for the gondola to Obergurgl can also build up late in the day as people start to head back home.

The same peak-season reporter also came across several trail bottlenecks, especially around the Nederhütte – possibly due to poor visibility higher up the mountain at the time. The blue runs from the top of the Wurmkogl lift and the long blue from the Festkogl to

---

the village can also get crowded.

MOUNTAIN RESTAURANTS
Little choice

Compared with most Austrian resorts, mountain huts are neither numerous nor very special. At Gaisberg the Nederhütte is jolly, and David's Skihütte is friendly, cheerful and good value. The 'traditional and welcoming' Schönwieshütte, a 10-minute walk from the trail, has excellent views, as does the small hut at the top of the Hohe Mut chair. At Hochgurgl, the tiny hut at Wurmkogl has stunning views into Italy and basic food. Many people return to one village or the other for lunch – some of the hotel restaurants have sun terraces.

SCHOOLS AND GUIDES
Mainly good news

We've had nothing but good reports of the Obergurgl school in the last couple of years, with good English spoken and excellent lessons and organization: 'highly efficient, very thorough testing of pupils before being put into a class', 'big effort to make school fun'. Class sizes are normally between 8 and 12 though we have received reports telling of 15 to a class at busy times.

FACILITIES FOR CHILDREN
Check out your hotel

Children's ski classes start at 5 years and children from age 3 can join Bobo's ski-kindergarten. There is also a non-skiing kindergarten for kids aged 3 and up. There's lunchtime supervision for ski school and kindergarten children alike. Many hotels offer childcare of one sort or another, and the Alpina has been particularly recommended.

Staying there

HOW TO GO
Plenty of good hotels

Most package accommodations are in hotels and pensions, but there are a number of comfortable apartments. Demand for rooms in Obergurgl exceeds supply, and for once it is true that you should book early to avoid disappointment.

Hotels Obergurgl's accommodations are of high quality: most hotels are 4-stars, and none is less than a 3-star. Hochgurgl's hotels include the most luxurious one in the area (the hotel Hochgurgl). Within each rating, hotels

GETTING THERE

Air Innsbruck, transfer 2hr. Salzburg, transfer 3hr. Munich, transfer 4hr.

Rail Train to Ötz; regular buses from station, transfer 1½hr.

Phone numbers
From elsewhere in Austria add the prefix 05256.
From abroad use the prefix +43 5256.

ACTIVITIES

Indoor Swimming pool (at Hotel Muhle, open to the public), saunas, whirlpools, steam baths, massage, bowling, pool and billiards, squash, table tennis
Outdoor Natural skating rink (open in the evenings), sleigh rides, snow-shoe outings

TOURIST OFFICE

Postcode A-6456
t +43 (5256) 6466
f 6353
info@obergurgl.com
www.obergurgl.com

are uniformly comfortable. Couples at the Deutschmann and at the Alpina have rightly been surprised to be asked to share a table.

A cheaper option is to stay down the valley in Untergurgl, where the 4-star Jadghof is recommended. It's worth remembering that some hotels still don't accept credit cards.

((((4) **Edelweiss und Gurgl** (6223) The focal hotel – biggest, oldest, one of the most appealing; on the central square, near the main lifts. Pool.

((((4) **Alpina de Luxe** (600) Big, smart chalet with excellent children's facilities. Pool.

((((4) **Hochfirst** (63250) Recommended by recent reporter. Good spa facilities, comfortable, four or five minutes from gondola.

((((4) **Jenewein** (6203) Recently refurbished, friendly staff, excellent food; good central position next to main lift.

((((4) **Berggasthof Gamper** (6545) Best rooms very comfortable, good food. Far end of town, past the square.

((((4) **Crystal** (6454) If you don't mind the ocean-liner appearance, it's one of the best near the Festkogel lift.

((((4) **Deutschmann** (6594) Popular choice with good food and facilities. Next to the Festkogel lift.

((((3) **Fender** (6316) Good all-rounder with friendly staff; central.

((((3) **Wiesental** (6263) Comfortable, well situated, good value.

((((3) **Granat-Schlössl** (6363) Amusing pseudo-castle, surprisingly affordable.

((((2) **Alpenblume** (6278) Good B&B hotel, well-placed for Festkogl lift.

((((2) **Haus Gurgl** (6533) B&B near Festkogl lift; friendly, pizzeria, same owners as Edelweiss und Gurgl.
Hochgurgl has equally good hotels.

((((5) **Hochgurgl** (6265) The only 5-star in the area. Luxurious, with pool.

((((3) **Sporthotel Ideal** (6290) Well situated for access to the slopes. Pool.

((((3) **Laurin** (6227) Well equipped, traditional rooms, excellent food.
Apartments/condos The Lohmann is a high-standard large modern apartment block, well placed for the slopes, less so for the village center below. The 3-star Pirchhütt has apartments close to the Festkogl gondola, and the Wiesental hotel has more central ones.

EATING OUT
Wide choice, limited range

Hotel dining rooms and à la carte restaurants dominate. The independent Pic Nic and Krumpn's Stadl are recommended. The Belmonte and the Romantika at the hotel Madeleine are popular pizzerias. Hotel Alpina has a particularly good reputation for its food – though a recent report says the Gotthard-Zeist and Hochfirst are 'just as good as the renowned Alpina'. The restaurant at the Berggasthof Gamper is pleasantly cozy. The two restaurants in the Edelweiss und Gurgl are reportedly 'superb'. Nederhütte and David's Skihütte up the mountain are both open in the evenings. Remember, credit cards are not accepted everywhere.

APRES-SKI
Lively early, quiet later

Obergurgl is more animated in the evening than you might expect. The Nederhütte mountain restaurant has lively tea dancing – you have to ski home afterwards though. All of the bars at the base of the Rosskar and Gaisberg lifts are popular at close of play – the Umbrella Bar outside the Edelweiss hotel is particularly busy in good weather. The Hexenkuchl at the Jenewein is also popular.

Later on, the crowded Krumpn's Stadl barn is the liveliest place in town with live music on alternate nights – it's also recommended for its fondues. The Josl, Jenewein and Edelweiss, and Gurgl hotels have atmospheric bars. The Bajazzo is a more sophisticated late-night haunt. The Edelweissbar and Austriakeller are discos (the latter with karaoke). There's now a casino at the Hochfirst.

Hochgurgl is very quiet at night except for Toni's Almhütte bar in the Olymp Sporthotel – one of three places with live music. There's also the African Bar disco.

OFF THE SLOPES
Very limited

There isn't much to do during the day, with few shops and limited public facilities. Innsbruck is over two hours away by post-bus. Sölden (20 minutes away) has a leisure center and shopping facilities. Pedestrians can walk to restaurants in the Gaisberg area to meet friends for lunch and there are 11km/7 miles of hiking paths. Many of the larger hotels have leisure facilities, though these are generally closed to non-residents – the Hochfirst health suite has been recommended.

Obertauern

1740m/5,710ft

Small but varied area, with great snow record

HOW IT RATES

The slopes

Snow	****
Extent	**
Experts	***
Intermediates	****
Beginners	*****
Convenience	****
Lines	****
Restaurants	***

The rest

Scenery	***
Resort charm	**
Off-slope	**

What's new

Last season the Kurvenlift T-bar up to the Edelweisshutte was replaced by a new fast quad, the Edelweissbahn.

MOUNTAIN FACTS

Altitude	1630m-2315m/ 5,350ft-7,600ft
Lifts	29
Trails	120km/75 miles
Blue	50%
Red	35%
Black	15%
Snowmaking	70km/ 43 miles

- ⊕ Excellent snow record
- ⊕ Well-linked, user-friendly circuit
- ⊕ Slopes for all standards
- ⊕ Good modern lift system
- ⊕ Good mountain restaurants
- ⊕ Lively après-ski scene
- ⊕ Short transfer from Salzburg

- ⊖ Village lacks traditional charm
- ⊖ Slopes have limited vertical and short runs
- ⊖ Lifts and snow can suffer from exposure to high winds

If you like the après-ski energy of Austria but have a hankering for the good snow of high French resorts, Obertauern could be just what you're looking for. The terrain is a bit limited by French standards, and the village is no Alpbach. But it's a lot prettier than Flaine – and if you've grown up on slush and ice in lower Austrian resorts moving up 1000m/3,000ft or so will be a revelation.

THE RESORT

In the land of postcard resorts grown out of rustic villages, Obertauern is different – a mainly modern development at the top of the Tauern pass road. Built in (high-rise) chalet style, it's not unattractive – but it lacks a central focus of shops and bars.

THE MOUNTAINS

The slopes and lifts form a ring around the village. The Tauern pass road divides them into two unequal parts; that apart, the slopes are well linked to make a user-friendly circuit that can be traveled clockwise or counter-clockwise in a couple of hours. Visitors used to big areas will soon start to feel they have seen it all. Vertical range is limited, and runs are short – most major lifts are in the 200m/600ft to 400m/1,300ft vertical range. Reporters complain about the trail map (which, unlike ours, takes a downward, bird's eye view of the area) and about poor trail marking that complicates navigation in bad weather.

Slopes Most trails are on the sunny slopes to the north of the road and village: a wide, many-faceted basin of mostly gentle runs, some combining steepish mogulled pitches with long schusses. The slopes on the other side of the road – on Gamsleitenspitze, to the south-west – have some of Obertauern's most difficult runs.

Snowboarding There is a fun-park at the mid-mountain lift junction of Hochalm.

Snow reliability The resort's key attraction is the exceptional snow reliability of its high bowl. But it is often windy, which can mean lifts close and snow blows away.

Experts Experts naturally incline towards the genuinely steep trails and off-trail runs from the Gamsleiten chair, but it is prone to closure. For more challenge, join an off-trail guided group.

Intermediates Most of Obertauern's circuit is of intermediate difficulty. Stay low for easier trails, or try the tougher runs higher up. The major mid-mountain lift base of the northern slopes is Hochalm, from where the Seekareck and Panorama chairs take you to challenging, often bumped runs. The chair to Hundskogel leads to a red and a black. And over at the Plattenkar quad there are two splendid reds.

Beginners Obertauern has very good beginner areas, close to the village. After the first couple of lessons you can go up the mountain, because the Schaidberg chair leads to a surface lift serving a high-altitude beginners' slope and there is an easy run to get you back to the village.

Cross-country There are 17km/11 miles of trails in the heart of the resort.

Liftlines When neighbouring resorts are not sharing Obertauern's good snow, non-residents arrive by the bus-load. However, the lift system is modern and impressive and is continually being upgraded. Seven new lifts in the last few years – including a six-pack on Schaidberg – are helping to eliminate the lines of the past and our most recent reporters experienced no serious lines.

The steep slopes on the south side of the village get some mornng sun, but are mainly shady →

Mountain restaurants Mountain restaurants are plentiful and good, but crowded. The smaller huts are more atmospheric ('Often full of groups of Germans singing,' says a reporter). The old Lürzer Alm at village level has been praised.

Schools and guides There are six schools. We have good reports of the Skischule Krallinger, despite large classes at peak times.

Facilities for children Most of the schools – including the Krallinger – take children.

STAYING THERE

Hotels Practically all accommodations are in hotels (mostly 3-star and 4-star) and guest houses. The following hotels have all been recommended: Petersbühel (7235); Enzian (7207-0); Steiner (7306); Das Schütz (7204-0); Edelweiss (7245); Gamsleiten (7286); and Alpina (73360).

Eating out The choices are mostly hotels (the Enzian is recommended) and the busy après-ski bars at the foot of the north-side lifts. The Hochalm restaurant at the top of the Grünwaldkopf quad sometimes serves early-evening meals.

Après-ski Obertauern has a lively and varied après-ski scene. The Latsch'n Alm has a terrace, music and dancing and is good at tea-time. Later, try the Lürzer Alm, which has farmyard-style decor and a disco. The Taverne has various bars, a pizzeria and disco.

Off the slopes There's an excellent, large sports center – with fitness room, tennis, squash and badminton, but no pool – but there's little else to do in the village in bad weather. However, Salzburg is an easy trip.

For lunch with friends, energetic non-skiers can get to the Kringsalm restaurant on foot.

Phone numbers
From elsewhere in Austria add the prefix 06456.
From abroad use the prefix +43 6456.

TOURIST OFFICE
Postcode A-5562
t +43 (6456) 7252
f 7515
info@ski-obertauern.com
www.ski-obertauern.com

Obertauern

87

Seekarspitze 2210m

Hundskogel 2135m

ekareck 2160m

Plattenspitze 2050m

Gamskarspitze 2030m

Hochalm 1945m

1980m

Kringsalm

1915m

Grünwaldkopf 1970m

1790m

Obertauern 1740m/5,710ft

1700m

1665m

1850m

Schaidberg 1630m

Gamsleitenspitze 2315m/7,600ft

1985m

Zehnerkarspitze 2190m

Saalbach-Hinterglemm 1000m/3,280ft

Attractive villages, lively nightlife and good intermediate runs

HOW IT RATES

The slopes

Snow	✱✱✱
Extent	✱✱✱
Experts	✱✱
Intermediates	✱✱✱✱
Beginners	✱✱✱
Convenience	✱✱✱✱
Liftlines	✱✱✱
Restaurants	✱✱✱✱

The rest

Scenery	✱✱✱
Resort charm	✱✱✱✱
Off-slope	✱✱

➕ Large, well-linked, intermediate circuit with open and tree-lined runs

➕ Saalbach is a big but pleasant, affluent village, lively at night

➕ Village main streets largely traffic-free

➕ Atmospheric mountain restaurants all over the mountain

➕ Sunny slopes

➕ Large snowmaking installation and excellent trail maintenance

➖ Large number of low, south-facing slopes that suffer from the sun

➖ Not much for experts

➖ Beginner areas in Saalbach are not ideal – sunny, and crowded in parts

➖ Saalbach spreads along the valley and some rooms are far from central

➖ Hinterglemm sprawls along a long street with no real center

➖ Can get rowdy at night

Like many Austrian resorts Saalbach-Hinterglemm has a pretty, traditional-style village and very lively nightlife, but unlike many it combines this with a very extensive circuit of slopes on both sides of a valley, and runs are linked by an efficient modern lift system. Its slopes resemble a French resort more than a traditional Austrian one – with the added advantage of excellent traditional mountain restaurants dotted around.

The main downside is the snow. Although it has impressive snowmaking, one side of the valley faces south and these slopes, especially the lower ones, deteriorate quickly in good weather.

Saalbach's après-ski is very lively – and can get rowdy – and is dominated by Scandinavian and German visitors. It rocks from 3pm until the early hours non-stop.

What's new

In 2000/01 two lifts on the south-facing slopes above Hinterglemm were replaced by high-speed chairs with bubbles for protection in cold weather. A six-seater replaced a slow old double chair to Spieleckkogel and a four-seater replaced a T-bar to Reiterkogel.

More snowmaking facilities were also installed on the Schattberg trails.

The resort

Saalbach and Hinterglemm, their centers 4km/2miles apart, expanded along a narrow dead-end valley floor until, a few years ago, they adopted a single identity. Their slopes are spread across north- and south-facing mountainsides, with lifts and runs connecting the villages via both sides.

Saalbach is one of the most attractive winter villages in Austria. Wedged into the narrow valley, with groomed slopes coming right down to the traffic-free

SAALBACH-HINTERGLEMM
TOURIST OFFICE

A perfect view looking towards Hinterglemm of the circuit's sunny south-facing slopes →

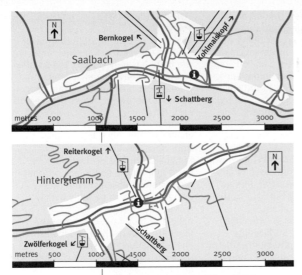

The slopes form a 'circus' almost exclusively suitable for intermediates, much of it on lightly wooded slopes. Few runs are likely either to bore the aggressive intermediate or worry the timid one. There are sufficient open sections and changes of pitch and direction to give trails variety, but not many genuinely black runs.

THE SLOPES
User-friendly circuit

The complete circuit of the valley can only be traveled counterclockwise – going clockwise at Vorderglemm there is no way up the slope on the opposite side of the valley. You can do a truncated clockwise circuit, crossing to the south side of the valley at Saalbach itself. The valley floor is very narrow, so there is very little walking necessary when changing sides. Where you end up at the end of the day is not important because of the excellent bus service, which runs every 20 minutes.

A good deal of the south-facing slopes is above 1400m/4,590ft, albeit with rather short runs. Five sectors can be identified – from west to east, **Hochalm**, **Reiterkogel**, **Bernkogel**, **Kohlmaiskopf** and **Wildenkarkogel**. The last connects via Schönleitenhütte to Leogang – a small, high, open area, leading to a long, narrow, north-facing slope down to Leogang village, broadening towards the bottom. An eight-person gondola brings you most of the way back.

The connections across Saalbach-Hinterglemm's south-facing slopes work well: when traversing the whole hillside you need to descend to the valley floor only once, in whichever direction you go. At Saalbach a very short walk across the main street gets you from the Bernkogel trail to the Kohlmaiskopf lift and vice versa. Both these runs are well endowed with

LIFT TICKETS

2001/02 prices in euros

Saalbach-Hinterglemm-Leogang
Covers all the lifts in Saalbach, Hinterglemm and Leogang, and the ski-bus.
Main ticket
1-day ticket 33
6-day ticket 155
(low season 140)
Senior citizens
Over 60: 6-day ticket 140
Children
Under 19: 6-day ticket 140
Under 14: 6-day ticket 78
Under 5: free ticket
Short-term tickets
Reduced price tickets in the morning from 9am to 12.30, and in the afternoon after 11.45.
Notes Can pay extra 10 euros for free use of indoor pool in Hinterglemm. Sun ticket for pedestrians: 7-day ticket 51 Euros. Points cards for beginners.
Senior citizen ticket for men and women over 60.

village center, its traditional-style buildings are huddled together around a classic onion-domed church. Most buildings are modern reproductions – the main exceptions are the Post Inn and the church – and the result is pretty close to Austrian charm with French convenience.

Saalbach is a strange mixture. The attractive, largely traffic-free, main street is lined with expensive, upscale hotels, restaurants and shops, festooned with twinkling lights, but further out there are more cheap and cheerful pensions. The clientele are similarly mixed, with rich BMW and Mercedes drivers rubbing shoulders in the bars and clubs with teenagers looking for a good time.

Hinterglemm is a more scattered, less appealing collection of hotels and holiday homes, with a small, virtually traffic-free zone in the center. It offers a cheaper, though not inexpensive, alternative to Saalbach, with far better access to the north-facing slopes.

Several resorts in Salzburg province are reachable by road – including Bad Hofgastein, Kaprun and Zell am See, the last a short bus-ride away.

boarding Saalbach is great for boarding. Slopes are extensive, lifts are mainly chairs and gondolas (though there are some connecting surface lifts), and there are trails to appeal to beginners, intermediates and experts alike. For experienced boarders there's good off-trail terrain, a large half-pipe on the Bernkogel above Saalbach, another below Hochalm and a terrain park on the north-facing slopes just above Hinterglemm. There are also dedicated 'carving' zones for boarders and skiers. And the nightlife is some of the liveliest in Europe.

MOUNTAIN FACTS

Altitude	930m-2095m/ 3,050ft-6,870ft
Lifts	52
Trails	200km/124 miles
Blue	50%
Red	33%
Black	17%
Snowmaking	30km/ 19 miles
Recco detectors used	

snowmaking to ensure the link normally remains open, and there is a choice of lifts going up, including a multi-cabin cable-way to Kohlmaiskopf.

The north-facing slopes are different in character – two distinct mountains, with long runs from both to the valley. Access from Saalbach is by a solitary, liftline-prone tram to **Schattberg**. The high, open, sunny slopes behind the peak are now served by a fast quad chair.

From Schattberg, long runs go down to Saalbach village, Vorderglemm and Hinterglemm. From the latter, lifts go not only to Schattberg but also to the other north-facing mountain, **Zwölferkogel**, served by a two-stage eight-person gondola. Surface lifts serve open slopes on the sunny side of the peak, and a high-capacity gondola provides a link from the south-facing Hochalm area.

SNOW RELIABILITY
Better than most of the Tirol
Saalbach's array of snowmaking guns cover several main runs on the lower half of the mountain, on both sides of the valley. The resort also claims to be in a 'snow pocket'. Good trail maintenance helps to keep the slopes in the best possible condition, but an altitude range of 930m to 2100m is only a slight advance on Kitzbühel. As 60% of runs face south, Saalbach suffers when the sun comes out. Both north and south sides can develop icy patches, as we found on our last January visit.

FOR EXPERTS
Little steep stuff
There are few challenging slopes. Off-trail guides are available, but snow conditions and forest tend to limit the potential. The north-facing slopes are steeper than those on the south-facing side of the valley. The long (4km) run beneath the length of the Schattberg tram is the only truly black run – a fine fast bash first thing in the morning if it has been groomed. The other long black from Zwölferkogel is really a red with just a couple of short, steeper pitches. The World Cup downhill run from Zwölferkogel is interesting, as is the 5km Schattberg West–Hinterglemm red (and its scenic 'ski route' variant).

FOR INTERMEDIATES
Paradise
This area is ideal for both the trail-basher, eager to rack up the miles, and the more leisurely cruiser. The south-facing trails have mainly been cut through the pine forest at an angle, allowing movement across the area on easy runs.

For those looking for more of a challenge, the most direct routes down from Hochalm, Reiterkogel, Kohlmaiskopf and Hochwartalm are good fun. All the south-facing slopes are uniformly pleasant and, as a result, everyone tends to be fairly evenly distributed over them. Only the delightful blue from Bernkogel to Saalbach gets really crowded at times. The alternative long ski route is very pleasant, taking you through forest and meadows.

The north-facing area has some more challenging runs, and a section of relatively high, open slopes around Zwölferkogel, which often have good snow. None of the black runs is beyond an adventurous intermediate, while the long pretty cruise from Limbergalm to Vorderglemm gets you away from lifts for most of the time and is particularly quiet and pleasant first thing in the morning.

Our favorite intermediate run was the long cruise down on excellent north-facing snow to Leogang – over 1000m/3,280ft of vertical.

FOR BEGINNERS
Best for improvers
Saalbach's two beginner areas are very well positioned for convenience, right next to the village center. But they are both south-facing, and the upper one gets a lot of intermediate traffic taking a short cut between the Kohlmaiskopf and Bernkogel areas. The lower one is very small, but the lift is free.

Alternatives are trips to the short, easy runs at Bernkogel and Schattberg. There is also a little slope at the foot of the Schattberg but the schools seem reluctant to use it – so it's great for messing around on your own at lunchtime. It's rather sunless and a little steeper than the other beginner areas, but perfectly usable.

Hinterglemm's spacious beginner area is separate from the main slopes. Being north-facing, it is much more reliable for snow later on in the season, but it consequently misses out on the sun in mid-winter.

There are lots of easy blue runs to move on to, especially on the south-facing side of the valley.

FOR CROSS-COUNTRY
Go to Zell am See
Trails run beside the road along the valley floor from Saalbach to Vorderglemm and between Hinterglemm and the valley end at Lindlingalm. In mid-winter these trails get very little sun, and are not very exciting. The countryside beyond nearby Zell am See offers more scope.

LIFTLINES
Crowded, but only one long delay
The Schattberg tram is an obvious problem, with waiting routine at peak periods. Otherwise, much depends on snow conditions. When all runs are in good shape there are few problems, other than small morning peak liftlines to leave Saalbach. If the snow is poor, the Bernkogel chair and the following surface lifts get very crowded, as do any lifts servicing the better snow.

Saalbach-Hinterglemm does not get as overrun at weekends as other Tirolean resorts – it's less accessible for the Munich hordes than the Ski Welt area and its neighbors.

MOUNTAIN RESTAURANTS
Excellent quality and quantity
The whole area is liberally scattered with attractive little huts that serve good food. Many have pleasant rustic interiors and a lively ambience.

On the south-facing slopes, the Panorama on the Kohlmaiskopf slope, Waleggeralm on Hochalm and Turneralm close to Bründelkopf serve particularly good food. The little Bernkogelalm hut, overlooking Saalbach, has a great atmosphere. Reporters recommend the Reider Alm adjacent to the beginner slopes ('table-service and very prompt') and the Bärnalm near the top of the Bernkogel chair ('good food, good value'). The Wildenkarkogel Hütte has a big terrace and possibly the loudest mountain-top music we've heard, with resident DJ from mid-morning.

On the north-facing slopes, the Bergstadl halfway down the red run from Schattberg West has stunning views and good food. Ellmaualm, at the bottom of the Zwölferkogel's upper slopes, is a quiet, sunny retreat with good food and 'palatial toilets'. The

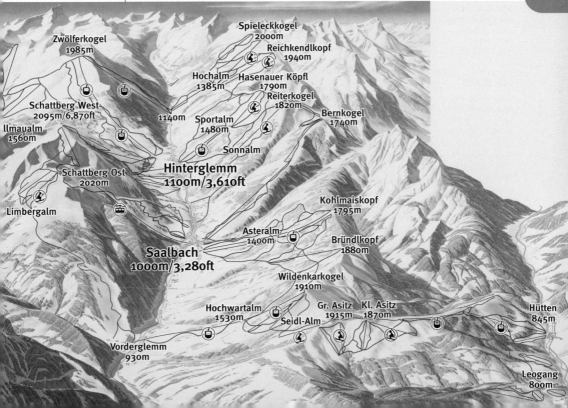

SCHOOLS/GUIDES

2001/02 prices in euros

Fürstauer

Classes 6 days
4hr: 10am-noon and 1pm-3pm
1 full day 44
6 full days 129

Children's classes
Ages: from 5
1 full day 44
6 full days 129

Private lessons
2hr and full-day
94 for 2hr, for 1 or 2 people; each additional person 10.

Snowboard classes
Half-day 50
6 half-days 137
3hr: 9am-noon or 1pm-4pm
1 half day 43
6 half days 145

Wolfgang Zink

Classes 6 days
4hr: 10am-noon and 1pm-3pm
1 full day 45
6 full days 123

Private lessons
2hrs and full-day
87 for 2hrs, for 1 to 2 people; each additional person 7.

Snowboard classes
3hr: 9am-noon or 1pm-4pm
3 half days 95

CHILDCARE

Some ski schools take children from age 4 or 5 and can provide lunchtime care.

Several hotels have kindergartens, and some in Hinterglemm are open to non-residents.

Phone numbers
From elsewhere in Austria add the prefix 06541.
From abroad use the prefix +43 6541.

GETTING THERE

Air Salzburg, transfer 2hr. Munich, transfer 3½hr.

Rail Zell am See; hourly buses from station, transfer 40 min.

12er Treff umbrella bar at the top of the Zwölferkogel gondola is good for lounging in the sun. The Simalalm at the base of the Limbergalm quad chair is 'great for the sun and the views'.

SCHOOLS AND GUIDES
An excess of choice

We're all in favor of competition between schools but visitors to Saalbach-Hinterglemm may feel that they are faced with rather too much of this good thing, with eight or nine to choose from. We have had good reports of the Wolf and Zink schools and the 'excellent' Snowboard Academy.

FACILITIES FOR CHILDREN
Hinterglemm tries harder

Saalbach doesn't go out of its way to sell itself to families, although it does have a ski kindergarten. Hinterglemm has some good hotel-based nursery facilities – the one at the Theresia is reportedly excellent.

Staying there

The walk to lifts from Saalbach's central hotels is minimal. But Saalbach has seen a fair amount of expansion in recent years, and many of the cheaper hotels are in the least convenient part of the village, some way from the nearest lift. In Hinterglemm, position isn't so important. Most of the accommodations are near a lift.

HOW TO GO
Cheerful doesn't mean cheap

Hotels There are a large number of hotels in both villages, mainly 3-star and above. Be aware that some central hotels are affected by disco noise – a real hazard in this lively resort.

Saalbach

((((4) **Alpenhotel** (6666) Luxurious, with open-fire lounge, disco, small pool.

((((4) **Berger's Sporthotel** (6577) Liveliest of the top hotels, with a daily tea dance, and disco. Good pool.

((((4) **Kendler** (6225-0) Position second to none, right next to the Bernkogel chair. Classy, expensive, good food.

((((4) **Saalbacher Hof** (7111-0) Retains a friendly feel despite its large size.

(((3) **Haider** (6228) Best-positioned of the 3-stars, right next to the main lifts.

(((3) **Kristiana** (6253) Near enough to lifts but away from night-time noise. 'Excellent food.' Sauna, steam bath.

(((3) **König** (6384) Cheaper 3-star and

---

more basic rooms.

Hinterglemm

((((4) **Theresia** (7414-0) Hinterglemm's top hotel, and one of the best for families. Out towards Saalbach, but beginner areas nearby. Pool.

(((3) **Wolf** (6346-0) Small but well-equipped 4-star in the nursery-sharing scheme. 'Especially good' food, excellent position. Pool.

((2) **Haus Ameshofer** (8119) Beside trail at Reiterkogel lift. 'Great value ski-in, ski-out B&B,' says a reporter.

Apartments/condos There's a big choice of apartments for independent travelers.

EATING OUT
Wide choice of hotel restaurants

Saalbach-Hinterglemm is essentially a half-board resort, with relatively few non-hotel restaurants. Peter's restaurant, at the top of Saalbach's main street, is atmospheric and serves excellent meat dishes cooked on hot stones. The Wallner Pizzeria on the main street is good value. The Auwirt hotel on the outskirts of Saalbach has a good à la carte restaurant.

APRES-SKI
It rocks from early on

Après-ski is very lively and can get very wild from mid-afternoon until the early hours. In Saalbach the rustic Hinterhagalm at the top of the main beginner area is packed by 3.30. When it closes around 6pm, the crowds slide down to Bauer's Skialm and try to get into the already heaving old cow shed to continue drinking and dancing. The tiny Zum Turn (next door to the church and cemetery) is an atmospheric former medieval jail that also gets packed around 4pm with many who are still there at 11pm.

Later on, The Pub on the main road out of town is packed with young Brits enjoying the karaoke. The Neuhaus Taverne and Crazy Bear have live music. Bobby's Bar is cheap, often full of British school kids, has bowling and serves Guinness. Kings Disco livens up after midnight. The Panther Bar has jungle decor, discreet music and well-heeled clientele. Zum Herrn'Karl, Hellis and Bergers are also popular. Arena disco has go-go dancers and is very popular. A reader recommends the Burgeralm as '3km/2 miles up the toboggan track, marvellous atmosphere and reindeer steaks before a 1am descent'.

ACTIVITIES

Indoor Swimming pools, sauna, massage, solarium, bowling, billiards, tennis (Hinterglemm), squash
Outdoor Floodlit tobogganing, sleigh rides, skating, ice hockey, curling, 35km/22 miles of cleared paths, paragliding

TOURIST OFFICE

Postcode A-5753
t +43 (6541) 680068
f 680069
contact@saalbach.com
www.saalbach.com

Leogang phone numbers
From elsewhere in Austria add the prefix 06583.
From abroad use the prefix +43 6583.

In Hinterglemm there are a number of ice bars which are crowded immediately after the lifts close, including the Gute Stube of Hotel Dorfschmiede in the center of town with loud music blasting out and people spilling into the street. The Tanzkimmel is an open, glass-fronted bar with a dance floor, next door to the Londoner, which is the biggest attraction later on – live and disco music, smart, friendly. The Hexenhausl near the Zwölferkogel gondola gets packed and has a mechanical model of a witch revealing her underclothes. A similar fascination with moving models is demonstrated at the rustic Goasstall just above town by the trail down from Sportalm, where a model goat is equally revealing (and where real goats graze behind glass near the men's room). Bla Bla is small, modern and smart, with reasonable prices. The Alm Bar has good music and some dancing.

Tour operator reps organize tobogganing, sleigh rides and bowling.

OFF THE SLOPES
Surprisingly little to do
Saalbach is not very entertaining if you're not into winter sports. There are few shops other than supermarkets and ski shops. Walks tend to be restricted to the paths alongside the shady cross-country trails or along the Saalbach toboggan run to Spielberghs. But there are excursions to Kitzbühel and Salzburg.

Leogang 800m/2,620ft

A much less expensive alternative to Saalbach-Hinterglemm.

THE RESORT
Leogang is an attractive, although rather scattered, quiet, farming community-cum-mountain resort, better placed than Saalbach for those with cars wanting to visit other resorts.

THE MOUNTAIN
The village is linked to the eastern end of the Saalbach-Hinterglemm ski circuit, rather out on a spur.
Slopes A gondola from Hütten takes you into the ski area. The local slopes tend to be delightfully quiet being off the main circuit.
Snow reliability The local slopes have some of the best snow in the region, being north- and east-facing, with snowmaking on the run home.

Snowboarding The whole area is great for boarding and there's a half-pipe here, though Leogang nightlife is deadly dull compared with Saalbach.
Experts Not much challenge here, except trying to get round the whole circuit and home again in a day.
Intermediates Great long red run cruise home from the top of the gondola. Plus the whole Saalbach-Hinterglemm circuit to explore.
Beginners Good beginner areas by the village, and short runs to progress to.
Cross-country The best in the area. There are 25km/16 miles of trails, plus a panoramic high-altitude trail which links through to other resorts.
Liftlines No local problems.
Mountain restaurants A couple of good local huts.
Schools and guides Leogang Altenberger school has a high reputation – 'excellent service and lessons; highly recommended'.
Facilities for children There is a non-ski day-care facility and children can start school at four years old.

STAYING THERE
It's best to stay at Hütten, near the lift.
Hotels The luxury Krallerhof (8246-0) has its own nursery lift, which can be used to get across to the main lift station. The 4-star Salzburgerhof (7310-0) is one of the best-placed hotels with sauna and steam, within a two-minute walk of the gondola.
Apartments/condos There are quiet apartments available.
Eating out Restaurants are hotel-based. The Krallerhof has the excellent food you would expect. The much cheaper Gasthof Hüttwirt has a high reputation for Austrian home cooking.
Après-ski The rustic old chalet Kralleralm is very much the focal tea-time and evening rendezvous.
Off the slopes Excursions to Salzburg are possible.

Schladming 745m/2,440ft

Pretty old town with extensive intermediate slopes

HOW IT RATES

The slopes

Snow	***
Extent	***
Experts	**
Intermediates	****
Beginners	****
Convenience	***
Lines	****
Restaurants	****

The rest

Scenery	***
Resort charm	****
Off-slope	****

➕ New lifts have linked extensive but previously fragmented slopes

➕ Excellent slopes for intermediates

➕ Extensive snowmaking operation and superb trail maintenance

➕ Very sheltered slopes, among trees

➕ Lots of good mountain restaurants

➕ Charming town with friendly people and a life independent of tourism

➕ New Ski Alliance Amadé lift ticket covers wide range of nearby resorts

➖ Beginner areas (at Rohrmoos) are inconvenient unless you stay beside them – and beginners are expected to pay for a full lift ticket

➖ Very little to entertain experts, on or off-trail

➖ Slopes lack variety – one mountain is much like the others

➖ Most runs are north-facing, so can be cold and shady in early season

Since its four previously separate mountains were linked by lifts and trails, Schladming has been able to compete with major resorts that are better known internationally. A keen intermediate who wants to make the most of the links can get a real sense of traveling around on the snow. And as our list of plus-points above suggests, we see many attractions in the place.

If you like your slopes to be reassuringly consistent, Schladming has a strong claim on your attention. If on the other hand you like the spice of variety and the thrill of a serious challenge, you might find it all rather tame.

94

What's new

The old gondola from Haus was upgraded to an eight-seater last season – eliminating the lines here. The slow double chair-lift from Rohrmoos on Hochwurzen was also replaced, by a fast six-person chair.

For 2001/02, the new Ski Alliance Amadé joint lift ticket is being introduced, covering more than 30 ski resorts in this part of Austria.

The resort

The old town of Schladming has a long skiing tradition – and it's well known to armchair skiers, having hosted World Cup races for many years.

The town sits at the foot of Planai, one of four mountains that are now linked by lifts and trails to offer 115km/71 miles of runs. A gondola starting close to the center goes most of the way up. A couple of km (around a mile) to the east is the small, rustic village of Haus, where a tram and gondola go up to the highest of the four linked mountains, Hauser Kaibling. From the western suburbs of Schladming there are chair-lifts back towards Planai and on towards the next mountain to the west, Hochwurzen. The latter chain of lifts passes through Rohrmoos, a quiet, scattered village set on what is effectively a giant beginner area.

The town (it is definitely not a village) has a charming, traffic-free main square, prettily lit at night, around which you'll find most of the shops, restaurants and bars (and some appealing hotels). The busy main road bypasses the town and is separated from it by a river. Many of the accommodations are close to the center, which is where we'd recommend staying – just a few minutes' walk from the Planai gondola. But some (mostly cheaper) hotels and most apartments are on the outskirts. The modern sports center and tennis halls are near the Sporthotel Royer, five minutes' walk from the center. Rohrmoos makes an excellent base for

SCHLADMING TOURIST OFFICE

← Woodland runs of easy red gradient are the norm on all four linked mountains

MOUNTAIN FACTS

Figures relate to the whole Sportregion Schladming-Ramsau/ Dachstein area

Altitude 745m-2015m/ 2,440ft-6,610ft

Lifts	88
Trails 167km/104 miles	
Blue	29%
Red	61%
Black	10%
Snowmaking	100%

Recco detectors used

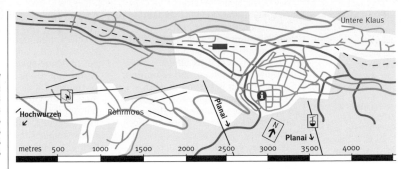

beginners who aren't looking for lively nightlife. Haus is preferable for those looking for more of a village atmosphere.

Despite the recently created links, it's still quicker to get to a particular hill by car, cab or the 'very efficient' ski-bus along the valley.

The new Ski Alliance Amadé lift ticket covers over 30 partially or wholly linked resorts in this part of Austria. Trips to Bad Gastein are feasible by rail but include at least one change. Drivers can also visit Wagrain/Flachau, Kleinarl and Maria Alm. Snow-sure Obertauern is not far away but is not included on the lift ticket.

The mountains

Most trails are on the wooded north-facing slopes above the main valley, with some going into the side valleys higher up, and there are some open slopes above the trees. The views from the limited Dachstein glacier (a 45-minute bus-ride) are superb.

THE SLOPES
Four linked sectors – and more

Each of the linked sectors is quite a serious mountain with a variety of lifts and runs to play on. **Planai** and **Hauser Kaibling** are linked at altitude via the high, wooded bowl between them. In contrast, the links with **Hochwurzen** and the fourth linked mountain, **Reiteralm,** are at valley level. So although the links offer the ability to travel around, getting around the whole area can take time – and involves skiing some runs you wouldn't choose to descend for fun. Although from Schladming it's perfectly practical to get to Hauser Kaibling or Hochwurzen, if you want to spend time on Reiteralm it's more practical to get the bus, or a cab, to the lift base at Pichl or Gleiming. The link between Planai and Hochwurzen involves riding a lift through a tunnel, whichever way you are traveling.

All the mountains have fairly similar terrain, with mainly red runs of much the same pitch down through heavily wooded north-facing slopes. The lack

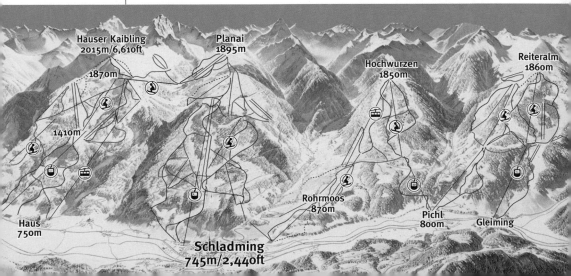

LIFT TICKETS

2001/02 prices in euros

Ski Alliance Amadé Ski ticket

The new joint lift ticket covers over 275 lifts in more than 30 ski resorts in this part of Austria: the Gastein valley and Grossarl; Salzburger Sportwelt (main areas: Flachau/ Wagrain/ St Johann and Zauchensee/ Kleinarl); Hochkönigs Winterreich (Maria Alm and neighbors). Buses, trains and road tolls between the resorts are covered by the ticket.

Main ticket

1-day ticket 32 (low season 29)
6-day ticket 150 (low-season 140)

Children

Under 15: 6-day ticket 75 (low season 70)
15-19: 6-day ticket 140
Under 6: free ticket

Notes Morning and afternoon tickets are also available (as are tickets from 11am, 1pm and 2pm on). 1½-day and 2½-day tickets are also possible.

of variety in the slopes is something of a drawback. Reporters have complained of poor trail signing and inaccuracies in the trail map.

There are five or six other identifiable mountains dotted around. Galsterbergalm is above Pruggern, along the valley to the east, beyond Haus. Fageralm is above Forstau, up a side valley to the east. North of the main valley, Ramsau has its own low slopes and access to the Dachstein glacier. And near Gröbming is the small area of Stoderzinken.

SNOW RELIABILITY
Excellent in cold weather

Schladming's impressive snowmaking operation makes it a particularly good choice for early holidays; and the northerly orientation of the slopes and superb maintenance help keep the slopes in better shape than in some neighboring resorts. They claim 100% artificial snow-cover, and certainly the main runs to the valley have full cover. Be wary of the steep bottom part of the World Cup downhill run back to town – it can get extremely icy. The best natural snow is usually found on Reiteralm and Hochwurzen.

FOR EXPERTS
Strictly intermediate stuff

Schladming's status as a World Cup downhill venue doesn't make it macho. The steep black finish to the Men's Downhill course and the moderate bump runs at the top of Planai and Hauser Kaibling are the only really challenging slopes. Hauser Kaibling's off-trail is good, although limited.

FOR INTERMEDIATES
Red runs rule

The area is ideal for intermediate cruising. The majority of runs are graded red but it's often difficult to distinguish them from the blues.

The open sections at the top of Planai and Hauser Kaibling have some more challenging slopes. And the two World Cup trails, and the red that runs

parallel to the Haus downhill course, are ideal for fast intermediates. Excellent trail grooming and quiet slopes at off-peak times allow you to get up some speed – the Women's World Cup run is great fun.

Hauser Kaibling has a lovely meandering blue running from top to bottom for the less confident intermediates, and Reiteralm has some gentle blues with good snow. Runs are well groomed, so intermediates will find the slopes generally flattering.

FOR BEGINNERS
Good slopes but poorly sited

Complete beginners generally start on the extensive but low-altitude Rohrmoos nursery area – fine if you are based there, not if you're not. Another novice area near the top of Planai is more convenient for most people and has better snow.

FOR CROSS-COUNTRY
Extensive network of trails

Given sufficient snow-cover, there are 300km/186 miles of trails in the region. The 1999 World Cross-country Championships were held at nearby Ramsau. There are local loops along the main valley floor and in the valleys between Planai and Hochwurzen. Further afield there are more snow-sure trails at Stoderzinken.

LIFTLINES
Only valley bottlenecks

The Planai gondola can suffer delays on peak-season mornings, but there are few other problems. The new gondola at Haus has relieved the pressure there, though the four-person chair at the top – essential for getting to Planai – still generates lines. The Reiteralm gondola is ancient and slow.

MOUNTAIN RESTAURANTS
Plenty of nice places

There are plenty of attractive rustic restaurants in all sectors, though Planai probably has the edge. Onkel Willi's is popular for its live music,

boarding *Schladming is popular with boarders. Most lifts on the spread-out mountains are gondolas or chairs, with some short surface lifts around. There are two terrain parks and half-pipes on the main linked area, with another terrain park on the Galsterbergalm. The Blue Tomato snowboard shop also runs a specialist school. The area is ideal for beginners and intermediates, except when the lower slopes are icy, though there are few exciting challenges for expert boarders bar the off-trail tree runs. Nightlife can be quite lively.*

SCHOOLS/GUIDES

2000/01 prices in euros
Tritscher and Hopl-Planai
Classes 5 days
4hr: 2hr am and pm
5 full days: 109
Children's classes
Ages: from 4
5 full days: 145
Private lessons
1hr, 2½hr or 4½hr
38 for 1hr; each additional person 12
Snowboard School Gerfried Schuller
Classes 5 days
5 full days: 116
Children's classes
Ages: from 5
Private lessons
1hr or 4hr
36 for 1hr; each additional person 7.

CHILDCARE

At Rohrmoos the nursery takes children from 18 months.

Children in ski school can be looked after all day.

GETTING THERE

Air Salzburg, transfer 1½hr.

Rail Mainline station in resort.

Phone numbers
From elsewhere in Austria add the prefix 03687.
From abroad use the prefix +43 3687.

ACTIVITIES

Indoor Swimming, sauna, bowling, indoor tennis court, squash, museum
Outdoor Ice skating, curling, 8km/5 mile floodlit toboggan run, sleigh rides, 50km/31 miles of cleared paths in the Schladming and surrounding area, paragliding

TOURIST OFFICE

Postcode A-8970
t +43 (3687) 222680
f 24138
touristoffice@
schladming.com
www.schladming.com

open fire, indoor nooks and crannies and large terrace, Mitterhausalm is good, and the Schladminger Hütte at the top of the Planai gondola has 'great food'. The Knapplhof at Hauser Kaibling is full of ski racing mementos.

SCHOOLS AND GUIDES
Satisfaction likely
There are two schools, and the only recent reports are on the Tritscher school: 'I was the only English speaker in the group but the instructor spoke good English and repeated everything,' says one. Boarders are well catered for by a specialist school.

FACILITIES FOR CHILDREN
Rohrmoos is the place
The extensive gentle slopes of Rohrmoos are ideal for building up youngsters' confidence. The nursery here takes children from 18 months.

Staying there

HOW TO GO
Lots of budget options
There are plenty of apartments for independent travellers.
Hotels Most of the accommodations are in modestly priced pensions but there are also a few more upscale hotels.
Sporthotel Royer (200) Big, smart and comfortable, a few minutes' walk from the main Planai lift. Pool.
Alte Post (22571) Picturesque old inn with great position on the main square. Very good food, but some rooms are rather small by 4-star standards. 'Excellent value' says a recent reporter.
Zum Stadttor (24525) Similarly priced, although less charming and well placed. 'Comfortable with excellent food,' says a reporter.
Neue Post (22105) Large rooms, friendly, good food, central.
Schladmingerhof (23525) Bright, modern chalet in peaceful position, out in Untere Klaus.
Apartments/condos Haus Girik (22663) is the best-positioned apartment house in town, close to the gondola.

EATING OUT
Some good places
Fritzi's Gasthaus is highly recommended by readers. Other recommendations include the Kirchenwirt hotel ('excellent home cooking'), Giovanni's (for pizza),

Gasthof Brunner ('good value'), Talbachschenke ('good grills and atmosphere') and Lisi's Landhausstüberl. Hotels Neue and Alte Post are 'good but pricey'.

APRES-SKI
Varied and quite lively
Some of the mountain restaurants are lively at the end of the afternoon, but reporters agree that down in the town there's a disappointing lack of after-ski animation. Charly's Treff (with umbrella bar) opposite the Planai gondola is the main exception (and has great photos of local hero Arnold Schwarzenegger inside). The Siglu (in a big plastic igloo-like bubble) also reportedly rocks from 3pm until late.

There is, however, no lack of options later on – a reporter found that many of the central bars open later on and stay open until dawn if necessary. Popular spots include the local brewpub Schwalbenbräu and Café Zauberkistl (translated as Magic Box), where the owner regularly performs conjuring tricks. Das Beisl is a smart, beautiful bar attracting a varied age group. Hanglbar has wooden decor and middle-of-the-road music and occasional karaoke. Ferry's Pub has a nautical theme, loud music and a quiet room at the rear. La Porta gets very crowded and has live music. The Gondl-Treff has an international soccer theme, with big-screen TV. The Sonderbar is a disco with international DJs and three bars.

OFF THE SLOPES
Good for all but walkers
Non-skiers are fairly well catered for. Some mountain restaurants are easily reached on foot. The town shops and museum are worth a look. Train trips to Salzburg are easy. Buses run to the old walled town of Radstadt. There's a public pool and ice rink.

Haus 750m/2,460ft

Haus is a real village with a life of its own. It has a fair number of accommodations (cheaper than in Schladming) plus its own ski schools and kindergartens. The user-friendly nursery area is handily set between town and gondola. There's a railway station for excursions, but off-slope activities and nightlife are very limited. Hotel Gürtl has been recommended for 'good food and ambience'.

Sölden
1380m/4,530ft

Good, extensive intermediate slopes with throbbing nightlife

98

HOW IT RATES

The slopes

Snow	*****
Extent	***
Experts	***
Intermediates	****
Beginners	**
Convenience	***
Liftlines	***
Restaurants	***

The rest

Scenery	***
Resort charm	**
Off-slope	**

➕ Excellent snow reliability, with access to two glaciers

➕ Fairly extensive network of slopes suited to adventurous intermediates

➕ Continually improving lift system

➕ Very lively nightlife

➕ Short transfers and day trips to nearby Innsbruck

➖ Sprawling, traffic-filled village

➖ Spread-out village means some central hotels are inconvenient for the two main lifts

➖ Inconvenient beginners' slopes

➖ Drink-fueled nightlife too rowdy for many visitors

➖ Limited off-slope activities

Sölden has invested massively in new lifts to link its home slopes, which suit adventurous intermediates best, with snow-sure runs on the Rettenbach and Tiefenbach glaciers. This is very good news – the Tiefenbach, in particular, is a serious 2km/1 mile-long slope – and may be enough to establish this quite impressive resort on the international market at last.

What's new

Previously closed in winter, in recent years Sölden's glaciers have been opened up to winter visitors by a series of fast new lifts – 'the golden gate to the glacier'. A new gondola was installed last season on the Tiefenbach glacier. Also new was a six-pack from Langegg – in the valley separating the two local sectors – to the Rotkoglhütte, greatly speeding access to the Rotkogl slopes for people based at the other end of the resort.

There is a new garage by the Giggijoch gondola with parking spaces for 600 cars.

The 2-seater Heidebahn chair from Gaislachalm up to the Gaislachkogl sector is being replaced by a fast quad for next season.

THE RESORT

Despite its traditional Tirolean-style buildings and tree-filled valley, Sölden is no beauty: it is a large, traffic-filled place that sprawls along both sides of a river and main road (particularly crowded at weekends). The resort attracts a young, lively crowd – mostly Dutch and German – bent on partying.

Gondolas from opposite ends of town go up to Sölden's home slopes – Gaislachkogl and Giggijoch. Staying in a hamlet near one of these lifts gets you away from the noisy main street (an efficient free shuttle-bus service runs between the two base stations). Or you could stay in tiny, remote Hochsölden (2090m/6,869ft), up on the Giggijoch slopes, provided evening isolation doesn't worry you.

THE MOUNTAINS

The two similar-sized sectors are linked by chair-lifts out of the Rettenbachtal that separates them. The Rettenbach and Tiefenbach glaciers – 15km/9 miles away by road, and until recently closed in winter – are now connected by a series of fast lifts from Rotkogl.

Slopes The Gaislachkogl runs are almost entirely red or black, but there are several blue runs around Giggijoch. Both main sectors have red runs through trees to the village.

The Rettenbach and Tiefenbach glacier slopes are gentler – blues and reds – and rise from 2685m/8,810ft to 3250m/10,660ft.

Trail marking and grooming are reportedly 'very good'.

Snow reliability Most of the area is over 2100m/6,860ft – a good height for Austria – and north-east-facing, so the slopes are generally reliable for snow. Now that there is access to the glaciers, Sölden is one of the best Alpine bets.

Snowboarding There are terrain parks and half-pipes at Giggijoch and on the Rettenbach glacier.

Experts Sölden's trails have little to challenge experts – three widely separated chair-lifts serve the only half-serious black runs. But off-piste is another story: there is a mountain guides' office in Sölden and there are extensive off-piste possibilities on both main mountains – particularly from the top of Gaislachkogl to the mid-station. And at the top of the valley is one of the Alps' premier touring areas.

Intermediates Most of Sölden's main slopes are red runs ideal for adventurous intermediates. There are several easy blacks, and the long, quiet piste down to Gaislachalm – floodlit on Wednesday nights – is ideal for high-speed cruising. Giggijoch and Rotkogl are good if you prefer a more moderate pace, but Sölden is not really for timid types.

Beginners The beginner areas are situated inconveniently – just above the village at Innerwald – and prone to poor snow. Near-beginners can use the blues at Giggijoch.

MOUNTAIN FACTS

Altitude 1380m-3250m
4,530ft-10,660ft

Lifts	34
Trails	141km/88 miles
Blue	32%
Red	52%
Black	16%
Snowmaking	27km/
	17 miles

Recco detectors used

Phone numbers
From elsewhere in
Austria add the prefix
05254.
From abroad use the
prefix +43 5254.

TOURIST OFFICE
Postcode A-6450
t +43 (5254) 5100
f 510520
info@soelden.com
www.soelden.com

Cross-country There are a couple of uninspiring cross-country loops by the river, plus small areas at Zwieselstein and Vent. The saving grace is altitude.

Liftlines Recent upgrades have done away with most of the liftlines, though one visitor reported late-afternoon bottlenecks for the return links from the glaciers.

Mountain restaurants The restaurants have improved in recent years, partly because they have increased in capacity. The self-service places around Giggijoch get very crowded. Gampealm, in the Rettenbachtal, is an atmospheric old hut. The Gaislachalm area is your best bet for avoiding the masses – the self-service Silbertal is recommended.

Schools and guides The only reports we have of the three ski schools tell of small class sizes.

Facilities for children There is no proper day-care nursery for children, but baby-sitters can be arranged. Children aged three and up can join the ski kindergarten. There are special lift ticket deals for families.

STAYING THERE

Hotels Sölden has some good hotels. The 5-star Central (22600) is the best and one of the biggest in town. The 4-star Regina (2301), by the Gaislachkogl lift is heartily recommended by a recent reporter. The Arno B&B (2488)

on the trail above the Giggijoch lift, and Gasthof Grüner (2214) in Ausserwald are also recommended. The apartments at the Posthäusl (31380) are good quality.

Eating out Café Hubertus caters for everything from snacks to full meals. The Nudeltopf and Corso are the best pizzerias, and the Hotel Birkenhof's restaurant is pleasantly traditional. S'Pfandl, and Hermann's – up the hill a little at the hamlet of See – are recommended.

Après-ski Sölden's après-ski is notorious. It starts up the mountain, notably at Giggijoch. The resort is full of bars, live bands and throbbing discos. It gets very loud and very rowdy. Even our keenest après-ski reporter was shocked on his last visit: 'Lots of drunks urinating and smashing glasses in the street. There is table dancing and striptease at Rodelhütte, and Lawine has great theme nights if you are into latex and leather.' Phillip's ice bar and disco are also popular and noisy. Somewhat tamer are the nightly toboggan evenings, with drinking and dancing before an exciting 6km/4 mile floodlit run back to town from the Gaislachalm mountain restaurant.

Off the slopes There's a new sports center and swimming pool complex, and an ice rink, too. Trips to Innsbruck and Igls are possible.

Sölden

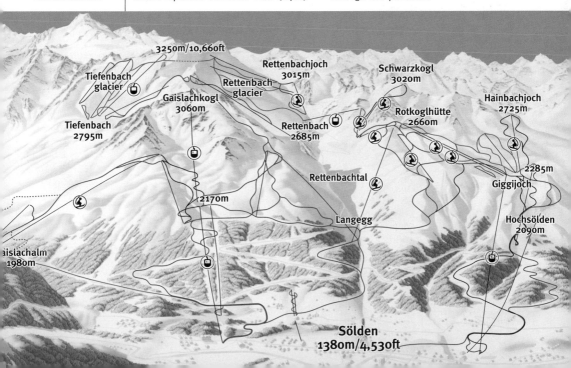

Small, lively village with large, easy ski and snowboard area

HOW IT RATES

The slopes

Snow	**
Extent	****
Experts	*
Intermediates	****
Beginners	***
Convenience	**
Lines	***
Restaurants	**

The rest

Scenery	***
Resort charm	***
Off-slope	**

What's new

The snowmaking capacity in the Ski Welt has been hugely increased in recent years. It now covers 130km/80 miles of trails (over half the trails in the Ski Welt) and is the largest snowmaking facility anywhere in Austria.

For 2000/01 the old single-seat chair to the Hohe Salve was replaced by a fast eight-seater gondola from Hochsöll, giving much quicker access to the steepest runs and to the Hopfgarten and Brixen areas (via a link that got new snowmaking for 2000/01, too).

In Hopfgarten, a liftline-prone T-bar (a key link on the Ski Welt circuit) was replaced by an eight-seater chair.

SKI WELT

If you are lucky and get fresh snow like this, the Ski Welt is an intermediates' paradise →

- ⊕ Part of Ski Welt, Austria's largest linked ski and snowboard area
- ⊕ Local slopes are the highest and steepest in the Ski Welt and north-facing so keep their snow well
- ⊕ Massive recent investment in snowmaking has paid off
- ⊕ Plenty of cheap and cheerful pensions for those on a budget
- ⊕ Pretty village with lively après-ski

- ⊖ Poor natural snow record
- ⊖ Long walk or infrequent bus-ride to the lifts
- ⊖ Little for experts or good intermediates
- ⊖ Ski Welt slopes can get busy at weekends and in high season
- ⊖ Local slopes are the most crowded in the Ski Welt
- ⊖ Mostly short runs in local sector

Söll has long been popular with groups of beginners and intermediates. Its pretty scenery, gentle slopes, small attractive traditional village, good-value accommodations and lively nightlife attract a mixture of young singles looking for fun and families looking for a quiet time. In the 1980s it gained notoriety as prime hard-drinking territory; it still has some loud bars but has calmed down a lot. Many visitors find the village surprisingly small and are disappointed by the distance between it and the slopes (and by the bus service).

Until recently its main drawback has always been snow – or lack of it. Because of its low altitude and sunny slopes, trails have often been slushy or bare, not just in Söll but also throughout the extensive Ski Welt circuit it is part of. But this problem has been tackled by a massive investment in snowmaking and half of the Ski Welt's 250km/155 miles of trails are now covered by snowmaking – more than in any other Austrian ski area. This ensures the region's main trails and links stay open, though it can't prevent slush and ice developing.

When the snow is good Söll can be a great place for a holiday, cruising the attractive and undemanding trails of Austria's largest linked area.

The resort

Söll is a small, pretty, friendly village – much smaller than you might expect by its reputation; you can explore it in a few minutes and there aren't many shops. New buildings are traditional in design and there's a huge church near the center which, according to a recent reporter, is well worth a visit at dusk as the graveyard is lit with candles. The pretty scenery adds to Söll's charm, and it benefits from being off the main road through the Tirol.

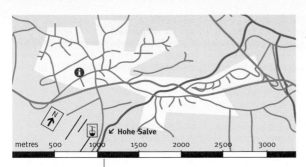

MOUNTAIN FACTS

Altitude 620m-1830m/
2,030ft-6,000ft
Lifts 93
Trails 250km/155 miles
Blue 43%
Red 48%
Black 9%
Snowmaking 130km/
80 miles

LIFT TICKETS

2001/02 prices in
euros

**Ski Welt Wilder
Kaiser–Brixental**
Covers all lifts in the
Wilder Kaiser-
Brixental area from
Going to Westendorf,
and the ski-bus.
Beginners Points
tickets (100 points
300). Most beginner
lifts cost from 3 to 10
points.
Main ticket
1-day ticket 29
6-day ticket 143
Children
Under 16: 6-days 81
Under 6: free ticket
Short-term tickets
Single ascent on
some lifts, tickets
from 11am, noon 2pm
to the end of the day.
Alternative periods
5 in 7 days, 7 in 10
days, 10 in 14 days.
Alternative tickets
Söll ticket (6-day
ticket for adults 117,
for children 68)
covers 12 lifts,
34km/21 mile trail).
Kitzbüheler Alpen-ski
ticket covers five ski
areas – Schneewinkel
(St Johann), Ski
Region Kitzbühel, Ski
Welt Wilder Kaiser,
Wildschönau and
Alpbachtal (adult 6-
day 160).

The slopes are a bus- or cab-ride or a 15-minute walk from the center, the other side of a busy road with a pedestrian tunnel underneath. The bus service has been criticized by most reporters as being too infrequent. Some accommodations are further away, though there are some near the lifts too.

The mountains

The Ski Welt is the largest linked area in Austria, but that doesn't make it a Trois Vallées. It covers Hopfgarten, Brixen, Scheffau and Ellmau, but is basically a typically small, low, pastoral Austrian hill multiplied several times. One section is much like another, and most slopes best suit low to average intermediates. Runs are short and scenery attractive rather than stunning – although the panoramic views from the Hohe Salve are impressive on a clear day.

Westendorf is separate, but covered by the area ticket. The Kitzbüheler Alpenski ticket also covers many other resorts easily reached by car including Kitzbühel, Schneewinkel (includes St Johann, Fieberbrunn, Steinplatte, Waidring), Niederau and Alpbach – an impressive total of 260 lifts and 680km/420 miles of trails.

THE SLOPES
Short run network
A gondola takes all but complete beginners up to the shelf of Hochsöll, where there are a couple of short lifts and connections in several directions.

An eight-person gondola (new for last season) takes you to the high

point of Hohe Salve. From here there are stunning views and runs down to Kälbersalve and Hopfgarten via Rigi. Rigi can also be reached by alternative chairs and trails without going to Hohe Salve – to which it is itself linked by chairs. Rigi is also the start of runs down to Itter. From Kälbersalve you can head down south-facing runs to Brixen or up to Zinsberg and Eiberg and towards the north-facing runs in the Ellmau sector.

A quicker way to Ellmau without taking as many south-facing slopes is by taking a tram from Hochsöll.

The whole area is vast and will easily keep a low or average intermediate amused for a week.

We have had lots of criticism of the trail map by recent reporters: 'Direction of runs/lifts and the links not clear' and 'Trail map did not correspond with lift numbers – generally a very bad map.'

SNOW RELIABILITY
Artificial help saves the day
With a very low average elevation, and important links that get a lot of sun, the snowmaking that the Ski Welt has installed in recent seasons is essential. At 125km/78 miles and covering half the area's trails, it is one of Austria's biggest artificial snow installations. We were there in January 1999, before any major snowfalls, and snowmaking was keeping the links open well. It did not, however, prevent slush and icy patches forming – usually slush on south-facing slopes, ice on north-facing ones.

FOR EXPERTS
Not a lot
The black run from Hohe Salve towards Hochsöll and the black run alongside the Brixen gondola are the only challenging trails. There are further blacks in Scheffau and Ellmau, but most experts will need to seek amusement off-trail – from Scheffau's Brandstadl down to Söll, for example.

FOR INTERMEDIATES
Mainly easy runs
With good snow, the Ski Welt is a paradise for early intermediates and those who love easy cruising. There

boarding *Söll is a good place to try out boarding: slopes are gentle and there are plenty of gondolas and chairs. For decent boarders it's more limited – the slopes of the Ski Welt are tame. But there is a terrain park and quarter-pipe near Hochsöll and lots of lively bars in the evening.*

SCHOOLS/GUIDES

2000/01 prices in euros

Söll-Hochsöll
Classes 5 days
2hr or 4hr: 10am-noon and 1.30-3.30
5 full days: 104
Children's classes
Ages: 5 to 14
5 full days: 100
Private lessons
Hourly or full day (4hr)
36 for 1hr; each additional person 13

Austria
Classes 6 days
4hr: 10am-noon and 1.30-3.30
5 full days: 95
Children's classes
Ages: 5 to 14
5 full days: 91
Private lessons
Hourly or daily
35 for 1hr; each additional person 11

ProSöll
Classes 5 days
4hr: 10am-noon and 1.30-3.30
5 full days: 104
Children's classes
Ages: 5 to 14
(younger than 5 years on request)
5 full days: 100
Private lessons
Hourly or daily
36 for 1hr; each additional person 13

are lots of blue runs and many of the reds in truth deserve a blue grading. It is a big area and you really get a feeling of traveling around – we skied it for two days in 1999 and felt we only scratched the surface. The main challenge you may find is when the snow isn't perfect – ice and slush can make even gentle slopes seem tricky. In general the most difficult slopes are those from the mid-stations to the valleys: the most direct of the runs between Brandstadl and Blaiken, the trails down to Brixen and the red run from Hochsöll back to Söll, for example. Higher up, the red from Hohe Salve to Rigi is a good cruise on relatively good snow.

FOR BEGINNERS
Excellent when snow is good

The big beginner areas between the main road and the gondola station are ideal when snow is abundant – gentle, spacious, uncrowded and free from good skiers whizzing past. But it can get icy or slushy. In poor snow the Hochsöll area is used. Near-beginners and fast learners can get home to the bottom station when the narrow blue from Hochsöll is not too icy.

FOR CROSS-COUNTRY
Neighboring villages are better

Söll has 35km/22 miles of local trails but they are less interesting than those between Hopfgarten and Kelchsau or the ones around and beyond Ellmau. Lack of snow-cover is a big problem.

LIFTLINES
Much improved

Continued introduction of new lifts has greatly improved this once line-prone area. The Blaiken gondola is to be avoided on weekend mornings. And when snow is poor, the linking lifts to and from Zinsberg and Eiberg get busy.

MOUNTAIN RESTAURANTS
Good, but crowded

There are quite a few little chalets dotted about, but we received a few complaints of insufficient seating and long lines this year. The atmospheric Stockalm (a converted cow shed), Kraftalm and Grundalm are all near Hochsöll. The Alpenrose, near the top of Hohe Salve, has a good sun terrace, generous portions and reasonable prices. Further afield, the Neualm, halfway down to Blaiken, is one of the best huts in the Ski Welt. The nearby Brantlalm has been recommended for lovely views. The Jochstubn at Eiberg is self-service but has a good atmosphere and excellent Tiroler Gröstl. The Filzalm above Brixen is a good place for a quick drink on the way back from the circuit. But our favorite is the Rübezahl above Ellmau – very rustic with wooden carvings, low doors, several rooms and good food.

SCHOOLS AND GUIDES
Three competing schools

The Austria school and the bigger Söll-Hochsöll school have fairly good reputations. But we had a recent report of an 'instructor with little patience'.

CHILDCARE

The ski schools take children from age 5 in special snow-gardens on the beginner areas from 9.45 to 4pm. Once they progress to Hochsöll, care has to be arranged with the instructor.

Next to the main ski kindergarten, the Söll-Hochsöll school operates a Mini Club for children aged 3 to 5 from 9.45 to 4pm.

GETTING THERE

Air Salzburg, transfer 2hr. Innsbruck, transfer 1½hr.

Rail Wörgl (13km/8 miles) or Kufstein (15km/9 miles); bus to resort.

Söll phone numbers
From elsewhere in Austria add the prefix 05333.
From abroad use the prefix +43 5333.

ACTIVITIES

Indoor Swimming, sauna, solarium, massage, bowling, squash
Outdoor Natural ice rink (skating, curling), sleigh rides, 3km/2 miles floodlit ski and toboggan runs, paragliding, hang-gliding

TOURIST OFFICE

Postcode A-6306
t +43 (5333) 5216
f 6180
info@soell.com
www.soell.com

FACILITIES FOR CHILDREN
Fast becoming a family resort

Söll has fairly wide-ranging facilities – the Söll-Hochsöll ski kindergarten, a Mini Club, which looks after children aged three to five who don't want to spend all day on the slopes, and a special kids-only surface lift and slope on the opposite side of the village to the main lifts. Reports welcome.

Staying there

There are some accommodations out near the lifts but most are in or around the village center – a free ski-bus-ride from the slopes. Being on the edge of town nearest the lifts is the best for those who are prepared to walk to the slopes. The other side of town has the advantage that you can board the bus there before it gets too crowded. Be aware that some guest houses are literally miles from the center and lifts, and that the ski-bus does not serve every part of this sprawling community.

HOW TO GO
Mostly cheap, cheerful gasthofs

There is a wide choice of simple gasthofs, pensions and B&Bs, and an adequate amount of better-quality hotel accommodations – mainly 3-star.

Hotels

⟨⟨3 **Greil** (5289) The only 4-star – attractive place, but out of the center on the wrong side for the lifts and pool.

⟨⟨3 **Postwirt** (5081) Attractive, central old 3-star with own bar and separate stube.

⟨⟨3 **Bergland** (5484) Small 3-star, well placed midway between the village and lifts.

⟨⟨3 **Panorama** (5309) 3-star far from lifts but with own bus stop; wonderful views; pleasant rooms; best cakes around.

⟨⟨3 **Tulpe** (5223) Next to the lifts.

⟨2 **Feldwebel** (5224) Central 2-star.

⟨2 **Schirast** (5544) Next to the lifts.

⟨2 **Garni-Tenne** (5387) B&B gasthof between center and main road.

Apartments/condos The central Ferienhotel Schindlhaus has nice accommodations, though the best apartments in town are attached to the Bergland hotel.

EATING OUT
A fair choice

Some of the best restaurants are in hotels. The Greil and Postwirt are

↑ Gentle, rolling, wooded slopes and lots of them is what the Ski Welt is all about

SKI WELT

good, but the Schindlhaus is said to be the best. Giovanni does excellent pizzas, while other places worth a visit include the Dorfstub'n and the Venezia, which received a glowing report from one guest last season.

APRES-SKI
Still some very loud bars

Söll is not as raucous as it used to be, but it's still very lively and a lot of places have live music. Pub 15 is a bit of a sleazy remnant of the old days, but is lively. The Whisky Mühle is a large disco that can get a little rowdy, especially after other bars close. The Postkeller sometimes has a singalong. Buffalo's Western Saloon is popular. There's a floodlit trail and separate toboggan run – both from top to bottom of the gondola. And for a romantic evening you can hire the Gerhard Berger VIP gondola, complete with leather upholstery, curtains and a champagne bucket.

OFF THE SLOPES
Not bad for a small village

You could spend a happy day in the wonderfully equipped Panoramabad: taking a sauna, swimming, lounging about. The large baroque church would be the pride of many tourist towns. There are numerous coach excursions, including trips to Salzburg, Innsbruck and even Vipiteno over in Italy.

Hopfgarten phone numbers
From elsewhere in Austria add the prefix 05335.
From abroad use the prefix +43 5335.

Hopfgarten 620m/2,030ft

Hopfgarten is an unspoiled, friendly and traditional resort tucked away several miles from the busy Wörgl road.

THE RESORT
The village is a good size: small enough to be intimate, large enough to have plenty of off-slope amenities. Most hotels are within five minutes' walk of the chair-lift to Rigi.

THE MOUNTAIN
Hopfgarten offers line-free access to Rigi and Hohe Salve – the high point of the Ski Welt.

Slopes When snow is good, the runs down to Hopfgarten and the nearby villages of Brixen and Itter are some of the best in the Ski Welt. But the fine, and relatively snowsure runs above Scheffau are irksomely distant.

For a change of scene, and perhaps less crowded trails, take a bus to Westendorf (see separate chapter) or Kelchsau, both on the Ski Welt ticket.

Snow reliability The resort's great weakness is the poor snow quality on the south-west-facing home slope.

Snowboarding A terrain park near Hochsöll can be accessed from the Hohe Salve above Hopfgarten.

Experts Experts should venture off-trail for excitement.

Intermediates The whole Ski Welt is great for intermediates.

Beginners There is a convenient beginners' slope in the village, but it is sunny as well as low, so lack of snow-cover is likely to mean excursions up the mountain to the higher blue runs – at the cost of a lift ticket.

Cross-country Hopfgarten is one of the best cross-country bases in the area. There are fine trails to Kelchsau (11km/7 miles) and Niederau (15km/9 miles), and the Itter–Bocking loop (15km/9 miles) starts nearby. Westendorf's trails are close.

Liftlines There's only a two-person chair out of the village, so lines can be a problem in the morning.

Mountain restaurants See Söll.

Schools and guides Partly because Hopfgarten seems to attract large numbers of Australians, English is widely spoken in the two schools.

Facilities for children Hopfgarten is a family resort, with a nursery and ski kindergarten.

STAYING THERE
How to go Cheap and cheerful gasthofs, pensions and little private B&Bs are the norm here.

Hotels The exceptions to the rule are the comfortable 4-star hotels Hopfgarten (3920) with pool, and Sporthotel Fuchs (2420), both well placed for the main lift.

Eating out Most of the restaurants are hotel-based, but there are exceptions, including Chinese food and a pizzeria.

Après-ski Après-ski is generally quiet.

Off the slopes Off-slope amenities include swimming, riding, bowling, skating, tobogganing and paragliding. The railway makes trips to Salzburg, Innsbruck and Kitzbühel possible.

Brixen 800m/2,620ft

It may not be pretty, but it has a line-free, high-capacity gondola up to the main Ski Welt slopes.

THE RESORT
Brixen im Thale is a very scattered roadside village at the south-east edge of the Ski Welt, close to Westendorf. The main hotels are near the railway station, a bus-ride from the lifts.

THE MOUNTAIN
When snow is good, Brixen has some of the best slopes in the Ski Welt.

Slopes All three runs leading down under the gondola are fine runs in different ways: an ungroomed route and a black and a red with snowmaking. There's a small area of north-facing runs, including beginner areas, on the other side of the village at Kandleralm.

Snow reliability A chain of snowmaking machines on the main south-facing trail helps to preserve the snow as long as possible.

Snowboarding See Söll..

Experts The black run alongside the Brixen gondola is one of the only challenging trails in the area.

Intermediates Some challenging local slopes for intermediates to tackle.

Beginners The beginner areas are secluded and shady, but meeting up with friends for lunch is a hassle – the area is a bus-ride from the village.

Cross-country Snow permitting, Brixen is one of the best cross-country villages in the Ski Welt. There is a long trail to Kirchberg, and more leisurely loops that circumnavigate nearby Westendorf. A 5km/3 mile loop up the

Brixen phone numbers
From elsewhere in Austria add the prefix 05334.
From abroad use the prefix +43 5334.

mountain at Hochbrixen provides fine views and fairly reliable snow.

Lines New lifts have improved the once line-prone area.

Mountain restaurants The Filzalm above Brixen has been recommended.

Schools and guides The ski school runs the usual group classes, and mini-groups for five to seven people.

Facilities for children Brixen is not as suitable as other Ski Welt resorts, but it has an all-day ski kindergarten with optional lunchtime supervision.

STAYING THERE

How to go There are plenty of hotels and pensions.

Hotels The hotel Alpenhof (88320) and the Sporthotel (8191) are both 4-star hotels with pools.

Eating out Restaurants are mainly in hotels.

Après-ski Après-ski is quiet, but livelier Westendorf is a short cab-ride.

Off the slopes Off-slope activities include tennis, hotel-based spa facilities and days out to Salzburg, Innsbruck and Kitzbühel. A free bus runs to Westendorf every 45 minutes.

Scheffau 745m/2,440ft

This is one of the most attractive of the Ski Welt villages.

Scheffau phone numbers
From elsewhere in Austria add the prefix 05358.
From abroad use the prefix +43 5358.

THE RESORT

Scheffau is a rustic little place complete with pretty white church. It is spacious yet not sprawling, and has a definite center. It is tucked away half a mile off the busy main Wörgl road, which increases its charm at the cost of slope convenience: the Ski Welt lifts are at Blaiken, on the opposite side of the main road. If convenience is all important to you, you have the option of staying in Blaiken, where there are several more hotels.

THE MOUNTAIN

Scheffau is well placed for the Ski Welt's best (and most central and snowsure) section of trails.

Slopes A gondola and parallel two-stage chair give rapid and generally line-free access directly to Brandstadl and the whole Ski Welt.

Snow reliability Nearby Eiberg is the place to go when snow is poor.

Experts The trails above Blaiken are some of the longest and steepest in the Ski Welt.

Intermediates This is as good a base as any in the area.

Beginners The beginner area is in the village, and is adequate when snow-cover is good enough. But this location means absolute beginners will be separated from those on the main Ski Welt slopes, and makes Scheffau a poor choice for mixed-ability parties – though one regular visitor finds even real beginners can make it up to Brandstadl by the end of the week.

Cross-country See Ellmau chapter.

Liftlines There can be weekend lines for the gondola. At such times the two-stage valley chair can be a useful alternative – though the VIP ticket for Scheffau guests means you can slide past day trippers in the line.

Mountain restaurants See Ellmau.

Schools and guides The school is well regarded, but groups can be large.

Facilities for children Both the ski kindergarten and non-ski nursery have good reputations.

STAYING THERE

Hotels The 4-star Kaiser (8000) and 3-star Alpin (8556-0) are the best hotels and both have pool, sauna and steam room. The Wilder Kaiser (8118), Waldhof (8122) and Blaiken (8126) are good value gasthofs near the Blaiken gondola.

Eating out There aren't many village restaurants, and those staying in B&B places are advised to book tables.

Après-ski Après-ski is unlikely to draw Blaiken residents up the hill.

Off the slopes Walking apart, there is little to do. Tour operators organise trips to Innsbruck and Salzburg.

Itter 700m/2,300

Itter is a tiny village halfway around the mountain between Söll and Hopfgarten, with beginner areas close to hand and a gondola just outside the village into the Ski Welt, via Hochsöll.

There's a hotel and half a dozen gasthofs and B&Bs. The school has a rental shop, and when conditions are good this is a good beginners' resort.

Get the next edition free!

Please send us reports on the resorts you visit this winter. You'll be helping us to make the next edition even more useful – and you may win one of the 100 free copies we'll be giving to the writers of the most helpful reports.

Where to Ski and Snowboard Worldwide is researched by a small team. There are too many resorts for us to visit them all every year, and in the resorts we do visit there are too many hotels, bars and mountain restaurants for us to see them all. What's more, there are some aspects of ski resorts that we can't sensibly assess by visiting at one particular time of the season – for example, whether there are serious liftlines at peak times, or congested trails. So we are very keen to encourage more readers to send in reports on their vacation experiences. We'll be giving 100 copies of the next edition to the writers of the best reports.

There are five main kinds of feedback we need:

• what you particularly **liked and disliked** about the resort

• what aspects of the resort came as a **surprise** to you

• your other suggestions for **changes to our evaluation** of the resort – changes we should make to the ratings, verdicts, descriptions etc

• your experience of **liftlines** and other weaknesses in the lift system, and of the **ski school** and associated childcare arrangements

• your feedback on **individual facilities** in the resort – the hotels, bars, restaurants (including mountain restaurants), nightclubs, equipment shops, sports facilities etc.

Please send your reports by e-mail to:

reports@snowfile.com

Don't forget to say when you visited the resort – and to include your mailing address, so that we can send you a free book next September. If you also include a short summary of your previous experience of ski resorts it will help us to interpret your reports correctly.

free books!

St Anton

Non-stop on- and off-slope action and pretty village base

HOW IT RATES

The slopes

Snow	****
Extent	****
Experts	*****
Intermediates	***
Beginners	*
Convenience	***
Lines	**
Restaurants	***

The rest

Scenery	***
Resort charm	****
Off-slope	***

➕ Extensive slopes for adventurous intermediates and experts

➕ Heavy snowfalls, backed up by snowmaking, generally give good cover despite sunny slopes

➕ Much-improved lift system has greatly reduced liftline problems

➕ Very lively après-ski

➕ Despite resort expansion, village retains distinct Tirolean charm

➖ Slopes not ideal for beginners or timid intermediates

➖ Most of the tough stuff is off-trail

➖ Trails can get very crowded

➖ Surprisingly little to amuse non-slope-users

➖ Nightlife can get rowdy, with noisy drunks in the early hours

The centre of St Anton looks like a typical Tirolean village. But it has become the most cosmopolitan resort in Austria and a Mecca for ski bums, who flock in from all over the world. That's because of the wonderful, tough off-trail runs available in the bowls below the Valluga – the best that Austria has to offer. In good snow conditions they are superb. Sadly, conditions are often less than perfect except just after a fresh snowfall, because of their south-facing aspect. But, if you are lucky with the snow you'll have the time of your life. There's a lot to offer adventurous intermediates too, both locally and at Lech and Zürs, a short bus-ride away.

There are lots of lively discos and bars, which keep going from 3pm to 2am. The resort is ideal for the hard-drinking, disco-loving, keen-for-action holidaymaker who can stand the pace of getting to bed late and being up for the first lift – it's not for those who like a quiet life and gentle, uncrowded trails.

Major improvements for last season's Alpine Skiing World Championships has left St Anton with much improved lifts from the resort, a smart new swimming pool and conference center and a less intrusive railway line.

The resort

MOUNTAIN FACTS

Altitude 1305m-2650m
4,280ft-8,690ft

Arlberg region

Lifts	83
Trails	260km/
	162 miles
Blue	25%
Red	50%
Black	25%
Snowmaking	65km/
	40 miles
Recco detectors used	

TVB ST ANTON AM ARLBERG

It is the high ungroomed bowls that good skiers and riders come for – but they are far from deserted →

St Anton is at the foot of the road up to the Arlberg pass, at the eastern end of a lift network that spreads across to St Christoph and above the pass to Rauz and Stuben. The resort is a long, sprawling mixture of traditional and modern buildings crammed into a narrow valley. It used to be sandwiched between a busy road and the mainline railway – but the railway was moved before the start of the 2000/01 World Championship season, and this area will now be landscaped into a park and ice rink.

It is an attractively bustling place, full of life, color and noise. Although it is crowded and commercialised, St Anton is full of character, and its traffic-free main street retains Alpine charm and traditional-style buildings.

The resort's main slopes start with a central tram into the Valluga area and

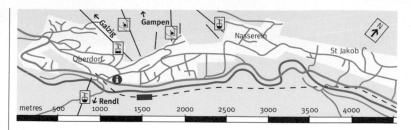

What's new

Major work for the 2001 World Championships benefited the resort enormously. A new eight-person gondola from Nasserein to Gampen has reduced the pressure on the central lifts and made Nasserein a good place to stay for a quieter time. The Fang fast quad from east of the central village has improved access for many accommodations too. These lifts have allowed demolition of the old funicular, making the home trail wider.

The railway line and station were moved to the outskirts of the town and the area is to be landscaped into a park with ice rink. For 2001/02 the Arlberg-well.com center, initially constructed for the World Championships, will be redeveloped to include an indoor pool, flume and waterfall, children's pool, outdoor pool, sauna and seminar and conference rooms.

a gondola and chair-lifts into Kapall. On the other side of the main road (served by free buses) a gondola goes to the Rendl area.

If you want to go further afield, regular buses go to Zürs, Lech and the less well-known Klösterle-Sonnenkopf area (which we had a rave review of), and are all covered by the Arlberg lift ticket. These buses can get busy and a reporter complained this year of struggling to get on the buses and lack of organization collecting payment and storing skis. Serfaus, Nauders, Ischgl and Sölden are also feasible outings by car.

The mountains

St Anton vies with Val-d'Isère for the title of 'resort with most undergraded slopes'. There are plenty of red trails that would be black in many other resorts, and plenty of blues that would be red. A few years ago, there were no black trails on the map. Now there are two, which have been regraded from red. There are many other very popular steep runs marked on the trail map,

but they are given off-trail status. Some are classified as 'high-alpine touring routes' – this means they are not marked, not groomed, not patrolled and not protected from avalanche danger. There are also some 'ski routes'. These have some markers, are groomed occasionally in part, but are not patrolled and are protected from avalanches only 'in the immediate vicinity of the markers'.

The trail map says that high-alpine touring routes require 'extensive mountain experience' and 'are only recommended when accompanied by an authorized guide'. Ski routes are recommended only for people with 'alpine experience or with a ski instructor'. And yet between these grades of run cover most of the best runs for experts. And they are commonly used by tourists without the services of an instructor or guide. One visitor commented, 'The lack of marked black runs is discouraging. When we were there the routes of the old black runs were clear and well used. It is entirely unreasonable to expect everyone to take guides on these

AUSTRIA

108

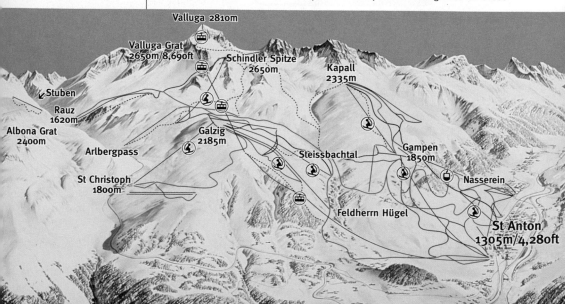

routes, and it seems irresponsible to ignore the fact that people will go on them. They run the risk of alienating those who want to move off red runs but are not quite ready to take on anything and everything. On some of the ski routes there were snow-guns. This doesn't fit with the theory that you are on your own.' A couple of years ago, a reporter told a worrying tale of being badly lost on an avalanched ski route that was not marked as closed at the start. But on our recent visits we found some ski route areas clearly roped off and marked closed in times of extreme avalanche danger – so it looks as if things might be improving in this respect.

The Arlberg region trail map is rather inadequate. One reporter commented on the poor clarity of the maps with the 'size of print being too small and the lengths and directions of the runs being unclear, which can be both misleading and dangerous'. Fortunately the on-mountain maps and signs are clearer. But reporters have complained of poor trail grooming and one of a blue run that was closed part way down with no prior warning, forcing him to take novice trails down the only alternative – a steep ungroomed run. Reporters have found the local cable TV, showing the state of some of the trails and lines, very useful.

THE SLOPES
Large linked area

St Anton's slopes are made up of several sectors, all except one of which are linked, on a predominantly south-facing mountain.

From the center, there's a two-stage tram up to **Galzig** and then **Valluga**, and a high-speed quad up to **Gampen**. From Gampen, trails lead back to St Anton and Nasserein, or in the opposite direction across to the links with the Valluga–Galzig area. Or you can go up higher to **Kapall** on the fast six-pack and head down ski routes or good cruising blues and reds.

A new eight-person gondola from Nasserein to Gampen opened last season. This is great for Nasserein residents and can also be reached by taking the relatively new Fang chair between the central lifts and Nasserein.

The high-speed quad that links Gampen to **Galzig** brings you out just above the mid-station of the tram up from St Anton. From here you can travel in most directions, including back to town, down to **St Christoph** (from where there's a high-speed quad back up) or back to the link between Galzig and Gampen (a slow chair can take you back to Gampen). At peak periods the trails down from Galzig are some of the most crowded we've come across.

From Galzig you can get up to St Anton's most famous slopes, the bowls below the **Valluga**, by taking the second stage of the tram or going up the Schindlergrat three-person chair, which delivers you to the same height but on a different peak. There's a tiny third stage of the Valluga tram which takes you up to 2810m/9,220ft, but this is mainly for sightseeing. The only run down from there is off the back, off-trail to Zürs. You are not allowed to take skis or a board up the lift without a guide.

From both the second stage of the tram and the Schindlergrat chair, you can take the long, beautiful but very crowded red run to Rauz, at the western end of St Anton's own slopes. From Rauz you cross the road and go along to Stuben, where a slow two-stage chair-lift takes you to the quiet, mainly north-facing **Albona** area.

The final area, **Rendl**, is separate and reached by gondola from just outside town (there are free buses from the village, but it's only a short

St Anton
05m/4,28oft

Gampberg
2405m/7,890ft

Riffel Scharte
2650m/8,690ft

Rendl

Brandkreuz
2100m

Moostal

LIFT TICKETS

2001/02 prices in euros

Arlberg Ski Ticket
Covers all St Anton, St Christoph, Lech, Zürs and Stuben lifts, and linking bus between Rauz and Zürs.
Beginners Limited ticket covering beginners' lifts.
Main ticket
1-day ticket 37
6-day ticket 171
(low season 154)
Senior citizens
Over 65: 6-day ticket 146
Children
Under 15: 6-day ticket 103
Short-term tickets
Single ascent tickets on some lifts throughout Arlberg. Half-day tickets (adults 28) from noon, afternoon 'taster' tickets (16) from 3pm.
Note Main ticket also covers Klösterle (10 lifts), 7km/4 miles west of Stuben. Discounts during wedel, firn and snow crystal weeks. Senior citizen ticket for women over 60.

walk). A number of lifts serve the west-facing runs at the top here, with a single north-facing trail returning to the gondola bottom station.

SNOW RELIABILITY
Generally very good cover

If the weather is coming from the west or north-west (as it often is), the Arlberg gets it first, and as a result St Anton and its neighbors get heavy falls of snow. They often have much better conditions than other resorts of a similar height, and we've had great fresh powder here as late as mid-April in recent years. But many of the slopes face south or south-east, causing icy or heavy conditions at times. It's vital to time your runs off the Valluga to get decent conditions.

The lower runs are now well equipped with snowmaking, which ensures the home runs remain open (but not necessarily enjoyable).

FOR EXPERTS
One of the world's great areas

St Anton vies with Chamonix, Val-d'Isère and a handful of others for the affections of experts. It has some of the most consistently challenging and extensive slopes in the world. The jewel in the crown is the variety of off-trail in the bowls beneath the Valluga – see feature panel opposite. Lower down, very difficult trails lead off in almost every direction from the Galzig summit. Osthang is an extremely tough, long bump run that leads down to Feldherrn Hügel. Not much less challenging are trails down to Steissbachtal, St Christoph and past Maiensee towards the road. These lower runs can be doubly tricky if the snow has been hit by the sun.

The World Championship courses are between Kapall, Gampen and town, and the previously red Fang run has been regraded black since the championships. There are countless opportunities for going off-trail in the Kapall–Gampen area, including the

beautiful Schöngraben unmarked route to Nasserein.

The Rendl area across the road has plenty of open space beneath the top lifts and, with an accompanying guide, there is some delightful fun to be had off the back of this ridge.

The Albona mountain above Stuben has north-facing slopes that hold powder well and some wonderful, deserted off-trail descents including beautifully long runs down to Langen (where you can catch the train) and back to St Anton. These are, however, 'high-alpine touring runs' and should be taken seriously. One of our reporters particularly liked the Klösterle/Sonnenkopf area down-valley from Stuben for its excellent off-trail route to Langen.

On top of all this, bear in mind that many of the red runs on the trail map are long and challenging, too.

The ultimate challenge, though, is perhaps to go with a guide off the back of the third stage of the Valluga. The initial pitch is very, very steep (if you fall you die, type of pitch). But once you have negotiated that, the run down to Zürs is very beautiful and usually deserted.

FOR INTERMEDIATES
Some real challenges

St Anton is well suited to good, adventurous intermediates. They will be able to try the Mattun run and the easier version of the Schindlerkar run from Valluga Grat (see feature panel on previous page). The run from Schindler Spitze to Rauz is very long (over 1000m/3,200ft vertical), tiring, varied and ideal for good (and fit) intermediates. Alternatively, turn off from this part way down and take the – usually very crowded – Steissbachtal to the lifts back to Galzig.

The Kapall–Gampen section is also interesting, with easy bumps among trees on the lower half. From Kapall to town (over 1000m/3,200ft vertical), following the downhill run is fun.

---

boarding *Though steeped in skiing tradition, St Anton is moving with the times and improving facilities for boarders. Although we don't really recommend it to beginners, it is one of the best free-ride areas in the world, with lots of steep terrain and natural hits. There is a terrain park and 100m/330ft half-pipe on Rendl. There are still a few T-bars around but fast chair-lifts are now the main ways around the mountains. Lessons are provided by the ski schools and the Snowboard Academy (part of the Arlberg school). A book could be written about the almost legendary nightlife.*

The off-trail runs in the huge bowl beneath the summit of the Valluga, and reached by either the Schindlergrat chair or the second stage of the Valluga tram, are justifiably world famous. In good snow, this whole area is an off-trail delight for experts.

Except immediately after a fresh snowfall, you can see tracks going all over the mountain – and some of the descents look terrifying. There are two main ski routes down marked on the trail map – both long, steep, often bumpy descents. The Schindlerkar is the first you come to and it divides into two – the Schindlerkar gully being the steeper option. For the second, wider and somewhat easier Mattun run, you traverse further at the top. Both these feed down into the Steissbachtal gulley where there are lifts back up to Galzig and Gampen. The Schweinströge starts off in the same direction as the red run to Rauz, but you traverse the shoulder of the Schindler Spitze and down a narrow gulley.

Less adventurous intermediates will find St Anton less to their taste. There are few easy cruising trails. The most obvious are the short blues on Galzig and the Steissbachtal (aka 'Happy Valley'). These are reasonably gentle but get uncomfortably crowded, particularly at peak times. The blue to St Christoph is generally quieter. The narrowish blues between Kapall and Gampen can have some challenging bumps. Intermediates looking for easy cruising will find the best by taking the bus to Lech.

In the Rendl area a variety of trails suitable for good and moderate intermediates criss-cross, including a lovely long tree-lined run (over 1000m/3,300ft vertical from the top) back to the valley gondola station. This is the best run in the whole area when visibility is poor, though it has some quite awkward sections.

FOR BEGINNERS
Far from ideal
St Anton has supposedly better beginner areas now, near the new Fang lift. But there are no easy, uncrowded runs for beginners to progress to. Experts and intermediates who are desperate to visit the Arlberg, but are taking novices on vacation, would be better off staying in Lech or Zürs and taking the bus to Rauz when they want to try St Anton.

FOR CROSS-COUNTRY
Limited interest
St Anton is not really a cross-country resort. There are a couple of uninspiring trails near town, another at St Jakob 3km/2 miles away, and a pretty trail through trees along the Ferwalltal to the foot of the Albona area. There is also a tiny little loop at St Christoph.

Snow conditions are usually good and trails total around 35km/22 miles.

LIFTLINES
Improved, but still a problem
Lines are not the problem they once were, since the replacement of several lifts by high-speed chairs. But they can still be tiresome in peak season and at weekends. There are useful 'singles entrances' at some lifts which enable you to cut the lines if you don't mind who you ride with – with taped announcements in several languages urging people to fill the chairs.

Perhaps worse than the lines in busy periods are the crowded trails that you'll encounter – we were there one March weekend and had to continuously look all round before making a turn to make sure we didn't hit anyone; we could have used rearview mirrors. And even in January, the Steissbachtal was uncomfortably crowded.

MOUNTAIN RESTAURANTS
Plenty of choice
Look out for the little table-service huts, which have much more going for them than the characterless cafeterias. Two of the best are just above town, the Sennhütte and Rodelhütte. The Rendl Beach is also worth a visit. The S'Gräbli was highly recommended by a recent reporter. The Mooserwirt serves typical Austrian food; the Krazy Kanguruh burgers, pizzas and snacks. The goulash soup at the Taps Bar next to Krazy Kanguruh has been recommended, and the Kaminstube

SCHOOLS/GUIDES

2001/02 prices in
euros

Arlberg
Manager Richard
Walter
Classes 6 days
4½hr: 2½hr am and
2hr pm, from 9.30
6 full days 181
Children's classes
Ages: 4 to 14
6 full days including
lunch 186
Private lessons
Half or full day
192 for full day; each
additional person 16

2000/01 prices in
euros

St Anton
Manager Franz
Klimmer
Classes 6 days
4½hr: 9.30-noon and
1pm-3pm
6 full days 174
Children's classes
Ages: 5 to 14
6 full days 125
Private lessons
Half or full day
182 for full day; each
additional person 15

Phone numbers
From elsewhere in
Austria add the prefix
05446.
From abroad use the
prefix +43 5446.

CHILDCARE

The kindergarten at
the Kinderwelt (2526)
takes toilet-trained
children aged 30
months to 14 years,
from 9.30 to 3.30. Ski
tuition with the
Arlberg ski school in
a special snow-garden
is available for
children aged 4.

gets beautiful sunset views.

Lunching in St Christoph or Stuben is also a useful idea. The St Christoph choices include the atmospheric Hospiz Alm (though we continue to receive reports of poor restaurant service), where instead of walking down to the toilets you can slide down a channel beside the stairs, the good value Almbar just above it, and Traxl's ice bar at the Maiensee Hotel. Reporters say that in Stuben the views from the Albonagrathütte are worth the short walk to get to it, that the Albona is quiet and friendly and that there are a couple of cozy places in the village for a good, quiet lunch, including the Berghaus just behind the church.

SCHOOLS AND GUIDES
Mixed reports
The relatively new St Anton school has brought much-needed competition to the Arlberg school. But we've had conflicting reports on the Arlberg school. 'Complete beginner group much too big despite our complaints and we learned more from our friends,' said one reporter. 'Superb teaching meant our novices had a great time and one was tackling red runs by the end of the week,' said another. 'Everyone in my chalet was very happy with the Arlberg school, with relatively small classes and good English,' says our most recent report.

Reporters who have hired a guide to the off-trail at the top of the Valluga have had a great day. And we ourselves have skied with excellent off-trail guides on the main ski area.

FACILITIES FOR CHILDREN
Getting better
St Anton might not seem an obvious resort for family holidays, but the resort works hard to accommodate families' needs: the youth center attached to the Arlberg school is excellent, and the special slopes both for toddlers (at the bottom) and bigger children (up at Gampen) are well done. Also the new Arlberg-well.com center should keep children entertained with its pools, flumes and waterfall.

Staying there

Staying near the attractive center is best if you want to hit the nightlife regularly. For a quieter time, the suburb of Nasserein is now a good base, with the fast new gondola up to Gampen. At night it is a short free bus-ride or 15-minute walk from the center. And many of the accommodations between Nasserein and the center have been made much more convenient by the new Fang chair.

St Anton spreads up the hill to the west of the center, towards the Arlberg pass. Places up here in and beyond Oberdorf can be 20 minutes' walk from the center – but quite convenient for the slopes, if snow-cover is good.

HOW TO GO
Lots of lodging options
There's a wide range of places to stay, from quality hotels to cheap and cheerful pensions and apartments.
Hotels There is one 5-star hotel and lots of 4- and 3-stars and B&Bs.
(((((5) **St Antoner Hof** (2910) Best in town, but its position on the bypass is less than ideal. Pool.
((((4) **Schwarzer Adler** (2244-0) Centuries-old inn on main street. Widely varying bedrooms.
((((4) **Alte Post** (2553) Atmospheric place on main street with lively après-ski bar. Endorsed by a reporter.
((((4) **Neue Post** (2213) Comfortable if uninspiring 4-star at the centre of affairs, close to both lifts and nightlife.
((((4) **Kertess** (2005) Charmingly furnished, further up the hill. Pool.
((((4) **Sport** (3111) Central position, with varied bedrooms, good food. Pool.
(((3) **Grischuna** (2304) Welcoming family-run place in peaceful position up the hill west of the town; close to the slopes, five minutes to the tram.
(((3) **Goldenes Kreuz** (22110) A comfortable B&B hotel halfway to Nasserein, ideal for cruising home.
Apartments/condos Plenty of apartments are available

STAYING DOWN THE VALLEY
Nice and quiet
Beyond Nasserein is the more complete village of St Jakob. It can be reached on snow, but is dependent on the free shuttle-bus in the morning.

Pettneu is a quiet village further down the valley. It's best for those with their own cars.

St Christoph is a collection of exclusive hotels and restaurants set high up by the Arlberg pass – convenient for the slopes but deadly quiet at night →

GETTING THERE

Air Innsbruck, transfer 1½hr. Zürich, transfer 3hr.

Rail Mainline station in resort.

ACTIVITIES

Indoor Swimming pool (also hotel pools open to the public, with sauna and massage), tennis, squash, bowling, museum, cinema in Vallugasaal

Outdoor Swimming pool, 15km/9 miles of cleared walks, natural skating rink (skating, curling), sleigh rides, tobogganing, paragliding

TOURIST OFFICE

Postcode A-6580
t +43 (5446) 22690
f 2532
st.anton@netway.at
www.stantonamlarlberg. com

EATING OUT
Mostly informal

You live fast and eat hard to make up for it in St Anton. Plain, filling fare is the norm, with numerous places such as the Fuhrmannstube, Trödlerstube and the Reselehof and Alt St Anton in Nasserein serving big portions of traditional Austrian food. A reporter recommends Dixies for pizza, pasta, steaks and fish, and Bobo's serves good Mexican. An atmospheric place for dinner is the wood-paneled Museum, where as well as enjoying upscale food and wine, you can learn the history of the resort. The toboggan run is floodlit and lift-served a couple of nights a week, and you can stop off at the Rodelalm above Nasserein for traditional food, beer and schnapps – booking is essential.

APRES-SKI
Throbbing till late

St Anton's bars rock from mid-afternoon until the early hours. A collection of bars on the slopes above town get packed by 3pm. The Krazy Kanguruh is probably the most famous. But, a bit lower down, the Mooserwirt and the S'Gräbli, opposite each other, are equally lively – live bands most days and dancing on the beams in ski boots. All this is followed by a slide down the trail in the dark. The bars in town are in full swing by 4pm, too. Most are lively with loud music – only sophisticates looking for a quieter more relaxed time are less well provided for. The Underground bar has a great atmosphere and live music, but gets packed. The Piccadilly pub and

Hazienda are equally popular. Recent reporters enjoyed the atmosphere at Scotty's, Jacksy's, Pub 37 and Funky Chicken. For late-night dancing, Kartouche and the Stanton in the center of town are the key places.

OFF THE SLOPES
Not very relaxing

St Anton is a sprawling resort, with little to offer non-slope users. Many of the most attractive mountain huts are not readily accessible by lift for pedestrians. The center is lively with a fair selection of shops. The new Arlberg-well.com center (see What's New) is a welcome addition. Getting by bus to the other Arlberg resorts is easy. Lech would arguably be a better, if pricier, base, with more to do. It's easy to visit Innsbruck by train.

St Christoph 1800m/5,910ft

A small, exclusive collection of hotels, restaurants and bars right by the Arlberg Pass, with surface-lifts for local slopes and a high-speed quad chair-lift to the heart of St Anton's slopes. It's home to Austria's elite academy for ski instructors. Good for a nice lunch, it's expensive and deadly quiet to stay in. The most expensive hotel of all is the huge 5-star Arlberg-Hospiz.

Zell am See — 755m/2,480ft

Charming lakeside town, varied slopes and glacier option

114

HOW IT RATES

The slopes

Snow	**
Extent	**
Experts	**
Intermediates	***
Beginners	***
Convenience	**
Liftlines	**
Restaurants	***

The rest

Scenery	***
Resort charm	***
Off-slope	****

- Pretty, tree-lined slopes with great views down to the lake
- Lively, but not rowdy, nightlife
- Charming old town center with beautiful lakeside setting
- Lots to do off the slopes
- Huge range of cross-country trails
- Kaprun glacier nearby
- Varied terrain including a couple of steep black runs

- Sunny, low slopes often have poor conditions despite snowmaking, which makes the area more limited
- Trek to lifts from many of the accommodations, and sometimes crowded buses
- Less suitable for beginners than most small Austrian resorts
- The Kaprun glacier gets horrendous liftlines when it is most needed

Zell am See is an unusual resort – not a rustic village like most of its small Austrian competitors, but a lakeside town with a charming old center that seems more geared to summer than winter visitors. It's a pleasant place, and – since a tunnel now takes through traffic to Schüttdorf – not plagued by traffic.

Zell's slopes have a lot of variety and challenging terrain for a small area, but not enough to keep a keen intermediate or better happy for long, especially if, as some reporters have found, there's a lack of snow. Zell is very near the Kaprun glacier, but so are many low-altitude resorts, all of which run buses there if snow is in short supply. The result can be horrendous liftlines.

Zell makes an attractive base for tourists who enjoy traveling around. Having a car makes it easy to visit numerous other resorts – including Saalbach-Hinterglemm, Bad Gastein-Bad Hofgastein, Wagrain, Schladming and Obertauern.

What's new

For 2001/02 in Kaprun, an additional gondola holding 24 people in each cabin will replace the funicular which suffered the tragic fire in autumn 2000. It will run parallel with and end at the existing gondola's top station for 2001/02 and be extended to the Alpincenter at the top of the defunct funicular for 2002/03. So for 2001/02 everyone will have to take a solitary high-speed quad chair to get to the main slopes from the top of the gondola – expect huge liftlines. But the following year, access should improve – the capacity of the new gondola will be 66% greater than the funicular (which will never be re-opened to the public).

In Zell am See for 2001/02, a quad chair will replace a T-bar up to Schmittenhöhe on the Sonnkogel side and snow-making will cover 70% of the lower slopes.

The resort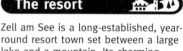

Zell am See is a long-established, year-round resort town set between a large lake and a mountain. Its charming, traffic-free medieval center is on a flat promontory, and the resort has grown up around this attractive core. A gondola at the edge of town goes up one arm of the horseshoe-shaped mountain, but Zell's trams are over a mile away. Most places to stay are a fair walk from the town gondola. Out by the tram station there are some accommodations, too. Access by another gondola at Schüttdorf is 3km/2 miles away; you can also stay here, close to the gondola (which goes directly to the top of the slopes), but the place is less appealing than Zell itself, especially for nightlife.

The mountains

Despite claims to the contrary, the extent of Zell's horseshoe of slopes is not large and the area is best suited to

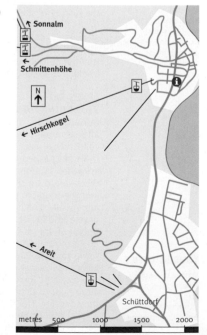

THE SLOPES
Varied but limited

The town gondola takes you to Mittelstation. From there it's either an easy or a steep run to the valley tram station. Or you can take a chair up to Hirschkogel to meet the gondola up from Schüttdorf – which you can ride up further and then take a T-bar to the Schmittenhöhe top-station. This is also where the main valley floor tram brings you. A gentle cruise and a single short surface lift moves you to Sonnkogel. Here several routes lead down to Sonnalm mid-station – where another tram from the valley arrives. A black trail runs from here to the valley floor. At the end of the day you can take a gentle trail from the top (Schmittenhöhe) tram back to town or ride one of the cars down.

SNOW RELIABILITY
Good snowmaking, but lots of sun

Zell am See's slopes get so much sun the snow can suffer as a result. Lots of slopes are now well covered by snow-guns, including the sunny home run to Schüttdorf and 70% of the lower slopes. But though reporters have seen 'lots of snowmaking in evidence', slush, ice and closed runs have still marred their holidays. The Kaprun glacier is snow-sure, but expect long liftlines there (and for buses to get there) when snow is short elsewhere.

↑ Zell am See on the far side of the lake with trails coming down into it

intermediates. The easiest runs are along the ridge, with steeper trails heading down to the valley. Kaprun's snow-sure glacier slopes are only a few minutes by bus; Saalbach and Bad Hofgastein are easily reached by bus and train respectively and, at a push, Wagrain, Schladming and Obertauern are car trips.

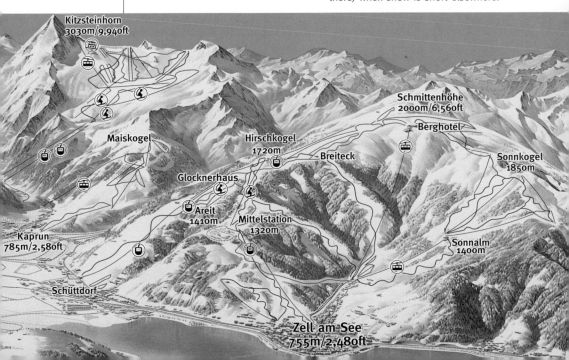

Kitzsteinhorn 3030m/9,940ft

Schmittenhöhe 2000m/6,560ft

Berghotel

Maiskogel

Hirschkogel 1720m

Breiteck

Sonnkogel 1850m

Glocknerhaus

Areit 1410m

Mittelstation 1320m

Sonnalm 1400m

Kaprun 785m/2,580ft

Schüttdorf

Zell am See 755m/2,480ft

MOUNTAIN FACTS

Altitude 760m-2000m/
2,490ft-6,560ft
Lifts 56
Trails 130km/81 miles
Blue 43%
Red 38%
Black 19%
Snowmaking 40km/
25 miles
Recco detectors used

LIFT TICKETS

2001/02 prices in
euros
**Europa–Sportregion
Kaprun–Zell am See**
Covers all lifts in Zell
and Kaprun, and
buses between them.
Beginners Points card
or limited ticket.
Main ticket
1-day ticket 33
6-day ticket 155
(low season 140)
Children
Under 15: 6 days: 78
Under 6: free ticket
Short-term tickets
Half-day ticket from
11.30 for Zell only.
Alternative periods
5 in 7 days and 10 in
14 days.
Notes Day ticket valid
at Zell am See only.

boarding *Zell is well suited to boarders. There's a high proportion of chairs, gondolas and trams and a terrain park and half-pipe. You'll also find plenty of life in the evenings. The Kaprun glacier also has a half-pipe and terrain park, with powder in its wide, open bowl. But it also has a high proportion of surface lifts – some beginners we heard from 'did a lot of walking'.*

FOR EXPERTS
Several blacks, but still limited
Zell has more steep slopes than most resorts this size, but can't entertain an expert for a week. When we were last there it was fabulous speeding down the immaculately groomed black runs 13 and 14 – they were deserted early in the morning. However, as a reporter points out, 'they are more like French reds'. Off-trail opportunities are limited.

FOR INTERMEDIATES
Bits and pieces for most grades
Good intermediates have a choice of fine, long runs, but this is not a place for mileage. All blacks are within a brave intermediate's capability, and there's a lovely cruising run between Areit and Schüttdorf when conditions are good. Some Sonnkogel trails are also suitable. The timid can cruise the ridge all day on quiet, attractive runs,

ZELL AM SEE TOURIST OFFICE

The slopes along the ridge from the top station to Schüttdorf are the easiest in the area ↓

or head past Mittelstation to Zell's trams on an easy blue. Kaprun's snow-sure glacier runs are also good 'especially trail 3 for early intermediates'.

FOR BEGINNERS
Two low novice areas
There are small beginner areas at the tram area and at Schüttdorf, both covered by snow-guns. Near-beginners and fast learners have plenty of short, easy runs at Schmittenhöhe, Breiteck and Areit. Some are used by complete beginners when snow conditions are poor lower down, but it means buying a lift ticket.

FOR CROSS-COUNTRY
Excellent if snow allows
The valley floor has extensive trails, including a superb area on the Kaprun golf course. At altitude there are just two short loops, one at the top of the Kaprun glacier, and the other at the top of the Zell gondola.

LIFTLINES
Not normally a problem
Zell am See doesn't have many problems except at peak times, when the Schmittenhöhe trams are generally the worst hit. A recent visitor found that getting to Schmittenhöhe via the Sonnalm tram is quieter.

When snow is poor there are few daytime liftlines at Zell – many people are away forming liftlines at Kaprun – but getting down by lift at the end of the day can involve delays.

MOUNTAIN RESTAURANTS
Plenty of little refuges
There are plenty of cozy, atmospheric huts. Among the best are Glocknerhaus, Kettingalm, Areitalm ('superb, freshly made strudel'), Pinzgauer and Brieteckalm. The Berghotel at Schmittenhöhe is good, but expensive. Its bar with loud music is lively (see Après-Ski). Over at the top of the Kaprun glacier the Aussichsrestaurant gets crowded, but 'has wonderful views and quite good food'.

SCHOOLS/GUIDES

2000/01 prices in euros
Zell am See
Classes 6 days
10am-noon, 1pm-3pm
5 full days: 125
Children's classes
Ages: from 4
5 full days: 125
Private lessons
Hourly: 44 for 1hr

CHILDCARE

The schools take children from age 4 and offer lunch-time care. The Areitbahn school runs a snow kindergarten from age 3, 9am to 4.30.

The village nursery is Ursula Zink (56343), which takes children from age 3, from 9.30 to 3.30.

ACTIVITIES

Indoor Swimming, sauna, solarium, fitness center, spa, tennis, squash, bowling, museum, art gallery, cinema, library, massage, ice skating
Outdoor Riding, skating, curling, floodlit toboggan runs, plane flights, sleigh rides, shooting range, swimming (Kaprun), ice-sailing, ice-surfing, tubing

GETTING THERE

Air Salzburg, transfer 2hr. Munich, transfer 3hr.

Rail Station in resort.

Phone numbers
From elsewhere in Austria add the prefix 06542.
From abroad use the prefix +43 6542.

TOURIST OFFICE

Postcode A-5700
t +43 (6542) 770
f 72032
zell@gold.at
www.zellamsee.com

SCHOOLS AND GUIDES
A wide choice
There is a choice of schools in both Zell am See and Kaprun. A reporter found boarding lessons from the main Zell school to be 'well-organized', though classes were a bit large, and English not always spoken fluently. There are also specialist Nordic centers at Schüttdorf and at Kaprun.

FACILITIES FOR CHILDREN
Schüttdorf's the place
We have no recent reports on the childcare provisions, but staying in Schüttdorf has the advantage of direct gondola access to the Areitalm snow-kindergarten, and the Ursula Zink nursery is at Zeller-Moos, just outside Schüttdorf. There's a children's adventure park on the mountain.

Staying there

Choice of location is tricky, and we have three favorite strategies. Stay in a beautiful lakeside setting (which gets you on the shuttle-bus before it's too crowded); at the upper edge of the town center (walking distance from the Zell gondola); or near the tram stations at the end of the valley.

Schüttdorf has easy access to the top of the mountain, but it is a characterless dormitory with little else going for it. Though closer to Kaprun, this is, perversely, a drawback unless you have a car. Trying to get on a glacier bus is tough, as they tend to be full when they leave Zell. Families wishing to use the Areitalm nursery and cross-country skiers stand to gain most from staying in Schüttdorf.

HOW TO GO
Choose charm or convenience
Lots of hotels, pensions and apartments.
Hotels A broad range of hotels (more 4- than 3-stars) and guest-houses.
((((4) **Salzburgerhof** (7650) Best in town – the only 5-star. Nearer lake than gondola, but has courtesy bus and pool.
((((4) **Tirolerhof** (7720) Excellent 4-star in old town. Good pool, hot tub and steam room. 'Food good, staff very friendly.'
((((4) **Eichenhof** (47201) On the outskirts of town, but popular and with a minibus service, great food and lake views.
((((4) **Alpin** (7690) Modern 4-star chalet next to the Zell gondola.

((((4) **Zum Hirschen** (7740) Comfortable 4-star, easy walk to gondola. Sauna, steam, splash pool, popular bar.
((((4) **Schwebebahn** (724610) Attractive 4-star in secluded setting by trams.
((((3) **Berner** (779) 4-star by the Zell gondola.
((2) **Hubertus** (72427) B&B near Zell gondola.
((2) **Margarete** (72724) B&B next to tram.
Apartments/condos The budget Karger Christine apartments are near the Zell gondola. Apartment Hofer is mid-range and close to the Ebenberg lift (linking to the gondola, but no boarders allowed). More comfortable are the 3-star Diana and Seilergasse (both in the old center) and the Mirabell, which is close to the Zell gondola.

STAYING UP THE MOUNTAIN
Three options
As well as the Berghotel (72489) at the top of the Schmittenhöhe tram, the Breiteckalm (73419) and Sonnalm (73262) restaurants have rooms.

EATING OUT
Plenty of choice
Zell has more non-hotel places than is usual in a small Austrian resort. The Ampere is quiet and sophisticated; Giuseppe's is a popular Italian with excellent food; and Kupferkessel and Traubenstüberl both do wholesome regional dishes. There are Chinese restaurants in Zell and Schüttdorf. Car drivers can try the good value Finkawirt, across the lake at Prielau, or the excellent Erlhof.

APRES-SKI
Plenty for all tastes
Après-ski is lively and varied, with tea dances and high-calorie cafes, plus bars and discos a-plenty. When it's sunny, Schnapps Hans ice bar outside the Berghotel at Schmittenhöhe really buzzes, with 'great music, a crazy DJ and dancing on tables and on the bar. All ages loved it.' The Diele disco bar rocks; Crazy Daisy on the main road has two crowded bars and 'the group loved it' says one reporter. Evergreen has a live band and 60s and 70s music. The Viva disco allows no under 18s; one reader proclaimed it 'excellent'. Or try the smart Hirschkeller, the cave-like Lebzelter Keller and the Sportstuberl with old ski photos on the walls.

OFF THE SLOPES
Lots of choices
There is plenty to do in this year-round resort. The train trip to Salzburg is a must, Kitzbühel is also well worth a visit and Innsbruck is within reach.

You can often walk across the frozen lake to Thumersbach, plus there are good sports facilities, a motor museum, sleigh rides and flights.

Kaprun 785m/2,580ft

THE RESORT
Kaprun is a spacious and quite lively village with lots of Tirolean charm.

THE MOUNTAIN
There is a small area of slopes on the outskirts of the village at Maiskogel best suited to early intermediates, and a separate nursery area. But most people will want to spend most of their time on the slopes of the nearby Kitzsteinhorn glacier or on Zell am See's slopes. Both are a crowded bus-ride away.

Slopes Investigations into last year's tragic fire on the funicular are still taking place and if it ever re-opens it will be for materials only, not for people. To take the strain a new 24-person gondola (Gletscherjet) has been built to run parallel with the existing eight-person gondola. The first stage of the project will be completed for 2001/02 and the Gletscherjet will start at the bottom station and run to Langwiedboden where it will be met by the quad chair. The second stage, which will take the gondola up to the Alpincenter (2450m/8,040ft) and main slopes, is due to be completed for 2002/03. The main slopes are in a big bowl above served by several T-bars and a couple of chairs. The area above the top of the Alpincenter is open for summer skiing and riding and is particularly good for an early pre-Christmas or late post-Easter break.

Snow reliability Snow is nearly always good. And with new snowmaking facilities from the Alpincenter at 2450/8,040ft to the top station of the Gratbahn at 2700m/8,860ft due to be finished for 2001/02, it should be even better.

Liftlines For 2001/02, before the second stage of the new gondola is built, expect huge liftlines at the quad chair at the top of the two access gondolas. Lines elsewhere on the mountain can be bad when crowds are bussed in if snow is poor in lower resorts.

Mountain restaurants There are a couple of decent mountain restaurants – one at the Alpincenter and another by the top of the gondolas.

Après-ski Nightlife is quiet, but the Baum and Nindl bars are lively.

Eating out Good restaurants include the Dorfstadl, the Bella Musica and the Schlemmerstuberl.

Snowboarding There's a terrain park on the glacier and some excellent natural half-pipes.

Experts There's little to challenge experts except for some good off-trail; the one slightly tough trail starts at the very top.

Intermediates trails are mainly gentle blues and reds and make for great easy cruising on usually good snow. From just below the top of the quad chair there is an entertaining red run down to the bottom of the chair. This is our favorite run on the mountain. But lines for the chair in the morning and crowds on the run in the afternoon may make it less pleasant for 2001/02 until the second stage of the new gondola is built.

Beginners There are a couple of beginner areas in the village and gentle blues on the glacier to progress to.

Cross-country The Kaprun golf course is superb, but at altitude there is just one short loop at the top of the glacier.

Schools and guides There are several ski schools offering the usual classes.

Facilities for children All of the schools offer children's classes and there's a kindergarten in the village.

STAYING THERE
Hotels The Orgler (8205), Mitteregger (8207) and Tauernhof (8235), are among the best hotels.

Off the slopes Off-slope activities are good, and include a fine sports center with outdoor rapids.

Kaprun phone numbers
From elsewhere in Austria add the prefix 06547.
From abroad use the prefix +43 6547.

France has the biggest lift-and-trail networks in the world; for those who like to cover as many miles in a day as possible, these are unrivalled. Most of these big areas are also at high altitude, ensuring high-quality snow for a long season. And French mountains offer a mixture of some of the toughest, wildest slopes in the Alps, and some of the longest, gentlest and most convenient beginner runs.

French resort villages can't be quite so uniformly recommended; but, equally, they don't all conform to the standard image of soulless, purpose-built service stations, thrown up without concern for appearance during the boom of the 1960s and 70s.

ANY STYLE OF RESORT YOU LIKE

The main drawback to France, hinted at above, is the monstrous architecture of some of the purpose-built resorts. But not all French resorts are hideous. Certainly, France has its fair share of Alpine eyesores, chief among them Les Menuires, central La Plagne, Flaine, Tignes, Isola 2000 and Les Arcs. The redeeming features of places like these are the splendid quality of the slopes they serve, the reliability and quality of the snow, and the amazing slope-side convenience of most of the accommodations.

But the French have learned the lesson that new development doesn't have to be tasteless to be convenient – look at Valmorel,

The most fashionable resort in France, and one of the best – Courchevel (1850) →

Getting around the French Alps

Pick the right gateway – Geneva, Chambéry or Grenoble – and you can hardly go wrong. The approach to Serre-Chevalier and Montgenèvre involves the 2058m/6,750ft Col du Lauteret; but the road is a major one and kept clear of snow or reopened quickly after a fall. Crossing the French–Swiss border between Chamonix and Verbier involves two closure-prone passes – the Montets and the Forclaz. When necessary, one-way traffic runs beside the tracks through the rail tunnel beneath the passes. The Mont-Blanc tunnel from Chamonix to Courmayeur is unlikely to reopen this season.

French purpose-built resorts are all about snow. The is the great freeway terrain on Bellevarde, above Val-d'Isère but just as easily reached from Tignes →

SNOWPIX.COM / CHRIS GILL

Belle Plagne and Les Coches, for example, and the newer parts of Isola 2000 or Flaine. Val-Thorens, always one of the more acceptable new resorts, is being extended sensitively, too.

If you prefer, there are genuinely old mountain villages to stay in, linked directly to the big lift networks. These are not usually as convenient for the slopes, but they give you a feel of being in France rather than a winter-holiday factory. Examples include Montchavin or Champagny for La Plagne, Vaujany for Alpe-d'Huez, St-Martin-de-Belleville for the Trois Vallées and Les Carroz, Morillon or Samoëns (a short drive from the slopes) for Flaine. There are also old villages with their own slopes that have developed as resorts while retaining some or all of their rustic ambience – such as Serre-Chevalier and La Clusaz. Megève deserves a special mention – an exceptionally charming little town combining rustic style with luxury and sophistication; shame about the traffic.

And France has Alpine centers with a long mountaineering and skiing history. Chief among these is Chamonix, which sits in the shadow of Mont Blanc, Europe's highest peak, and is the centre of the most radical off-piste terrain in the Alps. Chamonix is a big, bustling town, where skiing and boarding go on alongside tourism in general. At the opposite end of the vacation spectrum is tiny La Grave, at the foot of mountains that are almost as impressive – the highest within France – but with only a few simple hotels.

France has advantages in the gastronomic stakes. While many of its mountain restaurants serve fast food, most also do at least a plat du jour that is in a different league from what you'll find in Austria or the US. It is generally possible to find somewhere to get a half-decent lunch and to have it served at your table, rather than lining up repeatedly for every part of your meal. In the evening, most resorts have restaurants serving good, traditional, French food as well as regional specialities. And the wine is decent and affordable.

Many French resorts (though not all) have suffered from a lack of nightlife, but things have changed in recent years. In resorts dominated by apartments with few international visitors, there may still be very little going on after dinner, but places like Méribel are now distinctly lively in the evening.

Alpe-d'Huez

1860m/6,100ft

An impressive all-rounder; just a pity it faces south

HOW IT RATES

The slopes

Snow	****
Extent	****
Experts	****
Intermediates	****
Beginners	*****
Convenience	****
Liftlines	****
Restaurants	****

The rest

Scenery	****
Resort charm	*
Off-slope	***

➕ Extensive, high, sunny slopes, split interestingly into various sectors

➕ Huge snowmaking installation to keep runs open despite the sun

➕ Vast, gentle, sunny beginner areas right next to the resort

➕ Efficient, modern lift system, with few long waits

➕ Grand views of the peaks in the Ecrins national park

➕ Some good, surprisingly rustic mountain restaurants

➕ Short walks to and from the slopes

➕ More animated than most purpose-built resorts

➕ Pleasant alternative bases in outlying villages and satellites

➖ In late season the many south-facing runs can be icy early in the day and slushy in the afternoon

➖ Some main intermediate runs get badly overcrowded in high season

➖ Many of the tough runs are very high, and inaccessible or very tricky in bad weather

➖ Practically no woodland runs to retreat to in bad weather

➖ Run classifications tend to understate difficulty

➖ Messy, sprawling resort with a wide range of architectural styles, no central focus and very little charm

What's new

For 2000/01, a second stage was added to the Marmottes gondola, greatly speeding up access to some excellent challenging terrain. The tricky old Chatelard surface lift up to Auris was replaced by a double chair. And a lift from the Villard-Reculas parking lot up to the fast chair-lift was installed. The capacity of the Alpette gondola at Oz was also increased. And a second automatic snowmaking plant was installed.

Plans for 2001/02 include replacement of the glacier double chair by a quad starting lower down on the glacier. The capacity of the Marmottes 1 gondola is being increased. Snowmaking on the Rif Nel beginner area to les Bergers is being installed.

The proposed 3-star hotel in Les Bergers should now be ready for 2001/02.

There are few places to rival Alpe-d'Huez for extent and variety of terrain – in good conditions, it's one of our favorites. But, in late season at least, despite an ever-expanding snowmaking network, the 'island in the sun' suffers from the very thing it advertises: strong sun means that ice can make mornings miserably hard work, however alluring the prospect of slushy bumps in the afternoons.

The village has few fans, but if you don't like the sound of it you always have the alternative of staying in rustic Vaujany (with its mighty tram) or Villard-Reculas, or more modern Oz and Auris.

The resort

Alpe-d'Huez is a large village spread across an open mountainside, high above the Romanche valley, east of Grenoble. It was one of the venues for the 1968 Grenoble Winter Olympics, and then grew quickly in a seemingly unplanned way. Its buildings come in all shapes, sizes and designs (including a futuristic church which hosts weekly organ concerts) – and many now look scruffy and in need of renovation. It is a large, amorphous resort; the nearest thing to a central focus is the main Avenue des Jeux in the middle, where you'll find the swimming pool, ice skating and some of the shops, bars and restaurants. The rest of the resort spreads out in a triangle, with lift stations at two of the apexes.

AGENCE NUTS / OT ALPE D'HUEZ

The bowl immediately above the village has something for everyone, from beginner to expert – with the bonus of great views ➔

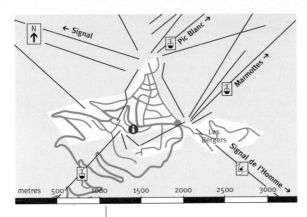

reclassified in the past few years, but the Signal runs are still a regular source of complaints.

THE SLOPES
Several well-linked areas

The slopes can be divided into four main sectors, with good connections between them.

The biggest sector is directly above the village, on the slopes of **Pic Blanc**. There is sport here for everyone, from excellent tough pitches at the top to vast, gentle beginner slopes at the bottom. The huge Grandes Rousses gondola, otherwise known as the DMC (a reference to its clever technology), goes up in two stages from the top of the village to 2700m/8,860ft. Above it, a tram goes up to 3330m/10,930ft on Pic Blanc itself – the top of the Sarenne glacier – where the runs are genuinely black. A lower area of challenging runs at Clocher de Macle, previously accessed by a slow chair, is much more attractive now that it is served by the recently extended Marmottes gondola.

The Sarenne gorge separates the main resort area from **Signal de l'Homme**. A spectacular down-and-up fast chair-lift accesses this area from the Bergers part of the village. From the top you can take excellent north-facing slopes back down towards the gorge, or head south to Auris or west to the old hamlet of Chatelard. The return from here is now by a new double chair-lift, instead of the famously tricky surface lift of old.

On the other side of town from Signal de l'Homme is the small **Signal** sector, reached by surface lifts next to the main gondola or by a couple of chairs lower down. Runs go down the other side of the hill to the old village of Villard-Reculas. Happily, the 1km/around 0.5 mile-long Signal blue run is now floodlit three nights a week.

The **Vaujany-Oz** sector consists largely of north-west-facing slopes, accessible from Alpe-d'Huez via good red runs from either the mid-station or the top of the big gondola. At the heart of this sector is Alpette, the mid-station of the two-stage tram from Vaujany. From here a disastrously sunny red goes down to Oz, and a much more reliable blue goes north to the Vaujany home slopes around Montfrais. The links back to Alpe-d'Huez are made by the top tram from Alpette, or a gondola from Oz.

LIFT TICKETS

2001/02 prices in euros

Grandes Rousses Covers all lifts in Alpe-d'Huez, Auris, Oz, Vaujany and Villard-Reculas.

Beginners Daily lift tickets for reduced areas. Beginner ticket covers 11 lifts (10), Altitude 2000 covers 26 lifts (17.5).

Main ticket
1-day ticket 32.5
6-day ticket 168

Senior citizens
Over 60: 6-day ticket 119
Over 70: free ticket

Children
Under 16: 6-day ticket 119
Under 5: free ticket

Notes ticket for 6 days or more includes one day's skiing at each of the Grande Galaxie resorts (Les Deux Alpes, Serre-Chevalier, Puy-St-Vincent and the Milky Way) and free entrance to the sports center.

Alternative tickets
tickets for Auris only (15 lifts), Oz-Vaujany only (20 lifts), Villard-Reculas only (8 lifts), and Altitude 2000 (26 lifts). Beginners tickets for the outlying villages are available.

The bus service around the resort is free with the main Visalp lift ticket, and there's a handy but slow open-air gondola (with a trail beneath it) running through the resort to get everyone up to the main lifts at the top.

A short distance from the main body of the resort (and linked by chair-lift) are the 'hamlets' – apartment blocks, mainly – of Les Bergers and L'Eclose. Les Bergers, at the eastern entrance to the resort is convenient for the slopes (with its own beginner area), but it's a trek from most of the other resort facilities. There are a couple of bar/restaurants and several shops near the slopes. L'Eclose, to the south of the main village, is the least convenient location and has even less to offer than Les Bergers.

There are accommodations down the hill in Huez, linked by lift to the resort.

Staying close to one of the main gondolas is useful. Or else it's worth being near the village gondola, though it is closed in the evenings.

Outings by road are feasible to other resorts covered on a week's lift ticket, including Serre-Chevalier, Les Deux-Alpes, Puy-St-Vincent and Montgenèvre. You can do a day-trip to Les Deux-Alpes by helicopter for a surprisingly modest fee.

The mountains

Alpe-d'Huez is a big-league resort, ranking alongside giants like Val-d'Isère or La Plagne for the extent and variety of its slopes. The trail classification system is unreliable; although it occasionally overstates difficulty, it more often does the opposite. A couple of runs have been

MOUNTAIN FACTS

Altitude	1120m-3320m
	3,670ft-10,890ft
Lifts	86
Trails	230km/143 miles
Green	35%
Blue	27%
Red	25%
Black	13%
Snowmaking	53km/
	33miles
Recco detectors used	

Since a trail was created from below Alpette to Enversin, just below Vaujany, an on-trail descent of 2200m/7,220ft has been possible – not the biggest vertical in the Alps, but not far short. The area does offer the longest trail in the Alps – the 16km/10 mile Sarenne on the back of the Pic Blanc (see the special feature box).

SNOW RELIABILITY
Affected by the sun
Alpe-d'Huez is unique among major purpose-built resorts in the Alps in having mainly south- or south-west-facing slopes. The strong southern sun means that in late season conditions may alternate between slush and ice on most of the area, with some of the lower runs being closed altogether. There are shady slopes above Vaujany and at Signal de l'Homme – and there is a small glacier area on the Pic Blanc, open in summer, but too small to pin all your hopes on in the winter. Overall, the orientation of the slopes is a real drawback of the area as a whole.

In more wintry circumstances the runs are relatively snow-sure, and the natural stuff is backed up by extensive snowmaking, covering the main runs above Alpe-d'Huez, Vaujany and Oz. An impressive number of snow-guns – 700-odd – covers 53km/33 miles of runs.

FOR EXPERTS
Plenty of blacks and off-trail
This is an excellent resort for experts, with long and challenging black runs (and reds that ought to be black) as well as serious off-trail options.

The slope beneath the Pic Blanc tram, usually an impressive bump-field, is reached by a 300m/980ft tunnel from the back side of the mountain. The tunnel exit was altered last season, supposedly creating a less awkward start to the actual slope; but it is still tricky. The slope itself is of ordinary black steepness, but can be very hard in the mornings because it gets a lot of sun. The run splits up part-way down – a couple of variants take you to the Lac Blanc two-seater chair back up to the Pic Blanc tram.

The long Sarenne run on the back of the Pic Blanc is described in a special feature box. There are several off-trail variants. There are also other very long off-trail descents over the bigger glaciers to the north and east, with verticals of 1900m/6,230ft to 2200m/7,220ft, for which guidance is essential. Some end up in Vaujany, others in Clavans (where you need a cab back), others in more remote spots where you need a helicopter back.

There is good off-trail in several other sectors, too – notably from Signal towards Villard-Reculas and Huez – and from Signal de l'Homme in various directions; the slopes above Auris are a particular favorite of locals.

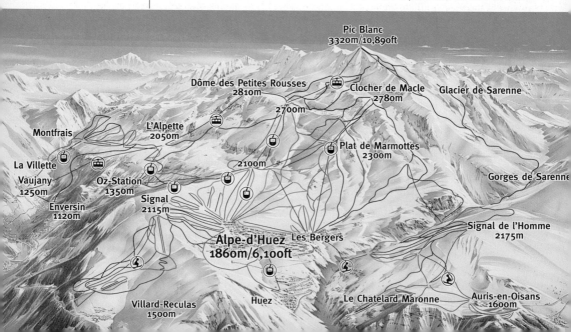

And there's abundant off-trail on the lower half of the mountain that is excellent in good snow conditions, including lovely runs through scattered trees at the extreme northern edge of the area above Vaujany. The trail map indicates some of the main off-trail routes, but don't be tempted to do them without a guide.

Some of the upper red trails are tough enough to give experts a challenge. These include the Canyon and Balme runs accessed by the Lièvre Blanc chair-lift from the gondola mid-station – runs which are unprepared and south-facing (late in the day, perhaps best tackled on a board), and steep enough to be graded black in many resorts. Above this, the Marmottes II gondola (which replaced the old Clocher chair last season) serves another series of steep black runs from Clocher de Macle including the beautiful, long, lonely Combe Charbonniere.

FOR INTERMEDIATES
Fine selection of runs

Good intermediates have a fine selection of runs all over the area. In good snow conditions the variety of runs is difficult to beat. Every section has some challenging red runs to test the adventurous intermediate. The most challenging are the Canyon and Balme runs, mentioned previously. There are lovely long runs down to Oz and to Vaujany. The off-trail among the trees above Vaujany, mentioned earlier, is a good place to start your off-trail career in good snow. The Villard-Reculas and Signal de l'Homme sectors also have long challenging reds. The Chamois red from the top of the gondola down to the mid-station is beautiful but quite narrow, and miserable when crowded and icy. Fearless intermediates should enjoy most of the super-long black runs from Pic Blanc.

For less ambitious intermediates, there are usually blue alternatives. The main Couloir blue from the top of the big gondola is a lovely run, well served by snowmaking guns, but it does get scarily crowded at times.

There are some great cruising runs above Vaujany; but it's not easy for early intermediates to get over to the Vaujany sector from Alpe-d'Huez. The blue down to the mid-station of the Vaujany gondola is picturesque and well served by snowmaking.

Early intermediates will also enjoy the gentle slopes leading back to Alpe-d'Huez from the main mountain, and the Signal sector.

FOR BEGINNERS
Good facilities

The large network of green runs immediately above the village is as good a beginner area as you will find anywhere – its only flaw is that it carries a lot of through-traffic. A large area embracing half a dozen runs has been declared a low-speed zone protégée, but the restriction is not policed and so doesn't achieve much. Add to the quality of the slopes the

---

THE LONGEST TRAIL IN THE ALPS – AND IT'S BLACK??

It's no surprise that most ski runs that are seriously steep are also seriously short. The really long runs in the Alps tend to be classified blue, or red at the most. The Parsenn runs above Klosters, for example – typically 12km/7 miles to 15km/9 miles long – are manageable in your first week. Even Chamonix's famously long Vallée Blanche off-trail run doesn't include steepness in its attractions.

So you could be forgiven for being sceptical about the 'black' Sarenne run from the top of the Pic Blanc to the Sarenne gorge that separates the resort from the Signal de l'Homme sector. Even though the vertical is an impressive 2000m/6,560ft, a run 16km/10 milesin length means an average gradient of only 11 per cent – typical of a blue run. Macho-hype on the part of the lift company, presumably?

Not quite. The Sarenne is a run of two halves. The bottom half is virtually flat (boarders beware) but the top half is a genuine black – a demanding and highly satisfying run (with stunning views) that any keen, competent skier will enjoy. The main challenge is the steep bump-field starting just below the top lift station; after that, things are much gentler, even before you get to the really flat bit. The run gets a lot of sun, so pick your time with care – there's nothing worse than a sunny run with no sun.

The main blue run
from the DMC
gondola gets
extremely crowded →

SNOWPIX.COM / CHRIS GILL

convenience, availability of good lessons, a special lift ticket covering 11 lifts and usually reliable snow, and Alpe-d'Huez is difficult to beat. There's another good beginners' area with gentle green runs at the top of the Vaujany gondola, and small slopes in Oz and Auris.

FOR CROSS-COUNTRY
High-level and convenient
There are 50km/31 miles of trails, with three loops of varying degrees of difficulty, all at around 2000m/6,500ft and consequently relatively snow-sure. All trails are within the Alpine domain and a cross-country user's ticket costs about 28 euros.

LIFTLINES
Generally few problems
Even in French holiday periods, the modern lift system ensures there are few long hold-ups. Lines can build up for the gondolas out of the village, but the DMC shifts its line impressively quickly. And the capacity of the Marmottes I is being increased for 2001/02, which should shorten waiting times next season. With the recently installed Lièvre Blanc quad and the new Marmottes II gondola, one of the old troublespots has been eliminated. The downside is that the Clocher de Macle area is no longer so secluded.

The small Pic Blanc tram is still line-prone and is often closed by bad weather. Although they may not cause lines, there are lots of old surface lifts scattered around. The small two-seater Lac Blanc chair-lift, back up to the Pic Blanc tram from the bottom of two of the black runs down from the Tunnel, gets very congested – though this can be avoided by taking an alternative variant.

A much greater problem than liftlines over much of the area is that the main trails can be unbearably crowded. The runs in the outlying satellites tend to be less crowded in peak periods.

MOUNTAIN RESTAURANTS
Some excellent rustic huts
Mountain restaurants are generally good – even self-service places are welcoming, and there are many more rustic places with table-service than you'd expect to find in French purpose-built resorts. One of our favorites is the cozy little Chalet du Lac Besson, on one of the cross-country loops north of the big gondola mid-station – the route to it now has trail status (the Boulevard des Lacs blue), but is no easier to follow in practice.

The pretty Forêt de Maronne hotel at Chatelard, below Signal de l'Homme, is delightful and has a good choice of traditional French cuisine. The Combe Haute, at the foot of the Chalvet chair

boarding *The resort suits experienced boarders well – the extent and variety of the mountains mean that there's a lot of good free-riding to be had. And, if there's good snow, the off-trail is vast and varied and well worth checking out with a guide. There's also a good terrain-park and a half-pipe near the main lift base as well as in Auris. Unfortunately for beginners, the main beginner areas are almost all accessed by surface lifts, but these can be avoided once a degree of control has been achieved. Planète Surf is the main snowboard shop and there are several cool bars – Freeride Café is recommended.*

SCHOOLS/GUIDES

2001/02 prices in euros

ESF
Classes 6 days
5½hr: 9.25-12.25 and
2.20-4.50
6 full days: 145
Children's classes
Ages: 4 to 16
6 full days: 130
Private lessons
(2000/01 prices)
Hourly. 29 for 1hr, for
1 or 2 people

2000/01 prices in euros

International
Classes 6 days
2½hr am, 2hr pm
6 full days: 202
Children's classes
Ages: 3 to 12
6 full days: 169
Private lessons
Hourly
30 for 1hr, for 1 or 2
people

CHILDCARE

The main schools run ski kindergartens

At Les Bergers the ESF Club des Oursons (0476 803169), takes children from age 4 during ski school hours.

The Eterlous day care center (0476 806785), in Les Bergers, has a private slope area and takes children aged 2 to 11 all day.

Les Crapouilloux day care center (0476 113923), next to the tourist information office, takes kids from 2 to 11.

The International school (0476 804277) runs the Baby-Club for children aged 3 to 4, and the Club des Marmottes for those aged 4 to 12.

Phone numbers
From abroad use the prefix +33 and omit the initial 'o' of the phone number.

---

in the gorge towards the end of the Sarenne run, is welcoming but gets very crowded. The Hermine, at the base of the Fontfroide lift, is recommended for basic but good-value food. The terrace of the Perce-Neige, just below the Oz-Poutran gondola mid-station, attracts crowds. The Plage des Neiges at the top of the beginner areas is one of the best places available to beginners. The Bergerie at Villard-Reculas has good views and is highly recommended by reporters. The Alpette and Super Signal places are also worth a visit. Chantebise 2100, at the DMC mid-station, offers slick and cheerful table service. The Cabane du Poutat, halfway down from Plat de Marmottes, is recommended for good food and service. Back in the village, lunch on the terrace at the Hotel Christina – by the top of the bucket lifts – is a pleasant option.

The restaurants in the Oz and Vaujany sectors tend to be cheaper. At Montfrais, Les Airelles is a rustic hut, built into the rock, with a roaring log fire, atmospheric music and excellent, good-value food.

SCHOOLS AND GUIDES
Contrasting views of the schools
We have a couple of reasonable reports on the ESF, which has apparently improved its act recently, 'good spoken English and good level of instruction'. However, class sizes are seemingly on the big side and we have witnessed classes of 12 students or more. Another recent report indicates that the International school operation has become a bit chaotic of late.

As usual, the best reports are saved for Masterclass, an independent operation run by British instructor Stuart Adamson: 'We cannot praise him too highly.' Class sizes are limited to eight. Advance booking during high season is advised. The Bureau des Guides also has a good reputation.

FACILITIES FOR CHILDREN
Mixed reports
We've had rave reviews in the past of the International school's classes for children ('started the week nervously snowploughing down greens, ended up skiing parallel down reds … only three in the class'). Reports on the ESF, on the other hand, have been mixed. Les Crapouilloux day care center is recommended.

HOW TO GO
Lots of low budget options
Hotels There are more hotels than is usual in a high French resort, and there's a clear downscale bias, with more 1-stars than 2- or 3-stars, and only two 4-stars. There is a huge Club Med at Les Bergers.

(((4 Royal Ours Blanc (0476 803550) Central. Luxurious, with lots of warm wood. Good food. Superb fitness center. Free minibus to the lifts.

(((3 Au Chamois d'Or (0476 803132) Good facilities, modern rooms, one of the best restaurants in town and well placed for main gondola.

(((3 Cimes (0476 803431) South-facing rooms, excellent food; close to cross-resort lift and trails.

(((3 Grandes Rousses (0476 803311) Comfortable but a bit dated and worn around the edges; close to lifts.

((2 Mariandre (0476 806603) Comfortable hotel with good food, recommended by readers. Some small rooms. Next to the bucket lift.

((2 Gentianes (0476 803576) Close to the Sarenne gondola in Les Bergers; a range of rooms, the best comfortable.

Apartments/condos There is an enormous choice of apartments available. The Pierre et Vacances residence near the Marmottes gondola in Les Bergers offers high standard accommodations with good facilities.

EATING OUT
Good value
Alpe-d'Huez has dozens of restaurants, some of high quality; many offer good value by French resort standards. The Crémaillère, at the bottom end of town, is highly recommended by a frequent visitor. Au P'tit Creux gets a similarly positive review for excellent food, ambience and value. The 'outstanding' Génépi is a friendly old place with good cuisine. The Pomme de Pin is also very popular. The Fromagerie, Rabelais and Edelweiss are others worth a try. And the Origan and Pinocchio pizzerias serve good, wholesome Italian fare.

APRES-SKI
Getting better all the time
The resort gets more animated each year and there's now a wide range of bars available, some of which get fairly lively later on. One complaint is that

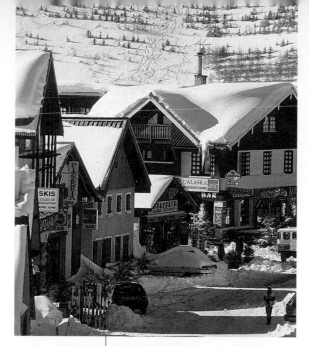

↑ There is a corner of the village that looks quite cute

GETTING THERE

Air Lyon, transfer 3hr. Geneva, transfer 4hr. Grenoble, transfer 1½hr.

Rail Grenoble (63km/39 miles); daily buses from station.

ACTIVITIES

Indoor Sports center (tennis, gym, squash, aerobics, climbing wall), library, movie theater, swimming pool, billiards, bridge **Outdoor** Artificial skating rink (skating and curling), 30km/19 miles of cleared paths, outdoor swimming pool, hanggliding, paragliding, all-terrain vehicles, quad-bikes

TOURIST OFFICE

Postcode 38750
t +33 476 114444
f 476 806954
info@alpedhuez.com
www.alpedhuez.com

they are widely dispersed, making pub crawls fairly time consuming.

The Roadhouse in Hotel Vallée Blanche, the Underground in Hotel Chamois, O'Sharkey's and the Pacific (sister bar to the one in Val d'Isère) are all popular. Smithy's does good Tex-Mex food and can get pretty rowdy late at night.

The little Avalanche bar attracts locals and visitors alike, and often has live music. The P'tit Bar de l'Alpe takes some beating for atmosphere, and also has live music. The Sporting is a large but friendly French rendezvous with a live band. The Etalon and Freeride cafes are also popular. And the Dutch-run Melting Pot does good tapas and is great for a relaxed drink, as is the Zoo.

The Stage One and Igloo discos liven up whenever the French are in town en masse.

OFF THE SLOPES
Good by purpose-built standards

There is a wide range of facilities, including a new indoor pool, an open-air pool (trunks, not swim shorts required), Olympic-size ice rink and splendid sports center. There's also an ice-driving school. Shops are numerous, but limited in range. The helicopter excursion to Les Deux-Alpes is amusing. It's a pity that the better mountain restaurants aren't easily accessible to pedestrians.

Vaujany 1250m/4,100ft

THE RESORT

Vaujany is a small village perched on the hillside opposite its own sector of the domain. Hydro-electric riches have financed huge continuing investment. There's a giant 160-person tram (that whisks you into the heart of the Alpe-d'Huez lift system), a superb new sports center, a huge snowmaking installation and apparently plans for a monorail within the village. Eventually, they are going to run out of things to buy. There are some tasteful new developments up the mountainside. A mile or two up the valley is the even smaller and more rustic hamlet of La Villette (just one tiny bar-restaurant).

THE MOUNTAINS

Although no slopes reach Vaujany itself, it is in practice a good base – its own slopes are not far away, and access to Alpe-d'Huez is speedy.

Slopes There are no village slopes, so even complete beginners have to ride the gondola to Montfrais, which has a mid-station at La Villette. There's a run back to La Villette, but you normally have to ride from there down to Vaujany. The alternative is the Fare black trail, ending below the village at a short lift.

Snowboarding Although there are some good beginner areas here, beginners will have difficulty negotiating the main surface lift up towards Alpette. And there's no easy route across to the main Alpe d'Huez sector except by riding down lifts.

Snow reliability A large snowmaking network and shady slopes help the area keep its snow-cover for longer.

Experts The huge tram offers quick line-free access up towards Lac Blanc and the Pic Blanc tram up to the resort high-point and the main body of expert terrain. Local challenges include some off-trail runs through the trees and a couple of black runs too.

Intermediates There's a nice variety of cruising runs in the local sector and the lack of crowds is a real bonus. A special lift ticket covering 20 lifts in Oz and Vaujany is available.

Beginners There are some good beginner areas at the top of the gondola and there are some nice cruisy blues to progress to. Complete beginners can buy a special ticket that covers the three Enversin lifts and one on Montfrais.

Cross-country The 20km/12 mile loop between Alpette and Alpe d'Huez is the most snow-sure circuit in the area.
Liftlines Vaujany gets some day visitors, but is generally a quiet spot. We've never seen the tram full.
Mountain restaurants The Airelles is probably the most atmospheric.
Schools and guides Vaujany has its own ski school – reports have all been very positive.
Facilities for children There's a big day nursery by the lift station.

STAYING THERE
How to go There's a handful of simple hotels in Vaujany.
Hotels The Rissiou is well situated for access to the tram. It has a popular bar, a pleasant dining room that serves excellent French cuisine (and good inexpensive wines), and fairly basic bedrooms. The staff are friendly and efficient. The hotel Cîmes (0476 798550), over the road, is another option but is less rustic.
Eating out There are a couple of restaurants in the village.
Après-ski The bar at the Rissiou is popular and frequented by the locals. The Cîmes is useful for a change of bar scenery. And the Etendard, by the lift station, has a lively après-ski bar. There are two nightclubs.
Off the slopes As well as the excellent sports center, there's an open-air ice rink, well-stocked sports shop and a small supermarket.

Oz-en-Oisans

1350m/4,430ft
The purpose-built ski station above the attractive old village of Oz-en-Oisans apparently now takes its parent's name. The village has the basics – ski school, sports shops, beginner areas, several bar-restaurants and a supermarket. There's also a large underground parking lot. A couple of large apartment blocks – built in a sympathetic style, with much use of wood and stone – stand between the two gondolas to make up the focus of the resort. Attractive new chalets have recently sprung up behind the center and more development is planned. A small hotel is under construction. To quote one recent visitor, Oz is now 'taking off'. But another complains that there is still no nightlife. The main run home is liberally endowed with snow-guns, but it needs to be.

Auris 1600m/5,250ft

Auris is a series of wood-clad, chalet-style apartment blocks with a few shops, bars and restaurants, pleasantly set close to the thickest woodland in the area. It's a fine family resort, with everything close to hand, including a nursery and a ski kindergarten. There's also a ski school. Beneath it is the original old village, complete with attractive, traditional buildings, a church and all but one of the resort's hotels. Staying here with a car you can drive up to the local lifts or make excursions to neighboring resorts such as Serre-Chevalier.

Unsurprisingly, evenings are quiet, with a handful of bar-restaurants to choose from. The Beau Site (0476 800639), which looks like an apartment block, is the only hotel in the upper village. A couple of miles down the hill, the traditional Auberge de la Forêt (0476 800601) gives you a feel of 'real' rural France.

Access to the slopes of Alpe-d'Huez is no problem, but there are plenty of local slopes to explore, for which there is a special lift ticket, covering 15 lifts and 45km/28 miles of trail. Most of the sport is intermediate, though Auris is also the best of the local hamlets for beginners.

Villard-Reculas

1500m/4,920ft
Villard is a secluded village, complete with an old church, set on a small shelf wedged between an expanse of open snowfields above and tree-filled hillsides below. Following the installation of a fast quad chair up to Signal (and the main Alpe d'Huez sector) a couple of years back, the village is becoming more popular as an access point and it is now beginning to find its feet as a 'resort'. Its 500 beds are mainly in self-catering apartments and chalets, though there is one 2-star hotel. There is a supermarket and a couple of bars and restaurants.

The local slopes have something for everyone, and there is now an ESF branch here. Snowmaking on the often icy and patchy home runs down to the village is planned for next season. A nursery is also planned.

Les Arcs 1600m-2000m/5,250ft-6,560ft

Purpose-built for a holiday on the slopes – and little else

HOW IT RATES

The slopes
Snow	****
Extent	***
Experts	****
Intermediates	****
Beginners	****
Convenience	****
Liftlines	***
Restaurants	**

The rest
Scenery	***
Resort charm	*
Off-slope	*

➕ Easy access to the slopes from most (but not all) of the apartments

➕ A wide range of runs to suit intermediates and experts

➕ Few serious liftlines

➕ Excellent woodland runs, mainly above Plan Peisey and Vallandry

➕ Opportunity for skiing beginners to learn by the évolutif method

➕ Splendid views of Mont Blanc massif

➕ Glowing recent reports of friendly locals – unusual for French resorts

➖ Main village centers range from the charmless to the positively tacky

➖ Few off-slope diversions

➖ Not the best resort for confidence-building green runs

➖ Still lots of slow old chair-lifts and surface lifts

➖ Very quiet in the evenings, and limited choice of bars/restaurants

➖ Some apartments are quite a walk from the nearest lifts

➖ Nearly all the accommodation is in apartments – there's a limited choice of alternatives

Les Arcs is a classic purpose-built French resort, with all the usual advantages and drawbacks. If altitude and a short walk from front door to lift base are your priorities – and not village charm or animation – put it on the short-list. A further attraction for some is that direct rail services to Bourg-St-Maurice connect with a funicular that takes you straight to Arc 1600 (though not to the other two Arcs).

The terrain isn't in quite the same league as the Three Valleys, La Plagne or Val-d'Isère/Tignes for sheer extent, but within its slightly smaller area it contains an impressive variety, including some of the longest descents in the Alps, plenty of steep stuff, and a very attractive area of woodland runs at one end of the area. For a keen mixed-ability group, it is a strong candidate.

What's new

Not much is happening on the lift front right now, presumably because of the imminent expense of the long-awaited link between the Les Arcs and La Plagne slopes. It is expected to be open for the 2002/03 season – a double-decker tram linking Plan-Peisey to Montchavin in only four minutes. The result will be the world's third biggest linked ski area.

The resort

Les Arcs is made up of three modern resort units, linked by road, high above the railway terminus town of Bourg-St-Maurice. The three villages have a lot in common: like many such resorts, they are purpose-built, apartment-dominated places, offering doorstep access to the snow with no traffic hazards, but lacking Alpine charm, off-slope activities, and evening animation. But reporters repeatedly comment on the friendliness of the natives.

Arc 1600 was the original Arc (it opened in December 1968). It has the advantage of a funicular railway up from Bourg-St-Maurice funicular, giving easy access from Paris by train. Above the village, a trio of chair-lifts fan out over the lower half of the slopes, leading to links to the other Arcs. 1600 is set in the trees and has a friendly, small-scale atmosphere; and it enjoys good views along the valley and towards Mont Blanc. The central area is particularly good for families: uncrowded, compact, and set on even ground. But things are even quieter here at night than during the day.

Much the largest of the three 'villages' is Arc 1800. It has three sections, though the boundaries are indistinct. Charvet and Villards are small, scruffy shopping centers, mostly open-air but still managing to seem as claustrophobic as the indoor arcades of neighbouring La Plagne. Both are dominated by apartment blocks the size of ocean liners (getting to the shops or the lifts may involve a much longer walk inside your apartment building than outside it). More pleasant on the eye is Charmettoger, with smaller, wood-clad buildings nestling among trees. Villards is the central component, and it's from here that the lifts depart – chair-lifts to mid-mountain, and the big Transarc gondola to Col de la Chal at the head of the Arc 2000 valley.

MOUNTAIN FACTS

Altitude 1200m-3225m
    3,940ft-10,580ft
Lifts   76
Trails 200km/124 miles
Green   8%
Blue   45%
Red   33%
Black   14%
Snowmaking   12km/
        7 miles
Recco detectors used

LIFT TICKETS

2000/01 prices in
euros
**Massif Aiguille Grive–
Aiguille Rouge**
Covers all lifts in Les
Arcs and Peisey-
Nancroix, including
funicular from Bourg-
St-Maurice.
Beginners Five free
lifts; one in 1600 and
two each in 1800 and
2000.
Main ticket
1-day ticket 35
6-day ticket 167
Senior citizens
Over 60: 6-day ticket
142
Over 75: free ticket
Children
Under 14: 6-day ticket
142
Under 7: free ticket
Short-term tickets
Half-day afternoon
(adult 25). Half-day
(am or pm) tickets for
each area (adult 18).
Single and return
tickets on most lifts
for walkers.
Notes All tickets over
1 day cover La Plagne
and allow 1 day in La
Rosière–La Thuile and
Tignes–Val-d'Isère. 6-
day ticket and over
allows one day each
in the 3V, Pralognan-
la-Vanoise and Les
Saises. 5% reduction
on presentation of
previous season's
ticket.
Alternative tickets
1- and 2-day tickets
(165, 305) are
available; one covers
Arc 2000 and
Villaroger (21 lifts),
the other Arc 1600
and 1800 (38 lifts).

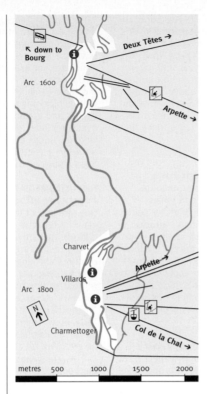

Arc 1800 is spreading up the
hillside, with more excellent
apartments coming on to the market in
Le Chantel.

Arc 2000 is just a few hotels,
apartment blocks and the Club Med,
huddled together in a bleak spot, with
little to commend it but immediate
access to the highest, toughest skiing.
There is only a handful of restaurants
and shops – and it's a serious bus-ride
to Arc 1600. A swanky new
development known as Arc 1950 or La
Daille d'Arc 2000 is now planned for
construction just below the original
village by the Canadian company
Intrawest, which if it comes off may be
much more compelling. There are lifts
all around 2000, but the main one now

is the Varet gondola up towards the
Aiguille Rouge.

At the southern end of the area,
linked by trails but reachable by road
only by descending to the valley, is
Peisey-Vallandry. Vallandry and Plan-
Peisey are the key components of this
composite resort – recently developed
lift-base resorts above the old village
of Peisey, which has a bucket lift up to
Plan-Peisey. Vallandry is reportedly a
bit more lively than 'very quiet' Plan-
Peisey. Chair-lifts go up from both
bases to mid-mountain. The long-
awaited tram link with Montchavin and
La Plagne will be built here.

There are a couple of alternative
places to stay down in the valley at
the other, northern end of the ski area
– see the end of this chapter.

The mountains

Les Arcs' trail network is not huge. But
its terrain is notably varied; it has
plenty of runs suitable for experts as
well as beginners and intermediates,
and a good mixture of high, snow-sure
slopes and accessible low-level
woodland runs ideal for bad weather.

THE SLOPES
Well planned, and varied
The slopes are very well laid out, and
moving around is quick and easy –
though direction-finding can be a
problem at times.

Arc 1600 and Arc 1800 share a west-
facing mountainside laced with runs
leading down to one or other village.
At the southern end is an area of
woodland runs – unusually extensive
for a high French area – down to Plan-
Peisey and Vallandry.

From various points on the ridge
above 1600 and 1800 you can head
down into the Arc 2000 bowl. On the
opposite side of this bowl, lifts take
you to the highest runs of the area,
from the Aiguille Rouge and the Grand
Col. As well as a variety of steep north-

Les Arcs

131

boarding *Les Arcs calls itself 'the home of the snowboard'. Local boy Regis
Rolland played a big part in popularizing the sport (not least with
his 'Apocalypse Snow' movies), and the resort is constantly developing its
boarding facilities. Some boarders are doubtless attracted by the budget
accommodations, but also by the great mix of terrain served mainly by boarder-
friendly lifts (though getting around can involve some long traverses on near-flat
catwalks). Arc 2000 and Vallandry have great smooth runs for beginners and
carvers, but some of the blues at 2000 are too flat for comfort. There's a park
and half-pipe, and a couple of specialist board schools and shops.*

SCHOOLS/GUIDES

2000/01 prices in euros

ESF
Classes 6 days
3hr am or pm
6 half-days 105
Children's classes
Ages: 3 to 14
6 half-days: 105
Private lessons
Hourly
29 for 1hr, for 1 or 2 people

Other schools
Arc Aventures (ESI)
Virages
Tip-Top (based in Bourg-St-Maurice)

west-facing runs back to Arc 2000, the Aiguille Rouge is the start of a lovely long run (over 2000m/6,500ft vertical and 7km/4 miles long) right down to the hamlet of Le Pré near Villaroger. Arc 2000 has runs descending below village level, to the lift-base, restaurant and parking lot at Pré-St-Esprit, about 200m/650ft lower. You can reach Le Pré from here, via a short surface lift (sometimes closed).

SNOW RELIABILITY
Good – plenty of high runs

A high percentage of the runs are above 2000m/6,500ft and when necessary you can stay high by using lifts that start around that altitude. Most of the slopes face roughly west – not ideal. Those from the Col de la Chal and down to Le Pré are north-facing. There is limited snowmaking on some runs back to 1600, 1800 and Peisey-Vallandry. Grooming has struck us and readers as 'economical'.

FOR EXPERTS
Challenges on- and off-trail

Les Arcs has a lot to offer experts – at least when the high lifts are open (the Aiguille Rouge tram, in particular, is often shut in bad weather).

There are a number of truly black trails above Arc 2000, and a couple in other areas. After a narrow shelf near the top, the Aiguille Rouge–Le Pré run is superb, with remarkably varying terrain throughout its vertical drop of over 2000m/6,500ft. There is also a great deal of off-trail potential, in

various parts. There are steep pitches on the front face of the Aiguille Rouge, and secluded runs on the back side, towards Villaroger – the Combe de l'Anchette, for example. A short climb to the Grand Col from the chair-lift of the same name gives access to several routes, including a quite serious couloir and a more roundabout route over the Glacier du Grand Col. The wooded slopes above 1600 are another attractive possibility – and there are open slopes all over the mountain.

FOR INTERMEDIATES
Plenty for all standards

One strength of the area is that most main routes have easy and more difficult alternatives, making it good for mixed-ability groups. There are plenty of challenges, yet less confident intermediates are able to move around without getting too many nasty surprises. An exception is the solitary Comborcières black from Les Deux Têtes down to Pré-St-Esprit. This long bump run justifies its rating and can be great fun for strong intermediates.

The woodland runs at either end of the domain, above Vallandry and Le Pré, and the bumpy Cachette red down to 1600, are also good for better intermediates. Those who enjoy speed will like the Vallandry area: its well groomed runs are remarkably uncrowded much of the time. Good intermediates can enjoy the Aiguille Rouge–Le Pré run (with red and blue detours available to avoid the toughest parts of the black trail).

CHILDCARE

The ESF branches in all three stations take children from 3. The International school's Club Poussin in 1800 starts at 4.

At Arc 1600 the Garderie at the Hotel de la Cachette (0479 077050) runs three clubs for children from 4 months to 11 years, from 8.30 to 6pm, with ski lessons available.

At Arc 1800 various schemes running from 8.45 to 5.45 are offered by the Pommes de Pin (0479 041530). The Nurserie takes children aged 1 to 3, the Garderie those aged 3 to 6, and children aged 3 to 9 can have lessons through the two clubs based at the Garderie.

At Arc 2000 Les Marmottons (0479 076425) takes children aged 2 to 6 from 8.30 to 5.45, with lessons for those aged 3 to 6.

Phone numbers
From abroad use the prefix +33 and omit the initial '0' of the phone number.

The lower half of the mountainside is good for mixed-ability groups, with a choice of routes through the trees. The red runs down from Arpette and Col des Frettes towards 1800 are quite steep but usually well groomed.

Cautious intermediates have plenty of blue cruising terrain. Many of the runs around 2000 are rather bland and busy. The blues above 1800 are attractive but busy. A favorite blue of ours is Renard, high above Vallandry, usually with excellent snow.

FOR BEGINNERS
1800 best for complete novices
There are beginner slopes conveniently situated just above all three villages. The ones at Arc 1600 are rather steep, while those at 2000 get crowded with intermediate through-traffic at times. The sunny, spacious runs at 1800 are best. There is a lack of attractive long green runs to move on to – La Forêt, above Vallandry, is just a winding woodland path. But the Mont Blanc above 1600 is a beautiful gentle blue, and you can take the gondola up to Col de la Chal and enjoy good snow on the easy runs towards 2000.

FOR CROSS-COUNTRY
Very boring locally
Short trails, mostly on roads, close to all three villages, is all you can expect unless you travel to Nancroix's 40km/25 miles of pleasant trails.

LIFTLINES
Few problems now
Reporters have few complaints about liftlines except in one or two places. In sunny weather, Arc 2000 attracts the crowds and there may be non-trivial lines for either the gondola or the chair to Col de la Chal. In bad weather, it's the lifts serving the woodland slopes above Vallandry that cause the problem. There are sometimes lengthy waits for the Aiguille Rouge tram. A bigger problem than liftlines is the time taken riding slow old chair-lifts, some of them very long. At holiday times overcrowded trails can be a problem, too.

MOUNTAIN RESTAURANTS
An adequate choice
Lunch isn't generally a highlight of the day unless you head for the hamlets at the extremes of the area. At the north end, the 500-year-old Belliou la Fumée at Pré-St-Esprit is charmingly rustic. La

Ferme and Aiguille Rouge down at Le Pré are both friendly, with good food. Chez Léa in Le Planay serves simple food in rustic surroundings. At the south end, a five-minute cab-ride from Vallandry will bring you to the Ancolie (0479 079320), a delightful auberge with superb Savoyarde food.

The restaurants scattered around the main slopes are mainly unremarkable. But the little Blanche Murée, just down from the Transarc mid-station, is consistently recommended – 'friendly service, fantastic food, reasonable prices' says one report this year. The Arpette is notable for its wide range of dishes.

SCHOOL AND GUIDES
Ski évolutif recommended
The ESF here is renowned for being the first in Europe to teach ski évolutif, where you start by learning parallel turns on short skis, gradually moving on to longer skis. We have a report this year of one beginner who astonished his experienced friends by 'doing perfect parallel turns on steep reds by the end of the week'. Private boarding lessons with the ESF have also been 'very highly recommended'. The International school (Arc Aventures) has impressed reporters over the years: 'Good instruction with English well spoken.' We have had glowing reports of the Optimum ski courses, using British instructors, based in a catered chalet in Le Pré. There are mountain guides available in the main villages.

FACILITIES FOR CHILDREN
Good reports
We have received good reports on the Pommes de Pin facilities in Arc 1800 – 'great care and attention', 'patient approach to teaching'. Comments on children's ski classes are favorable, too – 'nearly all instructors spoke English', 'classes went smoothly'.

Staying there 🔑

HOW TO GO
Apartments rule
Over three-quarters of the resort beds are in apartments.

Hotels The choice of hotels in Les Arcs is gradually widening, particularly at the upper end of the market. All-inclusive packages of full-board accommodation and lift ticket can be attractive.

GETTING THERE

Air Geneva, transfer 3½hr. Lyon, transfer 3½hr. Chambéry, transfer 2½hr.

Rail Bourg-St-Maurice; frequent buses and direct funicular to resort.

ACTIVITIES

Indoor Squash (3 courts 1800), Chinese gymnastics, saunas (1600, 1800), solaria, multi-gym (1800), cinemas, amusement arcades, music, concert halls, fencing (2000), bowling (1800)

Outdoor Natural skating rinks (1800 and 2000), floodlit skiing, speed skiing (2000), ski-jump, climbing wall (1800), organized snow-shoe outings, 10km/6 miles cleared paths (1800 and 1600), hang-gliding, horse-riding, sleigh rides, helicopter rides to Italy, ice grotto, paint balling

TOURIST OFFICE

Postcode 73706
t +33 479 071257
f 479 074596
lesarcs@lesarcs.com
www.lesarcs.com

(((④ **Mercure Coralia** (1800) (0479 076500) Newish, and locally judged to be worth four stars rather than its actual three.

((③ **Golf** (1800) (0479 414343) A pricey 3-star; the best in Les Arcs, with recently renovated rooms, sauna, gym, kindergarten and covered parking.

((③ **La Cachette** (1600) (0479 077050) Smartly renovated in the mid-1990s, with something of the style of an American resort hotel. But it can be 'dominated by kids' says one reporter.

(② **Aiguille Rouge** (2000) (0479 075707) Daily free ski guiding.

Apartments/condos The apartments are mostly tight on space, so you should generally rent one with more beds than you need. The recently built Alpages du Chantel apartments are exceptionally attractive, comfortable and spacious by French standards, with a pool, sauna and gym.

EATING OUT
Reasonable choice in Arc 1800

In Arc 1600 and 2000 there are very few restaurants, none of them discussed here. 1800 has a choice of about 15 restaurants; an ad-based (so not comprehensive) guide is given away locally. Le Petit Zinc restaurant in the Hotel du Golf has haute cuisine and high prices; it has a Friday evening seafood buffet. The Gargantus is a good informal place, although very cramped. Readers have been satisfied by 'enormous portions' at L'Equipage and 'good solid meals' at the Triangle Noir. Casa Mia is an excellent all-rounder with exceptionally friendly service. The Mountain Café does much more than the Tex-Mex it advertises, and copes well with big family parties. A popular outing is to drive half-way down the mountain to the welcoming and woody Bois de Lune at Montvenix, which has perhaps the best food in the area (reservations advised – 0479 071792).

APRES-SKI
Arc 1800 is the place to be

1800 is the liveliest center, though even so one reporter calls is 'very, very quiet'. The J.O. bar is open until the early hours and has a friendly atmosphere with live music. The friendly Red Hot Saloon has bar games and 'surprisingly good live music' some nights. The Fairway disco keeps rocking until 4 most mornings and the Apokalypse 'isn't terrible'. The cinemas

at 1800 and 1600 have English-language films once or twice a week. In 1600 the bar opposite (and belonging to) the Hotel La Cachette has games machines, pool and live bands, and can be quite lively even in low season. The Red Rock in 2000 is 'good for youngsters but too crowded for grown-ups'.

OFF THE SLOPES
Very poor

Les Arcs is not the place for an off-the-slopes holiday. There is very little to do; it doesn't even have a swimming pool. The main options available are a shopping trip to Bourg-St-Maurice (cheaper for buying ski equipment), preferably on Saturday for the market, and a few walks – nice ones up the Nancroix valley.

Bourg-St-Maurice
840m/2,760ft

Bourg-St-Maurice is a real French town, with cheaper hotels and restaurants and easy access to other resorts for day trips. The funicular goes straight to Arc 1600 in seven minutes. Hostellerie du Pt-St-Bernard has been reported to be a reasonable 2-star hotel. You can leave your skis or board and boots at a ski shop next to the bottom of the funicular.

Le Pré 1200m/3,940ft

A charming, quiet, rustic little hamlet with a chair-lift up towards Arc 2000. It has a couple of small bars and restaurants. Chalet Tarentaise (0479 069126) is a charming, rustic old chalet with basic rooms run by a British couple. We have received rave reviews from reporters. But Le Pré is not at all suitable for beginners.

Peisey-Vallandry
1550m/5,090ft

Peisey-Vallandry is a cluster of five small villages. Peisey, linked by lift to Plan-Peisey, dates back to AD1000, and its most striking feature is the fine baroque church. The other, mostly old, buildings house a small selection of shops, restaurants and bars. The hotel Vanoise in Plan-Peisey is repeatedly recommended by readers for its position, food and 'extremely friendly and helpful staff'.

Avoriaz

The best base on the Portes du Soleil circuit for snow

HOW IT RATES

The slopes

Snow	✭✭✭
Extent	✭✭✭✭✭
Experts	✭✭✭
Intermediates	✭✭✭✭
Beginners	✭✭✭✭
Convenience	✭✭✭✭
Liftlines	✭✭
Restaurants	✭✭✭✭

The rest

Scenery	✭✭✭
Resort charm	✭✭
Off-slope	✭

➕ Good position on the main Portes du Soleil circuit, giving access to very extensive, quite varied runs for all grades from novices to experts

➕ Generally has the best snow in the Portes du Soleil

➕ Accommodations right on the slopes

➕ Resort-level snow and ski-through, car-free village give Alpine ambience

➕ Good children's facilities

➖ Much of Portes du Soleil area is low for a major French area, with resulting risk of poor snow or bare slopes lower down

➖ Still a couple of lift bottlenecks and (especially in local Avoriaz area) some crowded trails

➖ Non-traditional architecture, which some find ugly

➖ Little to do off the slopes

➖ Few hotels

For access to the impressive Portes du Soleil trail network, Avoriaz has clear attractions. In a low-altitude area where snow is not reliable, it has the best there is – on relatively high, north-facing slopes of varying difficulty, including some of the most challenging terrain in the Portes du Soleil.

But there are drawbacks. First, the character of the village: we don't mind sleeping in purpose-built resorts to get instant access to high-altitude snow, but there is no really high-altitude terrain here. The Portes du Soleil has several attractive low-altitude villages, and we'd rather be based in one. Secondly, cost: Châtel and Morzine are cheap by French standards; Avoriaz is not. Liftlines can be a nuisance too, but they affect those exploring the Portes du Soleil from other bases as much as they affect those based in Avoriaz – more so, in fact.

What's new

Recent years have seen substantial investment in high-speed chairs (including some six-seaters) which have greatly reduced liftline problems.

For 2001/02 another high-speed, six-seater chair will replace the pair of surface lifts from Les Lindarets up to Avoriaz, cutting the liftlines at this bad bottleneck. A new trail will be built at the top to join the existing runs down to Les Lindarets.

For 2000/01 the gondola from Ardent to Les Lindarets was upgraded and the parking lot extended.

MOUNTAIN FACTS

for Portes du Soleil

Altitude	975m-2350m/ 3,200ft-7,710ft
Lifts	206
Trails	650km/400 miles
Green	13%
Blue	38%
Red	39%
Black	10%
Snowmaking	252 acres
Recco detectors used	

The resort

Avoriaz is a purpose-built, traffic-free resort perched above a dramatic, sheer rock face. From the edge of town horse-drawn sleighs or snow-cats transport people and luggage to the accommodations – or you can borrow a sled for a small deposit and transport your own! Traffic can be intrusive and fast moving but the problem of horse mess has been cut since they now wear 'diapers' and staff on snowmobiles scoop up what escapes! Cars are left in pay-for outdoor or underground parking – a reporter advises the latter to avoid a chaotic departure if it snows (it took him three hours). You can book your space in advance.

The village is set on quite a slope, but chair-lifts and elevators in buildings mean moving around is no problem except when paths are icy. Trails, lifts and off-slope activities are close to virtually all accommodations.

The village is all angular, dark, wood-clad, high-rise buildings, mostly apartments. The place at least has a distinct style, unlike the dreary cuboid blocks of Flaine and Les Menuires.

But the compact snow-covered village has a friendly Alpine feel despite the architecture. The evenings are not especially lively, but reporters have enjoyed the 'brilliant parade in half-term week, with a superb fire-eating display' in the past.

Avoriaz is above the valley resort of Morzine, to which it is linked by gondola (but not by trail). It also has good links to Châtel in one direction and Champéry in the other. Car trips are possible to Flaine and Chamonix.

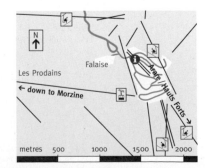

LIFT TICKETS

2001/02 prices in euros

Portes du Soleil
Covers all lifts in all 12 resorts, and shuttle-buses.
Main ticket
1-day ticket 33
6-day ticket 159
Senior citizens
Over 60: 6-day ticket 127
Children
Under 16: 6-day ticket 107
Under 5: free ticket
Alternative tickets
Day ticket for Avoriaz lifts only: 27.
Beginner's day ticket (limited area): 17.
Snowboarder ticket for terrain park and a few other areas: 20 per day; 6-day ticket 92.

The mountains

The slopes closest to Avoriaz are bleak and treeless, but snow-sure. They suit all grades from novice to expert and give quick access to the toughest runs in the Portes du Soleil. The whole circuit is easily done by intermediates of all abilities – and the booklet-style trail map makes for easy navigation. Reporters have also commented favorably on the system of Discovery Routes around the Portes du Soleil – choose an alpine animal that suits your ability and follow the signs displaying it. The circuit breaks down at Châtel, where you have to get a (frequent) shuttle-bus. The slopes of Morzine and Les Gets, accessed from the far side of Morzine, are part of the Portes du Soleil but not on the core circuit. An electronic lift ticket was introduced for 1999/2000, so you can now keep your ticket in your pocket.

THE SLOPES
Short runs and plenty of them

The village has lifts and trails fanning out in all directions. Staying in Avoriaz assures the comfort of riding mostly chairs – some other parts of the Portes du Soleil (especially on the Swiss side) have a lot of surface lifts. Facing the village are the slopes of **Arare-Hauts Forts** and, when snow conditions allow, there are long, steep runs down to Les Prodains.

The lifts off to the left go to the **Chavanette** sector on the Swiss border – a broad, undulating bowl. Beyond the border is the infamous Swiss Wall – a long, impressive bump slope with a tricky start, but not the terror it is cracked up to be unless it's icy (it gets a lot of sun). Lots of people doing the circuit (or returning to Champéry) ride the chair down. At the bottom of the Wall is the open terrain of Planachaux, above Champéry, with links to the still bigger open area around Les Crosets and Champoussin. There are several ways to return, but the most amusing is the chair up the Wall, with a great view of people struggling down it.

Taking a lift up from Avoriaz (or traversing from some of the highest accommodations) to the ridge behind the village is the way to the **Lindarets-Brocheaux** valley, from where lifts and runs in the excellent Linga sector lead to Châtel. Getting back is a matter of retracing your steps, although there are several options from Lindarets.

Morgins is the resort opposite Avoriaz on the circuit, and the state of the snow may encourage you to travel counter-clockwise rather than clockwise, so as to avoid the low, south-facing slopes down from Bec de Corbeau.

SNOW RELIABILITY
High resort, low slopes

Although Avoriaz town is high, its slopes don't go much higher – and some parts of the Portes du Soleil circuit are much lower. Considering their altitude, the north-facing slopes below Hauts Forts hold snow well. In general, the snow in Avoriaz is usually much better than over the border on the south-facing Swiss slopes.

Trail maintenance is 'erratic and it is quite common for runs not to be groomed overnight,' says a reporter. Snow-guns have been introduced in some areas, including on some blacks.

FOR EXPERTS
Several testing runs

Tough terrain is scattered about. The challenging runs down from Hauts Forts to Prodains (including a World Cup downhill) are excellent. There is a tough red, and several long, truly black runs, one of which cuts through trees – useful in poor weather. Two chair-lifts

Pointe de Mossettes 2275m

↓ Champéry

Chavanette   2215m   Hauts Forts 2465m/ 8,090ft

↙ Châtel

Col du Bassachaux 1920m

Avoriaz 1800m/5,900ft

Les Lindarets 1495m

Ardent

Les Prodains 1145m

Morzine 1000m/3,280ft

SCHOOLS/GUIDES

2001/02 prices in euros

ESF
Classes 6 days
5hr: 2½hr am and pm
6 full days: 130
Children's classes
Ages: 4 to 11
6 full days: 115
Private lessons
1hr, 1½hr or 2hr
29 for 1hr, for 1 to 2
people; 35 for 3 to 6

L'Ecole de Glisse
Classes 6 days
2hr, am or pm
6 half-days: 91
Private lessons
1hr or 2hr
32 for 1hr; 59 for 2hr

CHILDCARE

Les P'tits Loups (0450
740038) takes
children aged 3
months to 5, from
9am to 6pm; indoor
and outdoor games,
and so on. You have
to book in advance.

The Village des
Enfants (0450
740446) takes
children aged 3 to 16,
from 9am to 5.30.

The Club Med in
Avoriaz is one of their
'family villages', with
comprehensive
childcare facilities.

GETTING THERE

Air Geneva, transfer
2hr.

Rail Cluses
(42km/26miles) or
Thonon (45km/28
miles); bus and cable-
car to resort.

---

serve the lower runs, which snow-guns
help to keep open. The Swiss Wall at
Chavanette will naturally be on your
agenda, and Châtel is worth a trip.
The black runs off the Swiss side of
Mossette and Pointe de l'Au are worth
trying. It's not a great area for off-trail
adventures, but a recent reporter who
visited in less than ideal conditions
discovered a 'very good' ESF guide
who found 'great powder and off trail
and took us away from the crowds'.

FOR INTERMEDIATES
Virtually the whole area
Although some sections lack variety,
the Portes du Soleil is excellent for all
grades of intermediates when snow is
in good supply. Timid types not
worried about pretty surroundings
need not leave the Avoriaz sector;
Arare and Chavanette are gentle,
spacious and above the tree-line
bowls. The Lindarets area and on
down to Ardent is also easy, with
pretty runs through the trees.
Champoussin has a lot of easy runs,
reached without too much difficulty via
Les Crosets and Pointe de l'Au. Better
intermediates have virtually the whole
area at their disposal. The runs down
to Pré-la-Joux and L'Essert on the way
to Châtel, and those either side of
Morgins, are particularly attractive. The
long, sunny runs down to Grand-
Paradis near Champéry are a must
when snow conditions allow; they offer
great views. Good intermediates may
want to take on the Wall, but the chair
to Pointe de Mossette from Les
Brocheaux is an easier route to
Champéry.

FOR BEGINNERS
Convenient and good for snow
The beginner areas seem small in
relation to the size of the resort, but
are adequate because so many visitors
are intermediates. The slopes are
sunny, yet good for snow, and link
well to longer, easy runs.

FOR CROSS-COUNTRY
Varied, with some blacks
There are 45km/28 miles of trails, a
third graded black, mainly between
Avoriaz and Super-Morzine, with other
fine trails down to Lindarets and
around Montriond. The only drawback
is that several trails are not loops, but
'out and back' routes.

LIFTLINES
Main problems now gone
The lines for the lifts to Arare and
Chavanette have been more or less
eliminated by high-speed lifts. And for
2001/02 the bottleneck at Les Lindarets
to get back to Avoriaz should be
eliminated by a new six-pack. Peak
times will still see liftlines to get out of
Les Lindarets towards Châtel though.
Weekends can be crowded as people
pour into their holiday apartments.
Crowds on the trails (especially around
the village) can be worse than lines for
the lifts, with care having to be taken
to avoid collisions.

MOUNTAIN RESTAURANTS
Good choice over the hill
The charming, rustic chalets in the
hamlet of Les Lindarets are one of the
great concentrations of mountain
restaurants in the Alps. A particular
Lindarets favorite of ours is the
Crémaillière which has wonderful
chanterelle mushrooms and great
atmosphere. La Pomme de Pin is
recommended for its warm welcome
and friendly service. The rustic La
Grenuille du Marais near the top of the
gondola up from Morzine has good
value food, good views and
atmosphere. L'Abricotine, with table
service, at Les Brocheaux and
Chavanette at the top of the Swiss
Wall have also been recommended. As
has Le Yéti, at the top of town: 'Has a
terrace with a great view of a huge ski
jump (which sees lots of action).'

---

boarding *Avoriaz has always encouraged snowboarding, opening France's
first terrain park in 1993. There's now an excellent 1.5km/1 mile
terrain park and half-pipe – served by three lifts – and a special ticket for those
whose only interest is riding them. There's a specialist snowboard school and a
snowboard village for children aged 6 to 16. A micro terrain park specially for
children opened a couple of seasons ago. There's a Big Air competition on the
plateau every Wednesday. Only a few (mainly avoidable) surface lifts are left
after the lift upgrades. Nightlife revolves around the couple of bars that manage
an atmosphere.*

The main consideration in this steep village is whether you want to go out at night. By day you can get around by using chair-lifts, but at night it's a walk uphill – or nip in and out of apartment blocks using internal lifts.

HOW TO GO
Mostly apartments
Alternatives to apartments are few.
Chalets There are several available, comfortable and attractive but mainly designed for small family groups.
Hotels There is not much choice of hotels.
《《③ **Dromonts** (0450 740811) The original Avoriaz construction in the resort center, renovated for 2000/01.
《② **Falaise** (0450 742600) At the top of the village; encourages families.
Apartments/condos Some of the better apartments are in the Falaise area by the resort entrance. Reporters have said that some apartments badly need refurbishing – a real problem that is being addressed (the resort is giving owners incentives to spruce them up).

EATING OUT
Good; booking essential
There are more than 30 restaurants. The hotel Dromont's Table du Marché has a celebrity chef and excellent French cuisine. L'Igloo is also good. Le Bistro is recommended as 'good food at good value'. L'Ortolan is friendly and good value. You can buy meal vouchers for seven evening meals in a range of five good restaurants. 'Restricted menu but excellent value,' says a reporter.

APRES-SKI
Lively, but not much choice
A few bars have a good atmosphere, particularly in happy hour. Le Choucas and The Place are lively and have bands, Le Tavaillon (popular with Brits because tour op reps meet there) has a soccer theme and Le Fantastique is worth a visit. Midnight Express club (free entry, pricey drinks) is popular.

OFF THE SLOPES
Not much at the resort
Those not interested in the slopes are better off in Morzine, which has more shops and sports facilities – though Avoriaz does have the Altiform Fitness Center, with saunas and hot-tubs.

Phone numbers
From abroad use the prefix +33 and omit the initial 'o' of the phone number.

ACTIVITIES

Indoor Health center 'Altiform' (sauna, gym, hot-tub), squash, Turkish baths, cinema, bowling
Outdoor Paragliding, hang-gliding, snow-shoe excursions, ice diving, floodlit tobogganing, dog-sleigh rides, walking paths, sleigh rides, skating, snow-scooter excursions, helicopter flights

TOURIST OFFICE

Postcode 74110
t +33 450 740211
f 450 741825
info@avoriaz.com
www.avoriaz.com

↑ You can step straight on to the snow from all Avoriaz apartments
SNOWPIX.COM / CHRIS GILL

SCHOOLS AND GUIDES
Try BASS
The ESF has a good reputation, but classes can be large. The British Alpine Ski School has British instructors and has been highly recommended, especially for 'quite excellent children's lessons. Bookings are taken at Le Tavaillon bar in the high street'. Emery is a specialist snowboard school.

FACILITIES FOR CHILDREN
'Annie Famose delivers'
The Village des Enfants, run by ex-downhill champ Annie Famose, is a key part of the family appeal of Avoriaz. Its facilities are excellent – a chalet full of activities and special slopes complete with Disney characters for children aged 3 to 16. There's a snowboard village too, with special terrain, jumps etc. Car-free Avoriaz must be one of the safest villages in the Alps, but there are still sleighs, skiers, and snowcats to watch out for. Not to mention other tobogganing kids.

High drama among Europe's highest peaks

HOW IT RATES

The slopes

Snow	****
Extent	***
Experts	*****
Intermediates	**
Beginners	*
Convenience	*
Liftlines	**
Restaurants	**

The rest

Scenery	*****
Resort charm	****
Off-slope	*****

➕ A lot of very tough terrain, especially off-trail

➕ Amazing tram to the Aiguille du Midi, leading to the famous (not so tough) Vallée Blanche

➕ Amazing views of peaks and glaciers

➕ Town steeped in Alpine traditions, with lots to do off the slopes

➕ Well-organized and extensive cross-country trail system

➕ Easy access by road, rail and air

➖ Several separate mountains: mixed ability groups are likely to have to split up, and the bus service is far from perfect – we always take a car

➖ Trails in each individual area are quite limited

➖ Runs down to the valley floor are often closed due to lack of snow

➖ Popularity means crowds and liftlines, and lots of road traffic

➖ Bad weather can shut the best runs

Chamonix could not be more different from the archetypal high-altitude French resort. Unless you are based next to one mountain and stick to it, you have to drive or take a bus each day – although the tram now linking Le Brévent to La Flégère has improved things a little. There is all sorts of terrain, but it offers more to interest the expert than anyone else, and to make the most of the area you need a mountain guide rather than a trail map. Chamonix is neither convenient nor conventional.

But it is special. The Chamonix valley cuts deeply through Europe's highest mountains and glaciers. The views are stunning and the runs are everything really tough runs should be – not only steep, but high and long. If you like your snow and scenery on the wild side, give Chamonix a try. But be warned: there are those who try it and never go home – lots of them.

What's new

As we went to press the Mont Blanc tunnel, closed since the tragic fire in 1999, was officially due to re-open in the autumn of 2001. But the project has been delayed several times and locals predict that it won't open until December at the earliest, and maybe not until after the 2001/02 season.

The Charlanon surface lift, completing the Flégère-Brévent link, was upgraded to a fast quad last season. And a new mountain restaurant, La Bergerie, opened at Planpraz, on Le Brévent. There's also a new parking area at Le Brévent.

The resort

Chamonix is a long established tourist town that over the years has spread for miles along its valley in the shadow of Mont Blanc – the scale map below is one of the biggest in these pages.

On either side of the center, just within walking distance of it, are lifts to two of the dozen slope areas in the valley – the famous tram to the Aiguille du Midi, and a gondola to Le Brévent. Also on the fringe of the center is the

beginner area of Les Planards. All the other lift bases involve drives or bus-rides – the nearest being the tram to La Flégère at the village of Les Praz.

Chamonix is a bustling town with scores of hotels and restaurants, visitors all year round and a lively Saturday market. The car-free center of town is full of atmosphere, with cobbled streets and squares, beautiful old buildings and a fast-running river. Not everything is rosy: unsightly modern buildings have been built on

139

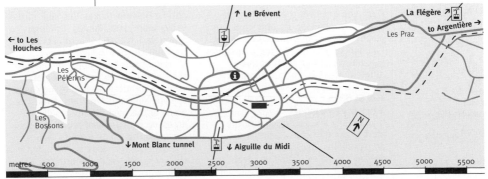

Downtown Chamonix is one of the most diverting ski towns, with a wide choice of shops and restaurants →

OT CHAMONIX-MONT BLANC

to the periphery (especially near the Aiguille du Midi tram station), some of the lovely old buildings have been allowed to fall into disrepair, and at busy times traffic clogs the streets around the pedestrianized center. The town squares and pavement cafes are crowded most of the day with shoppers and sightseers sipping drinks and staring at the glaciers above. It all makes for a very agreeable and 'cosmopolitan' feel, though the dominant language is English.

Chamonix's shops deal in everything from high-tech equipment to tacky souvenirs. But reporters often comment on the number and excellence of the former, and Chamonix remains essentially a town for mountain people rather than poseurs.

Strung out for 20km/12 miles along the Chamonix valley are several separate lift systems, some with attached villages, from Les Houches at one end to Argentière and Le Tour at the other. Regular buses link the lift stations and villages (there's an evening service too) but can get very crowded and aren't always reliable. Like many reporters, we rate a car as essential. A car also means you can get easily to other resorts covered by the Mont Blanc ticket, such as Megève and Les Contamines. (Courmayeur in Italy will again be a practical proposition if the Mont Blanc tunnel reopens for 2001/02.)

The obvious place to stay is in Chamonix itself – it's central, has all the amenities you could want and some of the slopes are close at hand. For those who intend to spend most of their time in one particular area such as Argentière, Le Tour or Les Houches, staying nearby obviously makes sense. Whatever the choice, no location is convenient for everything.

The mountains

Once you get over the fact that the place is hopelessly disconnected, you come to appreciate the upside – that Chamonix has a good variety of slopes available, and that each of the different areas is worth exploring.

THE SLOPES
Very fragmented
If you really like getting about, the Mont Blanc lift ticket covers 11 resorts, 25 mountains, over 200 lifts and 700km/435 miles of trail. It covers resorts far beyond the Chamonix valley – including St-Gervais, Megève, Les Contamines, and even Courmayeur.

The areas within the Chamonix valley – there are 11 in total – are either small, low, beginners' areas or are much higher up on the valley side, with tram or gondola access from the valley floor. If you are used to skiing from the door in more modern resorts, this may all seem very tedious.

The modern six-seater gondola for **Le Brévent** departs a short, steep walk from the center of town, and the tram above takes you to the summit at 2525m/8,280ft. At **La Flégère**, like Le Brévent, the runs are mainly between 1900m/6,230ft and 2450m/8,040ft, and the views of Mont Blanc are worth the price of the lift ticket. A new, fast chair recently replaced the old Trappe, and the 50-person tram linking La Flégère and Le Brévent makes this side of the valley more user-friendly – though reporters have said it's subject to frequent closure in high winds.

There have been improvements to the system at **Les Grands Montets** above Argentière, including increased snowmaking and remodelled runs, but much of the best terrain is still accessed by a tram of relatively low capacity. This costs extra to ride – though two free rides are included in a six-day ticket – but still attracts liftlines.

MOUNTAIN FACTS

Altitude	1035m-3840m
	3,400ft-12,600ft
Lifts	49
Trails	152km/94 miles
Green	21%
Blue	31%
Red	35%
Black	13%
Snowmaking	9km/
	6 miles
Recco detectors used	

LIFT TICKETS

2001/02 prices in euros

Cham'Ski ticket
Covers all areas in the Chamonix Valley and the bus services between them, except Les Houches. Includes a day in Courmayeur.
Beginners Cham'Start 6-day ticket covers all valley floor lifts (82), Cham'Baby 6-day ticket covers the same for 4- to 11-year-olds (60). You can buy day extensions to higher lifts.
Main ticket
1-day ticket 40
6-day ticket 168
Senior citizens
Over 60: 6-day ticket 143
Children
12 to 15:
6-day ticket 143
Under 12: 6-day ticket 118
Under 4: free ticket
Notes 6-day tickets include two ascents on the Grands Montets tram. Additional ascents cost extra (5 for 1 ascent, 73 for 20).
Alternative tickets
Ski-ticket Mont Blanc covers lifts in the 13 resorts of the Mont Blanc area (762km/473 miles of trails) and Courmayeur in Italy (6 days 200 for adults, 140 for children).

boarding *Chamonix is a place of pilgrimage for advanced boarders, but not the best place to learn. Head for Argentière and the Grands Montets for the hairiest action – the terrain-park and half-pipe host regular competitions. There's also a natural half-pipe/gully at Le Tour. Most of the ski areas are equipped mainly with trams, gondolas and chairs, though there are quite a few surface lifts at Le Tour. If you do the Vallée Blanche, be warned: the usual route is flat in places. If you're ready to tackle tougher off-trail, check out former British Champ Neil McNab's excellent Extreme Backcountry Camps (www.mcnab.co.uk). Staying in the town itself will certainly guarantee satisfactory nightlife.*

Le Tour, already quite extensive, doubled in size recently with the addition of new runs – an 8km/5 mile blue, a red and a black – above Vallorcine (which will eventually be linked by lift).

One of the valley-floor areas, Les Bossons, is open for floodlit skiing three nights a week.

The valley trail map is not sufficiently detailed to use for navigation. Use the little Cham'Ski handbook, which includes all of the local area trail maps with brief descriptions of each run and assessments of suitability for different standards of ability.

Most of our reporters have been surprised by the standard of trail grooming, but not with the signposting of the runs, or with 'rather antiquated chairs and surface lifts'.

SNOW RELIABILITY
Good high up; poor low down
The top runs on the north-facing slopes above Argentière are almost guaranteed to have good snow, and the season normally lasts well into May. The risk of finding the top lift shut because of bad weather is more of a worry (and is the excuse for not including the lift on the main ticket). The Col de Balme area above Le Tour has a snowy location and a good late-season record. The largely south-facing slopes of Brévent and Flégère suffer in warm weather, and runs to the resort are often closed. There's snowmaking on the Bochard trail on Les Grands Montets as well as some of the smaller areas. Several of the beginners' areas need snow-cover down to the valley floor to be operational.

FOR EXPERTS
One of the great resorts
Les Grands Montets above Argentière is justifiably renowned for its extensive steep terrain. To get the best out of

the area you really need to have a local guide. Without one you either stick to the relatively small number of trails or you put your life at risk.

The Grands Montets tram takes you up to 3235m/10,610ft; if you've got the legs and lungs, climb the 121 steep metal steps to the observation platform (3275m/10,740ft) and take in the stunning views. (But beware: it's 200 more steps down from the tram before you hit the snow.)

The ungroomed black trails from here – Point de Vue and Pylones – are long and exhilarating. The Point de Vue sails right by some dramatic sections of glacier, with marvellous views of the crevasses. The off-trail routes from the top are numerous and often dangerous; the Pas de Chèvre route is serious stuff, eventually joining the Vallée Blanche run. There are many routes down the Argentière glacier.

The Bochard gondola serves a challenging red and a moderate black. Alternatively, head directly down the Combe de la Pendant bowl for 1000m/3,000ft vertical of wild, ungroomed mountainside. The continuation down the valley side to Le Lavancher is equally challenging; it suffers frequently from lack of snow on the steep bits.

At Le Brévent there's more to test experts than the trail map suggests – there are a number of variations on the runs down from the summit. Some are steep and prone to ice, and the couloir routes are very steep and very narrow. The runs in the sunny Col de La Charlanon are uncrowded and include one marked red run and lots of excellent off-trail if the snow is good.

At La Flégère there are several good off-trail routes – in the Combe Lachenal, crossed by the linking tram, for example – and a pretty tough run back to the village when snow-cover permits. Le Tour boasts little tough terrain on-trail but there are good off-trail routes from the high points to the village and over the back towards Vallorcine or into Switzerland.

FOR INTERMEDIATES
It's worth trying it all
For less confident intermediates, the best areas are at the two extreme ends of the Chamonix valley. The Col de Balme area above Le Tour is good for easy cruising and usually free from crowds. And the slopes of the separate Prarion–Bellevue system above Les Houches are mostly gentle tree-lined blue and red runs, very unlikely to intimidate anyone – a good area for building confidence.

More adventurous intermediates will also want to try the other three main areas, though they may find the Grands Montets tough going (and crowded). The bulk of the terrain at Le Brévent and La Flégère provides a sensible mix of blue and red runs; at Le Brévent the slopes have been redesigned to achieve this. If the weather is good, book a guide and do the Vallée Blanche (see feature box).

A day trip to Courmayeur has traditionally made an interesting change of scene, especially when the weather's bad. It will become practical again if the Mont Blanc tunnel reopens for the forthcoming season.

FOR BEGINNERS
Best if there's snow in the valley
If there is snow low down, the beginner lifts at La Vormaine, Les Chosalets, Les Planards and Le Savoy are fine for teaching first-timers; learners will not be bothered by speed-merchants. The Planards and Glacier du Mont Blanc lifts both benefit from snowmaking. But the slopes on the south side of the valley can be dark and cold in winter. And the separation of beginners' slopes from the rest inhibits the transition to real runs, and makes lunchtime meetings of mixed groups impractical. Better to learn elsewhere, and come to Chamonix when you can appreciate the terrain.

FOR CROSS-COUNTRY
A good network of trails
Most of the 42km/26 miles of prepared trails lie along the valley between Chamonix and Argentière. There are green, blue, red and black loop sections and the full tour from Chamonix to Argentière and back is 32km/20 miles. All these trails are fairly low and fade fast in spring sun.

LIFTLINES
Fewer problems
There are still long lines for the top tram on Les Grands Montets. When

SCHOOLS/GUIDES

2000/01 prices in euros

ESF
In both Chamonix and Argentière
Classes 6 days
5hr: am and pm
6 full days: 183
Children's classes
Ages: 4 to 12
6 days: 9.30-5pm, including supervised lunch: 212
Private lessons
1hr, 2hr, half- or full day
37 for 1hr, for 1 or 2 people; 43 for 3 to 5 people

CHILDCARE

The ESF runs ordinary classes for children aged 6 to 12. For children aged 4 to 6 there are lessons in a snow-garden. And children in either category can be looked after all day (and amused when not on the slopes) from 8.30 to 5pm.

The day-care center at the Maison pour Tous (0450 533668) takes children aged 18 months to 6 years from 7.45 to noon and 2pm to 5.30.

The Panda Club takes children aged 10 months to 12 years. There is a nursery in Chamonix that takes children from 10 months (0450 558612). Older babies are taken here or to Argentière (0450 540476), where the club has its own slopes, open to children aged 3 or more.

Some of the more expensive hotels will provide child care.

they reach 30 minutes a booking system operates, so you can keep moving until it's your turn to ride.

At close of play, the lifts from the high-altitude areas to the valley floor get busy – especially the trams.

In poor weather Les Houches is most likely to be open. The lines for the Bellevue tram can be bad.

MOUNTAIN RESTAURANTS
Stunning views – not much else

The restaurants are a source of disappointment for many reporters – 'packed, pricey and soulless' was a recent description. The Panoramic at the top of Brévent enjoys the best views. The food's fine but the place is dull. Altitude 2000 provides table-service at rip-off prices. The new Bergerie at Planpraz – built in wood and stone – with self- and table-service has been recommended. There's a plain self-service joint at La Flégère.

On the Grands Montets the Plan Joran serves good food and does table- and self-service. The restaurant at Lognan has been smartly renovated. The rustic Chalet-Refuge du Lognan, off the beaten track overlooking the Argentière glacier, has marvellous food. Book in advance to guarantee a full menu.

SCHOOLS AND GUIDES
The place to try something new

The schools here are particularly strong in specialist fields – off-trail, glacier and couloir skiing, ski touring, snowboarding and cross-country. English-speaking instructors are plentiful. One second-week skier did report large classes and unimaginative teaching by the Evolution 2 school, though another near beginner had an 'excellent' private lesson with them. At the Maison de la Montagne in Chamonix is the main ESF office and the HQ of the Compagnie des Guides, which has taken visitors to the mountains for 150 years.

Competition is provided by a number of smaller, independent guiding and teaching outfits.

FACILITIES FOR CHILDREN
Better than they were

The Panda Club is used by quite a few British visitors and reports have been enthusiastic. The Argentière base can be inconvenient for meeting up with children for the afternoons.

Beware of children being kept on the valley beginner areas for the convenience of the school when they really should be getting some miles under their skis.

THE VALLÉE BLANCHE

This is a trip you do for the stunning scenery rather than the challenge of the run, which (although exceptionally long) is easy – well within the capability of the average intermediate. But be prepared for extreme cold at the top, for flat and uphill sections on the way down, and for hordes of people – going early on a weekday gives you the best chance of avoiding the worst of the crowds. Go in a guided group – despite the ease of the runs, dangerous crevasses lurk to swallow those not in the know. Book your guide or sign up for a group trip the day before at the Maison de la Montagne or other ski school offices.

The amazing Aiguille du Midi tram takes you to 3840m/12,600ft. Across the bridge from the arrival station on the Piton Nord is the Piton Central; the view of Mont Blanc from the cafe a stair-climb higher should not be missed – and gives you the opportunity to adjust to the dizzying altitude. A tunnel delivers you to the infamous ridge-walk down to the start of the run. There is a fixed guide-rope, and many parties rope up for this walk. You may still feel envious of those strolling nonchalantly down in crampons; you may wish you'd stayed in bed.

After that the run seems a stroll in the park; mostly effortless gliding down gentle slopes with only the occasional steeper, choppy section to deal with. So stop often and enjoy the surroundings fully. The views of the ice, the crevasses and seracs – and the spectacular mountains beyond – are simply mind-blowing. There are variants on the classic route, all more difficult and hazardous – the 'Vraie Vallée' and 'Envers du Plan' among them. Snow conditions may mean cutting short the full 24km/15miles run down to Chamonix, in which case you catch a train from the station at Montenvers (1910m/6,270ft). A short climb and gondola link the glacier to the station.

One of the delights of the Brévent and Flégère areas is their great views across the valley to peaks like the Grands Montets →

SNOWPIX.COM / CHRIS GILL

GETTING THERE

Air Geneva, transfer 1½hr. Lyon, transfer 3½hr.

Rail Station in resort, on the St Gervais-Le Fayet/Vallorcine line.

Direct TGV link from Paris on Friday evenings and weekends.

Phone numbers
From abroad use the prefix +33 and omit the initial 'o' of the phone number.

Staying there

HOW TO GO
Any way you like

There are all sorts of accommodations, and lots of them.

Hotels The place is full of hotels, many with fewer than 30 rooms and modestly priced. Hotel bookings for a day or two are easy to arrange since Chamonix's peak season is summer.

((((4) **Albert 1er** (0450 530509) Smart, traditional chalet-style hotel with 'truly excellent food' (two Michelin stars, Gault-Millau rating). Recent visitors loved the new half-indoor, half-outdoor swimming pool.

(((4) **Auberge du Bois Prin** (0450 533351) A small modern chalet with a big reputation; great views; bit of a hike into town; closer to Le Brévent.

(((4) **Mont-Blanc** (0450 530564) Central, luxurious.

(((4) **Jeu de Paume** (Lavancher) (0450 540376) Alpine satellite of a chic Parisian hotel: a beautifully furnished modern chalet half-way to Argentière.

(((3) **Alpina** (0450 534777) By far the biggest in town: modernist–functional place just north of center.

((3) **Labrador** (Les Praz) (0450 559009) Scandinavian-style chalet close to the Flégère lift. Good restaurant.

((3) **Sapinière** (0450 530763) Traditional hotel with good French food, run by long-established Chamonix family. Reasonable site on the Brévent side of town. Recommended by recent visitors.

((3) **Vallée Blanche** (0450 530450) Smart low-priced 3-star B&B hotel, handy for center and Aiguille du Midi.

((2) **L'Arve** (0450 530231) By the river, just off the main street; small newly decorated rooms.

((2) **Richemond** (0450 530885) Now rather faded and old-fashioned, but with good public areas.

((2) **Pointe Isabelle** (0450 531287) Not pretty, but central location; friendly staff, good plain food, well-equipped bedrooms.

((2) **Roma** Simple but satisfactory B&B hotel in hassle-free location on south side of center; friendly owner.

(1) **Faucigny** (0450 530117) Cottage-style; in center.

Apartments/condos Beware convenient but cramped and charmless blocks in Chamonix Sud. The Balcons du Savoy

ACTIVITIES

Indoor Sports complex (sports hall, gym, table tennis), indoor skating and curling rinks, ice hockey, swimming pool with giant water slide, saunas, six indoor tennis courts, two squash courts, fitness center, Alpine museum, casino, three cinemas, library, 10-pin bowling, climbing wall
Outdoor Ski-jumping, snow-shoe outings, mountain biking, hang-gliding, paragliding, flying excursions, heli-skiing, ice skating

TOURIST OFFICE

Postcode 74400
t +33 450 530024
f 450 535890
info@chamonix.com
www.chamonix.com

(0450 553232) look much better, are well situated and have use of a pool, steam room and solarium. The Splendid & Golf apartments in Les Praz (0450 559601) are charming and close to the Flégère tram.

EATING OUT
Plenty of quality places
The good hotels all have good restaurants – the Eden at Les Praz and Bois Prin in Chamonix are first-rate – and there are many other good places to eat. The Sarpé is a lovely 'mountain' restaurant and The Impossible is rustic but smart and features good regional dishes. Recent visitors have especially recommended Le Panier des Quatre Saisons ('Excellent food at reasonable prices. Wonderful atmosphere') and Le Crochon ('Good Savoyard fare, plus some varied and innovative dishes'). The Monchu is also good for Savoyard specialities. A recent reporter raves about the Cabane restaurant next to the Labrador hotel in Les Praz. There are a number of ethnic restaurants – Mexican, Spanish, Japanese, Chinese etc – and lots of brasseries and cafes.

APRES-SKI
Lots of bars and music
Many of the bars around the pedestrianized center of Chamonix get crowded for a couple of hours at sundown – none more so than the Choucas video bar. During the evening, The Pub, Wild Wallaby's, the Mill Street bar and the Bar du Moulin are busy. There's a lively variety of nightclubs and discos. The Choucas (again), and Dick's Tea bar are popular. The Cantina sometimes has live music and is open late. There are plenty of bars and brasseries for a quieter drink too.

OFF THE SLOPES
An excellent choice
There's more off-slope activity here than in many resorts. Excursion possibilities include Annecy and Geneva, plus Courmayeur and Turin. The Alpine Museum is 'excellent and very interesting' and there are good sports facilities. The sports center and 'excellent' swimming pool have been renovated after flood damage.

Argentière 1240m/4,070ft

The old village is in a lovely setting towards the head of the valley – the

Glacier d'Argentière pokes down towards it and the Aiguille du Midi and Mont Blanc still dominate the scene down the valley. There's a fair bit of modern development but it still has a rustic appeal. Le Tour, just beyond Argentière, is quiet and picturesque.

A number of the hotels are simple, inexpensive and handy for the village center – less so for the slopes – but the Grands-Montets (0450 540666) is a large chalet-style building, right next to the trail and the Panda Club for children. The family-run Montana (0450 541499) is recommended for 'lovely rooms, excellent food'.

Restaurants and bars are informal and inexpensive. The Office is the happening place in Argentière, from breakfast till late.

Les Houches 1010m/3,310ft

Les Houches, 6km/4 miles from Chamonix, is not on the valley ticket, but is covered by the regional Mont Blanc ticket. It's a pleasant village, sitting in the shade of the looming Mont Blanc massif – shady and cold in midwinter. There is an old core with a pretty church, but modern developments in chalet style have spread along the road up to Chamonix.

The area above Les Houches is served by a tram to **Bellevue** and a gondola to **Prarion**, the high-point at 1900m/6,230ft. Runs on the back of the mountain towards St-Gervais, and blue, red and black runs of 900m/3,000ft vertical down to Les Houches, make this the biggest single area of prepared runs in the Chamonix valley.

The almost entirely wooded slopes are popular when bad weather or the risk of avalanches closes other areas.

In good weather the slopes are quiet, and the views superb from the several attractive mountain restaurants. It is good for families, beginners and intermediates, with easy runs at the top of the mountain. Snow-cover on the lower slopes is not reliable, but there is a fair amount of snowmaking.

The village is quiet at night, but there are some pleasant bars and good restaurants. Recent visitors enjoyed staying in the Hotel du Bois (0450 545035), with its 'helpful staff and excellent restaurant – Le Caprice' and 'a good local band in the bar on Saturday'. Buses run in and out of Chamonix all evening.

A distinctively French base for touring the Portes du Soleil

HOW IT RATES

The slopes

Snow	**
Extent	*****
Experts	***
Intermediates	****
Beginners	**
Convenience	**
Liftlines	***
Restaurants	***

The rest

Scenery	***
Resort charm	***
Off-slope	**

What's new

For 2001/02 there will be a new boardercross course and terrain park built in the Linga area.

In 2000/01 the three-person chair from Les Combes to Cornebois was replaced by a high-speed quad. Improvements were made to some trails and to buses, roads and the ice rink. More avalanche protection equipment was installed.

MOUNTAIN FACTS

for Portes du Soleil

Altitude 975m-2350m/
3,200ft-7,710ft

Lifts	206
Trails	650km/
	400 miles
Green	13%
Blue	38%
Red	39%
Black	10%
Snowmaking	
	252 acres
Recco detectors used	

➕ Very extensive, pretty, intermediate terrain – the Portes du Soleil

➕ Wide range of cheap and cheerful, good-value accommodations

➕ Easily reached – close to Geneva, and one of the shortest drives from the Channel

➕ Pleasant, lively, French-dominated old village, still quite rustic in parts

➕ Local slopes relatively liftline-free

➕ Good views

➖ Both resort and top of skiing are low for a French resort, with resulting risk of poor snow – though extended snowmaking has helped

➖ Bus or gondola ride to most snow-sure beginner areas

➖ Liftlines can be a problem in parts of the Portes du Soleil circuit, particularly at weekends

➖ Village traffic can be congested at weekends and in peak season

Like neighboring Morzine, Châtel offers a blend of attractions that is uncommon in France – an old village with plenty of facilities, cheap accommodations by French standards, and a large ski area on the doorstep. Châtel's original rustic charm has been largely eroded by expansion in recent years, but some of it remains, and the resort has one obvious advantage over smoother Morzine: it is part of the main Portes du Soleil circuit.

The circuit actually breaks down at Châtel, but this works in the village's favor. Whereas those doing the circuit from other resorts have the inconvenience of waiting for a bus mid-circuit, Châtel residents have the advantage of being able to time their bus-rides to avoid waits and liftlines. Those mainly interested in the local slopes should also consider Châtel. For confident intermediates, Châtel's Linga has few equals in the Portes du Soleil, while the nearby Torgon section has arguably the best views. The Chapelle d'Abondance slopes are pleasantly uncrowded at weekends. Châtel has become more beginner-friendly with beginner areas at Super-Châtel and Pré-la-Joux, though these are a lift or bus-ride away.

The resort

Châtel lies near the head of the wooded Dranse valley, at the north-eastern limit of the French–Swiss Portes du Soleil ski circuit.

It is a much expanded and now quite large but nonetheless attractive old village. New unpretentious chalet-style hotels and apartments rub shoulders with old farmhouses where cattle still live in winter.

Although there is a definite center, the village sprawls along the road in from lake Geneva and the diverging roads out – up the hillside towards Morgins and along the valley towards the Linga and Pré-la-Joux lifts.

Lots of visitors take cars and the center can get clogged with traffic during the evening rush-hour – more so at weekends. Street parking is difficult but there is (pay-for) underground parking

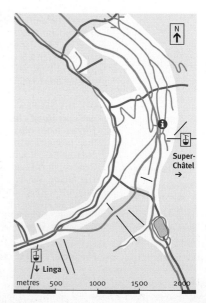

LIFT TICKETS

2001/02 prices in euros

Portes du Soleil
Covers all lifts in all 12 resorts, and shuttle-buses.
Main ticket
1-day ticket 33
6-day ticket 159
Senior citizens
Over 60: 6-day ticket 127
Children
Under 16: 6-day ticket 107
Under 5: free ticket
Short-term tickets
Morning/afternoon tickets for the Portes du Soleil (both 25), and for Châtel only (both 18 – 2000/01 price).
Alternative periods
5 non-consecutive-days ticket for Châtel only (adult 112 – 2000/01 price).
Alternative tickets
Châtel ticket covers 51 lifts in Châtel, Linga, Super-Châtel, Torgon, Barbossine, and the link to Morgins (adult 6-day ticket 114 – 2000/01 price).

and day parking lots at Linga and Pré-la-Joux. Other main French Portes du Soleil resorts – Avoriaz, Morzine – are easy to reach on skis or board, but not by road.

A few miles down the valley is the rustic village of La Chapelle-d'Abondance (see end of chapter).

The mountains

The Portes du Soleil is classic intermediate terrain, and Châtel's local slopes are very much in character. Confident intermediates, in particular, will find lots to enjoy in the Linga and Plaine Dranse sectors. If you travel the Portes du Soleil circuit the booklet-style trail map makes for easy navigation. Reporters have also commented favorably on the recently introduced system of Discovery Routes guiding you around the Portes du Soleil – choose an alpine animal that suits your ability and follow the signs displaying it. An electronic lift ticket was introduced for 1999, so you can now keep your ticket in your pocket.

THE SLOPES
The circuit breaks down here

Châtel sits between two sectors of the Portes du Soleil circuit – linked together by an 'excellent, practically

continuous', free bus service. **Super-Châtel** is directly above the village – an area of easy, open and lightly wooded beginner slopes, accessed by a choice of gondola or two-stage chair. From here you can cross the Swiss border, either to quiet Torgon or clockwise around the Portes du Soleil to Morgins, Champoussin and Champéry, before going back into France above Avoriaz.

Linga is a bus-ride away. For intermediates and better, the area has some of the most interesting runs in the Portes du Soleil, the best of them leading back towards Châtel. The fastest way to Avoriaz is to stay on the bus at Linga and go to Pré-la-Joux. From here a high-speed quad goes direct to Plaine Dranse; then it's one more lift and run to Les Lindarets, where there's a choice of lifts to Avoriaz.

SNOW RELIABILITY
The main drawback

The main drawback of the Portes du Soleil is that it is low, so snow quality can suffer when it's warm. Châtel is at only 1200m/3,940ft (600m/1,970ft lower than Avoriaz) and some runs home can be tricky or closed, especially from Super-Châtel. But a lot of snowmaking has been installed at Super-Châtel and on runs down from

Châtel

147

boarding *Avoriaz is the hardcore destination in the Portes du Soleil. But Châtel is not a bad place to learn or to go to as a budget option or as part of a mixed group of skiers and boarders. Most local lifts are gondolas or chairs and there's a terrain park, half-pipe and boardercross course at Super-Châtel. The Linga area has good varied terrain and off-trail possibilities – and will have a boardercross course and terrain park this year.*

↑ Châtel is a sprawling village with a good bus link between its central gondola and the Linga slopes (pictured here), served by another gondola

JEAN-FRANÇOIS VUARAND

CHILDCARE

The ESF's ski kindergarten is for children from age 4.

Le Village des Marmottons takes children from 2 to 8, from 8.30 to 5.30, with ski lessons for those aged 3 up.

Henri Gonon takes children over 6, as does the Ski and Surf International School and Snow Ride.

Francis Sports caters for 3 to 8 year olds at the Pitchounes.

Linga and to Pré-la-Joux. These last two are mainly north-facing and generally have the best local snow – a regular visitor tells us there is often good snow at Pré-la-Joux till May. But another told us of snow being like a 'damp pudding' in March and trails to Morgins and Les Lindarets being closed.

FOR EXPERTS
Some challenges
The best steep runs – on and off-trail – are in the Linga and Pré-la-Joux area. Beneath the Linga gondola and chair, there's a pleasant mix of open and wooded ground which follows the fall line fairly directly. And there's a bump run between Cornebois and Plaine Dranse which has been described as 'steeper and narrower than the infamous Swiss Wall' in Avoriaz. An ungroomed trail from Super-Châtel towards the village is also fun. And the challenging Hauts Forts sector beyond Avoriaz is within reach. There's also a great off-trail route from Tête du Linga down the valley of La Leiche – but you need a guide. Two trails recently created off the Rochassons ridge are both steep and kept well groomed.

Pierre Tardival's Extreme Clinics are held in Châtel and he doesn't seem to have any problem finding local, steep off-trail terrain (this is the man who climbed and skied Everest!).

FOR INTERMEDIATES
Some of the best runs in the area
When conditions are right the Portes du Soleil is an intermediate's paradise. Good intermediates need not go far from Châtel; Linga and Plaine Dranse have some of the best red runs on the circuit. But the Champéry-Avoriaz sector also beckons. The moderately skilled can do the circuit without problem, and will particularly enjoy runs around Les Lindarets and Morgins. Even timid types can do the circuit, provided they take one or two short-cuts and ride chairs down trickier bits. The chair from Les Lindarets to Pointe de Mossette leads to a red run into the Swiss area, which is a lot easier than the 'Swiss Wall' from Chavanette and also speeds up a journey round the circuit.

Leaving aside attempts to complete the circuit in both directions, there are rewarding out-and-back expeditions to be made clockwise to the wide open snowfields above Champoussin, beyond Morgins, and counterclockwise to the Hauts-Forts runs above Avoriaz.

FOR BEGINNERS
Go to Pré-la-Joux
The most snow-sure beginners' area is at Pré-la-Joux ('I loved it,' says a reporter), but you need to catch a bus there. There's also Super-Châtel or the low village beginner areas.

Phone numbers
From abroad use the prefix +33 and omit the initial '0' of the phone number.

SCHOOLS/GUIDES

2001/02 prices in euros

ESF
Classes 6 days
2½hr am or pm
6 half-days: 96
Children's classes
Ages: 5 to 16
6 half-days: 95
Private lessons
1hr or 1½hr
29 for 1hr, for 1 or 2 people

International
Classes 6 days
3hr: 9am-noon or 2pm-5pm; 2hr: noon-2pm
6 mornings: 102
Children's classes
Ages: from 8
6 afternoons: 108
Private lessons
1hr or 2hr
33 for 1hr, each additional person 5

Stages Henri Gonon
Courses can include 6 days' accommodation, ticket and 5 half-day lessons (2000/01 prices)
Classes 5 days
3hr per day
5 days: 95
Children's classes
Ages: 7 to 16
5 days: 83
Private lessons
1hr
22 for 1 or 2 people

Other schools include: Francis Sports, Snow Ride and Virages.

FOR CROSS-COUNTRY
Pretty, if low, trails
There are plenty of pretty trails along the river and through the woods on the lower slopes of Linga, but snow-cover can be a problem.

LIFTLINES
Bottlenecks being eased
Liftlines to get to Avoriaz have been eased by the high-speed quad at Pré-la-Joux. But there are still a couple of bottlenecks further afield, which tend to be worse at weekends (although we do have reports of few liftlines even during school holidays and New Year). At Les Lindarets, in particular, there is often a lengthy wait for the chair-lift to the Rochassons ridge on the way back to Châtel; but the liftline the other way up to Avoriaz should be eliminated for 2001/02 by the new six-pack – see Avoriaz chapter. You can face liftlines to get down from Super-Châtel if the slope back is shut by poor snow.

MOUNTAIN RESTAURANTS
Some quite good local huts
Atmospheric chalets can be found, notably at Plaine Dranse (Le Bois Prin, Chez Crépy, Tân o Marmottes and Chez Denis have been recommended). In the Linga area La Ferme des Pistes gets the thumbs up. The Perdrix Blanche at Pré-la-Joux scarcely counts as a mountain restaurant, but is an attractive (if pricey) spot for lunch. It does get crowded as there's nowhere else. At Super-Châtel the Portes du Soleil at the foot of the Coqs surface lift is much better than the big place at the top of the gondola. The Escale Blanche is worth a visit.

SCHOOLS AND GUIDES
Plenty of choice
There are now six ski and snowboard schools in Châtel. The International school has been recommended by a reporter and the ESF came in for praise this year for their 'very helpful and customer-focused instructors'. Ian McGarry, whose courses have received glowing reports from reporters, will be working with the ESF for part of this year. Bookings can be discussed directly (+35 312 859139), or via the ESF. Those tempted to join Pierre Tardival's Extreme Clinics, also bookable through Ski McGarry, should take the 'extreme' part seriously.

FACILITIES FOR CHILDREN
Increasingly sympathetic
The Marmottons nursery (now with their own snowmaking machine) has good facilities, including toboggans, painting, music and videos, and children are reportedly happy there. Francis Sports ski school have their own nursery area with a surface lift and chalet at Linga: 'Very organized, convenient and reasonably priced'. The ESF has had good reports: 'Small groups with excellent English spoken.'

Staying there

A central position gives you the advantage of getting on the ski-bus to the outlying lifts before it gets very crowded and simplifies après-ski outings. But there are accommodations near the Linga lift if that's the priority.

HOW TO GO
Simple hotels rule
Hotels Practically all of the hotels are 2-stars, mostly friendly chalets, wooden or at least partly wood-clad. None of the 3-stars is particularly well placed. Les Cornettes in La Chapelle (see end of chapter) is an interesting alternative. ⑬ **Macchi** (0450 732412) Modern chalet, most central of the 3-stars. ⑬ **Fleur de Neige** (0450 732010) Well-maintained, welcoming chalet on edge of center; Grive Gourmande restaurant does about the best food in town. ⑬ **Lion d'Or** (0450 813440) In center, 'basic rooms, good atmosphere'. ⑫ **Belalp** (0450 732439) Very comfortable, with excellent food. ① **Kandahar** (0450 733060) One for peace-lovers: a Logis by the river, a walkable distance from the center. ① **Rhododendrons** (0450 732404) 'Great service, friendly, comfortable, clean.'
Apartments/condos Many of the better places are available through Châtel and self-drive specialists. The Gelinotte (out of town but near the Linga lifts and children's village) and Les Erines (central and close to the Super-Châtel gondola) look good. The Flèche d'Or apartments are not well positioned for lifts or shops. The Aveniers is right by the Linga gondola. A couple of reporters have mentioned Châtel's supermarkets are small and over-crowded – worth shopping on the way if you're driving.

GETTING THERE

Air Geneva, transfer
1½hr.

Rail Thonon les Bains
(42km/26 miles).

ACTIVITIES

Indoor Swimming
pool, bowling,
cinema, library

Outdoor Skating rink,
horse-drawn carriage
rides, helicopter rides,
dog-sledding, snow-
shoe excursions, farm
visits, toboggan run,
floodlit skiing at Linga

TOURIST OFFICE

Postcode 74390
t +33 450 732244
f 450 732287
touristoffice@
chatel.com
www.chatel.com

EATING OUT
Fair selection

There is an adequate number and
range of restaurants. Les Cornettes in
La Chapelle-d'Abondance is one of our
favorites – amazingly good-value
menus with excellent food (but
'disappointing puddings' comments
one reporter). The Vieux Four, in an
old farm building, has a reputation for
the best steaks in Châtel. The Fleur de
Neige hotel has a good restaurant and
Le Fiacre is also popular. The Perrier
serves Savoyard specialities. La
Ripaille, almost opposite the Linga
gondola, was highly recommended by
a past reporter, especially for its fish.

APRES-SKI
All down to bars

Châtel is getting livelier, especially on
weekends. The Tunnel bar is very
popular and has a DJ or live music
every night. The Isba has apparently
slightly fallen from grace since its
supremo moved on last season to run
the new and very popular English-pub-
style Avalanche.
La Godille – close to the Super-Châtel
gondola and crowded at tea-time – has
a more French feel. The bar in the
hotel Soldanelles is also pretty lively.
The bowling alley, La Vielle Grange,
also has a good bar. The Jean'Club
disco at the Super-Châtel bubble is
crowded at weekends, and there's also
the Lagon Bleu in the same area. A
reporter has recommended the Saf
disco in Morgins.

OFF THE SLOPES
Better to stay in Morzine

Those with a car have some
entertaining excursions available:
Geneva, Thonon and Evian. Otherwise
there is little to do but take some
pleasant walks along the river, or visit
the cheese factory and the two theaters.
The tourist office organizes daily events
for non-slope users. But those not
using the slopes would find more to do
in Morzine. The Portes du Soleil as a
whole is less than ideal for those not
using the slopes who like to meet their
more active friends for lunch: skiers
and boarders are likely to be above at
some distant resort at lunchtime.

La Chapelle-d'Abondance
1010m/3,310ft

This unspoiled, rustic farming
community, complete with old church
and friendly locals, is 5km/3 miles
along a beautiful valley from Châtel. 'A
car and a bit of French is virtually
essential,' says a reporter this year. It's
had its own quiet little north-facing
area of easy wooded runs for some
years, but has more recently been put
on the Portes du Soleil map by a
gondola and three chair-lifts that now
link it to Torgon in Switzerland and,
from there, Super-Châtel. This section
is only a spur of the Portes du Soleil
circuit. But, taken together with
Chapelle's own little area, it is worth
exploring – good at weekends when
Châtel gets crowded and 'excellent for
beginners'.

Nightlife is virtually non-existent –
just a few quiet bars, a cinema and
torchlit descents.

The hotel Cornettes is an amazing
2-star with 2-star rooms but 4-star
facilities, including an indoor pool,
sauna, steam room, hot-tubs, excellent
restaurant (see Eating Out) and
atmospheric bar. Look out for
showcases with puppets and dolls and
eccentric touches, such as ancient old
doors that unexpectedly open
automatically. It has been run by the
Trincaz family since 1894. The Alpage
and Chabi are other hotel options. The
Airelles apartments have received a
favorable report.

Great for late-booking Francophiles

HOW IT RATES

The slopes

Snow	**
Extent	***
Experts	***
Intermediates	****
Beginners	****
Convenience	***
Liftlines	***
Restaurants	****

The rest

Scenery	****
Resort charm	****
Off-slope	***

➕ Mountain villages in a scenic setting, retaining traditional character

➕ Extensive, interesting slopes – trails best for beginners and intermediates

➕ Very French atmosphere

➕ Very short transfer time from Geneva

➕ Attractive mountain restaurants

➕ Good cross-country trails

➕ Slopes at La Clusaz and Le Grand-Bornand linked by shuttle-bus

➖ Snow conditions unreliable because of low altitude (by French standards)

➖ Not many challenging trails for experts – though there are good off-trail runs

➖ Crowded on weekends

Few other major French resorts are based around what are still, essentially, genuine mountain villages that exude rustic charm and Gallic atmosphere. Combine that with over 200km/125 miles of largely intermediate slopes, above and below the tree line, spread over five linked sectors in La Clusaz and the separate Le Grand-Bornand area, and there's a good basis for an enjoyable, relaxed week.

The area's one big problem is its height, or lack of it. Snowmaking has been installed in recent years and is continually increased, but it's still on a modest scale, and of course makes no difference in mild weather. So pre-booking a holiday here remains, as in other low resorts, a slightly risky business.

151

What's new

In La Clusaz, the surface-lift at the top of l'Aiguille was replaced by a quad chair-lift with a magic carpet last season.

New snowmaking was installed at the base of the Balme area.

In Le Grand-Bornand, the capacity of the Terres Rouges chair was upgraded with the installation of a magic carpet. And the snowmaking network was further extended.

Next season will see the replacement of the Lachat chair, to the resort high point, by a new six-pack, and the development of a new black run on the north-east side of the mountain.

The resort

La Clusaz was once frequented almost entirely by the French. But it has developed into a major international resort – summer and winter. As one of the most accessible resorts from Geneva and Annecy, it's good for short transfers, but it does get crowded, and there can be weekend traffic jams.

The village is built beside a fast-flowing stream at the junction of a number of narrow wooded valleys, and has had to grow in a rather rambling and sprawling way, with roads running in a confusing mixture of directions. But, unlike so many French resorts, La Clusaz has retained the charm of a genuine mountain village. (It's the kind of place that is as attractive in summer as under a blanket of snow in winter.)

In the center is a large old church, and other original old stone and wood buildings; and, for the most part, the new buildings have been built in chalet style and blend in well. Les Etages is a much smaller center of accommodations above the main town, where two of the mountain sectors meet.

La Clusaz has a friendly feel to it. The villagers welcome visitors every Monday evening in the main square with vin chaud and a variety of local cheeses. There's a weekly market, tempting food shops and a wide

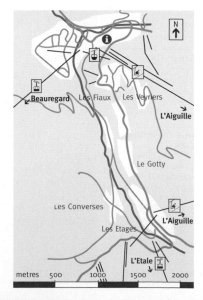

MOUNTAIN FACTS

La Clusaz

Altitude 1100m-2500m	
3,610ft-8,200ft	
Lifts	56
Trails 132km/82 miles	
Green	29%
Blue	32%
Red	29%
Black	10%
Snowmaking 50 acres	
Recco detectors used	

Le Grand-Bornand

Altitude 1000m-2100m	
3,280ft-6,890ft	
Lifts	39
Trails 82km/51 miles	
Green	32%
Blue	36%
Red	26%
Black	6%
Snowmaking 99 acres	
Recco detectors used	

LIFT TICKETS

2000/01 prices in euros

Aravis ticket
Covers La Clusaz and Le Grand-Bornand
Main ticket
6 days 133 (116 low season)
Senior citizens
Over 60: 6 days 113
Over 75: free ticket
Children
Under 15: 6 days 102
Under 5: free ticket

La Clusaz ticket
All lifts in La Clusaz.
Main ticket
1-day ticket 24
6-day ticket 125
(low season 105)
Senior citizens
Over 60: 6-days 102
Over 75: free ticket
Children
Under 15: 6-days 91
Under 5: free ticket

Le Grand-Bornand ticket
All lifts in Le Grand-Bornand.
Main ticket
1-day ticket 22
6-day ticket 107
(low season 96)
Senior citizens
Over 60: 6 days 101
(low season 91)
Over 75: free ticket
Children
Under 16: 6 days 88
Under 5: free ticket

choice of typically French bars.

For much of the season La Clusaz is a quiet and peaceful place for a holiday. But in peak season and on weekends the place gets packed with French and Swiss families.

Le Grand-Bornand, covered by the Aravis lift ticket, is an even more charming village than La Clusaz, with even more sense that it remains a mountain community. This is partly because most of the development as a winter sports resort has gone on up the road at the satellite village of Le Chinaillon, which has been developed in chalet style. Le Grand-Bornand and La Clusaz are linked by a free 10-minute bus-ride and buses run every 30 minutes during the day – these become more erratic in peak time traffic. Le Grand-Bornand has quite extensive slopes and is well worth exploring for a day or two or considering as an alternative, quieter base.

If you are taking a car, you might also consider basing yourself at **St-Jean-de-Sixt** – a small hamlet midway between La Clusaz and Le Grand-Bornand, with a small slope nearby, mainly used for sledding.

The mountains

Like the village, the slopes at **La Clusaz** are rather spread out – which makes them all the more interesting (and scenic). There are five main areas, each connecting with at least one other. At **Le Grand-Bornand** the slopes spread out along the mountainside and can be accessed from either the village or Le Chinaillon up the road.

The Aravis ticket, covering the lifts of both resorts, costs very little more than the La Clusaz ticket, but is a fair bit more than the Grand-Bornand one.

THE SLOPES
Pretty and varied

Several points in **La Clusaz** have lifts giving access to the predominantly west- and north-west facing slopes of **L'Aiguille**. Links between this sector and the slightly higher and shadier slopes of **La Balme** area have improved massively in recent years: a long red and a black trail have replaced the off-trail route from L'Aiguille towards La Balme, and last season a new gondola opened in the opposite direction, taking you up from the base of La Balme to Cote 2000 on

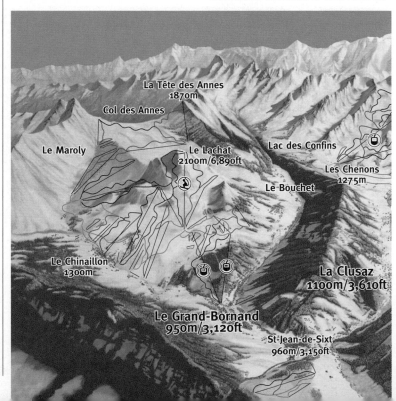

La Tête des Annes 1870m
Col des Annes
Le Maroly
Le Lachat 2100m/6,890ft
Lac des Confins
Les Chenons 1275m
Le Bouchet
Le Chinaillon 1300m
La Clusaz 1100m/3,610ft
Le Grand-Bornand 950m/3,120ft
St-Jean-de-Sixt 960m/3,150ft

L'Aiguille and cutting out the need to take a long, flat run back to La Clusaz. La Balme is a splendid, varied area with good lifts (a high-capacity gondola from the bottom linking to a quad chair); from the top there are wonderful views towards Mont Blanc.

Going the other way from L'Aiguille leads you to **L'Etale** via another choice of easy runs and the Transval tram, which shuttles people between the two areas. From the bottom of L'Etale, you can head back along another path to the village and the tram up to the fourth sector of **Beauregard** which, as the name implies, has splendid views and catches a lot of sunshine.

From the top of Beauregard you can link via another easy trail and a two-way chair-lift with the fifth area of **Manigod**. From here you can move on to L'Etale.

The main village at **Le Grand-Bornand** has two gondolas on the outskirts up to a gentle open area of easy runs (including beginner areas) lying between 1400m/4,600ft and 1500m/4,900ft. Chairs fan out above this point, one going up to the 2100m/6,890ft high point of **Le Lachat**, where there are serious red and black runs. Other lifts and runs go across the mountainside to the slopes above **Le Chinaillon** (1300m/4,270ft). Here there is a broad, open mountainside with a row of chairs and surface lifts serving blue and red slopes, and links to the rest of the domain – a wide area of blue and red runs.

SNOW RELIABILITY
Variable because of low altitude
Most of the runs are west- or north-west facing and tend to keep their snow fairly well, even though most of the area is below 2000m/6,500ft. The

boarding *Snowboarding is popular in La Clusaz, and although there are still a lot of surface-lifts, most are avoidable. There are some good beginner areas, served by chair-lifts, and great cruising runs to progress to. La Balme is a great natural playground for good free-riders. There's a terrain-park and a half-pipe on Aiguille and another in Le Grand-Bornand. During the week the resorts are fairly quiet, but La Clusaz livens up at the weekend.*

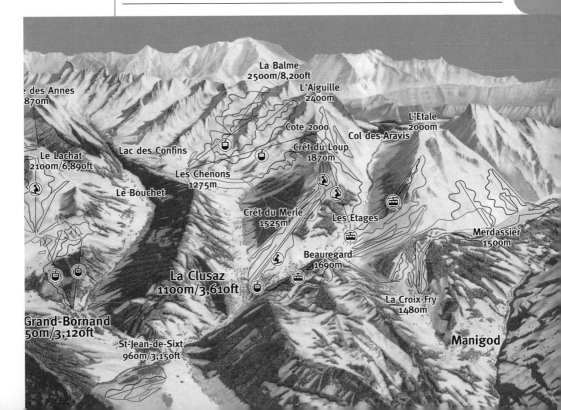

↑ Dramatic mountains and traditional chalet-style villages add up to an attractive resort
OT LA CLUSAZ / MP ROUGE-PULLON

best snow is usually on the north-west-facing slopes at La Balme, where a lift takes you up to 2500m/8,200ft. La Clusaz itself is at only 1100m/3,610ft and, in late season, the runs back can be dependent on artificial snow – of which there is now virtually blanket coverage. However, the long paths linking La Balme and l'Etale to the village are devoid of snow guns and can suffer from lack of snow. The main lifts to Beauregard and Crêt du Merle will carry people down as well as up. You can also ride the gondolas down to Le Grand-Bornand and the runs above Chinaillon have extensive snowmaking facilities.

FOR EXPERTS
Plenty to do, especially off-trail
The trail map doesn't seem to have a lot to offer experts, but the home resort of 1992 Olympic bumps champion Edgar Grospiron is not without challenges. Most of the sectors present off-trail variants to the trails, and there are more serious adventures to undertake – all the more attractive for being ignored by most visitors.

The best terrain is at La Balme, where there are several fairly challenging trails above mid-mountain. The black Vraille run, which leads to the speed skiing slope, is seriously steep. On the opposite side of the sector, the entirely off-trail Combe de Bellachat can be reached.

The Noire run down the face of Beauregard can be tricky in poor snow and is often closed. The Tetras on L'Etale and the Mur Edgar bumps run, below Crêt du Loup on L'Aiguille have been regraded as blacks, and rightly so. L'Aiguille has a good off-trail run down the neglected Combe de Borderan, and the trail map now shows the long new Lapiaz black run down the Combe de Fernuy – a continuation of the awkward black down from Cote 2000 to the parallel running Fernuy red.

In Le Grand-Bornand the steepest runs, including the black Noire du Lachat, go from the top of Le Lachat.

FOR INTERMEDIATES
Good if snow is good
Most intermediates will love La Clusaz if the snow conditions are good. Early intermediates will delight in the gentle slopes at the top of Beauregard and over on La Croix-Fry at Manigod, where there's a network of gentle tree-lined runs. And they'll be able to travel all over the area on the gentle, green linking trails, where poling or walking is more likely to be a problem than any fears about steepness.

SCHOOLS/GUIDES

2001/02 prices in euros

ESF

Classes 6 days
4hr: 9.30-11.30, 2.45-4.45
5 full days: 131
Children's classes
Ages: 5 to 12
5 full days: 119
Private lessons
Hourly
30 for 1 to 3 people;
42 for 4 or 5 people

Sno Academie
Classes
3½ hr a day
5 days: 116
Private Lessons
1 or 2 people:
2hr 58
3 or 4 people:
2hr 72

CHILDCARE

The ESF runs a ski kindergarten for children aged 5 to 12.

The two all-day kindergartens in La Clusaz operate 8.30 to 6pm. The Club des Mouflets (0450 326957) takes non-skiing children from 8 months to 4½ years. The Champions' Club (0450 326950) takes children 3½ to 6.

Le Grand-Bornand kindergarten takes children from 3 months.

GETTING THERE

Air Geneva, transfer 1½hr. Lyon, transfer 2½hr.

Phone numbers
From abroad use the prefix +33 and omit the initial '0' of the phone number.

L'Etale and L'Aiguille have more challenging but wide blue runs.

More adventurous intermediates will prefer the steeper red slopes and good snow of La Balme and the long linking red down the Combe du Fernuy from L'Aiguille.

Le Grand-Bornand is full of good cruising blue and red intermediate runs stretching in both directions above Le Chinaillon – well worth a visit for a day or two if you are staying in La Clusaz. Most visitors we hear from neglect Le Grand-Bornand and are missing out because of that.

FOR BEGINNERS
Splendid beginner slopes
There is a beginner area at village level at La Clusaz, and a couple of others just above it, but the best novice areas are up the mountain at the top of the Beauregard tram and at Crêt du Merle. The Beauregard area has lovely gentle blue runs to progress to, including one long run around the mountain right back to the village. There are also some greens at Le Grand-Bornand and St-Jean-de-Sixt.

FOR CROSS-COUNTRY
Excellent
The region has much better cross-country facilities than many resorts, with around 70km/40 miles of loops of varying difficulty. One good area is near the Lac des Confins, reached by bus. There's also a lovely sunny area at the top of the Beauregard tram. At Le Grand-Bornand there are extensive trails in the Vallée du Bouchet and towards Le Chinaillon. And there are further trails at St-Jean-de-Sixt.

LIFTLINES
Not a problem
Liftlines aren't a problem, except on peak weekends or if the lower slopes are shut because of snow shortage. The chair-lifts up the front face of L'Aiguille are the main weekend black spots – avoidable by taking other routes.

MOUNTAIN RESTAURANTS
High standard
Mountain restaurants are one of the area's strong points. There are lots of them and, for the most part, they are rustic and charming, and serve good, reasonably priced – often Savoyard – food. We have had excellent reports on the Télémark above the chair lift to

L'Etale and Les Chenons at the bottom of La Balme. There are several other good restaurants higher up in the Aiguille sector, of which the Bercail is said to be the best. Chez Arthur at Crêt du Merle has a calm little table-service restaurant tucked away behind the crowded self-service. The restaurant at Beauregard by the cross-country trail is sunny and peaceful, with good views. The Relais de L'Aiguille at Crêt du Loup and Le Neve at Le Rosay on Le Grand-Bornand are also recommended. The Vieille Ferme at Merdassier (see Eating out) is also open at lunchtime.

SCHOOLS AND GUIDES
Mixed reports
There are tales of large classes and poor instruction in ESF group lessons, but we've heard from some satisfied customers too – especially those who took private lessons. According to reports, the smaller Sno Academie – with smaller class sizes – is much more reliable.

FACILITIES FOR CHILDREN
Good – in theory
We have had mixed reports about the kindergarten in La Clusaz and none about those in Le Grand-Bornand. Generally, however, the resorts are places where families can feel at home.

Staying there

HOW TO GO
Good choice of hotels
Hotels Small, friendly 2-star family hotels are the mainstay of the area; luxury is not an option here.
《③ **Carlina** (0450 024348) A reporter says it's the best; central with pool and grounds.
《③ **Beauregard** (450 326800) Comfortable; on the fringe of the village. Pool. 'Fantastic for families, excellent food,' says a recent reporter.
《③ **Alp'Hôtel** (0450 024006) Comfortable modern chalet close to the center, with one of the better restaurants. Pool.
《③ **Alpen Roc** (0450 025896) Big but stylish, central and comfortable, although one reporter said his room was 'very cramped'. Pool.
《③ **Saytels** (0450 022016) Only 3-star in Le Grand-Bornand. Close to church.
《③ **Cimes** (0450 270038) 3-star in Le Chinaillon.
② **Aravis** (0450 026031) Traditional place with 'dated' rooms but 'great'

ACTIVITIES

Indoor Various hotels have saunas, massage, hot-tub, weights rooms, aerobics, sun beds and swimming pools

Outdoor Ice skating, paragliding, micro-light flights, snow-shoe excursions, ice carts, winter walks, horse-drawn carriage rides, quad-bikes, swimming pool.

TOURIST OFFICES

La Clusaz

Postcode 74220
t +33 450 326500
f 450 326501
infos@laclusaz.com
www.laclusaz.com

Le Grand-Bornand

Postcode 74450
t +33 450 027800
f 450 027801
infos@legrandbornand.
com
www.legrandbornand.
com

St-Jean-de-Sixt

Postcode 74450
t +33 450 027014
f 450 027878
infos@saintjeandesixt.
com
www.saintjeandesixt.
com

Vallées des Aravis

Postcode 74450
t +33 450 027874
f 450 023851
infos@aravis.com
www.aravis.com

OT LA CLUSAZ

Unlike so many French resorts, La Clusaz and Le Grand-Bornand retain the charm of being genuine mountain villages →

food, in la Clusaz center, close to lifts. ② **L'Alpage de Tante Pauline** (0450 026328) Dinky chalet at foot of L'Etale slopes (bus stop outside).

Apartments/condos There's quite a good choice, including fully equipped chalets as well as apartments. Some are out of town and best for those with a car.

EATING OUT
Good choice

There's a wide choice of restaurants, some a short drive away, including the Vieux Chalet, which is one of our favorites – good food and service in a splendid, creaky old chalet. It has a nice sunny terrace for a lunchtime blowout too. The St Joseph at the Alp'Hotel is regarded as the best restaurant in La Clusaz. L'Ecuelle is the place to go for Savoyard specialities. La Cordee and L'Outa are simple places giving great value for money. At the other end of the price scale is the more formal Symphonie restaurant in the hotel Beauregard – highly recommended by a recent reporter.

We're told some of the best food in the area is at the Ferme du Lormay in la Vallée du Bouchet, about 5km/3 miles on from Le Grand-Bornand. But another reporter rates the Vieille Ferme at Merdassier his favorite place in the Alps – an old farm building with 'serious food, classy staff, perfect atmosphere'. Le Foly, overlooking the Lac des Confins, is a firm favorite with both tourists and locals alike.

APRES-SKI
La Clusaz getting livelier

These resorts have always seemed to us typically quiet French family places, with the difference that La Clusaz is definitely the place to stay for a livelier time – especially on the weekend. Les Caves du Paccaly, in the center of La Clusaz, is a new place with woody decor and live music. Le Pressoir is a focal bar, popular for sports videos. Pub le Salto has draught Guinness. The Bali bar is a more French central recommendation. The Ecluse disco has a glass dance floor with a floodlit stream running beneath it. The Caffe Inn has DJs or live music, and Club 18 rocks, often with live bands.

OFF THE SLOPES
Some diversions

The villages are pleasant. It's easy for pedestrians to get around the valley by bus and to get up to several mountain restaurants for lunch. There are good walks along the valleys, and a day trip to the beautiful lakeside town of Annecy is possible.

STAYING UP THE MOUNTAIN
Cheap and panoramic

The Relais de l'Aiguille at Crêt du Loup has five adequate bedrooms that are about the cheapest in the resort. And there are no fewer than three places to stay at the top of Beauregard.

Courchevel 1300m-1850m/4,270ft-6,070ft

Gourmet skiing and boarding – and it needn't cost a fortune

HOW IT RATES

The slopes

Snow	****
Extent	*****
Experts	****
Intermediates	*****
Beginners	*****
Convenience	****
Liftlines	****
Restaurants	****

The rest

Scenery	***
Resort charm	**
Off-slope	***

➕ Extensive, varied local terrain to suit everyone from beginners to experts – plus the rest of the Three Valleys

➕ Great easy runs for near-beginners

➕ Lots of slope-side accommodations

➕ Impressive, continuously updated lift system, particularly above 1850

➕ Excellent trail maintenance, and widespread use of snowmaking guns

➕ Wooded setting is pretty, and useful in bad weather

➕ Choice of four very different villages

➕ Some great restaurants, and good après-ski by French standards

➖ Some trails get unpleasantly crowded (but they can be avoided)

➖ Rather soulless villages with intrusive traffic in places

➖ 1850 has some of the most expensive hotels, bars and mountain restaurants in the Alps (prices in the other villages are much lower)

➖ Losing a little of its very French feel as more and more overseas visitors discover its attractions

➖ Little to do away from the slopes (during the day, at least)

Courchevel 1850 – the highest of the five components of this big resort – is the favorite Alpine hangout of the Paris jet set, who fly directly in to the mini-airport in the middle of the slopes. Its top hotels and restaurants are among the best in the Alps, and the most expensive. But don't be put off: a holiday here doesn't have to cost a fortune (especially in the lower villages), the atmosphere is not particularly exclusive, and the slopes are excellent. Courchevel is the most extensive and varied sector of the whole Three Valleys, with everything from long gentle greens to steep couloirs. Many visitors never leave the Courchevel sector; but there is good access to the rest of the Three Valleys, too.

Le Praz is an overgrown, but still pleasant village, 1550 is quieter and good for families, 1650 has more of an old village atmosphere than it seems from the drive through, and the posh bits of 1850 are stylishly woody. But overall the resort is no beauty. Well, nothing's perfect. Courchevel's long list of merits is enough to attract more and more international visitors, but it remains much more French than Méribel, over the hill, as well as having better snow.

What's new

For 2001/02 a new high-speed six-seater chair will replace the long Pralong surface lift from the beginner slopes above 1850, speeding up the journey to 1650 and to La Vizelle via the high-speed Suisse chair. Another new high-speed six-pack will replace three surface lifts in 1650, making the journey to Signal and access to the underused red runs in that area from the 1850 area much quicker.

They are also adding to their grooming capacity with the aim of grooming two-thirds of all trails each night.

For 2000/01 the slow chair from Les Creux to La Vizelle was replaced by a high-speed six-seater and the start of the Creux Noir chair was moved up the mountain to avoid congestion at Les Creux and so that the lift serves only the steeper upper slopes of the red trail down.

The resort

Courchevel is made up of four varied villages, most known by their altitudes. A road winds up the hill, linking Le Praz (1300), 1550 and 1650 to 1850; free buses run between the villages.

1850 is the largest village, and the focal point of the area. It has the main lifts to the Three Valleys connections and most of the nightlife and shops. It's conspicuously upscale, with some very smooth hotels on the slopes just above the village center and among the trees of Jardin Alpin. There's also a spreading area of smart private chalets. However, the center of village is a bit of a messy sprawl.

While some readers 'couldn't afford a second week', others say, 'It's not as

upmarket as it's made out to be.' You can pay through the nose to eat, drink and stay, but more affordable places are not impossible to find.

The main road cuts through **1650** but there's also an attractive old village center, lively bars and quietly situated chalets. Its local slopes (whose main access is an escalator-served gondola) are relatively peaceful. 1650 isn't the most convenient base for the rest of the Three Valleys, but a day trip to Val-Thorens is well within reach, and 1650 is 'a pleasant start and end to the day'.

1550 is a quiet dormitory, a gondola ride from 1850. It has the advantage of having essentially the same position as 1850, with cheaper accommodations and restaurants. But it's a long trip to 1850 by road if you want to go there in

MOUNTAIN FACTS

For the Three Valleys

Altitude	1300m-3200m
	4,270ft-10,500ft
Lifts	200
Trails	600km/
	370 miles
Green	17%
Blue	34%
Red	37%
Black	12%
Snowmaking	90km/
	56 miles
Recco detectors used	

the evening. Some accommodations are a fair distance from the gondola.

Le Praz (or 1300) was once a traditional village set amid woodland. Still attractive, its charm has been undermined by expansion triggered by the 1992 Olympics, including the Olympic ski jump. It's quiet, 'excellent for children', with good links to 1850, and has tree-lined slopes on its doorstep for bad weather days. Near-beginners face rides down as well as up: the trails back to the village are red and black, and at this altitude snow conditions are often poor.

Champagny is an easy road outing, giving access to the La Plagne area.

The mountains

The local slopes are so well linked that Courchevel is essentially just one big network. The central 1850 area is suitable for all; wooded Le Praz suits experts best; while 1650 has mainly fairly easy slopes. Runs lead back to all the villages, but the runs to Le Praz are prone to close with lack of snow. Trail maintenance is superb and daily maps of which runs have been groomed overnight are available at major lift stations (a great idea which all American resorts adopt but which is very rare in Europe). Snowmaking guns are abundant and the major lifts are modern, fast and comfortable – though there are a number of ancient surface lifts, too. The area is also very well laid out. The main complaint we've had is that some slopes get busier than expected (but these can be avoided) and that the trail map is too small to

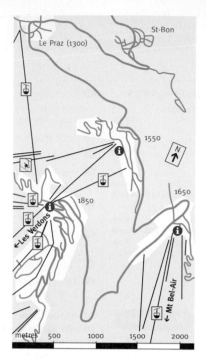

be clear (though it is cleverly designed to show the whole of the vast Three Valleys on one map).

Many reporters recommend buying only a Courchevel ticket ('I was still finding new runs after two weeks') and buying daily extensions when you want to try the rest of the Three Valleys.

THE SLOPES
Huge variety to suit everyone
A network of lifts and trails spreads out from **1850**, which is very much the focal

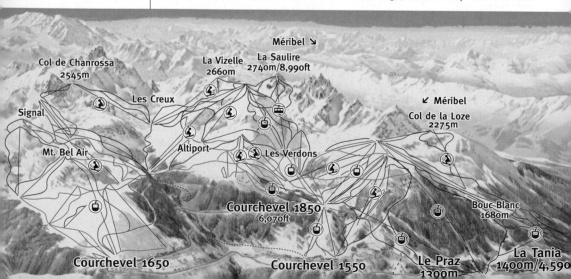

LIFT TICKETS

2001/02 prices in euros

Three Valleys
Covers all lifts in Courchevel, La Tania, Méribel, Val-Thorens, Les Menuires and St-Martin-de-Belleville.

Beginners 11 free lifts in the Courchevel valley.

Main ticket
1-day ticket 37
6-day ticket 182

Senior citizens
Over 60: 6-day ticket 146
Over 70: 6-day ticket 91
Over 75: free ticket

Children
Under 17: 6-day ticket 137
Under 10: 118
Under 5: free ticket

Short-term tickets
Half-day (from 12.30) for Courchevel valley (adult 23) and the Three Valleys (adult 28).

Notes 6-day ticket and over valid for one day each in Tignes-Val-d'Isère, La Plagne-Les Arcs, Pralognan-la-Vanoise and Les Saisies. Reductions for families.

Alternative tickets
Vallée de Courchevel ticket covers 67 lifts and 150km/93 miles of trail around Courchevel and La Tania (adult 6-day 148. One-day extension for Three Valleys, 17).

point of the area. The main axis is the Verdons gondola, leading to a second gondola to **La Vizelle** and a nearly parallel tram up to **La Saulire**. Both the high points give access to a wide range of intermediate and advanced terrain (including a number of couloirs), Méribel and all points to Val-Thorens. You can also get over to 1650 from here.

To the right looking up from 1850 the Chenus gondola goes towards a second departure point for Méribel, the **Col de la Loze**. Easy and intermediate runs go back to 1850, with more difficult runs in the woods above **La Tania** (see separate chapter) and **Le Praz** – splendid slopes when snow is in good supply.

To the left of the Verdons gondola is the Jardin Alpin gondola, which leads to some great beginner terrain, and serves the higher hotels and runs until 8pm. It also gives access to 1650.

1650 offers a good mix of beginner and intermediate slopes. Getting to and from Méribel and the rest of the Three Valleys involves slightly more effort than from the rest of Courchevel, since you have to go up and down another valley, but you can always catch the bus from 1850 if you run late on the way back.

SNOW RELIABILITY
Very good

The combination of Courchevel's orientation (its slopes are north- or north-east-facing), its height, an abundance of snowmaking guns and excellent trail maintenance usually guarantees good snow down to at least the 1850 and 1650 villages. On countless visits we have found that the snow is usually much better than in neighboring Méribel, whose slopes gets more direct sun.

FOR EXPERTS
Some black gems

There is plenty to interest experts, even without the rest of the Three Valleys.

The most obvious expert runs are the couloirs you can see on the right near the top of the Saulire tram. These used to be black trails (some of the steepest in Europe). But last season's trail map reclassified the Téléphérique (seriously narrow) and Emille Alais as itinéraires. The Grand Couloir is the widest and easiest and remains an official trail – but you have to traverse further along the narrow bumpy, precipitous access ridge to reach it.

There is a lot of steep terrain, on- and off-trail, on the shady slopes of La Vizelle, both towards Verdons and towards the link with 1650. Some of the reds on La Vizelle verge on black steepness and the black M trail is surprisingly little used. If you love bumps, don't miss the top of the black Suisses. Chanrossa, which comes towards 1850 from the top of 1650, is quite difficult – the off-trail just next to it is tougher. For a change of scene and a test of stamina, a couple of long (700m/2,300ft vertical), genuinely steep blacks cut through the trees down to Le Praz.

There is plenty of off-trail terrain to try with a guide and a bit of climbing – high, north-facing slopes right at the top of the 1650 sector, for example (the Vallée des Avals is a great run). Also ask about the mysterious Hidden Valley in 1650, and the huge bowl accessed from the Creux Noir chair.

La Saulire has some steep trails, and good off-trail routes →

↑ 1550 (foreground) is a short trip from 1850 (above it) by gondola or trail but a long trip by road

COURCHEVEL TOURIST OFFICE

CHILDCARE

There are kindergartens in 1850 (0479 080847) and 1650 (0479 083369) which take children from age 18 months, until 5pm. The ESF branches in all main parts of the resort have ski kindergartens.

FOR INTERMEDIATES
Paradise for all levels
The Three Valleys is the greatest intermediate playground in the world, but all grades of intermediates will love Courchevel's local slopes too.

Above 1650 novices have the wonderful long runs of Pyramide and Grand Bosses. Gentle blues such as Biollay in 1850 are fine, gentle slopes, leading to the two easy home runs on either side of the Jardin Alpin.

Those of average ability can handle most red runs without difficulty. Our favorite is the long, sweeping Combe de la Saulire from top to bottom of the tram. Very pleasant first thing, when it's well groomed and free of crowds, it's a different story at the end of the day – cut up snow and crowded. Creux, behind La Vizelle, is another splendid, fast long red (it gets bumpy though, and crowded with ski school groups). Marmottes from the top of Vizelle is quieter and more challenging.

The runs from Bouc Blanc through the trees towards La Tania are great – long, rolling cruises 'guaranteed to put a smile on your face'. The top of this section also has fine red runs down to 1850 and 1550, with easier blues alongside. Over at 1650, the reds on Mt Bel Air and Signal are excellent, if short, and usually quiet (though this may change with the new six-pack for 2001/02 – see What's new).

FOR BEGINNERS
Great graduation runs
There are excellent beginner areas above both 1650 and 1850. At the former, lessons are likely to begin on the short surface lifts close to the village, but quick learners will soon be able to go from close to the top of the 1650 area all the way down to the village. The best beginner area at 1850 is at Pralong, above the village, near the airstrip. A green path links this area with chairs to 1650, so adventurous novices have the opportunity to move far afield. The Bellecôte green run down into 1850 is an excellent, long, gentle slope – but does get crowded. It is served by the Jardin Alpin gondola, and a surface lift which is one of 13 free beginner lifts in Courchevel. 1550 and Le Praz have small beginner areas, but most people go up to 1850 for its more reliable snow.

FOR CROSS-COUNTRY
Long wooded trails
Courchevel has a total of 66km/41 miles of trails, the most in the Three Valleys. Le Praz is the most suitable village, with trails through the woods towards 1550, 1850 and Méribel. Given enough snow, there are also loops around the village.

LIFTLINES
There are always alternatives
Even at New Year and Easter, when 1850 in particular positively teems with people, lines are minimal, thanks to the excellence of the lift system. The Chenus, Verdons and Jardin Alpin gondolas have all had their capacity increased over the past few years, improving these old bottlenecks. However, as one reader points out, 'there can be a build-up at 1850 for the gondolas'. At such times 'it's best to avoid skiing back to 1850'. For example, try using the Plantrey chair, below 1850, or the Coqs chair, above it, to get over to Loze, Le Praz and La Tania. The Biollay chair is very popular with the ski school (who get priority) and can also

boarding *For an upmarket resort, Courchevel goes out of its way to attract boarders. There's a terrain-park and a half-pipe just below 1850 and the Verdons terrain park (all for skiers as well as boarders) just above 1850. Except above 1650, it's easy to get around the Three Valleys using chairs and gondolas. The big snowboard hangout is 'Prends ta luge et tire toi', a combined shop/bar/Internet cafe in the center of 1850.*

SCHOOLS/GUIDES

2000/01 prices in euros

ESF in 1850
Classes
6 full days:
Adults: 190
Children: 150
Children's classes
Ages: from 3
1 full day: 45
Private lessons
2½hr morning, 2hr lunchtime, 2½hr afternoon, 7hr full day
212 to 252 for full day.

ESF in 1650
Classes 6 days
6 full days: 125
Children's classes
Ages: from 3
Private lessons
9.15-4.45
244 for full day

ESF in 1550
Classes 6 days
Adults: 198
Children's classes
6 days, 183. Ages from 3 to 5

Ski Academie
Classes 5 days
2½hr: am
5 mornings: 115
Children's classes
Ages: from 4
5 mornings: 100

Ski Supreme 1850
2001/02 prices
Classes 12hr course
143
Children's classes
12hr course 135
Private lessons
1hr 55

New Generation
2000/01 prices in sterling

Classes 10 hr £90
Freeride clinic
7½hrs £85
Check Up clinic
4 hours £50
Private lessons
2 hours £75 for 1 to 2 people, £15 per additional person

Phone numbers
From abroad use the prefix +33 and omit the initial '0' of the phone number.

be worth avoiding. Lines for the huge Saulire tram have been all but eliminated by the upgrading of the parallel Vizelle gondola.

MOUNTAIN RESTAURANTS
Good but can be very expensive
Mountain restaurants are plentiful and pleasant by French standards, but it is sensible to check the prices and book for table-service restaurants.

The big Chalet de Pierres, on the Verdons trail just above 1850, is one of the highlights if you're inclined to extravagance – a comfortable, smooth place in traditional style, doing excellent food (including superb cakes) with high, high prices. Only a little way behind this for price comes the Cap Horn, near the airstrip. If you're feeling really flush, take a trip down to Bistrot du Praz at Le Praz for a blowout on a bad-weather day (treat yourself to the 'degustation de foie gras chaud'). The Bergerie on the Bellecôte trail is where the 'beautiful people' hang out.

For a good-value lunch above 1850 try the busy Altibar, with a fine terrace, good food and both self-service and table-service sections. The Verdons is well placed for trail-watching and La Soucoupe is an atmospheric self-service place, now with table-service upstairs too. The Panoramic at the top of Saulire was one of our favorites but was gutted by fire and closed for the 2000/01 season. Behind the main lift station at 1850 the Telemark terrace is a great suntrap, with good pizzas.

In 1650, Mont Bel-Air, at the top of the gondola, is our favorite Courchevel restaurant, with good food, friendly and efficient table-service, and a splendid tiered terrace. The Portetta hotel at the bottom has a good late-season sun terrace too. Down in 1550 try the Cortona – 'great pizza'.

SCHOOLS AND GUIDES
Size is everything
Courchevel's branches of the ESF add up to the largest ski school in Europe, with a total of almost 500 instructors. We've had bad reports on ESF 1850 in the past but this year a reporter says, 'They did a good job with a 17-year-old beginner in our party.' Another says, 'The jardin d'enfants of the ESF at 1850 was disorganised, with oversized classes and rude and arrogant staff. But our 7 and 10 year olds enjoyed their mainstream lessons.' A Bureau des Guides runs all-day excursions.

Ski Academie, an independent group of French instructors, was 'excellent for our 7 and 9 year olds,' says another reporter.

Supreme in 1850 is owned and staffed by British instructors and we've had good reports: 'Excellent. Our Scottish instructor was the best ever!'

New Generation is a school that started as Le Ski school in 1650, linked to the tour operator of the same name – but has now branched out into 1850 and Méribel too. It consists of highly qualified young British instructors committed to giving clients enjoyment as well as technique. We have nothing but rave reviews about them: 'Young and highly motivated. Adapt teaching to the clients' needs, not ski school dogma', 'I've taken five group classes now and not had a bad one ... this school is one reason I keep coming back to 1650', 'I did a check-up clinic (two afternoons) – very helpful, small group, personal attention, kept us busy'.

FACILITIES FOR CHILDREN
Bad report in 1850
There is a ski kindergarten in 1850 – but see comment under Schools.

Staying there

1850 is the swanky place, with the best hotels and chalets, the biggest choice of restaurants and nightlife and the jet set. 1650 is better value, 1550 is quiet and good for families. Le Praz is quiet and good value.

In all the resorts except Le Praz, there are lots of accommodations close to the lifts and runs. The prime place to stay is close to the main lift station at 1850, or on runs such as Bellecôte leading down to it.

HOW TO GO
Expensive in 1850
Hotels There are nearly 50 hotels in Courchevel, mostly at 1850 – including more 4-stars than anywhere else in France except Paris.

€€€€⑤ **Bellecôte** (1850) (0479 081019) Our favorite among the more swanky places – it offers some Alpine atmosphere as well as sheer luxury.

€€€€⑤ **Mélezin** (1850) (0479 080133) Superbly stylish and luxurious – and in an ideal position beside the bottom of the Bellecôte home slope.

€€€€⑤ **Carlina** (1850) (0479 080030) Luxury trail-side pad, next to Mélezin.

GETTING THERE

Air Geneva, transfer 3½hr. Lyon, transfer 3½hr. Chambéry, transfer 2½hr. Direct flights to Courchevel altiport from London at weekends only (contact tourist office for details). Also scheduled flights from Geneva to Courchevel.

Rail Moûtiers (24km/15 miles); transfer by bus or taxi.

ACTIVITIES

Indoor Artificial skating rink, climbing wall, bridge, chess, squash, swimming and saunas (hotels), gymnasium, health and fitness centers (swimming pools, sauna, steam-room, hot-tub, water therapy, weight-training, massage), bowling, exhibitions (galleries in 1850 and 1650), cinema, games rooms, billiards, language courses
Outdoor Hang-gliding, paragliding, flying lessons, parachuting, floodlit skiing, ski jumping, snow-shoe excursions, dog-sledding, snowmobile rides, 35km/22 miles cleared paths, 2km/1 mile toboggan run, curling, ice-climbing, flight excursions

TOURIST OFFICE

Postcode 73122
t +33 479 080029
f 479 081563
pro@courchevel.com
www.courchevel.com

((((⑤ **Byblos des Neiges** (1850) (0479 009800) Next to first stop on Jardin Alpin gondola; spacious public rooms, good pool, sauna, steam complex.
(((④ **Grandes Alpes** (1850) (0479 080335) On trail next to main lifts.
((((④ **Rond Point** (1850) (0479 080433) Family atmosphere, central position.
(((③ **Croisette** (1850) (0479 080900) Next to main lifts; recently refurbished. It contains the popular Le Jump bar.
(((③ **Courcheneige** (1850) (0479 080259) Pleasantly informal chalet in quiet position on the trail above the resort, with popular lunchtime terrace.
(((③ **Ducs de Savoie** (1850) (0479 080300) Pleasant, wood-built; well placed for skiing to the door, but only five minutes' walk from center.
(((③ **Sivoliere** (1850) (0479 080833) No beauty, but comfortable (though small lounge), pleasantly set among pines.
(((③ **Golf** (1650) (0479 009292) Rather impersonal 3-star, in a superb position on the trail next to the gondola.
(((③ **Ancolies** (1550) (0479 082766) 'A real find,' said a US visitor impressed by the friendly staff and excellent food.
((② **Edelweiss** (1650) (0479 082658) Simple, but 'great value', we're told.
((② **Peupliers** (1300) (0479 084147) Well placed and cheap by local standards.
Apartments/condos There's a large selection of apartments, though high-season dates can sell out early.

EATING OUT
Pick your price

There are a lot of good, very pricey French restaurants in Courchevel. Among the best, and priciest, are Le Chabichou (though a reporter calls it 'over-rated') and Le Bateau Ivre in 1850 – both with two Michelin stars. The 'friendly' Berçail also has a high reputation, notably for seafood. Other recommendations for Savoyard food include the cozy La Saulire (reservations essential) and La Fromagerie, the good-value L'Arbé, La Cloche ('good atmosphere') and Le Mazot – 'very traditional'. La Cendrée is a 'wonderful Italian'. The Smalto and Strada are good for pizza. Still in 1850, La Potinière does good, cheap pizzas, steaks and pasta. La Locomotive has a railway theme and a varied menu and Hotel Les Tovets has 'reasonable prices and delicious food'.

In 1550, L'Oeil du Boeuf is good for grills. La Cortona does good-value pizza.

In 1650 the Eterlou, Montagne and Le Petit Savoyard (all in the little square) do good traditional Savoyard food and cheaper pizza and pasta. In Le Praz, Bistrot du Praz is pricey but excellent – see 'Mountain restaurants'. Le Yaca is small and 'very French'.

APRES-SKI
1850 has most variety

If you want lots of nightlife, it's got to be 1850. But it doesn't have the same loud scene as Méribel complains one reporter. There are some exclusive nightclubs, such as La Grange and Les Caves, with top Paris cabaret acts and sky-high prices. The popular Kalico has DJs and cocktails and gets packed. The Bergerie does themed evenings – food, music, entertainment (but prices are high). The down-to-earth Bar L'Equipe seems to be readers' top nightspot.

Le Jump at the foot of the main slope is the place to be as the lifts close but it does get packed. El Gringo has theme nights. La Saulire (aka Jacques), Tee-Jay's and the cheap and cheerful Potinière are also popular.

Cinemas in 1850 and 1650 and La Tania sometimes show English-speaking films.

In 1650 Le Bubble is the hub, has satellite TV and internet access. Cheap bar prices, happy hour, strong Mutzig beer, with frequent live music it has a largely British clientele. Signal, on the main street, is quieter, has great views at the back and shuts at 9pm or so. Rocky's has satellite TV and loud music. Au Plouc is a tiny French bar. The Space Bar has pool, games and live music.

In 1550 the Chanrossa bar is British-dominated, with occasional live music, the Taverne 'French and friendly'.

OFF THE SLOPES
1850 isn't bad

The Forum sports center in 1850 includes a climbing wall in the shopping center – good for spectating too. There are a fair number of shops in 1850 and excellent markets at most levels. There's a fun ice-driving circuit and an ice-climbing structure. A pedestrian lift ticket for the gondolas and buses in Courchevel and Méribel make it easy for non-slope users to get around the area and meet companions for lunch on the slopes. And you can take joyrides from the altiport and try to spot friends below.

Les Deux-Alpes   1650m/5,410ft

Twin attractions of snow and fun

163

HOW IT RATES

The slopes

Snow	****
Extent	***
Experts	****
Intermediates	**
Beginners	***
Convenience	***
Liftlines	**
Restaurants	**

The rest

Scenery	****
Resort charm	**
Off-slope	**

What's new

The old Jandri 3 gondola from mid-mountain to the glacier was dismantled last season, putting extra pressure on the second stage of the Jandri express. A new eight-seater chair, to replace the original gondola, should be ready to relieve the resultant bottlenecks for 2001/02.

MOUNTAIN FACTS

Altitude 1300m-3570m
4,270ft-11,710ft

Lifts	58
Pistes	200km/ 124 miles
Green	24%
Blue	39%
Red	24%
Black	13%

Snowmaking 59 acres
Recco detectors used

- ➕ High, snow-sure slopes, including an extensive glacier area
- ➕ Varied high-mountain terrain, from freeway cruising to seriously steep blacks and off-trail slopes
- ➕ Efficient, modern lift system
- ➕ Excellent, sunny beginner areas
- ➕ Stunning views of the Ecrins peaks
- ➕ Lively, varied nightlife
- ➕ Wide choice of hotels

- ➖ Trail network modest by big French resort standards (we're sceptical about the claimed 200km/125 miles) and badly congested in places
- ➖ Only one easy run back home – a crowded zig-zag path; others are red or black, and often ruined by sun
- ➖ Virtually no woodland runs
- ➖ Spread-out, traffic-choked resort
- ➖ Few appealing mountain restaurants

We have a love–hate relationship with Les Deux-Alpes. We quite like the buzz of the town – arriving here is a bit like driving into Las Vegas from the Nevada desert – and we understand the appeal of its vibrant nightlife. We love the high-Alpine feel of its main mountain, and the good snow to be found on the north-facing runs in the middle of the mountain. But we're very unimpressed by the extent of those slopes, and we hate the trail congestion that results from most of the town's 35,000 visitors are crammed on to them. Crowding apart, keen intermediates spoiled by high-mileage French mega-resorts (and not up to the excellent off-trail) will simply find the usable area of slopes rather small.

The resort

Les Deux-Alpes is a narrow village sitting on a high, remote col. Access is from the Grenoble-Briançon road to the north or by gondola from Venosc. The village is a long, sprawling collection of hotels, apartments, bars and shops, most lining the busy main street and the parallel street that completes the one-way traffic system. Although there is no center as such, and lifts are spread fairly evenly along the village, a couple of focal points are evident.

The resort has grown haphazardly over the years, and there is a wide range of building styles, from old chalets through monstrous 1960s blocks to more sympathetic recent developments. France does have worse-looking resorts, though not many. Fans point out that it looks better as you drive out than as you drive in, because all the apartment buildings have their balconies facing the remote southern end of the resort. The lively ambience helps to distract you from the look of the place.

Alpe de Venosc, at the southern end of town, has many of the nightspots and hotels, the most character, the fewest cars, the best shops and the

Diable gondola up to the tough terrain around Tête Moute. More generally useful is the Jandri Express from the middle of the resort, where there is a popular outdoor ice rink and some good restaurants and bars. The village straggles north from here, becoming less convenient the further you go.

The free shuttle-bus service saves on some very long walks from one end of town to the other.

The six-day ticket covers a day in

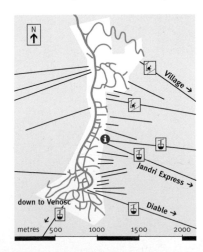

each of Alpe-d'Huez, Serre-Chevalier, Puy-St-Vincent and the Milky Way resorts from Montgenèvre to Sauze d'Oulx. All are easily reached by car, road conditions permitting. Helicopter trips to Alpe-d'Huez are good value at around 55 euros for a return trip. One recent reporter describes it as a 'must'. More economical is the shuttle-bus service on Wednesdays (15 euros for the round trip).

The mountains

For a big resort, Les Deux-Alpes has a disappointingly small trail area, despite recent improvements. Although extremely long and tall (it rises almost 2000m/6,560ft) the main sector is also very narrow, with just a few runs on the upper part of the mountain, served by a few long, efficient lifts.

THE SLOPES
Long, narrow and fragmented
The western **Pied Moutet** side of Les Deux-Alpes is relatively little-used, although recent improvements in the lift system and more snowmaking have helped to entice more people to the area. It is served by lifts from various parts of town but reaches only 2100m/6,890ft. As well as the short runs back to town which get the morning sun, there's an attractive,

longer north-facing red run down through the trees to the small village of Bons. This is one of only two tree-lined runs in Les Deux-Alpes – the other going down to another low village, Mont-de-Lans, and reachable from either sector.

On the eastern side of the resort, the broad, steep slope immediately above it offers a series of relatively short, challenging runs, down to the beginner areas ranged at the bottom. Most of these runs are classified as black, and rightly so: they aren't groomed and are usually bump-ridden, and often icy when not softened by the afternoon sun. As a result, many visitors are forced to take the gondolas or the long winding green back down in order to avoid the tricky home runs.

The ridge of **Les Crêtes** above the village has lifts and gentle runs along it, and behind it lies the deep, steep Combe de Thuit. Lifts span the combe to the main mid-mountain station at 2600m/8,530ft, at the foot of the slopes on **La Toura**. The middle section of the mountain, above and below this point, is made up primarily of blue cruising runs and is very narrow. At one point, there is essentially just a single run down the mountain – a broad ledge skirting the Combe de Thuit back to Les Crêtes. There is also the alternative of taking the

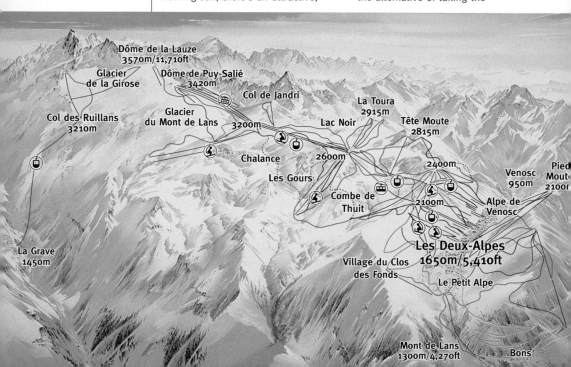

Dôme de la Lauze 3570m/11,710ft
Glacier de la Girose
Dôme de Puy-Salié 3420m
Col de Jandri
La Toura 2915m
Glacier du Mont de Lans 3200m
Lac Noir
Tête Moute 2815m
Col des Ruillans 3210m
Chalance
2600m
Les Gours
2400m
Venosc 950m
Pied Mout 2100r
Combe de Thuit
2100m
Alpe de Venosc
La Grave 1450m
Les Deux-Alpes 1650m/5,410ft
Village du Clos des Fonds
Le Petit Alpe
Mont de Lans 1300m/4,270ft
Bons

LIFT TICKETS

2001/02 prices in euros

Super ski ticket
Covers all lifts in Les Deux-Alpes, entry to swimming pool and skating rink.
Beginners 4 free lifts
Main ticket
1-day ticket 31
6-day ticket 150
(low season 135)
Senior citizens
Over 60: 6-day ticket 113 (low season 101)
Over 75: free ticket
Children
Under 13: 6-day ticket 113 (low season 101)
Under 5: free ticket
Short-term ticket
Half day tickets available.
Notes 6-day ticket includes one day's skiing in Alpe-d'Huez, Serre-Chevalier, Puy-St-Vincent and the Milky Way.
Alternative tickets
2 limited area tickets: 'Ski sympa' covers 21 lifts (15 per day), 'Grand ski' covers 32 lifts (25 per day). Les 2 Alpes/La Grave (39 per day) or an 8 euro supplement for this with a two-day or longer ticket.

roundabout (ie partly flat) blue Gours run to the bottom of the combe, where a chair-lift takes you up to Les Crêtes. This pleasant run passes the base of the Fée chair, serving an isolated (and neglected) black run.

The top **Glacier du Mont de Lans** section, served by surface lifts and the warmer underground funicular, has some fine, very easy runs which afford great views and are ideal for beginners and the less adventurous. You can go from the top here all the way down to Mont-de-Lans – a descent of 2268m/7,440ft vertical which, as far as we know, is the world's biggest on-trail vertical. A walk (or snowcat tow) in the opposite direction takes you over to the splendid La Grave area (a supplement is charged for the lifts).

SNOW RELIABILITY
Excellent on higher slopes

The snow on the higher slopes is normally very good, even in a poor winter – one of the main reasons for Les Deux-Alpes' popularity. Above 2200m/7,220ft most of the runs are north-facing, and the top glacier section guarantees good snow. You should worry more about bad weather shutting the lifts, or extremely low temperatures at the top, than about snow shortage. But the runs just above the village face west, so they get a lot of afternoon sun and can be icy at the beginning and end of the day. Snowmaking on some of the lower slopes helps keep them usable.

FOR EXPERTS
Off-trail is the main attraction

With good snow and weather conditions, the area offers wonderful off-trail sport. There are several good off-trail runs within the lift network, including a number of variations from underneath the top stage of the Jandri Express down to the Thuit chair-lift. The best-known ones are marked on the trail map. The Fée chair built a few years ago opened up new off-trail possibilities into the Combe de Thuit. There are also more serious routes that end well outside the lift network, with verticals of over 2000m/6,560ft.

The Super Diable chair-lift, from the top of the Diable gondola, serves the steepest black run around. The brave can also try off-trail variations here between the rocks.

If the conditions are right, an outing across the glacier to the largely off-trail slopes of La Grave is a must.

FOR INTERMEDIATES
Limited cruising

Les Deux-Alpes can disappoint keen intermediates. A lot of the runs are either rather tough – some of the blues could be reds – or boringly bland. The steep runs just above the resort put off many. As one of our reporters (who classes himself as an 'advanced' skier) said, 'I myself fell from top to bottom.

OT LES DEUX-ALPES

It's a long, long town, and ideally you don't want to be stuck out at the northern (right-hand) end ↓

SCHOOLS/GUIDES

2000/01 prices in euros

ESF
Classes 6 days
2¾hr am or pm
6 mornings: 115
Children's classes
Ages: 6 to 12
6 mornings: 96
Private lessons
2hr over lunchtime or full day Sunday
29 for 1hr, for 1 to 3 people

International St-Christophe
Classes 6 days
2½hr am or pm
6 mornings: 109
Children's classes
Ages: 6 to 12
6 mornings: 86
Private lessons
1hr over lunchtime
30 for 1hr, for 1 to 4 people

European Ski School
Classes 6 days
2hr am or pm
Children's classes
Private lessons

CHILDCARE

Both ski schools run kindergartens on more-or-less identical terms – taking children aged 4 to 6 until 5pm. The ESF (0476 792121) is slightly more expensive and does lunch only on request, but starts at 9.15, whereas the ESI de St Christophe (0476 790421) starts at 9.30. The Crèche du Village offers an excellent service for babies from 6 months to 2 years, from 8.30 to 5.30.
The Garderie du Bonhomme de Neige is for children aged 2 to 6 years.
A list of babysitters is available from the tourist office.

I was lucky. A girl in a different group broke her back. You cannot afford to be complacent here.'

The runs higher up generally have good snow, and aggressive intermediates can enjoy great fast cruising, especially on the mainly north-facing trails served by the chair-lifts off to the sides. You can often pick gentle or steeper terrain in these bowls as you wish, but avid trail-bashers will explore all there is to offer in a couple of days. Many visitors take the opportunity of excursions to Alpe-d'Huez and Serre-Chevalier.

Less confident intermediates will love the quality of the snow and the gentleness of most of the runs on the upper mountain. Their problem might lie in finding the trails too crowded, especially if snow is poor in other resorts and people are bussed in. At the end of the day, you can ride the Jandri Express down or take the long winding green back to town.

FOR BEGINNERS
Good slopes
The beginner areas beside the village are spacious and gentle. The run along the ridge above them is excellent, too. The glacier also has a fine array of very easy slopes – but bear in mind that bad weather can close the lifts.

FOR CROSS-COUNTRY
Needs very low-altitude snow
There are three small, widely dispersed areas. La Petite Alpe, near the entrance to the village, has a couple of snow-sure but very short trails. Given good snow, Venosc (950m/3,120ft), reached by a gondola down, has the only worthwhile picturesque ones. Total trail distance is 20km/12 miles. You can ski the Mont de Lans glacier with a qualified guide.

LIFTLINES
Can be a problem
Les Deux-Alpes has a great deal of hardware to keep liftlines minimal. But the village is large, and lines at the mid-morning peak can be 'diabolically' long for the Jandri Express and Diable gondolas. The Jandri liftline moves quickly and the new eight-seater chair from the mid-station to the glacier should get rid of the bottleneck for the second stage. Problems can also occur when people are bussed in when snow is in short supply. The top lifts are prone to closure if it's windy, putting pressure on the lower lifts. A recent visitor reported lines for the gondolas back to the village when large numbers of people declined to tackle the tricky blacks or the crowded green run back down. The narrow mid-section of the mountain, particularly the Grand Nord blue run, is a real bottleneck late in the day.

MOUNTAIN RESTAURANTS
On the up
There are mountain restaurants at all the major lift junctions, but they are generally pretty poor. La Pastorale, at the top of the Diable gondola, was for years the only recommendable place. But a few years ago the choice was doubled by the construction of the splendid Chalet de la Toura, in the middle of the domain at about 2600m/8,530ft, with a big terrace, a welcoming woody interior and efficient, if somewhat expensive, table-service. The Panoramic has been recommended.

SCHOOLS AND GUIDES
One of the better ESFs
The ski schools have a fairly good reputation for their lessons and English, although class sizes can be

boarding *Les Deux-Alpes has been catering to snowboarders for years, and has built up an excellent reputation. There's a specialist school and lots of boarder-friendly facilities. There's a terrain park with a boarder-cross, a half-pipe, music and a barbecue higher up the mountain in the Toura sector, where most of the lifts are chairs. This is relocated up to the glacier in the summer (access is by T-bar or funicular), which is where the Mondial du Snowboard competition is hosted each year. There's even a kids' park and the ESF offer freestyle classes, using trampolines and a huge air-bag to practice on. There's some great off-trail in the local area for free-riders and the link to La Grave offers some of the best off-trail terrain in the world for advanced riders – a guide is recommended. With cheap and plentiful accommodations, and noisy, lively nightlife in the bars and discos, it's a well-deserved reputation.*

GETTING THERE

Air Lyon, transfer 3½hr. Grenoble, transfer 2hr. Chambéry, transfer 3hr. Geneva, transfer 4½hr.

Rail Grenoble (70km/43 miles); 4 daily buses from station.

Phone numbers From abroad use the prefix +33 and omit the initial '0' of the phone number.

ACTIVITIES

Indoor 2 sports centers; Club Forme (squash, swimming pool, sauna, hot-tub), Tanking Center (flotation chambers, physiotherapy, pressotherapy, sauna, hot-tub, Turkish baths)

Outdoor Ice skating, swimming pool, ice driving lessons, ice gliders (dodgems), snow-shoe excursions

TOURIST OFFICE

Postcode 38860
t +33 476 792200
f 476 790138
les2alp@les2alpes.com
www.les2alpes.com

large. A recent report claims the European school was 'not very helpful'. There are several specialist courses available, as well as off-trail tours and trips to other resorts.

FACILITIES FOR CHILDREN
Fine for babies
Babies from six months to two years old can safely be entrusted to the village nursery. The kindergarten takes kids from two to six years. There are also four free T-bars for children at the village level.

Staying there

HOW TO GO
Stay at a hotel
Hotels There are over 30 hotels, of which the majority are 2-star or below.
《③ **Bérangère** (0476 792411) Most upscale in town, although dreary to look at, with an excellent restaurant and pool; on-trail, at less convenient north end of resort.
《② **Mariande** (0476 805060) Highly recommended, especially for its 'excellent' five-course dinners. At Venosc end of resort.
《② **Chalet Mounier** (0476 805690) Smartly modernized. Good reputation for its food, and well placed for the Diable bubble and nightlife.
《② **Souleil'or** (0476 792469) Looks like a lift station, but pleasant and comfortable, and well placed for the Jandri Express gondola. The rooms and food are reportedly 'fantastic'.
《② **Brunerie** (0476 792223) 'Basic and cheerful', large 2-star with plenty of parking and quite well positioned.
Apartments/condos Many of the apartments are stuck out at the north end of the resort – well worth avoiding.

EATING OUT
Plenty of choice
The hotel Bérangère has an excellent restaurant and the Chalet Mounier has a good reputation. La Petite Marmite has good food and atmosphere at reasonable prices. Bel'Auberge does classic French and is 'quite superb' – advance booking is advised. La Patate, Le Dahu and Crêpes à Gogo are also recommended. Visitors on a budget can get a relatively cheap Italian meal at either La Vetrata or La Spaghetteria.

APRES-SKI
Unsophisticated fun
Les Deux-Alpes is one of the liveliest of French resorts, with plenty of bars, several of which stay open until the early hours. The Rodéo has a mechanical bucking bronco which attracts great numbers of rowdy après-skiers. Mike's and the Windsor are other noisy enclaves. Corrigans, Smokey Joe's and Le Baron are recommended. Bar Brésilien has 'great music and tremendous atmosphere – teeming with Brits and Italians'. The Avalanche is the most popular of the discos. There are quieter places too – the 'cozy' Bleuets is recommended.

The resort has contrived a couple of ways of dining at altitude – you can snowmobile to the glacier and back, eating on the way (you're allowed one glass of wine), or at full moon you can ski or board back to town after dinner (accompanied by ski patrollers).

OFF THE SLOPES
Not recommended
Les Deux-Alpes is not a particularly good choice for people not hitting the slopes. It is quiet during the day, the shopping is uninspiring and the village is rather cut off, with little public transport for excursions. The pretty valley village of Venosc is well worth a visit by gondola, and you can take a scenic helicopter flight to Alpe-d'Huez (though there's even less to amuse you there). For the active there are plenty of sports facilities (including a 'very good pool') and lots of scenic walks. Several of the mountain restaurants are accessible to pedestrians – a good thing, as skiers and boarders will be very reluctant to descend the icy lower slopes to the village for lunch. Snowcat tours across the glacier provide wonderful views.

STAYING DOWN THE VALLEY
Worth considering
Close to the foot of the final ascent to Les Deux-Alpes are two near-ideal places for anyone thinking of traveling around to Alpe-d'Huez, La Grave and Serre-Chevalier, both Logis de France – the cheerful Cassini (0476 800410) at Le Freney, and the even more appealing Panoramique (0476 800625), at Mizoën.

Flaine

Wonderful ski area; bleak buildings but cute alternatives

HOW IT RATES

The slopes

Snow	****
Extent	****
Experts	****
Intermediates	*****
Beginners	*****
Convenience	*****
Liftlines	****
Restaurants	**

The rest

Scenery	****
Resort charm	*
Off-slope	*

➕ Big, varied area, with off-trail challenges for experts as well as extensive intermediate terrain

➕ Huge recent investment in new lifts

➕ Reliable snow in the main bowl

➕ Compact, convenient, mainly car-free village, right on the slopes

➕ Alternative of staying in traditional villages elsewhere in ski area

➕ Excellent facilities for children

➕ Scenic setting, and glorious views

➕ Very close to Geneva airport

➖ Bleak 1960s Bauhaus buildings are architecturally listed – but not to everyone's taste

➖ Main Flaine bowl has only a few short runs below the tree line, so bad weather can be a problem

➖ Links from one area to another are prone to closure by high winds

➖ No proper hotels in Flaine itself – only club hotels and apartments

➖ Not much nightlife

➖ Little to do off the slopes

So long as you don't care about the uncompromising architecture or narrow range of nightlife, Flaine has a lot going for it. It has slopes that intermediates will love, and lots of them – the area deservedly calls itself the Grand Massif and is the third biggest area of linked slopes in France. It also caters well to beginners, with free access to beginner area lifts – and the ski school has improved in recent years too. There is also challenging terrain for experts – particularly for those prepared to take guidance and go off-trail. Many visitors, especially those with children, love it.

The hotels have now all become club hotels run by tour operators. The only alternative is to rent an apartment. But we increasingly receive reports from satisfied guests who choose to stay in the more traditional outlying villages such as Samoëns, Morillon and Les Carroz. The only problems are that these lower villages may suffer poor snow conditions and that links with the high Flaine bowl may be cut off in bad weather.

What's new

For 2001/02, a new eight-seater gondola – the Grand Massif Express – will take you from Samoëns village to Samoëns 1600 in just eight minutes. This will greatly increase the attraction of Samoëns as a base because the lift into the slopes will no longer be a bus- or car-ride away.

A new high-speed quad from Morillon 1100 will serve the the Bergin run.

There will also be a new footpath between Flaine Forêt and Flaine Forum.

Over the last few years there has been huge investment in new high-speed lifts, including France's first high-speed eight-seater chair from the village at Flaine Forêt to Les Grands Vans for 2000/01.

In the longer term, there may be a new village development by Canadian company Intrawest at Vernant or close to the nearby lake.

The resort

We have to say we fall in the group that does not find Bauhaus architecture attractive. The concrete massifs that are Flaine's buildings were conceived in the sixties as 'an example of the application of the principle of shadow and light'. They look particularly shocking from the approach road – a mass of blocks nestling at the bottom of the impressive snowy bowl. From the slopes they are less obtrusive, blending into the rocky grey hillside. For us, the outdoor sculptures by Picasso, Vasarely and Dubuffet do little to improve Flaine's austere ambience.

In common with other French Alpine purpose-built resorts, Flaine has

PHOTOZOOM FLAINE

The scenic grandeur of Flaine's spectacular setting is quite a contrast to its stark Bauhaus architecture ➔

MOUNTAIN FACTS

Altitude 700m-2480m/
2,300ft-8,140ft

Lifts	75
Trails	260km/ 162 miles
Green	12%
Blue	41%
Red	38%
Black	9%
Snowmaking	25%
Recco detectors used	

LIFT TICKETS

2001/02 prices in euros

Grand Massif
Covers all the lifts in Flaine, Les Carroz, Morillon, Samoëns and Sixt.

Beginners Four free lifts. Ski ticket for beginners covers three more lifts (13 per day for adults, 9 for children aged 5-11, 10 for 12-15-year-olds).

Main ticket
1-day ticket 30
6-day ticket 151

Senior citizens
Over 60: 6-day ticket 127
Over 75: free ticket

Children
Under 12: 6-day ticket 110
Under 5: free ticket

Notes Discount on all ski-tickets for 12-15-year-olds: 6-day 119.

Alternative tickets
Flaine area only (1-day ticket 26 for adults, 21 for children)

Short-term tickets
A half-day Flaine area only from 11.30 costs 24 for adults, 19 for children aged 12-15 and 17 for those aged 5-11.

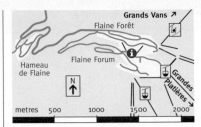

Grands Vans ↗
Flaine Forêt
Flaine Forum
Hameau de Flaine
Grandes Platières

metres 500 1000 1500 2000

improved its looks in recent years. The relatively new development of Hameau-de-Flaine is built in a much more attractive chalet style – but is inconveniently situated a good 15-minute walk or a short bus-ride from the slopes. Fortunately, the regular bus service is 'excellent'.

In Flaine proper, everything is close by: supermarket, sports rental shops, ski schools, main lifts out etc. The resort itself is also easy to get to – only 70km/43 miles from Geneva, and about 90 minutes from the airport.

There are two parts to the main resort. The club hotels, and some apartments, are set in the lower part, Forum. The focus of this area is a snow-covered square with buildings on three sides, the open fourth side blending with the slopes. Flaine Forêt, up the hillside and linked by lift, has its own bars and shops and most of the apartment accommodations.

There are children all over the place; they are catered for with play areas, and the resort is supposed to be traffic-free. This has become rather lax, in fact, and there is a fair amount of traffic; but the central Forum itself, leading to the trails, is pretty safe.

There are long-term plans to expand Flaine's bed base significantly. Intrawest (a Canadian company that owns Whistler and several other resorts with attractive villages) is now part owner of Flaine so let's hope they bring their flair for attractive village development to France.

It is possible to visit Chamonix by road, and get to Italy easily when the Mont Blanc tunnel is open.

The mountains

With its 260km/162 miles of trails, the Grand Massif claims to be the third largest resort in France (behind the Three Valleys and Espace Killy – the Franco- Swiss Portes du Soleil doesn't count). Certainly it is a genuinely impressive area, with plenty of scope for any level of skier or boarder, provided you can get to all of it – the greater part of the domain lies outside the main Flaine bowl and there are some fairly low altitude slopes.

THE SLOPES
A big white playground
The day begins for most people at the **Grandes Platières** jumbo gondola, which speeds you in a single stage up the north face of the Flaine bowl to the high-point of the Grand Massif, and a magnificent view of Mont Blanc.

Most of the runs are reds (though there are some blues curling away to the right as you look down the mountain, and one direct black). There are essentially four or five main ways down the barren, treeless, rolling terrain back to Flaine, or to chairs in the middle of the wilderness going back to the summit.

On the far right, the easy 14km/9 mile, picturesque Cascades blue run (one of the longest in the Alps) leads away from the lift system behind the Tête Pelouse and down to the outskirts of Sixt at 770m/2,530ft (giving a vertical drop of over 1700m/5,580ft). There is no lift back but there is a regular shuttle-bus service to the lifts at Samoëns or Morillon. Sixt has its own little west-facing area offering red and black slopes of 700m/2,300ft vertical – and is now linked to the Cascades run by surface lift.

On the other side of the Tête Pelouse, a broad cat-walk leads to the experts-only **Gers** bowl. At the bottom, a flat trail links with the Cascades run.

Back at Platières, the alternative is

boarding *Flaine suits boarders quite well – there's lots of varied terrain and plenty of off-trail with interesting nooks and crannies, including woods outside the main bowl. The key lifts are all now chairs or gondolas – with few unavoidable surface lifts. There's a big terrain park (called the JAM Park – standing for Jib and Air Maniacs) just below Les Grands Vans. The ESF runs a special 'Mini surf park' for kids, a great idea for a family-oriented resort like this. BlackSide is the local specialist shop, in the central Forum.*

↑The Flaine bowl seen from the approach road above

PHOTOZOOM FLAINE

to head left down the long red Méphisto (many of the runs in this area have diabolic names – Lucifer, Belzebuth etc) to the **Aujon** area. This opens up another sector of the bowl, again mostly red runs but with some blues further down. The lower slopes here are used as slalom courses. This sector is also reachable by gondola or surface lifts from below the resort.

The trails in the Flaine bowl are mostly punchy medium-length runs. For a collection of longer cruises, head out of the bowl via the Grands Vans chair (a new high-speed eight-seater for 2000/01), reached from Forum by means of a slow bucket lift (aka télébenne). From the top, you go over the edge of the bowl and have a choice of three different resorts to head towards, each with its own lifts and runs. Getting around this bowl below Les Grands Vans was made much quicker a couple of years ago by three new high-speed chair-lifts.

The lie of the land hereabouts is complicated, and the trail map does not represent it clearly. In good snow there is a choice of blues and reds winding down to **Les Carroz** or **Morillon**, the latter with a half-way point at 1100m/3,610ft. While there is a choice of blue, red and black runs on the top section above **Samoëns 1600**, the runs below here to Vercland are challenging blacks and reds.

Arrival back in Flaine can cause a problem: some reporters have said that it's difficult to get between the top of the resort and Forum. The trick is to loop round away from the buildings and approach from under the gondola – or catch the bucket down.

This season we have had reports of lifts breaking down too often and being too easily closed because of high winds, cutting off links with the lower villages. The very clear trail signs have, however, been praised.

SNOW RELIABILITY
Usually keeps its whiteness
The main part of Flaine's slopes lie on the wide north- and north-west-facing flank of the Grandes Platières. Its direction, along with a decent height, means that it keeps the snow it receives. There is snowmaking on the greater part of the Aujon sector and on the beginner areas. The runs towards Samoëns 1600 and Morillon 1100 are north-facing too, and some lower parts have snowmaking, but below here can be tricky or impossible. The Les Carroz runs are west-facing and can suffer from strong afternoon sun, but one of the runs has snowmaking. Recent reports have indicated a marked improvement in grooming.

FOR EXPERTS
Great fun with guidance
Flaine's family-friendly reputation tends to obscure the fact that it has some seriously challenging terrain. But much of it is off-trail and, although some of Flaine's off-trail runs look like they can safely be explored without guidance, this impression is mistaken. The Flaine bowl is riddled with rock crevasses and potholes, and should be treated with the same caution that you would use on a glacier. There have been some tragic cases of off-trail skiers coming across nasty surprises, including a British skier falling to his death only

yards from the trail.

All the black trails on the map deserve their grading. The Diamant Noir, down the line of the main gondola, is a challenging 850m/2,790ft descent, tricky because of bumps, narrowness and other people rather than because of great steepness; the first pitch is the steepest, with spectators applauding from the overhead chair-lift.

To the left of the Diamant Noir as you look down are several short but steep off-trail routes through the crags of the Grandes Platières.

The Lindars Nord chair serves a shorter slope that often has the best snow in the area, and some seriously steep gradients if you look for them.

The Gers surface lift, outside the main bowl beyond Tête Pelouse, serves great expert-only terrain. The trail going down the right of the surface lift is a proper black, but by departing from it you can find slopes of up to 45°. To the left of the surface lift is the impressive main Gers bowl – a great horseshoe of about 550m/1,800ft vertical, powder or bumps top to bottom, all off-trail. You can choose your gradient, from steep to very steep. As you look down the bowl, you can see more adventurous ways into the bowl from the Grands Vans and Tête de Veret lifts.

There are further serious trails on the top lifts above Samoëns 1600.

Touring is a possibility behind the Grandes Platières, and there are some scenic off-trail routes from which you can be retrieved by helicopter – such as the Combe des Foges, next to Gers.

FOR INTERMEDIATES
Something for everyone

Flaine is ideal for confident intermediates, with a great variety of trails (and usually the bonus of good snow conditions, at least above Flaine itself). The diabolically named reds that dominate the Flaine bowl are not really as hellish as their names imply – they tend to gain their status from short steep sections rather than overall difficulty, and they're great for improving technique. There are gentler cruises from the top of the mountain – Cristal, taking you to the Perdrix chair, or Serpentine, all the way home. The blues at Aujon are excellent for confidence-building, but the drag serving them is not.

The connections with the slopes outside the main bowl are graded blue but at least one blue-run reporter has found them tricky. Once outside the

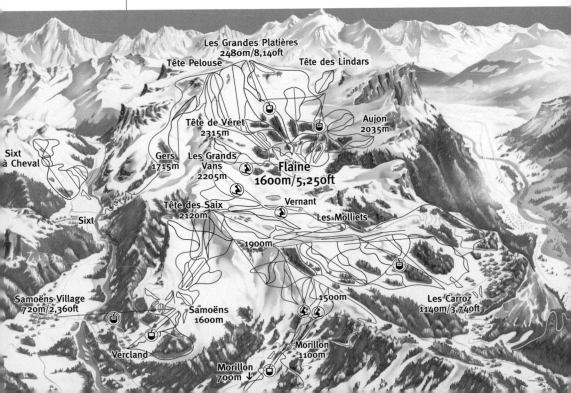

SCHOOLS/GUIDES

2001/02 prices in euros
International Classes 6 days
3hr per day
6 days 109
Children's classes
Ages: 6 to 12
6 days 86
Private lessons
1hr, 2hr or full day
30 for 1hr, for 1 to 2 people

ESF
2001/02 prices
Classes 6 days for 3hr per day
6 days: 105
Children's classes
Ages: 5 to 12
6 days 80
Private lessons
26 for 1hr, for 1 or 2 people

Flaine Super Ski
Advanced skiers only
0450 908288

Independent instructors
Rented by the day, hour or week;
contact Guy Pezet
0450 478454

CHILDCARE

Both schools operate ski kindergartens. The ESF's Rabbit Club (0450 908100) takes children aged 3 to 12, until 5pm. The SEI's Green Mouse Club (0450 908441) takes children aged 3 to 12, until 5pm. Club Med Flaine (0450 908166) has a nursery for babies aged from 4 months. The ESF's Rabbit Club will pick up children from Club Med for lessons, and deliver them at the end of the class. There is also an independent nursery, the Petits Loups (0450 908782) for children aged from 6 months to 4 years.

bowl, all intermediates will enjoy the long tree-lined runs down to Les Carroz, as long as the snow is good. The Morillon slopes are also excellent intermediate terrain.

FOR BEGINNERS
Very good
There are excellent beginner areas right by the village, served by free lifts which make a ticket unnecessary until you are ready to go higher up the mountain. There are no long green runs to progress to in the Flaine bowl – there is one above Morillon – but there are one or two gentle blues (see 'For intermediates').

CROSS-COUNTRY
Very fragmented
The Grand Massif claims 64km/40 miles of cross-country tracks but only about 10km/6 miles of that total is around Flaine itself. The majority is on the valley floor and dependent on low snow. There are extensive tracks between Morillon and Les Carroz, with some tough uphill sections. Samoëns 1600 has its own tracks and makes the best base for cross-country enthusiasts.

LIFTLINES
Few real problems
The massive recent investment in new lifts has eliminated the main trouble-spots. When the resort is full, the Grandes Platières gondola is prone to liftlines at the start of the day, but it is an efficient lift and the line moves quickly. Reporters say other liftlines are usually small, although some of the lifts are still somewhat antiquated, and the area does suffer a weekend influx because of its proximity to Geneva.

One reporter also said lines can be bad when the lifts out of the Flaine bowl are shut due to high winds or when the weather is warm and the lower resorts have poor snow.

MOUNTAIN RESTAURANTS
Back to base, or quit the bowl
In the Flaine bowl, there are few restaurants above the resort's upper outskirts. The Blanchot, at the bottom of the Serpentine run, is popular and rustic, with basic food, but it can get very crowded.

At Forum level, across the trail from the gondola, is a pair of chalets containing the welcoming Michet, with very good Savoyard food and table

service, and the self-service Eloge – friendly but with very limited food (lasagne and croque monsieurs recommended by one reporter). Up at Forêt level, Chalet Bissac has a good atmosphere, traditional decor and excellent plain food. The nearby Cascade is self-service, with a good terrace. The Chalet L'Epicéa near the end of the Faust trail has a rustic atmosphere, terrace and rave reviews (including 'Greek specialities').

Outside the Flaine bowl, we loved the remote Chalet du Lac de Gers (book in advance and call for a snowcat to tow you up from part way down the Cascades run) – simple food but splendid isolation and views of the frozen lake. Reporters recommend the Igloo above Morillon, the Chalet des Molliets beside the road up from Les Carroz and the Oreade at the top of the gondola from Les Carroz.

SCHOOLS AND GUIDES
Getting better
The few reports we've had in recent years on the ESF have been mixed. But this season reporters have praised the International school ('took time to assess people ... I would use them again') and the small specialist Super Ski school ('small class sizes, good instruction'). Nouvelle Dimension in Les Carroz and the ESF children's private lessons in Samoëns were both described as 'excellent'.

FACILITIES FOR CHILDREN
Parents' paradise?
Flaine prides itself on being a family resort, and the number of English-speaking children around is a bonus.

Club Med Flaine has good childcare facilities open to residents only. The Petits Loups nursery takes children from 6 months to 4 years. Some other accommodations have kids' clubs.

Staying there 🔑

As a purpose-built resort, Flaine is convenient regardless of where you stay, except in Hameau-de-Flaine.

HOW TO GO
Plenty of apartments
Accommodations are overwhelmingly in apartments.
Hotels There are no longer any normal hotels – you'll have to settle for a tour operator-run club hotel or go to one of the lower, more traditional villages.

GETTING THERE

Air Geneva, transfer 1½hr.

Rail Cluses (30km/19 miles); regular bus service.

ACTIVITIES

Indoor Top Form center (swimming pool complex with sauna, solarium, gymnasium, massage), arts and crafts gallery, cinema, auditorium, concerts, indoor climbing wall, cultural center with library (some books in English)

Outdoor Natural ice rink, snow-shoe excursions, hang-gliding, paragliding paraskiing, helicopter rides, snow scooters, high mountain outings, ice-driving car circuit

TOURIST OFFICE

Postcode 74300
t +33 450 908001
f 450 908626
flaine@laposte.fr
www.flaine.com

Phone numbers
From abroad use the prefix +33 and omit the initial 'o' of the phone number.

Apartments/condos The best apartments are out at Hameau. In Flaine Forêt, the recently renovated Forêt and Grand Massif apartment buildings are attractively woody inside and there are hotel facilities such as a restaurant, bar and kindergarten.

EATING OUT
Not many stars

The Perdrix Noire in Forêt is a good bet – smart, busy but friendly. Its bar is also popular. The Michet (see 'Mountain restaurants') is open in the evening. The Trattoria is a good Italian, Chez la Jeanne the best pizza restaurant. Chez Daniel offers a good range of Savoyard specialities, and has also been recommended for lunchtime crêpes and galettes. The Cîmes Rock is 'excellent, but it's best to go early because it gets very crowded' (see below).

APRES-SKI
Signs of life

Recent reports suggest that the après-ski scene is picking up. The resort is no longer limited to family groups, and some bars show signs of life.

The White Grouse pub is boisterous: extreme sports videos compete with rock music and punters trying to get pints in before the end of happy hour. Later, the more French Cîmes Rock is liveliest, with bands or karaoke. The 'seedy' Diamant Noir pool hall is open late, the Chaintre disco later.

OFF THE SLOPES
Curse of the purpose-built

As with most purpose-built resorts, there are few walks, and no town to explore. Not recommended for people who don't want to hit the slopes. But there is a great ice-driving circuit where you can take a spin (literally) in your own car or, more sensibly, have a lesson in theirs (as we did). Snowmobile tours and the weekly torchlight descent are popular, and there's a cinema, gymnasium and swimming pool.

Les Carroz 1140m/3,740ft

This is a spacious, sunny, traditional, family resort where life revolves around the village square with its sidewalk cafes and interesting little shops. It has a lived-in feel of a real French village, with more animation than Flaine – 'a delight' says a recent

visitor, who recommends the 3-star hotel Arbaron (0450 900267) for food, service and views. Also highly recommended is the 2-star Bois de la Char (0450 900618): 'It is perfectly situated beside the trail. The food was good, the staff friendly and it was excellent value for money.'

The gondola and chair-lift go straight into the Grand Massif area, but there's a steep 300m/98oft walk up from the center – the beginners' surface lift is a help.

Apartments make up a high percentage of the beds available.

The ski school's torchlit descent is apparently 'not to be missed' – it starts off with fireworks and ends with vin chaud and live jazz in the square.

Samoëns 720m/2,360ft

This is the only resort in France to be listed as a 'Monument Historique'. Medieval fountains, rustic old buildings, an ancient church – it's all there, although one recent reporter feels that it doesn't add up to a more charming village than Les Contamines, say. Despite the village's recent growth on the outskirts, the traditional-style bars and restaurants still give you a feel for 'real' rural France. A reporter recommends the Pizzeria Louisiana for its wood oven pizzas and 'highly alcoholic' ice creams. Another praises Chalet Fleurie ('five courses – 90 francs given 24 hours' notice') and Chardon Bleu, both a car-ride away in Verchaix.

A new gondola straight from village to the slopes should be open for the 2001/02 season, cutting out the need to take a bus to and from the lift. The local terrain is generally challenging and on the whole best suited to confident skiers – though there is a good beginners' area at Samoëns 1600.

Morillon 700m/2,300ft

Not quite in the Samoëns league, but still a pretty rustic village, Morillon makes an excellent base, with an efficient gondola (and a road) up to the mid-mountain mini-resort of Morillon 1100. Up here there is a large and 'delightful' ski kindergarten plus good slopes for adult beginners and brand new apartments right on the trail – it's 'dead as a dodo in the evenings', though, says a reporter.

La Grave

1450m/4,760ft

A superb mountain for good skiers and free-riders

➕ Legendary off-trail mountain

➕ Usually crowd-free

➕ Usually good snow conditions, with powder higher up

➕ Link to Les Deux-Alpes

➕ Good base for touring nearby resorts

➖ Rather drab, charmless village

➖ Poor weather spells regular lift closures – on average, two days per week

➖ Suitable for experts only, despite some easy slopes at altitude

➖ Nothing to do off the slopes

La Grave enjoys legendary status among experts. It's a quiet old village with around 500 visitor beds and just one serious lift – a small stop–start gondola serving a high, wild and predominantly off-trail mountainside. The result: an exciting, refreshingly crowd-free area. Strictly, you ought to have a guide, but in good weather hundreds of people risk it and go it alone. When the weather shuts the lift, you can head for Alpe-d'Huez, Les Deux-Alpes or Serre-Chevalier.

THE RESORT

La Grave is an unspoiled mountaineering village set on a steep hillside facing the impressive glaciers of majestic La Meije. It's rather drab, and the busy road through to Briançon doesn't help. But it still has a rustic feel, and prices in the handful of small hotels, food shops and bars are low by resort standards.

The village is small and most accommodation is convenient for the central lift station.

Storms close the slopes on average two days a week – so a car is useful for access to other resorts nearby.

THE MOUNTAIN

A slow two-stage 'pulse' gondola (with an extra station at a pylon halfway up the lower stage) ascends into the slopes and finishes at 3200m/10,500ft. Above that, a short walk and a surface lift give access to a second surface lift serving twin blue runs on a glacier slope of about 350m/1,150ft vertical – from here you can ski to Les Deux-Alpes. But the reason that people come here is to explore the legendary slopes back towards La Grave. These slopes offer no defined, patrolled, avalanche-protected trails – but there are two marked itinéraires (with several variations now indicated on the

← As well as fabulous views the refuge Chancel does a decent lunch, despite the fact that all ingredients and waste have to be backpacked in and out. Drop in during the morning to find out what's cooking and place your order.

What's new

La Grave does not change much, and that is half the charm of the place.

MOUNTAIN FACTS

Altitude 1400m-3550m
4,590ft-11,650ft
Lifts 4
Trails 5km/3 miles
Green/Blue 100%
The 'difficulty' figure relates to trails only; 90% of the slopes are off-trail
Snowmaking None
Recco detectors used

Phone numbers

From abroad use the prefix +33 and omit the initial '0'.

TOURIST OFFICE

Postcode 05320
t +33 476 799005
f 476 799165
ot.la.meije@wanadoo.fr
www.la.meije.com

'trail' map) of 1400m/4,590ft vertical down to the pylon lift station at 1800m/5,910ft. Top to bottom, the mountain offers a vertical of 2150m/7,050ft.

Slopes The Chancel route is mostly of red-run gradient; the Vallons de la Meije is more challenging but not too steep. People do take these routes without a guide or avalanche protection equipment, but we couldn't possibly recommend it.

There are many more demanding runs away from the itinéraires, including couloirs that range from the straightforward to the seriously hazardous, and long descents from the glacier to the valley road below the village, with return by cab, bus, or strategically parked car. The dangers are considerable, and guidance is essential. You can also descend southwards to St-Christoph, returning by bus and the lifts of Les Deux-Alpes.

Snow reliability The chances of powder snow on the high, north-facing slopes are good, but there are essentially no trails to fall back on if conditions are tricky. The biggest worry is poor weather keeping the mountain closed for several days at a time.

Experts La Grave's uncrowded off-trail slopes have earned it cult status among hard-core skiers. Only experts should contemplate a stay here – and then only if prepared to deal with bad

weather by sitting tight or struggling over the Col du Lautaret to the woods of Serre-Chevalier.

Intermediates The itinéraires get tracked into a trail-like state, and adventurous intermediates could tackle the Chancel. But the three blue runs at the top of the gondola won't keep anyone occupied for long. The valley stations of Villar d'Arène and Lautaret, around 3km/2 miles and 8km/5 miles to the east respectively, and Chazelet, 3km/2 miles to the north-west, offer very limited slopes with a handful of intermediate and beginner runs.

Beginners Novices tricked into coming here can go up the valley to the beginner slopes at Le Chazelet.

Snowboarding There are no special facilities for boarders, but advanced free-riders will be in their element on the open off-trail powder.

Cross-country There is a total of 30km/19 miles of loops in the area.

Liftlines There are short liftlines only at weekends – at the bottom station first thing, and at the mid-station later.

Mountain restaurants Surprisingly, there are three decent mountain restaurants; the best is the refuge on the Chancel itinéraire (see photo).

Schools and guides There are a dozen or so guides in the village, offering a wide range of services through their bureau.

Facilities for children Babysitting can be arranged through the tourist office.

STAYING THERE

How to go There are several simple hotels.

Hotels The Edelweiss (0476 799093) is a comfortable, friendly 2-star with a cozy bar and restaurant.

Apartments/condos Apartments can be booked through the tourist office.

Eating out Most people eat in their hotels, though there are alternatives.

Après-ski The standard tea-time après-ski gathering place is the central Glaciers bar, known to habitués as chez Marcel. O'Neill's Irish pub and Le Vieux Guide are crowded later. The Candy bar is another option.

Off the slopes Anyone not using the slopes will find La Grave much too small and quiet.

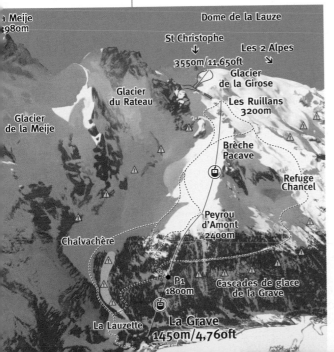

a Meije
3980m
Dome de la Lauze
St Christophe
↓
Les 2 Alpes
↘
3550m/11,650ft
Glacier de la Girose
Glacier du Rateau
Les Ruillans
3200m
Glacier de la Meije
Brèche Pacave
Refuge Chancel
Peyrou d'Amont
2400m
Chalvachère
P1
1800m
Cascades de glace de la Grave
La Lauzette
La Grave
1450m/4,760ft

Megève
1100m/3,610ft

One of the traditional old winter holiday towns

176

HOW IT RATES

The slopes

Snow	★★
Extent	★★★★★
Experts	★★
Intermediates	★★★★
Beginners	★★★
Convenience	★★
Liftlines	★★★★
Restaurants	★★★★★

The rest

Scenery	★★★
Resort charm	★★★★
Off-slope	★★★★

What's new

The resort has appointed fifty local representative ambassadors to provide visitors with information both on the slopes and around the village.

A new magic carpet lift was installed at the Princesse ski kindergarten.

Next season will see the introduction of a new hands-free lift pass system.

➕ Extensive slopes, with miles of easy trails, ideal for intermediates

➕ Scenic setting, with splendid views

➕ Charming old village center, with very swanky shopping

➕ Some lovely luxury hotels

➕ Gourmet mountain lunches in attractive surroundings

➕ Excellent cross-country trails, including some at altitude

➕ Different lift pass options cover other worthwhile resorts nearby

➕ Great for weekends – cooperative hotels and close to Geneva

➕ If it snows, deserted mountains

➕ Plenty to do off the slopes

➖ With most of the slopes below 2000m/6,560ft there's a risk of poor snow, especially on runs to the village – although the grassy terrain does not need a thick covering and snowmaking has improved a lot

➖ Three separate mountains, two linked by lift but not by trail and the third not linked at all

➖ Not many challenging trails – the few blacks are not extreme – but good off-trail potential

➖ Traffic jams and exhaust fumes at weekends and peak season

Megève is the essence of rustic chic. It has a medieval heart, but it was, in a way, the original purpose-built French ski resort – conceived in the 1920s as a French alternative to Switzerland's St Moritz. And although Courchevel took over as France's most fashionable winter sports resort ages ago, Megève's sumptuous hotels and chalets still attract plenty of 'beautiful people' with fur coats and fat wallets. Happily, you don't need either to enjoy it.

The risk of poor snow still makes us nervous about booking way ahead; but it is certainly true that a few inches of snow is enough to give skiable cover on the grassy slopes. And the list of plus-points above is as long as they come.

The resort

Megève is in a lovely sunny setting and has a beautifully preserved traditional medieval center, which is pedestrianised and comes complete with open-air ice rink, horse-drawn sleighs, cobbled streets and a fine church. Lots of upscale food, clothing, jewelry, and antique and gift shops add to the chic atmosphere.

The main Albertville–Chamonix road bypasses the center, and there are expensive underground parking lots. But the resort's clientele arrives mainly by car and the resulting traffic jams and exhaust fumes are a major problem. It's worst at weekends, but can be serious every afternoon in high season.

The clientele are mainly well-heeled French couples and families, who come here as much for an all-round winter holiday and for the people-watching

potential as for the slopes themselves. The nightlife is, as you'd expect, smart rather than lively.

A gondola within walking distance of central Megève gives direct access

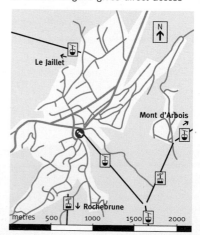

MOUNTAIN FACTS

Altitude	850m-2355m/ 2,790ft-7,730ft
Lifts	79
Trails	300km/ 186 miles
Green	17%
Blue	30%
Red	40%
Black	13%
Snowmaking 160 acres	
Recco detectors used	

LIFT PASSES

2000/01 prices in euros

Evasion Mont Blanc
Covers all lifts on Rochebrune, Mont d'Arbois, St-Gervais, Le Bettex, St-Nicolas, Le Jaillet, Combloux, Les Contamines and Bellevue.

Beginners Pay by the ride.

Main pass
1-day pass 29
6-day pass 136
(low season 121)

Senior citizens
Over 60: 6-day pass 121

Children
Under 13: 6-day pass 102
Under 5: free pass

Short-term passes
Half-day pass available in the afternoon.

Alternative passes
Mont Blanc pass covers all lifts in the resorts of the Mont Blanc area (700km/435 miles of trail and 190 lifts) and the buses between them, plus Courmayeur in Italy 6 days out of 6 (6 days 183 for adults and 128 for children). Jaco pass valid for Le Jaillet, Christomet and Combloux.

to one of the three mountains, Rochebrune. This sector can also be reached directly by a small tram from the southern edge of town. The main lifts for the bigger Mont d'Arbois sector start from an elevated suburb of the resort – though there is also a link from Rochebrune. The third sector, Le Jaillet, starts some way out on the north-west fringes of the town.

Staying close to one of the main lifts makes a lot of sense. Some accommodations are a long walk from the lifts and the free bus services are not super-convenient.

The mountains

The three different mountains provide predominantly easy intermediate cruising, much of it prettily set in the woods. But there are tough runs to be found, and large areas of off-trail that are neglected by most visitors. The wooded slopes make it a great resort to head for in poor weather.

There is a variety of different lift passes available, the widest-ranging covering Les Contamines, Les Houches

and Chamonix. A car is handy for visiting other resorts included on the various passes.

Plans to create a super ski area linking Megève, St-Gervais, Praz-sur-Arly, Nôtre-Dame-de-Bellecombe, Les Saisies, Flumet, Hauteluce and Crest-Voland, and eventually Les Contamines and Les Houches are under way. The first stage, two new chairs linking Megève and Praz-sur-Arly, should be ready for 2002/03. The whole area, labelled 'Espace Diamant', should cover 600km/373 miles of trails, making it one of the largest ski areas in the world.

THE SLOPES
Pretty but low

Two of the three areas of slopes are linked by lift, though not by trail.

The biggest, highest and most varied sector is **Mont d'Arbois**, accessible not only from the town but also by a gondola from La Princesse, way out to the north-east of town. It offers some wooded slopes but is mainly open, especially higher up.

Most of the slopes face more-or-less

boarding *Boarding doesn't really fit with Megève's traditional, rather staid, upscale image. But there is a terrain park and a half-pipe on Mont Joux – and free-riders will find lots of untracked off-trail powder for a few days after new snowfalls. It's a good place to try boarding for the first time, with plenty of fairly wide, gentle runs and a lot of chair-lifts and gondolas; though there are a fair number of surface lifts, they are generally avoidable. Nightlife tends to be rather sophisticated, but there are a few noisy bars as well.*

west, but there are north-east-facing slopes to Le Bettex and on down to St-Gervais. A two-stage gondola returns you to the top, with a mid-station at Le Bettex. You can work your way over to Mont Joux and up to the small Mont Joly area – Megève's highest slopes (2355m/7,730ft). And from there you can descend to the backwater village of St-Nicolas-de-Véroce; chair-lifts bring you back to Mont Joux. Directly behind Mont Joly, further up the same valley as St-Nicolas-de-Véroce, is the substantial resort of Les Contamines. You can get to it off-trail and a proper lift-and-trail link is envisaged.

From the Mont d'Arbois lift base, the Rocharbois tram goes across the valley to **Rochebrune**. Alpette is the starting point for Megève's historic downhill course. A network of gentle, wooded, north-east-facing slopes, served by surface and chair-lifts, lead across to the high-point of Côte 2000.

The third area, and much the quietest, is **Le Jaillet**, accessed by gondola from just outside the north-west edge of town. From the top of the gondola are predominantly easy, east-facing trails. The high point is Christomet, served by a long chair-lift. In the other directions, a series of long, tree-lined runs and lifts serves the area above Combloux.

Reporters claim that trail grading is inconsistent and that less advanced skiers should not be too complacent.

SNOW RELIABILITY
The area's main weakness
The problem is that the slopes are low, with very few runs above 2000m/6,560ft, and partly sunny – the Megève side of Mont d'Arbois gets the afternoon sun. So in a poor snow year, or in a warm spell, snow-cover and quality on the lower slopes can suffer badly – in which case you may need to ride the lifts back down.

Fortunately, the grassy slopes don't need much depth of snow, and the resort has made great strides in tackling this weakness, expanding its snowmaking network to 170 snow-guns at the last count. Some runs are now entirely covered, including the long red Olympique run at Rochebrune. There is also a high standard of trail grooming.

FOR EXPERTS
Off-trail is the main attraction
The Mont Joly and Mont Joux sections offer the steepest slopes. The top chair here serves a genuinely black run, and the slightly lower Epaule chair has some steep runs back down and also accesses some good off-trail runs, as well as trails, down to St-Nicolas.

The steep area beneath the second stage of the Princesse gondola can be a play area of powder runs among the trees. Côte 2000 has a small section of steep runs, including some off-trail.

The black run under the Christomet chair is no longer on the map and,

FRANCE

178

SCHOOLS/GUIDES

2000/01 prices in euros

ESF
Classes 6 days
4hr 9.30-11.30 and 3pm-5pm
6 afternoons 87
Children's classes
Ages: 5 to 12
6 afternoons: 78
Private lessons
Hourly or daily
32 for 1hr, for 1 or 2 people.
All-day classes are available.

International
Classes 5 mornings
2hr 10am-12.30: 108
Children's classes
Ages: 4 to 12
6 mornings: 119
Private lessons
Hourly or daily
1 to 5 people: 1 hr 38

CHILDCARE

There are three kindergartens dotted around the sprawling resort, all offering skiing. Age limits and hours vary. Caboche (0450 589765) at the Caboche gondola station: ages 3 to 10, until 5pm. Meg'Loisirs (0450 587784) is a comprehensive nursery: ages 3 to 6, until 6pm. Princesse (0450 930086), out at the Princesse gondola: ages 2½ to 6, until 6pm.

given decent snow, could be a good spot to practise off-trail technique.

FOR INTERMEDIATES
Superb if the snow is good

Good intermediates will enjoy the Mont d'Arbois area best. The black runs below the Princesse gondola are perfectly manageable. The runs served by the Grand Vorasset surface lift and the most direct route between Mont d'Arbois and Le Bettex are also interesting. Similarly challenging are the steepest of the Jaillet sector trails.

It's a great area for the less confident. A number of comfortable runs lead down to Le Bettex and La Princesse from Mont d'Arbois, while nearby Mont Joux accesses long, problem-free runs to St-Nicolas. Alpette and Côte 2000 are also suitable.

Even the timid can get a great deal of mileage in. All main valley-level lifts have easy routes down to them (although the Milloz trail to the Princesse mid-station is a little steep). There are some particularly good, long, gentle cruises between Mont Joux and Megève via Mont d'Arbois. But in all sectors, you'll find easy, blue runs.

FOR BEGINNERS
Good choice of beginner areas

There are beginners' slopes dotted all around at valley level, and more snow-sure ones at altitude on each of the main mountains. There are also plenty of very easy longer green runs to progress to.

FOR CROSS-COUNTRY
An excellent area

There are 75km/47 miles of varied trails spread throughout the area. Some are at altitude (1300m–1550m/4,270ft-5,090ft), making lunchtime meetings with Alpine skiers or walkers simple.

LIFTLINES
Few weekday problems

Megève is relatively line-free during the week, except at peak holiday time. But school holidays and sunny Sunday crowds can mean some delays. The Lanchettes surface lift between Côte 2000 and the rest of the Rochebrune slopes gets oversubscribed – as does the gondola linking the two mountains. Overcrowded trails at Mont Joux and Mont d'Arbois can also be a problem. Go out in falling snow and you'll have the mountain to yourself.

MOUNTAIN RESTAURANTS
The long lunch lives

Megève is one of the great gourmet lunch destinations. Many of the 30 restaurants have table-service and many of the terraces have magnificent views. Not surprisingly, they can be expensive. Booking ahead is advisable.

The Mont d'Arbois area is particularly well endowed. There are two suave places still owned by the Rothschilds, original promoters of Megève, both popular with poseurs with small dogs and fur coats – the Club House and the Idéal Sports. The Igloo, with wonderful views of Mont Blanc, has both self-service and table-service sections – recent reports of the self-service section are disappointing.

Above St-Nicolas are several little chalets offering great charm and good food at modest prices as well as glorious views.

At the base of the Mont Joux lift, Chez Marie du Rosay is recommended. On the back side of the hill, at Les Communailles, the Alpage was a key factor in one reader's decision to go back to Megève.

At the foot of the Côte 2000 slopes is a former farm, popular for its atmosphere, friendly service and good quality; Radaz, up the slope a little, enjoys better views and is similarly cozy, but the service can be slack. Alpette, atop the Rochebrune ridge, offers excellent all-round views outside, a comfortable lounge inside.

SCHOOLS AND GUIDES
Adventurous

The two schools offer expeditions to the Vallée Blanche and heli-skiing (in Italy) as well as conventional lessons. The International school appears to be more popular with readers than its rival, the ESF. A recent reporter found the ESF children's classes to be inefficient, with impatient instructors.

FACILITIES FOR CHILDREN
Language problems

A comfortable low-altitude resort like Megève attracts lots of families who can afford day care. The facilities seem impressive – the kindergartens offer a wide range of activities as an alternative to the slopes. Lack of English-speaking staff (and companions) could be a drawback.

↑ It's a low-rise town, but don't count on skiing to the door
MEGEVE TOURIST OFFICE

Phone numbers
From abroad use the prefix +33 and omit the initial 'o' of the phone number.

GETTING THERE

Air Geneva, transfer 1hr. Lyon, transfer 2½hr.

Rail Sallanches (13km/8 miles); regular buses from station.

Staying there

HOW TO GO
Some very stylish hotels

Hotels Megève offers a range of exceptionally stylish and welcoming hotels. There are simpler places, too.

((((4) Mont Blanc (0450 210202) Megève's traditional leading hotel – elegant and fashionable. Right in the center, and close to the main gondola.

((((4) Chalet du Mont d'Arbois (0450 212503) Prettily decorated, former Rothschild family home, now a Relais & Châteaux hotel in a secluded position above town, near the Mont d'Arbois gondola.

((((4) Fer à Cheval (0450 213039) French rustic-chic at its best, with a warmly welcoming wood-and-stone interior and excellent food. Close to the center.

(((3) Au Coin du Feu (0450 210494) 'Very well managed' chalet midway between Rochebrune and Chamois lifts.

(((3) Grange d'Arly (0450 587788) Wrong side of the road, but still quite close to the center and beautifully furnished.

(((3) Ferme Hôtel Duvillard (0450 211462) Smartly restored farmhouse, perfectly positioned for the slopes, at the foot of the Mont d'Arbois gondola.

((2) Gai Soleil (0450 210070) Comfortable family-run place – five minutes' walk from the center of town and the main gondola.

((2) Mourets (0450 210476) Poor location but repeatedly recommended by readers: 'basic but spacious accommodations with good food and wonderful views'; 'excellent hosts'.

Apartments/condos There are some very comfortable and well positioned apartments available – not cheap.

EATING OUT
Very French

Megève naturally has lots of high-quality, expensive restaurants – many of which are recommended in the top restaurant guides. The restaurants in all the best hotels – eg the Fermes de Marie, Chalet du Mont d'Arbois and Mont Blanc – are excellent but extremely expensive. Les Flocons de Sel, although quite pricey, is highly recommended for its quality and service. Michel Gaudin is one of the best in town – with very good-value set menus. The Taverne du Mont d'Arbois is a lovely woody chalet at the foot of the Mont d'Arbois lifts.

Some reporters wish for more variety of cuisine. The Phnom-Penh is one of the few possibilities. Mama Mia is a popular Italian restaurant though recent reports are mixed. The Pallas is recommended for burgers and pizzas.

ACTIVITIES

Indoor 'Palais des Sports' (climbing wall, swimming pool, sauna, solarium, skating, gym), judo, classical and contemporary dance classes, music lessons, bridge, tennis, bowling, archery, language classes, museum, library, cinemas, pottery, casino, concert and play hall, body-building hall, curling, tennis
Outdoor 50km/31 miles of cleared paths, snow-shoe excursions, skating rink, riding, sleigh rides, plane and helicopter trips, paragliding, hot-air ballooning, horse-riding, rock-climbing, ice driving, mountaineering

TOURIST OFFICE

Postcode 74120
t +33 450 212728
f 450 930309
megeve@megeve.com
www.megeve.com

APRES-SKI
Bit of a gamble?

The only recent reporter who has taken an interest in such things – and who was there in high season – reckons there is a shortage of lively après-ski bars. The Chamois has been recommended. The Puck is an atmospheric locals' bar, while Harry's Bar is an informal British rendezvous, popular for its wide range of beers, a weekly live band, karaoke and satellite TV. The casino, opened a few seasons ago, has more slot machines than blackjack tables. The Club de Jazz (aka Les 5 Rues) is something of an institution – a very popular, if rather expensive, jazz club-cum-cocktail bar, that gets some big-name musicians.

OFF THE SLOPES
Lots to do

There is something for most tastes, with an excellent sports center, an outdoor ice rink, plenty of outdoor activities and a weekly market. Trips to Annecy and Chamonix are possible. And St-Gervais is worth visiting for a spa treatment. Walks are excellent, with 50km/31 miles of marked paths, many at altitude. There is a special map of the paths, graded for difficulty. Meeting friends on the slopes for lunch is easy.

STAYING UP THE MOUNTAIN
Several possibilities

As well as mid-mountain Le Bettex (see St-Gervais), there are hotels further up on the slopes, near the summit of Mont d'Arbois. One is the 3-star Igloo (0450 930584), another the 2-star Chez la Tante (0450 213130).

St-Gervais 850m/2,790ft

St-Gervais is a handsome 19th-century spa town set in a narrow river gorge, halfway between Megève and Chamonix, at the entrance to the side-valley leading up to St-Nicolas and Les Contamines. It has direct access to the Mont d'Arbois slopes via a 20-person gondola from just outside the town.

It's a pleasant place to explore, with interesting food shops and cozy bars. Among its diversions are thermal baths and an Olympic skating rink. Prices are noticeably lower than over the hill in Megève. Two hotels convenient for the gondola are the Hostellerie du Nerey (0450 934521), a pleasantly traditional 2-star, and the 3-star Carlina (0450 934110), best in town. At the gondola mid-station is Le Bettex (1380m/4,530ft), a small collection of hotels, private chalets and new apartments, conveniently situated for the runs but with little evening animation.

You can go up on the opposite side of St-Gervais on a rack-and-pinion railway which in 1904 was intended to go all the way to the top of Mont Blanc but actually takes you to the slopes of Les Houches (see Chamonix chapter). Given enough snow, you can descend to St-Gervais off-trail.

Its position makes St-Gervais a good base for touring the different resorts covered by the Mont Blanc regional lift pass.

Other resorts

Praz-sur-Arly and Notre-Dame-de-Bellecombe are much cheaper options for independent car travellers – they are not part of the Megève lift network. Praz (1035m/3,400ft) is a small, quiet place, but has hotels, restaurants, bars, sports club, ski school and ski kindergarten. It has fair-sized slopes of its own, with short, mainly easy, north-facing runs. Notre-Dame (1130m/3,710ft) is further along the road past Praz, a pleasant village with mainly apartments , simple hotels, and several bars and restaurants. It has its own varied, pretty area.

St-Nicolas-de-Véroce is part of the lift network, and has a handful of simple small hotels.

One reporter spent a very rewarding few days based at the hotel Terminus (0450 936800) in Le Fayet, below St-Gervais, traveling to a different resort each day by coach.

Great slopes but horrendous buildings

HOW IT RATES

The slopes

Snow	★★★★
Extent	★★★★★
Experts	★★★★
Intermediates	★★★★★
Beginners	★★★
Convenience	★★★★★
Liftlines	★★★★
Restaurants	★★★

The rest

Scenery	★★★
Resort charm	★
Off-slope	★

+ Probably the cheapest place to stay in the famously extensive Three Valleys area – biggest in the world

+ Some great local slopes

+ Extensive snowmaking

+ Lots of slope-side accommodations

+ Trying hard to smarten the place up

− Possibly the ugliest resort in the Alps, but gradually improving

− Main intermediate and beginner slopes get a lot of sun

− No woodland slopes

− beginner areas are busy as well as overexposed to the sun

Les Menuires is trying hard to lose its reputation as the armpit of the Alps (see the What's New section for developments). But, whatever you may think of its appearance, it is certainly the bargain base for the Trois Vallées, with the bonus of immediate access to the excellent, challenging slopes on La Masse, rarely used by visitors from the other valleys.

What's new

For 2001/02, a new high-speed six-person chair-lift will go from the center of the village to mid-mountain, to be met by another new high-speed six-seater, which will whizz you to Mont de la Chambre and the links with Méribel and Val Thorens. This will eliminate liftlines for the rickety old gondola that used to be the main way up (the bottom section will still exist but the top section will be demolished).

Over the last few years all new building has been traditional Savoyard chalet-style (stone and wood) and several luxury developments have been built (with swimming pools, saunas etc). The latest for 2001/02 will form the new Hameau des Marmottes at Preyerand in the center and the Chalets de l'Adonis in the Bruyères area.

The shopping center in La Croisette will be given a facelift.

The resort

The resort is trying hard to lose its reputation as one of the ugliest in the Alps. But there is no getting away from the fact that the buildings that form the original center of the resort, La Croisette, are simply horrendous – the worst examples of huge buildings being thrown up in the building boom of the 1960s and early 70s. They look particularly vile when approached along the path from the St-Martin and Méribel directions. The main center has a claustrophobic indoor shopping complex (which we are told is being given a facelift). It is just a shame they cannot tear down the center and start again. Newer outposts such as Reberty and Les Bruyères are much better. And all new building is now in traditional Savoyard (stone and wood) style and

there are some luxury developments. The new outposts have their own shops and bars. Some pleasant bar and restaurant terraces face the slopes.

Three Valleys lift tickets for six days or more also give you a day in Val-d'Isère/Tignes, La Plagne or Les Arcs.

The mountains

Les Menuires has two main attractions: La Masse, a challenging and neglected mountain; and the swift links to the rest of the Trois Vallées.

THE SLOPES
A good base for the Trois Vallées
Les Menuires and St-Martin-de-Belleville share a local area with 160km/100 miles of runs and 43 lifts. The west-facing slopes have the vast bulk of the runs. The two new high-speed six-packs for 2001/02 will take you up from La Croisette to **Mont de la Chambre**, from where you can head back south to Val-Thorens or east over the ridge to the Méribel slopes. Chairs and surface lifts serve the local slopes, and you can head north to the old village of St-Martin.

The north-east-facing slopes of **La Masse** (2805m/9,200ft) usually have excellent snow on the top half and are served by high-capacity gondolas.

SNOW RELIABILITY
Cover guaranteed but not quality
La Masse's height and orientation ensure good snow for a long season. The opposite, west-facing slopes are supplied with abundant artificial snow

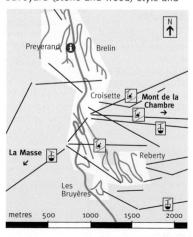

Preyerand
Brelin
Croisette
Mont de la Chambre →
La Masse
Reberty
Les Bruyères
metres 500   1000   1500   2000
N

MOUNTAIN FACTS

for the Three Valleys

Altitude	1300m-3200m
	4,27oft-10,5ooft
Lifts	200
Pistes	600km/
	370 miles
Green	17%
Blue	34%
Red	37%
Black	12%
Snowmaking	90km/
	56 miles
Recco detectors used	

LIFT TICKETS

2001/02 prices in euros
Three Valleys
See Méribel chapter.
Alternative tickets
Vallée des Belleville ticket covers 72 lifts and 300km/186 miles of trail in Val-Thorens, Les Menuires and St-Martin (adult 6-day 170). Les Menuires and St-Martin ticket covers 43 lifts and 160km/100 miles of trail (adult 6-day 147).

SCHOOLS/GUIDES

2001/02 prices in euros

ESF
Classes 6 half days: adult: from 95
Children's classes
Ages: up to 12
6 half days: from 86
Private lessons
Hourly 33 for 1 or 2 people

---

boarding

Les Menuires gets a fair number of boarding visitors – not surprising since it gives relatively economical access to such a huge area of terrain. There is plenty here for every style of rider. Lots of chairs and gondolas in the massive lift system make for comfortable travel, but be warned – there are some flattish sections of trail to negotiate in places. And we'd certainly recommend beginners to go somewhere with more secluded beginner areas and better snow. There's a terrain-park with a half-pipe just above the main village.

(the resort boasts 323 snow-guns). But although cover there is guaranteed – so long as the weather is cold enough to make snow – the snow lower down is often icy or slushy.

FOR EXPERTS
Hidden treasures
La Masse has some of the steepest and quietest trails in the Trois Vallées – most people doing the 'circuit' skip it. Long reds and a black come down beneath the top stage of the gondola. Other steep blacks, usually bumped, are the Dame Blanche and Lac Noir.

From the top there are also some marvellously scenic off-trail runs, some sporadically marked as itinéraires, others requiring guidance. The wide, sweeping, but not too steep, Vallon du Lou goes towards Val-Thorens. Others go in the opposite direction to various villages from which you need transport back, but the Les Yvoses run takes you back to the lifts.

There's easy access to the rest of the Trois Vallées: within an hour of your door are the steepest slopes of Méribel or Val-Thorens. Courchevel doesn't take much longer.

FOR INTERMEDIATES
600km/370 miles of trails to choose from
With good snow, you may find little reason for leaving the local slopes, which are virtually all blue and red. But because most slopes face west, the snow is often better elsewhere in the Trois Vallées. This is paradise for intermediates who like to travel. You can approach Méribel from five different peaks on the ridge. Even a second- or third-timer should have no problem cruising from valley to valley. In poor snow conditions the attractions of higher Val-Thorens become evident, and there's blue as well as red-run access.

FOR BEGINNERS
Try elsewhere
Although there are wide and gentle slopes for beginners and a special beginner's lift ticket, we think you'd be better off in a resort that has more of a real Alpine atmosphere and is easier on the eye. While others can get away from Les Menuires into beautiful Alpine scenery, beginners are stuck with it. The snow quality on the beginner

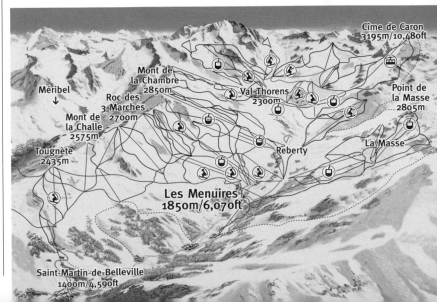

CHILDCARE

The ESF-run Village des Schtroumpfs (0479 006379) takes children aged 3 months to 12 years. It has a nursery for babies, a Baby Club for toddlers and a leisure center for older children, with activities and ski lessons for children aged 2½ or more.

At Reberty-les-Bruyères, the Marmottons offers similar facilities, but no nursery.

GETTING THERE

Air Geneva, transfer 3½hr. Lyon, transfer 3½hr. Chambéry, transfer 2½hr.

Rail Moûtiers (27km/17 miles); regular buses from station.

Phone numbers From abroad use the prefix +33 and omit the initial 'o' of the phone number.

ACTIVITIES

Indoor Library, movie theater, fitness centers, sauna **Outdoor** Two outdoor heated swimming pools, microlight flights, hang-gliding, guided walks, snow-scooters, artificial skating rink, snow-shoe excursions, paragliding, guided tours, tubing.

TOURIST OFFICE

Postcode 73440
t +33 479 007300
f 479 007506
lesmenuires@lesmenuires.com
www.lesmenuires.com

areas is a worry, and the blue slopes above the resort can get extremely crowded.

FOR CROSS-COUNTRY
Valley hike
There are 28km/17 miles of prepared trails along the valley floor between St-Martin and halfway between Les Menuires and Val-Thorens.

LIFTLINES
Big bottleneck goes
There could be big lines for the old gondola to Mont de la Chambre from La Croisette, especially when it broke down. The new high-speed six-packs for 2000/01 will eliminate that problem. There are few other local liftlines.

MOUNTAIN RESTAURANTS
A surprisingly atmospheric place
L'Etoile on the left of the main trail as you go down to La Croisette is one of the nicest stops in the Trois Vallées – a rustic old hut with smart terrace and good food served by waiters in berets and traditional dress. The restaurant at the top of the first stage of the La Masse gondola is fairly pleasant. But a lot of people prefer to head for the restaurants of the old village of St-Martin-de-Belleville – Les Airelles and Brewski's are recommended by reporters. The Bouitte, in nearby St-Marcel, is a serious restaurant. It's reachable off-trail, and they'll drive you to the lifts after lunch.

SCHOOLS AND GUIDES
Overcome language barrier
Reports tend to be positive, despite English not being widely spoken, and we have reports of children enjoying themselves in multinational classes.

FACILITIES FOR CHILDREN
All-embracing
This is very much a family resort, and the childcare arrangements seem well organized. The general view is that it is a good place for children to be introduced to the snow.

Staying there

Despite the fact that the resort is designed for convenient access to the slopes, you may wish to think about location. The central area around La Croisette is best for shops and après-ski. But the 'village' has several more attractive parts with fewer facilities, such as Reberty and Les Bruyères, and overall is nearly a mile in length.

HOW TO GO

Hotels None of the hotels are above 3-star grading.

⟨⟨3⟩ **Ours Blanc** (0479 006166) Best in town: a wood-clad, chalet-style 3-star on the slopes above Reberty 1850.

⟨⟨3⟩ **Latitudes** (0479 007510) 3-star on the lower fringe of Les Bruyères.

⟨2⟩ **Menuire** (0479 006033) Neat, well equipped place on southern fringe of the resort; but we have had some negative reports.

Apartments/condos The older apartments are cheap and small. But the newer ones are more attractive, spacious and luxurious. The Montagnettes and Alpages, both in Reberty, are among the best, the latter being an MGM development with a pool.

EATING OUT
Good authentic French cuisine
Though some restaurants lack atmosphere, there's no shortage of good food, including Savoyard specialities. Alternatives include Italian and Tex-Mex. The restaurant in the Ours Blanc and the rustic Ruade are recommended by reporters. L'Etoile (see Mountain Restaurants) is open in the evenings too.

APRES-SKI
Improving but still very limited
There isn't a huge après-ski scene. The Challenge bar has live music and La Mousse is popular. The Liberty and Passeport discos pick up later on.

OFF THE SLOPES
Forget it
Les Menuires is a resort for avid skiers and riders wanting to explore the world's most extensive slopes, though there are some pretty walks.

Méribel
1400m-1700m/4,690ft-5,580ft

The best-looking base for the wonderful Three Valleys

HOW IT RATES

The slopes

Snow	★★★★
Extent	★★★★★
Experts	★★★★
Intermediates	★★★★★
Beginners	★★★
Convenience	★★★
Liftlines	★★★★
Restaurants	★★★★

The rest

Scenery	★★★
Resort charm	★★★
Off-slope	★★★

What's new

For 2001/02, one of the few remaining bottlenecks in the Three Valleys will be sorted. The slow old Plan des Mains chair, from the bottom of Mont Vallon up to the Plattières gondola will be replaced by a high-speed six-seater chair. This chair is essential for those headed for Méribel and Courchevel from Mont Vallon or Val Thorens, who want to avoid the skate or pole along the alternative flat path to Mottaret.

The last couple of years has seen new eight- and six-seater high-speed chair-lifts in the Altiport area.

For 2000/01, a surface lift was installed in the floodlit Corbey slalom stadium. The snowpark at Arpasson was extended.

- ✚ In the center of the biggest linked trail network in the world – ideal for intermediates who love covering the miles, but plenty for experts, too
- ✚ Modern, constantly improved lift system means little waiting and rapid access to all slopes
- ✚ Good trail grooming and snowmaking
- ✚ Village purpose-built in pleasing chalet-style architecture

- ➖ Not the best snow in the Three Valleys, and trails can get crowded
- ➖ Main village spread out, straggling along a long, winding road, with many of the accommodations well away from the slopes
- ➖ Expensive
- ➖ Méribel–Mottaret and Méribel Village satellites are rather lifeless
- ➖ Not the place to go for real French atmosphere

For keen trail-bashers who dislike tacky purpose-built resorts, Méribel is difficult to beat. It is slap in the middle of the Three Valleys – the biggest interlinked winter sports area in the world. With 200 lifts and 600km/370 miles of trails, and endless off-trail possibilities, it is difficult to be bored in a two-week stay here. The orientation of Méribel's local slopes mean its snow is often not as good as in Courchevel and Val-Thorens. But its Mont Vallon area keeps its snow well and it is quick and easy to get to every part of the Three Valleys.

Méribel is built entirely in tasteful chalet-style, with wood-siding everywhere. And the center is very pleasant with raised walkways by the shops above the one-way road. The village has grown rapidly in recent years and now spreads widely over the mountainside. It is very popular with British visitors, many of whom own chalets here. And English can be more commonly heard than French on the slopes and in the bars. It remains decidedly upscale and it's not cheap. But regular visitors love it and wouldn't be seen anywhere else. And we still have a soft spot for it (one of us learned to ski here).

SNOWPIX.COM / CHRIS GILL

Méribel now spreads right along the mountainside, well away from its original center (near the right of this pic) ➜

The resort

Méribel occupies the central valley of the Three Valleys system and consists of two main resort villages.

The original resort of Méribel-les-Allues (now simply known as Méribel) is built on a single steepish west-facing hillside with the home trail running down beside it to the main lift stations at the valley bottom. All the buildings are wood-clad, low-rise and chalet style, making this one of the most tastefully designed of French purpose-built resorts. A road winds up from the village center at about 1400m/4,590ft to the Rond Point des Pistes at about 1650m/5,410ft, and goes on through woods to the outpost of the altiport (an airport with snow-covered runway for little planes with skis) at around 1700m/5,580ft.

The resort was founded by a British man, Peter Lindsay, in 1938, and has retained a strong British presence ever since. It has grown enormously over recent years, and although some accommodations are right on the trail, much of the newer building is more than a walk away. One clear exception is Belvédère, an upscale enclave built on the opposite side of the home trail (there's a tunnel for road access). There are collections of shops and restaurants at a couple of points on the road through the resort – Altitude 1600 and Plateau de Morel. The hotels and apartments of Altiport enjoy splendid isolation in the woods, and are convenient for some of the slopes.

The satellite village of Méribel-Mottaret was developed in the early 1970s. The original development was beside the trail on the east-facing slope, but in recent years the resort has spread up the opposite hillside and further up the valley. Both sides are served by lifts for pedestrians – but the gondola up to the original village stops at 7.30 and it's a long, tiring walk up. Mottaret looks modern, despite wood-siding on its apartment blocks. Even so, it's more attractive than many other resorts built for slope-side convenience. It has many fewer shops and bars and much less après-ski than Méribel, but reporters have found it makes a pleasant change, and enjoyed the convenience.

For the Olympics, a new gondola was built from Brides-les-Bains, an old spa town way down in the valley,

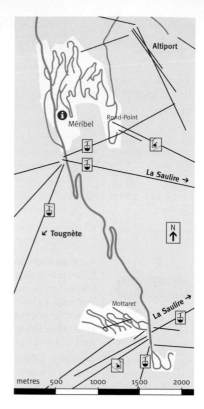

which served as the Olympic Village for the games, up to Méribel. There's a mid-station at the old village of Les Allues. Méribel-Village is a new development between Méribel and La Tania, with a chair-lift up to Altiport. There are some luxury chalets and apartments here but little else – no bars or restaurants in 2000/01.

The mountains

It's avid skiers who will get the best out of what Méribel has to offer. There's endless cruising to be had, as well as challenging terrain. The lift system is generally very efficient and is planned to cut walks and climbs. Trail grooming is not always reliable, however – reporters found 'some blues more difficult than some reds'.

To appreciate the merits of the whole Three Valleys region you'll need to read the entries for Courchevel, Les Menuires and Val-Thorens, too. Lift tickets for six days or more also give you a day in Val-d'Isère–Tignes (an hour and a half away), La Plagne or Les Arcs (an hour or so away).

MOUNTAIN FACTS
for the Three Valleys

Altitude	1300m-3200m
	4,270ft-10,500ft
Lifts	200
Trails	600km/
	370 miles
Green	17%
Blue	34%
Red	37%
Black	12%
Snowmaking	90km/
	56 miles
Recco detectors used	

THE SLOPES
Highly efficient lift system
The Méribel valley runs north–south. On the eastern side, gondolas leave both Méribel and Mottaret for **La Saulire** From here you can head back down towards either village or down the other side of the ridge towards Courchevel.

From Méribel a gondola rises to **Tougnète**, on the western side of the valley, from where you can get down to Les Menuires or St-Martin-de-Belleville. You can also head for Mottaret from here. From there, a fast chair then a surface lift take you to another entry point for the Les Menuires runs.

The Mottaret area has seen rapid mechanization over the last decade. The **Plattières** gondola rises up the valley to the south, ending at yet another entry point to the Les Menuires area. To the east of this is the big stand-up gondola to the top of **Mont Vallon**, where there are wonderful views from the top. A fast quad from near this area goes south up to **Mont de la Chambre**, giving direct access to Val-Thorens.

SNOW RELIABILITY
Not the best in the Three Valleys
Méribel's slopes aren't the highest in the Three Valleys, and they mainly face east or west, getting the full force of the morning or afternoon sun. So snow conditions are often better elsewhere.

And grooming seems to be rather better in neighboring Courchevel.

The lower runs now have substantial snowmaking and lack of snow is rarely a problem, but ice or slush at the end of the day can be. The west-facing La Saulire side gets the afternoon sun, and conditions deteriorate here first – but then you can always go over to Courchevel. The north-west-facing slopes above Altiport generally have decent snow.

At the southern end of the valley, towards Les Menuires and Val-Thorens, a lot of runs are north-facing and keep their snow well, as do the runs on Mont Vallon.

FOR EXPERTS
Exciting choices
The size of the Three Valleys means experts are well catered for. In the Méribel valley, head for Mont Vallon. The long, steep, Combe du Vallon run here is graded red; it's a wonderful long fast cruise when groomed, but presents plenty of challenge when bumpy. And there's a beautiful itinéraire (not marked on the trail map) in the next valley to the main trails, leading back to the bottom of the gondola.

The slopes down from the top of the Val-Thorens sector were all off-trail when we old hands first visited Méribel. Since the new lifts were installed up here, there are two trails back from Val-Thorens, but still plenty

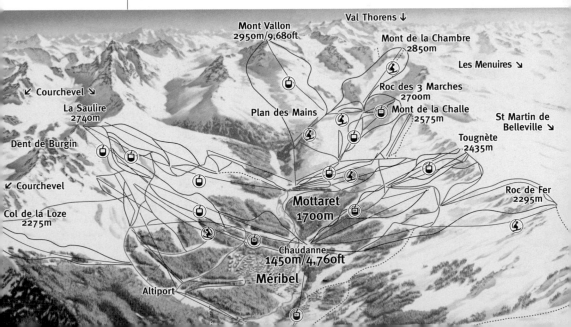

LIFT TICKETS

2001/02 prices in euros

Three Valleys
Covers all lifts in Courchevel, La Tania, Méribel, Val-Thorens, Les Menuires and St-Martin-de-Belleville.

Beginners Two free lifts in Méribel-Mottaret and two in Méribel; reduced price lift ticket with beginners' lessons.

Main ticket
1-day ticket 37
6-day ticket 182

Senior citizens
Over 60: 6-day ticket 146
Over 70: 6-day ticket 91
Over 75: free ticket

Children
Under 17: 6-day ticket 137
Under 10: 118
Under 5: free ticket

Short-term tickets
Half-day tickets (from 12.30) available for Vallée de Méribel (adult 23), Méribel Alpina (adult 20) and Three Valleys (adult 28).

Notes 6-day ticket and over valid for one day each in Tignes-Val-d'Isère, La Plagne-Les Arcs, Pralognan-la-Vanoise and Les Saisies. Reductions for families.

Alternative tickets
Vallée de Méribel ticket covers 150km/93 miles of runs in Méribel and Méribel-Mottaret (adult 6-day 148). One day Three Valleys extension 17).

of opportunity for getting off-trail in the wide open bowls.

A good bump run is down the side of the double Roc de Tougne surface lift which leads up to Mont de la Challe. And there is a steep black run all the way down the Tougnète gondola back to Méribel. Apart from a shallow section near the mid-station, it's unrelenting most of the way.

At the north end of the valley the Face run was built for the women's downhill in the 1992 Olympics. Served by a fast quad, it's a splendid cruise when freshly groomed, and you can terrify yourself just by imagining what it must be like to go straight down.

Nothing on the Saulire side is as steep or as demanding as on the other side of the valley. The Mauduit red run used to be black, however.

Throughout the area there are good off-trail opportunities. The ESF runs excellent-value guided groups.

FOR INTERMEDIATES
Paradise found
Méribel and the rest of the Three Valleys is a paradise for intermediates; there are few other resorts where an avid skier can cover so many miles so easily. Virtually every slope in the region has a good intermediate run down it, and to describe them would take a book in itself.

For less adventurous intermediates, the run from the second station of the Plattières gondola back to Mottaret is ideal, and used a lot by the ski school. It is a gentle, north-facing, cruising run and is generally in good condition.

Even early intermediates should find the runs over into the other valleys well within their capabilities, opening up further vast amounts of intermediate runs. Go to Courchevel or Val-Thorens for the better snow.

Virtually all the trails on both sides of the Méribel valley will suit more advanced intermediates. Most of the reds are on the difficult side.

FOR BEGINNERS
Not ideal
Méribel isn't ideal for beginners. The resort lacks good beginner areas set apart from the main areas. There is a small one at Rond Point, mainly used by the children's ski school.

The best area for beginners is at Altiport, accessible direct from the village at Altitude 1600 by chair-lift. There is a gentle out-of-the-way area here that can be treated as a beginner area. And you can progress to one of the best and most attractively situated green trails we know, the Blanchot – long, gentle, wide and tree-lined, and relatively quiet.

FOR CROSS-COUNTRY
Scenic routes
The main area is in the woods near Altiport. There is about 17km/11 miles of prepared track here, a pleasant introduction to those who want to try cross-country for the first time. There's also a loop around Lake Tueda, in the nature reserve, and for the more experienced an 8km/5 mile itinéraire from Altiport to Courchevel.

LIFTLINES
Easily avoided
Huge lift investment over the years has paid off in making the area virtually line-free most of the time, despite the huge numbers of people. The last big bottleneck at Plan des Mains will be eliminated for 2001/02 – see What's new. The excellent lift network means that if you do find a line, there is usually an alternative quieter route you can take. The Plattières gondola at Mottaret can get crowded at ski school time, when the schools gets priority – take the alternative Combes high-speed chair.

MOUNTAIN RESTAURANTS
Lots of choice but not cheap
There is lots of choice, but most places get very crowded. You might want to

boarding *Méribel is increasingly boarder-oriented. The terrain locally and further afield has lots to offer, you rarely have to take a surface lift, and there's one terrain-park with half-pipe, two quarter-pipes and boarder-cross below the second stage of the Plattières gondola, and another park with quarter-pipe and trick course near the Arpasson surface lift above the Tougnète gondola mid-station. The resort hosts a number of big-air and boarder-cross competitions. Specialist shops include Board Brains, Exodus and the Quiksilver snowboard shop, and you're bound to feel at home in at least one of the lively bars.*

2001/02 prices in euros

ESF
in Méribel and Méribel-Mottaret
Classes Adults
6 full days: 195
Children's classes
Ages: 5 to 13
6 full days: 156
Private lessons
1½hr from 47 for 1 or 2 people, 58 for 3 or 4 people
International section
In Méribel and Méribel-Mottaret
Classes Adults
6 mornings of 2½hr: 120
Children's classes
Ages: 5 to 13
6 mornings of 2½hr: 110

New Generation
2000/01 prices in sterling

Classes 10 hr £90
Freeride clinic
7½hr £90
Check Up clinic
4hr £50
Private lessons
2hr £75 for 1 or 2 people, £15 per additional person

take lunch early or late. The self-service Pierres Plates, at the top of the Saulire gondolas, has magnificent views, but the food and atmosphere are nothing special. Chardonnet, at the mid-station of the Mottaret gondola, has table-service and excellent food but is expensive. Rhododendrons, at the top of the Altiport surface lift, has a modern but atmospheric wooden dining room and 'reasonable, plentiful food'. The Altiport hotel has a great outdoor buffet in good weather and the 'best tarts in town' but, again, is expensive. Les Crêtes, below the top of the Tougnète gondola, is a cozy family-run hut with a terrace, has good service and is one of smallest mountain restaurants in the Three Valleys. La Sitelle, above the first section of the Plattières gondola, has decent self-service food and magnificent views towards Mont Vallon. Les Castors, at the main Méribel lift station, scarcely counts as a mountain restaurant, but earns praise for good, affordable food including 'exquisite' carbonara.

SCHOOLS AND GUIDES
No shortage of instructors
The main schools all have English-speaking instructors.

The ESF is by far the biggest, with over 300 instructors. It has a special international section with instructors speaking good English. Recent reports have been mixed, but we've heard tales of instructors behaving more like guides, and abilities being too mixed within a class. One reporter said the instructor was 'rude, arrogant and unhelpful' and gave 'poor lessons'.

The ESF offers useful alternatives to standard classes, such as off-trail groups, heli-skiing on the French/Italian border and 'Ski Discovery' tours of the Three Valleys.

Magic in Motion used to get rave reviews. 'Classes small, English spoken well, we were all pleased with our progress', was typical. But this year we received mixed reviews. One reporter said she and the rest of the group found their instructor very difficult to understand, resulting in him guiding more than instructing; while another claims their beginner group was

Méribel

189

From the Tougnète slopes on the far side of the Méribel valley you can go down to the village, to Mottaret, to St-Martin or to Les Menuires →

↑ The north-facing slopes above Altiport (see runway at top left of pic) keep their snow well

SNOWPIX.COM / CHRIS GILL

CHILDCARE

The ESF runs P'tits Loups kindergartens at both Méribel and Méribel-Mottaret, with snow-gardens (lifts, inflatable characters etc) for children aged 3 to 5. Open 9am to 5pm.

Les Saturnins in the Olympic Center building in Méribel takes children aged 18 months to 3 years, offering indoor games and handicrafts, sledging and other outdoor activities.

Phone numbers
From abroad use the prefix +33 and omit the initial 'o' of the phone number.

abandoned at the altiport as the instructor rushed off to his next class.

For 2001/02 New Generation school (which uses only top British instructors and has built up an excellent reputation in Courchevel) is starting a Méribel operation – see the Courchevel chapter for readers' reports and the advert opposite for advance booking details.

FACILITIES FOR CHILDREN
Lots of choice
Despite our fat file of reports on Méribel, none deals first-hand with the resort's childcare facilities.

Staying there

Pick where you stay with care. For easy access to the trail, Mottaret is hard to beat. For those who prefer chalets and a villagey ambience, the best place is around or just above the village center of Méribel. Check how far you will be from the trail – lots of places are a long hike up. You can rent a ski locker near the main lifts. Local buses are free (though some readers complain they are inadequate).

HOW TO GO
Huge choice but few bargains
Hotels Méribel has some excellent hotels, but they're not cheap.

(((((5) **Antares** (0479 232823) Best in town; beside the trail at Belvedere. Ambitious cooking. Pool, fitness, etc.
(((((5) **Chalet** (0479 232823) Luxurious, beautifully furnished wooden chalet at Belvedere, with lovely rooms and all mod cons – outdoor pool, fitness, etc.
((((4) **Grand Coeur** (0479 086003) Our favorite almost-affordable hotel in Méribel. Just above the village center. Welcoming, mature building with plush lounge. Magnificent food. Huge hot-tub, sauna, etc.
((((4) **Altiport** (0479 085754) Modern and luxurious hotel, isolated at the foot of the Altiport lifts. Convenient for Courchevel, not for Val-Thorens.
((((4) **Mont Vallon** (0479 004400) The best hotel at Mottaret; good food, and excellently situated for the Three Valleys trails. Pool, sauna, hot-tub, squash, fitness room, etc.
((((4) **Chaudanne** (0479 086176) One of the oldest Méribel hotels, renovated a few years ago, with a sports center. But a recent reporter says it has 'tiny rooms, tacky decor and arrogant staff'.
(((3) **Adray Télébar** (0479 086026) Welcoming trail-side chalet with pretty, rustic rooms, good food and popular sun terrace.
((2) **Roc** (0479 086416) A good value B&B hotel, in the center, with a bar-restaurant and crêperie below.
Apartments/condos There is a huge

GETTING THERE

Air Geneva, transfer 3½hr. Lyon, transfer 3½hr. Chambéry, transfer 2½hr.

Rail Moûtiers (18km/ 11 miles); regular buses to Méribel.

ACTIVITIES

Indoor Parc Olympique Méribel (skating rink, swimming pool), Forme Méribel (spa, sauna, gym, bowling, billiards, climbing wall), library, bridge, fitness centers, hot-tub, two cinemas, concert hall **Outdoor** Flying lessons and excursions, snow-mobiles, snow-shoe excursions, para-gliding, 20km/12 miles of cleared paths, motor-trikes, sleigh rides, hot air balloon

TOURIST OFFICE

Postcode 73551
t +33 479 086001
f 479 005961
info@meribel.net
www.meribel.net

number of apartments and chalets to let in both Méribel and Mottaret. Make sure the place you get is conveniently situated and has enough space.

EATING OUT
Fair choice

There is a reasonable selection of restaurants, from ambitious French cuisine to relatively cheap pizza and pasta. For the best food in town, in plush surroundings, there are top hotels – Cassiopée in the Antares, Grand Coeur ('so pleased, we ate there several times'), Allodis and Chaudanne. Other recommendations include: Chez Kiki – 'good food and atmosphere'; Jardin d'Hiver – 'great char grills'; Les Castors – 'best French fare'; La Taverne – 'surprisingly good'; the Tremplin – 'friendly service, reservations essential, reasonably priced'; and the Cactus Café – 'good food, makes children welcome'.

Alternatives include the Galette, the Glacier, the Refuge, the Cava, Plantin and Cro Magnon – all popular for raclette and fondue. A reporter recommends the Crocodile in the Hameau at Mottaret. Scott's does good American-style food, and there's even a Pizza Express for the homesick.

At Les Allues, the Croix Jean-Claude serves (eventually) good-value French food in a pretty dining room.

APRES-SKI
Méribel rocks – loudly

Méribel's après-ski revolves around British-run places and some readers complain there's nowhere to go if you don't like loud pubs. Dick's Tea Bar is now well established but is remote from the slopes. At day's end it's the trail-side Rond Point that's packed – happy hour starts around 4pm – and has live music. Jack's, with a sun terrace, is also very popular.

The ring of bars around the main square do good business at tea-time. La Taverne (run by the same company that owns Dick's Tea Bar) gets packed. Just across the square is The Pub, with videos, pool and sometimes a band. The Capricorne attracts a cosmopolitan crowd and Le Refuge (down the road towards the lifts) is that rare thing in Méribel: a place where you'll be understood if you use your French.

Later on, live music brings in the crowds at The Pub, Artichaud and Rond Point. There is late dancing at Scott's (next to The Pub) and, of course, there's Dick's Tea Bar (free

entry and sub-disco drinks prices until 11.30). Last season Pizza Express (above Dick's and under the same ownership, had a fabulous Beatles tribute band every Monday). El Poncho's serves Mexican dishes and Desperados (beer mixed with tequila).

In Mottaret the bars at the foot of the trails get packed at tea-time – Rastro and DownTown are the most popular, though reporters say that Zig Zag has lower prices. Later on, Plein Soleil sometimes has live music, and the Rastro disco gets going.

Both villages have a film theater.

OFF THE SLOPES
Flight of fancy

Méribel is not really a resort for people who want to languish in the village, but it is not unattractive. There's a good public swimming pool and an Olympic ice rink. You can also take joyrides in the little planes that operate from the altiport.

The pedestrian's lift ticket covers all the gondolas, trams and buses in the Méribel and Courchevel valleys, and makes it very easy for pedestrians to meet friends for lunch.

STAYING DOWN THE VALLEY
A few choices

If you want a quiet time, consider the old village of **Les Allues**, down the road from the resort and connected by the gondola up from Brides-les-Bains. There is a good-value, well renovated hotel – the Croix Jean-Claude (0479 086105). Rooms are small, though, and a reporter says the service is poor.

Brides-les-Bains is an old spa town that served as the Olympic village in 1992. It is very cheap compared with the higher resorts and has some simple hotels, shops and a casino. But it's dead in the evening. And the long gondola ride to and from Méribel is tedious and can be cold. If you are driving, it makes a good base for visiting other resorts.

The new development of **Méribel-Village** is linked by chair-lift to the Altiport area with a blue run back. There's not much to do in this quiet little place (no bar or restaurant last season). Having a car is advisable to reach nearby La Tania or Méribel proper as buses are infrequent. One reporter described the bus service to and from Méribel as 'appalling', with 'no bus after 9.40pm, and long liftlines in the mornings. A car is vital.'

A lively, year-round resort linked by lift to the Portes du Soleil

HOW IT RATES

The slopes

Snow	**
Extent	*****
Experts	***
Intermediates	****
Beginners	***
Convenience	**
Liftlines	***
Restaurants	***

The rest

Scenery	***
Resort charm	***
Off-slope	***

What's new

For 2000/01 the gondola up from Ardent to above Les Lindarets was upgraded to increase its capacity and the parking lot was also extended. In the local area, the Belvédère and Mouilles double chairs were replaced by quads and the area at the top of the Pleney gondola was rebuilt to make reaching the other lifts easier. More snowmaking was installed in the area of the Fys chair runs down to town, to improve links to Nyon.

MOUNTAIN FACTS

for Portes du Soleil

Altitude	975m-2350m/
	3,200ft-7,710ft
Lifts	206
Trails	650km/
	400 miles
Green	13%
Blue	38%
Red	39%
Black	10%
Snowmaking	
	250 acres
Recco detectors used	

➕ Part of the vast Portes du Soleil lift network

➕ Larger local trail area than other Portes du Soleil resorts

➕ Good nightlife by French standards

➕ Quite attractive old town – a stark contrast to Avoriaz

➕ Few liftlines locally (but see minus points)

➖ Takes a while to get to Avoriaz and main Portes du Soleil circuit

➖ Bus-ride or long walk to lifts from many of the accommodations

➖ Low altitude means there is an enduring risk of poor snow, though increased snowmaking has helped

➖ Low altitude or inconvenient beginner areas

➖ Not a great resort for experts

➖ Weekend crowds

Morzine is a long-established French resort, popular for its easy road access, traditional atmosphere and gentle tree-filled slopes, where children do not get lost and bad weather rarely causes problems. For avid skiers wanting to travel the Portes du Soleil circuit, the main drawback to staying in central Morzine is having to take a bus and tram or several lifts to get to Avoriaz and the main circuit. Morzine's local slopes can suffer from poor snow.

Such problems can be avoided by taking a car. The little-used Ardent gondola, a short drive from Morzine, gives access to a clockwise circuit via Châtel, missing out often crowded Avoriaz. If local snow is poor, you can visit nearby Flaine by car, which is better than Avoriaz at coping with crowds looking for snow.

The resort

Morzine is a traditional mountain town sprawling amorphously on both sides of a river gorge. Under a blanket of snow, its chalet-style buildings look

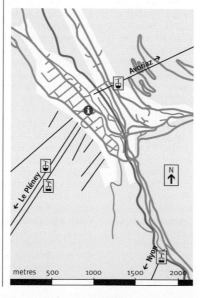

charming, and in spring the village quickly takes on a spruce appearance.

The old center is next to the river, but most resort amenities are clustered higher up around the Le Pléney lifts. Accommodations are widely scattered, and a good multi-route bus service links all parts of the town to outlying lifts, including those for Avoriaz.

Morzine is a family resort, and village ambience tends to be fairly subdued. Our view that the resort suits car drivers is widely shared. Roads are crowded, but parking problems have been somewhat relieved by new parking lots built for last season near Pléney.

The mountains

The local slopes suit intermediates well, with excellent areas for beginners and near-beginners too: 'More variety than expected,' said one recent visitor. 1999/2000 saw the introduction of an electronic lift ticket system, so you can now keep your ticket in your pocket – hold on to the card for a discount next time you visit. Reporters have commented favorably on the recently launched system of Discovery Routes around the Portes du Soleil – choose an alpine animal that suits your ability and follow the signs displaying it around the circuit.

There is floodlit skiing once a week.

THE SLOPES
No need to go far afield
Morzine is not an ideal base for the Portes du Soleil circuit (described in the Avoriaz, Châtel and Champéry chapters). But it has an extensive local area, shared with Les Gets.

A tram and parallel gondola rise from the edge of central Morzine to **Le Pléney**, where numerous routes return to the valley, including a run down to Les Fys – a quiet junction of chairs which access **Nyon** and, in the opposite direction, the ridge separating Morzine from the **Les Gets** slopes. Nyon can also be accessed by tram, situated a bus-ride from Morzine, and is connected to the slopes of Les Gets higher up the valley that separates the two, with a lift up from Le Grand Pré to Le Ranfolly. The Nyon sector has two peaks – Pointe de Nyon and Chamossière – accessible from Nyon and Le Grand Pré respectively.

From Le Ranfolly you can descend directly to Morzine without using a lift. To get to Morzine from the slopes above Les Gets you go first to the mid-mountain lift junction of Les Chavannes, then to the Folliets chair which takes you up to Le Pléney.

Beyond Les Gets is another small but worthwhile sector, on Mont Chéry. The short walk or 'petit train' shuttle through the village from the base of Chavannes takes about five minutes.

One means of access to the main Portes du Soleil circuit on the opposite side of the valley from Pléney is via a gondola from near the center of town – another handy 'petit train' shuttle service runs between this and the Le Pléney lifts. The gondola takes you up to **Super-Morzine**, and a series of trails and lifts lead to Avoriaz. A recent reporter found this route 'not worth the trouble', preferring the alternatives. These are a bus-ride or short drive to either Les Prodains (from where you can get a tram to Avoriaz or a chair-lift into the **Hauts Forts** slopes above it) or to Ardent, where the recently renovated gondola accesses Les Lindarets for lifts towards Châtel, Avoriaz or Champéry. The tree-lined slopes in this area are good in poor visibility. Car trips to Flaine and Chamonix are also feasible.

SNOW RELIABILITY
Poor
Morzine has a very low average height, and when snow disappears from the valley, the local slopes become very small and unconnected. There is some snowmaking, most noticeably on runs linking Nyon and Le Pléney, and on the reds and blues back to town. Les Gets recently benefited from extended snowmaking – but more is needed.

FOR EXPERTS
Limited on-trail
The run down from Pointe de Nyon is challenging, but for trail challenges the tram at Les Prodains is the place to head for, taking you up to Avoriaz. The Hauts Forts black runs, including the World Cup downhill course, are excellent. The above-the-tree-line slopes of Chamossière offer some of the best off-trail possibilities, and Mont Chéry is also well worth exploring. We've also had reports of great off-trail off the back of Col du Fornet down towards the Vallée de la Manche (but you'd need a guide).

FOR INTERMEDIATES
Something for everyone
Good intermediates will enjoy the challenging reds and blacks down from the Chamossière and Pointe de Nyon high points. Mont Chéry at Les Gets has some fine steepish runs.

Those of average ability have a great choice, though most runs are rather short. Le Ranfolly accesses a series of good cruisers on the Les Gets side of the ridge, and a nice trail back to Le Grand Pré. Le Pléney has a compact network of trails that are ideal for groups with mixed abilities: mainly

boarding *Avoriaz is the hard-core boarding HQ of the Portes du Soleil, with an excellent terrain-park and half-pipe – and a special ticket for those whose only interest is riding them. With interesting, tree-lined runs and few surface lifts, the local Morzine slopes are good for beginners and intermediates. There are a few lively bars.*

LIFT TICKETS

2001/02 prices in
euros
Portes du Soleil
Covers all lifts in all
12 resorts, and
shuttle buses.
Main ticket
1-day ticket 33
6-day ticket 159
Senior citizens
Over 60: 6-day ticket
127
Children
Under 16: 6-day ticket
107
Under 5: free ticket
Short-term ticketes
Half-day ticket for
Portes de Soleil (adult
25).
Also for Super-
Morzine-Avoriaz (adult
22) and Morzine-Gets
(adult 18).
Notes Discounts for
groups of 13 or more
and holders of the
Carte Neige.
Alternative tickets
Morzine-Les Gets
ticket covers 85 lifts
(adult 6-day 118, child
88).

moderate intermediate runs, but with
some easier alternatives for the more
timid, and a single challenging route
for the aggressive. Nyon's slopes are
rather fragmented for those not up to
at least the Chamossière runs.

Less experienced intermediates have
lots of options on Le Pléney, including
a snow-gun-covered cruise from the
top to the main lift station. Heading
from Le Ranfolly to Le Grand Pré is also
a nice run. And the slopes down to Les
Gets from Le Pléney are easy when
conditions allow (they face south).

And, of course, there is the whole of
the Portes du Soleil circuit to explore
by going up the opposite side of the
valley to Avoriaz or Les Lindarets.

FOR BEGINNERS
Good for novices and improvers
The village beginner areas are wide,
flat and convenient, and benefit from
snow-guns. Fast learners have the
inconvenience that the slightly longer,
steeper runs are over at Nyon.
However, adventurous novices also
have the option of easy trails around
Le Pléney. Near-beginners can get over
to Les Gets via Le Pléney, and return
via Le Ranfolly.

FOR CROSS-COUNTRY
Good variety
There is a wide variety of cross-country
trails, not all at valley level. The best
section is in the pretty Vallée de la
Manche beside the Nyon mountain up
to the Lac de Mines d'Or where there
is a good restaurant. The Pléney-
Chavannes loop is pleasant and
relatively snow-reliable.

LIFTLINES
Few problems when snow is good
Liftlines are not a problem in the local
area. The Nyon tram and Belvédère
chair-lift (Le Pléney) are weekend
bottlenecks. Liftlines to and from
Avoriaz are much improved in recent
times, but are still bad when snow is
in short supply.

MOUNTAIN RESTAURANTS
Within reach of some good huts
The nice little place at the foot of the
d'Atray chair is perhaps the best local
hut. On the Avoriaz side, Les Lindarets,
Les Marmottes and Plaine Dranse are
not too far and have some good
restaurants. Pommes de Pin at the top
of the télécabine d'Ardent is friendly
with reasonably priced food. The
Restaurant des Crêtes de Zore above
Super-Morzine is good.

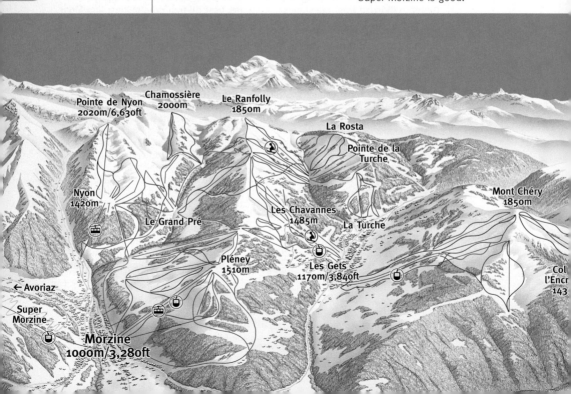

Gentle, pretty wooded slopes is what Morzine is all about – and if you get fresh snow like this, count yourself lucky →

OT MORZINE / G LANSARD

SCHOOLS/GUIDES

2001/02 prices in euros
ESF
Classes 6 days
5hr: 9.30-noon and 2.30-5pm; 2½hr: am or pm
6 half-days: 107
Private lessons
Hourly
30 for 1 or 2 people
Children's classes
Ages: 7 to 12
6 full days including lunch: 290

CHILDCARE

The Halte Garderie l'Outa (0450 792600) takes children aged 2 months to 6 years, from 8.30 to 6pm. From age 3 they can have one-hour introductory lessons. Les Pingouins Malins takes children aged 4 to 12, with ESF instruction and lunch provided (half or full days).

SCHOOLS AND GUIDES
British ski school here

The British Alpine Ski & Snowboard School, featuring BASI-qualified instructors, is based in Morzine and Les Gets and we have good reports on the lessons. Reports on the ESF are generally good except for some complaints about class sizes.

FACILITIES FOR CHILDREN
Lots of possibilities

The facilities of the Outa nursery are quite impressive, but we've received reports of poor spoken English and low staff ratios. A new childcare center, Les Pingouins Malins, opened last season, but we have no reports. The Dérêches Farm offers days learning about animals, snowshoeing and tobogganing. A recent reporter's three and five year olds were both happy with the ESF, making 'rapid progress with friendly, attentive instructors'

GETTING THERE

Air Geneva, transfer 1½hr. Lyon, transfer 3½hr.

Rail Cluses or Thonon (30km/19 miles); regular bus connections to resort.

Phone numbers
From abroad use the prefix +33 and omit the initial 'o' of the phone number.

ACTIVITIES

Indoor Skating, bowling, cinemas, massage, table tennis, fitness track
Outdoor Horse-riding, sleigh rides, snow-shoe classes, artificial climbing wall, tennis, paragliding

TOURIST OFFICE

Postcode 74110
t +33 450 747272
f 450 790348
touristoffice@morzine-avoriaz.com
www.morzine.com

Staying there

As the extensive network of bus routes implies, Morzine is a town where getting from A to B can be tricky. It is well worth making sure that your accommodations are near the lifts that you expect to be using, which for most visitors means the gondola and tram to Le Pléney, gondola to Super-Morzine or tram to Avoriaz.

HOW TO GO
Good-value hotels

Hotels The range of hotel accommodations is wider than it at first appears – the handful of 3-star hotels includes some quite smart ones. But the core of the resort is its modest accommodations – dozens of 2-stars and quite a lot of 1-stars. If there is a resort with more hotels in the Logis de France group, we have yet to find it.
(((④ **Dahu** (0450 791369) Upmarket 3-star; elegant public areas and good restaurant and pool. Some distance from all lifts and public buses except the Ardent route, but private shuttle.
(((④ **Airelles** (0450 747121) Central 3-star close to Pléney lifts and Prodains and Nyon bus routes. Good pool.
(((④ **Champs Fleuris** (0450 791444) Comfy 3-star next to Pléney lifts. Pool.
((③ **Tremplin** (0450 791231) Also next to the lifts; 'friendly staff, good food'.
((③ **Bergerie** (0450 791369) Rustic, old-fashioned chalet with a few rooms and many more studios, in center. Friendly staff. Pool and gym.
(② **Côtes** (0450 790996) Simple, upwardly-mobile 2-star, with more studios than rooms. Pool compensates for poor position on the edge of town.
(② **Equipe** (0450 791143) One of the best 2-stars; next to the Pléney lift.
Apartments/condos The Télémark apartments are high quality, and close to the Super-Morzine gondola. We're told those by the Prodains tram are excellent.

EATING OUT
A fine choice

Morzine is scarcely a gourmet's resort, but it has a wide choice of good restaurants. The expensive La Chamade has high-quality French cuisine, Café Chaud is popular and atmospheric, and does good fondue, Les Airelles has a fine restaurant (Les Jardins d'Ulysse), known for its hot buffets, and Le Dahu also has good food. The L'Etale is an excellent, atmospheric pizza joint, bedecked in soccer club memorabilia, also serving local specialities – booking is advisable. Reporters also recommend Clin d'Oeil, Le Don Camillo, the Gavottes, La Grange and the Combe á Zore.

APRES-SKI
One of the livelier French resorts

Nightlife is good by French standards. Le Dixie gets animated, with Eurosport, MTV, a great little cellar bar and some live music. At the Crépuscule, near the Pléney lifts, dancing on the tables in ski boots to deafening music seems compulsory at après time. Just below, the Cavern is popular with resort staff; the Buddha, with cozy Asian decor, is great for a quieter drink. The tiny Sherpa, on the outskirts of town, is also worth a try. L'Opéra, The Paradis du Laury's and La Caverne (a ten-pin bowling alley-cum-disco-cum-pool-hall-cum-bar) are the late night haunts. Cabs to outlying accommodations are said to be difficult to come by in the small hours. There are two cinemas.

OFF THE SLOPES
Quite good; excursions possible

There is an excellent ice rink, which stages ice hockey matches and skating galas. Some hotels have pools which non-residents can pay to use. Buses run to Thonon for shopping, and car owners can drive to Geneva, Annecy or Montreux. There are lots of very pretty walks, and other activities include horse-drawn sleigh rides, horse-riding, paragliding and a cheese factory visit.

Les Gets 1170m/3,840ft

Decent children's facilities, French ambience, convenience, nice village restaurants, fine beginner areas and reasonable prices make Les Gets a good choice for families and many others. Several reporters said that it feels tucked away and rather secret. But it's a major trek to get into the main Portes du Soleil circuit on snow.

THE RESORT

Les Gets is a little old village of mainly traditional chalet buildings, 6km/4 miles from Morzine. Although the village has a scattered appearance, most facilities are conveniently close to the main lift station. It is on a through-road, but traffic does not intrude too much. It is fairly quiet in the evenings except at weekends when the atmosphere becomes more chic.

The local ticket covers all Les Gets, Nyon and Pléney lifts, saves a fair bit on a Portes du Soleil ticket, and is worth considering by less experienced skiers and riders if the snow is good.

THE MOUNTAINS

Les Gets is not an ideal base for the Portes du Soleil, but its local slopes have far more trails than any of the resorts on the circuit.

Slopes As well as the local slopes that are linked to Morzine (see earlier in chapter), Les Gets has runs on Mont Chéry, accessed by gondola and parallel chair. The front slopes face south-east – bad news at this altitude; but the other two flanks are shadier.

Snowboarding The local Les Gets and Morzine slopes are good for beginners and intermediates. Experts are catered for by the excellent terrain-park in Avoriaz.

Snow reliability Despite having a slightly higher elevation than Morzine, snow conditions can again be erratic. Fifty snow-guns were installed recently, improving cover back to the resort.

Experts Black runs from the Chéry Nord chair are steep and challenging in parts.

Intermediates High-mileage skiers and riders will enjoy cruising the Portes du Soleil circuit, and the local slopes are not bad for the less adventurous.

Beginners The village beginner areas are convenient, but there are better, more snow-sure ones up at Chavannes. Progression is simple, with a very easy run between Chavannes and the resort and pleasant greens from La Rosta and to La Turche, mean confident novices can cover some miles.

Cross-country Morzine is better, with an excellent array of trails. But Les Gets has 46km/29 miles of good varied loops on Mont Chéry and Les Chavannes.

Liftlines Provided there's good snow, not much of a problem, though weekend crowds are a drawback.

Mountain restaurants See Morzine.

Schools and guides We've had mixed reports of the ESF, with tales of 'instructors shouting at our four-year-olds in French' but also of children enjoying 'a great instructor'. Beginners should, if conditions are less than perfect, try to have lessons at Chavannes.

Facilities for children There is a non-ski nursery for children aged three months to three years, and two ski kindergartens. Ski Espace's 'Ile des Enfants' is reputedly the better of the two. ESF's Club Fantaski has been criticised for inattentive supervision.

STAYING THERE

How to go Many visitors stay in private chalets.

Hotels All the hotels are 3-star and below, mostly cheap and cheerful old 2-stars. The 3-star Crychar (0450 758050), close to central Les Gets at the foot of the slopes, is one of the best. The 2-star Alpen Sports (0450 758055) is a friendly, family run hotel – 'excellent food and good value for money' says a reporter. We've also had good reports of the the Nagano (0450 797146) and the Marmotte (0450 758033) – both 3-star.

Apartments/condos The tourist office has a long list of apartments.

Eating out Les Gets has a wide variety of places to eat – including Le Boomerang, with an Australian flavour. Most hotels have good restaurants. The Tyrol and the Schuss are good for pizza. The rustic Vieux Chêne, for Savoyard specialities; the Flambeau and Tourbillon are also recommended.

Après-ski Après-ski is quiet, especially on weekdays. The Pub Irlandaise and Prings, an English-owned pub, get very crowded, and Bar les Copeaux has been recommended. The Igloo and Havana Noche are popular discos.

Off the slopes There's a well-equipped fitness center with a pool, and an artificial ice rink. Outings to Geneva, Lausanne and Montreux are possible.

TOURIST OFFICE

Postcode 74260
t +33 450 758080
f 797690
lesgets@lesgets.com
www.lesgets.com

A variety of villages spread across a vast playground

HOW IT RATES

The slopes

Snow	****
Extent	****
Experts	***
Intermediates	*****
Beginners	*****
Convenience	*****
Liftlines	**
Restaurants	**

The rest

Scenery	****
Resort charm	*
Off-slope	*

What's new

For 2000/01, the line-prone Grande Rochette gondola from Plagne-Centre was replaced by a new twin-cable gondola with three times the capacity. A 3-star hotel, Les Balcons, opened in Belle-Plagne.

2001/02 will see more snowmaking above outlying villages. The Jean-Luc Crétier slalom course will be equipped with new snowmaking and floodlighting. The Biolley two-seater chair-lift from Plagne Centre and the 1800 two-seater from Plagne 1800 to Aime-la-Plagne are being upgraded to quads.

The planned link to Les Arcs may be ready for 2002/03, but it may slide to 2003/04.

198

- ➕ Extensive intermediate slopes, plus plentiful off-trail terrain
- ➕ Good beginner areas
- ➕ High and fairly snow-sure – and blessed with some grand views
- ➕ Purpose-built resort units are convenient for the slopes, and some are not unpleasant
- ➕ Attractive, traditional-style villages lower down share the slopes
- ➕ Wooded runs of lower resorts are useful in poor weather
- ➕ Good cross-country trails

- ➖ Still some serious lift bottlenecks
- ➖ Trails in the main bowl don't have much to offer experts
- ➖ Lower villages can suffer from poor snow – Champagny especially
- ➖ Unattractive architecture in some of the higher resort units
- ➖ Not many green runs for nervous beginners to go on to – though some blues are very easy
- ➖ Nightlife very limited

In terms of size, La Plagne's terrain and lift network ranks alongside those of Val-d'Isère/Tignes and the Trois Vallées, yet the resort doesn't enjoy the same status. What it lacks is the macho factor: it has very few black runs, and scores of blues. For most intermediates that is, of course, just the ticket – a friendly area, offering a sensation of travel between the widely spread resort villages. And in fact the place is fine for experts who are prepared to head off-trail.

The resort is part-way through a major program of investment in new lifts. That's very welcome, but it reflects the fact that the lift system is still a weakness. The lifts to Roche de Mio and the Bellecôte glacier, in particular, are just inadequate, and there is no immediate sign of replacements.

The resort

La Plagne consists of no fewer than ten separate 'villages'; six are purpose-built at altitude in the main bowl, on or above the tree line and linked by road, lifts and trails; the other four are scattered around outside the bowl.

Even the core resorts vary considerably in style and character. The first to be built, in the 1960s, was Plagne-Centre, at around 2000m/6,60oft – still the focal point for shops and après-ski. Typical of its time, it consists of ugly blocks with dreary indoor 'malls' that house a reasonable selection of shops, bars and restaurants. Some new developments just above Plagne-Centre are more pleasing to the eye.

Lifts radiate from Centre to all sides of the bowl, the major one being the

Plagne-Centre: brutal on the outside, claustrophobic on the inside ➔

MOUNTAIN FACTS

Altitude 1250m-3250m
4,100ft-10,66oft
Lifts 111
Trails 215km/134 miles
Green 9%
Blue 58%
Red 28%
Black 5%
Snowmaking 50 acres
Recco detectors used

LIFT TICKETS

2001/02 prices in
euros
La Plagne
Covers all lifts in La
Plagne and
Champagny-en-
Vanoise.
Beginners Free baby-
lift in each center.
Main ticket
1-day ticket 35
6-day ticket 167
Senior citizens
Over 60: 6-day ticket
142
Over 72: free ticket
Children
Under 14: 6-day ticket
123
Under 5: free ticket
Short-term tickets
Half-day ticket (26).
Single ascent on
inter-area links.
Notes Standard 6-day
ticket and over allows
one day each in Les
Arcs, Tignes-Val-
d'Isère, the Three
Valleys, Pralognan-la-
Vanoise and Les
Saisies.
5% discount on
presentation of a La
Plagne ticket in your
name from the last
two seasons.
Family discounts are
also available.
Alternative tickets
Village area tickets
available for
Montchavin-Les
Coches, Plagne
Montalbert, or
Champagny.
Limited 'Discovery'
tickets in each area.

big new twin-cable gondola to Grande Rochette. Another is a tram up to the even more obtrusive 'village' of Aime-la-Plagne – a group of monolithic blocks that attract derisory comments from most reporters.

Below these two, and a bit of a backwater, is Plagne 1800, where the buildings are small-scale and chalet-style.

A little way above Plagne-Centre is the newest development, Plagne-Soleil, still small as yet, but with its own shops and some attractive new chalets. This area is officially attached to Plagne-Villages, which is a rather strung-out but otherwise attractive collection of small-scale apartments and chalets in traditional style, handy for the slopes but for nothing else.

The two other core resort units are a bus-ride away, on the other side of a low hill. The large apartment buildings of Plagne-Bellecôte form a wall at the foot of the slopes down to it. Some way above it is Belle-Plagne – as its name suggests, easy on the eye, with a Disneyesque neo-Savoyard look, and complete with entirely underground parking. Reporters have complained of exhaustion when moving between the different levels in Belle Plagne; the bars and other facilities are concentrated in the lower part.

Then there are the lower resorts in the valleys outside the bowl. At the northern extremity of the area are the old village of Montchavin and its recently developed neighbor Les Coches. At the southern extremity, not far from Courchevel, is the village of Champagny. And at the western extremity is the modern development of Montalbert. For a description of each, see the end of this chapter.

The efficient, free bus system between the core resorts within the bowl runs until after midnight and allows you to explore the après-ski in different areas – the lifts between some of the villages also run late into the evening. The outlying villages are effectively isolated in the evenings.

Day trips to Les Arcs are easy, trips to Val-d'Isère, Tignes or the Three Valleys more time-consuming – all are covered for one day each with a six-day ticket.

The mountains

The majority of the slopes in the main bowl are above the tree line, though there are trees scattered around most of the resort centers. The slopes outside the bowl are open at the top but descend into woodland. The exposed glacier slopes on Bellecôte, to the west of the main bowl, rise up to 3250m/10,66oft. The gondola is prone to closure by high winds or poor weather and the surface lifts are normally shut in winter.

THE SLOPES
Multi-centered; can be confusing
La Plagne boasts 215km/134 miles of trails over a wide area that can be broken down into seven distinct but interlinked sectors. From Plagne-Centre you can take a lift up to **Biolley**, from where you can head back to Centre, to Aime-la-Plagne or down gentle runs to **Montalbert**, from where you ride several successive lifts back up. But the main lift out of Plagne-Centre leads up to **Grande Rochette**. From here there are good sweeping runs back down and an easier one over to Plagne-Bellecôte, or you can drop over the back into the predominantly south-facing **Champagny** sector (from which a lift arrives back up at Grande Rochette and another brings you out much further east). From the Champagny sector there are great views over to Courchevel, across the valley.

From Plagne-Bellecôte and Belle-

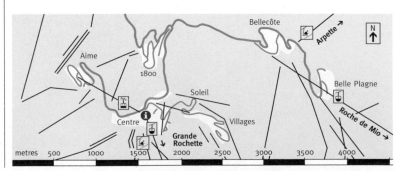

Plagne, a gondola heads up to **Roche de Mio**, where runs spread out in all directions – towards La Plagne, Champagny or **Montchavin/Les Coches.** Montchavin/Les Coches can also be reached by taking a chair from Plagne-Bellecôte. From Roche de Mio you can also take a gondola down to Col de la Chiaupe (there are no runs in that direction) then up to the **Bellecôte glacier**, start of some of the steepest slopes in the area. In good snow there is an easy off-trail run from the foot of Bellecôte at 2300m/7,550ft to Les Bauches, and the Montchavin slopes. Otherwise, you have to return to Roche de Mio.

The special 'evasion' map identifies five circuits of varying difficulty.

Several reporters have indicated that run classification is inconsistent; some runs are more difficult than their classification would suggest, while others are 'flattering'.

SNOW RELIABILITY
Good except in low-lying villages
Most of La Plagne's runs are snow-sure, being at altitudes between 2000m/6,560ft and 2700m/8,860ft on the largely north-facing open slopes above the purpose-built centers.

Runs down to the valley resorts can cause more problems, and you may have to take the lifts at times. This is particularly true of Champagny, where the two home runs are both south-facing. The runs down to Les Coches and Montchavin are north-facing and have snowmaking – these, and a few runs around Montalbert and Plagne-Bellecôte, are the main ones with snowmaking in the area, although the network is continually expanding.

FOR EXPERTS
A few good blacks and off-trail
In theory there are two potentially great black runs from Bellecôte to the chair-lift up to the gondola mid-station at Col de la Chiaupe – both beautiful long runs with a vertical of some 1000m/3,280ft that take you away from the lift system. But these are often closed due to too much or too little snow.

The long Emile Allais down from above Aime-la-Plagne through the forest, finishing at 1400m/4,590ft, is graded black only at its final stage. With a couple of surface lifts taking you back up, it is little used, although north-facing and very enjoyable in good snow. The shorter Coqs and Morbleu runs in the same sector are seriously steep.

The long, sweeping Mont de la Guerre red, with a 1250m/4,100ft

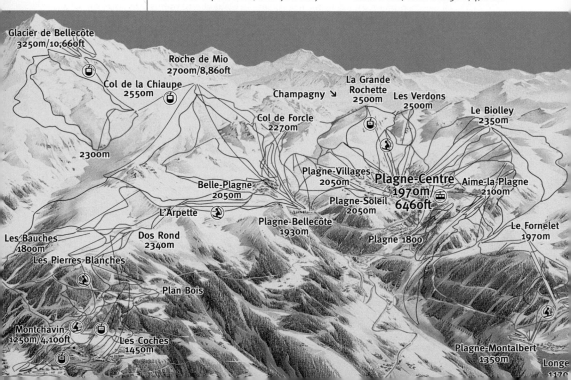

Glacier de Bellecôte
3250m/10,660ft

Roche de Mio
2700m/8,860ft

Col de la Chiaupe
2555m

2300m

Champagny ↘

Col de Forcle
2270m

La Grande
Rochette
2500m   Les Verdons
2500m

Le Biolley
2350m

Plagne-Villages
2050m   **Plagne-Centre** Aime-la-Plagne
2100m

Belle-Plagne
2050m

L'Arpette

1970m
Plagne-Soleil **6460ft**
2050m

Le Fornelet
1970m

Les Bauches
1800m

Les Pierres Blanches

Dos Rond
2340m

Plagne-Bellecôte
1930m

Plagne 1800

Plan Bois

Montchavin
1250m/4,100ft

Les Coches
1450m

Plagne-Montalbert
1350m

Longe
1170

Plagne-Centre
La Grande Rochette 2500m
s Verdons 2500m
Belle-Plagne
Plagne-Bellecôte ↓
Col de Forcle 2270m
Les Borseliers
Roche de Mio 2700m/8,86oft
Col de la Chiaupe 2550m
Bellecôte 3417m
Champagny-le-Haut
Le Planay
Champagny-en-Vanoise 1250m/4,100ft

vertical from La Grande Rochette–Les Verdons to Champagny, is also a beautiful run in good snow (a rare event).

There are other good long reds to cruise around on. But experts will get the best out of La Plagne if they employ a guide and explore the vast off-trail potential – which takes longer to get tracked out than in more 'macho' resorts. There are popular off-trail variants on the aforementioned black runs from Bellecôte down to Les Bauches (a drop of over 1400m/4,59oft). You can also head down off-trail to Peisey-Nancroix and take the lifts up to the Les Arcs slopes. Another beautiful and out-of-the-way off-trail run from Bellecôte is over the Col du Nant glacier towards Champagny-le-Haut.

In fresh snow, those who enjoy picking their way through woods in search of fresh light powder will not be disappointed by the forests above Montchavin and Montalbert.

FOR INTERMEDIATES
Great variety
Virtually the whole of La Plagne's area is a paradise for intermediates, with blue and red runs wherever you look. Your main choice will be whether to settle for one area for the day and explore it thoroughly, or just cruise around the trails that form the main arteries of the network.

For early intermediates there are plenty of gentle blue trails in the main La Plagne bowl, and a long, interesting run from Roche de Mio back to Belle Plagne, Les Inversins (involving a tunnel). The blue runs either side of Arpette, on the Montchavin side of the main bowl, are glorious cruises. In poor weather the best place to be is in the trees on the gentle runs leading down to Montalbert. The easiest way over to Champagny is from the Roche de Mio area rather than from Grande Rochette.

Better intermediates have lots of delightful long red runs to try. Roche de Mio to Les Bauches is a drop of 900m/2,95oft (the second half of this run is marked as a black). There are challenging red bump runs down from the glacier to the Col de la Chiaupe mid-station. And the main La Plagne bowl has enjoyable reds in all sectors. The Champagny sector has a couple of tough reds – Kamikaze and Hara-Kiri – leading from Grande Rochette. The Mont de la Guerre red is a satisfying run for adventurous intermediates.

FOR BEGINNERS
Excellent facilities for the novice
La Plagne is a good place to learn, with generally good snow and above-average facilities for beginners, especially children. Each of the main centers has beginner areas on its doorstep. There's a free surface lift in each resort as well. There are no long green runs to progress to, but no

SCHOOLS/GUIDES

2001/02 prices in
euros
ESF
Schools in all centers.
Prices vary; those for
Plagne Centre are
given here
Classes 6 days
2½hr, 3hr, 5hr, 6hr,
depending on center,
day and season
6 full days: 150
Children's classes
Ages: Up to 13 or 16
depending on village
6 full days: 131
Private lessons
1hr, 1½hr, 2hr
30 for 1hr

Eric Laboureix
In Belle-Plagne
Classes 6 days
am or pm
6 half days: 170
Children's classes
Ages: Up to 14
6 full days: 166
Private lessons
Hourly
31 for 1hr

Oxygène
Private school in
Plagne-Centre
Classes 6 days
am or pm
6 full days: 144
Children's classes
Ages: Up to 14
6 full days: 144
Private lessons
Hourly
32 for 1hr

Evolution 2
Private school in
Montchavin
Classes 5 days
5 days (3hr): 84
Children's classes
5 days (3hr): 76
Private lessons
Hourly
29 for 1hr

Antenne Handicap
Private lessons for
the disabled
31 for 1hr

boarding *La Plagne offers some pretty good terrain for all abilities of rider – there's a good mix of long, easy runs and high, open slopes with some fantastic off-trail variations that should be done with a guide. Whether on- or off-trail, be prepared for some flat areas, though. There are terrain-parks at Plagne-Bellecôte, Belle-Plagne and above Montchavin–Les Coches. The broad, gentle trails are ideal for beginners and carvers (crowds permitting). Most lifts are gondolas or chairs, though there are still some difficult-to-avoid surface lifts.*

shortage of easy blues. One reporter felt that the runs back into Plagne 1800 were a bit difficult for novices.

CROSS-COUNTRY
Open and wooded trails
There are 90km/56 miles of prepared and marked cross-country trails in La Plagne and its surrounding satellites. The most beautiful of these are the 30km/19 miles of winding track set out in the sunny valley around Champagny-le-Haut. The north-facing areas have more wooded trails that link the various centers. There is a 25km/16 mile route above Montchavin/Les Coches and an 18km/11 mile route above Montalbert. Plagne Bellecôte, Belle Plagne and Plagne Villages are similarly linked by a less arduous, 12km/7 mile route. Each of the trails has a beginners' circuit. Access is free (except at Champagny). A recent visitor points out that getting to the outlying loops can be time-consuming.

LIFTLINES
Bottlenecks in high season
When the resort is full there can be big liftlines to get out of the high-altitude centers at the start of the day. The old gondola from Plagne-Bellecôte via Belle-Plagne to Roche de Mio is still a bad bottleneck, despite the alternative ways available. The higher gondola is also overcrowded when snow is poor lower down. The new gondola from Plagne-Centre to Grande Rochette has

three times the capacity of the original, and reduces the lines impressively quickly. Two six-packs on the top slopes of the Champagny sector have greatly improved the links on that side. The fast Arpette chair from Plagne-Bellecôte towards Montchavin still causes liftlines, and there are several other lifts that can generate lines that you can't avoid, once you've descended to them – at Les Bauches for example. Crowds on the trails are as much of a problem as liftlines, particularly above Bellecôte in the afternoon.

MOUNTAIN RESTAURANTS
An improving choice
Mountain restaurants are numerous, varied and crowded only in peak periods, as many people prefer to descend to one of the resorts – particularly Champagny or Montchavin/Les Coches – at the end of the morning. Le Val Sante at Les Bauches is recommended. As are the Pierres Blanches, the Carroley, Plan Bois and Les Preizes on the Montchavin/Les Coches slopes. Two great rustic restaurants in which to hole up in poor weather for a long lunch of Savoyard dishes are Le Sauget, above Montchavin, and Au Bon Vieux Temps, just below Aime-la-Plagne. Reservations may be required at either. Chalet des Colosses above Plagne Bellecôte is also highly recommended, as is Roc des Blanchets at the top of

TRY THE OLYMPIC BOB-SLED RUN

If the thrills of a day on the slopes aren't enough, you can round it off by having a go on the 1992 Winter Olympics bob-sled run. The floodlit 1.5km/1 mile run drops 125m/400ft and has 19 bends. You can go in a proper four-man 'taxi-bob' (70 euros in 2000/01 – certain nights of the week only) or in a special padded driverless bob raft (30 euros). Most people find the bob raft's 80kph/50mph quite thrilling enough.

With the taxi-bob, you are one of three passengers wedged in behind the driver. You reach a maximum speed of 110kph/68mph and the pressure in turns can be as high as 3g – be sure your physical condition is up to it. You must be over 18. Additional insurance is available (yours may not be valid).

the Champagny gondola – friendly staff, both table- and self-service, beautiful views over to Courchevel from the terrace and good basic cooking. The little Breton cafe at the bottom of the Quillis lift at the start of the Levasset trail and the Borseliers (lower down) have also been highly recommended. The Forperet, above Montalbert, is also popular.

SCHOOLS AND GUIDES
Better alternatives to ESF
Each center has its own ESF school, offering classes for all abilities. Groups can be much too large (a recent visitor reports seeing classes of up to 20 students) and instructors speak English of varying standard. But reports about private lessons are generally positive. However, the consensus seems to be that the alternatives are preferable. The Oxygène school in Plagne-Centre continues to impress reporters. One recent report has nothing but praise for the sympathetic instructors and management of El Pro in Belle-Plagne. We have had good reports on Evolution 2 (based in Montchavin) – 'wonderful', says the parent of one junior pupil. Antenne Handicap offers private lessons for skiers with any kind of disability.

FACILITIES FOR CHILDREN
Good choice
Children are well catered for with facilities in each of the villages. The nursery at Belle-Plagne is 'excellent, with good English spoken'. However, one recent reporter complained that her daughter was the only English speaker in her ESF class.

Staying there

HOW TO GO
Mainly apartments
There are few hotels, but there are some attractive, simple 2-stars in the lower villages. Accommodations in the outlying satellite resorts are described at the end of the chapter. A reporter this year suggests checking out the resort website for special promotional deals.
Chalets There's a large number available – the majority are fairly simple, small, and located in 1800.
Hotels There are very few, all of 2-star or 3-star grading.
②② **Balcons** (0479 557655) Brand new 3-star at Belle Plagne. Pool.

②② **Eldorador** (0479 091209) Adequate hotel in Belle-Plagne – 'excellent food', according to several visitors.
②② **Terra Nova** (0479 557900) Big, new, 120-room 3-star hotel in Plagne-Centre.
Apartments/condos La Plagne is the ultimate apartment resort, but communal facilities are generally poor. The MGM apartments in Aime-la-Plagne were recently described as 'a real treat'. Two new 4-star residences – in Aime-La-Plagne and Plagne-Villages should also improve the general standard.

EATING OUT
Nothing fancy
Throughout the resort there is a good range of casual restaurants including pizzerias and traditional Savoyard places serving raclettes and fondue.

Reader recommendations in Plagne-Centre include La Métairie ('the most enjoyable we've encountered in the Alps') and Le Bec Fin. In Plagne-Villages, La Chevrette is recommended for pizzas and steaks. A recent reporter described his pizza at the Loup Garrou, next to the chair-lift in Plagne 1800, as 'the best he had ever tasted'. Au Bon

CHILDCARE
There are ESF ski kindergartens in all the high resort units, generally taking children from age 3. The ESF also runs all-day nurseries in most of the villages, mostly taking children aged 2 to 6 (18 months to 3 years in Belle Plagne). In Centre, independent nursery Marie Christine does much the same.

In Montchavin and Les Coches very young skiers go to the Nursery Club, the ESF taking over at age 4.

Phone numbers
From abroad use the prefix +33 and omit the initial 'o' of the phone number.

Aime-la-Plagne (on the skyline) isn't a 60s relic – it has expanded in recent years →

GETTING THERE

Air Geneva, transfer 3½hr. Lyon, transfer 3½hr. Chambéry, transfer 2½hr.

Rail Aime (18km/11 miles) and Bourg-St-Maurice (35km/22 miles) (Eurostar service to Bourg-St-Maurice and Aime available); frequent buses from station.

ACTIVITIES

Indoor Sauna and solarium in most centers, skating (Bellecôte and Aime-la-Plagne), squash (1800), fitness centers (Belle-Plagne, 1800, Centre, Bellecôte), cinemas, bowling

Outdoor Heated swimming pool (Bellecôte), bob-sleigh (La Roche), 30km/19 miles marked walks, paragliding, skidoos, climbing, skating, hang-gliding, snow-shoe excursions, dog sleigh tours

TOURIST OFFICE

Postcode 73211
t +33 479 097979
f 479 097010
ot.laplagne@wanadoo.fr
www.la-plagne.com

Vieux Temps (see also under Mountain restaurants) at Aime-la-Plagne is open in the evening, though a recent reporter was disappointed by his meal.

In Plagne-Bellecôte, La Ferme and Chalet des Colosses are recommended for Savoyard specialities. Le Matafan in Belle-Plagne is popular for Savoyard dishes (at lunch as well as dinner). The Cloche, Pappagone pizzeria and Maître Kanter have also been recommended.

APRES-SKI
Bars, bars, bars

Though fairly quiet during low season, La Plagne has a wide range of après-ski catering particularly to the younger crowd. In Belle-Plagne, Mat's and the Cheyenne are the main bars. The new Maître Kanter is also recommended. The King Café and the Luna are the liveliest bars in Plagne-Centre, and sometimes have live music. Plagne 1800 is fairly quiet at night – the Couleur Café and La Mine are popular. The Lincoln Pub in Plagne-Soleil is recommended. Plagne-Bellecôte is very limited at night, with only one real bar – Showtime. Aime-la-Plagne is also quiet. Neal's (Plagne-Centre), Le Jet 73 (Plagne-Bellecôte) and Le Saloon (Belle-Plagne) are the main discos recommended by local chalet staff.

OFF THE SLOPES
OK for the active

As well as the sports and fitness facilities, winter walks along marked trails in the March and April sunshine are particularly pleasant. It's also easy to get up the mountain on the gondolas, which both have restaurants at the top. The Olympic bob-sled run is a popular evening activity (see feature box). Excursions are limited.

STAYING IN THE LOWER RESORTS
A good plan

Montchavin (1250m/4,100ft) is a relatively unspoiled old farming community where wooden barns and sheds are much in evidence. Restaurant terraces set in orchards at the foot of the slopes add to the scene. There are adequate shops, a kindergarten and a school. Reaching the La Plagne slopes involves a series of lifts; but the local slopes have quite a bit to offer – the local lift ticket covers 30km/19 miles of mostly easy, pretty, sheltered runs, well endowed with snowmaking guns, with beginner areas at village level and up at Plan

Bois. Those who do venture further afield can return from Roche de Mio in one lovely long swoop (partly black). The more usual way home involves some of the trickiest blue runs we have encountered. Après-ski is quiet, but the village doesn't lack atmosphere and has a couple of nice little bars and a movie theater. The Bellecôte hotel (0479 078330) is convenient for the slopes.

Les Coches (1450m/4,760ft) is only a walk away, and shares the same slopes. It is a sympathetically designed modern mini-resort that several reporters have liked for its 'small, quiet and friendly' feel and its traffic-free center. It has its own school and kindergarten. The Last One pub is good for après-ski, with a big screen TV and regular live bands. La Poze and la Taverne du Monchu are recommended for eating out.

Montalbert (1350m/4,430ft) is a traditional but much expanded village with quicker access into the main area – though it's a long way from here across to the Bellecôte glacier. The local slopes are easy and wooded – a useful insurance against bad visibility. The Aigle Rouge (0479 555105) is a simple hotel.

Champagny-en-Vanoise (1250m/4,100ft) is a charming village in a pretty, wooded setting, with its modern expansion done sensitively. Champagny is better placed than any of the other outlying villages for access into the main bowl – and well placed for an outing by taxi or car to Courchevel (or the beautiful Vanoise national park with its 500km/310 miles of marked walking paths). Given good snow, there are lovely runs home from above Plagne-Centre but their southerly orientation means you may have to get a gondola instead. There are several hotels, of which the two best are both in the Logis de France consortium. The Glières (0479 550552) is a rustic old hotel with varied rooms, a friendly welcome and good food. L'Ancolie (0479 550500) is smarter, with modern facilities, 'high quality food and smiling staff'; it is very convenient for the gondola. The village is quiet in the evenings.

Portes du Soleil

Low altitude cross-border cruising

The Portes du Soleil vies with the Trois Vallées for the title of World's Largest Ski Area and claims 650km/400 miles of slopes. But these are not all linked, and they are very different from those of Méribel, Courchevel and neighbours. The Portes du Soleil's slopes are spread out over a large area and most of them are part of an extensive circuit straddling the French–Swiss border; you can travel the circuit in either direction, with a short bus-ride needed only at Châtel. There are smaller areas to explore slightly off the main circuit. The runs are great for enthusiastic intermediates who like to travel long distances and through different resorts. There are few of the tightly packed networks of runs that encourage you to stay put in one area – though there are exceptions. The area also has some nice rustic mountain restaurants, serving good food in pleasant, sunny settings.

The lifts throughout the area have been improved in recent years with several new high-speed chair-lifts eliminating some bad bottlenecks. But the slopes are low by French standards, with top heights in the range 2000m/6,600ft to 2300m/7,500ft and good snow is far from assured (though snowmaking has been expanded in recent years). When the snow is good you can have a great time racing all over the circuit (as we did in fresh powder on our last visit). But the slopes can get very crowded, especially on weekends and in the Avoriaz area. See separate chapters on

the main resorts: Avoriaz, Châtel (including La Chapelle d'Abondance), Morzine (including Les Gets) and Champéry (including Champoussin, Les Crosets and Morgins).

Purpose-built Avoriaz has the most snow-sure slopes and is especially good for families, with a big snow-garden right in the heart of the car-free village. But its local slopes do get crowded, especially on weekends when crowds pour in from nearby Geneva, and prices are rather high by local standards. The other French resort on the main circuit is Châtel. Given good snow, it has some of the best runs in the area. It is an old and quite picturesque village, but it's a busy, traffic-jammed place. It has a couple of good beginner areas both at resort level and up the mountain. Morzine is close to Avoriaz. It is linked by lift but there's no trail all the way back to town. It's a summer as well as a winter resort – a pleasant, bustling little town with good shops and restaurants, busy traffic and long walks to the lifts from many of the accommodations. The local slopes are extensive, and linked to those of the slightly higher, quieter, traditional village of Les Gets. But they

are low and good snow is certainly not assured. You can use Morzine as a base to ski the main Portes du Soleil circuit, but it's not ideal. Les Gets is even further off the main circuit.

On the Swiss side, Champéry is a classic charming mountain village – but again just off the main circuit. You have to take a tram down from the main slopes as well as up to them or, if there is enough snow, a bus from a trail which ends out of town.

Champoussin and Les Crosets are purpose-built mini-resorts set on the very extensive open slopes between Champéry and Morgins, with fairly direct links over to Avoriaz. Morgins, in contrast to Champéry, has excellent village slopes – but they are low and sunny, and although its higher local runs are enjoyable and prettily wooded, they are limited in extent.

On a spur off the main circuit are the resorts of La Chapelle d'Abondance (which has one of our favorite hotel-restaurants) in France and Torgon in Switzerland (which has splendid views over Lake Geneva). This area can be reached from above the Super-Châtel area and is usually quiet even when the rest of the circuit is packed.

SNOWPIX.COM / CHRIS GILL

Lifts spread out in all directions from Avoriaz ↓

Serre-Chevalier 1350m-1500m/4,430ft-4,920ft

Surprise! Big, French, but full of character

207

HOW IT RATES

The slopes

Snow	****
Extent	****
Experts	***
Intermediates	****
Beginners	****
Convenience	***
Liftlines	***
Restaurants	***

The rest

Scenery	****
Resort charm	***
Off-slope	**

➕ Big, varied mountain, with something for everyone

➕ Interesting mixture of wooded runs (ideal for blizzards) and open bowls (with acres of off-trail)

➕ One of the few big French areas based on old villages with character

➕ Good-value and atmospheric old hotels, restaurants and chalets

➕ Lift ticket covers days elsewhere

➕ Spectacular drive from Grenoble

➖ A lot of indiscriminate new building, which looks awful from the slopes

➖ Still lots of slow, old lifts, including many surface lifts – some of them vicious

➖ Serious liftlines on French holidays

➖ Busy road runs through the resort villages, with traffic jams at times

➖ Limited nightlife

➖ Inadequate trail map

➖ Few off-slope diversions

Serre-Chevalier is a big-league resort, but isn't as well known outside France as many of its rivals to the north and west. Maybe that's because it doesn't lend itself to marketing hype – the slopes are not super-high, the lifts are not super-efficient, the hotels are far from super-sophisticated. But we like it a lot: it's one of the few French resorts where you can find the ambience you might look for on a summer holiday – a sort of Provence in the snow, with lots of small, family-run hotels and restaurants housed in old stone buildings.

The slopes are equally likeable. Although there are runs on only one side of the long valley they are split into different segments, so you get a real sensation of travel. In good snow conditions there are excellent off-trail opportunities to keep experts happy, as well as intermediates. What really sets the area apart from the French norm is the woodland runs, making Serre-Chevalier one of the best places to be when snow is falling – though there are plenty of open runs, too.

What's new

For 2001/02 a new fast six-seater chair will replace the parallel Prorel surface lifts, linking the Chantmerle section to the Briançon slopes.

Other developments include floodlighting on the beginners' slopes at the Briançon gondola mid-station, a new terrain-park with a super-pipe at Alpage, above Villeneuve, and a new children's snow park at Bachas.

Snowmaking is being doubled – 300 guns will cover 30km/19 miles of trails for 2001/02 – the Vallons, Casse du Boeuf, Eychauda and Aya runs will all benefit from new artificial cover.

A new Club Med in Villeneuve is also planned for next season.

A free guest card – available at hotels and from the tourist office – gives access to a number of resort amenities.

The resort

The resort is made up of a string of 13 villages set on a valley floor running roughly north-west to south-east, below the north-east-facing slopes of the mountain range that gives the resort its name. From the north-west – coming over the Col du Lautaret from Grenoble – the three main villages are Le Monêtier (or Serre-Che 1500), Villeneuve (1400) and Chantemerle (1350), spread over a distance of 5km/3 miles. Finally, at the extreme south-eastern end of the mountain, is Briançon (1200) – not a village but a town (the highest in France). Nine smaller villages can be identified, and some give their names to the communes: Villeneuve is in the commune of La Salle les Alpes, for example. Confusing.

Serre-Chevalier is not a sophisticated or upscale resort, in any sense. Although each of its parts is based on a simple old village, there is a lot of modern development, which ranges from brash to brutal, and even the older parts are roughly rustic rather than conventionally pretty. (A ban on corrugated iron roofs would help.) Because the resort is so spread out, cars and buses are difficult to escape – indeed, in parts the place puts us in mind of some American resorts. But when blanketed by snow the older villages and hamlets do have an unpretentious charm, and we find the place as a whole easy to like.

There are no luxury hotels or swanky restaurants; on the other hand, there are more hotels in the Logis de France 'club' here than in any other ski resort. This is a family resort, which fills up (even more than most others) with French children in the February high season. You have been warned.

The heart of the resort is **Villeneuve**, which has two gondolas and a fast quad chair going up to widely separated points at mid-mountain. The central area of new development near the lifts is

← to Monêtier Villeneuve Chantemerle

Echaillon N to Briançon →

↙ Serre Ratier

metres 500 1000 1500 2000 2500 3000 3500 4000

brutal and charmless. But not far away is the peaceful and traditional hamlet of Le Bez, which has a third gondola, and across the main road and river is the old stone village of Villeneuve with its quiet main street lined by cozy bars, hotels and restaurants.

Not far down the valley **Chantemerle** gives access to opposite ends of the mid-mountain plateau of Serre Ratier via a gondola and a tram, both with second stages above. (The planned fast chair link from the village up to Prorel has been abandoned.) Chantemerle has some tasteless modern buildings in the center and along the main road. The old sector is a couple of minutes' walk from the lifts, with a lovely church and most of the restaurants, bars and small hotels.

At the top of the valley, **Le Monêtier** has one main access lift – a fast quad chair to mid-mountain, reached from the village by bus or a long and steepish walk, tricky when ice is around. Le Monêtier is the smallest, quietest and most unspoiled of the main villages, with a pronounced Provençal feel to its narrow streets and little squares, and new building mostly in sympathetic style. Sadly, the road to Grenoble, which skirts the other villages, bisects Le Monêtier; pedestrians stroll about bravely blocking the road, hoping the cars will avoid them.

Briançon has a gondola from right in the town to mid-mountain and on almost to the top. The area around the lift station has a wide selection of modern shops, bars, hotels and restaurants, but no character. In contrast, the lovely 17th-century upper quarter is a delight, complete with impressive fortifications, narrow cobbled streets and traditional restaurants, auberges and patisseries. Great views from the top, too.

Regular and reliable ski buses (covered on the free guest card) link all the villages and lift bases along the valley – but they finish quite early, and cabs aren't cheap.

A six-day area ticket covers a day in each of Les Deux-Alpes, Alpe-d'Huez, Puy-St-Vincent and the Milky Way (several reporters have enjoyed a day out to Montgenèvre, at the French end of that area). You also get a discount on a day at La Grave. All of these outings are possible by public transport, but are much more attractive to those with a car. If driving, you are likely to approach over the high Col du Lautaret, which is usually kept clear of snow but is occasionally closed by avalanche danger.

Air travellers are much better off using Turin airport than Lyon.

The mountains

Trees cover almost two-thirds of the mountain, providing some of France's best bad-weather terrain. The Serre-Chevalier massif is not particularly dramatic, but from the peaks and some other points there are fine views of the Ecrins massif, the highest within France (ie not shared with Italy).

The trail map is supposed to have

MOUNTAIN FACTS

Altitude	1350m-2780m
	4,430ft-9,120ft
Lifts	76
Trails	250km/
	155 miles
Green	19%
Blue	19%
Red	49%
Black	13%
Snowmaking	30km/
	19 miles
Recco detectors used	

boarding *Serre-Che is a snowboarding hot-spot, popular mainly with advanced boarders because of the off-trail powder and because the resort has invested in loads of fun features. There's big air in Briançon, boarder-cross in Villeneuve and Chantemerle and a half-pipe in Villeneuve, all with sound-systems. The diverse trails with open and tree-lined runs also suit intermediates, though there are annoying flat sections between some lifts and several tracks the less confident might find tricky. The main lifts are chairs and gondolas but there are a lot of difficult-to-avoid and violent surface lifts. Evenings are fairly quiet but there's at least one lively bar in each center.*

LIFT TICKETS

2001/02 prices in euros

Grand Serre-Chevalier
Covers all lifts in Briançon, Chantemerle, Villeneuve and Le Monêtier.

Main ticket
1-day ticket 30
6-day ticket 150

Senior citizens
Over 60: 6-day ticket 107
Over 70: free ticket

Children
Under 12: 6-day ticket 107
Under 6: free ticket

Notes Tickets of 6 days or more give one day in each of Les Deux-Alpes, Alpe-d'Huez, Puy-St-Vincent and Voie Lactée (Milky Way). Reductions for families.

Alternative tickets
Tickets covering individual areas of Serre-Chevalier. Adult 6-day ticket: Briançon, 95, Le Monêtier 109, Chantemerle / Villeneuve 129 Morning and afternoon tickets. Night-skiing ticket. Beginner's ticket. Non-skier's ticket.

been improved, but it remains infuriatingly unclear and imprecise in places. Readers have found navigation is made even more challenging by 'particularly poor' signposting and the tendency of runs to 'change color halfway down'. And last winter we found that the signposting at altitude is not up to the job when a storm socks in; take great care.

Trail grading is inclined to exaggerate difficulty – many reds, in particular, could be classified blue.

THE SLOPES
Interestingly varied and pretty
Serre-Chevalier's 250km/155 miles of trails are spread across four main sectors above the four main villages. The sector above Villeneuve is the most extensive, reaching back a good way into the mountains and spreading over four or five identifiable bowls. The main mid-station is Fréjus at 2100m/6,890ft. This sector is reliably linked to the slightly smaller Chantemerle sector at quite a low level – well below the tree line. The link from here to Briançon is over a high, exposed col and is now via a new six-pack. The link between Villeneuve and Le Monêtier is liable to closure by high winds or avalanche danger.

SNOW RELIABILITY
Good – especially upper slopes
Most slopes face north or north-east and so hold snow well, especially high up (there are lots of lifts starting above 2000m/6,600ft). The weather pattern is different from that of the northern Alps and even that of Les Deux-Alpes or Alpe-d'Huez, only a few miles to the west. It can get good snow when there is a shortage elsewhere (as it did in

the early part of 2001) and vice versa. There is snowmaking on long runs down to each village, and this is being doubled for next season – taking the snow-gun tally up to 300 for 30km/19 miles of trails.

FOR EXPERTS
Deep, not notably steep
There is plenty to amuse experts – except those wanting extreme steeps.

The broad black runs down to Villeneuve and Chantemerle are only just black in steepness, but they are fine runs with their gradient sustained over an impressive vertical of around 800m/2,600. One or the other may be closed for days on end for racing or training. The rather neglected Tabuc run, sweeping around the mountain away from the lifts to Le Monêtier, has a couple of genuinely steep pitches but is mainly a cruise; it makes a fine end to the day. For bumps, look higher up the mountain to the steeper slopes served by the two top lifts above Le Monêtier and the three above Villeneuve. The runs beside these lifts – on and off-trail – form a great playground in good snow. The more roundabout Isolée black is a readers' favorite – 'scenic and challenging'.

There are also plenty of more serious off-trail expeditions to be done. Highlights include: Tête de Grand Pré to Villeneuve (a climb from Cucumelle); off the back of L'Eychauda to Puy-St-André (isolated, beautiful, cab-ride home); L'Yret to Le Monêtier via Vallon de la Montagnolle; Tabuc (steep at the start, very beautiful) – and the Mecca of La Grave is nearby.

FOR INTERMEDIATES
Ski wherever you like

Serre-Chevalier's slopes ideally suit intermediates, who can buzz around without worrying about nasty surprises on the way. On the trail map red runs far outnumber blues – but most reds are at the easy end of the scale and the grooming is usually good, so even nervous intermediates shouldn't have problems with them.

There's plenty for more adventurous intermediates, though. Many runs are wide enough for a fast pace. Cucumelle in the Villeneuve sector is a favorite – a beautiful long red away from the lifts, with a challenging initial section. The red runs off the little-used Aiguillette chair in the Chantemerle sector are worth seeking out – quiet, enjoyable fast cruises.

If the reds are starting to seem a bit tame, there is plenty more to progress to. Unless ice towards the bottom is a problem, the blacks on the lower mountain should be first on the agenda, and the bumpier ones higher up can be tackled if snow is good.

FOR BEGINNERS
Best at Villeneuve

All three main villages have beginner areas (at Chantemerle it's small, and you generally go up to Serre Ratier or Grand Alpe). Villeneuve has excellent green runs to progress to above Fréjus. The Chantemerle sector is less suitable for confidence-building, but has some easy high runs, at Grand Alpe for instance. Both sectors have green paths winding down from mid-mountain. But they are narrow, and not enjoyable when the runs become rutted and others are speeding along. Le Monêtier's easy runs are at resort level, next to excellent beginner areas, and the area has been recommended by beginners for 'better snow and fewer people'.

FOR CROSS-COUNTRY
Excellent if the snow is good

There are 45km/28 miles of tracks along the valley floor, mainly following the gurgling river between Le Monêtier and Villeneuve and going on up towards the Col du Lautaret.

LIFTLINES
Avoid French school holidays

More than most resorts, Serre-Chevalier seems to fill up with French families in the February holidays, producing serious lines all over the place. The Aiguillette chair in the Chantemerle sector is a good place to escape to.

At other times a range of big lifts means there are few problems getting out of the valley. But old, slow lifts still cause lines at altitude. The Prorel

FRANCE

210

SNOWPIX.COM / CHRIS GILL
Le Monêtier is no Tirolean picture postcard, but it does still look like a mountain village ↓

Chantemerle may have been a mountain village originally, but it sure doesn't look like one any longer →

SNOWPIX.COM / CHRIS GILL

SCHOOLS/GUIDES

2001/02 prices in euros

ESF In all centers
Classes 6 days, 5hr: 3hr am and 2hr pm; half-day am or pm
6 full days: 170
Children's classes
Ages: up to 12
6 full days: 166
Private lessons
Hourly: 29

Ecole de Ski Buissonnière
Classes am or pm
6 mornings: 92
Children's classes
Ages: up to 12
6 mornings: 90
Private lessons
Hourly: 29

Génération Snow
6 mornings: 110
1½hr: 42

Montagne Adventure
Off-trail, ski-touring

Compagnie des Guides de l'Oisans
Off-trail, ski tours, ice-climbing, snow-shoes

Montagne à la carte
Off-trail, ski-touring, heli-skiing, climbing, snow-shoes

Montagne et Ski
Off-trail, ski-touring, heli-skiing, snow-shoes

David Legendre
Snow-shoes

GETTING THERE

Air Turin, transfer 2½hr. Grenoble, transfer 2½hr. Lyon, transfer 4hr.

Rail Briançon (6km/4 miles); regular buses from station.

double surface lift from Chantemerle towards Briançon – a regular bottleneck – is being replaced by a six-pack.

MOUNTAIN RESTAURANTS
Not a highlight
Mountain restaurants are quite well distributed, but the few good ones are mostly concentrated in the central sectors. If lunch is an important part of your day, plan it carefully; if it's a very important part, go elsewhere.

For a serious lunch, we head for Pi Maï in the hamlet of Fréjus, a little way below the Fréjus lift station. Its table-service meals are not cheap, but the food is good and the spacious, rustic restaurant with log fire is a fine place to retreat to on a bad day. Service may be charming, or not. Also in the Villeneuve sector is L'Echaillon, a lofty building with table-service food that we and some others have enjoyed; finding it is a bit of a challenge.

At Serre Ratier, above Chantemerle, is a big, popular and noisy self-service, with live entertainment. Higher up, the big Grand Alpe restaurant offers good value and good views but reportedly no longer offers table service.

In the Briançon sector, the little chalet just down from the top of Prorel, has great views of the Ecrins and is reasonably priced.

Above Le Monêtier the choice is between the unremarkable self-service

Bachas at mid-mountain and the cozy Peyra Juana much lower down, where we and readers alike have enjoyed excellent service, food and value.

SCHOOLS AND GUIDES
Nothing but praise
We have received a number of reports on the Ecole de Ski Buissonnière over the years – all of them full of praise. For example: 'We thoroughly enjoyed a two-hour introductory snowboarding class. Instructors speak good English and classes are small.' This year we also have an enthusiastic report on an ESF class in Le Monêtier that was 'almost like a private lesson'.

FACILITIES FOR CHILDREN
Facilities at each village
We have had no very recent reports, but the Ecole de Ski Buissonnière (see Schools and guides, above) also teaches children and has been praised in the past, as has Les Schtroumpfs in Villeneuve.

Staying there

HOW TO GO
Small family-run hotels
Hotels One of the features of this string of little villages is the range of attractive family-run hotels – many of them part of the Logis de France marketing consortium.

Phone numbers

From abroad use the prefix +33 and omit the initial 'o' of the phone number.

CHILDCARE

Each of the main villages has its own non-ski nursery that takes children all day (9am to 5pm). At Villeneuve, Les Schtroumpfs (0492 247095) caters for kids from age 6 months; meals not provided. At Chantemerle, Les Poussins (0492 240343) takes them from age 8 months; meals provided. At Le Monêtier, Garderie de Pré-Chabert (0492 244575) takes them from age 18 months (6 months out of school holiday times); meals not provided.

ACTIVITIES

Indoor Swimming pool, sauna, fitness centers, film theaters, bridge
Outdoor At Chantemerle: skating rink, paragliding, cleared paths, snow-shoe walks, snowmobiling. At Villeneuve: ice-driving circuit, skating rink, horse-riding, sleigh rides, cleared paths, paragliding, snow-shoe walks, snowmobiling. At Le Monêtier: skating rink, cleared paths, hang-gliding, hot springs, snow-shoe walks, ski-joring.

TOURIST OFFICE

Postcode 05240
t +33 492 249898
f 492 249884
contact@ot-serrechevalier.fr
www.serre-chevalier.com

In Monêtier:
((③ **Auberge du Choucas** (0492 244273) Smart wood-panelled rooms, and good food in stone-vaulted restaurant.
(② **Europe** (0492 244003) Simple but well run Logis in heart of old village, with pleasant bar and decent food.
(② **Alliey** (0492 244002) Our favorite place to eat (see Eating out).
In Villeneuve:
(② **Lièvre Blanc** (0492 247405) Former coaching inn, with a large, busy stone-vaulted bar and its own guide and rental shop.
(② **Christiania** (0492 247633) Traditional hotel on main road, crammed with ornaments.
(② **Vieille Ferme** (0492 247644) Stylish conversion on the edge of the village.
(② **Cimotel** (0492 247822) Modern and charmless, with good-sized rooms and 'excellent' food.
(① **Chatelas** (0492 247474) Prettily decorated simple chalet by river.
In Chantemerle:
(② **Plein Sud** (0492 241701) Modern; pool and sauna.
(② **Boule de Neige** (0492 240016) Comfortable, friendly, in the old center.
(① **Ricelle** (0492 240019) Charming, but across the valley from the slopes in Villard-Laté. Good food.
Apartments/condos There are plenty of modern apartment blocks in Villeneuve, Briançon and Chantemerle. Few have charm.

STAYING UP THE MOUNTAIN
Worth considering

Chalet-hotel Serre Ratier (0492 241581), at the mid-station of the Chantemerle tram, does full board at reasonable rates. A more seductive possibility is to stay at Pi Maï (0492 248363) in Fréjus, above Villeneuve (see Mountain restaurants).

EATING OUT
Unpretentious and traditional

In Le Monêtier, there are several good hotel-based options. Our favorite is the panelled restaurant of the Alliey, which offers excellent food at astoundingly moderate prices and an impressive wine list. The Auberge du Choucas considers itself best in town and is certainly the most expensive. The Europe has reliable French cooking at reasonable prices. The Boîte à Fromages does a 'magnificent' fondue.

In the old part of Villeneuve, La Pastorale is a crowded, cramped vault with a warm welcome, an open-fire grill and good-value menu. The Marotte, a tiny stone building with classic French cuisine, has been highly praised. The Noctambule and Le Refuge specialize in fondue and raclette. And there are good crêperies – try the Petit Duc, or La Manouille. Over in Le Bez, Le Bidule is said to have 'first-class food and service, at good value', while the Siyou in the old village of La Salle is good for 'local specialities at very reasonable prices'.

In Chantemerle, Le Couch'où is good value for fondue and raclette, and has a pizzeria upstairs. The candlelit Crystal is the most formal and expensive place in town. The Kandahar is a charming pizzeria and the rustic Ricelle offers amazing value.

APRES-SKI
Quiet streets and few bars

Nightlife seems to revolve around bars, scattered through the various villages.

In Le Monêtier the Alpen is a proper skiers' bar with Tirol-style U-shaped bench seats, a happy hour, free nibbles and welcoming staff. The British-run Rif Blanc bar is dreary but now rivals the Pub in popularity. If you want to forget you're in a ski resort (and see French smoking laws at their least effective), hit the Cibouit.

In Villeneuve the bar of the Lièvre Blanc is popular; the Iceberg is a pub-style bar frequented by teenagers. The Frog is cramped, but has 'good atmosphere'. In Chantemerle the Yeti and the Underground beneath it are focal. The Kitzbühel has a good atmosphere, particularly when sporting events are shown. After everything else has closed, a karaoke bar with 'an erratic door policy' may still let you in.

OFF THE SLOPES
Try the hot baths

Serre-Chevalier doesn't hold many off-slope attractions, and it's certainly not for avid shoppers, but the old town of Briançon is well worth a visit. Visitors have enjoyed walking in the valley on 'well-prepared trails', and the indoor-outdoor thermal bath in Le Monêtier (re-opened in 1999) makes a great place to watch the sun go down. The swimming pool in the hotel Sporting in Villeneuve is open to non-residents.

Ste-Foy-Tarentaise
1550m/5,090ft

Secret off-trail haven for those in the know

HOW IT RATES

The slopes

Snow	***
Extent	*
Experts	****
Intermediates	***
Beginners	**
Convenience	***
Lines	*****
Restaurants	*

The rest

Scenery	***
Resort charm	***
Off-slope	*

➕ No crowds

➕ Lots of excellent off-trail and untracked powder

➕ Cheap lift ticket and good value lodging

➕ Tarentaise mega-resorts nearby for a change of scene

➖ Tiny mountain hamlet offers few off-slope diversions

➖ Very limited trail network for high-mileage trail-bashers

➖ Few off-slope diversions

➖ Limited après-ski

This small area in the Tarentaise has been developed only since 1990. The millions who flock to the nearby mega-resorts of Val-d'Isère and Les Arcs never give it a thought. But those in the know are well rewarded. It's an uncrowded gem with some wonderful off-trail slopes for experts and intermediates.

What's new

Further development in keeping with the character of the resort is under way at the ski station, thanks to a new mayor with a commitment to expansion. Handsome new chalets are being built at the station for the coming season and there will be improvements to a couple of runs. More facilities and even more lifts are on the cards in the long run.

THE RESORT

There isn't much of one; that's part of the charm of this place – it's ideal for getting away from the crowds. The ski station of Ste-Foy, also known as Bonconseil, is a tiny mountain hamlet set 8km/5 miles off the main road between Val-d'Isère and Bourg-St-Maurice: turn off at La Thuile, just after the village of Ste-Foy. The largest building at the station houses the ticket office, a cafe/bar and the only equipment shop (Zigzags, which readers roundly condemn for its terrible service).

THE MOUNTAIN

Off-trail guides from Val regularly impress clients by bringing them to Ste-Foy's deserted slopes, accessed by three quad chairs, rising one above the other to the Col de l'Aiguille. Impressive as the off-trail can be, you may want to spread your wings from the tiny resort during a week's stay, particularly if the snow is unkind. Luckily Val-d'Isère, Tignes, Les Arcs (via Villaroger) and La Rosière are all within easy reach (with a car). You're entitled to a free day in La Rosière, and reduced prices in all the rest, with a current Ste-Foy six-day ticket – which at 82 euros last season was half the price of neighbouring Val d'Isère. A day ticket was a bargain 15 euros.

Slopes The top lift accesses almost 600m/1,970ft of vertical above the tree line and superb, long off-trail routes on the back of the mountain. The two lower chairs serve pleasant green, blue

MOUNTAIN FACTS

Altitude	1550m-2620m
	5,090ft-8,600ft
Lifts	5
Trails	25km/16 miles
Green	8%
Blue	15%
Red	54%
Black	23%
Snowmaking	None

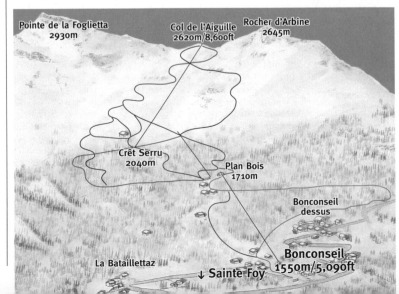

Pointe de la Foglietta 2930m
Col de l'Aiguille 2620m/8,600ft
Rocher d'Arbine 2645m
Crêt Serru 2040m
Plan Bois 1710m
Bonconseil dessus
Bonconseil 1550m/5,090ft
La Bataillettaz
↓ Sainte Foy

and red runs through trees and back to the base station. Don't come here for quality grooming or modern lifts, but this reporter didn't care: 'Most of my ski career I've been in Verbier, Zermatt and Vail. Skiing in Ste-Foy is better.'

Snow reliability The slopes face north or west. Snow reliability is good on the former but can suffer on the latter. But the lack of crowds means you can still make fresh tracks days after a storm.

Snowboarding Great free-riding terrain. A terrain park was built last year too.

Experts Experts can pass happy times on and off the sides of Ste-Foy's black and red runs, but it's the more serious off-trail you come for, for which you need a guide. There are wonderful runs down through deserted old villages to the road between Ste-Foy and Val-d'Isère and a splendid route off to the left which starts with a hike and takes you through trees and over a stream down to the tiny village of Le Crot. The ESF runs group off-trail trips, and arranges transport back to the station. There are three refuges in the area if you fancy an overnight adventure.

Intermediates Intermediates can enjoy 1000m/3,280ft vertical of uncrowded reds – ideal for confidence building and sharpening technique. The higher slopes are the more difficult – the red L'Aiguille is a superb test for confident intermediates, who should also try the off-trail (with a guide). Anyone who doesn't fancy experimenting with off-trail will tire of the limited runs in a day or so and be champing at the bit to get to Val d'Isère or Les Arcs.

Beginners Not the best place, but there is a small beginners' surface lift at the base. After that you can progress to a green run off the first chair – a pleasant, gentle track through trees – and a gentle blue off the second.

Cross-country No prepared trails, but ask the tourist office about marked itinerary routes such as Planay dessus.

Liftlines You have more chance of winning the lottery than finding a liftline at Ste-Foy.

Mountain restaurants There are two rustic mountain restaurants at the top of the first chair, Les Brevettes and Chez Léon. Recent reporters enjoyed the plat du jour at the latter but have been less complimentary about the former. La Ruelle, at the bottom of the first chair, is a good, rustic bar-restaurant, and La Maison à Colonnes, also at the base, gets good write-ups: 'Friendly, interesting menu, nice atmosphere.' There's also the Pitchouli for drinks and snacks in the main base building.

Schools and guides We've had good reports of ski school, especially for children (accepted from age four), There's a good chance classes will not be large.

Facilities for children There is a nursery, Les P'tits Trappeurs, which takes children from age three.

STAYING THERE

Drivers have most choice. If you don't have a car it's most convenient to stay at the ski station, since buses to and from Ste-Foy village run only every one to two hours (taking 20 minutes).

How to go Most people organize their own trip. Ste-Foy village is only about 20 minutes from the Eurostar terminal at Bourg St Maurice.

Hotels Auberge sur la Montagne (069583), just above the turn-off at La Thuile, sleeps 20, has excellent food and atmosphere and is run by an English couple. Yellow Stone Chalet (069606) is a Gîte de France at the station, run by an American and highly recommended by a recent reporter: 'Beautifully appointed, modern with good food.' Hotel Monal (069007), in Ste-Foy village, is a basic auberge.

Chalets Chalet Number One (UK number: 01572 717259), in the village of La Masure, is run by snowboarder Lloyd Rogers, serving good food in comfortable, rustic surroundings. Skiers are welcome. too!

Apartments/condos There are quite a few apartments and chalets to rent in the area, and there should be more at the station from this coming season – the tourist office has a list or there are rental agencies in Bourg St Maurice.

Après-ski Pretty quiet. There may be a short-lived après-ski scene in one of the bars at the station, and the bar of the Monal can get lively.

Eating out Book the excellent Chez Mérie, in the village of Le Miroir, well in advance. In La Thuile, book the Auberge sur la Montagne. In Ste-Foy village, the Monal does 'good food' and a reporter tells us that, at the station, La Ruelle opens in the evenings by arrangement.

Off the slopes Not a lot – snowshoeing and dog sledding.

Phone numbers
From abroad use the prefix +33 and omit the initial '0' of the phone number.

TOURIST OFFICE
Postcode 73640
t +33 479 069519
f 479 069509
www.sainte-foy-tarentaise.com

St-Martin-de-Belleville 1400m/4,590ft

Explore the Three Valleys from a traditional old village

HOW IT RATES

The slopes

Snow	★★★
Extent	★★★★★
Experts	★★★★
Intermediates	★★★★★
Beginners	★★★
Convenience	★★★
Liftlines	★★★★
Restaurants	★★★★

The rest

Scenery	★★★
Resort charm	★★★★
Off-slope	★

What's new

There are plans to build a gondola to replace the chair out of the village for the 2002/03 season. The surface lift on the slope up from the church will be moved to the side of the slope and made less vicious.

➕ Attractively developed traditional village with pretty church

➕ Easy access to the whole of the extensive Three Valleys network; very quick to get to Méribel and Les Menuires

➕ Long easy intermediate runs on rolling local slopes

➖ Snow reliability worse than in most other Three Valleys bases

➖ No green runs for beginners to progress to

➖ Limited après-ski

➖ Few off-slope diversions

St-Martin is a traditional Savoyard village, with old church (prettily lit at night), small square and wood and stone buildings, a few miles down the valley from Les Menuires. As a quiet, inexpensive, attractive base for exploration of the Three Valleys, it's unbeatable. All our reporters who stayed there have loved it. And it's a great spot to stop for lunch if you are cruising the slopes.

THE RESORT

In 1950 St-Martin didn't even have running water or electricity. Later, while new resorts were developed nearby, St-Martin was a bit of a backwater, though it remained the administrative center for the Belleville valley (which includes the resorts of Val-Thorens and Les Menuires). But in the 1980s chair-lifts were built, linking it to the slopes of Méribel and Les Menuires. The old village has been developed, of course, but the architecture of the new buildings fits in well with the old, and you can walk around it in a few minutes. The main feature of the center remains the lovely old 16th-century church – prettily floodlit at night. There are some good local shops and few 'touristy' ones.

THE MOUNTAINS

The whole of the Three Valleys can be easily explored from here.

Slopes Two chair-lifts – the upper one a fast quad – take you to a ridge from which you can access Méribel on one side and Les Menuires on the other.

Snow reliability Natural snow reliability is not the best in the Three Valleys – the local slopes face west and get the full force of the afternoon sun. But

215

OT LES MENUIRES /
PIERRE EXANDIER

→ New buildings blend in with old in picturesque St-Martin

MOUNTAIN FACTS

for the Three Valleys – see Les Menuires chapter for trail map

Altitude	1300m-3200m
	4,270ft-10,500ft
Lifts	200
Trails	600km/
	370 miles
Green	17%
Blue	34%
Red	37%
Black	12%
Snowmaking	90km/
	56 miles
Recco detectors used	

LIFT TICKETS

2001/02 prices in euros

Three Valleys
See Méribel chapter.

Alternative tickets
Vallée des Belleville ticket covers 72 lifts and 300km/186 miles trail in Val-Thorens, Les Menuires and St-Martin (adult 6-day 170). Les Menuires and St-Martin ticket covers 43 lifts and 160km/100 miles of trail (adult 6-day 147).

Phone numbers
From abroad use the prefix +33 and omit the initial 'o' of the phone number.

TOURIST OFFICE

Postcode 73440
t +33 479 089309
f 479 089171
lesmenuires@les
menuires.com
www.st-martin-belle
ville.com

there is now snowmaking from top to bottom of the main run.

Experts Locally there are large areas of gentle and often deserted off-trail. And access to La Masse for steep north-facing slopes is just one run away from the top of the local chairs.

Intermediates The local slopes are pleasant blues and reds, mainly of interest to intermediates – including one of our favorite runs in the Three Valleys: the long, rolling, wide Jerusalem red. The Verdet blue from the top of the Méribel lifts is a wonderful easy cruise with great views and is usually very quiet. The whole of the Three Valleys is, of course, an intermediate's paradise.

Beginners St-Martin is not ideal – there's a beginner area but no easy green runs to progress to.

Liftlines lines are not usually much of a problem – the local lifts can easily cope with the morning rush from the guest beds the village has. But we had a report in the past of a 20-minute liftline and 'line rage' from some 'embarrassingly pompous British'.

Cross-country There are 33km/21 miles of trails in the Belleville valley.

Snowboarding Some great local off-trail free-riding.

Mountain restaurants There are three atmospheric old mountain restaurants on the main run down to the village. Chardon Bleu and Corbelleys near the second chair-lift are good for lunch and La Loe, lower down, is popular as the lifts close. Brewski's (on the left, halfway down the local village slope with the surface lift – watch for the signs) does good-value pub food (pies are a speciality) and has sunny terraces with views down the valley – it attracts customers from all over the Three Valleys. La Bouitte in St-Marcel (an off-trail run away) is one of the best restaurants in the Three Valleys and features in the Gault-Millau gourmet guidebook – a traditional, welcoming, rustic French auberge (but not cheap).

Schools and guides The ski school is said to have instructors with good English. But a reporter said, 'They were kind and considerate to our children but my son struggled with French on his skiing lesson.'

Facilities for children We've had good reports of the kindergarten, which is housed in a new purpose-built building and takes children from three months.

STAYING THERE

How to go For such a small village there's a good variety of accommodations.

Hotels The Alp'Hôtel (0479 089282), at the foot of the slope by the main lift, got a rave review from a recent reporter: 'Second year there, good food and wine list, comfortable rooms; I've recommended it to *The Good Hotel Guide*.' Saint Martin (0479 008800) is right on the slope, and Edelweiss (0479 089667) is in the village itself. All are 3-stars. But the best value accommodations are offered at Brewski's B & B (0479 006234), again right on the slope with well furnished en suite rooms of various sizes. This also gives you the chance to try some of the excellent local restaurants.

Apartments/condos Les Chalets de St Martin has a variety of self-catered chalets and apartments to rent and plenty of others are available.

Après-ski Après ski centers around two bars. The Pourquoi Pas? piano bar is delightfully cozy with a roaring log fire and comfortable easy chairs and sofas (it was up for sale at the time we went to press). Brewski's has wooden chairs and tables, a pool table, activities such as karaoke, sumo wrestling or live bands most nights and photos of old pop stars – such as Frank Zappa, Cream, the Beatles, Tina Turner and the Sex Pistols – on the walls. One of the fun-loving Kiwi owners may do his Elvis impersonation if you buy him enough drinks.

Eating out For such a small village there is a good variety of restaurants nearby. Le Montagnard is in a rustic old building and has been highly recommended by a recent reporter: 'Very friendly, massive helpings of excellent traditional Savoyard specialities.' La Voute has reasonable prices and does good pizza. Brewski's does 'good pub grub and specializes in unusual pies (even lamb curry pie)'. Etoile de Neige is an upscale traditional restaurant. Le Lachenal is an intimate place with open fire and good food. Just down the road in St-Marcel is La Bouitte, the best restaurant in the valley – see Mountain Restaurants. A bit further at Les Granges is the rustic Chez Bidou, popular with locals for its traditional Savoyard food.

Off the slopes If you don't use the slopes, there are better places to base yourself. There are pleasant walks and a sports hall, but not much else.

La Tania

1400m/4,59oft

Small, family-friendly base for exploring the Three Valleys

HOW IT RATES

The slopes

Snow	★★★
Extent	★★★★★
Experts	★★★★
Intermediates	★★★★★
Beginners	★★
Convenience	★★★★
Liftlines	★★★★
Restaurants	★★★★

The rest

Scenery	★★★
Resort charm	★★★
Off-slope	★

What's new

For the 2001/02 season 38 snow-guns are to be installed on the blue piste back to La Tania. So when it is cold enough to make snow you'll be assured of being able to ski or ride all the way into the village.

➕ Part of the Three Valleys – the world's biggest linked ski area

➕ Quick access to Courchevel and Méribel

➕ Long, rolling, intermediate, wooded runs back to the village

➕ Good local beginner areas

➕ Attractively developed, small, traffic-free village

➖ Small development without much choice of après-ski

➖ Runs home can suffer when snow is poor, though new snowmaking should help

➖ Runs home too steep for beginners

La Tania does not try to compete with its more upscale neighbours, Courchevel and Méribel. It has carved out its own niche as a good-value, small, quiet, family-friendly base from which to hit the snow-sure slopes of Courchevel and to explore the whole of the Three Valleys. It is prettily set in the trees and the wood-sided buildings make it one of the more attractive French purpose-built resorts (it was started ten years ago, by which time lessons had been learned from the horrendous architecture of resorts that were developed in the 1960s and 70s). Though it has grown, it remains small. If you want lots of shops and varied après-ski you should choose another Three Valleys resort.

THE RESORT

La Tania is set just off the small road linking Courchevel Le Praz to Méribel (and, for those with a car, is much nearer to Méribel than Courchevel 1850, if you want to hit the shopping or nightlife). It was built for the 1992 Olympics and has grown into a quiet, attractive, car-free collection of mainly ski-in, ski-out chalets and apartments set among the trees, most with good views. There are few shops other than

food and sports shops and not much choice of bars and restaurants. You can walk around the place in a couple of minutes.

A gondola leads to the slopes, and there are two wonderful sweeping intermediate runs down. These aren't ideal for progressing beginners, but the beginner area is on your doorstep, and visitors say that La Tania is 'very child friendly'. Hourly buses go to Courchevel in the daytime.

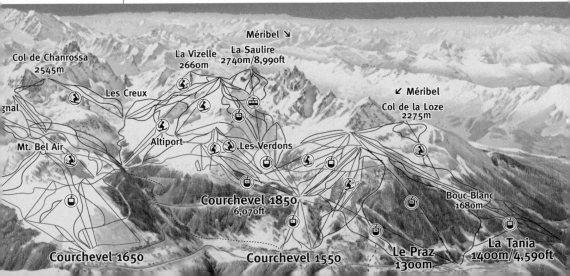

Méribel ↘
La Vizelle 266om
La Saulire 2740m/8,99oft
Col de Chanrossa 2545m
Les Creux
↙ Méribel
Col de la Loze 2275m
gnal
Mt. Bel Air
Altiport
Les Verdons
Courchevel 1850 6,07oft
Bouc-Blanc 168om
Courchevel 1650
Courchevel 1550
Le Praz 1300m
La Tania 1400m/4,59oft

MOUNTAIN FACTS

For the Three Valleys

Altitude	1300m-3200m
	4,270ft-10,500ft
Lifts	200
Trails	600km/
	370 miles
Green	17%
Blue	34%
Red	37%
Black	12%
Snowmaking	90km/
	56 miles
Recco detectors used	

THE MOUNTAINS

As well as good, though limited, local slopes, the whole of the Three Valleys can be explored easily from here, with just two lifts needed to get to either the Courchevel or Méribel slopes.

Slopes The gondola out of the village goes to Bouc Blanc. From here a surface lift takes you to Chenus and the slopes above Courchevel 1850 and a high-speed quad goes to the link with Méribel via Col de la Loze. An alternative way to the slopes above 1850 is to take two successive surface lifts from the village to Loze. From all these points, varied, interesting intermediate runs take you back into the La Tania sector.

Snow reliability Good snow-cover down to Bouc Blanc is usual all season. Below that the snow is less assured – you had to ride the gondola down for much of last season's poor snow. But things should be improved for 2001/02 by extra snowmaking covering the whole of the blue run back to the village.

Experts No local challenges but there's the whole of the Three Valleys to explore and some tough runs and good off-trail are close by in the Courchevel sector.

Intermediates There are two lovely, long, undulating intermediate runs back to La Tania. And the quick access to the rest of the Three Valleys' 600km/370 miles of well-groomed trails makes the area an intermediate's paradise.

Beginners There is a good beginner area and lift right in the village and novice children, in particular, are well catered to. But there are no very easy, long, local slopes to progress to; the intermediate runs back to the village are quite challenging.

Liftlines A line can build up for the village gondola but it is quick-moving. Elsewhere in the Three Valleys there are a few remaining bottlenecks – and those that do exist can easily be avoided by taking an alternative route.

Cross-country There are trails at altitude with links to Méribel and Courchevel.

Snowboarding There is no local terrain-park or half-pipe, but Courchevel's are easy to get to. There's a cheap place to stay that might appeal to boarders on a tight budget – see Staying there, below – and one lively local bar.

Mountain restaurants Bouc Blanc, near the top of the gondola, has friendly table-service, good food and a big terrace. Roc Tania at Col de la Loze is tiny but very pretty inside and has table-service.

Schools and guides Magic in Motion was 'absolutely wonderful' for the five children in a recent reporter's group.

Facilities for children The local kindergarten takes children from the age of three.

STAYING THERE

Hotels Montana (0479 088008) is a slope-side 3-star next to the gondola with a sauna and fitness club. It was said by a reporter to be 'Very good value, with friendly, English-speaking staff and excellent food.' The Mountain Centre opened last season (www.themountaincentre.com) and has 'cheap backpacker-style accommodations'.

Apartments/condos There are lots of apartments. We had a report in 2001 of the Pierre & Vacances apartments having 'incredibly cramped bedrooms and looking tired'. But the views and cleanliness were praised.

Après-ski Pub Le Ski Lodge is by far the liveliest place, with Murpheys on draft and frequent live bands and theme nights ('James Bond night was a good laugh,' said a reporter). L'Arbatt (a bar-tabac) and La Taïga (a bar-pizzeria) are quieter. But if you want a lively varied nightlife, go elsewhere – La Tania is too small.

Eating out La Ferme de la Tania and Le Farçon get generally good reviews for their Savoyard fare. Pub Le Ski Lodge has 'damn good chilli burgers'. La Taïga does 'very good pizzas and is friendly and quite cheap'.

Off the slopes Unless you have a car to travel around, La Tania will be deadly dull for anyone not intending to hit the slopes.

Phone numbers
From abroad use the prefix +33 and omit the initial '0' of the phone number.

TOURIST OFFICE

Postcode 73125
t +33 479 084040
f 479 084571
info@latania.com
www.latania.com

Great skiing and ... er, that's it

HOW IT RATES

The slopes

Snow	*****
Extent	*****
Experts	*****
Intermediates	*****
Beginners	**
Convenience	****
Liftlines	****
Restaurants	**

The rest

Scenery	***
Resort charm	**
Off-slope	*

- ➕ Good snow guaranteed for a long season – about the best Alpine bet
- ➕ One of the best areas in the world for lift-served off-trail runs
- ➕ Huge amount of terrain for all standards, shared with Val-d'Isère
- ➕ Many accommodations close to the slopes (though there are also quite a few that involves some walking)
- ➕ Swift access to Val-d'Isère slopes

- ➖ Resort buildings spoil the views from the slopes
- ➖ Bleak, treeless setting – no woodland runs, and many slopes liable to closure after heavy snow
- ➖ Still lots of long, slow chair-lifts
- ➖ Poor mountain restaurants
- ➖ Near-beginners have to go over to Val-d'Isère to find long green runs
- ➖ Limited après-ski

The appeal of Tignes is simple: good snow, spread over a wide area of varied terrain. Tignes and Val-d'Isère together form the enormous Espace Killy – a Mecca for experts, and ideal for adventurous intermediates. And in many ways Tignes makes the better base: appreciably higher, more convenient, surrounded by better intermediate terrain, with quick access to the Grande Motte glacier.

We prefer to stay in Val, which is a more human place. But the case for Tignes gets stronger as results flow from the resort's campaign to reinvent itself in a more cuddly form. Cars are being pushed underground, new buildings are being designed in traditional styles and old ones are getting a facelift. It all helps.

Although Tignes has invested in some impressive lifts in recent years, enjoyment of the expansive western side of the Tignes bowl – and large areas of the Val sector, too – is limited by the time you spend riding slow chair-lifts.

What's new

In 2000/01 the village centers became traffic-free and many hotels and apartments were renovated.

For 2001/02 there are plans for a tunnel under the road between the Chaudannes and the Paquis slopes and for a new restaurant at the top of the Chaudannes chair.

The slow Tommeuses lifts are due to be replaced by an eight-seater detachable chair, but no date has yet been specified.

219

The resort

Tignes was created before the French discovered the benefits of making purpose-built resorts look acceptable. Later than most of its contemporaries, it has now woken up to the demand for traditional Alpine ambience. Traffic is now under control, with pedestrian-only centers, and the villages are certainly more pleasant as a result. The downside is that your transfer bus may not be able to get close to your hotel.

The original and main village – Tignes-le-Lac – is still the hub of the lift system. Some of the smaller buildings in the central part, Le Rosset, are being successfully revamped in chalet style. But the place as a whole is dreary, and the blocks overlooking the lake from the quarter called Le Bec-Rouge will always be monstrous. Some attractive new buildings are being added on the fringes, in a suburb known as Les Almes. Recently added lifts have improved mountain access from here, and from the other suburb of Le Lavachet – a slightly more inviting area than Le Rosset.

Val-Claret (a mile or so up the valley, beyond the lake) was mainly developed after Le Rosset, and is a bit more stylish (though not at all traditional). There are major lifts up to the Grande Motte glacier here, as well as lifts accessing the sides of the bowl and the slopes of Val-d'Isère.

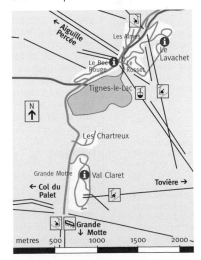

MOUNTAIN FACTS

For entire L'Espace
Killy area

Altitude 1550m-3455m
5,090ft-11,340ft

Lifts	97
Trails	300km/
	186 miles
Green	15%
Blue	46%
Red	28%
Black	11%
Snowmaking	24km/
	15 miles

Recco detectors used

LIFT TICKETS

2001/02 prices in
euros

L'Espace Killy
Covers all lifts in
Tignes and Val-
d'Isère.

Beginners Free lifts
on all main beginner
areas; special
beginners' half-day
ticket.

Main ticket
1-day ticket 35
6-day ticket 167

Senior citizens
Over 60: 6-day ticket
142
Over 75: free ticket

Children
Under 13: 6-day ticket
117
Under 5: free ticket

Short-term tickets
Half-day ticket from
12.30 (adult 25).

Alternative periods
14 non-consecutive
days ticket available.

Notes 6-day ticket
and over valid for one
day each in the Three
Valleys, Pralognan-la-
Vanoise, Les Saisies
and Valmorel. On 3-
to 15-day tickets,
ticket reimbursed if
all lifts are shut due
to bad weather.
Discount on new
tickets on
presentation of
previous season's
ticket. Extra discount
for senior citizens
aged 70 to 74.

Alternative tickets
Super Tignes ski
ticket covers the lifts
on the Tignes side of
the Espace Killy only
(adult 6-day 142).

Below the high valley of the main
resort villages are two smaller
settlements. Tignes-les-Boisses, quietly
set in the trees beside the road up to
the main Tignes villages, consists of a
barracks and a couple of simple hotels.
Lower Tignes-les-Brévières is a
renovated old village at the lowest
point of the slopes – a favorite lunch
spot, and a friendly place to stay.

Location isn't crucial, as a regular
and efficient free bus service connects
all the villages until midnight – though
in the daytime the route runs along the
bottom of Val-Claret, leaving residents
of central Val-Claret with some hiking.

A six-day ticket covers a day in
some other resorts, including Les Arcs
or La Plagne and the Three Valleys, all
most easily reached with the aid of a
car. Preserve your ticket and you'll get
a loyalty discount off next year's.

The mountains

The area's great weakness is that it
can become unusable in bad weather.
There are no woodland runs except
immediately above Tignes-les-Boisses
and Tignes-les-Brévières, heavy snow
produces widespread avalanche risk
and wind closes the higher chairs.

THE SLOPES
High, snow-sure and varied

Tignes' biggest asset is the **Grande
Motte** – and the runs from, as well as
on, the glacier. The underground
funicular from Val-Claret whizzes you
up to over 3000m/9,850ft in six
minutes. There are chairs and surface
lifts to play on, as well as beautiful
long runs back to the resort and a link
over to Val-d'Isère.

The main lifts towards Val-d'Isère
are efficient: a high-capacity gondola
from Le Lac to **Tovière**, and a fast
'bubble' chair from Val-Claret to **Col de
Fresse**. You can head back to Tignes
from either: the return from Tovière to
Tignes-le-Lac is via a steep black run
(not so difficult now the bumps are

regularly smoothed out), but there are
easier runs to Val-Claret.

Going up the opposite side of the
valley takes you to a quieter area
where a series of surface and chair-lifts
serve predominantly east-facing slopes
split into two main sectors, linked in
both directions – **Col du Palet** and
L'Aiguille Percée. From the latter, you
can descend to Tignes-les-Brévières, on
blue, red or black runs (but beware the
Chardons blue, which should be
classified red); there's an efficient
gondola back.

The Col des Ves chair-lift, at the
south end of the Col du Palet sector, is
not normally opened until high season
and several recent reporters have
commented that some lifts started later
in the day than advertised.

SNOW RELIABILITY
Difficult to beat

Tignes has all-year-round runs (barring
brief closures in spring or autumn) on
its 3455m/11,340ft Grande Motte
glacier. And the resort height of
2100m/6,890ft generally means good
snow-cover right back to base for most
of the long season. The whole region,
not just the glacier area, usually has
good cover from November to May.
The west-facing runs (especially those
from Tovière to Val-Claret) and the
Bleuets run down to Le Lac suffer from
the sun, although they now have
serious snowmaking.

FOR EXPERTS
An excellent choice

It is the off-trail possibilities that make
Tignes such a draw for experts. Go
with one of the off-trail groups that the
schools organize and you'll have a
great time (snow permitting).

One of the big adventures is to
head for Champagny (linked to the La
Plagne area) or Peisey-Nancroix (linked
to the Les Arcs area) – very beautiful
runs, and not too difficult. Your guide
will organize return transport.

Another favorite of ours is the Tour

boarding *This is a big area, with a big boarder reputation. Snow-sure (if a bit
flat) boarding on the glacier gives way to steep tree-hopping above the
lowest part, Tignes-les-Brévières. In between, the lift system relies more on chairs
and gondolas than surface lifts, and long, wide trails to blast down, with acres of
powder between them to play in. The glacier is a good place for near-beginners to
practice. And there are a couple of specialist snowboard schools/shops. You can
buy a specific ticket for the terrain-park and half-pipe. Hiring a guide and
exploring the off-trail is recommended for good free-riders.*

de Pramecou, from the Grande Motte glacier. After some walking and beautiful isolated runs, you end up on a steep, smooth north-facing slope that takes you back to Val-Claret. There are other descents across the glacier to the Leisse chair-lift.

The whole western side of the bowl has lots of off-trail possibilities. The terrain served by the Col des Ves chair is often excellent. To the left (looking up) there are wonderfully secluded, scenic and challenging descents. On the right, lower down, is a less heavily used and gentler area, ideal for off-trail initiation. To the north, there are excellent variants on the Sache run to Les Brévières (see below).

The schools and guides offer the bizarre French form of heli-skiing: mountaintop drops are forbidden, but from Tovière you can ski down towards the Lac du Chevril to be retrieved by chopper. Or you can be dropped over the border in Italy.

The only serious challenge within the trail network is the long black run from Tovière to Tignes-le-Lac, with steep, usually heavily bumped sections – though no longer so difficult at the bottom, according to this year's reporters. Parts of this run get a lot of afternoon sun. Our favorite black run is the Sache, from Aiguille Percée down a secluded valley to Tignes-les-Brévières, which can become very heavily bumped at the bottom.

A reporter recommends the black 'Silene' trail: 'big bumps – very challenging and enjoyable'.

FOR INTERMEDIATES
One of the best
For the avid intermediate, the Espace Killy is one of the top three or four areas in France, or the world.

Tignes' local slopes are ideal intermediate terrain. The red and blue runs on the Grande Motte glacier nearly always have superb snow. The glacier run from the top of the cable-car is a gentle blue. The Leisse run down to the chair-lift is now graded black and can get very bumpy but has good snow. The long red run all the way back to town is a delightful long cruise – though often crowded.

La Grande Motte
3455m/11,340ft

Col de la Leisse

Col des Ves
2840m

3015m

Col du Palet
2695m

Col de Fresse

L'Aiguille Percée
2705m

Tovière
2705m

Val-Claret

Tignes-le-Lac

Le Lavachet

Tignes
2100m/6,890ft

Tignes-les-Boisses
1850m

Tignes-les-Brévières
1550m/5,090ft

SCHOOLS/GUIDES

2001/02 prices in euros

ESF
Classes 5 days
5 half-days: 105
Children's classes
Ages: 5 to 14
5 half days: 105
Private lessons
Hourly or daily
30 for 1hr

Evolution 2
Classes 5 days
am or pm
5 half-days: 122
Children's classes
Ages: 5 to 14
5 half-days: 105
Private lessons
Hourly or daily
30 for 1hr

OTHER SCHOOLS

Tignes International
Snow Fun
Snocool
Kebra Surfing
Surf Feeling

From Tovière, the blue 'H' run to Val-Claret is an enjoyable cruise and generally well groomed. But again, it can get very crowded.

There is lots to do on the other side of the valley. We particularly like the uncrowded Ves red run reached by the low-capacity Col des Ves chair – the highest point of Tignes' non-glacier runs at 2840m/9,320ft. After an initial bump section (sometimes quite challenging) the run becomes an interesting undulating and curvy cruise, usually with good snow and a few bumps. The runs down from Aiguille Percée to Tignes-les-Boisses and Tignes-les-Brévières are also scenic and enjoyable. There are red and blue options as well as the beautiful Sache black run – adventurous intermediates shouldn't miss it. The runs down from Aiguille Percée to Le Lac are gentle, wide blues. The Bleuets blue from the top of the Aiguille Rouge chair is a more challenging alternative.

FOR BEGINNERS
Good beginner areas, but ...
The beginner areas of Tignes-le-Lac and Le Lavachet (which meet at the top) are excellent – convenient, snow-sure, gentle, free of through-traffic and served by a slow chair and a surface lift (free). The ones at Val-Claret are much less appealing – steep and served by a free surface lift. You can also ride the first stage of the Bollin chair for free.

For long green runs you have to go over to the Val-d'Isère sector – easy enough, but you need an Espace Killy ticket to use them, and you have to ride the gondola back down from Tovière. And in poor weather, the high Tignes valley is an intimidatingly bleak place – enough to make any wavering beginner retreat to a bar with a book.

FOR CROSS-COUNTRY
Interesting variety
The Espace Killy has 40km/25 miles of cross-country trails. There are tracks on the frozen Lac de Tignes, along the valley between Val-Claret and Tignes-le-Lac, at Les Boisses and Les Brévières and up the mountain on the Grande Motte.

LIFTLINES
Very few
The liftlines here depend on snow conditions. If snow low down is poor, the Grande Motte funicular generates

lines; the parallel high-speed chairs are often quicker. These lifts jointly transport a lot of people, with the result that the run down to Val-Claret can be seriously unpleasant. The worst lines now are for the cable-car on the glacier – half-hour waits are common.

Of course, if higher lifts are closed by heavy snow or high winds, the lifts on the lower slopes have big lines.

Lines can build up late in the day for the slow Tommeuses chairs (due for replacement, but no date as yet), bringing Tignes residents back from the Val slopes to Tovière – the Borsat fast quad to Col de Fresse is quicker.

MOUNTAIN RESTAURANTS
Head out of the bowl
Tignes' mountain restaurants are inadequate, especially on the west side of the bowl. Here there is one cafeteria – Le Palet – 'friendly, not as expensive as some and a good choice of food' – at the Col du Palet mid-mountain lift junction, and one pricey and crowded old hut, now being upgraded and rebuilt – the Savouna – just above Tignes-le-Lac.

The opposite side of the bowl is slightly better equipped, with the atmospheric chalet at the top of Tovière ('very good portions') and the newish but pleasantly woody Chalet du Bollin – just qualifying as a mountain restaurant, a few yards above Val-Claret. Both offer table-service as well as self-service.

The big restaurant at the top of the Grande Motte funicular has great panoramic views from its huge terrace, but it is traversed every few minutes by the next funicular-full of people. The new Alpage restaurant at the top of the Chaudannes lift is highly recommended for its 'good, if limited, food and friendly staff'.

There are lots of easily accessible places for lunch in the resorts. One ski-to-the-door favorite of ours is the ground-floor restaurant of the hotel Montana, on the left as you descend from the Aiguille Percée. La Place is reported to be 'a genuine delight with good food and real family hospitality' and a new bar in Val-Claret, the Fish Tank, is described as 'very good value'. In Les Brévières, a short walk round the corner into the village brings you to places much cheaper than the two by the trail.

The Grande Motte casts a long shadow over Val-Claret in January →

SNOWPIX.COM / CHRIS GILL

CHILDCARE

The hotel Diva in Val-Claret (0479 067000) has a nursery taking children from age 18 months.

The Marmottons kindergarten in Le Lac (0479 065167) takes children from 2 to 8, with skiing with Evolution 2 instructors for those aged 3½ or more.

Phone numbers
From abroad use the prefix +33 and omit the initial 'o' of the phone number.

GETTING THERE

Air Geneva, transfer 3½hr. Lyon, transfer 3½hr. Chambéry, transfer 2½hr.

Rail Bourg-St-Maurice (30km/19 miles); regular buses or cab from station.

SCHOOLS AND GUIDES
Enormous choice

There are half a dozen schools, plus various independent instructors. The ESF and Evolution 2 are the main ones, with sections in the main resort centers. Evolution 2 has received good reports with class sizes of eight and standards of English good – the chaos on registration days is also mentioned. The ESF also receives praise apart from the class sizes.

FACILITIES FOR CHILDREN
Mixed reports

In the past, we have had good reports on the Marmottons kindergartens, and on the 'experienced minders' of the Evolution 2 school in Le Lac. A reporter on the ESF considered the classes for five-year-olds too large.

Staying there

HOW TO GO
Unremarkable range of options

Hotels The few hotels are small and concentrated in Le Lac. Most are simple – there's nothing really swanky.
((3 **Campanules** (0479 063436) Smartly rustic chalet (since its makeover) in upper Le Lac, with well equipped rooms and a good restaurant, run by the friendly Reymond brothers.
((3 **Village Montana** (0479 400144) New, stylishly woody complex on the east-facing slopes above Le Lac, with suites and apartments as well as rooms. Outdoor pool, and spa treatments available. One reporter enthuses about the food but felt the accommodations were fairly 'ordinary'.

↑ Val Claret is no less obtrusive than the older parts, but a bit more stylish

FRANCE

ACTIVITIES

Indoor 'Vitatignes' in Le Lac (balneotherapy center with spa baths, sauna etc), 'Espace Forme' in Le Lac, 'Les Bains du Montana' in Le Lac, Fitness Club in Val-Claret (body-building, aerobics, squash, golf practice and simulation, sauna, hammam, Californian baths, hot-tub, swimming pool, massage), movie theaters, covered tennis court, bowling, climbing wall
Outdoor Natural skating-rink, hang-gliding, paragliding, helicopter rides, snow-mobiles, husky dog-sleigh rides, diving beneath ice on lake, heli-skiing, 'La Banquise' for children (ice skating, snow sliding, solarium, snow activities, climbing activities, ski-joring)

TOURIST OFFICE

Postcode 73321
t +33 479 400440
f 479 400315
information@tignes.net
www.tignes.net

Ⓐ **Arbina** (0479 063478) Well-run place close to the lifts in Le Lac, with lunchtime terrace, busy après-ski bar and one of the best restaurants.
Ⓐ **Terril Blanc** (0479 063287) Well run place next to the lake.
Ⓐ **Neige et Soleil** (0479 063294) Excellent family-run place in Le Lac – central, clean, cozy, comfortable, with good food.
Ⓐ **Marais** (0479 064006) Prettily furnished, simple little hotel in Tignes-les-Boisses.
Apartments/condos In upper Val-Claret, close to the Tovière chair, the Maeva 'Residence Le Borsat' apartments are about the best on offer – not too cramped, reasonably well equipped and with a communal lounge. The Chalet Club in Val-Claret is a collection of simple studios, but has the benefit of free indoor pool, sauna and in-house restaurant and bar. The supermarket at Tignes-le-Lac is reported to be 'comprehensive but very expensive'.

EATING OUT
Good places scattered about
Each of the main centers has a range of restaurants, although the options in Le Lavachet are rather limited. Advance booking is recommended for many restaurants. Finding anywhere with some atmosphere is difficult in Le Lac, though the food in some of the better hotels is good. We and readers have been impressed by the Arbina and the Campanules – 'a meal of the highest quality, excellent service and attention to detail'. In Val-Claret the Bouf'Mich is a favorite ('terrific food, reasonable

prices, helpful service, pretty interior'). The Cavern in Val Claret is recommended: 'Superb and there's entertainment – have to book.' Pizza 2000, also in Val-Claret, is recommended for 'reasonable prices, helpful staff, especially with large parties'. The Ski d'Or is a swanky Relais & Châteaux hotel. Les Terrasses du Claret is recommended for large groups. Those on a budget here should try the Italian at the Pignatta. The Cordée in Les Boisses is recommended – unpretentious surroundings, great traditional French food, modest prices.

APRES-SKI
Early to bed
Tignes is rather quiet at night, though there is no shortage of bars, some serving food as well. Val-Claret has some early-evening atmosphere and happy hours are popular – the 'pub-like' Crowded House hotel Curling gets most mentions, followed by the Wobbly Rabbit. Other recommendations include the Fish Tank, a new bar above the ski school meeting area – 'excellent audio visual system and satellite TV'.

Le Lac is a natural focus for immediate après-ski drinks, but don't expect anything too riotous. The bar of the hotel Arbina is our kind of spot – adequately cozy, spacious enough to absorb some groups, friendly service.

The most animated bar in Le Lavachet is Harri's – 'good atmosphere and ambience', 'always lively' are this year's verdicts. The satellite TV here is popular. The Alpaka Lodge is recommended as 'a relaxed place, great for conversation and cocktails'.

Les Caves du Lac, Café de la Poste and Jack's are popular late haunts.

OFF THE SLOPES
Forget it
Despite the range of alternative activities, Tignes is a resort for those who want to use the slopes, where anyone who doesn't is liable to feel like a fish out of water.

STAYING DOWN THE VALLEY
Only for visiting other resorts
See the Val-d'Isère chapter; the same considerations apply broadly here. But bear in mind that there are rooms to be had in simple hotels in Tignes-les-Boisses and Tignes-les-Brévières.

Les Trois Vallées

The biggest lift-linked ski area in the world

Despite competing claims, notably from the Portes du Soleil, with 200 lifts and 600km/370 miles of linked trails the sheer quantity of lift-linked terrain in Les Trois Vallées cannot be beaten. There is nowhere like it for a keen skier or boarder who wants to cover as much mileage as possible while rarely taking the same run repeatedly. And it has a lot to offer everyone, from beginner to expert.

The runs of Les Trois Vallées and their resorts are dealt with in six chapters. The four major resorts are Courchevel, Méribel, Les Menuires and Val-Thorens. St-Martin-de-Belleville, a small village along the mountainside from Les Menuires, gets its own chapter. And La Tania, a relatively new development on the slopes between Courchevel and Méribel, is also covered.

None of the resorts is cheap. **Les Menuires** is the cheapest but it is also the ugliest (though new developments around the original one are now being built in a much more acceptable style). The slopes around the village get too much sun for comfort, but close by across the valley are some of the best (and quietest) challenging trails in les Trois Vallées on its north-facing La Masse. Down the valley from Les Menuires is **St-Martin-de-Belleville**, a charming traditional Savoyard village which has been expanded in a sympathetic style. It has good-value accommodations and chair-lift links into the rest of the area.

Up rather than down the Belleville valley from Les Menuires, at 2300m/7,550ft **Val-Thorens** is the highest resort in the Alps, and at 3200m/10,500ft the top of its slopes is the high point of the Trois Vallées. The snow in this area is almost always good, and it includes two glaciers where good snow is guaranteed. But the setting is bleak and the lifts are vulnerable to closure in bad weather. The purpose-built resort is very convenient. Visually it is not comparable to Les Menuires, thanks to the smaller-scale design and more thorough use of wood to give the modern buildings a traditional veneer; but it still isn't to everyone's taste – especially the older parts.

Méribel is a two-part resort. The higher component, **Méribel–Mottaret**, is the best placed of all the resorts for getting to any part of the Trois Vallées system in the shortest possible time. It's now quite a spread-out place, with some of the accommodations a long way up the hillsides – great for access

to the slopes, less so for access to nightlife. **Méribel** itself is 200m/660ft lower and has long been a favorite. It is the most attractive of the main Trois Vallées resorts, built in chalet style beside a long winding road up the hillside. Parts of the resort are very convenient for the slopes and the village center; parts are very far from either. The new development of Méribel-Village has its own chair-lift into the system but is very isolated and quiet. A gondola leads up to Méribel from the old spa town of **Brides-Les-Bains** which has cheap accommodations but no trail back to it.

Courchevel has four parts. 1850 is the most fashionable resort in France, and can be the most expensive resort in the Alps (though it doesn't have to cost a fortune to stay there). The less expensive parts are Le Praz (aka 1300),

1550 and 1650. They don't have the same choice of nightlife and restaurants, and only 1550 enjoys the same central location in the lift system. Many people rate the slopes around Courchevel the best in the Trois Vallées, with runs to suit all abilities. The snow tends to be better than in neighboring Méribel, because many of the slopes are north-facing. And the trail grooming is the best in the Trois Vallées, if not the best in Europe.

La Tania was built for the 1992 Olympics, just off the small road linking Le Praz to Méribel. It has now grown into a quiet, attractive, car-free collection of chalets and chalet-style apartments set among the trees and is popular with families. It has a good beginner area and lovely long intermediate runs, but there are no very easy runs back to it.

It's quite a hike from the top of the Val-Thorens lifts to the Glacier de Gébroulaz, though the spectacular off-trail run down to Méribel makes it worth it →

Val-d'Isère

On- and off-trail playground with reliable snow

HOW IT RATES

The slopes

Snow	*****
Extent	*****
Experts	*****
Intermediates	*****
Beginners	***
Convenience	***
Liftlines	****
Restaurants	**

The rest

Scenery	***
Resort charm	***
Off-slope	**

➕ Huge area linked with Tignes, with lots of runs for all abilities

➕ One of the great resorts for lift-served off-trail runs

➕ High altitude of most slopes means snow is more or less guaranteed

➕ Wide choice of schools, especially for off-trail lessons and guiding

➕ For a high resort, the town is attractive, very lively at night, and offers a good range of restaurants

➕ Wide range of accommodations

➕ Trail grooming and staff attitudes have improved noticeably

➖ Trail grading understates the difficulty of many runs – though bumps on greens now uncommon

➖ You're quite likely to need the bus at the start or end of the day

➖ Most lifts and slopes are liable to close when the weather is bad

➖ Runs to valley level often tricky

➖ Beginner areas not ideal

➖ High-season crowds on some runs

➖ Still some lifts in need of upgrading

➖ Main off-trail slopes get tracked out very quickly

➖ Not the most distinctively French of French resorts

➖ Few good mountain restaurants

Val-d'Isère is one of the world's best resorts for experts – attracted by the extent of lift-served off-trail – and for confident, mileage-hungry intermediates. But you don't have to be particularly adventurous to enjoy the resort, and the village ambience has improved greatly in recent years.

The list of drawbacks above looks long, but they are mainly petty complaints, whereas the plus-points are mainly things that weigh heavily in the balance, both for us and for the many enthusiastic reporters we hear from. The last of the plus-points – the clear recent improvements in trail grooming and lift staff attitudes – is as welcome as it is surprising. If the lift company would make a serious attempt to classify its runs sensibly, Val would make more friends than it does at present among nervous intermediates who panic on bump fields.

Despite the unremarkable mountain restaurants, this is, in the end, simply one of our favorite resorts in the world.

What's new

2000/01 saw a new high-speed chair-lift replace the defunct Cascade and Pissaillas chairs on the Pissaillas glacier.

For 2001/02 the old Bellevarde cable car is being replaced by a giant gondola – each cabin seats 24 passengers. And the Glacier chair, an essential link from Solaise towards the Col de L'Iseran and the Pissaillas glacier is being upgraded to a six-pack.

The slow Tommeuses lifts are due to be replaced by an eight-seater detachable chair, but no date has yet been specified.

The resort

Val-d'Isère spreads along a remote valley, which is a dead end in winter. The road in from Bourg-St-Maurice brings you dramatically through a rocky defile to the satellite mini-resort of La Daille – a convenient but hideous slope-side apartment complex and the base of lifts into the major Bellevarde sector of the slopes. The outskirts of Val proper are dreary, but as you approach the center the legacy of the 1992 Olympics becomes more evident: new wood- and stone-siding, culminating in the tasteful pedestrian-only Val Village complex. The few remnants of the original old village are tucked away behind this. Many first-

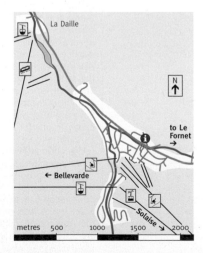

FRANCE

228

MOUNTAIN FACTS

For entire L'Espace Killy area

Altitude	1550m-3455m
	5,090ft-11,340ft
Lifts	97
Trails	300km/
	185 miles
Green	15%
Blue	46%
Red	28%
Black	11%
Snowmaking	24km/
	15 miles

Recco detectors used

time visitors find the resort much 'prettier' than they expect a big-name high resort to be, and returning visitors generally find things improving.

Turn right at the center and you drive under the beginner areas to Val's big lifts up to Bellevarde and Solaise; there is now a lot of development here, most of it beyond the lifts. Continue up the main valley instead, and you come to Le Fornet – an old village and the third major lift station.

There is a lot of traffic around, but the resort is working to get cars under control to make the center more pedestrian-friendly.

The location of your accommodations isn't crucial. Free shuttle-buses run along the main street linking the main lift stations. It is one of the most efficient bus services we've come across; even in peak periods, you never have to wait more than a few minutes. But in the evening frequency plummets and dedicated après-skiers will want to be within walking distance of the center. The development up the side valley beyond the main lift station is mainly attractive; some places are a pleasant stroll from the center, but the farthest-flung are a long slog – unless you're happy to pay for cabs, you need a car. La Daille and Le Fornet have their (quite different) attractions for those less concerned about nightlife.

A car is of no great value around the resort, but simplifies outings to other resorts. A six-day lift ticket gives a day in Les Arcs or La Plagne, plus the Trois Vallées. Other resorts nearby are Ste-Foy and La Rosière.

The mountains

Although there are wooded slopes above the village on all sectors, in practice most of the runs here are on open slopes above the tree line.

Last year's reporters thought that trail grooming had improved – this year's are mixed, ranging from 'no comparison to Méribel' to 'very good even after heavy snow'. A couple of readers complain about poor signage.

The local radio carries good weather reports in English as well as French.

THE SLOPES
Vast and varied

Val-d'Isère's slopes divide into three main sectors. **Bellevarde** is the mountain that is home to Val-d'Isère's famous downhill course – the OK trail, which opens each season's World Cup Alpine circus in early December. You can reach Bellevarde by funicular from La Daille; up to now this has been the favoured route, and even people based in central Val have taken the bus to La Daille at the start of the day. But for the coming season a powerful new gondola will replace the old tram from Val. From the top you can get back down to the main lifts, play on a variety of surface lifts and chairs at altitude or take a choice of lifts to the Tignes slopes.

Solaise is the other mountain accessible directly from Val-d'Isère. The Solaise Express fast quad chair-lift takes you a few feet higher than the parallel tram. Once up, a short surface lift takes you over a plateau and down to a variety of chairs that serve this

LIFT TICKETS

2001/02 prices in euros

L'Espace Killy
Covers all lifts in Tignes and Val-d'Isère.

Beginners 7 free beginners' lifts on main beginner areas.

Main ticket
1-day ticket 35
6-day ticket 167

Senior citizens
Over 60: 6-day ticket 142
Over 75: free ticket

Children
Under 13: 6-day ticket 117
Under 5: free ticket

Short-term tickets
Half-day ticket from 12.30 (adult 25).

Alternative periods
14 non-consecutive days ticket available.

Notes 6-day ticket and over valid for one day each in the Three Valleys, Pralognan-la-Vanoise and Les Saisies. On 3- to 15-day tickets, ticket reimbursed if all lifts are shut due to bad weather. Discount on new tickets on presentation of your lift ticket for any one of the previous three seasons. Extra discount for senior citizens aged 70 to 74.

very sunny area of predominantly gentle trails.

From near the top of this area you can catch a chair over to the third main area, above and below the **Col de l'Iseran**, which can also be reached by tram from Le Fornet in the valley. The chair-lift ride is spectacular or scary, depending on your head for heights: it climbs over a steep ridge and then drops suddenly down the other side. There is an alternative way over: a short and steep surface lift takes you to a narrow tunnel through the ridge, leading to an awkward black run which is often closed. The runs at Col de l'Iseran are predominantly easy, with spectacular views and access to the region's most beautiful off-trail sections. The defunct Cascade chair-lift has finally been replaced by a fast quad giving access to the runs on the Pissaillas glacier beyond the col.

SNOW RELIABILITY
Difficult to beat
In years when lower resorts have suffered, Val-d'Isère has rarely been short of snow. Its height means you can almost always get back to the village, especially because of the snowmaking facilities on the lower slopes of all the main routes home. But even more important is that in each sector there are lots of lifts and runs above mid-mountain, between about 2300m/7,500ft and 2900m/9,500ft. Many of the slopes face roughly north. And there is access to glaciers at Pissaillas or over in Tignes, although both take a while to get to.

FOR EXPERTS
One of the world's best
Val-d'Isère is one of the top resorts in the world for experts. The main attraction is the huge range of beautiful off-trail possibilities – see feature panel. There may be better resorts for really steep trails – there

are certainly lots in North America – but there is plenty to amuse the expert here, despite the small number of blacks on the trail map. Many of the red and blue runs are steep enough to get bumpy.

On Bellevarde the famous Face run is the main attraction – often bumpy from top to bottom, but not worryingly steep. Epaule is the sector's other black run – where the bumps are hit by long exposure to sun and can be slushy or rock-hard too often for our liking. There are several challenging ways down from Solaise to the village: all steep, though none fearsomely so. This has traditionally been classic bumps territory, but one of our regular reporters ruefully notes that the resort's new enthusiasm for grooming has extended even to these slopes: 'Solaise bumps the size of small cars are nothing now but a fond memory'.

FOR INTERMEDIATES
Quantity and quality
Val-d'Isère has even more to offer intermediates than experts. There's enough here to keep you interested for several visits – though there are complaints about crowded high-season trails, and the less experienced should be aware that many runs are under-graded. This remains a regular reporter complaint.

In the Solaise sector is a network of gentle blue runs ideal for building confidence. And there are a couple of beautiful runs from here through the woods to Le Laisinant, from where you catch the bus – these are ideal for bad weather, though prone to closure in times of avalanche danger.

Most of the runs in the Col de l'Iseran sector are even easier – ideal for early and hesitant intermediates. Those marked blue at the top of the glacier could really be graded green.

Bellevarde has a huge variety of runs ideally suited to intermediates of all abilities. From Bellevarde itself

Val d'Isère

229

boarding *Val-d'Isère is good for boarders, though Tignes is a more popular boarder destination. Most of the main lifts are trams, chair-lifts and gondolas, with very few surface lifts. But there are a few flat areas where you'll need to scoot or walk. Experts will revel in the off-trail. There's a terrain-park with a half-pipe on Bellevarde, under the Mont Blanc chair-lift, and another at La Daille. There are several specialist snowboard shops and schools. The village beginner area is ideal for trying boarding for the first time and Le Fornet is good to progress to. Val's nightlife – with its huge selection of bars – is difficult to beat.*

there is a choice of green, blue and red runs of varying pitch. And the wide runs from Tovière normally give you the choice of groomed trail or bumps.

A problem for early intermediates is that runs back to the valley can be challenging. The easiest way is to head down to La Daille, where there is a green run – but it should be classified blue (in some resorts it would be red), and it gets very crowded and bumpy at the end of the day. None of the runs from Bellevarde and Solaise back to Val itself is really easy. The blue Santons run from Bellevarde takes you through a long, narrow gun barrel which often has people standing around plucking up courage, making things even trickier. On Solaise there isn't much to choose between the blue and red ways down – and they're both narrow in places. At the top, there's no option other than the red run in full view of the lifts. Many early intermediates sensibly choose to ride the lifts down – take the chair for a spectacular view.

FOR BEGINNERS
OK if you know where to go

The beginner area right by the center of town is 95 per cent perfect; it's just a pity that the top is unpleasantly steep. The lifts serving it are free.

Once off the beginner areas, you have to know where to find easy runs; many of the greens should be blue, or even red. One local instructor admits: 'We have to have green runs on the map, even if we don't have so many green slopes – otherwise beginners wouldn't come to Val-d'Isère.'

Col Pers

3300m/10,830ft

Glacier de Pissaillas

Col de l'Iseran
2765m

2950m

2900m

Tigne

Col de Fresse
2770m

Tour Charvet

2325m

Le Manchet
1940m

Bellevarde
2705m

Solaise
2560m

Le Châtelard

Le Fornet
1930m

Le Laisinant

Val d'Isère
1850m/6,070ft

La Daille
1785m

A good place for your first real runs off the beginner areas is the Madeleine green run on Solaise – now served by a fast six-pack. The Col de l'Iseran runs are also gentle and wide, and not over-crowded. There is good progression terrain on Bellevarde, too, but no genuinely easy way back to the valley.

FOR CROSS-COUNTRY
Limited
There are a couple of loops towards La Daille and another out past Le Laisinant. More picturesque is the one going from Le Châtelard (on the road past the main tram station) to the Manchet chair. But keen cross-country enthusiasts should go elsewhere.

LIFTLINES
Few problems
Lines to get out of the resort have been kept in check by new lifts – first the funicular at La Daille, then fast chair-lifts as alternatives to the two main trams, and now replacement of the Bellevarde tram by a big gondola.

To get to Tignes, it's quicker to take the fast quad to Col de Fresse than the slow and often crowded Tommeuses chairs to Tovière. Coming back from Val-Claret at the end of the day is now much quicker thanks to a fast, dual-loading, six-person chair-lift direct to Col de Fresse, with a run down to Bellevarde. Make sure you get into the correct liftline: half the chairs stop part-way up the hill, serving runs back into Val-Claret.

The number of slow chair-lifts scattered about the area, particularly in Tignes, is a common complaint. Crowded trails is another.

At the end of the day, there's usually a wait for the chair back from Col de l'Iseran to Solaise (though you can always descend to Le Fornet instead). A reporter regularly found a line for the slow Lac chair that links the bottom of the Madeleine up to the Tête Solaise.

If you plan a return visit, keep your lift ticket – those with a week's ticket bought in the last three years are entitled to a 'loyal customer' discount.

OFF-TRAIL PARADISE

L'Espace Killy has some of the most extensive lift-served off-trail skiing in the world. There are dozens of classic off-trail runs waiting to be discovered, and all with endless variations. They are best explored with a professional guide because of the avalanche and other hidden dangers, such as cliffs to fall off and rivers to fall in. But many of the more popular runs are skied into an almost trail-like state soon after a fresh snowfall – here, again, a guide will be able to take you on less heavily skied routes. Our favorite off-trail routes include:

– Col Pers, from the top of the glacier above Le Fornet. You traverse over to a big, wide, fairly gentle bowl with glorious views. There are endless variants on the way down. Most bring you down via the very beautiful, narrow Gorges du Malpasset and the frozen river Isère back to the Le Fornet tram. This is a good area for spotting chamois grazing in the sun on the rocky outcrops above you.

– Tour de Charvet, from the top of the Grand Pré chair-lift in the Bellevarde sector. The easiest route starts with a long traverse in a huge bowl, before dropping into a narrow gorge which you ski along before the long run-out to the Manchet fast chair up to the Solaise sector.

– Tour de Pramecou, from the Grand Motte area in Tignes. After a long, flat section at the top and a couple of short climbs between downhill sections, you end up at the top of a long, steep, wide, north-facing slope (where the snow is usually excellent) and swoop down to the Carline trail back to the bottom of the Motte.

A seasoned reporter this year recommends the run from the back of Cugnai chair on Solaise: 'Good, steep slopes, excellent snow and a pretty run out by a stream through to the bottom of the Manchet fast chair.'

We recommend the Alpine Experience and Top Ski guided groups: you can join a group of your ability for off-trail skiing every morning (normally 9am until 1pm). Afternoons tend to be more conventional lessons to improve technique.

CHILDCARE

The new children's village, in the center of town by the beginner areas, takes children from 3 to 13, from 8.30 to 6.30.

The Petit Poucet (0479 061397) in the Residence les Hameaux at Val takes children from age 2, from 9am to 5.30.

Both provide indoor and outdoor activities and delivery to and collection from ski school.

Snowfun's Club Nounours takes children aged 3 to 6 for lessons of 1hr 30 min, 2hr or 3hr. Older children can be left in classes all day.

The ESF runs a ski nursery for age 4 up, with rope tows and a heated chalet.

A list of babysitters is available at the tourist office.

MOUNTAIN RESTAURANTS
Getting better

The mountain restaurants mainly consist of big self-service places with vast terraces at the top of major lifts.

La Fruitière at the top of La Daille gondola, decorated with stuff rescued from a dairy in the valley, continues to get good reports: 'Lovely food and friendly service. Very easy to rack up a large lunch bill here!' says one. La Folie Douce is a functional self-service place at the same spot – popular, though this year a visitor comments on the lack of variety. Other recommendations: Solaise ('great pizza bar, good crêpes'), Le Trifollet, about halfway down the OK run – 'efficient table-service, great pizzas', 'excellent'; Marmottes, in the middle of the Bellevarde bowl – big sunny terrace, self-service – 'a good coffee stop'; Le Signal at the top of the Le Fornet tram – 'excellent service and value, huge portions'; the 'small and friendly' Bar de L'Ouillette, at the base of the Madeleine chair-lift – 'good selection of snack meals'; the Datcha, at the bottom of the Cugnai lift – 'excellent salads, if expensive'; and La Tanière, a new restaurant between the two chairs going up Face de Bellevard – 'food well priced and service friendly, popular with liftline operators and ski patrols'.

There are restaurants on the lower

↑ Most of the slopes are above the tree line, but there are some below – this is the blue Mangard down to Le Fornet

OT VAL-D'ISERE / MARIO COLONEL

slopes at La Daille that are reachable on snow and by pedestrians. Les Tufs is 'a busy, friendly place that does rather a good pizza', and the Toit du Monde (formerly the Crêch'ouna), just across the slope from the funicular station at La Daille offers 'excellent service'. And of course there are lots of places actually in the resort villages.

Our favorite in Val-d'Isère is the big terrace of the Brussels, overlooking the beginner areas. When at Col de l'Iseran, one possible plan for lunch on a wintry day is to descend to the rustic Arolay at Le Fornet – good food, but 'rude service'. Lunch over in Tignes-les-Brévières is a popular option for those on a high-mileage mission.

SCHOOLS AND GUIDES
A very wide choice

There is a huge choice of schools and private instructors to choose from. We don't get many reports on the ESF adult classes. We've heard from lots of satisfied Snow Fun pupils: their guides seem to 'know their snow'. Reporters are also full of praise for Evolution 2: 'really good, with very encouraging instructors', 'excellent teachers'.

Several small outfits specialize in organizing small groups to go off-trail

SCHOOLS/GUIDES

2000/01 prices in euros

ESF

Classes 6 days
5½hr: 3hr am, 2½hr pm
6 full days: 180
Children's classes
Ages: from 4
6 full days: 165
Private lessons
1hr, mornings, afternoons, or whole day
31 for 1hr

Snow Fun

Classes 6 days
3hr am and 2½hr pm
5 mornings: 90
Children's classes
Ages: up to 13
6 full days: 158
Private lessons
Hourly or daily
29 for 1hr

Top Ski

Specializes in slalom, bump run and off-trail courses for small groups (max 6)
Classes 4 days
4hr: 9am-1pm; 2hr: 2pm-4pm
4 full days: 158
Private lessons
am (8.45-1pm), pm (2pm-4.30) or full day (8.45-4.30) 70 for 2 hours

Alpine Expérience

Specializes in off-trail guiding and teaching for small groups (max 6)

Other schools
Evolution 2
Ski Prestige
Mountain Masters
Altimanya

GETTING THERE

Air Geneva, transfer 4hr. Lyon, transfer 4hr. Chambéry, transfer 3hr.

Rail Bourg-St-Maurice (33km/21 miles); regular buses from station.

Phone numbers
From abroad use the prefix +33 and omit the initial '0' of the phone number.

– an excellent way to get off-trail safely without the cost of hiring a guide as an individual. Recent reports describe Evolution 2 as 'top class', Alpine Expérience as providing 'excellent off-trail lessons'. We have also had good reports on Ski Prestige and Top Ski. We've had great days ourselves with both Alpine Expérience and Top Ski. In peak periods it's best to book in advance. Mountain Masters offers private on- and off-trail lessons.

All the schools have teachers who speak good English – in many cases it's their native language. Heli-trips can be arranged – you are dropped over the border in Italy because heli-drops are banned in France.

FACILITIES FOR CHILDREN
Avoid the ESF

There's a 'children's village' for 3- to 13-year-olds, with supervised indoor and outdoor activities on the village beginner areas. It's open daily from 8.30 to 6.30. A reporter last season was 'very pleased' with the childcare there: 'The staff speak English, and are very organized, in particular about the children's safety.'

We have personal experience of the indifference of the ESF's handling of children, reinforced by a more recent report from the father of two children who were placed in classes of French pupils and subsequently 'abandoned in mid-class' by their instructors.

Staying there

HOW TO GO
Lots of choice

Hotels There are about 40 to choose from, mostly 2- and 3-star, but for such a big international resort surprisingly few are notably attractive.
((((④ **Christiania** (0479 060825) Recently renovated big chalet, probably best in town. Chic, with friendly staff. Sauna.
((((④ **Latitudes** (0479 061888) Modern, stylish. Piano bar, nightclub. Leisure center: sauna, steam room, whirlpool, massage.
((((④ **Blizzard** (0479 060207) Renovated for Olympics. Indoor-outdoor pool. Convenient. A non-resident praises the food very highly.
(((③ **Grand Paradis** (0479 061173) Excellent position. Good food.
(((③ **Savoyarde** (0479 060155) Rustic decor. Leisure center. Good food. Rooms a bit small.

(((③ **Kandahar** (0479 060239) Smart, newish building above Taverne d'Alsace on main street.
(((③ **Sorbiers** (0479 062377) Modern but cozy B&B hotel, not far from center. Due to be completely renovated in summer 2001.
(((③ **Samovar** (0479 061351) In La Daille. Traditional, with good food.
Apartments/condos There are thousands of properties to choose from. Local agency Val-d'Isère Agence has a good brochure. The local supermarkets are said to be well stocked to meet the needs of those cooking in.

EATING OUT
Plenty of good, affordable places

Restaurant standards are generally high. The 70-odd restaurants include Italian, Alsatian, Tex-Mex, even Japanese ones, but most offer good French dishes. In high season it is essential to book ahead.

There are plenty of pleasant mid-priced places. The Perdrix Blanche is popular, offering 'brilliant' fish dishes in particular, but reporters also comment that it is 'impersonal', 'too busy and noisy'. Better, perhaps, to head for the Taverne d'Alsace, another old favorite, with 'plenty of magnificent traditional food in a calm atmosphere'. The Tufs, a little way up the slopes at La Daille, is recommended, and will provide transport for groups. The Toit du Monde nearby (formerly the Crêch'ouna) offers Tibetan cuisine and is praised for 'making a real effort to be a bit different'. Le Canyon is recommended for 'great food with choice of traditional fare as well as pizza, pasta etc', 'very noisy and busy'.

But our favorite – and that of many reporters – for a special night out is the Chalet du Crêt, off the road on the northern edge of downtown Val. Set in a 300-year-old stone farmhouse, beautifully renovated by the Franco-British couple who run it, this place serves a fixed-price menu starting with a magnificent hors-d'oeuvres spread. It's not cheap, but it's highly satisfying.

Those on tight budgets should try Chez Nano (next to Dick's Tea Bar) – 'fantastic pizza and profiteroles'. The Melting Pot also gets good reviews for its interesting menu, which includes Thai dishes and 'a good selection of veggie options'. La Corniche and L'Olympique are recommended for being 'more French and less touristy'.

ACTIVITIES

Indoor Swimming pool, sports hall (basketball, volleyball, table tennis, badminton, trampoline and gymnastics), library, bridge, health centers in the hotels Christiania, Brussels and Le Val d'Isère (sauna, hammam, hot-tub, body building, massages, solarium etc), movie theater

Outdoor Walks in Le Manchet valley and Le Fornet, natural skating rink, hang-gliding, quad bikes, all-terrain karts, ice driving, snow-mobiles, paragliding, snow-shoe outings, heli-skiing, microlight trips, ice-climbing

TOURIST OFFICE

Postcode 73155
t +33 479 060660
f 479 060456
info@valdisere.com
www.valdisere.com

APRES-SKI
Very lively

Nightlife is surprisingly energetic, given that most people have spent a hard day on the slopes. There are lots of bars, many with happy hours followed by music and dancing later on.

La Folie Douce, at the top of the La Daille gondola, has become an Austrian-style tea-time rave, with music and dancing; normally you can ride the gondola down, but it can be closed by the weather, so it pays to keep the consumption of vin chaud within bounds. At La Daille the bar at the Samovar hotel is 'a good spot for a beer after skiing'. In downtown Val, Bananas (lively, busy, heated terrace, good happy hour prices), Café Face (very lively, excellent) and the Moris pub fill up as the slopes close, and Bar Jacques (also mentioned for its food) and the Perdrix Blanche bar are popular with locals. L'Aventure, next to Killy Sports, has household decor, including a fridge, a bath and a bed – it serves good food in a separate

eating area. Victor's bar is popular before it turns into a restaurant later on – black-and-white decor and stainless steel loos. The basement Taverne d'Alsace is quiet and relaxing. The famous Dick's Tea Bar (now 21 years old) was judged 'overpriced and overrated' by two reporters this year.

For those who like a quieter time, there are hotel bars, piano bars and cocktail lounges.

OFF THE SLOPES
Not much

Val is primarily a resort for those keen to get on to the slopes – though one non-skier this year was 'very satisfied' with the facilities. The swimming pool has been renovated, but the other sports facilities are not particularly impressive. The range of shops is better than in most high French resorts. Lunchtime meetings present problems: the easily accessible mountain restaurants are few, and your friends may prefer lunching miles away in places like Les Brévières.

OT VAL-D'ISERE / AGENCE NUTS

As far as the eye can see, there are skiable slopes – the main mountain here is Bellevarde, seen from above Le Fornet ➔

Val-Thorens

Europe's highest resort, with guaranteed good snow

HOW IT RATES

The slopes

Snow	*****
Extent	*****
Experts	****
Intermediates	*****
Beginners	****
Convenience	*****
Liftlines	***
Restaurants	****

The rest

Scenery	***
Resort charm	**
Off-slope	**

What's new

For 2001/02 a new jumbo gondola (the Fond 2 Funitel) will start from the bottom of the gondola towards Caron and take you to near the Col de la Montée du Fond, ending the need to walk to the Maurienne side (the Fourth Valley). A new black and a new red run will be built from the top on the Val Thorens side.

Two new successive quad chair-lifts in the Fourth Valley will take you from Plan Bouchet at the top of the gondola up from the Maurienne valley to Pointe du Bouchet, up a valley where a new black trail will replace the existing itinéraire run.

A 120m/400ft-long moving carpet will be built on the beginner Marmottons trail. The exit of the Caron tram will have a rubber walkway.

- ⊕ Extensive local slopes to suit all abilities, and good access to the rest of the vast Three Valleys
- ⊕ The highest resort in the Alps and one of the most snow-sure, with north-facing slopes guaranteeing good snow for a long season, even off the glacier
- ⊕ Not as much of an eyesore as most high, purpose-built resorts
- ⊕ Compact village with direct slope access from most accommodations

- ⊖ Can be bleak in bad weather – not a tree in sight
- ⊖ Parts of the village are much less attractive to walk through in the evening than to ski past in the day
- ⊖ Not much to do off the slopes
- ⊖ Some very busy trail intersections
- ⊖ Still some liftlines – especially for the Cîme de Caron tram.

For the enthusiast looking for the best snow in the Alps, it's difficult to beat Val-Thorens – especially given that it's also one of the least unpleasant purpose-built resorts. But we still prefer a cosier base elsewhere in the Three Valleys. That way, if a storm socks in, we can play in the woods around Méribel or Courchevel; if the sun is scorching, we have the option of setting off for Val-Thorens. The formula doesn't work the other way round.

The resort

Val-Thorens is built high above the tree line on a sunny, west-facing mountainside at the head of the Belleville valley, surrounded by peaks, slopes and lifts. The village streets are supposedly traffic-free. Practically all visitors' cars are banished to parking lots, except on Saturday. But workers' cars still generate a fair amount of traffic, and weekends can be mayhem with people entering and leaving the resort. One reporter recommends you leave 2½ hours to get to Moûtiers on a Saturday. Many parts of the resort are

designed with their 'fronts' facing the slopes, and their relatively dreary backs facing the streets. There are quite extensive shopping arcades, a fair choice of bars and restaurants, and a good sports center.

It is a classic purpose-built resort – compact, with lots of convenient slope-side accommodations. It's quite a complicated little village; but since it's quite compact, it doesn't matter much where you stay. At its heart is the snowy Place de Caron, where pedestrians mix with skiers and boarders. Many of the shops and restaurants are clustered here, along

235

OT VAL-THORENS / BASILE, MARK BUSCAIL

Snow wherever you look →

MOUNTAIN FACTS
for the Three Valleys

Altitude 1300m-3200m	
	4,270ft-10,500ft
Lifts	200
Trails	600km/
	370 miles
Green	17%
Blue	34%
Red	37%
Black	12%
Snowmaking	90km/
	56 miles
Recco detectors used	

with the best hotels, and the sports center is nearby. The village is basically divided in two by a little slope (with a surface lift) that leads down to the main slope running the length of the village. The upper half of the village is centered on the Place de Péclet. A road runs across the hillside from here to the new chalet-style Balcons development. The lower half of the village is more diffuse, with the Rue du Soleil winding down from the dreary bus station to the big Temples du Soleil apartments.

Seen from the slopes, it is not as hideous as many of its rivals. The buildings are mainly medium-rise and wood-sided; some are distinctly stylish.

The mountains

Take account of the height, the extent of its local slopes and the easy access to the rest of the Three Valleys, and the attraction of Val-Thorens becomes clear. The main disadvantage is the lack of trees. Heavy snowfalls or high wind can shut practically all the lifts and slopes, and even if they don't close, poor visibility can be a problem.

THE SLOPES
High and snow-sure
The resort has a wide trail going right down the front of it, leading down to a number of different lifts. The big **Péclet** gondola, with 25-person cabins, rises 700m/2,300ft to the Péclet glacier, with three red runs down. One links across

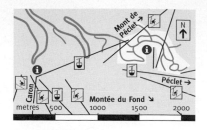

to a wide area of intermediate runs served by lifts to cols either side of the **Pointe de Thorens**. From one of these, the **Col de la Montée du Fond,** you can descend into the 'Fourth Valley', the **Maurienne**; for the 2001/02 season you will also be able to reach this point on a new jumbo gondola starting below the village. In the Maurienne valley a chair brings you back and serves red and blue slopes of 660m/2,170ft vertical and two new chairs and three new runs will be built for 2001/02.

The **Cîme de Caron** tram can be reached from the Pointe de Thorens area or by taking a gondola or fast chair from the same point as the new jumbo gondola. It rises 900m/2,960ft to the highest lift-served point in the Three Valleys, with red and black trails down the front of the mountain.

The two Boismint chairs from the lowest part of the domain serve an underused area of intermediate runs.

Chair-lifts heading north from the resort serve sunny slopes above the village and also lead to the Méribel valley. Les Menuires can also be

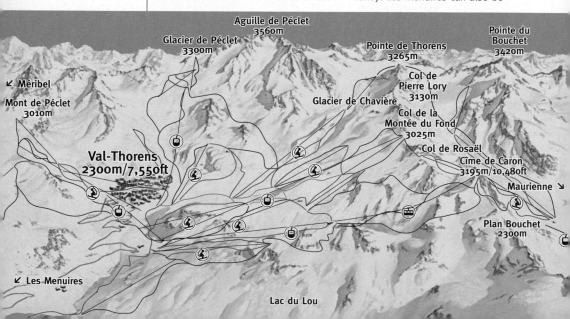

LIFT TICKETS

2001/02 prices in euros

Three Valleys
Covers all lifts in Courchevel, La Tania, Méribel, Val-Thorens, Les Menuires and St-Martin-de-Belleville.
Beginners 4 free lifts in Val-Thorens.
Main ticket
1-day ticket 37
6-day ticket 182
6-day low-season ticket 109
Senior citizens
Over 60: 6-day ticket 146
Over 70 6-day ticket 91
Over 75: free ticket
Children
Under 17: 6-day ticket 137
Under 10: 118
Under 5: free ticket
Short-term tickets
Half-day tickets (from 12.30) available for Val-Thorens lifts (adult 22) and the Three Valleys (adult 28).
Notes 6-day ticket and over valid for one day each in Tignes-Val-d'Isère, La Plagne-Les Arcs, Pralognan-la-Vanoise and Les Saisies. Reductions for families.
Alternative tickets
Vallée des Belleville ticket covers 72 lifts and 300km/186 miles trails in Val-Thorens, Les Menuires and St-Martin (adult 6-day 170). Val-Thorens-only ticket covers 30 lifts and 140km/87 miles of trails: adult 6-day 138.

reached via these lifts; the alternative Boulevard Cumin along the valley floor is nearly flat, and can be hard work.

SNOW RELIABILITY
Difficult to beat
Few resorts can rival Val-Thorens for reliably good snow-cover, thanks to its altitude and generally north-facing slopes. Snowmaking now covers 20% of the trails, including the crowded south- and west-facing runs on the way back from the Méribel valley.

FOR EXPERTS
Lots to do off-trail
Val-Thorens' local trails are primarily intermediate terrain. The runs down from the Cîme de Caron tram are the most challenging. The fast Cascades chair serves a good steep run that quickly gets bumpy but is not currently on the trail map. The sunny Marielle run is one of the easiest blacks we've come across.

The long Lac du Lou itinéraire goes from the Cîme de Caron to the lower Boismint chair. There is also a great deal of unmarked off-trail terrain to explore with a guide, particularly on the north-facing slopes reached from the Col, Fond, Deux Lacs and Boismint chairs. It is rocky terrain with serious hazards. You can also climb up from the top of the Péclet lifts and take a long off-trail run towards Méribel – a guide and fitness are essential.

FOR INTERMEDIATES
Unbeatable quality and quantity
The scope for intermediates throughout the Three Valleys is enormous. It will take a decent intermediate only 90 minutes or so to get to Courchevel at the far end, if not distracted by the endless runs on the way.

The local slopes in Val-Thorens are some of the best intermediate terrain in the region. Most of the trails are easy reds and blues, made even more

enjoyable by the excellent snow.

The snow on the red Col run is always some of the best around. The blue Moraine below it is gentle and popular with the schools. The runs on the top half of the mountain are steeper than those back into the resort. The Fond lifts serve a good variety of red runs. The Pluviometre from the Trois Vallées chair is a glorious varied red, away from the lifts. Adventurous intermediates shouldn't miss the Combe du Caron runs. The black run is not intimidating – it's very wide and usually has good snow.

FOR BEGINNERS
Good late-season choice
The slopes at the foot of the resort are very gentle and provide convenient, snow-sure beginner areas. There are no long green runs to progress to, but the blues immediately above the village are easy. The resort's height and bleakness make it cold in midwinter, and intimidating in bad weather.

FOR CROSS-COUNTRY
Try elsewhere
Val-Thorens is a poor base for cross-country, with only 4km/2.5 miles of local trails.

LIFTLINES
Persistent at the Cîme de Caron
Recent reports suggest few problems. But it is still common to wait 10 or 15 minutes for the Cîme de Caron tram, despite a scheme designed to speed up loading, and a March visitor found 40-minute-plus lines.

The Plein Sud six-pack chair-lift does a good job of getting the crowds back towards Méribel and Courchevel in the afternoon. The Côte Brune chair, on the Mottaret side, is a bottleneck for returning Val-Thorens residents.

When snow is in short supply elsewhere the pressure on the Val-Thorens lifts can of course increase.

boarding *The best resort-level snow in Europe appeals to boarders as well as skiers – and pulls in considerable numbers. There are trails to suit all abilities, and the good snow is great for beginners and carvers. There's plenty of off-trail choice for free-riders, though if you want trees you'll have to travel. The lifts are now mainly chairs and gondolas, though one or two surface lifts remain. The terrain-park towards the bottom of the Caron sector, served by a fast chair, has a half-pipe and a sound-system, and hosts weekly competitions. Nightlife centers around bars and a couple of discos that, because of all the young people in the resort (especially Scandinavians and Dutch), are usually noisy and entertaining.*

SCHOOLS/GUIDES

2001/02 prices in euros

ESF
Classes 6 days
3hr am or 2½hr pm
6 mornings 119
Children's classes
Ages: 4 to 12
6 mornings: 105
Private lessons
Hourly from 29 for 1 or 2 people

Ski Cool
2000/01 prices
Classes 6 days
3hr, am or pm
6 mornings: 107
Children's classes
5 days for 3 hours: 86
Private lessons
Hourly or daily
52 for 2hr, for 1 or 2 people

OTHER SCHOOLS
Pros Neige International

CHILDCARE

The ESF can provide all-day care and offers classes for children from age 2½. It also runs Mini Club nurseryies in two locations, at the top and bottom of the resort, taking children from age 3 months to 4 years.

Phone numbers
From abroad use the prefix +33 and omit the initial 'o' of the phone number.

GETTING THERE

Air Geneva, transfer 3½hr. Lyon, transfer 3½hr. Chambéry, transfer 2½hr.

Rail Moûtiers (37km/23 miles); regular buses from station.

The new chalet-style Balcons development in the upper part of the village is very attractive and has great views →

MOUNTAIN RESTAURANTS
Lots of choice

For a high, modern resort, the choice of restaurants is good. We like the Chalet de Génépi, on the run down from the Moraine chair – great views, an open fire and a wide range of good dishes. The Bar de la Marine, on the Dalles trail, does excellent food, but service can be slow. The Moutière, near the top of the chair of the same name, is one of the more reasonably priced of Val-Thorens' mountain huts (which are generally expensive). The Plan Bouchet refuge in the Maurienne valley is very popular and welcoming, but bar service can be slow. You can stay the night there, too. Chalet Plein Sud, below the chair of the same name, has excellent views but a 'rather limited menu'. The big Chalet de Thorens has been praised for its food and reasonable prices. Lots of people lunch in the village.

SCHOOLS AND GUIDES
A mixed bag

Like so many branches of the ESF, this one is incompetently run. One reporter speaks of two classes saddled with 'rude, unhelpful and unsympathetic' instructors. More alarmingly, we have yet another report of an ESF instructor losing a child – an incident about which the ESF 'could not have been more arrogant and unconcerned'. In contrast, a reporter found Pros Neige classes 'really excellent – my wife's skiing changed dramatically'.

We've had good reports of private lessons with the ESF and other schools. The ESF have a Trois Vallées group for those who want to cover a lot of ground while receiving lessons – available by the day or the week, and can include off-trail. Ski Cool class sizes are guaranteed not to exceed 10. They also have off-trail courses. But according to one reporter, they took someone with two days' experience down a bumped black run, causing him to injure his knee. There are several specialist guiding outfits.

FACILITIES FOR CHILDREN
Not up to much

We have conflicting reports of the ESF Mini-Club nursery. Some reporters are happy with it; others describe it as 'complete chaos' and report having to rescue children abandoned on the slopes.

Staying there

HOW TO GO
Surprisingly high level of comfort

Accommodations are of a higher standard than in many purpose-built resorts.

Chalets These are catered apartments, and many are quite comfortable.
Hotels There are plenty of hotels, mainly 3-stars.
((((5) **Fitz Roy** (0479 000478) Swanky but charming Relais & Châteaux place with lovely rooms. Pool. Well placed.
(((4) **Val Thorens** (0479 000433)

↑ You can slide to and from the door of virtually all Val-Thorens' accommodations

OT VAL-THORENS / BASILE, MARK BUSCAIL

ACTIVITIES

Indoor Sports center (tennis, squash, climbing wall, roller skating, golf simulator, swimming pool, saunas, hot-tub, volleyball, weight training, table tennis, fitness, badminton, football), games rooms, music recitals, movie theater, beauty center.
Outdoor Walks, snow-mobiles, paragliding, snowshoe excursions, toboggan run.

TOURIST OFFICE

Postcode 73440
t +33 479 000808
f 479 000004
valtho@valthorens.com
www.valthorens.com

Welcoming and comfortable; next door to Fitz Roy.
《《③ **Sherpa** (0479 000070) Highly recommended for atmosphere and food. Less-than-ideal position at the top of the resort.
《《③ **Bel Horizon** (0479 000477) Friendly, family-run 3-star, popular with reporters – 'cuisine wonderful'.
Apartments/condos The options include apartments of a higher standard than usual in France. The Temples du Soleil are recommended for good facilities.

EATING OUT
Surprisingly wide range

Val-Thorens has something for most tastes. The Fitz Roy and the Val Thorens hotels do classic French food. For something more regional, the best bets are the 'excellent' Vieux Chalet and the Chaumière. The Scapin is cosily done out in wood and stone, with 'good' food. Other reporters' recommendations include the Montana ('good food and service'), El Gringo's ('excellent but cramped Mexican'), Auberge des Balcons ('wonderful raclette'). The Galoubet has been praised for its steaks. The Blanchot is an unusually stylish wine bar with a simple but varied carte and of course an excellent range of wines. Several pizzerias are recommended, including that in the Temples du Soleil.

APRES-SKI
Livelier than you'd imagine

Val-Thorens is surprisingly lively at night. The Red Fox up at Balcons is busy at close of play, with karaoke. At the opposite extreme the Sherlock Holmes in the Temples du Soleil is 'always lively'. The Frog and Roast Beef at the top of the village is a cheerful British ghetto with a live band at tea-time and half-price beer while it plays. It claims to be the highest pub in Europe. Le Monde, Friends and the Viking pub are all lively bars on the same block. The Underground nightclub in Place de Péclet has an extended happy hour but 'descends into europop' when its disco gets going. Bloopers is another popular Scan-oriented bar-disco. The Malaysia cellar bar is recommended for good live bands, and gets very crowded after 11pm. Quieter bars include O'Connells (run by a Dane, of course), the cozy Rhum (aka Mitch's) and the St Pierre.

OFF THE SLOPES
Forget it

There's a good sports center, but the small pool can get crowded. You can get to some mountain restaurants by lift, and the 360° panorama from the top of the Cîme de Caron tram is not to be missed. But it is a pretty bleak place for non-slope-users.

Italy is a fun place to ski. It is the land of pasta and chianti, and there are lots of welcoming mountain huts to consume it in. Many of the resorts are set amid stunning scenery – Courmayeur at the foot of Mont Blanc, Cervinia at the foot of the Matterhorn and lots of resorts (such as Selva and Cortina d'Ampezzo) in the Dolomites, the most breathtaking backdrop for ski slopes that we've come across.

Italy has improved the attractions of its slopes enormously over the last decade or two. Powerful new lifts and huge amounts of snowmaking have been installed and trail grooming has improved greatly. And it remains the cheapest of the main Alpine countries for a vacation.

Although there aren't huge numbers of them (on the international market, at least), Italian resorts vary as widely in characteristics as they do in location – and they are spread along the length of Italy's northern border.

Sauze d'Oulx and Livigno are as cheap and cheerful as any resorts you'll find, attracting a youthful crowd to their cheap bars and clubs. Courmayeur in the Aosta valley and Cortina d'Ampezzo in the Dolomites are much more sophisticated, and attract rich Italian weekenders. Champoluc and Gressoney in the Monterosa region are little more than unspoiled mountain villages. Selva and neighbouring resorts in the Dolomites share an enormous linked ski circuit and have an Austrian rather than Italian feel – they used to be part of Austria. German is still the main language, most of the villages have both German and Italian names, and Austrian schnitzel

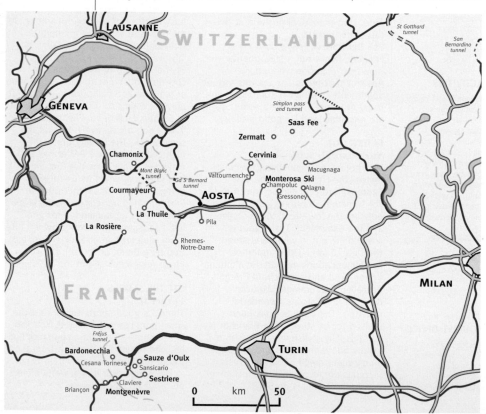

and bratwurst are as common as pasta and pizza.

One of Italy's weaknesses is its erratic natural snow record. It can have bumper seasons with huge snowfalls (such as 2000/01, when it had the best snow in Europe) and lean seasons (such as 1999/2000, when it had the worst snow in Europe). That's because it gets its snow from storms coming up from the south, whereas most of the Alps get their snow from the more frequent storms coming from the west. But most resorts have installed huge snowmaking systems, which in our experience work very effectively.

A lot of Italian runs seem flatteringly easy. This is partly because the trail grooming is immaculate and partly because trail classification seems to overstate difficulty.

We have also been struck by the way Italian resorts continue to be very weekend-oriented. Except in most of the Dolomites region (which depends largely on German visitors driving down for a week), resorts can be very quiet during the week, especially in low season, but come to life on Friday night or Saturday morning when the weekenders from Italy's affluent northern plain pour in by car. If, like us, you quite like having the trails and perhaps even the hotel bar to yourself, this is a real advantage.

In general, Italians don't take their skiing or boarding too seriously. Italian nightlife starts late and ends as dawn breaks – so even if the resort is full the trails are likely to be quiet until mid-morning. Some lifts may still close for lunch, and mountain restaurants are generally welcoming places serving satisfying food and wine, encouraging leisurely lunching. Pasta – even in the most

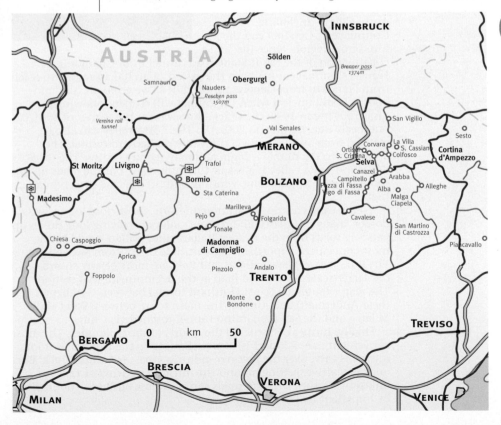

modest establishment – is delicious. And eating and drinking on the mountain is cheaper than in other Alpine countries.

DRIVING IN THE ITALIAN ALPS

There are four main, widely separated, geographical groupings of Italian resorts and moving from one area to another can involve some very long drives.

The handful of resorts to the west of Turin – Sauze d'Oulx, Sestriere and neighbours in the Milky Way region – are most easily reached from Turin airport (Milan is slightly further). They can also be reached from France via two major routes: the Fréjus tunnel from Modane, or via the good road over the pass from Briançon.

Further north, and again somewhat nearer to Turin than Milan, are the resorts of the Aosta valley – including Courmayeur, Cervinia and the Monterosa region. Since the

construction of the Mont Blanc road tunnel from Chamonix in France, Courmayeur has been the easiest of all Italian resorts to reach from France or from Geneva airport. But as we go to press in mid-2001 it is still unclear when the tunnel will reopen following the disastrous fire in 1999; the official line was for the winter of 2001/02, but locals were betting on 2002/03. The Aosta valley can also be reached from Switzerland via the Grand St Bernard tunnel. The approach to the tunnel is high, and may require chains. The road down the Aosta valley is a major toll motorway, but the roads up to some resorts are quite long, winding and (in the case of Cervinia) high.

To the east is a string of scattered resorts, most close to the Swiss border, many in isolated and remote valleys involving long drives up winding roads from the nearest Italian cities (Milan would be the most convenient airport), or high-altitude drives from Switzerland. The links between Switzerland and Italy are more clearly shown on our larger-scale Switzerland map at the beginning of that section. The major routes are the St Gotthard tunnel between Göschenen (near Andermatt) and Airolo – the main route between Basel and Milan – and the San Bernardino tunnel reached via Chur.

Finally, further east still are the resorts of the Dolomites. The most convenient major airport is Venice. Getting to the Dolomites from Austria is easy, over the Brenner motorway pass from Innsbruck. But once you arrive, getting around the intricate network of valleys linked by narrow, winding roads can be a slow business – not helped by impatient Italian driving.

Bormio

A tall, narrow mountain with a rather narrow appeal

HOW IT RATES

The slopes

Snow	★★★
Extent	★★
Experts	★
Intermediates	★★★
Beginners	★★
Convenience	★★★
Liftlines	★★★
Restaurants	★★★★

The rest

Scenery	★★★
Resort charm	★★★★
Off-slope	★★★★

➕ Good mix of high, open trails and woodland runs adding up to some good long runs

➕ Worthwhile neighboring resorts

➕ Attractive medieval town center – quite unlike any other winter resort

➕ Good mountain restaurants

➖ Slopes all of medium steepness

➖ Rather confined main mountain, with second area some way distant

➖ Still many slow old lifts

➖ Long airport transfers

➖ Crowds and liftlines on Sundays

➖ Central hotels inconvenient

If you like cobbled medieval Italian towns and don't mind a lack of Alpine resort atmosphere, you'll find the center of Bormio very appealing – though you're unlikely to be staying there. We'd plan on taking the free bus out to the Valdidentro area and perhaps make longer outings, to Santa Caterina at least.

What's new

A new fast quad is to replace the Isabella chair from Bormio 2000 next season. This should help reduce the liftlines for the second stage of the tram.

Bormio has been chosen to host the Alpine skiing World Championships in 2005, 20 years after it first staged them.

THE RESORT

Bormio is in a remote spot, close to the Swiss and Austrian borders (we're glad to hear that road improvements have cut the airport transfer to 3 hours). The 17th-century town center is splendid, with narrow cobbled streets and old stone façades. It began life as a Roman spa, and still has thermal baths. It's very colorful during the evening promenade.

The town center is a 15-minute walk from the tram and gondola stations across the river to the south. There are reliable free shuttle-buses, but many people walk. Closer to the lifts is a characterless suburban sprawl mainly made up of hotels built for skiers. Several major hotels are on Via Milano, leading out of town, which is neither convenient nor atmospheric.

THE MOUNTAINS

There's a nice mix of high, snow-sure trails and lower wooded slopes. The main slopes are tall (vertical drop 1800m/5,900ft) and narrow. Most trails face north-west and head to town.

Both the trail map and the trail marking are poor. Reporters complain about the many slow old lifts, and the resort policy of opening certain lift links only at weekends and busy times.

The Valdidentro area, a short bus-ride out of Bormio, shouldn't be overlooked. The open and woodland runs are very pleasant and usually empty (and have great views). Day trips to Santa Caterina (20 minutes by bus) and Livigno (90 minutes) are covered by the Alta Valtellina lift ticket. A six-day ticket includes a day in St Moritz (3 hours).

Slopes The two-stage Cima Bianca tram goes from bottom to top of the slopes via the mid-mountain mini-resort of Bormio 2000. An alternative gondola goes to Ciuk.

Snowboarding The slopes are too steep for novices, and there's little to attract experienced boarders either.

Snow reliability Runs above Bormio 2000 are usually snow-sure, and there is snowmaking on the lower slopes, though these were bare when we visited in late March. The Valdidentro area is more reliable, and the high, shaded, north-facing slopes of Santa Caterina usually have good snow.

Experts There are a couple of short black runs in the main area, but the main interest lies in off-trail routes from Cima Bianca to both east and west of the trail area.

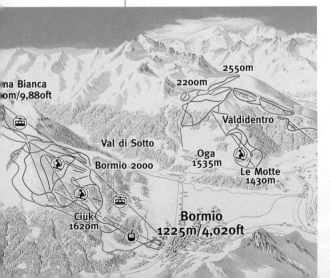

Cima Bianca
...m/9,880ft

2550m

2200m

Valdidentro

Val di Sotto

Oga
1535m

Le Motte
1430m

Bormio 2000

Ciuk
1620m

Bormio
1225m/4,020ft

MOUNTAIN FACTS

Figures relate to the Bormio, Valdidentro and Santa Caterina areas only

Altitude 1225m-3010m
4,020ft-9,880ft
Lifts 36
Trails 120km/75 miles
Blue 36%
Red 48%
Black 16%
Snowmaking 47km/
29 miles
Recco detectors used

Phone numbers
From abroad use the prefix +39 (and do **not** omit the initial 'o' of the phone number).

TOURIST OFFICE

Postcode 23032
t +39 (0342) 903300
f 904696
aptbormio@provincia.
so.it
www.valtellinaonline.it

MALCOLM RIDDOCH

A mix of open and wooded slopes ↓

Intermediates The men's downhill course starts with a steep plunge, but otherwise is just a tough red, ideal for strong intermediates. Stella Alpina, down to 2000, is also fairly steep. Many runs are less tough – ideal for most intermediates. The longest is a superb top-to-bottom cruise. The outlying mountains are also suitable for early intermediates.

Beginners The beginner areas at Bormio 2000 offer good snow, but there are no very flattering longer trails to move on to. Novices are better off at nearby Santa Caterina.

Cross-country There are some trails either side of Bormio, towards Piatta and beneath Le Motte and Valdidentro, but cross-country skiers are better off at snow-sure Santa Caterina.

Liftlines Both sections of the tram suffer delays in the morning peak period and on Sundays. A new fast quad from Bormio 2000 should help to relieve the pressure here for 2001/02. When the lower slopes are incomplete, lines form to ride down. Otherwise there are few problems outside carnival week.

Mountain restaurants The mountain restaurants are generally good. Even the efficient self-service at Bormio 2000 has a good choice of dishes. At La Rocca, above Ciuk, there is a welcoming chalet and a smart, modern place with table- or self-service. Cedrone, at Bormio 2000, has a good terrace and a play area for children. The very welcoming table-service Baita de Mario, at Ciuk, is a great place for a long lunch. The new San Colombano in Valdidentro is recommended.

Schools and guides We have received good reports of both the Alta Valtellina

and Nazionale schools.

Facilities for children The Bormio 2000 school has a roped-off snow garden at mid-mountain with moving carpet lift.

STAYING THERE

Hotels Most of Bormio's 40-plus hotels are 2- and 3-star places. The 4-star Palace (0342 903131) is the most luxurious in town. The Posta (0342 904753) is in the center of the old town – rooms range from adequate to very good. The Baita dei Pinti (0342 904346) is the best placed of the top hotels – on the river, between the lifts and center. The Ambassador (0342 904625) is close to the gondola.

Apartments/condos The Cristallo apartments have been recommended.

Eating out There's a wide selection of restaurants. The atmospheric Taulà does excellent modern food with great service. The Kuerc and the Vecchia Combo are also popular. There are excellent pizzerias, including the Jap.

Après-ski The après-ski scene starts on the mountain at La Rocca, and there are popular bars around the bottom lift stations. The Clem Pub, Gordy's, Cafe Mozart and the Auròra piano bar are popular spots. Shangri-La is a friendly bar. The King's Club is the best disco.

Off the slopes Diversions include thermal baths, riding and walks in the Stelvio National Park. There is also an excellent sports center, ice rink and 'superb' swimming pool. St Moritz and duty-free Livigno are popular excursions.

Staying up the mountain The modern Girasole, at Bormio 2000, is simple but well run by an Anglo-Italian couple, with lots of events.

Cervinia 2050m/6,730ft

Mile after mile of high-altitude, snow-sure cruising

➕ Extensive mountain with miles of long, consistently gentle runs – ideal for early intermediates and anyone wary of steep slopes or bumps

➕ High, sunny and snow-sure slopes amid impressive scenery

➕ Link with Zermatt in Switzerland provides even more spectacular views and good lunches

➖ Very little to interest good or aggressive intermediates and above

➖ Almost entirely treeless, with little to do in bad weather

➖ Lifts prone to closure by wind, particularly early in the season

➖ Link with Zermatt isn't quite as valuable as you might expect

➖ Village spoils some of the views

➖ Steep uphill walk to main lifts, followed by lots of steps in station

➖ Few off-slope amenities

What brings people to Breuil Cervinia (as the resort now styles itself) in winter in the 20th century is what brought climbers to the original village of Breuil in the 19th century: altitude. For climbers it was a launch pad for assaults on the nearby Matterhorn (Monte Cervino). For winter sports, it offers an unusual combination: slopes that are gentle and extensive, sunny and snow-sure.

For cruisers who like to cover the miles on flattering slopes with no worries about unexpected challenges, there is nowhere like it. But the more adventurous should steer clear: they'll find the slopes tame and the link with Zermatt disappointing because it doesn't access Zermatt's best slopes directly.

245

The resort

Cervinia is at the head of a long valley leading off the Aosta valley on the Italian side of the Matterhorn. The old climbing village developed into a winter resort in a rather haphazard way, and it has no consistent style of architecture. It's an uncomfortable hodgepodge, neither pleasing to the eye nor as offensive as the worst of the French purpose-built resorts. The center is pleasant, compact and traffic-free. But ugly surrounding apartment blocks and hotels make the whole place feel less friendly and welcoming.

A lot of people stay near the village center, at the foot of the beginner areas. You can take a series of surface lits from here to the slopes. But the main gondola and tram to Plan Maison at mid-mountain start an awkward uphill walk away, above the village. To avoid the walk to these lifts, choose a hotel with its own shuttle-bus. There are more accommodations further out at the Cieloalto complex and on the road up to it – but these buildings include some of the worst eyesores.

SNOWPIX.COM / CHRIS GILL

There is no better way to pack in the miles on-trail than to ride Cervinia's top tram repeatedly to Plateau Rosa →

MOUNTAIN FACTS

Altitude 1525m-3480m
5,000ft-11,420ft
Lifts   31
Trails   200km/
                125 miles
Blue   28%
Red   60%
Black   12%
Snowmaking   17km/
                11 miles
Recco detectors used

LIFT TICKETS

2001/02 prices in
euros
Breuil-Cervinia
Covers all lifts on the
Italian side of the
border including
Valtournenche.
Beginners 'First
bends' tickets
available.
Main ticket
1-day ticket 29
6-day ticket 152
(low season 122)
Senior citizens
Over 65: 6-day ticket
115
Children
Under 12: 6-day ticket
115
Under 8: free ticket
Short-term tickets
Half-day from noon
for Cervinia. Single
and return tickets on
some lifts.
Notes Daily extension
for Zermatt lifts at
Klein Matterhorn and
Schwarzsee (19) or for
all areas (25).
Alternative tickets
The International
Matterhorn ticket
includes Zermatt's
Klein Matterhorn and
Schwarzsee lifts: 6-
day ticket 178. The
International Zermatt
ticket covers all of
Zermatt: 6-day ticket
191. Limited area
tickets for Carosello
(four lifts) and
Carosello/ Cretaz
(seven lifts). Valle
d'Aosta ski ticket
covers all lifts in
Courmayeur, La
Thuile, Gressoney,
Alagna, Champoluc,
Pila, Cervinia and
Valtournenche (adult
6-day 155).

As well as the usual souvenir shops there are some smart clothes shops and jewellers. At peak periods, the resort fills up with day trippers and weekenders from Milan and Turin who bring cars and cell phones, making parts of the village traffic- and fume-ridden at times, and the hills alive with the sound of ringing tones.

The resort is relatively expensive by Italian standards, but reporters have found it good value recently because of the weak euro. There are surprisingly few off-slope amenities, such as kindergartens, marked walks and spa facilities.

The slopes link to Valtournenche further down the valley (covered by the lift ticket) and Zermatt over in Switzerland (covered by a daily supplement, or a more expensive weekly ticket). More about this later in the chapter.

Day trips by car are possible to Courmayeur, La Thuile and the Monterosa Ski resorts of Champoluc and Gressoney.

The mountains

Cervinia's main slopes are on a high, large, open and sunny west-facing bowl. It has Italy's highest trails and some of its longest (13km/8 miles from Plateau Rosa to Valtournenche – with only a short surface lift part-way). Nearly all the runs are accessible to intermediates. The weather is more of a problem than steepness. If it's bad, the top lifts often close because of high winds. And even the lower slopes may be unusable because of poor visibility. There are few woodland trails.

THE SLOPES
Very easy
Cervinia has the biggest, highest, most area of easy, well groomed trails we've come across – though we're very sceptical of the recent hike in the

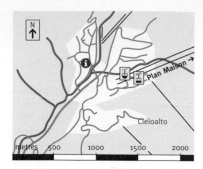

claimed total to 200km/125miles. The high proportion of red runs on the trail map is misleading: most of them would be graded blue elsewhere. The slopes just above the village are floodlit some evenings.

The main lifts take you to the mid-mountain base of **Plan Maison** (2555m/8,380ft). From there a further gondola then a giant tram go up to **Plateau Rosa** (3480m/11,420ft) and a link with Zermatt. Three successive fast quads (all with windshields) from Plan Maison go up to a slightly lower point on the border, where there is now a trail for Zermatt.

From the top you can ski back on some of Cervinia's easiest slopes to Plan Maison or down to the village. If instead you turn right at Plateau Rosa you take the splendid wide Ventina run. You can use the tram to do the top part repeatedly, or go all the way down to Cervinia (8km/5 miles and over 1400m/4,600ft vertical). Or you can branch off left down towards **Valtournenche** (1525m/5,000ft). The slopes here are served by a number of slow old lifts above the initial gondola from Valtournenche to Salette at 2245m/7,370ft. You can't get back to Plan Maison from this sector except by riding down the gondola.

There is also the small, little-used **Cieloalto** area, served by three lifts to the south of the tram at the bottom of the Ventina run. This has some of

boarding *Cervinia has great slopes for learning to snowboard – gentle, wide and usually with good snow. And the main lifts around the area are chairs, gondolas and trams, but beware, there are a lot of surface lifts (especially difficult to negotiate in high winds) and some long flat bits as well. There's not much to interest better boarders – just as there's not much to interest better skiers. The snowboarder-only trail and terrain park in the Cieloalto sector is open only on weekends during the peak season (the one in Zermatt is better but beware of long T-bars to get back if the Klein Matterhorn tram is closed). Nightlife is fairly limited.*

Cervino
Classes 6 days
2hr 45min: 10am-
12.45
6 days: 119
Children's classes
Ages: 5 to 7
Private lessons
Hourly
28 for 1 person; 31
for 2 people

Cervinia's steeper trails and can be very useful in bad weather as it has the only trees in the area.

Several reporters have criticized the fact that old lift stations and pylons have been left on the slopes as eyesores after the lifts have been scrapped. The trail map is another cause for complaint.

SNOW RELIABILITY
Superb
The mountain is one of the highest in Europe and, despite getting a lot of afternoon sun, can usually be relied on to have good snow conditions. Lift closures due to wind is a bigger worry. Several reporters have complained about the biting winds and one claims that every lift stopped due to high winds at some point in his holiday.

The village beginner areas and the bottom half of the Ventina run have snowmaking facilities. But the run below the top of the gondola to lower-lying Valtournenche doesn't – and is often closed later in the season.

FOR EXPERTS
Forget it
This is not a resort for experts. There are several black runs dotted about, but most of them would be graded red elsewhere. Many reporters head over to Zermatt for more challenging slopes but don't necessarily find them – more about this in the margin on this page.

FOR INTERMEDIATES
Miles of long, flattering runs
Virtually the whole area can be covered comfortably by average intermediates. And if you like wide, easy, freeway trails, you'll love Cervinia: it has more long, flattering runs than any other resort. The easiest slopes are on the left as you look at the mountain. From top to bottom here there are gentle blue runs and almost equally gentle reds in the beautiful scenery at the foot of the south face of the Matterhorn.

The area on the right as you look at the mountain is best for adventurous intermediates. The Ventina run is a particularly good fast cruise. The long run down to Valtournenche is easy for most of its length. Good intermediates will be capable of the black runs.

FOR BEGINNERS
Pretty much ideal
Complete beginners will start on the good village beginner area, and should graduate quickly to the fine flat area around Plan Maison and its gentle blue runs. Fast learners will be going all the way from the top to the bottom of the mountain by the end of the week.

FOR CROSS-COUNTRY
Hardly any
There are a couple of short trails, but this is not a cross-country resort.

Cervinia

247

M. Cervino
Matterhorn
4478m

Schwarzsee
2585m
Trockener Steg
2940m

Zermatt

Plateau Rosa
3480m/11,420ft

Colle Sup.
Cime Bianche
2980m

Cime
Bianche
2910m

Laghi
Cime Bianche
2810m

Colle Inf.
Cime Bianche
2825m

Plan Maison
2555m

Salette
2245m

Cretaz

Cervinia
2050m/6,730ft

Cieloalto

Valtournenche
1525m/5,000ft

THE ZERMATT CONNECTION

If the weather is good, you're bound to be tempted to go over to Zermatt. And quite right – the restaurants are simply the best, and it's only from the Swiss side that you get the classic view of the Matterhorn. But there are problems.

For a start, the two lift companies can't even convey clearly where you can cross over. Testa Grigia on one side of the joint map becomes Plateau Rosa on the other; Theodulpass becomes nameless. Pathetic.

Then there's the runs. You come first of all to even gentler glacier freeways than on the Cervinia side. There are more challenging trails once you get down to Schwarzsee. But there is no way to get to Zermatt's classic terrain on Stockhorn and Rothorn without making the long descent to the village, and bussing or walking its length to other lifts.

You could do this, but you couldn't do it enjoyably – partly because you have to set off back early on account of the lift links back to the border. Recent reporters tell of long afternoon liftlines for the Trockener Steg-Klein Matterhorn tram. And if this link is closed by high winds – as is often the case – there may be horrendous liftlines in grim conditions for the alternative route via two long, slow and very exposed T-bars.

You can get a taste of Zermatt from Cervinia, but you're unlikely to get your fill.

↑ The Matterhorn looks more spectacular from Zermatt, but Cervinia's setting is impressive by normal standards

SNOWPIX.COM / CHRIS GILL

LIFTLINES
Can still be problems

Although much improved recently, there are still some antiquated lifts, and the system still has drawbacks. The two main access lifts to Plan Maison can get crowded (twenty minute liftlines at peak times) and the alternative series of surface lifts and chairs need upgrading. The series of slow lifts back up from Valtournenche are another source of complaint. There can be lines for many lower lifts when upper lifts are shut due to high wind.

MOUNTAIN RESTAURANTS
Disappointing for Italy

The mountain restaurants are not as appealing as you might expect in an Italian resort (and the toilet facilities can be primitive), so some reporters prefer to head over to Zermatt's wonderful huts for lunch. However, the Châlet Etoile, beneath the Rocce Nerre chair-lift at Plan Maison, is highly praised by reporters – 'The best mountain restaurant I've been to,' says one – and it has a '1st class toilet'. Booking in advance is recommended. The Rocce Nere is also recommended. The British-run Igloo, at the top of the Bardoney chair just off the Ventina trail, serves huge burgers and has 'a UK-style loo'. Baita Cretaz, near the bottom of the Cretaz trails, is good value, but disappointed a recent visitor. The Bontadini, Teodulo, Pousset and Les Clochards are also recommended.

The restaurants are cheaper and less crowded on the Valtournenche side. The Motta, at the top of the surface lift of the same name, does excellent food including goulaschsuppe that is 'out of this world'.

CHILDCARE

The ski school runs a snow garden with mini-lift at the foot of the Cretaz slopes and one mini-lift in Plan Maison. Care arrangements 10am to 1pm. There is no non-ski kindergarten.

GETTING THERE

Air Turin, transfer 2½hr. Geneva, transfer 2½hr.

Rail Châtillon (27km/17 miles); regular buses from station.

Phone numbers From abroad use the prefix +39 (and do **not** omit the initial '0' of the phone number).

ACTIVITIES

Indoor Hotels with swimming pools and saunas, fitness center, bowling
Outdoor Natural skating rink (until March), paragliding, hang-gliding, mountaineering, skidoos, heli-skiing

TOURIST OFFICE

Postcode 11021
t +39 (0166) 949136
f 949731
breuil-cervinia@net
vallee.it
www.montecervino.it

SCHOOLS AND GUIDES
Getting better

Cervinia has two main schools, Cervino and Breuil. Reports on both are fairly positive.

FACILITIES FOR CHILDREN
Could be better

The Cervino ski school runs a ski kindergarten. And there's a babysitting and kindergarten area at Plan Maison. The slopes, with their long gentle runs, should suit families.

Staying there

HOW TO GO
Good choice of hotels

Hotels There are almost 50 hotels, mostly 2- or 3-star, with a few 4-stars.
((((⑤ **Cristallo** (0116 943411) Luxury 4-star quite a way from town with pool, sauna, massage, great views. Free bus to lifts. A change of ownership is apparently imminent.
(((④ **Hermitage** (0166 948998) Small, luxurious Relais et Château just out of the village on the road up to Cieloalto. Great views, pool, free bus to lifts.
(((④ **Punta Maquignaz** (0166 949145) Captivating chalet-style 4-star, in center near Cretaz lifts.
(((③ **Sporthotel Sertorelli** (0166 949797) Excellent food, sauna and hot-tub. Ten minutes from lifts.
(((③ **Europa** (0166 948660) Friendly and family run; near Cretaz lifts. Pool.
((② **Astoria** (0116 940062) Right by main lift station. Family run and simple. 'Comfortable but that's all,' says a reporter this year.
((② **Marmore** (0166 949057) Friendly, family run, with 'quite good food'; on main street – an easy walk to the lifts.
Apartments/condos There are many apartments in the resort. The Cristallino apartments are fairly simple, but guests have use of the fine facilities of the Cristallo next door, including the free bus.

EATING OUT
Plenty to choose from

Cervinia's 50 or so restaurants allow plenty of choice. The Chamois and Matterhorn are excellent, but quite pricey. The Grotta belies its name with good food. Casse Croute serves probably the biggest, and best, pizzas. The Copa Pan has a lively atmosphere and is again recommended by several reporters. La Bricole, Il Rustico and La Nicchia have also been recommended.

The Maison de Saussure does 'very good local specialities'. An evening out at the Baita Cretaz mountain hut makes a change.

APRES-SKI
Quiet for a large resort

Many looking for action find there isn't much to do except tour the mostly fairly ordinary bars. The Copa Pan (see Eating out) is lively, good value and serves generous measures. The Dragon Bar is popular with Brits and Scandinavians and has satellite TV and videos. Lino's (by the ice rink), the Yeti, Labatt and Café des Guides (with mementos of the owner's mountaineering trips to the Himalayas) are all recommended by reporters. The discos liven up at weekends – the Garage is reputedly the best. You can go snow-mobiling on the old bob-sled run and bowling.

OFF THE SLOPES
Little attraction

There is little to do. The pleasant town of Aosta is reached easily enough, but it's a four-hour round trip. Village amenities include hotel pools, a fitness center and a natural ice rink. The walks are disappointing. The mountain restaurants that are reachable by gondola or tram are not special.

STAYING UP THE MOUNTAIN
To beat the liftlines

Up at Plan Maison, the major lift junction 500m/1,640ft vertical above the resort, Lo Stambecco is a 50-room 3-star hotel ideally placed for early nights and early starts. Less radically, the Cime Bianche is a rustic 3-star chalet on the upper fringes of the resort (in the area known as La Vieille).

STAYING DOWN THE VALLEY
Great home run

Valtournenche, about five miles down the road, is cheaper than Cervinia, has a genuine Italian atmosphere and a fair selection of simple hotels, of which the 3-star Bijou (0166 92109) is the best.

The new gondola that opened in 1998 has cut the weekend waits. But the slow lifts above it mean it takes quite a time to reach Cervinia. The exceptionally long run back down, however, is a nice way to end the day – when it is all open. The main street through the village is very crowded with cars going to and from Cervinia.

Cortina d'Ampezzo

1225m/4,020ft

Simply the world's most beautiful winter playground

HOW IT RATES

The slopes

Snow	✱✱✱
Extent	✱✱✱
Experts	✱✱
Intermediates	✱✱✱
Beginners	✱✱✱✱✱
Convenience	✱
Liftlines	✱✱✱
Restaurants	✱✱✱✱

The rest

Scenery	✱✱✱✱✱
Resort charm	✱✱✱✱
Off-slope	✱✱✱✱✱

➕ Magnificent Dolomite scenery – perhaps the most dramatic of any winter resort

➕ Marvellous beginner areas and good long cruising runs, ideal for nervous intermediates

➕ Access to the vast area covered by the Dolomiti Superski ticket

➕ Attractive, although rather towny, resort, with lots of upscale shops

➕ Good off-slope facilities

➕ Remarkably uncrowded slopes

➖ Several separate areas of slopes, which are inconveniently spread around all sides of the resort and linked by buses

➖ Erratic snow record

➖ Expensive by Italian standards

➖ Gets very crowded during Italian holidays

➖ Very little to entertain experts

➖ Cell phones and fur coats may drive you nuts

Nowhere is more picturesque than chic Cortina, the most upscale of Italian resorts. Dramatic pink-tinged cliffs and peaks rise vertically from the top of the slopes, giving picture-postcard views from wherever you are.

Cortina's slopes are fine for its regular upscale visitors from Rome and Milan, many of whom have second homes here and enjoy the strolling, shopping, people-watching and lunching as much as the occasional leisurely excursion on to the slopes. For beginners and leisurely intermediates, the splendid beginner areas and long, easy, well-groomed runs are ideal. For avid skiers and riders, Cortina's fragmented areas can be frustrating, especially if snow is scarce and the area is fragmented even more; but the access to the Sella Ronda and other Dolomiti Superski resorts, though time-consuming, is some compensation – easiest by car. For experts, there are few tough runs, and the best of those are liable to poor snow conditions and closure because they face south.

What's new

Cortina has worked hard on much-needed snowmaking and now tells us that all trails below 2300m/7,550ft (which is most of the trails) are covered by snow-guns. But it still has to be cold enough for the guns to be able to work.

The Marmolada glacier lifts are now included in the Dolomiti Superski ticket.

Last season also saw the installation of a new two-seater chair-lift on the Socrepes beginner areas. A new board-park was created in Faloria and a second is planned at Cinque Torri for 2001/02.

250

CORTINA TURISMO / D G BANDION

Wherever you look there are towering cliffs and peaks ➔

The resort

In winter, more people come to Cortina for the clear mountain air, the stunning views, the shopping, the cafes and to pose and be seen than for the winter sports – 70% of all Italian visitors don't bother taking to the slopes. Cortina attracts the rich and famous from the big Italian cities. Fur coats and glitzy jewelry are everywhere.

The resort itself is a widely spread town rather than a village, with exclusive chalets scattered around the woods and the roads leading off into the countryside. The center is the traffic-free Corso Italia, full of chic designer clothes and jewelry shops, art galleries and furriers – finding a ski shop can seem tricky. The cobbles and picturesque church bell tower add to the Italian atmosphere. In early evening, the street is a hive of activity, with everyone parading up and down in their finery, window-shopping,

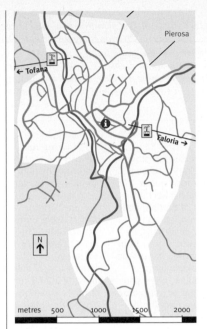

MOUNTAIN FACTS

Altitude 1225m-2930m
4,020ft-9,610ft
Lifts	51
Trails	140km/87 miles
Blue	33%
Red	62%
Black	5%
Snowmaking	133km
	83 miles

Recco detectors used

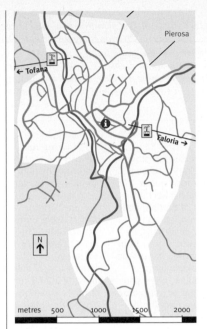

LIFT TICKETS

2000/01 prices in
euros
Dolomiti Superski
Covers 460 lifts and
1200km/746 miles of
trails in the
Dolomites, including
all Cortina areas.
Main ticket
1-day ticket 33
6-day ticket 162
(low season 142)
Senior citizens
Over 60: 6-day ticket
119
Children
Under 16: 6-day ticket
100

Alternative ticket
Cortina d'Ampezzo
Covers all lifts in
Cortina, San Vito di
Cadore, Auronzo and
Misurina, and ski-
buses.
Main ticket
1-day ticket 30
6-day ticket 148
(low season 130)
Senior citizens
Over 60: 6-day ticket
119
Children
Under 16: 6-day ticket
91
Under 8: free ticket

people-watching and finalizing their
clubbing arrangements on cell phones.
Seeing anyone dressed for the slopes
at 5pm is a rarity. But all this glamour
doesn't mean Cortina has to be
expensive.

Unlike the rest of the Dolomites,
Cortina is pure Italy. It has none of the
Germanic traditions of Selva and the
Sud Tirol, and doesn't attract many
German visitors.

Surrounding the center is a
horrendous one-way system, often
traffic-clogged and stinking of exhaust
fumes – a nasty contrast to the
stunning scenery everywhere else you
look. The lifts to the two main areas of
slopes are a fair way from the center,
and at opposite sides of town. Other
lifts are a lengthy bus-ride away.
There's a wide range of hotels in the
center and scattered in the outskirts.
To get the most out of the town,
staying centrally is the best bet –
though you could opt for one of the
main trams and base yourself near
that. The local bus service is good
(though it could do with being more
frequent). A car can be useful,
especially for getting to the outlying
areas – and certainly helps to make
the most of other areas on the
Dolomiti Superski ticket. San Cassiano
is not far to the west, with links from
there to Corvara and the other Sella
Ronda resorts.

Cortina first leapt to fame as host of
the 1956 Winter Olympics. At the time,
it was very modern; now its facilities
feel dated. There is a good mixture of
slopes above and below the tree line.

THE SLOPES
Inconveniently fragmented

All Cortina's smallish separate areas
are a fair trek from the town center.
The largest is **Socrepes**, accessed by
chair- and surface lifts a bus-ride away.
It links with **Tofana**, Cortina's highest
area, also reached by two-stage tram
from near the Olympic ice rink.

On the opposite side of the valley is
the tiny **Mietres** area. Another tram
from the east side of town leads to the
Faloria area, from where you can head
down to the chairs that lead up into
the limited but dramatic runs beneath
the **Cristallo** peak.

Other areas are reachable by road.
The tram from Passo Falzarego
(2150m/7,050ft) up to Lagazuoi
(2750m/9,020ft) accesses a beautiful
red run to Armenterola which takes
you away from all lifts and signs of
civilization and is called the Hidden
Valley. On the way to Passo Falzarego
is the tiny but spectacular Cinque Torri
area. Its excellent, north-facing slopes
are now accessed by a high-speed
quad.

Reporters praise the excellent
grooming and quiet slopes with few
liftlines, but complain about the trail
map not showing some runs, poor trail
marking, and World Cup races
disrupting January skiing. (Many of the
red runs on the map seem to have
been reclassified as blue recently.)

SNOW RELIABILITY
Lots of artificial help

The snowfall record is erratic – it can
be good here when it's poor on the
north side of the Alps (and vice versa).
But the resort has invested heavily in
snowmaking and over 90 per cent of
the trails are now covered, so cover
should generally be good if it is cold
enough to make snow. But last time
we visited, the link between Tofana
and Socrepes was closed because of
lack of snow on a key south-facing
slope – which made the areas even
more fragmented.

boarding *Despite its upscale chic, Cortina is a good resort for learning to board. The Socrepes beginner areas are wide, gentle and served by a fast chair-lift. And progress on to the resort's other easy slopes is simple because you can get around in all areas using just chairs and trams – though there are surface lifts, they can be avoided. There's a new half-pipe at Faloria and another is planned at Cinque Torri but there's little off-trail to interest experienced boarders.*

FOR EXPERTS
Limited
The run down from the second stage of the Tofana tram at Ra Valles goes through a gap in the rocks, and a steep, narrow, south-facing section gives wonderful views of Cortina, deep down in the valley. It's often tricky because of poor snow conditions.

Cortina's other steep run goes from the top of the Cristallo area at Forcella Staunies. A chair-lift takes you to a steep, south-facing couloir, often shut due to avalanche danger or poor snow.

Other than these two runs (both shut on our last visit) there's little to keep experts happy for a week.

Heli-skiing is available.

FOR INTERMEDIATES
Fragmented and not extensive
If you like cruising in beautiful scenery and don't mind repeating runs, you'll get the most out of Cortina.

The runs at the top of Tofana are short but normally have the best snow. The highest are at over 2800m/9,190ft and mainly face north. But be warned: the only way back down is by the tricky black run described above or tram. The reds from the linked Pomedes area are longer and offer good cruising.

Faloria has a string of fairly short north-facing runs – we loved Vitelli, around the back away from all lifts. And the Cristallo area has a long blue (formerly red), served by a fast quad.

It is well worth making the trip to Cinque Torri for wonderful, deserted fast cruising on usually excellent north-facing snow. The 'hidden valley' run from Lagazuoi at the top of the Passo Falzerego tram to Armenterola is a must – a very easy red and one of the most beautiful runs we've come across. It offers isolation amid sheer pink-tinged Dolomite peaks and frozen waterfalls. Make time to stop at the atmospheric Scotoni rifugio near the end, then it's a long pole, skate or walk to the welcome sight of a horse-drawn sled (with ropes attached) which tows the weary to Armenterola. Shared cabs take you back to Passo Falzerego (if you've time, try the slopes of Alta Badia, accessed from Armenterola).

FOR BEGINNERS
Wonderful beginner areas
The Socrepes area has some of the biggest beginner areas and best progression runs we have seen. Some of the blue forest paths can be icy and intimidating. But you'll find ideal gentle terrain on the main trails.

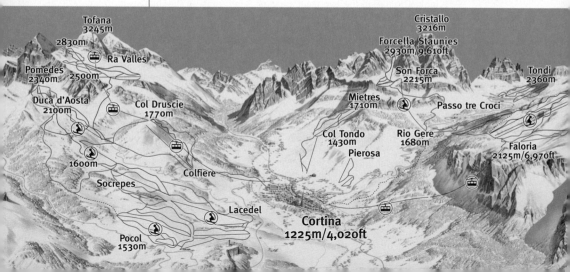

SCHOOLS/GUIDES

2000/01 prices in euros

Cortina
Classes 6 days
2½hr: 9.30-noon; 2hr: noon-2pm
6 2½hr days: 163
Private lessons
Hourly
35 for 1hr; each additional person 10

Azzurra Cortina
Classes 6 days
3½hr: 9.15-1pm;
6½hr: 9.15-4pm
6 3½hr days: 387
Private lessons
Hourly
39 for 1hr; each additional person 12

FOR CROSS-COUNTRY
One of the best

Cortina has around 75km/47 miles of trails, mainly in the woods towards Dobbiaco. There are also trails below the Cristallo area.

LIFTLINES
No problem

Most Cortina tourists rise late, lunch lengthily and leave the slopes early – if they get on them at all. That means few liftlines and generally uncrowded trails – a different world to the crowded Sella Ronda circuit. 'Lack of lines was one of the highlights of our holiday,' said one reporter.

MOUNTAIN RESTAURANTS
Good, but get in early

Lunch is a major event for many Cortina visitors. On weekends you often need to book or turn up very early to be sure of a table. Many restaurants can be reached by road or lift, and pedestrians arrive as early as 10am to sunbathe, admire the views and idle the time away on their cell phones.

Although prices are high in the fanciest establishments, we've found plenty of reasonably priced places, serving generally excellent food. In the Socrepes area, the Col Taron is highly recommended and the Piè de Tofana,

Phone numbers
From abroad use the prefix +39 (and do **not** omit the initial 'o' of the phone number).

CHILDCARE

There is non-skiing childcare, and schools offer all-day classes for children.

GETTING THERE

Air Venice, transfer 2½hr (free transfer available for hotel guests; advance booking required).

Rail Calalzo (35km/22 miles) or Dobbiaco (32km/20 miles); frequent buses from station.

ACTIVITIES

Indoor Swimming pool, saunas, museums, art gallery, cinema, indoor tennis court, public library
Outdoor Rides on Olympic bob run, snow rafting down Olympic ski jump, crazy sled for moonlit excursions, snow-shoe tours, all at Adrenalin center; Olympic ice-stadium (2 rinks), curling, ice hockey, sleigh rides, horse-riding school, 6km/4miles walking paths, toboggan run, heli-skiing

TOURIST OFFICE

Postcode 32043
t +39 (0436) 866252
f 867448
cortina@dolomiti.org
www.cortina.dolomiti.
org

Rifugio Pomedes and El Faral are also good. The Socrepes sector also has several hotels along the road at its edge – including the best restaurant in the resort, the Michelin-starred Tivoli.

At Cristallo the Rio Gere at the base of the quad chair and Son Forca, with fabulous views at the top of it, are both worth a visit.

The restaurants at Cinque Torri, the Scoiattoli and the Rifugio Averau, offer fantastic views as well as good food, and, unusually, are non-smoking. Rifugio Lagazuoi, a hike up from the top of the Passo Falzerego tram, also has great views and no smoking.

SCHOOLS AND GUIDES
Mixed reports

Of the four ski schools, we've had mixed reports of the 'Cortina' school. One couple had good classes in English-speaking groups. But there were other reports of a group that included six Brits being taught mainly in Italian, and a tired intermediate asking for a short rest and being left stranded at the top of the mountain. The Gruppo Guide Alpine offers off-trail and touring.

FACILITIES FOR CHILDREN
Better than average

By Italian standards childcare facilities are outstanding, with a choice of all-day care arrangements for children of practically any age. This is one resort where Mamma gets a break. Given the small number of British visitors, you can't count on good spoken English. And the fragmented area can make traveling around with children difficult.

 Staying there

HOW TO GO
Hotels dominate the market

Hotels There's a big choice, from 5-star luxury to 1-star and 2-star pensions.
(((((5) **Miramonti** (0436 4201) Spectacularly grand hotel, 2km/around 1 mile south of town. Pool.
((((4) **Poste** (0436 4271) Reliable 4-star, at the heart of the town.
((((4) **Ancora** (0436 3261) Elegant public rooms. On the traffic-free Corso Italia.
((((4) **Parc Victoria** (0436 3246) Rustic 4-star with small rooms but good food, at the Faloria end of the town center.
((((4) **Faloria** (0436 2959) Newish, near ski jump, splendid pool, good food.
(((3) **Olimpia** (0436 3256) Comfortable B&B hotel in center, near Faloria lift.

(((3) **Menardi** (0436 2400) Welcoming roadside inn, a long walk from center and lifts.
(((3) **Villa Resy** (0436 3303) Small and welcoming, just outside center, with British owner.
Apartments/condos There are some chalets and apartments – mostly out of town.

EATING OUT
Huge choice

There's an enormous selection, both in town and a little way out, doing mainly Italian food. The very smart and pricey El Toulà is in a beautiful old barn, just on the edge of town. Many of the best restaurants are further out – such as the Michelin-starred Tivoli, Meloncino, Leone e Anna, Rio Gere and Baita Fraina. Reasonably priced central restaurants include the Cinque Torri and Al Passetto for pizza and pasta.

APRES-SKI
Lively in high season

Cortina is a lively social whirl in high season, with lots of well-heeled Italians staying up very late. Don't go on the early evening walkabout if fur coats and cell phones annoy you.

Bar Lovat is one of several popular, high-calorie tea-time spots. There are three good wine bars: Enoteca has 700 different wines and good cheese and meats; Osteria has good wines and local ham; and Febar is a wine bar with good decor and is also crowded later. The liveliest bar is the Clipper, with a bob-sled in the door, and lots of designer beer. Discos liven up after 11pm.

OFF THE SLOPES
A classic resort

Along with St Moritz, Cortina rates as one of the leading resorts if you're happier off the slopes. The setting is stunning, the town attractive, the shopping extensive, the mountain restaurants easily accessible by road (a car is handy). And there's plenty more to do, including swimming, ice skating and dog-sledding. You can have a run (with driver!) down the Olympic bob-sled run. There's horse jumping and polo on the snow occasionally. There are several museums and art galleries.

Trips to Venice are easily and inexpensively organized.

Courmayeur

A seductive village on the sunny side of Mont Blanc

HOW IT RATES

The slopes

Snow	****
Extent	**
Experts	***
Intermediates	****
Beginners	**
Convenience	*
Liftlines	****
Restaurants	****

The rest

Scenery	****
Resort charm	****
Off-slope	***

➕ Charming, traditional village, with car-free center and stylish shops

➕ Stunning views of Mont Blanc massif

➕ Pleasant range of intermediate runs

➕ Comprehensive snowmaking

➕ Good mountain restaurants

➕ Lively, but not rowdy, après-ski

➕ Good base for heli-skiing

➖ Lack of beginner areas and easy runs for beginners to progress to

➖ No tough trails

➖ Relatively small area, with mainly short runs; high-mileage trail bashers will get bored in a week

➖ Slopes very crowded on Sundays

➖ Tiresome walk and tram journey between village and slopes

Courmayeur is very popular, especially at weekends, with the smart Italian set from Milan and Turin. It's easy to see why: it's very easy to get to and certainly the most captivating of the Val d'Aosta resorts.

The scenery, the charm of the village, the stylish bars and restaurants and the nightlife are big draws. The main slopes are fine but nothing special given their limited range of difficulty, inconvenient location across the valley from the village and their limited size; an avid skier will cover Courmayeur in a day. It is hoped that the Mont Blanc tunnel will re-open for this season, making the option of a quick trip to Chamonix feasible again. But don't bank on it until it has actually happened.

The resort could make a lively week for those who want to party as much as hit the slopes. It also appeals to those with quite different ambitions, who want to explore the spectacular Mont Blanc massif with the aid of a guide and other local peaks with the aid of a helicopter.

What's new

As we went to press the Mont Blanc tunnel was officially due to open in the autumn, after the tragic fire in 1999. But the project has been delayed several times and locals were predicting that it wouldn't open until December at the earliest and maybe not until after the 2001/02 season. Until it does re-open access will be quickest from Turin or Milan airports. From Geneva, the best route is via the Grand St Bernard tunnel.

The Cresta d'Arp tram can now be taken without a guide, to access the off-trail runs. And a heli-operation started where you can get picked up from right by the trail.

The resort

Courmayeur is a traditional old Italian mountaineering village that, despite the nearby Mont Blanc tunnel road (currently deserted) and modern hotels, has retained much of its old-world feel.

The village has a charming traffic-free center of attractive shops, cobbled streets and well-preserved buildings. An Alpine museum and a statue of a long-dead mountain rescue hero add to the historical feel.

The center has a great atmosphere, focused around the Via Roma. As the lifts close, people pile into the many bars, some of which are very civilized. Others wander in and out of the many small shops, which include a salami specialist and a good bookshop. On weekends people-watching is part of the evening scene, when the fur coats of the Milanese and Torinese take over.

The village is quite large and its huge tram is right on the edge.

Many of the mountain huts on the Zerotta side have stunning views like this ➜

MOUNTAIN FACTS

Altitude 1210m-2755m
3,970ft-9,040ft
Lifts 23
Trails 100km/62 miles
Blue 20%
Red 70%
Black 10%
Snowmaking 18km/
11 miles
Recco detectors used

LIFT TICKETS

2001/02 prices in
euros
**Courmayeur Mont
Blanc**
Covers all lifts in Val
Veny and Checrouit,
and the lifts on Mont
Blanc up to Punta
Helbronner.
Beginners Free
beginner lifts at Plan
Checrouit and top of
Val Veny tram (which
can be paid for by the
ride).
Main ticket
1-day ticket 30
(2000/01 price)
6-day ticket 161
(low season 145)
Short-term tickets
Single ascent on
some lifts and half-
day ticket (afternoon)
available.
Children
Under 12: 6-day ticket
121
Under 8: free ticket
with accompanying
adult
Notes tickets of two
or more days are
valid on the Mt Blanc
lift. Tickets of three or
more days cover all
lifts in the Aosta
Valley. Tickets of six
or more days are
valid for one day at
Pila and Verbier and
for two days in the
resorts of the Mont
Blanc region ski ticket
(including Chamonix,
Les Contamines, St
Gervais, Mégève).
Alternative tickets
Mont-Blanc ski region
ticket covers all lifts
in 13 resorts around
Mont Blanc.

The mountains

The trails suit intermediates, but are
surprisingly limited for such a well-
known, large resort. They are varied in
character, if not gradient. Trail marking
could be improved.

THE SLOPES
Small but interestingly varied
The slopes are separate from the
village: you have to ride a tram to
them and either take it down or take a
bus from Dolonne at the end of the
day. The tram arrives at the bottom of
the slopes at Plan Checrouit (where
you can store your equipment).

There are two distinct sections, both
almost entirely intermediate. The north-
east-facing **Checrouit** area accessed by
the Checrouit gondola catches morning
sun, and has open, above-the-tree-line
trails. The 25-person, infrequently
running Youla tram goes to the top of
Courmayeur's trails. There is a further
tiny tram to Cresta d'Arp. This serves
only long off-trail runs but it is no
longer compulsory to have a guide
with you to go up it.

Most people follow the sun over to
the north-west-facing slopes towards
Val Veny in the afternoon. These are
interesting, varied and tree-lined, with
great views of Mont Blanc and its
glaciers. Connections between the two
areas are good, with many alternative
routes. The Val Veny slopes are also
accessible by tram from Entrèves, a
few miles outside Courmayeur.

A little way beyond Entrèves is La
Palud, where a tram goes up in three
stages to Punta Helbronner, at the
shoulder of **Mont Blanc**. There are no
trails from the top, but you can do the
famous Vallée Blanche run to
Chamonix from here without the
horrific initial ridge walk on the
Chamonix side. But it's a long way
back if the Mont Blanc tunnel is
closed. Or you can tackle the tougher
off-trail runs on the Italian side of

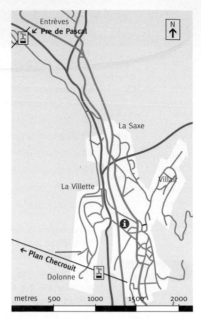

Mont Blanc. None of these glacier runs
should be done without a guide.

La Thuile and Pila are an easy drive
to the south, and Cervinia is reachable.

SNOW RELIABILITY
Good for most of the season
Courmayeur's slopes are not high –
mostly between 1700m/5,600ft and
2250m/7,400ft. Those above Val Veny
face north or north-west, so keep their
snow well, but the Plan Checrouit side
is rather too sunny for comfort in late
season. There is snowmaking on most
of the main runs, so good coverage in
midwinter is virtually assured.

FOR EXPERTS
Off-trail is the only challenge
Courmayeur has few challenging trails.
The only black – the Competizione, on
the Val Veny side – is not hard, and few
bumps form elsewhere. But if you're
lucky enough to find fresh powder – as
we have been several times – you can
have fantastic fun among the trees.

boarding *Courmayeur's trails suit intermediates, and most areas are easily
accessible by novices as the main lifts are trams, chairs and
gondolas – but it's all a bit steep for beginners. The biggest draws for the more
experienced are the off-trail routes to be done with a guide. Like a lot of Italian
resorts, Courmayeur has no terrain-park or half-pipe; but it still manages to
attract quite a few boarders, and you shouldn't find yourself in too much of a
minority. Nightlife is lively in a stylish way, and there's plenty of diversity in the
bars.*

Classic off-trail runs go from Cresta d'Arp, at the top of the lift network, in three directions – a clockwise loop via Arp Vieille to Val Veny, with close-up views of the Miage glacier; east down a deserted valley to Dolonne or Pré St Didier; or south through the Youla gorge to La Thuile.

On Mont Blanc, the Vallée Blanche is not a challenge (though there are more difficult variations), but the Toula glacier route on the Italian side from Punta Helbronner to Pavillon most certainly is, often to the point of being dangerous. There are also heli-drops available on a wide range of terrain.

FOR INTERMEDIATES
Ideal gradient but limited extent
The whole area is suitable for most intermediates, but it is small. The avid skier will find it very limited.

The open Checrouit section is pretty much go-anywhere territory, where you can choose your own route and make it as easy or difficult as you like. The blue runs here are about Courmayeur's gentlest. In Val Veny, the reds running the length of the Bertolini chair are more challenging and very enjoyable. They link in with the pretty, wooded slopes heading down to Zerotta.

The Zerotta chair dominates Val Veny, with lots of alternatives from the top – good for mixed abilities since runs of varying difficulty meet up at several places on the way down.

The Vallée Blanche, although off-trail, is easy enough for adventurous, fit intermediates to try. So is the local heli-skiing, where you are picked up on the trail so there's no wasted time.

FOR BEGINNERS
Consistently too steep
Courmayeur is not well suited to beginners. There are several beginner areas, none ideal. The area at Plan Checrouit gets crowded, and there are few easy runs for the near-beginner to progress to. The small area served by the short Tzaly surface lift, just above the Entrèves tram top station, is the most suitable beginner terrain, and it tends to have good snow.

FOR CROSS-COUNTRY
Beautiful trails
There are 35km/22 miles of trails scattered around the Courmayeur area. The best are the four covering 20km/12 miles at Val Ferret, to which there is a

Cresta d'Arp
2755m/9,040ft

Cresta Youla
2625m

Lago Checrouit
2255m

Colle Checrouit

Courba Dzeleuna

Val Veny

Plan Checrouit
1700m

Dolonne
1210m

Pre de Pascal
1910m

Zerotta
1525m

Courmayeur
1225m/4,020ft

La Palud
1370m

Entrèves

SCHOOLS/GUIDES

2000/01 prices in euros

Monte Bianco
Classes 6 days
3hr: 10am-1pm
6 half-days: 129
(106 low season)
Children's classes
Ages: from 4
6 full days incl snack
lunch: 258
(232 low season)
Private lessons
Hourly
36 for 1 person (26
low season); each
additional person 3

CHILDCARE

The Kinderheim at
Plan Checrouit (0165
842477) takes
children from the age
of 6 months, from
9.30 to 4pm. Children
taking lessons can be
deposited at the ski
school in Courmayeur
at 9am, and they will
be looked after for
the whole day (lesson
am, play pm). The
Kinderheim at the
Sports Center takes
children from the age
of 9 months.

Phone numbers
From abroad use the
prefix +39 (and do
not omit the initial '0'
of the phone
number).

GETTING THERE

Air Turin, transfer 2hr.

Rail Pré-St-Didier
(5km/3 miles); regular
buses from station.

bus service. Dolonne, across the valley,
has a couple of short trails.

LIFTLINES
Sunday crowds pour in
The lift system is generally excellent.
The Checrouit and Val Veny trams
suffer liftlines only on Sundays, and
even these can be beaten with an early
start. Patience is needed when waiting
for the infrequent Youla tram – 'Not
sure it's worth waiting more than 15
minutes for the one steep red,' said a
reporter. Overcrowded slopes on
Sundays, particularly down to Zerotta,
can also be a problem.

MOUNTAIN RESTAURANTS
Lots – some of them good
The area is lavishly endowed with 27
establishments ranging from rustic on-
trail huts to larger self-service places.
Most huts do table-service of delicious
pizza and pasta and it is best to book.
But there are also snack bars selling
more basic fare and relying on views
and sun to fill their terraces.

Several restaurants are excellent.
Maison Vieille, at the top of the chair
of the same name and run by the
charming mountain man Giacomo, is
our favorite – a friendly rustic place
with superb home-made pastas.
Chiecco, next to the surface lift with
the same name at Plan Checrouit, is
recommended for good food,
atmosphere, friendly service and good
views of struggling beginners. The pick
of the bunch at Plan Checrouit is the
Christiania – book a table downstairs,
where you can savour the superb food
(especially excellent pizzas) in peace.

On the other side of the mountain
in Val Veny is another clutch of places
worth noting – La Zerotta, at the foot
of the eponymous chair has a sunny
terrace and good food; the nearby
Petit Mont Blanc, the atmospheric
Monte Bianco climbing refuge, along
the mountainside, and the jolly Grolla,
further along still are also
recommended. One of the better snack
bars is Courba Dzeleuna, with
incredible views, at the top of
Dzeleuna chair.

SCHOOLS AND GUIDES
Good reports
We had a very enthusiastic report on
the Monte Bianco ski school last year:
'We had the best instructor for ages –
possibly ever.' There is a thriving
guides' association ready to help you

explore the area's off-trail; it has
produced a helpful booklet showing
the main possibilities.

FACILITIES FOR CHILDREN
Good care by Italian standards
Childcare facilities are well ahead of
the Italian norm, but Courmayeur is far
from an ideal resort for a young family.

Staying there

The tram station is on the southern
edge of town, a fair distance from
many of the accommodations. There is
no shuttle-bus alternative to walking,
but you can leave your skis, boards
and boots in lockers at the top –
highly recommended by most
reporters. There is another short walk
from the top to the other lifts before
you can get on the slopes.

Having accommodations close to
the village tram is handy. Parking at
the tram is very limited, but drivers can
go to Entrèves, a few miles away,
where there is a large parking lot at
the Val Veny tram. Buses, infrequent
but timetabled, link Courmayeur with
La Palud, just beyond Entrèves, for the
Punta Helbronner-Vallée Blanche tram.

HOW TO GO
Plenty of hotels
Hotels There are nearly 50 hotels,
spanning the star ratings.
(((4 Gallia Gran Baita (0165 844040)
Luxury place with antique furnishings,
panoramic views and 'superb food'.
Pool. Shuttle-bus to tram.
(((4 Pavillon (0165 846120)
Comfortable 4-star near tram, with a
pool. Friendly staff.
(((3 Auberge de la Maison (0165
869811) Small 3-star in Entrèves under
same ownership as Maison de Filippo
(see Eating Out).
(((3 Bouton d'Or (0165 846729) Small,
friendly B&B near main square.
(((3 Berthod (0165 842835) Friendly,
family-run hotel near center.
(((3 La Grange (869733) Rustic, stone-
and-wood farmhouse in Entrèves.
(((3 Triolet (0165 846822) 'Excellent
location close to lift. Comfy, well
furnished.'
((2 Edelweiss (0165 841590) Friendly,
cozy, good-value; close to the center.
((2 Lo Scoiattolo (0165 846721) Good
rooms, good food, shame it's at the
opposite end of town to the tram.
Apartments/condos There are quite a
lot available.

Courmayeur is full of well-groomed intermediate trails like this →

SNOWPIX.COM / CHRIS GILL

ACTIVITIES

Indoor Swimming pool and sauna at Pré-St-Didier (5km/3 miles), Alpine museum, cinema, library. Sports center with climbing, skating rink, curling, fitness center, indoor golf, squash, tennis, basketball, volley ball, sauna and turkish bath
Outdoor Walking paths in Val Ferret, paragliding, snow-biking, dog-sledding

TOURIST OFFICE

Postcode 11013
t +39 (0165) 842060
f 842072
apt.montebianco@psw.it
www.courmayeur.net

EATING OUT
Lively Italian evenings
There is a great choice, both in downtown Courmayeur and within taxi-range; there's a handy promotional booklet describing many of them (in English as well as Italian). The touristy but fun Maison de Filippo in Entrèves is famous for its fixed-price, 36-dish feast. We've been impressed by the traditional Italian cuisine of both Pierre Alexis ('good value') and Cadran Solaire. La Terrazza ('excellent pasta and very friendly, jolly service') is a rising star and has just been renovated. The Tunnel pizzeria and Mont-Frety ('good value', 'its antipasti is a must') have been recommended by reporters. Restaurants tend to be crowded, so book well in advance.

APRES-SKI
Stylish bar-hopping
Courmayeur has a lively evening scene, centered on stylish bars with comfy sofas or armchairs to collapse in. Our favorites are the Roma (reporters have been very taken with the free canapés), the back room of the Caffe della Posta and the Bar delle Guide.

The Cadran Solaire is where the big money from Milan and Turin hangs out. The American Bar has good music and an excellent selection of wines. The Red Lion is worth a visit if you like English pubs, though a recent reporter found it 'sadly empty'. Ziggy's is an internet cafe popular with local teenagers. There is a disco or two.

OFF THE SLOPES
Much improved for sporty types
If you're not interested in hitting the snow you'll find the village pleasant. You can go by tram up to Punta Helbronner, by bus to Aosta, or up the main tram to Plan Checrouit to meet friends for lunch. The large sports center is good but has no pool.

STAYING UP THE MOUNTAIN
Why would you want to?
Visiting Courmayeur and not staying in the charming village seems perverse – if you're that keen to get on the slopes in the morning, this is probably the wrong resort. But the Christiania at Plan Checrouit (see Mountain restaurants) has simple rooms; you need to book way in advance.

Lowish prices and highish altitude – a tempting combination

HOW IT RATES

The slopes

Snow	★★★★
Extent	★★
Experts	★★
Intermediates	★★★
Beginners	★★★★
Convenience	★★
Liftlines	★★★★
Restaurants	★★★

The rest

Scenery	★★★
Resort charm	★★★
Off-slope	★★

What's new

A new six-pack from Valfin on the Mottolino slopes to the top of Monte Della Neve has opened up a couple of new black runs.

260

MOUNTAIN FACTS

Altitude	1815m-2800m
	5,950ft-9,190ft
Lifts	31
Trails	115km/71 miles
Blue	35%
Red	48%
Black	17%
Snowmaking	70km/
	43 miles
Recco detectors used	

- ⊕ High altitude plus snowmaking ensures a long season and a good chance of snow to resort level
- ⊕ Large choice of beginners' slopes
- ⊕ Modern and improving lift system
- ⊕ Cheap by the standards of high resorts, with the bonus of duty-free shopping – a great place to treat yourself to new ski equipment
- ⊕ Cosmopolitan, friendly village with some Alpine atmosphere
- ⊕ Long, snow-sure cross-country trails

- ⊖ No difficult trails
- ⊖ Long airport transfers
- ⊖ Slopes split into two quite widely separated areas
- ⊖ Village is very long and straggling, and a bit rough round the edges
- ⊖ Few off-slope amenities
- ⊖ Bleak, windy setting – often resulting in upper lifts being shut
- ⊖ Nightlife can disappoint

Livigno offers the unusual combination of a fair-sized mountain, high altitude and fairly low prices. Despite its vaunted duty-free status, hotels, bars and restaurants are not much cheaper than in other Italian resorts, but shopping is – there are countless camera and clothes shops. As a relatively snow-sure alternative to the Pyrenees or to the smallest, cheapest resorts in Austria, Livigno seems attractive. But don't overlook the long list of drawbacks.

The resort

Livigno is an amalgam of three villages in a wide, remote valley near the Swiss border – basically a string of hotels, bars, specialist shops and supermarkets lining a single long street. The buildings are small in scale and mainly traditional in style, giving the village a pleasant atmosphere. The original hamlet of San Antonio is the

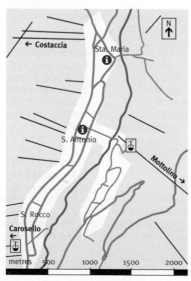

nearest thing Livigno has to a center. Here, the main street and those at right angles linking it to the crowded bypass road are nominally traffic-free. The road that skirts the 'traffic-free' area is constantly crowded, and becomes intrusive in the hamlets of Santa Maria, 1km/around half a mile to the north, and San Rocco, a bit further away to the south.

Lifts scattered along the length of the village access the western slopes of the valley. The main lift to the eastern slopes is directly across the flat valley floor from the center.

In such a long, strung out village, with fragmented slopes, the location of accommodations can be important. San Antonio is the best all-round location. San Rocco is a tiring uphill walk from the center. The bus services, on three color-coded routes, are free and fairly frequent, but can get overcrowded at peak times and stop early in the evening.

The lift ticket covers Bormio and Santa Caterina, an easy drive or free bus-ride if the high pass is open, and a six-day ticket entitles you to a discounted rate on a one-day ticket in St Moritz – reached via a road tunnel.

The airport transfer from Bergamo is long – five hours with a snack stop.

↑ There are woods, but most of the slopes are above or below them

APT LIVIGNO / L MARTINELLI

The mountain

The mainly open slopes, on either side of the valley, are extensive in comparison with many other cheap and cheerful destinations.

THE SLOPES
Improved links
There are three sectors, all of them suitable for moderate and leisurely intermediates, and two of them are reasonably well linked.

A two-seater chair from the beginner areas at the north end of the village take you up to **Costaccia** (2360m/7,740ft), where a long fast quad chair-lift goes along the ridge towards the **Carosello** sector. The blue linking run back from Carosello to the top of Costaccia is flat in places and may involve energetic poling if the snow conditions and the wind are against you. Carosello is more usually accessed by the optimistically named Carosello 3000 gondola at San Rocco, which goes up, in two stages, to 2750m/9,020ft. Most runs return towards the village, but there are a couple on the back of the mountain, on the west-facing slopes of Val Federia – served by a double surface-lift.

The ridge of **Mottolino** is reached by an efficient gondola from Teola, a tiresome walk or a short bus-ride across the valley from San Antonio. A slow antique chair from the top of the Mottolino gondola at Monte Sponda takes you to the top of Monte Della Neve. North-west-facing runs back towards Livigno are served by two fast chairs, and a couple of east-facing trails above Trepalle and Passo d'Eira on the road to Bormio are served by a third – an efficient setup.

Signposting is patchy and the trail map isn't always entirely accurate.

SNOW RELIABILITY
Very good, despite no glacier
Livigno's slopes are high (you can spend most of your time around 2500m/8,000ft), and with snow-guns on the lower slopes of Mottolino and Costaccia, the season is long.

FOR EXPERTS
Not recommended
The trail map shows a few black runs but these are not particularly steep. Even the all-black terrain served by the new six-pack on Monte Della Neve is really no more than stiff red in gradient. There is off-trail to be done, but guidance would be needed.

FOR INTERMEDIATES
Flattering slopes
Good intermediates will be able to tackle all of the blacks without worry. The woodland black run down from Carosello past Tea da Borch is narrow in places and can get bumpy and icy at the end of the day. The runs on the back of Carosello down to Federia are challenging, and bumpy. Moderate intermediates have virtually the whole area at their disposal. The long run beneath the Mottolino gondola is one of the best. Leisurely types have several long cruises available in all sectors. The run beneath the Valandrea-Vetta fast chair, at the top of the Costaccia sector, is a splendid slope for confidence-building – 1.5km/1 mile long, dropping only 260m/850ft.

FOR BEGINNERS
Excellent but scattered slopes
A vast array of beginner areas along

boarding *Livigno attracts a fair number of boarders and young people generally. There's a half-pipe and a good terrain-park/boarder-cross in the Mottolino area. And there are some good long, high runs for free-riders and carvers, as well as ample off-trail opportunities for intermediate riders. Most of the resort can be accessed by trams and chairs. However, the excellent beginner slopes are mainly served by surface lifts.*

SCHOOLS/GUIDES

2000/01 prices in euros

Livigno Inverno/Estate
Classes 6 days
2hr: 9am-11am or
11am-1pm
6 2hr days: 70
Children's classes
Ages: from 3
6 2hr lessons
Private lessons
Hourly
26 for 1hr; each
additional person 5

Azzurra Livigno
Classes 6 days
2½hr: 10am-12.30pm
6 2½hr days: 88
Private lessons
Hourly
26 for 1hr

OTHER SCHOOLS

Livigno Italy
Livigno Soc Coop
Top Club Mottolino

CHILDCARE

The Livigno school
runs the Alì Babà
kindergarten for
children aged 3 and
over. Lessons and
lunches available. The
staff speak English.

---

the sunny lower flanks of Costaccia, and other slopes around the valley, make Livigno excellent for novices – although some of the slopes at the northern end are on the steep side. There are lots of longer runs suitable for fast learners and near-beginners.

CROSS-COUNTRY
Good snow, bleak setting
Long snow-sure trails (40km/25 miles in total) follow the valley floor, making Livigno a good choice, though the scenery is bleak. There is a specialist cross-country school, and the resort organizes major cross-country races.

LIFTLINES
Few problems these days
Liflines are not usually a problem apart from short delays for the Carosello gondola in peak season. Investment in fast new chairs at Carosello and Mottolino has rid the area of any long liftlines. A bigger problem is that strong winds often close the upper lifts, causing overcrowding lower down. The slow old chair along the ridge to Monte Della Neve can be fiercely cold.

MOUNTAIN RESTAURANTS
More than adequate
Mottolino is the best bet for serious lunchers. The recently renovated refuge at the top of Mottolino is impressive with smart self- and table-service sections, a solarium and a nursery. And there are some more charming

---

places lower down. The welcoming Tea del Vidal is at the base of the same sector. Costaccia's Tea del Plan is pleasantly rustic and sunny, with good food and a great atmosphere. The self-service place at the top of Carosello is acceptable and Tea da Borch, in the trees lower down, serves great food in a Tirolean-style atmosphere, though the run down can be tricky. The rustic restaurants at Passo d'Eira and Trepalle are a good option for a quiet stop. Lunch in the valley at the hotel Sporting (near the Carosello gondola station) is popular. The terrace at the hotel Möta, at the base of the Costaccia lifts, is also recommended.

SCHOOLS AND GUIDES
Watch out for short classes
There are several schools. English is widely spoken, but recent reports are mixed. A common complaint is that most of the schools only offer short (two-hour) classes. Another complaint is that novices spend too long on the beginner areas before progressing up the mountain. It also seems to be the case that the schools on the Costaccia–Carosello side avoid the Mottolino sector altogether.

FACILITIES FOR CHILDREN
Bring your own
The schools run children's classes, and the Livigno school's Alì-Babà nursery offers all-day care.

GETTING THERE

Air Bergamo, transfer 5hr.

Rail Tirano (48km/30 miles), Zernez (Switzerland, 28km/17 miles); regular buses from station.

Phone numbers

From abroad use the prefix +39 (and do **not** omit the initial 'o' of the phone number).

ACTIVITIES

Indoor Sauna, gym, body-building, games room, bowling, cinema
Outdoor Cleared paths, skating rink, snow-mobiles, horse-drawn sleigh rides, paragliding, mountaineering

TOURIST OFFICE

Postcode 23030
t +39 (0342) 996379
f 996881
info@aptlivigno.it
www.aptlivigno.it

HOW TO GO
Lots of hotels, some apartments

Livigno has an enormous range of hotels and a number of apartments.
Hotels Most of the hotels are small 2- and 3-star places, with a couple of 4-stars out of the center.
Intermonti (0342 972100) Modern 4-star with all mod cons (including a pool); some way from the center, on the Mottolino side of the valley.
Bivio (0342 996137) The only hotel in central Livigno with a pool.
Steinbock (0342 970520) Nice little place, far from major lifts but a short walk from some beginner areas.
Teola (0342 996324) Quiet place, on the Mottolino side; recommended (despite small bedrooms) for good food and friendly staff.
Larice (0342 996184) Stylish little 3-star B&B well placed for Costaccia lifts and slopes.
Montanina (0342 996060) Good central 2-star.
Gimea (0342 997669) Quiet B&B 300m/980ft from Carosello gondola.
Camana Veglia (0342 996310) Charming old wooden chalet. Popular restaurant, well placed in Santa Maria.
Apartments/condos Most apartments are cheap and cheerful though some are more inconveniently situated than others.

EATING OUT
Value for money

Livigno has lots of traditional, unpretentious restaurants, many hotel-based. Hotel Concordia has some of the best cooking in town. Mario's has one of the largest menus, serving seafood, fondue and steaks in addition to the ubiquitous pizza and pasta. Bait dal Ghet and the Bivio restaurant are popular with the locals, and the Rusticana does wholesome, cheap food. Pesce d'Oro is good for seafood and Italian cuisine. The Bellavista, Ambassador, Mirage, Grolla and the Garden are also recommended.

APRES-SKI
Lively, but disappoints some

It's not that there isn't action in Livigno, but simply that the scene is quieter than some people expect in a duty-free resort. Also, the best places are scattered here and there, so the village lacks evening buzz. At tea-time many people return to their hotels for a quiet drink. But Tea del Vidal, at the bottom of Mottolino, gets lively, as does the Stalet bar at the base of the Carosselo gondola. The Caffé della Posta umbrella bar, near the center, is also popular. Nightlife only gets going after 10pm. Galli's pub, in San Antonio, is 'a full-on party pub', popular with Brits. The Kuhstall under the Bivio hotel is an excellent cellar bar with live music, as is the Helvetia, over the road. The San Rocco end is quietest, but Daphne's and Marco's are popular. The stylish Art bar is also recommended. Kokodi and Cielo are the main discos.

OFF THE SLOPES
Go shopping

Livigno does not have many off-slope amenities. Walks are uninspiring and there is no sports center or public swimming pool. However, the duty-free shopping more than makes up for this – it's a great place to equip yourself with some new ski equipment as well as picking up some designer labels at bargain prices. Trips to Bormio and St Moritz are popular.

Livigno

263

It may not look much like a pedestrian zone, but a least there's no through-traffic →

Monterosa Ski

1640m/5,380ft

Europe's best kept secret – an undiscovered gem

➕ Fairly extensive network of mainly intermediate trails

➕ Fabulous intermediate and advanced off-trail, including heli-skiing

➕ Beautiful scenery

➕ Good snow reliability and grooming

➕ Quiet, pretty, unspoiled, small villages

➖ Fragmented slopes

➖ Links to and from Alagna currently off-trail only

➖ Few off-slope diversions

➖ Limited après-ski

Monterosa Ski is Italy's little-known and less extensive answer to France's Trois Vallées and has a good lift system which is set for further big development over the next few years. Yet it is hardly heard of on the international market. It is popular with Italians on weekends, when they drive up for the day from Milan and Turin. But during the week it is deserted. The trails are mostly intermediate and they offer the same feeling of traveling around as the Three Valleys does, amid impressive scenery. And the off-trail is fabulous (and usually deserted). It is the only major ski area we have come across in Europe where there is no real well-developed resort to stay in. The villages that access the slopes have avoided commercialization and still retain a friendly, small-scale, local ambience. Our advice is to get there soon before all this changes.

What's new

The area is in the middle of an ambitious program to link Alagna properly by lifts and trail to Gressoney. For 2000/01 the ancient tram out of Alagna was replaced by a new gondola to Pianalunga, followed by a new chair-lift, which takes you to the top tram (still tiny and ancient) up to Punta Indren.

The next stage is to build a new tram followed by an eight-seater gondola from Pianalunga to Passo dei Salati and another tram from there to the Punta Indren area. The off-trail route from Passo dei Salati to Pianalunga will be converted into an official trail. The earliest all this is expected to happen is for 2002/03.

2000/01 also saw new high-speed chairs and more snowmaking at Antagnod and Orsia.

Monterosa's easy intermediate trails and fabulous off-trail slopes are set amid spectacular scenery ➔

MOUNTAIN FACTS

Altitude 1200m-3350m
3,940ft-10,990ft

Lifts	40
Trails	200km/
	125 miles
Blue	33%
Red	62%
Black	5%
Snowmaking	50km/
	31 miles

Recco detectors used

THE RESORTS

The main resorts are Champoluc in the western valley, Gressoney, in the central valley, and Alagna to the east. While Champoluc and Alagna have a very Italian ambience, Gressoney shows more Swiss-German influence, even having some signs in German.

Champoluc is towards the end of a long, winding road up from the Aosta valley highway. It is strung out along the road for quite a distance but retains a certain quiet charm and very Italian feel. The first part you come to is the attractive old village center with the church and a fast-running river.

Small shops and hotels line the road (part of a one-way traffic system) between here and the gondola station, several minutes' walk away. You can store boots and skis/board there overnight. More accommodations are on the road to Frachey, where there is a chair-lift into the slopes.

Gressoney La Trinité is a quiet, neat little village, with cobbled streets, wooden buildings and an old church. It is about 800m/2,620ft from the chair-lift into the slopes, where there are a few convenient hotels. It is a bus-ride from the outpost of Stafal at the head of the valley, which is the link between the Gressoney and Champoluc slopes and has a few rather soulless apartment blocks. Gressoney St Jean, a bigger village, is 3 miles down the valley and has its own separate slopes. Local buses are covered by the lift ticket.

The main resort in the east valley is Alagna, a strange place with some large, deserted and dilapidated buildings as well as smaller charming wooden buildings and church.

Trips to Cervinia, La Thuile and Courmayeur (covered by the Aosta Valley ticket) are possible by car.

THE MOUNTAINS

The slopes of Monterosa Ski are relatively extensive, and very scenic. The trails are almost all intermediate (and well groomed), and the lifts are mainly chairs and gondolas, with few surface lifts. The terrain is undulating and fragmented; runs are attractively varied and long, but many lifts serve only one or two trails. The trail map is poor: 'Woefully inadequate,' said a reporter.

Slopes A gondola from Champoluc followed by a couple of slow chairs takes you up to the steep, narrow, bumpy link with the rest of the slopes. Taking the bus to the Frachey chair is a quicker way into the main cruising runs and the link via Colle Bettaforca with Stafal in the Gressoney valley.

At Stafal a tram followed by a high-speed chair take you back to the Champoluc slopes and a two-stage 12-person gondola opposite takes you up to Passo dei Salati. From there runs lead back down to Stafal and to Gressoney La Trinité and Orsia, both served by more chair-lifts. Or you can head down towards Alagna on an easy, popular off-trail run (due to become a trail in the next couple of years).

From Alagna a new gondola goes to

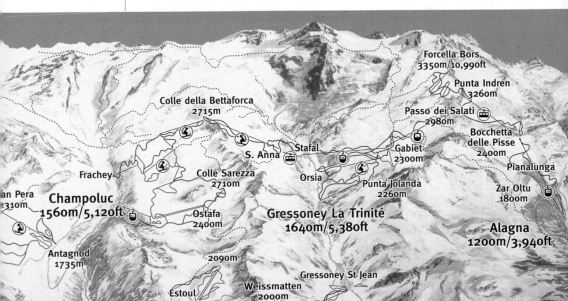

Pianalunga at mid-mountain, where a new two-person chair-lift carries you up to a tiny, ancient tram, which accesses the high slopes around Punta Indren. There are a couple of surface lifts and short trails up here but the only ways back to Gressoney are off-trail. On the Alagna side there is lots of off-trail and an ungroomed black run that leads to an old bucket lift that you jump into while it is still moving (it takes you back to the tram).

Gressoney St Jean and Antagnod near Champoluc have their own small areas of slopes.

Snowboarding There is no terrain park or half-pipe but great off-trail free-riding.

Snow reliability Good, thanks to the high altitude, extensive snowmaking and good grooming.

Experts The attraction is the off-trail, with great runs from the high-points of the lift system in all three valleys and some excellent heli-drops.

A mountain guide is essential for getting the best out of the area. We had a fabulous day last season with Claudio from Gressoney (all the younger guides speak good English) skiing down to Alagna and then exploring the amazing, deserted off-trail bowls above Gressoney. Snow can lie untracked for days here. Alagna is a cult area for expert off-trail, with couloirs, cornices and cliffs you have to be roped down. There is an epic run down to the Champoluc valley from the top of the Cervinia–Zermatt area.

There are a few black trails but none of them really deserve their grading. And many of the reds would be blue in other resorts.

Intermediates For those who like to travel on easy, undemanding trails, the area is great, with long cruising runs from the ridges down into the valleys. There isn't much on-trail challenge for more demanding intermediates, but those willing to take a guide and explore some of the gentler off-trail will have a great time. If you stick to the trails, a weekend rather than a full week might be worth trying: 'It's great for a short break,' said a recent reporter.

Beginners The high beginner areas at the top of the gondola at Champoluc are better than the lower ones at La Trinité. But easy runs to progress to are best accessed by the Frachey chair or going to Antagnod.

Cross-country There are long trails around St Jean, and shorter ones up the valley; Brusson, in the Champoluc valley, has the best trails in the area.

Liftlines Only on weekends, when the hordes from Turin and Milan arrive, are there any liftlines. The worst bottleneck is the tiny top tram on the Alagna side, where waits of over an hour are possible. Trails can get crowded at weekends, too, but the off-trail is still delightfully quiet.

Mountain restaurants The mountain restaurants are good and cheap. The Chamois at Punta Jolanda, Bedemie on the way to Gressoney from Gabiet, Del Ponte above Gabiet, Vieux Crest and Belvedere, above Champoluc, and the Guglielmina, Lys and Gabiet refuges are recommended.

Schools and guides We have had decent reports on the ski schools and excellent ones of the Gressoney and Alagna mountain guides.

Facilities for children There is a special kids' ski school and snow park at Antagnod near Champoluc and a mini-club at Gressoney St Jean.

STAYING THERE

Hotels At Champoluc the Castor (0125 307117) in the old center is 'an absolute gem' and is managed by a British guy. At the amazing Hotel California (0125 307977 – the owners speak no English) – every room is dedicated to a pop star or group (eg The Byrds, Bob Dylan, Joan Baez, the Doors) and their music plays whenever you turn on the light. It's quite a way out of the center. The new Relais des Glaciers (0125 308721) near the center has a spa complex, but a reporter had 'a chilly room, very slow service'.

At Gressoney La Trinité reporters recommend the Jolanda Sport (0125 366140) and Dufour (0125 366139); in Alagna, the Monterosa (0163 923209) and Cristallo (0163 91285).

Eating out Both Gressoney and Champoluc have a few stand alone restaurants, but most are in hotels.

Après-ski Après-ski is quiet. At weekends, the disco beneath Hotel California in Champoluc gets going. The bar of the Hotel Castor is cozy.

Off the slopes There is little to amuse those who don't head for the slopes.

Phone numbers
From abroad use the prefix +39 (and do **not** omit the initial 'o' of the phone number).

TOURIST OFFICE

Postcode 11020
t +39 (0125) 303111
f 303145
kikesly@tin.it
www.monterosa-ski.com

Sauze d'Oulx

1510m/4,950ft

'Suzy does it' still, but with more dignity than in the past

267

HOW IT RATES

The slopes

Snow	**
Extent	*****
Experts	**
Intermediates	****
Beginners	**
Convenience	**
Liftlines	***
Restaurants	***

The rest

Scenery	***
Resort charm	**
Off-slope	*

What's new

Turin has been chosen to host the 2006 Olympic Winter Games; most of the Alpine events will be held at Sansicario and Sestriere, and freestyle competitions at Sauze d'Oulx.

Snowmaking has been improved on the Clotes run and more is planned.

➕ Extensive and uncrowded slopes, great intermediate cruising

➕ Linked into Milky Way network

➕ Mix of open and tree-lined runs is good for all weather conditions

➕ Entertaining nightlife

➕ Some scope for off-trail adventures

➕ One of the cheapest major resorts there is – and more attractive than its reputation suggests

➖ Still lots of ancient lifts, making progress around the slopes slow

➖ Erratic snow record – and still far from comprehensive snowmaking

➖ Crowds at weekends

➖ Brashness of resort will not suit everyone

➖ Very few challenging trails

➖ Mornings-only classes, and the best beginner areas are at mid-mountain

➖ Steep walks around the village, and an inadequate shuttle-bus service

If you're looking for a cheap holiday in a resort with extensive slopes, put **Sauze** on your shortlist. In the 1980s it gained a reputation for drunken and rowdy behaviour by young visitors (mainly British) on a budget. But it always had a more up-market side too, thanks to mature second-home owners from Turin. These days the drunkeness and rowdiness are not so marked. It still has lively bars and a youthful clientele but sober adults need not stay away. Whenever we visit we like it more than we expect to – as do many reporters.

We are slightly haunted, though, by the memory of the bare slopes of our first visit, in the mid-1980s. Thin cover two seasons ago brought it all back: Sauze is a resort that needs comprehensive snowmaking, and doesn't yet have it.

The resort

Sauze d'Oulx sits on a sloping mountain shelf facing north-west across the Valle di Susa, with impressive views of the towering mountains forming the border with France. Most of the resort is modern and undistinguished, made up of block-like hotels relieved by the occasional chalet, spreading down the steep hillside from the foot of the slopes to the village center and beyond. The center is still lively at night; the late-closing bars are usually quite full, and the handful of discos do brisk business at the weekend, at least.

It's not immediately obvious, but Sauze also has an attractive old core, with narrow, twisting streets, the occasional carved stone fountain and houses with huge stone slabs serving as roof slates.

Traffic roams freely through the village, which can be congested morning and evening as cars vie for convenient parking spaces or the quickest way out of town. The roads become slushy during the day and icy and treacherous at night – hazardous, as there are few sidewalks.

Out of the bustle of the center, where most of the bars and nightclubs are located, there are quiet, wooded residential areas full of secluded apartment blocks, and a number of good restaurants are also tucked out of the way of the front line. Chair-lifts go from the top of the village and from two points on its fringes. There's also a chair from nearby Jouvenceaux.

Most of the hotels are reasonably central, but the Clotes lift is at the top of the village, up a short but steep hill,

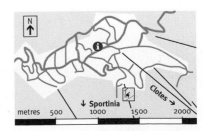

MOUNTAIN FACTS

Figures relate to the whole Milky Way area

Altitude	1390m-2825m
	4,560ft-9,270ft
Lifts	92
Trails	400km/
	250 miles
Blue	12%
Red	67%
Black	21%
Snowmaking	75km/
	47 miles

and the Sportinia chair is an irritatingly long walk beyond that. Buses (not covered by the lift ticket) run around the resort, but the service is infrequent and can't cope with high-season crowds. The service around lunch-time is particularly poor, signposting of stops is unclear; and the service to Jouvenceaux stops inconveniently early, at 5pm.

The mountains

Sauze's mountains provide excellent intermediate terrain. The trail grading fluctuates from year to year, if you believe the resort's map – and we're never sure we've caught up with the latest changes from blue to red and red to blue. But most reporters agree that many runs graded red or even black should really be graded blue; challenges are few and far between. (The same might be said of the whole extensive Milky Way area, of which Sauze is one extreme.)

THE SLOPES
Big and varied enough for most
Sauze's local slopes are spread across a broad wooded bowl above the resort, ranging from west- to north-facing. The main lifts are chairs, from the top of the village up to **Clotes** and from the western fringes to **Sportinia** – a sunny mid-mountain clearing in the

woods, with a ring of restaurants and hotels (see Staying up the mountain) and a small beginner area.

The high point of the system is **Monte Fraiteve**. From here you can travel west on splendid broad, long runs to **Sansicario** – and on to chair-lifts near **Cesana Torinese** that link with **Clavière** and then **Montgenèvre**, in France, the far end of the Milky Way (both are reached more quickly by car).

You normally get to **Sestriere** from the lower point of Col Basset, on the shoulder of M Fraiteve. The alternative of descending the sunny slope from M Fraiteve itself has been reinstated after a few years of closure; but snow here is not reliable, which we're told is why the old lift from Sestriere up this slope was removed some years ago. You can make the link via the gondola but this is prone to closure in bad weather.

As in so many Italian resorts, trail marking, direction signing and trail map design are not taken particularly seriously.

The slopes of Montgenèvre and Sestriere are dealt with in separate chapters. If you have a car, you can go beyond Montgenèvre to Briançon, Serre-Chevalier and Bardonecchia.

SNOW RELIABILITY
Can be poor, affecting the links
The area is notorious for erratic snowfalls – though it did fairly well last

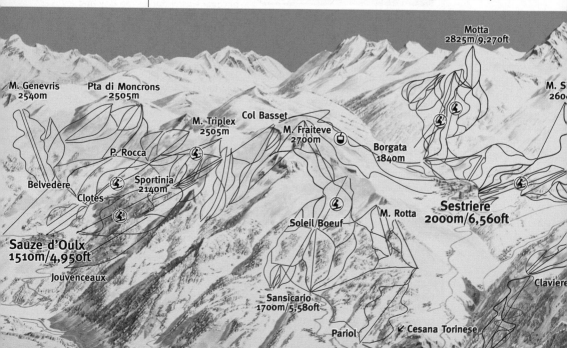

Motta
2825m/9,270ft

M. Genevris
2540m

Pta di Moncrons
2505m

M. S
260

M. Triplex
2505m

Col Basset

M. Fraiteve
2700m

P. Rocca

Borgata
1840m

Belvedere

Sportinia
2140m

Clotes

Soleil/Boeuf

M. Rotta

Sestriere
2000m/6,560ft

Sauze d'Oulx
1510m/4,950ft

Jouvenceaux

Claviere

Sansicario
1700m/5,580ft

Pariol

Cesana Torinese

LIFT TICKETS

2000/01 prices in euros

La Via Lattea
Covers all lifts in Sauze d'Oulx, Sestriere, Sansicario, Cesana and Clavière.

Beginners Points book (80 points 72), with lifts costing from 1 to 12 points.

Main ticket
1-day ticket 25
6-day ticket 137 (low season 111)

Senior citizens
Over 60: 6-day ticket 126

Children
Under 12: 6-day ticket 126
Under 8: free ticket

Short-term tickets
Some single ascent tickets and afternoon ticket.

Notes Includes one free day in each of: Alpe-d'Huez, Les Deux Alpes, Serre-Chevalier and Puy-St-Vincent. One day extension for Montgenèvre (12). One day extension for Pragelato and Bardonecchia available.

Alternative tickets
La Via Lattea VIP card also covers Montgenèvre and Pragelato.

boarding *Sauze has good snowboarding slopes – it's got local tree-lined slopes (with space in the trees, too), high, undulating, open terrain, and links to other resorts in the Milky Way. But although it has a fair number of chair-lifts, there are also lots of surface lifts – a serious drawback for novice riders. There's no park or pipe, but the amount and variety of terrain makes up for this. Sauze's mainly young visitors ensure lively, entertaining nightlife.*

year, it received very little snow two seasons ago. Another problem is that many of the slopes get a lot of afternoon sun. At these modest altitudes, late-season conditions are far from reliable. Reporters have found icy, bare slopes at vital link points earlier in the season, too – particularly from M Fraiteve. There's snowmaking on a couple of slopes, notably the key home run from P Rocca via Clotes to the village.

FOR EXPERTS
Head off-trail
Very few of the trails are challenging. The best slopes are at virtually opposite ends of Sauze's local area – a high, north-facing run from the shoulder of M Fraiteve, and the sunny slopes below M Moncrons.

The main interest is in going off-trail. There are plenty of minor opportunities within the trail network, but the highlights are long, top-to-bottom descents of up to 1300m/4,270ft vertical from M Fraiteve, ending (snow permitting) at villages dotted along the valleys. The best-known of these runs (which used to be marked on the trail map but is no longer) is the Rio Nero, down to the road near Oulx. When snow low down is poor, some of these runs can be cut short at Jouvenceaux or Sansicario.

FOR INTERMEDIATES
Splendid cruising terrain
The whole area is ideal for confident intermediates who want to chalk up the miles. For the less confident, the trail map doesn't help because it picks out only the very easiest runs in blue – there are many others they could manage. The Belvedere and Moncrons sectors at the east of the area are served only by surface lifts but offer some wonderful, uncrowded high cruising, some of it above the tree line.

The long runs down to Sansicario and down to Jouvenceaux are splendid, confidence-boosting intermediate terrain. Getting back to Sauze involves

tackling some of the steepest terrain in the area – the black run from M Fraiteve to the Col Basset lifts at Malafosse. This presents a problem for many intermediates and is a serious shortcoming in the circuit. The run down to Sestriere gets a lot of sun but is worth it for the somewhat more challenging intermediate terrain on the opposite side of the valley. If conditions are too poor, you can always ride the gondola down.

At the higher levels, where the slopes are above the tree line, the terrain often allows a choice of route. Lower down are pretty runs through the woods, where the main complication can be route-finding. The mountainside is broken up by gullies, and trails that appear to be quite close together may in fact have no easy connections between them.

FOR BEGINNERS
There are better choices
Sauze is not ideal for beginners: its village-level slopes are a bit on the steep side and the main beginner area is up the mountain, at Sportinia. Equally importantly, the mornings-only classes don't suit everyone.

FOR CROSS-COUNTRY
Severely limited, even with snow
There is very little cross-country skiing, and it isn't reliable for snow.

LIFTLINES
Slow lifts the biggest problem
There can be 10-minute waits at Sportinia when school classes are setting off or immediately after lunch, but otherwise the system has few bottlenecks. The main problem with the network is that, despite the recent introduction of three high-speed quads, most of the lifts are ancient and terribly slow. Amazingly, they haven't yet replaced the museum-piece chair-lift from the village to Clotes which requires you to carry your skis in your lap and hit the ground running at the top. Although it links to a fast

SCHOOLS/GUIDES

2000/01 prices in euros

Sauze Sportinia
Classes 6 days
3hr: 10am-1pm
6 3hr days: 108
Children's classes
Ages: from 6
6 3hr days: 108
Private lessons
Hourly
26 for 1hr

Sauze d'Oulx
Classes 6 days
3hr: 10am-1pm
6 3hr days: 103
Children's classes
Ages: from 6
6 3hr days: 103
Private lessons
Hourly
27 for 1hr

Sauze Project
Italian-speaking only school.

CHILDCARE

The village kindergarten, Little Dumbo, has English and Italian staff and takes children up to 6 years, from 9am to 5pm. You have to provide lunch, but it can be heated up.

GETTING THERE

Air Turin, transfer 2hr.

Rail Oulx (5km/3 miles); frequent buses.

Phone numbers
From abroad use the prefix +39 (and do **not** omit the initial '0' of the phone number).

quad which takes you the rest of the way to the top, this lift is still hugely inadequate for such an important link; it can create long bottlenecks and makes the uplift seem interminable. Breakdowns on elderly surface lifts may also be a nuisance.

MOUNTAIN RESTAURANTS
Some pleasant possibilities
Restaurants are numerous and generally pleasant, though few are particularly special. One place that's certainly worth picking out is the hotel Capricorno, at Clotes – one of the most civilized and appealing lunch-spots in the Alps. It is not cheap, though. There are more modest mid-mountain restaurants across the mountainside, with the main concentration at Sportinia. The Capannina and the Belvedere are popular. And the Ciao Pais, at the top of the Clotes chair-lift, the Chalet Pian della Rocca and the Chalet Clot Bourget have been recommended.

SCHOOLS AND GUIDES
Lessons variable, large classes
Recent reporters have found a lack of good English spoken and large classes. Some found the lessons satisfactory, others were disappointed. Classes are only half a day, but last three hours. Reporters on the school in Sansicario have found the instruction enthusiastic and useful, with good spoken English.

FACILITIES FOR CHILDREN
Adequate
There is a resort kindergarten with English-speaking staff,

Staying there

HOW TO GO
Mainly budget hotels
Hotels Simple 2-star and 3-star hotels form the core of the holiday accommodations, with a couple of 4-stars and some more basic places.
③ **La Torre** (0122 850020) Cylindrical landmark 200m/660ft below center. Excellent rooms; mini-buses to lifts.
② **Hermitage** (0122 850385) Neat chalet-style hotel in about the best spot for the slopes – beside the home trail from Clotes.
② **Gran Baita** (0122 850183) Comfortable place in quiet, central backstreet, with excellent food and good rooms, some with spectacular sunset views from their balconies.

② **Biancaneve** (0122 850021) Pleasant, with smallish rooms. Near the center.
② **Des Amis** (0122 858488) Down in Jouvenceaux, but near bus stop; simple hotel run by Anglo-Italian couple.
Apartments/condos There are apartments and chalets available.

EATING OUT
Caters for all tastes and pockets
Typical Italian banquets of five or six courses can be had in the upscale Don Vincenzo and Il Cantun restaurants. The Del Falco does a particularly good three-course 'skiers' menu'. In the old town, the Del Borgo and La Griglia are popular pizzerias. Il Lampione is the place to go for good-value Chinese, Mexican and Indian food. Sugo's spaghetteria provides delicious, filling and economic fare. Le Pecore Nere also gets good reviews. A number of reporters have suggested booking restaurants in advance to avoid disappointment.

APRES-SKI
Suzy does it with more dignity
Once favoured almost solely by large groups of youngsters, some of whom were very rowdy, the number and atmosphere of Sauze's bars now impress reporters young and old.

The Assietta terrace is popular for catching the last rays of the sun at the end of the day. The excellent New Scotch bar is also recommended. As is Il Lampione, in the old town.

After dinner, more places warm up. One of the best is the smart, atmospheric cocktail bar Moncrons, which holds regular quiz nights. We also like the late-night Village Café (aka Osteria da Gigi), which is popular with Italians and workers. The Cotton Club provides good service, directors' chairs, video screen and draught cider. The Rock Café has as many Italian clients as British. Paddy McGinty's is especially popular with resort staff and has a lively atmosphere. Gran Trün has live music and reminded us of a Majorcan barbecue venue, with bottles on the wall and white stucco decor. The Derby is nice for a quiet drink in a relaxed setting. Of the discos, Il Bandito is a walk away, and popular with Italians. Schuss runs theme nights and drink promotions – entrance is normally free.

↑ The ideal base for exploration of the whole Milky Way – not Sauze but Sansicario

LAPRESSE

ACTIVITIES

Indoor Bowling, cinema, sauna, massage
Outdoor Artificial skating rink, torchlit descents, heli-skiing, ice-climbing, snow-shoeing

TOURIST OFFICE

Postcode 10050
t +39 (0122) 858009
f 850700
sauze@montagnedoc.it
www.montagnedoc.it

OFF THE SLOPES
Go elsewhere
Sauze is not a particularly pleasant place in which to while away the days if you don't want to hit the slopes. Shopping is limited, there are no gondolas or trams for pedestrians and there are few off-slope activities. Turin or Briançon are worth a visit.

STAYING UP THE MOUNTAIN
'You pays your money ... '
In most resorts, staying up the mountain is an amusing thing to do and is often economical – but usually you pay the price of accepting simple accommodations. Here, the reverse applies. The 4-star Capricorno (0122 850273), up at Clotes, is one of the most comfortable hotels in Sauze, certainly the most attractive and by a wide margin the most expensive. It's a charming little chalet beside the trail, with a smart restaurant and terrace (a very popular spot for a good lunch on the mountain) and only eight bedrooms.

Not quite in the same league are the places up at Sportinia. Reporters who stayed here enjoyed the isolation and easy access to the slopes – but you can't get down to town after 4pm, making it more suitable for groups providing their own entertainment or those for whom nightlife matters little.

Sansicario 1700m/5,580ft

If any resort is ideally placed for exploration of the whole Milky Way, it is Sansicario. It is a modern, purpose-built, self-contained but rather soulless little resort, mainly consisting of apartments linked by monorail to the small shopping precinct. The 45-room Rio Envers (0122 811333) is a reasonably comfortable, pricey hotel. Visitors recommend the Chalmettes for its views and food at lunch-time, and the Enoteca in the evening for fondue and grappa. The whole place will doubtless get a bit of a boost from the 2006 Olympics – downhill and super G races will be held here.

Spectacular Dolomite resort ideal for intermediates

HOW IT RATES

The slopes

Snow	****
Extent	*****
Experts	***
Intermediates	*****
Beginners	****
Convenience	***
Liftlines	***
Restaurants	****

The rest

Scenery	*****
Resort charm	***
Off-slope	***

What's new

For 2000/01 a new fast quad replaced the surface lift from Piz Seteur, in Plan de Gralba, up to Passo Sella. And in Canazei, two chairs on Belvedere were upgraded – to a six-pack and a quad.

Other developments in the area include a new gondola up to Col Pradat in Colfosco's local area, and a new quad chair at Bufaure di Sotto in Val di Fassa.

The Marmolada glacier lifts are now included in the Dolomiti Superski ticket.

272

- Vast network of connected slopes – suits intermediates particularly well
- Stunning, unique Dolomite scenery
- Superb snowmaking and grooming
- Lively mountain huts with good food
- Many new lifts have cut out all but a few bad bottlenecks on the famous Sella Ronda circuit
- Good beginner areas
- Excellent value

- Small proportion of tough runs
- Lifts and slopes can be crowded, especially on Sella Ronda circuit
- High proportion of short runs, not so many long ones
- Selva is not a particularly attractive village, nor especially convenient
- Erratic snow record; slopes vulnerable to warm weather

This is an area unlike any other. The Sella Ronda is an amazing circular network of lifts and trails taking you around the spectacular Gruppo Sella – a mighty limestone massif with villages scattered around it, the biggest of them being Selva (or Selva Val Gardena / Wolkenstein, to give the resort its Sunday name and alternative German form). As well as this impressive main circuit, there are major lift systems leading off it at four main points. In overall scale, the network rivals the famed Trois Vallées in France. And the Superski lift ticket covers dozens of other resorts reachable by road. So there's plenty to keep you busy.

The scenery is fabulous – almost a match for nearby Cortina. But the Dolomite landscape that provides the visual drama also dictates the nature of the slopes. Sheer limestone cliffs rise out of gentle pastureland; you spend your time on the latter, gazing at the former. There is scarcely a black run to be seen, and runs of more than 500m/1,600ft vertical are rare. Runs of under 300m/1,000ft vertical are not.

Although we hinge this chapter on Selva, you certainly shouldn't overlook the several alternative bases around the circuit. For experts, in particular, Arabba has clear attractions. It's here that the classic Dolomite landscape gives way to a more familiar kind of terrain, with longer, steeper slopes. For nervous intermediates, on the other hand, the obvious alternative to Selva is Corvara.

Selva sits at the foot of the towering Sassolungo →

The resort

Selva is a long roadside village, almost merged with the next village of Santa Cristina. It suffers from traffic but has traditional-style architecture and an attractive church. The area is famed for wood carvings – you'll see them all over.

The village enjoys a lovely setting under the impressive pink-tinged walls of Sassolungo and the Gruppo Sella – a fortress-like massif about 6km/ 4 miles across that lies at the hub of the Sella Ronda circuit (see the feature box later in the chapter). Despite its World Cup fame (as Val Gardena, the name of the valley) and animated atmosphere, Selva is neither upscale nor brash. It's a good-value, civilized family resort – and is undoubtedly the biggest and liveliest of the places to stay right on the Sella Ronda circuit.

For many years the area was under Austrian rule, and reporters admire the Tirolean charm of the resort. German is the main language, not Italian, and most visitors are German, too. Selva is also known as Wolkenstein and the Gardena valley as Gröden. The local dialect is Ladino, which has resisted being absorbed into German or Italian.

Ortisei is the administrative center of Val Gardena – pretty, and more of a complete community – but it is not so convenient for the Sella Ronda slopes. For a brief description of the other villages on or near the circuit, see the end of this chapter.

From Selva, gondolas rise in two directions. One goes east from the top of the beginner areas towards Colfosco and Corvara and the clockwise Sella Ronda route. The other takes you south from the village to Ciampinoi and the counter-clockwise route. The most convenient position is near one of these gondolas. There is a free, regular bus service throughout the valley until early evening, but reporters

say this can get very oversubscribed. Some prefer to share cheap cabs. Others suggest a beer or two before heading for home, to avoid the rush.

The Dolomiti Superski ticket covers not only the Sella Ronda resorts but dozens of others. It's an easy road trip to Cortina – worth it for the fabulous scenery alone. But many other drives in this area are very tortuous and slow – it's often quicker on skis.

The mountain

The slopes cover a vast area, all amid stunning scenery and practically all ideally suited to intermediates who don't mind shortish runs. There are different trail maps for different areas, and a common complaint is that they are inadequate. Trail marking and signage also come in for criticism.

THE SLOPES
High mileage trail excursions

A gondola and parallel-running chair go up from Selva to **Ciampinoi**, from where several trails, including the famous World Cup Downhill run, spread out across the mountain and lead back down to Selva, **Santa Cristina** and **Plan de Gralba**. From Plan de Gralba, you can head off towards **Passo Sella**, **Canazei** and the rest of the Sella Ronda.

Across the valley from the Ciampinoi gondola is a chair that links with the Dantercëpies gondola. This accesses the Sella Ronda in the opposite direction or you can return to Selva on the Ladies Downhill. From the top you head down to **Colfosco**, then lifts link with **Corvara**, and you go on to **Arabba** and the rest of the Sella Ronda.

At Passo Pordoi between Canazei and Arabba is the one breach in the defences of the Gruppo Sella: a tram goes up to Sass Pordoi at 2950m/9,680ft, giving access to off-trail routes as well as spectacular

MOUNTAIN FACTS

Altitude	1235m-2520m
	4,050ft-8,270ft
Lifts	81
Trails	175km/
	109 miles
Blue	30%
Red	60%
Black	10%
Snowmaking	140km/
	87 miles
Recco detectors used	

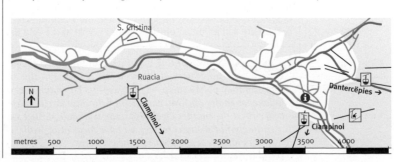

LIFT TICKETS

2000/01 prices in euros
Dolomiti Superski
Covers 460 lifts and 1200km of trails in the Dolomites, including all Sella Ronda resorts.
Main ticket
1-day ticket 33
6-day ticket 162
(low season 142)
Senior citizens
Over 60: 6-day ticket 129
Children
Under 16: 6-day ticket 113

Alternative ticket
Val Gardena ticket covers all lifts in Selva Gardena, S Cristina, Ortisei and Alpe di Siusi.

views.

There are several linked areas that are not directly on the Sella Ronda circuit that are worth exploring. The biggest is the **Alta Badia** area to the west of Corvara, from which you can get down to **San Cassiano** and **La Villa**.

Local to Selva is the **Seceda** area, accessed by a gondola, a bus-ride from town and on the outskirts of Santa Cristina. You can head back down to the bottom or go on to **Ortisei**. And from Ortisei a tram goes up the other side of the valley to **Alpe di Siusi** – a gentle elevated area of quiet, easy runs, cross-country and walks.

The Marmolada glacier near Arabba is open most of the winter and is now included on the main lift ticket. One reader recommends it 'for the spectacular views rather than for the typically boring glacier slopes.'

SNOW RELIABILITY
Excellent when it's cold
The slopes are not high – there are few above 2200m/7,220ft and most are between around 1500m/5,000ft and 2000m/6,500ft. And natural snowfalls are erratic. But we have experienced excellent trails here in times of severe natural snow shortage – the area has invested heavily in snowmaking and now has one of the largest capacities in Europe, covering 140km/87 miles of runs. Most areas have snow-guns on the main runs to the resorts, and almost all Selva's local trails are well endowed. Good trail grooming adds to the effect.

Problems arise only in poor snow years when temperatures are too high to make snow.

FOR EXPERTS
A few good runs
In general, experts may find the region too tame, especially if they're looking for lots of steep challenges or bumps.

Arabba has the best steep slopes (and snow). North-facing blacks and reds from Porta Vescovo back to Arabba are served by an efficient high-

capacity gondola and are great fun. The Val Gardena World Cup trail, the 'Saslonch', is one of several steepish runs between Ciampinoi and both Selva and Santa Cristina. Unlike many World Cup trails it is kept in racing condition for Italian team practices, but it is open to the public much of the time. It's especially good in January, when it's not too crowded. The ungroomed trail down to Santa Cristina, accessed from the Florian chair on Alpe di Siusi, is not difficult, but pleasantly lonely.

Overall, off-trail is limited because of the sheer-drop nature of the tops of the mountains in the Dolomites, but for the daring there is excitement to be found with a guide. The itinerary from Sass Pordoi back to the tram station is not too difficult; the much longer route to Colfosco ends in a spectacular narrow descent through the Val de Mesdi.

FOR INTERMEDIATES
A huge network of ideal runs
The Sella Ronda region is famed for easy slopes. For early or timid intermediates, the runs from Dantercëpies to Colfosco and Corvara, and over the valley from there in the Alta Badia, are superb for cruising and confidence-boosting. They're easy to reach from Selva, but returning from Dantercëpies may be a little daunting. Riding the gondola down is an option.

Nearer to Selva, the runs in the Plan de Gralba area are gentle. The Alpe di Siusi runs above Ortisei are rather flat, but a recent visitor found this area 'a much underrated winter wonderland. It took our breath away for scenery and quiet, good blue runs'.

Average intermediates have a very large network of suitable trails, though there are few long runs. The beautiful swoop down the far side of the Seceda massif from Cuca to Ortisei is a favorite with recent reporters. The Plan de Gralba area, the runs on either side of the Florian chair on Alpe di Siusi, and the main trails to San Cassiano and La Villa in the Alta Badia area are other

boarding *Snowboarding is not particularly big in the area. There was a small park at Piz Sella last season, but this was made by the local riders and may not be there for next season. The main lifts out of Selva are all gondolas or chairs and you can do the Sella Ronda clockwise using only one surface lift – the counter-clockwise route has more. Either way, there are some frustratingly flat sections where you have to scoot or walk. There are enough lively bars to have a good time in the evenings.*

recommended cruises.

Several reporters also enjoyed the area above Canazei, below the Belvedere: 'Well served with efficient lifts, and good snow. The red to Lupo Bianco is an especially beautiful run through the trees.'

The runs back down to the valley direct from Ciampinoi are a bit more challenging, as are the descents from Dantercëpies to Selva. And, of course, most intermediates will want to do the Sella Ronda circuit at least once during a week – see feature panel. The spectacular 'Hidden Valley' is also worth a visit. It's reached via a tram at Lagazuoi, which you get to via a bus or shared cab from Armentarola. See the Cortina chapter for details.

FOR BEGINNERS
Great slopes, but ...
Near-beginners have numerous runs, and the village beginner areas are excellent – spacious, convenient, and kept in good condition. There are splendid gentle runs to progress to.

Visiting beginners have thoroughly recommended the area in the past. However, we have varying reports about the school – see 'Schools and Guides' section.

FOR CROSS-COUNTRY
Beautiful trails
There are over 70km/43 miles of trails, all enjoying wonderful scenery. The 12km/7 mile trail up the Vallunga–Langental valley is particularly attractive, with neck-craning views all around. The largest section of trails (40km/25 miles) has the advantage of being at altitude, running between Monte Pana and Seiseralm, and across Alpe di Siusi.

LIFTLINES
Much improved: a few problems
New lifts have vastly improved the area and bottlenecks are no longer as common, except in peak periods. That said, we still get complaints about parts of the Sella Ronda circuit. And you may find the crowds on the trails

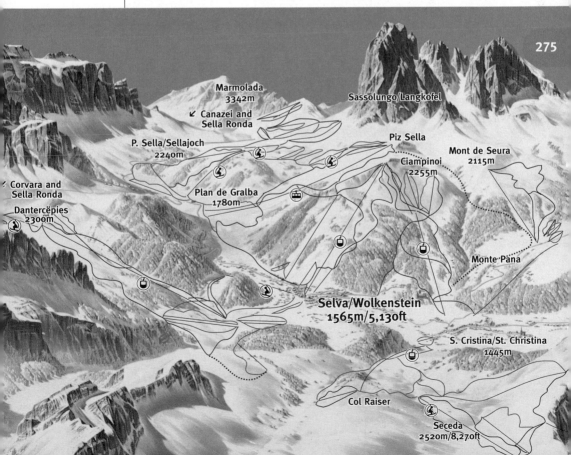

worse than the lines for the lifts. One recent peak-period visitor was appalled by pushy liftlines.

In busy periods the chair-lifts from Arabba in both directions have been a problem, as have the long, cold surface lifts from Colfosco to Selva.

MOUNTAIN RESTAURANTS
One of the area's highlights
Our reporters are unanimous in their praise for the mountain huts – there are lots of them all over the area, and virtually all of them are lively, offer good food, atmosphere and value for money.

In Val Gardena the Panorama is a small, cozy, rustic suntrap at the foot of the Dantercëpies surface lift. On the way down to Plan de Gralba from Ciampinoi, the Vallongia Rolandhütte is tucked away on a corner of the trail. In the Plan de Gralba area the top station of the tram does excellent pizza slices; the Comici is atmospheric with a big sun terrace. Further west the Sanon, above Col Raiser, 'has bags of atmosphere. It's cozy on bad days, and it's lovely to sit out on the terrace in the sun'.

The trio of little huts in the Colfosco area – Forcelles, Edelweiss and Pradat – are all very pleasant.

At Alta Badia the Piz Sorega above San Cassiano gets very crowded. Pride of place must go to Trappers' Home – a Wild West mountain hut with totem pole, teepee, country music and a Harley Davidson in the basement. Cherz above Passo di Campolongo has great views of Marmolada.

THE SELLA RONDA

The Sella Ronda is one of the world's classic intermediate circuits. The journey around the Sella massif is easily managed in a day by even an early intermediate. The slopes you descend are almost all easy, and take you through Selva, Colfosco, Corvara, Arabba and Canazei. You can do the circuit in either direction by following very clear colored signs. We prefer the clockwise route; it is slightly quicker, avoids a tedious series of surface lifts from Colfosco towards Selva, and offers more interesting slopes. But why not do both? There are two free maps of the circuit available; for map-literate people, the better bet is the proper topographical one with contour lines.

The runs total around 23km/14 miles and the lifts around 14km/9 miles. We've done it in three and a half hours plus some diversions and hut stops, though five or six hours may be more realistic during busy periods. The lifts take about two hours (plus any waiting in line). On busy days it can be crowded (on the trails and the lifts). If possible, choose low season or a Saturday, and set out early.

Not everyone likes it. 'It's a bit of a slog,' said one reporter. Others have found the circuit 'boring', and 'a bit of a rat race' but agree that 'it is a good way to get to other areas'. To make the journey more enjoyable we suggest experts take time out for some diversions. Among the most entertaining segments are the long runs down from Ciampinoi to Santa Cristina and Selva, from Dantercëpies to Selva, from the top of the Boe gondola back down to Corvara and from the top of the Arabba gondola. Take in all those in a day doing the circuit and you'll have had a good day.

Intermediates could take time out to explore the off-the-circuit Alta Badia area from Corvara. Groups of different abilities can do the circuit and arrange to meet along the way. There are plenty of welcoming rifugios at which to take a break.

SCHOOLS/GUIDES

2000/01 prices in euros

Selva Gardena
Classes 6 days
6 4hr days: 132
Children's classes
Ages: 4 to 12
6 6hr days: 201
(includes lunch)
Private lessons
Hourly
29 for 1hr for 1 person

Ortisei
Classes 5 days
2 half-days (3hr) and 3 full days (6½hr): 132
Children's classes
Ages: from 3
5 6½hr days: 188
Private lessons
Hourly
29 for 1hr for 1 person

S Cristina
Classes 6 3½hr days: 127
Children's classes
Ages: from 2½
1 day: 119
Private lessons
Hourly
29 for 1hr for 1 person

CHILDCARE

The ski schools run a kindergarten for children aged 1 to 4, with skiing available for the older children. Those attending proper ski school classes can be looked after all day.

Phone numbers
From abroad use the prefix +39 (and do **not** omit the initial '0' of the phone number).

Around Arabba, Bec de Roces and Col de Burz are both suntraps. The rifugio at the top of the Porta Vescovo lifts has been recommended as 'modern, clean, bright, efficient and with excellent food'. Capanna Bill, on the long run down to Malga Ciapela, has stunning views of the Marmolada glacier.

On Alpe di Siusi the rustic Sanon Refuge gets a good review, particularly since 'the barman came out to serenade us with his Tirolean accordion'. And the Wilhelms Hutte at the top of the Florian chair has 'superb views under Sassopiatto'.

Above Canazei there are at least six huts scattered around the Belvedere bowl. Lower down, Lupo Bianco is a notable rendezvous point and suntrap. As well as restaurants, there are lots of little snow bars for a quick grappa.

SCHOOLS AND GUIDES
Mixed views

The Selva school is capable of good instruction, provided you get into a suitable group. One recent visitor was very pleased with her lessons and made 'good progress' in her class of six. However, another was 'very unimpressed' when all the English speakers, of varying abilities, were lumped in the same class due to a lack of English speaking instructors.

FACILITIES FOR CHILDREN
Good by Italian standards

There are comprehensive childcare arrangements, but German and Italian are the main languages here and English is not routinely spoken. That said, in the past we have had reports of very enjoyable lessons and of children longing to return.

Staying there

HOW TO GO
A reasonable choice

Hotels There are a dozen 4-stars, over 30 3-stars and numerous lesser hotels. Few of the best are well positioned.
(((③ **Gran Baita** (0471 795210) Large, luxurious sporthotel, with lots of mod cons including indoor pool. A few minutes' walk from center and lifts.
(((③ **Aaritz** (0471 795011) Best-placed 4-star, opposite the Ciampinoi gondola, and with an open fire.
((② **Astor** (0471 795207) Family-run chalet in center, below beginner areas. Good value.
((② **Continental** (0471 795411) 3-star situated right on the beginner areas.
((② **Olympia** (0471 795145) Well positioned 3-star.
((② **Solaia** (0471 795104) 3-star chalet, superbly positioned for lifts and slopes.
Apartments/condos There are plenty to choose from. We have had excellent reports of the Villa Gardena (0471 794602) and Isabell (0471 794562) apartments over the years.

EATING OUT
Plenty of good-value choices

Selva offers the best of both Austrian and Italian food at prices to suit all

GETTING THERE

Air Verona, transfer 3hr; Bolzano, transfer 45min; Innsbruck, transfer 3hr.

Rail Chiusa (27km/17 miles), Bressanone (35km/22 miles), Bolzano (40km/25 miles); frequent buses from station.

ACTIVITIES

Indoor Swimming, sauna, solaria, bowling alley, squash, artificial skating rink, ice hockey, museum, concerts, movie theater, billiards, tennis, climbing wall, fitness center
Outdoor Sleigh rides, torch-light descents, snow-shoeing, toboggan runs, paragliding, horse-riding, extensive cleared paths around Selva Gardena and above S Cristina and Ortisei

TOURIST OFFICE

Postcode 39048
t +39 (0471) 795122
f 794245
selva@val-gardena.com
www.valgardena.it

pockets. The higher-quality restaurants are mainly hotel-based. The Antares and Laurin have especially good menus. The Bellavista is recommended for good pasta and Doug and Dagi's Costabella for Tirolean specialities. Rino's has 'excellent pizza'.

APRES-SKI
Above average for a family resort
Nightlife is lively and informal, though the village is so scattered there is little on-street atmosphere. La Stua is an après-ski bar on the Sella Ronda route, with accordion music later on. The Igloo at Plan de Gralba is also 'good fun for those first few beers before heading back to Selva in virtual darkness'. For a civilized early drink try the good value ski-school bar at the base of the Dantercëpies trail. Or the Costabella is cozy, serving good gluwein. Café Mozart on the main street is highly recommended for ice cream and cakes.

Ardent après-skiers should visit the Posta Zirm in Corvara. 'The ski-boot tea dance was excellent,' recommends one reporter.

For thigh-slapping in Selva later on, the Laurinkeller has good atmosphere though it's 'quite expensive', while the Luislkeller gets 'a very rowdy German and Scandinavian clientele'.

La Bula 'has live music every night, and gets quite lively later'. The disco of the hotel Stella next door has a 'good crowd and is well used by the British'.

OFF THE SLOPES
Good variety
There's a sports center, lovely walks and sleigh rides on Alpe di Siusi; and snow-shoeing around Chertz is reputed to be good. The charming town of Ortisei is well worth a visit for its large hot-spring swimming pool, shops, restaurants and lovely old buildings.

Pedestrians can reach numerous good restaurants, nicely scattered around the mountains, by gondola or tram. Car drivers have Bolzano and Innsbruck within reach and tour operators do trips to Cortina.

Ortisei 1235m/4,050ft

Ortisei is a market town with a life of its own, and its local slopes aren't on the main Sella Ronda circuit. It's full of lovely buildings, pretty churches and pleasant shops. The lift to the south-facing slopes is very central, and the north-facing Alpe di Siusi lifts are only

slightly further out. The nursery area, school and kindergarten are at the foot of these slopes, but there's a fair range of family accommodations on the trail side of the road. The fine public indoor pool and ice rink are also here.

There are hotels and self-catering to suit all tastes and pockets and many good restaurants, mainly specializing in local dishes. Après-ski is quite lively, and many bars keep going till late.

Corvara 1570m/5,150ft

Corvara is the most animated Sella Ronda village east of Selva, with plenty of hotels, restaurants, bars and sports facilities.

It's well positioned, with village lifts heading off to reasonably equidistant Selva, Arabba and San Cassiano. The main shops and some hotels cluster around a small piazza, but the rest of the place sprawls along the valley floor.

Colfosco 1645m/5,400ft

Colfosco is a smaller, quieter version of Corvara, around 2km/1 mile away. It has a fairly compact center with a sprawl of large hotels along the road towards Selva. It's connected to Corvara by a horizontal-running chair-lift. In the opposite direction, a series of surface lifts head off to the Passo Gardena and on to Selva.

Several large hotels between them provide plenty of services.

San Cassiano

1530m/5,020ft
San Cassiano is a pretty little village, set in an attractive, tree-filled valley. It's a quiet, slightly upscale resort, full of well-heeled Italian families and comfortable hotels. The local slopes, the Alta Badia, though sizeable and fully linked, are something of a spur of the main Sella Ronda. Adventurers who want to do the circuit will find it a tiresome business.

The best hotel in town is the 4-star Rosa Alpina (0471 849500). The tea dance in Corvara's Posta Zirm is a must if you want something lively. Stop there at the end of the day, cab home afterwards. Later nightlife is very limited: the Rosa Alpina has dancing and there's a bowling alley. Walking in the pretty scenery is the main off-slope activity; swimming is the other. There is no nursery or ski kindergarten.

La Villa 1435m/4,710ft

La Villa is similar to neighboring San Cassiano in most respects – small, quiet, pretty, unspoiled – but it is slightly closer to Corvara, making it rather better placed for the main Sella Ronda circuit. There is a home trail that features on the World Cup circuit, and village amenities include a pool, bowling and skating on a frozen lake.

Canazei 1440m/4,720ft

Canazei is a sizeable, bustling, pretty, roadside village of narrow streets, rustic old buildings, traditional style hotels and nice little shops, set in the Sella Ronda's most heavily wooded section of mountains. There's plenty going on generally – and it has been recommended by many reporters.

A 12-person gondola is the only mountain access point, but it shifts the liftlines (which can be long) quickly.

A single trail back to the village is linked to runs returning from both Selva and Arabba, but it is often closed. The local Belvedere slopes are uniformly easy with scattered mountain restaurants. The village beginner area is good but inconveniently located and is unlikely to be used after day one. The Bella Vista at the top of the gondola has a lovely sun terrace and is recommended for 'excellent food and wine'.

Lack of spoken English in the school can be a problem. Children have an all-day ski nursery. But again the lack of spoken English could pose problems.

There are no really luxurious hotels, but the grand 3-star Dolomiti (0462 601106) in the middle of town is one of the original resort hotels. The chalet-style Diana (0462 601477) is charming and five minutes from the village center. The 4-star Astoria (0462 601302) has a pool and minibus transfers to and from the gondola.

There are numerous restaurants. The Stala, Melester and Te Cevana are all worth a try. And après-ski is reasonably animated. La Stua dei Ladins serves good local wines. The Husky and Roxy bars are worth a visit.

Off-slope entertainment consists of beautiful walks and shopping. There's also a pool, sauna, Turkish baths and skating in neighboring Alba.

Campitello 1445m/4,740ft

Campitello is smaller and quieter than next-door Canazei and still unspoiled. By Sella Ronda standards, the village is nothing special, particularly when there's little snow – which is much of the time – but it's still pleasant.

It's remarkably quiet during the day, having no slopes to the village. A tram takes you up into the Sella Ronda circuit. If you don't wish to return by lift, take the trail to Canazei and catch a bus.

The Rubino (0462 750225) is an elegant 4-star with a pool and close to the tram. The 4-star Park Diamant (0462 750440) next door is under the same management. Campitello is quite lively – we've had trouble getting near the bar of the throbbing Da Giulio in the early evening. Neighboring Pozza has ice skating and floodlit slopes. There are no children's facilities.

Arabba 1600m/5,250ft

Arabba is a small, traditional, still uncommercialized village. But the lifts into the Sella Ronda in both directions make it very convenient. The high north-facing slopes have the best natural snow and steepest trails in the Dolomites. The 4-star Sport (0436 79321) is the best hotel, and reporters recommend the large, 3-star Portavescovo (0436 79139): 'Excellent hotel, wonderful food, nicely furnished rooms and a well-equipped fitness center'. It has the only pool in town.

Venues for eating out are limited. 7 Sass and Ru De Mont are cheap and cheerful pizzerias. The après-ski is also limited – but cheap. The atmospheric Rifugio Plan Boe is good for a last drink on the trails before heading back to the village. Bar Peter and hotel bars are the focal points. The Delmonego family's bar-caravan, at the bottom of the trail, is the tea-time rendezvous.

Modern resort with access to the Milky Way

HOW IT RATES

The slopes

Snow	***
Extent	****
Experts	***
Intermediates	****
Beginners	***
Convenience	****
Liftlines	***
Restaurants	**

The rest

Scenery	***
Resort charm	*
Off-slope	*

➕ Part of the extensive Franco-Italian Milky Way area

➕ Snow reliability is usually good, with extensive snowmaking backup

➕ Local slopes suitable for most levels, with some tougher runs than most neighbouring resorts

➖ Much of the purpose-built village is scruffy, though likely to improve for the 2006 Winter Olympics

➖ Situated at one extreme of the Milky Way area – so inconvenient for exploration of the whole network

➖ Weekend and peak-period liftlines

➖ Little après-ski during the week

Sestriere was built for snow – high, with north-west-facing slopes – and it has very extensive snowmaking, too. So even if you are let down by the notoriously erratic snowfalls in this corner of Italy, you should be fairly safe here – certainly safer than in Sauze d'Oulx, over the hill.

What's new

Turin has been chosen to host the 2006 Olympic Winter Games; Sestriere will host many of the Alpine events.

The terrain park is being improved and expanded for 2001/02. And the village beginner lifts are being improved.

280

MOUNTAIN FACTS

Figures relate to the whole Milky Way area

Altitude	1390m-2825m
	4,560ft-9,270ft
Lifts	92
Trails	400km/
	250 miles
Blue	12%
Red	67%
Black	21%
Snowmaking	75km/
	47 miles
Recco detectors used	

TRAIL MAP

Sestriere is covered on the Sauze d'Oulx map.

LAPRESSE

Club Med: Distinctive? Yes. Attractive? Well ... ➜

THE RESORT

Sestriere was the Alps' first purpose-built resort. It sits on a broad, sunny and windy col at 2000m/6,560ft. Neither the site nor the village, with its large apartment blocks, looks very hospitable, though the buildings have benefited from recent investment, and they'll doubtless get more in the run-up to the Olympics. There are some interesting buildings, but much of the village still seems rather scruffy.

This is not the most convenient of purpose-built resorts, but location is not crucial. Borgata is less convenient for nightlife and the shops and a recent report suggests that buses to and from Sestriere are infrequent.

THE MOUNTAINS

Sestriere is at one extreme of the big Franco-Italian Milky Way area. The local slopes have two main sectors: Sises, directly in front of the village, and more varied Motta, above Borgata – to the north-east and 225m/740ft higher.

Slopes There are mainly surface and chair-lifts on the local north-west-facing slopes. Access to Sansicario and the rest of the Milky Way is via gondola from Borgata to Col Basset, at the top of the Sauze d'Oulx area, and a surface lift back up to Monte Fraiteve. Snow permitting, the return to Sestriere is via a long red from the top of the gondola at Col Basset – or the newly restored red run down from Monte Fraiteve. But it more often depends on riding the gondola down. Signposting and the trail map are poor.

Snow reliability With most of the local slopes facing north-west and ranging from 1840m/6,040ft to 2820m/9,250ft, and an extensive snowmaking network covering most of the Sises sector and half of Motta, snow-cover is usually reliable for most of the season. The notoriously erratic snowfalls in the

Milky Way often leave the rest of the area seriously short of snow while the extensive snowmaking in Sestriere provides fairly reliable cover. The sunny runs down from Sauze suffer from poor snow and do not benefit from any snowmaking backup.

Experts There is a fair amount to amuse experts – steep trails served by the surface lifts at the top of both sectors, and off-trail slopes in several directions from here and Monte Fraiteve.

Intermediates Both sectors also offer plenty for confident intermediates, who can explore practically all of the Milky Way areas, conditions permitting.

Beginners The terrain is good for beginners, with several beginnerareas and the gentlest of easy runs down to Borgata. However, one reporter points out that there is a lack of easy intermediate runs to progress to.

Cross-country There are two loops covering a total of 10km/6 miles.

Snowboarding The terrain park next to the Cit Roc chair on Sises is being improved and expanded for 2001/02.

Liftlines The lifts are mainly modern though there are still some inadequate old ones. But lines for the main lifts occur at the weekends and holidays. The lifts from Borgata to Sestriere can be a bottleneck at the end of the day. Liftlines occur when poor weather closes the gondola link to Sauze. A recent visitor reported a large proportion of lift closures at the end of March, despite good snow.

Mountain restaurants The local ones could only be described as 'fair' – the one at Sises is best – but there are better ones further afield.

Schools and guides Lack of spoken English can be a problem.

Facilities for children There are no special facilities for children.

STAYING THERE

How to go Most accommodations are in apartments.

Hotels There are a dozen hotels, mostly of 3-star or 4-star status. Just out of the village (but not far from a lift) is the luxurious Principi di Piemonte (0122 7941). The Savoy Edelweiss (0122 77040) is a central, attractive 3-star. The distinctive round towers in the center are the Club Med quarters.

Eating out There are plenty of options. Try Lu Peirol for home-made ravioli and atmosphere. Tre Rubineti has been highly recommended for 'outstanding Italian cooking' and an enormous wine list. Last Tango and La Baita are also well regarded.

Après-ski Après-ski is quiet during the week but becomes lively at weekends: the Black Sun pub-cum-disco and the Tabatà club are great fun, and the Prestige and Palace are two of the many little bars that liven up. The Pinky is one of the best of the bars that double as eateries, with lots of low sofas in the classic Italian casual-chic style.

Off the slopes There's quite a bit to do, but it isn't a very attractive place, despite some upscale shops.

Phone numbers
From abroad use the prefix +39 (and do **not** omit the initial 'o' of the phone number).

TOURIST OFFICE

Postcode 10058
t +39 (0122) 755444
f 755171
sestriere@montagne doc.it
www.sestriere.it
www.vialattea.it

M Sises provides world-class slalom slopes directly facing the village →

Switzerland is home to some of our favorite resorts. For sheer charm and spectacular scenery, the 'traffic-free' villages of Wengen, Mürren, Saas-Fee and Zermatt can't be beat. Many resorts have impressive slopes too – including some of the biggest, highest and toughest runs in the Alps, as well as a lot of reassuring intermediate terrain. For fast, efficient, liftline-free lift networks, Swiss resorts rarely match French standards – but the real black spots are gradually disappearing. And there are compensations: the world's best mountain restaurants, for example. People always seem to associate Switzerland with high prices. Barring some catastrophic accident to the Swiss franc, prices are never going to be low, but usually they are not greatly different from prices in major French resorts; and what you get for your money is first class.

While France is the home of the purpose-built resort, Switzerland is the home of the traditional mountain village that has transformed itself from farming community into year-round holiday center. Many of Switzerland's most famous mountain resorts are as popular in the summer as in the winter, or more so. This creates places with a much more lived-in feel to them, and a much more stable local community. Many are still run and dominated by a handful of families who were lucky or shrewd enough to get involved in the early development of the area.

This has its downside as well as advantages. The ruling families are able to stifle competition and prevent newcomers from taking a slice of their action. Alternative ski schools, competing with the traditional school and pushing up standards, are much less common than in other countries, for example.

SNOWPIX.COM / CHRIS GILL

Saas-Fee is one of the classic Swiss resorts – cozily traditional in style, free of traffic except for a few electric taxis, and set high up at the foot of glaciers tumbling from the shoulders of a ring of 4000m/ 13,000ft peaks ↓

Switzerland is associated with high living, and the swanky grand hotels of St Moritz, Gstaad, Zermatt and Davos are beyond the dreams of most ordinary vacationers. And even in more modest resorts, nothing is cheap. But the quality of the service you get for your money is generally high. Swiss hotels are some of the best in the world. The trains run like clockwork to the advertised timetable (and often they run to the top of the mountain, doubling as ski-lifts). The food is almost universally of good quality and much less stodgy than in neighboring Austria. In Switzerland you get what you pay for: even the cheapest wine, for example, is not cheap; but it is reliable – bad bottles are very rare.

Perhaps surprisingly for such a long-established, traditional, rather staid skiing country, Switzerland has gone out of its way to attract snowboarders by developing the facilities they look for. Even stuffy resorts like Davos cater to boarders thoroughly.

GETTING AROUND THE SWISS ALPS

Access to practically all Swiss resorts is fairly straightforward when approaching from the north – just pick your highway. Many of the high passes that are perfectly sensible ways to get around the country in summer are closed in winter, which can be inconvenient if you are moving around from one area to another. There are car-carrying trains linking the Valais (Crans-Montana, Zermatt etc) to Andermatt via the Furka tunnel and Andermatt to the Grisons (Flims, Davos etc) via the Oberalp pass – closed to road traffic in winter but open to trains except after very heavy snowfalls.

St Moritz is more awkward to get to than other resorts, as well as being further away. The main road route is over the Julier pass. This is normally kept open, but at 2284m/7,490ft it is naturally prone to heavy snowfalls that can shut it for a time. The fallback is the car-carrying rail tunnel under the Albula pass. A major new rail tunnel opened in November 1999, offering an alternative route. The Vereina tunnel runs for 19km/12 miles from Klosters to a point near Susch and Zernez, down the Inn valley from St Moritz.

These car-carrying rail services are painless unless you travel at peak times, when there may be long lines – particularly for the Furka tunnel from Andermatt, which offers residents of Zürich the shortest route to Zermatt and the other Valais resorts. Another rail tunnel service that's very handy is the Lötschberg tunnel, linking Kandersteg in the Bernese Oberland with Brig in the Valais. Apart from helicopters, there's no quicker way from Wengen to Zermatt.

There is a car-carrying rail tunnel linking Switzerland with Italy – the Simplon. But most of the routes to Italy are kept open by means of road tunnels. See the Italy introduction.

To use Swiss highways (and it's difficult to avoid doing so if you're driving serious distances) you have to buy a permit to stick on your windshield (costing SF40 last time we asked). They are sold at the border, and are for all practical purposes compulsory.

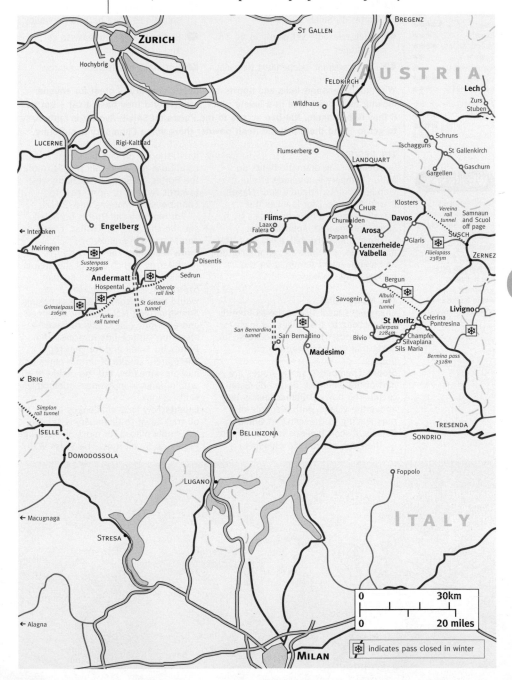

Champéry
1050m/3,440ft

Picture-postcard village, with access to the Portes du Soleil

286

HOW IT RATES

The slopes

Snow	**
Extent	*****
Experts	***
Intermediates	****
Beginners	**
Convenience	*
Liftlines	****
Restaurants	***

The rest

Scenery	****
Resort charm	****
Off-slope	***

What's new

There are plans to replace old double chair-lifts from Grand Paradis and at Planachaux by fast six-packs. But when we went to press it had not been confirmed if this would happen for 2001/02 or 2002/03.

➕ Charmingly rustic mountain village

➕ Tram takes you into very extensive Portes du Soleil slopes

➕ Quiet, relaxed – yet plenty to do off the slopes

➕ Easy access for independent travelers

➖ Local slopes suffer from the sun

➖ No runs back to the village – and sometimes none back to the valley

➖ Beginner areas not easy to get to and not that gentle

➖ Not many tough slopes nearby

With good transport links and sports facilities, Champéry is great for anyone looking for a quiet time in a lovely place, especially if they have a car – but not if they're beginners. Not bad access to the Portes du Soleil: Avoriaz is fairly easy to get to – and there may be fresh powder there when Champéry is suffering.

THE RESORT
Set beneath the dramatic Dents du Midi, Champéry is a village of old wooden chalets. Friendly and relaxed, it would be ideal for families if it wasn't separated from its slopes by a steep, fragmented mountainside.

Down a steepish hill, away from the main street, are the tram, sports center and a convenient terminus for the narrow-gauge railway.

THE MOUNTAINS
Champéry's local slopes are as friendly and relaxing as the village, at least for intermediates. There's an electronic lift ticket that you can keep in your pocket.

Slopes Champéry's sunny slopes are part of the extensive Portes du Soleil circuit. The bowl of **Planachaux** is way above the village, with a couple of runs leading to the valley at **Grand Paradis**, a short bus-ride from Champéry.

There are no trails to Champéry

itself, though on rare occasions local conditions allow off-trail trips. Explore the Portes du Soleil by heading west towards Avoriaz or north-east to Champoussin, Morgins and Châtel.

For more on the Portes du Soleil, see the chapters on Avoriaz, Châtel and Morzine in France.

Snow reliability The snow on the north-facing French side of the area is usually better than on the sunnier Swiss side to the south. The area would benefit from more snowmaking.

Snowboarding Not ideal for beginners, and everyone else needs to have mastered surface lifts to access the Portes du Soleil and tougher terrain. There are a couple of terrain-parks and half-pipes nearby, but the daddy of all terrain-parks is in Avoriaz – definitely worth a look.

Experts Few local challenges unless the off-trail down to Champéry is skiable, and badly placed for most of the tough Portes du Soleil runs. The Swiss Wall,

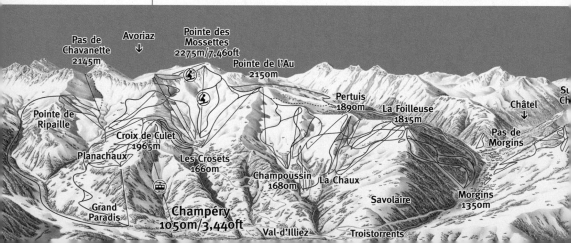

MOUNTAIN FACTS

Altitude 975m-2350m
3,200ft-7,710ft

Lifts	219
Trails	650km
	400 miles
Blue	51%
Red	40%
Black	9%

Snowmaking
522 acres
Recco detectors used

on the Champéry side of Chavanette, is intimidatingly long and steep, but not that terrifying. There's scope for off-trail at Chavanette and on the broad slopes of Les Crosets and Champoussin.

Intermediates Confident intermediates have the whole Portes du Soleil at their disposal. Locally, the runs home to Grand Paradis are good when the snow conditions allow and Les Crosets is a junction of several fine runs.

Also worth trying are the slightly tougher trails down from Mossette and Grand Conche, the runs back from Pointe de l'Au, Champoussin's leisurely cruising and runs to Morgins – delightful tree-lined meanders.

Beginners Go elsewhere if you can. Despite a good school, Champéry is far from ideal – even the Planachaux runs, where lessons are held, are steepish.

Cross-country Advertised, but very unreliable snow.

Liftlines Few local problems. If snow is good, avoid end-of-the-day lines for the tram down by taking the Grand Paradis run to the valley floor and getting the free bus back to town.

Mountain restaurants Chez Coquoz at Planachaux and Chez Gaby above Champoussin are recommended. The tiny Lapisa on the way to Grand Paradis is delightfully rustic. Further afield, try the Les Lindarets refuges (see Avoriaz).

Schools and guides The few reports that we've had are free of criticism.

Facilities for children The tourist office has a list of baby sitters. The Swiss ski school takes three- to seven-year-olds.

STAYING THERE

Although it's a small village, most hotels are some way from the tram.

How to go Limited packages available. Easy access for independent travelers.

Phone numbers
From elsewhere in Switzerland add the prefix 024.
From abroad use the prefix +41 24.

Hotels Wide choice from 3-star down. Prices low compared with smarter Swiss resorts. The Champéry (479 1071) is the best – a comfy chalet on the main street. Beau Séjour (479 1701) is at the southern end. The National (479 1130) has 'friendly staff, lovely breakfast'.

Apartments/condos Some apartments are available to independent travellers.

Eating out A fair choice. Two of the best for local specialities are just outside the village: Cantines des Rives is a beautiful traditional chalet; the Grand Paradis is excellent, if pricey, and decorated with stuffed animals.

Locally, try the the Farinet or the 'excellent' restaurant in the Hotel du Nord. Mitchell's bar also has a good

TOURIST OFFICE

Postcode CH-1874
t +41 (24) 479 2020
f 479 2021
champery-ch@portes dusoleil.com
www.champery.ch

restaurant and the Café du Centre will serve Asian food this season. Two evenings a week, when the slopes are floodlit, the restaurant at the top of the tram opens.

Après-ski Mitchell's has big sofas, fireplace and a great atmosphere till late. Below the 'rather seedy' Pub, the Crevasse disco is one of the liveliest places in town. The underground Mines d'Or nightclub has 'ridiculously high' drink prices. The Café du Centre will be run by a Scot and have its own micro brewery. Other suggestions are the bars in the hotel Suisse Golden Tulip, the Bar des Guides and the Farinet's spacious cellar nightclub – fun when there are enough people to give it atmosphere, mostly on weekends.

Off the slopes Walks, particularly along to Val d'Illiez, are pleasant, and the narrow-gauge railway allows excursions to Montreux, Lausanne and Sion. There's a decent sports center.

Les Crosets 1660m/5,450ft

A good base for a quiet time and slopes on the doorstep. Good snow and a prime position on the Portes du Soleil. Not much here, but the Hotel Télécabine (479 1421) is homely, serving great food in a lovely rustic dining room.

Champoussin

1680m/5,510ft

Champoussin is, theoretically, a good family choice – no through traffic, convenient for the slopes, no noisy late-night revelers and the comfortable Royal Alpage Club hotel – pool, gym, disco, two restaurants (476 8300).

Morgins 1350m/4,430ft

A fairly scattered but attractive resort with some nightlife. Suits those with a car, who can easily get to the higher slopes and bars of Châtel. The Hotel Bellevue (477 8171) and the Pension de Morgins (477 1143) are well thought of.

Crans-Montana
1500m/4,920ft

Sun-soaked slopes with stunning views and big town base

HOW IT RATES

The slopes

Snow	**
Extent	***
Experts	**
Intermediates	****
Beginners	***
Convenience	**
Liftlines	***
Restaurants	***

The rest

Scenery	****
Resort charm	**
Off-slope	****

What's new

The separate lift companies have merged, and there is now a single lift ticket for the whole area – including the glacier.

288

➕ Large trail area suitable for all, except if you prefer black runs

➕ Splendid wooded setting with magnificent panoramic views

➕ Fair number of woodland slopes – good in bad weather

➕ Modern, well-designed lift system, with few liftlines

➕ Golf course provides excellent, gentle beginner areas

➕ Very sunny slopes (but see right)

➕ Excellent cross-country trails

➖ Snow badly affected by sun except in early season

➖ Large town (rather than village) composed partly of big chalet-style blocks but mainly of dreary cubic blocks – and therefore entirely without Alpine atmosphere

➖ Bus or car rides to lifts from many of the accommodations

➖ Not many challenging trails

When conditions are right – clear skies above fresh, deep snow – Crans-Montana is hard to beat. The mountains you bounce down with the midday sun full on your face are charmingly scenic, the slopes broken up by rock outcrops and forest. The mountains you gaze at – Zermatt's Matterhorn just discernible among them – are mind-blowing. When conditions are right, mountain-lovers may forgive Crans-Montana anything – in particular, its inconvenient, linear layout and the plain, towny style of its twin resort centers.

Sadly, conditions are more often wrong than right. Except in the depths of winter, the strong midday sun quickly bakes the trails. For someone booking six months ahead, this is enough to keep Crans-Montana off the shortlist. For those who can time a visit according to the weather – and are more interested in impressive distant views than cozy immediate surroundings – the resort is worth serious consideration.

The resort

Crans-Montana celebrated 100 years as a resort in 1993, but is far from being a picturesque Swiss chocolate-box village. Set on a broad shelf facing south to the great mountains across the Rhône valley, it is really two villages, their centers a mile apart and their fringes now merging. Strung along a busy road, the resort's many hotels, villas, apartments and upscale shops are mainly dull blocks with little traditional Alpine character.

Fortunately, the resort's many trees help to screen the buildings, and they make some areas positively attractive. And its wonderful setting means you get a lot of sun as well as superb views. There are several lakes and two golf courses, one home to the Swiss Open.

The resort is reached by good roads, and by a fast funicular railway up from Sierre to Montana. It depends heavily on summer conference business, which sets the tone even in winter. Hotels tend to be comfortable and fairly formal, village facilities varied but daytime-oriented, and visitors middle-aged and dignified. In the evenings there's little Alpine-village atmosphere.

Gondolas go up to the main slopes from both villages. Crans is the more upscale, with expensive jewelry shops, a casino, and a high fur-coat count. It is well situated for the pretty golf course area, which has baby lifts for complete beginners, a cross-country trail and lovely walks. Montana has somewhat cheaper restaurants and bars.

There are other gondola base stations and places to stay further east: at Violettes in Les Barzettes (the lift from here connects directly to the top glacier lift and is the fastest way to the top) and at Aminona.

MOUNTAIN FACTS

Altitude	1500m-3000m
	4,920ft-9,840ft
Lifts	35
Trails	160km
	100 miles
Blue	38%
Red	50%
Black	12%
Snowmaking	17km
	11 miles
Recco detectors used	

LIFT TICKETS

2001/02 prices in Swiss francs

Crans-Montana-Aminona
Covers all lifts in Crans-Montana and Aminona and the ski-bus.
Beginners Points card
Main ticket
1-day ticket 54
6-day ticket 253
Senior citizens
Over 65 (men), 62 (women) 6-day ticket 215)
Children
Under 15: 6-day ticket 152
Under 6: free ticket
Short-term tickets
Half day from 11 (adult 45) or 12.30 (adult 36).
Alternative periods
6 non-consecutive days (adult 292).

The mountains

Although it has achieved some prominence in ski-racing, Crans-Montana has slopes that suit intermediates well, with few challenges and no nasty surprises. Beginners are well catered to.

THE SLOPES
Interestingly fragmented
Crans-Montana's 160km/100 miles of trails are spread over three well-linked areas, all equally suitable for intermediates of varying abilities and persuasions. The upper runs are wide and good but many of those down to the valley are narrow woodland paths.

Cry d'Er is the largest sector – an open bowl descending into patchy forest, directly above Montana. Cry d'Er itself is the meeting point of many lifts and the starting point of the lift up to the sector high point of Bella-Lui (2545m/8,350ft). Cry d'Er is served directly by two gondolas – a newish eight-person one from just above Crans, and another from just above central Montana, which has a useful mid-station where beginners can get off and access high-altitude beginner areas. A third gondola goes from the west side of Crans to Chetseron, with a surface lift above going on to Cry d'Er.

The next sector, reached by another powerful gondola directly from Les Barzettes (labelled 'Violettes' on the resort trail map), is focused on Les Violettes, starting point of the jumbo gondola up to the Plaine Morte glacier. There are three linking routes from Cry d'Er to the **Violettes–Plaine Morte** sector. The highest, starting at Bella-Lui (or, strictly, at Col du Pochet, a short run and surface lift beyond) used to be off-trail but is now an official red run. Bella-Lui is also the start of the Men's Downhill course (Piste Nationale) that goes past Cry d'Er to Les Barzettes.

The third **Petit Bonvin** sector is served by a gondola up from Aminona at the eastern end of the area. This is linked to Les Violettes by red and blue runs passing the surface and chair lifts at La Toula.

Reporters complain of confusion caused by poor signage.

Anzère is nearby to the west, though the slopes aren't linked. You can make expeditions to Zermatt, Saas Fee and Verbier by road or rail.

SNOW RELIABILITY
The resort's main drawback
Crans-Montana's slopes go up to glacier level at 3000m/9,840ft, but this is misleading; the runs on the Plaine

boarding *Despite Crans-Montana's staid, middle-aged image, boarding is very popular. There are plenty of broad, smooth trails, lots of underexploited off-trail, and good specialist facilities. Aminona is a good area for experienced boarders and has a terrain-park, and there's a half-pipe in the more central Cry-d'Er area. There are a number of specialist shops and the Stoked snowboard school. The main lifts are chairs and gondolas, and the surface lifts are usually avoidable with good planning. It is a good place for beginner and intermediate boarders – and, of course, slush is not such a problem for novice boarders to navigate as it is for novice skiers! But avoid the ice first thing in the morning. Nightlife tends to be a fairly civilized affair, though; the George & Dragon can get quite lively and has a 'typical' pub atmosphere.*

Morte glacier are very limited and, excellent though it is, the solitary run down from there does not make this a snow-sure area as a whole. Few of the other slopes are above 2250m/7,38oft, and practically all get a lot of direct sun. Late in the season, at least, this makes for slush in the afternoons, rock-hard ice in the mornings, and a tendency for snow to disappear. There is now snowmaking on the main runs down from both Violettes and Cry d'Er to Montana, from Cry d'Er to Crans and the bottom part of the run from Chetseron. We applaud these efforts; but it is a losing battle. We have never experienced good snow on the runs down to the valley.

FOR EXPERTS
Lacks challenging trails

There are few steep trails and the only decent bumps are on the short slopes at La Toula. There's plenty of off-trail in all sectors, but particularly beneath Chetseron and La Tza; guides are usually easy to book. The off-trail tour from Plaine Morte to Aminona is recommended.

The Piste Nationale course is far

from daunting taken at 'normal' speed, but has some enormous jumps just above Les Marolires. The direct run from La Tza to Plumachit is in places fairly challenging, especially when icy.

FOR INTERMEDIATES
Lots of attractive, flattering runs

Crans-Montana is very well suited to intermediates. Trails are mostly wide, and many of the red runs don't justify the classification. They tend to be uniform in difficulty from top to bottom, with few nasty surprises for the nervous. Avid skiers and riders enjoy the length of many runs, plus the fast lifts and good links that allow a lot of varied mileage.

The 11km/7 mile run from Plaine Morte to Les Barzettes starts with superb top-of-the-world views and powder snow, and finishes among pretty woods. But many people love the top half so much ('my favorite run in Europe') they do it repeatedly, curtailing their descent halfway down at either the Barmaz or Cabane de Bois chair-lifts to Les Violettes, for quicker access to the top gondola. Because of the gondola's high capacity the run

Plaine Morte
3000m/9,84oft

Mt. Bonvin
2995m

Petit Bonvin
2400m

Bella-Lui
2545m

Cry d'Er
2265m

Les Violettes
2250m/7,38oft

La Toula

La Tza

Mt. Lachaux
2140m

Chetseron
2100m

Pas du Loup
2000m

Plumachit

Merbé
1900m

Verdets
Grand
Signal

Les Marolires

Aminon
1500m

Plans Mayens

Arnouvaz

1700m

Les Barzettes

Montana

Crans

Crans-Montana
1500m/4,920ft

SCHOOLS/GUIDES

2000/01 prices in Swiss francs

Swiss
Classes 6 days
3hr: 9.30-12.30
6 days: 170
Children's classes
Ages: from 3
9.30-12.30 or 9.30-4pm
Half day 45
1 day with meal 80
Private lessons
Hourly
60 for 1hr

Ski & Sky
Private lessons
Hourly
60 for 1hr

Stoked Snowboard
Classes Half day: 50

CHILDCARE

The Montana ski school runs a kindergarten with skiing available up at Signal and the Crans school on the golf course for children aged 3 to 6, from 9.30 to 4.30.

There are several other kindergartens. In Montana, Fleurs des Champs takes children aged 3 months to 7 years; and Zig-Zag takes children from 2 to 6 years.

GETTING THERE

Air Sion, transfer 30min. Geneva, transfer 3hr.

Rail Sierre (15km/9 miles), Sion (22km/14 miles); regular buses to resort.

Phone numbers
From elsewhere in Switzerland add the prefix 027.
From abroad use the prefix +41 27.

---

can get crowded.

The short runs from Bella-Lui to just below Cry d'Er have some of the best snow and quietest slopes in the area, and provide fine views of awesome Montagne de Raul. The Piste Nationale is a good test of technique, with plenty of bumps but also lots of room. The quietest area, and good for groups of varying intermediate standards, is the Petit Bonvin sector.

FOR BEGINNERS
Plenty to offer the first-timer

There are three excellent beginner areas, with slopes of varying difficulty. Complete beginners have very gentle slopes on the golf course next to Crans. Cry d'Er has an area of relatively long, easy runs, with up-the-mountain views and atmosphere as well as better snow. But the runs aren't just for beginners, and you do need a full lift ticket. The Verdets–Grand Signal run is steeper, and the surface lift can get terribly icy. Near-beginners can try the little run up at Plaine Morte.

FOR CROSS-COUNTRY
Excellent high-level trails

There are 40km/25 miles of cross-country trails altogether. There are some pretty, easy trails (skating-style as well as classic) on and around the golf course. But what makes Crans-Montana particularly good for cross-country is its high-level route, in and out of woods, across the whole mountainside from Plans Mayens to beyond Aminona. 10km/6 miles of trails at Plaine Morte are open when the lower trails are closed.

LIFTLINES
Few problems

The resort's big investment in new gondolas – notably the jumbo 'Funitel' gondola from Les Violettes to the Plaine Morte glacier slopes and the lift out of Crans – has greatly alleviated any liftline problems – though bottlenecks can occur at the Nationale surface lift. Recent reporters say you rarely wait longer than five minutes – except occasionally if snow lower down is in poor condition. More of a problem can be bottlenecks on some trails, including the top glacier run. The resort does not get weekend crowds.

MOUNTAIN RESTAURANTS
A good choice

There are 20 mountain restaurants, many offering table-service. The Merbé, at the Crans–Cry d'Er gondola mid-station, is one of the most attractive, with good food in a pleasant setting just above the tree line. Advance reservations are recommended because it does get busy. Bella-Lui's terrace (with service) offers good views. The Chetseron eatery has fine views.

Petit Bonvin, at the top of the Aminona sector, has self-service and table-service sections, with superb views. There is not much choice in the Violettes sector, but we had a good meal on the table-service terrace of the main restaurant. And the small self-service Cabane des Violettes, just below this, gets rave reviews for food and views (be there early for a seat).

SCHOOLS AND GUIDES
Good reports

Both local branches of the Swiss school have mainly attracted favorable comments over the years.

FACILITIES FOR CHILDREN
Adequate, but few reports

The resort facilities for children seem to be adequate, especially in Montana, but we have no recent reports.

Staying there

Crans-Montana is quite sprawling. A free shuttle-bus links the villages and satellite lift stations during the day but can get very crowded – one reporter recommends taking a car. The main Crans and Montana gondola stations are above the main road and a tiring walk away. Many people store their equipment at lift stations overnight.

HOW TO GO
Lots of choice

There is a wide choice of hotels and apartments.
Hotels This conference resort has over 50 mainly large, comfy, expensive hotels. Most have three or more stars.
((((**Crans-Ambassador** (485 4848) Health spa, with some rooms a bit shabby for its 5-star rating. Excellent treatments such as plant baths, mud packs. Just above Montana gondola.
((((**Pas du l'Ours** (485 9333) Our favorite. Chic, attractive, wood and stone Relais & Chateaux place with nine individually designed suites.

ACTIVITIES

Indoor Hotel swimming pools, tennis, bowling, bridge, chess, golf simulator, squash, concerts, film theaters, casino, curling, ice skating, galleries
Outdoor Toboggan run, ski-bob, horse-riding, ice skating, paragliding, balloon flights

TOURIST OFFICE

Postcode CH-3962
t +41 (27) 485 0404
f 485 0460
info@crans-montana.ch
www.crans-montana.ch

((((④ **Aïda Castel** (485 4111) Beautifully furnished in chic rustic style. Between the two resort centers. Outdoor pool.
(((③ **La Forêt** (480 2131) Highly recommended. Almost at Les Barzettes, with minibus to lifts. Pool, good views.
(((③ **National** (481 2681) Perfectly placed for the Crans-Cry d'Er gondola; 'quiet, comfortable, good food'.
(((③ **Curling** (481 1242) Comfortable, near center of Montana.
(((③ **Robinson** (481 1353) B&B only; well placed near the National, in Crans.
Apartments/condos There are many apartments available.

EATING OUT
Plenty of alternatives

There is a good variety of restaurants from French to Lebanese. The best is the Michelin-starred Bistrot in the Pas de l'Ours hotel. Almost all the cheaper places are in Montana. The Dent Blanche is recommended for fondues. We had a good, simple Italian meal at Il Padrino in Crans. La Nouvelle Rotisserie is reputed to be excellent. The Gréni is a friendly restaurant on the western fringe of Montana. Cervin up at Vermala is unusually rustic.

APRES-SKI
Can be ritzy, but otherwise quiet

Crans-Montana visitors tend to prefer quiet meals and drinks to raucous nightlife. Amadeus 2006 and Chez Nanette are tents on Cry d'Er serving end-of-day vin chaud. The George & Dragon in Crans is one of the liveliest, most crowded bars with 'the cheapest beer in town'. Reporters recommend Bar 1900, La Grange, Le Constellation and Indiana Café. The outdoor ice rink in Montana is 'fun'. The film theater has films in English. Bridge is played in the hotels Royal and Aïda.

OFF THE SLOPES
Excellent, but little charm

There are plenty of off-slope activities including lovely walks. Swimming is available in several hotels.

Sierre is easily reached for shopping, and the larger Sion is only a few minutes further. Montreux is within reach. Mountain restaurants are mainly at gondola and tram stations.

One of the chair-lifts back to Violettes from the end of the glacier run – and the ever-present view over the Rhône valley ➔

Davos

A big town surrounded by a great Alpine playground

HOW IT RATES

The slopes

Snow	★★★★
Extent	★★★★★
Experts	★★★★
Intermediates	★★★★★
Beginners	★★
Convenience	★★
Liftlines	★★
Restaurants	★★★

The rest

Scenery	★★★★
Resort charm	★★
Off-slope	★★★★★

What's new

For 2000/01 the Dorftälli surface lift up to Weissfluhjoch was replaced by a six-seater chair-lift, starting at the mid-station of the Parsennbahn railway. Plans to replace the railway have been abandoned.

- Very extensive slopes
- Some superb, long and mostly easy runs away from the lifts
- Lots of accessible off-trail terrain, with many marked itineraries and some short tours
- Good cross-country trails
- Plenty to do off the slopes – excellent sports facilities, pretty walks, good range of shopping
- Some captivating mountain restaurants above Klosters
- Klosters is an attractively villagey alternative base

- Dreary block-style buildings of Davos spoil the views
- Davos is a huge, city-like resort, rather plagued by traffic and lacking Alpine atmosphere
- The slopes are spread over five or six essentially separate areas
- Some access lifts are old and out-of-date, with long liftlines – especially the main funicular from Davos Dorf
- Only one trail (black) back to Davos Dorf, which finishes 500m/one-third of a mile from town

Davos was one of the original mega-resorts, with slopes on a scale that few resorts can better, even today. But it's a difficult resort to like. It's easy to put up with slopes spread over separate mountains and relatively ancient, line-prone lifts if that's the price of staying in a captivating Alpine village. But Davos is far from that.

Whether you forgive the flaws and fall for the resort depends on how highly you value three plus-points: the distinctive, super-long intermediate runs of the Parsenn area; being able to visit a different sector every day; and the considerable off-trail potential. We value all three, and we always look forward to visiting.

You don't have to stay in Davos to enjoy its slopes: Klosters offers a much more captivating alternative. Despite royal connections, it is not exclusive – on the contrary, it has exceptionally friendly places to stay. But it is less well placed than Davos for exploring all the mountains.

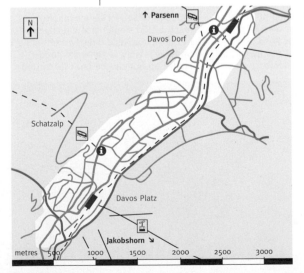

The resort

Davos is set in a high, broad, flat-bottomed valley, with its lifts and slopes either side. Arguably it was the very first place in the Alps to develop its slopes. The railway up the Parsenn was one of the first built for skiers (in 1931), and the first surface lift was built on the Bolgen beginner areas in 1934. But Davos was already a health resort; many of its luxury hotels used to be sanatoriums.

Sadly, that's just what they look like. There are still several specialist clinics and these, along with major conferences (including the World Economic Forum) and top international sporting events, are what the town of Davos has become well known for. It is also a popular destination for athletes

MOUNTAIN FACTS

Altitude	810m-2845m/ 2,66oft-9,33oft
Lifts	54
Trails	320km/ 200 miles
Blue	30%
Red	50%
Black	20%
Snowmaking	18km 11 miles
Recco detectors used	

wanting to train at high altitude.

It has two main centers, Dorf and Platz, about a mile apart. Although transport is good, with buses around the town as well as the railway linking Dorf and Platz to Klosters and other villages, location is important. Easiest access to the slopes is from Dorf to the main Parsenn area, via the funicular railway; Platz is better placed for the Strela and Jakobshorn areas, the big sports facilities, the smarter shopping and evening action.

Davos shares its slopes with the famously royal resort of Klosters, down the valley – an attractive village with good links into the Parsenn area and its own separate sector, the sunny Madrisa. Klosters is described in more detail at the end of this chapter.

Trips are possible by car or rail to St Moritz (the Vereina rail tunnel offers access to the Engadine area without having to negotiate the snowy Flüelapass) and Arosa, and by car to Flims-Laax and Lenzerheide.

The mountains

The slopes here have something for everyone, though experts and nervous intermediates need to choose their territory with care. You could hit a different mountain in Davos every day for a week. In practice, the minor areas tend to be neglected by most visitors – and so are much quieter.

THE SLOPES
Vast and varied

The ancient Parsennbahn funicular from Davos Dorf takes you to the major lift junction of Weissfluhjoch, at one end of the **Parsenn**. At the other end is Gotschnagrat, reached by tram from Klosters. Between the two is the wide, open Parsenn bowl. From Davos Platz, a funicular takes you up to Schatzalp, at the base of the **Strela** area. Follow this with a long, two-person chair, a tram and finally a T-bar, and you will eventually gain access to the Weissfluhjoch.

Across the valley, **Jakobshorn** is reached by tram from Davos Platz; this is the main snowboarders' hill. **Rinerhorn** and **Pischa** are reached by bus or (in the case of Rinerhorn) train.

Beyond the main part of Klosters, a gondola goes up from Klosters Dorf to the sunny, scenic **Madrisa** area.

There is a small floodlit slope area at the Jakobshorn.

SNOW RELIABILITY
Good, but not the best

Davos is high by Swiss standards. Its mountains go respectably high too – though not to glacial heights. Not many of the slopes face directly south, but not many face directly north either. Snow reliability is generally good higher up but can be poor lower down

LIFT TICKETS

Top Card
Covers all Davos and
Klosters, the railway
in the whole region
and buses between
the resorts.

Beginners Single and
return tickets on main
lifts in each area.

Main ticket
1-day ticket 57
6-day ticket 279

Children
6-16: 6-day ticket 168
Under 6 (with adult):
free ticket

Notes
A confusing array of
tickets are available
for individual areas
(Parsenn, Gotschna,
Schatzalp,
Jakobshorn,
Rinerhorn, Gotschna
and Madrisa) and
combined areas, from
a half day to 17 days.
Several reporters
have complained that
not all tickets are
available at each base
station.

boarding *Although the beginner areas are not ideal, the long easy runs of
the Parsenn are good for near-beginner boarders and you can
avoid surface lifts if you plan your runs. But intermediate and advanced boarders
will get the most out of Davos's vast terrain and off-trail potential. The
established boarder mountain is the Jakobshorn, with its half-pipe, terrain-park,
boarder-cross course and funky Jatz Bar nearby. The Rinerhorn and Pischa each
have a terrain-park. There are several cheap and cheerful hotels specially for
boarders, including the 180-bed Bolgenhof hotel near the Jakobshorn, the
Snowboardhotel Bolgenschanze and the Snowboarder's Palace.*

– you may have to take the lifts down
after using the Parsenn slopes.
Snowmaking has been added on some
lower runs.

FOR EXPERTS
Plenty to do, on- and off-trail

A glance at the trail map may give the
misleading impression that this is an
intermediate's resort – there aren't
many black runs. But there are some
excellent runs among them – the
Meierhofer Tälli run to Wolfgang is a
favorite – and there are also nine or
ten off-trail itineraries (marked on the
map and on the ground, but not
prepared or patrolled). These are a key
feature, adding up to a lot of expert
terrain that can be tackled without
expensive guidance. Some are on the
open upper slopes, some in the woods
lower down, some from the peaks right
to the valley. Two of the steepest runs
go from Gotschnagrat directly towards
Klosters – around the infamous
Gotschnawang slope. The Wang run is
a seriously steep ski route (and rarely
open, in our experience). Drostobel is
less scary, though the overall gradient
is little different.

There is also excellent 'proper' off-
trail terrain for which guidance is
needed, and some short tours. Arosa
can be reached much more quickly on
snow than by road or rail, but requires

a return by rail via Chur. From Madrisa
you can make tours to Gargellen in
Austria's Montafonal. This means an
exhausting one-hour walk on skins on
the way back.

FOR INTERMEDIATES
A splendid variety of runs

For intermediates of any temperament,
this is a great area. There are good
cruising runs on all five mountains, so
you would never get bored in a week.
This variety of different slopes taken
together with the wonderful long runs
to the valleys makes it a compelling
area with a unique character.

The epic runs to Klosters and other
places (described in the feature box)
pose few difficulties for a confident
intermediate or even an ambitious
near-beginner (one of your editors did
the run to Klosters on his third day on
skis, and we have heard from reporters
who did the run to Kublis on their
second holiday). And there are one or
two other notable away-from-the-lifts
runs to the valley. In particular, you
can travel from the top of Madrisa
back to Klosters Dorf via the beautiful
Schlappin valley.

FOR BEGINNERS
Platz is the more convenient

The Bolgen beginner area is
adequately spacious and gentle, and a

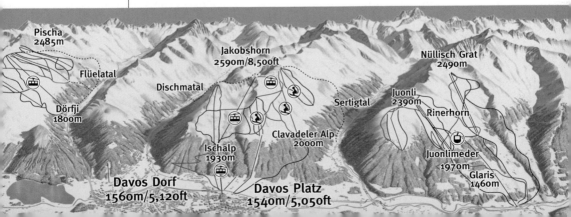

The runs from Weissfluhjoch that head north, on the back of the mountain, make this area special for many visitors. The trails that go down to Schifer and then to Küblis, Saas and Serneus, and the one that curls around the mountain to Klosters, are graded red but are not normally difficult – though a reporter this year found the latter parts challenging because they were not groomed. What marks them out is their sheer length (10-12km/6-7 miles) and the sensation of travel they offer.

Until the late 1980s, only the very top 2.5km/1.5 miles and 400m /1,300ft vertical of this enormous snowfield was served by a lift; once below Kreuzweg, you had to go down to the valley and catch the train home. Usually, you did it towards the end of the day, dawdling in the rustic restaurants in the woods on the lower reaches. The long Schiferbahn gondola changed all that – you can now descend the 1100m/3,600ft vertical to Schifer as often as you like. Some long-standing visitors regret the change, but there is the added advantage that the lower runs, below Schifer, are quieter – especially if you do them early in the day rather than as your last run.

There are even longer marked but unpatrolled routes to Fideris and Jenaz, the latter being 18km/11 miles from Weissfluhjoch, according to official figures. But these are not continuous runs: they require skins or snow-shoes for a couple of short ascents, and payment for the use of the lifts at Fideriser Heuberge on the way. And they are often closed because of shortage of snow low down.

bearable walk from the center of Platz. But Dorf-based beginners face more of a trek out to Bünda – unless staying out at the hotel of the same name.

There is no shortage of easy runs to progress to, spread around all the sectors. The Parsenn sector probably has the edge, with long, early intermediate runs in the main Parsenn bowl, as well as in the valleys down from Weissfluhjoch.

FOR CROSS-COUNTRY
Long, scenic valley trails
Davos has a total of 75km/47 miles of trails running in both directions along the main valley and reaching well up into Sertigtal, Dischmatal and Flüelatal. There is a cross-country ski center and special ski school on the outskirts of town.

LIFTLINES
Still a problem in the valley
The ancient Parsennbahn railway – the only way out of Davos Dorf – is a relic that generates some of the longest lines remaining in the Alps: a reporter this year tells us of waiting 90 minutes. And when snow on the lower slopes is poor you have to wait to come down at the end of the day as well. So we are very disappointed that its planned replacement has been cancelled. We assume that the six-pack built in parallel with the top section

last season will be followed by another chair on the lower mountain.

MOUNTAIN RESTAURANTS
Stay low down
The main high-altitude restaurants are dreary self-service affairs, but the Strelapass hut is recommended as particularly enjoyable on a warm sunny day, with good views and 'excellent' food (although it's a five-minute climb). There are other compelling places lower down – notably the rustic Conterser Schwendi ('excellent choice of rösti') and Serneuser Schwendi in the woods on the way down to the Klosters valley from the Parsenn. These are fun places to end up as darkness falls – Klosters Schwendi, at least, sells wax torches to illuminate your final descent to the village. The Skilife, down from Totalp, is self-service, has very loud pop music and is popular with hordes of school children. The Jatzhütte near the boarders' terrain-park on Jakobshorn is wild – with changing scenery such as mock palm trees, parrots and pirates. A reporter this year recommends the restaurant at Weissfluhjoch for 'Indian/Chinese food freshly cooked to order on Sunday afternoons – a great treat'. The restaurant Gotschnastübli at the base of the Gotschna tram was criticized by a reporter for its 'officious waiter service and confusing menu options'.

SCHOOLS/GUIDES

2001/02 prices in Swiss francs

Classes

4hr: 2hr am and pm
5 full days: 210

Children's classes

Ages: 4 to 16
5 full days: 210

Private lessons

Half day or full day
175 for half day or
280 for full day

Phone numbers

From elsewhere in Switzerland add the prefix 081.
From abroad use the prefix +41 81.

CHILDCARE

The Bobo-Club (formerly Pinocchio nursery) at Bünda takes children aged between 4 and 7 from 10am to noon and from 2pm to 4pm, and offers a 'playful approach to snow and skiing'. Lunch supervision possible.

The day nursery Kinderhotel Muchetta at Wiesen takes children from 3 years. There is also a day nursery for babies from 6 months.

GETTING THERE

Air Zürich, transfer 2hr by car, 3hr by rail or bus.

Rail Stations in Davos Dorf and Platz. 20 minutes from Davos to Klosters.

Davos is a big town, but you can quickly escape its streets on to paths and trails →

Both restaurants on the Madrisa slopes were pronounced 'disappointing' in terms of food choice and quality. On the Rinerhorn, the Hubelhütte at the top of the surface lift was preferred by one reporter to the main restaurant on the Rinerhorn. The Erika at Schlappin below Madrisa is noted for cheese fondue at lunchtime.

SCHOOLS AND GUIDES
Don't count on English

The Davos Swiss ski school has been renamed the Swiss Snowsportschool to emphasise the variety of instruction available. Given the small number of English-speaking visitors that Davos attracts these days, it's not surprising to find that classes are often German-dominated. A Davos regular tells us that the school is well organized, but that the instructors vary widely. A reporter this year was very happy with the school – 'friendly instructors (who will drop you off at your hotel), good English spoken'. There is an alternative ski school called New Trend and a choice of three schools for snowboarding.

FACILITIES FOR CHILDREN
Not ideal

Davos is a rather spread-out place in which to handle a family – and indeed the school's nursery is in a slightly isolated spot, at Dorf's Bünda beginner area, inconvenient for dropping off and picking up. A recent reporter tells us the school is 'well organized, but even good instructors forget at times that your child doesn't speak German'.

HOW TO GO
Hotels are the norm

Hotels A dozen 4-star places and about 30 3-stars form the core of the Davos hotel trade, though there are a couple of 5-stars and quite a few cheaper places, including bed and breakfast houses. You can book any hotel by phoning the central reservations service number (415 2121).

((((5 **Flüela** (410 1717) The more atmospheric of the two 5-star hotels, in central Dorf, and quite well placed to beat the Parsenn liftlines. Pool.

(((4 **Golfhotel Waldhuus** (416 8131) As convenient for winter langlaufers as for summer golfers. Quiet, modern, tasteful. Pool.

(((4 **Davoserhof** (415 6666) Best in town. Small, old, beautifully furnished, with excellent food; well placed in Platz. But will be under new management for 2001.

(((4 **Sunstar Park** (413 1414) At far end of Davos platz. Pool, sauna, games room. Recommended for 'excellent' food.

((3 **Parsenn** (416 3232) Right opposite the Parsenn railway in Dorf. An attractive chalet marred by the big McDonald's on the ground floor.

((3 **Bahnhof Terminus** (413 2525) Friendly, three restaurants including a great Chinese, good sauna, right by bus stop in Platz.

((3 **Berghotel Schatzalp** (415 5151) Converted sanatorium on the tree line 300m/1,000ft above Platz and reached by funicular (free to guests).

Davos

297

Downtown Davos is
no beauty →

Phone numbers
From elsewhere in
Switzerland add the
prefix 081.
From abroad use the
prefix +41 81.

ACTIVITIES

Indoor Artificial
skating rink, fitness
center, tennis,
squash, swimming,
sauna, film theater,
museums, galleries,
libraries, massage,
badminton, golf-
driving range
Outdoor Over
80km/50 miles of
cleared paths (mostly
at valley level), snow-
shoe trekking, full-
moon skiing,
toboggan run, snow
volleyball, natural
skating rink, curling,
horse-riding, mule-
trekking, sleigh rides,
hang-gliding,
paragliding

TOURIST OFFICE

Postcode CH-7270
t +41 (81) 415 2121
f 415 2100
davos@davos.ch
www.davos.ch

② **Alte Post** (413 5403) Traditional and cozy; in central Platz. Popular with boarders.
② **Hubli's Landhaus** (417 1010) 5km/3 miles out at Laret, towards Klosters. Quiet country inn with sophisticated, expensive food.
① **Snowboarder's Palace** Close to Schatzalp lift, offers good-value dormitory accommodations.

EATING OUT
Wide choice, mostly in hotels
Most of the better restaurants are in hotels. The Davoserhof's two restaurants are among the best in town, both for food and ambience. There is a choice of two good Chinese restaurants – the lavish Zauberberg in the Europe and the Goldener Drachen in the Bahnhof Terminus.

Good-value places include the Pizzeria Al Ponte, La Carretta (good for home-made pasta) and the small and cozy Gentiana (with an upstairs stübli). An evening excursion for dinner out of town is popular. Schatzalp (reached by a funicular), the Schneider and Landhaus in Frauenkirch have also been recommended.

APRES-SKI
Lots to offer, but quiet clientele
There are plenty of bars, discos and nightclubs, and a large casino in the hotel Europe. But we're not sure how some of them make a living – Davos guests tend to want the quiet life. At tea-time, mega-calories are consumed at the Weber, and Scala has a popular outside terrace.

The liveliest place in town is the rustic little Chämi bar (popular with locals); it has 'the best atmosphere later in the evening', according to one of this year's reporters. The Ex Bar is a smart mixture of Parisienne Brasserie

with a touch of Pancho Villa and attracts a mixed age group.

Nightclubs tend to be sophisticated, expensive and lacking atmosphere during the week. The most popular are the Cabanna (in the hotel Europe), the Rotliechtli, Cava Grischa, Millennium! Bar Senn and for live music Grand-Café.

Bolgenschanze and Bolgen are popular boarder hang-outs.

OFF THE SLOPES
Great apart from the buildings
Provided you're not fussy about building style, Davos can be unreservedly recommended for off-slope fun. The towny resort has shops and other diversions, and transport along the valley and up onto the slopes is good – though the best of the mountain restaurants are well out of range for pedestrians. The sports facilities are excellent; the natural ice rink is said to be Europe's biggest, and is supplemented by artificial rinks, both indoor and outdoor.

Spectator sports include speed skating as well as hockey (most noteworthy is the Spengler Cup held in December). And there are lots of walks up on the slopes as well as around the lake and along the valleys.

Klosters 1190m/3,900ft

In a word association game, Klosters might trigger 'Prince of Wales'. The world's TV screens have shown him skiing there countless times. In 1988 he was almost killed there in an off-trail avalanche on the Gotschnawang slope that did kill one of his companions, and now the enlarged tram to Gotschna – which takes you to the Parsenn area shared with Davos – is named after him.

Don't be put off. We don't know why HRH likes to ski in Klosters particularly, but it is certainly not because the place is the exclusive territory of royalty. Most of the really smart socializing goes on behind closed doors, in private chalets.

THE RESORT

Klosters is a comfortable, quiet village with a much more appealing Alpine flavour than Davos, despite its lower altitude. Klosters Platz is the main focus – a collection of upscale, traditional-style hotels around the railway station, at the foot of the steep, wooded slopes of Gotschna. The road to Davos passes through, and traffic is a problem (although they are building a bypass).

The village spreads along the valley road for quite a way before fading into the countryside; there's then a second concentration of building in the even quieter village of Klosters Dorf.

THE MOUNTAIN

Slopes A tram takes you to the Gotschnagrat end of the Parsenn area and a gondola from Klosters Dorf takes you up to the scenic Madrisa area.

Snow reliability It's usually reliable higher up but can be poor lower down – you may have to take the lifts down after using the Parsenn slopes.

Snowboarding Boarders are better off staying in Davos since Jakobshorn is the established boarder mountain.

Experts The off-trail possibilities are the main appeal for experts.

Intermediates There are excellent cruising runs in all five ski areas – see in particular the feature box on the Parsenn's super-runs.

Beginners There are some beginners' lifts at valley level, but the wide sunny slopes of Madrisa are more appealing.

Cross-country There are 35km/22 miles of trails and a Nordic ski school offers lessons.

Liftlines Lines for the Gotschna tram have been reduced by a doubling of its capacity, but can still be a problem on weekends. A reporter tells of hour-long lines at the beginning of the day.

Mountain restaurants There are a number of atmospheric huts in the woods above the village – the Conterser Schwendi is particularly recommended for its 'excellent' food.

Schools and guides There is a choice of three ski and snowboard schools, and Klosters is well known for excellent mountain guides.

Facilities for children The ski schools offer classes for children from the age of four.

STAYING THERE

Hotels There are some particularly attractive hotels – all bookable on the central reservations phone number, 410 2020. The central Chesa Grischuna (422 2222) is irresistible, combining traditional atmosphere with modern comfort – and a lively après-ski bar. The Cresta (422 2525) is a popular 3-star described as 'very pleasant and friendly' by a reporter this year.

The less central but very cozy Wynegg (422 1340) is popular with British visitors, with good-value bedrooms. The Sport hotel in Dorf (423 3030) has also been recommended.

Eating out Good restaurants abound, but a reporter comments that there is a shortage of the cheap and cheerful variety. Top of the price bracket for eating out is the Walserhof, while Alberto's is the best pizzeria in town. The Chesa Selfranga is 20 minutes' walk from the center of town, but is noted for fondue, both cheese and Chinoise.

Après-ski In the village, the Chesa Grischuna is a focus of activity from tea-time onwards, with its piano bar, bowling and restaurant. A reporter advises that drinks are much cheaper at the Gotschnastübli. The newly rebuilt hotel Vereina is recommended for its piano bar.

Gaudy's at the foot of the slopes is a popular pit stop after skiing, as is the lively bar at the four-star Alpina and the warmly panelled Wynegg.

In the late evening the bar of the hotel Kaiser is popular. The Casa Antica is a small but popular disco – though a reporter this year found only four people there at 11.30 on a Friday night in February. The Kir Royale, under the hotel Silvretta Park, is bigger and more brash. The Funny Place, under the Piz Buin, is more grown-up and expensive.

Off the slopes Klosters is an attractive base for walking and cross-country skiing. There is a sport and leisure center, and some hotels have pools – the pool and spa/fitness room at the Vereina were available for use by non-residents at a charge of 60 swiss francs per day in 2000/01. An excursion by train to the spa at Scuol Tarasp is recommended by one reporter.

A splendid, spacious area that deserves to be better known

HOW IT RATES

The slopes

Snow	★★★
Extent	★★★★
Experts	★★★
Intermediates	★★★★★
Beginners	★★★★
Convenience	★★★
Liftlines	★★★
Restaurants	★★★

The rest

Scenery	★★★
Resort charm	★★★
Off-slope	★★★

- ⊕ Extensive, varied slopes suitable for all but experts
- ⊕ Impressive lift system
- ⊕ Virtually liftline-free on weekdays
- ⊕ Fair number of slopes above 2000m/6,500ft, partly offsetting effects of their sunny orientation
- ⊕ Lots of wooded runs for bad-weather days
- ⊕ Just 90 minutes from Zürich airport

- ⊖ Though well intentioned, the unique trail grading system is confusing
- ⊖ Sunny orientation can cause icy or slushy trails and shut lower runs
- ⊖ Buses or long walks to lifts from many of the accommodations
- ⊖ Very subdued in the evenings
- ⊖ Village very spread out, which detracts from its charm
- ⊖ Weekend crowds

Flims/Laax has an impressive 220km/137 miles of mainly intermediate trails. The resort is very popular with weekenders and has some high-capacity lifts which help it cope. It can be very quiet during the week, and is virtually unknown outside the Swiss and German markets. It deserves better. Don't be put off by the unfortunate (for English-speakers) local name for 'peak', which is 'crap'. All the mountain-tops are called crap, a top après-ski venue is the Crap Bar and the tourist office has used the slogan 'Flims is crap' in promotions.

There are very long runs, ideal for adventurous intermediates, amid stunning scenery. And there's plenty to play around on in all areas. For us there have always been two main drawbacks: a sunny orientation which can spoil the snow on the lower part of the mountain, and the lack of real Alpine charm in the villages. Now there's a third: their new trail map uses a unique classification system unlike any other we have seen. Formerly black and red runs have become green (to signify 'Allround Slope'), red now means 'Freestyle Slope', off-trail areas are shaded yellow, black diamonds have appeared. Confused? We are.

What's new

A new Slope System trail map has been introduced which uses a unique trail grading system unlike any other we've seen. It may be okay when you've got used to it. But at first sight it is confusing.

For 2000/01 a Pipe & Park ticket and limited area beginners' ticket were introduced. The snowboard park on Crap Sogn Gion got a new lift, the children's Dreamlands was extended and a second Riders Palace opened at Murschetg. Another New Technology Center – see The Resort section – opened in Falera. And you can now view and book rental apartments on the website.

The resort

Flims is made up of two parts nearly a mile apart on a sunny, wooded mountain terrace. Dorf sprawls along a busy road lined with shops, hotels, restaurants, bars and the main lift station. Waldhaus is a sophisticated, sedate huddle of hotels quietly set in the trees. Both parts look traditional, with wooden chalet-style buildings.

The slopes spread across the mainly south-east-facing mountain to another lift base-station at Murschetg (1.5km/1 mile from Waldhaus), an outpost of Laax. From here there's an efficient jumbo gondola and a less efficient tram – this is the easiest entry point for those with cars. There's also a high-speed quad at Falera, 5km/3 miles from Waldhaus.

Most hotels are a bus-ride from the slopes but a combination of resort, hotel and post buses works well.

New Technology Centers, now at all three lift bases, offer a package of ski clothing and equipment rental by the day – turn up in city clothes and get all you need from SF115, including lift ticket and a shower after you finish.

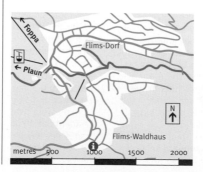

Foppa
Flims-Dorf
Plaun
Flims-Waldhaus
metres 500 1000 1500 2000
N

The mountains

Flims has extensive, underrated, varied slopes: some long runs and some high, exposed peaks (which can be very windswept), including a small glacier.

MOUNTAIN FACTS

Altitude 1100m-3020m
3,610ft-9,910ft

Lifts	28
Trails	220km
	137 miles
Blue	29%
Red	45%
Black	26%

(% refers to old map
and conventional
color gradings – see
right for new system)

Snowmaking   13km
8 miles

Recco detectors used

LIFT TICKETS

2000/01 prices in
Swiss francs

Alpine Arena
Covers all lifts and
buses between Flims,
Laax and Falera.

Main ticket
1-day ticket 59
6-day ticket 301

Senior citizens
Over 65 (men) or 62
(women): 6-day ticket
241

Children
Under 18: 6-day ticket
241
Under 13: 6-day ticket
151
Under 6: free ticket

Short-term tickets
Half day from 12.15
(adult 48).

Alternative tickets
One day Pipe & Park
ticket for Crap Sogn
Gion 35.
Beginner tickets for
limited lifts in Flims,
Laax (both 35) and
Falera (30).

Notes Free Alpine
Arena Clubcards can
get you discounts on
tickets – register on
the internet at
www.alpenarena.ch/
clubcard/eng/register.
htm or in resort. You
need a Clubcard to
claim senior citizen or
child lift ticket
discounts. You get
extra points on the
Clubcard when you
spend money in the
Alpine Arena, which
can be exchanged for
further discounts.

Because of its sunny aspect, lower runs can deteriorate quickly making it difficult to get back to Flims on snow (there is some snowmaking). In poor visibility there are plenty of tree-lined runs. Trips are possible to Lenzerheide, Davos–Klosters and Arosa.

Flims now grades its slopes according to its own innovative system: yellow for 'backcountry' (or off-trail), red for 'freestyle', blue for 'beginner' and green for 'allround'. Difficult slopes are indicated by black diamonds – two for difficult and three for very difficult. So, for instance, the formerly black Sattel run from the Vorab glacier is marked green with two black diamonds. Useful once you understand, but rather open to confusion. One of our reporters certainly had trouble: 'Undoubtedly the most confusing map ever – grading verges on dangerous.' In our map, we have continued to use the conventional grading of the resort's previous trail map.

The new map does, however, show the time it takes to ride each lift – an excellent idea that makes meeting others on time very easy – and marks some flattish trails as 'traverses'.

THE SLOPES
Impressive and well planned

There are essentially four sectors, each good for all grades but expert. Slopes are well planned, and getting around is easy but can mean a lot of traversing.

The gondola from Flims has two mid-stations, the first at Plaun, where you change cabins or catch a fast six-person chair to **Crap Sogn Gion** at the heart of the Laax slopes. From here you can go towards Murschetg, Laax or Falera or catch a tram up to **Crap Masegn**. This is the biggest area.

If, instead, you continue in the gondola there's another mid-station at Scansinas before the top at Nagens – alighting at either will allow you to get over to **La Siala,** from where there's a run to the high **Vorab glacier.**

There is also a link via a two-way, two-stage gondola (which can be closed by wind) between the Vorab glacier and Crap Masegn. And there's a slope linking Crap Masegn with Plaun.

The **Cassons** sector above Flims Dorf is the smallest, particularly when runs to the village are incomplete. It is reached via two chairs and a tram and linked to Nagens and Grauberg.

SNOW RELIABILITY
Good higher up

The upper runs are generally snow-sure. But due to the sunny aspect, the runs back to Flims itself can suffer. There is snowmaking on three main runs from Crap Sogn Gion, including the splendid black race course run right down to Murschetg. There is also snowmaking from Segnes-Hütte to Flims and on the bottom part of the run to Alp Ruschein.

FOR EXPERTS
Bits and pieces

There is a fair amount to challenge, but it's rather scattered here and there, with the added frustration that some of it is on short sections of otherwise easy trails. The toughest run is the steep, ungroomed Cassons run to the bottom of its cable car, reached by a steep climb from the top of the tram. Other off-trail trips from this summit might look tempting, but we'd recommend hiring a guide (they get three black diamonds on the new trail map). Throughout the area the off-trail is generally between trails (and is now marked in yellow on the trail map).

One of the great pleasures of the area is the men's World Cup Downhill course (formerly a black run, now marked green on the trail map) from Crap Sogn Gion to Murschetg. It's so long (1000m/3,300ft vertical) and pretty that doing it repeatedly using

boarding *Flims/Laax is a snowboard hot spot. Crap Sogn Gion is a popular meeting point, with plenty of loud music from the outdoor Rock Bar and the No-Name Café, which overlook two of four half-pipes on the mountain – their walls can be built to an amazing 6.7m/22ft with the worldbeating Pipe Monster. A Pipe & Park day ticket is available if that's all you're into, but the slopes are well suited to all levels of rider. As the slopes close, the Crap Bar at Murschetg is popular. The Arena in Flims is good for live gigs. The Riders Palaces in Murschetg and Mountain Hostel up the mountain at Crap Sogn Gion have great value accommodations. Flims/Laax also hosts lots of international snowboarding events.*

the Murschetg tram doesn't get boring. And the Sattel trail from Vorab – see For Intermediates – is long and beautiful. The Nagens–Startgels run is short but steep.

FOR INTERMEDIATES
Paradise for all
In general this is a superb area for all intermediates. When conditions allow, the area just above Flims is splendid for easy cruising. But a real highlight for early intermediates is a trip to the Vorab glacier and back on easy intermediate runs. On the way back you can take the tram down from Grauberg to Startgels to avoid steeper slopes.

For more adventurous intermediates there's a wonderful descent of over 1700m/5,6ooft vertical if you start at La Siala and go all the way down to Flims. One of the two ungroomed runs from Cassons is a lovely trip along the shoulder of the mountain into a valley and on to Startgels – but check snow conditions first and be warned, there's a hike to get to it. The run from Crap Sogn Gion to Larnags via Curnius is also great fun.

Good intermediates will enjoy the superb, long and beautiful Sattel run from the glacier to Ruschein at the extreme west of the area. It starts with a challenging bump field but develops into a fast cruise.

The Crap Sogn Gion to Plaun routes are interesting, being quite steep and sheltered – and are some of the few runs not to directly face the sun.

Less confident intermediates should note that some easy runs have short steep sections. The links from Nagens towards Flims can be intimidating.

FOR BEGINNERS
Plenty of options
There's a good beginner area in Dorf, and alternatives at Startgels and Nagens if snow is poor. The Foppa and Naraus areas have good confidence-building runs to move on to. Getting the bus to the lovely easy runs above Falera is another option for those just off the beginner areas. There are plenty of lessons in English.

FOR CROSS-COUNTRY
One of the best
An excellent choice. There are 70km/43 miles of beautiful, well marked, mainly forest trails. Loops range from 3km/2 miles to 20km/12 miles. Another fine 60km/37 miles network starts near Laax. The ski school, centered at Waldhaus, has a good reputation and organizes group classes. 3km/2 miles of trail are floodlit. The only drawback is the possibility of poor snow.

LIFTLINES
Some delays
There is generally little waiting during the week, but we have had a report of long waits for the Cassons, Crap Sogn Gion and Crap Masegn trams. On weekends, with coach loads of day visitors arriving at Murschetg, the lifts there get crowded. But delays out of Flims in the morning are rare. The chair

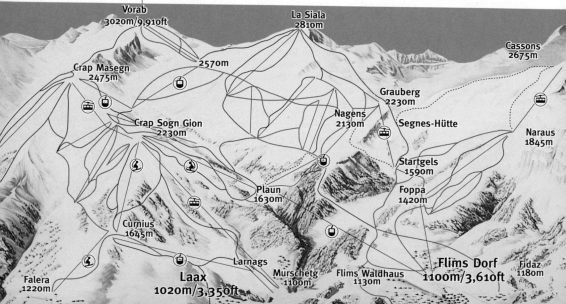

Trust snowboarders to try to ruin your photo of one of the bars outside Crap Sogn Gion →

SWISS-IMAGE / MOUNTAIN MARKETING AG

Phone numbers
From elsewhere in Switzerland add the prefix 081.
From abroad use the prefix +41 81.

GETTING THERE

Air Zürich, transfer 1½hr.

Rail Chur (22km/14 miles); regular buses to resort.

SCHOOLS/GUIDES

2000/01 prices in Swiss francs

Swiss
Classes 5 days 4hr
5 full days: 350
Children's classes
Ages: up to 12
5 full days: 350 with lunch
Private lessons
Full day 320

CHILDCARE

The ski school runs ski kindergartens (Dreamlands) taking children from age 4 – in Flims, Laax and Falera from 9.30 to 11.30 and 1.30 to 3.30.

Several hotels claim special facilities for children – the Park Hotel Waldhaus has its own nursery.

towards La Siala can generate lines, as can the slow two-person Alp Ruschein chair and some T-bars. Lifts closing because of wind (especially up to Cassons) has been a common complaint among reporters.

MOUNTAIN RESTAURANTS
Good, wide selection
Mountain restaurants are numerous and generally good. The large cafeterias at Curnius, Sogn Gion and Vorab are clean, efficient and serve good wholesome food. Nagens has a place with great views, a sun terrace and live music, but the nicest refuges are lower down, such as The Spaligna below Foppa and the Startgels Hütte above Foppa. We had a great lunch (with electronic ordering) in the rustic Tegia by the Murschetg gondola mid-station at Larnags. The Runcahöhe, where the Stretg trail flattens out and crosses the path down from Startgels, is another good cozy cabin. For a more expensive menu the restaurant at Crap Masegn is highly recommended.

SCHOOLS AND GUIDES
Plenty of English lessons
The school has a good reputation and standards of English are reported to be good too. They offer Early Bird specials on empty trails followed by breakfast – a great North American concept not generally available in Europe.

FACILITIES FOR CHILDREN
Good Dreamland centers
Children aged three and over (skiers or not) can be looked after at one of three Dreamland centers in Dorf, Murschetg and Falera. The facilities are to be extended for 2001/02, but there

were no details as we went to press. For children under three the resort can recommend qualified nannies.

Staying there

It may seem best to stay near the lifts in Dorf, but in practice the better hotels in Waldhaus (and remote bits of Dorf) run efficient courtesy buses to and from the slopes. These satisfy most guests, especially as there's not much to tempt you into town after dinner.

HOW TO GO
Few tour operators
Only a handful of tour operators feature Flims.
Hotels The majority are either 3-star or simple B&B places. Of six top hotels, five are in Waldhaus.
((((⑤ **Park** (928 4848) Enormous and very comfortable, but rather institutional, 5-star in wooded grounds at Waldhaus. Efficient courtesy bus. Pool.
(((④ **Adula** (928 2828) Big 4-star in Waldhaus, highly recommended by recent reporters. Good pool. 'Superb food and service,' says reporter.
(((④ **Sunstar Surselva** (911 1121) Part of the reliable Sunstar chain but run in a rather more institutionalized way than most. Quiet situation in Waldhaus with excellent new spa facilities.
((③ **Grischuna** (911 1139) Pretty little 3-star just outside Dorf, close to lifts.
((③ **Cresta** (911 3535) Rave review: 'Helpful staff, fabulous spa facilities and food, unpretentious family hotel.'
((③ **Curtgin** (911 3566) Attractive, quiet place on edge of town, quite near lifts.
((③ **Albana Sporthotel** (911 2333) Modern 3-star beside lifts, with focal après-ski bar.

Flims

303

Phone numbers
From elsewhere in
Switzerland add the
prefix 081.
From abroad use the
prefix +41 81.

ACTIVITIES

Indoor Large public
swimming pool and
over 20 hotel pools
(many open to the
public), saunas, 4
indoor tennis courts,
covered hall with ice
skating and 4 curling
rinks, fitness centers
(including Prau La
Selva), table tennis,
whirlpool, solarium
Outdoor 60km/37
miles of cleared
paths, riding, natural
skating rinks, curling,
sleigh rides, toboggan
runs, ski-bob,
paragliding, hot-air
ballooning, hang-
gliding, snow-
shoeing, helicopter
flights and night
skiing

TOURIST OFFICE

Postcode CH-7017
t +41 (81) 920 9200
f 920 9201
tourismus@alpen
arena.ch
www.alpenarena.ch

((C3)) **Waldeck** (911 1228) Neat 3-star in
Waldhaus, with pleasant restaurant.
Apartments/condos The tourist office
has a long list of available apartments,
which you can view and book on the
website.

EATING OUT
Varied options
Most Flims restaurants are in hotels.
The National, by the bus station, has
good fish dishes. The Meiler hotel
restaurant also has a good reputation.
For something a bit different, go up to
the Spaligna mountain restaurant and
use the toboggan run to get home.
Little China is a good Chinese, and the
Alpina Garni (Waldhaus) is very good
value, does good pizzas and is 'busy
and fun', says a recent reporter.

APRES-SKI
Not a strong point
Flims is very quiet après-ski. The
Spaligna trip mentioned under Eating
Out is the highlight of the week. The
Iglou bar at the base of the Flims
gondola is packed when the slopes
close, as is the Stenna-Bar, opposite,
which has a tea dance. Just across the
road the Albana Pub is popular with a
young crowd. Later, the focal spot is
also in Dorf, at the hotel Bellevue's
Caverna, an atmospheric old wine
vault. The Angel is a late-night club.
The Park hotel is the center of limited
action in Waldhaus, having an old
cellar with entertainer, and the Chadafo
bar with dancing to live music. At
Murschetg, the Crap Bar is lively when
the slopes close and Casa Veglia has
live bands and dancing.

OFF THE SLOPES
Lots to do
There are plenty of things to do. The
enormous sports center has a huge
range of activities, including shooting –
and 'guest cards' from hotels and the
tourist office provide a discount. Flims
also has some of the best and most
extensive (60km/37 miles) marked
walks of any winter resort, some into
and through the ski areas. Historic
Chur is a short bus-ride away. Other
good trips are to the impressive church
at Zillis, and to the Rhine canyon,
which is nature at its best. The Glacier
Express train from Chur to Andermatt
takes you through some wonderful
scenery.

STAYING UP THE MOUNTAIN
Hostel St John
The Crap Sogn Gion Mountain Hostel,
1100m/3,600ft above Murschetg in the
center of the slopes, has budget 4-
bedded rooms as well as single and
double. You can also stay above Flims
in the more traditional Berghaus
Nagens.

Laax 1020m/3,350ft

Laax is a quiet, spacious old farming
community which has retained a lot of
its original character. Most of its
modern development has taken place
a short bus-ride away at Murschetg, a
modern, functional complex at the
base of the lifts. The oldest house in
Laax dates from 1615, and the setting
is pleasant enough, but the old village
is no more than routinely charming.
   Laax has its own school and ski
kindergarten.
   The Laaxerhof (920 8200) and
Signina (927 9000) are Murschetg 4-
stars. The 4-star Arena Alva (927 2727)
is a more attractive building in the old
village, with transport to the lifts. The
charming, central old Posta Veglia (921
4466) has a lively stubli and piano bar.
A good central B&B is the Cathomen
(921 4545). The two Riders Palaces
(927 9000) offer dormitory
accommodations at a bargain price at
the base station.
   Restaurants and bars are mostly
hotel-based. The Laaxer Bündnerstuben
in the Posta Veglia is best for a meal
in traditional surroundings. The limited
nightlife centers around the Bistro Bar
in the Capricorn hotel, live music in the
Vallarosa Bar or Laaxerhof and, again,
the Posta Veglia. At Murschetg the
Crap Bar gets packed when the lifts
close – popular with snowboarders.

Falera 1220m/4,000ft

Along the road from Flims, beyond
Laax, lies the tiny village of Falera, a
quiet traffic-free place, with two old
churches. Sitting on a sunny plateau, it
has good views over three valleys. Two
successive fast quad chairs take you to
the heart of the slopes.
   Accommodations are mostly in
apartments, but La Siala (927 2222) is
a large 3-star hotel with pool. Its
Spielkeller is the only real nightspot.

Grindelwald 1035m/3,400ft

Traditional mountain town in spectacular scenery

HOW IT RATES

The slopes

Snow	**
Extent	***
Experts	**
Intermediates	*****
Beginners	***
Convenience	**
Liftlines	**
Restaurants	***

The rest

Scenery	*****
Resort charm	****
Off-slope	****

➕ Dramatically set in magnificent scenery directly beneath the towering north face of the Eiger

➕ Lots of long, gentle runs, ideal for intermediates, with links to Wengen

➕ Pleasant old village with long mountaineering history, though the tourist trade now sets the tone

➕ Fair amount to do off the slopes, including splendid walks and recently expanded toboggan runs

➖ Village gets very little midwinter sun

➖ Few challenging trails for experts

➖ Inconvenient for visiting Mürren

➖ Snow-cover unreliable

➖ Major area accessed by a slow gondola, liftline-prone especially on weekends, and by very slow and infrequent trains – life revolves around timetables

For stunning views from your hotel window and from the trails, there are few places to rival Grindelwald, and two of them are just over the hill. The village is nowhere near as special as Wengen or Mürren, but staying here does give you direct access to Grindelwald's own First area. But you can spend hours waiting for or sitting in the gondola or trains up into the Kleine Scheidegg area shared with Wengen. (The gondola ride takes over half an hour.) Grindelwald regulars accept all this as part of the scene, and some elderly skiers even find it adds to the holiday by enforcing a slow pace.

The resort

MOUNTAIN FACTS

Altitude	945m-2970m
	3,100ft-9,740ft
Lifts	45
Trails	205km
	127 miles
Blue	30%
Red	50%
Black	20%
Snowmaking	30km
	19 miles
Recco detectors used	

Grindelwald is set either side of the road along the foot of a narrow valley. Buildings are primarily traditional Swiss-chalet style. Towering mountains rise steeply from the valley floor, and the resort and main slopes get very little sun in January.

Grindelwald can feel very convivial at times, such as during the ice-carving festival in January, when large and beautiful tableaux are on display along the main street. The village is livelier at night than the other Jungfrau resorts of Wengen and Mürren. There's live music in several bars and hotels, but it isn't a place for dancing until dawn.

The major lifts into the slopes shared with Wengen are at Grund, right at the bottom of the sloping village. Near the opposite end of the village, a gondola goes up to the separate First area. There are trains between the center and Grund, and shuttle-buses linking the lift stations – but these get congested at times.

The most convenient place to stay for the slopes is at Grund. But this is out of the center and rather charmless. There's a wide range of hotels in the heart of the village, handy enough for everything else, including the First area, at the foot of which are beginner

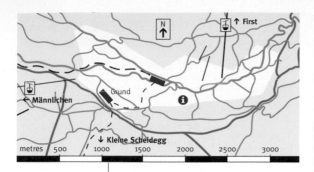

LIFT TICKETS

2000/01 prices in Swiss francs

Jungfrau Top Ski Region
Covers all lifts in Wengen, Mürren and Grindelwald, trains between them and Grindelwald ski-bus.

Beginners Points card (adult 100 points 48, lifts cost 4 to 10 points).

Main ticket
1-day ticket 52
6-day ticket 254

Senior citizens
Over 62: 6-day ticket 229

Children
16 to 19: 6-day ticket 203
Under 16: 6-day ticket 127
Under 6: 6-day ticket 25

Short-term tickets
Single ascent tickets for most lifts. Half-day ticket available for each of First, Kleine Scheidegg-Männlichen and Mürren-Schilthorn (adult 40).

Alternative periods
3 days in 7 ticket is available (156).

Notes Day ticket price is for Kleine Scheidegg-Männlichen area only (102km/63 miles of trails, 21 lifts), as Jungfrau Top Ski Region ticket is only available for 2 days or over.

Alternative tickets
1- and 2-day tickets available for each of First, Mürren-Schilthorn and Kleine Scheidegg-Männlichen (adult 2-day 95).

areas, ski school and kindergarten.

Trips to other resorts are not very easy, but you can drive to Adelboden. Getting to the tougher, higher slopes of Mürren is a lengthy business unless you go to Lauterbrunnen by car.

The mountains

The major area shared with Wengen offers a mix of wooded slopes and open slopes higher up. The smaller First area is mainly open, though there are wooded runs to the village.

THE SLOPES
Broad and mainly gentle
From Grund, near the western end of town, you can get to **Männlichen** by an appallingly slow two-stage gondola or to **Kleine Scheidegg** by an even slower cog railway. The slopes of the separate south-facing First area are reached by a long, slow three-stage gondola starting a bus-ride east of the center. From all over the slopes there are superb views, not only of the Eiger but also of the Wetterhorn and other peaks. Trail marking is poor, and one reporter complains that from First it is difficult to determine which run you are on and therefore easy to end up at the wrong point in the valley, a bus-ride from where you want to be.

SNOW RELIABILITY
Poor
Grindelwald's low altitude (the slopes go down to below 1000m/3,300ft and few are above 2000m/6,600ft) and the lack of snowmaking mean this is not a

resort to book up months in advance. And it's not the place for a late-season holiday. First is sunny, and so even less snow-sure than the main area.

FOR EXPERTS
Very limited
The area is quite limited for experts. The black run on First beneath the gondola back to town is quite tough, especially when the snow has suffered from too much sun – late in the season, the run is one of the first to close. See also the Wengen chapter.

Heli-trips with mountain guides are organized if there are enough takers.

FOR INTERMEDIATES
Ideal intermediate terrain
In good snow, First makes a splendid intermediate playground, though the general lack of trees makes the area less friendly than the larger Kleine Scheidegg–Männlichen area, and many of the lifts are T-bars. The runs to the valley are great fun, but naturally popular in the afternoon. Nearly all the runs from Kleine Scheidegg are long blues or gentle reds. On the Männlichen there's a choice of gentle runs down to the mid-station of the gondola up from Grindelwald Grund. In good snow, you can get right down to the bottom on easy red runs – 'barely deserving the grade', says a reporter (and one of these runs used to be marked black).

For tougher trails, head for the top of the Lauberhorn lift and the runs to Kleine Scheidegg, or to Wixi (following the start of the downhill course). You could also try the north-facing run from Eigergletscher to Salzegg, which often has the best snow late in the season.

FOR BEGINNERS
In good snow, wonderful
The beginner area is friendly and scenic, just above the village, but in late season it can suffer from the sun and low altitude. There are splendid longer runs served by the railway to Kleine Scheidegg, notably the easy scenic blue Mettlen-Grund run, right from the top to the bottom.

boarding *This isn't prime boarder territory though there is a terrain-park and a half-pipe at Oberjoch on First. Intermediates will enjoy the area most – the beginners' slopes can be bare, while experts will hanker for the steep, off-trail slopes of Mürren. Nightlife caters mainly to the more affluent, middle-aged visitors.*

SCHOOLS/GUIDES

2000/01 prices in
Swiss francs

Swiss
Classes 5 days
4hr: 10am-noon and
2pm-4pm
5 full days: 214
Children's classes
Ages: 3 to 14
5 full days: 214
Private lessons
2½hr or 5hr
170 for 2½hr
288 for 5hr

CHILDCARE

The ski school takes
children from age 3,
and they can be
looked after at
lunchtime in the
Children's Club
kindergarten at the
Bodmi beginner
areas. This takes
children from age 3,
from 9.30 to 4pm. It
apparently ceases to
function if snow
shortage closes the
beginner areas.

The Sunshine nursery
on First takes children
from 1 month from
8.30-5pm.

From Kleine Scheidegg you can take a train through the heart of the Eiger to the highest railway station in Europe – Jungfraujoch at 3454m/11,332ft.

The journey itself is a bit tedious – you're in a tunnel most of the time. You stop part way up to look out of a viewing gallery carved into the sheer north face of the Eiger, with magnificent views down the valley and over to Männlichen. At the top is a big restaurant complex. There's a fascinating 'ice palace' carved in the glacier with beautiful ice sculptures and slippery walkways, an outdoor 'plateau' to wander around and a panoramic viewing tower called the Sphinx.

The return trip cost SF48 in 2000/01 if you had a Jungfrau lift ticket for three days or more, but around three times that if you didn't. Watch out for the effects of altitude. At these altitudes the air is thin, and we met people having breathing and balance problems.

FOR CROSS-COUNTRY
Good but shady
There are over 25km/16 miles of prepared tracks. Almost all of this is on the valley floor, so it's very shady in midwinter and may have poor snow later in the season.

LIFTLINES
Can be dreadful at peak times
The lines for the gondola and train at Grund can be very bad in high season, especially when weekend visitors pour in. One Christmas week reporter experienced half-hour waits for the Männlichen gondola last season. The popular Oberjoch chair-lift is a bottleneck. Lines for the rest of the upper lifts build up only when snow is short lower down. (The same Christmas visitor experienced 15-minute liftlines higher up and also reported long waits for the gondola back down from First as all the lower runs were closed.)

MOUNTAIN RESTAURANTS
Wide choice
See the Wengen chapter for restaurants around Kleine Scheidegg. Brandegg, on the railway, is recommended for its 'wonderful' apple fritters. Berghaus Bort does very good rösti, but the 'best rösti anywhere' is at the Jägerstubli, 500m/1,640ft up the road from the Aspen, off the Rennstrecke trail.

Grindelwald

307

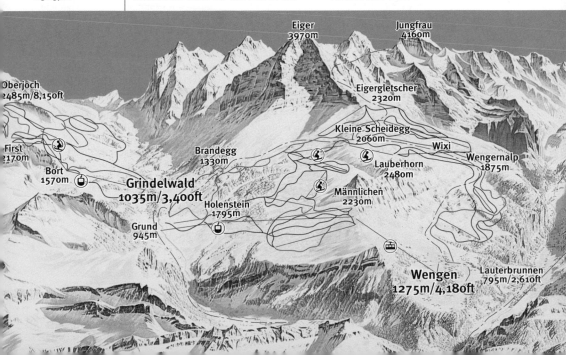

GETTING THERE

Air Zürich, transfer 3hr. Bern, transfer 1½hr.

Rail Station in resort.

Phone numbers
From elsewhere in Switzerland add the prefix 033.
From abroad use the prefix +41 33.

ACTIVITIES

Indoor Sports center (swimming pool, sauna, solarium, table tennis, fitness room, climbing room, games room), indoor skating rink, curling, bowling, movie theater
Outdoor 80km/50 miles of cleared paths, train rides to Jungfraujoch, tobogganing, snowshoe excursions, sleigh rides, paragliding, heli-skiing and boarding, open-air ice skating, snowrafting, glacier tours, devalkarts

TOURIST OFFICE

Postcode CH-3818
t +41 (33) 854 1212
f 854 1210
touristcenter@
grindelwald.ch
www.grindelwald.ch

SCHOOLS AND GUIDES
One of the better Swiss schools
A recent report declares the Swiss school 'very good'; spoken English is normally excellent. It now has some competition in the form of private lessons from the Buri Sport school.

FACILITIES FOR CHILDREN
Good reputation
A past reporter who put four children through the Grindelwald mill praised caring and effective instructors, and a recent reporter rates them 'brilliant'. The First mountain restaurant runs a day nursery, which is a neat idea.

Staying there

HOW TO GO
Something for every budget
Traditional little B&B pensions and apartments are widely available to those who book independently.
Hotels One 5-star, a dozen 4-stars, and a good range of more modest places are available.
(((((5) **Regina** (854 8600) The one 5-star. Big and imposing; right next to the railway station. Nightly music in the bar. Pool.
(((4) **Belvedere** (854 5454) Family-run, recently renovated, close to station and with a 'wonderful' pool.
(((4) **Schweizerhof** (853 2202) Beautifully decorated 4-star chalet at west end of center, close to station. Pool.
(((4) **Bodmi** (853 1220) Little chalet right on the village beginner areas.
(((3) **Hirschen** (854 8484) Family-run 3-star in central position at foot of beginner areas. Good food. Security can be a problem – one recent visitor had skis stolen from the ski room.
(((3) **Fiescherblick** (854 5353) Hospitable chalet on eastern fringe of village, five minutes from the First gondola.
(((3) **Derby** (854 5461) Popular, modern 3-star next to station, with 'first-class' service, good food and great views.
((2) **Tschuggen** (853 1781) Modest chalet in central position below beginner areas.
(1) **Hotel Wetterhorn** (853 1218) Cozy, simple chalet way beyond the village, with great views of the glacier.
Apartments/condos One independent reporter recommended the apartments of the hotel Hirschen for comfort and space.

EATING OUT
Hotel based
There's a wide choice of good hotel restaurants, but cheaper pizzeria-style places are in short supply. The Latino does home-made Italian cooking. Among the more attractively traditional places are: the Swiss Chalet in the Eiger; Schmitte in the Schweizerhof; Challi-Stübli in the Kreuz; and the Alte Post. The Fiescherblick's Swiss Bistro is repeatedly recommended – 'brilliant but expensive'. The Kirchbühl and Oberland are good for vegetarians, the Bahnhof in the Derby for fondue and raclette. Hotel Spinne has many options: Italian, Mexican, Chinese and the candlelit Rôtisserie for a special romantic meal.

APRES-SKI
Relaxed
A delightful way to end the day is to have a drink or two at Kleine Scheidegg before skiing home. Nightlife is not the special subject of our reporters, but we can say that there are at least three discos and a handful of bars that aim to keep going late. There's also a movie theater, plus ice hockey and curling matches to watch. There's an excellent sports center with pool. Tobogganing and tubing are organized on First, and Thursday to Friday a 'Sledge Express' train takes people up to Brandegg/Alpiglen for fondues and tobogganing.

OFF THE SLOPES
Plenty to do, easy to get around
There are many cleared paths with magnificent views, especially around the First area – and there's a special (though expensive) pedestrian bus/lift ticket. A trip to Jungfraujoch is spectacular (see previous page), and excursions by train are easy to Interlaken and possible to Bern. Tobogganing has recently undergone a bit of a renaissance, with runs up 15km/9 miles on First (Europe's longest) and 70km/43 miles of runs in total. Helicopter flights from Männlichen are recommended.

STAYING UP THE MOUNTAIN
Several possibilities
See the Wengen chapter for details of rooms at Kleine Scheidegg. The Berghaus Bort (853 1762), at the gondola station in the middle of the First area (1570m/5,160ft), is an attractive alternative.

Gstaad

Surprisingly unpretentious, with extensive, pretty slopes

HOW IT RATES

The slopes

Snow	*
Extent	****
Experts	**
Intermediates	***
Beginners	***
Convenience	*
Liftlines	***
Restaurants	***

The rest

Scenery	***
Resort charm	****
Off-slope	****

➕ Traditional village, traffic-free in center, without the towny feel of other fashionable Swiss resorts

➕ Lift ticket covers large area of slopes

➕ Good long runs for intermediates

➕ Lively après-ski scene

➕ Wide range of off-slope diversions, including swanky shops

➖ Fragmented slopes, none convenient for central hotels – so you are always using buses and trains

➖ Unreliable snow-cover, except on the limited (and distant) Diablerets glacier slopes

➖ No budget accommodations

➖ Few challenges for experts

Gstaad is renowned as a jet-set resort, but for 'ordinary' holidaymakers, too, it has attractions – especially for those with a relaxed outlook, who can happily spend time on trains looking at the landscape without feeling it's precious trail time wasted.

What's new

Last season saw further improvements to the glacier lifts – the Mazot-Meilleret and Scex-Rouge chairlifts are the latest lifts to have been upgraded.

MOUNTAIN FACTS

Altitude	950m-3000m
	3,120ft-9,840ft
Lifts	67
Trails	250km
	155 miles
Blue	48%
Red	36%
Black	16%
Snowmaking	12km
	7 miles

THE RESORT

Gstaad is a traditional, year-round resort in a spacious, sunny setting surrounded by a horseshoe of wooded mountains. The main street, lined with hotels, smart shops and cafes, has a pleasant and relaxed feel now that it's traffic-free. The Montreux–Oberland–Bernois (MOB) railway station is only yards away, and accesses the numerous surrounding villages. These are smaller (and cheaper), and with their own lifts form good alternative bases to Gstaad itself. Three areas of slopes are accessed via lifts scattered around the fringes of Gstaad and served by a regular shuttle-bus service.

THE MOUNTAINS

There are four main areas of slopes, covered by a single map that is a confusing mess. Most of the slopes are below the tree line, with just the top sections reaching above that.
Slopes Wasserngrat (to the east of the village) and Wispile (to the south) are both small areas with one or two main lifts and runs alongside them. Eggli (to the west) is more complex, and leads via the valley of Chalberhöni to the crags of Videmanette, also accessible by gondola from the rustic village of Rougemont, just over the border into French-speaking Switzerland.

The fourth and largest sector is accessed from the lift stations at Saanenmöser and Schönried. The slopes here have for years been linked with those above St Stephan, over the mountain, and more recently have been linked to those above

Zweisimmen. Saanenmöser and Schönried are no more inconvenient than Gstaad's local lift stations, given a train timetable. Schönried also has a separate sunny area of slopes on the opposite side of the valley.

The Glacier des Diablerets is covered by the local area ticket but is 15km/9 miles away to the south, with lifts at Reusch and Col du Pillon. There are excellent runs below glacier level, but the glacier itself is limited. Slightly further afield, past Rougemont, but

Gummfluh and La Videmanette (on the right) introduce a bit of drama into the landscape ↓

included on the map and connected by rail, are Château d'Oex and Les Moulins – both with their own small ski areas.

Snowboarding There's a terrain-park at Eggli and a half-pipe at Zweisimmen.

Snow reliability A lack of altitude means that snow-cover can be unreliable except on the glacier, but most of the slopes are roughly north-facing and there is now quite a lot of artificial snowmaking.

Experts Few runs challenge experts. Black runs rarely exceed red difficulty, and some should be blue. There are off-trail possibilities – steep ones on the wooded flanks of Wispile and Eggli.

Intermediates Given good snow, this is a superb area for intermediates, with long, easy descents in the major area to the villages dotted around its edges – that to St Stephan being rather more challenging than most. The run to Rougemont from the top of the Eggli sector is lovely, with no lifts in view. The adventurous should take a trip to the Diablerets glacier for the splendid shady red run down the lift-free Combe d'Audon – an Alpine classic.

Beginners The beginner areas at the bottom of Wispile are adequate, and there are plenty of runs to progress to.

Cross-country The 60km/37 miles of trails are very pretty, and there are some epic journeys to be done given the stamina. Most loops are low down and can suffer from poor snow; but there are higher loops, notably at the special langlauf center at Sparenmoos.

Liftlines Time lost on buses or trains is more of a problem than lines, except at peak times and weekends.

Mountain restaurants Mountain restaurants are plentiful, and most are attractive, although pricey.

Schools and guides English is widely spoken by the ski school. It has a good reputation, too.

Facilities for children The kindergarten offers limited hours.

STAYING THERE

How to go Gstaad is certainly exclusive, with over three-quarters of its accommodations in private chalets and apartments. The remainder of the beds are in 3-star hotels and above.

Hotels The 5-star Palace (748 5000) is extravagantly swish, in secluded grounds. The Bernerhof (748 8844) and Christiana (744 5121) are recommended 4-stars. The Olden (744 3444) is a charming, central, chalet-style building.

Apartments/condos There is a wide choice of self-catering accommodations locally.

Eating out Restaurants are mainly hotel-based, and pricey. The rustic Chlösterli – a massive 350-seat establishment a short drive out – is a popular place to eat and dance. Hotel Rössli is reasonably priced and the locals' bar in the Olden has filling, value-for-money meals.

Après-ski In season nightlife is lively both at tea-time and later on.

Off the slopes Gstaad's activities are wide-ranging. The tennis center and swimming pool complex are impressive, and there are 50km/30 miles of pretty cleared walks. Getting around is easy, and excursions by rail to Montreux and Interlaken or even further afield are possible.

Phone numbers
From elsewhere in Switzerland add the prefix 033.
From abroad use the prefix +41 33.

TOURIST OFFICE
Postcode CH-3780
t +41 (33) 748 8181
f 748 8183
gst@gstaad.ch
www.gstaad.ch

And La Videmanette gives a grand view over the gentler mountains east of Gstaad ➔

Mürren

Stupendous views, an epic run, and a chocolate-box village

HOW IT RATES

The slopes

Snow	***
Extent	*
Experts	***
Intermediates	***
Beginners	**
Convenience	***
Liftlines	***
Restaurants	**

The rest

Scenery	*****
Resort charm	*****
Off-slope	***

➕ Tiny, charming, traditional 'traffic-free' village, all snowy paths and chocolate-box chalets

➕ Stupendous scenery, best enjoyed on the challenging run from the panoramic Schilthorn

➕ Good sports center

➕ Good snow high up, even when the rest of the region is suffering

➖ Extent of local trails very limited no matter what your level of expertise

➖ Lower slopes can be in poor condition and are served by some awkward T-bars

➖ Quiet, limited nightlife

➖ Like all other Swiss 'traffic-free' villages, Mürren is gradually admitting more service vehicles

Mürren is one of our favorite resorts – for a short visit, at least. There may be other Swiss mountain villages that are equally pretty, but none of them enjoys views like those from Mürren across the deep valley to the rock faces and glaciers of the Eiger, Mönch and Jungfrau: simply breathtaking. And then there's the Schilthorn run, which draws us back like a magnet – 1300m/4,270ft vertical that combines varied terrain and glorious views like no other run we know.

Our visits are normally one-day affairs; vacationers, we concede, are likely to want to explore the extensive intermediate slopes of Wengen and Grindelwald, across the valley. And you have to accept that getting there takes time.

It was in Mürren that the British more or less invented modern skiing. Sir Arnold Lunn organised the first ever slalom race here in 1922. Some 12 years earlier his father, Sir Henry, had persuaded the locals to open the railway in winter so that he could bring the first winter package tour here. Sir Arnold's son Peter, who first skied here in November 1916, now skis here with his children and grandchildren. Mürren's that kind of place.

The resort

Mürren is set on a shelf high above the Lauterbrunnen valley floor, across from Wengen, and is reached from Stechelberg (via Gimmelwald) by tram or from Lauterbrunnen by funicular and then railroad. Once there, you can't fail to be struck by Mürren's tranquillity and beauty. The tiny village is made up of paths and narrow lanes weaving between tiny wooden chalets and a handful of bigger hotel buildings. All is normally snow-covered.

Two further stages of the tram take you up to the high slopes of Birg and the Schilthorn, nearby lifts go to the main lower slopes, and a newly modernized funicular halfway along the village accesses the other slopes.

KVV MÜRREN

The views of the Eiger, Mönch and Jungfrau are quite amazing →

Although in our summary above we protest against the gradual 'traffic' increase, Mürren still isn't plagued by electric carts and taxis as most other traditional 'traffic-free' resorts now are.

It's not the place to go for lively nightlife, shopping or showing off your latest gear to admiring hordes. It is the place to go if you want tranquillity and stunning views.

The village is so small that location is not a concern. Nothing is more than a few minutes' walk.

The mountain

Mürren's local slopes aren't extensive (53km/33 miles in total). But it has something for everyone, including one of our favorite runs, and a vertical of some 1300m/4,270ft. And those happy to take the time to cross the valley to Wengen– Grindelwald will find plenty of options. These resorts are covered by the Jungfrau lift ticket.

THE SLOPES
Small but interesting

There are three connected areas around the village, reaching no higher than 2145m/7,040ft. The biggest is **Schiltgrat**, served by a fast quad chair behind the tram station. You can also get there from the top of the modernized funicular that goes from the middle of the village to the beginner area at **Allmendhubel** – from where a run and a surface lift take you to the slightly higher **Maulerhubel**. Runs go down from here to the Winteregg stop on the railway, too. These lower slopes take you up to around 2000m/6,600ft.

Much more interesting are the higher slopes reached by tram. The first stage takes you to Birg and the **Engetal** area, where an old T-bar serves short, steep, shady slopes. Two chair-lifts below the Engetal now serve some snow-sure intermediate slopes. But plans for a third chair, back up to Birg, have been shelved. To get back to the Birg tram station and avoid the tricky black run down to the village, you face an annoying walk up from these chairs to the old T-bar.

The final stage of the tram takes you up to the 2970m/9,740ft summit of the **Schilthorn** and the Piz Gloria revolving restaurant, made famous by the James Bond film *On Her Majesty's Secret Service*. In good snow you can go all the way from here (via the Engetal and the Maulerhubel surface lift) to Lauterbrunnen at 795m/2,610ft – a distance of almost 16km/10 miles.

MOUNTAIN FACTS

Altitude	945m-2970m
	3,100ft-9,740ft
Lifts	45
Trails	205km
	127 miles
Blue	30%
Red	50%
Black	20%
Snowmaking	30km
	19 miles
Recco detectors used	

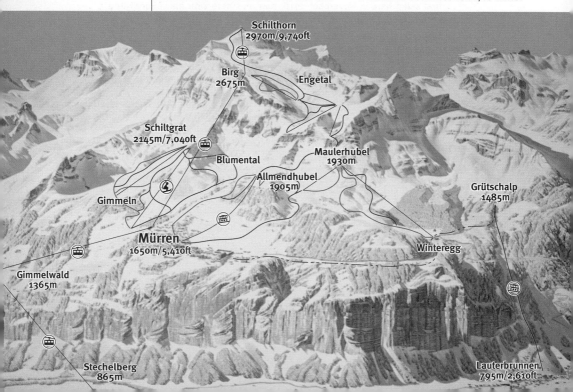

Schilthorn
2970m/9,740ft

Birg
2675m

Engetal

Schiltgrat
2145m/7,040ft

Blumental

Maulerhubel
1930m

Allmendhubel
1905m

Grütschalp
1485m

Gimmeln

Mürren
1650m/5,410ft

Winteregg

Gimmelwald
1365m

Stechelberg
865m

Lauterbrunnen
795m/2,610ft

LIFT TICKETS

Jungfrau Top Ski Region
Covers all lifts in Wengen, Mürren and Grindelwald, trains between them and Grindelwald ski-bus.
Beginners Points card (adult 100 points 48, lifts cost 4 to 10 points).
Main ticket
1-day ticket 52
6-day ticket 254
Senior citizens
Over 62: 6-day ticket 229
Children
16 to 19: 6-day 203
Under 16: 6-day ticket 127
Under 6: 6-day ticket 25
Short-term tickets
Single ascent tickets for most lifts. Half-day ticket for Mürren-Schilthorn (adult 40).
Alternative periods
3 days in 7 ticket is available (156).
Notes Day ticket price is for Mürren-Schilthorn area only (53km/33 miles of trails, 12 lifts), as Jungfrau Top Ski Region ticket is only available for 2 days or over.
Alternative tickets
1- and 2-day tickets available for Mürren-Schilthorn (adult 2-day 95) and Kleine Scheidegg-Männlichen (adult 2-day 95).
4-, 5- and 6-day tickets available for non-skiers (adult 6-day 189).

SCHOOLS/GUIDES

Swiss
Classes 6 days
2hr: 9.45-11.45
6 days 135
Children's classes
Ages: from 4
2hr: 6 days 135
Private lessons
Half day (2hr) or full day (5hr)
from 110 for 2hr

boarding *Like other Swiss resorts, Mürren has a traditional image, but it is trying to move with the times and offer a more snowboard-friendly attitude. This may be at odds with the resort's usual clientele, but they build a half-pipe every season, and the major lifts are trams and chair-lifts (though there are some key surface lifts too). The terrain above Mürren is suitable mainly for good free-riders – it's steep, with a lot of off-trail routes. Intermediates will find the area tough and limited, but nearby Wengen is ideal and is much better for beginners. At night, Mürren is quiet, with not much scope for raving.*

The Inferno race (see box over the page) takes place over this course, conditions permitting. But below Winteregg it's all boring paths.

The Jungfrau trail map doesn't deal with Mürren's slopes at all well. The one used in the Mürren brochures (on which our own is based) is better.

SNOW RELIABILITY
Good on the upper slopes
The Jungfrau region does not have a good snow record – but Mürren always has the best snow in the area. When Wengen–Grindelwald (and Mürren's lower slopes) have problems, the Schilthorn and Engetal often have packed powder snow because of their height orientation – north-east to east. A recent reporter confirms that trail grooming and marking are poor.

FOR EXPERTS
One wonderful trail
The run from the top of the Schilthorn starts with a steep but not terrifying slope, in the past generally bumpy but now often groomed. It flattens into a schuss to Engetal, below Birg. Then there's a wonderful, wide run with stunning views over the valley to the Eiger, Mönch and Jungfrau. Since the chair-lifts were built here you can play on these upper runs for as long as you like. Below the lifts you hit the Kanonenrohr (gun barrel). This is a very narrow shelf with solid rock on one side and a steep drop on the other – protected by nets. After an open slope and scrappy zig-zag path, you arrive at the 'hog's back' and can descend towards the village on either side of Allmendhubel.

From Schiltgrat a short, serious bump run – the Kandahar – descends towards the village, but experts are more likely to be interested in the off-trail runs into the Blumental – both from here (the north-facing Blumenlucke run) and from Birg (the sunnier Tschingelchrachen) – or the adventurous runs from the Schilthorn.

FOR INTERMEDIATES
Limited, but Wengen nearby
Avid skiers and riders will want to make a few trips to the long cruising runs of Wengen–Grindelwald. The best easy cruising run in Mürren is the north-facing blue down to Winteregg. The reds on the other low slopes can get bumpy, and snow conditions can be poor. The area below the Engetal normally has good snow, and you can choose your gradient.

FOR BEGINNERS
Not ideal, but adequate
The beginner areas at Allmendhubel, at the top of the funicular, are on the steep side. And there are not many easy runs to graduate to – though the blue down the Winteregg chair is easy, and the Schilt-Apollo blue served by the long Gimmeln surface lift and the less tiring Schiltgrat chair are ideal.

FOR CROSS-COUNTRY
Forget it
There is one small loop above the village in the Blumental, and more extensive loops down at Lauterbrunnen or Stechelberg. But snow is unreliable at valley height.

LIFTLINES
Generally not a problem
Mürren doesn't get as crowded as Wengen and Grindelwald, except on sunny Sundays. There can be lines for the trams – usually when snow shortages bring in refugees. The top stage has only one cabin. The new Allmendhubel funicular goes at twice the speed of the old one.

MOUNTAIN RESTAURANTS
Disappointing at altitude
Piz Gloria revolves once an hour, displaying a fabulous 360° panorama of peaks and lakes. Don't expect particularly good food, or a small bill. By the 'new' Engetal chair-lifts, the Schilthorn Hutte is small and rustic.

Lower down, the Suppenalp in the

CHILDCARE

The ski school takes children from age 4.

For the last few years there has been non-skiing childcare in the sports center. But lack of demand has meant that it may not be available in the coming seasons. The tourist office staff suggest you contact them for the latest situation.

GETTING THERE

Air Zürich, transfer 3½hr. Bern, transfer 1½hr.

Rail Lauterbrunnen; transfer by mountain railway and tram.

ACTIVITIES

Indoor 'Alpine Sports Center Mürren' swimming pool, whirlpool and children's pool, library, children's playroom, gymnasium, squash, sauna, solarium, steam bath, massage, fitness room
Outdoor Artificial skating rink (curling, skating), toboggan run to Gimmelwald, 15km/9 miles cleared paths

Phone numbers
From elsewhere in Switzerland add the prefix 033.
From abroad use the prefix +41 33.

TOURIST OFFICE

Postcode CH-3825
t +41 (33) 856 8686
f 856 8696
info@muerren.ch
www.wengen-muerren.ch

Blumental is rustic and quietly set, does 'excellent food' but gets no sun in January. Sonnenburg is sunnier. Gimmelen is a self-service place with a large terrace, famous for its apple cake. Winteregg does something similar, as well as 'the best burger east of the Rockies'. Both have little playgrounds to amuse kids.

SCHOOLS AND GUIDES
Small, not perfectly formed
Recent reports speak of good progress for beginners, but also of one English speaker who had a rather lonely week in a group with six Germans – the kind of thing that happens in a small resort.

FACILITIES FOR CHILDREN
Adequate
There is a baby slope with rope tow. There may be a children's club at the sports center but the tourist office staff suggest you contact them in advance to see if it will be open. The ski school takes children from four years.

Staying there

HOW TO GO
Mainly hotels
Hotels There are fewer than a dozen hotels, ranging widely in style.
(((④ **Palace** (855 2424) Victorian pile near station – recently renovated.
(((④ **Eiger** (856 5454) Plain-looking 'chalet' blocks next to railway station, widely recommended; good blend of efficiency and charm; good food; pool.
(((③ **Alpenruh** (856 8800) Attractively renovated chalet next to the tram.
(((③ **Edelweiss** (855 1312) Block-like but friendly; good food and facilities.
(((③ **Jungfrau** (856 4545) Perfectly placed for families, in front of the baby slope and close to the funicular.

(② **Alpenblick** (855 1327) Simple, small, modern chalet near station.
Apartments/condos There are plenty of chalets and apartments in the village for independent travelers to rent.

EATING OUT
Mainly in hotels
The main alternative to hotels is the rustic Stägerstübli – a bar as well as restaurant. The locals eat in the little diner at the back. The food at the Eiger hotel is good, and the Bellevue and Alpenruh get good reports.

APRES-SKI
Not devoid of life
The tiny Stägerstübli is cozy, and the place to meet locals. Other activities are hotel-based. The Palace's Balloon bar is an attempt at a trendy cocktail bar; it also has a weekend disco, the Inferno. The Bliemli Challer disco in the Blumental caters to kids, the nightly Tachi disco in the Eiger to a more mixed crowd.

OFF THE SLOPES
Tranquillity but not much else
There isn't a lot to amuse people who don't want to hit the slopes. But there is a very good sports center, with an outdoor ice rink. Excursions by car or train to Interlaken and to Bern are easy to undertake. It's no problem for friends to return to the village for lunch. The only problem with meeting at the top of the tram instead is the expense.

STAYING DOWN THE VALLEY
A cheaper option
Lauterbrunnen is a good budget place to stay. It has a resort atmosphere and access to and from both Wengen and Mürren until late.

THE INFERNO RACE

Every January 1,800 amateurs compete in the spectacular Inferno race. Conditions permitting, and they usually don't, the race goes from the top of the Schilthorn at 2970m/9,740ft right down to Lauterbrunnen at 795m/2,610ft – a vertical drop of 2175m/7,140ft and a distance of almost 16km/10 miles, incorporating a short climb at Maulerhubel. The racers start in pairs at 30-second intervals and the fastest finish the course in around 15 minutes, but anything under half an hour is very respectable.

The race was started by Sir Arnold Lunn in 1928 when he and his friends climbed to the top of the Schilthorn, spent the night in a mountain hut and then raced down in the morning. For many years the race was organized by the British-run Kandahar Club, and there is still a strong British presence among the competitors.

Saas-Fee

Beautiful, car-free village with slopes on top of the world

HOW IT RATES

The slopes

Snow	*****
Extent	**
Experts	***
Intermediates	****
Beginners	*****
Convenience	***
Liftlines	***
Restaurants	***

The rest

Scenery	****
Resort charm	*****
Off-slope	****

What's new

A new family offer was introduced for 2000/01 – children aged up to 16 ski for free if two adults buy a 6-day or 5-days-in-7 ticket.

- ➕ Spectacular setting amid peaks and glaciers – slopes open year-round
- ➕ Traditional, 'traffic-free' village
- ➕ Good percentage of high-altitude, snow-sure slopes
- ➕ Powerful lift access to highest slopes for year-round skiing
- ➕ Good off-slope facilities are banned

- ➖ Disappointingly small area of slopes, with mainly easy runs
- ➖ Glacier stops off-trail exploration
- ➖ Much of the area is in shadow in midwinter – cold and dark
- ➖ Bad weather can shut the slopes
- ➖ Long village can mean quite a bit of walking to and from the slopes

Saas-Fee is one of our favorite places. It oozes Swiss charm, and the setting is stunning – spectacular glaciers and 4000m/13,000ft peaks surround the place. And good snow is guaranteed, even late in the season: the altitude you spend most of your time at – between 2500m/8,200ft and 3500m/11,500ft – is unrivalled in the Alps.

But we tend to drop in for a couple of days at a time, so the limited extent of the slopes never becomes a problem; for a week's holiday, it would. Top to bottom there is an impressive 1800m/5,900ft vertical – but there aren't many alternative ways down. Keen, mileage-hungry intermediates should look elsewhere, as should experts (except those prepared to go touring). For the rest, it's a question of priorities and expectations. Over to you.

The resort

Like nearby Zermatt, Saas-Fee is a high-altitude mountain village centered on narrow streets lined by attractive old chalets and free of cars (there are parking lots at the resort entrance) but not free of electric carts posing as cabs. On most other counts, Saas-Fee and its more exalted neighbor are a long way apart in style.

There are some very upscale hotels (plus many more modest ones) and plenty of good eating and drinking places. But there's little of the glamour and greed that, for some, spoil Zermatt – and even the electric cabs here are driven at a more considerate pace. Saas-Fee still feels like a village, with its cow sheds more obviously still containing cows. The village may be chilly in January, but when the spring sun is beating down, Saas-Fee is a quite beautiful place in which to just stroll around and relax, admiring the impressive view.

Depending on where you're staying and which way you want to go up the mountain, you may do more marching than strolling. It's a long walk from one end of the spread-out village to the other, though your hotel may run a courtesy bus to and from the lifts.

Three major lifts start from the southern end of the village, at the foot of the slopes, and lots of the hotels and apartments are half a mile or more away from there.

The village center has the school and guides' office, the church and a few more shops than elsewhere, but doesn't add up to much. On a sunny day, though, the restaurant terraces fronting the beginner areas at the far end of the village are a magnet, with breathtaking views of the surrounding peaks – you can see why the village is called 'The Pearl of the Alps'.

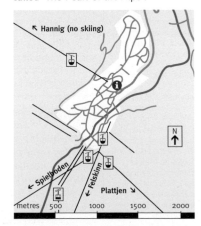

Saas-Fee's highest slopes are on and around the glaciers →
SNOWPIX.COM / CHRIS GILL

MOUNTAIN FACTS

Altitude	1800m-3620m
	5,910ft-11,880ft
Lifts	27
Trails	100km/60 miles
Blue	25%
Red	50%
Black	25%
Snowmaking	10km
	6 miles
Recco detectors used	

LIFT TICKETS

2000/01 prices in Swiss francs

Saas-Fee area
Covers all lifts in Saas-Fee only.
Beginners Village area ticket covers 5 beginners' lifts. 1-day 20, 6 days 90
Main ticket
1-day ticket 58
6-day ticket 270
Children
Under 16: 6-day ticket 162
Under 6: free ticket
Short-term tickets
Single and return tickets on most main lifts. Half-day ticket from noon (adult 46).
Notes Discount for groups of 20 or more.
Alternative tickets
Separate tickets for each of the other ski areas in the Saastal (Saas-Grund, Saas-Almagell, Saas-Balen). Ticket for all four villages in the Saastal also available, and includes ski-bus between them. 6-day ticket, 294.

Staying near a main lift makes most sense. If you do end up at the wrong (north) end of the village – and most budget accommodations are there – ease the pain by storing your gear near the lifts.

The modest slopes of Saas-Almagell and more extensive ones of Saas-Grund are not far away, and you can buy a lift ticket that covers all four resorts and buses between them. Day trips to Zermatt, Grächen and Crans-Montana are also realistic options for those itching for a change.

The mountain

The area has been steadily improved by the installation of new lifts, but the slopes are still a bit fragmented. Many visitors complain about this, and about the number of cold surface lifts. But the reason for these complaints is also Saas-Fee's strong point – its snow-sure glacier slopes. The glacier can move downhill by 100m/330ft a year and surface lift pylons can be moved to cope, but chair-lifts are not practicable.

The upper slopes are largely gentle, while the lower mountain, below the glacier, is steeper and rockier.

Saas-Fee is one of the leading resorts for mountaineering and ski-touring. Several nearby peaks can be climbed, and the extended Haute Route from Chamonix ends here.

THE SLOPES
A glacier runs through it

The main **Felskinn** area can be reached in three ways. The efficient 30-person Alpin Express jumbo gondola takes you to Felskinn at 3000m/9,840ft, starting across the river from the main village. It has a mid-station at Maste 4 (where you have to change cabins).

The Felskinn tram, starting a short surface lift away from the foot of the main trails and beginner areas at the southern end of the village, also takes you to Felskinn.

From Felskinn, the Metro Alpin (an underground funicular) hurtles to the thin air at Mittelallalin (3500m/11,480ft). From below here the top two surface lifts access the high point of 3620m/11,880ft.

Also from the south end of the village, a gondola leaves for Spielboden. This is met by a tram which takes you up to **Längfluh**.

Between Felskinn and Längfluh is an off-limits glacier area. A very long surface lift from Längfluh takes you to a point where you can get down to the Felskinn area. These two sectors are served mainly by surface lifts, and you can get down to the village from both.

Another gondola from the south end of the village goes up to Saas-Fee's smallest area, **Plattjen**.

SNOW RELIABILITY
Good at the highest altitudes

Most of Saas-Fee's slopes face north and many are above 2500m/8,200ft, making this one of the most reliable resorts for snow in the Alps. The glacier is open most of the year. Visitors tell us that the substantial

boarding *Saas-Fee encourages boarding in a big way. In summer, in particular, its glacier slopes are dominated by boarders. Facilities include a half-pipe, a terrain-park and a boarder-cross. The nearby Maste 4 snow-bar is the place for a break. While the gentle glacier slopes are ideal for learning, only main access lifts are boarder-friendly (gondolas, trams and a funicular); nearly all the rest are surface lifts. There are a couple of specialist schools. Expert free-riders may be frustrated by the limits imposed on off-trail riding by the glacier. For nightlife the Popcorn board shop and bar is popular.*

recent investment in snow-guns still doesn't completely ensure good coverage on the rocky lower slopes below glacier level, though trail grooming is 'excellent'. Conversely, after heavy snowfalls you may find yourself limited to the beginner area for a while.

FOR EXPERTS
Not a lot to keep your interest
There is not much steep stuff, except on the bottom half of the mountain where the snow tends not to be as good. The highest surface lift on the left near Felskinn serves two short, steep blacks and one easy one. The slopes around the top of Längfluh often provide good powder and there are usually bumps above Spielboden. The blacks and trees on Plattjen are worth exploring. The glacier puts limits on the local off-trail even with a guide – crevasse danger is extreme. But there are extensive touring possibilities, especially late in the season.

FOR INTERMEDIATES
Great for gentle cruising
Saas-Fee is ideal for early intermediates and those not looking for much of a challenge. For long cruises, head for Mittelallalin. The top of the mountain, down as far Längfluh in one direction, and as far as Maste 4 in the other, is ideal, with usually excellent snow. Gradients range from gentle blues to slightly steeper reds which can build up smallish bumps.

Recent visitors loved the 'beautiful, wide blue and red cruising runs accessed by the surface lift between Maste 4 and Felskinn'.

The 1800m/5,900ft vertical descent from Mittelallalin (via Felskinn or Längfluh) to the village is a great test of stamina – or, if you choose, an enjoyable long cruise with plenty of view stops. The lower runs have steepish, tricky sections and can have poor snow, especially if it isn't cold enough to make snow – timid intermediates might prefer to take a lift down from mid-mountain.

Plattjen has a variety of runs, all of them fine for ambitious intermediates and often underused.

FOR BEGINNERS
Usually a nice place to start
There's a good, large, out-of-the-way beginner area at the edge of the village. Those ready to progress can head for the gentle blues on Felskinn

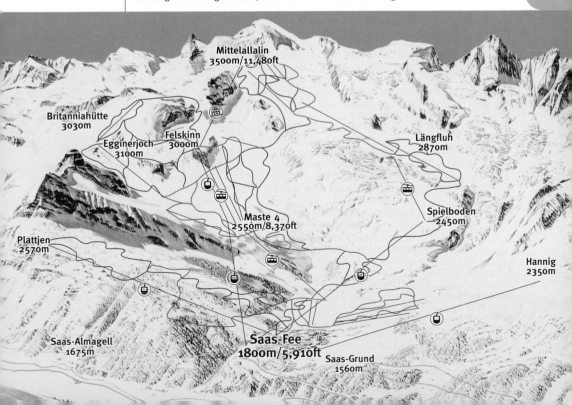

Mittelallalin
3500m/11,480ft

Britanniahütte
3030m

Egginerjoch
3100m

Felskinn
3000m

Längfluh
2870m

Spielboden
2450m

Maste 4
2550m/8,370ft

Plattjen
2570m

Hannig
2350m

Saas-Almagell
1675m

Saas-Fee
1800m/5,910ft

Saas-Grund
1560m

Sadly, the sun terrace doesn't revolve. They're working on a system of mirrors so that the view moves but you never have to turn away from the sun ➔

SNOWPIX.COM / CHRIS GILL

EUROPE'S HIGHEST LUNCH?

There is something beautifully Swiss about the idea of a revolving restaurant – and all three pivoting pubs in the Alps are in Switzerland. 'Customers not getting a share of the views? Can't have that. Only one thing for it: spin the whole restaurant about once an hour.' Actually, they spin only the bit of floor with the tables on it; the stairs stay put (along with the windows – watch your gloves).

Two years after Saas-Fee built the Alps' highest funicular railway in 1984, it crowned that with the world's highest revolving restaurant – a good 500m/1,650ft higher than the famous original on Mürren's Schilthorn. We don't rate the views from Mittelallalin so highly. But it's an amusing novelty that most visitors enjoy. To reserve a table next to the windows phone 957 1771. And the third spinning speisesaal? At Leysin.

---

just above Maste 4 – it's best to return by the Alpin Express. There are also gentle blues at the top of the mountain, from where you can head down to Längfluh. Again, use the lifts to return to base.

A useful beginners' ticket covers all the short lifts at the village edge, for those not ready to go higher.

FOR CROSS-COUNTRY
Good local trail and lots nearby
There is one short (8km/5 mile) pleasant trail at the edge of the village. It snakes up through the woods, providing about 150m/500ft of climb and nice views. There are more options in the valley.

LIFTLINES
Only if snow is poor elsewhere
Lift improvements seem to have done their job and lines are now rare: 'Considering it was semester break, and the weather wonderful with excellent snow, we were relieved at how little we had to wait.' But things change if snow

is poor elsewhere, not an uncommon thing late in the season – as one recent Easter visitor found: 'The worst I'd seen for years – half-hour waits for the Felskinn tram and 25-minute waits for the Alpin Express – and it got worse as the week went on.'

MOUNTAIN RESTAURANTS
Fair choice, but not like Zermatt
The restaurants at the main lift stations are functional. The best places are slightly off the beaten track: the Berghaus Plattjen (just down from Plattjen) and the Gletschergrotte, halfway down from Spielboden (watch for the path from the trail). Both have good food in old huts. If you're up for a trek, the Britanniahütte is a real mountain refuge, with atmosphere and views. The new restaurant at the top of Plattjen has 'friendly service and the best rösti in the resort'. At Spielboden there's 'good food', a terrace and views of tricky slopes. At Längfluh the large terrace has views of huge crevasses, and Popcorn Plaza nearby is

SCHOOLS/GUIDES

2000/01 prices in Swiss francs

Swiss
Classes 5 days
3hr: 10am-1pm, 45
5 days (15hr): 168
Children's classes
5-day ski courses including lunch, from age 3
Private lessons
Hourly or daily
56 for 1hr for 1 or 2 people

CHILDCARE

The Bären-Klub (Bears Club) kindergarten takes infants for full days or half days. From age 3, they can go here in the morning and to ski school in the afternoon. Full junior ski school starts at age 4. Lunchtime care and meals can be provided with all programs.

There's also a children's day center for kids aged 2 to 6 in Saas Grund.

GETTING THERE

Air Sion, transfer 1hr. Geneva, transfer 3½hr. Zürich, transfer 4hr. Milan, transfer 3hr.

Rail Brig (38km/24 miles); regular buses from station.

Phone numbers
From elsewhere in Switzerland add the prefix 027.
From abroad use the prefix +41 27.

ACTIVITIES

Indoor Bielen leisure center (swimming, hot-tub, steam bath, whirlpool, solarium, sauna, massage, tennis, gym), movie theater, museum, concerts, badminton
Outdoor 20km/12 miles cleared paths, natural skating rink (skating, curling, ice hockey), toboggan run, paragliding

TOURIST OFFICE

Postcode CH-3906
t +41 (27) 958 1858
f 958 1860
to@saas-fee.ch
www.saas-fee.ch

popular with a 'really good atmosphere'. Maste 4 has 'cheap and very good' pizza. Back in the village, the sunny, trail-side terrace of the Waldesruh Hotel serves 'wonderful' rösti and the terrace of the Belmont is a popular sunbathing spot.

SCHOOLS AND GUIDES
Good reports
For skiing, it's the Swiss school or nothing. In the past we've received complaints of 'arrogant attitude', but recent reporters seem better pleased: 'excellent' says one, 'had a good private lesson and felt I was skiing better afterwards,' says another.

FACILITIES FOR CHILDREN
Seem adequate
The school takes children from four years old, and the reports we have had have been positive – 'Most classes quite small and English spoken'. One solution for younger ones is to stay at a hotel with an in-house kindergarten – see reports below.

Staying there

HOW TO GO
Check the location
Hotels There are 50-plus hotels, so lots of choice.
(((((5) **Fletschhorn** (957 2131) Elegant chalet in woods, with original art and individual rooms, a trek from the village and lifts, but fabulous food.
((((4) **Walliserhof** (958 1900) Excellent 4-star. Superb, friendly welcome and service, delicious dinners, champagne breakfast. Spa.
((((4) **Schweizerhof** (957 5159) Stylish place in quiet position above the center. 'Fantastic food, friendly staff, excellent kindergarten.' Pool.
(((3) **Beau-Site** (958 1560) 'First-rate' but quiet 4-star in central, but not convenient, position. Good food. Pool.
(((3) **Saaserhof** (957 3551) Modernized old chalet in good position, over river from beginner areas. Sauna, whirlpool.
(((3) **Ambassador** (957 1420) Modern chalet, close to beginner areas.
(((3) **Alphubel** (957 1112) At the wrong end of town, praised by reporters for its own 'brilliant nursery'.
(((3) **Waldesruh** (957 2232) Strongly recommended by a reporter: 'Best situation in Saas-Fee for the Alpin Express.'

(((3) **Hohnegg** (957 2268) Small rustic alternative to the Fletschhorn, in a similarly remote spot.
((2) **Belmont** (958 1640) The most appealing of the hotels looking directly on to the beginner areas.
Apartments/condos There are plenty of apartments but check the location before booking.

EATING OUT
No shortage – some high class
Gastronomes will want to head for the highly acclaimed Fletschhorn – expensive but excellent. Our favourite is the less formal Bodmen along a path into the woods. It has great food (from rösti to fillet steak) and rustic ambience. We had a delicious Thai meal in one of the Walliserhof's several restaurants. Boccalino is cheap and does pizzas – book or get there early. Alp-Hitta specializes in rustic food and surroundings. The hotel Dom's restaurant specializes in endless varieties of rösti. Arvu-Stuba, Zur Mühle, La Gorge, Feeloch, Skihütte and La Ferme have all been recommended.

APRES-SKI
Excellent and varied
Late afternoon, Nesti's ski-bar, Zur Mühle and the little snow-bars such as Black Bull, near the lifts, are all pretty lively, especially if the sun's shining. Later on, Nesti's and the Underground keep going till 1am. Popcorn is packed and praised for 'lively atmosphere, brilliant music and catering for all ages'. The Art Club is smarter and more sophisticated, with live music. The Metro Bar is like being in a 19th-century mine shaft; Why Not pub is popular; The Metropol has the Crazy Night disco and a couple of other bars.

OFF THE SLOPES
A mountain for pedestrians
The whole of the Hannig mountainside is dedicated to eating, drinking, walking, tobogganing and paragliding – skiers and boarders are banned. In the village, the splendid Bielen leisure center boasts a 25m pool, indoor tennis courts and a lounging area with sunlamps. There's also the 'interesting' Saas museum and the Bakery Museum, where children can make bread. Don't miss the largest ice pavilion in the world, which is carved out of the glacier at Mittelallalin and includes a wedding chapel.

Luxury living – on and off the flatteringly easy slopes

320

HOW IT RATES

The slopes

Snow	****
Extent	*****
Experts	****
Intermediates	****
Beginners	**
Convenience	**
Liftlines	**
Restaurants	****

The rest

Scenery	****
Resort charm	*
Off-slope	*****

What's new

The World Alpine Ski Championships are to be held in St Moritz in 2003, and have heralded much improvement in the resort, including road access, lift updating, more snowmaking and recent refurbishment of all the 5-star hotels.

For 2001/02 on Corviglia, the Plateau Nair T-bar from Marguns will be replaced by a high-speed quad chair. For 2002/03 the ancient, tiny Piz Nair cable car will be rebuilt to increase its capacity.

Always a center for teaching blind skiers, St Moritz is now offering the same to blind snowboarders.

⊕ Beautiful panoramic scenery

⊕ Off-slope activities second to none – including the Cresta Run, horse-racing and lots of varied festivals

⊕ Extensive, largely intermediate slopes

⊕ Fairly snow-sure, thanks to altitude and extensive snowmaking

⊕ Good après-ski, for all tastes

⊕ Good mountain restaurants, some with magnificent views

⊕ Painless rail access via Zürich

⊖ Some hideous block buildings

⊖ A sizeable town, with little traditional Alpine character

⊖ No proper beginner areas at resort level – except at Celerina

⊖ Several unlinked mountains, with a bus, train or car needed to most

⊖ Runs on two main mountains all fairly easy and much the same

⊖ Expensive

St Moritz is Switzerland's most famous 'exclusive' winter resort: glitzy, pricey, fashionable and, above all, the place to be seen – it's the place for an all-round winter holiday with an unrivalled array of different diversions, including such wacky pursuits as polo, golf and cricket on snow and gourmet and music festivals. The slopes on the two main mountains are almost uniformly easy intermediate – we don't rate it highly for complete beginners, and experts must be prepared to venture off-trail. But for cross-country, it is superb.

The town of St Moritz doesn't have the chocolate-box image of a Swiss mountain resort, all wooden huts and cows with bells round their necks. Many of the buildings are uncompromisingly rectangular and plain.

But you may find, as some readers have, that St Moritz's spectacular setting, beside the lowest in a long chain of lakes at the foot of the 4000m/13,000ft Piz Bernina, blinds you to the town's aesthetic faults. This is one of those areas where our progress on the mountain is regularly interrupted by the need to stand and gaze. It may not have quite the drama of the Jungfrau massif, or the Matterhorn, or the Dolomites, but its wide and glorious mountain landscapes are equally special. And the langlauf, walking and other activities on the frozen lake give it a real 'winter wonderland' feel.

The resort

St Moritz has two distinct parts. Dorf is the fashionable main part, on a steep hillside above the lake. It's a busy, compact town with two main streets lined with boutiques selling Rolex watches, Cartier jewelry and Hermes scarves, a few side lanes and a small main square. A funicular takes you from Dorf to the main slopes of Corviglia, also reached by gondola from down the road at Celerina, and by tram from Dorf's other half, the spa resort of St Moritz Bad, spread around one end of the lake.

Everything in Bad is less prestigious. Many of the modern buildings are uncompromisingly rectangular and spoil otherwise superb views. In winter the lake is used for eccentric activities including horse and greyhound racing, show jumping, polo, 'ice golf' and even cricket. It also makes a superb setting for walking and cross-country skiing.

Other downhill slopes, at Corvatsch, are reached via lifts at Surlej and Sils Maria. Cross-country skiing is the main activity around the outlying villages of Samedan and Pontresina.

The town clientele is typified by the results of a Cresta Run race we saw on one of our visits. In the top 29 were three Lords, one Count, one Archduke and a Baronet – but the race was won by a Swiss, without a title.

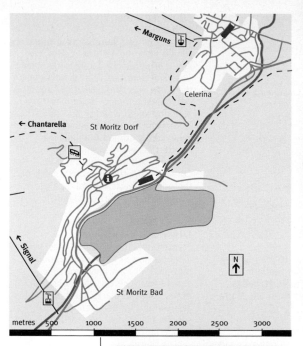

Big beautiful mountains make up for St Moritz's distinct lack of chocolate-box charm ↗

VERKEHRSVEREIN ST MORITZ

MOUNTAIN FACTS

Altitude 1730m-3300m
  5,680ft-10,830ft
Lifts 57
Trails 350km
  217 miles
Blue 16%
Red 71%
Black 13%
Snowmaking 45km
  28 miles
Recco detectors used

The mountains

Like the resort, most of the slopes are made for posing. There are lots of long and generally wide flatteringly well-groomed runs, with varied terrain. There's an occasional black run, but few are seriously steep. But there is tough off-trail, and it doesn't get tracked out as it does in more macho resorts. Beginners' slopes are few and far between. Trips to other resorts such as Klosters, Davos (both around 90 minutes by train or car) and Livigno (an hour by car) are also possible.

THE SLOPES
Big but broken up
The several distinct areas add up to a substantial 350km/217 miles of trails. The main slopes, shown on our maps, are nearby Corviglia–Marguns and Corvatsch– Furtschellas, a bus-ride

away (although you can get back to Bad on snow). Diavolezza, Piz Lagalb, Alp Languard and a few more distant bits and pieces make up the rest. Some of these are well worth an outing. It helps to have a car, although the free bus service is reported to be fairly efficient.

From St Moritz Dorf a two-stage monorail goes up to **Corviglia**, a fair-sized area with slopes facing east and south. The peak of Piz Nair, reached from here by an ancient tram, splits the area – sunny runs towards the main valley, and less sunny ones to the north. From Corviglia you can head down (snow permitting) to Dorf and Bad, and via the lower lift junction of Marguns to Celerina.

From Surlej, a few miles from St Moritz, a two-stage tram takes you to the north-facing slopes of **Corvatsch**. From the mid-station at Murtèl you

boarding *Despite the high prices and its glitzy image, the terrain in St Moritz turns out to be quite favorable and the resort produces a special booklet with recommended 'secret spots', 'natural freestyle' and beginner areas. Above the town on Corviglia there is a terrain-park and half-pipe in the Signal area and there are two terrain-parks in the Corvatsch/Furtschellas area. The Corvatsch area has links that rely on surface lifts – otherwise, most lifts are chairs, gondolas, trams and trains. The well-groomed cruising runs should appeal to any hard-boot rider, and there are several specialist snowboard shops. At night, there are a few places you don't have to wear a dinner jacket to get in.*

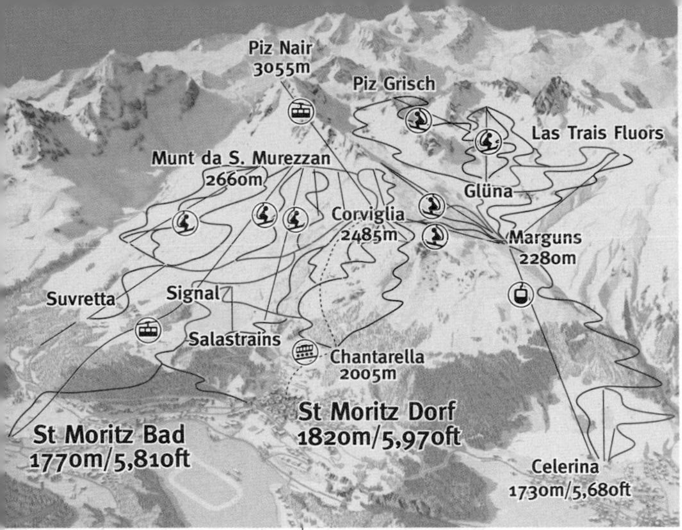

Map labels (top image):
Piz Nair 3055m
Piz Grisch
Las Trais Fluors
Munt da S. Murezzan 2660m
Glüna
Corviglia 2485m
Marguns 2280m
Suvretta
Signal
Salastrains
Chantarella 2005m
St Moritz Dorf 1820m/5,970ft
St Moritz Bad 1770m/5,810ft
Celerina 1730m/5,680ft

have a choice of reds to Margun-Vegl and Alp Margun. From the latter you can work your way to **Furtschellas**, also reached by tram from Sils Maria, and to Bad.

Diavolezza (2980m/9,780ft) and Lagalb (2960m/9,710ft), the main additional areas, are on opposite sides of the road to the Bernina pass to Italy, less than half an hour away by bus. **Diavolezza** has excellent north-facing trails of 900m/2,950ft vertical, down under its big 125-person tram, and a very popular 'amazing' off-trail route, off the back of the mountain, across a glacier and down a valley beneath Piz Bernina to Morteratsch. **Lagalb** is a smaller area with quite challenging slopes, with an 80-person tram serving the west-facing front slope of 850m/2,790ft vertical.

SNOW RELIABILITY
Reasonable

This corner of the Alps has a rather dry climate, but the altitude means that any precipitation is likely to be snowy – several reporters told us how good the snow was throughout the 2000/01 season, when many other resorts were suffering warm weather and rain. There is snowmaking in every sector: several easy slopes around Corviglia are covered, as is an excellent 800m/2,600ft vertical red run on Corvatsch (Murtèl to Surlej), much of the 900m/2,950ft vertical face of Diavolezza and part of Lagalb.

FOR EXPERTS
Dispersed challenges

If you're looking for challenges, you're liable to find St Moritz disappointing on-trail. Red runs (many of which should really be classified blue) far outnumber the black, and bump fields are few and far between. The few serious black runs are scattered about in different sectors.

The blacks at Lagalb and Diavolezza are the most challenging trails. The direct Minor run down the Lagalb tram has 850m/2,800ft vertical of non-stop bumps.

There are plenty of opportunities to venture a little way off-trail in search of challenges – there is an excellent north-facing slope immediately above the Marguns lift junction, for example. Experts often head for the tough off-trail runs on Piz Nair or the Corvatsch summit. More serious expeditions can be undertaken – such as down the

Map labels (bottom image):
Piz Corvatsch 3450m
3305m/10,840ft
Culöz das las Furtschellas 2800m
Fuorcla Surlej 2760m
Murtèl 2700m/8,860ft
Val Fex
Giand'Alva 2645m
Margun-Vegl 2405m
Hahnensee 2155m
Alp Margun 2270m
Furtschellas 2310m
Surlej 1870m
Sils Maria 1795m
St. Moritz Bad 1770m/5,810ft

LIFT TICKETS

2001/02 prices in Swiss francs

Upper Engadine
Covers all lifts in St Moritz, Celerina, Surlej, Sils Maria, Maloja, Lagalb, Diavolezza, Pontresina, Punt Muragl, Samedan, Müsella and Zuoz, and the swimming pools in St Moritz and Pontresina.
Main ticket
1-day ticket 65
6-day ticket 305
Children/teenagers
Age 16-20: 6-day ticket
275
Under 16: 6-day ticket
153
Under 6: free ticket
Short-term tickets
Half-day ticket from 11.45 (adult 53).
Notes Prices are for high season. Mid-season adult 6-day ticket 290; low season 261. Child reductions too. Deposit of SF5 gets you a hands-free ticket. Six-day ticket gives one day's skiing in Livigno.
Alternative tickets
Half-day and day tickets for individual areas within the Upper Engadine.

SCHOOLS/GUIDES

2000/01 prices in Swiss francs

St Moritz
Classes 6 days
4hr: 10am-noon and 1.30-3.30
1 half day 45
6 full days: 250
Children's classes
Ages: from 5
6 full days 250
Private lessons
Half-day (2hr) or full-day (5hr)
160 for half-day

Suvretta
Small groups of 4 to 6 people
Classes 6 days
2hr, 3hr, 4hr or full-day (5hr)
Half day: 42
6 full days 250-310

---

splendid Roseg valley from Corvatsch. The off-trail potential is all the better for being relatively little exploited.

FOR INTERMEDIATES
Good but flattering
St Moritz is great for intermediates. Most trails are easyish reds that could well have been classified blue. Reporters enjoyed 'marvellous GS ground' around Corviglia and Murezzan, for example.

One of the finest runs is Hahnensee, from the northern limit of the Corvatsch lift system at Giand'Alva down to St Moritz Bad – a black run that is of red difficulty for most of its 6km/4 mile length and 900m/2,950ft vertical drop. It's a five-minute walk from the end of the run to the tram up to Corviglia.

Diavolezza is mostly intermediate. There is an easy open slope at the top, served by a fast quad, and a splendid long intermediate run back down under the lift. The popular off-trail run to Morteratsch requires a bit of energy and nerve. After a gentle climb, you cross the glacier on a narrow ledge, with crevasses waiting to gobble you up on the right. When we last did it, there were ice-picks and shovels at intervals along the path, put there by the enterprising proprietors of the beautifully laid out, welcoming ice bar which greets you at the end of the 30-minute slog. After that, it's downhill through the glacier, with splendid views. Lagalb has more challenging trails.

FOR BEGINNERS
Not much to offer
St Moritz is not ideal for beginners. It sits in a deep, steep-sided valley, with very little space for beginner areas at the lower levels. Beginners start up at Salastrains or Corviglia, or slightly out of town, at Suvretta. Celerina has good, broad beginner areas at village level. Progression from the beginner areas to

intermediate runs is rather awkward – these always include a difficult section.

FOR CROSS-COUNTRY
Excellent; go to Pontresina
The Engadine is one of the premier regions in the Alps for cross-country, with 150km/90 miles of trails of all levels, including floodlit loops, amid splendid scenery and with pretty reliable snow. The famous Engadine Ski Marathon is held here every March – over 12,000 racers take part. Pontresina makes a great base, with lots of other activities.

LIFTLINES
Crowds can be a problem
St Moritz has invested heavily in new lifts lately. High-speed quad chairs are common on Corviglia and there are some six-seaters. But the area as a whole is over-dependent on trams – many not huge – both for getting up the mountain from the resort and for access to peaks from mid-mountain. Liftlines can result, though reporters have had good experiences lately – the enlarged tram from Surlej to Murtèl is a big improvement, as will be the one to Piz Nair when it happens. Happy reporters comment that St Moritz's visitors are often late risers, and that lunch can signal the end of skiing – leaving the slopes pretty clear at the start and end of the day.

MOUNTAIN RESTAURANTS
Some special places
Mountain restaurants are plentiful, and include some of the most glamourous in Europe. Prices can be high, and reservations are advisable. But there are plenty of cheaper places too.

On Corviglia, the gourmet highlight is the Marmite; but it is outrageously expensive. And it is housed in the Corviglia lift station, known locally as the highest post office in Switzerland

---

THE CRESTA RUN

No trip to St Moritz is really complete without a visit to the Cresta Run. It's the last bastion of Britishness (until recently, payment had to be made in sterling) and male chauvinism (women have been banned since 1929 – unless you can secure an invitation from a club member for the last day of their season).

Any adult male can pay around SF500 for five rides on the famous run (helmet and lunch at the Kulm hotel included). Watch out for the Shuttlecock corner – that's where most people come off, and the ambulances ply for trade. You lie on a toboggan (aptly called a 'skeleton') and hurtle head-first down a sheet ice gully from St Moritz to Celerina. Fancy giving it a go?

GETTING THERE

Air Zürich, transfer 3hr (or fly into small Upper Engadine airport 5km/3 miles away).

Rail Mainline station in resort.

CHILDCARE

The St Moritz ski school operates a pick-up service for children. St Moritz and Suvretta schools provide all-day care.

Children aged 3 or more can be looked after in hotels – there are nurseries in the Carlton, the Parkhotel Kurhaus and the Schweizerhof, open from 9am to 4.30 or 5.30.

ACTIVITIES

Indoor Curling, swimming, sauna, solarium, tennis, squash, museum, health spa, movie theatre (with English movies), aerobics, beauty farm, health center, Rotary International club **Outdoor** Ice skating, sleigh rides, ski jumping, toboggan run, hang-gliding, golf on frozen lake, Cresta run, 150km/90 miles cleared paths, greyhound racing, horse-riding and racing, polo tournaments, cricket tournaments, ski-bob run, paragliding, skydiving, curling

Phone numbers
From elsewhere in Switzerland add the prefix 081.
From abroad use the prefix +41 81.

---

because of its bright yellow paint. Much better for charm is the Paradiso, with glorious panoramic views from the terrace, and the Lej de la Pesch behind Piz Nair. A reader recommends Mathis for 'first-class food and wine'.

On the Corvatsch side, we've heard good reports about the self-service place at the top and the sunny Sternbar, with live music, at the bottom of Rabguisa. Fuorcla Surlej is delightfully secluded, as is Hahnensee, on the lift-free run of the same name down to Bad – a splendid place to pause in the sun on the way home. On stormy days, most captivating is the rustic Alpetta, at Alp Margun (table-service inside).

The hotel-restaurant up at Muottas Muragl, between Celerina and Pontresina, is well worth a visit. It has truly spectacular views overlooking the valley, as well as good food.

Morteratsch restaurant (at the end of the off-trail run from Diavolezza) is splendid – sunny, by the cross-country area and tiny railway station, and with excellent, good-value food.

SCHOOLS AND GUIDES
Internal competition

As well as the St Moritz and Suvretta schools, there is The Wave snowboarding school and The St Moritz Experience, for heli-trips. A free 'ski safari' is offered on Thursdays, something we've only seen in North America before. Some hotels have their own instructors for private lessons.

FACILITIES FOR CHILDREN
Hotel-based nurseries

Children wanting lessons have a choice of schools, but others must be deposited at one of the hotel nurseries: the Parkhotel Kurhaus near the tram in Bad, or the Schweizerhof in Dorf. Club Med has its usual good facilities.

Staying there

For high society and a better choice of bars and restaurants, stay in Dorf. Bad has the advantage that you can get back to it from Corvatsch and Corviglia. Celerina is another option.

HOW TO GO
A few good-value options

Hotels Over half the hotels are 4-stars and 5-stars – the highest concentration of high-quality hotels in Switzerland.

We don't like any of the famous 5-stars or their jacket-and-tie policies.

If made to choose we'd prefer the glossy, secluded Carlton or even more secluded Suvretta House to the staid Kulm or Gothic Badrutt's Palace.

(((④ **Crystal** (836 2626) Big 4-star in Dorf, as close to the Corviglia lift as any. Recently renovated and now part of the 'Small Luxury Hotels' group.
(((④ **Schweizerhof** (837 0707) 'Relaxed' 4-star in central Dorf, five minutes from the Corviglia lift, with 'excellent food and very helpful staff'.
(((④ **Albana** (833 3121) 4-star in Dorf, with walls adorned with big game trophies bagged by proprietor's family.
(((③ **Monopol** (837 0404) Good value (for St Moritz) 4-star in center of Dorf. Excellent buffet breakfasts. Pool, sauna.
(((③ **Nolda** (833 0575) One of the few chalet-style buildings, close to the tram in St Moritz Bad.
((② **Bellaval** (833 3245) A two-star between the station and the lake, offering bargain double rooms from SF60 per person per night last season.

EATING OUT
Mostly chic and expensive

It's easy to spend SF125 a head eating out in St Moritz – without wine – but you can eat more cheaply, as reporters love to tell us. We liked the excellent Italian food at the down-to-earth, atmospheric Cascade in Dorf and the three restaurants in the Chesa Veglia. Hauses and the Veltlinerkeller are recommended by locals. But the best food is supposed to be out at Champfer, at Jöhri's Talvo.

Try an evening up at Muottas Muragl for a splendid sunset and dinner in the hotel's unpretentious restaurant.

APRES-SKI
Caters for all ages

There's a big variety of après-skiing age groups here. The fur coat count is high – people come to St Moritz to be seen.

At tea-time, if you can tear yourself away from the mountain bars, the key venue is the famous Hanselmann's, for 'fabulous tea and strudels'. We've also heard good things about Café Hauser.

The pub-style Bobby's Bar, which has internet connection, keeps the younger crowd happy, as do the Prince, with a 'disco/lounge', and the loud music of the Stübli, one of three bars in the Schweizerhof: the others are the Muli, with a country and western theme and live music, and the chic Piano Bar. The Cresta, at the Steffani, is popular with the British, while the Cava below it is louder, livelier and younger. It is also amusing to put on a jacket and tie and explore bars in Badrutt's Palace and the Kulm.

The two most popular discos are Vivai (expensive) at the Steffani, and King's at Badrutt's Palace (even more expensive; jackets and ties required). And if they don't part you with enough cash, try the St Moritz Casino.

OFF THE SLOPES
Excellent variety of pastimes
Even if you lack the bravado or masculinity for the Cresta Run, there is lots to do. In midwinter the snow-covered lake provides a playground for bizarre events (see earlier in chapter) but in March the lake starts to thaw. There's an annual 'gourmet festival', with chefs from all over the world, a new library with some English books and a couple of museums.

Some hotels run special activities, such as a curling week, health spa week or even rock and roll courses.

Other options are hang-gliding, indoor tennis and even trips to Italy (Milan is four hours away by car). The public pool in Bad is worth a visit.

St Moritz gets a lot of sun – 322 sunny days a year, they claim – so lounging on sunny terraces is popular.

STAYING UP THE MOUNTAIN
Excellent possibilities
Next door to each other at Salastrains are two chalet-style hotels, the 3-star Salastrains (833 3867), with 60 comfy beds, and the slightly simpler and much smaller Zauberhütte (833 3355). Great views, and no lines.

Celerina 1730m/5,680ft

At the bottom end of the Cresta Run, Celerina is unpretentious and villagey, if quiet, with good access to Corviglia. It is sizeable, with a lot of second homes, many owned by Italians (the upper part is known as Piccolo Milano). There are some appealing small hotels (reporters suggest Chesa Rosatsch 837 0101) and a couple of bigger 4-stars.

Pontresina 1805m/5,920ft

Pontresina is small and sedate and an excellent base for the extensive cross-country skiing on its doorstep.

It's a sheltered, sunny village with one main street, spoiled by the usual sanatorium-style architecture. All downhill slopes are a bus-ride away. Towards Celerina is Muottas Muragl, where a funicular serves a tiny mountain-top area with one long run to the bottom. Pontresina's own hill, Languard, has a single long trail.

Much is made of Pontresina being cheaper to stay in than St Moritz, but cheaper doesn't mean cheap. Dining is mostly hotel-based and nightlife is quiet.

TOURIST OFFICE

Postcode CH-7500
t +41 (81) 837 3333
f 837 3377
information@stmoritz.ch
www.stmoritz.ch

SNOWPIX.COM / CHRIS GILL

The popular glacier run from Diavolezza to Morteratsch goes through spectacular scenery ↓

Verbier

1500m/4,920ft

Paradise for nightlife-loving powder hounds with cash

HOW IT RATES

The slopes

Snow	★★★
Extent	★★★★★
Experts	★★★★★
Intermediates	★★★
Beginners	★★
Convenience	★★
Liftlines	★★★
Restaurants	★★★

The rest

Scenery	★★★★
Resort charm	★★★
Off-slope	★★★

What's new

For 2001/02 the first two stages of the gondola from Le Châble to Les Attelas, via Verbier and Les Ruinettes, will be upgraded – though the capacity will still be modest.

➕ Extensive, challenging slopes with a lot of off-trail potential and some good bump runs

➕ Lively, varied nightlife

➕ Sunny, panoramic setting, and great views from the highest slopes

➕ Hardly any surface lifts in Verbier (though still lots in linked resorts)

➕ Fewer liftlines than there used to be

➕ Good advanced-level lessons

➕ Much improved trail grooming in recent seasons

➖ Overcrowded trails in certain areas

➖ Sunny lower slopes will always be a problem, even with snowmaking

➖ Easily accessed off-trail slopes get tracked out very quickly

➖ Still some serious liftlines, particularly on 4 Valleys links

➖ Trail map and direction signposting still hopelessly inadequate

➖ Busy traffic (and fumes) in center

➖ Some long walks/rides to lifts

➖ The 4 Valleys network is no rival for the Three Valleys

➖ Pretty expensive

There is no doubt that Verbier is trying hard to retain its international visitors, improving over the last few years its grooming, snowmaking, ski school and lifts – most notably with the overdue replacement three years ago of the Tortin gondola. But major complaints remain. Some are down to the organization of the resort – the kind of trail signs shown later in the chapter would be comical if it were not infuriating – but others are down to the lie of the land.

For experts prepared to pay a guide in order to explore off-trail, Verbier is one of the big names. With its 4 Valleys lift network and a claimed 400km/250 miles of trails, Verbier also seems at first sight to rank alongside the French mega-resorts such as Courchevel or La Plagne for trail skiers. But it doesn't; the 4 Valleys is an inconveniently sprawling affair, while Verbier's local trails are surprisingly confined. Of course, trail skiers can have a satisfying vacation here – but you can do that in scores of modest resorts from Alpbach to Zell am See. Whether they can match Verbier's famously vibrant nightlife is another question.

The resort

Verbier is an amorphous sprawl of chalet-style buildings, without too much concrete in evidence, and with an impressive setting on a wide, sunny balcony facing spectacular peaks. It's a fashionable, but informal, very lively place that teems with a youngish, cosmopolitan clientele. But it's no longer exclusive. The resort attracts a broad range of tourists, including plenty of British and Scandinavians.

Most of the smart shops and hotels (but not chalets) are set around the Place Centrale and along the sloping streets stretching down the hill in one direction and up it in the other to the main lift station at Medran 500m/1,600ft away. Much of the nightlife is here, too, though bars are

SNOWPIX.COM / CHRIS GILL

The views from the top lifts (this is from Mont-Fort at the very top) are superb ➔

rather scattered. These central areas get unpleasantly packed with cars at busy times, especially weekends.

More chalets and apartments are built each year – which means building sites spoil the views in places – with newer properties inconveniently situated along the road to the lift base for the secondary Savoleyres area, about a mile from Medran.

Staying at the top of the resort, close to the Medran lift station, is convenient for the slopes and sufficiently distant from nightlife to avoid late evening noise. If nightlife is not a priority, staying somewhere near the upper (north-east) fringes of the village may mean that you can almost ski to your door – and there is a trail linking the upper beginner areas to the one in the middle of the village.

But in practice most people just get used to using the free buses, which run efficiently on several routes until 7pm. Some areas have quite an infrequent service. We are told that from 7pm to 8.30 there is a special cab service that will drop you at any of the usual bus stops within the resort for five francs per person.

Verbier is at one end of a long, strung-out series of interconnected slopes, optimistically branded the 4 Valleys and linking Verbier to the resorts of Nendaz (described at the end of this chapter), Thyon and Veysonnaz. Other small areas reached by bus are covered by the lift ticket, including Bruson – also reached by riding a gondola down to Le Châble and taking a bus from there. Chamonix and Champéry are within reach by car. But a car can be a bit of a nuisance in Verbier itself. Parking is tightly controlled; your chalet or hotel may not have any or may not have enough, which means a hike from the free parking at the sports center or paying for garage space.

MOUNTAIN FACTS

Altitude 1500m-3330m
    4,920ft-10,930ft
Lifts   100
Trails   410km
    255 miles
Blue   32%
Red   42%
Black   26%
Snowmaking   50km
    31 miles
Recco detectors used

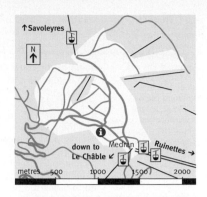

The mountains

Essentially this is high-mountain terrain. There are wooded slopes directly above the village, but the runs here are either bumpy itinéraires or winding paths. There is more sheltered skiing in other sectors – particularly above Veysonnaz.

THE SLOPES
Very spread out

Savoleyres is the smaller area, mainly suited to intermediates and reached by a gondola from the north-west end of town. This area is underrated and generally underused. It has open, sunny slopes on the front side, and long, pleasantly wooded, shadier runs on the back. When conditions are good you can get back to Verbier on south-facing slopes, but in sunny weather these deteriorate quickly.

You can take a catwalk across from Savoleyres to the foot of Verbier's main slopes. These are served by lifts from Medran, at the opposite end of town. Two gondolas rise to **Les Ruinettes** and then on to **Les Attelas**. From Les Attelas a small tram goes up to Mont Gelé, for steep off-trail runs only. Heading down instead, you can go back westwards to Les Ruinettes,

Verbier

boarding *As with its skiing, Verbier is one of Europe's best off-trail and extreme boarding resorts for those able and willing to pay for a guide or join a group. The main area is served by gondolas, trams and chairs, with no surface lifts at all. There are two terrain-parks (the Swatch-sponsored boarder-cross course at La Chaux and another one at La Tournelle) and a half-pipe at Col des Gentianes. Less experienced boarders should try Savoleyres, though there are a few surface lifts. To see some real experts in action, hang around the resort in late March, when the world's best congregate here for the Red Bull Xtreme contest, on the cliff-like north face of the Bec des Rosses. There is a specialist snowboard school and a couple of specialist snowboard shops. And then there's the nightlife, which gets pretty wild at times.*

LIFT TICKETS

2000/01 prices in
Swiss francs
4 Valleys/Mont-Fort
Covers all lifts and
ski-buses in Verbier,
Mont-Fort, Bruson,
Champex-Lac, La
Tzoumaz, Nendaz,
Veysonnaz and
Thyon.
Beginners Station
ticket covers five
beginner lifts.
Main ticket
1-day ticket 58
6-day ticket 294
Senior citizens
Over 65: 6-day ticket
176
Children
Under 16: 6-day ticket
176
Under 6: free ticket
Short-term tickets
Half-day ticket from
11am (adult 53) or
12.30 (adult 46).
Notes Reductions for
families and groups.
Alternative tickets
Limited tickets for
Savoleyres-La
Tzoumaz, Bruson, and
Verbier only.

south to La Chaux or north to Lac des
Vaux. From here chairs go back to Les
Attelas and on to Chassoure, the top
of a wide, steep and shady off-trail
bump field leading down to **Tortin**,
with a gondola back.

La Chaux is served by two slow
chair-lifts and is the departure point of
a jumbo tram up to Col des Gentianes
and the glacier area. A second, much
smaller tram then goes up to **Mont-Fort,** the high point of the 4 Valleys at
3330m/10,930ft. From the glacier is
another off-trail route down to Tortin, a
north-facing run of almost
1300m/4,300ft vertical. A tram returns
to Col des Gentianes.

Tortin is the gateway to the rest of
the 4 Valleys. From there you head
down to **Siviez**, where one chair goes
off into the long, thin **Nendaz** sector
and another heads for the **Thyon** and
Veysonnaz sectors, reached by a
couple of lifts and a lot of catwalk
skiing. Both these sectors suit
intermediates best.

Allow plenty of time to get to and
from these remote corners – you don't
want to be stranded in the wrong
valley. It's an expensive cab-ride.

SNOW RELIABILITY
Improved snowmaking
The slopes of the Mont-Fort glacier
always have good snow. The runs to
Tortin are normally snow-sure too. But
nearly all of this is steep, and much of

it is formally off-trail. Most of Verbier's
main local slopes face south or west
and are below 2500m/8,000ft – so they
can be in poor condition at times.
Snowmaking on the lower slopes has
improved a lot in recent years. The
north-facing slopes of Savoleyres and
Lac des Vaux are normally much better.

FOR EXPERTS
The main attraction
Verbier has some superb tough slopes,
many of them off-trail and needing a
guide. The very extreme couloirs
between Mont Gelé and Les Attelas
and below the Attelas gondola are
some of the toughest. There are safer,
more satisfying off-trail routes from
Mont Gelé to Tortin and La Chaux.

There are hardly any conventional
black trails – most of the runs that
should have this designation are now
defined as itinéraires, which means in
theory they are not patrolled. The
blacks that do exist are mostly
indistinguishable from nearby reds.

The front face of Mont-Fort is a
conspicuous exception: a wonderful
tough bump field, all of black
steepness but with a choice of gradient
from seriously steep to intimidatingly
steep. Occasionally you can get from
Mont-Fort all the way to Le Châble off-trail. You can also head off-trail down
to Siviez via one of two spectacular
couloirs off the back of Mont-Fort. The
North Face of Mont-Fort is one of the

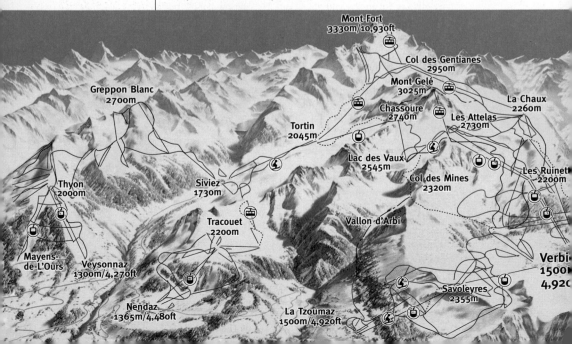

Mont-Fort
3330m/10,930ft

Col des Gentianes
2950m

Mont Gelé
3025m

La Chaux
2226m

Greppon Blanc
2700m

Chassoure
2740m

Les Attelas
2730m

Tortin
2045m

Lac des Vaux
2545m

Les Ruinet
2200m

Col des Mines
2320m

Thyon
2000m

Siviez
1730m

Vallon d'Arbi

Verbi
1500m
4,920

Tracouet
2200m

Mayens-
de-L'Ours

Veysonnaz
1300m/4,270ft

Savoleyres
2355m

Nendaz
1365m/4,480ft

La Tzoumaz
1500m/4,920ft

hottest of expert runs.

The two itinéraires to Tortin are both excellent in their different ways. The one from Chaussoure is just one steep slope, normally a huge bump field. The north-facing itinéraire from Gentianes is longer, less steep, but feels much more of an adventure. Those willing to walk up a steep slope near the start (known as the Highway to Heaven) are rewarded by usually good powder in a quiet valley parallel to the main run. Les Attelas is the start of shorter runs towards the village.

A couple of long, but easy, off-trail routes go from Lac des Vaux via Col des Mines. One is a popular route back to Verbier, the other a very beautiful run through Vallon d'Arbi to La Tzoumaz. They are not always open: a trail-basher needs to form a ledge across a steep slope to the Col – otherwise the traverse is scary.

The World Cup run at Veysonnaz is a steepish, often icy, red, ideal for really speeding down. There is also an entertaining off-trail run from Greppon Blanc at the top of the Siviez–Thyon sector down to Leteygeon. There are 'memorable' heli-trips.

FOR INTERMEDIATES
Go to Savoleyres

Many mileage-hungry intermediates find Verbier disappointing. The intermediate slopes in the main area are concentrated between Les Attelas and the village, above and below Les Ruinettes, plus the little bowl at Lac des Vaux and the sunny slopes served by the chairs at La Chaux. This is all excellent and varied intermediate territory, but there isn't much of it – to put it in perspective, this whole area is no bigger than the slopes of tiny Alpbach – and it is used by the bulk of the visitors staying in one of Switzerland's largest resorts. So it is often very crowded, especially the otherwise wonderful sweeping red from Les Attelas to Les Ruinettes served by the big gondola. Even early intermediates should taste the perfect snow on the glacier (provided you don't mind T-bars). The red run from Col des Gentianes to La Chaux is not too difficult, but its high-mountain feel can be unnerving and it's no disgrace to ride the tram down instead.

Intermediates should make much more use of the Savoleyres area. This has good intermediate trails, usually better snow and far fewer people (especially on Sundays). It is also a good hill for mixed abilities, with variations of many runs to suit most abilities of intermediate.

The area as a whole presents some difficulties for early intermediates, as the editorial daughter, Laura (then aged 8), found a couple of seasons back. There is excellent easy blue-run

---

FINDING YOUR WAY AROUND THE SLOPES OF VERBIER

It isn't easy. The main area is complicated, and difficult to represent on a single map. A couple of years back the lift company, Téléverbier, dropped its hopeless map and produced a booklet of maps dealing separately with each sector. This, too, was hopeless. Now we seem to be back with one hopeless map.

Direction signs on the mountain are equally frustrating. There are two problems. One is a strange faith in the kind of 'highway' signs shown here. We and our readers find these impossible to relate to the real choices of route. The second is that although the signs religiously use trail numbers there are no such numbers on the trail map. So how do you connect the two?

Navigation is further complicated by confusion over where it is prudent to go. For years now, runs that once were black trails have been defined as 'itinéraires à ski' (eg both runs down to Tortin) or 'itinéraires de haute-montagne' (eg the Col des Mines run home from Lac des Vaux). We've long campaigned for these runs to be restored to trail status, but at least their non-trail status needs to be clear.

With patience, you can work out that neither is patrolled, and possibly deduce that 'itinéraires de haute-montagne' are 'not protected against mountain dangers' (ie avalanches) and should be tackled only in the company of an experienced mountaineer or a guide. But it is far from clear.

No other resort finds all this so difficult to resolve. All it takes is a modest budget, some awareness of visitors' needs and half a brain. Which does Téléverbier lack?

330

skiing at La Chaux, but there is no easy way back to Les Ruinettes from there. From Savoleyres there is an easy way across to Medran but there may be no easy way down to that link from the top of Savoleyres. In both cases, we had to take quite challenging red runs. Laura managed it, but in a properly run resort the difficulties would have been eliminated.

FOR BEGINNERS
Progression is the problem
There are sunny beginner areas close to the middle of the village and at Les Esserts, at the top of it. These are fine provided they have snow (they have a lot of snowmaking, which helps). The problem is what you do after the beginner areas. There are easy blues on the back side of Savoleyres, and at La Chaux, but they are not easy to get back from (see above).

FOR CROSS-COUNTRY
Surprisingly little on offer
Verbier is limited for cross-country. There's a 4km/2.5 mile circuit in Verbier, 4km/2.5 miles at Les Ruinettes–La Chaux and 30km/19 miles down at Le Châble/Val de Bagnes.

LIFTLINES
Not the problem they were
It's clear that Verbier's liftline problems have been greatly eased by recent

investment. The jumbo gondola to Les Attelas has virtually eliminated lines at Les Ruinettes, but it has increased the overcrowding on the trails back down. The mega lines at Tortin for Chassoure are a thing of the past, thanks to the new eight-seater gondola. The new fast chair at Lac des Vaux has greatly eased the bottleneck there. But the tram from Tortin to Col des Gentianes can produce lines, and the Mont-Fort tram above it can still generate very long ones.

Lines at the main village lift station at Medran persist, especially when day visitors are filling one of the gondolas by boarding down in the valley at Le Châble. The upgrade of this gondola for the coming season will help – but it is getting only a 50% boost to its present tiny capacity.

But the main complaints from this year's reporters are of lines for inadequate surface lifts in the outlying 4 Valleys resorts – and a La Chaux when crowds descend from the glacier.

MOUNTAIN RESTAURANTS
Disappointing in main area
There are not enough huts, which means liftlines and overcrowding in high season. Savoleyres is the best area. The hotel by the Tzoumaz chair takes some beating for value and lack of crowds. Also worth trying are Chez Simon ('simple and cheap'), Le Mayen

(beneath the Combe 1 chair) and the rustic Marmotte ('wicked, excellent rösti'), just below the Sud surface lift. Le Sonalon, on the fringe of the village beneath the gondola, is 'excellent, with great views', but reached off-trail.

In the main area, the rustic Chez Dany at Clambin, on the off-trail run down from the Chaux area, is about the best, and gets packed despite being a bit tricky to get to at times. Carrefour is popular and well situated at the top of the village, above the golf course. The restaurants at Les Ruinettes – table-service upstairs – have big terraces with splendid views. L'Olympique at Les Attelas is a good table-service restaurant.

Everyone loves the Cabane Mont Fort – a proper mountain refuge off the run to La Chaux from Col des Gentianes); great views, but very crowded – get there early.

SCHOOLS AND GUIDES
Good reports
Verbier is an excellent place for advanced skiers, in particular, to get lessons. Several reporters have been complimentary about the off-trail lessons with the Swiss ski school. More than 20 guides are available for heli-trips, which include trips to Zermatt and the Aosta valley. The Vallée Blanche at Chamonix and a trip to Zinal are cheaper excursions. Verbier is also quite big on snowboard and telemark lessons. The consensus is that the Swiss school's standards have improved generally, partly thanks to the replacement of some old-timers by keen new recruits. Of the others, the Adrénaline international school gets rave reviews, particularly for its private lessons.

FACILITIES FOR CHILDREN
Wide range of options
The Swiss school's facilities in the resort are good, and the resort attracts quite a lot of families. The playground up at La Chaux has also received favourable reports. Space on the bus back is limited, and priority is given to school groups. The possibility of leaving very young babies at the Stroumpfs nursery is valuable. There are considerable discounts on the lift ticket price for families on production of your passports.

HOW TO GO
Plenty of options
Given the size of the place there are surprisingly few apartments and pensions available in Verbier, though those on a budget have inexpensive B&B options in Le Châble. Hotels are expensive in relation to their grading. Given a sleeping bag you can bed down at the sports center for about SF25 a night – and that includes the use of the pool.

Hotels There are half a dozen 4-star places, a dozen 3-star and a handful of simpler places.

((((4) **Rosalp** (771 6323) The place to stay if you can afford it, not least for the food in Roland Pierroz's Michelin-starred restaurant, which is the best you'll find in a Swiss resort. Good position midway between center and lifts.

((((4) **Montpelier** (771 6131) Very comfortable 4-star, but out of town (a courtesy bus is provided).

(((4) **Vanessa** (775 2800) Central 4-star with spacious apartments as well as rooms; 'excellent' food.

(((3) **Rotonde** (771 6525) Much cheaper, well positioned 3-star between center and lifts; some budget rooms.

(((3) **Chamois** (771 6402) 3-star close to lifts.

(((3) **Poste** (771 6681) Well placed 3-star midway between center and lifts; the only hotel pool. Some rooms rather small.

(((3) **de Verbier** (771 6688) Central 3-star, renowned for good food; atmospheric and traditional, with helpful owners and staff.

((2) **Farinet** (771 6626) Central 3-star hotel, now British-owned, with a focal après-ski bar on its elevated terrace.

Apartments/condos The comfortable Richemont and Troika apartments are close to the beginner areas, a trek from the main lifts. The similar standard Blizzard is midway between Place Centrale and lifts.

EATING OUT
Very big choice
There is a very wide range of restaurants. Hotel Rosalp is clearly the best (and most expensive) in town, and among the best in Switzerland, with an awesome wine cellar to match its excellent Michelin-starred food – splurge on the seven-course Menu

Phone numbers
From elsewhere in Switzerland add the prefix 027.
From abroad use the prefix +41 27.

SCHOOLS/GUIDES
2000/01 prices in Swiss francs
Swiss Ski School
Classes 6 days
2½hr: 9.15-11.45
5 half days: 148
Children's classes
Ages: 3 to 12
5 half days: 136
Private lessons
Hourly, half or full day
120 for 2hr for 1 or 2 people

OTHER SCHOOLS
Fantastique
Adrénaline

CHILDCARE
The ski school's Kids Club kindergarten (771 6333), on the slope at Les Moulins, has its own surface lift and takes children from aged 3 from 8.30 to 5pm.

The Schtroumpfs non-ski kindergarten (771 6585), close to the middle of the resort, takes children of any age up to 4 years (older ones by arrangement), from 8.30 to 5.30.

GETTING THERE

Air Geneva, transfer 2hr.

Rail Le Châble (7km/4miles); regular buses to resort or gondola.

ACTIVITIES

Indoor Sports center (swimming, skating, curling, squash, sauna, solarium, steam bath, hot-tub), movie theater, ice hockey, indoor golf
Outdoor Ski-bob, 25km/16 miles cleared walking paths, paragliding, hang-gliding, mountaineering, sledding

Gastronomique if you can afford it. The Pinte bistro in the hotel basement is a less pricey option – worth trying out.

The Grotte à Max does a vast variety of rösti plus unusual meats such as ostrich and kangaroo. The popular King's bar developed a restaurant a couple of years back, and its innovative food ('not a fondue in sight') quickly gained favour. An equally refreshing newcomer is the stylish Millénium, above the Toro Negro steak-house.

The Farinet restaurant is atmospheric and has good food at affordable prices. For Swiss specialities, try the Relais des Neiges, Le Robinson, Le Caveau, Au Vieux-Verbier by the Medran lifts or Les Esserts by the beginner areas. Le Fer à Cheval is a very popular and lively place for pizza and other simple dishes. Arguably the best-value Italian food in town is at Al Capone's out near the Savoleyres gondola. The Hacienda Café is another inexpensive place. Harold's is Verbier's burger joint.

You can snowmobile up to Chez Dany or La Marmotte for an evening meal, followed by a torchlit descent.

APRES-SKI
Throbbing but expensive

It starts with a 4pm visit to the Offshore Café at Medran, for people-watching. The nearby Big Ben is 'great and lively on a sunny afternoon'. Au Mignon at the bottom of the golf course has become popular since it was given a large sun deck.

Then if you're young and loud it's on to the Pub Mont Fort – there's a widescreen TV for live sporting events. The Nelson is popular with locals. The Farinet is particularly good in spring, its live band playing to the audience on a huge, sunny terrace – there's now a conservatory-type cover over it when it's cold. Au Fer à Cheval is a fun place

full of locals and regular Verbier-ites.

After dinner the Pub Mont Fort is a very lively pick-up joint, (the shots bar in the cellar is worth a visit). Crok No Name has good live bands or a DJ and is entertaining for its cosmopolitan crowd. Murphy's Irish pub in the Garbo hotel is popular, with a good resident DJ. The much-loved King's is a quiet candlelit cellar bar with 60s decor – 'hip crowd, good music'. Bar New Club is a sophisticated piano bar, with comfortable seating and a more discerning clientele. Jacky's is a classy piano bar frequented by big spenders on their way to the Farm Club – an outrageously expensive nightclub which inexplicably is very popular, especially with balding geriatrics with much younger girls in tow (tables are difficult to book). It's packed with rich Swiss paying SF220 for bottles of spirits on Fridays and Saturdays.

More within the average pocket is the noisy, glitzy Marshalls Club, which sometimes has live music. Taratata is a friendly club that seems to be growing in popularity. Scotch is the cheapest disco in town and popular with teenagers and snowboarders. Big Ben is another cheaper, young place.

The beginner area at Les Esserts is floodlit for tubing etc on Saturday and Sunday evenings.

OFF THE SLOPES
No great attraction

Verbier has an excellent sports center and some nice walks, but otherwise very little to offer if you don't want to hit the slopes. Montreux is an enjoyable train excursion from Le Châble, and Martigny is worth a visit for the Roman arena and museums. Various mountain restaurants are accessible to pedestrians. Both toboggan runs – on the shady side of Savoleyres and from Les Ruinettes – are an impressive 10km/6 miles long.

STAYING IN OTHER RESORTS
A lot going for them
There are advantages to staying in the other resorts of the 4 Valleys. For a start, you can avoid the worst of the morning liftlines if you set off early, spend the day in the Verbier area and wave to the crowds on your way home.

Secondly, they are substantially cheaper for both accommodations and incidentals. What you lose is the Verbier ambience and its range of restaurants, bars and nightlife.

Nendaz is a sizeable and quite rounded resort, described below.

Veysonnaz and Thyon are both small resorts, with mainly apartment accommodations. Veysonnaz is by far the more attractive – an old village complete with church. It has adequate bars, cafes and restaurants, a disco, sports center with swimming pool, and school and guides. Thyon is a functional, ugly, purpose-built place.

Le Châble is a village a gondola-ride below Verbier. As changing gondola cars is not necessary for moving on to Les Ruinettes and Les Attelas, access to the slopes can be just as quick (or even quicker) from the liftline-free valley. Le Châble is particularly convenient for those traveling by train, and for drivers who want to visit other resorts.

Nendaz 1365m/4,480ft

Nendaz is a big resort with over 17,000 beds and handily placed for exploring all of the 4 Valleys. It deserves more attention, especially if you want a cheaper base from which to use Verbier's slopes – but avoid the Sloanes and other Brits it attracts. Airport transfers are quick.

THE RESORT
Nendaz itself is a large place on a shelf above and with great views of the Rhône valley. Most of the resort is modern but built in traditional chalet-style and the original old village of Haute-Nendaz is still there, with its narrow streets, old houses and barns, and baroque chapel dating from 1499.

THE MOUNTAIN
Nendaz has a central and convenient location in the 4 Valleys and allows you to avoid some of the worst liftlines.

Slopes There's a 12-person gondola straight to the top of the local north-facing slopes at Tracouet (2200m/7,220ft). Here there are good, snow-sure beginner areas plus blue and red intermediate runs back to town through the trees.

Intermediate and better skiers and boarders can head off down the back of Tracouet to a tram which takes you to Plan de Fou at 2430m/7,970ft. From there you can go down to Siviez and the links to Tortin, Mont Fort and the local Verbier slopes in one direction and Thyon and Veysonnaz in the other.

Snow reliability Nendaz sits on a north-facing shelf so its local slopes don't get the sun that affects Verbier.

Snowboarding There is also a snowboard terrain-park.

Experts Access to the tough stuff is a bit slower from here than from Verbier.

Intermediates Nendaz makes an excellent base for 4 Valleys exploration. Coming back to Nendaz you have to use an ungroomed ski route but intermediates can take the Plan de Fou tram down instead. Or you can take a shuttle-bus between Nendaz and Siviez.

Beginners There are good beginners' slopes at Tracouet.

Cross-country There are 17km/11 miles of cross-country tracks.

Liftlines There may be lines at Siviez at the end of the day.

Mountain restaurants The most compelling are in the Verbier area.

Schools and guides A reporter tells us that families seemed pleased with the school.

Facilities for children The school has a nursery area at Tracouet.

STAYING THERE
Accommodations are mainly in apartments but there are a few friendly and traditional hotels.

Hotels Reporters recommend the Sourire – 'simple, but good food'.

Apartments/condos There is no shortage of apartments bookable locally or through Interhome.

Eating out There are several good restaurants; readers recommend the hotel Sourire and the nearby Mont Rouge restaurant.

Après-ski There are plenty of bars and four discos; a 17-year-old reporter recommends the Cactus and the Bodega as the liveliest spots.

Off the slopes Nendaz has 70km/43 miles of winter walks, an open-air ice rink, a fitness center and squash courts.

TOURIST OFFICE

Postcode CH-1936
t +41 (27) 775 3888
f 775 3889
info@verbier.ch
www.verbier.ch

Verbier

Villars
1300m/4,270ft

Let the train take the strain

HOW IT RATES

The slopes

Snow	**
Extent	**
Experts	**
Intermediates	***
Beginners	****
Convenience	***
Lines	***
Restaurants	***

The rest

Scenery	***
Resort charm	****
Off-slope	****

What's new

For 2001/02 a six-seater chair will link from La Rasse to Chaux Ronde, replacing a surface lift and slow chair.

⊕ Pleasant, relaxing year-round resort

⊕ Fairly extensive intermediate slopes linked to Les Diablerets

⊕ Good beginner areas

⊕ Quite close to Geneva airport

⊕ Good range of off-slope diversions

⊖ Unreliable snow cover

⊖ Overcrowded mountain restaurants

⊖ Main lift a bus-ride from the town centre

With its mountain railway and gentle low-altitude slopes, Villars is the kind of place that has been overshadowed by modern mega-resorts. But for a relaxing and varied family holiday the attractions are clear – and improved lifts and links with Les Diablerets have added to the appeal.

THE RESORT

Villars sits on a sunny shelf at 1300m/4,270ft, looking across the Rhône valley to the mountains of the Portes du Soleil. A busy main street lined with all sorts of shops gives Villars the air of a pleasant small town; all around are chalet-style buildings, with just two or three block-like large hotels. You can reach Villars by a cog railway from the valley, and it goes on up into the slopes from a station at one end of the town. But a gondola at the other end is the main lift; it's worth staying nearby if possible – there are reliable shuttle-buses, but they get crowded at the peaks. There is an alternative way into the lift system via a gondola at Barboleuse, near Gryon (so you'll see the resort marketed as Villars-Gryon).

The lift system links with Les Diablerets (much more conveniently than it once did), and outings to Leysin and Champéry are possible by rail or road. Many other resorts (such as Verbier) are within driving distance.

334

Villars

335

Intermediates The local slopes offer a good range of variety, and with the slopes of Les Diablerets there is a fair amount of terrain to explore. The adventurous should take a trip to the Diablerets glacier for the splendid red run down the Combe d'Audon.

Beginners Beginners will feel comfortable on the village beginner slopes, and riding the train to Bretaye. There are gentle slopes here, too, but also lots of people speeding through a crowded area.

Snowboarding There are terrain-parks at both Bretaye and Les Chaux.

Cross-country The trails up the valley past La Rasse are long and pretty, and there are more in the depression beyond Bretaye (44km/27 miles in all).

Liftlines Lines appear for the lifts at Bretaye mainly at weekends.

Mountain restaurants The mountain restaurants are often overcrowded. The Golf Club is pricey but gets excellent reports, as does the Col de Soud ('best rösti ever'); Lac des Chavonnes (open weekends and peak periods) is worth the walk involved. Les Vioz in Les Diablerets is also recommended.

Schools and guides Villars' Ecole Moderne (still using the ski évolutif method) and the Swiss ski school both get positive reports. Riderschool is a specialist snowboard outfit. The Bureau des Guides organizes heli-trips.

Facilities for children Both ski schools run children's classes. There is also a non-ski nursery for children up to six.

STAYING THERE

Hotels The hotel du Golf (495 2477) is popular and has recently been upgraded to a 4-star ('great, family tries hard'). The 4-star Eurotel Victoria (495 3131) lacks character but not space – it has huge rooms.

Eating out Many of the restaurants are hotel-based. The neo-rustic Vieux-Villars is popular for local specialities.

Après-ski Charlie's, the Central and the Mini-Pub are popular bars. El Gringo and Fox are the discos.

Off the slopes There's plenty to keep you active: tennis courts, walks, swimming, skating and curling; or trips on the train – to Lausanne for instance.

MOUNTAIN FACTS

Altitude	1130m-3000m
	3,710ft-9,840ft
Lifts	46
Trails	125km
	78 miles
Blue	40%
Red	50%
Black	10%
Snowmaking	17km
	11 miles
Recco detectors used	

Phone numbers
From elsewhere in Switzerland add the prefix 024.
From abroad use the prefix +41 24.

TOURIST OFFICE

Postcode CH-1884
t +41 (24) 495 3232
f 495 2794
information@villars.ch
www.villars.ch

THE MOUNTAINS

There's a good mix of open and wooded slopes throughout the area.

Slopes The railway goes up to the col of Bretaye, which has intermediate slopes on either side, with a maximum vertical of 300m/1,000ft back to the col and much longer runs back to the village. To the east, easier open slopes (very susceptible to sun) go to La Rasse (1350m/4,430ft) and the link to the otherwise separate Les Chaux sector. Beyond Les Diablerets the village is Les Diablerets the glacier-equipped mountain, covered by the lift ticket. The main interest is the slopes descending from the glacier (see 'Intermediates').

Snow reliability Low altitude and sunny orientation mean that Villars' snow reliability is not good, though new mobile snowmaking guns have helped.

Experts The main interest for experts is in exploring off-trail. There is plenty of worthwhile terrain reachable from the Chaux de Conches, for example.

Charm, stunning views and extensive intermediate terrain

HOW IT RATES

The slopes

Snow	**
Extent	***
Experts	**
Intermediates	****
Beginners	***
Convenience	***
Liftlines	***
Restaurants	****

The rest

Scenery	*****
Resort charm	*****
Off-slope	****

➕ Some of the most spectacular scenery in the Alps

➕ Traditional, 'traffic-free' Alpine village, reached only by cog railway

➕ Lots of long, gentle runs, ideal for intermediates, leading down to Grindelwald

➕ Rebuilt tram now an attractive alternative to trains up to the slopes

➕ Beginner areas in heart of village

➕ Calm, unhurried atmosphere

➖ Limited terrain for experts

➖ Despite some snowmaking, snow conditions are unreliable – especially on the sunny home run and village beginner area

➖ Trains to slopes from here and from Grindelwald are slow and infrequent – you have to plan your movements with the aid of timetables

➖ Getting to Grindelwald's First area can take hours

➖ Subdued in the evening, with little variety of nightlife

Given the charm of the village, the friendliness of the locals and the drama of the scenery, it's easy to see why some people – including numbers of middle-aged people who have been going for decades – love Wengen. But non-devotees should think carefully about the lack of challenge, the unreliable snow and the dependence on cog railways before signing up.

The last of these drawbacks is slightly less serious than it was. The Männlichen tram station, destroyed in the devastating avalanches of 1999, was rebuilt in the heart of the village, where it is not only less vulnerable to avalanche but also much more convenient. Of course, the tram is now more popular, and gets lines. So those willing to gear their holiday activities to timetables – or to accept half-hour waits for trains – will still mainly rely on the railway. The rest of us will probably conclude that life is too short, and go elsewhere.

The resort

Wengen is set on a shelf high above the Lauterbrunnen valley, opposite Mürren, and reached only by a cog railway, which carries on up the mountain as the main lift. Wengen was a farming community long before skiing arrived; it is still tiny, but it is dominated by sizeable hotels, mostly of Victorian origin. So it is not exactly pretty, but it is charming and relaxed, and almost traffic-free. The only traffic is electric hotel taxi-trucks, which gather at the station to pick up guests, and a few ordinary gas-engined cabs. (Why, we wonder?)

The short main street is the hub of the village. Lined with chalet-style shops and hotels, it also has the ice rink and village beginner areas right next to it. The beginner areas double as the venue for floodlit ski-jumping and parallel slalom races.

The views across the valley are stunning. They get even better higher

up, when the famous trio of peaks comes fully into view – the Mönch (Monk) protecting the Jungfrau (Maiden) from the Eiger (Ogre).

The main way up the mountain is the regular, usually punctual trains from the southern end of the street to Kleine Scheidegg, where the slopes of Wengen meet those of Grindelwald. The tram is a much quicker way to the Grindelwald slopes, and now starts conveniently close to the main street.

Wengen is small, so location isn't as crucial as in many other resorts. The main street is ideally placed for the station. There are hotels on the home trail, convenient for the slopes. Those who don't fancy a steepish morning climb should avoid places down the hill below the station.

You can get to Mürren by taking the train down to Lauterbrunnen, and a funicular and connecting train up the other side. The Jungfrau lift ticket covers all of this. Outings farther afield aren't really worth the effort.

The mountains

MOUNTAIN FACTS

Altitude	945m-2970m
	3,100ft-9,740ft
Lifts	45
Trails	205km
	127 miles
Blue	30%
Red	50%
Black	20%
Snowmaking	30km
	19 miles
Recco detectors used	

Although it is famous for the fearsome Lauberhorn Downhill course – the longest and one of the toughest on the World Cup circuit – Wengen's slopes are best suited to early intermediates. There are no seriously steep trails and the scariest part of the Downhill course, the Hundschopf jump, is shut to tourists. Most runs are gentle blues and reds, ideal for cruising.

THE SLOPES
Picturesque playground

Most of the slopes are on the Grindelwald side of the mountain. From the railway station at Kleine Scheidegg you can head straight down to Grindelwald or work your way across the mountain with the help of a couple of lifts to the top of the Männlichen. This area is served by surface and chair-lifts, and can be reached directly from Wengen by the improved tram.

There are a few runs back down towards Wengen from the top of the **Lauberhorn** (2480m/8,140ft), but below Kleine Scheidegg there's really only one.

SNOWPIX.COM / CHRIS GILL

It's not surprising that sightseeing helicopter tours around the Jungfrau massif are in great demand →

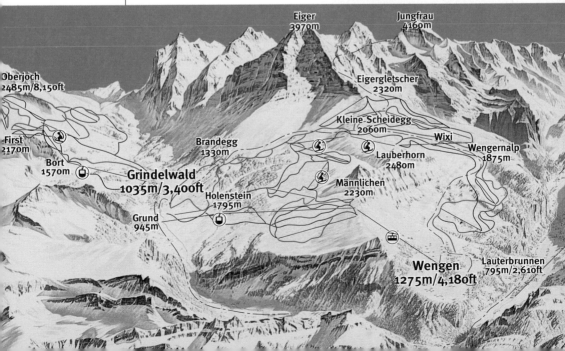

Eiger 3970m

Jungfrau 4160m

Oberjoch 2485m/8,150ft

Eigergletscher 2320m

First 2170m

Kleine Scheidegg 2060m

Wixi

Brandegg 1330m

Lauberhorn 2480m

Wengernalp 1875m

Bort 1570m

Grindelwald 1035m/3,400ft

Männlichen 2230m

Holenstein 1795m

Grund 945m

Wengen 1275m/4,180ft

Lauterbrunnen 795m/2,610ft

LIFT TICKETS

2000/01 prices in Swiss francs

Jungfrau Top Ski Region
Covers all lifts in Wengen, Mürren and Grindelwald, trains between them and Grindelwald ski-bus.
Beginners Points card (adult 100 points 48, lifts cost 4 to 10 points).
Main ticket
1-day ticket 52
6-day ticket 254
Senior citizens
Over 62: 6-day ticket 229
Children
16 to 19: 6-day ticket 203
Under 16: 6-day ticket 127
Under 6: 10
Short-term tickets
Single ascent tickets for most lifts. Half-day ticket for First (adult 40), Kleine Scheidegg-Männlichen (adult 40) and Mürren-Schilthorn (adult 40).
Alternative periods
3 days in 7 ticket available (156).
Notes
Day ticket price is for Kleine Scheidegg-Männlichen area only (102km/63 miles of trails 21 lifts), as Jungfrau Top Ski Region ticket is only available for 2 days or over.
Discounts for groups.
Alternative tickets
1- and 2-day tickets available for First (adult 2-day 95), Mürren-Schilthorn (adult 2-day 95) and Kleine Scheidegg-Männlichen (adult 2-day 95).
4-, 5- and 6-day tickets available for non-skiers (adult 6-day 189)

SNOW RELIABILITY
Why not use the guns?

Most slopes are below 2000m/6,500ft, and at Grindelwald they go down to less than 1000m/3,300ft. Very few slopes face north and Wengen's snowmaking facilities are not up to protecting them. The real shame is that the snowmaking that exists isn't always used when it's needed.

All this can mean problems, and while we've found wonderful snow a couple of times in late March, we've also struggled to find decent snow to ski on in January.

FOR EXPERTS
Few challenges

Wengen is quite limited for experts. The one genuine black run in the area takes you from Eigergletscher to Wixi. For most of its length, the Lauberhorn Downhill course is merely of intermediate red run gradient.

The main challenges are off-trail runs such as Oh God from near Eigergletscher to Wixi (and even that is now classified as a 'free-ride trail') and White Hare from under the north face of the Eiger. There are a number of more adventurous off-trail runs from the Jungfraujoch late in the season. For more challenges it's well worth going to nearby Mürren, an hour away by train and funicular. Heli-trips with mountain guides are organized if there are enough takers.

FOR INTERMEDIATES
Wonderful if the snow is good

Wengen and Grindelwald share superb intermediate slopes. Nearly all are long blue or gentle red runs – see Grindelwald chapter. The run back to Wengen is a relaxing end to the day, as long as it's not too crowded.

For tougher trails, head for the top of the Lauberhorn lift and then the runs to Kleine Scheidegg, or to Wixi (following the start of the Downhill course). You could also try the north-facing run from Eigergletscher to Salzegg, which often has the best snow late in the season.

FOR BEGINNERS
Not ideal

There's a beginner area in the center of the village – it's convenient and gentle, but the snow is unreliable. A small part of it is now served by a moving carpet lift, ideal for children. There's a beginner area at Wengernalp, but to get back to Wengen you either have to climb up to the train or tackle the run down, which can be tricky. There are plenty of good, long, gentle slopes to progress to.

FOR CROSS-COUNTRY
There is none

There's no cross-country skiing in Wengen itself. There are tracks down in the Lauterbrunnen valley, but the snow there is unreliable.

LIFTLINES
Improving, but a long way to go

The new Männlichen tram has helped cut the lines for the trains but both can still suffer from horrific bottlenecks in peak periods, as well as daily scrambles to board the trains that the school uses. Weekend invasions can increase the crowds on the Grindelwald side, especially. Liftlines up the mountain have been alleviated a lot in the last few years by the installation of fast quad chairs on the Grindelwald side – though plenty of old lifts remain.

MOUNTAIN RESTAURANTS
Plenty of variety

A popular but expensive place for lunch is Wengernalp, where the rösti is excellent and the views of the Jungfrau are superb. The highest restaurant is at Eigergletscher. If you get there early on a sunny day, you can grab a table on the narrow outside balcony and enjoy magnificent views of the glacier. The station buffet at Kleine Scheidegg gets repeated rave reviews, so it's not surprising that it also gets packed – the take-out rösti and sausage are a popular option. The Grindelwaldenblick is a worthwhile trudge uphill from Kleine Scheidegg, with great food and

boarding *Wengen is not a bad place for gentle boarding – the beginner area is not ideal, but beginners have plenty of slopes to progress to, with lots of long blue and red runs served by the train and chair-lifts. Getting from Kleine Scheidegg to Männlichen means an unavoidable surface lift though. There's a terrain-park at Wengernalp but experts will tire quickly of the area, and hanker after the steeper slopes of Mürren.*

The cog railway remains the main way up the mountain for Wengen residents →

SCHOOLS/GUIDES

2000/01 prices in Swiss francs

Swiss
Classes 6 days
3hr: am
6 half days: 219
Children's classes
Ages: 4 to 12
6 half days: 219
Private lessons
2hr, 3hr or 5hr
135 for 2hr

CHILDCARE

The kindergarten on the first floor of the Sport Pavilion takes children from 18 months from 8.30 to 5pm, Sunday to Friday. Children can be taken to and from lessons with the ski school, which starts at age 4.

A couple of 4-star hotels have their own kindergartens.

GETTING THERE

Air Zürich, transfer 3½hr. Bern, transfer 1½hr.

Rail Station in resort.

views of the Eiger. In the village, the Gruebi cafe, a short walk from the tram station, is highly recommended. For restaurants down towards Grindelwald, see the Grindelwald chapter.

SCHOOLS AND GUIDES
Healthy competition
A reporter says, 'The Swiss school is definitely trying harder than a few years ago.' The lessons and the standard of English are usually good. The independent Privat school has been recommended for private lessons.

Snowboarders are well served. And guides are available for heli-trips and powder excursions.

FACILITIES FOR CHILDREN
Apparently satisfactory
Our reports on children's facilities are from observers rather than participants, but are all favorable. It is an attractive village for families, with the baby slope in the center.

The train gives easy access to higher slopes.

Staying there 🔑

HOW TO GO
Wide range of hotels
Most accommodations are in hotels. Apartments are few.
Hotels There are about two dozen hotels, mostly 4-star and 3-star, with a handful of simpler places.
((((4) **Wengener Hof** (855 2855) No prizes for style or convenience, but recommended for peace, helpful staff and spacious, spotless rooms with good views.
((((4) **Sunstar** (856 5111) Modern hotel on main street. Comfortable rooms; lounge has a log fire. Live music some nights. Pool with views. Food very good. Friendly.
((((4) **Regina** (855 1512) Quite central. Smart, traditional atmosphere. 'Best food in Wengen.' Carousel nightclub.
((((4) **Silberhorn** (856 5131) Comfortable, modern 4-star in excellent central position, with choice of restaurants.

Wengen

339

THE BRITISH IN WENGEN

There's a very strong British presence at Wengen. Many Brits have been returning to the same rooms in the same hotels in the same week, year after year, and treat the resort as a sort of second home. There is an English church with weekly services, and a British-run club, the DHO (Downhill Only) – so named when the first Brits persuaded the locals to keep the summer railway running up the mountain in winter so they would no longer have to climb up in order to ski down again. That greatly amused the locals, who until then had regarded skiing in winter as a necessity rather than a pastime to be done for fun. The DHO is still going strong and organizes regular events throughout the season.

Phone numbers
From elsewhere in Switzerland add the prefix 033.
From abroad use the prefix +41 33.

ACTIVITIES

Indoor Swimming pool (in Beausite Park and Sunstar hotels), sauna, solarium, whirlpool, massage (in hotels), movie theater (with English films), billiards

Outdoor Skating, curling, 50km/30 miles cleared paths, toboggan runs, paragliding, glacier flights, sledging excursions, hang-gliding

TOURIST OFFICE

Postcode CH-3823
t +41 (33) 855 1414
f 855 3060
info@wengen.ch
www.wengen-muerren.ch

((((④ **Caprice** (855 4141) Small, smartly furnished chalet-style hotel across the tracks from the Regina. Kindergarten. 'Comfortable and friendly' according to a recent guest.

(((③ **Bellevue** (855 1121) Some way out, but does have the best views as well as 'friendly staff and excellent food'.

(((③ **Alpenrose** (855 3216) Small, simple rooms, but good views; 'first-class' food; friendly staff. Eight minutes' climb to the station.

(((③ **Eiger** (855 1131) Very conveniently sited, right next to the station. Focal après-ski bar. Rebuilt with comfy modern rooms.

(((③ **Falken** (856 5121) Further up the hill, with lots of regular guests who affectionately call it 'Fawlty Towers'.

Apartments/condos The hotel Bernerhof's decent Résidence apartments (855 2721) are well positioned just off the main street, and hotel facilities are available to guests.

EATING OUT
Lots of choice

Most restaurants in the village are in the hotels. They offer good food and service, and are open to non-residents. Recent recommendations include the Eiger, with a traditional restaurant and a stube with Swiss and French cuisine, the Sunstar ('high quality, not such high prices') and the Bernerhof ('good-value honest cooking'). The little hotel Hirschen has 'the best steaks'. There's no shortage of fondues in the village. Several bars do casual food, including good-value pizza at Sina's. You could eat at Wengernalp's excellent restaurant – but you have to get back on skis or on a toboggan.

APRES-SKI
It depends on what you want

People's reactions to the après-ski scene in Wengen vary widely, according to their expectations and appetites. If you're used to raving in Kitzbühel or Les Deux Alpes, you'll rate Wengen dead, especially for young people. If you've heard it's dead, you may be pleasantly surprised to find that there is a handful of bars that do good business both early and late in the evening. But it is only a handful of small places. The Schnee-Bar, at the Bumps section of the home run, is a popular final run stop-off. And the stube at the Eiger and the tiny, 'always welcoming' Eiger Bar are popular at the end of the day, especially with

Germans and Scandinavians. The traditional Tanne and the funky Chilli's are almost opposite on the main street, and generally lively. Sina's, a little way out by Club Med, usually has live music. The Caprice bar is also recommended as is the new Mister Mac bar and disco. There are discos and live music in some hotels. The movie theater often shows English-language films.

OFF THE SLOPES
Good for a relaxing time

Wengen is a superb resort for those who want a completely relaxing holiday, with its unbeatable scenery and pedestrian-friendly trains and tram (there's a special, though expensive, five-day ticket). There are some lovely walks, ice skating and a curling club. Several hotels have health spas. Excursions to Interlaken and Bern are possible by train, as is the trip up to the Jungfraujoch (see the Grindelwald chapter). Helicopter flights from Männlichen are recommended.

STAYING UP THE MOUNTAIN
Great views

You can stay at two points up the mountain reached by the railway: the pricey Jungfrau (855 1622) at Wengernalp and at Kleine Scheidegg, where there's a choice of rooms in the big Scheidegg-Hotels (855 1212) or dormitory space above the Grindelwaldblick restaurant and the station buffet. The big restaurant at Männlichen also has rooms.

STAYING DOWN THE VALLEY
The budget option

Staying in a 3-star hotel like the Schützen (855 2032) or Oberland (855 1241) in Lauterbrunnen will cost about half as much as similar accommodations in Wengen. The train from Wengen runs until 11.30pm and is included in your lift ticket. Staying in Lauterbrunnen also improves your chances of getting a seat on the train to Kleine Scheidegg rather than joining the scramble at Wengen – though of course it also means a longer journey time. Lauterbrunnen is also much better placed for Mürren.

You can save even more by staying in Interlaken. Choose a hotel near Interlaken Ost station, from which you can catch a train to Lauterbrunnen (22 minutes) or Grindelwald (36 minutes). Driving can take longer at weekends.

Magical in many respects – both on and off the slopes

HOW IT RATES

The slopes

Snow	★★★★
Extent	★★★★
Experts	★★★★★
Intermediates	★★★★
Beginners	★
Convenience	★
Liftlines	★★★
Restaurants	★★★★★

The rest

Scenery	★★★★★
Resort charm	★★★★★
Off-slope	★★★★

What's new

For the 2000/01 season moving carpets were installed from the tunnel at Sunnegga to the Eisfluh T-bar and in the snowboard training area at Blauherd.

A fabulous new terrain-park and half-pipe were built near Riffelberg, an ice cave opened on Klein Matterhorn and winter hiking along a 2.5km/1.5 mile trail made possible on Gornergrat.

The extended and refurbished 5-star Riffelalp resort hotel reopened at 2222m/7,290ft.

A much-needed new ski school (now called StokedAG-The Ski-School Zermatt) opened to compete with the existing school, which has a poor reputation.

- ➕ Wonderful, high and extensive slopes for experts and intermediates, with three separate and interestingly different areas
- ➕ Spectacular high-mountain scenery, dominated by the Matterhorn
- ➕ Charming, if rather sprawling, old mountain village, largely traffic-free
- ➕ Reliable snow at altitude
- ➕ World's best mountain restaurants
- ➕ Extensive helicopter operation
- ➕ Nightlife to suit most tastes
- ➕ Smart shops
- ➕ Linked to Cervinia in Italy

- ➖ Getting to main lift stations may involve a long walk, crowded (but free) bus or expensive cab-ride
- ➖ Main ski school has poor reputation (but new rival school just started)
- ➖ Beginners should go elsewhere
- ➖ One-way link only between Klein Matterhorn and the other two areas
- ➖ Getting up the mountain and around the different areas can be slow
- ➖ Annoying electric cabs detract from the otherwise relaxed, car-free village ambience

You must try Zermatt before you die. Few places can match its combination of excellent advanced and intermediate slopes, reliable snow, magnificent scenery, Alpine charm and mountain restaurants with superb food and stunning views.

Many people complain that the car-free village is spoiled by intrusive electric carts and cabs; some complain about the time it takes to get to the top of the mountain; others say that the atmosphere is of Swiss efficiency and international tourism rather than mountain-village friendliness. But friendliness and service have definitely improved – we had fewer complaints about liftlines this year and there's a magical feel to both the village and the mountains.

Zermatt's flaws are minor compared to its attractions, which come close to matching perfectly our notion of the ideal winter resort. It's one of our favorites.

The resort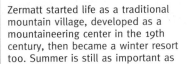

Zermatt started life as a traditional mountain village, developed as a mountaineering center in the 19th century, then became a winter resort too. Summer is still as important as winter here.

Be warned: Zermatt is big business and most restaurants and hotels are owned by a handful of families. Many of the workers are brought in from outside Switzerland – but that is probably one of the reasons many reporters have remarked on the increased friendliness and improved service in recent years.

The village sprawls along either side of a river, mountains rising steeply on each side. It is a mixture of chocolate-box chalets and modern buildings, most in traditional style. You arrive by rail or cab from Täsch, where cars have to be left, for a fee. They can be left

for free at more distant Visp, from where you can also get a train. The main street runs past the station, lined with luxury hotels and shops.

Zermatt doesn't have the relaxed, quaint feel of other car-free resorts, such as Wengen and Saas-Fee. That's partly because the electric vehicles are

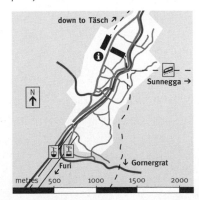

341

LIFT TICKETS

2000/01 prices in
Swiss francs
Area ticket
Covers all lifts on the
Swiss side of the
border.
Main ticket
1-day ticket 64
6-day ticket 318
Senior citizens
Over 65 (male), 62
(female): 6-day ticket
239
Children
Under 16: 6-day ticket
159
Under 9: free ticket
Short-term tickets
Single ascent tickets
for most lifts.
Notes Daily
supplement available
to cover all lifts in
Cervinia and
Valtournenche (33).
Alternative tickets
tickets for any period
available for each
area of Zermatt
(Gornergrat-
Stockhorn, Sunnegga-
Rothorn, Trockener
Steg-Klein
Matterhorn-
Schwarzsee), and
combinations of
areas. Ticket available
for Zermatt, Cervinia
and Valtournenche (1-
day: 64; 6-day: 366).

more intrusive and aggressive, and
partly because the clientele is more
overtly part of the jet set, with large
contingents from the US and Japan.

For a resort with such good and
extensive slopes, there's a remarkably
high age profile. Most visitors seem to
be over 40, and there's little of the
youthful atmosphere you get in rival
resorts with comparable slopes, such
as Val-d'Isère, St Anton and Chamonix.

The main street, with the station
square near one end, is the focal point
of village life. The cog railway to the
Gornergrat area leaves from opposite
the main station, and the underground
funicular to the Sunnegga area is a few
minutes' walk away. From here the
gondola to the Klein Matterhorn area
(and the link to Cervinia) is a 15-
minute trek, crowded bus-ride or
expensive cab ('The best daily SF20
investment of the trip,' said a reader).

The school and guides office, the
tourist office and many hotels, shops,
restaurants, bars and nightspots are on
or near the main street. Another main
street runs along the river. To each side
are narrow streets and paths; many are
hilly and treacherous when icy.

Bill Baker in Julen Sport is one of
the best boot fitters in the world – pay
him a visit if your boots are giving
you problems.

The mountains

There are slopes to suit all abilities
except absolute beginners, for whom
we don't recommend the resort. For

intermediates and experts Zermatt has
few rivals, with marvellously groomed
cruising trails, some of the best bumps
around, long, beautiful scenic runs out
of view of the lift system, exciting heli-
trips and off-trail possibilities, as well
as the opportunity to get down into
Italy for the day and lunch on pasta
and chianti. The hands-free, electronic
lift ticket system means you never
have to get it out of your pocket.

THE SLOPES
Beautiful and varied
Zermatt consists of three separate
areas, two of which are now well
linked. The **Sunnegga–Blauherd–
Rothorn** area is reached by the
underground funicular starting about
five minutes' walk from the station.
This shifts large numbers rapidly but
can lead to lines for the subsequent
gondola – you can take a run down to
a high-speed quad alternative.

From the top of this area you can
make your way – via south-facing
slopes served by snowmaking guns –
to Gant in the valley between
Sunnegga and the second main area,
Gornergrat–Hohtälli–Stockhorn. A new
125-person tram opened a few seasons
ago linking Gant to Hohtälli in just
seven minutes – a vast improvement
on the two gruelling steep T-bars that
were the only links before. A gondola
makes the link back from Gant to
Sunnegga.

Gornergrat can be reached direct
from Zermatt by cog railway trains
which leave every 24 minutes and take

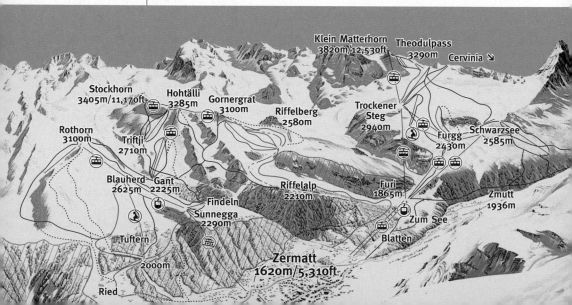

A great view of the Klein Matterhorn (top right) and the slopes between Trockener Steg and Furgg →

MOUNTAIN FACTS

Altitude	1620m-3820m
	5,310ft-12,530ft
Lifts	71
Trails	250km
	155 miles
Blue	22%
Red	50%
Black	28%
Snowmaking	43km
	27 miles
Recco detectors used	

30 or 40 minutes to get to the top – arrive at the station early to get a seat on the right-hand side and enjoy the stupendous views.

From Gornergrat, there's a trail, followed by a short walk, to Furi to link up with the third and highest area, **Klein Matterhorn–Trockener Steg-Schwarzsee**. But you can't do the journey in the opposite direction: once on the Klein Matterhorn, moving to a different mountain means heading down and getting from one end of the village to the other to catch a lift up. The Klein Matterhorn gives access to Cervinia – you need to buy an 'international ticket' or pay a daily supplement to your Zermatt lift ticket and the high lifts are sometimes shut because of high winds.

There are trails back to the village from all three areas – though some of them can be closed or tricky due to poor snow conditions at times.

SNOW RELIABILITY
Good high up, poor lower down
Zermatt has rocky terrain and a relatively dry climate. But it also has some of the highest slopes in Europe, and quite a lot of snowmaking.

All three areas go up to over 3000m/10,000ft, and the Klein Matterhorn tram is the highest in Europe, ending at over 3800m/12,500ft and serving a summer glacier. There are loads of runs above 2500m/8,200ft, many of which are north-facing, so guaranteeing decent snow except in freak years.

Artificial snowmaking machines serve some of the trails on all three areas, from around 3000m/10,000ft to under 2000m/6,500ft. The runs back to the village can still be patchy, but we've had noticeably better reports on trail maintenance and marking lately.

FOR EXPERTS
Good – with superb heli-trips
If you've never been, Zermatt has to be on your shortlist. If you have been, we're pretty sure you'll want to return.

If you love long, fluffy bump pitches, the slopes at Triftji, below Stockhorn, are the stuff of dreams. From the top of the Stockhorn tram there's a run down to the T-bar that serves another two steep 2km/1 mile runs – one each side of the lift. The whole mountainside here is one vast bump field – steep, but not extremely so. Being north-facing and lying between 3400m/11,150ft and 2700m/8,860ft, the snow is usually the best around, which makes the huge bumps so forgiving that even we can enjoy them. The snag in early season is that this whole area is unlikely to open until well into January, and possibly later.

You can continue down from here to

343

boarding *Boarders in soft boots have one big advantage over skiers in Zermatt – they have much more comfortable walks to and from the lift stations! Even so, there aren't many around. The slopes are best for experienced free-riders, because tough trail and off-trail action is what Zermatt is really about. There are acres of underused powder to ride, plus a world-class new terrain-park and half-pipe near Riffelberg and another park and pipe on Klein Matterhorn. The main lifts are boarder-friendly: train, funicular, gondolas and trams, but there are T-bars too. The resort is not ideal for learning, just as it isn't ideal for first-time skiers. Evenings have something for all.*

Gant and catch the gondola up to Blauherd. On that mountain there are a couple of wonderful off-trail 'downhill routes' from Rothorn, which have spectacular views down towards the village and over to the Matterhorn.

On the Klein Matterhorn, the best area for experts is Schwarzsee, from where there are several steep north-facing gullies through the woods. Unfortunately, you can't try these repeatedly without taking the beautiful, but slightly boring, track down to Furi and catching the tram up again.

There are marvellous off-trail possibilities from the top lifts in each sector, but they aren't immediately obvious to those without local knowledge. They are also dangerous because of rocky and glacial terrain.

We don't recommend anyone going off-trail without a guide. You can join daily ski touring groups but there aren't standard off-trail groups as there are in resorts such as Val-d'Isère and Méribel. Unless you join The Ski School Zermatt off-trail free-ride classes, you have to employ a guide privately for a full day, and that's expensive unless you have a fair-sized group. The Ski Club of Great Britain usually hires a guide for off-trail skiing once a week – we joined that on our last visit and had a great day.

Zermatt is the Alps' biggest heli-trip center; the helipad resembles a bus station at times, with choppers taking off every few minutes. There are only three main drop-off points, so this can mean encountering one or two other groups on the mountain, even though there are multiple ways down. From all three points there are routes that don't require great expertise. The epic is from Monte Rosa, at over 4000m/ 13,000ft, down through wonderful glacier scenery to Furi. If there isn't much snow you may need the help of a rope that's fixed at the almost vertical, icy end of the glacier to get down.

FOR INTERMEDIATES
Mile after mile of beautiful runs
Zermatt is ideal for adventurous intermediates. Many of the blue and red runs tend to be at the difficult end of their grading. There are very beautiful reds down lift-free valleys from both Gornergrat and Hohtälli to

THE WORLD'S BEST MOUNTAIN RESTAURANTS

We once met a man who had been coming here for 20 years simply because of the mountain restaurants. The choice is enormous (the tourist information says 38, but it seems more). Most have table-service, nearly all of those we've tried have excellent food and many are in spectacular settings. It is impossible to list here all those worth a visit – so don't limit yourself to those we mention. It is best to book – and check the prices are within your budget when you do so!

The restaurants at Fluhalp (live music and 'great glühwein and chocolate mit rum') and Grünsee have beautiful isolated situations and good food. The large terrace at Sunnegga has decent food and great views. Up at Rothorn, the restaurant has excellent food – we had wonderful lamb – and views. Down at Findeln are several attractive, busy, rustic restaurants, including Findlerhof (aka Franz & Heidy's), Chez Vrony ('this year's must'), Paradies and Enzian ('less crowded than others'). And the restaurant at Tuftern sells good Heida white wine from the highest vineyard in Europe – just down the valley at 1200m/3,940ft.

At Furi, the Restaurant Furi, Aroleid above it and Simi's on the road below all have large sun terraces and good food. The hotel at Schwarzsee is right at the foot of the Matterhorn, with staggering views and endless variations of rösti. Round the back from here Stafelalp is simple but charmingly situated. Up above Trockener Steg Gandegghütte has stunning views of the glacier and 'good polenta'. On the way back to the village below Furi, Zum See is a charming old hut serving the best mountain food in Zermatt (which means it is world-class: we had delicious beef, lamb and raspberry tart here last season). Blatten is good too.

The Kulmhotel, at 3100m/10,170ft at Gornergrat, has both self-service and table-service restaurants with amazing views of lift-free mountains and glaciers.

Wherever you go, don't miss the local alcoholic coffee – in its many varieties!

Gant – we love these first thing in the morning, before anyone else is on them. A variant to Riffelalp ends up on a narrow wooded path with a sheer cliff and magnificent views to the right.

On Sunnegga, the 5km/3 mile Kumme run, from Rothorn to the bottom of the Patrullarve chair, also gets away from the lift system and has an interesting mix of straight-running and bump pitches. On Klein Matterhorn, the reds served by the Hörnli and Garten surface lifts and the fast four-person chair from Furgg are all long and gloriously set at the foot of the Matterhorn.

For less adventurous intermediates, the blues on Sunnegga and above Riffelberg on Gornergrat and the runs between Klein Matterhorn and Trockener Steg are best. Of these, the Riffelberg area often has the best combination of good snow and easy cruising, and is popular with the school. Sunnegga gets a lot of sun, but the snowmaking means that bare patches are less of a problem than deep heavy snow near the bottom.

On the Klein Matterhorn, most of the runs, though marked red on the trail map, are very flat and represent the easiest slopes Zermatt has to offer, as well as the best snow. The problem here is the possibility of bad weather because of the height – high winds, extreme cold and poor visibility can make life very unpleasant. To get to Cervinia, you set off from Testa Grigia with a choice of two routes – even an early intermediate should find the easier 10km/6 mile route (on the left as you look at the Cervinia trail map) down to the village manageable. The red Ventina run is a delightful cruise for better intermediates.

Beware of the run from Furgg to Furi at the end of the day, when it can be tricky and very crowded.

FOR BEGINNERS
Learn elsewhere
Zermatt is to be avoided by beginners. The easiest slopes are outlined above. And there's no decent beginner area area. Unless you have a compelling reason to start in Zermatt, don't.

FOR EVERYONE
A spectacular tram ride
The Klein Matterhorn tram is an experience not to miss if the weather is good. The views down to the glacier and its crevasses, as the car swings steeply into its hole blasted out of the mountain at the top, are stupendous. When you arrive, you walk through a long tunnel, to emerge on top of the world for the highest trail in Europe – walk slowly, the air is thin here and some people have altitude problems. The top surface lifts here are open in the summer.

FOR CROSS-COUNTRY
Fairly limited
There's a 4km/2.5 mile loop at Furi, 3km/2 mile near the bottom of the gondola to Furi, and 12 to 15km/7 to 9 miles down at Täsch (don't count on there being snow). There are also some 'ski walking trails' – best tackled as part of an organized group.

LIFTLINES
Some bottlenecks, and slow lifts
Zermatt used to have one of the worst reputations for liftlines in the Alps. Many major problems have now been eliminated but there can still be a lengthy scramble for the gondola out of town towards Klein Matterhorn at the start of the day, followed by long waits for the two successive trams to the top – one reporter complained the whole journey took two and a half hours. Buses back to town from Klein Matterhorn at the end of the day are also overcrowded. The other problem is the Gornergrat train – you may find there's only standing room.

But some reporters had largely line-free stays, even in mid-February, and raved about the empty runs. And one thing we love about Zermatt is that the lifts start at 8am. Get out early and you can enjoy deserted slopes for at least two hours.

SCHOOLS AND GUIDES
Welcome competition at last
The main Swiss school has a poor reputation and one reporter said: 'Awful – in three days, the instructor taught our early intermediate no technique, spoke no English and used the follow-me method the whole time.' But another praised the half-day private lessons his wife had: 'Excellent English and her skiing improved dramatically.'

There's a separate Stoked snowboard school, which we have good reports of. This has now combined with a new ski school which started last season and is made up of talented young instructors, all of whom

SCHOOLS/GUIDES
2000/01 prices in Swiss francs

Swiss
Classes 5 days
6hr: 3hr am and pm
5 full days: 280
Children's classes
Ages: 4-6 and 6-12
5 full days including lunch: 270-330
Private lessons
1hr, 2hr or full-day
full day: 330 for 1 or 2 people; each additional person 15

The Ski School
Classes 5hr: 9.3-12 and 1-3.30
5 full days: 410
Children's classes 5 full days including lunch: 485
Private lessons
half or full-day
full day: 360 for 1; each additional person 25

CHILDCARE

There are nurseries in two upscale hotels. The one in the Nicoletta (966 0777) takes children aged 2 to 8, from 9am to 5pm. The Kinderclub Pumuckel at the Ginabelle (966 5000) takes children from 30 months, from 9am to 5pm, and ski lessons are available on the spot. The Kinderparadies (967 7252) takes children from 3 months from 9am to 5pm. Private babysitters are available, too.

Ski school lessons start at age 4.

Phone numbers
From elsewhere in Switzerland add the prefix 027.
From abroad use the prefix +41 27.

speak good English. They were called 4Synergies last season and a reporter who took a private instructor highly recommends them. Next season they will be called the The Ski School Zermatt and have 25 full-time instructors. Their program includes off-trail free-ride classes and freestyle classes (learning tricks in the terrain-park) as well as standard lessons.

FACILITIES FOR CHILDREN
Good hotel nurseries
The Nicoletta and Ginabelle hotels have obvious attractions for families who can afford them (though their nurseries are open to others). Despite our fat file of reports on Zermatt, we have no first-hand reports on them.

 Staying there

Choosing where to stay is very important in Zermatt. The solar-powered shuttle-buses are crowded, but at least they are now large, free to lift-ticket holders and more frequent than they used to be. Walking from one end of the village to the furthest lifts can take 15 to 20 minutes and can be unpleasant because of treacherous icy paths.

The best spot for most people is near the Gornergrat and Sunnegga railways, near the end of the main street. Some accommodations are up the steep hill across the river from the center in Winkelmatten. This is less isolated than it appears say reporters – you can ski back to it from all areas and the bus to town is reliable.

Getting up to the village from Täsch is no problem. The trains run on time and have automatically descending ramps that allow you to wheel luggage trolleys on and off. You are met at the other end by electric and horse-drawn cabs and hotel shuttles.

HOW TO GO
A wide choice
Hotels There are over 100 hotels, mostly comfortable and traditional-style 3-stars and 4-stars, but taking in the whole range.
Mont Cervin (966 8888) Biggest in town. Elegantly traditional. Good pool.
Zermatterhof (966 6600) Traditional 'grand hotel' style with piano bar and pool.
Riffelalp Resort (966 0555) Up the mountain, newly refurbished and extended, pool and spa, own evening trains.

Alex (966 7070) Close to station. Good facilities, including a pool. Reporters love it.
Ambassador (966 2611) Peaceful position near Gornergrat station. Large pool; sauna.
Monte Rosa (966 0333) Well-modernized original Zermatt hotel, near southern end of village – full of climbing pictures and mementos.
Ginabelle (966 5000) Smart pair of chalets not far from Sunnegga lift; great for families – on-the-spot ski nursery as well as day care.
Nicoletta (966 0777) Modern chalet quite close to center, with nursery.
Sonne (966 2066) Traditionally decorated, in quiet setting away from main street; 'Roman Bath' complex.
Butterfly (966 4166) 'Small, friendly, close to and as well furnished as the Alex, but much better food,' says a recent reporter.
Julen (966 7600) Charming, modern-rustic chalet over the river, with Matterhorn views from some rooms.
Atlanta (966 3535) No frills, but good food; close to center, with Matterhorn views from some rooms.
Alpina (967 1050) Modest but very friendly, and close to center.
Apartments/condos There are a lot of apartment accommodations. The tourist office can provide a list of apartments and tell you availability.

STAYING UP THE MOUNTAIN
Comfortable seclusion
There are several hotels at altitude, of which the pick is the Riffelalp Resort at the first stop on the Gornergrat railway (see Hotels above), which re-opened as a luxury hotel last season – but you might find its limited evening train service a bit restricting. At the top of the railway, at 3100m/10,170ft, is the Kulmhotel Gornergrat – a rather austere building with basic accommodations.

STAYING DOWN THE VALLEY
Attractive for drivers
In Täsch, where visitors must leave their cars, there are five 3-star hotels, costing less than half the price of the equivalent in Zermatt. The Täscherhof (967 1818) is next to the station; the City (967 3606) close by. It's a 13-minute ride from Zermatt, with trains every 20 minutes for most of the day; the last train down is 11.10.

GETTING THERE

Air Geneva, rail transfer 4hr. Zürich, rail transfer 5hr. Sion, transfer 1 1/2hr.

Rail Station in resort.

ACTIVITIES

Indoor Sauna, tennis, hotel swimming pools (some open to public), salt water pool, keep-fit center, squash, billiards, curling, bowling, gallery, excellent Alpine museum, movie theater, indoor golf
Outdoor Skating, curling, sleigh rides, 30km/19 miles cleared paths, helicopter flights, paragliding, cycling, ice-diving

TOURIST OFFICE

Postcode CH-3920
t +41 (27) 966 8100
f 966 8101
zermatt@wallis.ch
www.zermatt.ch

EATING OUT
Huge choice at all price levels

There are over 100 restaurants to choose from, ranging from top-quality haute cuisine, through traditional Swiss food, Chinese, Japanese and Thai to egg and chips and even a McDonald's.

'Enzo, Vrony' has superb food and unique decor (combining new with old), with the kitchen in full view in the center. Booking is essential.

The Mazot is highly rated and highly priced. All the top hotels have classy restaurants open to non-residents. At the other end of the scale, Café du Pont has good-value pasta and rösti.

The Schwyzer Stübli has local specialities and usually live Swiss music and dancing. The Bahnhof Buffet has been rebuilt and serves reasonable food in a dining room built like a panoramic railway carriage.

Da Mario, Casa Rustica, Baku (see Après-ski) and the Spaghetti Factory (in the Hotel Post complex) have all been recommended by readers.

APRES-SKI
Lively and varied

A good mix of sophisticated and informal fun, though it helps if you have deep pockets. On the way back from the Klein Matterhorn there are lots of restaurants below Furi for a last drink and sunbathe – and delicious fruit tarts at Zum See. Recent visitors rave about the new Baku, on the way back to Winkelmatten. It's got a wigwam outside so you can't miss it: 'The staff are friendly, some of the food is exceptional and there is a great atmosphere.' On the way back from Sunnegga, Othmar's Hutte is popular and the Olympia Stübli often has live music. Near the church at Winkelmatten, the Sonnenblick is 'a great place to watch the sun set'. In town the Papperla is one of the few popular early places (it's crowded after dinner, too). Elsie's bar is atmospheric and gets packed with an older crowd both early and late. The North Wall is frequented by seasonal workers and Murphy's Irish pub is the place if you're interested in 'loud music and beer'. Promenading the main street checking out expensive shoes and watches is popular.

Later on, the remarkable Hotel Post complex has something for everyone, from a quiet, comfortable bar (David's Boathouse) to a lively disco (Le Broken); Pink Elephant has live music (jazz, Irish

etc) and a selection of restaurants.

Grampi's has dancing and is worth a visit. Z'Alt Hischi and the Little Bar are good for a quiet drink. The Hexenbar is cozy too. The hotel Alex draws a mature clientele for eating, drinking and dancing, with 'middle-of-the-road music and candlelit tables'.

The Vernissage is our favorite bar in town for a quiet evening drink. It is an unusual and stylish modern place, with the projection room for the movie theater built into the upstairs bar and displays of art elsewhere.

OFF THE SLOPES
Considerable attractions

Zermatt is an easy place to spend time (and money). And, if lunch up the mountain appeals, this is a great resort for pedestrians. The Alpine museum is recommended – as is a helicopter trip around the Matterhorn. There is an 'excellent' movie theater, and a reader tells us the free village guided tour is 'well worth doing'. You can also try ice-diving at Trockener Steg.

Zermatt has rustic old buildings in its lanes – amazingly there's no electric cab racing down this one ↓

347

We love skiing and riding in the USA. Many of the reasons are set out in the 'Transatlantic differences' chapter near the start of the book – start there if you haven't visited many North American resorts. But don't fall into the trap of thinking that US resorts are all the same. Those in New England are totally different from those in Colorado. We have grouped American resorts by region or state, each with a short introductory chapter. But even within one state, resort towns and resort mountains vary widely in character. Telluride, Keystone, Vail and Aspen in Colorado, for example, are about as varied as you can get.

If you want the best chance of fresh untracked powder, head for Utah, Colorado or one of the other western states (but bear in mind that average snowfall varies appreciably from resort to resort). If you want cute resort villages, it's difficult to beat Colorado. The silver-mining and gold-mining boom of the late 1800s created many 'Wild West' towns in the mountains. They subsequently hit hard times but, set at the foot of ideal snow-covered mountains, they were revived and restored to their former glory when the new 'white gold' boom saw them transformed into winter sports resorts.

New England and California are dominated more by day or weekend visitors from the nearby coastal cities than by destination visitors staying for a few days or a week. Their resorts are much more sprawling, having grown up to meet the needs of visitors arriving by car and using that car to get around.

If you rent a car, you can easily tour several resorts during a vacation. There are clusters of resorts west of Denver and east of Salt Lake City where distances are short. But wide-ranging tours are also possible, especially if you use 'open-jaw' flights and one-way rental.

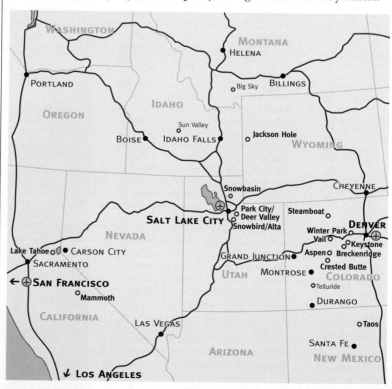

California

California has the highest mountains in continental USA and they usually have reliable snow from November to May (Mammoth has often stayed open until the Independence Day holiday, the 4th of July). Many accommodations are great value for money here because they are geared up for the summer market and winter is their low season. The main reservation we have about the resorts is the lack of charming slope-side villages – but that is changing.

California's mountains get a lot of snow, and in several recent seasons Californian resorts have recorded the deepest snow-cover in North America. A common allegation is that the snow that falls here is wet 'Sierra Cement' that can't compete with the light, dry powder of Colorado and Utah. Our fat file of reports from visitors has some complaints about that – especially late in the season – but most people have found the snow just fine, as we have.

Heavenly, Squaw Valley and Mammoth, in particular, are impressive mountains, with something for all abilities of skier or boarder. Our main reservation has been the character of the resorts themselves; they don't have the traditional mountain-town ambience or pedestrian-friendly 'village centers' that we like if we are staying somewhere for a few days or a week; they are aimed more at summer tourists and at visitors with cars who are happy to drive around to get to shops and restaurants.

But there are compensations. Because winter is low season, many of the accommodations offer good-value deals to keep a contribution coming in towards their overheads. The scenery, particularly around Lake Tahoe, is simply stunning – much more spectacular than you find in most US resorts. And Heavenly offers uniquely big-time entertainment in its casinos.

The resorts have recognized that the lack of attractive villages is a drawback for destination visitors looking to stay somewhere for a few days or a week. So now several new 'pedestrian villages' are being developed.

Last season in Heavenly there was a new gondola from the center of town right into the heart of the slopes – and work on the new car-free village at the gondola base has now started. The first stage of the new village at Squaw Valley will be open at the base of the slopes for the 2001/02 season. A couple of smaller Lake Tahoe resorts – Kirkwood and Northstar-at-Tahoe – have small, attractive slope-side villages. Mammoth has new slope-side accommodations, and redevelopment has started on part of Mammoth Lakes to form a village that will eventually be linked to the slopes by gondola.

If you go to California for a stay of a week or more, consider a two-center trip – taking in Lake Tahoe and Mammoth. Or just go to Tahoe and rent a car. The area has several ski and snowboard areas that are well worth visiting. And the views as you drive around the lake are superb.

HEAVENLY SKI RESORT / CHACO MAHLER

The views in the Lake Tahoe region are stunning→

Heavenly

1995m/6,540ft

Knockout lake views, and gambling until dawn

HOW IT RATES

The slopes

Snow	****
Extent	***
Experts	***
Intermediates	****
Beginners	****
Convenience	*
Liftlines	****
Restaurants	*

The rest

Scenery	****
Resort charm	*
Off-slope	**

- ➕ Amazing views across Lake Tahoe and arid Nevada
- ➕ Fair-sized mountain which offers a sensation of traveling around – common in the Alps, not in the US
- ➕ Lots of easy off-trail among trees
- ➕ Some serious challenges for experts
- ➕ Numerous other worthwhile areas within driving distance
- ➕ A unique après-ski scene
- ➕ Impressive snowmaking facilities

- ➖ The base-town of South Lake Tahoe is quite unlike a traditional resort, and not attractive – though things are changing with the construction of a new resort village near the existing downtown area
- ➖ Very little traditional après-ski activity – though this may soon change as well
- ➖ If natural snow is in short supply, most of the challenging terrain is likely to be closed

What's new

In December 2000 the long-awaited eight-person gondola from the center of South Lake Tahoe into the middle of Heavenly's slopes opened. This means that anyone staying downtown no longer has to drive or catch a bus to and from the slopes.

Work on a 34-acre pedestrian village around the new gondola base is under way, with two new hotels, an ice rink and shopping village planned.

There's a new tubing hill at the top of the gondola, and new scenic cross-country and snow-shoe trails here should be ready for 2001/02. Two new gladed runs are opening for 2001/02 in the upper Nevada area off Skyline Trail.

Two more new lifts from the top of the gondola, three new runs and a new restaurant are planned but not until 2002/03 at the earliest.

A resort called Heavenly invites an obvious question: just how close to heaven does it take you? Physically, close enough: with a top height of 3060m/10,040ft and vertical of 1065m/3,500ft, it's the highest and biggest of the resorts clustered around scenic Lake Tahoe (see Lake Tahoe chapter). Metaphorically, it's not quite so close. The slopes have something for all abilities, and having another dozen resorts within easy reach by car means that an interestingly varied holiday is assured. But anyone who (like us) is drawn to the place by its amazing views across the lake is likely to be dismayed by the appearance and atmosphere of the town of South Lake Tahoe, at the foot of the slopes, dominated as it is by a handful of high-rise hotel-casinos and a straggle of rather tacky motels.

But things are changing: the shabby Park Avenue area has been flattened to make way for a new 34-acre resort village with luxury accommodations, shops, restaurants, bars and an ice-rink – all built in a more sympathetic style. And an eight-seat gondola, new last season, runs the two-and-a-half miles from here to the center of the slopes.

The resort

Heavenly is at the south end of Lake Tahoe, on the borders of California and Nevada, east of San Francisco. Heavenly's base-town – South Lake Tahoe – is unlike any other resort we know. The Stateline area at its center is dominated by a handful of monstrous hotel-casinos (located just inches over the Nevada side of the line). These brash but comfortable hotels offer good-value accommodations (subsidized by the gambling) and big-name entertainment as well as slot machines, roulette wheels, craps and endless card games. They are a conspicuous part of the amazing lake views from the lower slopes (though not from above mid-mountain, nor on the Nevada side). The area around the casinos is currently strangely devoid of 'downtown' atmosphere (never mind mountain resort atmosphere); there are few bars or shops, and the center is bisected by US Highway 50. The rest of the town consists of low-rise motels, stores, wedding chapels and so on, spreading for miles along this crowded, pedestrian-hostile highway; many are rather shabby, though this is partly camouflaged by the tall trees that surround most of them. The Heavenly Village project – a new, sympathetically designed resort village just on the California side of the stateline – will greatly improve the town's appeal as a base for a holiday.

The new gondola direct from Heavenly Village to the slopes means you no longer need a car or bus to get to the slopes if you stay downtown. But many of South Lake Tahoe's

MOUNTAIN FACTS

Altitude 1995m-3060m
6,540ft-10,040ft

Lifts	29
Trails	4,800 acres
Green	20%
Blue	45%
Black	35%

Snowmaking
500 acres

LIFT TICKETS

2000/01 prices in dollars

Heavenly
Covers all lifts on Heavenly mountain.
Beginners 3-day learn to ski packages include lift ticket and rental (adult 233).
Main ticket
1-day ticket 57
6-day ticket 306
Senior citizens
Over 65: 6-day ticket 144
Children
13 to 18: 6-day ticket 246
Under 13: 6-day ticket 144
Under 5: free ticket
Short-term tickets
Half-day tickets available from 12.30 to 4pm (adult 42)
Notes Tickets of three days or more allow one non-skiing day; 6-day ticket valid for 7 days, with one non-skiing day.

accommodations are more than walking distance away and having a car is still handy to explore the other resorts around Lake Tahoe – and to get to many of the best bars and restaurants.

South Lake Tahoe is surprisingly downscale. The casinos have some swanky restaurants, but basically exist to attract gamblers. The accommodations away from the center are not particularly upscale. But most of them conform to American norms, and (except on weekends) all are under-used in winter, which is one reason why you can get cheap deals.

You reach the slopes from the new downtown gondola or from any of the base lodges, which can easily be reached by road. The new Heavenly Village will ultimately be the main base area. But California Lodge, up a heavily wooded slope a mile out of South Lake Tahoe, beside a huge parking lot, will remain the main base for people staying outside the downtown area. Boulder and Stagecoach base lodges lie around the mountain in Nevada. There is an 'excellent' free shuttle-bus service to the three out-of-town bases.

The mountain

Most of Heavenly's slopes suit intermediates perfectlly, but there are also good beginner slopes at the California base, and some splendid easy runs to progress to. Experts can find genuine challenges at the two extremes of the area – as well as lots of fun in acre upon acre of easy off-trail wooded terrain. Keep in mind that

there are other worthwhile areas [within] easy reach by car or bus (or pad[dle] steamer!). You'll want to try at le[ast a] couple during your stay – see th[e] Tahoe chapter.

The Hornblower boat shuttle across the lake to Squaw Valley and Alpine Meadows is a pleasant alternative to driving. It costs $87 including lift ticket and there's a good live band on the way back. But you lose two hours on the slopes – you don't arrive at Squaw until 11am.

THE SLOPES
Interestingly complex

Heavenly's mountain is quite complicated, and getting from A to B requires more careful navigation than is usual on American mountains.

There is a fairly clear division between the California side (the lifts and runs directly above South Lake Tahoe) and the Nevada side (above Stagecoach Lodge and Boulder Lodge).

From the top of the new gondola it's short walk to the Tamerack Express six-seater chair, which allows you to access either side. Or slide down to the Sky high-speed quad: this goes to the top of the California side and the tedious Skyline Trail traverse takes you to the top of the Nevada side. Near the border you can see beautiful views over Lake Tahoe in one direction and the arid Nevada 'desert' in the other.

From the top of the Sky chair you can play on greens, blues and blacks on the top half of the mountain on the Californian side – served by four other lifts as well. The lower half of the Californian side has unrelenting steep

HEAVENLY / SCOTT MARKEWITZ

The locals get blasé about the lake views after a while; but visitors can't take their eyes off them →

black runs down the front face, often heavily bumped, with the alternative of the narrow, blue Roundabout trail snaking its way down the mountain. Right at the California Lodge base is a great beginner area. From here uplift is by a mid-sized tram and the recently upgraded Gunbarrel fast quad.

On the Nevada side there are three main bowls. The central one, above East Peak Lodge, is an excellent intermediate area served by two fast quad chairs, with a downhill extension of the bowl served by the Galaxy chair. On one side of this central bowl is the steeper, open terrain of Milky Way Bowl, leading to the seriously steep Mott and Killebrew canyons, served by the Mott Canyon chair. On the other side is the North Bowl, with lifts up from Nevada's two base lodges.

There are no really easy runs on the Nevada side, apart from limited beginner areas at the base.

SNOW RELIABILITY
No worries

Heavenly suffered from drought in the early 90s. That, no doubt, prompted it to install a very impressive snowmaking system that now covers around 70% of the trails and ensures

that most sections are open most of the time. In recent years Californian resorts have consistently recorded some of the deepest snow cover of any North American resorts; and when we last visited most of the snow-guns were invisible – entirely buried underneath natural snow.

FOR EXPERTS
Some specific challenges

Although the area as a whole suits intermediates better, there are genuine challenges for the more advanced. The runs under the California base lifts – including The Face and Gunbarrel (often used for bump competitions) – are of proper black steepness, and very challenging when the snow is hard. Ellie's, at the top of the mountain, may offer continuous bumps too.

The really steep stuff is on the Nevada side. Milky Way Bowl offers a fairly gentle introduction to this terrain. At the extremity of the bowl the seriously steep Mott and Killebrew canyons have roped gateways. The less expert are steered to lower gates.

All over the mountain, there is excellent off-trail terrain among widely spaced trees, which offers tremendous

ridge towards the Sky Deck restaurant. The confident intermediate may want to spend more time on the Nevada side, where there is more variety of terrain. Recent visitors enjoyed 'fast blues off the Dipper Express chair'. You should also head for some of the long, quite challenging runs down to the base stations and to the Galaxy chair.

FOR BEGINNERS
An excellent place to learn
The California side is more suited to beginners, with gentle green runs served by the Pioneer surface lift and the Powderbowl chair-lift at the top of the tram. There are good beginner areas at base lodge level.

FOR CROSS-COUNTRY
A separate world
The Spooner Lake Cross Country Area located close to Tahoe is an extensive meadow area of over 100km/60 miles in 21 prepared trails. There are ample facilities for instruction and rental. Organized moonlit tours are a popular alternative to the noise and bright lights of the casinos.

LIFTLINES
Some on weekends
Liftlines are generally not a problem, except during some weekends and public holidays when the entire Tahoe area is swamped with weekenders and day trippers. Thanks to the new gondola, the key lifts moving people out from the base lodges are now under less pressure on busy days.

MOUNTAIN RESTAURANTS
Several options, none exciting
Two restaurants can be recommended on the California side. At The Top of the Tram is a table-service restaurant which makes up for its simple food with a calm atmosphere and the famous lake view (reservations necessary). The Sky Deck at the heart of the California slopes has a good

↑ Heavenly's slopes, seen from across the lake

HEAVENLY

fun when the conditions are right.

FOR INTERMEDIATES
Lots to do
Heavenly is excellent for intermediates, who are made to feel welcome and secure by excellent trail grooming and signage. The California side offers a progression from the relaxed cruising of the long Ridge Run, starting right at the top of the mountain, to more challenging blues dropping off the

SCHOOLS/GUIDES

2000/01 prices in dollars

Perfect Turn
Clinics 7 days
2³/₄hr: from 10am or 1pm
5 half days: 185
Children's clinics
Ages: 4 to 13
5 5hr days including ticket, rental and lunch: 493
Private clinics
1hr, 2hr, 4hr and 6hr
85 for 1hr

boarding *Lake Tahoe is quickly becoming known as the snowboarding hub of North America and, as you would expect, boarders are very well catered to at Heavenly. There are good terrain-parks and half-pipes on both the California and Nevada sides. The off-trail in trees and double-black-diamond bowls make a great playground for good free-riders. Beginners and intermediates will enjoy great cruising runs and the easy-to-ride chair-lifts. There are a couple of specialist board shops in South Lake Tahoe, but quite an absence of lively boarder-friendly bars.*

CHILDCARE

Heavenly's state-of-the-art Day Care Center opens at 8.30 to care for children between the ages of 2 months and 4 years. Book ahead.

Children between 4 and 13 can enrol in the Perfect Kids program. It offers skiing from age 4 and a snowboarding option from 8 upwards. It is an all-inclusive day of supervision, lessons, lunch, lift access, equipment and snacks. The program is based at California Lodge (which includes an indoor play area) or at Boulder Lodge.

GETTING THERE

Air San Francisco, transfer 3½hr. Reno, transfer 75 min. South Lake Tahoe, transfer 15 min.

ACTIVITIES

Indoor 6 casinos, 6 movie theaters, cheap factory shops, ice skating, bowling, gyms, spas, Western museum
Outdoor Boat cruises, snowmobiling, horse-drawn sleigh rides, horse riding, ice skating, hot springs, ghost town tours

Phone numbers

The state line runs through Heavenly, so two different area codes are used. For this chapter only, therefore, the area code is included with the hotel's number.

From distant parts of the US, add the prefix 1. From abroad, add the prefix +1.

TOURIST OFFICE

Postcode NV 89449
t +1 (775) 586 7000
f 588 5517
info@skiheavenly.com
www.skiheavenly.com

barbecue, where California-style rock music blasts and cool dudes hang out.

In Nevada, East Peak Lodge has a terrace and barbecue plus interesting views over arid Nevada, but it gets hideously overcrowded when the weather drives people indoors. There's an Italian-themed place at Stagecoach Lodge, and a Tex-Mex at Boulder.

SCHOOLS AND GUIDES
Good system
The Perfect Turn ski and ride programs build on your strengths rather than focusing on your weaknesses and are highly regarded.

FACILITIES FOR CHILDREN
Comprehensive
The Perfect Kids learning center in the California Base Lodge is expanded by 30% for 2001/02. It attracted particular praise from one reporter: 'This was an excellent facility – very convenient and very professionally run. I would thoroughly recommend it.'

Staying there 🔑

Give careful consideration to your plans for evenings as well as daytime. If you have a car, your options are numerous; for example, you could base yourself out at one of the Nevada lift stations, and drive when you want entertainment. Night owls can scarcely do better than to stay in a casino.

HOW TO GO
Hotel or motel?
Accommodations in the South Lake Tahoe area are abundant and range from the glossy casinos to small, rather ramshackle motels. Hotel and motel rooms are easy to find midweek, but can be sold out on busy weekends.
Hotels Caesars (775 558 3515), Harrah's (558 6611), Horizon (775 558 6211), (775 558 2411) and Harveys are the main casino hotels. Rooms booked on the spot are expensive.
(((4) **Embassy Suites** (530 544 5400) Luxury suites in a new, traditional-style building next to the casinos.
((2) **Tahoe Chalet Inn** (530 544 3311) Clean, friendly, near casinos. Back rooms (away from highway) preferable.
((2) **Best Western Timber Cove Lodge** (530 541 6722) Bland but well run, with lake views from some rooms.
Apartments/condos Plenty of choice. We've had a rave report about The Ridge Tahoe condos near Stagecoach

Lodge: 'Luxury accommodations. The bathroom was big enough for waltzing.' There's an indoor–outdoor pool, hot-tub and a private gondola to whisk you to the slopes.

EATING OUT
Good value
The casino hotels offer fantastic value in their buffet-style all-you-can-eat dining. They have some more ambitious 'gourmet' restaurants too – some high enough up their towers to give superb lake views (try Harrah's 18th floor). The sprawling resort area offers a great choice of international dining, from cozy little pizza houses to large, traditional American diners, Mexican tequila-and-tacos joints, and English and Irish pubs. Visitors' suggestions include Paul Kennedy's steakhouse, and Fresh Ketch at Tahoe Keys Marina for 'wonderful fresh fish and harbour views – though don't expect snazzy presentation'. The Riva Grill is also recommended, as are Bandanas and the Driftwood Café for breakfast. The Tudor Pub is better than it sounds.

APRES-SKI
Extraordinary
What makes the area unique is the casinos on the Nevada side of the stateline. These aren't simply opportunities to throw money away on roulette or slot machines: top-name entertainers, pop and jazz stars, cabarets and Broadway revues are also to be found in them – designed to give gamblers another reason to stay. We saw a great show by acrobats and trapeze-artists on our last visit.

You can dance and dine your way across the lake aboard an authentic paddle steamer.

OFF THE SLOPES
Luck be a lady
You're in luck if gambling is your weakness. Or then again, perhaps not. If you want to get away from the bright lights, try a boat trip on Lake Tahoe, snowmobiling a short drive from South Lake Tahoe, or a hot-air balloon ride.

Pedestrians can use the existing tram or the new gondola to view the lake and mountains below.

Lake Tahoe   1890m/6,200ft

Slopes everywhere you look – and magnificent lake views

What's new

At Squaw, work on a new base village is progressing. For the 2001/02 season the first phase of accommodations, shops, restaurants and underground parking should be in use. Over the next few years, the size of the village will quadruple.

At Kirkwood, the small base village will see a new ice rink and recreation center.

TOURIST OFFICE

Alpine Meadows

Postcode CA 96145
t +1 (530) 583 4232
f 583 0963
info@skialpine.com
www.skialpine.com

Kirkwood

Postcode CA 95646
t +1 (877) 547 5966
f (209) 258 8899
kwd-info@
ski-kirkwood.com
www.kirkwood.com

Squaw Valley

Postcode CA 96146
t +1 (530) 583 6985
f 581 7106
squaw@squaw.com
www.squaw.com

Northstar-at-Tahoe

Postcode CA 96160
t +1 (530) 562 1010
f 562 2215
northstar@
boothcreek.com
www.skinorthstar.com

Set high in the mountains 200 miles east of San Francisco, on the borders of California and Nevada, Lake Tahoe has the highest concentration of resorts in the US, with 14 downhill and seven cross-country centers. It is a very beautiful region, ideal for driving around on a tour, visiting a different area each day – though the major mountains are worth devoting a few days each to.

THE RESORTS

The resorts of the Lake Tahoe region are mostly not fully fledged resorts in the European sense. Some have no accommodations, others few. Most of the areas attract weekend or day trippers. There are lots of B&Bs and motels scattered around the lake, and a couple of quite pleasant small towns.

Then there is South Lake Tahoe, at the foot of the Heavenly slopes (the biggest resort in the area), which is a small town unlike any other ski resort we have seen (see Heavenly chapter). It has boomed on the back of gambling, which is a big industry on the Nevada side of the stateline that cuts through the town. (At the northern end of the lake, though, the stateline has not generated an equivalent gambling phenomenon.)

The next biggest resort is Squaw Valley, about a 90-minute drive from South Lake Tahoe. It has had some accommodations for years but now a real resort village is being built – the first phase of which is due to open for the 2001/02 season.

THE MOUNTAINS

The choice of **slopes** around the lake is enormous, with more than enough to keep even the keenest skier or boarder happy for a couple of weeks. With a car you can make the best of the weather, heading for less exposed resorts when a storm socks in, for example.

Snow reliability hasn't been a problem in the last few years – which have seen massive falls. The area also has huge amounts of snowmaking capacity.

Heavenly, at the southern end of the lake, has the greatest vertical drop of the region, with slopes to suit all abilities and splendid lake views. See the Heavenly chapter for details.

Nearby **Sierra-at-Tahoe** is a smaller, tree-lined area – sheltered, so useful in bad weather, mainly easy cruising plus a few bump fields. Unusually, it offers some free lessons (or did last season) – two instructors am and pm.

Kirkwood, also at the south end of the lake, is renowned for its powder, steep runs and uncrowded slopes. It also has fine intermediate groomed trails and a small new mountain village with ski-in, ski-out accommodations. A new ice rink and a recreation center with outdoor heated pool, spa and sun deck will be ready for 2001/02. The lift system is also being developed – the new high-speed quad, Cornice Express, takes you to the top of the mountain in four minutes. Adventurous intermediates can tackle some of the great off-trail – Thunder Saddle to Eagle Bowl is a must.

The major resort at the north end of the lake is **Squaw Valley**, with 4,000 acres of open, above-the-tree-line bowls on six linked mountains. It is unusual in having no trails marked on its map. Instead it has green, blue and black graded lifts. The possibilities for experts here are phenomenal, with lots of steep slopes, chutes and big bump fields – many extreme skiing and boarding movies are made here. But it is good for intermediates, with lovely long groomed runs including a top-to-bottom three-mile cruise, and a superb beginner area at altitude. Squaw is a big snowboarding center and at night a terrain-park, half-pipe and run (for skiers too) down from mid-mountain is floodlit. Massive recent investment has resulted in a very slick lift system, including North America's first twin-cable jumbo Funitel gondola (as in Verbier and Crans-Montana) and high-speed six-seater chairs. For 2001/2, the first phase of the new car-free village will open at the base of the mountain – with accommodations, shops, restaurants and underground parking. When this is completed, it will be a compelling place to stay – it is being

MOUNTAIN FACTS

Alpine Meadows

Altitude 2085m-2630m
6,840ft-8,640ft

Lifts	12
Trails	2,000 acres
Green	25%
Blue	40%
Black	35%
Snowmaking	
	185 acres
Recco detectors used	

Kirkwood

Altitude 2375m-2985m
7,800ft-9,800ft

Lifts	12
Trails	2,300 acres
Green	15%
Blue	50%
Black	35%
Snowmaking	55 acres
Recco detectors used	

Squaw Valley

Altitude 1890m-2760m
6,200ft-9,050ft

Lifts	30
Trails	4,000 acres
Green	25%
Blue	45%
Black	30%
Snowmaking	
	360 acres
Recco detectors used	

Northstar-at-Tahoe

Altitude 1930m-2625m
6,330ft-8,610ft

Lifts	12
Trails	2,420 acres
Green	25%
Blue	50%
Black	25%
Snowmaking	
	1,200 acres

developed by Intrawest, owners of Whistler and several other resorts.

Alpine Meadows has the longest season and some of the most varied terrain in the Tahoe region – snow conditions can still be good in July some years. This area is excellent for all abilities, with green runs and beginner slopes at the bottom, top-to-bottom blues and some varied blacks, including high bowls and tree-covered terrain. The mountain has slopes facing in all directions, giving good conditions whatever the weather. There is a new terrain-park and half-pipe.

Northstar-at-Tahoe is a fairly small, largely easy-to-intermediate mountain close to Squaw. The nine or so black runs on the back-side (served by a single fast quad) vary little in character and are really good long advanced intermediate cruises. A new chair-lift for 2000/01 opened up another five black runs on Lookout Mountain. Previously, this area had been accessible only by snowcat. The whole area is very sheltered and good for bad-weather days. For 2001/02 there will be even more snowmaking, covering over 50% of the mountain. There are some accommodations and a pleasant shopping, restaurant and bar area at the bottom of the mountain.

Those are the six areas we'd most recommend visiting. But there are eight other areas in the Tahoe region in case you get bored, most of which are marked on our map. A regular visitor to the region who is particularly keen on the north shore recommends Diamond Peak for its 'breathtaking views and fab restaurant', Mount Rose for its 'great snow always and carving runs', and both for quiet slopes and zero liftlines. There are also **cross-country** possibilities at most of the downhill areas as well as in dedicated cross-country areas.

Liftlines are rare in all the areas, except at peak weekends when people pour in from San Francisco and Los Angeles. We have few reports of the **schools** or facilities for **children**, but doubtless they are up to the usual high US standards.

STAYING THERE

We'd recommend spending a few days at each end of the lake.

At the southern end the main options are the brash and rather tacky town of South Lake Tahoe (see the chapter on Heavenly), or the quiet mountain village at Kirkwood.

At the northern end there's more choice. Squaw Valley has a handful of hotels and the first phase of a new village. Squaw's tram runs in the evenings to serve the floodlit slopes and the dining facilities at High Camp. This is an incredible mid-mountain complex, with several restaurants and bars, outdoor pool, ice skating, tennis and bungee jumping. The new resort village at the base will massively increase Squaw's attraction for a week's stay.

Northstar has very convenient hotel rooms and condominiums. It would be a good family choice for a quiet stay.

An alternative is to stay in the small town of Tahoe City, right on the lake, a short drive from both the Squaw Valley and Alpine Meadows areas and a little bit further from Northstar. It has a fair number of hotels and bars, and some good restaurants.

Our regular Tahoe reporter suggests Incline Village (which comes a close second to Tahoe City for choice of bars and restaurants) for its 'country charm and ambience, and friendly people'. Incline Village is handy for Diamond Peak and Mount Rose, a bit of a drive from Squaw and Alpine Meadows, but under an hour from Heavenly.

Mammoth Mountain 2425m/7,950ft

California sun and snow with extensive, varied terrain

HOW IT RATES

The slopes

Snow	****
Extent	***
Experts	****
Intermediates	****
Beginners	****
Convenience	**
Liftlines	****
Restaurants	*

The rest

Scenery	***
Resort charm	**
Off-slope	*

What's new

Work has started on a new car-free village at the core of Mammoth Lakes, eventually with a gondola link to the slopes.

The restaurant at the top of the Panorama gondola will be open for table-service dining for 2001/2.

For 2000/01 the two lifts up from Juniper Springs were replaced by the Mammoth's first fast six-seater.

MAMMOTH MOUNTAIN

You can ski and board all over Mammoth's mammoth mountain ↓

➕ One of North America's biggest and best mountains, with steep bowls at the top and easy/intermediate cruises lower down, in the trees

➕ Can get a lot of snow – and there's extensive snowmaking

➕ Deserted slopes during the week

➕ Good children's facilities

➕ Excellent daytime bus service

➕ Lots of recent resort improvements

➖ Mammoth Lakes is a rather sprawling place with no focus, where it helps to have a car

➖ Most accommodations are miles from the slopes

➖ Weekend crowds from Los Angeles

➖ Runs not clearly marked on map or mountain, especially high up

➖ Wind can close high lifts, and upper runs can be icy and windblown

Mammoth lives up to its name, more or less. It may not be giant in Alpine terms, but it is much bigger than most resorts in the US, and big enough to provide a week's amusement for most people. It has everything from steep, high, experts-only chutes and bowls (with magnificent views) to long, easy cruising runs in the trees. What it lacks, more than anything else, is a real village at the base.

Enter Intrawest, owner of Whistler and now of various key plots of land here, plus a majority share in Mammoth Mountain. Intrawest is investing heavily in transforming the resort infrastructure and plans to create 10,000 more guest beds over the next decade. It opened the first stage of a new slope-side development at Juniper Springs a couple of years ago. But plans for a new pedestrian village center in the town of Mammoth Lakes, to be linked to the mountain by gondola, will take longer to realize. For now, the mountain is the attraction. But it is quite a mountain.

The resort

Most people stay in Mammoth Lakes, a small year-round resort town four miles from the main lift base. There is no 'downtown' area yet, though one is under construction: hotels, bars, restaurants and little shopping centers are scattered along Main Street, the very wide highway running through the resort, and Old Mammoth Road at right angles to it. The buildings are generally rustic in style, and are set among trees, so although Mammoth Lakes may be short on resort ambience it has a pleasant enough appearance. Even McDonald's has been tastefully designed. The 'village' is usually under a blanket of snow, which also helps.

There are also accommodations at the main base area at the Mammoth Mountain Inn complex, along with some restaurants. And along the road up to the slopes lie several hotels and condos. Shuttle-buses run efficiently on several routes serving the lift bases, but they are limited after 5.30pm and a car is useful, especially for getting to June Mountain for a change of scenery.

The five- or six-hour drive up from Los Angeles, along a very good road, is spectacular. You pass through the San Bernardino mountains and Mojave Desert before reaching the Sierra Nevada range, of which Mammoth is part. Light aircraft can fly into Mammoth Lakes' own airport.

MOUNTAIN FACTS

Altitude 2425m-3370m
7,950ft-11,050ft
Lifts 27
Trails 3,500 acres
Green 30%
Blue 40%
Black 30%
Snowmaking
450 acres
Recco detectors used

LIFT TICKETS

2001/02 prices in
dollars
Mammoth Mountain
Covers all lifts at
Mammoth.
Beginners 69 a day
learn-to-ski packages
include ticket, lessons
and rental.
Main ticket
1-day ticket 56
6-day ticket 293
Senior citizens
Over 65: 6-day ticket
145
Over 80: free ticket
Children
13-18: six day ticket:
218
Under 13: 6-day ticket
145
Under 6: free ticket
Short-term tickets
Scenic Mammoth
Gondola ride (adult
16); afternoon ticket
(adult 45)
Notes Main ticket also
covers the eight lifts
at June Mountain.
Tickets of over 2 days
allow for one non-
skiing day – 5-day
ticket is valid for 6
days, with one non-
skiing day, and
tickets over five days
allow for 2 non-skiing
days.

The mountain

Although Mammoth is one of the US's largest areas, its claim to have 150 trails should not be taken too seriously. The slightest variant of a run is given a separate name. Nevertheless, the 27 lifts access an impressive area suitable for all abilities. The highest runs are almost exclusively steep bowls and chutes for experts. In general, the lower down you go the easier the terrain.

Finding your way around is something else. The lifts are mainly known by numbers, allocated as they were built, so the system has no geographic logic: chair 17 is between chairs 7 and 8 and below chair 22, and so on. New lifts are now being given names, though, which is starting to make things easier. However, the trail map still shows trails by means of symbols and names, not continuous lines, so it's difficult to see where a particular run takes you. On the lower part of the mountain this doesn't matter a lot: head downhill, and you'll eventually come to a lift. But higher up there are real dangers, especially in poor visibility.

Though Intrawest is now the majority owner, Dave McCoy, who built the first lift here in the 1940s, still has the final say about mountain development. People told him it was too high, too remote and too stormy here to make it as a resort, so he is naturally proud that he has seen it developed into a top American resort.

THE SLOPES
It's all here

There are three major lift-stations along the foot of the slopes, which mainly face north-east. An isolated fourth base – Juniper Springs – is growing in importance.

Main Lodge has the biggest choice of lifts. The newly upgraded two-stage Panorama gondola goes via Mid Chalet, the site of a huge restaurant,

right to the top. The views are great, with Nevada to the north-east and the jagged Minarets to the west.

From the top, there are essentially three ways down. The first, on which there are countless variations, is down the front of the mountain, which ranges from steep to very steep – or vertical if the wind has created a cornice, as it often does. The second is off the back, down to **Chair 14 Outpost**, whence chairs 14 or 13 bring you back to lower points on the ridge. The third is to follow the way down to the Main Lodge area. This route brings you past an easy area served by chair 12, and a very easy area by the Discovery fast quad. But finding the way you intend from the top is tricky because of poor signage and the amazingly unhelpful trail map.

Mid Chalet can also be reached using the Stump Alley fast chair from **The Mill Cafe**, on the road up from town. Other lifts from here, including the fast Gold Rush quad, take you into the more heavily wooded eastern half of the area. This has long, gentle runs served by lifts up from **Canyon Lodge** and the new **Juniper Springs Lodge** and seriously steep stuff as well as some intermediate terrain on the subsidiary peak (nameless, of course) served by lifts 25 and 22.

A separate ski area called **June Mountain** is 30 minutes' drive away and is covered by the lift ticket.

SNOW RELIABILITY
A long season

Mammoth has an impressive snow record – an annual average of 380in, which puts it in the second rank, ahead of major Colorado resorts and about on a par with Jackson Hole (but a long way behind Alta and Snowbird). Thanks to both its height and ever-expanding snowmaking, it enjoys a long season – staying open as late as July 4th in many years. But the upper mountain can get icy and windswept.

boarding *Mammoth initially set out to attract boarders to its sister mountain June, where there's a good terrain-park and half-pipe. But Mammoth itself now has three impressive 'Unbound' terrain parks and half-pipes for different abilities. The main one is served by the high-speed Thunder Bound Express lift, with the Quarter Pipe Cafe half-way up the slope. The rest of Mammoth's slopes are ideal for all abilities, with some excellent free-riding in the high bowls and perfect beginner and intermediate runs below. All but one tiny lift are chairs or gondolas. There are some good bars in town, lively on weekends.*

SCHOOLS/GUIDES

2000/01 prices in dollars

**Mammoth Mountain
Classes** 7 days
3hr: 10am-1pm 52
5 full days: 180
Children's classes
Ages: 4 to 14
5 full days including
lunch: 380
Private lessons
1hr, 3hr or 6hr
110 for 1hr; each
additional person 12

FOR EXPERTS
Some very challenging terrain
The steep bowls that run the width of the mountain top provide wonderful opportunities for experts. There are one or two single-diamond slopes, but most are emphatically double-diamond runs requiring a lot of courage. The snow up here can suffer from high winds and it can be difficult to find your way – marking is virtually non-existent, so take great care.

The steep chutes either side of lift 22 are also very challenging, and being relatively sheltered are often open in bad weather when the top is firmly shut. Above Main Lodge is another steep area ideal for advanced skiers.

Many of the lower trails are short, but you can go virtually from top to bottom all day entirely on black runs.

FOR INTERMEDIATES
Lots of great cruising
Mammoth's trail maintenance is generally good, and many slopes that might become intimidatingly bumpy are kept easily skiable. And there is plenty for all levels of intermediate.

Some of the mountain's longest runs, served by chairs 9 and 25, are ideal for good intermediates. And a couple of lovely, fairly steep, tree-lined trails run from the top of the Goldrush chair down to The Mill Cafe.

The tree-lined runs above Juniper Springs Lodge are flattering, and there are several easy cruises – notably the slopes converging on The Mill Cafe.

A reporter recommends the quiet little Santiago bowl at the western extremity of the slopes down to Chair 14 Outpost: 'The whole group

enjoyed runs like Arriba, Surprise and Oops.'

The less adventurous have some good, wide runs through trees in the triangle between Main Lodge, The Mill Cafe and Mid Chalet.

June mountain is great for a leisurely day out. Most of its runs are overrated. Blues are easy cruisers, single blacks groomed and double blacks advanced rather than expert.

FOR BEGINNERS
Good lessons
'Excellent for beginners,' says one visitor. 'Good beginner areas and lots of marvellous improving slopes, such as Sesame Street West, Lower Road Runner and Bridges.' Excellent lessons, fine trail grooming and snow quality usually make progress speedy.

FOR CROSS-COUNTRY
Very popular
Two specialist centers, Tamarack and Sierra Meadows, provide lessons and tours (the Sierra Meadows trails aren't groomed). There are 70km/43 miles of trails in all, including some through the pretty Lakes Basin area, and lots of scenic ungroomed tracks.

LIFTLINES
Weekend invasions
During the week the lifts and slopes are usually very quiet, with no lines. But even the efficient lift system can struggle when 15,000 visitors arrive from LA on fine weekends. That's the time to try June Mountain – it is remarkably uncrowded. But as one reporter put it, 'The weekend rush was like a quiet day in the Alps.'

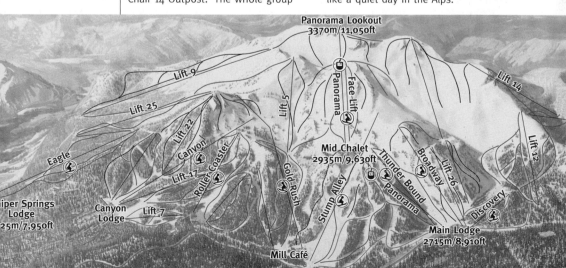

Panorama Lookout
3370m/11,050ft

Lift 9

Lift 25

Lift 22

Lift 5

Lift 14

Lift 12

Eagle

Canyon

Lift 17

Roller Coaster

Gold Rush

Mid Chalet
2935m/9,630ft

Face-lift

Panorama

Panorama

Thunder Bound

Broadway

Lift 26

Discovery

iper Springs
Lodge
25m/7,950ft

Canyon
Lodge

Lift 7

Stump Alley

Panorama

Main Lodge
2715m/8,910ft

Mill Café

CHILDCARE

Children's classes are handled by the Woollywood Ski and Snowboard School in the Panorama gondola building, which 'interfaces' with Small World Child Care (934 0646) based at the nearby Mammoth Mountain Inn. Small World Child Care takes children from newborn to age 12, from 8am to 5pm.

GETTING THERE

Air Los Angeles, transfer 5hr. Reno, transfer 3hr. Mammoth Lakes, transfer 20 minutes.

ACTIVITIES

Indoor Mammoth museum, art galleries, theater, mini golf
Outdoor Snowmobiling, ski touring, bob-sled, dog-sledding, ice skating, tobogganing, sleigh rides, hot air balloon rides, snow-shoe tours

Phone numbers
From distant parts of the US, add the prefix 1 760.
From abroad, add the prefix +1 760.

TOURIST OFFICE

Postcode CA 93546
t +1 (760) 934 0745
f 934 0616
woolly@mammoth-mtn.com
www.mammoth
mountain.com

MOUNTAIN RESTAURANTS
Lots of new venues

The giant functional cafeteria at Mid Chalet used to be the only on-mountain option. But for 2001/02 the new Top of the World restaurant, at the top gondola station, will offer table-service and views at Mammoth's highest point. Many people eat at the bases, where there are several options. The Mill Cafe boasts 'gourmet sandwiches'. Or choose from Mexican, Italian, Asian and more at the revamped Canyon Lodge. Sun decks and music are the norm. There are outdoor BBQs at Juniper Springs Lodge and Chair 14 Outpost. There's also a sun deck at the Yodler at Main Lodge.

SCHOOLS AND GUIDES
Excellent reports

Mammoth has a high reputation for lessons. Our most recent reporter rated his three-hour advanced class 'excellent'. And we have reports of beginners making 'excellent progress' as well. There are also some special camps (eg steep terrain and racing) for experts, and for seniors and women.

FACILITIES FOR CHILDREN
Family favorite

Mammoth is keen to attract families. The children's Woollywood school, now based in the new Panorama gondola station, works closely with the nearby Small World childcare center. We've had glowing reports; one reporter noted the 'family feel of the resort'.

Staying there

Staying near Main Lodge or at the new condo complexes at Canyon Lodge or Juniper Springs Lodge is convenient for the slopes but not much else. The efficient bus service from Mammoth Lakes means staying in town and getting to the slopes is easy.

HOW TO GO
Plenty of choice

A good choice of hotels (none very luxurious or expensive) and condos. The condos tend to be out of town, near the lifts or on the road to them.
(((4) **Mammoth Mountain Inn** (934 2581) Motel/hotel/condo complex at Main Lodge. Comfortable, spacious bedrooms. Rather gloomy common rooms.
(((3) **Quality Inn** (934 5114) Good main street hotel with a big hot-tub.

(((3) **Alpenhof Lodge** (934 6330) Comfortable and friendly, in central location. Shuttle-bus stop and plenty of restaurants nearby.
(((3) **Austria Hof** (934 2764) Ski-out location near Canyon Lodge, recommended by a reporter despite modest-sized rooms.
(((3) **Sierra Nevada Inn** (934 2515) Central, good value, 'excellent spa'.
Apartments/condos The new Juniper Springs Lodge opened for 1999/2000. Close to the Canyon Lodge base-station, the 1849 Condominiums are spacious and well equipped. The Mammoth Ski and Racquet Club, a 10-minute walk from the same lifts, is very comfortable.

EATING OUT
Outstanding choices

There are over 50 restaurants in town, scattered around over a wide area, catering for most tastes and pockets. We've had delicious dinners at Nevados and Skadi (both 'modern American' food). Other good places are the atmospheric Slocums and lively Whiskey Creek. The Yodler does good hearty food at the Main Lodge area. Roberto's offers Mexican food; the Shogun Japanese (and karaoke). The Mogul, Alpenrose, Giovanni's, Berger's, Mountainside Grill, Angel's, Ocean Harvest and Grumpy's have all been recommended. For delicious breakfasts and pastries try Schat's Bakery.

APRES-SKI
Lively at weekends

The liveliest immediate après-ski spot is the Yodler, at the Main Lodge base – a chalet transported from Switzerland (so they say). Nightlife in town is essentially bars, which come to life on weekends (one reporter warns that during the week they'll be pushing you out at 12.30am). Whiskey Creek is the liveliest. It has live bands and gets packed. Slocums is popular with locals while Gringo's does great margaritas. Grumpy's is a good sports bar (big screen TVs etc).

OFF THE SLOPES
Mainly sightseeing

The main diversion is sightseeing by car (preferably 4WD), which can be spectacular. Sights include the pretty Mono Lake, the beautiful Yosemite and other National Parks and the mining ghost-town of Bodie. There are some diverting clothes shops.

Colorado

Colorado has America's densest network of attractive 'destination' resorts where we can wholeheartedly recommend going for a stay of a week or more. It has an alluring combination of attractive resort villages, slopes to suit all abilities and excellent, reliable snow – dry enough to justify its 'champagne powder' label.

Colorado has amazingly dry snow. Even when the snow melts and refreezes, the moisture seems to be magically whisked away, leaving it in soft powdery condition. The snow is good even in times of unusual snow shortage; in December a couple of years ago, when very little snow had fallen so far that season, we had a great week cruising on magical man-made snow in Breckenridge and Keystone.

Colorado resorts vary enormously, both in the extent and variety of slopes and in the character of the villages themselves. If you want beautifully restored buildings from the mining boom days of the late 1800s, try the dinky old towns of Telluride or

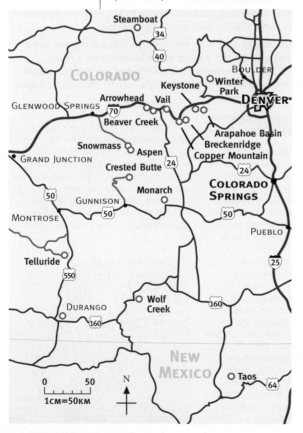

Crested Butte (but beware: both these have separate, modern mountain villages, too) or the much grander and larger-scale Aspen (which also has its modern outpost at Snowmass).

If you are planning a stay of a few days or more, consider resorts that have easy access to other major mountains nearby, which will add variety and interest to your stay (eg Breckenridge, Keystone and Copper Mountain). Some others, such as Steamboat, Crested Butte and Telluride, are rather isolated.

It is an easy state in which to put together a 'ski safari' – driving from resort to resort and spending a day or two in each. As well as the destination resorts we feature in the full chapters that follow, there are lots of resorts that have few accommodations but are well worth visiting for a day. Our favorite in this category for good skiers and riders is funky Berthoud Pass (see the Winter Park chapter). But there are many others which are more conventional – such as Monarch near Crested Butte, Loveland on the road from Denver to Vail and Ski Cooper between Vail and Leadville.

The two biggest Colorado resorts, Vail and Aspen, both have substantial amounts of terrain suitable for every ability – and even an avid skier or boarder would not get bored here in a week. Both have also been developing their exciting ungroomed terrain in recent years – Vail has opened up Blue Sky Basin, with usually excellent snow in the trees, while Aspen has extended its high, steep, open bowls at the top of Aspen Highlands.

Resorts that have been busy developing new attractive car-free village centers in the last few years include Copper Mountain and the River Run area of Keystone – both with the help of Intrawest, the Canadian company that specializes in resort development that is in sympathy with its surroundings. (Intrawest owns several resorts including Copper Mountain, Whistler and Tremblant.)

Aspen

Don't be put off by its ritzy image; it's our favorite US resort

HOW IT RATES

The slopes

Snow	★★★★★
Extent	★★★★
Experts	★★★★★
Intermediates	★★★★★
Beginners	★★★★★
Convenience	★★
Liftlines	★★★★
Restaurants	★★★★

The rest

Scenery	★★★
Resort charm	★★★★
Off-slope	★★★★

What's new

Snowboarders can rejoice as boarding is now allowed on Aspen Mountain, after 54 years of being a skiers-only mountain.

At Highlands, even more steep terrain is to be added in Highland Bowl near the Y, B and recently opened G zones.

The base lodge at Highlands Village is ready. It will house a new bar and restaurant, and Ritz Carlton club.

For 2000/01, Snowmass got a new children's training area with its own lift, kids' trails, snowcat sculpted bumps, a race area, a picnic area, and a video analysis center.

Buttermilk built a two-mile long terrain-park for 2000/01 with numerous hits and jumps, a boardercross course and a 400-foot long superpipe.

➕ Endless slopes to suit all abilities, with a vertical drop at Snowmass of 1343m/4,406ft – biggest in the US

➕ Notably uncrowded slopes, even by American standards

➕ Attractive, picturesque, old mining town, with lots of upscale shops

➕ Lively, varied nightlife and a great range of restaurants in the town

➕ Some of the best 'gourmet' mountain restaurants in the States

➕ Large numbers of slope-side accommodations at Snowmass

➖ Four mountains are widely separated (though there's efficient, free transport between them)

➖ Some accommodations in Aspen town are a long walk or a bus-ride from the local lifts

➖ Can be very expensive (although certainly doesn't have to be)

Aspen is our favorite American resort for a week-long stay. We reached that view three editions back, and subsequent visits have simply confirmed it. Its four separate mountains have something for every ability of skier and rider. And the town is delightful, with beautifully renovated old buildings and a good choice of bars and restaurants to suit every budget. Convenience-freaks will find it a nightmare, but that really is the only serious drawback, and nowhere else comes close to matching the combination of plus-points listed above.

Worried by the film-star image? Forget it. Yes, the resort has many rich and famous guests, with their private jets parked at the local airport, and for connoisseurs of cosmetic surgery it can be a fascinating place. But most celebs are keen to keep a low profile and, like all other 'glamorous' ski resorts, Aspen is actually filled by ordinary tourists.

The resort

In 1892 Aspen was a booming silver-mining town, source of one-sixth of the USA's silver, with 12,000 inhabitants, six newspapers, an opera house and a red-light district. But Aspen's fortunes took a nose-dive when the silver price plummeted in 1893, and by the 1930s the population had shrunk to 700 or so. Handsome Victorian buildings – such as the Wheeler Opera House and the Hotel Jerome – had fallen into disrepair. Development of the skiing started on a small scale in the late 1930s. The first lift (then the world's longest chair-lift) was opened shortly after the Second World War, and Aspen hasn't looked back since. Now, the historic center has been beautifully renovated to form the core of the most fashionable ski town in the Rockies. There's a huge variety of shops, bars, restaurants and galleries – some amazingly upscale. Spreading out from this center, you'll find a mixture of developments, ranging from the homes of the super-rich to the mobile homes for the workers. Though the town is full of traffic, pedestrians seem to have priority in much of the central area.

Twelve miles away is Snowmass, with its own mountain and modern accommodations right on the slopes.

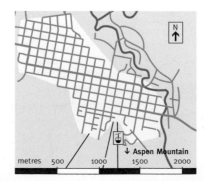

↓ Aspen Mountain

metres	500	1000	1500	2000

Some of Aspen Highlands' steep terrain, seen from Aspen Mountain →
SNOWPIX.COM / CHRIS GILL

Ski Area Boundary

The mountains

Aspen has lots for every ability; you just have to pick the right mountain. All of them have regular free guided tours, given by excellent amateur ambassadors, and other guest services on the slopes such as free sunscreen, drinks and biscuits. The ratio of acres to visitor beds is high, and the slopes are usually blissfully uncrowded.

MOUNTAIN FACTS

Altitude	2400m-3815m
	7,870ft-12,510ft
Lifts	44
Trails	4,780 acres
Green	13%
Blue	44%
Black	43%
Snowmaking	
	566 acres
Recco detectors used	

THE SLOPES
Widely dispersed

There are four mountains, only one accessible directly from Aspen town. Each is big enough to keep you amused for a full day or more, but Snowmass is in a league of its own – almost five miles across, with over 60% of Aspen's total skiable acreage and the biggest vertical in the US. Getting around between the areas by free bus is easy, and for $3 you can have your equipment ferried from one mountain to another overnight.

The Silver Queen gondola takes you from the edge of town to the top of **Aspen Mountain** in 14 minutes. A series of chairs serves the different ridges – Gentleman's Ridge along the eastern edge, the Bell in the center, and Ruthie's to the west – with gulches in between. In general, there are long cruising blue runs along the valley floors and short steep blacks down from the ridges. There are no greens.

Snowmass is a separate resort some 12 miles west of Aspen, opened in 1967. Chair-lifts fan out from the purpose-built village at the base towards four linked sectors – Elk Camp, High Alpine, Big Burn and Sam's Knob. Since 1995 there has also been access to the Elk Camp sector via the Two Creeks lift base, which is much nearer to Aspen, and has free slope-side parking. There are free shuttle-buses between here and Aspen, as there are between all four mountains. Many of the Snowmass runs are wide, sweeping cruisers. But it also has some of the toughest terrain.

Buttermilk is the least challenging mountain. The runs fan out from the top in three directions. The West Buttermilk and Main Buttermilk areas are almost all gentle; Tiehack, to the east, is a bit more demanding – ideal for an intermediate keen to progress.

Aspen Highlands was, until 1993, separately owned. Since then, Aspen Skiing Company has transformed the

---

GET THE BEST OF THE SNOW, ON- AND OFF-TRAIL

Aspen offers several special experiences for small numbers of skiers or riders.

Fresh Tracks *The first eight skiers to sign up each day get to ride the gondola up Aspen Mountain at 8am the next morning, and to get first tracks on perfect corduroy or fresh powder. Free!*

Off-trail Tours *On Wednesdays and Fridays, backcountry guides lead expert skiers and riders around the famous double-black terrain of Highlands (eg the Y and B Zones) and Snowmass (eg Hanging Valley). 9am–2.30pm, $99 (2000/01).*

Powder Tours *Spend the day exploring the backcountry beyond Aspen Mountain, with a 10-passenger heated snowcat as your personal lift. Away from the lifts and other people, your two guides search out untracked snow – there's 1,500 acres to choose from. You're likely to squeeze in about 10 runs in all. At midday, you break for lunch at an old mountain cabin. Full day, $275 (2000/01).*

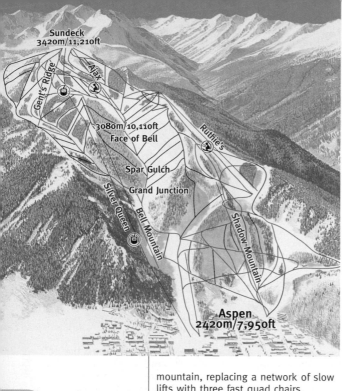

Sundeck
3420m/11,210ft

Gent's Ridge

Ajax

3080m/10,110ft
Face of Bell

Ruthie's

Spar Gulch

Grand Junction

Silver Queen

Bell Mountain

Shadow Mountain

Aspen
2420m/7,950ft

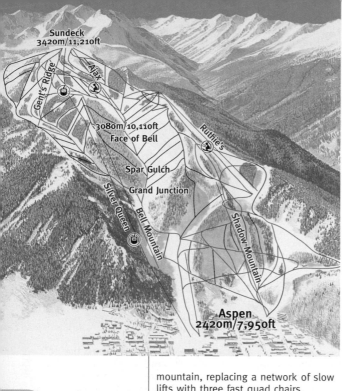

West Summit
3015m/9,900ft

ASPEN HIGHLANDS

Cliffhouse
2965m/9,720ft

Buttermilk West

Upper Tiehack

BUTTERMILK

West
Buttermilk
2655m/8,710ft

Summit

Tiehack
2450m/8,040ft

Main
Buttermilk
2400m/7,890ft

mountain, replacing a network of slow lifts with three fast quad chairs. Broadly, the mountain consists of a single ridge, with easy and intermediate slopes along the ridge itself and steep black runs on the flanks – very steep ones at the top. And beyond the lift network is the Highland Bowl, where gates give access to a splendid open bowl of entirely double-black gradient and the Y, B and G zones. The views from the

upper part of Highlands are the best that Aspen has to offer – the famous Maroon Bells that appear on countless postcards. A new base lodge with underground parking and a Ritz-Carlton condotel is now finished.

SNOW RELIABILITY
Rarely a problem

Aspen's mountains get an annual average of 300in of snow – not in the front rank, but not far behind. In addition, all areas have substantial snowmaking. Immaculate grooming adds to the quality of the trails.

FOR EXPERTS
Buttermilk is the only soft stuff

There's plenty to choose from – all the mountains except Buttermilk offer lots of challenges. Consider joining a guided group as an introduction to the best of Snowmass or Highlands.

Aspen Mountain has a formidable array of double-black-diamond runs. From the top of the gondola, Walsh's, Hyrup's and Kristi are double-diamonds on a lightly wooded slope that link up with Gentleman's Ridge and Jackpot to form the longest black run on the mountain. A series of steep glades drop down from Gentleman's Ridge. The central Bell ridge has less extreme single-diamonds on both its flanks. On the opposite side of Spar Gulch is another row of genuine double-blacks collectively called the Dumps, because slag was dumped here in the silver-mining days.

At Snowmass, our favorite area is around the Hanging Valley Wall and Glades – beautiful scenery and wonderful tree-covered slopes, and steep enough everywhere to satisfy the keenest – well worth the short hike. The other seriously steep area is the Cirque. The Cirque surface lift takes you well above the tree-line to Aspen's top altitude of almost 3815m/12,510ft. The Headwall is open and not terrifyingly steep, but there are also narrow, often rocky, chutes – Gowdy's is one of the steepest in the whole area. All these runs funnel into a pretty, lightly wooded valley.

At Highlands there are challenging runs from top to bottom of the mountain. Highland Bowl, beyond the top lift, is superb in the right conditions: a big open bowl with pitches from a serious 38° to a terrifying 48° – facts you can check in the very informative Highlands Extreme

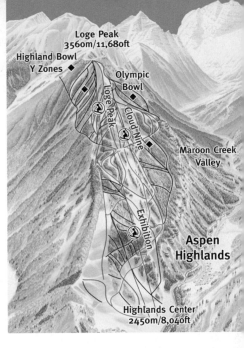

LIFT TICKETS

2000/01 prices in dollars

Four Mountain ticket
Covers Aspen Mountain, Aspen Highlands, Buttermilk and Snowmass, and shuttle-bus between the areas.

Beginners Included in price of beginners' lessons; 219 for 3-day learn-to-ski or snowboard lessons and rental.

Main ticket
1-day ticket approx 65 (depends on season and snow conditions) 6-day ticket 342

Senior citizens
Over 65: 6-day ticket 312
Over 70: season ticket 149.

Children
Under 12: 6-day ticket 231
Under 7: free ticket

Advance purchase
Big savings can be made if you buy lift tickets well in advance or through certain tour operators. Book by 1 December for an adult 6-day ticket from $294, over 70s 6-day from 119, under 14 6-day 234, under 12 six-day 186.

Skiing Guide leaflet. If you're lucky, the ski patrol may be running free snowcat rides from Lodge Meadow to the first access gate of Highland Bowl; otherwise, it's a 20-minute hike. More of this terrain – the furthest-out G Zone – opened for 2000/01. Within the lift system, the Steeplechase area consists of a number of parallel natural avalanche chutes, and their elevation means the snow stays light and dry. The Olympic Bowl area on the opposite flank of the mountain has great views of the Maroon Bells peaks and some serious bumps. The Thunderbowl chair from the base serves a nice varied area that's often underused.

FOR INTERMEDIATES
Grooming to die for

Snowmass is the best mountain for intermediates, and the Big Burn is definitely the first place to head for. The huge lightly wooded area is a cruising paradise. The runs merge into each other, though there's a satisfying variety of terrain and some trees to add interest – and the tempting Powerline Glades for the adventurous. The easiest intermediate slopes are reached from the Elk Camp lift. There's a choice of runs from the top, through spruce trees, and long runs all the way down to Two Creeks. Long Shot is a glorious, ungroomed, three-mile run, lost in the forest, and well worth the short hike up to get to the start. In the center of the area, the two chair-lifts below High Alpine serve yet more intermediate slopes – a little trickier

and more varied. The Sam's Knob sector offers slightly more advanced challenges, including some regularly groomed single-black runs. Finally, Green Cabin, at the top of the High Alpine lift, is a magical intermediate run cruising from top to bottom of the mountain, with spectacular views.

Most intermediate runs on Highlands are concentrated above the mid-mountain Merry-Go-Round restaurant, many (including the very popular Scarlet's Run) served by the Cloud Nine fast quad chair. But there

are good slopes higher up and lower down – don't miss the vast, neglected expanses of Golden Horn, on the eastern limit of the area.

Aspen Mountain has its fair share of intermediate slopes, but they tend to be tougher than on the other mountains. Copper Bowl and Spar Gulch, running between the ridges, are great cruises early in the morning but can get crowded later. Upper Aspen Mountain, at the top of the gondola, has a dense network of well-groomed blues. The unusual Ruthie's chair – a fast double, apparently installed to rekindle the romance that quads have destroyed – serves more cruising runs and the popular Snow Bowl, a wide, open area with bumps on the left but groomed on the right and center.

The Main Buttermilk runs offer good, easy slopes to practice on. And good intermediates should be able to handle the relatively easy black runs in the Tiehack area.

FOR BEGINNERS
Can be a great place to learn
Buttermilk is a great mountain for beginners. West Buttermilk has beautifully groomed, gentle runs. The easiest slopes of all, though, are at the base of the Main Buttermilk sector – on Panda Hill. The easiest beginner slope at Snowmass is the wide Assay Hill, at the bottom of the Elk Camp area. Right next to Snowmass Village Mall is the Fanny Hill fast quad and beginners' run. Further up, from Sam's Knob, there are long, gentle cruises.

Despite its macho image, Highlands boasts the highest concentration of green runs in Aspen.

FOR CROSS-COUNTRY
Backcountry bonanza
There are 80km/50 miles of groomed trails between Aspen and Snowmass in the Roaring Fork valley – the most extensive maintained cross-country system in the US. And the Ashcroft Ski Touring Center maintains around 30km/20 miles of trails around Ashcroft, a mining ghost-town. Take the opportunity of eating at the Pine Creek Cookhouse: excellent food and accessible by ski, board or dogsled only. In addition, there are limitless miles of ungroomed trails. Aspen is at one end of the famous Tenth Mountain Division Trail, heading 230 miles north-east almost to Vail, with 13 huts for overnight stops.

LIFTLINES
Few problems
There are rarely major liftlines on any of the mountains. At Aspen Mountain, the gondola can have delays at peak times, but you have alternative lifts to the top. Snowmass has so many alternative lifts and runs that you can normally avoid any problems. But some long, slow chairs can be cold in mid-winter, and the home slope gets very crowded. Aspen Highlands is almost always line-free, even at peak times. The two lifts out of Main Buttermilk sometimes get congested.

MOUNTAIN RESTAURANTS
Good places on each mountain
On Aspen Mountain the new Sundeck at the top has quite a stylish self-service section with a good range of food, but the table-service Benedict's restaurant is unappealing (unless the terrace is in operation). Sadly the swanky lunch club that shares the new building is strictly for members. The mid-mountain restaurant formerly called Ruthie's is now Gwyn's; as well as a self-service section it has an exceptionally civilized table-service restaurant with excellent food and good views over Aspen.

At Snowmass, Gwyn's High Alpine is an elegant restaurant serving excellent food. The best views are from Sam's Knob, where there is a self-service and a new and impressive Italian table-service restaurant, Finestra.

SCHOOLS/GUIDES
2000/01 prices in dollars

Aspen Skiing Company
Snowmass and Buttermilk for all abilities; Aspen Mountain and Aspen Highlands for intermediate and advanced only
Mountain Explorers
4 days
5hr: 10am-3pm;
4 full days: 339
Private lessons
449 for full day
309 for half day
(up to 5 people)
Other options
Beginner's Magic
1 full day: 99
3 full days incl lift ticket: 249
Small group lessons
Approx four skiers
99 for full day
Off-trail tours
Full day 99
Children's classes
Ages: 18 months to 19
Age: 18 months
1 hr private lesson 99
Beginners
Ages: 7-19
One day 79

boarding *Aspen has great snowboarding for every ability. And at last the ban on snowboarders on Aspen Mountain was lifted on April 1, 2001. Aspen bowed to pressure after becoming one of just five major areas in the world open to skiers only. All four mountains are served almost entirely by chairs or gondolas and there are lots of special boarder facilities – Aspen Mountain will even have a special Spring Jam terrain-park on Little Nell in the spring. Buttermilk has a new two-mile long terrain-park with numerous hits and jumps, a boardercross course and a 400-foot long superpipe. Snowmass has two terrain-parks and a half-pipe. Some of the bars can be quite entertaining at night.*

FACILITIES FOR CHILDREN
Choice of nurseries
There is no shortage of advertised childcare arrangements. We have no recent first-hand reports, but reporters' observations were that, as usual in the US, all the kids were having the time of their lives. And past reports have always been first class. Young children based in Aspen town are taken from the gondola building each morning around 9am by the Max the Moose bus to Buttermilk's very impressive Fort Frog – a wooden frontier-style fort, with lookout towers, flags, old wagons, a jail, a saloon and a native American teepee village – and delivered back at 4pm. Snowmass has its own facilities. The Kids' Trail Map is a great way to get them used to finding their way around using maps.

Staying there

Aspen town is the liveliest place to stay, and near the gondola is the most convenient location. Buses for the other areas also leave from nearby. Snowmass offers ski-out convenience at 95% of its properties, and buses from Aspen run until 1am or later.

CHILDCARE
The childcare possibilities are too numerous to list in detail.

There's a children's 'learning center' at Buttermilk with a special children's shuttle-bus from Aspen. The Powder Pandas classes there take children aged 3 to 6. At Snowmass, the Big Burn Bears ski kindergarten takes children from age 3½, and children aged 6 weeks to 3½ have the Snow Cubs playschool. The Nighthawks program looks after children aged 3 to 10 from 4pm to 11pm.

There are several all-day non-skiing nurseries.

Phone numbers
From distant parts of the US, add the prefix 1 970.
From abroad, add the prefix +1 970.

↑ Highland Bowl has fabulous open terrain with pitches from a serious 38° to a terrifying 48°
ASPEN / KEN MISSBRENNER

At Highlands the Cloud Nine 'Alpine bistro' is the nearest thing you will find in the States to an Alpine chalet with Alpine views and excellent food – thanks to an Austrian chef. The Merry-Go-Round has the biggest terrace in the valley.

On Buttermilk the mountaintop Cliffhouse is known for its 'Mongolian Barbecue' stir-fry bar and great views.

SCHOOLS AND GUIDES
Special programs
There's a wide variety of specialized instruction – bumps, powder, mountain exploration groups, backcountry groups, and so on. A reporter raves about the semi-private lessons, with maximum four pupils per group. On Snowmass and Aspen Mountain there are performance centers where your alignment is tested and adjusted, and you can test any number of skis. A new addition is the Wizard Ski Deck – an indoor ski and snowboard simulator. It claims to be 'Safe, enjoyable and comfortable'.

HOW TO GO
Accommodations for all pockets
There's a mixture of hotels, inns, B&Bs, lodges and condos.
Hotels There are places for all budgets.
((((5) **St Regis** (920 3300) Opulent city-type hotel, near gondola. Fitness center, outdoor pool, hot-tubs, sauna.
((((5) **Little Nell** (920 4600) Stylish, modern hotel right by the gondola with popular bar. Fireplaces in every room, outdoor pool, hot-tub, sauna.
((((5) **Jerome** (920 1000) Step back a century: Victorian authenticity combined with modern-day luxury. Several blocks from the gondola.
(((4) **Sardy House** (920 2525) Elegantly furnished, intimate hotel 10 minutes from the gondola. Small outdoor pool, hot-tub.
(((4) **Lenado** (925 6246) Smart modern B&B place with open-fire lounge, individually designed rooms.
(((4) **Silvertree** (923 3520) Large slope-side hotel at Snowmass. Pools.
(((3) **Innsbruck Inn** (925 2980) Consistently liked by reporters. Tirolean-style hotel, 10 mins from lifts.
(((3) **Stonebridge Inn** (923 2420) Good-value hotel close to Snowmass slopes; nice restaurant, pool, hot-tub.

GETTING THERE

Air Aspen, transfer ½hr. Eagle, transfer 1½hr. Denver, transfer 4hr.

Rail Glenwood Springs (63km/40 miles).

Phone numbers

From distant parts of the US, add the prefix 1 970.
From abroad, add the prefix +1 970.

ACTIVITIES

Indoor Aspen Athletic Club (racquetball, swimming, free weights, aerobics classes, sauna, steam, hot-tubs), skating, museum.
Outdoor Ballooning, paragliding, snowcat tours, snow-shoe tours, sleigh rides, dog-sledding, snow-tubing, snowmobiles, tours of mines

TOURIST OFFICE

Postcode CO 81612
t +1 (970) 925 1220
f 920 0771
intlres@skiaspen.com
www.aspensnowmass.com

⟨⟨③ Hotel Aspen (925 3441) Best 'moderate' place in town, 10 minutes from the gondola; comfortable motel-style rooms, pool, hot-tubs.
② Skier's Chalet (920 2037) Closest 'economy' lodging to the lifts.
Apartments/condos The standards here are high, even in US terms. Many of the smarter developments have their own free shuttle-buses. The Gant is luxurious and close to the gondola. Chateau Roaring Fork and Eau Claire, four blocks from the gondola, are spacious and well-furnished. A reader says the two small supermarkets are are 'exceptionally well stocked'.

EATING OUT
Dining dilemma

You can dine in whatever style you like in Aspen town. As you'd expect, there are excellent upscale places, but also plenty of cheaper options.

Piñons serves innovative American food in South-Western surroundings. Syzygy is a suave upstairs place with live jazz from 10pm. On our last visit we particularly enjoyed the 'fierce American food' at Jimmy's. Conundrum (modern American food, expensive) and Pacific (seafood) are top-notch. Poppie's Bistro Cafe is famous for its breads and desserts. L'Hostaria, The Mother Lode, Campo de Fiori and Farfalla are good Italians. Cache Cache does good-value Provençal. Ute City is in the upscale surroundings of an old bank and good for local game.

Cheaper recommendations include: Boogie's (a 50s-style diner, great for families), Hard Rock Cafe, Main Street Bakery, Mezzaluna, O'Leary's, Red Onion, Rusty's Hickory House and the Skier's Chalet steak house. At Snowmass, the choice is adequate.

APRES-SKI
Party time (later)

As the lifts shut, a few bars at the bases do reasonable business. At Snowmass, the slope-side Cirque Cafe has live bands most days. In Aspen a the Ajax Tavern is popular. But it's after dinner that Aspen town livens up.

Many of the restaurants are also bars – Ajax, Jimmy's (spectacular stock of tequila), Mezzaluna, O'Leary's, Red Onion, and Ute City, for example. The J-bar of the Jerome hotel still has a traditional feel. Shooters is a splendid country-and-western dive with pool and line-dancing. Maxfield's is a popular pool bar. For pool in more suave circumstances, there's Aspen Billiards adjoining the fashionable Cigar Bar, with its comfortable sofas (and smoking permitted!). The Double Diamond has live bands most nights (from 11pm). Popcorn Wagon is the place for munchies after the bars close at 2am. You can get a week's membership of 426, a club appealing to 30-somethings. Old timers like us prefer to get an evening's use of the Caribou club for the price of dinner.

OFF THE SLOPES
Silver service

Aspen has lots to offer, especially if you've got a high credit card limit. There are literally dozens of galleries, as well as the predictable clothes and jewelry shops. Just wandering around town is pleasant. It's a shame that all the best mountain restaurants are awkward for pedestrians to get to. Most hotels have excellent spa facilities. There's tubing at Snowmass.

ASPEN / DOUG CHILD

The atmospheric old mining town sits right at the foot of Aspen Mountain's slopes ➔

Smoother than Vail, and in many respects more attractive

HOW IT RATES

The slopes

Snow	*****
Extent	***
Experts	****
Intermediates	****
Beginners	*****
Convenience	****
Lines	*****
Restaurants	**

The rest

Scenery	***
Resort charm	***
Off-slope	***

What's new

An extra 30 acres of snowmaking was installed for 2000/01.

Village development projects in Arrowhead and Bachelor Gulch continue – a new Ritz-Carlton hotel in Bachelor Gulch will be ready in 2002.

➕ Blissfully quiet slopes, in sharp contrast to nearby Vail

➕ Mountain has it all, from superb novice runs through fast cruisers to long, daunting bump fields

➕ Compact, largely traffic-free village center (though with spacious suburbs beyond it)

➕ Some very convenient lodgings

➖ Rather urban feel to the village core

➖ Expensive

➖ Disappointing mountain restaurants – the best ones are exclusive members-only affairs

In contrast to its better-known neighbor, Vail, Beaver Creek is a haven of peace – both on and off the slopes. It gets rather overshadowed by big sister, but we wouldn't dream of making a trip to Vail without spending a day or two at The Beav, and there's a lot to be said for doing it the other way round – if you can live with the prices in this most exclusive of Colorado resorts.

THE RESORT

Beaver Creek, ten miles to the west of Vail, was developed by Vail Resorts in the 1980s. It is unashamedly exclusive, with a choice of top-quality hotels and condos right by the slopes. It centers on a large pedestrian square featuring escalators to the slopes, exclusive shops, exquisite bronze statues and an open-air ice rink. Lifts go up to the slopes from three points around the village, so choice of location isn't of great importance.

The lift system spreads across the mountains to Arrowhead – a secluded area of luxurious chalets 'nearing completion'. And Bachelor Gulch, half-way to Arrowhead, is also being developed into a village base – a hotel will be open here next year.

Nightlife and choice of bars and restaurants is much more limited than in Vail, a 25-minute bus-ride away. The complimentary resort shuttle-bus and taxi service is excellent.

THE MOUNTAINS

Beaver Creek, Bachelor Gulch and Arrowhead offer a small-scale version of the linked lift networks of the Alps. Free mountain tours are available four days a week.

Slopes The slopes immediately above Beaver Creek (where the men's downhill and super-G were held in the 1999 World Championships) divide into two sectors, each accessed by a fast quad chair. The major sector is centered on Spruce Saddle, with lifts

above it reaching 3490m/11,440ft. The other is lower and smaller, but forms the link with **Bachelor Gulch** and **Arrowhead**. Up the valley a little, and between these two sectors, is Grouse Mountain.

Resorts within a two-hour drive include Breckenridge and Keystone (owned by Vail Resorts and covered by multi-day lift tickets), Aspen, Steamboat and Copper Mountain.

Snow reliability In addition to an exceptional natural snow record, Beaver Creek has extensive snowmaking facilities, normally needed only in early season. The Grouse Mountain slopes can suffer from thin snow cover (some locals call it Gravel Mountain). Grooming is excellent.

Snowboarding Good riders will love the excellent gladed runs, perfect carving slopes and three terrain parks. The resort is great for beginners too.

Experts There is quite a bit of intimidatingly steep double-diamond terrain. In the Birds of Prey area and Grouse Mountain areas most runs are long, steep and bumped from top to bottom. The Larkspur Bowl area has three short steep bump runs.

Intermediates There are marvelous long, quiet, cruising blues almost everywhere, including top to bottom runs with a vertical of over 1000m/3,300ft. The Larkspur chair and the chairs going west from the village serve further cruisers – and lead to yet more ideal terrain served by the Bachelor Gulch and Arrowhead chairs.

MOUNTAIN FACTS

Altitude	2255m-3490m
	7,400ft-11,440ft
Lifts	13
Trails	1,625 acres
Green	34%
Blue	39%
Black	27%
Snowmaking	
	605 acres

Phone numbers
From distant parts of the US, add the prefix 1 970.
From abroad, add the prefix +1 970.

TOURIST OFFICE
PO Box 7, Vail, CO 81658
t +1 (970) 845 5745
bcinfo@vailresorts.com
www.beavercreek.com

Beginners There are excellent beginner slopes at resort level and higher up. And there are plenty of easy longer runs to progress to, including runs from top to bottom of the mountains.

Cross-country There's a splendid, extensive, mountain-top network of tracks at McCoy Park (over 32km/20 miles), reached via the Strawberry Park lift.

Liftlines The slopes are delightfully deserted and virtually line-free, even at peak times – it is amazing that more skiers don't come here from Vail.

Mountain restaurants There's not much choice. Spruce Saddle at mid-mountain is the main place – a food court in a spectacular log and glass building. Redtail Camp does decent barbecues. Rendezvous Bar and Grill at the foot of the main slope is very civilized, with good food. The Broken Arrow at Arrowhead is recommended.

Schools and guides The school has an excellent reputation.

Facilities for children The facilities for young children look excellent, and we've had good reports on the children's school. There are splendid children's areas with adventure trails and themed play areas.

STAYING THERE

Hotels There are lots of classy places. The luxury Inn at Beaver Creek (845 7800) has ski-in/ski-out convenience and a pool. And the Hyatt Regency (949 1234) has impeccable service, a lively bar and one of the major spas.

Apartments/condos There's a wide choice of condos available. However, one recent reporter complained that grocery shopping is very limited – a drive to Avon to stock up is advised.

Staying up the mountain Trappers Cabin is a luxurious private enclave up the mountain, which a group can rent (for a small fortune) by the night.

Staying along the valley Avon, a mile away at the foot of the approach road, has budget motels. The Minturn Inn in Minturn is a stylish B&B.

Eating out The SaddleRidge is a luxurious wooden building packed with photos and Wild West artifacts. The Mirabelle, at the bottom of the access road, is also rather special. The sleigh ride to Beano's Cabin makes a good evening out – like Allie's, a beautifully built cabin that is a members-only club at lunchtime but open for dinner. Toscanini's, the Golden Eagle, Dusty Boot, and Blue Moose are all recommended.

Après-ski There is a handful of bars – Rendezvous is recommended – but otherwise it's fairly quiet. Vail is the place to head to for a lively time.

Off the slopes Upscale boutiques and art galleries are good for window shopping. There's an impressive ice rink, and some great shows and concerts at the 500-seat Vilar Center. Hot-air balloon rides are popular. There are three seriously indulgent spas.

We've redrawn our map to take in the whole of Beaver Creek's new terrain, stretching across to Arrowhead

Summit Elevation
3490m/11,440ft

Grouse Mountain
3260m/10,690ft

Birds of Prey

Rose Bowl

Westfall

Larkspur Bowl
3160m/10,370ft

Spruce Saddle
3110m/10,200ft

Grouse Mountain

Larkspur

Cross-country and snowshoe park

Centennial

Red Tail Camp

Strawberry Park

Arrowhead Mountain
2775m/9,100ft

Bachelor Gulch

Elkhorn

Arrow Bahn

Beaver Creek Village
2470m/8,100ft

Bachelor Gulch
2470m/8,100ft

Arrowhead
2255m/7,400ft

Breckenridge

Popular introduction to Colorado

HOW IT RATES

The slopes

Snow	★★★★★
Extent	★★
Experts	★★★★
Intermediates	★★★★
Beginners	★★★★
Convenience	★★★
Lifts	★★★★
Restaurants	★★

The rest

Scenery	★★★
Resort charm	★★★
Off-slope	★★★

What's new

The Bell Tower Mall at the foot of Peak 9 has been replaced by a Hyatt timeshare complex.

A vast new indoor ice skating rink opened for 2000/01.

In the longer term there are proposals to build new villages at both Peak 7 and Peak 8 and to link them to town by gondola.

➕ Varied local mountains, with something for all abilities

➕ Good snow record and lots of snowmaking

➕ Shared lift ticket with nearby Keystone and Arapahoe Basin and not-so-nearby Vail and Beaver Creek

➕ Efficient lifts mean few liftlines

➕ Lively bars, restaurants and nightlife by US standards

➕ Based on restored Victorian mining town, with many new buildings in attractive 19th-century style

➕ One of the nearest major resorts to Denver, so relatively short transfer

➖ The local area is rather small, with few long runs

➖ Best advanced slopes can be windy

➖ At this extreme altitude there is an appreciable risk of sickness for visitors coming straight from lower altitudes (although the lift-accessed terrain does not go super-high, at 2925m/9,600ft the village is one of the highest you will encounter)

➖ The 19th-century style gets a bit overblown in places, and there are some out-of-place modern buildings that detract from its charm

➖ Main Street is just that – always crowded with traffic

Breckenridge is very popular with first-time visitors to Colorado. It's easy to see why: it is one of the closest resorts to Denver Airport, has slopes for all abilities, usually excellent dry snow, good facilities for families, relatively lively nightlife and good-value slope-side accommodations. Add to that the image of a restored Wild West mining town and you have a compelling package.

It is true that the slopes do not cover a huge area and that the town is rather spoiled by out-of-style buildings in parts and a rather Disneyesque feel to other parts. But it has skiing and boarding for all abilities, and there are lots of other areas to try on day trips, some covered by a shared lift ticket (Vail, Beaver Creek, Keystone and Arapahoe Basin), some not (such as Copper Mountain) – much more than you could cover in a week or 10 days. But take heed of the altitude warnings; drink plenty of water and stay well hydrated.

BOB WINSETT / VAIL RESORTS, INC

Peak 8 in the center and Peak 7 on the right have good advanced bowls high up accessed by a T-bar and a hike or traverse ➔

MOUNTAIN FACTS

Altitude 2925m-3700m
9,600ft-12,140ft
Lifts 23
Trails 2,043 acres
Green 14%
Blue 26%
Black 60%
Snowmaking
516 acres
Recco detectors used

The resort

Breckenridge was founded in 1859 and became a booming gold-mining town. The old clapboard buildings have been well renovated and form the bottom part of Main Street. New shopping malls and buildings have been added in similar style – though they are obvious modern additions.

The town center is lively in the evening, with over 100 restaurants and bars. Christmas lights and decorations remain throughout the season, giving the town an air of non-stop winter festivity. This is enhanced by a number of real winter festivals such as Ullr Fest – a carnival honoring the Norse God of Winter – and Ice Sculpture championships, which leave sculptures for weeks afterwards.

Hotels and condominiums are spread over a wide, wooded area and are linked by regular free shuttle-

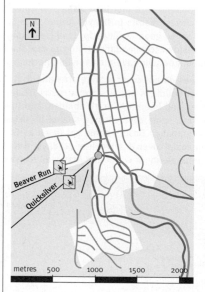

metres 500   1000   1500   2000

buses. If you stay in a condo and don't have a car, shopping at the local supermarket can be hard work – it is not in the center of town. Breckenridge boasts more slope-side lodging than any other Colorado resort.

The mountains

There are four separate peaks, linked by lift and trail. Boringly, they are named Peaks 7, 8, 9 and 10 – going from right to left as you look at the mountain. Though there's something for all abilities, the keen skier or rider will want to explore other resorts too. Breckenridge and Keystone were bought in 1996 by the owners of Vail and Beaver Creek (around an hour away); a multi-day lift ticket covers these four resorts and Arapahoe Basin, also nearby. Copper Mountain is not covered by the same ticket. All six of these resorts are linked by regular buses (free except for a $10 return fare for Vail and Beaver Creek). Steamboat and Winter Park are both less than two hours' drive away.

THE SLOPES
Small but fragmented
Two high-speed chair-lifts go from the top end of town up to **Peak 9**, one accessing mainly green runs on the lower half of the hill, the other mainly blues higher up. From there you can get to **Peak 10**, which has a large number of blue and black runs served by one high-speed quad.

The other flank of Peak 9 takes you to a lift up into the **Peak 8** area – tough stuff at the top, easier lower down. The base lifts of Peak 8 at the Bergenhof can also be reached by the town shuttle-bus or the Snowflake lift from the edge of town. From the top T-bar of Peak 8, you can traverse to the all-black **Peak 7** slopes and back bowls which have no lifts of their own – you

boarding *Breckenridge is pretty much ideal for all abilities of boarder and plays host to several major US snowboarding events. Beginners have ideal beginner areas and easy greens to progress to, and intermediates have great cruising runs, all served by chairs. For good boarders there's one of the best terrain-parks in the US on Peak 9, with a series of great jumps, obstacles and an enormous championship half-pipe on Peak 8, which one reporter described as 'massive, steep, well kept and awesome'. The powder bowls at the top of Peaks 7 and 8 make for great riding – unfortunately accessed only by an awkward T-bar, which is less attractive. Nearby Arapahoe Basin is another area for hardcore boarding in steep bowls and chutes.*

LIFT TICKETS

2000/01 prices in dollars

Breckenridge-Keystone
Covers all lifts in Breckenridge, Keystone and Arapahoe Basin. Tickets for 3 days or more also cover Vail and Beaver Creek.

Beginners
3 beginners' lifts. Beginners and novices have a reduced area ticket in ski school.

Main ticket
1-day ticket 57
6-day ticket 294

Senior citizens
Over 65: 1-day ticket 39 6-day ticket 234
Over 70: 99 for a season ticket

Children
Under 13: 6-day ticket 150
Under 5: free ticket

Alternative periods
Tickets of 2 days and over allow one non-skiing day, eg 6-day ticket valid for a 7-day period, with one non-skiing day.

---

go back to the base of Peak 8.

For the end of the day three trails lead back to town from Peak 8. A regular free shuttle runs around the resort to the Peak 9 and Peak 8 lifts. The grooming is excellent and the signage very clear.

SNOW RELIABILITY
Excellent
With the village at almost 3000m/10,000ft (the highest of the main North American resorts), the lifts going up to almost 3700m/12,140ft and a lot of east and north-east-facing slopes, Breckenridge boasts an excellent natural snow record. That is supplemented by substantial snowmaking.

FOR EXPERTS
Quite a few short but tough runs
A remarkable 60% of Breckenridge's runs are classified as 'most difficult' (single-black-diamond) or 'expert' (double-black-diamond) terrain. That's a higher proportion than the famous 'macho' resorts, such as Jackson Hole, Taos and Snowbird. But remember that Breckenridge is not a big area by European standards, so most experts there for a week or more will want to spend some of their time exploring the other nearby resorts.

Peak 7 is an entirely black-run area, which is reached by traversing or hiking up from the top of the T-bar. It has great steep runs with good snow on north-east-facing slopes. Peak 8 has some good open terrain in

Horseshoe and Contest bowls, where the snow normally remains good; and you can hike up to the steepest slopes in Imperial Bowl and Lake Chutes.

We particularly liked the back bowls of Peak 8. This is basically terrain among a thin covering of trees and bushes. Lots of runs, such as Lobo, Hombre, Amen and Adios, are marked on the trail map. But in practice you can easily skip between them and invent your own way down. It's picturesque and not too steep. Steep black bump fields lead down under chair 4 to the junction with Peak 9.

Peak 9 itself has nothing to offer experts except very steep blacks from the top down under chair E.

Peak 10 offers much more interest. Off to the right of the chair, at the edge of the area, is a network of interlinking black bump runs by the side of the downhill course – consistently steep and bumpy. To the left of the chair is a lovely, lightly wooded off-trail area called The Burn.

FOR INTERMEDIATES
Nice cruising, limited extent
Breckenridge has some good blue cruising runs for all standards of intermediate. But dedicated skiers and riders will find it limited and will want to visit the other nearby resorts.

Peak 9 has the easiest terrain. It is nearly all gentle, wide, blue runs at the top and almost flat, wide, green runs at the bottom. Timid intermediates will find it reassuring to see the ski patrol enforcing slow-speed skiing in narrow

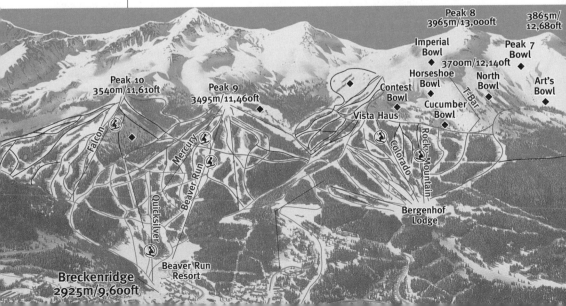

Breckenridge
2925m/9,600ft

SCHOOLS/GUIDES

2000/01 prices in
dollars

Breckenridge
Classes 7 days
5hr: 9.45-12.15 and
1.30-4pm; 2½hr: am
or pm
2 full days: 130
Children's classes
Ages: 3 to 12
6 full days 378
(including lunch for 3
to 5 year-olds)
Private lessons
1hr, 3hr or 6hr –
prices are per
instructor regardless
of 1 to 6 persons.
1hr: 115; 3hr: 260
6hr: 425.

CHILDCARE

At each major lift
base there is a resort-
run Children's Center
(453 3258), with a
complex array of
options for all-day
care from 8.30 to
4.30. Children aged 6
to 14 go into ordinary
children's school, but
all-day care is
available at Kid's
Castle meeting areas
at each lift base.

At Beaver Run there is
also an independent
childcare option called
Kinderhut for ages six
weeks to six years
(453 0379). Their
hours are 8.15 to 4pm
and from Tuesday to
Friday they are also
open from 6pm to
10pm.

Phone numbers
From distant parts of
the US, add the prefix
1 970.
From abroad, add the
prefix +1 970.

GETTING THERE

Air Denver, transfer
2½hr.

and crowded areas. Peak 10 has a
couple of more challenging runs
graded blue-black, such as Crystal and
Centennial, which make for good fast
cruising.

Peak 8 has a choice of blues down
through trails cut close together in the
trees. More adventurous intermediates
will also like to try some of the high
bowl runs (see 'For Experts'). And
Keystone, Vail, Beaver Creek and
Copper Mountain all offer miles of
excellent intermediate terrain.

FOR BEGINNERS
Excellent

The bottom of Peak 9 has a big,
virtually flat area and some good
gentle beginner areas. There's then a
good choice of green runs to move on
to. Beginners can try Peak 8 too, with
another selection of green runs and a
choice of trails back to town. Reporters
praise the good-value beginner
package which includes lessons,
equipment rental and lift ticket.

FOR CROSS-COUNTRY
Specialist center in woods

Breckenridge's Nordic Center is prettily
set in the woods between the town
and Peak 8 (and is served by the
shuttle-bus). It has 38km/24 miles of
trails.

LIFTLINES
Not normally a problem

Breckenridge's six high-speed chair-lifts
(three on Peak 9, two on Peak 8 and
one on Peak 10) make light work of
peak-time crowds. We've never come
across serious lines, and neither have
our reporters, except at exceptional
times, such as President's Day
weekend and on powder days – when
the T-bar at Peak 8 can get crowded.

MOUNTAIN RESTAURANTS
Varied but nothing special

Breckenridge is making an effort to
improve on the standard US cafeterias.

Ten Mile Station, situated between
Peaks 9 and 10, is the newest and
best, with a heated outdoor deck as
well as indoors. Border Burritos is in
the Bergenhof at the base of Peak 8.
Spencer's at Beaver Run does an all-
you-can-eat breakfast and lunch menu.
Vista Haus, at the top of Peak 8, has a
couple of restaurants.

SCHOOLS AND GUIDES
Excellent reports

Our reporters are unanimous in their
praise for the school: classes of five to
eight; doing what the class, not the
instructor, wants. Special clinics
include bumps, telemark and powder.

FACILITIES FOR CHILDREN
Excellent facilities

Every report on the children's school
and nursery bubbles with praise.
Typical comments: 'nothing but praise
for the children's ski school',
'excellent, combining serious coaching
with lots of fun', 'our boys loved it'.

 Staying there

Breckenridge is quite spread out.
Although there are a lot of slope-side
accommodations, there are also a fair
number away from Main Street and the
lift base-stations. Free shuttle-buses
serve most of the area well, but less
reliably in the evening than the day.

HOW TO GO
Lots of choice

Hotels There's a good choice of style
and price range.
((((4) **Great Divide** (453 4500) Used to
be the Hilton but is now owned by Vail
Resorts. Prime location, vast rooms
and recently renovated – although a
recent report complains of 'terrible
service, poor cleaning and dirty
hallways'. Pool, tubs.
((((4) **Lodge at Breckenridge** (453
9300) Stylish luxury spa resort set out
of town among 32 acres, with great
views. Private shuttle-bus. Pool, tubs.
((((4) **Little Mountain Lodge** (453 1969)
Luxury B&B near ice rink.
(((3) **Beaver Run** (453 6000) Huge,
resort complex with 520 spacious
rooms. Great location, by one of the
main lifts up Peak 9. Pool, hot-tubs.
(((3) **Williams House** (453 2975)
Beautifully restored, charmingly
furnished four-room B&B on Main St.
((2) **Fireside Inn** (453 6465) Dormitory-
style rooms. Historic part of town. Tub.
(1) **Breckenridge Wayside Inn** (453
5540) Friendly budget place out of
town. Tub.
Apartments/condos There is a huge
choice of condominiums, many set
conveniently off the aptly named Four
O'Clock run.

Ten Mile Station with its heated deck is the newest and best of Breck's mountain restaurants →

VAIL RESORTS, INC / TODD POWELL

ACTIVITIES

Indoor Sports clubs, swimming, sauna, massage, hot-tubs, theater, movie theater, art gallery, library, indoor miniature golf course, ice skating, good leisure center (pool, tubs, gym, climbing wall) on the outskirts of town – accessible by bus

Outdoor Horse- and dog-sleigh rides, fishing, snow-mobiles, toboggans, scooters, mountain biking, snow-shoeing, ice skating, hot-air balloon rides

TOURIST OFFICE

Postcode CO 80424
t +1 (970) 453 5000
f 453 3202
international@vail resorts.com
www.breckenridge.com

STAYING DOWN THE VALLEY
Good for exploring the area
Staying in Frisco makes sense for those touring around or on a tight budget. It's a small town with decent bars and restaurants. There are cheap motels, a couple of small hotels and some B&Bs (Hotel Frisco is recommended (668 5009).

EATING OUT
Over 100 restaurants
There's a very wide range of eating places, with pretty much everything you'd expect, from typical American food to 'fine-dining'. Pick up a copy of Breckenridge Dining Guide which lists a full menu of most places.

The Brewery is famous for its enormous portions of appetisers such as Buffalo Wings – as well as its splendid brewed-on-the-spot beers. We particularly liked the Avalanche beer.

We also liked Poirier's Cajun Café and the sophisticated food at both Café Alpine and Pierre's Riverwalk Café. Sushi Breck and Mi Casa (Mexican) have had good reviews. The Hearthstone has been recommended for 'lovely food in good surroundings'. And Michael's Italian is recommended for 'good food, extensive menu, large portions and reasonable prices'.

APRES-SKI
The best in the area
The Breckenridge Brewery, Shamus O'Toole's and Tiffany's are popular hangouts. The Gold Pan saloon dates from gold rush days, and is reputedly the oldest bar west of the Mississippi. Cecelia's has good cocktails and The Liquid Lounge and Sherpa & Yetti's are also popular. The Underworld is a trendy disco bar. But one of the locals' best kept secrets is Mount Java – a relaxed cafe-cum-bookshop with Internet access. More unusually, The O2 Lounge is an Oxygen bar, where you can snort different flavours of oxygen – the trick is to 'have a few beers beforehand and you'll leave sober'.

OFF THE SLOPES
Pleasant enough
Breckenridge is a pleasant place to wander around with plenty of souvenir and gift shops. Silverthorne (about 30 minutes away and connected by a free bus service) has excellent bargain factory outlet stores such as Levi, Gap and Ralph Lauren. It is easy to get around and visit other resorts.

Great all-rounder above a born-again resort

HOW IT RATES

The slopes

Snow	*****
Extent	**
Experts	****
Intermediates	****
Beginners	****
Convenience	****
Liftlines	****
Restaurants	*

The rest

Scenery	***
Resort charm	**
Off-slope	*

➕ Convenient purpose-built resort undergoing exciting renaissance

➕ Fair-sized mountain, with good runs for all abilities

➕ Excellent snow reliability

➕ Efficient lift system – few lines

➕ Several other good resorts nearby

➖ One fast-food mountain restaurant

➖ Limited vertical on black-diamond bowls at the top

➖ Village still rather limited when compared with established resorts

➖ Appreciable risk of altitude sickness for visitors arriving directly from much lower altitudes

Copper's slopes are some of Colorado's best, and last season saw the birth of the all-new slopeside resort centre – 'The new village at Copper' – to match the quality of the slopes. As a result, Copper now makes a much more attractive destination – but watch out for that altitude sickness.

What's new

Intrawest's new car-free 'Village at Copper' was opened for last season.

Passage Point, a fifth building in the new village complex, will be ready for 2001/02. The new development will house some new restaurants and more lodgings.

Copper's snowmaking capacity is being doubled for next season.

376

THE RESORT

Copper Mountain was originally built rather like the French resorts of the 1960s – high on convenience, low on charm. Because of that it never took off on the international market. But it has always had one of Colorado's best ski areas. And the resort has now been transformed by its new owners, Intrawest. Last season saw the opening of 'The new village at Copper' – four new impressive wood-and-stone-clad buildings with shops, restaurants and car-free walkways and squares, forming the new heart of the resort. The new village is based at the foot of the main intermediate area, with two fast quads up to the heart of the skiing. This follows the opening, two seasons ago, of the new base lodge and accommodations at East Village – with easy access to the resort's expert and intermediate terrain. A regular free shuttle-bus runs between the two main bases and the family skiing and beginners' area at Union Creek.

Keystone, Breckenridge and Arapahoe Basin are all nearby, and Vail, Steamboat and Winter Park are within an hour or two.

MOUNTAIN FACTS

Altitude 2960m-3750m
9,710ft-12,300ft

Lifts	23
Pistes	2,450 acres
Green	21%
Blue	25%
Black	54%
Snowmaking	
	400 acres

Tucker Mountain
Union Peak 3750m/12,300ft
Copper Peak
Copper Bowl
Union Meadows
3750m/12,300ft
Union Bowl
Spaulding Bowl
Upper Enchanted Forest
3655m/11,990ft
356om/11,68oft
Excelerator
Solitude Station
3485m/11,44oft
Timberline
3300m/10,83oft
Super Bee
American Flyer
American Eagle
The New Village at Copper
2960m/9,700ft
East Village
Union Creek
Cross-country and Snowshoe Center

Experts There is a lot of good expert terrain, especially in the steep and wild Copper Bowl on the back side of Copper's mountain and in the bump runs through the trees below Spaulding Bowl.

Intermediates Good intermediates will find long steep runs in the Copper Peak section on the left of the mountain. The slightly less proficient can enjoy gentler runs on the middle section of mountain, while early intermediates have gentle cruisers in the Union Peak area on the right.

Beginners The beginner slopes are excellent, and there are plenty of very easy green runs to graduate to.

Snowboarding There is excellent terrain for all abilities and there's also a terrain park and two half-pipes.

Cross-country There are 25km/15 miles of trails through the White River forest.

Liftlines Copper is popular with day visitors from Denver but lines are rare because of the efficient lift system.

Mountain restaurants Grim. The main place is a fast food court at Solitude Station. The alternatives are outdoors – a soup shack and a burger bar.

Schools and guides The school offers a wide variety of courses and has a fine reputation, especially for teaching children.

Facilities for children The Belly Button childcare facility, at the Schoolhouse at Union Creek, takes children from two months old and ski school starts from age three.

STAYING THERE

Hotels There are no identifiable hotels, but some of the condo buildings are hotel-like in style and look splendidly luxurious, with outdoor hot-tubs, etc.

Après-ski In the past – because the resort mainly catered for day trippers – après-ski was lively at lift closing time, but quiet later on. However, the new resort developments mean that many visitors will now stay overnight. Endo's Adrenaline cafe in the main village, and Molly B's, in the East village, are popular new venues.

Eating out Beachside pizza and pasta is new in the main village. Endo's and Molly B's are also popular. Evening sleigh rides take people out to Western-style dinners in tents.

Off the slopes Facilities include a fine sports club, with a huge pool and indoor tennis, and an ice rink. There's also a multi-screen movie theater nearby.

↑ There is some great terrain in the high bowls

COPPER MOUNTAIN / BEN BLANKENBURG

Central reservations
Call 968 2882 (from distant parts of the US, add the prefix 1 970; from abroad, add the prefix +1 970)

Toll-free number (from within the US) 1 888 219 2441.

TOURIST OFFICE
Postcode CO 80443
t +1 (970) 968 2882
f 968 2711
international@ski-copper.com
www.ski-copper.com

THE MOUNTAIN
The area is quite sizeable by American standards, and has great runs for all ability levels. Mountain tours with a Copper guide are available daily.

Slopes As you look up at the mountain, the easiest runs are on the right-hand side and the forested terrain gradually gets steeper and more challenging the further left you go. Above the forest, a series of steeper open bowls is served by two chairs and a surface lift on the front of the mountain and two further chairs on the back side (not very clearly shown on our single trail map, unfortunately).

Snow reliability Height and an extensive snowmaking operation give Copper an early opening date each season and excellent snow reliability. Grooming is excellent.

Crested Butte

Surprises galore in a Jekyll and Hyde resort

HOW IT RATES

The slopes
Snow	****
Extent	**
Experts	****
Intermediates	***
Beginners	****
Convenience	***
Liftlines	*****
Restaurants	*

The rest
Scenery	***
Resort charm	****
Off-slope	**

➕ Lots of 'extreme' and expert terrain

➕ Excellent for beginners and for near-beginners, with long easy runs

➕ Charming, tiny, restored Victorian mining town with good restaurants

➕ Convenient 'village' at lift base

➕ Excellent school

➕ Attractive scenery, for Colorado

➖ Limited for confident intermediate skiers and riders

➖ Old town is 10 minutes from resort village by shuttle-bus

➖ Remote location, away from mainstream Colorado resorts

➖ Only one satisfactory mountain restaurant

Among experts who are at home on steep, unprepared runs – and 'extremists' who like their mountains as steep as possible – Crested Butte enjoys cult status. Meanwhile, the commercial success of the place depends on beginners and timid intermediates, who love the long, gentle slopes of the main area. These two groups can safely include Crested Butte on their shortlists. But keen, mileage-hungry intermediates will find there isn't enough suitable terrain.

What's new

The Teocalli Bowl debate is still ongoing but should be resolved this year. This 274 acres of expert terrain at the top of the Extreme Limits area has been closed for several years due to patrolling problems and ski boundary discrepancies.

The Crested Butte Marriot Resort hotel at the foot of the slopes was reopened as a Club Med 'village' last season.

THE RESORT

Crested Butte is a small resort in a remote corner of Colorado. It takes its name from the local mountain – an isolated peak (a butte, pronounced 'beaut') with a distinctive shape. It started life as a coal-mining town in the late 1800s and is now one of the most attractive resorts in the Rockies – a few narrow streets with beautifully restored wooden buildings and sidewalks, a tiny town jail and a classic general store – straight out of a Western movie.

The town is a couple of miles from the mountain, linked by regular free shuttle-bus. But at the foot of it is the resort 'village' of Mount Crested Butte – modern and characterless, with a cluster of bars and restaurants at the foot of the slopes, a couple of big hotels and a sprawling area of houses and condos. There are some accommodations in the town, but most are at the resort village. You can stroll to the lifts from some of them; but from many condos you need the bus.

MOUNTAIN FACTS

Altitude	2775m-3620m
	9,100ft-11,880ft
Lifts	14
Pistes	1,058 acres
Green	14%
Blue	32%
Black	54%
Snowmaking	
	300 acres
Recco detectors used	

THE MOUNTAIN

It's a small area, but it packs in an astonishing mixture of perfect beginner slopes, easy cruising runs and expert terrain. There are free daily mountain tours for intermediates or better.

Slopes Two fast quad chairs leave the base. The Silver Queen takes experts to black runs and links with lifts to the steepest runs. The Keystone lift takes

you to the easiest runs. Intermediates can access cruising blue runs from either of these two lifts.

Snow reliability The resort apparently benefits from snowstorms from several directions, and has a substantial snowmaking installation.

Snowboarding There's lots of extreme terrain and a terrain-park for good riders. Beginners have a large section of long, wide green runs to the base.

Experts For those who like steep, ungroomed terrain, Crested Butte is

Phone numbers
From distant parts of the US, add the prefix 1 970.
From abroad, add the prefix +1 970.

idyllic – the 448 acres of the Extreme Limits at the top of the mountain offer seriously steep but prettily wooded and safe terrain. But the area needs a lot of snow cover – it is not unusual for it to be closed until late January. Guided tours of the North Face are available. Though there are also some 'ordinary' black runs, these are few.

Irwin Lodge, a few miles away, runs a snowcat skiing and riding operation on its secluded slopes (details below).

Intermediates Good intermediates are likely to find the area limited. For early intermediates, there are lots of wide, fairly gentle, well groomed and normally uncrowded cruising runs.

Beginners There are excellent beginner areas near the village and lots of good long runs to progress to.

Cross-country There are 30km/ 20 miles of cross-country trails near the old town of Crested Butte, and backcountry tours are available in Elk Mountain and the Gunnison National Forest.

Liftlines Virtually non-existent.

Mountain restaurants Most people go back to the base for lunch. The restaurant at the base of the Paradise lift is fairly civilized, though, with a table-service restaurant as well as a cafeteria and barbecue.

Schools and guides The school has an excellent reputation.

Facilities for children Parents praise the teaching and separate kids' area.

STAYING THERE

Hotels You have a broad range of options, from international-style comfort to homely character. In the resort village, the Sheraton Crested Butte Resort (349 2333) is one of the smartest options, with a pool and outdoor hot-tub and great views. The Nordic Inn B&B (349 5542) is a short walk from the lifts: 'Full of character, charming hosts', outdoor hot-tub and large rooms. On the outskirts of the old town, the 'Scandinavian-style' Inn at Crested Butte (349 1225) is a non-smoking hotel with an outdoor hot-tub. Elk Mountain Lodge B&B (349 7533) is a renovated miners' hotel.

Apartments/condos There are thousands of apartments available in the village.

Eating out Top of the pile is Soupçon, a tiny place in an old log cabin just off the main street in the old town, serving refined French food. Le Bosquet and Timberline run it close, and Bacchanale is a good Italian. The Idle Spur micro-brewery is popular. In the resort village, the WoodStone Grille is recommended. Bubba's and Twister, on the mountain, are open at night.

Après-ski Kochevar's, in the old town, is an amusing Wild West saloon. The Wooden Nickel and The Powerhouse are recommended. At the resort village, Rafters and Casey's are popular.

Off the slopes Activities are limited, though there are some galleries, a theater and a movie theater.

Staying up the mountain Nowhere near the main mountain, but well worth knowing about, is Irwin Lodge (349 2773) – a great wooden barn in a remote backcountry area, used as the base of a snowcat skiing operation and reached in winter only by snowcat or snowmobile. It has an outdoor hot-tub, great views and simple rooms above a huge sitting room with open fire.

TOURIST OFFICE

Postcode CO 81225
t +1 (970) 349 2286
f 349 2250
info@cbmr.com
www.crestedbutte
resort.com

SNOWPIX.COM / CHRIS GILL

← Condos spread widely around the valley from the lift base

3620m/11,88oft
The Headwall
3390m/11,120ft
High Lift
North Face
Spellbound Bowl
Third Bowl
The North Face
The Glades
Phoenix Bowl
Paradise
Twister
Silver Queen
Teocalli
3140m/10,300ft
East River
Keystone
2775m/9,100ft
Gold Link
Town of **Crested Butte**
Mountain Resort 2886m/9,38oft
2930m/9,61oft

Pampered cruising in the trees

HOW IT RATES

The slopes

Snow	*****
Extent	**
Experts	***
Intermediates	****
Beginners	****
Convenience	**
Liftlines	****
Restaurants	***

The rest

Scenery	***
Resort charm	**
Off-slope	**

What's new

For 2001/02 two new hotel-condominium buildings will open in River Run, including the ski-in, ski-out Lone Eagle next to the gondola.

Everyone staying at a resort-owned property receives a free mountain passport with over $500-worth of free activities (such as tubing, ice skating, yoga classes and wine tastings).

2000/01 saw a new six-pack, Ruby Express, on the back of Keystone Mountain – speeding up the return from North Peak.

380

➕ Good mountain for everyone but the double-diamond diehard; extensive, immaculately groomed intermediate slopes are a particular strength

➕ Huge night-skiing operation – almost half the runs are floodlit and open until 8pm

➕ Lots of other nearby resorts, and a shared lift ticket with Breckenridge, Vail and A-Basin

➕ Efficient lift system – few lines

➕ Luxurious condominiums set in woods (with good-value rates)

➕ Very impressive childcare facilities

➖ Very quiet in the evenings

➖ Very high – altitude sickness can be a problem for some visitors

➖ Few slope-side properties, and most involve bus-rides to and from lifts

➖ Resort lacks village atmosphere except in the newish River Run development

➖ Poor shops for self-catering

➖ Limited choice of restaurants

Keystone's slopes are impressive from many points of view. If there was a village at the foot of them like Vail or Breckenridge, Keystone's stable-mates, it would be easily recommendable. But what Keystone offers at present is less compelling. River Run – a joint venture with Whistler's Canadian owner, Intrawest – is developing into something like a recognisable resort village, but it still has some way to go before a week of evenings spent there could be called an attractive prospect. And the appeal of Keystone's other 'neighborhoods' – all less entertaining, all but one further from the lifts – is difficult to see.

Perhaps it is price: you may find some of Keystone's lodgings offer exceptional value. Rent a car to simplify shopping, and plan on eating in more than out.

The resort

Keystone is a sprawling resort of condominiums spread over wooded countryside at the foot of Keystone Mountain, beside the Snake River and the highway to Loveland Pass. As yet it has no clear center, but is nominally divided into seven 'neighborhoods', with regular buses between them (although one reporter says 'the routes can be very roundabout'). Some consist of little more than groups of condos, while others have shops, restaurants and bars (though no supermarkets or liquor stores – they are out on the main highway).

At River Run, at the base of the main gondola, an attractively designed, car-free development is taking shape that is destined to become the new focal point of the resort. A second lift base area half a mile to the west, Mountain House, is much less of a village. Another mile west is Keystone Village, set around the picturesque lake – a huge natural ice rink in winter. These and some other 'neighborhoods' are shown on our resort plan; Ski Tip (with famous Lodge) is off to the east.

The mountains

Keystone's terrain has expanded rapidly in the last few years and by US standards now offers extensive intermediate slopes and some challenging steeper stuff.

Keystone is owned by Vail Resorts, who also own Vail, Beaver Creek and Breckenridge. Lift tickets between the four resorts are interchangeable, and

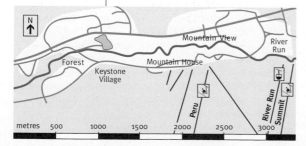

↑ Keystone is best-known for its groomed cruising, but it has excellent advanced terrain too

KEYSTONE / DAVE NAGEL

MOUNTAIN FACTS

Altitude	2835m-3720m/ 9,300ft-12,000ft
Lifts	22
Trails	1,861 acres
Green	12%
Blue	34%
Black	54%
Snowmaking	956 acres

there is bus transport between them. Copper Mountain is nearby and Arapahoe Basin (or A-Basin as it is known locally) a few minutes by road, but both are separately owned. Your lift ticket covers a trip to A-Basin, but not to Copper. In contrast to Keystone's superb modern lifts, A-Basin is still served by a series of slow old chairs.

THE SLOPES
A keen intermediate's dream
Three tree-lined, interlinked mountains form Keystone's local slopes. The only one directly accessible from the resort is **Keystone Mountain**, to which lifts depart from Mountain House or River Run. The front face of the mountain has Keystone's biggest network of lifts and runs by far, mainly of easy and intermediate gradient. From the top you can drop over the back down to Keystone Gulch, where there are lifts back up to Keystone Mountain and on to the next hill, **North Peak.** Or you can ride the Outpost gondola directly to the top of North Peak. From North Peak you can get back to the bases of both Keystone Mountain and the third peak, known as **The Outback**. This area is served by another high-speed quad.

SNOW RELIABILITY
Not a natural strength
Keystone's annual snowfall is low by Colorado standards – 230in, whereas many other resorts get 300in or more. But shortage of snow is rarely a problem, not least because Keystone has one of the world's biggest snowmaking systems as back-up.

One of the main reasons for the snowmaking is to help form an early-season base. Keystone traditionally vies with Killington to be the first US resort to open its runs for the season – normally in October.

A-Basin has no need for artificial snow. It has the highest lift-served terrain in the US, at around 4000m/ 13,000ft, and the base-station is at an impressive 3285m/10,780ft. The slopes are normally open well into June.

FOR EXPERTS
Some steeps, no super-steeps
Keystone has a reputation for great groomers, but it also has a lot of steeper ungroomed terrain (though none of it gets a double-diamond grading).

Windows is a 60-acre area of experts-only glade runs on Keystone Mountain's back side, opened in 1998. The trail map identifies around 10, but on the ground they are not clearly defined. All three mountains have some good bump runs, such as Ambush and Geronimo, and there are splendid glade runs on both North Peak and The Outback. Traversing from the top of the lift on The Outback takes you to open and glade runs in the North Bowl and the South Bowls, which are basically ski-anywhere areas.

Arapahoe Basin, up the road, is a good place for those looking for more of a challenge. The East Wall here has some splendid steep chutes. And the opposite side of the bowl is riddled with steep bump runs – although none of the runs is particularly long.

boarding *Until five years ago, snowboarding was banned at Keystone. Then they invested $2.5 million in facilities – these include the 20-acre Jackwhacker terrain-park and adjoining Area 51 half-pipe, on the front side of Keystone Mountain – floodlit to make the biggest night-snowboarding operation in Colorado (you can actually ride from 8.30am to 8pm – if you've got superhuman stamina, that is). Keystone as a whole is ideal for beginners and intermediates, with mainly chair-lifts and gondolas, good beginner areas (there are a couple of easily avoidable surface lifts here) and superb cruising runs. Experienced riders will love The Outback and the bowls and chutes of nearby A-Basin, a favorite area with hardcore boarders. Evenings are quiet.*

South Bowl

The Outback
3650m/11,98oft

North Bowl

Keystone
Mountain
3550m/
11,64oft

Windows

Outpost

North Peak
3555m/11,66oft

Wayback

Outback

Keystone
2835m/
9,300ft

Summit

River Run

Montezuma

Ruby

Santiago

3190m/10,46oft

Peru

Keystone
Gulch
3060m/10,04oft

LIFT TICKETS

2000/01 prices in dollars

Keystone-Breckenridge
Covers all lifts in Breckenridge, Keystone and Arapahoe Basin. Tickets for 3 days or more also valid for Vail and Beaver Creek.

Beginners Beginners and novices have a reduced area ticket in ski school.

Main ticket
1-day ticket 57
6-day ticket 294

Senior citizens
Over 65: 1-day ticket 39 6-day ticket 234
Over 70: 99 for a season ticket

Children
Under 13: 6-day ticket 150
Under 5: free ticket

Alternative periods
Tickets of 2 days and over allow one non-skiing day, eg 6-day ticket valid for a 7-day period, with one non-skiing day.

Copper Mountain, Breckenridge, Vail and Beaver Creek have some good challenging terrain, for those prepared to travel around.

FOR INTERMEDIATES
A cruiser's paradise

Keystone is ideal for intermediates. The front face of Keystone Mountain itself is a network of beautifully groomed blue and green runs through the trees. Enthusiastic skiers and riders will love it.

The Outback and North Peak also have easy cruising blues, and The Outback has some of the steepest blue runs, including a couple of blue-blacks through the trees that are pretty much off-trail and unmarked.

On top of that, Vail, Beaver Creek and Copper Mountain all have some great intermediate terrain.

FOR BEGINNERS
Nice gentle greens

There are good beginner areas (floodlit in the evening) at the top and bottom of Keystone Mountain, which also has some excellent long green runs to progress to – one of them, Schoolmarm, goes right from top to bottom of the mountain. There's another long green on North Peak, accessible by gondola.

FOR CROSS-COUNTRY
Extensive facilities

The special Cross-Country and Touring Center between Keystone and A-Basin is served by a shuttle-bus. There are 16km/10 miles of groomed trails. And 50km/31 miles of unprepared trails

take you through spectacular scenery in the Montezuma area, with great views of the Continental Divide. Some trails lead to old mining ghost-towns. The Cross-Country and Touring Center runs guided tours, including a Full Moon evening tour.

LIFTLINES
Not a problem

Keystone has an efficient, modern lift system, and, except at the morning peak, there are few line problems. Last time we tried the night skiing the River Run gondola stopped running and the parallel high-speed chair made for a mind-numbingly cold ride. The trails are usually beautifully quiet, except for Mozart, the only blue run down from Keystone Mountain to North Peak and The Outback.

MOUNTAIN RESTAURANTS
A resort of extremes

There are two mountain restaurant complexes. Summit House at the top of Keystone Mountain has a food court, a pizza place and a bar, all inclined to get overcrowded – 'Eat at the base,' says a reporter. The Outpost Lodge at the top of North Peak is beautifully designed in wood, with high ceilings, picture windows and a big terrace. Its Timber Ridge food court is strictly for refuelling, but the table-service Alpenglow Stube is something else. It has a luxury atmosphere rarely found in mountain restaurants, even in Europe – but it is, of course, expensive. There's a simple cabin and outdoor grill at Keystone Gulch, at the foot of North Peak.

There are lots of luxurious condos set in the trees with use of pool or hot-tub →

SCHOOLS/GUIDES

2000/01 prices in dollars

Keystone
Classes 7 days
2¹/₂hr: 10.30-1pm or 1.30-4pm; 2hr evening: 4.30-6.30 half-day 40
Children's classes
Ages: 3 to 14
Full day including lunch, equipment rental and ski-ticket: 84
Private lessons
1¹/₂hr, 2hr, half- or full-day
130 for 1¹/₂hr

Phone numbers
From distant parts of the US, add the prefix 1 970.
From abroad, add the prefix +1 970.

CHILDCARE

The Children's Center at the base of the mountain caters for children aged 2 months to 12 years and is open from 8am to 9pm. They can also provide evening babysitting in your own room. From age 3, children can join in the Snowplay programs.

The school's Mini Minor's Camp takes children aged 3 to 4, the Minor's Camp those from 5 to 12.

SCHOOLS AND GUIDES
Advanced classes a bargain
As well as the normal lessons, there are bumps, race, women-only and various other advanced classes. There are also special courses run by Olympic medallists Phil and Steve Mahre, designed specially for experienced adult skiers. Reporters have been very impressed by the school's advanced classes, partly because they found themselves in tiny groups or even receiving one-to-one attention for the price of a group lesson.

FACILITIES FOR CHILDREN
Excellent
Childcare facilities are excellent, with programs tailored to specific age groups, and nursery care going on into the evening. Children have their own teaching areas, with 'magic carpet' lifts. Ske-cology classes are designed to teach children about the environment and the resort's ecology while learning to ski.

Staying there

The most convenient places to stay are near the Mountain House or River Run lifts. But all the accommodations are served by free shuttle-buses.

HOW TO GO
As you please
It's easy to fix your own lodgings, and regular shuttles operate from Denver airport. There are hotels but most accommodations are in condominiums.
Hotels There isn't a great choice but they're all of a high standard.
《《《④ **Chateaux d'Mont** (496 4500) Luxury condo-hotel near the lifts; only 15 suites, with private hot-tubs and other luxuries.
《《《④ **Keystone Lodge** (496 2316) Large, recently renovated hotel in Keystone Village. All rooms have mountain views. Pool and fitness center.
《《③ **Inn at Keystone** (496 4242) Modern, comfortable, resort-owned hotel. Hot-tubs with great views. Liked by reporters who stayed there.
《《③ **Ski Tip Lodge** (496 4202) Former stagecoach halt and home of

GOURMET NIGHT SKIING

Keystone has the biggest floodlighting operation in the US, covering Keystone Mountain top to bottom. When the light begins to fade, the floodlights come on and you can continue skiing or riding up to 8pm. A gondola, high-speed quad and surface lift serve 17 green and blue runs (longest top-to-bottom trail over three miles long) and a 20-acre terrain park. Cruising through falling snow illuminated by the bright lights can be delightful. On a clear night, though, it can be bitter.

You can combine the action with dinner on the mountain. The Alpenglow Stube, at the top of North Peak (reached by gondola), stays open until 8.15 to serve haute cuisine with a Colorado flavor for pedestrians, skiers and snowboarders. Slippers are provided. A cheaper option is next door's Der Fondue Chessel which features fondue, raclette and 'Bavarian' music and dancing.

GETTING THERE

Air Denver, transfer 2hr.

ACTIVITIES

Indoor Swimming, hot-tubs, tennis
Outdoor Floodlit ice skating, sleigh and stagecoach rides, snowmobiling, horse-riding, tubing, night skiing, snow-shoeing, cross country skiing, winter fly fishing, star gazing workshops, weekly firework display, torch-light descents, dog-sledding, evening gondola trips

TOURIST OFFICE

Postcode CO 80424
t +1 (970) 496 6772
f 453 3202
international@vail resorts.com
www.keystoneresort.com

Keystone's founder, Max Dercum, who restored and extended it and used broken ski tips found on the slopes as door handles – hence the name. Atmospheric old rooms, bar and lounge with log fires. 'Superb food and very attentive service,' reports one visitor.

Apartments/condos All the condominiums we've seen or heard about are large and luxurious – and we've stayed in some fabulous ones with nice touches, such as log fires and two-story floor-to-ceiling windows. Most condos have use of a pool and hot-tub. Except for their position, we particularly liked the Lakeside condos (near the lake!). The equally comfortable and well positioned Frostfire condos have fewer amenities, but each unit has an en suite whirlpool bath. Cinnamon Ridge at Mountain View, Slopeside at Mountain House and Flying Dutchman in the Forest 'neighborhood' are other recommended places. There are lots of condos at the River Run development.

STAYING DOWN THE VALLEY
Possible, good for exploring

A few years ago a couple of reporters stayed in **Silverthorne**. The Days Inn was thought comfortable but basic. The Alpen Hutte was friendly and had its own private bus transfer. **Frisco** is a good center for visiting other nearby resorts – reporters recommend the Alpine Inn, Lake Dillon Lodge and Hotel Frisco.

EATING OUT
Not the widest choice

You can have your evening meal up the mountain. The Summit House, at the top of the gondola on Keystone Mountain, remains busy at the end of the normal day because of the floodlit sessions at night. There's live country and western entertainment and simple food – hamburgers, ribs and so on. The Outpost, on North Peak, is a hive of dining activity including the Alpenglow Stube (see Mountain restaurants).

There are some good upscale places at valley level too. We've eaten well at the Ski Tip Lodge by the cross-country track (the menu changes daily) – a charming former stagecoach halt. The Keystone Ranch, well outside the resort, serves six-course dinners in a building based on a 19th-century homestead. The Garden Room of

Keystone Lodge overlooks the lake and reports are favorable: 'Small menu but good food.'

River Run and Keystone Village each offer half a dozen options, including steak houses and pizza places. But there isn't the range of mid-market restaurants that makes eating out such a pleasure in many American resorts – and it's in the nature of the place that the restaurants are scattered around in different parts of the resort. Paisano's is an 'excellent' Italian at River Run, where there are also two taverns. The cozy Snake River Saloon in the Mountain View neighborhood is recommended for grills. The Bighorn Steakhouse in Keystone Lodge is well worth avoiding – lousy service in a dreary room.

APRES-SKI
Pretty quiet in the evenings

Immediately after coming off the slopes, it can be quite lively. The Summit House at the top of the gondola has live music and caters to people using the slopes at night as well as après-skiers. The Kickapoo Tavern at River Run has a sunny deck and eight Colorado microbrews on tap, and Montezuma has rock 'n roll. Some of the eateries double as bars with live music. The Snake River Saloon has a happy hour, 5–7pm, and is thoroughly recommended by a reporter: 'Brilliant restaurant and lively bar – including a fire-eating barman.' Ida Belle has ragtime music and a miners' tavern decor; and Dillon Inn has Country and Western.

However, places empty out quite early and Keystone isn't really the place for late-night revellers.

The Inxpot is a quiet, laid-back coffee house, cum bar, cum bookstore, with comfy armchairs and a great selection of books. Other popular hangouts with the locals are The Goat and Out of Bounds.

OFF THE SLOPES
OK if you want a peaceful time

Keystone makes it easy for pedestrians to get around the mountain, with both mountain restaurant complexes easily accessible by gondola. It's also easy to get to Breckenridge and Vail.

There are plenty of other activities, including skating on the frozen lake (the largest outdoor maintained rink in the US) and indoor tennis.

Steamboat

Something for everyone above a cowboy town

HOW IT RATES

The slopes

Snow	****
Extent	***
Experts	***
Intermediates	****
Beginners	*****
Convenience	***
Liftlines	****
Restaurants	***

The rest

Scenery	***
Resort charm	**
Off-slope	**

What's new

Steamboat's terrain has expanded a lot in recent years – first into Morningside Park and then into the Pioneer Ridge area. Another lift and another 500 acres of terrain are planned to open at some stage.

A new 'Super-Pipe' is planned for the Dude Ranch snowboard area for 2001/02.

And a new Grand Summit condo-hotel at the base of the mountain, opened in time for the 2000/01 season. It is a large complex of rooms, condos and suites with extensive facilities (pool, hot-tubs, fitness room, conference center, ballrooms and restaurants).

STEAMBOAT

You have to be there at the right time in January to experience the amazing Cowboy Downhill →

➕ Now a fair-sized mountain, with a decent amount of black-diamond terrain to go with its excellent beginner and early intermediate runs

➕ Famed for its gladed powder terrain

➕ Plenty of slope-side lodging

➕ Town of Steamboat Springs has some Western character – though it's less of a wild cowboy town than the hype leads you to expect

➕ Good snow record combined with modest altitude – sickness problems are very unlikely

➖ Old town is a couple of miles from the slopes, and the resort as a whole sprawls over a large area

➖ Modern resort 'village' at the foot of the slopes is rather a mess, with some big eyesore buildings

➖ Mountain lacks distinctive character

➖ Not enough tough blue/easy black runs to amuse keen intermediates for a week

➖ Not a huge amount of double-black terrain – some of it a hike away

➖ Green runs tend to be winding catwalks rather than proper runs

Steamboat's brochures routinely feature horse-riding, Stetson-wearing, lasso-wielding cowboys. There are working cowboys around, but as Steamboat the ski resort has grown it has rather swamped Steamboat Springs the cattle town – without itself developing much of a village atmosphere.

Steamboat's mountain may not be a match in extent and challenge for some Colorado neighbors – experts and avid skiers and riders going for a week or more might do well to plan a two-resort vacation. But Steamboat is one of the best resorts for powder fun among the trees. Recent expansions have added to its appeal in this respect.

The resort

The resort is a 10-minute bus-ride from the old town of Steamboat Springs – a long drive or short flight from Denver. Near the gondola station there are a couple of shop- and restaurant-lined multi-level squares. Some of the accommodations are up the sides of the trail, but the resort also sprawls across the valley.

The old town can be a bit of a disappointment after the hype of the brochures. It may be a working cattle town – it's certainly a great place to buy a Stetson (at the famous FM Light & Son). But the Wild West isn't much in evidence except in January when the Cowboy Downhill brings cowhands into town from the National Western Stock Show and Rodeo in Denver to compete in a fun race, lassoing and saddling competition.

The main (and almost only) street in the old town is very wide, with multiple lanes of traffic each way – it was built that way to allow cattle to be driven through town. It is lined with

MOUNTAIN FACTS

Altitude 2100m-3220m
6,900ft-10,570ft

Lifts	20
Trails	2,939 acres
Green	13%
Blue	56%
Black	31%
Snowmaking	
	438 acres

LIFT TICKETS

2000/01 prices in dollars

Steamboat
Covers all lifts at Steamboat only.
Beginners One free lift at base (Preview); day ticket for beginners covers two extra lifts (adult 36).
Main ticket
1-day ticket 59
6-day ticket 306
(low season 264)
Senior citizens
Over 65: 6-day ticket 210
Over 70: free ticket
Children
Under 13: 6-day ticket 204 – but can be free, see Notes below
Under 5: free ticket
Short-term tickets
Afternoon tickets from 12.15 (adult 47) and from 2pm (adult 34). Single ascent on Silver Bullet Gondola for non-skiers only (adult 17).
Alternative periods
3-day ticket is valid for 4 days with one non-skiing day. Tickets of 4 days and over allow two days' non-skiing, so 4 days' skiing in 6, 6 in 8.
Notes Children up to 12 ski free when parents buy full lift ticket and stay for 5 days or more (one child per parent). Discounts for groups.

bars, hotels and shops, built at various times over the last 120 years, in a wide mixture of styles, from old wooden buildings to modern concrete plazas.

The town got its name in the mid-1800s, when trappers going along by the Yampa river heard a chugging they thought was a steamboat. It turned out to be the bubbling of a hot spring.

The mountain

Located in the Routt National Forest, Steamboat's slopes are prettily set among trees, with views over rolling hills below. On our last late-season visit we even glimpsed a black bear and her cubs ambling across a trail.

It claims to be one of Colorado's biggest areas, and with its recent ongoing expansion, there's now more terrain for better skiers in particular. But even when the expansion is finished it still won't rival places such as Aspen and Vail.

With an Early Bird ticket ($11 including breakfast) you can ride the gondola at 8.15am, and get fresh tracks when the slopes open at 8.30 before having a buffet breakfast at Thunderhead when the crowds arrive.

There are various complimentary guided tours. Mountain hosts do tours of blue and black runs daily at 10.30. Olympic medallist Billy Kidd takes groups down the mountain most days at 1pm. Nelson Carmichael, bronze medallist at the Albertville Olympics, runs a free bump clinic on Sundays at 1pm. There are nature ski tours three times a week. And five days a week at 9am local guides lead groups of over-50s on a 'mellow cruise' of groomed runs. There are also snow-shoeing tours on Thursdays and Saturdays.

Vacationers generally overlook Steamboat Springs' little local hill, Howelsen. In addition to a row of ski jumps, it has a modest area of trails, floodlit most evenings.

If you have a car, Vail, Beaver Creek, Copper Mountain, Keystone, Breckenridge and Winter Park are all less than a two-hour drive.

THE SLOPES
Five different flanks

The slopes divide naturally into five sectors, and most have runs to suit all abilities. The gondola from the village rises to **Thunderhead**. From here you can choose the runs back to the village and a variety of chairs. Or you can go down to the left to catch a chair up to **Storm Peak** or to the new **Pioneer Ridge** area. From Storm Peak you can drop over the back into **Morningside Park** area. If you turn right from Thunderhead you can catch a chair up to **Sunshine Peak**.

SNOW RELIABILITY
Good despite 'low' altitude

Steamboat is relatively low by Colorado standards; it goes from 2100m/6,900ft to 3220m/10,570ft. So its highest slopes are below the height of the base of Arapahoe Basin. Despite this it has an excellent snow record, with an annual average of 334 inches – more than most of the higher resorts. This is where they invented the term Champagne Powder™. There is also snowmaking from top to bottom of the mountain.

FOR EXPERTS
Powder glades are the highlight

The main attraction of Steamboat for experts is the challenging 'off-trail' terrain in the forest glades. The trees are fantastic with fresh powder though, sadly, conditions have never been perfect on our visits.

A great area is on Sunshine Peak below the Sundown Express and Priest Creek lifts. You simply take off through the aspens and choose a route where the trees are spaced as you like them – wide or narrow. Of the marked black

boarding *Steamboat is ideal for first-time boarders – there's a special learning area, ideal gentle slopes to progress to, and you can get all over the mountain using chair-lifts and the gondola. The snowboard school even offers another lesson free if you can't ride from the top of the beginners' area after the first. Steamboat is also great for experienced boarders, with two terrain-parks: The Beehive, especially for kids, and the competition-standard Dude Ranch half-pipe and terrain-park (which will have a new superpipe for 2001/02). And riding the glades in fresh powder is unbeatable. There's also a choice of specialist snowboard shops, and benches and tools at the top of lifts.*

runs in this area, the two to the left of the lifts as you go up – Closet and Shadows – are only loosely trails: the trees have just been thinned out a bit. On the right of the lift as you go up are some clearer marked black runs.

Morningside Park and Pioneer Ridge also have excellent gladed terrain, without any scary gradients.

The scary gradients are reached via the lift back from Morningside – the three numbered chutes are easily accessed, and a short hike gets you to the tree skiing of Christmas Tree Bowl.

Most other marked blacks are easy for good intermediates and make great fast runs if they've been groomed. For bumps, try the series of runs off Four Points – including Nelson's, named after local hero Nelson Carmichael.

Steamboat Powder Cats (aka Blue Sky West) run snowcat skiing tours over 15 square miles of backcountry.

FOR INTERMEDIATES
Some long cruises
Much of the mountain is ideal intermediate territory, with long cruising blue runs such as Buddy's Run, Rainbow and Ego on Storm Peak and High Noon and One O'Clock on Sunshine Peak. Some black runs, such as West Side and Lower Valley View,

also make good, challenging intermediate runs when the bumps have been groomed out of them.

Morningside Park is a great area for easy black as well as blue slopes. And don't ignore Thunderhead – there are lots of good runs that are easy to miss if you always head straight to the top. The runs on Sunshine at the far right-hand side of the area are very gentle – Tomahawk and Quickdraw are marked blue but are perfectly possible for those who normally stick to green.

For keen intermediates the area is limited – not really enough to keep you interested for a week unless you enjoy repeating the same runs.

FOR BEGINNERS
Excellent learning terrain
There's a big, gentle beginner area at the base of the mountain served by several lifts. You progress from this to the Christie chairs to a variety of gentle green runs such as Yoo Hoo and Giggle Gulch. A green run winds all the way down from Thunderhead, but there is rather a shortage of 'proper' green runs up the mountain for those not ready for the psychological leap to the easy blues on Sunshine.

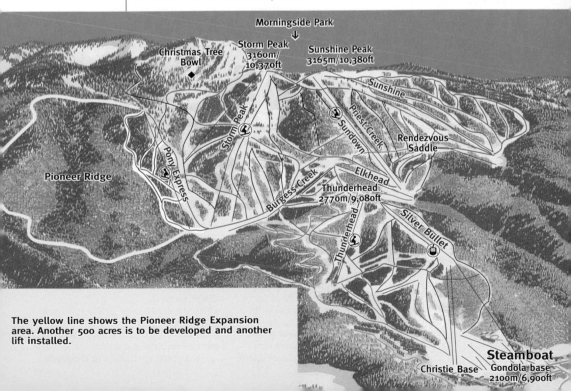

The yellow line shows the Pioneer Ridge Expansion area. Another 500 acres is to be developed and another lift installed.

Morningside Park

Christmas Tree Bowl

Storm Peak 3160m/10,370ft

Sunshine Peak 3165m/10,380ft

Sunshine

Storm Peak

Sundown

Priest Creek

Rendezvous Saddle

Pioneer Ridge

Pony Express

Burgess Creek

Elkhead

Thunderhead 2770m/9,080ft

Thunderhead

Silver Bullet

Steamboat

Christie Base

Gondola base 2100m/6,900ft

SCHOOLS/GUIDES

2000/01 prices in dollars

**Steamboat
Classes** 5 days
2hr 30min: 11.15am-1.45pm
5 half days: 197
Children's classes
Ages: 6 to 15
5 5hr days including lunch: 325
Private lessons
1hr, 2hr, 3hr or full-day
100 for 1hr

Phone numbers
From distant parts of the US, add the prefix 1 970.
From abroad, add the prefix +1 970.

CHILDCARE

The Kids' Vacation Center is run by the resort in the lower gondola station. The Kiddie Coral nursery takes children aged 6 months to 6 years, all day. Those aged 2 can opt for the Buckaroos program with a one-hour private lesson (ski rental not included). Older children go on to the Mavericks and Sundance Kids group classes.

The school has Rough Rider and Desperados programs for children up to 15, with their own skiing skills area and lunchtime supervision.

The Adventure Club at Night offers evening childcare in the Vacation Center for ages 4 to 12, from 6pm to 10pm. Reservations necessary.

The Steamboat Grand has childcare facilities.

FOR CROSS-COUNTRY
Plenty out of town

There's no cross-country in Steamboat itself but a free shuttle service takes you to the Touring Center, where there are 30km/20 miles of groomed tracks and lessons available. There are also Forest Service trails around Rabbit Ears Pass – many quite challenging, apparently.

LIFTLINES
A problem in the morning

Lines can form for the gondola at the start of the day; at least they are well organized. New fast quad chairs have cut out the worst bottlenecks up the mountain, though the slow Sunshine lift serving the easiest top-of-the-mountain runs can be crowded.

MOUNTAIN RESTAURANTS
Good by US standards

There are two main restaurant complexes on the mountain, both of which include excellent table-service restaurants. At Thunderhead there's a choice of the big BK Corral self-service food court, a barbecue on the sun deck, or table-service in the pub-style Stoker bar or more elegant Hazie's restaurant. At Rendezvous Saddle there's a slightly smaller alternative, which has a two-floor self-service section including a pizza bar, another sun deck and barbecue and Ragnar's table-service Scandinavian restaurant. You can book for Ragnar's and Hazie's. There's also a snack bar and sun deck at Four Points.

SCHOOLS AND GUIDES
Lots of variety

The program includes special workshops such as powder, bumps and style clinics. Reports on the school are very positive: 'A fantastic tree skiing lesson.' There's a First Tracks option at 8am for $35 for 90 minutes – great on a powder day. The Guided Demo Center at the top of the gondola provides not only the latest skis to test but instructors to help you get the best out of them, for $10/hr.

FACILITIES FOR CHILDREN
Kids Go Free

Steamboat has a Kids Go Free scheme – free lift ticket for one child of up to age 12 per parent buying a ticket for at least five days. The school has a variety of courses for different abilities and age groups. Recent comments include 'Louis (aged four) pleaded with

us to up his half day to a full day,' and 'the camaraderie between instructors and pupils is great'. Childcare arrangements are comprehensive, including evening entertainment or excursions from 6pm.

Staying there 🗝

Our preference is to stay on the slopes and make occasional excursions to Steamboat Springs. The free shuttle-buses are very efficient.

HOW TO GO
Choose between town and resort

Hotels The more upscale hotels out at the resort have less character than some of the in-town options.

(((④ **Steamboat Grand** (871 5500) New 330-room resort-owned condo-hotel close to the lifts, with pool, hot-tubs and child care.

((((④ **Best Western Ptarmigan Inn** (879 1730) Ideally situated just above the gondola station and right on the trail, with an outdoor pool and hot-tub, a sauna and good après-ski bar.

(((④ **Sheraton** (879 2220) Big, comfortable but impersonal hotel near the gondola, with a pool and hot-tub.

((③ **Harbor** (879 1522) The oldest hotel in the old town. Rooms vary in size and style; sauna, steam room and two hot-tubs.

(② **Bristol** (879 3083) Traditional little hotel on main street of old town, with 'small but fairly priced' rooms.

(② **Alpiner Lodge** (879 1430) Bavarian style economy in old town.

(② **Rabbit Ears Motel** (879 1150) Recommended by reporter: 'Excellent. Family run, comfortable rooms.'

Apartments/condos There are countless apartment developments, many with good pool/tub facilities and shuttle-buses. Recommendations include Bear Claw condos at the top of the beginner area; Timber Run, a short shuttle-ride from the center with multiple hot-tubs; The Lodge at Steamboat, close to the gondola station; Thunderhead Lodge & Condominiums; and the aptly named Ski Inn. Storm Meadows condos at Christie Base are 'wonderful'.

EATING OUT
Huge variety

There's a wide choice of places to suit all pockets – over 70 bars and restaurants. Pick up a dining guide booklet to check out menus.

Steamboat specializes in mountain-

GETTING THERE

Air Yampa Valley regional airport, transfer ¾hr. Denver, transfer 3½hr.

ACTIVITIES

Indoor Ice skating, hot-tubbing, swimming pools, tennis, gym, weights room, climbing wall, museum

Outdoor Ice driving school, dog-sledding, snowmobiling, ballooning, hot springs, dinner sleigh rides, horse-riding, skating, ice and rock climbing, fly-fishing, snowcat skiing, snow-shoeing, cross-country skiing, tubing

TOURIST OFFICE

Postcode CO 80487
t +1 (970) 879 6111
f 879 7844
steamboat-info@steamboat-ski.com
www.steamboat-ski.com

top dining, in three restaurants accessed via the gondola to Thunderhead. Five nights a week the Western BBQ does an all-you-can-eat buffet, with country and western music and dancing. Or you can have a gourmet treat at Hazie's, where the menu goes somewhat upscale from lunchtime. Three nights a week you can take a sleigh hauled by a snowcat to Ragnar's at Rendezvous Saddle for a Scandinavian meal with live music.

In the resort, the Slopeside Grill has a good selection of pizza and pasta dishes and doubles as a bar, with live music some nights. The plush Steamboat Grand has two options: Chaps, a popular cowboy-style bar and grill and The Cabin, which 'does seriously good food'.

In downtown Steamboat Springs try L'Apogee for fine French-style food, or the cheaper Harwig's Grill on the same premises. The Steamboat Yacht Club on the river bank is recommended for seafood and views of ski-jumping. Antares is deservedly popular for its excellent international cuisine. The Steamboat Brewery has a wide-ranging menu as well as its own beers. For more traditional fare try the popular Old West Steakhouse – 'very charming, reasonably priced, great food' – or the Ore House at the Pine Grove. Cantina is recommended for Tex-Mex and Cugino's for Italian. The Cottonwood Grill offers 'superb' Pacific Rim Cuisine. For a real budget buy, head for the barbecue food at the Double Z, popular with locals.

APRES-SKI
Fairly lively

Restaurants apart, the old town is quiet in the evening. The Old Town Pub has live music on weekends. The Tap House has 30 TVs as well as the best draft beer choice in town.

The base lodge area is livelier. Popular places at day's end are the Slopeside Grill and the Inferno, in the gondola square, both with live music and a happy hour. The mountain hosts regularly serve up free hot apple cider and hot chocolate at the base of the gondola in the afternoons. The Inferno is the place for dancing to loud live music – and on Sundays it has a very popular 'Disco Inferno' night. Dos Amigos and the Tugboat Tavern are popular bars for drinks by the pitcher. The Ptarmigan Inn offers a rather more sophisticated atmosphere. While The Stoker Comedy Club up at Thunderhead has live stand-up comedy from 7 until 10pm.

Evening activities include watching floodlit ski-jumping in the old town and tubing on the floodlit beginner area at the main ski area.

OFF THE SLOPES
Lots to do

Getting up to Thunderhead restaurant complex is easy for pedestrians. Visiting town is, too. And you can go and relax in outdoor Strawberry Park Hot Springs six miles from town. The snowmobiling terrain around Rabbit Ears Pass looks great to our untutored eye. The ice rink is Olympic size.

Steamboat has great skiing among the trees as well as on the open trails ➔

Telluride

Cute old town, massive expansion of slopes for 2001/02

HOW IT RATES

The slopes

Snow	****
Extent	**
Experts	****
Intermediates	***
Beginners	*****
Convenience	****
Liftlines	*****
Restaurants	*

The rest

Scenery	****
Resort charm	****
Off-slope	**

What's new

For 2001/02 three new high-speed chair-lifts (Prospect Bowl, Gold Hill and Ute Park) will give access to an additional 733 acres of terrain in Prospect Bowl – this is a 70% increase and includes 20 new runs.

Two further lifts are planned for 2002/03.

A new mountain restaurant with a Ute Indian theme (teepees etc) is planned for 2001/02.

Telluride ski area was sold in March 2001 and the new owner is Hideo 'Joe' Morita (son of Sony founder Akio Morita).

390

➕ Charming restored Victorian silver-mining town with a real Wild West atmosphere

➕ Skiing for all abilities, including long, serious bump slopes

➕ Dramatic, craggy mountain scenery – unusual for Colorado

➖ Isolated location

➖ Remains to be seen whether the new terrain merits a week's stay

➖ Mountain Village a bit of an eyesore

➖ Limited mountain restaurants (but another planned)

We have always loved the old town of Telluride – it has lots of character, lovely old buildings, good restaurants and shops and dramatic views of the San Juan mountains. Our only criticism has been the limited extent of the lift-served slopes. But all that will change for 2001/02, with a 70% expansion of the slopes and new intermediate and advanced runs. We can't wait to go and try them!

THE RESORT

Telluride is an isolated resort in south-west Colorado. The town first boomed when gold was found – some say its name is a shortened version of 'To hell you ride', but in fact it's more probably due to the presence of tellurium in the rock. The old wooden buildings and sidewalks have been well-restored and it has more Wild West charm than any other US resort. The shops and restaurants have gone decidedly up-scale since its 'hippy' days of a few years ago. But it is still small-scale and friendly. Up on the slopes, Mountain Village is a model American leisure resort with modern buildings. A free gondola (running in the evenings as well as in the day) links the two.

THE MOUNTAINS

There is some fearsomely steep terrain, and also ideal beginner and intermediate areas.

Slopes Chair-lifts and a gondola serve the steep wooded slopes directly above the town, and give access to the bowl beyond which leads down to Mountain Village. This has steep slopes at the top from the Giuseppe's area, intermediate terrain in the middle and ideal, gentle beginner slopes beyond the village down to Big Billie's and the long runs served by the Sunshine Express lift. The new terrain for 2001/02 will be great steep runs on Gold Hill (previously accessed by a 20-minute hike) and intermediate and advanced terrain in Prospect Bowl.

↑ Runs down the front lead right back into the cute old town of Telluride

TELLURIDE SKI & GOLF CO / GUS GUSCIORA

MOUNTAIN FACTS

Altitude	2660m-3735m
	8,730ft-12,250ft
Lifts	16
Trails	1,700 acres
Green	22%
Blue	38%
Black	40%
Snowmaking	
	204 acres
Recco detectors used	

Central reservations phone number

For all resort accommodations ring 728 7507 (from distant parts of the US, add the prefix 1 970; from abroad, add the prefix +1 970)

Toll-free number (from within the US) 1 888 827 8050.

TOURIST OFFICE

Postcode CO 81435
t +1 (970) 728 3041
f 728 6475
skitelluride@telski.com
www.telski.com

Snowboarding The Surge Air Garden Terrain Park, located next to Gorrono Ranch, is the largest terrain park in the Southwest. Its 13 acres include 23 hits, a 'rail garden' and a 12ft half-pipe.

Snow reliability With a high average snowfall and lots of well-placed snowmaking, snow reliability is good.

Experts The double-black bump runs directly above the town are what has given the area its expert reputation and there are steep gladed runs from all along the ridge between Giuseppe's and Gold Hill – no longer a hike away. You can also go heli- and snowcat skiing or boarding.

Intermediates There are ideal blue cruising runs with awesome views right from the top down to Mountain Village (including the aptly-named See Forever). But avid skiers and riders could get bored with their limited extent after a couple of days. The new terrain in the Prospect Bowl area should mean more to keep you interested. The main easy way back down to town is a winding path.

Beginners There are ideal runs in the Meadows below Mountain Village, and splendid long greens and blues served by the Sunshine Express chair.

Cross-country The scenic beauty of the area makes it splendid for cross-country – the Telluride Nordic Center runs over 35km/22 miles of trails.

Liftlines These are rarely a problem – there are no weekend crowds, and the lift system is increasingly impressive.

Mountain restaurants Gorrono Ranch is the main on-mountain restaurant, with a big terrace, live music and a BBQ. Another at the top of the Sunshine Express lift with a Ute Indian Village theme (teepees etc) will open for 2001/02.

Schools and guides In addition to the usual, the ski school offers day-long outback adventures by snowcat and a biomechanical private lesson where your equipment is adjusted to suit you.

Facilities for children The Adventure Club provides indoor and outdoor play before and after lessons.

STAYING THERE

Thanks to the gondola link between the town and Mountain Village, it doesn't much matter where you stay.

How to go There is the usual range of accommodations.

Hotels The 4-star Hotel Telluride, in the old town, promises to be the most luxurious in the resort. The New Sheridan is one of the town's oldest hotels. Skyline Guest Ranch is a lovely old ranch-house with excellent food, a few minutes' drive from Mountain Village. The big Peaks hotel in the Mountain Village is a bit anonymous but has good spa facilities.

Apartments/condos There are also plenty of condos and houses.

Eating out There is a cosmopolitan choice of restaurants, from Sushi to French to Tex-Mex. Harmon's (in the old station) is one of the best. Allred's at the top of the gondola is a private club for lunch but offers gourmet dining in the evenings.

Après-ski There's a lively bar-based après-ski scene. Leimgruber's is popular in the early evening, but closes early. The New Sheridan has a lovely old bar. The Swede Finn and the Last Dollar have been recommended by locals. The Fly Me to the Moon Saloon has live music and stays open late.

Off the slopes There's quite a lot to do around town if you are not skiing or boarding, such as dog sledding, horse riding, ice skating and glider rides.

Luxury living and the US's biggest and ever-improving area

HOW IT RATES

The slopes

Snow	*****
Extent	****
Experts	****
Intermediates	*****
Beginners	*****
Convenience	***
Liftlines	**
Restaurants	**

The rest

Scenery	***
Resort charm	***
Off-slope	***

What's new

The 2000/01 season saw another high-speed quad and another 125 acres of terrain open in Blue Sky Basin.

The snowmaking network has been upgraded.

Several prime hotels have been renovated. The Vail Village Inn and Chateau Vail will remain closed for the 2001/02 season.

➕ Biggest area in the US – great for confident intermediates

➕ The Back Bowls are big areas of treeless terrain – unusual in the US

➕ Fabulous new area of ungroomed, wooded slopes recently opened at Blue Sky Basin

➕ Largely traffic-free resort village, with great bus service

➖ Slopes can be crowded by American standards, with some liftlines even in low season

➖ The famous Back Bowls may be closed in early season – and can suffer from the sun

➖ Inadequate mountain restaurants

➖ Big, sprawling resort, more like a city than a village

➖ Expensive

Blue Sky Basin, Vail's new area of shady, wooded, largely ungroomed slopes, has transformed Vail's attraction for good skiers and riders. Not only does it bring a much-needed bit of spice to the resort, but it gets you away from the crowds that are Vail's most serious drawback.

Vail's slopes are now undeniably compelling, especially when you take account of nearby sister-resort Beaver Creek (which has a separate chapter). What continues to push Vail down our American shortlist is its style and atmosphere – a curious mixture of pseudo-Tirol and anonymous suburbs. The resort works well, largely thanks to the efficient buses. But if you hope to be captivated, Vail can't compete with the distinctive Rockies resorts based on old mining towns or cowboy towns. If we're going that far West, we like it to be a bit Wild.

The resort

Standing in the center of Vail Village, surrounded by chalets and bierkellers, you could be forgiven for thinking you were in Austria's Tirol – which is what Vail's founder, Pete Seibert, intended back in the 1950s. But Vail Village is now just part of an enormous resort, mostly built in anonymous modern style, stretching for miles beside the I-70 freeway – the main route westwards through the Rockies from Denver.

The vast village benefits from a free and efficient bus service, which makes choice of location less than crucial. But there's no denying that the most convenient – and expensive – places to stay are in mock-Tirolean Vail Village, near the Vista Bahn fast chair, or in functional Lionshead, near the gondola. There are a lot of accommodations further out – the cheapest tend to be across I-70.

Beaver Creek, ten miles away, is covered by the lift ticket and is easily reached by bus (see separate chapter). Other resorts within a two-hour drive include Breckenridge and Keystone (both owned by Vail Resorts and covered by the lift ticket), Aspen, Steamboat and Copper Mountain.

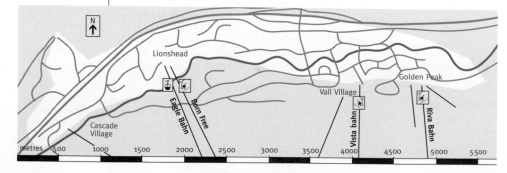

It doesn't look much, but Blue Sky Basin has lots to offer the expert and the adventurous intermediate →

MOUNTAIN FACTS

Altitude	2475m-3525m
	8,120ft-11,570ft
Lifts	33
Trails	5,289 acres
Green	18%
Blue	29%
Black	53%
Snowmaking	
	380 acres
Recco detectors used	

The mountains

Vail has the biggest area of slopes in the US, with immaculately groomed trails and ungroomed powder skiing in open bowls and among the trees. There are runs to suit every taste. The main criticism is that some of the runs (especially blacks) are overrated.

THE SLOPES
Something for everyone
The slopes above **Vail** can be accessed via three main lifts. From right next to Vail Village, the Vista Bahn fast chair goes up to the major mid-mountain focal point, Mid-Vail; from Lionshead, the Eagle Bahn gondola goes up to the Eagle's Nest complex; and from the Golden Peak base area just to the east of Vail Village, the Riva Bahn fast chair goes up towards the Two Elk area.

The front face of the mountain is largely north-facing, with well-groomed trails cut through the trees. At altitude the mountainside divides into three bowls – Mid-Vail in the center, with Game Creek to the south-west and Northeast Bowl to the, er, north-east. Lifts reach the ridge at three points, all giving access to the **Back Bowls** (mostly ungroomed and treeless) and through them to the new **Blue Sky Basin** area (mostly ungroomed and wooded or gladed).

The slopes are patrolled by yellow-jacketed 'speed patrollers' who stop slope users skiing or riding recklessly fast. There's a 'new technology center' at mid-mountain where you can test the latest equipment.

SNOW RELIABILITY
Excellent, except in the Bowls
In addition to an exceptional natural snow record, Vail and Beaver Creek both have extensive snowmaking, normally needed only in early season. Although snow in the Back Bowls is often poor because of its largely south-facing aspect, Blue Sky Basin is largely north-facing and sheltered from sun by trees – so the snow quality can be expected to be excellent, with powder lasting for days after the latest fall.

FOR EXPERTS
Transformed by Blue Sky Basin
Vail's Back Bowls are vast areas, served by three chair-lifts and a couple of short surface lifts. You can go virtually anywhere you like in the half-dozen identifiable bowls, trying the gradient and terrain of your choice. There are interesting lightly wooded areas as well as the open slopes that dominate the area. The Bowls are practically all rated black but are not particularly steep, and they have disappointed some of our more confident reporters.

Blue Sky Basin has some great adventure runs in the trees.

On the front face there are some genuinely steep double-black-diamond runs which usually have great snow; they are often bumpy but sometimes groomed to make wonderful fast cruising. The Highline lift on the extreme east of the area serves three. And Prima Cornice, served by the Northwoods Express, is one of the steepest runs on the front side.

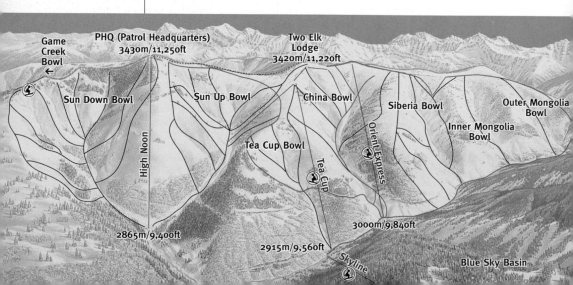

Two Elk Lodge
3420m/11,220ft

Summit
3430m/11,250ft

Wildwood
3345m/10,980ft

Game Creek Bowl

Northeast Bowl

Northwoods

Mountaintop

Wildwood

Game Creek

Highline

Mid-Vail
3095m/10,150ft

Avanti

Eagle's Nest
3155m/10,350ft

Riva Bahn

Vista Bahn

Pride

Born-Free

Eagle Bahn

Golden Peak

Vail Village
2500m/8,200ft

Lionshead
2475m/8,120ft

Cascade Village

boarding

Vail has been wooing boarders with excellent facilities and a positive attitude for years. With beautifully groomed, gentle slopes and lots of high-speed chairs, this is a great area for beginners, and there's plenty for experts too including some wonderful gladed runs and an excellent terrain-park and super-pipe on Golden Peak. There are specialist board shops and good lessons and a Burton test center at the top of Vail mountain. The lively bars and nightlife are another draw.

Game Creek Bowl
←

PHQ (Patrol Headquarters)
3430m/11,250ft

Two Elk Lodge
3420m/11,220ft

Sun Down Bowl

Sun Up Bowl

China Bowl

Siberia Bowl

Outer Mongolia Bowl

Inner Mongolia Bowl

High Noon

Tea Cup Bowl

Tea Cup

Orient Express

2865m/9,400ft

2915m/9,560ft

Skyline

3000m/9,840ft

Blue Sky Basin

A sense of adventure combined with safety is what Blue Sky Basin provides →

VAIL RESORTS, INC / JACK AFFLECK

LIFT TICKETS

2000/01 prices in dollars

Vail and Beaver Creek
Covers all Vail and Beaver Creek lifts, and ski-bus around resort. Multi-day tickets also cover Breckenridge, Keystone and Arapahoe Basin.

Main ticket
1-day ticket 57
6-day ticket 342

Senior citizens
Over 65: 6-day ticket 330
Over 70: season ticket 99

Children
Under 13: 1-day ticket 21
Under 5: free ticket

Short-term tickets
Half-day ticket from noon available.

Notes
Discounts may be available if you buy a lift ticket in advance. Return trips available on some lifts for foot passengers only. A 10-day ticket, entitles you to an extra 4 days free. Full-day lesson and lift ticket 109.

BLUE SKY BASIN

This is the biggest new development in any Colorado ski area for years – and the prospect of it caused outrage among environmental groups; protesters burned down the Two Elk mountain restaurant, the ski patrol HQ and some lift stations in protest. The first 520 acres of it, served by two high-speed quads, opened in January 2000. Last season saw the addition of Pete's Express (named after Vail's founder Pete Seibert), another fast quad, accessing a further 125 acres of gentler terrain – making up 645 acres in total.

We skied the Basin two months after opening and loved it. The area is almost entirely ungroomed and the runs are among the trees – some widely spaced, some very tight. Few of the runs are very steep, but because you are basically finding your own way much of the time, there is a great feeling of adventure. The snow will generally be much better than in the Back Bowls because of the shelter given by the trees and the generally north-facing aspect. We had hoped the slightly adventurous nature of the area would mean that the Vail crowds would stay away, but reports suggest that we were wrong.

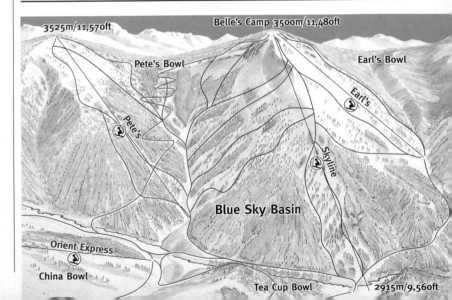

SCHOOLS/GUIDES

2000/01 prices in dollars

Classes 7 days
Full day: 5hr 45 min: 9.45-3.30 with lunch break
Half day: 3hr: am or pm
1 full day: 82
Children's classes
Ages: 3 to 14
Full day: 5hr 45 min including lift ticket, lunch
1 full-day: 93
Private lessons
1hr, 2hr, half and full day
1hr: 120, for 1 to 6 people
Half day: 335, for 1 to 6 people

CHILDCARE

School lessons are based at Children's Ski Centers located at Golden Peak and Lionshead. There are separate programs to suit children of different ages and competence – Mini-Mice for children aged three, Mogul Mice and Superstars for those aged four to six.

Small World Play School, located at Golden Peak, provides day care for children aged two months to six years, from 8am to 4.30.

DANN COFFEE

If you don't fancy skiing or boarding, climb on an inner tube at Eagle's Nest
→

If the snow is good, try the backcountry Minturn Mile – you leave the ski area through a gate in the Game Creek area for a European-style off-trail run starting with a powder bowl and finishing on a path by a river – ending up in the atmospheric Saloon (see Après-ski).

FOR INTERMEDIATES
Ideal territory

The majority of Vail's front face is great intermediate territory, with easy cruising runs. On the western side of the area, especially, there are excellent long, relatively quiet blues – Born Free and Simba both go from top to bottom. Game Creek Bowl, nearby, is excellent, too.

As well as tackling some of the easier front-face blacks, intermediates will find plenty of interest in the Back Bowls. Some runs are groomed. Several of the runs are graded blue, including Silk Road, which loops around the eastern edge of the domain, with wonderful views. Some of the ungroomed slopes make the ideal introduction to powder. Confident intermediates will also enjoy Blue Sky Basin – choose the clearly marked blue runs to start with.

FOR BEGINNERS
Difficult to beat

There are excellent beginner areas at resort level and at altitude. And there are plenty of easy longer runs to progress to – not only winding catwalk runs but also proper green runs that go from top to bottom.

FOR CROSS-COUNTRY
Some of the best

Vail's cross-country areas are at the foot of Golden Peak and at the Nordic Center on the golf course.

LIFTLINES
Can be bad

Vail has some of the longest liftlines we've hit in the US, especially on weekends because of the influx from Denver. Most lines move quickly. But at Mid-Vail waits of 15 minutes are common and we have reports of 45-minute waits.

MOUNTAIN RESTAURANTS
Surprisingly poor

As other major American resorts are gradually improving their mountain restaurants, Vail's are slipping further behind: demand is increasing to the point where the major self-service restaurants can be unpleasantly crowded from 11am to 2pm. There's table-service (with limited menu) at Eagle's Nest – book ahead.

SCHOOLS AND GUIDES
Among the best in the world

The Vail-Beaver Creek school has an excellent reputation. All the reports we've had of it have again been glowing. Class sizes are usually small – as few as four is not uncommon. Having tried three different instructors, we can vouch for the high standard. There are specialist half-day workshops in, for example, bumps and powder and adventure tours of Blue Sky Basin. You can sign up on the mountain.

FACILITIES FOR CHILDREN
Excellent

The comprehensive arrangements for young children look excellent, and we've had good reports on the children's school. There are splendid children's areas with adventure trails and themed play areas.

Staying there

HOW TO GO
Fair choice

Hotels Vail has a fair choice of hotels, ranging from luxurious to budget. The Vail Village Inn and Chateau Vail are currently closed for renovation.

(((((5) **Vail Cascade** One of the best in town. A resort within a resort – lots of facilities and a chair-lift right outside.

(((((5) **Sonnenalp Bavaria Haus** Very upscale and central. Large spa and splendid piano bar-lounge.

(((((5) **Lodge at Vail** Owned by Vail Resorts, right by the Vista Bahn in Vail Village. Some standard rooms small. Huge buffet breakfast. Outdoor pool.

(((3) **Evergreen** Between Vail Village and Lionshead. Giant indoor hot tub, outdoor pool. Lively sports bar.

((2) **Roost Lodge** One of the cheapest in Vail. Basic. Poor position, out of town in west Vail. Indoor pool.

Apartments/condos For those who want lots of in-house amenities, the Racquet Club at East Vail is superb. The Mountain Haus has high-quality condos in the center of town. There are plenty of cheaper options, and several tour operators have allocations conveniently close to the Lionshead gondola.

STAYING UP THE MOUNTAIN
Great if you can afford it

Game Creek chalet above Vail (like Trappers Cabin at Beaver Creek) is a luxurious private enclave up the mountain, which a group can rent by the night (for a small fortune). You ski in at the end of the day to a champagne welcome, soak in an outdoor hot-tub and enjoy a gourmet dinner. The cabin-keeper then leaves, returning in the morning to prepare breakfast.

STAYING ALONG THE VALLEY
Cheaper but quiet

Staying out of central Vail is certainly cheaper but not so lively. If you rent a car, staying out of town and visiting nearby resorts makes for an interesting holiday. East Vail and West Vail both have reasonably priced lodging.

EATING OUT
Endless choice

Whatever kind of food you want, Vail has it – but most of it is not cheap. 'All restaurants require a fat wallet' and 'high standards but at New York [...] are typical comments from report[...] Booking in advance is essential.

Recommended fine-dining optio[...] include the Wildflower, in the Lodg[...], Ludwig's, in the Sonnenalp Bavaria Haus, and La Tour.

For a budget option we liked the Hubcap Brewery in Vail Village, with local ales and decent food.

Recommendations from readers include May Palace (Chinese) in West Vail, Blu's (good value), Montauk (seafood) at Lionshead, the Bistro at the Racquet Club, Los Amigos, Russell's, La Bottega and Vendetta's.

APRES-SKI
Fairly lively

Gravity at Lionshead is convenient for the end of the day and has live music. Garfinkel's has a DJ and happy hour. The Red Lion in the village center is popular, with big-screen TVs and huge portions of food. The George tries to be an English-style pub. The Ore House serves 'mean margaritas and very hot chicken wings'.

The Swiss Chalet attempts to recreate European 'gemütlichkeit'; King's Club is the place to go for high-calorie cakes, and becomes a piano bar later; and Los Amigos and the Hubcap Brewery are other lively places at four o'clock.

You can have a good night out at Adventure Ridge at the top of the Eagle Bahn gondola. In addition to bars and restaurants, there's ice skating, tubing, snowmobiling, snow-shoeing and snowbiking – though a reporter reckons the tubing hill is boring and badly run compared with Keystone's.

Later on, Club Chelsea is a popular disco. 8150 is also good, with a suspended floor that moves with the dancing; the Bully Ranch at the Sonnenalp is famous for its 'mudslide' drinks; Nick's is a snowboard hangout; Vendetta's does good pizza and beer.

Out of town in Minturn, the Saloon is worth a trip – genuine old-west style with photos of famous skier patrons on the wall.

OFF THE SLOPES
A lot to do

Getting around on the free bus is easy, and there are lots of activities to try. Balloon rides are popular. The factory outlets at Silverthorne are a must for shopaholics who can't resist a bargain.

Central reservations phone number
For all resort accommodations call 1 800 270 4870 (toll-free from within the US).

GETTING THERE

Air Eagle, transfer 1hr. Denver, transfer 2½hr.

ACTIVITIES

Indoor Athletic clubs and spas, massage, museum, theater, movie theater, tennis courts, artificial skating rink, library, galleries
Outdoor Hot-air ballooning, skating, ice hockey, sleigh rides, fishing, mountaineering, snowmobiles, snow-shoe excursions, snowcat tours, dog-sledding, paragliding, tubing hill, ski biking, thrill sledding, laser tag

TOURIST OFFICE

PO Box 7, Vail, CO 81658
t +1 (970) 496 9090
international@vail resorts.com
www.vail.com

Good value, great terrain, huge snowfalls, unpretentious town

HOW IT RATES

The slopes

Snow	*****
Extent	***
Experts	****
Intermediates	****
Beginners	*****
Convenience	***
Liftlines	****
Restaurants	***

The rest

Scenery	***
Resort charm	**
Off-slope	*

What's new

The first phase of Winter Park's new slope-side village is now complete. The Zephyr Mountain Lodge condos at the base of the slopes have Slopeside and Riverside buildings, with lodging, shopping and dining.

Land has been purchased to build a gondola from the town to the slopes, but it's still in the planning stages and won't be ready for a few years yet.

➕ The best snowfall record of all Colorado's major resorts

➕ Slopes to suit all abilities, from superb beginner terrain to countless challenging bump slopes

➕ Great expert terrain and great untracked snow at Berthoud Pass

➕ Quiet on weekdays, and impressive lift system copes with weekends

➕ Leading resort for teaching people with disabilities to ski and ride

➕ Good views by US standards

➕ Largely free of the inflated prices and glitz you expect in a resort

➖ Also largely free of the range of restaurants and shops you expect in a big international resort

➖ Town is a bus-ride away from the slopes – though there is now the option of staying in the new development at the main lift base

➖ The nearest big resort to Denver, so can get crowded on weekends – mainly a problem on runs close to the base, and in rental shops

Winter Park was developed to amuse the residents of Denver, only a 90-minute drive away, and still belongs to the city. But it has developed into a mountain (if not yet a resort) of world class. If variety of shops and restaurants is not important to you, and value for money and snow are more important than glamour, the place should be high on your Colorado shortlist. Especially now that the first stage of a new pedestrian village at the foot of the slopes is complete.

For good skiers and riders, Winter Park's secret weapon is actually another 'resort' a few miles away – Berthoud Pass. It has no lodgings and only two chair-lifts, but they serve large amounts of wild terrain, the snow approaches Utah's exalted standards and is mostly untracked. It's unreal.

The resort

Winter Park started life around the turn of the century as a railway town, when Rio Grande railway workers climbed the slopes to ski down. One of the resort's mountains, Mary Jane, is named after a legendary 'lady of pleasure' who is said to have received the land as payment for her favors.

The railway still plays an important part in Winter Park's existence, with a station right at the foot of the slopes where trains deposit day trippers from Denver every Saturday and Sunday.

In the last couple of years, stylish accommodations have been developed at or near the foot of the slopes, most recently a car-free mini-resort known variously as The Village or Winter Park Resort. But most accommodations are a shuttle-bus-ride away in spacious condos scattered around either side of the road through downtown Winter Park – US highway 40, which continues

WINTER PARK RESORT

Winter Park's new Zephyr Mountain Lodge condos are pretty convenient to the slopes! ➔

boarding *The great boarder facilities on Winter Park Mountain make it a favorite with many riders. The half-pipe, just above Snoasis, is great for both experts and novices. The Big Air Park and The Rolls terrain-parks have enough jumps, ramps, winding gullies and tabletops to satisfy any big-air thrill seeker. Special 'Terrain Park Ambassadors' are often available to demonstrate tricks. There is some great advanced and extreme boarding terrain. Winter Park is also an ideal beginner and intermediate boarder area, with excellent terrain for first steps on a board, a good school and a network of lifts that is entirely chairs. Though there's no longer a ride guide to the mountain, signs indicate the most boarder-friendly routes to take. The bars get crowded and lively on weekends – and boarders tend to hang out at Slade's Underground downtown.*

MOUNTAIN FACTS

Altitude 2740m-3675m
9,000ft-12,060ft

Lifts	22
Trails	2,886 acres
Green	9%
Blue	34%
Black	57%
Snowmaking	
	294 acres

LIFT TICKETS

2001/02 prices in US dollars
Winter Park Resort
Covers all lifts in Winter Park.
Main ticket
1-day ticket 55
6-day ticket 252
(low season 210)
Senior citizens
Over 61: 6-day ticket 180
Over 70: free ticket
Children
Under 14: 6-day ticket 90
Under 6: free ticket
Short-term tickets
Half-day tickets up to 12.45: 25
from 12.00 35
Alternative periods
Tickets of 2 days and over allow one non-skiing day, eg 6-day ticket valid for 7 days with one day off. 8- and 9- day tickets allow 2 non-skiing days.
Notes Special rates for disabled skiers. Reduction for all skiing before Dec 3 and after April 2.

to the nearby town of Fraser. There are also motels, bars and restaurants along the road, and at night Winter Park resembles an established ski resort town – but in the daytime it's clear that the place doesn't amount to much. Reporters complain there's no real 'town center'. Confusingly, an area between the mountain and the town is known as Old Town.

Shuttle-buses run regularly between the town and the lift base, and the hotels and condos also provide shuttle services. But a car does simplify day trips to Denver or to other resorts – within a two-hour drive are Steamboat, Breckenridge, Copper Mountain, Keystone and Vail, and experts should not miss Berthoud Pass (see later in this chapter).

The mountains

Winter Park has a mountain that's big by US standards, and an excellent mix of terrain that suits all abilities. 'I would recommend it to anyone visiting Colorado for the first time,' says a reporter; we're inclined to agree, so long as you don't want a fancy village.

THE SLOPES
Interestingly divided
There are five very distinct, but well-linked, areas. From the main base, a high-speed quad takes you up the original **Winter Park** mountain to the Sunspot restaurant area at 3260m/10,700ft. From there, you can descend in all directions. Runs lead back towards the main base and over to the **Vasquez Ridge** area on the far right. This is served by a high-speed quad which allows you to use that area continuously or get back to the Winter Park mountain. Both areas are mainly beginner and intermediate terrain.

From the top of Winter Park mountain you can get to **Mary Jane** mountain, which has much tougher runs. Mary Jane is served by six lifts, including four from its own separate base area. From the top you can head up to **Parsenn Bowl** via the slow double Timberline chair, which has intermediate terrain above and in the trees. From here, conditions permitting, you can now get a tow by snowmobile (the 'Ridge Ride') for $5 (or hike for up to half an hour) to access the advanced and extreme slopes of **Vasquez Cirque**. A long ski-out takes you to the bottom of Vasquez Ridge and the Pioneer lift.

SNOW RELIABILITY
Among Colorado's best
'Copious amounts of beautiful, dry powder,' enthuses a reporter. Winter Park's position, close to the watershed of the Continental Divide, gives it an average yearly snowfall of over 350in – the highest of any major Colorado resort. As a back-up, snowmaking covers a high proportion of the runs on Winter Park mountain.

FOR EXPERTS
Some hair-raising challenges
Mary Jane has some of the steepest bump runs, chutes and hair-raising challenges in the US. The fearsome runs of Mary Jane's back side are accessed by a control gate off a long black run called Derailer. Hole in the Wall, Awe Chute, Baldy's Chute and Jeff's Chute are all steep, narrow and bordered by rocks. More manageable are the wider black bump fields such as Derailer, Long Haul and Brakeman. There are good blue/black runs on Mary Jane's front side and some good challenges on Winter Park Mountain.

When it's open, Vasquez Cirque has excellent ungroomed expert terrain

If you are able-bodied, the most striking and humbling thing you'll notice as you ride your first chair-lift is the number of people with disabilities hurtling down the mountain faster than many of us could ever hope to. There are blind skiers, skiers with one leg, no legs, paralysis – whatever their disability, they've overcome it.

That's because Winter Park is home to the US National Sports Center for the Disabled (NSCD) – the world's leading center for teaching skiing and snowboarding to people with disabilities. In addition to full-time instructors, there are 1,000 trained volunteers who help in the program. People are placed with instructors trained to teach people with their particular disability – more than 40 disabilities are specially catered to.

If you are disabled and want to learn to ski or snowboard, there's no better place to go. It's important to book ahead so that a suitable instructor is available. The NSCD can help with travel and arrangements for lodgings:

NSCD, PO Box 36, Winter Park, CO 80482, USA. Tel: 726 1540.

Phone numbers
From distant parts of the US, add the prefix 1 970.
From abroad, add the prefix +1 970.

COLORADO

400

with extensive views. To get to the best of it you no longer have to earn your turns with a 20- to 30-minute hike around the cirque: if you part with $5, you can get a pull from a snowmobile. You don't get much vertical before you hit the forest, though. One way to explore the area is on the Improvement Center's three-hour Cirque Adventure Tour.

FOR INTERMEDIATES
Choose your challenge
From pretty much wherever you are on Winter Park mountain and Vasquez Ridge you can choose a run to suit your ability. Most are well groomed every night giving you perfect early morning cruising on the famous Colorado 'corduroy' trails.

For bumps try Mary Jane's front side, where 'the blue/blacks are particularly enjoyable'. Parsenn Bowl

SCHOOLS/GUIDES

2000/01 prices in dollars

Intermediate and advanced classes
6 days
2½hr: from 9.30 or 12.45
6 2½hr days: 234

Beginner classes
6 days
2½hr: from 9.30 or 12.45
6 2½hr days: 150

Children's classes
Ages: 3 to 13
6 full days including ticket and lunch: 425

Private lessons
1½hr, 3hr or 6hr
100 for 1½hr, for 1 or 2 people

National Sports Center for the Disabled
Special program for disabled skiers and snowboarders

Private lessons
3hr or 6hr, with ticket and special equipment
40 for 3hr; 80 for 6hr

CHILDCARE

The ski school runs special classes for children aged 3 to 13 and provides lunch. The Children's Center has a popular non-skiing program for children aged 2 months to 5 years. You can rent out bleepers to keep in touch. Book early to ensure a place. The Children's Center is open 8am to 4pm. Lessons are 10am to 3pm.

has grand views and some gentle cruising trails as well as more challenging ungroomed terrain. It's an intermediate paradise and an ideal place to try your hand off-trail.

FOR BEGINNERS
The best we've seen
Discovery Park is a 25-acre dedicated area for beginners, reached by a high-speed quad and served by two more chairs. As well as a beginner area and longer green runs, it has an adventure trail through trees and a special terrain park. Once out of the Park, there are easy runs back to base.

FOR CROSS-COUNTRY
Lots of it
There are several different areas, all with generally excellent snow, adding up to well over 200km/125 miles of groomed trails, as well as backcountry tours.

LIFTLINES
Rarely a problem
During the week the mountain is generally quiet, though there may be a crowd waiting for the opening of the

Zephyr Express from the main base and there can be lines on the old double Timberline chair. On weekends the Denver crowds arrive – even then the network of more than twenty lifts (including eight fast quads) makes light work of the crowds.

MOUNTAIN RESTAURANTS
Some good facilities
The highlight is the Lodge at Sunspot, at the top of Winter Park mountain. This wood and glass building has a friendly bar with a roaring log fire, a table-service restaurant and very good self-service. The Club Car at the bottom of Mary Jane is good and Snoasis is self-service. Lunch Rock Cafe at the top of Mary Jane does quick snacks.

SCHOOLS AND GUIDES
A good reputation
Recent visitors have been 'impressed by the standard of instructors'. As well as standard classes there are ideas such as Family Private, for different abilities to learn together; themed lessons such as Mogul Mania; and Quick Tips, a 'quick fix' video analysis of your main weaknesses (only $5).

DON'T PASS ON BERTHOUD PASS

The drive to Winter Park from Denver – unusual for an American resort – involves a winding climb. It takes you to the summit of Berthoud Pass, where there is a small parking lot – usually near-empty – and a couple of chair-lifts. Continue on over the pass to your destination, right? Wrong. Well, wrong if you press on and don't come back during your stay. And if you like deep untracked snow.

You've heard of heli-skiing and cat-skiing. Well, Berthoud offers something damn-near as good: bus-skiing. The chair-lifts – a triple and a quad – lift you a modest few hundred feet vertical above the pass, but you descend to much lower points on highway 40, where beaten-up buses (with classic 60s pop playing) pick you up.

There are runs to suit every ability, but in practice this is a mountain for good skiers and riders. The slopes down to the road are steep, and sometimes very steep. The runs back to the summit of the pass are easier, but hardly any of them are groomed, and they can be quite tricky if there is a substantial snowfall. And there often is: Berthoud is on the Continental Divide, and claims for its annual snowfall from 400in to 500in a year. This is Jackson Hole/Alta territory.

The terrain and the snowfall are two key elements. The third is the lack of people. There is a limit of 400 day tickets, and there are about 200 season ticket holders. In practice, it's normal to have between 100 and 200 people on the slopes, which cover 1,100 acres. That's something on the order of 10 acres each. Enough?

In the base lodge, as well as a ski shop, there is the highest pub in North America and a pleasant table-service restaurant – so a day here can be quite a civilized affair. And it won't cost a lot: the price of a day ticket is low, and depends on the snow – $34 if there's 4in of fresh powder, $30 if there's no fresh for two days (2000/01 prices). Winter Park's tickets are flexible (eg 5 days out of 6) so it's easy to slot in a day at Berthoud. But you may want to make it more than one.

There are easier ways into Vasquez Cirque than this, thank goodness →

WINTER PARK RESORT

GETTING THERE

Air Denver, transfer 1½ hr.

Rail Leaves Denver Sat and Sun at 7.15am and returns at 4.15pm. Journey time 2 hr.

Phone numbers
From distant parts of the US, add the prefix 1 970.
From abroad, add the prefix +1 970.

ACTIVITIES

Indoor movie theater, swimming pool, roller skating, amusement arcade, health club, comedy club, aerobics, racquetball
Outdoor Dog-sledding, sight-seeing flights, snow-shoe, sleigh rides, 'tubing', ice skating, snowmobiling, snowbiking, snowcat tours, ice fishing, hot springs

TOURIST OFFICE

Postcode CO 80482
t +1 (970) 726 5514
f 726 1572
wpinfo@mail.skiwinterpark.com
www.winterparkresort.com

FACILITIES FOR CHILDREN
Some of the best
The Children's Center at Winter Park base area houses day-care facilities and is the meeting point for children's classes, which have their own areas, including 'magic carpet' lifts. A recent reporter was very impressed with the lessons and said there's even a 'warming tent' – what a great idea.

Staying there

Most accommodations are down in town, but the choice at or near the base has improved a lot.

HOW TO GO
Fair choice
Hotels There are a couple of outstanding hotel/condo complexes. (((④ **Iron Horse Resort** (726 8851) Slope-side, comfortable, condo-style. (((④ **Vintage** (726 8801) Near resort entrance; good facilities but some poor recent reports of it. (((③ **Mountain Lodge** (726 4211) Across the valley from the lifts; micro-brewery above the bar; good atmosphere.
Apartments/condos There are a lot of comfortable condo complexes, including the new slope-side Zephyr Mountain Lodge.

EATING OUT
Lots of choices
Reporters are enthusiastic about the long-established Deno's – seafood, steaks etc. Try the Crooked Creek Saloon in Fraser for atmosphere and typical American food; Smokin' Moe's for ribs, New Hong Kong for Chinese, the Divide Grill for pasta, seafood and grills are all in the new Cooper Creek Square area; The Shed for Mexican and Fontenot's for Cajun. Hernandos is a 'fairly rustic but busy' Italian place. Rome on the Range is good for steaks, seafood and pasta plus 20 beers on tap. Gasthaus Eichler does German food.

APRES-SKI
If you know where to go ...
Use the Black Diamond Nightlife Tour Map, which also gets you two-for-one drink deals. At day's end, there's action at the Derailer Bar at the main lift base and the Club Car at the base of Mary Jane. Later on, try The Slope (in Old Town) for live music and dancing, or Adolph's, just across the road. Try downtown Rome on the

Range for country and western. The Shed can be lively. The Crooked Creek is popular with locals. Randi's Irish Saloon is 'a pleasant and lively bar'.

OFF THE SLOPES
Mainly the great outdoors
Most diversions involve getting about on snow in different ways. If you like shopping, visit Silverthorne's factory outlet stores (90 minutes away on I-70).

The massive snowfalls and the world's best lift-served powder skiing and riding are the main reasons for taking a vacation in Utah. But the region will get massive publicity this winter for a different reason: Salt Lake City and the Utah resorts will host the 2002 Winter Olympics from February 8 to 24. The Paralympics will follow from March 7 to 16.

'The Greatest Snow on Earth' – that's what Utah claims. (Until recently it made the claim on every car license plate, but it now seems to be targeting broader markets.) It's a debatable claim: the Colorado resorts say that their famous powder is drier, and have figures to prove it. What they can't dispute is that some Utah resorts do get huge dumps of snow – up to twice the amount, over the season, that falls on some big-name Colorado resorts. In any case, by European standards the snow here is wonderful stuff. If you like the steep and deep, you should make the pilgrimage to Utah.

There are differences in snowfall though. The biggest dumps are reserved for Snowbird and Alta (an average of 500 inches a year), close together in Little Cottonwood Canyon. The snow record of these small resorts makes them the powder capitals of the world. And the big news for the 2001/02 season is that their slopes will be linked and they will offer a shared lift ticket for the first time. They are not holding any Olympic events because of access problems with their avalanche-prone road and their lack of suitable infrastructure.

Park City, the main 'destination' resort of the area, and neighboring Deer Valley will host the lion's share of the Olympic events. These and The Canyons nearby are only a few miles, as the crow flies, from Alta and Snowbird, but they get 'only' 300 to 350 inches (still more than most Colorado resorts). But it's unknown Snowbasin (400 inches) that gets the prestige downhill and super-G Olympic events. Separate chapters follow on these six resorts.

But there are other Utah resorts that are well worth visiting too. If you enjoy seeing different resorts, renting a car, staying in Park City (by far the liveliest

SNOWPIX.COM / CHRIS GILL

One of four fast six-packs that whizz you around the mountain at Park City

403

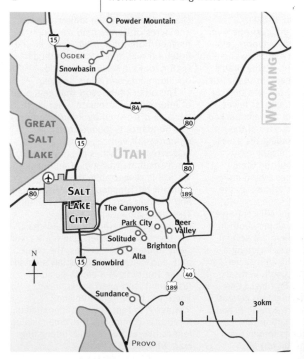

↑The Utah Interconnect is a not-to-be-missed off-trail day tour between Park City and Snowbird (see Park City chapter). This is the Highway to Heaven traverse from Solitude to Alta

SNOWPIX.COM / CHRIS GILL

Solitude phone number
From distant parts of the US, add the prefix 1 801.
From abroad, add the prefix +1 801.

resort) or Salt Lake City (with a big city rather than a ski resort ambience) and driving to a different resort each day makes a compelling vacation. The roads are generally good.

Brighton (2670m/8,760ft, vertical 530m/1,750ft, 7 lifts, 64 runs, 850 acres), right at the end of Big Cottonwood Canyon (the next one over from Little Cottonwood Canyon), gets as much snow as Alta and Snowbird – which may help to explain why Utah's first ski-lift was built here, in 1936. But the snow gets tracked out less quickly because the resort attracts far fewer visitors. There are a lot of trails packed into quite a small area. Two of the three major lifts – including the area's one fast quad – serve mostly easy-intermediate slopes, but the Great Western slow quad goes over a more challenging slope that represents the resort's full vertical of 530m/1,750ft, and the separate Mount Millicent area has some good steep slopes, both in and out of bounds. There are several accommodation options, including a slope-side lodge, cabins and chalets.

Solitude (2435m/7,990ft, vertical 625m/2,050ft, 7 lifts, 63 runs, 1,600 acres), next door to Brighton, gets as much snow and covers a much bigger area, even without counting the excellent out-of-bounds terrain that you can get to from the top lift.

Basically, the slopes here get steeper as you go up the mountain – except that the area's one fast quad, Eagle, serves a slightly separate ridge that is almost entirely blue in gradient, and starts slightly down the valley from the main base. We haven't yet had a chance to explore the entirely black 400 acres of Honeycomb canyon, reached from the top lift. There is one hotel – the 46-room Inn at Solitude (536 5700) – a few small condo developments and some houses.

The other Utah resort that gets a bit of international attention – not least because it's owned by Robert Redford – is **Sundance** (1860m/6,100ft, 655m/2,150ft vertical, 4 lifts, 41 runs, 450 acres, 320 inches of snow a year). It's a small, narrow mountain but the vertical is respectable, the setting beneath Mt Timpanogos is spectacular and there is terrain to suit all abilities. The lower mountain is easy-intermediate, served by a quad chair, the upper part steeper: one triple chair serves purely black slopes, the other blue and black trails. Bearclaw's Cabin, at the top of it, is a small, basic restaurant with spectacular views. There are beautifully furnished 'cottages' to rent, and grander chalets. A reporter commends the 'emphasis on renewable resources' and 'interesting craft workshops'.

Alta
2600m/8,530ft

Cult resort with fabulous powder and new link with Snowbird

HOW IT RATES

The slopes
Snow	*****
Extent	***
Experts	*****
Intermediates	***
Beginners	***
Convenience	****
Liftlines	***
Restaurants	**

The rest
Scenery	****
Resort charm	**
Off-slope	*

What's new

For 2001/02, Alta is at last emerging from its time-warp. It is installing its first high-speed quad to replace the slow triple Sugarloaf lift.

From the top of this lift you will be able to ski down into Snowbird's Mineral Basin to access the whole of Snowbird's terrain as well as Alta's on a joint area lift ticket. A new quad the other side will bring you back. The terrain available will be more than doubled to 4,700 acres, making it the biggest lift-linked area in Utah and one of the biggest in the US. The resorts will keep separate ownership and operation, and Alta is still refusing to allow snowboarding.

The double chair to Point Supreme will become a triple.

ALTA
Powder is what Alta is all about (but not if you are on a snowboard) →

- Phenomenal snow record
- Cult status among powderhounds
- New link to Snowbird making one of the largest ski areas in the US
- Very cheap local lift ticket
- Ski-almost-to-the-door convenience
- Easy to get to Salt Lake City and other Utah resorts (so long as access road open)

- No resort village as such – a handful of scattered lodges
- No snowboarding allowed
- Old-fashioned lift network
- Limited groomed runs for intermediates, though the new link with Snowbird doubles the terrain
- Not much après-ski atmosphere
- Few off-slope diversions

Alta is famous for remarkable amounts of powder snow arriving with great regularity, for a stubborn refusal to develop or modernize the area and for one of the cheapest lift tickets around. This year sees a new lift and trail link with neighboring Snowbird which also gets phenomenal powder and makes the joint area one of the top powder-pig paradises in the world and one of the US's biggest lift-linked areas. But snowboarders will still be banned from Alta's slopes.

THE RESORT
Alta sits at the craggy head of Little Cottonwood Canyon, a mile beyond Snowbird and less than an hour's drive from downtown Salt Lake City. The peaceful location was once the scene of a bustling and bawdy mining town. The 'new' Alta is a strung-out handful of lodges and parking areas, and nothing more; life revolves around the two separate lift base areas – Albion and Wildcat – linked by a bi-directional rope tow along the flat valley floor.

THE MOUNTAINS
Alta's slopes haven't changed much in the last 20 years and are served by mainly slow double and triple chairs. As Alta's mayor explained to us: 'Alta's philosophy is old-fashioned quality. Keeping slow, old chair-lifts means you never have too many people on the slopes, so you have a quality skiing environment.' It will be interesting to see how that philosophy and environment changes now they have agreed to a high-speed quad and the link with Snowbird.

Slopes The dominant feature of Alta's terrain is the steep end of a ridge that separates the area's two basins. To the left, above Albion Base, the slopes stretch away over easy green terrain towards the black runs of Point Supreme and Devil's Castle; to the right is a more concentrated bowl with blue runs down the middle and blacks

either side. These two sectors are linked at altitude, and by a flat rope tow along the valley floor.

Snowboarding Boarding is banned.
Snow reliability The quantity and quality of snow that falls here, and the northerly orientation of the slopes, put Alta among the world's best.
Experts Even without a link with Snowbird, Alta had cult status among

MOUNTAIN FACTS

For Alta and Snowbird combined area

Altitude 2365m-3355m
7,760ft-11,000ft

Lifts	26
Trails	4,700 acres
Green	25%
Blue	37%
Black	38%

Snowmaking
150 acres

Recco detectors used

Phone numbers

From distant parts of the US, add the prefix 1 801.
From abroad, add the prefix +1 801.

TOURIST OFFICE

Postcode UT 84092
t +1 (801) 359 1078
f 799 2340
info@alta.com
www.alta.com

local experts, who flocked to the high ridges after a fresh snowfall. There are dozens of steep slopes and chutes throughout the area. The new link will mean the area will be the world's best for powderhounds.

Intermediates Adventurous intermediates who are happy to try ungroomed slopes and learn to love powder should like Alta, too. There are good blue bowls in both Alta and Snowbird and not so tough blacks to progress too. But if it is miles of perfectly groomed trail you are after there are plenty of better resorts.

Beginners Timid intermediates and beginners will be happy on the Albion side, where the lower runs are broad, gentle and well groomed.

Cross-country There's little provision for cross-country skiing; but the surrounding backcountry offers adventures for those with guidance.

Liftlines Bottlenecks are not unknown at Alta – the snow record, easy access from Salt Lake City and the slow, old chair-lifts see to that – especially in spring and on sunny weekends. It will be interesting to see what effect the new link with Snowbird has.

Mountain restaurants There's a mountain restaurant in each sector of the slopes – Collins Grill on the Wildcat side has table-service – and several places in the valley are open for lunch.

Schools and guides The famous Alf Engen ski school naturally specializes in powder lessons – though all the regular classes and clinics are also available. The ski school organizes children's lessons.

Facilities for children Day care for those over 3 months old is available at the Children's Center at Albion Base.

STAYING THERE

There are about a dozen places to stay – simple hotels and apartments.

How to go None of the hotels is luxurious in US terms. Most get booked up well in advance by repeat visitors. Unusually for America, most lodges are half-board deals with dinner included.

Hotels The Alta Lodge (742 3500) is one of Alta's oldest, and feels rather like an over-crowded chalet-hotel in the Alps. Rustler Lodge (742 2200) is more luxurious, with a big outdoor pool, but impersonal. The comfortable, modern Goldminer's Daughter (742 2300) and the basic Peruvian Lodge (742 3000) are cheaper.

Eating out Eating in is the routine.

Après-ski This rarely goes beyond a few drinks and possibly a sports film in the lodges. The Goldminer's Daughter has the main après-ski bar.

Off the slopes There are few options other than a trip to Salt Lake City.

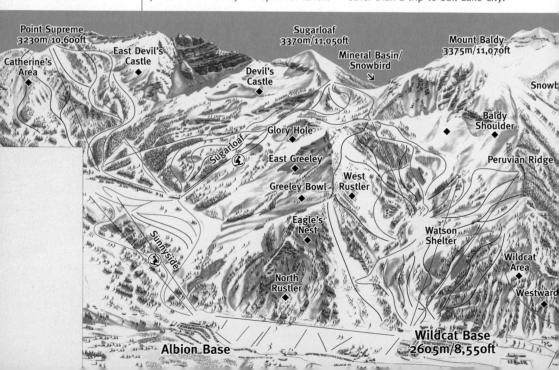

The Canyons

2075m/6,800ft

Potentially the biggest mountain in the US

HOW IT RATES

The slopes

Snow	****
Extent	***
Experts	***
Intermediates	***
Beginners	***
Convenience	****
Liftlines	****
Restaurants	***

The rest

Scenery	***
Resort charm	**
Off-slope	**

What's new

For 2001/2 there will be a new fixed-grip three-person chair between Dreamscape and Peak 5, with five new intermediate trails as well as tree runs.

A new terrain park will be built near the Red Hawk lift at the base area.

A new beginners-only area has been made behind Red Pine Lodge.

New snowmaking will be on the main run from Dreamscape to Tombstone.

For 2000/01 an open-air gondola opened to take you from the parking area to the resort village in three minutes.

⊕ Extensive ski area with slopes for all abilities – potentially the biggest in the US

⊕ Brand new lift system

⊕ Convenient new purpose-built resort village

⊕ Excellent snow reliability

⊕ Few liftlines

⊕ Nearby Park City is an entertaining alternative base

⊕ Park City and Deer Valley slopes only a short drive away

⊕ Easy access to Salt Lake City and other Utah resorts

⊖ Snow often not up to usual Utah standards on the many south-facing slopes

⊖ Because the area is a series of canyons (valleys) many runs are short and the area is a bit disjointed

⊖ Resort village is still being built – though the first part is finished

⊖ Limited après-ski and dining possibilities at resort village

⊖ Few off-slope diversions at resort village

The Canyons is the new kid on the Park City block. Formerly a small locals' area known as Park West and then Wolf Mountain, it was taken over and renamed by the American Skiing Company in 1997. (The company itself has been taken over since.) But ambitious plans remain to make the slopes the biggest in the US, and the area has already more than doubled in size and benefited from a virtually new lift system. The first part of a new slope-side resort village is open.

THE RESORT

When we visited in March 1999 there wasn't a resort – just a muddy parking lot and building site. On our return in March 2000, the car-free village was really taking shape. But a reporter this year still describes it as 'a muddy mess'. Most people visit The Canyons from a base in Park City.

THE MOUNTAINS

The Canyons gets its name from the valleys between the various mountains (now eight of them) that make up the ski area.

Slopes Red Pine Lodge, at the heart of the slopes, is reached by an eight-person gondola from the village base. From here you can move in either direction across a series of ridges – and the valleys between them. These ridges range from Dreamscape to the south (closest to Park City) to Murdock Peak to the north. Runs come off both sides of each ridge, meaning that they generally face north or south (see Snow reliability section). Most runs finish in the valley floors with some long, relatively flat run-outs. Five of the major lifts are high-speed quads, all put in – along with the gondola – since

THE CANYONS / MARK MAZIARZ

One of the green runs leading down to Red Pine Lodge that can get crowded →

MOUNTAIN FACTS

Altitude 2075m-3045m
6,800ft-9,999ft

Lifts	15
Trails	3,650 acres
Green	14%
Blue	44%
Black	42%
Snowmaking	
	150 acres
Recco detectors used	

**Central reservations
phone number**
For all resort
accommodations call
1 800 472 6309
(toll-free from within
the US)

TOURIST OFFICE

Postcode UT 84098
t +1 435 649 5400
f 649 7374
info@thecanyons.com
www.thecanyons.com

1997. Complimentary mountain tours are offered twice daily.

Snowboarding It's a great area to snowboard in, with lots of natural hits, five natural half-pipes and a great terrain-park and half-pipe. Canis Lupis (aka James Bond trail) is a mile-long, tight, winding natural gulley with high banked walls and numerous obstacles – like riding a bob-sled course. For beginners and intermediates there's easy cruising served by chair-lifts.

Snow reliability Snow reliability is not the best in Utah. The Canyons gets as much snow on average as next-door Park City and Deer Valley. But although the north-facing slopes are normally in good condition, the south-facing ones suffer in sunny late-season conditions.

Experts There is steep terrain all over the mountain. We particularly liked the north-facing runs off Ninety-Nine-90, with steep double-black-diamond runs plunging down through the trees to a pretty but almost flat run-out trail. Go south at the top of the lift and (when the gate is open) you can legally enter the backcountry – with the right gear and guidance, of course.

Intermediates There are lots of groomed blue runs for intermediates on all the main sectors except Ninety-Nine-90. Some are quite short, but you can switch from valley to valley easily for added interest, and you can contrive some longer runs.

Beginners There's a new area just for beginners behind Red Pine Lodge. But the run you progress to is a popular route that gets crowded.

Cross-country There are prepared trails on the Park City golf course and the Homestead Resort course. There is also lots of scope for backcountry trips.

Liftlines We've heard of no problems.

Mountain restaurants The central Red Pine Lodge is a large, new, attractive log-and-glass building with a busy self-service cafeteria and a table-service restaurant. The Lookout Cabin has wonderful views, and we've had excellent table-service food there. Sun Lodge, with decks, is another option.

Schools and guides The ski school uses the American Skiing Company's Perfect Turn formula, which focuses on an individual's strengths and builds on them (rather than correcting faults).

Facilities for children There's day care for children from 18 months.

STAYING THERE

Although there are now some convenient accommodations at the resort village, staying in Park City is a more attractive option – regular shuttle-buses run to the resort.

How to go Accommodations at the resort village are still fairly limited, but you do have the choice of hotel or condo.

Hotels The luxurious Grand Summit is right at the base of the gondola.

Apartments/condos The new Sundial Lodge condos are part of the resort village.

Après-ski The Grand Summit contains several bars, and there are many more in Park City.

Eating out The Cabin restaurant, in the Grand Summit hotel, serves eclectic American cuisine. And there are many more options in Park City.

Off the slopes There's a fair bit going on in Park City – shops, galleries etc – and Salt Lake City has some good concerts, shopping and sights. Balloon rides and snowmobiling are popular.

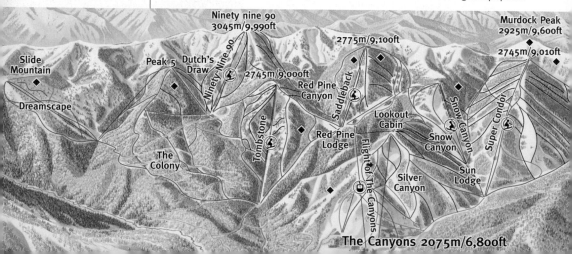

Deer Valley

The ultimate upscale ski resort

HOW IT RATES

The slopes

Snow	****
Extent	**
Experts	***
Intermediates	****
Beginners	****
Convenience	****
Liftlines	****
Restaurants	****

The rest

Scenery	***
Resort charm	***
Off-slope	**

What's new

A much-needed new day lodge and restaurant at the bottom of the Empire and Ruby lifts will be open for 2001/02.

The Quincy triple chair will be replaced by a high-speed quad.

There will be increased snowmaking.

And a 10,000-seat stadium will be built for viewing the Olympic events.

MOUNTAIN FACTS

Altitude 2000m-2915m
    6,570ft-9,570ft

Lifts	19
Trails	1,750 acres
Green	15%
Blue	50%
Black	35%
Snowmaking	
	500 acres

Recco detectors used

DEER VALLEY

Although Deer Valley prides itself on its grooming, it has good bump, bowl and tree skiing too →

- ⊕ Highly convenient, upscale luxury resort with superb skier services
- ⊕ Immaculate trail grooming, good snow record and lots of snow-guns
- ⊕ Good tree skiing
- ⊕ No liftlines
- ⊕ Slopes of Park City and The Canyons very close and access to Salt Lake City and other Utah resorts is easy

- ⊖ No snowboarding allowed
- ⊖ Relatively expensive
- ⊖ Deer Valley itself is quiet at night

Deer Valley prides itself on pampering its guests. Free valet ski storage, gourmet dining, immaculately groomed slopes, limits on numbers of skiers on the mountain, no snowboarding. But there's more to it than that – it has some remarkably good slopes, with interesting terrain for all abilities. It will be hosting the freestyle and slalom competitions in the 2002 Olympics.

THE RESORT

Just a mile from the end of Park City's Main Street, Deer Valley is unashamedly upscale and famed for the care and attention lavished on both slopes and guests. Valets will unload your equipment before you park your car – it's very obviously aimed at people who are used to being pampered and can pay for it. Luxurious private chalets are scattered around the slopes. The hotels are particularly luxurious.

There is not much of a village to stroll around. There are a few shops, hotels and restaurants at Silver Lake Lodge (mid-mountain but accessible by road), but for any real animation you need to head for Park City's Main Street – easily reached by free buses.

THE MOUNTAINS

The slopes are varied and interesting. Deer Valley's reputation for immaculate grooming is justified, but there is also a lot of exciting tree skiing (great when it is snowing) – and some steep bump runs too. There is a special experts' trail map with extra information on the chutes, bowls and glades.

Slopes Two high-speed quads take you up to Bald Eagle Mountain, just beyond which is the mid-mountain focus of Silver Lake Lodge. You can ski from here to the isolated Little Baldy Peak, served by a gondola and a quad chair-lift, with mainly easy blue and green runs to serve property being developed there. But the main skiing is on three linked mountains above Silver Lake Lodge. From left to right these are Bald Mountain, Flagstaff Mountain and Empire Canyon. Empire is serviced by a fast quad – the top of which is just a few yards from the runs of the Park City ski area and could easily be linked. Empire also has a family area with a three-seater chair.

Snowboarding Boarding is banned.
Snow reliability As you'd expect in Utah, snow reliability is excellent, and there's plenty of snowmaking too.

Experts Despite its image of pampered luxury there is excellent expert terrain on all three main mountains, including fabulous glade skiing as well as bumps, defined chutes and open bowl slopes. And because the place doesn't attract many hotshots the snow doesn't get skied out quickly.

Intermediates There are lots of immaculately groomed blue runs all over the mountains.

Beginners There are beginners' slopes at Silver Lake Lodge as well as the base, and gentle green runs to progress to on all the mountains.

Cross-country There are prepared trails on the Park City golf course and the Homestead Resort course, just out of town. There is also lots of scope for backcountry trips.

Liftlines Waiting in liftlines is not something that Deer Valley wants its guests to experience, so it limits the number of lift tickets sold.

Mountain restaurants There are attractive wood-and-glass self-service places run by the resort at both Silver Lake Lodge and the base lodge, with free valet ski storage. The food is fine (though expensive). There will be a much-needed new restaurant at Empire Canyon for 2001/02 – which should relieve the overcrowding at Silver Lake. We recommend you pamper yourself by taking table-service at the Stein Eriksen Lodge or the Goldener Hirsch.

Schools and guides The ski school is doubtless excellent.

Facilities for children Deer Valley's Children's Center gives parents complimentary pagers.

STAYING THERE

Many visitors prefer to stay in livelier Park City. But if it's plush hotels and pampering you want, it's worth staying in Deer Valley itself.

How to go A car is useful for visiting the other nearby Utah resorts, though Deer Valley, Park City and The Canyons are all linked by regular shuttle-buses.

Hotels The Stein Eriksen Lodge and Goldener Hirsch at Silver Lake Village are two of the plushest hotels in any ski resort.

Apartments/condos There are many luxury apartments and houses to rent.

Après-ski The Lounge of the Snow Park Lodge at the base area is the main après-ski venue, with live music. There are lively bars and restaurants around Main Street, in Park City.

Eating out Of the gourmet restaurants, the Mariposa is the best. The Seafood Buffet and McHenry's grill are also recommended. Park City has a number of good restaurants.

Off the slopes Park City has lots of shops, galleries etc. Salt Lake City has good concerts, sights and shopping. Balloon rides and snowmobiling are popular.

Central reservations phone number
For all resort accommodations call 645 6528 (from distant parts of the US, add the prefix 1 435; from abroad, add the prefix +1 435)

TOURIST OFFICE
Postcode UT 84060
t +1 (435) 649 1000
f 645 6939
marketing@deervalley.com
www.deervalley.com

Empire Canyon 2915m/9,570

Flagstaff Mt. 2775m/9,100ft

Bald Mt. 2865m/9,400ft

Heber City

Ruby

Quincy

Northside

Empire

Wasatch

Silver Lake Lodge 2470m/8,100ft

Bald Eagle Mt. 2560m/8,400ft

Little Baldy Peak 2425m/7,950ft

Carpenter

Silver Lake

Deer Valley Resort

Jordanelle

Snow Park Lodge 2195m/7,200ft

Park City 2105m/6,900ft

Jordanelle 2000m/6,570ft

An entertaining base for excursions into Utah's deep powder

HOW IT RATES

The slopes

Snow	****
Extent	***
Experts	****
Intermediates	****
Beginners	****
Convenience	***
Liftlines	****
Restaurants	**

The rest

Scenery	***
Resort charm	***
Off-slope	***

What's new

For 2000/01 a new base lodge – Legacy Lodge – opened. The building reflects the area's mining history and houses a food court restaurant, pub, ski and board rental facilities and shops.

An Olympic half-pipe has been added, making a total of two terrain parks and two half-pipes. Snowmaking facilities have also been recently extended.

- ➕ Increasingly touristy Wild West-style main street, convenient for slopes
- ➕ Lots of bars and restaurants make nonsense of Utah's image as a puritanical Mormon state
- ➕ Well maintained slopes, good snow record, and lots of snowmaking
- ➕ Good lift system including four fast six-packs
- ➕ Good base for visiting other major Utah resorts – Deer Valley and The Canyons are effectively suburbs and other resorts less than an hour away

- ➖ Rest of town doesn't have same charm as main street – lots of recent building has created an enormous sprawl (and building continues)
- ➖ The blue and black runs tend to be rather short – most lifts give a vertical of around 400m/1,300ft
- ➖ Although the snowfall record is impressive by normal standards, it comes nowhere near that of Alta and Snowbird, a few miles away
- ➖ Lack of spectacular scenery

You'll be hearing a lot about Park City this season. For the 2002 Olympics, it is hosting the giant slalom and the snowboarding events, and next-door Deer Valley is hosting the slalom and freestyle events. The bob-sled, luge and Nordic events will take place down the road in the new winter sports park.

For a holiday, Park City has clear attractions, particularly if you ignore its sprawling suburbs and stay near the center to make the most of the lively bars and restaurants in its beautifully restored and developed main street. But the place really comes into its own as a base for touring other resorts as well. Deer Valley is separated from Park City's slopes by a fence between the tops of two lifts, and by separate ownership with quite different objectives. All that is required to link them is to remove the fence – a bizarre situation. The Canyons is only a little further, on the outskirts of town, and reached by free buses. Both are excellent mountains, well worth exploring. And then there are the famously powdery resorts of Snowbird and Alta, less than an hour away by car or bus. All four are covered in separate chapters. If that's not enough, the quiet resorts of Brighton, Solitude and Sundance and the Olympic downhill slopes of Snowbasin (see separate chapter) are within easy reach if you have a car.

411

PARK CITY / LORI ADAMSKI-PEEK

Though not usually this deserted, Park City has a lot of easy runs like this ➔

MOUNTAIN FACTS

Altitude 2105m-3050m
6,900ft-10,000ft

Lifts	14
Trails	3,300 acres
Green	18%
Blue	44%
Black	38%
Snowmaking	
	475 acres

Recco detectors used

Park City is in Utah's Wasatch Mountains, about 45 minutes by road from Salt Lake City. It was born with the discovery of silver in 1872. By the turn of the century it boasted a population of 10,000, a red-light district, a Chinese quarter and 27 saloons. Careful restoration has left the town with a splendid historic center-piece in Main Street.

The old wooden sidewalks and clapboard buildings are now filled with a colorful selection of art galleries, shops, boutiques, bars and restaurants – though it is getting rather touristy, with some tacky shops selling T-shirts and souvenirs. New buildings have been tastefully designed to blend in smoothly. But away from the center

the resort lacks charm, sprawls over a wide area and is still expanding.

There is a lift up to the slopes from the heart of the town, but the main lift base area is Resort Center, on the fringes with modern buildings and its own bars, restaurants and lodgings.

Deer Valley and The Canyons are almost suburbs of Park City, but all three retain quite separate identities. They are linked by free shuttle-buses, which also go around town and run until late. A trolley-bus runs along Main Street. A car is useful for visiting other ski areas on the good roads.

The mountain

Mostly the area consists of blue and black trails cut through the trees on the flanks of rounded mountain ridges, with easier runs running along the ridges and the gullies between. The challenge for experts is in the lightly wooded bowls and ridges at the top of the resort's slopes.

THE SLOPES
Bowls above the woods

A fast six-seat chair-lift whisks you up from Resort Center, and another beyond that up to Summit House, the main mountain restaurant.

Most of the easy and intermediate runs lie between the Summit House and the base area, and spread along the sides of a series of interconnecting ridges. Virtually all the steep terrain is above Summit House in a series of ungroomed bowls, and accessed by the new McConkey's six-pack and the old Jupiter double chair.

There are a few old wooden mine buildings left scattered about the slopes, which add extra atmosphere. Daily mountain tours of the historical sites are offered free of charge – as are the twice a week black-diamond tours for advanced skiers.

A floodlit run – the longest in the Rockies – is available until 9pm, together with a floodlit half-pipe.

SNOW RELIABILITY
Not quite the Greatest on Earth

Utah resorts make a lot of fuss about the quality and quantity of their snow. Park City's record doesn't match those of Alta and Snowbird, but an annual average of 350in is still impressive, and ahead of most Colorado figures. And there's snowmaking on about 15% of the terrain.

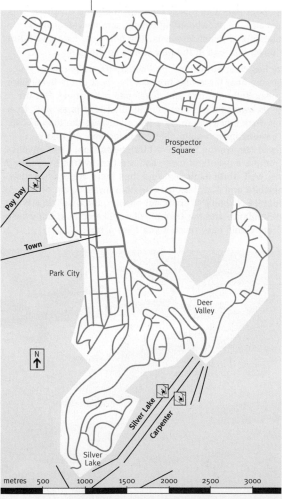

Prospector Square

Pay Day

Town

Park City

Deer Valley

Silver Lake

Carpenter

Silver Lake

N

metres 500 1000 1500 2000 2500 3000

UTAH

412

LIFT TICKETS

2000/01 prices in dollars

Park City
Covers all lifts in Park City Mountain Resort, with free ski-bus.

Main ticket
1-day ticket 60
6-day ticket 282

Senior citizens
Over 65: 1-day 30
Over 70: free ticket

Children
Age 7-12: 6-day ticket 126
6 and under: free

Short-term tickets
Half-day tickets from 1pm to 4pm (adult 44). Twilight skiing ticket 1pm-9pm (50). Night ticket 4pm-9pm 24.

Notes All multi-day tickets are good for one week, allowing for days off. Reductions for groups but not students.

Alternative tickets
Multi-area passport is available through UK tour operators.

boarding

Boarding was banned on Park City's slopes until a few years ago. But now the Olympic boarding events are being held here and the resort has fully embraced boarding, with two terrain-parks and half-pipes – one floodlit at night. It has wonderful free-ride terrain, its higher lifts giving access to some great powder bowls. Beginners have their own excellent area, good easy cruising and a lift system which is entirely chair-lifts. Intermediates have to put up with fairly short cruising runs. The town has plenty of bars to keep you going.

FOR EXPERTS
Lots of variety

There is a lot of excellent advanced and expert terrain at the top of the lift system. It is now all marked as double-diamond on the trail map but there are many runs that deserve only a single-diamond rating – so don't be put off. We particularly like the prettily wooded McConkey's Bowl, served by a six-pack and offering a range of open pitches and gladed terrain. The old Jupiter lift accesses the highest bowls, which include some serious terrain – with narrow couloirs, cliffs and cornices – as well as easier wide-open slopes. The Jupiter bowl runs are under the chair, but there is a lot more terrain accessible by traversing and hiking – turn left for West Face, Pioneer Ridge and Puma Bowl, right for Scotts Bowl and the vast expanse of Pinecone Ridge, stretching literally for miles down the side of Thaynes Canyon.

Lower down, the side of Summit House ridge, serviced by the Thaynes and Motherlode chairs, has some little-used black runs, plus a few satisfying trails in the trees. There's a zone of steep runs towards town from further round the ridge. And don't miss Blueslip Bowl near Summit House – so called because ski company employees who skied it in the past when it was out of bounds were handed a blue slip which meant they were fired.

Good skiers (no snowboarders, due to some long flat run-outs and hikes) should not miss the Utah Interconnect (see feature panel). For bigger budgets, Park City Powder Guides offers heli-skiing on 20,000 acres of private backcountry land.

FOR INTERMEDIATES
Many better places

There are blue runs served by all the main lifts, apart from Jupiter. The areas around the King Con high-speed quad and Silverlode high-speed six-pack

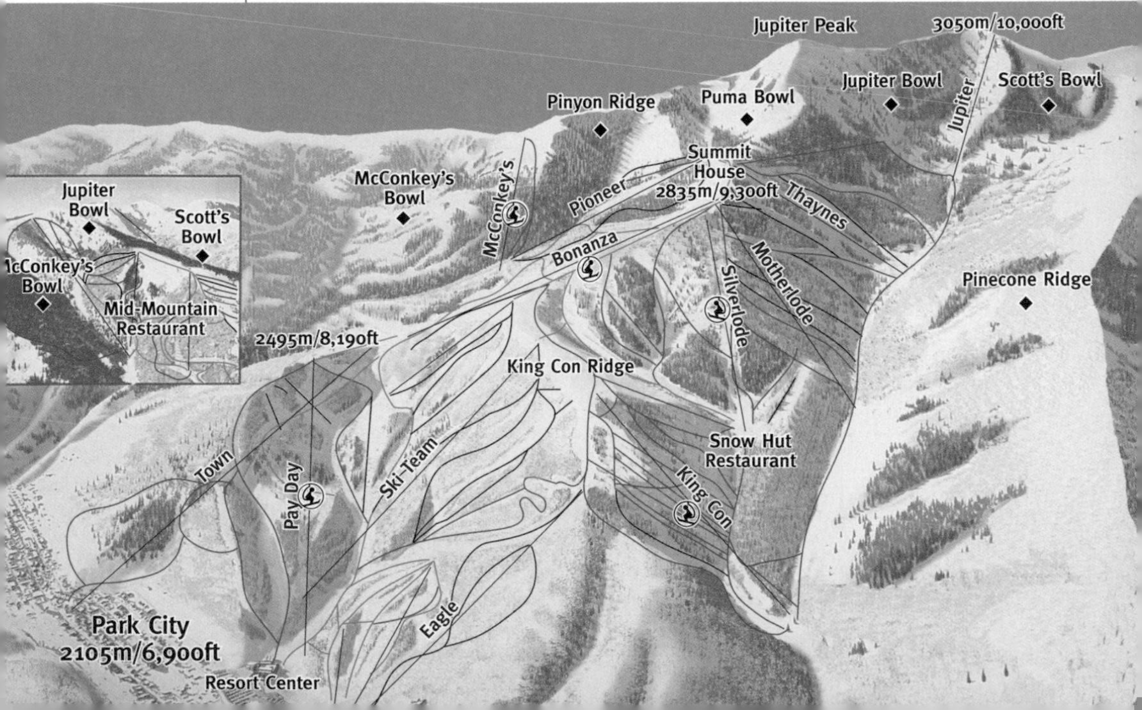

SCHOOLS/GUIDES

2000/01 prices in dollars

Park City

Classes 5 days
3hr: 9.30-12.30 or
1pm-4pm 290; 3 3hr
days: 175
Children's classes
Ages: 7 to 12
Full day 105 (incl lunch)
Private lessons
1hr, 2hr, half- or full-day
95 for 1hr; 450 for full day; additional cost for more than one person

CHILDCARE

The ski school's Mountain School takes children aged from 3 to 6, from 8.30 or 9.30 to 4.30, mixing skiing instruction with other indoor and outdoor activities. $115 per day or $330 for three days. There are several different nurseries in the town.

have a dense network of great (but fairly short) cruising runs. There are also more difficult trails close by, for those looking for a challenge.

But the avid intermediate skier or rider who might be happy at Vail or Snowmass won't be so happy here. There are few long, fast cruising runs – most trails are in the 1km to 2km/ around a mile region and many have long, flat run-outs. The Pioneer and McConkey's chair-lifts are off the main drag and serve some very pleasant, often quiet runs. A reporter complains of too many ungroomed bump runs, 'leaving a choice of ultra-easy cruising or bump-running, with little in-between'.

Intermediates will certainly want to visit The Canyons and Deer Valley for a day or two (see separate chapters) and may be tempted further to try the famous Alta/Snowbird powder.

FOR BEGINNERS
A good chance for fast progress
Novices get started on short lifts and a dedicated beginner area near the base lodge. The beginners' classes graduate up the hill quite quickly, and there's a good, very gentle and wide 'easiest way down' – the three-and a half-mile Home Run – clearly marked all the way from Summit House. It's easy enough for most beginners to manage after only a few lessons. The Town chair can be ridden down.

FOR CROSS-COUNTRY
Some trails; lots of backcountry
There are prepared trails on both the Park City golf course, next to the downhill area, and the Homestead Resort course, just out of town. There is lots of scope for backcountry trips.

LIFTLINES
Peak period problems only
Liftlines aren't normally a problem with all the high-speed six-seat chairs in the area. But it can get pretty crowded (on some trails as well as the lifts) on busy weekends.

MOUNTAIN RESTAURANTS
Standard self-service stuff
The Mid-Mountain Lodge is a 19th-century mine building which was heaved up the mountain to its present location near the bottom of Pioneer chair. The food is standard self-service fare but most reporters prefer it to the alternatives. The Summit House is cafe-style – serving chilli, pizza, soup etc. The Snow Hut is a smaller log building and usually has an outdoor grill. The Skiosk is an on-mountain yurt (a tent) serving snacks, halfway down the Bonanza chair-lift. There's quite a choice of restaurants back at the base area including the food court at the new Legacy Lodge.

SCHOOLS AND GUIDES
Thorough, full of enthusiasm
The school offers performance workshops (Dealing with the Diamonds, Moguls and Beyond) and Power Clinics (for strong intermediates) as well as beginner and private lessons.

FACILITIES FOR CHILDREN
Well organized; ideal terrain
There are a number of licenced caregivers who operate either at their own premises or at visitors' lodgings. The ski school takes children from the age of 3. Book in advance.

THE UTAH INTERCONNECT

Good skiers should not miss this excellent guided backcountry tour that runs four days a week from Park City to Snowbird. (Three days a week it runs from Snowbird, but only as far as Solitude.) When we did it we got fresh tracks in knee-deep powder practically all day. After a warm-up run to weed out weak skiers, we headed up to the top of the Jupiter chair, went through a 'closed' gate in the area boundary and skied down a deserted, prettily wooded valley to Solitude. After taking the lifts to the top of Solitude we did a short traverse, then down more virgin powder towards Brighton. After more powder runs and lunch back in Solitude, it was up the lifts and a 30-minute hike up the Highway to Heaven to north-facing, tree-lined slopes and a great little gully down into Alta. How much of Alta and Snowbird you get to ski depends on how much time is left.

The price ($150) includes two guides – one leading, another at the rear – lunch, lift tickets for all five resorts you pass through and transport home.

Staying there

If you're not renting a car, pick a location that's handy for Main Street and the Town chair or the free bus.

GETTING THERE

Air Salt Lake City, transfer ½hr.

Phone numbers

From distant parts of the US, add the prefix 1 435.
From abroad, add the prefix +1 435.

ACTIVITIES

Indoor Park City Racquet Club (4 indoor tennis courts, 2 racquetball courts, heated pool, hot-tub, sauna, gym, aerobics, basketball), Silver Mountain Spa (racquetball courts, weights room, swimming pool, aerobics, spa, massage and physical therapy, whirlpool, sauna), art galleries, concerts, theater, martial arts studio, bowling
Outdoor Snowmobiles, ballooning, sleigh rides, ski jumping, ice skating, bob-sled and luge track, snow tubing, sports and recreation opportunities for disabled children and adults

TOURIST OFFICE

Postcode UT 84060
t +1 (435) 649 8111
f 647 5374
info@pcski.com
www.parkcitymountain.
com

HOW TO GO
Check the location
Park City is the busiest and most atmospheric of the Utah resorts, and a good base for visiting the others.
Hotels There's a wide variety, from typical chains to individual little B&Bs.
((((₄ **Silver King** (649 5500) Deluxe hotel/condo complex at base of the slopes, with indoor-outdoor pool.
((((₄ **Radisson Inn Park City** (649 5000) Excellent rooms and indoor-outdoor pool, but poorly placed for nightlife (out of town on main road).
((((₄ **Yarrow** (649 7000) Recently renovated with big welcoming lobby, outdoor pool and hot-tub. Free shuttle.
((((₄ **Washington School Inn** (649 3800) 'Absolutely excellent' historic inn in a great location near Main Street, with free wine and snacks creating a thriving après-ski social scene.
(((₃ **Best Western Landmark Inn** (649 7300) Way out of town near The Canyons and factory outlet mall. Swimming pool. 'Good place to stay with car to visit other resorts.'
(((₃ **Old Miners' Lodge** (645 8068) 100-year-old building next to Town lift, restored and furnished with antiques.
((₂ **Chateau Apres Lodge** (649 9372) Close to the slopes: comfortable, faded, cheap.
((₂ **1904 Imperial Inn** (649 1904) Quaint B&B at the top of Main Street.
Apartments/condos There's a big range available. The Townlift studios near Main Street and Park Avenue condos are both modern and comfortable and the latter have outdoor pool and hot-tubs. Silver Cliff Village is adjacent to the slopes and has spacious units and access to the facilities of the Silver King Hotel. Blue Church Lodge is a well-converted 19th-century Mormon church with luxury condos and rooms.

EATING OUT
Book in advance
There are over 100 restaurants but they all get crowded, so book in advance. Zoom is the old Union Pacific train depot, now a trendy restaurant owned by Robert Redford. The Riverhorse is in a beautiful, high-ceilinged first-floor room with live music. Chimayo has

great south-west cuisine. The Juniper at the Snowed Inn has won awards. Chez Betty is small and has perhaps the best food in town – expensive though. Cheaper places include the US Prime Steakhouse ('best steak ever'), the Grub Steak Restaurant at Prospector Square, Cisero's and Grappa (Italian), Jambalaya (Cajun), Wasatch Brew Pub (good value and an interesting range of beers) and Baja Cantina (Mexican).

APRES-SKI
Better than you might think
Although there are still some arcane liquor laws in Utah, provided you're over-21 and have your ID handy the laws are never a serious barrier to getting a drink. At the bars and clubs that are more dedicated to drinking (ie don't feature food but do serve spirits) membership of some kind is required. This may involve handing over $5 or more – one member can introduce numerous 'guests' – or else there'll be some old guy at the bar already organized to 'sponsor' you (sign you in) for the price of a beer. But a recent reporter points out that the system can be very expensive if you visit different resorts most days and just want a quick beer before hitting the road.

As the slopes close, the Pig Pen in the new lodge is the place to head for at the Resort Center – but you can of course make directly for Main Street. The Wasatch Brew Pub makes its own ale. The Claimjumper, JB Mulligans and the scruffy Alamo are lively places and there's usually live music and dancing on weekends. Harry O's and Cisero's nightclub are good too.

OFF THE SLOPES
Should be interesting
There's a factory outlet mall near The Canyons. Scenic balloon flights and excursions to Nevada for gambling are both popular. Snowmobiling is big. In January there's Robert Redford's Sundance Film Festival.

There are lots of shops and galleries and the museum and old jail house are worth a visit. Salt Lake City has some good concerts and shopping and a few points of interest, many connected with its Mormon heritage. The Capitol Building is open until 8pm and gives 'an interesting perspective on the State' and good views of the city.

You might like to learn to ski-jump or try the Olympic bob track at the Winter Sports Park down the road.

Coming shortly to a screen near you

HOW IT RATES

The slopes

Snow	*****
Extent	***
Experts	****
Intermediates	****
Beginners	**
Convenience	*
Lines	*****
Restaurants	*

The rest

Scenery	****
Resort charm	**
Off-slope	*

What's new

Before the Olympics, the new base lodge will be complete, built in the same plush wood and glass-style as the River Run lodge at Sun Valley. It will include restaurants, bars and a ski school desk. There will also be a skier services lodge nearby for tickets, rentals, children's ski school and, they hope, a daycare center.

There will be two new on-mountain restaurants with sun decks – at the top of the Middle Bowl gondola and at John Paul chair-lift – also in plush Sun Valley-style.

A new access road has been built, reducing the journey time from Salt Lake City.

The Strawberry gondola serves easy blue runs – but you can also hike from the top to the line of chutes seen in the background here ➔

➕ Fair-sized ski area

➕ Impressive new lift system

➕ Under an hour from Salt Lake City and other Utah resorts

➖ No resort village as yet

➖ The nearest accommodations are down in nearby Ogden or Huntsville

➖ Not really suitable for beginners

Snowbasin? If you haven't heard of it you soon will. The four Olympic downhill events (men's and women's downhills, plus the downhill elements of the combined) and the two super giant slaloms will be held here in February 2002. It's a great hill, and it gets great snow (usually). All it needs is a great village.

THE RESORT

There is no resort, in the European sense of a village where you can stay. There will be one day: the mountain is under the same ownership as Sun Valley, and big investment in hotels and other accommodations is expected over the next few years. But for now you have to stay elsewhere. Ogden is the closest big town. It's also possible to stay nearer the mountain in (or close to) the backwater town of Huntsville. But we'd recommend staying in another Utah resort and making a day trip to Snowbasin in a rental car. A reporter made the 60-mile trip from Park City in less than an hour. It is 40 miles from Salt Lake City.

THE MOUNTAINS

Snowbasin's slopes cover a lot of pleasantly varied terrain and are served by nine lifts including a fast quad chair and two gondolas, all three installed in 1998. And there are other attractions. Not the least is the amazing view over the ridge at the top of the Strawberry Express gondola across the Great Salt Lake and surrounding plain. Another is the excursion to cutely named Powder Mountain, a few miles away across the other side of the Huntsville basin. This has (as you might hope) a reputation for powder and has an extensive snowcat skiing operation.

Slopes A new base lodge in the plush style of those at Sun Valley will be ready 'before the Olympics'. From this main base, the Middle Bowl gondola goes up to the area's central core, which has lots of different slopes and gullies presenting different challenges. The John Paul fast quad chair goes up to the right from the base and serves great black slopes, on- and off-trail, with just one blue alternative way down. Above it, a mini-tram goes up to Allen's Peak and the dramatic start of the Olympic men's downhill course. The Strawberry gondola serves good blue runs at the opposite end of the ski area.

Snow reliability At 400 inches the average snowfall is in the usual Utah class. And there's lots of snowmaking.

MOUNTAIN FACTS

Altitude 1785m-2850m
5,860ft-9,350ft

Lifts	9
Trails	3,200 acres
Green	13%
Blue	49%
Black	38%
Snowmaking	
	580 acres
Recco detectors used	

Accommodations phone number

For accommodations information call the Ogden Chamber of Commerce on 627 8228 (from distant parts of the US, add the prefix 1 801; from abroad, add the prefix +1 801).

TOURIST OFFICE

Postcode UT 84317
t +1 (801) 399 1135
f 399 1138
info@snowbasin.com
www.snowbasin.com

Experts This is a great mountain for experts. All the lifts serve worthwhile terrain – even Strawberry has some severe chutes reached by hiking from the top, but most of the steep stuff is at the other end of the area. The mini-tram serves a short black slope that was bumped up when we were there but will be glass-smooth when it serves as the start of the Olympic downhill race course. The course has been designed by Bernhard Russi – who else? It drops 902 metres/2,959ft and is already claimed to be a modern classic. The parts of it that were open when we visited were certainly impressive. Between the race course and the area boundary is a splendid area of off-trail wooded glades and gullies. This is where most good skiers and riders will want to spend their time, riding the fast chair.

Intermediates It's also a good mountain for intermediates. Strawberry accesses mainly long open blue runs but also leads to a lightly wooded steeper slope at the extremity of the area. Middle Bowl is great terrain for the adventurous.

Beginners A place like this can't seriously be recommended for beginners from afar, but there is a beginner area, and a few green runs.

Snowboarding Although there are no specific facilities for boarders, there is some excellent free-ride terrain.

Cross-country Nordic Valley is nearby.

Liftlines Lines are unlikely.

Mountain restaurants For 2001/02, there will be two – see What's New.

Schools and guides The school has special women's clinics as well as the normal offerings.

Facilities for children The plans for the new base include a daycare center.

STAYING THERE

Ogden and Huntsville are the two closest towns to Snowbasin.

Hotels Ogden has various standard-issue hotels and motels. Huntsville has a small hotel, a couple of small B&Bs and Utah's oldest tavern (opened in 1879), the Shooting Star – a splendid scruffy relic of times past. On the walls are not only stuffed moose and elk but a stuffed St Bernard dog – apparently a beast of record-breaking enormity.

Après-ski The new base lodge will have a couple of bars and eating places. Otherwise it's back into town for evening entertainment.

Eating out The Shooting Star, in Huntsville, is famous for its huge Starburgers, which come with sausage as well as multiple burger patties etc.

Off the slopes Visits to Ogden, Park City or Salt Lake City are the options – you'll probably stay in one of them!

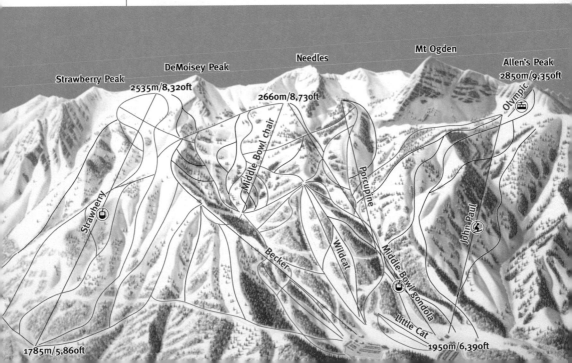

Snowbird

2470m/8,100ft

One of the world's top places for powderhounds

HOW IT RATES

The slopes
Snow	*****
Extent	***
Experts	*****
Intermediates	***
Beginners	**
Convenience	*****
Liftlines	**
Restaurants	*

The rest
Scenery	***
Resort charm	*
Off-slope	*

What's new

For 2001/02, the Alta and Snowbird areas will be officially linked for the first time. A second high-speed quad in Mineral Basin will take you to the Sugarloaf saddle area above Alta's Albion Base. The return will be from the same area, reached by Alta's new Sugarloaf high-speed quad. A joint Snowbird-Alta lift ticket will be available to skiers (but not boarders, as Alta bans them). The joint area will cover 4,700 acres.

There are plans for a new restaurant at the top of the Tram on Hidden Peak, but these are the subject of an ongoing court battle with anti-development groups.

MOUNTAIN FACTS

for Snowbird and Alta combined area

Altitude 2365m-3355m
7,760ft-11,000ft
Lifts	26
Trails	4,700 acres
Green	25%
Blue	37%
Black	38%

Snowmaking
150 acres
Recco detectors used

- ⊕ Quantity and quality of powder snow unrivalled except by next-door Alta
- ⊕ New link to Alta for 2001/02 makes one of the largest ski areas in the US
- ⊕ Fabulous ungroomed slopes, with steep and not-so-steep options
- ⊕ Luxurious accommodations with excellent facilities
- ⊕ Slopes-at-the-door convenience
- ⊕ Easy to get to Salt Lake City and other Utah resorts (so long as access road open)

- ⊖ Limited groomed runs for intermediates, though the new link with Alta doubles the terrain
- ⊖ Tiny, claustrophobic resort 'village'
- ⊖ Uncompromising modern architecture
- ⊖ Frequent lines for main tram
- ⊖ Area is very prone to avalanches, which can close the road as well as the slopes and keep you indoors
- ⊖ Very quiet at night

There can be few places where nature has combined the steep with the deep better than at Snowbird and neighboring Alta, and even fewer places where there are also lifts to give you access. At long last the two resorts have agreed to a shared lift ticket – and lifts and trails to link the two have been built. The combined area will be one of the top powder-pig paradises in the world (with an average snowfall of 500 inches a year) and one of the US's biggest lift-linked ski areas. So it is a shame that Snowbird's concrete, purpose-built 'base village' is so lacking in charm and animation. If you are planning on a week's stay, you may prefer the more traditional (but equally quiet) Alta next door. Snowboarders are banned from Alta's slopes so cannot take advantage of the joint lift ticket.

The resort

Snowbird lies 40km/25 miles south-east of Salt Lake City in the Wasatch mountains, up Little Cottonwood Canyon – just before Alta. The setting is rugged and rather Alpine – and both the resort and (particularly) the approach road are prone to avalanches and closure: visitors are sometimes confined indoors for safety. The resort buildings are mainly block-like and dull – but they provide high-quality lodging and are convenient for the slopes.

The resort area and the slopes are spread along the road on the south side of the narrow canyon. The focal Snowbird Center is towards the eastern, up-canyon end; much of the rest consists of car-parking areas.

The mountain

Snowbird's new link with Alta (see separate Alta chapter) forms one of the largest ski areas in the US.

THE SLOPES
Looming above the resort
The north-facing slopes rear up from the edge of the resort. Five access lifts are ranged along the valley floor, the main one being the 125-person tram (the Aerial Tram) to Hidden Peak. The toughest terrain is on the flanks of the ridge beneath the line of the Tram. To the west, in Gad Valley, there are runs ranging from very tough to nice and easy – and six chair-lifts. Mineral Basin, on the back of Hidden Peak, opened in 1999/2000 with a new fast quad and

boarding *Unfortunately for snowboarders, the joint Alta-Snowbird ticket is not available for them as Alta still bans boards. But ask any Utah boarder where the best place to ride is and you'll get the same answer, 'the Bird's the word'. Competent free-riders will have a wild time in Snowbird's legendary powder and there is a terrain park and half-pipe. However, Snowbird's attractions would be wasted on beginners. And the nightlife's deadly dull.*

LIFT TICKETS

2001/02 prices in dollars
Snowbird
Covers lifts and Aerial Tram in Snowbird.
Beginners Chickadee chair ticket (11 per day).
Main ticket
1-day ticket 56
6-day ticket 258
Senior citizens
Over 65:
1-day ticket 43
Children
Under 12: free (chair-lifts only, up to 2 children per adult; upgrade to Tram is 9)
Short-term tickets
Half-day (am or pm) ticket available (adult 48)
Alternative tickets
Joint Snowboard-Alta ticket prices had not been agreed at press time.
Day and half-day tickets for Snowbird chair-lifts only (47 per day for adults, 35 for seniors, free for two children under 12 with an adult)

SCHOOLS/GUIDES

2001/02 prices in dollars
Snowbird
Classes 5 days
Half- (pm only) or full-day. 5 full days: 360
Children's classes
Ages: 3 to 15
5 full days including lunch: 400
Private lessons
1hr, 3hr or 6hr
75 for 1hr, for 1 or 2 people, 100 for 3-6 people

CHILDCARE

The Camp Snowbird day camp, in the Cliff Lodge, takes children from 3 to 12, from 8.30 to 4.30. The nursery takes infants from 6 weeks to 3 years.

The Chickadees ski classes start at age 3. Evening babysitting is available.

500 acres of terrain for all abilities. Another new quad there for 2001/02 will form the link with Alta.

The First Tracks program allows you to ride the Tram to the top at 8am so as to be first up on the mountain. Numbers limited: book ahead ($20).

SNOW RELIABILITY
Exceptional
With Little Cottonwood Canyon's huge snowfalls, north-facing slopes and all runs above 2365m/7,760ft, snow reliability is very good. Snowbird and Alta typically average 500 inches of snowfall a year – twice as much as some Colorado resorts and around 50% more than nearby Park City.

FOR EXPERTS
Steep and deep – superb
Snowbird was created for experts, with a lot of tough terrain. The trail map is liberally sprinkled with double-black-diamonds, and some of the gullies off the Cirque ridge – Silver Fox and Great Scott, for example, are exceptionally steep and frequently neck-deep in powder. Lower down lurk the bump runs, including Mach Schnell – a great run straight down the fall line through trees. There is some wonderful ski-anywhere terrain in the bowl beneath the high Little Cloud chair, and the Gad 2 lift opens up some attractive tree runs. Mineral Basin has added more expert terrain. Backcountry tours are available, and Wasatch Powderbird Guides offer heli-skiing and boarding. And now there's the whole of Alta's slopes to enjoy if you are a skier.

FOR INTERMEDIATES
Quality, not quantity
The winding Chip's Run on the east side of the Cirque ridge provides the only comfortable route down from the top for intermediates – at 5km/3 miles, it's Snowbird's longest run. For adventurous intermediates wanting to try powder skiing, the bowl below the Little Cloud lift is a must – you'll rarely find better powder than this. There are some challenging runs through the trees off the Gad 2 lift. There are also some nice long cruises in Mineral Basin and from the new link with Alta. But if you are after miles of groomed trails, there are plenty of better resorts.

FOR BEGINNERS
Better than you'd expect
Beginners have the Chickadee lift right down in the resort – and then there's a small network of trails to progress to.

FOR CROSS-COUNTRY
Go elsewhere
There are no prepared cross-country trails at Snowbird. All-terrain skiers can hike into the backcountry, but for loops you need to go elsewhere.

LIFTLINES
Avoid the Tram
For much of the season lines of up to 40 minutes for the Tram are common. The Gadzoom fast quad and the Little Cloud chair above it – sadly, also rather line-prone – get you almost as high as the Tram. The lift back from Mineral Basin arrives at the same height as the Tram.

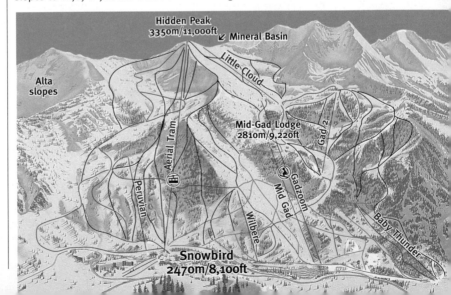

Hidden Peak
3350m/11,000ft — Mineral Basin
Little Cloud
Alta slopes
Mid-Gad Lodge
2810m/9,220ft
Aerial Tram
Gad 2
Peruvian
Gadzoom
Mid Gad
Wilbere
Baby Thunder
Snowbird
2470m/8,100ft

↑ The Cliff Lodge is not pretty – but it has great facilities and is right on the slopes

SNOWBIRD / DEREK SMITH

Central reservations phone number
For all resort accommodations call 1 800 640 2002 (toll-free from within the US)

GETTING THERE

Air Salt Lake City, transfer ½hr.

ACTIVITIES

Indoor Snowbird Canyon Racquet Club (tennis, racquetball, squash, climbing wall, aerobics, weight training, fitness room), hot-tubs, The Cliff Spa (fitness room, aerobics, beauty center, sauna, steam room, solarium), conference centre, art gallery **Outdoor** Swimming pools, hot-tubs, ice skating, tubing, snow-shoeing

TOURIST OFFICE

UT 84092-9000
t +1 (801) 742 2222
f 933 2298
info@snowbird.com
www.snowbird.com

MOUNTAIN RESTAURANT
Note the use of the singular
It's the Mid Gad self-service cafeteria – or 'fuel stop', to use the resort's own description – or else it's back to base. One reporter complains that even at the base it's crowded and limited.

SCHOOLS AND GUIDES
Something for everyone
The ski school offers a progressive range of lessons and speciality clinics – such as women-only clinics, over-50s lessons, bumps and diamonds lessons, and experts-only programs ('A life-altering experience,' said a reporter).

FACILITIES FOR CHILDREN
All ages well cared-for
The 'kids ski free' program allows two children (12 and under) to ski for free ($9 a day extra for use of the Tram) with each adult buying an all-day lift ticket. There are occasional evening distractions like parties, games and movies to keep the kids happy.

Staying there

All the lodgings and restaurants are within walking distance of each other. The Tram station is central and the Gad lifts can be reached on snow. There are shuttle-bus services linking the lodgings, the lifts and the parking lots, and a regular service up to Alta.

HOW TO GO
Package or independent
Salt Lake City airport is close, and well set up to handle independent travelers. There are several companies offering frequent transfers. If you plan to visit several other resorts, you'll want to rent a car, and it's worth considering Salt Lake City as a base – not least because avalanche danger

can close Little Cottonwood Canyon after heavy snowfalls, in which case you can be stuck in your Snowbird hotel room.
Hotels There are several lodges, and smaller condominium blocks.
⟨⟨⟨4 **Cliff Lodge** (800 640 2002 for Snowbird Central Reservations). The main place: a huge luxury hotel and restaurant complex just up the beginner slopes from the Snowbird Center. There's a rooftop pool and hot-tub, sauna, steam room and gym. Prices here are understandably high, but if you can bear to share a four-bed 'dorm' room they're great value, considering the facilities you can use.

EATING OUT
A reasonable choice
Generally eating out revolves around the Cliff Lodge and the Snowbird Center – both house a number of restaurants. It's advisable for at least one member of a party to pay a few dollars to join the Club at Snowbird (guests at the Cliff Lodge are automatically registered) as most of the better restaurants are classed as private clubs. The Aerie and the Wildflower are quite upscale venues, the Mexican Keyhole Junction and the Forklift are easier on the pocket and better for families.

APRES-SKI
Very quiet weekdays
Après-ski in Snowbird tends to be a bit muted, especially during the week. The Tram Club under the Tram itself was rocking with live music as the slopes closed when we were there. The Keyhole Cantina also has a good atmosphere at end-of-day. A sunset swim and a few cocktails at the rooftop pool in Cliff Lodge is relaxing. It's quite feasible to head into Salt Lake City for the occasional night out – lots of live bands and so on.

OFF THE SLOPES
Head down-canyon
People not using the slopes will be bored at Snowbird once they've tried the Cliff Spa and its treatments. You could head towards the city – the Racquet Club down the valley is owned by Snowbird and has superb tennis facilities, and there are some attractions downtown, particularly around Temple Square.

The Rest of the West

This section covers a varied group of isolated resorts in different parts of the great Rocky Mountain chain that stretches the length of the United States from Montana and Idaho down through Wyoming and Colorado to New Mexico. Each has its own unique character – and each is well worth knowing about.

Sun Valley, Idaho, was America's first purpose-built resort, developed in the 1930s by the president of the Union Pacific Railway. It quickly became popular with the Hollywood jet set and has managed to retain its stylish image and ambience over the years. It hasn't become a big international destination, because of its rather isolated location, limited hotel accommodations and poor reputation for snow – although this has largely been rectified by the huge snowmaking installation. But if you want to indulge yourself a little and be pampered, bear it in mind – it has one of our favorite luxury hotels.

If you don't mind a bit of a cross-state drive, you might combine a visit to Sun Valley with a visit to the famously snowy resorts of Utah or to Jackson Hole in Wyoming – another resort with an impressive snow record. Jackson is the nearest there is to a resort with a genuine Wild West cowboy atmosphere. The old town is lined with wooden sidewalks and there are lively saloons, where modern-day working cowboys drink, play pool and dance to country music. The mountain is a 15-minute drive away and offers some of America's most extreme terrain, with steeps, jumps and bumps to suit all – a sharp contrast to the tame, immaculately groomed runs typical of many US resorts. It does have easier runs, but that's not why most people go there.

A little way north of both Sun Valley and Jackson, just inside Montana, is Big Sky, not to be confused with Big Mountain at the far northern end of the state, or indeed Big White, over

the Canadian border in British Columbia. Big Sky has one of the biggest verticals in America (1275m/4,180ft) thanks to its Lone Peak tram, going way above the tree line to 3405m/11,170ft. Its extensive slopes have something for everyone, from extreme steeps at the top to countless gentle cruises at the bottom. But there's not much to do here except ski and board.

Taos, New Mexico, is the most southerly major resort in America, and because of its isolation is relatively unknown on the international market. There's a tiny resort development called Taos Ski Valley at the foot of the slopes, which are set high above the traditional adobe town of Taos, 18 miles away in the arid valley and full of art galleries, museums, restaurants and bars. There are lots of accommodations down in town and along the road between it and the resort. The area was developed in the 1950s by European, Ernie Blake, and is still family-run, with a friendly feel to it. It is one of the few resorts still to ban snowboarders.

The first thing you see is Al's Run, a mogul field of formidable steepness rising sheerly out of the resort. Founder Ernie Blake put up a sign saying 'Don't panic! You're looking at 1/30 of Taos Ski Valley. We have many easy runs too.' They do, but Taos still suits experts best with some very steep runs through trees and great powder fields that you have to hike to, including the 75-minute plus hike to Kachina Peak. Taos ski school has an excellent reputation.

421

JACKSON HOLE / GORAN ASSNER

In many ways the Best of the West – Jackson Hole →

Big Sky

2285m/7,500ft

Vast and empty slopes for all abilities

422

HOW IT RATES

The slopes

Snow	★★★★
Extent	★★★
Experts	★★★★★
Intermediates	★★★★
Beginners	★★★★
Convenience	★★★★
Liftlines	★★★★★
Restaurants	★

The rest

Scenery	★★★
Resort charm	★★
Off-slope	★★

MOUNTAIN FACTS

Altitude 2125m-3405m
6,970ft-11,170ft

Lifts	18
Trails	3,600 acres
Green	10%
Blue	47%
Black	43%
Snowmaking	
	350 acres

Recco detectors used

- ⊕ Extensive ski area with runs for all abilities
- ⊕ Excellent snow reliability
- ⊕ Big vertical by US standards
- ⊕ No liftlines, empty slopes
- ⊕ Some slope-side accommodations

- ⊖ No real resort village as yet
- ⊖ Inadequate on-mountain dining facilities
- ⊖ Quite a few slow, old chair-lifts

Big Sky is renowned for its powder, steeps and big vertical, and has lots of blissfully empty gentler slopes. At present, there's no real village, just a very small collection of shops, restaurants and accommodation units – and nightlife is limited to say the least. If that's what you like, go soon – the owners have big expansion plans which include a complete village overhaul and enough extra terrain to put Big Sky in the first rank.

THE RESORT

Big Sky, now over 25 years old, has started to attract a few international visitors who have heard of its huge snowfalls and deserted slopes.

The resort is set amid the wide open spaces of Montana, one hour's drive from the airport town of Bozeman. At the foot of the slopes is Mountain Village – the obvious base, with some slope-side condominiums and lodges. Despite efficient free buses, condos scattered around a golf course 10km/6 miles east at Meadow Village hold little appeal. Renting a car is recommended.

Bridger Bowl is less than two hours' drive away, and makes a worthwhile outing – a broad, lightly wooded mountain of 600m/2,000ft vertical.

THE MOUNTAINS

The slopes cover a big area spread over two linked mountains, with long runs for all abilities. Lone Mountain, with steep open upper slopes and a wooded base, dominates. Andesite mountain is a much more modest

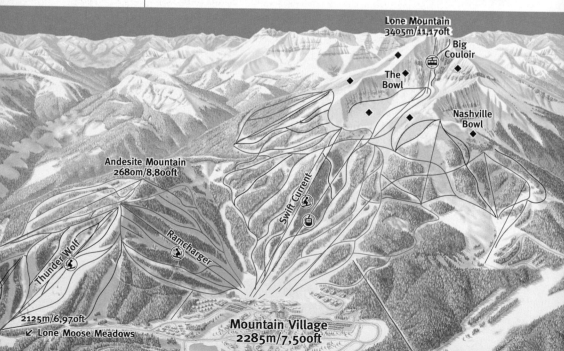

Lone Mountain
3405m/11,170ft

Big Couloir

The Bowl

Nashville Bowl

Andesite Mountain
2680m/8,800ft

Swift Current

Ramcharger

Thunder Wolf

2125m/6,970ft
↙ Lone Moose Meadows

Mountain Village
2285m/7,500ft

What's new

A new 80-room Mountain Inn hotel in the Mountain Village will be ready for 2001/02. Four new gladed runs will be created on Andesite.

A 10-year expansion plan has now been approved – developments will include an enhanced mountain village with over 100 shops and restaurants, a spa, conference facilities, 1,800 acres of new terrain and an extra six fast lifts.

Central reservations phone number
For all resort accommodations call
1 800 548 4486
(toll-free from within the US).

TOURIST OFFICE

Postcode MT 59716
t +1 (406) 995 5000
f 995 5001
info@bigskyresort.com
www.bigskyresort.com

wooded hill of 400m/1,300ft vertical. Although there are three fast quads, most of the chair-lifts are old triples and doubles. There are daily free mountain tours.

Slopes Half-a-dozen chairs and a gondola serve the wooded lower half of Lone Mountain (with a vertical of about 500m/1,650ft). The Lone Peak chair accesses a few blue slopes at the bottom of the main bowl and leads to the Lone Peak Tram – a tiny 15-person tram to the top, which serves great experts-only terrain all around the top bowl. The longest run – from the top of the Tram, down through Liberty Bowl round the back of the mountain, to the village – is about six miles long.

Snowboarding There is a good terrain park and half-pipe on Andesite and a gentler one on Lone Mountain.

Snow reliability Snowfall averages 400+ inches, which puts Big Sky ahead of most Colorado resorts and alongside Jackson Hole. Grooming is good, too.

Experts The terrain accessed from the Tram is great, including narrow couloirs and wide powder fields. Castro's Shoulder is the steepest route at 50°. There are good black slopes lower down, around the tree line.

Intermediates There is lots of cruising terrain – the shady runs on Andesite from the Ramcharger chair are splendid, but practically all the lower lifts serve worthwhile blue runs.

Beginners It's excellent, with a beginner area at the base and long greens on both mountains.

Cross-country There are 65km/40 miles of trails at Lone Mountain Ranch. There are also trails at West Yellowstone.

Liftlines Waiting in lines is unheard of unless high winds close the upper lifts, and the runs seem deserted. There are 3,600 skiable acres; on an average day they sell 2,000 lift tickets; do the math.

Mountain restaurants The Dug-Out, on Andesite, is the only mountain restaurant – fast food and barbecues. You can head back to base to eat.

School and guides The ski school receives excellent reviews. A recent reporter described his children's lessons as a '100% success'.

Facilities for children Handprints nursery in the slope-side Snowcrest lodge takes children from age six months ('It was perfection – four to an adult,' says a reporter). Children under 10 years ski for free.

STAYING THERE

How to go Condos are the norm at the slope-side Mountain Village.

Hotels In Mountain Village, Huntley Lodge (highly recommended by a reporter), Shoshone and the new slope-side Summit are the most convenient hotels, with good facilities. Mountain Inn will be open for 2001/02.

Apartments/condos There are lots of condos available for rent – the well-equipped Stillwater condos in the resort village are 'excellent'.

Après-ski Chet's bar has live music, pool and poker games. The Carabinier lounge in the Summit, Roosters and Scissorbill's are also popular.

Eating out In Mountain Village, Huntley Lodge has a smart restaurant, The Peaks and Dante's Inferno are popular. You can take a shuttle-bus or a restaurant courtesy car to Meadow Village: Buck's T-4, First Place, Café Edelweiss and Rocco's get good reports. 320 Guest Ranch at Gallatin Canyon is also recommended.

Off the slopes The main things to do are snowmobiling, horse riding, sleigh riding, visiting Yellowstone national park and shopping in Bozeman.

Big Sky

Wild West cowboy town close to wild, exciting slopes

HOW IT RATES

The slopes

Snow	****
Extent	***
Experts	*****
Intermediates	**
Beginners	***
Convenience	***
Liftlines	***
Restaurants	*

The rest

Scenery	***
Resort charm	****
Off-slope	***

MOUNTAIN FACTS

Altitude	1925m-3185m
	6,310ft-10,450ft
Lifts	11
Trails	2,500 acres
Green	10%
Blue	40%
Black	50%
Snowmaking	
	160 acres
Recco detectors used	

424

JACKSON HOLE / BOB WOODALL / FPI

The Million Dollar Cowboy Bar in the center of Jackson has saddles as bar stools and a stuffed grizzly bear staring at drinkers ↓

➕ Big, steep mountain, with some real expert-only terrain and one of the US's biggest verticals: 1260m/4,140ft

➕ Jackson town has an entertaining Wild West ambience

➕ Unspoiled, remote location with some impressive scenery nearby

➕ Excellent snow record

➕ Even more snow (and astonishingly empty slopes) 90 minutes away at Grand Targhee – with snowcats

➕ Low altitude, so no altitude sickness

➕ Cheap lodgings (winter is off-peak)

➕ Plenty to do off the slopes

➕ Airport is only minutes from town

➖ Intermediates lacking the confidence to tackle black runs (often with deep snow) will be more-or-less confined to the minor Apres Vous mountain

➖ Inadequate mountain restaurants

➖ The tram serving the top runs still generates long lines

➖ Low altitude, and slopes face roughly south-east, so snow can be poor on the lower slopes

➖ Jackson town is 15 minutes from the mountain, although Teton Village offers accommodations at the base

For those who like the idea of steep slopes smothered in deep powder or plastered with big bumps, Jackson Hole is Mecca. Like many American mountains, Jackson has double-diamond steeps that you can't find in Europe except by going off-trail with a guide. What marks it out from the rest is the sheer quantity of black-graded terrain, and the scale of the mountain.

Utah devotees will tell you that the snow here isn't as light as at Alta/Snowbird; but it's light enough, and falls in quantities somewhere between those found in Colorado and those famously found in Alta – the average annual total is around 400in, but in recent seasons it has often been around or above the 500in mark.

With its wooden sidewalks, country-music saloons and pool halls, tiny Jackson is a determinedly Western town – great fun, if you like that kind of thing. We do.

The resort

The town of Jackson sits at the south-eastern edge of Jackson Hole – a high, flat valley surrounded by mountain ranges, in the north-west corner of Wyoming. This is real 'cowboy' territory, and the town strives to maintain its Wild West flavor, with traditional-style wooden buildings and sidewalks, and a couple of 'cowboy' saloons. Jackson gets many more visitors in summer than winter (thanks to the nearby national parks), which accounts for the many clothing and souvenir shops, alongside the more upscale galleries appealing to affluent second-home owners. But in winter it's basically a ski town with a Western feel.

The slopes, a 15-minute drive north-east, rise abruptly from the flat valley floor. At the base is Teton Village – a small purpose-built collection of lodgings, shops and restaurants in a pleasantly woody setting, some neo-Alpine but increasingly in local style. The public bus service to the mountain ($2 single) is reported to be irregular and slow.

What's new

A couple of seasons ago Jackson Hole opened gates into the wild backcountry of Grand Teton and Bridger Teton National Parks, making it an even more compelling destination for expert skiers and riders. But don't dream of trying this without a guide.

For 2000/01, the old Union Pass surface lift that brought you back to the base area after doing the Hobacks was replaced by a fixed-grip quad chair. Another quad was built from the Moose Creek condo area of Teton Village to give guests access to the Union Pass chair rather than having to walk to the base area

The big news for 2001/02 is in the nearby resort of Grand Targhee. 500 acres of what was formerly snowcat skiing will now be served by a high-speed quad, opening great ungroomed powder as well as new groomed runs. That will still leave 1000 acres for snowcat guests only.

The mountains

Jackson Hole has long been recognized as one of the world's most compelling resorts for advanced and expert skiers. With recent improvements to the lifts and some of the buildings at Teton Village, the resort may seem less of a cult destination for hard-core experts and more of a conventional resort, with something for everyone. Don't be fooled: the beginner slopes are fine, but intermediates wanting to build up confidence should look elsewhere.

THE SLOPES
One big mountain, one small one

Trail ratings are accurate at Jackson: our own small map doesn't distinguish black from double-black-diamond runs, but the distinction matters once you are there – 'expert only' tends to mean just that. Some of the double-black runs are simply steep; but there are also cliffs, bumps, jumps and couloirs, including the infamous Corbet's.

One big mountain makes Jackson Hole famous – **Rendezvous**. The summit, accessed by the Tram, provides a 1260m/4,140ft vertical drop – exceptional for the US. And the vertical is usable: conditions and thighs permitting, you can go from top to almost bottom on black slopes. From the top of the Tram you can now access the backcountry of Cody Bowl.

To the right looking up is **Apres Vous** mountain, with half the vertical and mostly much gentler runs, accessed by the short Teewinot and the longer Apres Vous fast quads.

Between these two peaks is a broad mountainside split by gullys, accessed since 1997 by the **Bridger gondola**. This opened up new terrain, and gives speedy access to the Thunder and Sublette quad chairs serving some of the steepest terrain on Rendezvous.

Hosts offer complimentary tours of the mountains, starting from the Host building at 9.30. And at 1.30 on weekdays you can usually take a tour with Olympic gold medallist Pepi Stiegler – Jackson's director of skiing.

Snow King is a separate area right next to Jackson town. Locals use it in their lunch-hour and in the evening (it's partly floodlit).

Grand Targhee, famous for its powder snow, is just 90 minutes' drive from Jackson Hole – buses run daily. See end of chapter.

SNOW RELIABILITY
Steep lower slopes can suffer

The claimed average of 402in of 'mostly dry powder' snow is much more than most Colorado resorts claim – and for a core three-month season conditions are likely to be reasonable. But the base elevation here is relatively low for the Rockies, and the slopes are quite sunny – they basically face south-east. If you're unlucky, you may find the steep lower slopes like the Hobacks in poor shape, or even shut. Happily, much of the best expert terrain is relatively shady. And snowmaking covers top-to-bottom runs from the gondola and on Apres Vous.

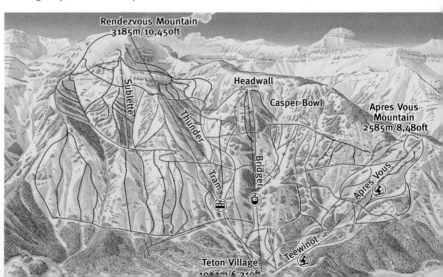

Rendezvous Mountain
3185m/10,450ft

Headwall

Casper Bowl

Apres Vous Mountain
2585m/8,480ft

Sublette

Thunder

Bridger

Tram

Apres Vous

Teewinot

Teton Village

↑ The infamous Corbet's Couloir – leap in and impress the tram crowd by surviving to brag about it

LIFT TICKETS

2001/02 prices in dollars
Jackson Hole
Covers all lifts and includes 'Tram'.
Main ticket
1-day ticket 59
7-day ticket 343
Senior citizens
Over 65: 7-day ticket 172
Children
15 to 21: 7-day ticket 257
Under 15: 7-day ticket 172
Short-term tickets
Afternoon ticket from 12.30 (adult 44)
Notes 5-year-olds and under have free use of some lifts.

FOR EXPERTS
Best for the brave

For the good skier or boarder who wants challenges without the expense of hiring a guide to go off-trail, Jackson is one of the world's best resorts – maybe even the best.

Rendezvous mountain offers virtually nothing but black and very black slopes.

The routes down the main Rendezvous Bowl are not particularly fearsome; but some of the alternatives are. Go down the East Ridge at least once to stare over the edge of the notorious Corbet's Couloir. The Tram passes right above it, providing a great view of people throwing themselves off the lip. It's the jump in that's special; the word is that the slope you land on is a mere 50° to the horizontal.

Below Rendezvous Bowl, the wooded flanks of Cheyenne Bowl offer serious challenges, at the extreme end of the single-black-diamond spectrum.

If instead you take the ridge run that skirts this bowl to the right, you get to the Hobacks – a huge area of open and lightly wooded slopes, gentler than those higher up, but still black.

Corbet's aside, most of the seriously steep slopes are more easily reached from the slightly lower quad chairs. From Sublette, you have direct access to the short but seriously steep Alta chutes, and to the less severe Laramie Bowl beside them. Or you can track over to Tensleep Bowl – pausing to inspect Corbet's from below – and on to the less extreme (and less chute-like) Expert Chutes, and the single black Cirque and Headwall areas). Casper Bowl – accessed through gates only – is recommended for untracked powder. Thunder chair serves further steep, narrow, north-facing chutes.

Again, the lower part of the mountain here offers lightly wooded single-black slopes.

The gondola serves terrain not without interest for experts. In particular, Moran Woods is a splendid under-utilized area. And even Apres Vous itself has an area of serious single blacks in Saratoga bowl.

The gates into the backcountry access over 3,000 acres of amazing terrain and you should hire a guide to take you there. There are some heli-ski and heli-board operations.

FOR INTERMEDIATES
Exciting for some

There are great cruising runs on the front face of Apres Vous, and top-to-bottom blues from the new gondola also offer quite gentle runs. But they don't add up to a great deal of mileage, and you shouldn't consider Jackson unless you want to tackle the blacks. It's then important to get guidance on steepness and snow conditions. The steepest single blacks are steep; intimidating when bumpy and fearsome when hard. The daily grooming map is worth consulting.

boarding *Jackson Hole is a cult resort for expert snowboarders, just as it is for expert skiers. The steeps, cliffs and chutes make for a lot of high-adrenalin thrills for competent free-riders. There's a terrain-park and a half-pipe, and Dick's Ditch is a natural pipe. It's not a bad resort for novices either, with the beginner slopes served by a high-speed quad. Intermediates not wishing to venture off the groomed runs will find the resort a bit limited. There are some good snowboard shops, including the Hole-in-the-Wall at Teton Village. The nightlife in the bars around the town square is reasonably lively.*

SCHOOLS/GUIDES

2000/01 prices in dollars

Jackson Hole
Classes Full day: 65
Half-day: 50
First Tracks (8.30am)
4 hours: 85
Children's classes
Ages: 3 to 6 (inc lunch and lift ticket):
Full day 75
Half day 50
Ages: 7 to 17 (inc lunch and lift ticket):
Full day: 95
Private lessons
1-5 people
Early tram (8.30), Full day (7 hr): 415
Half day (4 hr): 310
All day from 9am 395
Backcountry Guiding
1-5 people
Full day 415
Half day am 310
Half day pm 225

CHILDCARE

The Kids' Ranch (739 2691) in the Cody House at Teton Village takes children aged 2 months to 6 years, from 8.30 to 4.30, with indoor and outdoor games and one-to-one ski lessons from age 3. Kids use the Fort Wyoming snow-garden, with 'magic carpet' lift.

GETTING THERE

Air Jackson, transfer ½hr.

Phone numbers
From distant parts of the US, add the prefix 1 307.
From abroad, add the prefix +1 307.

FOR BEGINNERS
Fine, up to a point
There are a few broad, gentle runs: fine for getting started. The progression to the blue Werner run off the Apres Vous chair is gradual enough – but what then? Most of the blues are traverses and the exceptions will not help build a novice's confidence.

FOR CROSS-COUNTRY
Lots of possibilities
There are three centers in the valley, offering trails of various lengths and difficulty. The Spring Creek Nordic Center has some good beginner terrain and offers moonlight tours. The Nordic Center at Teton has 17km/11 miles of trails and organizes trips into the National Parks.

LIFTLINES
Always lines for the Tram
The Bridger gondola has relieved some of the pressure on the 30-year-old Tram. But the Tram is still the quickest way up Rendezvous, still the only way to the very top and still not able to keep up with demand; there may be lines all day.

MOUNTAIN RESTAURANTS
Head back to base
There's only one real restaurant on the mountain – at the base of the Casper chair-lift; it does a good range of self-service food, but gets very crowded. There are simple snack-bars at four other points on the mountain. At the base, Nick Wilson's in the Clocktower, the Alpenhof restaurant and the Mangy Moose are favorites.

SCHOOLS AND GUIDES
Learn to tackle the steeps
As well as the usual lessons, there are also First Tracks classes on steep and deep slopes. On certain dates, special steep skiing and boarding, freestyle and backcountry camps are held. Backcountry guides can be hired.

FACILITIES FOR CHILDREN
Just fine
The area may not seem to be one ideally suited to children, but in fact there are enough easy runs and the 'Kids' Ranch' care facilities are good.

Staying there

HOW TO GO
In town or by the mountain
Teton Village is convenient. But stay in Jackson for cowboy atmosphere.
Hotels There's something to suit most tastes. Because winter is low season, prices are low.
((((⑤ **Amangani Resort** (734 7333) Hedonistic (expensive) luxury in isolated position way above the valley.
(((④ **Alpenhof** (733 3242) Our favorite (and our readers') in Teton Village. Tirolean-style, with rooms of varying standard and price. Good food. Pool, sauna, hot-tub.
((((④ **Wort** (733 2190) Brick-built hotel right in the center of town, above the lively Silver Dollar Bar. 'Very comfortable.' Hot-tub.
(((④ **Rusty Parrot Lodge** (733 2000) A stylish place in Jackson town, with a rustic feel and handcrafted furniture. Hot-tub.
(((④ **Snake River Lodge & Spa** (733 3657) At Teton Village. Upscale and friendly as well as comfortable and convenient, with fine new spa facilities.
((((④ **Spring Creek Ranch** (733 8833) Exclusive retreat midway between town and slopes; cross-country trails nearby.
((((④ **Huff House Inn** (733 4164) Charming old inn – the best of Jackson's many luxury B&B places.
((((④ **Painted Porch** (733 1981) Gorgeous B&B full of antiques.
((③ **Lodge at Jackson Hole** (733 2992) Western-style place on fringe of Jackson town. Comfortable mini-suite rooms, and free breakfast/après-ski munchies. Pool, sauna, hot-tubs.
((③ **Parkway Inn** (733 3143) Friendly, family-run place in town; nice pool.
(② **Trapper Inn** (733 2648) Friendly, good value, a block or two from Town Square. Hot-tubs.
Apartments/condos There is lots of choice at Teton Village, within Jackson and at more isolated locations.

EATING OUT
It's a pleasure in Jackson
Teton Village has pizza, Mexican, a steakhouse and a number of hotel restaurants. Most people favor the Mangy Moose – good value, good fun. In Jackson there are lots of places to try (but book ahead). The cool art-deco Cadillac Grille does good food – in the attached bar as well as the restaurant. The Range is excellent for trendy

ACTIVITIES

Indoor Art galleries, ice skating, movie theaters, swimming, theater, concerts, wildlife art museum

Outdoor Snowmobiles, mountaineering, horse riding, snow-shoe hikes, snowcat tours, floodlit skiing, heli-skiing, sleigh rides, dog-sledding, walks, wildlife safaris and tours of Yellowstone National Park

TOURIST OFFICE

Postcode WY 83001
t +1 (307) 733 7182
f 733 1286
info@jacksonhole.com
www.jacksonhole.com

American regional cuisine. The Blue Lion is small, cozy and casually stylish. The 'saloons' do hearty meals, and a reporter reckons the Million Dollar does 'the best steaks and ribs in town'. A good budget place is the Snake River brew-pub – not to be confused with the pricey, over-rated Snake River Grill. The 'Greek-inspired' food at the cute log-cabin Sweetwater is recommended. There's also Italian, Cajun, Chinese (Lame Duck), Indian, Tex-Mex and sushi (Masa Sushi).

APRES-SKI
Amusing saloons

For immediate après-ski festivities at Teton Village, the biggest draw is the Mangy Moose – a big, happy, noisy place, often with good live music. In sharp contrast is the calm and friendly Dietrich's bar, at the Alpenhof.

In Jackson there are two famous 'saloons'. The Million Dollar Cowboy Bar features saddles as bar stools and a stuffed grizzly bear, and is usually the liveliest place in town, with good food and live music some nights (and sometimes line-dancing, with classes, too). The Silver Dollar around the corner is more subdued; there may be ragtime playing as you count the 2032 silver dollars inlaid into the counter.

The Rancher is a huge pool-hall. The Shady Lady saloon at Snow King sometimes has live music – country and western of course. The Virginian saloon is a quieter watering hole.

For a night out of town, join the local ravers at the Stagecoach Inn at Wilson, especially on Sundays.

OFF THE SLOPES
'Great' outdoor diversions

The famous Yellowstone National Park is 100km/60 miles to the north. You can tour the park by snowcat or snowmobile, but you'll be roaring along the snowy roads in the company of several hundred other snowmobiles – 'more like a Grand Prix than a wilderness', as a recent reporter puts it. There is much more rewarding snowmobiling to be done elsewhere, eg at Goosewing Ranch and along the Gros Ventre river – much quieter and more wildlife.

The National Elk Refuge, next to Jackson and across the road from the National Museum of Wildlife Art, has the largest elk herd in the US. In town there are some 40 galleries and museums and a number of outlets for Indian and Western arts and crafts. There is, believe it or not, a branch of Ripley's Believe It or Not®.

A DAY OUT IN GRAND TARGHEE 2440m/8,000ft

We'd recommend any adventurous visitor to make the hour-and-a-half trip over the Teton pass to sample Grand Targhee's fabled powder. The average snowfall here is over 500in – 25% greater than Jackson, and on a par with Utah's best. Locals call it Grand Foggee, because there is often low cloud even when it's not snowing. This may be just as well, because the slopes generally face south-west, which is about the worst orientation in the book for sun damage.

On the main Fred's Mountain, the 1,500 acres of slopes are blissfully empty. A central fast quad serves a wide area of open and lightly wooded blue and black runs with a respectable 670m/2,200ft vertical. Off to the left, a slow quad chair serves an excellent area of short green runs, and beyond that a longer slow double serves another splendid area of tough blues and easy blacks – deserted when we visited.

Next-door Peaked Mountain offers slopes that are similar in extent, but were previously only accessible by snowcat. For 2001/02 it will be accessed by a new high-speed detachable quad. About a third of the new terrain will be groomed, but pristine glade skiing and open bowls will be left untouched. For those (like us) who loved the Targhee snowcat trips, there are still over 1,000 acres kept just for this. On Peaked Mountain, the vertical is slightly greater, at 860m/2,820ft, than on Fred's; and the lower part of the mountain is more heavily wooded.

Daily buses to Targhee pick up at various points around town and Teton Village. A combined bus/lift ticket costs $56. The snowcat operation costs $240 a day, $175 a half-day. You can take an instructor along, for a premium. You can also stay at Grand Targhee – there's a small, quiet, modern village right at the base.

Sun Valley
1755m/5,750ft

Stylish resort with slopes to flatter its rich and famous guests

HOW IT RATES

The slopes

Snow	★★★
Extent	★★★
Experts	★★★
Intermediates	★★★★
Beginners	★★★
Convenience	★★
Liftlines	★★★★
Restaurants	★★★★

The rest

Scenery	★★★
Resort charm	★★★
Off-slope	★★★

➕ Luxury resort built around the atmospheric old mining town of Ketchum

➕ Ideal intermediate terrain

➕ Wonderful luxurious mountain restaurants and base lodges

➕ Great restaurants and atmospheric bars for dining out, après-ski, and star-spotting

➕ Lots of off-slope diversions

➖ Expensive

➖ Erratic snow record though extensive snowmaking back-up

➖ Shuttle-buses between two separate mountains and from most accommodations

Millions of dollars have been spent in recent years building new facilities – high-speed chair-lifts, a huge computerized snowmaking system, splendid base lodges and mountain restaurants – to maintain Sun Valley's reputation as the US's original luxury purpose-built winter sports resort. For a peaceful, relaxing time, it's hard to beat. For skiing and boarding alone, there are better resorts.

MOUNTAIN FACTS

Altitude	1755m-2790m
	5,750ft-9,150ft
Lifts	13
Trails	2,067 acres
Green	38%
Blue	45%
Black	17%
Snowmaking	
	600 acres

There are three luxury lodges like River Run on Bald Mountain ↓

THE RESORT

Sun Valley is based around the old mining village of Ketchum. It was built in the 1930s by Averell Harriman, President of the Union Pacific Railway, and became a favorite with stars such as Clark Gable and Judy Garland. Its current owner, Earl Holding, has pumped millions of dollars into the mountain to restore it to state-of-the-art luxury and Sun Valley now attracts stars like Clint Eastwood and Arnie Schwarzenegger. The town of Ketchum retains its old-world charm and has atmospheric bars, restaurants and shops. But it's not cheap: 'More expensive than Aspen. I didn't buy, but I enjoyed looking in the high-quality shops,' says a reporter.

THE MOUNTAINS

There are two separate mountains – Bald Mountain, with the main body of runs, and the smaller Dollar Mountain.
Slopes The main slopes of Bald Mountain (known locally as Baldy) are accessed from one of two luxurious base lodge complexes at River Run and Warm Springs, a shuttle-bus-ride from most accommodations. Of the 13 lifts, seven are high-speed quads. One reporter complained of 'dangerous icy trails that should have been closed, and trails crossing each other, causing more collisions than I have seen anywhere'. The separate Dollar Mountain has good beginner terrain.
Snowboarding Snowboarders are now allowed and the chair-lifts make getting about easy.
Snow reliability The resort has an erratic natural snow record, so it has installed 600 acres of snowmaking, covering over 70% of the groomable runs.
Experts There are a few tough runs and bowls for experts, but nothing beyond single-black-diamond pitch, including the two most famous bump runs, Exhibition and Limelight. Heli-skiing is available locally.
Intermediates Most of the terrain is ideal, with lots of runs at a similar consistent pitch. There are good blue bowl runs with great views from the top ridge as well as groomed cruisers through the trees.

What's new

Sun Valley's owner Earl Holding has invested millions in high-speed lifts, new runs, a huge computer-controlled snowmaking system and plush on-slope restaurant complexes and base lodges. Currently he is plowing money into his new baby, Snowbasin in Utah, which will host the downhill events in the 2002 Olympics. So development in Sun Valley on hold.

Central reservations phone number
For all resort accommodations call 1 800 634 3347 (toll-free from within the US).

TOURIST OFFICE

Postcode ID 83340
t +1 (208) 726 3423
f 726 4533
ski@sunvalley.com
www.sunvalley.com

Beginners Dollar is the place to be, with gentle, long green runs to progress to. Baldy's greens are tougher.

Cross-country 40km/25 miles of prepared trails start at the Nordic Center, with more along the valley.

Liftlines These are rarely a problem, with Sun Valley's network of high-speed quads whisking people around.

Mountain restaurants The mountain restaurants and base lodges have to be seen to be believed, with floor-to-ceiling windows, beautiful wooden decor, heated terraces so snow instantly melts, and marble public restrooms with gold-plated taps. One reporter enjoyed 'the piano and violin players and people-watching at River Run base' at the end of the day.

Schools and guides We have no reason to believe that the lessons are not up to the usual high standards found in most North American resorts.

Facilities for children The ski school takes children from age 3, and under 16s staying with parents in certain lodgings get a free lift ticket.

STAYING THERE

Shuttle-buses from most accommodations make your choice of location less of an issue.

How to go There are some wonderful smart hotels to stay in, and there are plenty of cheaper options as well, including motels and condos.

Hotels One of our favorite hotels in any resort is the stylish Sun Valley Lodge. As well as magnificent rooms, there are a big outdoor ice rink and a pool, and the corridors are lined with photos of film-star guests. Ernest Hemingway wrote *For Whom the Bell Tolls* here.

Eating out There are over 80 restaurants and Sun Valley was rated number one in the US by readers of *Gourmet* magazine. We had excellent food at the relaxed Evergreen Bistro and a great breakfast at The Knob Hill Inn. A reporter recommends Chandlers, too.

Après-ski Atmospheric places include the Sawtooth Club (popular with locals), Whiskey Jaques for live music and dancing, and the Pioneer Saloon, popular for its prime rib and Clint Eastwood spotting.

Off the slopes You can have a fine time relaxing off the slopes, including sleigh rides, walking, snowmobiling, ice skating, swimming, fishing, gliding, paragliding and strolling round the galleries and shops. There's a special snow-shoe trail, too.

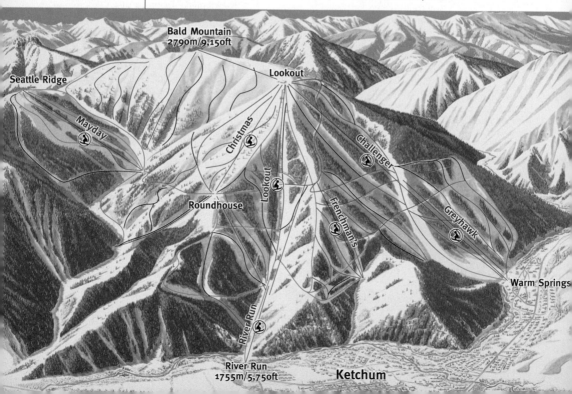

New England

You go to Utah for the deepest snow, to Colorado for the lightest powder and swankiest resorts, to California for the mountains and low prices. You go to New England for ... well, for what? Extreme cold? Rock-hard artificial snow? Mountains too limited to be of interest beyond New Jersey? Yes and no: all of these preconceptions have some basis, but they add up to an incomplete and unfair picture.

Yes, it can be cold: one of our reporters recorded −27°C/−17°F, with wind chill producing a perceived temperature of −73°C/−99°F. Early in the season, people wear face masks to prevent frostbite. It can also be warm – another reporter had a whole week of rain that washed away the early-season snow. The thing about New England weather is that it varies. The locals' favorite expression is: 'If you don't like the weather in New England, wait two minutes.' But we got routine winter weather on both our visits – one in January, one in February.

New England doesn't usually get much super-light powder or deep snow to play in. But the resorts have big snowmaking installations, designed to ensure a long season and to help the slopes to 'recover' after a thaw or spell of rain. They were the pioneers of snowmaking technology; and 'farming' snow, as they put it, is an art form and a way of life – provided the weather is cold enough. And they make and groom their snow to produce a superb surface. Many of the resorts get impressive amounts of natural snow, too – and they did get some huge dumps last season.

Sure, the mountains are not huge in terms of trail mileage. But several have verticals of over 800m/2,600ft (on a par with Colorado resorts such as Keystone) and most have over 600m/2,000ft, and are worth considering for a short stay, or even for a week if you like familiar runs. For more novelty, a two- or three-center trip is the obvious solution. You won't lack challenge – most of the double-black-diamond runs are seriously steep. And you won't lack space: most Americans visit on weekends, which means deserted slopes on weekdays – except at peak periods such as New Year and during the President's Day holiday, in February. It also means the resorts are keen to attract long-stay visitors.

But the big weekend and day-trip trade also means that few New England resorts have developed atmospheric resort villages – just a few condos and a hotel, maybe, with places to stay further out geared to suit car drivers who ski, eat, sleep, ski, go home.

There are some pretty towns to visit, with their clapboard houses and big churches. If you are travelling a long way to ski or snowboard in New

Killington is New England's most impressive resort, at least in terms of its terrain and trails →

England, you might also like to consider spending a day or two in Boston – one of America's most charming cities.

We cover four of the most popular resorts in the separate chapters that follow. But there are many other small areas, too. And if you are going for a week or more, we recommend renting a car and visiting a few resorts. In the rest of this introduction, we outline the attractions of the main possibilities.

From Killington (by far the biggest resort), you can go south to a range of smaller resorts. **Okemo** competes with Smugglers' Notch for the family market. Okemo mountain has southern Vermont's biggest vertical (655m/ 2,150ft) and longest trail (over 7km/4.3 miles). The slopes, on several flanks of a single peak, are largely intermediate or easy – though there are a dozen black runs and a couple of short double-black-diamonds. Boarders are well catered to, with an extensive park leading into a half-pipe. There is almost 100% snowmaking cover – and the product is said to be among the best in the east.

Mount Snow is another one-peak resort, with a long row of lifts on the front face serving easy and intermediate runs of just over 500m/ 1,640ft vertical, and a separate area of black runs on the north face – including one short but serious double-black. (The sister resort of **Haystack**, a short drive away, has more steep slopes in its Witches area.) Mount Snow has a huge snowboard park – one of the best in the east.

Stratton offers something like the classic European arrangement of a village at the foot of the lifts. It's an upscale, modern development with a pedestrian shopping street. The slopes – mostly easy and intermediate, with some blacks and some short double-black pitches – is spread widely around the flanks of a single peak, served by modern lifts, including a 12-person gondola and a fast six-seat chair. Stratton calls itself the 'snowboarding capital of the east', claiming the best terrain park, half-pipe, instruction and (of course) attitude.

You may find more interest in **Sugarbush**, to the north of Killington on the way to Smugglers' Notch.

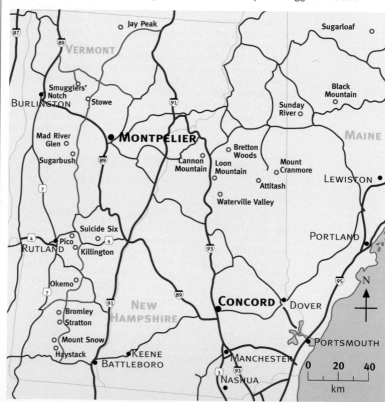

Sugarbush, midway between Killington and Stowe, is a fast-developing resort with one of the larger ski areas. The main sector is an extensive bowl below Lincoln Peak, with lifts up to six points on the rim; a long up-and-over chair-lift links the Mt Ellen area – smaller, but with more altitude and more vertical (808m/2,650ft). The easy skiing is confined to the lower slopes; higher up, the direct runs are seriously steep. There are snowboard parks in both areas. Most of the accommodations are in the historic village of Waitsfield, but the American Skiing Company is building a village at the base.

Mad River Glen next door is a cult resort with local skiers (snowboarding is not allowed), with some tough ungroomed terrain, a few well-groomed intermediate trails and old-fashioned lifts – including an old single-person chair-lift.

Further north, near the Canadian border, is **Jay Peak**. It gets busy at weekends (with Canadian as well as American visitors) but is quiet in the week. It has Vermont's only cable-car, which takes you to the summit and to views of four states plus Canada. It gets a lot of snow for New England and has some good runs for advanced skiers and adventurous intermediates.

Sugarloaf in Maine already has a much better developed village than most small New England resorts. But the mountain is small and a keen trail-basher could ski it out in a day or two. Very popular with day and weekend skiers and boarders, it was very noticeable on our visit how safety conscious the local slope-users were. There was a higher proportion of people wearing protective helmets here than any other resort we have visited – and these included all age groups, from children to octogenarians. Even teenage and twenty-something skiers and boarders were comfortable in their helmets – a sign of things to come elswhere perhaps? Sugarloaf is another resort that is now owned by the American Skiing Company (Killington, Mount Snow, Sugarbush, Sunday River and Attitash Bear Peak are its other New England resorts).

New Hampshire has several small resorts dotted along the Interstate 93 highway. **Bretton Woods** is one of the smaller areas, 460m/1,510ft vertical on a single mountain face, but it is highly rated, particularly by families, who relish the top-to-bottom easy trails.

There is a good mix of terrain, and snowmaking is comprehensive. Snowboarders have a park and a half-pipe. There are a few places to stay near the base, with more five miles away at Twin Mountain.

Cannon is a ski area and nothing more – lifts from two base areas close to I-93 converge on the summit 650m/2,130ft above, serving mainly intermediate slopes; there are quite a few black runs, but no double-blacks and not much that is genuinely easy. It's only a few minutes' drive to Franconia in one direction and Lincoln in the other.

Loon Mountain Resort is a small, smart, modern resort just outside the sprawling town of Lincoln. The mountain (640m/2,100ft vertical) is mostly of intermediate difficulty, though some fall-line runs merit their black grading. There is a large snowboard park.

Waterville Valley is a compact area with runs dropping either side of a broad, gentle ridge rising 615m/2,020ft above the lift base. There are a couple of short but genuine double-black-diamond bump fields, but most of the slopes are intermediate. Boarders are well catered to. The village is a Disneyesque affair a couple of miles away down on the flat valley bottom.

Killington

670m/2,200ft

Good slopes, great après-ski, no village (yet)

HOW IT RATES

The slopes

Snow	***
Extent	**
Experts	***
Intermediates	***
Beginners	****
Convenience	*
Liftlines	****
Restaurants	*

The rest

Scenery	***
Resort charm	**
Off-slope	*

What's new

Killington has grand plans for a resort village at the Snowshed lift base, where the Grand Resort Hotel and Conference Center were built a couple of years back – work is due to start in summer 2001.

Following a couple of very bad seasons for natural snow, snowmaking was increased by 30% for 2000/01.

434

➕ The biggest mountain in the East, matching some Colorado resorts, with terrain to suit everyone

➕ Lively après-ski, with lots of bar-restaurants offering happy hours and late-night action

➕ Excellent beginner areas

➕ Comprehensive and very effective snowmaking

➕ Good childcare, although it's not a notably child-oriented resort

➖ No resort village: hotels, condos and restaurants are widely spread, mostly along the five-mile access road – a car is almost a necessity

➖ New England weather – highly changeable and can be very cold

➖ The trail network is complex, and there are lots of trail-crossings

➖ Boring for anyone who is not a skier or boarder

It's difficult to ignore Killington. It claims to have the largest mountain in the East (whether gauged in trail length, accessible area, vertical drop or top altitude), the largest number of quad chairs in the East, the world's biggest snowmaking installation and the East's largest grooming fleet. (As a result it claims to have the longest season in the East – it tries to be the first resort in America to open, in October, but often shuts again shortly after.) It also claims to have America's longest lift and longest trail (a winding 16km/10 miles for a drop of 960m/3,150ft) and New England's steepest bump slope (Outer Limits – 800m/2,620ft long for a drop of 370m/1,210ft). Impressive, by local standards.

A slope-side village is only now starting to take shape at the lift base, but even when it is completed, for most visitors life will continue to revolve around driving. But once you get used to that, it's not an unpleasant place. The vibrant nightspots weigh in the balance, even for us: in the early evening they're lively places to eat, even if you're visiting with kids.

The main problem, in the end, is the unpredictable New England weather.

The resort

Most of Killington's hotels and restaurants are spread along a five-mile approach road. The nearest thing you'll find to a focus is the occasional set of traffic lights with a cluster of shops, though there is a concentration of buildings along a two-and-a-half mile stretch of the road. The resort caters mainly to day and weekend visitors who drive in from the East-Coast cities (including a lot of New Yorkers). The car is king; provided you have one, getting around isn't that much of a hassle. There's also a good free shuttle-bus service during the day – it costs a dollar after 5pm.

A new resort village is slowly taking shape around Snowshed, one of the main lift bases. Practically all the other lodges are a drive from a lift station – either this one or the Skyeship gondola station on the main Highway

100, leading past the resort. Staying near the end of the access road is convenient for this and for outings to Pico, a separate little mountain owned by Killington, to be linked one day to Killington's Ram's Head mountain.

The mountains

Runs spread over a series of wooded peaks, all quite close together but giving the resort a basis for claiming to cover six mountains – or seven if you count Pico. A huge number of runs and impressive number of lifts are crammed into a modest area. The result is a very complex network of runs, and signs aren't always very clear. To some extent the terrain on its six sectors suits different standards. But there are also areas where a mixed ability group would be quite happy, and there are easy runs from top to bottom of each peak. Some runs of all

MOUNTAIN FACTS

Altitude	325m-1285m
	1,070ft-4,220ft
Lifts	32
Trails	1,182 acres
Green	30%
Blue	39%
Black	31%
Snowmaking	
	752 acres

LIFT TICKETS

2001/02 prices in dollars

Killington Mountain Ticket

Covers all lifts in the Killington and Pico ski areas.

Beginners See Schools/Guides

Main ticket

1-day ticket 58

6-day ticket 276

Senior citizens

Over 64: 6-day ticket 168

Children

Under 6: free

6-12: 6-day ticket 168

13-18: 6-day ticket 240

levels are left to form bumps; there is half-and-half grooming on selected trails; and terrain features – ridges, bumps, quarter-pipes – are created.

Killington has also created areas that are called Fusion Zones – thinned-out forest areas, where you pick your own line. These areas are not groomed or patrolled – and they come in blue and single- and double-black-diamond grades. We found them great fun.

The trail map is one of the largest and most fact-packed we've ever come across. But this makes it unwieldy and awkward to handle.

THE SLOPES
Complicated

The Killington Base area has chairs radiating to three of the six peaks – **Snowdon**, **Killington** (the high-point of the area) and **Skye** – the last also accessible by gondola starting beside US Highway 4. Novices and families head for the other main base area, which has two parts: Snowshed, at the foot of the main beginner slope, served by several parallel chairs; and Rams Head, just across the road up to Killington Base, where there's a Family Center at the foot of the entirely gentle **Rams Head** mountain.

The two remaining peaks are behind Skye Peak; they can be reached by trails from Killington and Skye, but each also has a lift base accessible by road. **Bear Mountain** is the expert's hill, served by two quad chairs from its mid-mountain base area. The sixth 'peak', **Sunrise**, is a slight blip on the mountainside, with a short triple chair

up from the Sunrise Village condos area. The area below Sunrise Village is used for snowmobile tours – from the old lift base just off Highway 4.

SNOW RELIABILITY
Good if it's cold

Killington has a good snowfall record and a huge snowmaking system. But even that is no good if temperatures are too high to operate it. Bad weather can ruin a vacation even in mid-season. A reporter who had new powder each night in March 1999 went back at the same time in 2000 to find people skiing in shorts and T-shirts on the few runs that were open. A February visitor told of 'everything from frostbite to pouring rain'.

FOR EXPERTS
Some challenges

The main areas that experts head for are Killington Peak, where there is a handful of genuine double-diamond fall-line runs under the two chair-lifts, and Bear Mountain. Most of the slopes here are single blacks but Outer Limits, under the main quad chair, is a double-diamond claimed to be 'the steepest bump slope in the East'. We suspect there are steeper runs at Stowe and Smugglers' Notch. There are two or three worthwhile blacks on Snowdon, too. The Fusion Zones on Skye and Snowdon are well worth seeking out. But one reporter thought many of the black runs overrated: 'Some would be red in Europe and comfortably skied by an intermediate.'

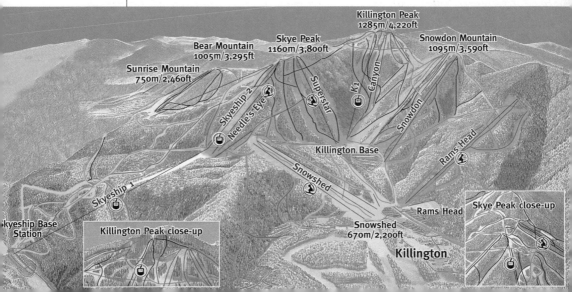

435

SCHOOLS/GUIDES

2001/02 prices in dollars
Perfect Turn clinics
7 days
2hr: from 9.30, 10.15, or 1.30: 31
Learn to ski clinics
(incl lift ticket, equipment and use of Discovery Center)
1 day: 65
3 days: 150
Children's classes
Ages: 4 to 6 (incl lift ticket)
half day: 8.30-12
noon or 12.30-4pm: 59
full day: 89
Ages: 7 to 12 (excl lift ticket)
half day: 9.30-11.30 or 1pm-3pm: 71
full day: 101
Private lessons
1hr, 2hr, half or full day
78 for 1hr (115 for 2 people)
202 for half day of 3hr (270 for 2 people)

CHILDCARE

A Family Center at Rams Head was built a few years ago. The Friendly Penguin nursery takes kids from age six weeks to six years – reservations required. Outside the door is the Snow Play Park, with magic carpet lift and handle tow-lift. There are ski classes for several age groups.

FOR INTERMEDIATES
Navigation problems?

There are lots of easy cruising blue and green runs all over the slopes, except on Bear Mountain, where the single blacks present a little more of a challenge for intermediates. Snowdon is a splendid area for those who like to vary their diet. There's a blue-rated Fusion Zone on Rams Head. Finding your way around the complicated network of trails may be tricky, though. One reporter liked Pico a lot but complained that the blue run down was more difficult than some blacks.

FOR BEGINNERS
Splendid

The facilities for complete beginners are excellent. The Snowshed slope is one vast beginner area served by three chair-lifts and a very slow surface lift. Rams Head also has excellent gentle slopes. The ski school runs a special, purpose-built Discovery Center just for first-time skiers and boarders – they introduce you to the equipment, show you videos and provide refreshments.

FOR CROSS-COUNTRY
Two main options

Extensive cross-country loops are available at two specialist 'resorts' – Mountain Meadows down on US Highway 4, and Mountain Top Ski Touring, a short drive away at Chittenden.

LIFTLINES
Weekend crowds

Killington gets a lot of weekend and public holiday business, but at other times the slopes and lifts are likely to be quiet. One New Year reporter told of 'a madhouse with overcrowded slopes, and a 20-minute crawl up the access road', and the gondola to Killington Peak and the Rams Head chair can get crowded. Overcrowded slopes are more of a problem than liftlines.

MOUNTAIN RESTAURANTS
Bearable base lodges

There are only two real mountain restaurants. We have mixed reports on the one at the top of Killington Peak, in what was the top station of the old gondola. Max's Place, on Sunrise, has table-service burgers, pasta, salad etc, and is highly recommended by a reporter for 'escaping the squalor of the other on-mountain eating places'. Each of the lift base stations has an eatery, of which the one at Killington Base Lodge is the least dreary and crowded.

SCHOOLS AND GUIDES
In search of the Perfect Turn

The philosophy of the Perfect Turn school is to build on your strengths rather than correct your mistakes, and it seems to work for most people. There is a special Discovery Center for beginners, where you start and finish in a dedicated building with easy chairs, coffee, videos and help with choosing and fitting your equipment.

FACILITIES FOR CHILDREN
Fine in practice

There is a Family Center at the Rams Head base, which takes kids from six weeks and will introduce them to skiing from age two years. The editorial daughter is a graduate of this institution and approves of it.

Staying there

HOW TO GO
Wide choices

There is a wide choice of places to stay.
Hotels There are a few places near the lifts, but most are a drive or bus-ride away, down Killington Road or on US4.
(((4 **Cortina Inn** 20 minutes away on US4, near Pico; pool, 'excellent food, but poor soundproofing'.
(((4 **Grand Resort** Swanky resort-owned place at Snowshed, with outdoor pool and health club.

---

boarding *A cool resort like Killington has to take boarding seriously, and it does. There are three terrain-parks, a super-pipe and a boarder-cross course. And there are terrain features scattered around the area, and parts of the mountain have been reshaped to cut out some of the unpleasant flats on contouring green runs. Several big-name board events are held here. For less competent boarders, there are excellent beginner slopes, and plenty of friendly high-speed (ie slow-loading) chair-lifts – and the Perfect Turn Discovery Center caters just to beginners.*

There are now some accommodations close to the lifts (this is the Rams Head chair), and it is set to increase →

Central reservations phone number
For all resort accommodations call 1 800 621 6867 (toll-free from within the US).

GETTING THERE

Air Boston, transfer 2½hr.

ACTIVITIES

Indoor Killington Grand Resort Hotel has massage, fitness center, outdoor pool, hot-tub, sauna, aerobics. movie theaters and bowling at Rutland
Outdoor Skating, floodlit tubing and snowboarding, sledding, sleigh rides, cross-country, snowshoe tours

TOURIST OFFICE

Postcode VT 05751
t +1 (802) 422 3333
f 422 4391
info@killington.com
www.killington.com

Inn of the Six Mountains Couple of miles down Killington Road; 'spacious rooms, good pool'.
Red Rob Inn Short drive from slopes – 'good restaurant, a cut above the usual motel style'.
North Star Lodge Well down Killington Road; 'good budget accommodations'.

EATING OUT
You name it

There are all sorts of restaurants spread along the Killington Road, from simple pizza or pasta through to 'fine dining' places. They get very crowded on weekends and many don't take reservations. Many of the nightspots mentioned below serve food for at least part of the evening.

The local menu guide is essential reading. Claude's Choices, the Grist Mill, Charity's and the Cortina and Red Rob Inns have been recommended by recent reporters.

APRES-SKI
The beast of the east

Killington has a well-deserved reputation for a vibrant après-ski scene; many of its short-stay visitors are clearly intent on making the most of their few days (or nights) here.

Although there are bars at the base lodges, keen après-skiers head down Killington Road to one of the lively places scattered along its five-mile length. From 3pm it's cheap drinks and free munchies, then in the early evening it's serious dining time, then later on the real action starts (and admission charges kick in). Most of the places mentioned here would also rate a mention in Eating Out.

The train-themed Casey's Caboose is said to have the best 'wings' in town. Charity's is another lively bar, with an interior apparently lifted from a turn-of-the-century Parisian brothel. The Wobbly Barn is a famous live-music place that rivals Jackson's Mangy Moose for the position of America's leading après-ski venue. The Pickle Barrel caters to a younger crowd, with theme nights and loud music. The Outback complex has something for everyone, from pizzas and free massages to disco and live bands.

OFF THE SLOPES
Rent a car

If there is a less amusing resort in which to spend time doing things other than skiing or boarding, we have yet to find it. Make sure you have a car, as well as a book.

Fine fun for families

HOW IT RATES

The slopes

Snow	***
Extent	*
Experts	***
Intermediates	***
Beginners	****
Convenience	*****
Liftlines	****
Restaurants	*

The rest

Scenery	***
Resort charm	**
Off-slope	*

➕ Excellent children's facilities

➕ Lots of slope-side accommodations

➕ Varied slopes with runs for all abilities

➕ Link to Stowe, over the hill

➕ No liftlines

➕ Great for beginners, with excellent ski school

➖ Family orientation may be too much for some

➖ New England weather – highly changeable, and can be very cold

➖ Limited local slopes

➖ No proper mountain restaurants

➖ No hotels – condos only

➖ No après-ski atmosphere

➖ Few off-slope diversions

Smuggs hits the family target squarely, with a constant round of early-evening activities, sympathetic instructors, comprehensive childcare, a generally child-friendly layout and some long, quiet, easy runs. There are challenging slopes, too, but mileage-hungry intermediates should go elsewhere.

What's new

Snowmaking was extended by 40% for 2000/01 and a new water reservoir will increase the capacity further for 2001/02.

Four new gladed trails were opened on Sterling Mountain last season and two more are planned for 2001/02.

The construction of new condos goes on.

438

THE RESORT

Smugglers' Notch is about the nearest thing you'll find in the US to a French-style purpose-built family resort – except that it doesn't look so bad. The village isn't genuinely traffic-free – you may have to tangle with traffic to get to the childcare center, even – but it comes close, and once installed in your condo you can happily do without a car (much of the accommodations are near to or on the slopes). Those not afflicted with children could find the family orientation of the resort a bit overpowering: you may find it's difficult to get away from Billy Bob Bear and pals.

The resort is energetically managed and produces a constant flow of developments designed to tighten its grip on the market. Yet again it has been voted 'North American family resort of the year' by at least one American skiing publication.

THE MOUNTAIN

Smuggs has varied and satisfying slopes, spread over three hills – Morse, above the village (with the newish Morse Highlands area off to the left), and Madonna and Sterling off to the right, reached by green links.

Slopes There are some real challenges as well as easy cruising, and a worthwhile vertical of 800m/2,610ft. It's blissfully quiet on the mountain except on weekends and holidays. It's undeniably a small area, though. You can get to Stowe's Spruce Peak by an intermediate trail from the top of Sterling, and guests staying two nights or more get a free day in Stowe.

Snow reliability Snow reliability is good, subject to the inherent variability of New England weather. And the snowmaking is being further improved.

Beginners It's a great area for beginners. One of the chair-lifts out of the village runs at half speed, and the

SMUGGLERS' NOTCH

We never saw this many people on one trail when we visited Smuggs →

MOUNTAIN FACTS

Altitude	315m-1110m/
	1,030ft-3,640ft
Lifts	9
Trails	1,000 acres
Green	22%
Blue	53%
Black	25%
Snowmaking	
	159 acres

TOURIST OFFICE

Postcode
VT 05464-9537
t +1 (802) 644 8851
f 644 2713
smuggs@smuggs.com
www.smuggs.com

runs it accesses are of an ideal gradient. Morse Highlands adds another tailor-made novice area. And the higher lifts take you to long easy runs that even 'never-evers' can tackle during their first week.

Intermediates There are intermediate runs of every type; there just aren't many of them. The link with Stowe adds variety.

Experts There are challenges for experts. We were impressed by the two or three double-diamond runs on Madonna, and they have recently opened The Black Hole – the only triple-diamond run in the east, they say. You can go off through the trees anywhere within the resort boundary – but these areas are not patrolled.

Snowboarding Smuggs encourages snowboarding; it has impressive terrain-parks and a half-pipe.

Cross-country The 23km/15 miles of trails may be a bit limited for experts.

Liftlines We encountered no lines, and apart from weekends we'd be surprised if anyone else did.

Mountain restaurants There are no real mountain restaurants, but there is a new warming hut with snacks at the top of the Prohibition Park half-pipe and the new lodge at Morse Highlands serves food. Most people go back to base for lunch.

Schools and guides At least one reporter judges the ski school (or 'Snow Sport University') to be 'outstanding', and it has often been voted the best in North America.

Among its bright ideas are private lessons for a parent and child, with the idea that the parent learns how to help the child develop while having fun.

Facilities for children Smuggs aims to be simply the best for children. The mountain is child-friendly, offering excitement with safety – with a special kids' trail map. There's a terrain park for kids, and little forest glades where even pre-schoolers can be taken 'off-trail'. Alice's Wonderland Child Enrichment Center is a comprehensive nursery. The school arrangements are very good, too, with childcare before and after sessions, and carriage to the kids' chair-lift by horse-drawn sleigh.

STAYING THERE

How to go There are no hotels in the resort itself – though there are some within driving distance.

Apartments/condos There are lots of comfortable condos on or near the slopes, none very far from the snow.

Eating out There are a couple of restaurants in the resort, including the cozy Hearth and Candle, and others a short drive down the road to the outside world – we and the kids enjoyed an outing to Banditos. Babysitters can be arranged.

Après-ski The adult après-ski possibilities are about the most limited we have come across. We hear good reports of the teen center.

Off the slopes There is very little to do off the slopes. Organized day tours of Vermont or to Montreal are possible.

Madonna Mountain
1110m/3,640ft

Sterling Mountain
925m/3,040ft

Stowe

Mid Station

Morse Mountain
685m/2,250ft

Mid Stations

Morse
Highlands

Smugglers' Notch
315m/1,030ft

Stowe

475m/1,560ft

Charming Vermont town, small but serious mountain

➕ Cute tourist town in classic New England style

➕ Some good slopes for all abilities, including serious challenges

➕ Few liftlines

➕ Link to Smugglers' Notch, over the hill

➕ Excellent cross-country trails

➕ Great children's facilities

➖ Town is a shuttle-bus or short drive from the slopes

➖ One of the mountains is a short shuttle-bus-ride from the other two

➖ New England weather – highly changeable, and can be very cold

➖ Limited local slopes

➖ Weekend liftlines

➖ No après-ski atmosphere

Stowe is one of New England's cutest little towns, its main street lined with dinky clapboard shops and restaurants; you could find no sharper contrast to the other New England resorts we feature. Its mountain, six miles away, is another New England classic: something for everyone, but not much of it.

What's new

The new Burton Method Center has created a 'Learn to Ride' program involving new teaching techniques and special beginner equipment.

STOWE MOUNTAIN RESORT / LANDEWEHRLE STUDIO

Stowe is a picture-postcard town ↓

THE RESORT

Stowe is a picture-postcard New England town – a real community and a popular spot for tourists year-round, with cute little 'specialty' shops lining its sidewalks and more 3- and 4-diamond hotels and restaurants than any other place in New England except Boston. The slopes of Mount Mansfield, Vermont's snow-capped (though mainly wooded) highest peak, are a 15-minute drive away and much of the resort's accommodations are along the road out to it. There's a good day-time shuttle-bus service but a car is recommended for flexibility.

THE MOUNTAIN

There are three different sectors, two linked by blue runs mid-mountain and green ones at the base, the third (Spruce Peak) a short shuttle-ride away (there are plans for a lift link, but it's not imminent).

Slopes The main sector, served by a trio of chair-lifts from Mansfield Base Lodge, is dominated by the famous Front Four – a row of seriously steep double-black-diamond runs. But there is plenty of easier stuff, too, including long green runs down to the alternative lift base at Toll House.

A fast eight-seat gondola serves the next sector: easy-intermediate runs with one black alternative – plus the short but very steep Waterfall, under the gondola at the top.

The third area, Spruce Peak, has the main beginner area at the bottom, with a slow chair-lift to mid-mountain and another beyond that. 'Possibly the slowest chairs in the world,' says a reporter. The top of this sector links with Smugglers' Notch, over the hill, though the link isn't widely used – it's not particularly easy and involves a walk or scoot across a frozen lake. Guests staying for two nights or more get a free day at Smuggs.

There are free daily mountain tours with a mountain host.

Snowboarding Stowe attracts many snowboarders and has two terrain-parks and a half-pipe. Beginners learn on special customized boards at the Burton Method Center on Spruce Peak.

Snow reliability Snow reliability is helped by snowmaking on practically all the blue (and some black) runs of the main sectors, and on lower Spruce Peak.

Experts The Front Four and their

MOUNTAIN FACTS

Altitude	390m-1110m
	1,280ft-3,640ft
Lifts	11
Trails	480 acres
Green	16%
Blue	59%
Black	25%
Snowmaking	
	350 acres

Central reservations phone number
For all resort accommodation call
1 877 317 8693
(toll-free from within the US)

TOURIST OFFICE

Postcode VT 05672
t +1 (802) 253 3500
f 253 3406
info@stowe.com
www.stowe.com

variants on the top half of the main sector present a real challenge.

Intermediates The usual New England reservation applies: the terrain is limited in extent; there's also a severe shortage of ordinary black runs (as opposed to double diamonds).

Beginners The beginner areas and long green runs are great. 'Spruce Peak is one of the best beginner/early skier areas we've seen,' says a report. Progression to longer green runs means moving over to Mount Mansfield, where there are splendid long greens down to Toll House.

Cross-country There are excellent cross-country centers scattered around the landscape (including the musically famous Trapp Family Lodge), with lots of connected trails – 35km/22 miles of groomed and 40km/25 miles of back country trails.

Liftlines The area is largely free of lines mid-week but we've had reports of 25-minute liftlines at weekends.

Mountain restaurants Cliff House, at the top of the gondola, is a lofty room with table-service and good food and views. Midway Café near the base of the gondola has a BBQ deck and table-service inside. The Octagon Web Café, at the top of the main sector, is a small cafeteria.

Schools and guides A recent reporter was disappointed by the ski school – but this was partly because he had a different instructor every day, which is common in the US.

Facilities for children There are excellent facilities and the nursery takes children from age six months to six years.

STAYING THERE

How to go There are hotels in and around Stowe itself and various points along the road to the slopes, some with Austrian or Scandinavian names and styles.

Hotels 1066 Ye Olde England Inne is recommended by reporters (despite the appalling name). Stowehof Inn and Green Mountain Inn are also recommended. The smart Inn at the Mountain, at the Toll House lift base of Mount Mansfield, provides the only slope-side accommodations, with chair-lift access to the main sector of slopes.

Apartments/condos There is a reasonable range of condos available for rent.

Eating out There are restaurants of every kind. The Cliff House at the top of the gondola is open for dinner.

Après-ski Après-ski is muted – Stowe reportedly goes to bed early. There's a good movie theater with new releases.

Off the slopes Stowe is a pleasant town in which to spend time off the slopes – at least if you like shopping. A trip to the Burlington shopping mall is recommended (you need a car).

Sunday River

The biggest snowmaking system in New England

HOW IT RATES

The slopes

Snow	***
Extent	**
Experts	**
Intermediates	****
Beginners	****
Convenience	***
Liftlines	****
Restaurants	***

The rest

Scenery	***
Resort charm	**
Off-slope	*

➕ Some convenient slope-side accommodations

➕ Some good runs for all abilities

➕ Decent natural snow record with extensive snowmaking

➕ Lots of scope for cross-country skiing in the area

➕ No lines

➖ Scattered slope-side developments mean no village atmosphere

➖ Relatively small slopes

➖ No real mountain restaurants

➖ Quiet après-ski scene

➖ Limited off-slope diversions

Sunday River was one of the pioneers of snowmaking, and over 90% of its trails are served by it. So the snow should be as good here as anywhere in the East. The terrain is varied and quite extensive. But it lacks village ambience.

What's new

For the 2000/01 season a new terrain-park called Nebula – claimed to be 'the largest in the East'. It is designed for expert skiers and riders looking to catch big air and perform aerial tricks.

For 2001/02 the half-pipe is being made into an 18-feet-deep superpipe. More snowmaking guns are due to be added too.

442

THE RESORT

Sunday River is where the American Skiing Company (which owns eight other US resorts) started and where it still has its HQ. Despite this, there isn't really a slope-side village yet – there are various developments scattered around the slopes – so there isn't much village ambience.

The plan is for the area around the Jordan Grand hotel to become the focus of the resort with shops, bars, restaurants, theater, nightclub and even a village green and pond. For now, Bethel is the nearest small town, a 10-minute drive away; it's a pleasant place with a few shops and a handful of restaurants and bars.

THE MOUNTAINS

The slopes range over about 5km/3 miles from east to west and across eight different peaks. It does feel like a reasonably extensive network of trails and glades – 127 at the last count – and there are numerous base areas,

parking lots and accommodations scattered around.

Slopes The White Cap base marks the eastern extremity of the system and is handy for the Grand Summit hotel, the half-pipe and other evening activities. The peaks around the main base areas are fairly packed with lifts and trails. The Jordan Grand hotel is at the western limit of the system, and in general the western sector (Aurora, Oz and Jordan Bowl) has far fewer lifts and runs and a more remote and backwoods feel.

Snow reliability Snow reliability is good: a decent natural snow record is backed up by a high-capacity, high-tech system for making and grooming machine-made stuff. Last season was a vintage one for natural snow.

Experts There are challenging narrow, often bumped double-blacks on White Cap and Barker Mountain, and there is excellent glade skiing on Aurora, Oz and Jordan Bowl. Indeed, 40% of the trails are graded black.

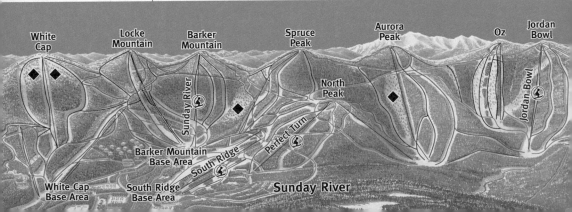

↑ Sunday River's trails spread right along the slopes of eight linked peaks, with lots of car parking for day visitors

SUNDAY RIVER / NORM HERSOM

MOUNTAIN FACTS

Altitude	245m-955m/ 800ft-3,140ft
Lifts	18
Trails	660 acres
Green	25%
Blue	35%
Black	40%
Snowmaking	
	607 acres

Central reservations phone number
For all resort accommodations call 1 800 543 2754 (toll-free from within the US)

TOURIST OFFICE
Postcode ME 04217
t +1 (207) 824 3000
f 824 5110
snowtalk@sunday river.com
www.sundayriver.com

Intermediates It's generally a good resort for intermediates who will enjoy cruising around on a series of nice rolling blues (often deserted in mid-week). There are some not too fearsome glades to tempt the bold.

Beginners South Ridge is a well-organized area for beginners, with good, easy runs to progress to.

Snowboarding Boarders will find no fewer than five terrain parks (including the largest in the eastern US, called Nebula) and three half-pipes (including a competition standard one, which is floodlit for evening use). For 2001/02 the half-pipe is to be made even bigger and promoted to superpipe status.

Cross-country In and around Bethel there are three cross-country centers with a total of around 140km/90 miles of trails.

Liftlines Mid-week lines are non-existent – indeed most lifts and slopes are deserted. Even on busy weekends you should be okay if you stick to the four high-speed quads.

Mountain restaurants There are no real mountain restaurants, but there are good, civilized table-service places at the Jordan Grand and Grand Summit hotels as well as the usual self-service places.

Schools and guides Ski school is not a term they use at Sunday River but there is a series of 'Perfect Turn' clinics available. A reporter who took a group of 40 schoolchildren in February said the ski instructors were 'overstretched at but still superb, and one even

bought his class baseball caps'.

Facilities for children The Grand Summit and South Ridge Center house the main children's facilities. There's also a family entertainment center called the White Cap (see Après-ski).

STAYING THERE

There are some slope-side accommodations but many people prefer to stay in Bethel – a 10-minute drive from the ski area.

How to go There are numerous inns, lodges, motels and B&Bs in and around Bethel.

Hotels The main slope-side hotels are the Jordan Grand and the Grand Summit. There's a dorm as well as normal rooms at the Snow Cap Inn.

Apartments/condos The Brookside condos have been recommended. There are plenty of others too.

Après-ski Après-ski in Sunday River is quiet. Bumps pub often has live bands. A recent reporter recommends the Foggy Goggle bar, which also has live music, and the Matterhorn Steak Bar in Bethel (large steaks, local beers, good atmosphere). There are two brew pubs. The White Cap Fun Center has floodlit tubing, sledding and ice skating. There are guided snow-shoe tours on two evenings a week. And there's a games arcade.

Eating out There's a handful of restaurants in Bethel.

Off the slopes Apart from the likes of snowmobiling, tubing, ice-fishing and swimming, there are a few antique and craft shops.

The winter of 2000/01 was exceptional for Canada. While the eastern resorts in Québec got hammered with frequent snowstorms, the western resorts of Alberta and British Columbia had their worst year for snow in living memory. We took a trip through eight western resorts during the February 2001 snow drought, and the locals were moaning like mad about conditions. But compared with a normal year in the Alps the snow on the groomed runs was just fine in most places. What we missed was gliding through knee-deep powder – something that is normally an everyday experience in western Canada. That's what Canada in a normal season is all about to us: deep, deep, snow and lots of it. That plus the North American service culture that is missing in Europe. Plus the spectacular mountain scenery that is missing in the US. Plus great value for money because of the weak Canadian dollar.

A few seasons ago we drove from Whistler to Banff, stopping by lots of smaller resorts on the way. The whole trip took two weeks and for eight consecutive days in the middle it snowed. It snowed and snowed and snowed. It made driving from resort to resort tricky as we insisted on driving at night after getting in a full day on the slopes. But the skiing was spectacular – day after day of dry, light powder. That's a normal winter in western Canada.

In an average year Whistler, for example, gets 360 inches of snow and it snows (or rains at resort level!) for half the days in the season. When you reach Banff–Lake Louise you might not get quite the same frequency of snow, but it stays in great condition because it is further inland, the air is drier and temperatures are colder. You get a better chance of blue skies there – but also a higher chance of a day or two of very low temperatures of –20°C/ –4°F or less.

So you go to western Canada for the skiing or boarding, not the sunbathing. If you prefer long lunches on sun-drenched restaurant terraces, stick to March in the Alps. If you want a good chance of hitting powder, put Canada high on your list of possible destinations.

If you really want untracked powder and are feeling rich, there is nothing to beat Canada's amazing heli- and snowcat skiing operations. The main difference is that the former is faster paced and more expensive than the latter. But with both, you are taken to the middle of nowhere in a deserted mountain wilderness and then let loose with a guide who takes you down untracked slopes to another spot in the middle of nowhere, where you are picked up and taken to the top of another mountain and another untracked run. And so it goes on! You can do it by the day, but the hedonistic luxury option is to book a few days or a week in a luxury lodge run by the heli-skiing or snowcat operation, eating gourmet dinners and stepping out of the door each morning straight into the chopper or snowcat.

If you can't afford the US$4,000 plus a week that this would cost, you can always try a day for US$300 plus. But if you resist heli-skiing or snowcat heaven, you'll find a holiday in Canada can be very affordable, largely because of the weak Canadian dollar.

In the west you'll also find spectacular scenery and an amazing variety of wildlife, especially in the Banff and Jasper areas and in the interior of British Columbia.

For us, the main attraction of eastern Canada is that the resorts are in the heart of the province of Québec, where the French influence is predominant – language, cuisine and culture are all dominated by French-Canadians and it makes for a unique ambience. But it does have the disadvantage of extremes of weather.

Western Canada

For international visitors to Canada, the main draw is the west. It has fabulous scenery, good snow and a wonderful sense of the great outdoors. We have full chapters on the three resorts best established on the international market (Whistler, Banff and Lake Louise) and five smaller resorts. But there are lots of other worthwhile smaller resorts that more adventurous travelers are now starting to explore. We recommend renting a car and combining two or more of these resorts, perhaps with a couple of days on virgin powder served by helicopters or snowcats as well. You'll have the vacation of a lifetime.

Our map shows the area we're covering in this section.

Five of the smaller resorts where you're most likely to want to stay for a while now get their own chapters. Big White is BC's highest ski area, and second in size to Whistler. It has a reputation for powder, and the small slope-side village is developing fast. Access isn't easy unless you fly into Kelowna airport. Fernie, in the same ownership as Lake Louise, has a deserved reputation for great powder and is fast developing. Jasper is a spectacular three-hour drive from Lake Louise through the Banff and Jasper National Parks; the ski area of Marmot Basin is a 30-minute drive from the tiny town. Panorama, in the same ownership as Whistler, has a big

vertical and an attractive village developing at the foot of the slopes. Kicking Horse is the new kid on the block. Formerly known as Whitetooth, the mountain has been transformed by the installation of a single-stage gondola serving a vertical of 1,150m/ 3,775ft – possibly a world record. With an impressive snow record to boot, this is a coming place. But at present you have to stay down in Golden.

There are quite a few other resorts that you might want to include in a tour of this area.

Kimberley Alpine Resort is the most accessible – about 90 minutes from Fernie and three hours from Banff. Like Fernie, it's a recent addition to the portfolio of Resorts of the Canadian Rockies, owners of Lake Louise.

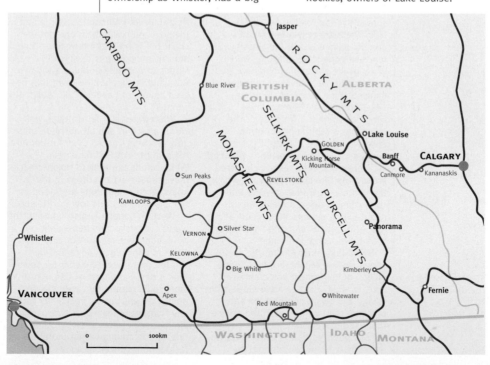

At the mountain there are in practice two base areas. The original one is not quite at the bottom of the hill; there are two old chairs and a T-bar here (though they are no longer regularly used), and a range of lodgings including the 'lovely' NorthStar Chalets (condos). On the flat ground below this, a new village is being built, served by a new fast quad that is now the resort's staple lift. This set-up may work eventually, but at present it requires everyone using the new chair to descend a steep, traffic-polished and congested final slope to the lower level. Not ideal.

The new village is at present very limited, but includes the comfortable and very convenient Trickle Creek Residence Inn by Marriott (catchy, eh?), the 'superb' Polaris condos and a couple of restaurants.

The town of Kimberley, about five minutes' drive away, is known for its synthetic and indescribably tasteless 'Bavarian theme', but is reported to contain some good restaurants.

Kimberley's terrain offers a mix of blue and black runs (plus the occasional green) and a vertical of 700m/2,300ft. In addition to the lifts up the front there are basically two other slow chairs (one is a double discarded from Lake Louise). The runs – all in forest of varying density – are spread over two rather featureless hills. There are only a few short double-diamonds, but the classification tends to understate difficulty, and many of the single-diamonds are quite challenging. We – and our reporters – enjoyed some excellent skiing on deserted runs last winter, when conditions were far from ideal; the resort has a reputation for good powder, although it doesn't get huge amounts. Further expansion is planned.

There are several resorts clustered around the Okanagan valley, of which Big White is one. Probably the least compelling is **Apex**, a family-oriented resort with a modern mini-resort at the foot of its slopes and good views from the top, 610m/2,000ft higher.

Sun Peaks, near Kamloops, was known as Tod Mountain. Now C$100 million of investment has created a cute, car-free, Tirolean-style slope-side village and good intermediate and beginner terrain to go with the steeps that used to dominate. The 880m/2,900ft vertical is claimed to be the biggest in the BC interior; the

mountain, open at the top and densely wooded lower down, has a balance of blue and black runs at top and bottom and a couple of areas of genuinely double-black stuff. Novices are safely tucked away on their own hill.

Silver Star, above the town of Vernon, is a newly developed 'gaslight-era' 1890s-style village right on the slopes. The wooded mountain has two separate but linked faces: the south face around the village has mainly easy and intermediate slopes served by a fast quad of 480m/1,570ft vertical; the back north face is a splendid wooded bowl of easy runs along the rim and black and double-black trails dropping into the middle to meet the 630m/ 2,070ft vertical fast quad.

Finally, there are a couple of resorts tucked away in the mountains close to the US border.

Red Mountain is up there with Fernie and other cult powder paradises in our estimation. There are green and red runs, but it's the black and double-black stuff that is the real attraction, coupled with superb powder. We loved the terrain here – mostly in trees, and as steep as you can handle. Granite Mountain is a conical peak with more-or-less separate faces of blue, black and double-black steepness, and a total vertical of 880m/2,890ft – all served by a couple of triple chairs. Next-door Red Mountain itself is half the size and has only a lone double chair, but is no less interesting. There are accommodations close to the slopes or a couple of miles away in Rossland, a simple little town that has bred countless Canadian ski racers. No wonder.

Whitewater, not far away, is well worth a look in and an absolute must after a storm. Tucked even further into the ranges than Red Mountain, Whitewater's bottomless powder elicits rave responses from those in the know. Accommodations are found in the charming historic town of Nelson.

Western Canada is also home to the world's most famous **heli-skiing** operations, where you can stay for a week in a luxurious lodge and be whirled up to virgin powder for several runs a day – at a cost of C$5,400 or more (plus flights from your starting point). Or you can try heli-skiing for a day from many resorts. A cheaper alternative is snowcat skiing where you ride up the mountain in a more relaxed fashion in a converted snowcat.

Banff

A winter wonderland with wildlife

HOW IT RATES

The slopes

Snow	****
Extent	****
Experts	****
Intermediates	****
Beginners	***
Convenience	*
Liftlines	****
Restaurants	***

The rest

Scenery	****
Resort charm	***
Off-slope	*****

What's new

For 2001/02 Sunshine's old access gondola will be replaced by a new eight-seater, almost doubling the capacity and cutting the journey time to Sunshine Village by over 40% to under 13 minutes.

For 2000/01 two new quad chairs were installed between Goat's Eye and Sunshine Village. The Wolverine fast quad has replaced the old Wheeler chair. The new Jackrabbit quad place and has replaced the Fireweed T-bar. This cuts out a long flat section of the green run down the length of the gondola.

A couple of seasons ago Sunshine reopened (after 14 years) the Delirium Dive area of extreme terrain.

SUNSHINE VILLAGE

Looking down over Sunshine's Delirium Dive (the steep bits are out of shot below the photo!) to Goat's Eye →

- ➕ Spectacular high-mountain scenery – quite unlike the Colorado Rockies
- ➕ Three widely separated mountains adding up to a lot of terrain
- ➕ Excellent snow record at Sunshine
- ➕ Lots of wildlife around the valley
- ➕ Lots of touristy shops
- ➕ Good value lodging because winter is the area's low season

- ➖ You need to drive or take a bus to get to the slopes – between 10 and 45 minutes to the three local areas
- ➖ Can be very cold – and most lifts offer no protection
- ➖ Lack of traditional ski resort atmosphere

Banff and its surrounding ski areas are spectacularly set in Banff National Park, amid a landscape of glaciers, jagged peaks and magnificent views. The valleys are full of wildlife such as elk and long-horned sheep. Add to that the fact that winter is low season in the area, so room prices are low and value-for-money is high, and you have a compelling destination for an all-round winter vacation.

The big drawback – and one that our reporters frequently complain about – is that you have to drive or catch buses to the slopes. Once you reach them, the slopes have something for everyone, from steep couloirs to gentle cruising. The snow is some of the coldest, driest and most reliable you'll find anywhere in the world, and there's usually a lot of it (at Sunshine Village, at least). And there are the standard Canadian assets of people who are friendly, and low prices for meals and other on-the-spot expenses.

For us, these factors count for more than the drawbacks. But then we, luckily, have not encountered the extremely low temperatures (–30°C/–22°F is not unknown) that have left some early-season reporters feeling less convinced.

The resort

Banff is a big summer resort that happens to be within driving distance of three separate ski and snowboard areas. Norquay is a small nearby area overlooking the town. Sunshine Village, 20 minutes away, is a bigger mountain; despite the name, it's not a village (nor is it notably sunny) – it has just one small hotel at mid-mountain. Lake Louise is 45 minutes away (see separate chapter).

Banff is in a spectacular setting, with several towering peaks rising up around its outskirts. There is lots of

MOUNTAIN FACTS

NORQUAY, SUNSHINE & LAKE LOUISE

Covered by the Tri-area ticket

Altitude	1635m-2730m
	5,370ft-8,950ft
Lifts	30
Trails	7,558 acres
Green	25%
Blue	45%
Black	30%
Snowmaking	
	1,700 acres

NORQUAY

Altitude	1635m-2135m
	5,370ft-7,000ft
Lifts	5
Trails	162 acres
Green	20%
Blue	36%
Black	44%
Snowmaking	90%

SUNSHINE

Altitude	1660m-2730m
	5,440ft-8,950ft
Lifts	12
Trails	3,168 acres
Green	20%
Blue	50%
Black	30%
Snowmaking	none

wildlife around; don't be surprised to find a herd of elk or long-horned sheep outside your hotel (though we are told that the town is now trying to keep elk away). In spring there may be bears along the highways.

Banff town has grown substantially since 1990, when it became independent of the Banff National Park authority. But it still consists basically of one long main street and a small network of side roads built in grid fashion, lined by clothing and souvenir shops (aimed mainly at summer visitors) and a few ski shops. The buildings are low-rise and some are attractively wood-sided. The town is pleasant enough, but it lacks genuine charm; it's a tourist town, not another Aspen or Telluride.

A car can be helpful here, especially in cold weather. The buses to Sunshine, Norquay and Lake Louise (free to Tri-area lift ticket holders) are frequent and generally reliable, although a reporter points out that, depending on the number of pickups, the bus-rides can take twice as long as advertised. Buses are also organized to more distant Panorama and Kicking Horse, and the small resorts of Nakiska and Fortress. Day-trip heli-skiing and boarding can be organized.

The mountains

The amount of skiing within reach is huge, and the views from the slopes are the most spectacular that the Rockies have to offer.

THE SLOPES
Lots of variety

The slopes of **Sunshine Village** are set right on the Continental Divide and as a result get a lot of snow and can be very cold and bleak during a snowfall or cold snap. The main slopes are not visible from the base station: you ride a two-stage gondola, first to the base of the recently developed Goat's Eye Mountain, and then on to Sunshine Village itself. The old slow gondola (the subject of many reporters' complaints) is due to be replaced by a fast new one for 2001/02. Most of the

BANFF-MOUNT NORQUAY

Norquay is the nearest area to Banff town and has short runs for all abilities ↓

boarding

Boarders will feel at home in Banff. The nearby mountains have good terrain-parks and half-pipes and some excellent free-riding terrain for experienced riders. Norquay offers a snowboard park lift ticket for those wishing to use only the park and pipe. We have had mainly positive reports about the lessons. Beware green trails, however, as they can be really flat and require some walking. Banff is quite lively for nightlife.

LIFT TICKETS

2001/02 prices in Canadian dollars
Tri-area lift ticket
Covers all lifts and transport between Banff, Lake Louise, Norquay and Sunshine Village, available for 3 days or more.
Main ticket
3-day ticket 175
6-day ticket 350
Children
6-12: 6-day ticket 128
Beginners First time ski packages including rental, ticket and lessons available
Day tickets
2000 prices
Day tickets excluding transport to/from individual areas (10 return)
Sunshine Village: 54
Norquay: 47
with reductions for senior citizens (over 65 at Sunshine, over 55 at Norquay), teenagers (13-17), children (6-12). Kids aged five and under are free.
Short-term tickets
Half-day ticket for individual areas of Sunshine Village: 43
Mount Norquay: 35
(or hourly rate at any time of day, minimum 2hr: 25). Night skiing also available here on Friday evenings.

slopes above the village are above the tree line. Although there is a wooded sector served by the second section of the gondola and a couple of chairs, in bad weather you're better off elsewhere.

Goat's Eye is served by one lift, a fast quad chair rising 580m/1,900ft. Although there are some blue runs, this is basically a black mountain, with some genuine double-blacks at the extremities. There has been talk of building an additional fast quad up the middle of the slopes to a point more or less on the tree line; this would make the area more useful in bad weather, but the plan is still awaiting approval.

Lifts fan out in all directions from Sunshine Village, with short runs back from Mount Standish and longer ones from Lookout Mountain. Lookout is where the Continental Divide is, with the melting snow flowing in one direction to the Pacific and in the other to the Atlantic. From the top of here experts can pass through a gate (you need an avalanche transceiver to get through) and hike up to the extreme terrain of Delirium Dive.

Many people ride the gondola down at the end of the day. But the 2.5km/1.5 mile green run to the bottom is a pretty cruise. If you go down while the lifts are running you can take the new Jackrabbit chair to cut out a flat section, but the run gets crowded and is much more enjoyable if you delay your descent a bit. The black-diamond Canyon run provides a fun alternative for more advanced skiers and riders.

Norquay is much smaller. But it's worth a visit, especially in bad weather – it has wooded slopes to suit all abilities served by a row of five lifts. It is often overlooked by visitors who head for the bigger areas, and so the trails can be delightfully quiet. One trail is floodlit on weekends.

Lake Louise (see separate chapter) is about 45 minutes' drive from Banff.

SNOW RELIABILITY
Excellent
Sunshine Village claims '100% natural snow', a neat reversal of the usual snowmaking hype. Certainly, the lack of snowmaking there has never been a problem in our experience other than in last season's exceptionally poor snow year – when the blues were still fine but the blacks remained rocky during our February visit. 'Three times the snow' is another Sunshine slogan – a cryptic reference to the fact that the average snowfall here is 360 to 400 inches (depending on which figures you believe) – as good as anything in Colorado, and rivalling Jackson Hole – compared with a modest 140 inches at Lake Louise and 120 inches on Norquay. But we're told the Sunshine figures relate to Lookout, and that Goat's Eye gets less. There is snowmaking on 90% of trails at Norquay. So all in all, lack of snow is unlikely to be a problem.

FOR EXPERTS
Pure pleasure
Both areas have satisfying terrain for good skiers and boarders.

Sunshine has plenty of open runs of genuine black steepness above the tree line on Lookout, but Goat's Eye Mountain makes this area much more compelling. It has opened up a great area of expert double-black-diamond trails and chutes, both above and below the tree line – one reporter enjoyed the area so much that he and his party kept 'going back again and again'. But the slopes are rocky and need good cover, and the top can be windswept. There are short, steep runs on Mount Standish, too. One particular novelty is a pitch, near the mid-station, known as the Waterfall run – because you do actually ski down over a snow-covered frozen fall.

Real experts will want to get to grips with the recently reopened Delirium Dive on Lookout Mountain's north face. You are only allowed to hike up to it if you have a companion, an avalanche transceiver and a shovel

– and a guide is recommended. ('Book in advance,' says a disappointed reporter.) But a local expert says: 'The patrol neurotically carpet-bombs the entire cirque and closes Delirium upon sighting the first tiny fog-bank, making Delirium about the safest off-trail on the planet. The mandatory transceiver routine is pure theater.' The area was closed on our 2001 visit, but we did take a look at it, and it is suitably impressive, with pitches over 40°.

Norquay's two main lifts give only 400m/1,300ft vertical, but both serve black slopes and the North American chair accesses a couple of double-diamond runs that justify their ranking.

Heli-skiing is available from bases outside the National Park in British Columbia – roughly two hours' drive.

FOR INTERMEDIATES
Ideal runs
Half the runs on Sunshine are classified as intermediate. Wherever you look there are blues and greens – some of the greens as enjoyable (and pretty much as steep) as the blues.

We particularly like the World Cup Downhill run, from the top of Lookout to the mid-mountain base. Don't ignore the Wawa T-Bar, which gives access to the often quiet Wawa Bowl and Tincan Alley. There's a delightful wooded area under the second stage of the gondola served by Jackrabbit and Wolverine chairs. The blue runs down Goat's Eye are good cruises too.

The Pathfinder fast quad at Norquay serves a handful of quite challenging tree-lined blues and a couple of sometimes-groomed blacks – great for a snowy day or a 'first day of the vacation' warm-up.

FOR BEGINNERS
Pretty good terrain
Sunshine has a good area by the mid-mountain base, served by a rope tow. The long Meadow Park Green is a great, long, easy run to progress to.

Norquay has a good small beginner area with a magic carpet and gentle greens served by the Cascade chair.

Banff is not the ideal destination for a mixed party of beginners (who may want to stay in one area) and more experienced friends (who are likely to want to visit other places).

FOR CROSS-COUNTRY
High in quality and quantity
It's a good area for cross-country. There are trails near Banff, around the Bow River, and on the Banff Springs golf course. But the best area is around Lake Louise. Altogether, there are around 80km/50 miles of groomed trails within Banff National Park. Beware of the wildlife though: last season a cross-country skier was killed by a mountain lion.

LIFTLINES
Should not be a problem
Half the slope-users come for the day from cities such as Calgary – so it's fairly quiet during the week. The old gondola up to Sunshine was line-prone in the mornings but the new one should solve that problem.

SCHOOLS/GUIDES
2001/02 prices in Canadian dollars

Club Ski and Club Snowboard
3 days of guided lessons of the three areas

Club Program
4½hr per day
3 full days 169
(incl lunch for Club Junior Program for age 6-12)

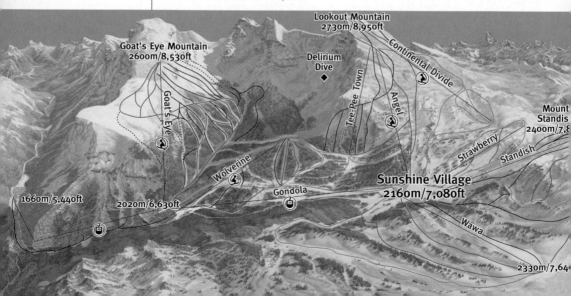

Lookout Mountain
2730m/8,950ft

Goat's Eye Mountain
2600m/8,530ft

Delirium Dive ◆

Continental Divide

Tee-Pee Town

Angel

Mount Standis
2400m/7,8

Strawberry

Standish

Goat's Eye

Sunshine Village
2160m/7,080ft

1660m/5,440ft

2020m/6,630ft

Wolverine

Gondola

Wawa

2330m/7,64

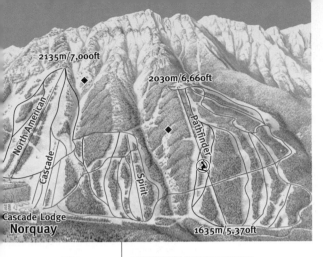

2135m/7,000ft

2030m/6,660ft

1635m/5,370ft

North American

Cascade

Spirit

Pathfinder

Cascade Lodge
Norquay

CHILDCARE

The nurseries at
Sunshine Village and
Norquay's Cascade
Lodge take children
aged 19 months to 6
years, from 9am to
4pm. Children aged 3
or more can take
short ski lessons.

SUNSHINE VILLAGE

Coming down into
Sunshine Village and
its beginner area ↓

MOUNTAIN RESTAURANTS
Quite good

Sunshine Village has a choice of eating
places at its mid-mountain base. The
Day Lodge now has quite a choice of
three different styles of food on three
floors (table service in the top floor
Lookout Lodge, with great views). Mad
Trapper's Saloon is a lively western-
style place in Old Sunshine Lodge,
serving different food on its two levels
(though reporters have criticized its
disposable plates). The Sunshine Inn
hotel has the best food – table-service

snacks in the Chimney Corner Lounge
or a full lunch in the Eagle's Nest
Dining Room. The Java Hut (actually a
tent), at the bottom of Goat's Eye
Mountain, has had mixed reports.

At the base of Norquay, the big,
stylish, timber-framed Cascade Lodge
is excellent – it has great views and a
table-service restaurant upstairs as well
as a self-service cafeteria.

SCHOOLS AND GUIDES
Some great ideas

Both mountains have their own school.
But recognizing that visitors wanting
lessons won't want to be confined to
just one mountain, the resorts have
organized an excellent Club Ski and
Club Snowboard Program – three-day
courses starting on Mondays and
Thursdays that take you to Sunshine,
Norquay and Lake Louise on different
days, offering a mixture of guiding and
instruction and including free video
analysis, a fun race and a group photo.
We'd recommend this to anyone who
wants to see the whole area while
improving his or her technique.
Reporters rave about it: 'absolutely
brilliant' and 'improved more in three
days than in a week anywhere else'. All
abilities are catered to, including
beginners. We also have a fat file full
of praise for the free mountain tours
by friendly local volunteer snow hosts.

FACILITIES FOR CHILDREN
Excellent

One reporter who used Sunshine,
Norquay and Lake Louise said: 'I'd
recommend all three.'

Staying there 🔑

Unless you stay mid-mountain on
Sunshine, it will be a drive or bus-ride
to the slopes. Don't expect resort
ambience or too much nightlife. Some
of the Banff lodgings (even on the
main Banff Avenue) are quite a
distance from downtown, but there's a
good bus service.

HOW TO GO
Superb-value packages

A huge number of accommodations are
available – both hotels and condos
Hotels Summer is the peak season
here. Prices are cut in half for the
winter – so you can stay in luxury at
bargain rates.
(((④ **Fairmont Banff Springs** (762 2211)
A turn-of-the century, castle-style

GETTING THERE

Air Calgary, transfer 1½hr.

Phone numbers
From distant parts of the Canada, add the prefix 1 403.
From abroad, add the prefix +1 403.

ACTIVITIES

Indoor Film theater, museums, galleries, swimming pools (one with water slides), gym, squash, racquetball, weight training, bowling, hot-tub, sauna, mini-golf, climbing wall
Outdoor Swimming in hot springs, ice skating, heli-skiing, horse-drawn carriage rides, sleigh rides, dog-sled rides, snowmobiles, curling, ice hockey, ice fishing, helicopter tours, night skiing, snow-shoe tours

TOURIST OFFICE

Postcode ToL oCo
t +1 (403) 762 4561
f 762 8185
info@sblls.com
www.sblls.com

Canadian Pacific property, well outside town. It's virtually a town within itself – it can sleep 2,000 people, has over 40 shops, numerous restaurants and bars, a nightclub and a superb health club and spa (which costs extra).

((((**Rimrock** (762 33560)
Spectacularly set, out of town, with great views and a smart health club. Luxurious.

(((**Sunshine Inn** (762 6550) On the slopes at Sunshine Village. Luggage transported for you in the gondola while you hit the slopes. Rooms vary in size. Big outdoor hot-pool. Sauna. Good restaurant.

(((**Inns of Banff** (762 4581) About 20 minutes' walk from town; praised by reporters for large rooms, room service and fitness facilities.

(((**Banff Park Lodge** (762 4433) Best-quality central hotel, with hot-tub, steam room and indoor pool.

((**Banff Caribou Lodge** (762 5887) On the main street, slightly out of town. It has a variety of wood-sided, interestingly and individually designed rooms, a sauna and hot-tub complex and a good restaurant and bar. Repeatedly recommended by reporters.

((**Banff King Edward** (762 2202) Right in the town center, set above shops; large rooms and surprisingly quiet for its position.

Apartments/condos The Banff Rocky Mountain Resort is set in the woods on the edge of town; facilities include indoor pool, squash and hot-tubs. Reporters have also recommended the Douglas Fir resort for families – though 'a bit out of town' – and Woodland Village.

EATING OUT
Lots of choice

Banff boasts over 100 restaurants, from McDonald's to fine dining in the Banff Springs hotel. Reporters praise lots of places but complain about them being crowded and many places not taking reservations. Many places do huge portions that you can share. Regular recommendations include the new Maple Leaf (Canadian, relatively expensive), Earl's (burgers and ethnic dishes, very popular and lively), Magpie and Stump (Mexican, with Wild West decor), Giorgio's (Italian), Rose & Crown (pub food), the Keg (steaks, two branches – one in town and one in Caribou Lodge), Seoul Country (Korean), Wild Bill's (burgers, grills, Tex Mex, dancing), Grizzlies Fondue House.

APRES-SKI
Livens up after dark

One of the drawbacks of the area is that après-ski is limited because the villages are a drive from the slopes. But Mad Trapper's Saloon at the top of the Sunshine Village gondola is popular during afternoon happy hour (with endless free peanuts). In town later in the evening, Wild Bill's has live country and western music and line dancing. The Rose & Crown has live music and gets crowded. The Works and the Barbary Coast nightclubs are popular. And Outabounds attracts a young lively crowd, while Aurora is for more serious clubbing. The St James Gate Irish pub has 'great atmosphere, good-value food and a wide range of beers'.

OFF THE SLOPES
Lots to do

For someone who does not intend to hit the slopes, Banff has to be one of the best resorts there is: there are so many other things to do and lots of wildlife to see. There are lovely walks, including organized ice canyon walks, and you can go snow-shoeing, dog-sledding, skating and tobogganing. You can go on sightseeing tours and visit natural hot springs as well.

There are museums to visit such as Banff Park Museum, the Whyte Museum of the Canadian Rockies, the Natural History Museum, the Canadian Ski Museum West and the Buffalo Nation's Luxton Museum of the Indians of the Northern Plains.

There are hundreds of shops, though most of them are overtly aimed at the tourist trade.

STAYING UP THE MOUNTAIN
Worth considering

At Sunshine Village, the Sunshine Inn is the only slope-side hotel (see Hotels, above).

Big White — 1755m/5,760ft

Big by local standards, white by any standard

HOW IT RATES

The slopes

Snow	****
Extent	***
Experts	*****
Intermediates	****
Beginners	****
Convenience	****
Liftlines	*****
Restaurants	*

The rest

Scenery	***
Resort charm	**
Off-slope	**

What's new

Last season saw the opening of the new Happy Valley adventure area, with a huge tubing hill, a skating rink, paths, kids' beginner area and a day lodge, all linked to the village by a new eight-person gondola. More accommodations were also added.

Much more development is planned, and 2001/02 should see more lodgings as well as new slopes. Four new trails are being cut on the black-graded terrain off the Ridge Rocket chair.

MOUNTAIN FACTS

Altitude	1510m-2285m
	4,950ft-7,500ft
Lifts	13
Trails	2,200 acres
Green	18%
Blue	56%
Black	26%
Snowmaking	none

BIG WHITE / KLAUS GRETZMACHER

This shot shows only the 'front face' of Big White – the Gem Lake chair and its runs are off to the left ➜

➕ BC's highest ski area, with a good snow record

➕ Mainly fast lifts, with few liftlines

➕ Extensive, varied slopes, deserted except on weekends and holidays

➕ Convenient, purpose-built village with mainly ski-in/ski-out accommodations and car-free center

➕ Excellent kids' facilities

➖ Few off-slope diversions – and isolated without a car

➖ Upper mountain is very exposed – and is known for freezing fog

➖ No mountain restaurants

➖ Limited après-ski

'It's the snow,' says the Big White slogan. And as slogans go, it's right on. If all you want to do is ski or ride, with a fair chance of doing it in deep snow, put Big White high on the shortlist. If other things enter into your holiday equation, the attractions are less clear, despite current improvements. That's if you're planning a week-long stay in one place; for anyone planning a tour of BC resorts, Big White should be an automatic choice.

THE RESORT

Big White is a modern, purpose-built resort above the Okanagan valley. It is built on a sloping hillside, slightly above the three main chair-lift bases so that many of the accommodations are ski-in/ski-out. A lot of the resort's business comes from day visitors, who can park near these lift bases or at the more remote base of Westridge, but these days are most likely to park at the newly created Happy Valley activity area, where a powerful new gondola gives access to the village center. This is a rather piecemeal affair (Intrawest-style urban planning not in evidence) but attractive in wood and stone.

Big White is only 45 minutes from Kelowna airport (but a long drive from bigger gateways). Other candidates for inclusion in a tour along with Big White are Silver Star and Red Mountain (see Western Canada introduction).

THE MOUNTAINS

Much of the terrain is heavily wooded though the trees thin out towards the summits, leading to almost open slopes in the bowls at the top. There's at least one green option from the top of each lift so beginners need not be intimidated by any one sector. Grooming is excellent.

Slopes Fast chairs run from points below village level to above mid-mountain, serving the main area of wooded beginner and intermediate runs above and beside the village. Slower lifts – a T-bar and two chairs – serve the higher slopes. Quite some way across the mountainside is the Gem Lake fast chair, serving a range of long top-to-bottom runs to its base at Westridge; with its 710m/2,330ft vertical, this lift is in a different league from the others. There are free daily mountain tours and floodlit skiing.

453

Central reservations phone number
For all resort accommodations call 765 8888 (from distant parts of Canada, add the prefix 1 250; from abroad, add the prefix +1 250)

Toll-free number (from within Canada) 1 800 663 1772.

TOURIST OFFICE

Postcode V1X 4K5
t +1 (250) 765 8888
f 765 1822
bigwhite@bigwhite.com
www.bigwhite.com

Snowboarding There's some excellent free-riding terrain and three terrain-parks and pipes. Novices are well catered to with long, chair-lift-served green runs.

Snow reliability Big White has a reputation for great powder; average snowfall is about 300 inches, which is not quite Alta or even Fernie class, but not far short. There is no snowmaking.

Experts There is lots to do, especially if you get good snow. The main bowl off the side of the T-bar is of serious double-black pitch. The Sun-Rype bowl at the opposite edge of the ski area is more forgiving. There are some superb long blacks off the Gem Lake chair and several shorter ones off the Powder and Ridge Rocket chairs – with more in the latter area for this season. In most of these areas there are extensive glades to explore, too.

Intermediates The resort is excellent for cruisers and families, with long blues and greens all over the hill.

Beginners There's a good dedicated beginner area in the village and lots of long easy runs to progress to.

Cross-country There are 25km/15 miles of trails in total.

Liftlines With four fast quads and few visitors still, lines are pretty rare. However, the Alpine T-bar can be a bottleneck on sunny days.

Mountain restaurants The nearest thing to a mountain restaurant is the Westridge base warming hut.

School and guides The ski school offers some interesting options.

Facilities for children The excellent 'Kids' Center' takes children from 18 months. And there's a dedicated beginner area with a magic carpet lift at the new Happy Valley area. Evening activities are organized.

STAYING THERE

Hotels The White Crystal Inn, Coast Resort and Chateau Big White are recommended – all are convenient for the slopes.

Apartments/condos There's a reasonable choice of accommodations. Grocery shopping is very limited.

Eating out The choice of restaurant is gradually widening. Snowshoe Sam's is good for casual dining. Other recommendations include Powder Keg (Greek), Swiss Bear in the Chateau Big White (Swiss!), China White Wok, Loose Moose (steaks and grills), and Coltino's in the Hopfbrauhaus (Italian).

Après-ski The atmospheric Snowshoe Sam's is a focal point, with a DJ and live entertainment. Powder Keg, Loose Moose and Grizzly Bear are also recommended, and Raakel's is good for families.

Off the slopes The brand new Happy Valley adventure park features western Canada's largest tubing hills and ice skating, and is the launch pad for snowmobiling, snow-shoeing and dog-sledding. Helicopter tours and the two health spas are also popular.

Fernie

Lots of snow, and lots of steeps

HOW IT RATES

The slopes

Snow	****
Extent	***
Experts	*****
Intermediates	**
Beginners	****
Convenience	****
Liftlines	****
Restaurants	*

The rest

Scenery	****
Resort charm	**
Off-slope	**

➕ Good snow record, with less chance of rain than at Whistler, and less chance of Arctic temperatures than at Lake Louise

➕ Great terrain for those who like it steep and deep, with lots for confident intermediates and beginners, too

➕ A couple of snowcat operations nearby

➕ Good on-slope accommodations becoming increasingly available in small, friendly mountain resort

➖ Lift system poor, with a primitive rope tow and hikes and traverses to some of the best terrain

➖ After a dump it can take time to make the black bowls safe

➖ Little groomed cruising for timid or average intermediates

➖ No decent mountain restaurants

➖ Mountain resort is still small and under construction with very limited evening options, and town of Fernie (a short drive away) is not particularly appealing either

455

What's new

The new mountain village has started to take shape with the opening of new condo-hotels, restaurants, a couple of shops and a nursery, and development continues.

The Bear T-bar was replaced by a fast quad for 2000/2001, improving access to both Lizard and Cedar Bowls.

SNOWPIX.COM / CHRIS GILL

The center of Fernie Alpine Resort with the new Cornerstone Lodge on the right ↓

Fernie has long had cult status among Alberta and BC skiers for its steep gladed slopes and superb natural snow. In 1998 the operation was bought by Charlie Locke, owner of Lake Louise. There has since been a lot of investment in the development of the village at the foot of the slopes – though it still remains small without many facilities, and for much of last winter it seemed like a muddy construction site. Some visitors would rather see more investment in the mountain, to speed up the lifts, cut down the amount of hiking and traversing, and to hasten reopening after a serious snowfall. We see their point, but most reports we get are dominated by excitement at Fernie's combination of snow and terrain. 'Just like Jackson Hole', said two reporters independently this year. When we went to press Charlie Locke's company had hit financial problems and further investment was on hold.

The resort

Fernie Alpine Resort is set at the lift base a little way up the mountainside from the flat Elk Valley floor and a couple of miles from the little town of Fernie. It has grown from nothing in the last two or three years. But there's still not much there other than convenient accommodations and a few places to eat. It is quiet at night. Several reporters commented that it lacked charm and resembled a muddy building site. But we were there when there was snow on the ground and found it okay. Owner Charlie Locke has been good at attracting crowds to his flagship resort of Lake Louise and is now doing the same in Fernie. It remains to be seen how his financial difficulties affect further development.

The town of Fernie is named after William Fernie – a prospector who discovered coal here and triggered a boom at the turn of the century. Much of the town was destroyed by fire in 1908 but some downtown stone and brick buildings survived and are still there. We thought it a nondescript spot on our first visit three years ago but noticed a few more tourist shops on our 2001 visit. One reporter described it as 'a bit like staying in an industrial estate' – a bit unfair, we thought, but you can't describe it as 'charming'.

The mountains

Fernie's 2,500 acres pack in a lot of variety, from superb green terrain at the bottom to ungroomed chutes (that will be satisfyingly steep to anyone but the extreme specialist) and huge numbers of steep runs in the trees. A lot of the runs have the rare quality of consistently steep pure fall lines.

THE SLOPES
Bowl after bowl
What you see when you arrive at the lift base is a trio of impressive bump slopes towering above you. The Deer chair approaches the foot of these slopes, but goes no further. You get to them by traversing and hiking from the main Lizard Bowl, on the right. This is a broad snowfield reached by a series of lifts: a slow quad (which one reporter found stopped 'on average four times per uplift'); a fast quad (which replaced the old T-bar last season); and finally the short Face Lift, a dreadful rope tow that wasn't working when we were there in February 2001 because lack of snow meant it was high above the ground – it also 'shredded' one reporter's gloves. This is also the main way into lift-free Cedar Bowl (where a reporter came across a moose) and to Snake Ridge beyond it. There is a mini-bowl between Lizard and Cedar, served by the 500m/1,640ft vertical Boomerang chair.

The Timber Bowl fast quad chair gives access to Siberia Bowl and the lower part of Timber. But for access to the higher slopes and to Currie Bowl you must take the White Pass Quad. A long traverse from the top gets you to the steeper slopes on the flanks of Currie (our favorite area), which are otherwise reached by hiking from the main Lizard Bowl. From there you have to go right to the bottom, and it takes quite a while to get back for another go.

There are excellent, free, hosted tours of the area in groups of different abilities for two hours twice a day. These may be a good way to get your bearings, as several readers found the signposting 'minimal', and we found both signs and trail map dangerously inadequate. Indeed, when we tried to find the long, black Diamond Back run from the top of the White Pass quad, we failed and ended up in narrowly spaced trees on a slope of triple-diamond steepness – pretty scary.

Outings to Kimberley are possible; a coach does the trip every Thursday (there's also a helicopter option). Buses back to Fernie town at the end of the day are 'excellent' for C$2.50, and a reporter said they were dropped off at their lodging if they asked.

SNOW RELIABILITY
A key part of the appeal
Last year's exceptionally poor year apart, Fernie has an excellent snow record – with an average of 350 inches per year, better than practically all of Colorado. But the altitude is modest – rain is not unknown, and in warmer weather the lower slopes can suffer. There is very little snowmaking, and reporters said trail maintenance was poor in last season's snow drought.

FOR EXPERTS
Wonderful – deep and steep
The combination of heavy snowfalls and abundant steep terrain with the shelter of trees makes this a superb mountain for good skiers. There are about a dozen identifiable faces

MOUNTAIN FACTS

Altitude	1070m-1925m
	3,500ft-6,320ft
Lifts	10
Trails	2,500 acres
Green	30%
Blue	40%
Black	30%
Snowmaking	25 acres
Recco detectors used	

Phone numbers
From distant parts of the Canada, add the prefix 1 250.
From abroad, add the prefix +1 250.

RIDE THE SNOWCATS AT ISLAND LAKE LODGE

Any good skier who relishes off-trail should consider treating themselves to three or four days staying at Island Lake Lodge (423 3700). Book as far in advance as you can as we've heard they can be booked up to three years in advance! You can do single days without lodging, but only on a standby basis; we did this three years ago but could not get in on our 2001 visit. The Lodge is a cozy chalet 10km/6 miles from Fernie, amid 7,000 acres of spectacular bowls and ridges. It has 36 beds, and four snowcats to act as lifts. In a day you might do eight powder runs averaging around 500m/1,500ft vertical, taking in all kinds of terrain from gentle open slopes to some very Alpine adventures – maybe not as exciting as heli-skiing, but in its way just as rewarding. Three-day packages cost around C$1,500. There are other snowcat operations in the region, less well-known and so less likely to be booked solid.

boarding

Fernie is a fine place for boarders (and there are a lot of local experts here). Lots of natural gullies, hits and endless off-trail opportunities – including some adrenalin-pumping tree-runs and knee-deep powder bowls – will keep free-riders of all abilities grinning from ear to ear. There's also a good terrain-park and half-pipe. Snowcat operators can take you to some excellent untouched powder. There are a couple of decent bars in the town, and Frozen Ocean and Board Stiff are the main board shops.

LIFT TICKETS

2000/01 prices in Canadian dollars
Main ticket
1-day ticket 54
6-day ticket 300
Senior citizens
Over 65: 6-day ticket 228
Children
13-17: 6-day ticket 228
Under 13: 6-day ticket 90
Under 6: free ticket
Short-term tickets
Half-day ticket from noon (adult 43)
Notes
Mighty Moose lift tickets available for beginners: 15

offering genuine black or double-black slopes, each of them with several alternative ways down. Currie and Timber Bowls both have some serious double-diamonds but mainly have single-diamonds. However, one of our regular reporters says, 'The majority of the single blacks are tough. Some of them are so steep that I can't work out how you could get anything harder without falling off the mountain ... just like Jackson Hole but without the cliffs.' Even where the trail map shows trees to be sparse, expect them to be close enough together, and where there aren't any, expect alder bushes unless there's lots of snow.

There are also backcountry routes you can take with guidance and snowcat operations to try. If you can't get in at Island Lake – see feature panel – try Fernie Wilderness Adventures.

FOR INTERMEDIATES
Far from ideal
Although there are intermediate runs both low down and high up, they don't add up to a lot of mileage. Most high runs are not groomed, and one reporter said, 'The blues in all bowls except Timber would be black in most resorts.' Adventurous, strong intermediates willing to give the ungroomed terrain a try will enjoy the area. The blue/green Falling Star run (a short hike up from the top of the Timber Bowl chair) is often completely deserted and has good snow, although near the bottom it is narrow and it gets a bit flat. But if you want miles of groomed cruising, go elsewhere.

FOR BEGINNERS
Excellent
There's a good beginner area and the lower mountain served by the Deer and Elk chairs has lots of wide, smooth trails to gain confidence on. But most runs from the top of the mountain have tough parts to them.

FOR CROSS-COUNTRY
Some possibilities
There are 14km/9 miles of trails marked out in the forest adjacent to the resort, and the Fernie golf and country club allows enthusiasts on to their white fairways.

Fernie

457

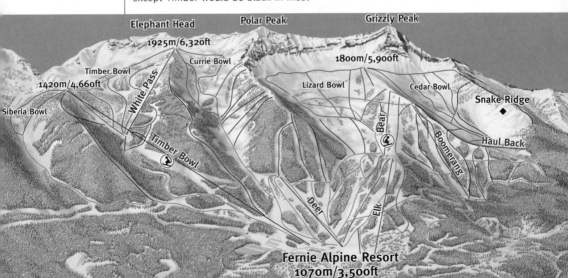

Elephant Head
Polar Peak
Grizzly Peak
1925m/6,320ft
Currie Bowl
1800m/5,900ft
Timber Bowl
White Pass
Lizard Bowl
Cedar Bowl
1420m/4,660ft
Snake Ridge
Siberia Bowl
Bear
Haul Back
Timber Bowl
Boomerang
Deer
Elk

Fernie Alpine Resort
1070m/3,500ft

SCHOOLS/GUIDES

2000/01 prices in Canadian dollars
Fernie
Classes
1¹/₄hr: 10am and 1.30
Half day: 27
Multi half days: 23
Children's classes
Ages 3 to 4 years and 5 to 12 years
Multi full day: 38
Private lessons
2 hr: 92 (22 for each additional person)

CHILDCARE

The resort day care center takes children of all ages. It is open daily from 9am to 4pm.

ACTIVITIES

Indoor Museum, galleries, aquatic center, saunas, bowling, fitness center, ice skating, movie theater, curling **Outdoor** Sleigh rides, snowmobiling, dog-sledding, snow-shoe excursions, ice fishing, cross-country skiing.

GETTING THERE

Air Calgary, transfer 3¹/₂hr.

Central reservations phone number
For all resort accommodations call 1 800 258 7669 (toll-free from within Canada).

TOURIST OFFICE

Postcode V0B 1M6
t +1 (250) 423 4655
f 423 6644
info@skifernie.com
www.skifernie.com

LIFTLINES
Not usually a problem

Unless there is a weekend invasion from Calgary, liftlines are rare. Last year's poor snow kept numbers down but in a normal year we guess that the new fast Bear quad chair will lead to lines at the inadequate and atrocious Face Lift tow (if it is working). If heavy snow keeps part of the mountain closed, there can be lines elsewhere.

MOUNTAIN RESTAURANTS
What mountain restaurants?

Bear's Den at the top of the Elk chair is an open-air fast-food kiosk. So it's back to base for lunch – the ancient Day Lodge is grim but cheap and serves good soups and sandwiches to order. Or see Eating Out.

SCHOOLS AND GUIDES
'Lessons for all abilities'

Reporters have praised the ski school and its small classes. One tried telemarking and described the lessons as 'outstanding' and 'best ever', with only two people in the class. 'First Tracks' gets you up the mountain at 8am for two hours, but when we tried it the instructor didn't know which lifts were open and there was a lot of wasted time.

FACILITIES FOR CHILDREN
New day care center

There's a new day care center in the Cornerstone Lodge, which a reporter found 'very well run'. There are also 'Kids' Activity Nights'.

Staying there

You're going for the snow, so our advice would be to stay on or close to the hill. A reader warns that if you're staying in a condo in the village, the only decent food shopping is in the town. It's cheaper to stay in the town, where there is a wider choice of restaurants, bars and other diversions, and a much wider choice of shops.

HOW TO GO
Hotels and condos

As the resort develops, the choice is widening and shifting up-scale.
(((4 **Lizard Creek Lodge** New luxury ski-in/ski-out condo hotel. Spa, outdoor pool and hot-tub. We stayed there and highly recommend it.
(((3 **Cornerstone Lodge** New condo hotel in the village core.

(((3 **Griz Inn** Condo-hotel with good facilities. Pool.
(((3 **Wolf's Den Lodge** 'Adequate but uninspiring' with 'simple' rooms say reporters. Indoor hot-tub, games room and small gym. At base of slope.
((2 **Timberline Village** Very comfortable condos a shuttle-ride from the lifts.
((2 **Cedar Lodge** Motel on road to town. 'Comfortable and clean, but not very welcoming,' said reporters.
((2 **Alpine Lodge** New B&B recommended by reporter.

EATING OUT
Not a highlight

At the base, the Lizard Creek Lodge is expensive but serves the best gourmet food in the district (in small portions). Kelsey's (part of a chain) is more casual and offers good food and large servings, with Asian dishes as well as standard burgers, steaks, pasta, The Powderhorn in the Griz Inn does 'good, reasonably priced' food. Gabriella's Pasta Place is cheap but nothing special.

In Fernie, the restaurants at the Royal and Grand Central hotels are recommended, as is Rip n' Richard's Eatery – south-western food and a lively atmosphere. The Old Elevator is in a converted grain store and does good grills and pasta; Jamocha's is a coffee house that does meals. The Cottage has a 'nice ambience, friendly staff and good food'. Coltraynes is very lively with an interesting menu and international food. The Curry Bowl has recently opened and is very good.

APRES-SKI
Have a beer

The Grizzly bar in the Day Lodge and the Powderhorn, in the nearby Griz Inn, are quite lively when the lifts close – the latter with live bands sometimes. During the week, the bars are pretty quiet later on, but one reporter recommends Kelsey's. In town, the bar of the Royal hotel is popular with locals. Other recommendations are the Park Place Lodge Pub and the bar in the Grand Central hotel.

OFF THE SLOPES
Get out and about

There is a heritage walking tour of historic Fernie. The old railroad station is now the Art Station. The main diversion is the great outdoors.

Jasper

Small area of slopes set amid glorious scenery and wildlife

HOW IT RATES

The slopes

Snow	****
Extent	*
Experts	**
Intermediates	**
Beginners	****
Convenience	*
Liftlines	****
Restaurants	**

The rest

Scenery	***
Resort charm	***
Off-slope	***

What's new

A new quad chair-lift will be ready for the 2001/02 season. The new chair, starting just below mid-mountain, will open up twenty new runs on Eagle East and Chalet Slope on either sides of Eagle Ridge – previously accessible only by taking the high traverse from the top of the Knob chair-lift. It will also provide a more direct route to the Knob chair-lift.

MOUNTAIN FACTS

Altitude	1705m-2600m
	5,590ft-8,530ft
Lifts	8
Trails	1,000 acres
Green	35%
Blue	35%
Black	30%
Snowmaking	10 acres

Marmot Basin's slopes are quiet but not huge – in either extent or vertical drop
→

➕ Lots of lovely walks and drives in National Park land

➕ Spectacular scenery and wildlife

➖ Slopes are a long way from town and limited in size, especially for intermediates

➖ Town rather spread out and lacks charm

Set in the middle of Jasper National Park, the small railroad town is surrounded by spectacular scenery and wildlife. There's a small area of slopes 30 minutes away, but Jasper best suits those looking for an all-round winter vacation. It would be best combined with a stay in Whistler, Banff or Lake Louise.

THE RESORT

Jasper is an unremarkable, growing railway town that started life as a stopover for fur traders. There's little more to it than a couple of main streets. Most accommodations are out of town or on the outskirts and the local slopes are 30mins drive away.

Its main attractions are the beautiful scenery and drives and walks in the surrounding unspoiled National Park land. One of the most beautiful drives in the world is the three-hour trip to Lake Louise on the Columbia Icefields Parkway through the Banff and Jasper National Parks – past glaciers, frozen waterfalls and lakes.

This makes Jasper a good place to stay for a couple of days as part of a two-center holiday. You can travel from Whistler to Jasper by overnight train from Vancouver and wake up to spectacular Rocky Mountains scenery.

Although there are buses to and from the slopes, it would be handy to have a car (to explore the surrounding area as well as reach the slopes).

THE MOUNTAINS

The slopes are at Marmot Basin, in the heart of the unspoiled National Park.
Slopes A high-speed quad takes you to mid-mountain, with three slow chairs above that and a new one to Eagle Ridge for 2001/02. The highest chair ends way below the 2600m/ 8,530ft peak that the area includes in its claim of almost 900m/2,950ft vertical.
Snow reliability Snow reliability is reputed to be good, but cover has been sparse on both our visits and there is little snowmaking capacity.
Experts There are some decent bump runs on the top and bottom halves of the mountain, and some entertaining off-trail on the top half. For those willing to hike up from the top of the Knob chair and take the High Traverse, virtually the whole of the left-hand side of the mountain, as you look up, is made up of black-diamond runs. But unless you hit excellent snow the area is very small and limited.
Intermediates Keen trail-bashers will cover all the groomed runs in half a

day and find the area very small unless they are prepared to brave the ungroomed blacks. Less adventurous intermediates will be happy to cruise the greens and blues for a day or two.

Beginners The area around the base is very gentle, and there are greens to progress to from a T-bar and the quad.

Snowboarding There's a terrain-park below Caribou Ridge.

Cross-country Over 300km/185 miles of trails make this one of the best areas in Canada, with good trails near Jasper.

Liftlines These are rarely a problem.

Mountain restaurants At mid-mountain the Paradise Chalet has a big self-service cafe and the connected Eagle Chalet is a cozy table-service place. At the base the rebuilt Caribou Chalet is another option. Catering is run by the Jasper Park Lodge (see Hotels).

Schools and guides These are doubtless up to the usual high Canadian standards.

Facilities for children The Little Rascals nursery takes children from 19 months.

STAYING THERE

Hotels The Fairmont Jasper Park Lodge (852 3301) is a beautiful collection of luxurious log cabins set 5km/3 miles out of town around a lake in the middle of 1,000 acres of land rich with wildlife. Room service is delivered on bicycles and you may well have to walk around grazing elk to reach your room or visit the outdoor pool and other facilities. On the edge of town, the Royal Canadian Lodge (852 5644) has some comfortable rooms and indoor pool.

Eating out There's plenty of choice – from fine dining at the Jasper Park Lodge to Cajun, pizza and Japanese. We had good seafood and steak at the Fiddle River on the main road.

Après-ski The bar in the base lodge is crowded at the end of the day. In town, try Astoria, O'Shea's and Nick's.

Off the slopes, There is lots to do, including beautiful walks, ice skating and snow-shoeing, and there is a fine indoor sports complex.

Phone numbers

From distant parts of Canada, add the prefix 1 780.
From abroad, add the prefix +1 780.

TOURIST OFFICE

Postcode T0E 1E0
t +1 (780) 852 3816
f 852 3533
info@skimarmot.com
www.skimarmot.com

460

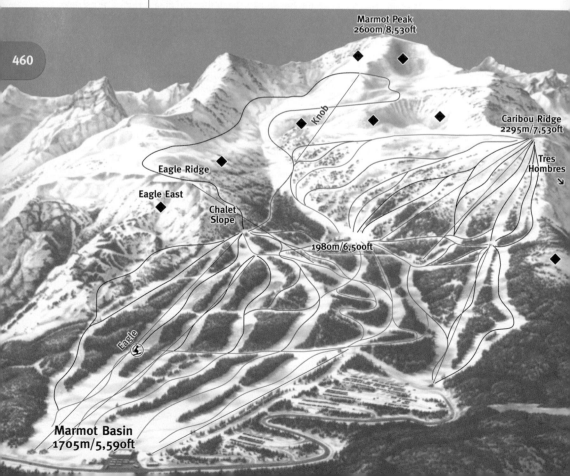

Marmot Peak
2600m/8,530ft

Knob

Caribou Ridge
2295m/7,530ft

Tres Hombres

Eagle Ridge

Eagle East

Chalet Slope

1980m/6,500ft

Eagle

Marmot Basin
1705m/5,590ft

Kicking Horse

Heli-skiing for the rest of us

HOW IT RATES

The slopes

Snow	****
Extent	***
Experts	****
Intermediates	***
Beginners	***
Convenience	*
Liftlines	*****
Restaurants	**

The rest

Scenery	***
Resort charm	*
Off-slope	*

➕ A good bet for powder snow

➕ Some great terrain for experts and adventurous intermediates

➕ Big vertical served by one fast lift

➕ Splendid mountaintop restaurant

➖ No resort village yet

➖ Golden, the resort substitute, is neither attractive nor convenient

➖ Single-stage gondola suits summer visitors, not skiers and riders

➖ Few groomed intermediate runs

Two years ago, this was Whitetooth, the local ski hill of the nondescript logging town of Golden: two old lifts, open on the weekend, serving modest wooded slopes beneath high bowls used by the local heli-skiing operation. Enter a Dutch–Canadian consortium, bringing with it vision, capital and a cute name. Within months, in go a new access road, a gondola rising 1150m/3,770ft to the heart of the heli-terrain, and smart base and mountaintop restaurants. Soon, in will go a designer mountain village at the lift base, making this a real destination resort. Meanwhile, any competent skier or rider staying in Banff or Lake Louise should give Kicking Horse a shot.

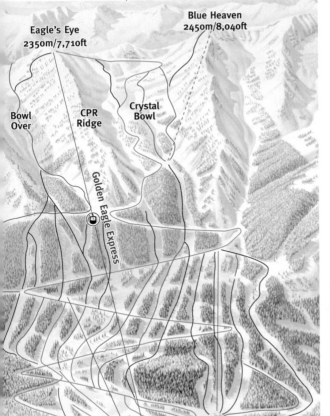

Blue Heaven
2450m/8,040ft

Eagle's Eye
2350m/7,710ft

Bowl Over

CPR Ridge

Crystal Bowl

Golden Eagle Express

Kicking Horse
1200m/3,940ft

THE RESORT
Eight miles from the small logging town of Golden, Kicking Horse is nothing but a lift base station. When we visited early in 2001, the developers planned to open the first phase of a mountain village in time for the 2001/02 season, but this has now been postponed to 2002/03.

Golden is a spread-out place beside the transcontinental highway that climbs up into the main Rockies range to the east. It has no real center – it's the kind of place where you travel from motel to restaurant to shops by car.

THE MOUNTAINS
The lower two-thirds of the hill is wooded, with trails cut in the usual style. The upper third is a mix of open and lightly wooded slopes.

Slopes The only way up to the top of the mountain is by the eight-seater gondola to Eagle's Eye. Despite the serious vertical of 1150m/3,770ft, this lift goes up in a single stage – to give summer sightseeing visitors a quick ascent. In winter, the lack of a mid-station is a real drawback: you have to make the full descent regardless of the conditions and your own preferences. The lift accesses runs on both sides of the central CPR ridge. As well as the marked runs there are literally hundreds of ways down through the bowls, chutes and trees. The plan is that hardly any of the terrain will be groomed – making the area a paradise

From this point at Eagle's Nest, you can descend into Crystal Bowl or spend half an hour hiking up to Blue Heaven to tackle it from there. The descent is less steep than it looks →

SNOWPIX.COM / CHRIS GILL

What's new

The resort started operating last season, 2000/01. As we go to press it is unclear when the chair-lift to Blue Heaven or the first developments at the mountain village will be open.

MOUNTAIN FACTS

Altitude	1200m-2450m	
	3,940ft-8,040ft	
Lifts		4
Trails	4,000 acres	
Green		20%
Blue		45%
Black		35%
Snowmaking		None

Phone numbers
From distant parts of Canada, add the prefix 1 250.
From abroad, add the prefix +1 250.

TOURIST OFFICE

Postcode V0A 1H0
t +1 (250) 439 5400
f 5401
www.kickinghorse resort.com

for powder pigs. A new chair-lift – shown dotted on our map – is planned to go from the bottom of Crystal Bowl to the slightly higher peak of Blue Heaven for 2002/03 – so this part of the higher terrain, at least, will then be skiable without descending to the base. Two chair-lifts from near the base serve the lower runs that formed the original Whitetooth ski area.

Snow reliability Excellent: until recently the top half of the mountain was heli-skiing terrain, and it gets almost 300 inches of snow a year. We were there in the February 2001 snow drought and had excellent skiing in powder in the bowls even though much of the middle of the mountain was closed.

Experts It's advanced skiers and riders who will get the most out of the area. From the ridge under the gondola, drop off to skier's right through trees or to skier's left through chutes – there are endless options. The lower half of the mountain has fine black runs on cleared trails through the trees, some with serious bumps. Do six or seven laps on the gondola in a day and you'll have had a fine time. If you detect signs of the powder getting tracked out, you can spend 30 minutes hiking up the ridge to Blue Heaven for a different approach to Crystal Bowl. From the top you can also take off (with guidance) into the next bowl, which is still part of the terrain used by Purcell heli-skiing (in Golden).

Intermediates Adventurous intermediates will have a fine time at Kicking Horse, learning to play in the powder up in Crystal Bowl. But don't expect many groomed runs. Trail-bashers and timid intermediates should go elsewhere. The only easy, groomed way down the mountain is a boring winding road.

Beginners There are some excellent beginner slopes and gentle green trails on the lower mountain.

Snowboarding Free-riders will love this powder paradise. But there's no terrain-park or half-pipe.

Cross-country There are 12km/7 miles of trails at Dawn Mountain nearby, and a 5km/3 mile loop on the golf course.

Liftlines No problem at the moment – and you won't see many people on the slopes either.

Mountain restaurants The Eagle's Eye table-service restaurant at the top of the gondola serves excellent food in stylish log cabin surroundings and has fine views. The base lodge is also

newly built with logs and beams; its small self-service restaurant seems likely to prove inadequate before long.

Schools and guides Surprise, surprise: the school specializes in powder lessons and runs two-hour 'powder tune-up' group lessons.

Facilities for children The school teaches children from the age of three.

STAYING THERE

How to go For 2001/02, you'll have to do a day-trip from a nearby resort such as Panorama, Lake Louise or Banff, or stay in Golden – a dull prospect for more than a night or two.

Hotels The Prestige Inn (344 7990), a neat, functional hotel with a small pool just off the Trans Canada Highway, is probably the best in town. Sisters and Beans (344 2443) has some well kept rooms – see below.

Eating out There are several restaurants in Golden; we enjoyed the cozy Sisters and Beans (pasta, steaks, Asian dishes) run by sisters of Swiss origin. Eagle's Eye at the top of the gondola opens some nights.

Après-ski The Mad Trapper is the main drinking spot in town – a lively high-ceilinged pub.

Off the slopes There is lots of local snowmobiling and you can go ice-climbing and dog-sledding. But for someone who isn't going to hit the slopes, Golden is a dire place to stay.

Lake Louise   1645m/5,400ft

Knockout scenery and the Banff area's biggest mountain

➕ Spectacular high-mountain scenery – the best of any North American resort

➕ Local slopes are the largest area in the Banff region

➕ Lots of wildlife around the valley

➕ Good value for money

➖ Local slopes are a short drive away, other Banff areas further

➖ Can be very cold – and lifts offer no protection

➖ 'Village' little more than a collection of buildings around a road junction with little to offer

Lake Louise's slopes are the biggest of Banff's three local areas and have good terrain for all ability levels. Many week-long visitors will want to spend two or three days there. The views from the slopes are stunning; and those of the lake itself and the Victoria Glacier behind it from the Chateau Lake Louise hotel must be among the most spectacular in the world. Owner Charlie Locke has done a good job marketing his slopes and they tend to be the busiest in the Banff area. It is a shame that the 'resort' of Lake Louise is basically a collection of disparate buildings around a road junction with no character or resort feeling. It has a couple of picturesque hotels, and if you are happy to relax in their pools and hot-tubs, you'll enjoy your stay. But if you want a choice of shops, bars, restaurants and nightlife or some streets to stroll around, you should stay in Banff. Banff is also more convenient for reaching the other two local areas of slopes.

What's new

For 2000/01 the Glacier triple chair from the base was replaced by an additional high-speed quad to eliminate any peak period waits at the bottom of the mountain.

SKI BANFF / LAKE LOUISE

The views from Lake Louise's slopes are the most spectacular of any North American resort ↓

The resort

Lake Louise is a resort of parts. First, there's the lake itself, in a spectacular mountain setting beneath the Victoria Glacier. Tom Wilson, who discovered it in 1882, declared, 'As God is my judge, I never in all my exploration have seen such a matchless scene.' Neither have we – it is simply stunning. And it can be appreciated from many of the

rooms of the monster Chateau Lake Louise hotel on the shore. Then there's Lake Louise 'village' – a shapeless little collection of hotels, condominiums, gas station, supermarket, liquor store and a few shops, a couple of miles away on a road junction down in the main valley, close to the railroad and highway from Banff to Jasper. Finally, a mile or two across the valley is the lift base station (1645m/5,400ft). A car can be helpful especially in cold weather. Buses to the Lake Louise ski area are frequent, but a lot less so to Sunshine and Norquay (free to Tri-area lift ticket holders). You can also organize trips to the more distant major resorts of Panorama and Kicking Horse and the small resorts of Nakiska and Fortress. Day-trip heli-skiing and boarding can also be organized.

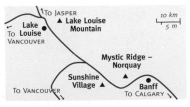

The mountains

The Lake Louise ski area is big, and the views are the most spectacular that the Rockies have to offer. There are plenty of slopes to suit every level of skill. Reporters are full of praise for the free guided tours of the area given by volunteer 'Ski Friends'.

THE SLOPES
A wide variety

A choice of two high-speed quads (one new for last season) take you up the **Front Face** to mid-mountain and are met by another which goes to the top. From here, as elsewhere, there's a choice of green, blue or black runs to other lifts. The tree line comes about halfway up the top lift, but there are alternative lifts that stop a bit lower, so you can stay in the trees in bad weather. From mid-mountain, a surface lift takes you to the high-point of the area (2635m/8,650ft), at the shoulder of Mount Whitehorn.

Temple Lodge at the bottom of the Larch area, with the Ptarmigan glades on the far side ↓

From the top there's a stunning view of the high peaks and glaciers of the Continental Divide, including Canada's uncanny Matterhorn lookalike, Mount Assiniboine.

From either the top chair or the surface lift you can go over the ridge and into Lake Louise's treeless **Back Bowls**. The bowls are predominantly north-facing and so keep their snow well.

From the bottom of the bowls you can take a lift back to the top again or up to the separate **Larch** area, served by a fast quad chair. With a vertical of 375m/1,230ft it's not huge, but it has pretty wooded runs of all levels. From the bottom you can return to the top of the main mountain via the Ptarmigan chair or take a long green path back to the main base area.

SNOW RELIABILITY
Usually excellent

Lake Louise gets around 140 inches a year on the front face, and there is snowmaking on 40% of the trails. The backside is north-facing, so it holds the snow pretty well. Lack of snow is unlikely to be a problem, except in an exceptionally poor snow year such as 2000/01 (when one reporter was annoyed to have to take his skis off and walk over a bare patch of slope on a trail that was described as open).

FOR EXPERTS
Widespread pleasure

There are plenty of steep slopes. On the front face, as well as a score of marked black-diamond trails in and above the trees, there is the alluring West Bowl, reached from the Summit surface lift – a wide open expanse of snow outside the area boundary. Because this is National Park territory, you can in theory go anywhere. But outside the boundaries there are no patrols and, of course, no avalanche control. A guide is essential. Inside the boundaries there are also areas permanently closed because of avalanche danger. Going over to the back bowls opens up countless black bump/powder runs. Try the recently opened avalanche-prone Whitehorn 2 area directly behind the peak (marked 'Occasional Openings' on the trail map). It gave our Australian editor what she called 'some of the most exciting in-bounds skiing in North America' – a row of extreme chutes, half a mile long.

464

MOUNTAIN FACTS

SUNSHINE, NORQUAY & LAKE LOUISE

Covered by the Tri-area pass

Altitude 1635m-2730m	
	5,35oft-8,95oft
Lifts	30
Trails	7,558 acres
Green	25%
Blue	45%
Black	30%
Snowmaking	
	1,700 acres

LAKE LOUISE

Altitude 1645m-2635m	
	5,400ft-8,650ft
Lifts	13
Trails	4,200 acres
Green	25%
Blue	45%
Black	30%
Snowmaking	40%
Recco detectors used	

LIFT TICKETS

2001/02 prices in Canadian dollars
Tri-area lift ticket
Covers all lifts and transport between Banff, Lake Louise and Sunshine Village, available for 3 days or more.
Main ticket
3-day ticket 175
6-day ticket 350
Children
6-12: 6-day ticket 128
Beginners First time ski packages including rental, ticket and lessons available
Day tickets
2000/01 prices
A day ticket for Lake Louise is 54, with reductions for senior citizens (over 65), teenagers (13-17) and students with ID (13-25).
Short-term tickets
Half-day ticket for Lake Louise 43

The Top of the World quad takes you to the very popular Paradise Bowl, served by its own triple chair – one run is marked on the map but there are endless variants. From the Summit surface lift you can access wide open slopes that take you right away from all signs of lifts. Again, there are endless variations. The seriously steep slope served by the Ptarmigan quad chair provided many of the logs for the new base lodge, and offers great glade terrain as a result. The Larch area has some steep double-diamond stuff in the trees, and open snowfields at the top for those with the energy to hike up above the lift. Heli-skiing is available from bases outside the National Park in British Columbia – roughly two hours' drive.

FOR INTERMEDIATES
Some good cruising

Almost half the runs are classified as intermediate. But from the top of the Front Face the blue runs down are little more than paths in places, and there are only two blue and two green routes marked in the Back Bowls. Once you get part way down the Front Face the blues are much more interesting. And when groomed, the Men's and Ladies' Downhill black runs are great fast cruises on the lower half of the mountain. Juniper and Juniper Jungle are wonderful cruising runs in the same area. Meadowlark is a beautiful tree-lined run from the top of the Eagle chair to the base area. The Larch area has some short but ideal intermediate runs. And the adventurous should try the blue-graded Boomerang, which

465

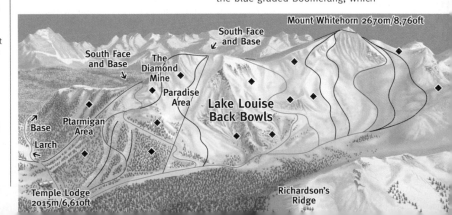

↑ Easy green runs at the bottom of the slopes lead to the splendid Lodge of the Ten Peaks amid the scenic grandeur
SNOWPIX.COM / CHRIS GILL

starts with a short hike from the top of the Summit surface lift, and some of the ungroomed Back Bowls terrain.

FOR BEGINNERS
Excellent terrain

Louise has a good beginner area near the base, served by a short T-bar; progress to the gentle, wide Wiwaxy (designated a slow skiing zone) and the slightly more difficult Deer Run or Eagle Meadows on the upper mountain. There are even greens round the back bowls and in the Larch area – worth taking for the views.

FOR CROSS-COUNTRY
High in quality and quantity

It's a very good area for cross-country, with around 80km/50 miles of groomed trails within Banff National Park. There are excellent trails in the local area (and on Lake Louise itself). And Emerald Lake Lodge 40km/25 miles away has some lovely peaceful trails and has been highly recommended as a place to stay for a peaceful time.

LIFTLINES
Not unknown

Half of the area's visitors come for the day from nearby cities such as Calgary – so it's fairly quiet during the week. Lake Louise is so sure of its lift system that it offers vouchers, to be used within the year, if you have to wait in line for over ten minutes. A new chair on the front side was installed for 2000/01 to be on the safe side. But a recent reporter encountered weekend liftlines of up to ten minutes on the back of Lake Louise, not the front.

MOUNTAIN RESTAURANTS
Good base facilities

The Lodge of the Ten Peaks at the base is a hugely impressive, spacious, airy, modern, log-built affair with various eating, drinking and lounging options. The neighboring, refurbished Whiskeyjack building has the good Northface table-service restaurant and buffet. Beavertails, at the Gazebo, is popular with reporters for a quick lunch, though it can get very crowded.

boarding *Lake Louise is a great mountain for free-riders, with all the challenging terrain in the bowls and glades. Unless you are proficient, avoid the one surface-lift, which is a tricky one to ride. The resort claims that its terrain-park is now the biggest in Canada, and it's certainly impressive, as is the half-pipe. The bars at the base are the liveliest at the end of the day of any of the Banff areas, but the village is deadly dull at night.*

SCHOOLS/GUIDES

2001/02 prices in Canadian dollars

Club Ski and Club Snowboard
3 days of guided lessons of the three areas

Club Program
4½hr per day
3 full days 169
(incl lunch for Club Junior Program for age 6-12)

CHILDCARE

The nursery at Lake Louise takes children aged 18 days to six years, from 8am to 4.30. Children aged three or more can take short ski lessons.

GETTING THERE

Air Calgary, transfer 1½hr.

Phone numbers

From distant parts of Canada, add the prefix 1 403.
From abroad, add the prefix +1 403.

ACTIVITIES

Indoor Mainly hotel-based pools, saunas and hot-tubs
Outdoor Ice-skating, walking, cross-country skiing, ice fishing on the lake, swimming in hot springs, heli-skiing, sleigh rides, dog-sled rides, snowmobiles, helicopter tours, snowshoe tours

TOURIST OFFICE

Postcode ToL oCo
t +1 (403) 762 4561
f 762 8185
info@sblls.com
www.sblls.com

Up the mountain, Temple Lodge, near the bottom of the Larch lift, is built in rustic style with a big terrace. It too can get very crowded, but options include a calm table-service restaurant and a well-priced buffet (buffalo stew a speciality). Whitehorn Lodge, at mid-mountain on the front face, has good views from its balcony.

SCHOOLS AND GUIDES
Excellent reports

'The best lesson we've encountered' is how a reporter described his 'bumps' lesson at Lake Louise. See the Banff chapter for details on the excellent three-day, three-mountain Club Ski and Club Snowboard Program.

FACILITIES FOR CHILDREN
First-class

A reporter who used Lake Louise, Sunshine and Norquay facilities said: 'I'd recommend all three and advise booking in advance at Lake Louise.'

Staying there

Lake Louise village is handy for the slopes, which are 10 minutes' drive away. But don't expect resort ambience or much nightlife.

HOW TO GO
Superb-value packages

Hotels Summer is the peak season here. Prices halve for the winter – so you can stay in luxury at bargain rates.
Fairmont Chateau Lake Louise (522 3511) Isolated position with stunning views over frozen Lake Louise, 500 rooms, lots of shops, groups of tourists (lots of Japanese groups), indoor pool, steam room and hot-tub.
Post Hotel (522 3989) Small, comfortable Relais & Châteaux place in village with good restaurant and indoor pool, hot-tub, sauna.
Lake Louise Inn (522 3791) The cheaper option in the village, with pool, hot-tub and sauna. 'Comfortable rooms' and an efficient shuttle-bus, but 'disappointing restaurants'.
Deer Lodge (522 3747) Charming old hotel next to the Chateau, good restaurant, rooftop hot-tub with amazing views.
Apartments/condos A limited number are available.

EATING OUT
Limited choice

The Post hotel has the best cuisine in the Banff region. The Outpost (also in the Post hotel) does good inexpensive pub food. The Station Restaurant is in an atmospheric old station building, but we were disappointed with the food there. The small bakery/coffee shop in the village has had praise from reporters and is good for breakfast.

APRES-SKI
Lively at teatime, quiet later

There are several options at the bottom of the slopes. The Sitzmark Lounge in Whiskeyjack Lodge is a popular – with an open fire and often a live band. The upstairs part of The Lodge of the Ten Peaks has lovely surroundings, an open fire, a couple of bars and a relaxed atmosphere. Beavertails has a good sun terrace. A few times a week there are weekly parties with live music and dancing and an excellent buffet dinner at the mid-mountain Whitehorn Lodge. You ski or ride there as the lifts close and the evening ends with a torchlit descent. We loved it.

Later on, things are fairly quiet. For most guests, it's a leisurely dinner followed by bed. But the Glacier Saloon, in Fairmont Chateau Lake Louise, with traditional Wild West decor, often has live music until late. Explorer's Lounge, in the Lake Louise Inn, has nightly entertainment. The Post hotel's Outpost Pub has been recommended.

OFF THE SLOPES
Beautiful scenery

Lake Louise makes a lovely, peaceful place to stay for someone who does not intend to hit the slopes. The lake itself makes a stunning setting for walks, snow-shoeing, cross-country skiing and ice skating. There are plenty of other things to do and lots of wildlife to see. You can go on organized ice canyon walks, sleigh rides and sightseeing tours, and you can go dog-sledding and tobogganing, and visit natural hot springs.

For a more lively day or for shopping you can visit Banff.

Lake Louise is near one end of the Columbia Icefields Parkway, a three-hour drive to Jasper through National Parks, amid stunningly beautiful scenery of high peaks and glaciers – one of the world's most beautiful drives.

Panorama
1160m/3,800ft

Vertically challenging and fast developing

What's new

➕ Increasing number of slope-side accommodations, and the lower village is now linked by lift

➕ Fairly extensive slopes with big vertical and challenging runs for all abilities

➕ Runs are usually deserted

➕ Heli-skiing by the day on hand

➖ May be too challenging for timid intermediates – not many cruisers

➖ Snowfall record not impressive by high local standards

➖ Mainly slow lifts, including T-bars

➖ Some liftlines

➖ No real mountain restaurants

➖ Few off-slope diversions

You can expect to hear more and more about Panorama. Its dynamic owner, Intrawest, has big plans for it, and the mountain has great potential. Its vertical of 1220m/4,000ft is one of the biggest in North America, and less than half of the available terrain is in use at present. Like Fernie's, the slopes are not as good for the intermediate trail-basher as for the novice and the expert or the confident intermediate.

THE RESORT
Panorama is a small (but growing) purpose-built resort above the lakeside town of Invermere in eastern BC, about two hours' scenic drive south-west of Banff. Accommodations are concentrated mainly in two car-free areas. Recently, lodges have been built at the foot of the main slopes but a lot of accommodations are in a 'lower village'. This is now linked to the lift base area by a bucket lift. There are also houses spread widely around the hillside.

Outings by car are possible to Kimberley, less than two hours south, or to Lake Louise or Kicking Horse, slightly further away to the north.

THE MOUNTAIN
The slopes basically follow three ridges, joined at top and bottom. At the top, between the left and central ridges, is the double-black-diamond Extreme Dream Zone. Almost all of the terrain is wooded. Daily mountain tours are available.

Slopes From the upper village, a fast quad goes over gentle slopes to mid-mountain. Above this a double-chair followed by two T-bars opens up intermediate and expert slopes. From the summit there are long runs down the two outer ridges as well as the central one. Those on the right bring you to a triple-chair up to mid-mountain, which also serves its own bunch of runs. Either way, the whole vertical is usable. 2000/01 saw the opening of the new 'Outback' area in Taynton Bowl, off the back of the summit area – 700 acres of lightly wooded expert terrain (previously used for heli-skiing) funnelling down to a single blue run back to the village.

Snowboarding The extensive powder bowls and tree runs are ideal for good riders, and there's also the Show Zone terrain-park and pipe (open in the

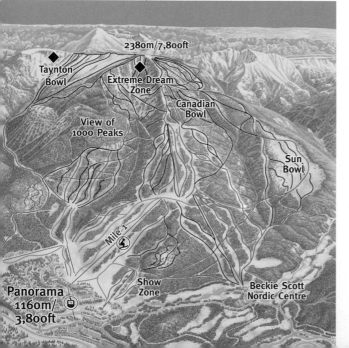

Taynton Bowl

2380m/7,800ft

Extreme Dream Zone

View of 1000 Peaks

Canadian Bowl

Sun Bowl

Mile 1

Show Zone

Beckie Scott Nordic Centre

Panorama
1160m/
3,800ft

MOUNTAIN FACTS

Altitude 1160m-2380m
3,800ft-7,800ft

Lifts	10
Trails	2,847 acres
Green	15%
Blue	55%
Black	30%
Snowmaking	
	800 acres

Central reservations phone number
Call 1 800 663 2929
(toll-free from within Canada)

TOURIST OFFICE

Postcode VoA 1To
t +1 (250) 342 6941
f 341 6262
paninfo@panorama resort.com
www.skipanorama.com

INTRAWEST / SCOTT ROWED

From higher up they say you can see 1,000 peaks ↓

evening too). Beginners have several good long green runs to practice on, but the two main beginner areas are served by surface lifts.

Snow reliability Snow reliability could be better – the annual snowfall is less than half of the Fernie/Whistler figure. But snowmaking covers 40% of the area, and most slopes are not over-sunny. And grooming is excellent.

Experts There are genuine black runs scattered all over the mountain, but also some areas of special interest for experts. At the very top of the mountain and accessed by a gateway is the Extreme Dream Zone – seriously steep trails complicated by cliffs as well as tight trees, said to contain the best snow on the mountain. Off the back of the summit, is the new Taynton Bowl area offering challenging but less extreme expert terrain. There are often good bumps on the blacks at mid-mountain. On the extreme right of the mountain is an area of gentler glades, where you can pick the density of trees and steepness of slope to suit yourself. And RK Heli-Skiing operates from a base right next to the village.

Intermediates For adventurous intermediates the terrain is excellent – there are easy blacks all over the mountain, some of them regularly groomed. The View of 1000 Peaks (now regraded black) and Schober's Dream are beautiful and long for North America (up to 3.5km/2 miles). But for the less experienced it may be uncomfortably challenging. The blues in the center of the area are excellent – the new Millennium (black running into

blue) is a great roller-coaster – but they don't add up to a lot.

Beginners There are a couple of beginners' lifts and access to good, longer runs served by the lower lifts.

Cross-country There are 17km/10 miles of trails out at the Nordic Centre.

Liftlines There can be lines for the double-chair from mid-mountain and the T-bars above it, though the trails are usually deserted.

Mountain restaurants There are no real mountain restaurants, just two huts offering basic refreshments. But there's a good coffee shop and the Ski Tip day lodge at the base is an excellent modern affair.

Schools and guides The Bilodeau School of Skiing and Snowboarding (SOS) was 'universally agreed as superb by all who tried it', says one reporter. Another reporter was pleased with his private bumps class.

Facilities for children Wee Wascals is the childcare center, taking children from 18 months. Evening babysitters are also available.

STAYING THERE

How to go There's an increasing choice of hotels and condos. The better places are the newer ones up on the beginner area level.

Hotels Ski Tip, Tamarack and the new Panorama Springs have all been recommended. And the new slope-side stone and timber-clad Taynton Lodge looks impressive. The Pine Inn is 'a high standard' budget option.

Apartments/condos There are plenty of condo blocks and town homes. The store is inadequate, so stock up in Invermere.

Eating out Eating out options are mainly in the lodges – the Toby Creek restaurant is good (though a bit gloomy for some tastes), and the Starbird Steak House does a good buffet breakfast. The Heliplex restaurant offers good value. There's also an evening shuttle-bus to the restaurants down in Invermere.

Après-ski Après-ski revolves around the Kicking Horse bar in the Pine Inn and the Jackpine pub in the Horsethief Lodge. The Ski Tip Lodge terrace is popular on sunny afternoons. The Glacier is the night club.

Off the slopes The new hot pools facility, with different thermal baths, a swimming pool, slides and sauna, is a welcome addition but gets rather taken over by kids.

Whistler

North America's biggest mountain set in Alpine-style scenery

HOW IT RATES

The slopes

Snow	★★★★
Extent	★★★★
Experts	★★★★★
Intermediates	★★★★★
Beginners	★★★★
Convenience	★★★★
Liftlines	★★★
Restaurants	★★

The rest

Scenery	★★★
Resort charm	★★★
Off-slope	★★

➕ North America's biggest mountain, both in area and vertical (1609m/5,280ft)

➕ Good slopes for all abilities, with an unrivalled combination of high open bowls and woodland trails

➕ Good snow record

➕ Almost Alpine scenery, unlike the rounded Rockies of Colorado

➕ Attractive modern village at the foot of the slopes, car-free in the center, with lively après-ski

➕ Good range of restaurants and bars (though not enough of them)

➕ Excellent heli-operation nearby

➖ Proximity to the ocean means a lot of cloudy weather and, with the low altitude, when it's snowing on the mountain it's often raining at resort level

➖ Two separate mountains are linked only at resort level

➖ Some runs get very crowded

➖ Liftlines are often a problem

➖ Mountain restaurants are mostly functional (and overcrowded)

➖ Whistler is in danger of becoming a victim of its own success – attracting more people than the mountain or the village facilities (restaurants in particular) can cope with

Provided you go to Whistler prepared for cloudy skies and rain at the base, you'll love it. Last season was an unusually poor snow year for the whole of western Canada and meant more blue sky days than usual – we had virtually a whole week of them in a December visit. But Whistler still got more snow than most places and reporters were generally happy with it throughout the season. Whatever the weather, Whistler's combination of wonderful varied and extensive terrain, big vertical, reliable snow and good lifts is unrivalled, and for a purpose-built resort the village is attractive. Most readers love it, though waiting in line is becoming more of a problem, as are overcrowded runs and restaurants. Extracts from this year's crop of reports: 'Enough terrain to satisfy any expert.' 'Awesome.' 'Charming, pretty and friendly.' But a touch of scepticism has crept in too: 'Just like Disneyland on snow – highly organized, good at extracting money from you and prone to the odd line for the best attractions!'

WHISTLER RESORT ASSOCIATION / PAUL MORRISON

Whistler gets a lot of snow – in the village as well as on the mountain if you are lucky ↓

The resort

Whistler Village sits at the foot of its two mountains, Whistler and Blackcomb, a scenic 120km/75-mile drive inland from Vancouver on Canada's west coast. Whistler started as a locals' ski area in 1966 with a few ramshackle buildings in what is now Whistler Creek. Whistler Village was developed in the late 1970s, and a village spread up the lower slopes of Blackcomb Mountain in the 1980s. Whistler has now annexed Blackcomb's village, a 10-minute walk away, and it's now called Upper Village.

Both centers are traffic-free. The architecture is varied and, for a purpose-built resort, quite tasteful. There are lots of chalet-style apartments on the hillsides. The centers have individually

A couple of seasons ago, two much-needed fast quad chairs opened on Whistler mountain, making an alternative route up from the base to the often overcrowded gondola, bringing Whistler's total number of fast lifts to 15. The funky Chic Pea restaurant opened near the top, and additional gladed runs were cut beneath the higher Garbanzo chair-lift. Whistler Mountain's Nintendo 64 terrain-park doubled in size to 26 acres.

Whistler Creek continues to be developed, making it less of an outpost and more a suitable place to stay in its own right.

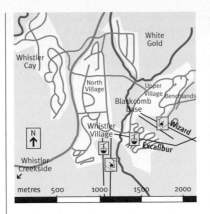

designed wood and concrete buildings, blended together in a master plan around pedestrian streets and squares. There are no monstrous high-rise blocks – but there are a lot of large five- or six-story hotel and apartment buildings. Whistler Village has most of the bars, restaurants and shops, and the two main gondolas. Whistler North, further from the lifts, is newer and has virtually merged with the original village, making a huge car-free area of streets lined with shops, condos and restaurants. Upper Village is much smaller and quieter, but its huge Chateau Whistler hotel dominates the views of the village from the mountain.

Whistler Creek, a 10-minute bus-ride from Whistler Village, is rather out on a limb, with limited bars and restaurants. But it's changing fast – a five-year development project is well under way and more readers are staying there.

There is a free bus between Whistler and Upper Village but it's just as quick to walk. Staying further out means paying for buses (C$1.50) or cabs – which are inexpensive.

Whistler is very cosmopolitan, with many visitors from Japan and Australia as well as Europe and the US. But it is now getting very crowded and reporters have complained of rowdy behaviour (over 100 arrests on New Year's Eve and fights at the taxi stand).

The mountains

The area has acquired a formidable and well-deserved reputation among experts. But both Whistler and Blackcomb also have loads of well-groomed intermediate terrain. Together they have over 200 marked trails, and form the biggest area of slopes, with the longest runs, in North America.

Many reporters are enthusiastic about the mountain host service and the 'go slow' patrol – some find the latter 'over zealous', but crowded slopes, especially on the runs home ('a human slalom'), mean they're often needed.

THE SLOPES
The best in North America
Whistler Mountain is accessed from Whistler Village by a two-stage, 10-person gondola that rises over 1100/3,800ft to the Roundhouse Lodge, the main mid-mountain base at 1850m/6,070ft. There is an alternative of two consecutive fast quads, which take you slightly lower.

Runs back down through the trees fan out from the top of the gondola – cruises to the Emerald and Big Red fast chairs on the flanks, longer runs to the gondola mid-station.

From Roundhouse you can see the jewel in Whistler's crown – magnificent above-the-tree-line bowls below the peak, served by the fast Peak and Harmony quads. The bowls have some groomed trails, but are mostly go-anywhere terrain for experts.

A six-person gondola from Whistler Creek also accesses Whistler mountain.

Access to **Blackcomb** from Whistler Village is by an eight-seater gondola, followed by a fast quad. From Upper Village you take two consecutive fast quads up to the main Rendezvous restaurant. From the arrival points you can go left for great cruising terrain and the Glacier Express quad up to the Horstman Glacier area, or right for

MOUNTAIN FACTS

Altitude 655m-2285m
2,140ft-7,490ft

Lifts	33
Trails	7,071 acres
Green	18%
Blue	55%
Black	27%
Snowmaking	
	530 acres
Recco detectors used	

boarding *Both mountains are excellent for every ability of boarder. All the main lifts are chairs and gondolas and terrain ranges from gentle green runs to wide open bowls and heart-stopping cliff drops and chutes. The Whistler terrain-park and half-pipe is a good place to hone your skills before trying the more difficult park on Blackcomb. The resort regularly hosts big snowboard events so it's not uncommon to see pro riders. There are T-bars on the glacier, but they're not vicious and any discomfort is worth it for the powder! It's popular with snowboarders and well known for its summer boarding camps.*

LIFT TICKETS

2000/01 prices in
Canadian dollars
**Whistler/Blackcomb
Lift Ticket**
Covers all lifts on
both Whistler and
Blackcomb
mountains.
Main ticket
1-day ticket 61
6-day ticket 336
Senior citizens
Over 65: 6-day ticket
286
Children
Age 13-18: 6-day
ticket 286
Age 7-12: 6-day ticket
168
Under 7: free ticket
Short-term tickets
Half-day ticket 46
Notes
Whistler/Blackcomb
ticket of 5 days or
over gives one non-
skiing day; 6-day
ticket valid for 7 days
with one day non-
skiing. Further
discounts for groups
of over 25.

steeper slopes, the terrain park or the 7th Heaven chair. The 1609m/5,280ft vertical from the top of this chair to the base is the largest in North America (and big even by Alpine standards). Or you can go into the glacier area. A T-bar from the Horstman Glacier brings you (with a very short hike) to the Blackcomb Glacier in the next valley – a beautiful run which takes you away from all lifts.

Fresh Tracks is a deal that allows you to ride up Whistler mountain (at extra cost) at 7.30, have a buffet breakfast and hit the slopes as soon as they open – very popular with many of our reporters. A good tip is to hit the slopes first and breakfast after – otherwise you may miss the quietest time on the slopes. Blackcomb has floodlit beginner slopes a couple of nights a week. Free guided tours of each mountain are offered twice a day.

SNOW RELIABILITY
Excellent at altitude

Snow conditions at the top are usually excellent – the place gets around 360 inches of snow a year, on average. The 2000/01 season was a surprising exception to the rule, but reporters still had few complaints. Even in a good year, since the resort is low and close to the Pacific, the bottom slopes can be wet, icy or unskiable. People may

'download' from the mid-stations due to poor snow, especially in late season.

FOR EXPERTS
Few can rival it

Whistler Mountain's bowls are enough to keep experts happy for weeks. Each has endless variations, with chutes and gullies of varied steepness and width. The biggest challenges are around Glacier, Whistler and West Bowls, with runs such as The Cirque and Doom & Gloom – though you can literally go anywhere in this high, wide area.

Blackcomb has challenging slopes too; not as extensive as Whistler's, but some are more difficult. From the top of the 7th Heaven lift, traverse to Xhiggy's Meadow, for good sunny bowl runs.

If you're feeling brave, go in the opposite direction and drop into the extremely steep chutes down towards Glacier Creek, including the infamous 41° Couloir Extreme, which had bumps the size of elephants at the top when we last visited. Or try the also serious, but less frequented, steep bowls reached by hiking up Spanky's Ladder, after taking the Glacier Express lift.

Both mountains have challenging trails through the trees. The adventurous can explore the 'Peak to Creek' trails, from below Whistler's West Bowl to Whistler Creek – still

From the top of Harmony Express there are bowls in every direction

INTRAWEST / RANDY LINCKS

the Harmony Express lift is a favorite with many of our reporters. The blue path round the back from the top of The Peak chair, which skirts West Bowl, has beautiful views over a steep valley and across to the rather phallic-shaped Black Tusk mountain.

Lower down the mountain there is a vast choice of groomed blue runs with a series of efficient fast chairs to bring you back up to the top of the gondola. It's a cruiser's paradise – especially the aptly named Ego Bowl. A great long run is the fabulous Dave Murray Downhill all the way from mid-mountain to the finish at Whistler Creek. Although marked black on the map, it's a wonderful fast and varied cruise when it has been groomed.

FOR BEGINNERS
Great if the sun shines
Whistler has excellent beginner areas by the mid-station of the gondola – and Blackcomb down at the base area. Both have facilities higher up too.

On Whistler, after progressing from the beginner slopes, there are some gentle first runs from the top of the gondola, except for other people speeding past. You can return by various chairs or carry on to the base area on greens. Check the latter are in good condition first, and maybe avoid them at the end of the day, when they can get very crowded.

On Blackcomb, Green Line runs from the top of the mountain to the bottom. The top part is particularly gentle, with some steeper pitches lower down.

Our main reservation is – you guessed – the weather. Beginners don't get a lot out of heavy snowfalls, and might be put off by rain.

FOR CROSS-COUNTRY
Picturesque but low
There are over 28km/18 miles of cross-country tracks, starting in the valley by the river, on the path between Whistler and Blackcomb. But it is low altitude, so conditions can be unreliable. Keen cross-country skiers can catch the train to better areas.

LIFTLINES
An ever-increasing problem
Whistler is becoming a victim of its own success. Even with 15 fast lifts – more than any other resort in North America – the mountains are line-prone, especially on weekends when people pour in from Vancouver. There

outside the area boundary at present, so rescues are costly.

If all this isn't enough, there's also local heli-skiing available by the day.

FOR INTERMEDIATES
Ideal and extensive terrain
Both mountains are an intermediate's paradise. In good weather, good intermediates will enjoy the less extreme variations in the bowls on both mountains.

One of our favorite intermediate runs is the Blackcomb Glacier from the top of the mountain to the bottom of the Excelerator chair over 1000m/ 3,300ft below. This 5km/3 mile run away from all lifts starts with a two-minute walk up from the top of the Showcase T-bar. You drop over the ridge into a wide, wide bowl – not too suddenly or you'll get a short, sharp shock in the very steep double-diamond Blowhole. The further you traverse, the shallower the slope.

You are guaranteed good snow on the Horstman Glacier too, and typically gentle runs. Lower down there are lots of perfect cruising runs through the trees – ideal when the weather is bad.

On Whistler Mountain, there are easy blue trails in Symphony, Harmony and Glacier bowls, which allow even early intermediates to try the bowls, always knowing there's an easy way down. The Saddle run from the top of

There's nowhere better in North America for ungroomed bowl skiing and riding amidst spectacular scenery →

is a cute system for displaying waiting times at strategic points, but most people would prefer shorter lines. Some reporters have signed up with the ski school to get lift priority. Others have visited Vancouver on the weekend to avoid the crowds. The fast chairs in parallel with the Whistler gondola have helped but lines still form at the base in the morning, especially for the Blackcomb gondola. Whistler Creek is less of a problem. Some of the chairs up the mountain also produce lines (up to 30 minutes) – especially Harmony ('Even the singles liftline doesn't make it quicker,' says a reporter) – and several on Blackcomb build lines, too.

MOUNTAIN RESTAURANTS
Overcrowded
The main restaurants sell decent, good-value food but are charmless self-service stops with long lines. They're huge, but not huge enough. 'Seat-seekers' are employed to find spaces, but success is not guaranteed. In the past, reporters have stressed the need to lunch early. That no longer works – 'they're packed by 11.30'. 'Try a big breakfast followed by a 2.30 lunch instead,' suggests a recent visitor.

Blackcomb has the Rendezvous, mainly a big (850-seat) self-service place but also home to Christine's, a table-service restaurant – the best on either mountain. Glacier Creek Lodge, at the bottom of the Glacier Express, is a better self-service place. But even this (1,496 seats) gets 'incredibly busy'. Whistler has the massive (1,740-seat) Roundhouse Lodge; Steeps Grill is its table-service refuge.

Reporters generally prefer the smaller places – but they're still packed unless you time it right. On Blackcomb Crystal Hut at the top of the Crystal Ridge chair and Horstman Hut at the top of the mountain are tiny Alpine-style huts with great views.

On Whistler Raven's Nest, at the top of the Creekside gondola, is a small and friendly deli/cafe. And the Chic Pea near the top of the Garbanzo chair-lift is 'funky and rustic' for pizza and barbecue. You can of course descend to the base – the table-service Dusty's at Whistler Creek has good sandwiches and soup.

SCHOOLS/GUIDES
2000/01 prices in Canadian dollars

Whistler and Blackcomb
Guided instruction with Ski Esprit course
Classes 3 or 4 days
Full day from 9.45
3 days: 249
4 days: 289
Children's classes
Ages: 3 to 6
5 6hr days including lunch, lift ticket and equipment rental: 445
Private lessons
Half day: 305
Full day: 469

CHILDCARE
Whistler Kids takes non-skiing children aged 3 months to 3 years, as well as acting as the base for ski lessons.

Whistler Kids offers various skiing and snowboarding programs to children of all ability levels, aged 3 to 17. The Kids' Adventure Camp is a 5-day camp for 3 to 12 year olds. Ride Tribe is the teen program for ages 13 to 17.

Après-ski programs – with a 'Kids' Night Out' – are offered during the season.

SCHOOLS AND GUIDES
A great formula
Ski Esprit and Ride Esprit programs run for three or four days and combine instruction with showing you around the mountains – with the same instructor daily. Many of our reporters have joined these groups (usually small), and all reports are glowing: 'Big improvement in confidence and skill' is typical. There are specialist clinics and snowboard classes, too.

We have rave reviews of Extremely Canadian's challenging free-skiing clinics (938 9656) for experts.

FACILITIES FOR CHILDREN
Impressive
Blackcomb's base area has a special slow-moving Magic Chair to get children part-way up the mountain. Whistler's gondola mid-station has a splendid kids-only area. A reporter found the staff were 'friendly and instilled confidence'. The drawback for young children is the risk of bad weather.

Staying there

The most convenient place to stay is Whistler Village as you can go straight up either mountain by gondola. A lot of accommodations are an inconvenient walk or bus-ride from the villages and slopes. Whistler Creek, though convenient for Whistler's slopes, is less so for Blackcomb and is pretty quiet.

A number of recent visitors have found the central area around Village Square very noisy in the early hours.

HOW TO GO
Vast choice of hotels and condos
Hotels There is a very wide range.
((((⑤ **Fairmont Chateau Whistler** (938 8000) Modern but in traditional Canadian Pacific château-hotel style, at the foot of Blackcomb mountain. Indoor-outdoor pool and tubs. The Entree Gold floor is expensive and indulging.
((((⑤ **Westin Resort & Spa** (905 5000) New luxury all-suite hotel at foot of Whistler mountain next to lifts.
(((④ **Pan Pacific Lodge** (905 2999) Luxury all-suite place at Whistler Village base. Pool/sauna/tub.
(((④ **Lost Lake Lodge** (932 2882) 'Excellent' place: studios and suites, out by the golf course. Pool/tub.
(((④ **Crystal Lodge** (932 2221) 'Comfortable, friendly, convenient', in Whistler Village. Pool/sauna/tub.
((③ **Glacier Lodge** (932 2882) In Upper Village. Pool/tub.
Apartments/condos There are plenty of spacious, comfortable condominiums in both chalet and hotel-style blocks.

EATING OUT
High quality and plenty of choice
Reporters are enthusiastic about the range, quality and value of places to eat, but do book well ahead: there simply aren't enough restaurant seats to meet demand. Some cheaper places won't take bookings for small groups, meaning long waits. Bars serve decent food, too. If you've got kids, as one reporter found, '60% of restaurants don't allow under-19s in, or even to sit outside, and we had to wait up to two hours elsewhere.'

At the top of the scale, Umberto's in Whistler Village has classy Italian cuisine. The Rimrock Café at Whistler Creek serves 'the best seafood we have ever eaten'.

Good mid scale Whistler Village places include Araxi (Italian/Pacific), the Keg (steak and seafood), Teppan Village (Japanese), Mongolie (Asian) and Kipriaki Norte (Greek). Crab Shack has good-value seafood. In Village North: the good-value Brewhouse has great atmosphere (steaks, burgers), Caramba has 'good Mediterranean food at reasonable prices' and the Tandoori Grill has 'Indian just like at home'. Hy's Steakhouse has the best steaks. Sushi-Ya, and Quattro (Italian) are good.

There are plenty of budget places, including the bars mentioned under après-ski. Uli's Flipside and The Old Spaghetti Factory have been recommended for pasta.

APRES-SKI
Something for most tastes
With over 50 bars, night-clubs and restaurants, Whistler is very lively. Most of the après bars seem to compete to see who can serve the biggest trash can lid of nachos. Popular at Whistler are the Longhorn, with a huge terrace, and the Garibaldi Lift Company. The Dubh Linn Gate Irish pub has 'great live music and Guinness'. Black's is good for a quiet drink while Tapley's seems 'the nearest thing to a locals' bar'. Merlin's is the focus at Blackcomb base, and Dusty's at Whistler Creek – good beer, loud music.

Later on, Buffalo Bills is lively and loud and the Amsterdam is worth a look. The Cinnamon Bear in the Delta Resort hotel is a sports bar with some live music. Tommy Africa's vies with the Savage Beagle, Maax Fish and Garfinkel's for the clubbing crowd, and Moe Joe's has been recommended. The bizarre AlpenRock House has all sorts of games (from glow-in-the-dark bowling to virtual reality), restaurants and bars – all in a neo-Swiss setting. ('Excellent for the kids.') Try the Mallard bar in Chateau Whistler and the Crystal Lodge piano bar for a relaxed time.

OFF THE SLOPES
Not ideal
Whistler is a long way to go if you don't ski or ride. Meadow Park Sports Center has a full range of fitness facilities. There are also several luxurious spas. Excursions to Squamish (famous for its eagles) are easy. A day trip to Vancouver is recommended.

GETTING THERE

Air Vancouver, transfer 2hr.

Phone numbers
From distant parts of Canada, add the prefix 1 604.
From abroad, add the prefix +1 604.

ACTIVITIES

Indoor Ice skating, museum, tennis, hot-tubs
Outdoor Flightseeing, heli-skiing, snow-shoe excursions, snowmobiling, paragliding, fishing, horse-riding, sleigh rides, guided tours

TOURIST OFFICE

Postcode V0N 1B4
t +1 (604) 932 3928
f 932 7231
reservations@tourism whistler.com
www.whistler-black comb.com

For us the main attraction of skiing or riding in eastern Canada is the French culture and language that are predominant in the province of Québec. It really feels like a different country from the rest of Canada – as indeed many of its residents want it to become. Tremblant is the main destination resort and is one of the cutest purpose-built resorts we've seen. The other main base is Québec city, which dates from the 17th century and is full of atmosphere and Canadian history. The slopes of the main resorts are small both in extent and in vertical drop, and the weather can be brutally cold in early and mid-winter. But at least this means that the extensive snowmaking systems that all the resorts have can be effective for a long season. Be prepared for variable snow conditions and don't go expecting light, dry powder – if that's what you want, head west.

There are lots of ski and snowboard areas in Ontario – Canada's most populated province – but most of them are tiny and cater just to locals. For people headed on vacation for a week or more, eastern Canada really means the province of Québec. Québec – and its capital, Québec city – are heavily dominated by the French culture and language. Notices, menus, trail maps and so on are usually printed in both French and English. Many ski area workers will be bilingual or just French-speaking. And French cuisine abounds.

The weather is very variable, rather like New England's – but it can get even colder. Hence the snow, though pretty much guaranteed by snowmaking, can vary enormously in quality. When we were there in April we were slush skiing in Tremblant one day and rattling along on a rock hard surface in Mont-Ste-Anne the next. Last season one of our reporters visited Mont-Ste-Anne, Stoneham and Le Massif in late January and experienced mild temperatures and several perfect blue sky days.

The main destination resort is Tremblant (see separate chapter), about 90 minutes' drive from Montreal. Other areas near here popular with locals include **Mont Blanc** (with only 300m/980ft of vertical, hardly a competitor to the Franco-Italian version) and the **Saint-Sauveur** valley (five areas, each with around 200m/660ft of vertical and with interchangeable lift tickets).

INTRAWEST

One of the best addresses in Tremblant: Chateau Mont Tremblant ↓

The other main place to stay for easy access to several ski resorts is **Québec city**. Old Québec, at the city's heart, is North America's only walled city and is a World Heritage site. Within the city walls are narrow, winding streets and 17th and 18th century houses. It is situated right on the banks of the St Lawrence river. In January/February there is a famous two-week carnival, with an ice castle, snow sculptures, dog-sled and canoe races, night parades and grand balls. But most of the winter is low season for Québec city, with good-value rooms available in big hotels.

There are several ski and snowboard areas close to Québec city. There's now a Carte Blanche pass which covers the three main areas: a total of 106 runs and 26 lifts and including Canada's largest night skiing area. A car is handy, but there are buses to some areas.

The biggest and most varied area (though easily skied in a day by a good skier) is **Mont-Ste-Anne**, 30 minutes away and with some accommodations of its own. A gondola takes you to the top, and slopes lead down the front (south) and back (north) sides. There are intermediate cruising runs on both sides and some steep blacks (including World Cup runs) through the trees on the front among its 63km/39 miles of trails. There are some easy top-to-bottom runs and good beginner areas at the base. The views from the front over the ice-flows of the St Lawrence are spectacular. Fourteen trails are floodlit until 10pm five nights a week. Over 80% of the runs are covered by snowmaking. It also has the largest cross-country center in Canada, with 223km/139 miles of trails. In the spring you can stop by the Taffi hut and try fresh maple toffee, made to order.

Stoneham is the closest resort to Québec city, around 20 minutes away. It also has its own small village with accommodations and an impressive base lodge with bar, restaurant and big wooden deck. Après-ski in the lodge can be lively, and there is sometimes live music. It is a small area, with only around 30km/19 miles of runs spread between three faces and a vertical of 420m/1,380ft. But it is very sheltered in a sunny setting protected from wind. It suits families well, with mainly intermediate and beginner terrain. Snowboarders, freestylers and freeskiers are attracted to the area by the resort's impressive terrain-park and half mile long permanent boarder-cross course. A reporter who went there last season raved about how addictive it was. Stoneham also has the biggest night-skiing operation in Canada, with two of the three faces lit top-to-bottom. Some 95% of the area has snowmaking.

Le Massif is around an hour away from Québec city and is a cult area with locals. It is in a UNESCO World Biosphere Reserve, and is just yards from the St Lawrence. The views of the ice-flows are stunning, and you feel you are heading straight down into them when you are on the pretty, tree-lined trails.

The area of slopes, though small, has the largest vertical drop in the east. There are a couple of steep double-black-diamond runs and some good, well-groomed black and blue cruising runs. But it suits experts and good intermediates best – beginners and timid intermediates would be better off elsewhere.

Major new development is due to be complete for the 2001/02 season. Two new quad chair-lifts will supplement the three existing lifts. A new lodge is being built with a 1,500 capacity car park, accessed by a new road. The area of slopes will increase by a third, with up to 10 new trails, including one designed to meet International Ski Federation World Cup standards.

Where to Ski and Snowboard is an annual publication – don't rely on an old edition

Resorts change every year as new lifts are built, new slopes are opened up, more snowmaking is installed, ski schools come under new management, hotels, bars and restaurants change hands. We revise the book annually to keep up with these developments. And the book itself is constantly developing, with new features and new resorts being added. (For this edition, for example, we have added 40 new trail maps.)

Tremblant

265m/87oft

Charming new village below surprisingly small area of slopes

HOW IT RATES

The slopes

Snow	****
Extent	**
Experts	***
Intermediates	***
Beginners	****
Convenience	****
Liftlines	***
Restaurants	**

The rest

Scenery	***
Resort charm	****
Off-slope	***

What's new

For 2001/02 there will be a new two-acre beginner area by the village with two magic carpet lifts of 420ft and 210ft, a heated rest area with washrooms, an observation deck and a fire pit.

Better snowmaking facilities, a new half-pipe grinder and a new rental shop are also planned for 2001/02.

➕ Charming purpose-built village

➕ Slope-side accommodations

➕ Good snow reliability with extensive artificial back-up

➕ Some good runs for all abilities

➕ Good variety of restaurants and bars

➖ Limited area for high-mileage trail-bashers

➖ Can be perishingly cold in early and mid-winter

➖ Weekend liftlines and overcrowding can be a problem

Tremblant is eastern Canada's main destination resort. But for avid skiers and riders the limited slopes don't really do justice to the cute and lively little village, which has been built in traditional style.

THE RESORT

Tremblant has been transformed in recent years from a day or weekend ski area for locals to being eastern Canada's leading ski resort and cutest resort village. Intrawest (which also owns Whistler and several other North American resorts) has developed a charming purpose-built village in the same traditional style as the original old village. Buildings in bright, vibrant colors line narrow, cobbled traffic-free streets and squares, with lots of galleries, boutiques, patisseries and cafes. It has a very French feel to it and large ski-in, ski-out hotels and condos blend in unobtrusively, as does a C$4 million Acquaclub pool complex built to resemble a lake set in a forest.

THE MOUNTAINS

In its small area, Tremblant has a good variety of terrain.

Slopes A heated gondola takes you to the top, from where there are good views over the village and a 14km/9 mile lake on the so-called south side and over National Park wilderness on the north side. The north side is really north-east facing and gets the morning sun – a high-speed quad brings you back and there are two other chairs to play on. In 2000/01 a new beginner run was made, stretching from top to bottom of the north side. The Edge lift accesses another summit, serving mainly expert terrain. Back on the south side (really south-west facing and so good for the afternoon sun) you can go right back to town on blue or green runs, or use two high-speed quads to explore the top and bottom halves. The Versant Soleil area is more directly south-facing and has one top-to-bottom blue run with all the rest being black runs and tree runs.

Snow reliability Over 70% of the terrain is covered by snowmaking –

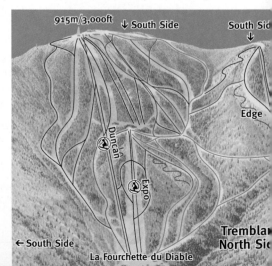

From Edge ↓   North Side ↓ 915m/3,000ft ↓ North Side

South Side

TGV

Versant Soleil

Le Soleil

Flying Mile

Tremblant 265m/ 87oft

Domaine de La Forêt   North Side →

915m/3,000ft ↓ South Side   South Side ↓

Edge

Duncan

Expo

← South Side

La Fourchette du Diable

Tremblan North Side

The charming purpose-built village is right next to the slopes →

MOUNTAIN FACTS

Altitude	265m-915m
	870ft-3,000ft
Lifts	12
Trails	81km/50 miles
Green	20%
Blue	25%
Black	55%
Snowmaking	
	440 acres

Central reservations phone number
For all resort accommodations call 425 8681 (from distant parts of Canada, add the prefix 1 819; from abroad, add the prefix +1 819)

TOURIST OFFICE
Postcode JOT 1ZO
t +1 (819) 681 2000
f 5990
info_tremblant
@intrawest.com
www.tremblant.ca

The central Place St-Bernard square is usually lively, with a band playing or something going on →

claimed to be 'the most powerful in North America'.

Experts Over half the runs are graded as suitable for advanced skiers and riders. But we found a few of the blacks rather overgraded. There are steep top-to-bottom bump runs on the north side and great tree runs off the Edge lift. The south side has some shorter challenging runs. The Versant Soleil area has more black runs and some tough runs in the trees.

Intermediates Both north and south sides have good cruising and we found the north side rather less crowded. There are blue-graded runs in the trees as well as on groomed trails.

Beginners The new beginner area for 2001/02 will be a huge improvement on the previously inadequate facilities. There are long, easy top-to-bottom green runs to progress to on both north and south sides.

Snowboarding The slopes are good, with mostly chairs, and the excellent gravity terrain-park and half-pipe are on the top half of the north side.

Cross-country There are around 100km/60 miles of trails.

Liftlines On weekends there can be lines but they tend to move quickly. We found crowds on the main run back to the village more of a problem.

Mountain restaurants The main Grand Manitou restaurant has good views back over town and decent food but can get crowded. Many people go back to town for lunch – La Diable was recommended by a reporter for its own micro-brewed beer and huge portions of poutine (a local speciality: chips, melted cheese and gravy).

Schools and guides There's a wide variety of options and a reporter recommends the 90-minute Super Group 4 (maximum of four people): 'Very impressed with instructors and small group was brilliant.'

Facilities for children Children from age one can be looked after during the day and until 9.30pm.

STAYING THERE

Hotels and condos Many of our reporters stayed at the luxurious Fairmont (formerly Chateau) Tremblant and praise it highly. Others stayed at the Plaza condos – 'central', 'comfortable' and 'well equipped' but warned of 'very limited food shopping – best to have a car'.

Eating out There is a good variety of restaurants.

Après-ski There are several lively bars, and there was live music in the main square when we were there in April. There are floodlit slopes some nights.

Off the slopes You can go ice climbing, horseback-riding, snow-shoeing, ice skating, snowmobiling, dog-sledding and swimming – and visit Montreal.

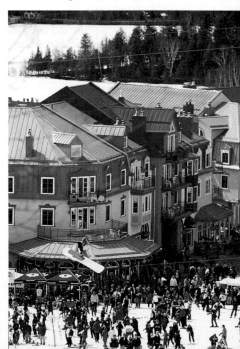

Andorra

- Excellent choice for beginners and early intermediates, with good instruction, good trail grooming and plenty of gentle slopes
- Lots of efficient, modern lifts
- Good combination of altitude and extensive snowmaking with strong southern sunshine
- Lively nightlife, with cheap duty-free drinks and generous measures
- Cheap package holidays in some resorts, competing with those in inferior resorts in eastern Europe
- Resorts close enough to each other – and some are now physically linked – so you can sample at least one other during a week

- Most resorts have little in the way of charm, and Soldeu and Pas de la Casa are sited on the busy main road through the country
- Nightlife tends to revolve around bars – not much variety, and some places can get rowdy
- Potential for a really impressive linked lift network is not exploited – no shared lift ticket
- There seems to be no end to the construction work

It's tempting to generalize about a small duty-free country like Andorra, with only a handful of resorts all within an hour's drive of the capital, and the generalizations above should help you decide whether it's the place for you. But there are differences between the resorts that make things a bit more complicated.

These days the major resorts – Soldeu and Pas de la Casa – compete more with middle-market Alpine resorts than with the budget destinations of eastern Europe. They have impressive mountains with efficient lifts, their hotels include some attractively upscale places, and package prices are no lower than those in mid-market resorts in the Alps. Not surprisingly, the clientele they attract is not as youthful, impecunious and party-oriented as it once was.

The less impressive resorts of Arinsal and Pal, and the valley towns of La Massana and Encamp, are considerably less attractive from most points of view. But prices here are appreciably cheaper, and do still compete with Bulgaria, Romania and Slovenia for the business of those on the tightest of budgets.

Soldeu, Pas de la Casa and Arinsal have their own separate chapters; this introduction includes some comments on the valley towns, and on the excellent out-of-the-way day skiing area of Arcalis.

Andorra attracts many international visitors away from Austrian and Italian resorts partly because of its relatively reliable snow record. Its situation close to both the Atlantic and the Mediterranean oceans, together with the high altitude of its resorts, means it usually gets substantial natural snowfalls. It has also invested heavily in snowmaking. This combination means you can book Andorra months in advance with some confidence. And an early reservation is necessary: late bookers can have difficulty.

As we've explained, prices vary between resorts. So, to a degree, do prices once you arrive. But prices for drinks and extras such as instruction and ski rental are generally lower than in the Alps. Some reporters have been disappointed to find duty-free luxury goods not the super-bargain they had expected.

Duty-free prices and large, unmeasured measures of spirits mean that nightlife can be very lively. But in our recent experience you will equally have no trouble avoiding rowdy scenes, and finding more civilized places in which to celebrate your day on the slopes.

The sight of cranes is not

uncommon, as the Andorrans continue to build hotels and apartments as fast as they can to keep up with the demand. It is no longer true to say (as it once was) that the resorts resemble giant construction sites, but they all have construction sites within them. Perhaps more irritating is the fact that the Andorrans don't seem to feel any obligation to finish the construction or renovation of a hotel in time for the season. They may still be installing lights, or even staircases, in hotels in mid-season.

Adjacent resorts have begun to link their areas together, meaning bigger ski areas and a bit more variety. Pas de la Casa's and Soldeu's slopes have been physically linked by lift and trail for a couple of seasons. But there seems to be no immediate prospect of a joint lift ticket, which is incredibly frustrating for keen intermediates who would relish the chance to explore the two adjacent areas. Arinsal and Pal in the west were linked by a new tram for the 2000/01 season – and have had a joint lift ticket for some years.

STAYING DOWN THE VALLEY

Several valley towns can be used as bases either to use the slopes of one resort or to explore several resorts in the course of a week.

The obviously strong candidate here is **Encamp**, which now has a powerful gondola giving a quick way into the Pas de la Casa slopes. From the top of it you can actually ski into the Soldeu area as well, but you would need to have a day ticket for that area before you set off. Encamp seemed to us the least attractive of the towns, but we can't claim to have examined it closely.

La Massana is a more appealing town, and has the considerable attraction of being quite well placed for access to Arcalis – an excellent but lodging-free ski area directly to the north, described later in this chapter. La Massana is more often used as a base for Pal and Arinsal, which are much closer – and the hotel-owning mayor is apparently planning a gondola link directly into the Pal slopes. **Ordino** is slightly nearer Arcalis, and pleasantly rustic.

The capital of **Andorra la Vella** is not far down the valley from Encamp (and the gondola into Pas de la Casa slopes) but is a much more attractive

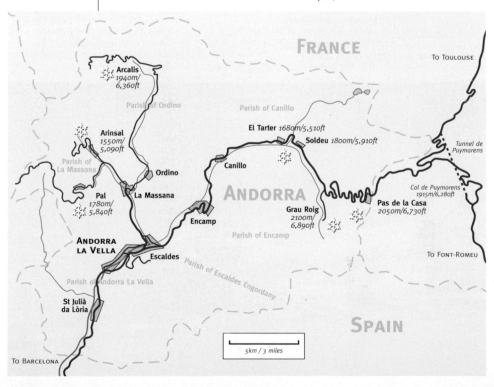

FRANCE

To Toulouse

Arcalis
1940m/
6,360ft

Parish of Ordino

Parish of Canillo

El Tarter 1680m/5,510ft

Soldeu 1800m/5,910ft

Tunnel de Puymorens

Arinsal
1550m/
5,090ft

Parish of
La Massana

Ordino

Canillo

ANDORRA

Col de Puymorens
1915m/6,280ft

Pas de la Casa
2050m/6,730ft

Pal
1780m/
5,840ft

La Massana

Grau Roig
2100m/
6,890ft

Encamp

Parish of Encamp

ANDORRA
LA VELLA

Escaldes

Parish of Escaldes Engordany

To Font-Romeu

Parish of Andorra La Vella

St Julià
da Lòria

SPAIN

5km / 3 miles

To Barcelona

↑ We've never seen anything quite as daft as this: a single trail splits into two, one way leading to the Soldeu lifts and the other to the Pas de la Casa lifts – and no lift-ticket sharing arrangements

SNOWPIX.COM / CHRIS GILL

SNOWPIX.COM / CHRIS GILL

Approaching Pas from the slopes, it's not an attractive prospect ↓

base, especially for someone wanting a more rounded holiday. The duty-free shopping could fill a page, but probably the most interesting place is Caldea spa. The interior is laid out in a 'Hanging Gardens of Babylon' style, and the facilities are very impressive – indoor–outdoor pools, with fountains and waterfalls, saunas, hot-tubs, Turkish baths, hydrotherapy, sunbeds, massage ... even a grapefruit bath!

There are plenty of high-quality, if relatively expensive, hotels. Andorra la Vella is not a big place, and most hotels are within easy walking distance of the center of the town.

There is plenty of choice when it comes to dining out. Andorrans love seafood, and the traditional Catalan restaurants delight in providing it, which seems odd in the mountains; it is delivered fresh from the coast daily.

Nightlife is also well catered to – there are plenty of bars and nightclubs, and most stay open until 4am. However, the clientele is generally a more sophisticated bunch, mainly Andorrans and Spaniards, and the 'drink-until-you-drop' attitude of the mountain resorts is rare.

What's new

2000/01 saw the extension of the snowmaking network and new signposting was installed around the mountain.

A new magic carpet conveyor belt has replaced the old rope tow in the children's snow playground.

MOUNTAIN FACTS

Altitude 1940m-2640m
6,36oft-8,66oft

Lifts	14
Trails	26km/16 miles
Green	24%
Blue	24%
Red	44%
Black	8%
Snowmaking	10km
	6 miles

Recco detectors used – helicopter based

TOURIST OFFICE

t +376 850121
f 850440
ito@andorra.ad
www.andorra.ad/comuns/ordino

SNOWPIX.COM / CHRIS GILL

There are some excellent challenging runs from the central ridge back down into the Cercle d'Arcalis ➔

Arcalis 1940m/6,36oft

Arcalis is the most remote resort in Andorra, tucked away at the head of a long valley. But it makes a very worthwhile day trip – the variety of the terrain is better than most of the other resorts, and the snow is usually the best you will find. There are no accommodations at the mountain, but increasing numbers along the Vall d'Ordino leading up to it.

THE RESORT

Arcalis resembles some of the smaller New World resorts in having nothing at the lift base apart from day lodge buildings and a lot of parking lots – the resort is very popular with weekenders, both from Andorra and Spain. There are actually two lift bases: Els Planells is up the hill from Arcalis itself, reached by a winding road that provides additional parking.

THE MOUNTAIN

The slopes are made up of two bowls, with lifts meeting at the ridge that separates them. The lower slopes of the main bowl, above the the resort base, are lightly wooded, but all the higher slopes are open.

Slopes Chair-lifts from both bases – a fast one from the lower base – cross the main bowl, the Cercle d'Arcalis, to reach the central ridge at 2550m/8,37oft. Long red and black runs come back down. On the left-hand side of this bowl, red and blue runs are served by a chair and several surface lifts. From the dividing ridge, blue and red runs descend into the bowl, the Cercle de la Coma, which is entirely tree-free (its floor is at 2200m/7,22oft). On the far side of this second bowl, a recently added chair-lift goes up to the area high point at 2640m/8,66oft, with just one red trail back down. From the Cercle de la Coma, there are three ways back to the base: a long red to Arcalis, a long green to Els Planells, or off-trail itineraries off the shoulder of the dividing ridge, reached by a short surface lift.

Snow reliability This is good. Artificial snow covers the base area and some trails leading into it. The height of the area, which starts a good 400m/1,30oft higher than Arinsal, also adds to the length of the season.

Snowboarding We're not aware of any special facilities. Beware flat sections on the trails in the Cercle de la Coma.

Experts Of all the resorts in Andorra, Arcalis has the most to offer experts. The black run that leads from the ridge back down towards the base is steep, and often bumped, while the red run it connects to starts from the top of the main chair, going through a spectacular gully before widening out. There is also plenty of space between runs for off-trail forays, especially in the Cercle de la Coma. There must be some good routes down from the new chair on the far side of it. Arcalis is well known for heli-skiing; the mountains facing the area are favored by the guides.

Intermediates You are well catered to here, with smooth, long blues and reds being the main feature of the slopes in both bowls.

Beginners The beginners' slopes are conveniently located near the upper base lodge, with a couple of surface lifts leading to some longer blue runs.

Liftlines There are no problems with liftlines midweek, when you can explore the resort and see hardly anyone. On the weekend the area is much busier, especially in good weather, and you may encounter a long wait at the bottom in the morning, especially if racers take over one of the lifts.

Mountain restaurants The base stations have a restaurant and bar. Up the mountain choices are limited; there is a snack bar at the top of the main lift, and a self-service restaurant in the Cercle de la Coma.

Schools and guides We have no reports on the ski school, but it seems well run, with a good range of options.

Facilities for children There is a day nursery for children aged 1 to 5, and a ski kindergarten for 5- to 12-year-olds.

Andorra's bargain basement just got better

➕ Good value

➕ Plenty of lively bars

➕ New tram link with Pal is very good news for non-beginners

➕ Newish gondola from village center gives easy access to the slopes

➖ Very confined local slopes

➖ Runs to village need good snow to be open, and don't lead to gondola station

➖ Long, linear and rather dreary village, with no focus

➖ Obtrusive construction sites

Before the new link with Pal, Arinsal had little going for it except cheap prices, lively bars and a good ski school. That's why it attracts lots of young people on a budget and on their first skiing or snowboarding vacation, looking for lively alcohol-fuelled evenings as well as a fun time on the slopes. The village has few other attractions, being long and strung-out, with no real focus or charm. And if it is a more attractive village and better slopes that you're interested in we'd recommend going to Soldeu instead.

THE RESORT

Arinsal is a long, narrow village of grey, stone-clad buildings, near the head of a steep-sided valley north of Andorra la Vella. Development in recent years has been rapid, and it continues, giving the place a building-site appearance.

There are some accommodations at Pal, but they are a bus-ride from the lift base. Staying in Arinsal (preferably close to the gondola station) and accessing the Pal slopes via the new tram link makes better sense for most visitors. Since 1998/99 a gondola from the village center has given access to the slopes; for most guests, the alternative chair-lift half a mile out of town is now happily irrelevant – though you can stay next to it and ski to the door in good conditions.

There are attractive accommodations in the lower town of La Massana (see the introductory chapter to Andorra). A gondola link from here to the Pal slopes is planned, possibly for 2002/03; La Caubella is 700m/2,300ft above the town.

THE MOUNTAIN

The very small local area above Arinsal's gondola is a narrow, east-facing bowl of open slopes. Pal's slopes, in contrast, are the most densely wooded of the Andorran resorts, calling to mind American resorts. They mainly face east, those down to the link with Arinsal north.

Slopes Arinsal's slopes consist essentially of a single, long, narrow bowl above the upper gondola station at Comallenpla, with runs leading straight back towards that point served by a complex network of chairs and surface lifts. Almost at the top is the tram station for the link to Pal. Again, these slopes present a sharp contrast – the runs are widely spread around the mountain with four main lift bases, all reachable by road. The main one, La Caubella, is at the opposite extreme from the linking tram.

Snow reliability With most runs above 1950m/6,400ft, north-easterly orientation and an impressive 350 snow-guns, snow is relatively assured.

Snowboarding It's possible to get around much of the area without using surface lifts. Arinsal has a new terrain-park.

Experts These aren't great mountains for experts, but there are short, sharp black slopes at Arinsal, and quite long and testing reds (and one black) at Pal – where there is also some off-trail scope.

Intermediates Arinsal offers a reasonable range of difficulty, but any confident intermediate is going to want to explore the Pal slopes, which are much more interesting, varied and extensive. There are easy cruises, and a variety of challenges in the central and Seturia sections.

Beginners Almost half the guests here are beginners. Arinsal and Pal both have gentle beginner areas apart from the main runs; they can get very crowded at peak times. There are long easy runs to progress to.

Cross-country There isn't any.

Liftlines Although there is only one lift out of the center, liftlines are not a problem on weekdays; however, Spanish weekenders and local children can hit the slopes en masse at times. Most of the higher lifts are surface lifts, keeping the mountain open when it's windy – the new tram link can easily be closed by wind.

Mountain restaurants These are not a highlight. They are mainly functional self-service places, doing routine snack food, and are often crowded.

Schools and guides Arinsal's ski school is its pride and joy. It offers technically sound, patient instruction. Over half the instructors are native English-speakers. Class sizes can, however, be very large in peak season. English speaking is not so widespread in the Pal school.

Facilities for children There is a ski kindergarten and a non-skiing nursery for younger children.

STAYING THERE

Hotels Rooms in the hotel Arinsal (835640) are not large, but it is well run, ideally placed and has a pleasant bar. The Princesa Parc (836699) is a big new glossy 4-star place, also close to the gondola, with a swanky spa. The Xalet Verdu (737140) is a smooth little 4-star, a little further from the gondola. The Micolau (835052) is a picturesque stone house, close to the

center, with simple rooms and a jolly beamed restaurant. If there is snow to the valley, the Crest (835866), up at the old chair-lift station, has the attraction that you can ski to the door.

Apartments/condos There is a reasonable choice of places. Aparthotel Sant Andreu (836164) offers simple but comfortable apartments, with a relaxed bar-restaurant on site. There are also apartments attached to the new Princesa Parc hotel.

Eating out There is a fair range of restaurants for a small resort. The Surf disco-pub is a lively spot doing open-fire grills. Cisco's is a central Tex-Mex place in a lovely wood and stone building serving Mexican food. The Rocky Mountain, up at the top of the village, is popular for steaks. The Micolau does very satisfying meals. Borda Callisa does Indian.

Après-ski Arinsal has plenty of animated bars and discos. The Surf, Cisco's and Rocky Mountain, mentioned above, all have lively bars. The liveliest places when we visited are only a short stagger apart – the Quo Vadis (a pub) and El Cau (big, noisy, with disco lights, full of kids). El Derbi was also hopping on karaoke night. If, like us, you prefer something quieter, head for Borda Callisa – out of the way and pleasantly relaxed – or the bar of the hotel Arinsal.

Off the slopes Arinsal has few facilities off the slopes. The main thing to do is to shop in Andorra la Vella, half an hour away by infrequent bus.

Phone numbers
From abroad use the prefix +376.

TOURIST OFFICE
Pal
t +376 737000
f 835904
Arinsal
t +376 737020
f 836242
pal@arinsal.ad
www.palarinsal.com

Arinsal

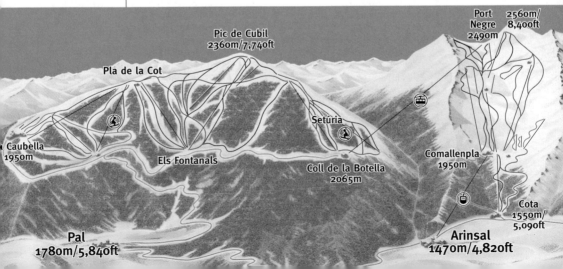

Pic de Cubil
2360m/7,740ft

Pla de la Cot

Port Negre 2490m   2560m/8,400ft

Caubella
1950m

Els Fontanals

Setúria

Coll de la Botella
2065m

Comallenpla
1950m

Cota
1550m/5,090ft

Pal
1780m/5,840ft

Arinsal
1470m/4,820ft

Pas de la Casa

2100m/6,890ft

Andorra's biggest ski mountain

HOW IT RATES

The slopes

Snow	***
Extent	***
Experts	*
Intermediates	***
Beginners	****
Convenience	****
Liftlines	***
Restaurants	***

The rest

Scenery	**
Resort charm	*
Off-slope	*

What's new

For 2000/01 the Font Negre surface lift above Pas de la Casa was replaced by a six-pack – the new lift now extends up towards the top of the Pic Blanc ridge. And two of the three Llac del Cubill surface lifts to the Grau Roig area from the Encamp side have also been upgraded to a six-pack.

Next season's developments include the expansion of the Pas de la Casa beginner area, extra snowmaking and improvements to the terrain-park and boarder-cross.

MOUNTAIN FACTS

Altitude	2050m-2640m
	6,730ft-8,660ft
Lifts	31
Trails	100km/62 miles
Blue	25%
Red	55%
Black	20%
Snowmaking	23km
	14 miles
Recco detectors used	

- ⊕ Slopes to match many mid-sized resorts in the Alps
- ⊕ High altitude means relatively reliable snow
- ⊕ Andorra's liveliest nightlife
- ⊕ Encamp (linked by gondola) is a cheaper but even more dreary base
- ⊕ Grau Roig is a more attractive, quiet base (if you can afford it)
- ⊕ Equally worthwhile Soldeu area is physically linked, but ...

- ⊖ No shared lift ticket with Soldeu, although runs overlap
- ⊖ Pas is an eyesore – an uncompromisingly commercial frontier town – and the center suffers from traffic (and fumes)
- ⊖ Very few woodland slopes, and none directly above the village – unpleasant in bad weather

Pas de la Casa is Andorra's wildest party resort. Having driven through it and skied down to it, we are quite happy to stay over the hill in Soldeu – or, for ideal access to the Pas slopes, secluded Grau Roig.

THE RESORT

Sited right on the border between Andorra and France, Pas de la Casa owes its development as much to duty-free sales to the French as to skiing. It is a sizeable collection of concrete-box-style apartment blocks and hotels, a product of the rapid development Andorra saw in the late 1960s and early 1970s. Some thought has gone into its layout, if not its appearance, with most accommodations conveniently placed near the lift base and slopes. The town center boasts plenty of cheap shops and bars, as well as a sports center. Reporters complain that it's starting to look a little shabby and that the heavy traffic generates exhaust fumes.

The resort attracts a lot of French visitors (so beware the February school holidays) and Spanish families.

The lift system spreads from Pas over three adjacent valleys. The furthest from Pas has nothing but a lift station, but in the attractively wooded middle one is Grau Roig ('Rosh'). This is a mini-resort that acts as the access point for day visitors arriving by road from central Andorra and Spain, but it also makes a good base.

The road through from France goes on over the Port d'Envalira towards Soldeu and central Andorra. There are accommodations at the pass, which we suggest you avoid.

THE MOUNTAINS

Pas de la Casa boasts the most extensive slopes in Andorra, and has the Soldeu slopes right next door. With the exception of a couple of attractively wooded slopes in the central valley, the slopes are all open, and vulnerable to bad weather. There's floodlit skiing every Wednesday night.

Slopes The treeless local slopes, facing north-east, descend from a high, north–south ridge; lifts go up to it at four points. Runs on the far side of the ridge converge on Grau Roig, where there is some wooded terrain at the head of the valley. And a single lift goes on further west to the bowl of Llac del Cubill, where the Pas area adjoins the Soldeu one. On the far side of this bowl is the arrival station of the new 6km/4 mile gondola up from Encamp.

Snow reliability Heavy investment in artificial snowmaking equipment, coupled with the area's height, means a good snow reliability record and a season that often reaches late April.

Snowboarding Boarding is popular with the young crowd that Pas de la Casa attracts, and there is a small, lift-served board-park and half-pipe on the Grau Roig side of the mountain.

Experts There are few challenges on-trail – the black runs are rarely of serious steepness, and bumps are rare. But there seem to be plenty of off-trail slopes inviting exploration when fresh snow arrives.

Central reservations phone number
For all resort accommodations call 801060.

From abroad, add the prefix +376.

TOURIST OFFICE
t +376 801060
f 801070
info.reserves@pasgrau.com
www.pasgrau.com

Intermediates The slopes cater to confident intermediates far better, with plenty of top-to-bottom reds and blues on the main ridge, though they do rather lack variety.

Beginners There are beginner slopes in both Pas and Grau Roig. The Pas area is a short but inconvenient bus-ride out of town. Progression to longer runs is easier in Grau Roig, too.

Snowboarders There's a terrain park with half-pipe and boarder-cross at Grau Roig. Surface lifts are usually avoidable.

Cross-country Although they get very little attention, there are loops totalling 12km/7 miles below Grau Roig.

Liftlines Liftlines are rarely serious, now that there are two fast chairs out of Pas – one of them a six-pack. But during French school holidays some bottlenecks can develop.

Mountain restaurants There are routine places at the ridge above Pas and the top of the gondola from Encamp, but the Rifugi dels Llacs dels Pessons at the head of the Grau Roig bowl is far from routine: as well as a bar it has a cozy beamed table-service restaurant with excellent food.

Schools and guides The ski school has an excellent reputation, with good English spoken.

Facilities for children There are ski kindergartens at Pas and Grau Roig, and a non-ski one at the latter.

STAYING THERE

Hotels We don't have any special recommendations in Pas. The Grau Roig hotel is in a league of its own for comfort and seclusion. (Beware: some operators list it under Soldeu, presumably because it seems a bit out of place alongside brash Pal.)

Apartments/condos We have no particular recommendations.

Eating out There are doubtless various possibilities, but we rarely get reports on them. 'There are no really good restaurants,' says a reporter.

Après-ski 'The après-ski is very lively' and 'Nightspots get very crowded' say reporters. The Billboard is 'by far the best club', and the Milwaukee is one of the most popular bars. The Safari bar is 'a good place to chill out'.

Off the slopes Off-slope activity is limited to shopping ('Electrical goods and perfume are good buys,' says one reporter), visiting the leisure center or taking a trip to Andorra la Vella for more of the same.

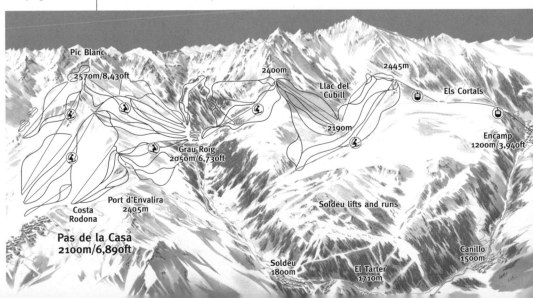

Pic Blanc

2570m/8,430ft

2400m

2445m

Llac del Cubill

Els Cortals

2190m

Encamp
1200m/3,940ft

Grau Roig
2050m/6,730ft

Port d'Envalira
2405m

Costa Rodona

Soldeu lifts and runs

Pas de la Casa
2100m/6,890ft

Canillo
1500m

Soldeu
1800m

El Tarter
1710m

Andorra's best all-rounder

HOW IT RATES

The slopes

Snow	***
Extent	**
Experts	*
Intermediates	***
Beginners	****
Convenience	***
Liftlines	***
Restaurants	*

The rest

Scenery	***
Resort charm	*
Off-slope	*

What's new

The slopes above El Forn were developed for last season.

For 2001/02, the Riba Escorxada beginners' area is being improved – a new quad is being added. There will also be a couple of new runs.

The Espiolets beginner area is being further improved and a new surface lift installed.

A new black run is planned for the Canillo slopes.

The El Tarter terrain park is being improved. New trail signing and information boards are also planned.

MOUNTAIN FACTS

Altitude	1710m-2560m
	5,610ft-8,400ft
Lifts	28
Trails	88km/55 miles
Green	24%
Blue	32%
Red	36%
Black	8%
Snowmaking	25km
	16 miles

Recco detectors used – helicopter based

⊕ Slopes to match many mid-sized resorts in the Alps

⊕ Impressively efficient lift system

⊕ Not at all the rowdy resort it once was

⊕ Ski school has excellent British-run section for English-speaking visitors

⊕ Equally worthwhile Pas de la Casa area is physically linked, but ...

⊖ No shared lift ticket with Pas de la Casa, although runs overlap

⊖ Village is over-run by traffic on main road through from France to Andorra la Vella

⊖ Packages not particularly cheap

⊖ Not much to do off the slopes

If we were planning a vacation in Andorra, it would be in Soldeu (unless it was in the isolated hotel at Grau Roig, up the road – covered in the Pas de la Casa chapter). Despite the traffic, it is the least unattractive village, and its slopes are the most interestingly varied. Mind you, we would make expeditions to the Pas de la Casa slopes, too, even if it meant spending more on lift tickets. Bear in mind the alternative bases of El Tarter and Canillo, which may be cheaper.

For many people the trickier question is whether to come here or to go somewhere completely different. Soldeu no longer competes on price with the bargain basements of eastern Europe, so the alternatives are more likely to be in Austria or Italy. It's easy to find villages there that are a lot prettier than Soldeu, scenery that is more impressive, and off-slope diversions that are more, well, diverting. But you would often have to settle for less extensive and interesting slopes, and less carefully organized ski lessons.

The resort

The village is a small, though ever-growing, ribbon of modern buildings – not pretty, but mainly given a stone veneer in traditional style – on a steep hillside, lining the busy road that runs through Andorra from France to Spain. Most of them are hotels, apartments or bars, with the occasional shop; for serious shopping – or for any other off-slope diversions – you have to head down to Andorra la Vella.

The steep hillside leads down to the river, and the ski slopes are on the opposite side of it. The practicalities of skiing here were transformed a few years back, when a new gondola station was built in the heart of Soldeu, next to the main road, and the slopes were extended to the bottom of this new station by a wide bridge across the river, with elevators to take you up to the gondola.

For many years El Tarter, a few miles by road and 200m/66oft vertical down the valley, has offered an alternative way into the slopes. From last year the same is true of Canillo,

another 200m/66oft lower – though there is no proper shared lift ticket. Nor is there one with Pas de la Casa, whose trail network actually overlaps that of Soldeu. Keen skiers and riders will want to explore the Pas area, and will tailor their ticket buying accordingly. There is easy access at Grau Roig, a few miles up the valley.

The mountain

The main local slopes are on open mountainsides above the woods, though there are runs in the woods back to all of the resort lift bases.

THE SLOPES
Pleasantly varied

The gondola rises over wooded, north-facing slopes to Espiolets, a broad shelf that is virtually a mini-resort – the ski school is based here, and there are extensive beginner areas. A gentle run to the east takes you to an area of long, easy runs served by one of Soldeu's three six-packs. And beyond that is an extensive area of more varied slopes, served by a quad and

488

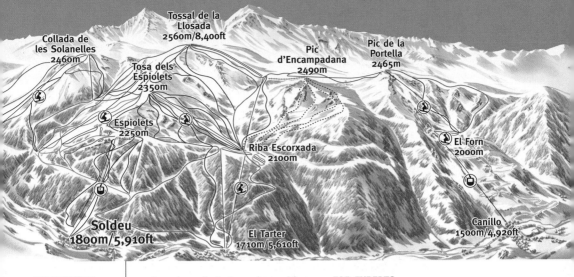

Tossal de la Llosada 2560m/8,400ft — Collada de les Solanelles 2460m — Tosa dels Espiolets 2350m — Pic d'Encampadana 2490m — Pic de la Portella 2465m — Espiolets 2250m — Riba Escorxada 2100m — El Forn 2000m — Soldeu 1800m/5,911ft — El Tarter 1710m/5,610ft — Canillo 1500m/4,920ft

LIFT TICKETS

2000/01 prices in euros

Soldeu El Tarter
Covers all lifts in Soldeu El Tarter.
Main ticket
1-day ticket 26
6-day ticket 123
Over 65: 10 (1 day)
Over 75: free ticket
Children
Under 12: 6-day ticket 98
Under 6: free ticket
Short-term tickets
Half-day ticket 19
Notes
A supplement is charged for the El Forn area: 3 euros for 1 day or 15 euros for 6 days.
Alternative tickets
The 5-day Ski Andorra ticket covers all five resorts and costs around 115 euros.

another six-pack, that overlaps with the Pas de la Casa area – hence the extraordinary signs shown in our introduction to Andorra. Going west from Espiolets takes you to the open bowl of Riba Escorxada and the arrival point of the lift up from El Tarter. From here, the third six-pack serves sunny slopes on Tosa dels Espiolets, while a slow quad leads off southwards towards surface lifts serving the high-point of Tossal de la Llosada and the little-used link with the slopes above Canillo.

SNOW RELIABILITY
Not at all bad

Soldeu enjoys fairly reliable snow. Most slopes are north-facing, with artificial snow on the descents to Soldeu. The snowmaking is expanded each year, but even if runs to the village are incomplete, the area as a whole is not unduly affected.

FOR EXPERTS
Hope the snowcat's going

It's a limited area for experts, at least on-trail. The black runs down to Soldeu and El Tarter more or less justify their grading, and the one at the top of the Canillo sector looked like fun but was short of snow when we visited. The blacks on Tosa dels Espiolets are indistinguishable from the neighboring (and more direct) red and blue. One intriguing possibility that we were not able to explore last winter is that when conditions permit a snowcat takes people up to Pic d'Encampadana whence a range of off-trail routes (shown dotted on our map) descend to Riba Escorxada. There is plenty of other off-trail potential, given the necessary guidance – notably in the bowl above Riba Escorxada, in the area where Soldeu meets Pas, and above El Forn.

SNOWPIX.COM / CHRIS GILL

Espiolets is a regular little mini-resort, though there are no accommodations up here ➔

boarding

There's a well-equipped terrain-park and half-pipe for snowboarders, which is easier to get to due to a new six-seater chair. Competent free-riders should be among the first in line for the snowcat service when it's running (see For experts).

SCHOOLS/GUIDES

2000/01 prices in euros

Soldeu El Tarter school

Classes 5 or 6 days 15 hours: 79

Children's classes 15 hours: 67

Private lessons Hourly: 26 for 1 or 2 people, 32 for 3 or 4 people.

CHILDCARE

The three nurseries, at Espiolets, Riba Escorxada and El Forn, take children from 3 to 10.

FOR INTERMEDIATES
Pity about the ticket position

There is plenty to amuse all but the keenest intermediates. The area east of Espiolets is splendid for building confidence, while those who already have it will be able to explore the whole mountain. Riba Escorxada is a fine section for mixed ability groups, and the new link to Canillo/El Forn and newly created runs there allow for more cruising mileage completely free of crowds. The great frustration for mileage-hungry intermediates is the lack of a joint Soldeu/Pas ticket.

FOR BEGINNERS
One of the best

This is a good resort for beginners. It is relatively snow-sure, and there are numerous easy trails to move on to. The Espiolets beginner area and playground has recently been expanded by 50%, and two new rope tows have been added. A bar, cafeteria, and nursery are soon to be located inside a new building there.

FOR CROSS-COUNTRY
Er, what cross-country?

If there is any cross country here we've neither seen it nor heard about it. There is some not far away at Grau Roig (covered in the Pas de la Casa chapter), but Andorra's serious cross-country resort is at La Rabassa, some distance away in the south-west corner of the country, close to Spain – 20km/12 miles of loops at an altitude of 2000m/6,600ft.

LIFTLINES
Weekends only

The lift system is a mixture of the old and the impressively new and powerful – there aren't many resorts in the Alps with three six-packs – which seems to be able to cope with those staying locally. When there is an influx on weekends, there can be waits up the mountain.

MOUNTAIN RESTAURANTS
Not a highlight

The mountain restaurants are crowded, not because they stimulate trade but because there aren't enough. There is a choice of places at Espiolets, with one restaurant doing service at crowded refectory tables. Reporters favor descending to El Tarter, particularly to the snack bar El Clos.

SNOWPIX.COM / CHRIS GILL

El Tarter is an increasingly popular alternative to Soldeu, with equally good access to the shared slopes ↓

GETTING THERE

Air Toulouse, transfer 3½hr.

Rail L'Hospitalet-Près-L'Andorre (25km/16 miles); buses and taxis to Soldeu

ACTIVITIES

Indoor Ice skating, swimming, gym, squash, tennis
Outdoor Thermal spas, snowmobiling, tobogganing

Central reservations phone number
For all resort accommodations call 890501.

From abroad, add the prefix +376.

TOURIST OFFICE

t +376 890500
f 890509
soldeu@soldeu.ad
www.soldeu.ad

SCHOOLS AND GUIDES
Great for English-speakers

The ski school is effectively run as two units, the one dealing with English-speaking clients headed by an Englishman and largely staffed by native-English-speaking instructors. 40% of the pupils are beginners, and the school has devised a special 'team teaching' scheme to cope with the challenge of helping this number of beginners to find their feet and sorting them into aptitude groups. The school has an excellent reputation for quality of lessons and friendliness.

FACILITIES FOR CHILDREN
With altitude

Children are looked after at the mid-mountain stations. We lack recent reports, but given the way the ski school is run we would expect the child-care to be competent too.

Staying there

HOW TO GO
Some comfortable hotels

Hotels The best hotels are very civilized, and far removed from the standards of a decade ago.
((((4) **Sport Hotel Village** Clearly best in town, with a style and spaciousness to the public areas that is rare. Directly over the gondola station. But no ski room – you share with the Sport.
(((3) **Sport** Comfortable and pleasant, with good lounge areas, a lively bar and a popular basement disco-bar used for ski school presentations. Over the road from the gondola.
(((3) **Piolets** Pleasant enough, with a pool and other amenities. Central.
((2) **Himalaia** Recently refurbished, central.
Apartments/condos The Edelweiss apartments are spacious and generally pleasant, and well placed opposite the Sport hotel, the facilities of which are available.

EATING OUT
Some gourmand delights

Last winter we enjoyed excellent, satisfying meals at two cute rustic restaurants – Fat Albert's in downtown Soldeu and 'Snails and Quails', 3km/2 miles up the road in Bordes d'Envalira. The Pussycat and El Squirol (Indian) are recommended by readers.

APRES-SKI
Lively

Although après-ski is lively, it consists mainly of bars. The bar at Fat Albert's (see above) has a great atmosphere, with videos shot on the mountain and often a live band. The long-established Pussycat is a good late-night place, with changing party themes. The Piccadilly under the Sport hotel is popular. Aspen is the main snowboard hang-out. The Naudi has a quieter locals' bar. The El Duc is the best disco. Expect noise from late-night revelers on the streets.

OFF THE SLOPES
Head downhill

There is little to amuse non-skiers in Soldeu itself. Down the valley in Canillo is the upscale Palau de Gel (see below), and in Escaldes (effectively Andorra la Vella) there are other diversions including the impressive Caldea spa, and some very serious shopping opportunities. There are several small museums scattered around the country. Some of the bigger hotels have excellent sports facilities.

El Tarter 1710m/5,610ft

El Tarter has grown over recent years to the point where it now seems no smaller than Soldeu; but it is quieter. There is no shortage of places to stay here. A recent reporter recommends the resort, the Hotel del Tarter and the local ski school. El Mosquit is a recommended pizzeria; a new British-run bar, Peanuts, beneath it seems set to monopolize the British custom.

Canillo 1500m/4,920ft

If you like the idea of deserted local slopes and don't mind riding a gondola down at the end of the day, consider Canillo, which looked an acceptably pleasant spot as we repeatedly drove through it on a recent tour. It has the attraction of the impressive Palau de Gel – an Olympic ice-rink plus swimming pool, gym and other amenities.

Spain

It's difficult to generalize about Spanish resorts – which is why we don't provide the lists of ✚ and ➖ points that we do for other second-division countries. Most resorts are in the Pyrenees, and some of these are well equipped with fine, snow-sure slopes that compare favorably with mid-sized resorts in the Alps – and with the competing resorts of Andorra. Two resorts are decidedly upscale – Sierra Nevada and Baqueira-Beret are both frequented by the King of Spain. Winter sports are becoming more popular with the prosperous Spanish themselves, and as a result many of the smaller resorts are continually improving.

The general ambience of Spanish resorts is attractive – not unlike that of Italy. There's plenty of animation, with eating, posing and partying taken seriously. Large families often lunch together, creating much merriment while huge amounts of food are consumed. Dinner and nightlife start late in Spain and many non-Spaniards have difficulty getting used to the late hours – eating at 11pm and going clubbing at 1am is quite normal. The Spanish make up the sleep by taking a nap after the immediate 4pm après-ski.

Sierra Nevada (2100m/6,890ft) – also known as Sol y Nieve – in the extreme south of Spain suffers from extremely unpredictable weather conditions. The much-fêted 1995 World Championships had to be canceled at the eleventh hour due to a lack of snow-cover, with high temperatures rendering the resort's state-of-the-art snowmaking installation useless (fortunately better conditions permitted the Champion-ships to take place in 1996).

The resort's natural snow arrives via completely different weather patterns from those supplying the Alps and the Pyrenees; in 1990, when the Alps were disastrously snowless, Sierra Nevada had the best conditions in Europe.

The mostly intermediate slopes are very exposed to the elements. When the wind blows, as it does, the slopes close, and the strong sun makes the trails either icy or soft in late season. On a good day, however, visitors are treated to a fantastic view from the top of the highest point at Veleta, across the Med, all the way to the Atlas mountains in Morocco.

The resort is very ugly but user-friendly, and its restaurants, bars and shops are nicely gathered around a central square. Granada's proximity means good outings but overcrowding on weekends and holidays. Hotels are comfortable and good value, but a recent visitor recommends staying in Granada and driving up each day.

The best of the Pyrenean resorts is Baqueira-Beret, on the northern slope of the range (see next chapter).

There is a group of worthwhile resorts in the western Pyrenees, between Pau and Huesca.

Formigal is working hard to improve its standing as a winter resort. There has been recent expansion and a number of lift improvements but the 56km/35 miles of trails are windswept. When the wind blows, retreat to nearby **Panticosa** – a charming old village with sheltered but limited slopes that have recently doubled in size to 34km/21 miles of trails. **Candanchu** and nearby **Astún**, with almost 100km/62 miles of trails between them, are popular on the Spanish market. They offer a wide range of lodging set in some of the Pyrenees' most stunning scenery. Candanchu has a reputation for tough runs.

The other resorts of international interest are just east of Andorra. The 44km/27 miles of runs at **La Molina** and its purpose-built satellite **Supermolina** (1700m/5,580ft) are now linked to those of **Masella**, over the mountain, via a gondola and six-pack. The whole area, called Alp 2500, now extends over 100km/62 miles of mainly intermediate skiing.

Baqueira-Beret   1500m/4,920ft

Spain's leading winter resort – fit for their king

493

HOW IT RATES

The slopes

Snow	★★★
Extent	★★★
Experts	★★★
Intermediates	★★★★
Beginners	★★
Convenience	★★★
Liftlines	★★★
Restaurants	★★

The rest

Scenery	★★★
Resort charm	★★
Off-slope	★

➕ Compact modern resort

➕ Efficient lifts with few liftlines

➕ Reasonable snow reliability

➕ Some good off-trail potential

➕ Lots of good intermediate slopes

➕ Friendly, helpful locals

➕ Good restaurants and bars for après-ski

➖ Drab high-rise blocks dominate the main village, though new developments are more attractive

➖ Resort is not cleverly laid out, and suffers from traffic around the lift base station

➖ Few off-slope diversions other than walks

Baqueira is in a different league from other resorts in the Spanish Pyrenees – a smart family-oriented resort with a wide area of north-facing slopes that gives a real feeling of travel. It attracts an almost entirely Spanish clientele (which regularly includes the royal family), so don't count on English being spoken.

What's new

For 2000/01 a new fast chair and surface lift opened up a new area facing the main Beret slopes. And a new chair in the Bonaigua sector has opened up a couple of new blue runs. Snowmaking has been further extended.

Two new hotels opened last season, and another is to follow for the coming season.

MOUNTAIN FACTS

Altitude	1500m-2510m
	4,920ft-8,230ft
Lifts	27
Trails	86km/53 miles
Green	8%
Blue	8%
Red	37%
Black	47%
Snowmaking	35km
	22 miles

BAQUEIRA TOURIST OFFICE

Baqueira's lift base is just above the village
➔

THE RESORT

Baqueira was purpose-built in the 1960s and has its fair share of drab, high-rise blocks; these are clustered below the road that runs through to the high pass of Port de la Bonaigua, while the main lift base is just above it. But up the steep hill from the main base are some newer, smaller-scale stone-clad developments. At the very top is an alternative chair-lift into the slopes. The most convenient base is close to the main chair-lift, but the village is small enough for location not to be too much of an issue. There are a lot of accommodations spread down the valley, and a big parking lot with road-train shuttle up to the lift base.

THE MOUNTAINS

There is an extensive area of long, mainly intermediate, runs, practically all of them on open treeless slopes. There are long-term plans to extend the slopes to the sunny side of the Bonaigua pass.

Slopes The slopes are split into three distinct but well-connected areas – Baqueira, Beret and Bonaigua. From the base station at Baqueira, a fast quad (which you load without skis on – you put them in ski carriers on the back of the chair in front) takes you up to the beginner areas at 1800m/5,910ft. Fast chairs go on up to Cap de Baqueira. From here there is a wide variety of long runs, served by chairs and surface lifts. From several points you can descend into the Argulls valley and the Bonaigua sector, leading over to the summit of the Bonaigua pass. From the opposite extremity at Orri a triple chair takes you off to the Beret sector, where a series of more-or-less parallel chairs serve mainly blue and red runs. A new fast quad and a surface lift serve a new fourth sector across the valley from the Beret slopes, with new red and blue trails. Beret, Orri and Bonaigua are accessible by road.

Snowboarding There's a permanent half-pipe at Bonaigua. The beginner areas are served by surface lifts and some of the blues are a bit tricky for novices.

Snow reliability Mainly north-west-facing slopes above 1800m/5,910ft and extensive snowmaking make the area fairly snow-sure. But the latitude means strong sun in late season.

Experts Experts will find few on-trail challenges, but there's plenty of off-trail if you hire a guide. The infamous Escornacrabes itinerary, from the top of Cap de Baqueira, is steep and narrow. Cheap heli-lifts are available.

Intermediates It's excellent for intermediates, with lots of varied blues and some classic long red runs such as Mirador. The excursion to Port de la Bonaigua has a nice air of adventure. Less daring intermediates will enjoy the long blue from the Dossau ridge to Beret, and the Argulls valley runs.

Beginners There are some good beginners' runs, but on the main mountain progression is not easy – some of the blues can be a bit tough; there are gentler blue runs at Beret, but you'd need to take a cab to them.

Cross-country There is 7km/4 miles of cross-country skiing between Orri and Beret.

Liftlines The network of modern lifts means few lines most of the time. But at peak times, when French and Spanish tourists flood into the resort, some waits can be 10 minutes.

Mountain restaurants Most are cheap and charmless, but with good-value food and pleasant terraces. You can get table service at Cap del Port, at the Bonaigua pass.

Schools and guides The school gets good reports – some spoken English.

Facilities for children The kindergarten takes children from three months to three years. Lack of spoken English is a problem in the kindergartens. Ski school classes start from age four, and English is less problematic here.

STAYING THERE

How to go There is a reasonable choice of hotels and apartments locally.

Hotels In the main village three hotels have been recommended – the 4-star Montarto (973 639001) and the 3-star Tuc Blanc (973 644350) and Val de Ruda (973 645258). The 5-star Tryp Royal Tanau at the top of the resort looks good (973 644446). There is a Parador (973 640801) down the valley in Arties.

Eating out The more interesting restaurants are down the valley in Salardu and Arties. Reporters have enjoyed the local tapas bars.

Après-ski There are lots of pubs and discos in the valley. Tiffany's and Pacha are in the main village. They get going very late (ie in the early hours).

Off the slopes Pool and spa facilities are available in several hotels, but not much else. Viehla, 15km/9 miles away, has a good sports center.

Phone numbers
From abroad use the prefix +34.

TOURIST OFFICE
Postcode 25530
t +34 973 639000
f 973 644488
baqueira@baqueira.es
www.baqueira.es

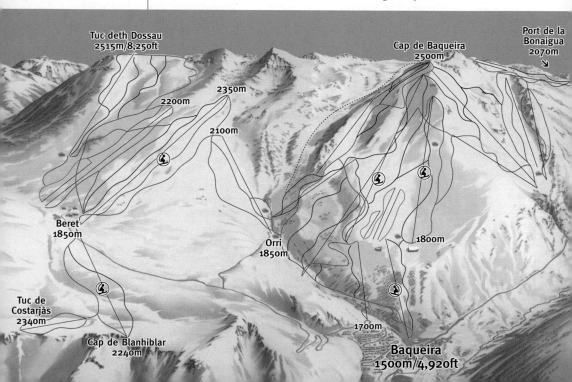

Bulgaria

- ➕ Very cheap
- ➕ A different winter holiday, with the chance to experience a fascinating, although depressed, culture
- ➕ Very friendly, welcoming people
- ➕ Good ski schools

- ➖ Not enough snowmaking
- ➖ Poor trail and lift maintenance
- ➖ Problems with theft of equipment
- ➖ Borovets hotels and food poor
- ➖ Archaic airports, airline and coaches can cause long travel delays

Bulgaria attracts tourists on a tight budget: hotels, equipment rental, school and lift ticket are all very cheap. Drawbacks include limited slopes, old lifts, and food that can be dreadful. But there are compensations: reporters are struck by the friendliness of the people, the ski schools are excellent, the nightlife is good fun, and from Borovets an excursion to Sofia is recommended.

But keen trail-bashers, gourmets, posers, and those wanting creature comforts should look elsewhere or be prepared for a shock.

The flow of readers' reports has dried up over the last few seasons, but we have surfed the internet for vacation reports. Most – at least from absolute beginners – are extremely positive, enthusing about the benefits mentioned above, but others tell worrying tales of burgled rooms and stolen ski equipment (mainly in Borovets). And those who have skied elsewhere tend to be more critical.

Bulgaria's two main resorts are some way apart, served by different airports, with similarly short transfer times (less than two hours). They are similar places in that both have good instruction and a poor selection of quality restaurants, but they suit different levels of ability.

Pamporovo 1650m/5,410ft

THE RESORT
Despite the bus-ride to the lifts, families praise Pamporovo. The purpose-built village has 'everything to hand'.

THE MOUNTAIN
Pamporovo is Bulgaria's best bet for beginners and early intermediates, with mostly easy runs. Others are likely to find 17.5km/11 miles of mainly short runs too limited.
Slopes The slopes are pretty and sheltered, with trails starting at a high point of 1925m/6,320ft and cutting through pine forest. Getting lost is difficult even in the worst weather.
Snow reliability Late-season snow-cover is unreliable.
Snowboarding The Snow Shack is best for snowboard rentals and instruction.
Experts Experts will find little to challenge them in this limited ski area.
Intermediates The slopes are too limited for most intermediates.
Beginners The terrain is ideal for

learning to ski or snowboard. Booking lessons and equipment rental in advance can save you money compared with on-the-spot prices.
Mountain restaurants The best bets are the Lodge and the Spider restaurant.
Schools and guides The ski schools are repeatedly praised by reporters – instructors are patient, enthusiastic and speak good English, and class sizes are usually quite small.
Facilities for children The English-speaking nursery is well regarded.

STAYING THERE
The main hotels are in the center of the handy purpose-built village.
Hotels Hotel Pamporovo was new for 1999/2000 and offers the best accommodations in the resort. It's close to the village center, and facilities include an indoor swimming pool, a hot-tub and a gym. More basic are the Perelik (also with a pool) and Mourgavets – both in the center.
Eating out The food can be poor. You are best off sticking to local Bulgarian stew dishes, gyuvech and kavarma, which can be delicious. The breakfast buffets offer a fair choice.
Après-ski The nightlife is fairly lively, although limited to a handful of bars and discos – BJ's, the White Hart, Dax and the Havana club are popular.
Off the slopes The organized evening events are recommended by reporters.

Borovets 1300m/4,270ft

THE RESORT

Borovets is a collection of large, modern hotels, with bars, restaurants and shops housed within them. There is a ramshackle selection of quirkier bars, shops and eating places. The beautiful wooded setting provides a degree of Alpine-style charm, and trees hide some of the worst architectural excesses. A cluster of large hotels is at the main village lift (a gondola) up to two of the three ski sectors. A couple of minutes' walk takes you to the top of the resort, where an enormous hotel overlooks the remaining village lifts.

THE MOUNTAIN

The 40km/25 miles of trails are spread over three sectors – two are loosely linked.

Slopes The two largest sectors have fairly steep and awkward slopes. The gondola rises over 1000m/3,280ft to service both the small, high, easy slopes of Markoudjika (up to 2700m/8,860ft), and the mainly long, steepish Yastrebets trails. A little surface-lift and path connect the two. The third Baraki sector is accessed by several lifts. Runs are short, with a range of just 550m/1,800ft up to a top station at 1850m/6,070ft.

Snow reliability Reliable cover is by no means guaranteed.

Experts There's little of real challenge.

Intermediates The runs are best suited to good intermediates. Less confident skiers may find the mainly tough red runs a bit intimidating.

Beginners The slopes are not particularly suitable for novices. The beginner areas are inadequate and Markoudjika is good for near beginners, but progress beyond that means going on to reds.

Liftlines When snow is poor and when the resort is full, liftlines can be bad – 'unruly and pushy'. Reporters suggest an early start to avoid the worst of the gondola lines – the main bottleneck. Erratic grooming and poor signing are other common complaints.

Mountain restaurants Mountain restaurants are mostly basic little snack bars with limited seating, serving large portions of very simple fare.

Schools and guides 'Brilliant,' says a reporter with children aged 6 and 9.

Facilities for children Reports of the ski kindergarten have been complimentary. The non-ski nursery is in the Rila hotel.

STAYING THERE

Hotels A report says of the Rila: 'Clean, good food, rooms secure.' The Samokov is popular and its pool is a major asset. The Breza and Edelweiss get reasonable reviews.

Eating out Alpin Hotel, Krima, Bulgarian Dish, La Bamba, Ela Tavern and Franco's are better than the rest.

Après-ski The nightlife is very lively, catering well to an 18–30 type crowd. The Black Tiger pub (with karaoke), the Buzz Bar, Titanic and Bonkers have been recommended.

Off the slopes Excursions to the Rila monastery by coach and to Sofia by coach or helicopter are interesting.

Vitosha 1810m/5,940ft

No more than a few widely scattered hotels with very limited, bland runs and a top height of 2290m/7,510ft. The hotels are fairly dreary, and most are a bus-ride from the lifts. The resort is just over 20km/12 miles from the center of Sofia, allowing for short transfers and easy excursions, but the slopes get overrun on weekends. The slopes are north-facing and have a decent snow record.

Romania

- ➕ Extremely cheap
- ➕ Interesting excursions and friendly local people
- ➕ Good standard of affordable lessons

- ➖ Primitive facilities
- ➖ Uninspiring food
- ➖ Limited slopes with few real challenges

Like Bulgaria, Romania sells mainly on price. Local prices are very, very low. Provided you have correspondingly low expectations – and provided you go to Poiana Brasov and not Sinaia – you may be content. If you have any interest in good living, and particularly good lunching, stay away. It's a place for beginners and near-beginners – the slopes are limited in extent and challenge, but lessons are good (and cheap, of course).

There is another possible dimension to a vacation here, which is the experience of visiting (and supporting) an interesting and attractive country with a traumatic recent history. Reporters have commented on the friendliness of the people, and most recommend exploring beyond the confines of the resorts. Bucharest is 'not to be missed'.

It's some years since we visited the country. The abiding impression we brought back then was one of resources stretched to their limits. To judge by the few reports we have since received, post-revolutionary Romania has, sadly, not made much progress.

Romania's two main resorts are in the Carpathian mountains, about 120km/75 miles north-west of the capital and arrival airport, Bucharest. They are very different places, but have one or two things in common apart from prices: patient instruction, with excellent spoken English, and small classes; and very basic mountain restaurants, with extremely primitive toilets that, according to one report, would 'shock the toughest of characters'.

The main resort is **Poiana Brasov** (1030m/3,380ft), near the city of Brasov. It is purpose-built, but not designed for convenience: the hotels are dotted about a pretty, wooded plateau, served by regular buses and cheap cabs. There is nothing resembling a real village – the place has the air of a spacious holiday camp.

The main slopes (approximately 17km/11 miles of trails in total) consist of decent intermediate tree-lined runs of about 750m/2,460ft vertical, roughly following the line of the main tram and gondola, plus an open beginner area at the top. There are also some beginners' lifts at village level. A black run takes a less direct route down the mountain, which means that on average it is less steep than the red run under the lifts; it has one steepish pitch towards the end. The more adventurous would need to seek opportunities to go off-trail. The resort gets weekend business from Brasov and Bucharest, and the main lifts can suffer serious lines as a result.

The recently refurbished Bradul and Sport hotels are handy for the lower beginner slopes and for one of the trams. The Capra Neagra and Tyrol are brand new and the Alpin gets good reports. The Ciucas is a 'good, basic' place with satellite TV. Après-ski revolves around the hotel bars and discos and can be quite lively at times. The nightclub puts on cheap cabarets. Off-slope facilities are limited; there is a good-sized pool, and bowling. A trip to the Carpathian Stag in Brasov for an evening of wine tasting in the wine cellars, dinner and a folklore show is recommended. An excursion to nearby Bran Castle (Count Dracula's home) is also popular.

You may be offered holidays in **Sinaia** – a small town on the busy road from Bucharest to Brasov. When we visited it some years ago we were impressed by the modest intermediate slopes, on largely treeless hills next to the town. The town seemed to us a rather depressing place, and reporters since have been shocked and saddened by the evident poverty. But a new 4-star Holiday Inn hotel and new chalets may help to attract your much-needed cash.

Slovenia

- ✚ Good value for money
- ✚ Beautiful scenery
- ✚ Good beginners' slopes and lessons
- ✚ Good off-slope diversions and excursions

- ➖ Limited, mainly easy slopes
- ➖ Mainly antiquated lifts
- ➖ Uninspiring food

Slovenia offers good value for money 'on the sunny side of the Alps'. An attractive idea would be to arrange a trip which combines a stay in the Slovenian mountains with a stay in the vibrant city of Ljubljana. It would be easy add this on to a stay in the Italian Dolomites or the Austrian Alps.

Kranjska Gora and Bohinj are the best-known resorts and both are popular with international visitors, giving the resorts a cosmopolitan feel.

Slovenia is a small country bordering Italy to the west and Austria to the north. It was the first state to break away from former Yugoslavia and has managed to escape the turmoil that engulfed the Balkans. The economy is improving steadily, and there is a positive feel to the resorts – along with a warm and hospitable welcome.

The main resorts are within two and a half hours' bus-ride of the capital, Ljubljana.

The ski areas are generally small, with fairly antiquated lifts but few lines. The mountain restaurants are mainly unappealing, while the ski schools are of a high standard and cheap, with good English encountered by our most recent reporter. Hotel star ratings tend to be a trifle generous, but high standards of service and hygiene are observed. Snow reliability is not particularly good, but some resorts have snowmaking.

Kranjska Gora (810m/2,660ft), a few miles from the Austrian and Italian borders, is the best-known resort. The pretty village is dominated by the majestic Julian Alps. The Lek, Kompass and Larix hotels – with pools – are the best placed for slope-side convenience.

There are around 30km/20 miles of mainly intermediate slopes, rising up to 1623m/5,325ft. The only challenging slopes are a couple of short, demanding runs in the Podkiron area and the World Cup slalom run. For those wanting a change of slopes, trips to Arnoldstein in Austria are available. Snow reliability is not good, despite artificial backup and a northerly exposure. The lift system is rather antiquated (most of the 23 lifts are surface lifts), but at least lines are rare.

Mountain restaurants are poor and most people choose to lunch in the village. There are 40km/25 miles of cross-country trails. There is a good selection of bars and discos for Austrian-style après-ski.

Vogel (1540m/5,050ft), in the beautiful **Bohinj** basin, has the best slopes and conditions in the area. The 36km/22 miles of slopes are reached by a tram up from the valley. There's a collection of small hotels and restaurants at the base. Trails of varying difficulty run from the high point at 1800m/5,910ft back into a central bowl with a small beginner area. When conditions permit, there is a long run to the bottom tram station. For a change of scene, **Kobla**, with 23km/14 miles of wooded runs, is a short bus-ride away.

Bled, with its beautiful lake and fairly lively nightlife, is an attractive base. Its local slopes are very limited indeed, but there are free buses to Vogel (about 20km/12 miles) and Kobla (slightly nearer). The Grand Hotel Toplice and the Park are among the best lakeside hotels.

Kanin (2200m/7,220ft), near the village of **Bovec**, 17km/11 miles from Italy, offers the only high Alpine skiing – 15km/9 miles of trails between 980m/3,220ft and 2300m/7,550ft.

Slovenia's second city, **Maribor** (325m/1,070ft), in the north-east, is 6km/4 miles from its local slopes – the biggest ski area in the country, with 64km/40 miles of runs and 20 lifts. Accommodations are cheap and there are some atmospheric old inns serving good, Hungarian-influenced food.

Turkey

- ✚ Exotic curiosity value
- ✚ Cultural interest
- ✚ Very friendly, welcoming people
- ✚ Turkish baths after skiing
- ✚ Short transfer (to Palandöken)

- ➖ Small ski areas
- ➖ Not as cheap as other fringe destinations

Tourists who have enjoyed the Turkish summer – for its warm welcome and low prices, seasoned with history and haggling to taste – may be tempted to repeat the experience in winter. Of Turkey's 13 ski areas, which are widely spread around the vast country, only two have attracted international attention. If you are travelling a long distance to reach Turkey, you will probably want to combine a stay on the slopes with a visit to Istanbul and perhaps other Turkish cities or resorts.

The most developed of them is Uludag, a fashionable weekend escape from Istanbul above the old city of Bursa, with a small ski area on the upper slopes of Turkey's Mount Olympus, also known as Zirve. More than a thousand kilometres/six hundred miles further east, the remote Anatolian city of Erzurum's local ski area of Palandöken has higher, bigger and better slopes and a small local airport less than half an hour from them.

Recent investment in new lifts and hotels is starting to attract a few international visitors to the resort. It is hoped that they will give a boost to Erzurum's down at heel economy. That's the plan, anyway.

Palandöken's slopes are good and – as is usually the case in Turkey – the locals are super-keen to make visitors feel welcome. But this is a Moslem country, so don't expect to find the cheap alcohol that is such an

INGHAMS

The Dedeman hotel is in the middle of Palandöken's slopes at 2450m/8,040ft ↓

important ingredient of the success of Bulgaria, Romania and Andorra.

Erzurum is a famously cold and windy outpost in winter, and claims an absolute snow guarantee for the treeless slopes of nearby **Palandöken**. These give around 1000m/3,300ft vertical of varied skiing from a top lift station (3125m/10,250ft) that overlooks the city and include the longest run in Turkey at about 12km/7 miles. But on the evidence of last winter, when the first serious snow arrived in late February, Anatolia may not be immune from the effects of global warming.

The ski area is not new, but has been transformed by new lifts and two big hotels. The smart and well-equipped, if somewhat anonymous, 5-star Polat Renaissance is at the foot of the slopes, and has an excellent pool, Turkish spa and all you need for a business conference. The less luxurious 4-star Dedeman has a small pool and sauna at the heart of the ski area (2450m/8,040ft), where the altitude is quite noticeable. These hotels are self contained mini-resorts, each with ski rental and in-house child care. The Dedeman's après ski cafe and night club are popular with the Russian visitors who have made up the bulk of Palandöken's foreign custom until now.

The seven lifts include a gondola and three new chair lifts, a single-seater chair and a couple of beginners' surface lifts outside the Dedeman hotel. Most of the 17 trails are easy, or would be, if well groomed. Trail marking and mapping are a bit sketchy too. The run down to the Polat is a snow-covered road, but the higher slopes offer steeper terrain: black 18 beneath the top chair-lift is an excellent slope of sustained pitch and the off-trail is quite steep enough to pose an avalanche risk. The Dedeman cafe is convenient for lunch, and the new Café Ejder at the summit has an

open fire and overhead electric heaters – much needed on a windy day.

On the not too distant frontier with Armenia and Iran, Mount Ararat (over 5000m/16,500ft) is talked of as a potential heli-ski excursion. But don't count on it.

Erzurum is the biggest city in eastern Turkey and on first impression (shoddy tower blocks on the ring road) may seem less than enchanting. But the center is rich in historic interest. It is a good place to shop for rugs, so long as you enlist local help and have a few hours to spare for the haggling. The other speciality is jet-black local stone used for bracelets, worry beads and other jewelry. A traditional lie-down lunch or supper at the Erzurum Houses restaurant is not to be missed.

Uludag is 250km/155 miles from Istanbul and 32km/20 miles, by long hairpin climb, from Bursa. It is easily – indeed inevitably – combined with a visit to Istanbul and makes an attractive twin-center proposition for Easter, when the Alpine resorts are overcrowded and Turkish skiers are enjoying sizzling kebab lunches out of doors. Most of its 13 lifts are short surface lifts and chairs serving unremarkable if pleasant intermediate and easy skiing; the vertical range is modest – 1800m/5,910ft to 2250m/7,380ft. The resort is a cluster of modern hotels at the tree line, with several swimming pools between them, at least one ice rink and a backless squash court. Most people eat and spend the evening in their hotels, where the atmosphere is cheerful on weekends, otherwise quiet.

Bursa was the home of the Ottoman dynasty and is well worth a visit, with fine mosques, a splendid public hammam (Turkish bath), and good shopping. Access, if not by car, is by bus from Istanbul, or bus and ferry across the Sea of Marmara.

Norway

- ➕ Probably the best terrain and facilities in Europe for serious cross-country skiing
- ➕ The home of telemark – plenty of opportunities to learn and practice
- ➕ Complete freedom from the glitziness often associated with downhill resorts, and from the ill-mannered liftlines of the Alps
- ➕ Quiet atmosphere that suits families and older people
- ➕ Impressive snowboard parks
- ➕ Usually reliable snow conditions throughout a long season

- ➖ Very limited downhill areas – small, and mostly with few challenges
- ➖ Mountain restaurants are basic and disappointing
- ➖ Prohibitively high prices (because of high taxes) for alcoholic drinks
- ➖ Unremarkable scenery
- ➖ Après-ski is either deadly dull or irritatingly rowdy
- ➖ Short daylight hours in midwinter
- ➖ Highly changeable weather
- ➖ Limited off-slope activities

Norway and its resorts are very different from the Alps, or indeed the Rockies. Some people find the place very much to their taste. For cross-country there is nowhere like it; and for downhillers who dislike the usual resort trappings, and prefer a simpler approach to winter holidays, it could be just the place. For families with young children, in particular, the drawbacks are less pronounced than for others; you'll have no trouble finding junk food for the kids to eat – the mountain restaurants serve little else.

Speaking for ourselves, any one of the first three ➖ points we've listed above would probably be enough to put us off; when these are combined in a single destination – and when you add in the other negative points – you can count us out.

International interest in Norway as a winter vacation destination was stimulated by the country hosting the 1994 Olympic Winter Games in Lillehammer. We have to say that our visits have left us underwhelmed by both the quality of the experience and the warmth of the welcome. But at least English is widely spoken – universally spoken, in our experience.

For the Norwegians and Swedes, skiing is a weekend rather than a special vacation activity, and not an occasion for extravagance. So at lunchtime they tend to haul sandwiches out of their backpacks, and in the evening they cook in their apartments. Don't expect a wide choice of restaurants.

Many Norwegians have a problem with alcohol. Walk into an après-ski bar at 5pm on a Saturday and you may find young men already inebriated – and by that we mean not merry but incoherent. And this is despite – or, some say, because of – prohibitively high taxes on booze. Restaurant prices for wine are ludicrous, and on our last visit we were unable to check out shop prices because the resort (Hemsedal) had no state-controlled liquor store. Our one attempt at eating in (well, OK, our one takeout meal) was an unusually sober affair as a result.

Other prices are generally not high by Alpine standards, and those for ski equipment rental and ski school are relatively low.

Cross-country skiing comes as naturally to Norwegians as walking; and even if you're not that keen, the fact that cross-country is normal, and not a wimp's alternative to 'real' skiing, gives Norway a special appeal. Here, cross-country is both a way of getting about the valleys and a way of exploring the hills. Although you can plod around short valley circuits as you might in an Alpine resort, what distinguishes Norway for the keen cross-country skier is the network of long trails across the gentle uplands, with refuges along the way where backpackers can pause for refreshment or stay overnight. This network of mountain huts offers basic but cheap accommodations which can turn touring into a week-long adventure away from the crowds.

More and more Norwegians are taking to telemarking (a bit like cross-country, with a free-heel binding, but with broader skis) for both downhill and backcountry skiing trips.

Snowboarding is very popular, particularly with local youths who swarm on to the slopes and impressive terrain-parks at weekends.

For downhill skiing, the country isn't nearly so attractive. Despite the fact that it is able to hold downhill races, and despite the successes of its Alpine racers during the 1990s, Norway's Alpine areas are of limited appeal.

The most rewarding resort for downhillers is Hemsedal, which we cover in detail in the next chapter.

The site of the 1994 Olympics, the little lakeside town of **Lillehammer** (200m/660ft), is not actually a downhill resort at all. There is plenty of cross-country terrain around, but the nearest downhill runs are 15km/9 miles north at Hafjell (230m/750ft). This is a worthwhile little area, with a vertical of 830m/2,720ft, 11 lifts, and trails totalling 25km/16 miles with a longest run of 4.5km/2.8 miles. The Olympic slalom events were held here; but the planned women's downhill and super-G races were moved elsewhere after the racers judged the course too easy. They went to Kvitfjell, about 35km/ 22 miles further north, developed specially for the men's downhill and super-G. It's steeper but a bit smaller – 23km/14 miles of trails.

Norway's other internationally known resort is **Geilo** (800m/2,620ft) – a small, quiet, unspoilt community on the railroad that links Bergen, on the coast, to Oslo. It provides all the basics of a resort – a handful of cafes and shops clustered around the train station, 10 hotels more widely spread around the wide valley, children's facilities and a sports center.

Geilo is a superb cross-country resort. As the Bergen–Oslo railroad runs through the town it is possible to go for long tours and then catch the train back at the end of the day.

But Geilo is very limited for downhillers. The 28km/17 miles of trails are spread over two small hills – one, Vestlia, a bus-ride away from Geilo, with a good, informal hotel and restaurant at its foot – offering a maximum vertical of 380m/1,250ft and a longest run of 2km/1.2 miles. None of the runs is really difficult.

Clearly the best hotel, and one of the attractions of staying in Geilo, is the Dr Holms Hotel – attractively white-painted outside, beautifully furnished and spacious inside. This is the center for après-ski, but prices are high. All the other hotels we have seen can be safely recommended. The resort is quiet at the end of the day, but the main hotels often provide live entertainment.

A long way north of the other resorts is **Oppdal** (550m/1,800ft), with more downhill runs than any of its rivals (58km/36 miles). The total vertical is 790m/2,590ft, but this is misleading as most of the runs are short.

There are almost equally extensive slopes at **Trysil** (460m/1,510ft), off to the east on the border with Sweden, and the runs are longer (up to 4km/ 2 miles and 685m/2,250ft vertical). The runs here are all around the conical Trysilfjellet, some way from Trysil itself – though there are some accommodations at the hill.

In complete contrast to all of these resorts is **Voss** (50m/160ft), a sizeable lakeside town quite close to Bergen and the sea. A tram links the town to the slopes on Hangur and Slettafjell, with a total of 40km/25 miles of trails. Snow reliability can be poor. There are plenty of excursion possibilities, in particular the spectacular Flåm railway, which plunges down the side of a mountain to fjord (sea) level. From there you can take a boat trip to link up with a bus back to Voss. Nearby Bergen is a pleasant city that is worth a visit.

Hemsedal 650m/2,130ft

Norway's best Alpine resort

HOW IT RATES

The slopes

Snow	****
Extent	*
Experts	**
Intermediates	****
Beginners	***
Convenience	**
Liftlines	****
Restaurants	*

The rest

Scenery	**
Resort charm	**
Off-slope	*

➕ Impressive snow reliability because of northerly location

➕ Increasing amounts of convenient slope-side accommodations

➕ Extensive cross-country trails compared to the Alps

➕ Some quite challenging slopes, and mountains with a slightly Alpine feel

➖ Not much of a village

➖ Infrequent shuttle-bus service to the slopes

➖ Limited slopes for keen trail-bashers

➖ Exposed upper mountain prone to closure because of bad weather

➖ Weekend liftlines

➖ Poor mountain restaurants

➖ No liquor store for miles

➖ Après-ski limited during the week and rowdy on weekends

Hemsedal's craggy terrain, 800m/2,500ft vertical, proper black runs and worthwhile off-trail terrain are reminiscent of a small-but-serious Alpine resort. Most people not resident in Scandinavia would be better advised to go for the real thing, but if you like the sound of Norway, Hemsedal is the place for downhill skiing.

THE RESORT
Hemsedal is both an unspoiled valley and a village, also referred to as Trøym and Sentrum ('Center'), which amounts to very little – a couple of hotel/apartment buildings, a few shops, a bank and a gas station. Though there has been talk of a lift from Trøym to the slopes, for now the lift base is a mile or two away, across the valley. There are apartments beside the slopes and in a separate cluster a walkable distance down the hill from the lifts. A ski-bus links these points, and others in the valley, but the service is inadequate; really, the place is geared to weekend visitors arriving by car or by coach.

THE MOUNTAINS
Hemsedal's slopes pack a lot of variety into a small space.
Slopes With no less than four fast chairs to play on, you can pack a lot of runs into the day. The lift ticket also covers smaller Solheisen, a few miles up the valley. A small supplement is required to ski at Geilo, an hour away.
Snow reliability The combination of northerly latitude and reasonable altitude makes for impressive snow reliability. It's a good bet for a late vacation; the season runs until the first weekend in May.
Snowboarding There's a terrain-park and two half-pipes.

What's new

2000/01 saw 50 new ski-in/ski-out apartments at the mountain base. The children's area and beginner area have been extended and two new baby lifts have been added. The snowmaking network is being extended for next season. And more ski-in/ski-out accommodations are being built. New facilities will include a new restaurant/bar, nightclub and bowling alley.

SNOWPIX.COM / CHRIS GILL

The mountains hereabouts are more craggy than in most Norwegian resorts ➜

MOUNTAIN FACTS

Altitude 670m-1455m
2,200-4,770ft
Lifts 16
Trails 42km/26 miles
Green 32%
Blue 47%
Black 21%
Snowmaking 12km
7 miles

Phone numbers
From abroad use the prefix +47.

TOURIST OFFICE

Postcode N-3561
t +47 320 55030
f 320 55031
hemsedal@hemsedal.
net
www.hemsedal.com

Experts There is quite a bit to amuse experts – two or three black trails of 450m/1,480ft vertical served by a fast triple chair from the base, and wide areas of gentler off-trail terrain served by surface lifts above the tree line.

Intermediates Mileage-hungry trail-bashers will find Hemsedal's 42km/ 26 miles of runs very limited, but others will find good variety in the blue and red runs, and the easier blacks.

Beginners There's a gentle new area for absolute beginners. And there are splendid long green runs (up to 6km/ 4 miles), but they get a lot of traffic, some of it irresponsibly fast. Some long blues and reds also suit near-beginners.

Cross-country The steep mountainsides that make this a worthwhile Alpine resort mean that it is not classic Norwegian cross-country skiing terrain. But by Alpine standards there is still lots to do, both in the valley and at altitude, and a few miles down the valley at the Gravset cross-country centre – 90km/56 miles in all.

Liftlines Hemsedal is Norway's premier downhill resort, and is only a three-hour drive from Oslo, the capital. Good weekend weather fills the parking lots, leading to lines for the main access lifts, and possibly for others. But midweek it is quiet. The upper lifts are very exposed, and are easily closed by bad weather.

Mountain restaurants There's one functional self-service mountain restaurant doing dreary fast food, plus two or three kiosks with benches.

Schools and guides Our most recent reporter on the ski school was not particularly impressed, except by the spoken English.

Facilities for children The facilities at the lift base are good, with day care for children over three months. The kids' beginner area is admirably gentle but not particularly convenient.

STAYING THERE

How to go Most of the accommodations are in apartments, varying widely in convenience.

Hotels The best hotel is the Skogstad (320 60333) in central Hemsedal – comfortable, but noisy on weekends.

Apartments/condos The Alpin apartments, (320 55700) a walk from the lift base, are satisfactory, provided you don't fill all the beds. The adjacent Tinden (320 55700) ones are quite upscale.

Eating out There are half-a-dozen restaurants in the village.

Après-ski It's minimal in the early and middle parts of the week, rowdy on weekends and holidays.

Off the slopes There are some diversions, including sleighs drawn by horses or dogs. The pool at the hotel Skogstad is open to the public.

Sweden

- ➕ Snow-sure from December to May
- ➕ Unspoiled, beautiful landscape
- ➕ Uncrowded trails and lifts
- ➕ Vibrant (but regimented) après-ski
- ➕ Good range of non-skiing activities

- ➖ Limited challenging downhill terrain
- ➖ Small areas by Alpine standards
- ➖ Lacks the dramatic peaks and vista of the Alps
- ➖ Short days during the early season

Sweden's landscape of forests and lakes and miles of unspoiled wilderness is entirely different from the Alps' grandeur and traffic-choked roads. Standards of accommodations, food and service are good and the people welcoming, lively and friendly. There are plenty of off-slope activities, but most of its downhill areas are limited in size and challenge. Sweden is likely to appeal to those who want an all-round winter vacation in a different environment and culture. Don't be put off by the myths that Sweden is expensive, dark and cold – see below.

Vacationing in Sweden is a completely different experience, culturally as well as physically, from a holiday in the Alps. The language is generally incomprehensible and, although virtually everyone speaks good English, the menus and signs are often written only in Swedish. The food is delightful, especially if you like fish and venison.

One of the myths about Sweden is that it is expensive. Sweden is significantly cheaper than neighboring Norway, especially for alcohol, and prices are pretty much on a par with the main Alpine countries.

Another myth is that it is dark. It is true that the days are very short in December and early January. But from early February the lifts generally work from 9am to 4.30pm and by March it is light until 8.30pm. And most resorts have floodlit trails for night skiing.

On the down side, downhill slopes are generally limited in both challenge and extent and the lift systems tend to be dominated by T-bars. But there is lots of cross-country and backcountry skiing. Snowboarding is also popular, with parks and pipes in most resorts.

Après-ski is taken very seriously – with live bands from mid- to late-afternoon. But it all stops suddenly, dinner is served and then the nightlife starts and the bands are back. There is plenty to do off the slopes: snowmobile safaris, ice fishing, ice climbing, dog-sled rides, and saunas galore. You can visit a local Sami (the politically correct name for Lapp) village. And resorts are very family-friendly.

The main resort is Åre (see separate chapter). **Sälen** is Scandinavia's largest winter sports area – and is made up of four separate sets of slopes totalling 144km/89 miles of trails. Most slopes are very gentle, suiting beginners and early or timid intermediates best, though there are 31 black runs listed, including the locally notorious 'Wall' in Hundfjället. Lindvalen and Högfjallet are vaguely linked by a lift and a long cross-country slog. But you need the unreliable bus service to the others.

Vemdalen has two separate areas of slopes 18km/11 miles apart by road. **Björnrike** is great for families, beginners and early intermediates, with eight lifts and 15km/9 miles of mainly gentle trails. The Country Club hotel is right on the slopes and built in modern Scandinavian style. **Vemdalsskalet** has more advanced intermediate terrain, which is served by 10 lifts and 13km/8 miles of trails. The Högfjällshotell at the base is large, dates from 1936 and prides itself on its lively après-ski.

Riksgränsen, 250km/150 miles north of the Arctic Circle, is an area of jagged mountain peaks and narrow fjords. The season starts in mid-February and ends in June – when you can be on the slopes under the midnight sun. There are only six lifts and 21km/13 miles of trails. But there is some good off-trail and midnight heli-skiing.

Björkliden, also above the Arctic Circle, is famous for its subterranean skiing inside Scandinavia's largest cave system. You need to go with a guide.

Ramundberget is a good, small, quiet family resort with ski-in, ski-out accommodations. It gets large amounts of snow and its 22km/14 miles of trails are mainly easy or intermediate cruising runs. There is a special children's area with its own lift.

Åre

380m/1,250ft

Sweden's best slopes strung out along a frozen lake

HOW IT RATES

The slopes
Snow	★★★
Extent	★★
Experts	★★
Intermediates	★★★★
Beginners	★★★★
Convenience	★★★
Liftlines	★★★★
Restaurants	★★★

The rest
Scenery	★★★
Resort charm	★★★
Off-slope	★★★

What's new

For 2001/02 there will be two new red and two new blue slopes (all with snowmaking) in the central area above the town.

There are plans for two new high-speed six-seater chair-lifts to replace T-bars and open up some easy off-trail for the following season.

For 2000/01, a new 1.4km/almost 1 mile boarder- and skier-cross course was built.

506

➕ Cute little town center

➕ Good snow reliability

➕ Ideal intermediate and beginner runs

➕ Extensive cross-country trails

➕ Excellent children's facilities

➕ Lively après-ski scene

➕ Lots of off-slope diversions

➖ Lots of T-bars

➖ Exposed upper mountain prone to closure because of bad weather

➖ High winds detrimental to snow conditions

➖ Few expert challenges

➖ High season liftlines

Åre has the biggest area of linked slopes in Sweden and some of its most challenging terrain. But it suits beginners, intermediates and families best. It has a dinky little town center and a long area of slopes set along a frozen lake.

THE RESORT
Åre is a small town made up of old, pretty, colored wooden buildings and some larger, modern additions. When we were there the main square had a roaring open fire to warm up by. In addition to accommodations in town, there are lots spread out along the valley, with a concentration in the Duved area. All the slopes and accommodations are set on the shore of a huge, long lake, frozen in the winter months.

THE MOUNTAINS
The terrain is mainly green and blue tree-lined slopes, with a couple of wind-swept bowls above the trees.
Slopes There are two main areas. The largest is accessed by a funicular from the center of town or a chair or tram a short climb above it. This takes you to the hub of a network of runs and T-bars that stretches for 10km/6 miles from end to end. The tram is often shut because it goes to the top of the above-the-tree-line slopes (known as

the 'high zone'), which often suffers from howling gales. A gondola also accesses the high zone from a different point. You can get back on-trail right into the town square. A separate area of slopes is above Duved, the other main bed base, now served by a high-speed chair. There are four floodlit slopes, each open on a different night.
Snow reliability Snow reliability is good from November to May. More of a problem is the wind, which can blow fresh snow away. It also means that artificial snow is often deliberately made wet so that it doesn't blow away – it then compacts to a hard, icy surface (and certainly had when we tried the Olympia night skiing area – the top part was sheet ice).
Experts Experts will find Åre's slopes limited, especially if the 'high zone' is closed. If it is open, there is a lot of off-trail available, including an 8km/5 mile run over the back accessed by a snowcat service in high season. On the main lower area the steepest (and iciest when we were there) trails are in

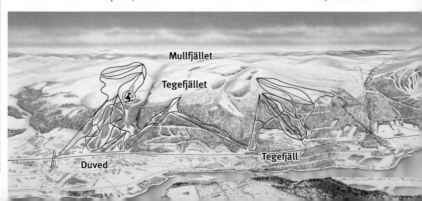

Most of Åre's runs are easy and intermediate and cut through the trees with great views of the frozen lake →

MOUNTAIN FACTS

Altitude	380m-1275m/
	1,250ft-4,18oft
Lifts	44
Trails	93km/58 miles
Green	11%
Blue	43%
Red	36%
Black	5%
Unpatrolled	5%
Recco detectors used	

Central reservations phone number

For all resort accommodations call 17700.
From elsewhere in Sweden add the prefix 0647.
From abroad use the prefix +46 647 .

TOURIST OFFICE

Postcode 830 13
t +46 (647) 17720
f 17712
info@areresort.se
www.areresort.se

the Olympia area. There are also steep black and red runs back to town.
Intermediates The slopes are ideal for most intermediates with pretty blue runs through the trees. Because they tend to be more sheltered, the blue runs also often have the best snow. You can get a real sense of traveling on the main area – from hill to hill and valley to valley.
Beginners There are good facilities for beginners, both on the main area and at Duved.
Cross-country The area has an amazing 300km/200 miles of cross-country trails, both on prepared tracks and unprepared trails marked with red crosses. Some trails are floodlit in the evening.
Liftlines In high season there can be lines for some lifts, especially in the central area immediately above Åre.
Mountain restaurants There are some good mountain restaurants. Our favorite was the rustic Buustamons, tucked away in the woods near Rödkulleomradret.
Schools and guides The ski school has a very good reputation – and this, the easy terrain and excellent childcare facilities make it a good area for families and children.
Facilities for children There are special children's areas and under 11-year-olds get free lift tickets if wearing helmets. There's a kindergarten that takes children from the age of two.

STAYING THERE

There are plenty of cabins and apartments as well as some hotels.
Hotels The main central hotels are the delightful old Åregarden and the simpler Diplomat Ski Lodge. The big Sunwing is right on the slopes, but a bit out of town. The Renen in Duved is very popular with families.
Apartments/condos There is plenty of choice.

Eating out Our favorite restaurant was Sames, with excellent Swedish food. There are plenty of alternatives.
Après-ski Après-ski is amazingly lively – the Sunwing on the slopes and the Diplomat in town are packed from 3pm onwards (both have live bands). Later on, the Diplomat, the Country Club and Bygget all have live bands and there are plenty of bars for a quiet drink.
Off the slopes Lots to do including dog- and reindeer-sled rides, skating, ice fishing, tobogganing, ice driving, ice climbing and snowmobiling.

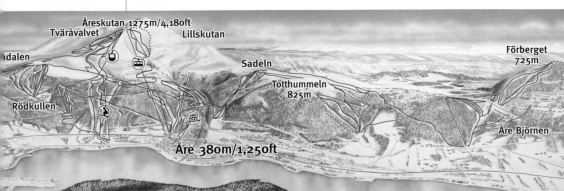

- Offers skiing and boarding during the northern hemisphere's summer
- In one holiday you can also take in a visit to tropical northern Australia
- Some of the resorts are year-round destinations offering sophisticated upscale accommodations

- It's a long way from anywhere except New Zealand and south-east Asia
- Mountains are rather low, and lift/trail networks are small by Alpine standards

Even more than New Zealand, Australia offers resorts that are basically of local interest, but which might amuse people with other reasons to travel there – catching up with those long-lost relatives, say. The mountains are certainly more entertaining than most of the glacier areas that snow-starved northern hemisphere dwellers must normally rely on in the summer. Skiing among the snow-laden gum trees is also a unique experience, plus there is often the chance to see kangaroos, emus and wombats. The resorts mainly offer some accommodations close to the slopes (unlike those in New Zealand), and ski schools are sizeable and professional.

The major resorts are concentrated in the populous south-east corner of the country, between Sydney and Melbourne, with the largest in New South Wales (NSW) – in the National Park centered on Australia's highest mountain, Mt Kosciusko (2230m/7,320ft), about six hours' drive from Sydney. Skiing has been going on here since the early years of last century – as in the next-door state of Victoria, where there are several resorts within three or four hours' drive of Melbourne. Visitors to Tasmania may want to check out the possibilities there, too.

The season generally runs from early June to mid-October, but may be extended at either end if snow conditions allow.

Last year's big news was the construction of a commercial airport just 20 minutes' drive from Mount Hotham in Victoria. Qantas started twice-weekly flights in 2000, effectively making the resort the closest to a major city: 90 minutes from Sydney, under an hour from Melbourne. Mount Hotham doubled its terrain three years ago, putting it on a par with NSW's Thredbo.

Thredbo is a long-established and relatively upscale alpine village in NSW. It hosted the only World Cup race event held in Australia thanks to its size and vertical of 670m/2,200ft.

Thredbo is rather like a small and quite upscale French purpose-built resort – user-friendly, and mostly made up of modern apartments (and lodges run by clubs). But there are many more bars than you would find in the French equivalent. There is an Austrian flavor to some of the lodges and bars, due to the early influx of Europeans. It's a steep little place, with stiff climbs to get around from one part to another. Road access is easy, but the toll is high. It costs A$60 just to enter the park. Once you're there it's A$75 a day to ski, the same as its long-standing rival Perisher Blue.

The slopes, prettily wooded with gum trees, rise up across the valley from the village, served by a regular shuttle-bus through the resort. The runs are well laid out, with better connections between slopes than in many areas – and the resort as a whole gives the impression of good organization. The dozen lifts include four fast quad chairs, and the trails include Australia's highest (2035m/6,680ft) and longest (6km/4 miles). While the blacks are not difficult, they offer some variety, and on the higher lifts there are off-trail variants.

Since 1987 A$100 million has been poured into Thredbo by its owners. The result is an abundance of luxurious apartments, an attractive pedestrian mall with good shopping and some high-class restaurants both on and off the mountain. There is also an impressive four-year-old Australian Institute of Sport training complex open to the public, with an Olympic-size pool, waterslide, traverse climbing wall, squash and tennis courts, gym, and basketball courts. On the hill a 700m/2,300ft bob-sled track for the public is popular all year round. You can take the Crackenback gondola to the mountain top for dinner.

On the other side of the mountain range is the **Perisher Blue** resort complex, with a pass covering 51 lifts – more than anywhere else in Australia – but a vertical of less than 400m/1,310ft. The main area is **Perisher/Smiggins**, where lifts and runs – practically all easy or intermediate – range over three lightly wooded sectors. The resort is reachable by road, but is also served by the Skitube, a rack railway that tunnels its way up from Bullocks Flat and goes on to the second area, **Blue Cow/Guthega**, where the slopes offer more challenges.

Perisher Blue has been doing its best to catch up with Thredbo by upgrading hotels and building more facilities, but it remains spread out and does not have the cozy village atmosphere that Thredbo fans adore. On the other hand, Perisher Blue has more ski-in ski-out accommodations. Its main advantage over Thredbo is its snow, thanks to its position further within the mountain ranges and its altitude: Perisher Blue's lifts start at about the same elevation as Thredbo's mid-station.

Many people also stay in apartments or hotels in the lakeside town of Jindabyne, a half-hour drive from both Thredbo and Perisher, or in cozy chalets along the Alpine Way, which leads to Thredbo.

From Perisher, a snowcat can take you on an 8km/5 mile ride to the isolated chalets of Australia's highest resort, **Charlotte Pass** (1760m/5,770ft), with five lifts but only 200m/660ft vertical. People visit the Pass more for its charm than the skiing, although it is a favorite with families. The major hotel is the historic and turreted Kosciusko Chalet, a good spot for romantic weekends.

In Victoria, resorts are not as high as in NSW but many have good snow since they are set well within the ranges. The aforementioned **Mount Hotham** has a reputation for powder

snow. The 11 lifts serve a complete range of runs with plenty of variety. The longest run is 2.5km/1.5 miles and there is more consistently steep terrain here than at any other area in Australia.

Mount Hotham is unique among the Australian fields in that the village is built along the top of a ridge, with the slopes below it. The focus of the village is Mount Hotham Central, comprising apartments, shops and a choice of eateries, including several excellent restaurants catering to the rising champagne factor in the village. Mount Hotham skiers can also stay 15 minutes' drive away at Dinner Plain, a settlement of architect-designed chalets set prettily among gum trees. There are a few restaurants and bars here, and many cross-country trails.

There is also a 10-minute helicopter link from Mount Hotham to another resort nearby (and covered by the same lift pass), **Falls Creek**, that costs all of A$59. Falls Creek is the most alpine of Australia's resorts, completely snow-bound in winter. Guests not arriving by chopper are taken by snowcat to their ski-in ski-out lodge. There are 18 lifts, though the area is smaller than Mount Hotham's.

The other Victorian resort of note is **Mt Buller**. This place is to Melbourne what Cape Cod is to Manhattan – a magnet for old money and a place to be seen. Drive time from Melbourne is just three hours. Big-time entrepreneurs have poured millions into infrastructure surrounding Mt Buller's isolated peak, creating a proper resort village with a luxury hotel, and even a university campus. Draped around the mountain are 25 lifts – the largest network in Victoria, including 13 chair-lifts. There's also a tubing hill, snow-shoeing, cross-country, telemarking lessons and tobogganing.

2000 brought snowcat skiing on Australia's steepest mountain, **Mt McKay**, and in 2001 the mountain's true expert terrain hosted the country's first real extreme skiing contest. Snowmobiling and dog-sled rides are also possible.

Mt Buffalo is worth visiting mainly to stay in the historic Mt Buffalo Chalet, with its dramatic views over the craggy Victorian alps. The slopes, a short drive away, are in an alpine basin surrounded by boulders, with five lifts almost purely for beginners.

➕ For northern hemisphere dwellers, good for a vacation in the southern hemisphere combining sight-seeing with some skiing or boarding

➕ For Australians, conveniently close, with flights from Sydney

➕ Huge areas of off-trail terrain accessible by helicopter on the South Island

➕ Some spectacular views

➖ It's a long way from anywhere except Australia

➖ Limited mountain facilities – mountain restaurants are mostly very basic

➖ Generally long drives from accommodations up to the ski areas

➖ Highly changeable weather

➖ No trees, so skiing in bad weather is virtually impossible

The number of keen skiers and boarders from New Zealand found kicking around the Alps gives a clue that there must be some decent slopes back home – and indeed there are. The resorts are rather different from those of the Alps or the Rockies, and the networks of lifts and runs are rather limited by those exalted standards. However desperate you are for snow during the northern summer, we wouldn't advise traveling halfway round the world from North America or Europe just to get access to the likes of Coronet Peak, Mount Hutt or Whakapapa. But the heli-skiing around the Mt Cook region on the South Island is definitely worth writing home about. For visitors already spending a lot to travel to New Zealand, the extra cost of a day or two's heli-drops is well worth while. If you are traveling a long way, New Zealand's ski resorts could make an interesting part of a wider-ranging visit to the country; they may be the best skiing or boarding option you have if you're starting from somewhere nearer.

The big news is that Whakapapa and Turao have joined forces to offer a shared lift ticket. A linking lift is being planned, creating arguably the most impressive network in the southern hemisphere.

There are exceptions but, broadly speaking, the system in New Zealand is that you stay in towns at fairly low altitude – usually below the snow line – and drive up each day to a base lodge where there will be a simple restaurant, ski rental and one or two shops as well as the main lifts, but usually no accommodations.

There are resorts on both North Island and South Island. The main concentration on South Island is around the lakeside town (and year-round resort) of Queenstown, covered in detail in a separate chapter after this one. Queenstown has become known as the adrenalin capital of New Zealand – and probably the world – by offering a range of dangerous (or at least thrilling) activities, of which the best known is bungee jumping. Most of these are available in winter as well as summer.

In what follows, we describe the most prominent resorts (apart from Queenstown and its two local mountains), but there are a number of other possibilities. The main commercial ones are described briefly in our directory at the back of the book, but there are also other ski-areas run by clubs. By all means enquire about what's available on the club area front, but don't expect groomed trails or other luxuries: club areas are pretty primitive, involving long walks to get to the base and crude rope tows when you get there. You even have to bring your own food and drink. If you must visit any club area, Craigieburn on the South Island, near Mt Hutt, wins the vote for the most impressive terrain out of the selection.

Any of the major resorts is worth a day or two of your time if you're in the area and the conditions are right. But if your credit card is also in good condition, don't miss the heli-skiing; even if you're no expert off-trail; with powder skis it's easy, and tremendously satisfying. There are several companies operating on South Island, based in Queenstown, Wanaka and Methven. Methven Heli Ski arguably has the most impressive terrain on offer, operating in steep and spectacular ranges surrounding New Zealand's highest peak Mt Cook. Harris Mts Heli-Ski, operating out of Queenstown and Wanaka, caters mainly to the large Japanese market, and the three-run days are generally very easy skiing with long waits in between lifts. The other major Queenstown operation, Southern Lakes Heli-Ski, is more amenable to exciting skiing. Try to leave the arrangements loose, to cope with the highly changeable weather. A heli-ski day NZ-style usually starts with a 7.30 phone call to let you know if the weather's suitable.

An alternative adventure is to fly by plane to ski 10km/6 miles down the length of the Tasman Glacier. Be aware that this is quite a costly venture for a gentle schuss down a very mild slope, with few areas to lay real turns. The main drawcard of the Tasman is the immense grandeur of the place, along with the ski-plane flights over stunning blue ice-flows and the close proximity of Mt Cook. The Tasman is also one of the few glaciers in the world where it is possible to walk through the eery ice-blue glacial caves – quite a surreal experience.

As in the northern hemisphere, the season doesn't really get under way until about midwinter – mid or late June; it runs until some time in October. Mount Hutt aims to open first, in mid-May, and disputes the longest-season title with Whakapapa, which generally stays open until mid-November.

Snowboarding is very popular in New Zealand, and most of the major resorts have special terrain parks including half-pipes, as well as boarding classes and equipment rental.

Whakapapa (pronounced Fukapapa) is on the slopes of the active volcano Mt Ruapehu, which has occasionally erupted in recent years, leaving the slopes black with volcanic ash. Until the late 1990s the volcano had not caused havoc since the 1950s, when an eruption carried away a bridge.

Mt Ruapehu is in the middle of the North Island and within four hours' drive of both Auckland and Wellington. Whakapapa, New Zealand's largest ski field, is located on the north-facing slopes with a top height of 2300m/7,550ft and a vertical of 675m/2,210ft served by 20 lifts including one fast quad. Terrain is typified by large, wide open cruisers plus challenging off-trail. Next to the base lodge is an extensive beginner area, Happy Valley, with half a dozen rope tows and snowmaking that allow this particular section to open early in the season. The resort's lifts and runs range across craggy terrain made especially interesting because of the unpredictable twists, turns and drops of the solidified lava on which it sits. There is a mix of deep gullies, superb natural half-pipes for snowboarders and narrow chutes. There is a handful of mountain restaurants.

Accommodations are 6km/4 miles away at Whakapapa village, with the

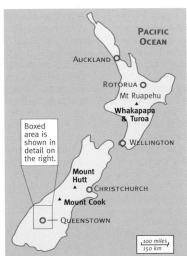

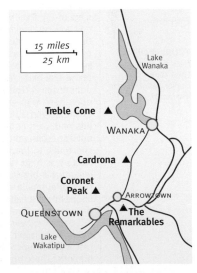

TREBLE CONE MOUNTAIN FACTS

Altitude	1200m-1860m
	3,940ft-6,100ft
Lifts	5
Trails	1,359 acres
Green	15%
Blue	45%
Black	40%
Snowmaking	
	125 acres

TOURIST OFFICE

t +64 (3) 443 7443
f 443 8401
tcinfo@treblecone.co.nz
www.treblecone.co.nz

CARDRONA MOUNTAIN FACTS

Altitude	1505m-1895m
	4,940ft-6,220ft
Lifts	7
Trails	790 acres
Green	20%
Blue	55%
Black	25%
Snowmaking	none

TOURIST OFFICE

t +64 (3) 443 7411
f 443 8818
info@cardrona.com
www.cardrona.com

MOUNT HUTT MOUNTAIN FACTS

Altitude	1420m-2075m
	4,660ft-6,810ft
Lifts	10
Trails	902 acres
Green	25%
Blue	50%
Black	25%
Snowmaking	
	103 acres

TOURIST OFFICE

t +64 (3) 308 5074
f 308 5076
marketing@nzski.com
www.nzski.com

best middle-of-the-road property being a motel named the Skotel. A complete anomaly in this area of rustic lodges is the Chateau, a hotel in the grand style of the 1920s, with overly high ceilings, sweeping drapes over picture windows, a marble foyer and formal dining room with grand piano.

Worth knowing about is the hike to Mt Ruapehu's fizzing Crater Lake. Ask ski patrol for directions or better still talk them into taking you on a guided trip. This involves about a half-hour hike up from the top of the highest T-bar, and then a long traverse across a large flat tundra-like area. A few lefts and rights and you are staring into the mouth of a volcano. Awesome views and neighbouring volcanos give this area an other-worldly feel.

On the south-western slope of Mt Ruapehu is **Turoa** – now under the same ownership as Whakapapa and soon to be joined by lift and trail. (At present it is reachable on snow by going off-trail from Whakapapa after a stiff climb.) Turoa is smaller, but with an impressive 720m/2,360ft vertical – the biggest in Australasia. The longest run is 4km/2.5 miles. There's plenty of scope off-trail away from the gentle intermediate runs, plus the chance to ski on the Mangaehuehu Glacier. Accommodations are 20 minutes away in Ohakune.

The South Island has 15 ski areas, including five club areas. **Mt Hutt**, an hour west of Christchurch in the northern part of the island, has a 670m/2,200ft vertical and some of the country's most impressive, consistently steep, wide-open terrain – all within view of the Pacific Ocean. On a clear day you can even see the sandy beaches in the distance beyond the patchwork Canterbury plains. The lift system is half the size of Whakapapa's and a few more fast chair-lifts would not go amiss. The main area is an open bowl with gentle terrain in the centre served by chairs and surface lifts and steeper terrain around the outside, some of which requires a short hike to the top. A large new base lodge was built for the 2000 season, including a big carpeted cafe and brasserie, plus a well stocked rental shop. Mt Hutt Helicopters offers six-run days in the mountains beyond for NZ$600. The helicopter departs from the heli-pad right in the parking lot – just wander up to the heli hut and book in. There are no accommodations

on-mountain – most people stay in the quiet little town of Methven, where there are several truly comfortable upscale B&Bs as well as motels and apartments. The very British South Island capital of Christchurch, an hour and a half away, is also an option for accommodations.

About six hours' drive south of Christchurch is the quiet lakeside town of Wanaka, which is also 90 minutes from Queenstown, and there are two resorts accessible from here.

Treble Cone, 20km/12 miles from Wanaka, has more advanced slopes than any other NZ ski area, plus the advantage of a better lift system including the first six-seater chair-lift in the southern hemisphere. There are two well maintained intermediate trails, one 3.5km/2 miles, the other 2km/1.2 miles. Both on the main flank and off to the side in Saddle Basin there are long natural half-pipes which are great fun when snow is good, as well as smooth, wide runs for cruising. Treble Cone is reached by a long and winding dirt track that adds to the excitement. The ski field offers stunning views across Lake Wanaka, its shores usually free of snow, with snowcapped Alpine-style peaks in the distance. There's an adequate cafe at the lift base.

Cardrona, 34km/21 miles from Wanaka, is famous for its dry snow. The terrain is noted for its well-groomed, flattering cruisers. But there are some serious if short chutes, and the middle basin, Arcadia, hosts the New Zealand Extreme Skiing Championships. The total vertical is a modest 390m/1,280ft. Millions have been poured into the resort by its family owners over the past few years, resulting in a large base area focused around an impressive, if odd, clock tower. There's a bar and brasserie-style restaurant, large rental facility and a licenced childcare center, plus several neat and modern self-contained apartments at the base (but bring all your own supplies). There are four half-pipes for boarders. Learners are looked after well, with three magic carpet lifts.

Queenstown 310m/1,020ft

A lively base for sampling a range of resorts

➕ For northern hemisphere dwellers, more interesting than summer skiing on glaciers

➕ For Australians, conveniently close, with flights from Sydney

➕ Huge areas of off-trail terrain accessible by helicopters

➕ Lots to do off the slopes, especially for adrenalin junkies

➕ Lively town, with lots going on and good restaurants

➕ Grand views locally, and the spectacular 'fjord' country nearby

➖ Slopes (in two separate areas locally) are a drive from town

➖ Limited lift-served slopes in each area

➖ It's a long way from anywhere except Australia

➖ No real mountain restaurants – just basic cafés at the lift bases

➖ Highly changeable weather

➖ No trees, so skiing in bad weather virtually impossible

SKYLINE QUEENSTOWN

Queenstown has a gondola but it doesn't access slopes – just Remarkable views across Lake Wakatipu ↓

If you want a single destination in New Zealand – as opposed to visiting a few different mountains on your travels – Queenstown is probably it, especially if you can cope with the cost of a few heli-drops. Although the resorts of North Island are impressive, the Southern Alps are, in the end, more compelling – and their resorts are free of volcanic interruptions. Mount Hutt may be a slightly more impressive area than either of Queenstown's local fields – Coronet Peak and The Remarkables – but it's a rather isolated field. From Queenstown you have a choice of the two local fields plus the option of an outing to Treble Cone and Cardrona. The best way to take them in would be to plan on a night or two in Wanaka, an hour or two away (see Introduction to New Zealand).

boarding

Boarding is popular in New Zealand, and although the two mountains close to Queenstown don't seem to have quite such a hold on the boarding market as Cardrona (see New Zealand introduction), they have everything you need, including equipment, lessons and new terrain-parks and half-pipes. You needn't go anywhere near a surface lift, and there are no flats to worry about except on the lowest green run at The Remarkables.

What's new

A magic carpet conveyor-belt now connects the parking lot at The Remarkables with the main lift stations.

CORONET PEAK MOUNTAIN FACTS

Altitude	1210m-1650m
	3,970ft-5,410ft
Lifts	7
Trails	690 acres
Green	20%
Blue	45%
Black	35%
Snowmaking	
	200 acres

TOURIST OFFICE

t +64 (3) 442 4620
f 442 4624
admin@coronetpeak.co.nz
www.nzski.com

THE REMARKABLES MOUNTAIN FACTS

Altitude	1620m-1980m
	5,310ft-6,500ft
Lifts	5
Trails	543 acres
Green	30%
Blue	40%
Black	30%
Snowmaking	25 acres

TOURIST OFFICE

t +64 (3) 442 4615
f 442 4619
admin@theremarkables.co.nz
www.nzski.com

The resort

Queenstown is a winter-and-summer resort on the shore of Lake Wakatipu. (There is a map of the area in the introductory chapter.) Although the setting is splendid, with views to the peaks of the aptly named Remarkables range beyond the lake, the town itself is no beauty – it has grown up to meet tourists' needs, and has a very commercial feel. In recent years much effort has been put into sprucing up the town, with such additions as the classy new Steamer Wharf complex by the lake and luxury accommodations. It has a lively, relaxed feel, and makes a satisfactory base, with some good restaurants, plenty of entertaining bars and lots of touristy clothes shops.

The mountains

There are four lift-served mountains – all small by North American or European standards – that you can get to from Queenstown. The two described here – Coronet Peak and The Remarkables – are close by. The others – Cardrona and Treble Cone – are a more serious drive away, near Wanaka. At each base area you'll find a mini-resort – a ski school, a ski rental shop, a functional self-service restaurant, but no accommodations except at Cardrona.

All these areas have something for all abilities of skier or boarder, with off-trail opportunities as well as prepared and patrolled trails. These areas use the American green/blue/black convention for run gradings, not the European blue/red/black.

THE SLOPES
Not the height of convenience

The Remarkables, true to their name, are a dramatic range of craggy peaks visible across the lake from some parts of Queenstown. The slopes are tucked in a bowl behind the peaks, a 40-minute drive from town.

Two chairs go up from the base. The slow Alta lift serves easy runs and accesses the higher Sugar Bowl chair, which serves mainly long, easy runs plus a couple of black chutes. The Shadow Basin chair accesses steeper terrain, including three hike-accessed, expert-only chutes that drop down to Lake Alta, and the Homeward Run – a broad, fairly gentle, unprepared slope down to the resort access road, where a shuttle-truck takes you back to the base. The Remarkables is also home to New Zealand's first snowcat operation in the bowls behind the main slopes.

Coronet Peak, about 25 minutes' drive from Queenstown, is a far more satisfying resort, especially for intermediates and above. Again, there are three main chair-lifts, one a fast quad that accesses practically all the runs. The main mountainside is a pleasantly varied intermediate slope, full of highly enjoyable rolling terrain that snowboarders adore, though it steepens near the bottom. A fourth lift, a T-bar, serves another mainly intermediate area to one side. There are also surface lifts for beginners. Night skiing runs from July to September on Fridays and Saturdays.

SNOW RELIABILITY
Good at Coronet

The New Zealand weather is highly variable, so it's difficult to be confident about snow conditions. Coronet tends to receive sleet and/or rain even when it's snowing in The Remarkables. But Coronet Peak has snowmaking on practically all its intermediate terrain, and boosted the system's capacity by 30% last season.

FOR EXPERTS
Challenges exist

Both areas have quite a choice of genuinely black slopes. Coronet's Back Bowls is an experts-only area, and there are other black slopes scattered around the mountain. The main enjoyment comes from venturing off-trail all over the place. The Remarkables' Shadow Basin chair serves some excellent slopes.

CHILDCARE

At both areas there is a Skiwiland Club for children aged 4 to 6 with morning and afternoon sessions. The Queenstown Crèche can take younger children all day. There is a licensed nursery at the Remarkables, taking children from 2 to 4.

FOR INTERMEDIATES
Fine, within limits

There are some very enjoyable intermediate trails in both areas – appreciably more at Coronet, where there are also easy blacks to go on to. But remember: these are very small areas by North American or European standards.

FOR BEGINNERS
Excellent

There are gentle slopes at both areas served by rope tows, and longer green runs served by chairs. And there are many other diversions if you decide skiing and boarding are not for you.

FOR CROSS-COUNTRY
Unremarkable

There is a short loop around a lake in the middle of The Remarkables area, but the only serious cross-country area is the elevated plateau of Waiorau Snow Farm, near Cardrona.

LIFTLINES
It depends

Coronet and The Remarkables can suffer a little from high-season crowds – there are certainly enough beds locally to lead to liftlines at peak times. But they aren't a major worry.

MOUNTAIN RESTAURANTS
Er, what mountain restaurants?

Both areas have a simple cafeteria at the base, and Coronet has a brasserie, but nothing up the mountain.

SCHOOLS AND GUIDES
All the usual classes

The schools are well organized, with a wide range of options, including 'guaranteed' beginner classes.

FACILITIES FOR CHILDREN
Look good

Childcare looked OK to us.

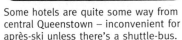

Staying there

Some hotels are quite some way from central Queenstown – inconvenient for après-ski unless there's a shuttle-bus.

HOW TO GO
Stay out of town?

There are lots of big, upscale but rather impersonal places built to meet the big summer demand for beds in this popular lakeside resort.
Hotels The hotels range from the very simple to the glossily pretentious Millennium. Aim to get a room with a view across Lake Wakatipu and the mountains – the view is worth the extra dollars. One of the most welcoming places – with more of a 'ski-lodge' atmosphere – is Nugget Point, a few miles out.

EATING OUT
Lots of choice

There are over 100 restaurants – Chinese, Italian, Malaysian, Lebanese ... you name it. The Moa is a particularly stylish bar-restaurant, with live music sometimes. Solero Vino has delicious Mediterranean food and a

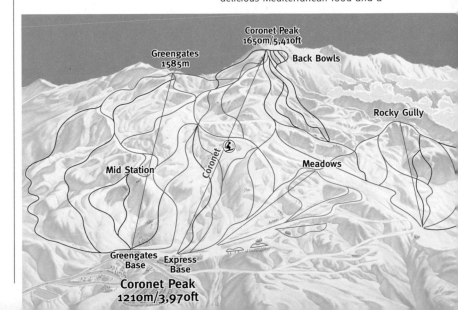

Greengates
1585m

Coronet Peak
1650m/5,410ft

Back Bowls

Rocky Gully

Mid Station

Coronet

Meadows

Greengates Base

Express Base

Coronet Peak
1210m/3,970ft

rustic bar, and McNeill's is an excellent brew-pub housed in a stone cottage, with a range of tasty beers. The Bunker does excellent local cuisine such as Bluff oysters and lamb. At the other end of the scale, pizza-lovers crowd into The Cow, a cozy barn-like place where you sit on logs around a fire waiting for tables or takeaways. Lone Star offers big servings of satisfying American-style food.

APRES-SKI
Lively little town
Queenstown has a good range of bars and clubs that stay open late with disco or live music. A small upscale casino opened in 1999 in the plush Steamer Wharf, which also holds a classy cigar bar.

OFF THE SLOPES
Scare yourself silly
There are lots of scary things to do – see below. Just to the west is New Zealand's spectacularly scenic 'fjord country', and you can go on independent or guided walks. By all reports, the Milford Sound sightseeing flights by plane or helicopter are to be preferred to the slow, lumbering bus-ride from Queenstown – but be aware that the weather can ruin your plans. Arrowtown is interesting for a quick visit – a cute, touristy old mining town where you can equip yourself to go panning for gold. The Winter Festival, held in mid-July, is an annual 'action-packed week of mayhem on the mountain and in the town'.

GET THAT ADRENALIN RUSH

The streets of Queenstown are lined by agencies offering various artificial thrills.

AJ Hackett's bungee jump at Kawarau Bridge is where this crazy activity got off the ground – you plunge towards the icy river, but are pulled up short by your bungee cord and lowered into an inflatable boat.

The Shotover Jet Boat experience is less demanding. You get chauffeured at high speed along the rocky river in a boat that can get along in very shallow water, execute high-speed 360° turns and pass very close to cliffs and trees. It's probably more fun in summer than in freezing winter temperatures.

The whitewater rafting is genuinely thrilling – and not as uncomfortable as you'd expect, thanks to the full wet-suit, helmet, boots and gloves, and to the exertion involved. The rivers have some exciting rapids. One route even passes through a tunnel excavated in the gold-mining days, after which comes a small but steep waterfall where your souvenir shots are snapped.

Resort index / directory

This is an index to the resort chapters in the book; you'll find page references for about 400 resorts described elsewhere. But you'll also find brief descriptions here of another 700 resorts, most of them much smaller than those we've covered in full, but often still worth a short visit.

Key

⛷ Lifts
🎿 Pistes
✉ UK tour operators

49 Degrees North USA
Inland area with best snow in Washington State, including 120-acre bowl reserved for powder weekends.
1195m; slopes 1195–1760m
3,920ft; slopes 3,920–5,770ft
⛷5 🎿 780 acres

Abetone Italy
Resort in the exposed Appennines, less than two hours from Florence and Pisa.
1390m; slopes 1390–1900m
4,560ft; slopes 4,560–6,230ft
⛷25 🎿 50km

Abtenau Austria
Sizeable village in Dachstein-West region near Salzburg, on plain ideal for cross-country.
710m; slopes 710–1260m
2,330ft; slopes 2,330–4,130ft
⛷6 🎿 10km

Achenkirch Austria
Unspoilt, low-altitude Tirolean village close to Niederau and Alpbach. Beautiful setting overlooking a lake.
930m; slopes 930–1800m
3,050ft; slopes 3,050–5,910ft
⛷10 🎿 25km

Adelboden Switzerland
Charming old village with several areas of mainly intermediate skiing; linked to Lenk.
1355m; slopes 1070–2355m
4,450ft; slopes 3,510–7,730ft
⛷55 🎿 166km

Les Aillons France
Traditional village near Chambéry. Nicely sheltered slopes.
1000m; slopes 1000–1900m
3,280ft; slopes 3,280–6,230ft
⛷24 🎿 40km

Akakura Japan
Old spa of some oriental charm, 150km/95 miles from Tokyo; modern lift system and easy runs.
770m; slopes 770–1500m
2,530ft; slopes 2,530–4,920ft
⛷41 🎿 85km

Alagna 264
Small resort on the western fringe of Monterosa Ski area.

Alba Italy
Picturesque Dolomite village with a small, quiet area; access to the Sella Ronda at nearby Canazei.
1515m; slopes 1515–2440m
4,970ft; slopes 4,970–8,010ft
⛷5 🎿 10km

Alleghe Italy
Dolomite village near Cortina in a pretty lakeside setting close to numerous areas.
980m / 3,220ft ⛷24 🎿 80km

Alpbach Austria
Exceptionally pretty and friendly old village with limited but quite varied skiing, mostly a bus-ride away.
1000m; slopes 670–2025m
3,280ft; slopes 2,200–6,640ft
⛷19 🎿 45km

Alpe-d'Huez 122

Alpe-du-Grand-Serre France
Tiny resort near Alpe-d'Huez and Les Deux-Alpes. Good for bad-weather days.
1400m; slopes 1400–2200m
4,590ft; slopes 4,590–7,220ft
⛷20 🎿 55km

Alpendorf
Hamlet-cum-base-station 4km from St Johann im Pongau. Linked to Wagrain and the extensive Salzburger Sportwelt Amadé lift network.
850m; slopes 850–2185m
2,790ft; slopes 2,790–7,170ft
⛷100 🎿 350km

Alpine Meadows 355

Alps Korea
Korea's most northerly, snowsure resort, near Seoul. ⛷5

Alta 405

Altenmarkt Austria
Unspoilt village well placed just off the Salzburg–Villach autobahn for numerous resorts including snowsure Obertauern and Wagrain.
855m; slopes 855–2130m
2,810ft; slopes 2,810–6,990ft
⛷23 🎿 150km

Alto Campoo Spain
Barren, desolate place with undistinguished slopes, but with magnificent wilderness views.
1700m; slopes 1650–2175m
5,580ft; slopes 5,410–7,140ft
⛷10

Alt St Johann Switzerland
Old cross-country village with Alpine slopes connecting into Unterwasser area near Liechtenstein.
900m; slopes 900–2260m
2,950ft; slopes 2,950–7,410ft
⛷21 🎿 50km

Alyeska USA
Alaskan area 60km/35 miles from Anchorage, with luxury hotel. Spring best for weather.
75m; slopes 75–1200m
250ft; slopes 250–3,940ft
⛷9 🎿 785 acres

Aminona 288
Purpose-built resort on the eastern side of the Crans-Montana network.

Andalo Italy
Atmospheric Dolomite village near Madonna, with low wooded slopes well equipped with snowmakers; best for novices.
1050m; slopes 1035–2125m
3,440ft; slopes 3,400–6,970ft
⛷17 🎿 60km

Andermatt Switzerland
Picturesque old village, isolated at the heart of Switzerland, with excellent steep skiing on the Gemsstock.
1445m; slopes 1445–2965m
4,740ft; slopes 4,740–9,730ft
⛷13 🎿 56km

Andorra la Vella 480

Angel Fire USA
Intermediate area near Taos, New Mexico. Height usually ensures good snow.
2620m; slopes 2620–3255m
8,600ft; slopes 8,600–10,680ft
⛷6 🎿 455 acres

Les Angles France
Attractive resort with one of the best ski areas in the Pyrenees. Pretty, tree-lined, mostly easy skiing.
1600m; slopes 1650–2400m
5,250ft; slopes 5,410–7,870ft
⛷23

Annaberg-Lungötz Austria
Peaceful village in a pretty setting, sharing a sizeable area with Gosau. Close to Filzmoos.
775m; slopes 775–1620m
2,540ft; slopes 2,540–5,310ft
⛷33 🎿 65km

Antagnod Italy
Weekend day-tripper area on the road up to Champoluc, above Aosta valley. No village.
1710m; slopes 1710–2000m
5,610ft; slopes 5,610–6,560ft
⛷4 🎿 7km

Anzère Switzerland
Sympathetically designed modern resort on a sunny balcony near Crans-Montana, with slopes suited to leisurely intermediates.
1500m; slopes 1500–2460m
4,920ft; slopes 4,920–8,070ft
⛷13 🎿 40km

Apex 445

Aprica Italy
Ugly, straggling village between Lake Como and the Brenta Dolomites, with bland slopes and limited facilities.
1180m; slopes 1180–2310m
3,870ft; slopes 3,870–7,580ft
⛷24 🎿 40km

Arabba 272
Tiny village with the Sella Ronda's highest, steepest skiing on its doorstep.

Aragnouet-Piau France
Purpose-built mid-mountain satellite of St-Lary, best suited to families, beginners and early intermediates.
1850m; slopes 1420–2500m
6,070ft; slopes 4,660–8,200ft
⛷32 🎿 80km

Berwang   Austria
Unspoiled village nestling in a spacious valley, close to Lermoos.
1335m; slopes 1335–1740m
4,380ft; slopes 4,380–5,710ft
⛷ 13   🚡 40km

Bessans   France
Old cross-country village near Modane. Well placed for touring Maurienne valley resorts such as Val-Cenis.
1710m; slopes 1740–2200m
5,610ft; slopes 5,710–7,220ft
⛷ 4   🚡 5km

Besse   France
Charming old village built out of lava, with purpose-built slope-side satellite Super-Besse. Beautiful extinct-volcano scenery.
1050m; slopes 1350–1800m
3,440ft; slopes 4,430–5,910ft
⛷ 21   🚡 80km

Bethel   USA
Pleasant, historic town very close to Sunday River, Maine. Attractive alternative to the slope-side resort.

Le Bettex   **176**
Small base at the gondola mid-station above St-Gervais, with links to the Megève network.

Bettmeralp   Switzerland
Central village of the sizeable Aletsch area near Brig, perched high above the Rhône valley, amid spectacular glacial scenery.
1955m; slopes 1925–2710m
6,410ft; slopes 6,320–8,890ft
⛷ 31   🚡 90km

Beuil-les-Launes   France
Alpes-Maritimes resort closest to Nice. Shares area with Valberg.
1400m; slopes 1400–2100m
4,590ft; slopes 4,590–6,890ft
⛷ 26   🚡 90km

Bezau   Austria
Virtually no slopes of its own but main village lies in low Bregenzerwald region north-west of Lech.
650m; slopes 1210–1650m
2,130ft; slopes 3,970–5,410ft
⛷ 2

Biberwier   Austria
Limited little village with a small area of its own. Best as a quiet base from which to cover the Zugspitz area.
1000m; slopes 1000–1880m
3,280ft; slopes 3,280–6,170ft
⛷ 5   🚡 25km

Bichlbach   Austria
Smallest of the Zugspitz villages with very limited slopes of its own. Suitable as an unspoiled base for visiting the rest of the area.
1070m; slopes 1070–1620m
3,510ft; slopes 3,510–5,310ft
⛷ 3   🚡 7km

Big Mountain   USA
Impressive ski area close to Montana's Glacier National Park, with good snow, a fun town and low prices.
1370m; slopes 1370–2135m
4,490ft; slopes 4,490–7,000ft
⛷ 10   🚡 3000 acres

Big Powderhorn   USA
Area with the most 'resort' facilities in south Lake Superior region - and the highest lift capacity too. The area suffers from winds.
370m; slopes 370–560m
1,210ft; slopes 1,210–1,840ft
⛷ 10   🚡 250 acres

Big Sky   **422**

Big White   **445**

Bischofshofen   Austria
Working town and mountain resort near St Johann im Pongau with very limited local runs and the main slopes starting nearby at Muhlbach.
545m; slopes 545–1000m
1,790ft; slopes 1,790–3,280ft
⛷ 2   🚡 2km

Bivio   Switzerland
Quiet village near St Moritz with easy slopes opened up by a few lifts.
1775m; slopes 1780–2600m
5,820ft; slopes 5,840–8,530ft
⛷ 4   🚡 40km

Bizau   Austria
One of two main areas in the low Bregenzerwald region north-west of Lech.
680m; slopes 680–1700m
2,230ft; slopes 2,230–5,580ft
⛷ 6   🚡 24km

Björkliden   **505**

Björnrike   **505**

Blackcomb   **470**

Blatten-Naters   Switzerland
Stunning glacial scenery, immediately above Brig, with larger Aletsch slopes nearby.
675m; slopes 1325–2880m
2,210ft; slopes 4,350–9,450ft
⛷ 9   🚡 60km

Bled   **498**

Blue Cow   **508**

Blue Mountain   Canada
Largest area in Ontario, with glorious views of Lake Huron. High-capacity lift system and 100% snowmaking.
230m; slopes 230–450m
750ft; slopes 750–1,480ft
⛷ 15   🚡 275 acres

Blue River   Canada
Base of world-famous Mike Wiegele heli-ski operation in Cariboo and Monashee mountains.

Bluewood   USA
Particularly remote area even by American north-west standards. Worth a visit if you're in Walla Walla.
1355m; slopes 1355–1725m
4,450ft; slopes 4,450–5,660ft
⛷ 3   🚡 530 acres

Bogus Basin   USA
Sizeable area overlooking Idaho's attractive, interesting capital, Boise.
1760m; slopes 1760–2310m
5,770ft; slopes 5,770–7,580ft
⛷ 8   🚡 2600 acres

Bohinj   **498**

Bois-d'Amont   France
One of four resorts that make up Les Rousses area in Jura region.
1050m; slopes 1120–1680m
3,440ft; slopes 3,670–5,510ft
⛷ 40

Bolognola   Italy
Tiny area in Macerata region near the Adriatic Riviera.
1070m; slopes 1070–1845m
3,510ft; slopes 3,510–6,050ft
⛷ 7   🚡 5km

Bolton Valley   USA
Resort near Stowe with mostly intermediate slopes.
465m; slopes 465–960m
1,530ft; slopes 1,530–3,150ft
⛷ 6   🚡 155 acres

Le Bonhomme   France
One of several areas with snowmakers near Strasbourg.
830m; slopes 830–1235m
2,720ft; slopes 2,720–4,050ft
⛷ 9   🚡 12km

Bonneval-sur-Arc   France
Unspoiled, remote old village in the Haute Maurienne valley with many of its slopes at high altitude. Pass to neighbouring Val-d'Isère is closed in winter.
1800m; slopes 1800–3000m
5,910ft; slopes 5,910–9,840ft
⛷ 18   🚡 25km

Bons   **163**
Rustic, unspoiled old hamlet linked to Les Deux-Alpes' skiing, conveniently placed down the valley for day trips to La Grave, Alpe-d'Huez and Serre-Chevalier.

Boreal   USA
Closest area to north Lake Tahoe town, Truckee. Limited slopes, best for novices.
2195m; slopes 2195–2375m
7,200ft; slopes 7,200–7,790ft
⛷ 9   🚡 380 acres

Bormio   **243**

Borovets   **495**

Bosco Chiesanuova   Italy
Weekend day tripper's place near Verona. A long drive from any other resort.
1105m; slopes 1105–1805m
3,630ft; slopes 3,630–5,920ft
⛷ 18   🚡 20km

La Bourboule   France
Spa and cross-country village with the slopes of Le Mont-Dore nearby. Spectacular extinct-volcano scenery.
850m; slopes 1050–1850m
2,790ft; slopes 3,440–6,070ft
⛷ 41   🚡 80km

Bourg-d'Oisans   France
Pleasant valley town on main Grenoble-Briançon road. Cheap base for visits to Alpe-d'Huez and Les Deux-Alpes.

Bourg-St-Maurice   **130**
French valley town, useful as a base for visiting nearby resorts and with a funicular to Les Arcs.

Bovec   **498**

Boyne Highlands   USA
Area with impressive, high-capacity lift system for weekend Detroit crowds. Fierce winds off Lake Michigan a major drawback.
225m; slopes 225–390m
740ft; slopes 740–1,280ft
⛷ 10   🚡 240 acres

Boyne Mountain   USA
Resort popular with weekend Detroit crowds. Not as windy as sister resort Boyne Highlands.
190m; slopes 190–340m
620ft; slopes 620–1,120ft
⛷ 12   🚡 115 acres

Bramans   France
Old cross-country village near Modane. Well placed for touring numerous nearby resorts such as Val-Cenis and Valloire.
1230m / 4,040ft ⛷ 1

Brand Austria
Family resort, less popular now, perhaps because it lacks the charm to compensate for its small, low area.
1050m; slopes 1050–1920m
3,440ft; slopes 3,440–6,300ft
⛷ 8 ↗ 30km

Les Brasses France
Collective name for six traditional hamlets with some of the closest slopes to Geneva, but best known for cross-country.
900m; slopes 900–1600m
2,950ft; slopes 2,950–5,250ft
⛷ 17 ↗ 50km

Braunwald Switzerland
Sunny but limited area, a funicular ride above Linthal.
1300m; slopes 1300–1910m
4,270ft; slopes 4,270–6,270ft
⛷ 8

Breckenridge 371

Brentonico Italy
Little resort just off Verona-Trento motorway.
1160m; slopes 1160–1520m
3,810ft; slopes 3,810–4,990ft
⛷ 16

La Bresse France
Largest of ski areas near Nancy and Strasbourg.
900m; slopes 900–1350m
2,950ft; slopes 2,950–4,430ft
⛷ 21 ↗ 62km

Bretton Woods 431

Briançon 207
Part of the Serre-Chevalier ski area.

Brian Head USA
Utah area south of Salt Lake City, too far from Park City for a day trip.
2925m; slopes 2925–3445m
9,600ft; slopes 9,600–11,300ft
⛷ 10 ↗ 500 acres

Brides-les-Bains 185
Quiet, unattractive old spa town with a long gondola connection up to Méribel.

Bridger Bowl 422
Montana area near Big Sky. Only a third of area is groomed. Good powder.

Brighton 403

Brixen im Thale 100
Best equipped of Grossraum villages, with gondola access to the slopes, shared with Söll and Ellmau.

Brodie Mountain USA
Largest Massachusetts area. 100% snowmaking and mostly easy slopes.
440m; slopes 440–820m
1,440ft; slopes 1,440–2,690ft
⛷ 6 ↗ 250 acres

Bromley USA
New York City weekend retreat, reputedly the warmest place to ski in chilly Vermont.
595m; slopes 595–1000m
1,950ft; slopes 1,950–3,280ft
⛷ 9 ↗ 300 acres

Bromont Canada
Purpose-built resort an hour east of Montreal, with one of the best small areas in eastern Canada, popular for its night skiing.
slopes 405–575m
slopes 1,330–1,890ft
⛷ 6 ↗ 135 acres

Bruck Austria
Low, two-lift beginners' resort, but would suit intermediates looking for a small, quiet base from which to visit nearby Zell am See.
560m; slopes 560–600m
1,840ft; slopes 1,840–1,970ft
⛷ 2

Brundage Mountain USA
Remote, uncrowded Idaho area with glorious views across lake towards Hell's Canyon. Mostly intermediate slopes. Also has a snowcat operation.
1760m; slopes 1760–2320m
5,770ft; slopes 5,770–7,610ft
⛷ 5 ↗ 1300 acres

Bruson Switzerland
Relaxing respite from Verbier's crowds, on the other side of Le Châble. Well placed for car trips to Chamonix and Champéry.
1080m; slopes 820–2200m
3,540ft; slopes 2,690–7,220ft
⛷ 7 ↗ 15km

Burke Mountain USA
Uncrowded, isolated family resort in Vermont with mostly intermediate slopes. Great views from the top.
385m; slopes 385–995m
1,260ft; slopes 1,260–3,260ft
⛷ 4 ↗ 130 acres

Bürserberg Austria
Undistinguished valley town near Brand.
900m; slopes 1035–1850m
2,950ft; slopes 3,400–6,070ft
⛷ 5 ↗ 16km

Cairngorm Scotland
Ski area 14km/9 miles from its dreary but well equipped modern resort (Aviemore).
635m; slopes 550–1100m
2,080ft; slopes 1,800–3,610ft
⛷ 16 ↗ 37km

Caldirola Italy
Genoese weekend day-tripper spot in a remote region off the motorway to Turin.
1010m; slopes 1010–1460m
3,310ft; slopes 3,310–4,790ft
⛷ 4 ↗ 5km

Camigliatello Italy
Tiny area on the foot of the Italian 'boot' near Cosenza. Weekend/day-trip spot.
1270m; slopes 1270–1750m
4,170ft; slopes 4,170–5,740ft
⛷ 4 ↗ 6km

Campitello 272
Linked to the Sella Ronda, with quick connections to the interesting Arabba section.

Campitello Matese Italy
The only slopes near Naples. Surprisingly large area when snowcover is complete. Weekend crowds.
1440m; slopes 1440–2100m
4,720ft; slopes 4,720–6,890ft
⛷ 8 ↗ 40km

Campo di Giove Italy
Highest slopes in L'Aquila region east of Rome.
1070m / 3,510ft
⛷ 6 ↗ 23km

Campodolcino Italy
Valley town with new funicular up to the fringe of Madesimo's slopes.
1070m; slopes 1545–2880m
3,510ft; slopes 5,070–9,450ft
⛷ 15 ↗ 45km

Campo Felice Italy
Easiest resort to reach from Rome, off Aquila motorway. One of the better lift systems in the vicinity.
1410m; slopes 1520–2065m
4,630ft; slopes 4,990–6,770ft
⛷ 14 ↗ 40km

Campo Imperatore Italy
One of the best of many little areas east of Rome in L'Aquila region.
1980m / 6,500ft
⛷ 8 ↗ 20km

Canazei 272
Sizeable and lively rustic village in the Sella Ronda's most heavily wooded section of mountain.

Candanchu/Astún 492

Canillo 488
Small, quiet town, with good sports facilities and newly developed lifts and slopes, linked to Soldeu.

Canmore Canada
Old frontier town on the way to Nakiska/Fortress, well placed for touring the region and an attractive alternative to staying in Banff.

Cannon 431

The Canyons 407

Cardrona 510

Les Carroz 168
An attractive, spacious village on a sunny shelf on the road up to Flaine.

Caspoggio Italy
Attractive, unspoiled village north-east of Lake Como, with easy slopes (and more at nearby Chiesa).
1100m; slopes 1100–2155m
3,610ft; slopes 3,610–7,070ft
⛷ 8 ↗ 22km

Castel S Angelo Italy
Tiny area in Macerata region near Adriatic Riviera.
805m / 2,640ft
⛷ 4 ↗ 2km

Cauterets France
Historic Pyrenean spa town with easy/intermediate open bowl slopes above it. 36km/ of snow-sure cross-country tracks.
935m; slopes 1400–2500m
3,070ft; slopes 4,590–8,200ft
⛷ 15 ↗ 30km

Cavalese Italy
Unspoiled medieval town with its own pretty slopes and close to the Sella Ronda.
1000m; slopes 975–2265m
3,280ft; slopes 3,200–7,430ft
⛷ 9 ↗ 70km

Ceillac France
Tight cluster of rustic old buildings near Serre-Chevalier. Not far from the highest village in Europe, St-Veran.
1600m; slopes 1600–2400m
5,250ft; slopes 5,250–7,870ft

Celerina 320
Quiet, unpretentious village, with links up to St Moritz's Corviglia sector.

Cerler Spain
Very limited, purpose-built resort with a compact ski area similar to that of nearby Andorra's Arinsal.
1500m; slopes 1500–2630m
4,920ft; slopes 4,920–8,630ft
⛷ 14 ↗ 35km

Le Cernix France
Hamlet near Megève where Les Saisies' slopes link to those of Crest-Voland. Uncrowded retreat.
1250m; slopes 1150–1950m 4,100ft; slopes 3,770–6,400ft
⛷ 24 ☂ 100km

Cerrato Lago Italy
Very limited area near the coastal town of La Spezia.
1270m; slopes 1270–1890m 4,170ft; slopes 4,170–6,200ft
⛷ 5 ☂ 3km

Cerro Castor Argentina
Ski area near Tierra del Fuego – the most southerly ski slopes in the world.

Cervinia 245

Cesana Torinese Italy
Little Italian village linking the Sauze d'Oulx, Sestriere and Sansicario side of the Milky Way to the Clavière, Montgenèvre side.
1350m ; slopes 1850–2680m 4,430ft ; slopes 6,070–8,790ft
⛷ 39 ☂ 100km

Le Châble 326
Small village below Verbier, linked by gondola.

Chacaltaya Bolivia
Highest ski area in the world, reached by four-wheel drive vehicle from nearby La Paz. Primitive facilities.
5190m; slopes 5220–5420m 17,030ft; slopes 17,130– 17,780ft
⛷ 1 ☂ 2km

Chaillol France
Cross-country base on the edge of the beautiful Ecrins National Park, near Gap. Small Alpine area, lots of snowmakers.
1600m; slopes 1450–2000m 5,250ft; slopes 4,760–6,560ft
⛷ 11

Chamois Italy
A good choice when higher areas are affected by bad weather. Close to Valtournenche and Cervinia.
1815m; slopes 1815–2270m 5,950ft; slopes 5,950–7,450ft
⛷ 8 ☂ 20km

Chamonix 139

Champagny-en-Vanoise 198
Charming village with pretty, south-facing local slopes linking to the La Plagne network.

Champéry 286

Champex Switzerland
Lakeside hamlet tucked away in the trees above Orsières. A nice quiet, unspoiled base from which to visit Verbier's area.
1470m; slopes 1470–2220m 4,820ft; slopes 4,820–7,280ft
⛷ 4 ☂ 8km

Champfér 320
Lakeside hamlet between St Moritz and Silvaplana with speedy access to the Corvatsch lifts.

Champoluc 264
Unspoiled, inexpensive village at one end of the the Monterosa Ski area.

Champoussin 286
Quiet mountainside village with convenient links to the rest of the Champéry slopes.

Chamrousse France
Functional family resort near Grenoble, with good, sheltered slopes.
1650m; slopes 1400–2255m 5,410ft; slopes 4,590–7,400ft
⛷ 26 ☂ 77km

Chandolin Switzerland
Picturesque, unspoiled village near equally delightful Zinal and Grimentz. Magnificent scenery. Extensive intermediate slopes.
1935m; slopes 1660–2895m 6,350ft; slopes 5,450–9,500ft
⛷ 15 ☂ 70km

Chantemerle 207
One of the main valley villages with direct access to Serre-Chevalier's slopes.

Chapelco Argentina
Only ski area in South America with a gondola. Year-round resort, 15 km/9 miles from sizeable town of St Martin de Los Andes.
slopes 1250–1980m slopes 4,100–6,500ft ⛷ 9

La Chapelle-d'Abondance 146
Unspoiled village 5km/3 miles down the valley from Châtel, with lift access to the Portes du Soleil network.

Charlotte Pass 508

Château d'Oex Switzerland
Pleasant village at the opposite end of the White Highlands ski area to Gstaad.
970m; slopes 950–3000m 3,180ft; slopes 3,120–9,840ft
⛷ 69 ☂ 250km

Châtel 146

Le Chatelard France
Small resort in remote Parc des Bauges between Lake Annecy and Chambéry.

Chiesa Italy
Attractive 'learn to ski' venue with a fairly high plateau of easy runs above the resort.
1000m; slopes 1700–2335m 3,280ft; slopes 5,580–7,660ft
⛷ 10 ☂ 25km

Le Chinaillon 151
Modern, chalet-style village at base of lifts above Le Grand-Bornand.

Chiomonte Italy
Tiny resort on the main road east of Bardonecchia and Sauze d'Oulx. A good half-day trip from either.
745m; slopes 745–2210m 2,440ft; slopes 2,440–7,250ft
⛷ 6 ☂ 10km

Chonmasan Korea
Dreary, purpose-built resort only 50 minutes from Seoul so it can get very crowded.
⛷ 7

Chsea Algeria
Largest of Algeria's skiable areas, 135km/84 miles south-east of coastal town of Alger in the Djur Djur mountains.
1860m; slopes 1860–2510m 6,100ft; slopes 6,100–8,230ft

Churwalden Switzerland
Hamlet on fringe of Lenzerheide-Valbella area.
1230m; slopes 1230–2865m 4,040ft; slopes 4,040–9,400ft
⛷ 35 ☂ 155km

Clavière Italy
Small Italian village linked to Montgenèvre (in France) and the rest of the Milky Way ski area.
1760m; slopes 1850–2680m 5,770ft; slopes 6,070–8,790ft
⛷ 39 ☂ 100km

La Clusaz 151

Les Coches 198
Small, purpose-built village, linked to the La Plagne ski area.

Cogne Italy
One of Aosta valley's larger villages. Small area worth a short visit from nearby Pila.
1530m; slopes 1530–2245m 5,020ft; slopes 5,020–7,370ft
⛷ 5 ☂ 8km

Colfosco 272
Small but sprawling village that makes up part of the Sella Ronda circuit.

Colle di Tenda Italy
Dour, modern resort that shares a good area with much nicer Limone. Not far from Nice.
1400m; slopes 1120–2040m 4,590ft; slopes 3,670–6,690ft
⛷ 33 ☂ 80km

Colle Isarco Italy
Brenner Pass area – and the bargain-shopping town of Vipiteno is nearby.
1095m; slopes 1095–2720m 3,590ft; slopes 3,590–8,920ft
⛷ 5 ☂ 15km

Le Collet-d'Allevard France
Ski area of sizeable summer spa Allevard-les-Bains in remote region east of Chambéry–Grenoble road.
1450m; slopes 1450–2100m 4,760ft; slopes 4,760–6,890ft
⛷ 13 ☂ 35km

Collio Italy
Tiny area of short runs in a remote spot between lakes Garda and d'Iseo.
840m; slopes 840–1715m 2,760ft; slopes 2,760–5,630ft
⛷ 14

Combelouvière France
Quiet hamlet tucked away in the trees at the foot of Valmorel's slopes.
1250m; slopes 1200–2550m 4,100ft; slopes 3,940–8,370ft
⛷ 56 ☂ 153km

Combloux 176
Quiet, unspoiled alternative to linked Megève.

Les Contamines France
Unspoiled village, up the valley from St-Gervais and on the fringe of the Mont Blanc ski area. The local skiing is best for intermediates.
1160m; slopes 1165–2485m 3,810ft; slopes 3,820–8,150ft
⛷ 26 ☂ 120km

Copper Mountain 376

Le Corbier France
Purpose-built tower-block resort with an extensive but low intermediate area linked with La Toussuire, off the Maurienne valley.
1500m; slopes 1500–2260m 4,920ft; slopes 4,920–7,410ft
⛷ 24 ☂ 75km

Coronet Peak 513

Corrençon-en-Vercors France
Charming, rustic village at foot of Villard-de-Lans ski area. Good cross-country, too.
1160m; slopes 1160–2170m 3,810ft; slopes 3,810–7,120ft
⛷ 29 ☂ 130km

Etna Italy
Scenic, uncrowded, short-season area on the (erupting as we go to press) volcano's flank, 20 minutes from Nickolossi.
1800m; slopes 1800–2350m
5,910ft; slopes 5,910–7,710ft
⬆ *5km*

Evolène Switzerland
Charming rustic village in unspoiled, attractive setting south of Sion. Own little area, with Verbier's slopes accessed at nearby Les Masses.
1380m; slopes 1300–3330m
4,530ft; slopes 4,270–10,930ft
⬆ *100* ⬆ *400km*

Faak am See Austria
Limited area, one of five overlooking town of Villach.
550m; slopes 840–1045m
1,800ft; slopes 2,760–3,430ft
⬆ *2* ⬆ *2km*

Fairmont Hot Springs Canada
Major luxury spa complex ideal for a relaxing holiday with some gentle skiing thrown in.
1280m; slopes 1280–1585m
4,200ft; slopes 4,200–5,200ft
⬆ *2* ⬆ *60 acres*

Faistenau Austria
Cross-country area close to Salzburg and St Wolfgang. Limited Alpine slopes.
785m; slopes 785–1000m
2,580ft; slopes 2,580–3,280ft
⬆ *6* ⬆ *3km*

Falcade Italy
Largest of many little ski areas close to but not part of the Sella Ronda.
1145m; slopes 1145–2170m
3,760ft; slopes 3,760–7,120ft
⬆ *11* ⬆ *39km*

Falera 300
Small, rustic village, with improved access to big ski area shared by Flims and Laax.

Le Falgoux France
One of the most beautiful old villages in France, set in the very scenic Volcano National Park. Several ski areas nearby.
930m; slopes 930–1350m
3,050ft; slopes 3,050–4,430ft

Falkertsee Austria
Base area rather than a village, with bleak, open slopes in contrast to nearby Badkleinkirchheim.
1690m; slopes 1690–2385m
5,540ft; slopes 5,540–7,820ft
⬆ *5* ⬆ *15km*

Falls Creek 508

Farellones Chile
One of Chile's best ski areas, an hour from Santiago. Crowded at weekends.

La Feclaz France
One of several little resorts in the remote Parc des Bauges.

Fernie 455

Fieberbrunn Austria
Friendly old traditional village, an inconvenient distance from its small but attractive ski area.
800m; slopes 800–2020m
2,620ft; slopes 2,620–6,630ft
⬆ *14* ⬆ *30km*

Fiesch Switzerland
Traditional Rhône valley resort close to Brig, with a lift into the beautiful Aletsch area.
1060m; slopes 1050–2870m
3,480ft; slopes 3,440–9,420ft
⬆ *10*

Filzmoos Austria
Charming, unspoiled, friendly village with leisurely slopes that are ideal for novices. Good snow record for its height.
1055m; slopes 1055–1645m
3,460ft; slopes 3,460–5,400ft
⬆ *12* ⬆ *32km*

Finkenberg 76
Between Mayrhofen and Hintertux, with a large area of mainly intermediate skiing

Fiss Austria
Nicely compact, quiet traditional village with a sunny area well protected by snowmakers and linked to Serfaus.
1435m; slopes 1200–2540m
4,710ft; slopes 3,940–8,330ft
⬆ *17* ⬆ *70km*

Flachau Austria
Quiet village in a pretty setting. Linked to Wagrain and extensive Salzburger Sportwelt Amadé lift network.
925m; slopes 925–2185m
3,030ft; slopes 3,030–7,170ft
⬆ *100* ⬆ *350km*

Flachauwinkl Austria
Well placed within the Salzburger Sportwelt Amadé area, but with the Salzburg-Villach autobahn running through it.
930m; slopes 800–2185m
3,050ft; slopes 2,620–7,170ft
⬆ *100* ⬆ *350km*

Flaine 168

Flims 300

Flumet France
Large resort, well placed for whole Mont Blanc area. Cheap, big-village alternative to Megève.
1000m; slopes 1000–1600m
3,280ft; slopes 3,280–5,250ft
⬆ *10* ⬆ *40km*

Flumserberg Switzerland
Collective name for the villages sharing a varied area an hour south-east of Zürich.
1220m; slopes 1220–2220m
4,000ft; slopes 4,000–7,280ft
⬆ *17*

Folgaria Italy
Largest of several resorts east of Trento. Old lift system.
1165m; slopes 1185–2005m
3,820ft; slopes 3,890–6,580ft
⬆ *38* ⬆ *70km*

Folgarida Italy
Pleasant Dolomite village, with links to Madonna di Campiglio's extensive area.
1270m; slopes 1270–2180m
4,170ft; slopes 4,170–7,150ft
⬆ *23*

Foncine-le-Haut France
Major cross-country village with extensive trails.

Fonni Gennaragentu Italy
Sardinia's only 'ski area' – and it's tiny.
⬆ *1* ⬆ *5km*

Font-Romeu France
Family resort set in woodland, with the biggest snowmaking set-up in the Pyrenees.
1800m; slopes 1650–2250m
5,910ft; slopes 5,410–7,380ft
⬆ *29* ⬆ *45km*

Foppolo Italy
Relatively unattractive but user-friendly village, a short transfer from Bergamo.
1510m; slopes 1610–2160m
4,950ft; slopes 5,280–7,090ft
⬆ *10* ⬆ *45km*

Forca Canapine Italy
Limited area near the Adriatic and Ascoli Piceno. Popular with weekend day-trippers.
1450m; slopes 1450–1690m
4,760ft; slopes 4,760–5,540ft
⬆ *11* ⬆ *20km*

Formazza Italy
Cross-country base with some downhill slopes.
1280m; slopes 1275–1755m
4,200ft; slopes 4,180–5,760ft
⬆ *8km*

Formigal 492

Le Fornet 227
Rustic, old hamlet 3km/2 miles further down the valley from Val-d'Isère.

Forstau Austria
Secluded hamlet above Radstadt-Schladming road. Very limited area with old lifts, but nice and quiet.
930m; slopes 930–1885m
3,050ft; slopes 3,050–6,180ft
⬆ *7* ⬆ *14km*

Fortress Mountain Canada
Primitive, wild little mountain between Banff and Calgary, renowned for powder snow, dramatic scenery and uncrowded slopes.
2040m; slopes 2040–2370m
6,690ft; slopes 6,690–7,780ft
⬆ *7* ⬆ *325 acres*

La Foux-d'Allos France
Purpose-built resort that shares a good intermediate area with Pra-Loup.
1800m; slopes 1800–2600m
5,910ft; slopes 5,910–8,530ft
⬆ *53* ⬆ *230km*

Frabosa Soprana Italy
One of numerous little areas south of Turin, well placed for combining winter sports with Riviera sightseeing.
850m; slopes 860–1740m
2,790ft; slopes 2,820–5,710ft
⬆ *40km*

Frisco 371
Small town based on a Victorian settlement, down the valley from Breckenridge.

Frontignano Italy
Best lift system in the Macerata region, near the Adriatic Riviera.
1340m; slopes 1340–2000m
4,400ft; slopes 4,400–6,560ft
⬆ *8* ⬆ *10km*

Fügen Austria
Unspoiled village with limited area best suited to beginners. Poorly placed for other Zillertal resorts.
560m; slopes 560–2400m
1,840ft; slopes 1,840–7,870ft
⬆ *19* ⬆ *48km*

Fulpmes 54

Funäsdalen Sweden
Cross-country Mecca, home of the world's longest ski trails, with 600m/1,970ft vertical of Alpine runs. Top-class facilities throughout.
600m; slopes 600–1200m
1,970ft; slopes 1,970–3,940ft
⬆ *30* ⬆ *85km*

524

Furano *Japan*
Small Hokkaido resort, one of the few Japanese areas to get reasonable powder.
235m; slopes 235–1065m
770ft; slopes 770–3,490ft
⛟ 17

Fusch *Austria*
Cheaper, quiet place to stay when visiting Zell am See. Across golf course from Kaprun and Schuttdorf.
805m; slopes 805–1050m
2,640ft; slopes 2,640–3,440ft
⛟ 2 ⛷ 5km

Fuschl *Austria*
Attractive, unspoiled, lakeside village close to St Wolfgang and Salzburg, 30 minutes from its slopes. Best suited to part-time skiers who want to sightsee as well.
670m / 2,200ft

Gala *Norway*
Base for downhill and cross-country skiing, an hour's drive north of Lillehammer.
930m / 3,050ft ⛟ 7

Gallio *Italy*
One of several low resorts near Vicenza and Trento. Popular with weekend day-trippers.
1100m; slopes 1100–1550m
3,610ft; slopes 3,610–5,090ft
⛟ 11 ⛷ 50km

Galtür 58
Charming traditional village near Ischgl, in the news in 1998/99 due to a tragic avalanche disaster.

Gambarie d'Aspromonte *Italy*
Italy's second most southerly ski area (after Mt Etna), On the 'toe' of the Italian 'boot' near Reggio di Calabria.
1310m; slopes 1310–1650m
4,300ft; slopes 4,300–5,410ft
⛟ 3

Gantschier *Austria*
No slopes of its own but particularly well placed for visiting all the Montafon areas.
700m / 2,300ft

Gargellen *Austria*
Quiet, tiny and secluded village tucked up a side valley in the Montafon area, with a small but varied local area that is blissfully quiet.
1425m; slopes 1425–2300m
4,680ft; slopes 4,680–7,550ft
⛟ 8 ⛷ 33km

Garmisch-Partenkirchen *Germany*
Large twin resort; unspoiled, traditional Partenkirchen much the prettier. Superb main area of wooded runs when the unreliable snowcover allows.
700m; slopes 700–2830m
2,300ft; slopes 2,300–9,280ft
⛟ 38 ⛷ 118km

Gaschurn *Austria*
Attractive, unspoiled village with the largest of the pretty Montafon areas, well suited to intermediates.
1000m; slopes 1000–2300m
3,280ft; slopes 3,280–7,550ft
⛟ 15 ⛷ 100km

Geilo 501

Gérardmer *France*
Sizeable resort near Strasbourg with plenty of amenities. Night skiing, too.
665m; slopes 750–1150m
2,180ft; slopes 2,460–3,770ft
⛟ 20 ⛷ 40km

Gerlitzen Alpe *Austria*
A gondola ride above Villach and with good views. A worthwhile excursion from Badkleinkirchheim.
500m; slopes 1003–1911m
1,640ft; slopes 3,290–6,270ft
⛟ 14 ⛷ 20km

Gerlos *Austria*
One of Austria's few inexpensive but fairly snow-sure resorts, linked to Zell im Zillertal as well as Konigsleiten to form a fair-sized intermediate area.
1250m; slopes 1250–2300m
4,100ft; slopes 4,100–7,550ft
⛟ 23 ⛷ 70km

Les Gets 192
Sprawling chalet resort on low pass near Morzine, on the periphery of the Portes du Soleil area.

La Giettaz *France*
Small resort between La Clusaz and Megève with no particular attractions.

Gitschtal/Weissbriach *Austria*
One of many little areas near Hermagor in eastern Austria, close to Italian border.
690m; slopes 690–1400m
2,260ft; slopes 2,260–4,590ft
⛟ 4 ⛷ 5km

Glaris *Switzerland*
Hamlet base station for the uncrowded Rinerhorn section of the Davos slopes.
1455m; slopes 1455–2490m
4,770ft; slopes 4,770–8,170ft
⛟ 5 ⛷ 30km

Glencoe *Scotland*
Limited slopes in moody and magnificent setting close to Aonach Mor. Only one hotel nearby.
305m; slopes 305–1110m
1,000ft; slopes 1,000–3,640ft
⛟ 7 ⛷ 20km

Glenshee *Scotland*
Scotland's most varied ski area, 40km/25 miles from pretty Blairgowrie, but runs are short and it gets crowded at weekends.
610m; slopes 610–1070m
2,000ft; slopes 2,000–3,510ft
⛟ 26 ⛷ 40km

Going 48
Small local ski area near Ellmau, linked to the huge Ski Welt area.

Goldegg *Austria*
Year-round resort famous for its lakeside castle. Limited slopes but Wagrain (Salzburger Sportwelt Amadé) and Grossarl (Gastein valley) are nearby.
825m; slopes 825–1250m
2,710ft; slopes 2,710–4,100ft
⛟ 4 ⛷ 12km

Golden *Canada*
Small logging town, the place to stay when visiting Kicking Horse resort 15 minutes away. Also the launch pad for Purcell heli-skiing.

Gore Mountain *USA*
One of the better areas in New York State. Near Lake Placid, sufficiently far north to avoid worst weekend crowds. Intermediate terrain.
455m; slopes 455–1095m
1,490ft; slopes 1,490–3,590ft
⛟ 9 ⛷ 290 acres

Göriach *Austria*
Hamlet with trail connecting into one of longest, most snow-sure cross-country networks in Europe.
1250m / 4,100ft

Gortipohl *Austria*
Traditional village in pretty Montafontal.
920m; slopes 900–2395m
3,020ft; slopes 2,950–7,860ft
⛟ 62 ⛷ 209km

Gosau *Austria*
Straggling village with plenty of pretty, if low, runs. Snow-sure Obertauern and Schladming are within reach.
765m; slopes 765–1800m
2,510ft; slopes 2,510–5,910ft
⛟ 37 ⛷ 65km

Göstling *Austria*
One of Austria's easternmost resorts, between Salzburg and Vienna. A traditional village in wooded setting.
530m; slopes 530–1800m
1,740ft; slopes 1,740–5,910ft
⛟ 12 ⛷ 20km

Götzens *Austria*
Valley village base for Axamer Lizum area.
870m / 2,850ft

Grächen *Switzerland*
Quiet little family village with a scenic but small intermediate area. Tricky access road.
1615m; slopes 1615–2890m
5,300ft; slopes 5,300–9,480ft
⛟ 13 ⛷ 50km

Le Grand-Bornand 151

Grand Targhee 424
Powder skiing paradise an hour from Jackson Hole.

Grangesises *Italy*
Small satellite of Sestriere, with lifts up to the main slopes.

Grau Roig 486
Mini-resort at foot of Pas de la Casa's only woodland runs, with one smart hotel and abundant day-tripper parking.

La Grave 174

Gray Rocks *Canada*
Very popular family resort, 130km/80 miles north of Montreal; renowned for its ski school.
250m; slopes 250–440m
820ft; slopes 820–1,440ft
⛟ 4 ⛷ 200 acres

Great Divide *USA*
Area near Helena, Montana, best for experts. Mostly bowls; plus near-extreme Rawhide Gulch.
1765m; slopes 1765–2195m
5,790ft; slopes 5,790–7,200ft
⛟ 6 ⛷ 720 acres

Gresse-en-Vercors *France*
Resort south of Grenoble. Sheltered slopes worth noting for bad-weather days.
1250m; slopes 1250–1800m
4,100ft; slopes 4,100–5,910ft
⛟ 16

Gressoney-la-Trinité 264
Smaller and higher of the two villages in the central valley of the Monterosa Ski area.

Gressoney-St-Jean 264
Larger and lower of the two villages in the central valley of the Monterosa Ski area.

Grimentz Switzerland
Captivating, unspoiled rustic village with high, varied runs served by modern lifts. Near the Valais town of Sierre.
1570m; slopes 1570–3000m
5,150ft; slopes 5,150–9,840ft
⚡12 ⛷ 50km

Grindelwald 305

Grossarl 41
Secluded village linked to Dorfgastein in the Gastein valley.

Grosskirchheim Austria
Very limited area near Heiligenblut.
1025m; slopes 1025–1400m
3,360ft; slopes 3,360–4,590ft
⚡2 ⛷ 3km

Grouse Mountain Canada
The Vancouver area with the largest lift capacity. Superb city views from mostly easy slopes; night skiing.
880m; slopes 880–1245m
2,890ft; slopes 2,890–4,080ft
⚡11 ⛷ 120 acres

Grünau Austria
Spacious riverside village in a lovely lake-filled part of eastern Austria. Nicely varied area, but very low.
525m; slopes 600–1600m
1,720ft; slopes 1,970–5,250ft
⚡14 ⛷ 40km

Gryon 334
Village below Villars, with which it shares a ski area.

Gstaad 309

Gunstock USA
One of the New Hampshire resorts closest to Boston, popular with families. Primarily easy slopes. Gorgeous Lake Winnisquam views. 98% snowmaking.
275m; slopes 275–700m
900ft; slopes 900–2,300ft
⚡8 ⛷ 220 acres

Guthega 508

Hallanrinteet Finland
Collective name for twin ski areas 20 minutes apart. Good lake views and short intermediate runs. ⚡14

Happo One Japan
European-style resort in same the vicinity as Nagano (Shiga Heights). One of Japan's more challenging areas.
750m; slopes 750–1830m
2,460ft; slopes 2,460–6,000ft
⚡34

Harrachov Czech Republic
Closest resort to Prague, with enough terrain to justify a day trip. No beginner area.
685m; slopes 650–1020m
2,250ft; slopes 2,130–3,350ft
⚡4 ⛷ 8km

Hasliberg Switzerland
Four rustic hamlets on a sunny plateau overlooking Meiringen and Lake Brienz. Two of them are the bottom stations of a varied intermediate area.
1055m; slopes 600–2435m
3,460ft; slopes 1,970–7,990ft
⚡16 ⛷ 60km

Haus in Ennstal 94
Village next to Schladming, with good local slopes connected to the rest of the network.

Haystack 431

Heavenly 350

Hebalm Austria
One of many small areas in Austria's easternmost ski region near Slovenian border. No major resorts in vicinity.
1350m; slopes 1350–1400m
4,430ft; slopes 4,430–4,590ft
⚡6 ⛷ 11km

Heiligenblut Austria
Picturesque village in beautiful surroundings with mostly high terrain. Its remote position west of Bad Gastein ensures that it remains uncrowded.
1300m; slopes 1300–2900m
4,270ft; slopes 4,270–9,510ft
⚡14 ⛷ 55km

Hemlock Resort Canada
Area 90km/55 miles east of Vancouver towards Sun Peaks, Mostly intermediate terrain and snowfall of 600 inches a year. Lodging is available at the base area.
1000m; slopes 1000–1375m
3,280ft; slopes 3,280–4,510ft
⚡4 ⛷ 350 acres

Hemsedal 503

Heremence Switzerland
Quiet village in unspoiled attractive setting south of Sion. Verbier's slopes are accessed a few minutes' drive away at Les Masses.
1250m; slopes 1300–3330m
4,100ft; slopes 4,270–10,930ft
⚡100 ⛷ 400km

Hermagor Austria
Carinthian village below the Sonnenalpe ski area, rated one of the best areas in Austria by champion skier Franz Klammer.
600m; slopes 1210–2005m
1,970ft; slopes 3,970–6,580ft
⚡29 ⛷ 101km

Himos Finland
Varied Alpine and cross-country area.
80m; slopes 80–220m
260ft; slopes 260–720ft ⚡10

Hintersee Austria
Easy slopes very close to Salzburg. Several long top-to-bottom runs and lifts means the size of the area is greatly reduced if the snowline is high.
745m; slopes 750–1470m
2,440ft; slopes 2,460–4,820ft
⚡9 ⛷ 40km

Hinterstoder Austria
Quiet, unspoiled traditional village, 80km/50 miles east of Salzburg, with a good snow record for its height.
600m; slopes 600–1860m
1,970ft; slopes 1,970–6,100ft
⚡14 ⛷ 35km

Hintertux 51

Hippach 76
Hamlet near a crowd-free lift into Mayrhofen's main area.

Hochgurgl 81
Quiet mountain-side hotel-village with a gondola connection to Obergurgl's slopes.

Hochpillberg Austria
Peaceful hamlet with fabulous views towards Innsbruck and varied terrain. Virtually traffic-free.
1330m / 4,360ft
⚡5 ⛷ 10km

Hochsölden 98
Quieter mountain-side satellite above lively, sprawling Sölden, with links to the whole network.

Hochybrig Switzerland
Purpose-built complex only 64km/21oft south of Zürich, with facilities for families.
1050m; slopes 1050–2200m
3,440ft; slopes 3,440–7,220ft
⚡16 ⛷ 50km

Hohuanshan Taiwan
Limited ski area with short season in high wild inaccessible Miitaku mountains.
3275m / 10,740ft ⚡1

Hollersbach Austria
Pass Thurn hamlet near Mittersill. Uncrowded base from which to visit Kitzbühel if snowline is low – or Kaprun, Gerlos, Matrei and Uttendorf if high.
805m; slopes 805–1000m
2,640ft; slopes 2,640–3,280ft
⚡2 ⛷ 5km

Homewood USA
Area with unsurpassed Lake Tahoe views, near Tahoe City. Most sheltered slopes in the vicinity so a good choice in bad weather.
1895m; slopes 1895–2400m
6,220ft; slopes 6,220–7,870ft
⚡10 ⛷ 1260 acres

Hoodoo Ski Bowl USA
Typical Oregon area with sizeable but short runs. Snow record isn't as good as its competitors near Portland.
1420m; slopes 1420–1740m
4,660ft; slopes 4,660–5,710ft
⚡5 ⛷ 800 acres

Hopfgarten 100
Small chalet village with lift link into extensive Ski Welt area shared with Söll.

Horseshoe Resort Canada
Toronto region resort with high-capacity lift system and 100% snowmaking. The second mountain – The Heights – is open to members only.
310m; slopes 310–405m
1,020ft; slopes 1,020–1,330ft
⚡7 ⛷ 60 acres

Hospental Switzerland
Small village connected to Andermatt by road and rail and with local slopes of its own.
1455m; slopes 1445–2965m
4,770ft; slopes 4,740–9,730ft
⚡13 ⛷ 56km

Les Houches 139
Varied, tree-lined area above spread-out village at the entrance to the Chamonix valley.

Hovden Norway
Big, modern luxury lakeside hotel in wilderness midway between Oslo and Bergen. Cross-country venue with some Alpine slopes.
760m; slopes 760–1205m
2,490ft; slopes 2,490–3,950ft
⛷ 2

Huez 122
Charming old hamlet on the road up to Alpe-d'Huez with lift into ski area.

Hunter Mountain USA
Popular New Yorkers' area so it gets very crowded at weekends.
485m; slopes 485–975m
1,590ft; slopes 1,590–3,200ft
⛷ 14 ⛷ 230 acres

Hüttschlag Austria
Hamlet in dead-end valley with lifts into Gastein area at nearby Grossarl.
1020m; slopes 840–1220m
3,350ft; slopes 2,760–4,000ft
⛷ 2 ⛷ 5km

Hyundai Sungwoo Korea
Massive high-rise monstrosity, two hours from Seoul. 21 slopes. ⛷ 8

Idre Sweden
Collective name for four areas – snow-sure but only 305m/1,000ft vertical.
710m; slopes 710–890m
2,330ft; slopes 2,330–2,920ft
⛷ 30 ⛷ 28km

Igls 54

Iizuna Japan
Tiny area one hour from Nagano and four hours from Tokyo. ⛷ 5

Incline Village 355
Large village on northern edge of Lake Tahoe - reasonable stop-off if touring.

Indianhead USA
South Lake Superior area with the most snowfall in region. Winds are a problem.
395m; slopes 395–585m
1,300ft; slopes 1,300–1,920ft
⛷ 12 ⛷ 195 acres

Inneralpbach Austria
Small satellite of Alpbach, 3km/2 miles up the valley.
1050m; slopes 670–2025m
3,440ft; slopes 2,200–6,640ft
⛷ 19 ⛷ 45km

Innerarosa Switzerland
The prettiest part of Arosa.
1800m; slopes 1800–2655m
5,910ft; slopes 5,910–8,710ft
⛷ 14 ⛷ 70km

Innsbruck 54

Interlaken 336
Large lakeside summer resort at entrance to the valleys leading to Wengen, Grindelwald and Mürren.

Ischgl 58

Ishiuchi Maruyama-Yuzawa Kogen Japan
Sizeable resorts offering the largest ski area in the central Honshu region.
255m; slopes 255–920m
840ft; slopes 840–3,020ft
⛷ 36

Isola 2000 France
Small purpose-built family resort 90km/55 miles from Nice, with a compact ski area and an improving range of amenities.
2000m; slopes 1840–2610m
6,560ft; slopes 6,040–8,560ft
⛷ 24 ⛷ 120km

Isoyöte Finland
The most southern downhill skiing area in Finland. Mostly easy slopes, and the main hotel is at the top of the mountain.
430m; slopes 240–430m
1,410ft; slopes 790–1,410ft
⛷ 11 ⛷ 21km

Itter 100
Next to Söll, skiing linked to Hopfgarten and Brixen, and to the whole of the Ski Welt region.

Jackson USA
Classic New England village, and a major cross-country base. A lovely place from which to ski New Hampshire's Alpine areas.

Jackson Hole 424

Jasper 445

Jay Peak 431

Jochberg 63
Straggling village, 8km/ 5 miles from Kitzbühel. Shares its varied, snow-sure ski area with Pass Thurn.

La Joue-du-Loup France
Purpose-built little ski-in/ski-out family resort. Shares sizeable intermediate area with Superdévoluy.
1500m; slopes 1500–2510m
4,920ft; slopes 4,920–8,230ft
⛷ 31 ⛷ 100km

Jouvenceaux 267
Less boisterous base from which to ski Sauze d'Oulx's splendid cruising terrain.

Jukkasjärvi Sweden
Centuries-old resort with unique ice hotel - rebuilt every December out of 3,000 tons of snow and ice.

June Mountain USA
Well liked by day-visitors from nearby Mammoth. Quiet slopes and superb school.
2300m; slopes 2300–3090m
7,550ft; slopes 7,550–10,140ft
⛷ 8 ⛷ 500 acres

Juns 51
Small, spread out village between Lanersbach and Hintertux, with its own tiny beginners' area.

Kals am Grossglockner Austria
Village in remote valley north of Lienz.
1325m; slopes 1325–2305m
4,350ft; slopes 4,350–7,560ft
⛷ 7 ⛷ 15km

Kaltenbach Austria
One of the larger, quieter Zillertal areas, with plenty of high-altitude slopes.
560m; slopes 560–2300m
1,840ft; slopes 1,840–7,550ft
⛷ 16 ⛷ 60km

Kananaskis Canada
Small area near Calgary, nicely set in woods, with slopes at Nakiska and Fortress Mountain.
slopes 1525–2465m
slopes 5,000–8,090ft
⛷ 12 ⛷ 605 acres

Kandersteg Switzerland
Good cross-country base set amid beautiful scenery near Interlaken.
1175m; slopes 1175–2000m
3,850ft; slopes 3,850–6,560ft
⛷ 7 ⛷ 13km

Kanin 498

Kaprun 114
Classic Austrian charmer of a village. Extensive sheltered slopes at nearby Zell am See.

Les Karellis France
Resort with slopes that are more scenic, challenging and snow-sure than those of better-known Valloire, nearby.
1600m; slopes 1600–2550m
5,250ft; slopes 5,250–8,370ft
⛷ 19 ⛷ 60km

Kastelruth Italy
Charming picturesque village in the south Tirolean Italian Dolomites with good cross-country trails. Near the Sella Ronda circuit.

Kasurila Finland
Siilinjarvi ski area popular with boarders. ⛷ 5

Katschberg Austria
Lovely hamlet above St Michael in southern Austria.
1140m; slopes 1650–2220m
3,740ft; slopes 5,410–7,280ft
⛷ 15 ⛷ 80km

Keystone 380

Kicking Horse Mountain 445

Killington 434

Kimberley 445

Kirchberg 63
Lively little town close to Kitzbühel, with which it shares its slopes.

Kirchdorf Austria
Attractive village a bus-ride from St Johann in Tirol, with good local beginner slopes.
640m; slopes 640–1000m
2,100ft; slopes 2,100–3,280ft
⛷ 2 ⛷ 5km

Kirkwood 355

Kitzbühel 63

Kleinarl Austria
Secluded traditional village up a pretty side valley from Wagrain, with lifts into the Flachau section of the Salzburger Sportwelt Amadé.
1015m; slopes 800–2185m
3,330ft; slopes 2,620–7,170ft
⛷ 100 ⛷ 350km

Klippitztorl Austria
One of many little areas in Austria's easternmost ski region near Slovenian border.
1460m; slopes 1460–1820m
4,790ft; slopes 4,790–5,970ft
⛷ 6 ⛷ 25km

Klosters 293
Quiet, affluent chalet village with much-improved access to the huge ski area it shares with Davos.

Kobla 498

Kolsass-Weer Austria
Once a fashionable resort, but with low, inconvenient and limited slopes.
555m; slopes 555–1010m
1,820ft; slopes 1,820–3,310ft
⛷ 3 ⛷ 14km

Königsleiten
Quiet, high resort sharing fairly snowsure area with Gerlos, now also linked to Zell im Zillertal to form a fair-sized area.

Kopaonik Serbia
Modern, sympathetically designed family resort in a pretty setting.
1770m; slopes 1110–2015m
5,810ft; slopes 3,640–6,610ft
⛷ 21 ⛷ 57km

Koralpe   Austria
Largest and steepest of many gentle little areas in Austria's easternmost ski region near the Slovenian border.
1550m; slopes 1550–2050m
5,090ft; slopes 5,090–6,730ft
⛷ 10   🚶 25km

Korea Condo   Korea
A single condo complex built some way from the three slopes. ⛷ 2

Kössen   Austria
Village near St Johann in Tirol with low, scattered and limited local slopes.
600m; slopes 600–1700m
1,970ft; slopes 1,970–5,580ft
⛷ 11   🚶 25km

Kötschach-Mauthen   Austria
One of many little areas near Hermagor in eastern Austria, close to the Italian border.
710m; slopes 710–1300m
2,330ft; slopes 2,330–4,270ft
⛷ 4   🚶 6km

Kranjska Gora   498

Krimml   Austria
Sunny area, high enough to have good snow usually. Shares regional pass with Wildkogel resorts (Neukirchen).
1075m; slopes 1640–2040m
3,530ft; slopes 5,380–6,690ft
⛷ 8   🚶 33km

Krispl-Gaissau   Austria
Easy slopes very close to Salzburg. Several long top-to-bottom lifts mean the size of the area is greatly reduced if the snowline is high.
925m; slopes 750–1570m
3,030ft; slopes 2,460–5,150ft
⛷ 11   🚶 40km

Kühtai   Austria
Huddle of good hotels (and little else) with a small, snowsure area suited to intermediates. Only 35km/ 22 miles from Innsbruck.
2020m; slopes 2010–2520m
6,630ft; slopes 6,590–8,270ft
⛷ 11   🚶 40km

Kurumayama Kogen   Japan
Remote resort, six hours from Osaka. Probably the least crowded slopes in Japan. ⛷ 11

Kusatsu Onsen   Japan
Spa village with attractive hot springs, three hours from Tokyo. ⛷ 15

Laax   300
Old farming community with a lot of character and some new development nearby - linked to Flims.

Ladis   Austria
Smaller alternative to Serfaus and Fiss, with lifts that connect into the same varied ski area.
1200m; slopes 1200–2540m
3,940ft; slopes 3,940–8,330ft
⛷ 4   🚶 18km

Le Laisinant   227
Tiny hamlet a short bus-ride down the valley from Val-d'Isère.

Lake Louise   447

Lake Tahoe   355

Lanersbach   51
Attractive village with charming little ski area of its own, plus Hintertux glacier nearby.

Lans-en-Vercors   France
Village close to Villard-de-Lans and near Grenoble. Highest slopes in region; few snowmakers.
1020m; slopes 1400–1805m
3,350ft; slopes 4,590–5,920ft
⛷ 16   🚶 24km

Lauterbrunnen   311
Valley town in the Jungfrau region, with a funicular and rail connection up to Mürren.

Le Lavancher   139
Quiet village between Chamonix and Argentière, with off-trail runs home for the insane.

Lavarone   Italy
One of several areas east of Trento, good for a weekend day-trip.
1195m; slopes 1075–1555m
3,920ft; slopes 3,530–5,100ft
⛷ 13   🚶 12km

Leadville   USA
Old mining town full of historic buildings. Own easy area (Ski Cooper) plus snowcat operation. Picturesque inexpensive base for visiting Copper Mountain, Vail and Beaver Creek.

Lech   69

The Lecht   Scotland
Gentle area of easy, short runs with the nearest hotel 5km/3 miles away.
640m; slopes 610–825m
2,100ft; slopes 2,000–2,710ft
⛷ 14   🚶 20km

Lélex   France
Family resort with pretty wooded slopes between Dijon and Geneva.
900m; slopes 900–1680m
2,950ft; slopes 2,950–5,510ft
⛷ 29   🚶 50km

Las Leñas   Argentina
Euro-style resort, 3 hours south of Mendoza, with varied, beautiful terrain. Peak season crowds.
2240m; slopes 2240–3430m
7,350ft; slopes 7,350–11,250ft
⛷ 12   🚶 65km

Lenk   Switzerland
Traditional village that shares a sizeable area of easy, pretty terrain with Adelboden.
1070m; slopes 1070–2355m
3,510ft; slopes 3,510–7,730ft
⛷ 55   🚶 166km

Lenzerheide   Switzerland
Spacious village, separated by a lake from Valbella and sharing a large intermediate area.
1500m; slopes 1230–2865m
4,920ft; slopes 4,040–9,400ft
⛷ 35   🚶 155km

Leogang   88
Quiet, spread-out village with over-the-mountain link to Saalbach-Hinterglemm.

Lermoos   Austria
Focal resort of the Zugspitz area, a delightful base for beginners and for cross-country enthusiasts.
1005m; slopes 1005–2250m
3,300ft; slopes 3,300–7,380ft
⛷ 10   🚶 29km

Lessach   Austria
Hamlet with trail connecting into one of longest, most snow-sure cross-country networks in Europe.
1210m / 3,970ft

Leukerbad   Switzerland
Major spa resort of Roman origin, with spectacular scenery and high runs including a World Cup downhill course.
1410m; slopes 1410–2700m
4,630ft; slopes 4,630–8,860ft
⛷ 17   🚶 60km

Leutasch   Austria
Traditional cross-country village with limited slopes but a pleasant day trip from nearby Seefeld or Innsbruck.
1130m; slopes 1130–1605m
3,710ft; slopes 3,710–5,270ft
⛷ 4   🚶 9km

Levi   Finland
Finland's most rapidly developing and most Alpine-like resort. Slope-side village with several hotels and easy to get to – Kittila airport is only 10 minutes away.
205m; slopes 205–530m
670ft; slopes 670–1,740ft ⛷ 15

Leysin   Switzerland
Large resort near Aigle, with a good range of facilities, but low, sunny terrain.
1400m; slopes 1400–2300m
4,590ft; slopes 4,590–7,550ft
⛷ 19   🚶 60km

Lienz   Austria
Pleasant town in pretty surroundings.
675m; slopes 730–2290m
2,210ft; slopes 2,390–7,510ft
⛷ 12   🚶 55km

Lillehammer   501

Limone   Italy
Pleasant old town not far from Turin, with a pretty area, but far from snow-sure.
1010m; slopes 1030–2050m
3,310ft; slopes 3,380–6,730ft
⛷ 29   🚶 80km

Lincoln   431

Lindvallen-Hogfjallet   Sweden
Largest ski area (but two unlinked mountains) in Scandinavia. The start of Vasalopp, world's largest cross-country race.
800m; slopes 800–1000m
2,620ft; slopes 2,620–3,280ft
⛷ 72   🚶 85km

Le Lioran   France
Auvergne village with purpose-built satellite above. Spectacular volcanic scenery.
1160m; slopes 1160–1850m
3,810ft; slopes 3,810–6,070ft
⛷ 24   🚶 60km

Livigno   260

Lizzola   Italy
Small base development in remote region north of Bergamo. Several other little areas nearby.
1250m; slopes 1250–2070m
4,100ft; slopes 4,100–6,790ft
⛷ 9   🚶 30km

Llaima   Chile
Exotic and popular ski touring area (Alpine and Nordic) around and below a mildly active volcano.
1500m / 4,920ft

Loch Lomond   Canada
Steep, narrow, challenging slopes near Thunder Bay on the shores of Lake Superior. Candy Mountain is nearby.
215m; slopes 215–440m
710ft; slopes 710–1,440ft
⛷ 3   🚶 90 acres

Lofer Austria
Quiet, traditional, village close
to Salzburg with a small area
of its own, and Waidring's
relatively snow-sure
Steinplatte nearby.
640m; slopes 640–1745m
2,100ft; slopes 2,100–5,720ft
⛷ *13* ⬈ *46km*

Longchamp France
Dreary purpose-built resort
with little to commend it over
pretty Valmorel, with which it
shares its ski area.
1650m; slopes 1200–2550m
5,410ft; slopes 3,940–8,370ft
⛷ *56* ⬈ *153km*

Loon Mountain 431

Lost Trail USA
Remote Montana area, open
only Thursday to Sunday and
holidays. Mostly intermediate
slopes.
2005m; slopes 2005–2370m
6,580ft; slopes 6,580–7,780ft
⛷ *6* ⬈ *800 acres*

Loveland USA
High, varied slopes, a day trip
from Keystone and renowned
for snow. Long season, good
for all abilities.
3220m; slopes 3220–3730m
10,560ft; slopes 10,560–12,240ft
⛷ *11* ⬈ *836 acres*

Luchon France
Sizeable village with plenty of
amenities, with gondola (8
minutes) to its ski area and to
purpose-built Superbagnères.
630m; slopes 1440–2260m
2,070ft; slopes 4,720–7,410ft
⛷ *16* ⬈ *35km*

Lurisia Italy
Sizeable spa resort, a good
base for visits to surrounding
little ski areas and to Nice.
750m; slopes 850–1800m
2,460ft; slopes 2,790–5,910ft
⬈ *30km*

Luz-Ardiden France
Spa village below its ski area.
Cauterets and Barèges
nearby.
710m; slopes 1730–2450m
2,330ft; slopes 5,680–8,040ft
⛷ *19* ⬈ *60km*

Macugnaga Italy
Pretty, two-part village set
amid stunning scenery. Novice
and intermediate slopes,
1330m; slopes 1330–2970m
4,360ft; slopes 4,360–9,740ft
⛷ *12* ⬈ *40km*

Madesimo Italy
Remote valley village, with
limited area of mainly
intermediate runs, and a
famous itinerary route.
1545m; slopes 1545–2880m
5,070ft; slopes 5,070–9,450ft
⛷ *15* ⬈ *45km*

Madonna di Campiglio Italy
Large modern village in the
western Dolomites with a
large area of easy and
intermediate skiing.
1520m; slopes 1550–2505m
4,990ft; slopes 5,090–8,220ft
⛷ *51* ⬈ *150km*

Mad River Glen 431

La Magdelaine Italy
Close to Cervinia, and good
on bad-weather days.
1645m; slopes 1645–1870m
5,400ft; slopes 5,400–6,140ft
⛷ *4* ⬈ *4km*

Maishofen Austria
Cheaper place to stay when
visiting equidistant Saalbach
and Zell am See.
765m / 2,510ft

Malbun Liechtenstein
Quaint user-friendly little
family resort, 16km/10 miles
from the capital, Vaduz.
Limited slopes and short easy
runs.
1600m; slopes 1595–2100m
5,250ft; slopes 5,230–6,890ft
⛷ *6* ⬈ *16km*

Malcesine Italy
Large summer resort on Lake
Garda with a fair area of
slopes.
1430m; slopes 1430–1830m
4,690ft; slopes 4,690–6,000ft
⛷ *8* ⬈ *12km*

Malga Ciapela Italy
Resort at the foot of the
Marmolada glacier massif,
with a link into the Sella
Ronda. Cortina is nearby.
1445m; slopes 1445–3270m
4,740ft; slopes 4,740–10,730ft
⛷ *8* ⬈ *18km*

Mallnitz Austria
Village in a pretty valley close
to Slovenia, with two varied
areas providing a fine mix of
wooded and open runs.
1200m; slopes 1300–2650m
3,940ft; slopes 4,270–8,690ft
⛷ *5* ⬈ *30km*

Mammoth Mountain 357

Manigod France
Small valley village over the
Col de la Croix-Fry from La
Clusaz.

Marble Mountain Canada
Area near the charming
Newfoundland town Corner
Brook and Gros Morne
National Park. It has one of
the east coast's highest
snowfall records.
85m; slopes 85–570m
280ft; slopes 280–1,870ft
⛷ *5* ⬈ *126 acres*

Maria Alm Austria
Charming unspoiled village
east of Zell am See with a
varied area that spreads
impressively over five linked
mountains.
800m; slopes 800–2000m
2,620ft; slopes 2,620–6,560ft
⛷ *36* ⬈ *150km*

Mariapfarr Austria
Village at the heart of one of
the longest, most snow-
reliable cross-country
networks in Europe. Sizeable
Mauterndorf-St Michael Alpine
area and Obertauern area are
nearby.
1120m / 3,670ft
⛷ *7* ⬈ *30km*

Mariazell Austria
Traditional Styria village with
an impressive basilica.
Limited slopes.
870m; slopes 870–1265m
2,850ft; slopes 2,850–4,150ft
⛷ *5* ⬈ *11km*

Maribor 498

Marilleva Italy
Small resort with direct links
to Madonna di Campiglio's
extensive intermediate slopes.

Masella 492

La Massana 480

Le Massif 476

Matrei in Osttirol Austria
Large market village south of
Felbertauern tunnel. Mostly
high slopes.
1000m; slopes 1000–2400m
3,280ft; slopes 3,280–7,870ft
⛷ *6* ⬈ *29km*

Mauterndorf Austria
Village near Obertauern with
tremendous snow record.
1120m; slopes 1075–2360m
3,670ft; slopes 3,530–7,740ft
⛷ *10* ⬈ *25km*

Maverick Mountain USA
Montana resort with plenty of
terrain accessed by few lifts.
Cowboy Winter Games venue
- rodeo one day, ski races the
next.
2155m; slopes 2155–2800m
7,070ft; slopes 7,070–9,190ft
⛷ *2* ⬈ *500 acres*

Mayens de Riddes 326
Tiny hamlet next to La
Tzoumaz with its links up to
Savoleyres and the Verbier
network.

Mayens-de-Sion 326
Tranquil hamlet off road up to
Les Collons - part of Verbier
area.

Mayrhofen 76

Méaudre France
Small resort near Grenoble
with good snowmaking to
make up for its low altitude.
1000m; slopes 1000–1600m
3,280ft; slopes 3,280–5,250ft
⛷ *10* ⬈ *18km*

Megève 176

Meiringen Switzerland
Varied terrain, a good outing
from the nearby Jungfrau
resorts or Interlaken. Conan
Doyle's deathplace of
Sherlock Holmes.
600m; slopes 600–2435m
1,970ft; slopes 1,970–7,990ft
⛷ *16* ⬈ *60km*

Les Menuires 182

Merano Italy
Purpose-built base on a high
plateau near Bolzano.
2000m; slopes 2000–2240m
6,560ft; slopes 6,560–7,350ft
⛷ *18* ⬈ *28km*

Méribel 185

Métabief-Mont-d'Or France
Twin villages in the Jura
region, not far from Geneva.
900m; slopes 880–1430m
2,950ft; slopes 2,890–4,690ft
⛷ *22* ⬈ *42km*

Methven 510

Mijoux France
Pretty wooded slopes
between Dijon and Geneva.
Lélex nearby.
1000m; slopes 900–1680m
3,280ft; slopes 2,950–5,510ft
⛷ *29* ⬈ *50km*

Mission Ridge USA
Area in dry region that gets
higher-quality snow than
other Seattle resorts but less
of it. Good intermediate
slopes.
1390m; slopes 1390–2065m
4,560ft; slopes 4,560–6,770ft
⛷ *6* ⬈ *300 acres*

Misurina Italy
Tiny village near Cortina. A
cheap alternative base.
1755m; slopes 1755–1900m
5,760ft; slopes 5,760–6,230ft
⛷ *4* ⬈ *13km*

Mount Baldy   Canada
Tiny area, but a worthwhile
excursion from Big White.
Gets ultra light snow – great
glades/powder chutes.
slopes 1705–2150m
slopes 5,590–7,050ft
⛷2 ⛷ 150 acres

Mount Baldy   USA
Some of the longest and
steepest runs in California.
Near Los Angeles, but 20%
snowmaking and antiquated
lifts are major drawbacks.
1980m; slopes 1980–2620m
6,500ft; slopes 6,500–8,600ft
⛷4 ⛷ 400 acres

Mount Baw Baw   Australia
Small but entertaining
intermediate area in attractive
woodland, with great views.
Closest area to Melbourne
(2.5 hours). Nearest town is
Noojee.
1480m; slopes 1340–1565m
4,860ft; slopes 4,400–5,130ft
⛷8 ⛷ 61 acres

Mount Buffalo   508

Mount Buller   508

Mount Dobson   New Zealand
Mostly intermediate slopes in
a wide, treeless basin, with
good snow-cover and good
views of Mt Cook and the
Pacific. Long runs by NZ
standards.
1630m; slopes 1630–2045m
5,350ft; slopes 5,350–6,710ft
⛷4 ⛷ 990 acres

Mount Hood Meadows   USA
One of several sizeable areas
amid magnificent Oregon
scenery. Impressive snowfall
record but snow tends to be
wet, and weather damp.
1375m; slopes 1375–2535m
4,510ft; slopes 4,510–8,320ft
⛷12 ⛷ 2150 acres

Mount Hood Ski Bowl   USA
Sizeable area set amid
magnificent Oregon scenery.
Weather can be damp.
1095m; slopes 1095–1540m
3,590ft; slopes 3,590–5,050ft
⛷9 ⛷ 960 acres

Mount Hotham   508

Mount Hutt   510

Mount Lemmon   USA
Southernmost area in North
America. close to famous Old
West town Tombstone,
Arizona. Reasonable snowfall.
2500m; slopes 2500–2790m
8,200ft; slopes 8,200–9,150ft
⛷3 ⛷ 70 acres

Mount Lyford   New Zealand
Limited but developing area
close to the superb whale-
and seal-watching centre,
Kaikoura, north of
Christchurch.
1200m; slopes 1200–1640m
3,940ft; slopes 3,940–5,380ft
⛷6 ⛷ 395 acres

Mount McKay   508

Mount Olympus   Greece
Ski mountaineering site with
a chain of huts on both faces.
Late winter is the best time to
visit.

Mount Rose   USA
Only 35km/22 miles from
Reno. Good slopes of its own
and well placed for trips to
other Tahoe resorts.
2515m; slopes 2515–2955m
8,250ft; slopes 8,250–9,690ft
⛷5 ⛷ 900 acres

Mount Selwyn   Australia
Popular with beginners and
families 6 hours from Sydney.
Good lift system.
1520m; slopes 1490–1610m
4,990ft; slopes 4,890–5,280ft
⛷13 ⛷ 111 acres

Mount Snow   431

Mount Spokane   USA
Little intermediate area
outside Spokane (Washington
State).
1160m; slopes 1160–1795m
3,810ft; slopes 3,810–5,890ft
⛷5 ⛷ 350 acres

Mount St Louis / Moonstone
                             Canada
Premier area in Toronto
region, spread over three
peaks. Very high-capacity lift
system and 100%
snowmaking.
⛷13 ⛷ 175 acres

Mount Washington Resort
                             Canada
Scenic area in remote part of
Vancouver Island; the base
village has lodging.
Impressive snowfall record
but rain is a problem.
1110m; slopes 1110–1590m
3,640ft; slopes 3,640–5,220ft
⛷6 ⛷ 970 acres

Mount Sunapee   USA
Closest area of any size to
Boston; primarily intermediate
terrain.
375m; slopes 375–835m
1,230ft; slopes 1,230–2,740ft
⛷10 ⛷ 210 acres

Mount Waterman   USA
Small Los Angeles area where
children ski free. The lack of
much snowmaking is a
drawback.
2135m; slopes 2135–2440m
7,000ft; slopes 7,000–8,010ft
⛷3 ⛷ 210 acres

Mühlbach   Austria
Village near Bischofshofen, a
short bus-ride from one end
of an impressive five-
mountain area that spreads
for miles towards Maria Alm.
855m; slopes 790–1825m
2,810ft; slopes 2,590–5,990ft
⛷23 ⛷ 80km

Mühltal   Austria
Small village halfway between
Niederau and Auffach in the
Wildschönau. No local skiing
of its own.
780m; slopes 830–1900m
2,560ft; slopes 2,720–6,230ft
⛷29 ⛷ 42km

Muhr   Austria
Village by Katschberg tunnel
well placed for visiting St
Michael, Badkleinkirchheim,
Flachau and Obertauern.
1110m / 3,640ft

Muju   Korea
Largest area in Korea and the
furthest from Seoul (more
than three hours south). Not
as ugly or crowded as most
Korean resorts. ⛷13

Mürren   311

Mutters   54

Myoko Kogen   Japan
Japan's best all-round area.
Extensive slopes spread over
five distinct, interconnected
sections with longer, wider
runs than normal for Japan.
⛷57

Nakiska   Canada
Small area of wooded runs
between Banff and Calgary,
with state-of-the-art
snowmaking.
1525m; slopes 1525–2215m
5,000ft; slopes 5,000–7,270ft
⛷5 ⛷ 230 acres

Nasserein   107
Quiet suburb of St Anton, a
short bus ride from the lifts.

Nauders   Austria
Attractive village on Italian
border with a high, sunny
intermediate area and with
lots of snowmakers.
1400m; slopes 1400–2750m
4,590ft; slopes 4,590–9,020ft
⛷16 ⛷ 65km

Nax   Switzerland
Quiet, sunny village in a
balcony setting overlooking
the Rhône valley. Own little
area and only a short drive
from Veysonnaz.
1300m; slopes 1300–3330m
4,270ft; slopes 4,270–10,930ft
⛷100 ⛷ 400km

Nendaz   326
Enormous apartment
development offering quiet
alternative to Verbier.

Neukirchen   Austria
Quiet, pretty beginners' resort
with a fairly snow-sure
plateau at the top of its
mountain. The nearby Ziller
valley suits intermediates.
855m; slopes 855–2150m
2,810ft; slopes 2,810–7,050ft
⛷14 ⛷ 35km

Neustift   54

Nevegal   Italy
Weekend place near Belluno,
south of Cortina.
1030m; slopes 1030–1650m
3,380ft; slopes 3,380–5,410ft
⛷14 ⛷ 28km

Nevis Range   Scotland
Highest and newest Scottish
ski area, on the slopes of
Aonach Mor and with good
views of Ben Nevis. 6km/
4 miles from Fort William.
90m; slopes 655–1220m
300ft; slopes 2,150–4,000ft
⛷12 ⛷ 35km

Niederau   Austria
Amorphous chalet-style village
in the Wildschönau region.
830m; slopes 830–1900m
2,720ft; slopes 2,720–6,230ft
⛷29 ⛷ 42km

Niedernsill   Austria
Crowd-free alternative to
Kaprun when the snowline is
high, Also well placed for
visiting uncrowded, snowy
Gerlos and Matrei.
770m; slopes 770–1000m
2,530ft; slopes 2,530–3,280ft
⛷3

Niseko Kogen   Japan
Hokkaido's main resort – a
small exposed area with very
short runs and unpredictable
weather. ⛷22

Nordic Valley   USA
Utah cross-country area close
to Salt Lake City. Powder
Mountain and Snowbasin are
nearby Alpine areas.

Nordseter Norway
Cluster of hotels in deep forest north of Lillehammer. Basic Alpine facilities but best for cross-country.
1000m / 3,280ft

Norefjell Norway
Norway's toughest run, a very steep 600m/1,970ft drop. 120km/75 miles north-west of Oslo.
750m; slopes 185–1185m
2,460ft; slopes 610–3,890ft
11

La Norma France
Traffic-free, purpose-built resort near Modane and Val-Cenis, with mostly easy terrain.
1350m; slopes 1350–2750m
4,430ft; slopes 4,430–9,020ft
18 65km

Norquay 447

North Conway USA
Attractive factory-outlet-shopping town in New Hampshire close to Attitash and Cranmore ski areas.

Northstar-at-Tahoe 355

Nosawa Onsen Japan
Shinetsu spa village with good hot springs. The runs are cut out of heavy vegetation.
500m; slopes 500–1650m
1,640ft; slopes 1,640–5,410ft
27

Nôtre-Dame-de-Bellecombe 176
Pleasant village spoiled by the busy Albertville-Megève road. Inexpensive base from which to visit Megève, though it has fair slopes of its own.

Nova Levante Italy
Little area used mostly by weekend day-trippers.
1180m; slopes 1180–2200m
3,870ft; slopes 3,870–7,220ft
14 20km

Nub's Nob USA
One of the most sheltered Great Lakes ski areas (many suffer fierce winds). 100% snowmaking; weekend crowds from Detroit. Wooded slopes suitable for all abilities.
275m; slopes 275–405m
900ft; slopes 900–1,330ft
8 245 acres

Oberau Austria
Very pretty village in the Wildschönau region.
935m; slopes 830–1900m
3,070ft; slopes 2,720–6,230ft
29 42km

Obereggen Italy
Tiny resort used mainly by weekend day-trippers.
1550m; slopes 1550–2200m
5,090ft; slopes 5,090–7,220ft
6 10km

Obergurgl 81

Oberlech 69
Car- and crowd-free family resort alternative to Lech. Snow-sure due to height, snow-pocket position and snow-guns.

Oberndorf Austria
Quiet hamlet with beginners' area and a chair connecting it to St Johann's undemanding ski area.
700m; slopes 670–1700m
2,300ft; slopes 2,200–5,580ft
17 60km

Oberstdorf Germany
Attractive winter-sports town near the Austrian border with three small areas. Famous ski-jumping hill.
815m; slopes 800–2220m
2,670ft; slopes 2,620–7,280ft
31 30km

Obertauern 86

Ochapowace Canada
Main area in Saskatchewan, east of Regina. It doesn't get a huge amount of snow but 75% snowmaking helps.
4 100 acres

Ohau New Zealand
Some of NZ's steepest slopes, with great views of Lake Ohau.
1425m; slopes 1425–1825m
4,680ft; slopes 4,680–5,990ft
3 310 acres

Okemo 431

Oppdal 501

Orcières-Merlette France
Good family resort with convenient, snow-sure beginner slopes. Longer runs mostly funnel safely back to town.
1850m; slopes 1850–2650m
6,070ft; slopes 6,070–8,690ft
27 80km

Ordino 480
Valley village near La Massana, on the road to Arcalis.

Oropa Italy
Little area just off the Aosta–Turin motorway. An easy change of scene from Courmayeur.
1180m; slopes 1200–2390m
3,870ft; slopes 3,940–7,840ft
15km

Les Orres France
Friendly modern resort with great views and varied intermediate terrain, but the snow is unreliable, and it's a long transfer from Lyon.
1550m; slopes 1550–2720m
5,090ft; slopes 5,090–8,920ft
23 62km

Orsières Switzerland
Traditional, sizeable winter resort near Martigny. Well-positioned base from which to visit Verbier and the Chamonix valley.
900m / 2,950ft

Ortisei 272
Charming, lively, old market town in the Italian Dolomites with indirect links to the Sella Ronda.

Oslo Norway
Capital city with cross-country ski trails in its parks. Alpine slopes and lifts in Nordmarka region, just north of city boundaries.

Otre il Colle Italy
Smallest of many little resorts near Bergamo.
1100m; slopes 1100–2000m
3,610ft; slopes 3,610–6,560ft
7 7km

Oukaimeden Morocco
Slopes 75km/45 miles from Marrakesh with a surprisingly long season.
2600m; slopes 2600–3260m
8,530ft; slopes 8,530–10,700ft
8 15km

Ovindoli Italy
One of the smallest areas in L'Aquila region east of Rome, but it has higher slopes than most and one of the better lift systems.
1375m; slopes 1375–2220m
4,510ft; slopes 4,510–7,280ft
9 10km

Ovronnaz Switzerland
Pretty village set on a sunny shelf above the Rhône valley, with a good pool complex. Limited area but Crans-Montana and Anzère are close.
1350m; slopes 1350–2080m
4,430ft; slopes 4,430–6,820ft
10 25km

Owl's Head Canada
Steep mountain rising out of a lake, in a remote spot bordering Vermont, away from weekend crowds.
7 90 acres

Oz-en-Oisans 122
Attractive old village with higher satellite at base of lifts into Alpe-d'Huez.

Pal 484
Prettily wooded mountain, now linked with slopes of Arinsal and soon to be accessible from valley town of La Massana.

Palandöken 499

Pamporovo 495

Panarotta Italy
Smallest of the resorts east of Trento. It is at a higher altitude than nearby Andalo, so it is worth a day out from there.
1500m; slopes 1500–2000m
4,920ft; slopes 4,920–6,560ft
6 7km

Panorama 468

Panticosa 492

Park City 411

Parnassus Greece
Biggest and best area in Greece with surprisingly good slopes and lifts, Wonderful sea views.
slopes 1600–2250m
slopes 5,250–7,380ft 10

Parpan Switzerland
Pretty village linked to the large intermediate area of Lenzerheide.
1510m; slopes 1230–2865m
4,950ft; slopes 4,040–9,400ft
35 155km

Partenen Austria
Traditional village in a pretty setting at the end of Montafontal. Slopes start at Gaschurn, and there are lots more in the vicinity.
1100m; slopes 700–2300m
3,610ft; slopes 2,300–7,550ft
25 100km

La Parva Chile
One of Chile's best ski areas, an hour from Santiago. Crowded at weekends.
2815m; slopes 2815–3570m
9,240ft; slopes 9,240–11,710ft
14

Pas de la Casa 486

Passo Lanciano Italy
Closest area to Adriatic. Weekend crowds visit from nearby Pescara when the snow is good.
1305m; slopes 1305–2000m
4,280ft; slopes 4,280–6,560ft
13

Passo Tonale   Italy
Ugly resort in a bleak setting
with guaranteed snow at a
bargain price. Pretty Madonna
is nearby.
*1885m; slopes 1885–3025m
6,180ft; slopes 6,180–9,920ft*
⛟ 30   ⛷ 80km

Pass Thurn   **63**
Road-side lift base for
Kitzbühel's most snow-sure,
but unconnected, ski area.

Pebble Creek   USA
Small area on Utah-Jackson
Hole route. Blend of open and
wooded slopes.
*1920m; slopes 1920–2530m
6,300ft; slopes 6,300–8,300ft*
⛟ 3   ⛷ 600 acres

Pec Pod Snezkou   Czech
Republic
Collection of hamlets spread
along the valley road leading
to the main lifts and the very
limited ski area.
*770m; slopes 710–1190m
2,530ft; slopes 2,330–3,900ft*
⛟ 5   ⛷ 12km

Peisey-Nancroix   **130**
Small village linked to the Les
Arcs network via a five-minute
gondola ride to Plan-Peisey-
Vallandry.

Pejo   Italy
Unspoiled traditional village
in a pretty setting, with a
limited area. A cheap base for
nearby Madonna.
*1340m; slopes 1340–2800m
4,400ft; slopes 4,400–9,190ft*
⛟ 6   ⛷ 15km

Perisher/Smiggins   **508**

Pescasseroli   Italy
One of numerous areas east
of Rome in L'Aquila region.
*1250m; slopes 1250–1945m
4,100ft; slopes 4,100–6,380ft*
⛟ 6   ⛷ 25km

Pescocostanzo   Italy
One of numerous areas east
of Rome in L'Aquila region.
*1395m; slopes 1395–1900m
4,580ft; slopes 4,580–6,230ft*
⛟ 4   ⛷ 25km

Pettneu   **107**
Snow-sure specialist
beginners' resort with an
irregular bus link to nearby St
Anton.

Petzen   Austria
One of many little areas in
Austria's easternmost ski
region near Slovenian border.
*600m; slopes 600–1700m
1,970ft; slopes 1,970–5,580ft*
⛟ 6   ⛷ 13km

Peyragudes-Peyresourde
    France
Small Pyrenean resort with its
ski area starting high above.
*1000m; slopes 1600–2400m
3,280ft; slopes 5,250–7,870ft*
⛟ 15   ⛷ 37km

Pfunds   Austria
Picturesque valley village
close to several resorts in
Switzerland and Italy, as well
as Ischgl in Austria.
970m / 3,180ft

Phoenix Park   Korea
Golf complex with 12 ski
slopes in winter. Two hours
from Seoul. ⛟ 7

Piancavallo   Italy
Uninspiring yet curiously
trendy purpose-built village,
an easy drive from Venice.
*1270m; slopes 1270–1830m
4,170ft; slopes 4,170–6,000ft*
⛟ 17   ⛷ 45km

Piani delle Betulle   Italy
One of several little areas
near the east coast of Lake
Como.
*730m; slopes 730–1850m
2,390ft; slopes 2,390–6,070ft*
⛟ 6   ⛷ 10km

Piani di Artavaggio   Italy
Small base complex rather
than a village. One of several
little areas near Lake Como.
*875m; slopes 875–1875m
2,870ft; slopes 2,870–6,150ft*
⛟ 7   ⛷ 15km

Piani di Bobbio   Italy
Largest of several tiny resorts
above Lake Como.
*770m; slopes 770–1855m
2,530ft; slopes 2,530–6,090ft*
⛟ 10   ⛷ 20km

Piani di Erna   Italy
Small base development – no
village. One of several little
areas above Lake Como.
*600m; slopes 600–1635m
1,970ft; slopes 1,970–5,360ft*
⛟ 5   ⛷ 9km

Piau-Engaly   France
User-friendly St-Lary satellite
in one of the best areas in
the Pyrenees.
*1850m; slopes 1420–2500m
6,070ft; slopes 4,660–8,200ft*
⛟ 21   ⛷ 40km

Piazzatorre   Italy
One of many little areas in
the Bergamo region.
*870m; slopes 870–2000m
2,850ft; slopes 2,850–6,560ft*
⛟ 5   ⛷ 25km

Pico   **434**
Low-key little family area (no
resort) close to Killington in
central Vermont.

Piesendorf   Austria
Cheaper, quiet place to stay
when visiting Zell am See.
Tucked behind Kaprun near
Niedernsill.
*780m; slopes 780–1275m
2,560ft; slopes 2,560–4,180ft*
⛟ 3   ⛷ 3km

Pievepelago   Italy
Much the smallest and most
limited of the Appennine ski
resorts. Less than 2 hours
from Florence and Pisa.
*1115m; slopes 1115–1410m
3,660ft; slopes 3,660–4,630ft*
⛟ 7   ⛷ 8km

Pila   Italy
Purpose-built mountain resort
in the Aosta valley linked by
gondola to its historical valley
village. Varied, snowsure
terrain.
*1800m; slopes 1550–2710m
5,910ft; slopes 5,090–8,890ft*
⛟ 13   ⛷ 70km

Pilion   Greece
Pleasant slopes cut out of
dense forest, only 15km/
10 miles from the holiday
resort of Portaria above town
of Volos. ⛟ 3

Pinzolo   Italy
Atmospheric village with
slopes well equipped with
snowmakers. Cheap base for
nearby Madonna.
*800m; slopes 780–2100m
2,620ft; slopes 2,560–6,890ft*
⛟ 8   ⛷ 29km

Pitztal   Austria
Long valley with good glacier
area at its head, accessed by
underground funicular.
*1250m; slopes 1735–3440m
4,100ft; slopes 5,690–11,290ft*
⛟ 12   ⛷ 40km

Pla-d'Adet   France
Limited purpose-built complex
at the foot of the St-Lary ski
area (the original village is
further down the mountain).
*1680m; slopes 1420–2450m
5,510ft; slopes 4,660–8,040ft*
⛟ 32   ⛷ 80km

La Plagne   **198**

Poiana Brasov   **497**

Pomerelle   USA
Small area in Idaho on the
Utah–Sun Valley route.
*2430m; slopes 2430–2735m
7,970ft; slopes 7,970–8,970ft*
⛟ 3   ⛷ 300 acres

Pontechianale   Italy
Highest, largest area in a
remote region south-west of
Turin. Day-tripper place.
*1600m; slopes 1600–2680m
5,250ft; slopes 5,250–8,790ft*
⛟ 8   ⛷ 30km

Ponte di Legno   Italy
Attractive sheltered
alternative to bleak, ugly
neighbour Passo Tonale.
Linked by piste and bus.
*1255m; slopes 1255–1920m
4,120ft; slopes 4,120–6,300ft*
⛟ 5   ⛷ 15km

Pontresina   **320**
Small, sedate base linked to
nearby St Moritz by road, with
extensive cross-country trails.

Porter Heights   New Zealand
Closest skiing to Christchurch
(one hour). Open, sunny bowl
offering mostly intermediate
skiiing – with back bowls for
powder.
*1300m; slopes 1300–1980m
4,270ft; slopes 4,270–6,500ft*
⛟ 5   ⛷ 200 acres

Porterillos   Argentina
Limited area near Mendoza,
just over the border from
renowned Chilean resort
Portillo.

Portes du Soleil   **205**

Portillo   Chile
Luxury hotel 150km/93 miles
north-east of Santiago, with
slopes that are more snow-
sure and less crowded than
those of Las Leñas in
Argentina.
*2880m; slopes 2510–3290m
9,450ft; slopes 8,230–10,790ft*
⛟ 12   ⛷ 25km

Powderhorn   USA
Area in west Colorado
perched on world's highest
flat-top mountain, Grand
Mesa. Sensational views. Day
trip from Aspen.
*2490m; slopes 2490–2975m
8,170ft; slopes 8,170–9,760ft*
⛟ 4   ⛷ 300 acres

Powder King   Canada
Remote resort in British
Columbia, between Prince
George and Dawson City. As
its name suggests, it has
great powder. Plenty of
lodging.
*880m; slopes 880–1520m
2,890ft; slopes 2,890–4,990ft*
⛟ 3   ⛷ 160 acres

Powder Mountain   USA
Sizeable Utah area, a feasible
day out from Park City.
Wonderfully uncrowded locals'
secret, renowned for bowls of
fluffy virgin powder. Snowcat
operation too.
2315m; slopes 2315–2710m
7,600ft; slopes 7,600–8,890ft
⏚ 6 ⏚ 1600 acres

Pozza di Fassa   Italy
Pretty Dolomite village with
its own slopes, three other
small areas close by, and
access to the Sella Ronda at
nearby Campitello.
1340m; slopes 1340–2155m
4,400ft; slopes 4,400–7,070ft
⏚ 6 ⏚ 20km

Pragelato   Italy
Inexpensive base, a short
drive east of Sestriere. Its
own area is worth a try for
half a day.
1535m; slopes 1535–2580m
5,040ft; slopes 5,040–8,460ft
⏚ 35km

Prägraten am Grossvenediger
                                    Austria
Traditional mountaineering/ski
touring village in lovely
setting south of Felbertauern
tunnel. The nearest Alpine ski
slopes are at Matrei nearby.
1310m; slopes 1310–1490m
4,300ft; slopes 4,300–4,890ft
⏚ 2 ⏚ 3km

Prali   Italy
Tiny resort east of Sestriere –
a worthwhile half-day trip.
1455m; slopes 1450–2500m
4,770ft; slopes 4,760–8,200ft
⏚ 6 ⏚ 25km

Pralognan-la-Vanoise France
Unspoiled traditional village
overlooked by spectacular
peaks. Champagny (La
Plagne) and Courchevel are
close by.
1410m; slopes 1410–2355m
4,630ft; slopes 4,630–7,730ft
⏚ 14 ⏚ 25km

Pra-Loup   France
Convenient, purpose-built
family resort with an
extensive, varied intermediate
area linked to La Foux-d'Allos.
1500m; slopes 1500–2600m
4,920ft; slopes 4,920–8,530ft
⏚ 32 ⏚ 73km

Prati di Tivo   Italy
Weekend day-trip place east
of Rome and near the town of
Teramo. A sizeable resort by
southern Italy standards.
1450m; slopes 1450–1800m
4,760ft; slopes 4,760–5,910ft
⏚ 6 ⏚ 16km

Prato Nevoso   Italy
Purpose-built resort with
rather bland slopes.
Mountain-top transfer to and
from Artesina by skidoo.
1500m; slopes 1500–1950m
4,920ft; slopes 4,920–6,400ft
⏚ 13 ⏚ 30km

Prato Selva   Italy
Tiny base development (no
village) east of Rome near
Teramo. Weekend day-trip
place.
1370m; slopes 1370–1800m
4,490ft; slopes 4,490–5,910ft
⏚ 4 ⏚ 10km

Le Praz   157
The lowest and most
attractive of the Courchevel
resorts, with direct access to
the slopes.

Les Praz   139
Quiet hamlet 4km/2 miles
from Chamonix, with
convenient lift link to the
varied Flégère area.

Praz-de-Lys   France
Little-known snow-pocket
area near Lake Geneva that
can have good snow when
nearby resorts (eg La Clusaz)
do not.
1500m; slopes 1200–2000m
4,920ft; slopes 3,940–6,560ft
⏚ 23 ⏚ 60km

Praz-sur-Arly   176
Traditional village in a pretty,
wooded setting just down the
road from Megève, with its
own varied slopes.

Le Pré   130
Charming, rustic hamlet with
lifts up to Arc 2000 and
excellent runs back down.

Predazzo   Italy
Small quiet place between
Cavalese and the Sella Ronda
resorts. Well positioned for
touring the Dolomites area.
1015m; slopes 995–2205m
3,330ft; slopes 3,260–7,230ft
⏚ 8 ⏚ 17km

Premanon   France
One of four resorts that make
up Les Rousses area in Jura
region.
1050m; slopes 1120–1680m
3,440ft; slopes 3,670–5,510ft
⏚ 40

La Presolana   Italy
Large summer resort near
Bergamo. Several other little
areas nearby.
1250m; slopes 1250–1650m
4,100ft; slopes 4,100–5,410ft
⏚ 6 ⏚ 15km

Puy-St-Vincent   France
Modern apartment complex
above an old village south of
Briançon; convenient access
to a modest but quite varied
area. Relatively inexpensive
and popular with families.
1400m; slopes 1400–2700m
4,590ft; slopes 4,590–8,860ft
⏚ 16 ⏚ 62km

Pyhä   Finland
Steep slopes, popular with
good skiers and boarders.
Youthful atmosphere in its
only hotel. *⏚ 6*

Pyrenees, French   France
The ski areas of the Pyrenean
resorts can't compete with the
mega-resorts of the Alps, but
hotels, meals and drinks are
relatively cheap, and many of
the resorts have a rustic, rural
Gallic charm.

Pyrenees 2000   France
Tiny resort built in pleasing
manner. Shares pretty area of
short runs with Font-Romeu.
Impressive snowmaking.
2000m; slopes 1750–2250m
6,560ft; slopes 5,740–7,380ft
⏚ 32 ⏚ 52km

Québec   476

Queenstown   513

Radium Hot Springs   Canada
Summer resort offering an
alternative to the purpose-
built slope-side resort of
Panorama.
slopes 975–2135m
slopes 3,200–7,000ft
⏚ 8 ⏚ 300 acres

Radstadt   Austria
Interesting, unspoiled
medieval town near
Schladming that has its own
small area, and the
Salzburger Sportwelt Amadé
accessed from nearby
Zauchensee or Flachau.
855m; slopes 855–2185m
2,810ft; slopes 2,810–7,170ft
⏚ 100 ⏚ 350km

Rainbow   New Zealand
Northernmost ski area on
South Island, 90 minutes from
Nelson. Wide, undulating,
treeless area, best for
beginners and intermediates.
1440m; slopes 1440–1760m
4,720ft; slopes 4,720–5,770ft
⏚ 4 ⏚ 865 acres

Ramsau am Dachstein Austria
Charming village overlooked
by the Dachstein glacier.
Renowned for cross-country, it
also has Alpine slopes locally,
on the glacier and at
Schladming.
1200m; slopes 1100–2700m
3,940ft; slopes 3,610–8,860ft
⏚ 18 ⏚ 30km

Ramundberget   505

Rauris   Austria
Old roadside village close to
Kaprun and Zell am See, with
a long, narrow area that has
snowmakers on the lower
slopes.
950m; slopes 950–2200m
3,120ft; slopes 3,120–7,220ft
⏚ 10 ⏚ 30km

Ravascletto   Italy
Resort in a pretty wooded
setting near Austria, with
most of its terrain high above
on open plateau.
920m; slopes 920–1735m
3,020ft; slopes 3,020–5,690ft
⏚ 12 ⏚ 40km

Reallon   France
Traditional-style village, with
splendid views from above
Lac de Serre-Ponçon.
1560m; slopes 1560–2115m
5,120ft; slopes 5,120–6,940ft
⏚ 6 ⏚ 20km

Red Lodge   USA
Picturesque Old West
Montana town. Ideal for
combined trip with Big Sky or
Jackson Hole.
1800m; slopes 2155–2860m
5,910ft; slopes 7,070–9,380ft
⏚ 8 ⏚ 1600 acres

Red Mountain   445

Red River   USA
New Mexico western town –
complete with stetsons and
saloons – with intermediate
slopes above.
2665m; slopes 2665–3155m
8,740ft; slopes 8,740–10,350ft
⏚ 7 ⏚ 270 acres

Reichenfels   Austria
One of many small areas in
Austria's easternmost ski
region near the Slovenian
border.
810m; slopes 810–1400m
2,660ft; slopes 2,660–4,590ft

The Remarkables   513

Rencurel-les-Coulumes France
One of seven little resorts just
west of Grenoble. Unspoiled,
inexpensive place to tour.
Villard-de-Lans is main resort.

Reutte   Austria
500-year old market town with many traditional hotels, and rail links to nearby Lermoos.
855m; slopes 855–1900m
2,810ft; slopes 2,810–6,230ft
🚡 9   🎿 18km

Revelstoke   Canada
Town from which you can heli-ski in Monashees or cat-ski locally at a lower cost.
460m / 1,510ft

Rhêmes-Notre-Dame   Italy
Unspoiled village in the beautiful Rhêmes valley, south of Aosta. Courmayeur and La Thuile within reach.
🚡 2   🎿 5km

Riederalp   Switzerland
Pretty, vehicle-free village perched high above the Rhône valley amid the glorious scenery of the Aletsch area. Access by lift from near Brig.
1900m; slopes 1900–2710m
6,230ft; slopes 6,230–8,890ft
🚡 32   🎿 90km

Rigi-Kaltbad   Switzerland
Resort on a mountain rising out of Lake Lucerne, with superb all-round views, accessed by the world's first mountain railroad.
1440m; slopes 1195–1795m
4,720ft; slopes 3,920–5,890ft
🚡 9   🎿 30km

Riihivuori   Finland
Finnish area with its 'base' at the top of the mountain. The city of Jyvaskyla is nearby. 🚡 4

Riksgränsen   **505**

Riscone   Italy
Dolomite village sharing a pretty area with San Vigilio. Good snowmaking. Short easy runs.
1200m; slopes 1200–2275m
3,940ft; slopes 3,940–7,460ft
🚡 35   🎿 40km

Risoul   France
Small, convenient family resort linked with Vars to form a sizeable skiing area.
1850m; slopes 1660–2750m
6,070ft; slopes 5,450–9,020ft
🚡 56   🎿 180km

Rivisondoli   Italy
Sizeable mountain retreat east of Rome, with one of the better lift systems in the vicinity.
1350m; slopes 1350–2050m
4,430ft; slopes 4,430–6,730ft
🚡 7   🎿 16km

Rjukan   Norway
Gateway to the cross-country region of Hardanger Vidda. Trails to Voss take a week.
300m / 980ft

Roccaraso   Italy
Largest of the resorts east of Rome – at least when snow-cover is complete.
1280m; slopes 1280–2200m
4,200ft; slopes 4,200–7,220ft
🚡 12   🎿 56km

Rohrmoos   **94**
Situated below small mountain in Dachstein-Tauern region, next to Schladming.

La Rosière   France
Small village linked to La Thuile on the Italian side. Skiing mostly for intermediates and beginners.
1850m; slopes 1175–2640m
6,070ft; slopes 3,850–8,660ft
🚡 35   🎿 150km

Rossland   Canada
Town with an excellent range of restaurants, the place to stay when skiing Red Mountain, 5km/3 miles away.

Rougemont   **309**
Only 7km/4.5 miles from Gstaad, and part of the Gstaad super ski region.

Ruka   Finland
Spacious area by Finnish standards with snow-guns on most of its slopes. 🚡 18

Russbach   Austria
Secluded village tucked up a side valley and linked into the Gosau-Annaberg-Lungotz area. The slopes are spread over a wide area.
815m; slopes 780–1620m
2,670ft; slopes 2,560–5,310ft
🚡 33   🎿 65km

Saalbach-Hinterglemm   **88**

Saalfelden   Austria
Ideally placed for touring eastern Tirol. Maria Alm and Saalbach are nearby.
745m; slopes 745–1550m
2,440ft; slopes 2,440–5,090ft
🚡 3   🎿 3km

Saanen   Switzerland
Cheaper and more convenient alternative to staying in Gstaad – but there's much less going on.
slopes 950–3000m
slopes 3,120–9,840ft
🚡 69   🎿 250km

Saanenmöser   **309**
Small village with local slopes and rail/road links to Gstaad.

Saas-Almagell   Switzerland
Compact village up the valley from Saas-Grund, with good cross-country trails and walks, and a limited Alpine area.
1670m / 5,480ft   🚡 6

Saas-Fee   **315**

Saas-Grund   Switzerland
Sprawling valley village below Saas-Fee, with a separate, small but high Alpine area.
1560m; slopes 1560–3100m
5,120ft; slopes 5,120–10,170ft
🚡 7   🎿 45km

Saddleback   USA
Small area between Maine's premier resorts. High slopes by local standards.
695m; slopes 695–1255m
2,280ft; slopes 2,280–4,120ft
🚡 5   🎿 100 acres

Sahoro   Japan
Ugly, purpose-built complex on Hokkaido island. A limited area, but one of the most exotic package destinations.
400m; slopes 400–1100m
1,310ft; slopes 1,310–3,610ft
🚡 9   🎿 15km

Les Saisies   France
Traditional-style cross-country venue in a pretty setting, surrounded by varied four-mountain Alpine slopes.
1650m; slopes 1150–2000m
5,410ft; slopes 3,770–6,560ft
🚡 24   🎿 40km

Sälen   **505**

Salt Lake City   USA
Underrated base from which to ski Utah. 30 minutes from Park City, Deer Valley, The Canyons, Snowbird, Alta, Snowbasin. Cheaper and livelier than the resorts.

Salzburg-Stadt   Austria
A single, long challenging run off the back of Salzburg's local mountain, accessed by a spectacular lift-ride from a suburb of Grodig.
425m / 1,390ft

Samedan   Switzerland
Valley town, just down the road from St Moritz.
1720m; slopes 1740–2570m
5,640ft; slopes 5,710–8,430ft
🚡 3   🎿 7km

Samnaun   **58**
Shares large ski area with Ischgl.

Samoëns   **168**
Beautiful rural valley village, a bus-ride from lifts into Flaine's skiing.

San Bernardino   Switzerland
Pretty resort south of the road tunnel, close to Madesimo.
1625m; slopes 1600–2595m
5,330ft; slopes 5,250–8,510ft
🚡 8   🎿 35km

San Candido   Italy
Austrian border resort on the road to Lienz.
1175m; slopes 1175–1580m
3,850ft; slopes 3,850–5,180ft
🚡 4   🎿 15km

San Carlos de Bariloche   Argentina
South America's only year-round resort, with five areas nearby.
790m; slopes 1050–2300m
2,590ft; slopes 3,440–7,550ft
🚡 29   🎿 26km

San Cassiano   **272**
Pretty village linked to the Sella Ronda.

Sandia Peak   USA
World's longest lift-ride ascends from Albuquerque. Mostly gentle slopes; children ski free.
slopes 2645–3165m
slopes 8,680–10,380ft
🚡 7   🎿 100 acres

San Grée di Viola   Italy
Easternmost of resorts south of Turin, surprisingly close to Italian Riviera.
1100m; slopes 1100–1800m
3,610ft; slopes 3,610–5,910ft
🎿 30km

San Martin de los Andes   Argentina
Limited area on the slopes of Cerro Chapelco, near to main resort Bariloche. 🚡 6

San Martino di Castrozza   Italy
Plain village in the southernmost Dolomites with varied slopes in four disjointed areas, none very extensive.
1465m; slopes 1465–2610m
4,810ft; slopes 4,810–8,560ft
🚡 20   🎿 50km

Sansicario   **267**
Small, stylish, modern resort, well placed in the Milky Way near to Sauze d'Oulx.

San Simone   Italy
Tiny development north of Bergamo, close to unappealing Foppolo area.
2000m; slopes 1105–2300m
6,560ft; slopes 3,630–7,550ft
🚡 9   🎿 45km

Santa Caterina   Italy
Pretty, user-friendly village near Bormio, with a snow-sure intermediate area.
1740m; slopes 1740–2725m
5,710ft; slopes 5,710–8,940ft
⛷8 ☂ 25km

Santa Cristina   **272**
Quiet village on the periphery of the Sella Ronda.

Santa Fe   USA
One of America's most attractive and interesting towns. Varied slopes – glades, bowls, cruiser pistes, desert views. Great excursion from Taos.
3145m; slopes 3145–3645m
10,320ft; slopes 10,320–11,960ft
⛷7 ☂ 600 acres

Santa Maria Maggiore   Italy
Resort south of the Simplon Pass from the Rhône valley, and near Lake Maggiore.
820m; slopes 820–1890m
2,690ft; slopes 2,690–6,200ft
⛷5 ☂ 10km

San Vigilio   Italy
Charming, atmospheric Dolomite village with a delightful, sizeable area well covered by snow-guns.
1200m; slopes 1200–2275m
3,940ft; slopes 3,940–7,460ft
⛷33 ☂ 40km

San Vito di Cadore   Italy
Sizeable, alternative place to stay to Cortina. Negligible local slopes, though.
1010m; slopes 1010–1380m
3,310ft; slopes 3,310–4,530ft
⛷9 ☂ 12km

Sappada   Italy
Isolated resort close to the Austrian border below Lienz.
1215m; slopes 1215–2050m
3,990ft; slopes 3,990–6,730ft
⛷17 ☂ 50km

Sappee   Finland
Resort within easy reach of Helsinki, popular with telemarkers and boarders. Lake views. ⛷4

Sarnano   Italy
Main resort in the Macerata region near Adriatic Riviera. Valley village with ski slopes accessed by lift.
540m / 1,770ft
⛷9 ☂ 11km

Le Sauze   France
Fine area near Barcelonnette, sadly remote from airports.
1400m; slopes 1400–2440m
4,590ft; slopes 4,590–8,010ft
⛷23 ☂ 65km

Sauze d'Oulx   **267**

Savognin   Switzerland
Pretty village with a good mid-sized area; a good base for the nearby resorts of St Moritz, Davos/Klosters and Flims.
1200m; slopes 1200–2715m
3,940ft; slopes 3,940–8,910ft
⛷17 ☂ 80km

Scheffau   **100**
Rustic beauty not far from Söll.

Schia   Italy
Very limited area of short runs – the only ski area near Parma. No village.
1245m; slopes 1245–1415m
4,080ft; slopes 4,080–4,640ft
⛷7 ☂ 15km

Schilpario   Italy
One of many little areas near Bergamo.
1125m; slopes 1125–1635m
3,690ft; slopes 3,690–5,360ft
⛷5 ☂ 15km

Schladming   **94**

Schönried   **309**
A cheaper and quieter resort alternative to staying in Gstaad.

Schoppernau   Austria
A scattered farming community, one of two main areas in Bregenzerwald north-west of Lech.
860m; slopes 860–2050m
2,820ft; slopes 2,820–6,730ft
⛷8 ☂ 37km

Schröcken   Austria
Bregenzerwald area village close to the German border.
1260m; slopes 1260–2100m
4,130ft; slopes 4,130–6,890ft
⛷16 ☂ 60km

Schruns   Austria
Pleasant little town at the heart of the Montafon region, south-west of Lech.
700m; slopes 700–2380m
2,300ft; slopes 2,300–7,810ft
⛷13 ☂ 40km

Schüttdorf   **114**
Ordinary dormitory satellite of Zell am See, with easy access to the shared ski area.

Schwarzach im Pongau   Austria
Riverside village with rail links. There are limited slopes at Goldegg, and Wagrain (Salzburg Sportwelt) and Grossarl (Gastein valley) are also nearby.
600m / 1,970ft

Schweitzer   USA
In Idaho but near Spokane (Washington State) and an easy combined trip with Fernie (in Canada). Good snowfall record; uncrowded, varied slopes.
1215m; slopes 1215–1945m
3,990ft; slopes 3,990–6,380ft
⛷6 ☂ 2350 acres

Scopello   Italy
Low area close to the Aosta valley, worth considering for a day trip in bad weather.
slopes 690–1740m
slopes 2,260–5,710ft
⛷9 ☂ 26km

Scuol   Switzerland
Year-round spa resort close to Austria and Italy, with an impressive range of terrain.
1250m; slopes 1250–2785m
4,100ft; slopes 4,100–9,140ft
⛷15 ☂ 80km

Searchmont Resort   Canada
Ontario area with modern lift system and 95% snowmaking. Fine Lake Superior views.
275m; slopes 275–485m
900ft; slopes 900–1,590ft
⛷4 ☂ 65 acres

Sedrun   Switzerland
Charming, unspoiled old village on the Glacier Express rail route close to Andermatt, with fine terrain amid glorious scenery.
1440m; slopes 1450–2350m
4,720ft; slopes 4,760–7,710ft
⛷12 ☂ 50km

Seefeld   **54**

Le Seignus-d'Allos   France
Close to La Foux-d'Allos (which shares large area with Pra-Loup) and has own little area, too.
1400m; slopes 1400–2425m
4,590ft; slopes 4,590–7,960ft
⛷13

Sella Nevea   Italy
Limited but developing resort in a beautiful setting on the Slovenian border. Summer glacier nearby.
1140m; slopes 1190–1800m
3,740ft; slopes 3,900–5,910ft
⛷11 ☂ 8km

Selva/Sella Ronda   **272**

Selvino   Italy
Closest resort to Bergamo.
960m; slopes 960–1400m
3,150ft; slopes 3,150–4,590ft
⛷6 ☂ 20km

Semmering   Austria
Long-established winter sports resort set in pretty scenery, 100km/62 miles from Vienna, towards Graz. Mostly intermediate terrain.
1000m; slopes 1000–1340m
3,280ft; slopes 3,280–4,400ft
⛷5 ☂ 14km

Seoul   Korea
Small, unattractive, barren area 25 minutes from the capital. Three very crowded slopes. ⛷3

Les Sept-Laux   France
Ugly, user-friendly family resort near Grenoble. Pretty slopes for all grades.
1350m; slopes 1350–2400m
4,430ft; slopes 4,430–7,870ft
⛷25 ☂ 100km

Serfaus   Austria
Charming traffic-free village (with underground people-mover) at the foot of a long, narrow ski area, mainly easy and intermediate. Linked to Fiss.
1425m; slopes 1200–2700m
4,680ft; slopes 3,940–8,860ft
⛷19 ☂ 80km

Serrada   Italy
Very limited area near Trento.
slopes 1250–1605m
slopes 4,100–5,270ft ⛷5

Serre-Chevalier   **207**

Sesto   Italy
Dolomite village on the road to Cortina, surrounded by pretty little areas.
1310m / 4,300ft
⛷31 ☂ 50km

Sestola   Italy
Appennine village a short drive from Pisa and Florence with its pistes, some way above, almost completely equipped with snowmakers.
900m; slopes 1280–1975m
2,950ft; slopes 4,200–6,480ft
⛷23 ☂ 50km

Sestriere   **280**

Shames Mountain   Canada
Remote spot inland from coastal town of Prince Rupert and with impressive snowfall record. Deep powder.
670m; slopes 670–1195m
2,200ft; slopes 2,200–3,920ft
⛷3 ☂ 183 acres

Shawnee Peak USA
Small area near Bethel and Sunday River renowned for its night skiing. Spectacular views. Mostly groomed cruising.
185m; slopes 185–580m
610ft; slopes 610–1,900ft
⛷5 🚡 225 acres

Shemshak Iran
Most popular of the three mountain resorts within easy reach of Teheran. Packed at weekends, though few go to ski.

Shiga Heights Japan
Largest area in Japan, the site of Nagano's 1998 Olympic skiing events, Happo One is nearby.
930m; slopes 1220–2305m
3,050ft; slopes 4,000–7,560ft
⛷73 🚡 130km

Showdown USA
Intermediate area in Montana cut out of forest north of Bozeman. 50km/30 miles to the nearest hotel.
2065m; slopes 2065–2490m
6,770ft; slopes 6,770–8,170ft
⛷4 🚡 640 acres

Sierra-at-Tahoe 355
Sierra Nevada 492
Sierra Summit USA
Sierra Nevada area accessible only from the west. 100% snowmaking.
2160m; slopes 2160–2645m
7,090ft; slopes 7,090–8,680ft
⛷8 🚡 250 acres

Silbertal Austria
Low secluded village in the Montafon area, linked to Schruns. A good base for touring numerous areas.
890m; slopes 700–1450m
2,920ft; slopes 2,300–4,760ft
⛷3 🚡 6km

Sils Maria 320
Pretty lakeside village, linked to the St Moritz Corvatsch slopes via a lift to Furtschellas.

Silvaplana 320
Pretty lakeside village near St Moritz, a short drive from the lift connections.

Silver Creek USA
Child-oriented resort close to Winter Park. Low snowfall record for Colorado.
2490m; slopes 2490–2795m
8,170ft; slopes 8,170–9,170ft
⛷5 🚡 250 acres

Silver Mountain USA
Northern Idaho area near delightful resort town of Coeur d'Alene. Best for experts, but plenty for intermediates too.
1215m; slopes 1215–1915m
3,990ft; slopes 3,990–6,280ft
⛷6 🚡 1500 acres

Silver Star 445
Silverthorne USA
Factory outlet town on main road close to Keystone and Breckenridge. Good budget place for skiing Vail and BeaverCreek.

Sinaia 497
Sipapu USA
Great little New Mexico area that would be better known if it had more reliable snow-cover. Mostly tree-lined runs. Nice day out from Taos when conditions are good.
slopes 2500–2765m
slopes 8,200–9,070ft
⛷3 🚡 40 acres

Siviez 326
A quieter and cheaper base for skiing Verbier's Four Valleys circuit.

Sixt 168
Traditional village near Samoëns, at foot of a new run down from the Flaine area. Own little area across the valley, too.

Sjusjoen Norway
Cluster of hotels in deep forest close to Lillehammer. Basic Alpine facilities but better for cross-country.
885m / 2,900ft

Ski Apache USA
Apache-owned area south of Albuquerque noted for groomed steeps. Panoramic views. Nearest lodging in charming Ruidoso.
2925m; slopes 2925–3505m
9,600ft; slopes 9,600–11,500ft
⛷11 🚡 750 acres

Ski Cooper USA
Small area close to historic Old West town of Leadville. Good ski/sightseeing day out from nearby Vail, Beaver Creek and Copper Mountain.
slopes 3200–3565m
slopes 10,500–11,700ft ⛷4

Ski Windham USA
2 hours from New York City and second only to Hunter for weekend crowds. Decent slopes by eastern standards.
485m; slopes 485–940m
1,590ft; slopes 1,590–3,080ft
⛷7 🚡 230 acres

Smokovec Slovakia
Spa town near Poprad, with three small areas known collectively as High Tatras.
1000m; slopes 1000–1500m
3,280ft; slopes 3,280–4,920ft
⛷5

Smugglers' Notch 438
Snowbasin 416
Snowbird 418
Snowbowl (Arizona) USA
One of America's oldest areas, near Flagstaff, Arizona, atop an extinct volcano and with stunning desert views. Good snowfall record.
2805m; slopes 2805–3505m
9,200ft; slopes 9,200–11,500ft
⛷5 🚡 135 acres

Snowbowl (Montana) USA
Montana area renowned for powder, outside lively town of Missoula. Intermediate pistes plus 700 acres of extreme slopes. Grizzly Chute is the ultimate challenge.
1520m; slopes 1520–2315m
4,990ft; slopes 4,990–7,600ft
⛷4 🚡 1400 acres

Snowmass 362
Purpose-built village with big mountain near Aspen.

Snow Summit USA
San Bernardino National Forest ski area near Palm Springs. Lovely lake views. 100% snowmaking. High-capacity lift system for weekend crowds.
2135m; slopes 2135–2500m
7,000ft; slopes 7,000–8,200ft
⛷12 🚡 230 acres

Snow Valley USA
Area quite near Palm Springs. Fine desert views. High-capacity lift system copes with weekend crowds better than nearby Big Bear.
2040m; slopes 2040–2390m
6,690ft; slopes 6,690–7,840ft
⛷11 🚡 230 acres

Solda Italy
The other side of the Stelvio Pass from Bormio. Very long airport transfers.
1905m; slopes 1905–2625m
6,250ft; slopes 6,250–8,610ft
⛷19 🚡 25km

Sölden 98
Soldeu 488
Solfonn Norway
Tiny development two hours west of Geilo with some of Norway's most challenging Alpine slopes. Extensive, interesting cross-country trails too.
550m; slopes 550–760m
1,800ft; slopes 1,800–2,490ft
⛷2

Solitude 403
Söll 100
Sommand France
Purpose-built base that shares area with Praz-de-Lys.
1420m; slopes 1200–1800m
4,660ft; slopes 3,940–5,910ft
⛷22 🚡 50km

Sorenberg Switzerland
Popular weekend retreat between Berne and Lucerne, with a high proportion of steep, low runs.
1165m; slopes 1165–2350m
3,820ft; slopes 3,820–7,710ft
⛷18 🚡 50km

South Lake Tahoe 355
Tacky base for skiing Heavenly, with cheap lodging, traffic and gambling.

South Tatras Slovakia
An area covering both sides of Mount Chopok near Poprad. There's no resort.
slopes 1240–2005m
slopes 4,070–6,580ft
⛷19 🚡 20km

Spindleruv Mlyn Czech Republic
Largest Giant Mountains region resort but with few facilities serving several little low areas.
750m; slopes 750–1300m
2,460ft; slopes 2,460–4,270ft
⛷9 🚡 25km

Spital am Pyhrn Austria
Limited village east of Schladming, 4km/2 miles from its easy intermediate slopes. Nearby Hinterstoder is more interesting.
650m; slopes 810–1885m
2,130ft; slopes 2,660–6,180ft
⛷10 🚡 18km

Spittal/Drau Austria
Historic Carinthian town with a limited area starting a lift-ride above it. A good day trip from Bad Kleinkirchheim or from Slovenia.
555m; slopes 1650–2140m
1,820ft; slopes 5,410–7,020ft
⛷12 🚡 22km

Sportgastein 41
Mountain village with some of the more interesting skiing in the Badgastein valley.

Squaw Valley 355

Srinagar India
Himalayan resort in Kashmir, with a small ski area and excellent heli-skiing.
2720m; slopes 2645–3645m
8,920ft; slopes 8,680–11,960ft
7 5km

Stafal 264
Tiny, isolated village, with good access to the Monterosa Ski area.

St Andrä im Lungau Austria
Valley-junction village ideally placed for one of the longest, most snow-sure cross-country networks in Europe. Close to the Tauern pass and to St Michael.
1045m / 3,430ft

St Anton 107

St Cergue Switzerland
Limited resort less than an hour from Geneva, good for families with young children.
1045m; slopes 1045–1700m
3,430ft; slopes 3,430–5,580ft
9 20km

St Christoph 107
Small village on Arlberg pass above St Anton.

St-Colomban-des-Villards
France
Small resort in next side valley to La Toussuire. Good base for visiting largest areas in vicinity (Valloire and Val-Cenis).

Steamboat 385

Sainte-Foy-Tarentaise 213

Steinach Austria
Pleasant village in picturesque surroundings, just off the autobahn near the Brenner Pass. An easy outing from Innsbruck,
1050m; slopes 1050–2205m
3,440ft; slopes 3,440–7,230ft
6 16km

Stevens Pass USA
A day trip from Seattle, and accommodation 60km/35 miles away in Bavarian-style town Leavenworth. Low snowfall and no snowmakers. Mostly intermediate slopes,
1235m; slopes 1235–1785m
4,050ft; slopes 4,050–5,860ft
14 1125 acres

St-François-Longchamp France
Sunny, gentle slopes, with a couple of harder runs. Linked to Valmorel.
1400; slopes 1200–2550m
4,590ft; slopes 3,940–8,370ft
56 153km

St Gallenkirch Austria
Smaller, less attractive village than Gaschurn, with which it shares a sizeable intermediate area in the Montafon valley.
900m; slopes 900–2370m
2,950ft; slopes 2,950–7,780ft
27 100km

St-Gervais 176
Small town sharing its ski area with Megève and Chamonix.

St Jakob in Defereggen
Austria
Unspoiled traditional village in a pretty, sunny valley close to Lienz and Heiligenblut, and with a good proportion of high-altitude slopes.
1390m; slopes 1390–2520m
4,560ft; slopes 4,560–8,270ft
9 35km

St Jakob in Haus Austria
Snowy village with its own slopes. Fieberbrunn, Waidring and St Johann are nearby.
855m; slopes 855–1500m
2,810ft; slopes 2,810–4,920ft
7 22km

St-Jean-de-Sixt 151
Traditional hamlet, a cheap base for La Clusaz and Le Grand-Bornand (3km/2 miles to both).

St-Jean-Montclar France
Small village at the foot of thickly forested slopes. Good day out from nearby Pra-Loup.
1300m; slopes 1300–2500m
4,270ft; slopes 4,270–8,200ft
18 50km

St Johann im Pongau Austria
Bustling, lively town with a small area of its own, but the impressive Salzburger Sportwelt Amadé area starts only 4km/2 miles away at Alpendorf.
650m; slopes 800–2285m
2,130ft; slopes 2,620–7,500ft
100 350km

St Johann in Tirol Austria
Busy valley town near Kitzbühel, at the foot of a small area of easy and intermediate skiing. Enormous range of mountain huts.
650m; slopes 670–1700m
2,130ft; slopes 2,200–5,580ft
17 60km

St Lary Espiaube France
Satellite of St-Lary-Soulan in the Pyrenees
830m; slopes 1700–2450m
2,720ft; slopes 5,580–8,040ft
32 90km

St-Lary-Soulan France
Well preserved old stone Pyrenean village, a lift-ride below its fine intermediate area.
830m; slopes 1700–2450m
2,720ft; slopes 5,580–8,040ft
32 90km

St Leonhard in Pitztal Austria
Village beneath a fine glacier in the Oetz area, accessed by underground funicular.
1250m; slopes 1735–3440m
4,100ft; slopes 5,690–11,290ft
12 40km

St Luc Switzerland
Quiet, unspoiled rustic village on the south side of the Rhône valley, with plenty of high, easy slopes.
1650m; slopes 1650–3025m
5,410ft; slopes 5,410–9,920ft
15 75km

St Margarethen Austria
Village near Obertauern in remarkable snow pocket.
1065m; slopes 1075–2210m
3,490ft; slopes 3,530–7,250ft
14 50km

St Martin bei Lofer Austria
Traditional cross-country village in a lovely setting beneath the impressive Loferer Steinberge massif. Alpine slopes at Lofer.
635m / 2,080ft

Saint-Martin-de-Belleville 215

St Martin in Tennengebirge Austria
Highest village in the Dachstein-West region near Salzburg. It has limited slopes of its own but nearby Annaberg has an interesting area.
1000m; slopes 1000–1350m
3,280ft; slopes 3,280–4,430ft
5 4km

St-Maurice-sur-Moselle France
One of several areas near Strasbourg. No snowmakers.
550m; slopes 900–1250m
1,800ft; slopes 2,950–4,100ft
8 24km

St Michael im Lungau Austria
Quiet, unspoiled village in the Tauern pass snowpocket with an uncrowded but disjointed intermediate area. Close to Obertauern and Wagrain.
1075m; slopes 1075–2360m
3,530ft; slopes 3,530–7,740ft
25 60km

St Moritz 320

St-Nicolas-de-Véroce 176
Small hamlet with a handful of simple hotels on the northern fringes of the Megève network.

St-Nizier-du-Moucherotte France
One of seven little resorts just west of Grenoble. Unspoiled, inexpensive place to tour. Villard-de-Lans is main resort.

Stoneham 476

Stoos Switzerland
Small, unspoiled village an hour from Zürich. Overcrowded at weekends. Magnificent views of Lake Lucerne.
1300m; slopes 570–1920m
4,270ft; slopes 1,870–6,300ft
7

Storlien Sweden
Small family resort amid magnificent wilderness scenery, One hour from Trondheim, 30 minutes from Åre.
600m; slopes 600–790m
1,970ft; slopes 1,970–2,590ft
7 15km

Stowe 440

St-Pierre-de-Chartreuse France
Locals' weekend place near Grenoble. Unreliable snow.
900m; slopes 900–1800m
2,950ft; slopes 2,950–5,910ft
14 35km

Stratton 431

Strobl Austria
Close to St Wolfgang in a beautiful lakeside setting. There are slopes at nearby St Gilgen and Postalm.
545m; slopes 545–1510m
1,790ft; slopes 1,790–4,950ft
9 12km

St Stephan Switzerland
Unspoiled old farming village at the foot of the largest area in the Gstaad Super Ski region.
995m; slopes 950–2155m
3,260ft; slopes 3,120–7,070ft
69 250km

Stuben 69
Small, unspoiled village linked to St Anton.

St Veit im Pongau Austria
Spa resort with limited slopes at Goldegg, but Wagrain (Salzburg Sportwelt Amadé) and Grossarl (Gastein valley) are nearby.
765m / 2,510ft

St-Veran France
Said to be the highest traditional village in Europe, full of charm. Close to Serre-Chevalier and the Milky Way. Snow-reliable cross-country skiing.
*2040m; slopes 2040–2800m
6,690ft; slopes 6,690–9,190ft*
≜15 ≛30km

St Wolfgang Austria
Charming lakeside resort near Salzburg, some way from any slopes, best for a relaxing winter holiday with one or two days on the slopes.
*540m; slopes 665–1350m
1,770ft; slopes 2,180–4,430ft*
≜9 ≛17km

Sugar Bowl USA
Exposed area north of Lake Tahoe with highest snowfall in California, best for experts. Lodging in Truckee but Squaw Valley nearby. Weekend crowds.
*2095m; slopes 2095–2555m
6,870ft; slopes 6,870–8,380ft*
≜8 ≛1500 acres

Sugarbush 431

Sugarloaf 431

Summit at Snoqualmie USA
Four areas – Summit East, Summit Central, Summit West and Alpental – with interlinked lifts. Damp weather and wet snow are major drawbacks.
*slopes 915–1645m
slopes 3,000–5,400ft*
≜24 ≛2000 acres

Sun Alpina Japan
Collective name for three tiny areas four hours from Tokyo, three hours from Osaka. ≜23

Sundance 403

Sunday River 442

Sunlight Mountain Resort USA
Quiet little area worth the easy trip from Vail to get away from its crowds for a day. Varied terrain. Good snowboard park.
*2405m; slopes 2405–3015m
7,890ft; slopes 7,890–9,890ft*
≜4 ≛460 acres

Sun Peaks 445

Sunrise Park USA
Arizona's largest area, operated by Apaches. Slopes are spread over three mountains; best for novices and leisurely intermediates.
*2805m; slopes 2805–3500m
9,200ft; slopes 9,200–11,480ft*
≜12 ≛800 acres

Sunshine Village 447

Sun Valley 429

Suommu Finland
A lodge (no village) right on the Arctic Circle with a few slopes but mostly a ski-touring place.
*140m; slopes 140–410m
460ft; slopes 460–1,350ft*

Super-Besse France
Purpose-built resort amid spectacular extinct-volcano scenery. Shares area with Mont-Dore. Limited village.
*1350m; slopes 1300–1850m
4,430ft; slopes 4,270–6,070ft*
≜22 ≛45km

Superdévoluy France
Ugly, purpose-built, user-friendly family resort, an hour south-east of Grenoble, with a sizeable intermediate area.
*1500m; slopes 1500–2510m
4,920ft; slopes 4,920–8,230ft*
≜32 ≛100km

Supermolina 492

Tahko Finland
Largest resort in southern Finland. Plenty of intermediate slopes in an attractive, wooded, frozen-lake setting. ≜8

Tahoe City 355
Small lakeside accommodation base for visiting nearby Alpine Meadows and Squaw Valley.

Talisman Mountain Resort Canada
One of the best areas in the Toronto region, but with a relatively low lift capacity. 100% snowmaking.
*235m; slopes 235–420m
770ft; slopes 770–1,380ft* ≜8

Tamsweg Austria
Large cross-country village with rail links in snowy region close to Tauern Pass and St Michael.
1025m / 3,360ft

La Tania 157

Taos 421

Tärnaby-Hemavan Sweden
Twin resorts with own airport. Snow-sure.
*slopes 265–830m
slopes 870–2,720ft*
≜7 ≛44km

El Tarter 488
Relatively quiet, convenient alternative to Soldeu, with which it shares its slopes.

Tarvisio Italy
Interesting, animated old town bordering Austria and Slovenia. A major cross-country base with fairly limited Alpine slopes.
*750m; slopes 750–1860m
2,460ft; slopes 2,460–6,100ft*
≜12 ≛15km

Täsch 341
The final base accessible by road on the way to car-free Zermatt – you take the train the rest of the way.

Tauplitz Austria
Traditional village at the foot of an interestingly varied area north of Schladming.
*900m; slopes 900–2000m
2,950ft; slopes 2,950–6,560ft*
≜18 ≛25km

Tazawako Japan
Small area four hours from Tokyo. One of the few Japanese areas to get reasonable powder. ≜10

Telluride 390

Temu Italy
Sheltered hamlet near Passo Tonale. Worth a visit in bad weather.
*1155m; slopes 1155–1955m
3,790ft; slopes 3,790–6,410ft*
≜4 ≛5km

Tengendai Japan
Tiny area three hours from Tokyo with one of Japan's best snow records, including occasional powder. ≜5

Termignon France
Traditional rustic village with good slopes of its own. A good base for touring Maurienne valley resorts such as Valloire and Val-Cenis.
*1300m; slopes 1300–2500m
4,270ft; slopes 4,270–8,200ft*
≜6 ≛35km

Terminillo Italy
Purpose-built resort 100km/62 miles from Rome with a worthwhile area when its lower runs have snowcover.
*1500m; slopes 1500–2210m
4,920ft; slopes 4,920–7,250ft*
≜15 ≛40km

Cedars Lebanon
The largest of Lebanon's ski areas, 130km/80 miles inland from Beirut. Good, open slopes with a surprisingly long season.
*1850m; slopes 2100–2700m
6,070ft; slopes 6,890–8,860ft*
≜5

Thollon-les-Mémises France
Attractive base for a relaxed holiday. Own little area and close to Portes du Soleil.
*1000m; slopes 1600–2000m
3,280ft; slopes 5,250–6,560ft*
≜19 ≛50km

Thredbo 508

La Thuile Italy
Old mining village turned smart ski resort, with a fair-sized ski area linked to that of La Rosière. Uncrowded.
*1450m; slopes 1175–2640m
4,760ft; slopes 3,850–8,660ft*
≜35 ≛150km

Thyon 2000 326
Extremely limited ski-from-the-door mid-mountain resort above Veysonnaz in the Verbier ski area.

Tignes 219

Timberline (Palmer Snowfield) USA
East of Portland, Oregon, and the only lift-served summer skiing in the US: winter snow maintained by spreading vast amounts of salt to harden it.
*slopes 1830–2600m
slopes 6,000–8,530ft*
≜6 ≛2500 acres

Togari Japan
One of several areas close to the 1998 Olympic site Nagano. ≜16

Torgnon Italy
Resort near Cervinia, good for bad weather.
*1500m; slopes 1500–1965m
4,920ft; slopes 4,920–6,450ft*
≜4 ≛6km

Torgon Switzerland
Old village in a pretty wooded setting, with a lift connection to the Portes du Soleil.
*1150m; slopes 975–2275m
3,770ft; slopes 3,200–7,460ft*
≜219 ≛650km

Le Tour France
Charming, unspoiled hamlet at the head of the Chamonix valley.
*1465m; slopes 1465–2185m
4,810ft; slopes 4,810–7,170ft*
≜9 ≛40km

La Toussuire France
Dreary, modern resort off the Maurienne valley with a large, uncrowded intermediate area.
1800m; slopes 1400–2225m
5,910ft; slopes 4,590–7,300ft
⛷19 ⛓45km

Trafoi Italy
Quiet, traditional (Austrian-style) village near Bormio, worth a day-trip if snow is good at low levels.
1570m; slopes 1570–2550m
5,150ft; slopes 5,150–8,370ft
⛷6 ⛓10km

Treble Cone 510

Tremblant 478

Les Trois Vallées 225

Troodos Cyprus
A good outing from Greek-sector coastal resorts, with interesting old villages en route. Pretty, wooded slopes and fine views.
1920m / 6,300ft
⛷4 ⛓5km

Trysil 501

Tschagguns Austria
Village with a varied little area of its own but part of Montafon valley area.
700m; slopes 700–2100m
2,300ft; slopes 2,300–6,890ft
⛷13 ⛓32km

Tsugaike Kogen Japan
Sizeable resort four hours from Tokyo, three hours from Osaka. Helicopter service to the top station.
800m; slopes 800–1700m
2,620ft; slopes 2,620–5,580ft
⛷28

La Tuca Spain
Purpose-built development near Viella with a lift to the slopes. Worthwhile excursion from nearby Baqueira-Beret, especially in bad weather.
1050m; slopes 1270–2250m
3,440ft; slopes 4,170–7,380ft
⛷7

Tulfes 54

Turoa 510

Turracherhöhe Austria
Tiny, unspoiled resort on a mountain shelf, with varied intermediate slopes above and below it. A good outing from Bad Kleinkirchheim.
1765m; slopes 1400–2200m
5,790ft; slopes 4,590–7,220ft
⛷11 ⛓30km

Tyax Mountain Lake Resort Canada
Heli-skiing operation in the Chilcotin mountains – transfers from Whistler or Vancouver.

Uludag 499

Unken Austria
Traditional village hidden in a side valley. Closest slopes to Salzburg.
565m; slopes 1000–1500m
1,850ft; slopes 3,280–4,920ft
⛷4 ⛓8km

Untergurgl 81
Valley-floor alternative to staying in more expensive Hochgurgl or Obergurgl.

Unternberg Austria
Riverside village with trail connecting into one of longest, most snow-sure cross-country networks in Europe. Large St Margarethen Alpine area close by.
1030m / 3,380ft

Unterwasser Switzerland
Old but not especially attractive resort 90 minutes from Zürich. Fabulous lake and mountain views. The more challenging half of the area shared with Wildhaus.
910m; slopes 900–2260m
2,990ft; slopes 2,950–7,410ft
⛷21 ⛓50km

Uttendorf-Weiss-See Austria
Astute alternative to crowded Kaprun when the snowline is high.
805m; slopes 1485–2600m
2,640ft; slopes 4,870–8,530ft
⛷9 ⛓20km

Vail-Beaver Creek 392

Valbella Switzerland
Convenient but ordinary village sharing large intermediate Lenzerheide area.
1540m; slopes 1470–2865m
5,050ft; slopes 4,820–9,400ft
⛷35 ⛓155km

Valberg France
Large Alpes-Maritimes resort (bigger than better-known Isola 2000) close to Nice.
1650m; slopes 1430–2100m
5,410ft; slopes 4,690–6,890ft
⛷26 ⛓90km

Val-Cenis France
Two pleasant villages in the Haute Maurienne, over the Iseran pass (closed in winter) from Val-d'Isère.
1400m; slopes 1400–2800m
4,590ft; slopes 4,590–9,190ft
⛷22 ⛓80km

Val d'Illiez Switzerland
Peaceful, unspoiled village a few minutes below Champoussin. Open-air thermal baths. Good views of impressive Dents du Midi.
950m; slopes 1050–2280m
3,120ft; slopes 3,440–7,480ft
⛷228 ⛓650km

Val-d'Isère 227

Val Ferret Switzerland
Old climbing village near Martigny, with spectacular views. Own tiny area.
1600m / 5,250ft ⛷4

Valfréjus France
A small and unusual modern resort in the Maurienne valley – built in the woods, with most of the slopes higher up above the tree line.
1550m; slopes 1550–2735m
5,090ft; slopes 5,090–8,970ft
⛷12 ⛓52km

Val Gardena 272
Valley area of Selva, Ortisei and Santa Cristina – part of the Sella Ronda circuit.

Vallandry 130
Family-friendly satellite of Les Arcs with direct access to the main slopes.

Valloire France
Old village above the Maurienne valley, with a fair-sized area of mainly intermediate skiing spread over two mountains.
1430m; slopes 1430–2595m
4,690ft; slopes 4,690–8,510ft
⛷36 ⛓150km

Valmeinier France
Spread out resort in the Maurienne valley, with links over a ridge to Valloire.
1500m; slopes 1430–2595m
4,920ft; slopes 4,690–8,510ft
⛷36 ⛓150km

Valmorel France
Prettily designed purpose-built resort with a fair-sized area of varied skiing shared with St-François-Longchamp.
1400m; slopes 1200–2550m
4,590ft; slopes 3,940–8,370ft
⛷56 ⛓153km

Val Senales Italy
Top-of-the-mountain hotel, the highest in the Alps, in the Dolomites near Merano.
3250m; slopes 2005–3250m
10,660ft; slopes 6,580– 10,660ft
⛷10 ⛓24km

Val-Thorens 235

Valtournenche 245
Cheaper alternative to Cervinia, with genuine Italian atmosphere, and access to the extensive area.

Vandans
Sizeable working village well placed for visiting all the Montafon areas.

Vars France
Large, convenient purpose-built resort linked to Risoul.
1650m; slopes 1660–2750m
5,410ft; slopes 5,450–9,020ft
⛷56 ⛓180km

Vaujany 122
Tiny, rustic village with lift accessing the heart of the Alpe-d'Huez ski area.

Las Vegas Resort USA
Area formerly known as Lee Canyon, cut from forest only 50 minutes' drive from Las Vegas. Height and snowmaking gives fairly reliable snow. Night skiing too.
2590m; slopes 2590–2840m
8,500ft; slopes 8,500–9,320ft
⛷3 ⛓200 acres

Vemdalen 505

Vemdalsskalet 505

Vent Austria
High, remote Oztal village with just enough skiing to warrant a day trip from nearby Obergurgl.
1900m; slopes 1900–2680m
6,230ft; slopes 6,230–8,790ft
⛷4 ⛓15km

Ventron France
One of several areas near Strasbourg. No snowmakers.
630m; slopes 900–1110m
2,070ft; slopes 2,950–3,640ft
⛷8 ⛓15km

Verbier 326

Verchaix France
Charming hamlet in lovely surroundings, next to Morillon, at the foot of the Flaine area.
700m; slopes 700–2560m
2,300ft; slopes 2,300–8,400ft
⛷80 ⛓260km

Verditz Austria
One of several small, mostly mountain-top areas overlooking the town of Villach.
675m; slopes 675–2165m
2,210ft; slopes 2,210–7,100ft
⛷5 ⛓17km

Wildhaus   Switzerland
Undeveloped farming
community in stunning
scenery near Liechtenstein;
popular with families and
serious snowboarders.
1100m; slopes 1100–2075m
3,610ft; slopes 3,610–6,810ft
⛷ *9* 🚡 *50km*

Wildschönau   Austria
Wildschönau is the dramatic-
sounding brand name
adopted by a group of
attractive small resorts in the
Tirol – Niederau, Oberau and
Auffach.
830m; slopes 830–1900m
2,720ft; slopes 2,720–6,230ft
⛷ *29* 🚡 *42km*

Wiler   Switzerland
Main village in particularly
remote, picturesque dead-end
valley near Lotschberg rail
tunnel north of Rhône valley.
Very limited slopes.
1380m; slopes 1380–2700m
4,530ft; slopes 4,530–8,860ft
⛷ *6*

Willamette Pass   USA
US speed skiing training base
in national forest near
beautiful Crater Lake, Oregon.
Small but varied slopes
popular with weekenders.
1560m; slopes 1560–2035m
5,120ft; slopes 5,120–6,680ft
⛷ *7* 🚡 *550 acres*

Williams   USA
Tiny area above the main
place to stay for the Grand
Canyon.
slopes 2010–2270m
slopes 6,590–7,450ft
⛷ *2* 🚡 *50 acres*

**Windischgarsten und
Umgebung**   Austria
Large working village linked
by rail to Schladming. Its
slopes are at nearby
Hinterstoder and Spital.
600m; slopes 810–1870m
1,970ft; slopes 2,660–6,140ft
⛷ *11* 🚡 *18km*

Winter Park   **398**

Wolf Creek   USA
Remote area with highest
snowfall record in Colorado.
Uncrowded; wonderful
powder. Great stop en route
between Taos and Telluride.
3155m; slopes 3155–3590m
10,350ft; slopes 10,350–11,780ft
⛷ *6* 🚡 *800 acres*

Xonrupt   France
Cross-country venue only 3km
from nearest Alpine slopes at
Gérardmer.
715m; slopes 666–1150m
2,350ft; slopes 2,190–3,770ft
⛷ *20* 🚡 *40km*

Yangji Pine   Korea
Modern, ever-growing resort
40 minutes south of Seoul,
with runs cut out of dense
forest. Gets very crowded. ⛷ *7*

Ylläs   Finland
Largest ski centre in the Arctic
area, not far from from
Lapland's capital Rovaniemi.
Unusually open slopes for
Finland, popular with
boarders and telemarkers.
255m; slopes 255–715m
840ft; slopes 840–2,350ft
⛷ *18*

Yong Pyeong   Korea
Largest resort in Korea,
200km/125 miles east of
Seoul, with snowmakers on
all 18 of its short runs.
750m; slopes 750–1460m
2,460ft; slopes 2,460–4,790ft
⛷ *16* 🚡 *20km*

Zakopane   Poland
An interesting old town near
Cracow and Auschwitz. Mostly
intermediate slopes.
830m; slopes 1000–1960m
2,720ft; slopes 3,280–6,430ft
⛷ *20* 🚡 *10km*

Zao   Japan
Three interconnected areas
with unpredictable weather
and very cold temperatures.
Renowned for 'chouoh' –
pines frozen into weird
shapes.
780m; slopes 780–1660m
2,560ft; slopes 2,560–5,450ft
⛷ *42*

Zauchensee   Austria
Purpose-built resort with lifts
spreading out into the
Salzburger Sportwelt Amadé
area that surrounds it.
855m; slopes 800–2185m
2,810ft; slopes 2,620–7,170ft
⛷ *100* 🚡 *350km*

Zell am See   **114**

Zell im Zillertal   Austria
Sprawling valley town with
slopes on two nearby
mountains. Linked to higher
Gerlos and Konigsleiten to
form a fair-sized area.
580m; slopes 930–2410m
1,900ft; slopes 3,050–7,910ft
⛷ *22* 🚡 *47km*

Zermatt   **341**

Zinal   Switzerland
Pretty, rustic village with high
slopes. For some, the modern
buildings are incongruous.
168om; slopes 1680–2895m
5,510ft; slopes 5,510–9,500ft
⛷ *9* 🚡 *70km*

Zug   **69**
Tiny village in scenic location
with Lech's toughest skiing on
its doorstep.

Zürs   **69**
High, smart but soulless
village on road to Lech, with
which it shares extensive
skiing.

Zweisimmen   **309**
Limited but inexpensive base
for slopes around Gstaad,
with its own delightful little
easy area too.

MONEY BACK VOUCHER

To be sent to
SkiEurope
1535 West Loop South 319, Houston, TX 77027, USA

Name

Address

E-mail address

Daytime phone number

Departure date

I have bought a copy of Where to Ski and Snowboard Worldwide and
claim a refund of the cover price. I understand this amount will be
deducted from the cost of the vacation I am booking through SkiEurope
to be taken during the 2001/02 or 2002/03 winter seasons.

Signature   **Date**

WHERE *to* SKI
AND Snowboard

WHERE *to* SKI
AND Snowboard

WHERE *to* SKI
AND Snowboard

WHERE *to* SKI
AND Snowboard

WHERE *to* SKI
AND Snowboard